Personal Identifiable Information and Data Breaches

PERSONAL IDENTIFIABLE INFORMATION AND DATA BREACHES

UNITED STATES GOVERNMENT ACCOUNTABILITY OFFICE

Nova Science Publishers, Inc.
New York

For permission to use material from this book please contact us:
Telephone 631-231-7269; Fax 631-231-8175
Web Site: http://www.novapublishers.com

LIBRARY OF CONGRESS CATALOGING-IN-PUBLICATION DATA

United States. Government Accountability Office.
Personal identifiable information and data breaches / GAO.
p. cm.
Includes index.
ISBN 978-1-60692-061-9 (softcover)
1. United States--Officials and employees--Crimes against--Prevention. 2. United States--Officials and employees--Protection--Technological innovations. 3. Identity theft--United States--Prevention. I. Title.
JK850.E49U6 2009
352.3'87--dc22

2008052167

Published by Nova Science Publishers, Inc. ✢ New York

CONTENTS

PREFACE

The centerpiece of the federal government's legal framework for privacy protection, the Privacy Act of 1974, provides safeguards for information maintained by federal agencies. In addition, the E-Government Act of 2002 requires federal agencies to conduct privacy impact assessments for systems or collections containing personal information.

The author was asked to determine whether laws and guidance consistently cover the federal government's collection and use of personal information and incorporate key privacy principles. The author was also asked, in doing so, to identify options for addressing these issues.

Chapter 1

DATA BREACH NOTIFICATION*

WHAT GAO FOUND

Based on the experience of VA and other federal agencies in responding to data breaches, GAO identified the following lessons learned regarding how and when to notify government officials, affected individuals, and the public:

- Rapid internal notification of key government officials is critical.
- Because incidents vary, a core group of senior officials should be designated to make decisions regarding an agency's response.
- Mechanisms must be in place to obtain contact information for affected individuals.
- Determining when to offer credit monitoring to affected individuals requires risk-based management decisions.
- Interaction with the public requires careful coordination and can be resource-intensive.
- Internal training and awareness are critical to timely breach response, including notification.
- Contractor responsibilities for data breaches should be clearly defined.

These lessons have largely been addressed in guidance issued in 2006 from the Office of Management and Budget (OMB), which is responsible for overseeing security and privacy within the federal government. However, guidance to assist agency officials in making consistent risk-based determinations

* Excerpted from GAO Report 07-657, dated April 2007.

about when to offer credit monitoring or other protection services has not been developed. Without such guidance, agencies are likely to continue to make inconsistent decisions about what protections to offer affected individuals, potentially leaving some people more vulnerable than others.

WHY GAO DID THIS STUDY

A May 2006 data breach at the Department of Veterans Affairs (VA) and other similar incidents since then have heightened awareness of the importance of protecting computer equipment containing personally identifiable information and responding effectively to a breach that poses privacy risks. GAO's objective was to identify lessons learned from the VA data breach and other similar federal data breaches regarding effectively notifying government officials and affected individuals about data breaches. To address this objective, GAO analyzed documentation and interviewed officials at VA and five other agencies regarding their responses to data breaches and their progress in implementing standardized data breach notification procedures. The cases at the other agencies were chosen because, like the VA case, they involved loss or theft of computing equipment and relatively large numbers of affected individuals (10,000 or more).

WHAT GAO RECOMMENDS

To better ensure that individuals who are at risk of identity theft are offered consistent levels of support, GAO is recommending that the Director of OMB develop guidance for agencies on when to offer credit monitoring and when to contract for an alternative form of monitoring, such as data breach monitoring, to assist individuals at risk of identity theft. In written comments on a draft of this report, OMB and VA concurred with GAO's recommendation.

ABBREVIATIONS

HHS	Department of Health and Human Services
OMB	Office of Management and Budget
PII	personally identifiable information
VA	Department of Veterans Affairs

April 30, 2007
Congressional Requesters

In May 2006, the Department of Veterans Affairs (VA) announced that computer equipment containing personally identifiable information (PII) [1] on approximately 26.5 million veterans and active duty members of the military was stolen from the home of a VA employee. Until the equipment was recovered, veterans did not know whether their information was likely to be misused. In addition to concerns about protecting personal information, the incident highlighted unclear policy about security breach notification procedures. The VA data breach coupled with recent reports of other federal data breach incidents have heightened awareness of the need for agencies to be prepared to effectively respond to a breach that poses privacy risks.

While existing laws generally do not require agencies to notify affected individuals of data breaches, such notification appears to be consistent with agencies' responsibilities under the Privacy Act of 1974 and promotes accountability for privacy protection [2]. When data breaches occur, notification has clear benefits such as allowing the affected individuals the opportunity to take steps to protect themselves from identity theft or other misuse of their personal information.

However, as we noted in June 2006, public notification of data breaches presents challenges as well as benefits [3]. Determining the specific criteria for incidents that merit notification involves these important considerations:

- Notification of a breach when there is little or no risk of harm might create unnecessary concern and confusion.
- Sending too many notices, based on overly strict criteria, could render all such notices less effective, because consumers could become desensitized to them and fail to act when risks are truly significant.
- The costs associated with notification are not insignificant for either agencies or individuals.

As agreed with the requesters' staff, our objective was to identify lessons learned from the VA data breach and other similar federal data breaches regarding effectively notifying government officials and affected individuals about data breaches.

To address our objective, we analyzed documentation capturing lessons learned from VA's data breach, including reports on actions taken and planned to address the data breach and to protect personal information. We interviewed VA officials regarding how they decided to address data breach notification and their plans and progress in implementing standardized data breach notification procedures. We also analyzed current federal guidance on data breach notification procedures and interviewed cognizant officials about the guidance. In addition, we examined similar data breach cases at five other agencies—the Departments of Agriculture, Defense, Education, Health and Human Services (HHS), and Transportation—to determine their notification practices and lessons learned regarding how and when to notify affected individuals or the public. These cases were chosen because, like the VA case, they involved relatively large numbers of affected individuals (10,000 or more) and also involved circumstances similar to VA's—the loss or theft of computing equipment containing PII. The cases at Agriculture, Education, and HHS involved data breaches of information held by contractors. We conducted our review in accordance with generally accepted government auditing standards from August 2006 through February 2007.

On March 9, 2007, we provided staff of requesters with a briefing on the results of our study. The slides from that briefing, with minor technical clarifications, are included as appendix I of this report. The purpose of this report is to provide the published briefing slides to you and to officially transmit our recommendation to the Office of Management and Budget (OMB) In summary, based on the experience of VA and other federal agencies in responding to data breaches, we identified the following lessons learned regarding how and when to notify government officials, affected individuals, and the public:

- *Rapid internal notification of key government officials is critical.* Internal delays prevented key VA officials, including the Secretary, from being aware of the data breach until as long as two weeks after it occurred. Because of these delays, the department's decision about how to respond was also delayed. As a result, affected individuals were denied the opportunity to take prompt steps to protect themselves against the dangers of identity theft. Prompt internal notification would help ensure that future data breaches are addressed promptly, maximizing the opportunity for affected individuals to effectively take precautions.
- *Because incidents vary, a core group of senior officials should be designated to make decisions regarding an agency's response.* In the VA incident, a variety of key decisions needed to be made including, what information had been compromised and what risks the theft posed, and how affected individuals should be notified. Cognizant officials at VA were initially unsure about who should be involved in decision making about the incident. Establishment of core management groups within

agencies that can be convened in the event of a breach to evaluate the situation and guide the agency's response should help ensure that future data breaches are addressed consistently.

- *Mechanisms must be in place to obtain contact information for affected individuals.* VA and other agencies faced challenges in identifying addresses for all individuals affected by their data breaches. If proper public notices as required by the Privacy Act are made in advance, key agencies will more likely be in a better position to assist in responding to data breaches by providing address or other contact information to affected agencies.
- *Determining when to offer credit monitoring to affected individuals requires risk-based management decisions.* Agencies have made varying decisions about how and when to offer credit monitoring. As a result, affected individuals may not always receive a consistent level of support from the federal government when their personal information is compromised. Until guidance is available to promote consistent decision making by federal agencies, protections offered to affected individuals are likely to remain inconsistent.
- *Interaction with the public requires careful coordination and can be resource-intensive.* VA invested substantially in facilities to help address follow-on inquiries and provide information to support affected individuals after notifications were issued to affected individuals. Other agencies have also taken a variety of actions to establish call centers to interact with the public.
- *Internal training and awareness are critical to timely breach response, including notification.* The slow response to the May 2006 VA incident highlighted the need for personnel to be more aware of the agency's privacy and security procedures, including incident response and reporting procedures. Because a prompt response is critical, agency personnel must be prepared in advance with an understanding of their roles and responsibilities in responding to a data breach.
- *Contractor responsibilities for data breaches should be clearly defined.* While the VA data breach did not involve contractors, the issue of contractor responsibilities has figured prominently in three other recent incidents (at Agriculture, Education, and HHS). Contractor obligations for taking steps, such as notifying affected individuals or providing credit monitoring, may be unclear unless specified in the contract.

These lessons have largely been addressed in guidance from OMB, which is responsible for overseeing security and privacy within the federal government. However, guidance to assist agency officials in making consistent risk-based determinations about when to offer credit monitoring or other protection services has not been developed. Without such guidance, agencies could make inconsistent decisions about what protections to offer affected individuals, potentially leaving some more vulnerable than others.

CONCLUSIONS

VA's data breach of May 2006 and other recent federal data breaches provide valuable lessons learned for agencies about responding to such incidents. Key government officials need to be informed promptly, and a designated group of agency officials must be ready to make prompt decisions about notification, which can be challenging if address information is not readily available. Careful planning is needed to be able to interact effectively with the public, training and awareness are critical, and contractor roles and responsibilities must be defined.

To its credit, OMB responded to the VA data breach by issuing guidance and forwarding recommendations by the ID Theft Task Force that largely address these lessons. However, the issue of how to make risk-based determinations on when to offer credit monitoring and when to contract for an alternative form of monitoring, such as data breach monitoring, has not been addressed in guidance. Without such guidance, agencies are likely to continue to make inconsistent decisions about what protections to offer affected individuals.

RECOMMENDATION FOR EXECUTIVE ACTION

We recommend that the Director of OMB develop guidance for federal agencies on conducting risk analyses to determine when to offer credit monitoring and when to contract for an alternative form of monitoring, such as data breach monitoring, to assist individuals at risk of identity theft as a result of a federal data breach.

AGENCY COMMENTS AND OUR EVALUATION

We received written comments on a draft of this report from OMB Administrator of the Office of E-Government and Information Technology and from the Secretary of Veterans Affairs. (These written comments are reproduced in apps. II and III.) OMB agreed with our recommendation and noted that while it is important that individuals receive consistent responses and levels of support from federal agencies, the same response or type of support will not be appropriate in every situation. We agree that appropriate responses must be tailored to address the circumstances of the breach and believe additional guidance from OMB can facilitate consistent agency decision making about such responses. In addition, OMB commented that our definition of PII is similar to one it has used and noted that its definition of PII is likely to be revised in the future. However, we believe the definition we have used is appropriate for the material discussed in this report.

In written comments on the draft of this report, the Secretary of VA agreed with our findings and our recommendation to OMB. The Secretary also stated that VA is finalizing its new data breach regulation that implements the Veterans Benefits, Health Care, and Information Technology Act of 2006, Public Law 109-461 [4]. This act requires VA to issue interim regulations for the provision of certain services, including notification, in the event that a data breach of veterans' sensitive personal information results in a determination that a reasonable risk exists for the potential misuse of the information.

We are sending copies of this report to interested congressional committees; the Secretary of Veterans Affairs; the Director, OMB; and other interested parties. We will also make copies available to others upon request. In addition, the report will be available at no charge on the GAO Web site at www.gao.gov.

Should you have any questions on matters contained in this report, please contact me at (202) 512-6240 or by e-mail at koontzl@gao.gov. GAO staff who made major contributions to this report are included in appendix IV.

Linda D. Koontz
Director, Information Management Issues

List of Requesters

The Honorable Harry Reid
Majority Leader
United States Senate

The Honorable Daniel K. Akaka
Chairman, Committee on Veterans' Affairs
United States Senate

The Honorable Joseph I. Lieberman
Chairman, Committee on Homeland Security and Governmental Affairs
United States Senate

The Honorable Bob Filner
Chairman
Committee on Veterans' Affairs
House of Representatives

The Honorable Hillary Rodham Clinton
United States Senate

The Honorable Byron L. Dorgan
United States Senate

The Honorable Patty Murray
United States Senate

The Honorable Barack Obama
United States Senate

The Honorable John D. Rockefeller,
IV United States Senate

The Honorable Ken Salazar
United States Senate

The Honorable Charles E. Schumer
United States Senate

Appendix I: Briefing to Staff of Congressional Requesters

Introduction

In May 2006, the Department of Veterans Affairs (VA) announced that computer equipment containing personally identifiable information (PII) [1] on approximately 26.5 million veterans and active duty members of the military was stolen from the home of a VA employee.

In June, VA sent notices to the affected individuals that explained the breach and offered advice on steps to take to reduce the risk of identity theft.

The equipment was eventually recovered, and forensic analysts concluded that it was unlikely that the personal information contained therein was compromised [2].

Until the equipment was recovered, veterans did not know whether their information was likely to be misused.

In addition to concerns about protecting personal information, the incident highlighted unclear policy about security breach notification procedures.

The Senate Majority Leader, the Chairman, Senate Committee on Veterans Affairs, and other Congressional requesters asked us to review lessons learned from the VA data breach about how to effectively notify government officials and the public about security breaches.

Objective, Scope, and Methodology

As agreed with the requesters' staff, our objective was to identify lessons learned from the VA data breach and other similar federal data breaches regarding effectively notifying government officials and affected individuals about data breaches.

To address our objective, we

- Analyzed documentation capturing lessons learned from VA's data breach, including reports on actions taken and planned to address the data breach and to protect personal information.
- Interviewed VA officials regarding how they decided to address data breach notification and their plans and progress in implementing standardized data breach notification procedures.

- Analyzed current federal guidance on data breach notification procedures and interviewed cognizant officials about the guidance.
- Examined similar data breach cases at five other agencies—the Departments of Agriculture, Defense, Education, Health and Human Services (HHS), and Transportation—to determine their notification practices and lessons learned regarding how and when to notify affected individuals or the public. The cases were chosen because, like the VA case, they involved relatively large numbers of affected individuals (10,000 or more) and also involved circumstances similar to VA's—the loss or theft of computing equipment containing PII. The cases at Agriculture, Education, and HHS involved data breaches of information held by contractors.

We conducted our review in accordance with generally accepted government auditing standards from August 2006 through February 2007.

RESULTS IN BRIEF

Based on the experience of VA and other federal agencies in responding to data breaches, we identified the following lessons learned regarding how and when to notify government officials, affected individuals, and the public:

- Rapid internal notification of key government officials is critical.
- Because incidents vary, a core group of senior officials should be designated to make decisions regarding an agency's response.
- Mechanisms must be in place to obtain contact information for affected individuals.
- Determining when to offer credit monitoring to affected individuals requires risk-based management decisions.
- Interaction with the public requires careful coordination and can be resource-intensive.
- Internal training and awareness are critical to timely breach response, including notification.
- Contractor responsibilities for data breaches should be clearly defined.

These lessons have largely been addressed in guidance from the Office of Management and Budget (OMB), which is responsible for overseeing security and privacy within the federal government. However, guidance to assist agency officials in making consistent risk-based determinations about when to offer credit monitoring or other protection services has not been developed. Without such guidance, agencies are likely to continue to make inconsistent decisions about what protections to offer affected individuals, potentially leaving some more vulnerable than others.

To better ensure that individuals who are at risk of identity theft are offered consistent levels of support, we are recommending that the Director, OMB, develop guidance for agencies on when to offer credit monitoring and when to contract for an alternative form of monitoring, such as data breach monitoring, to assist individuals at risk of identity theft as a result of a federal data breach.

An OMB Policy Analyst in the Information Policy and Technology Branch provided an e-mail message stating that OMB concurred with our recommendation.

In oral comments on a draft of this briefing, VA officials, including the VA/GAO Liaison, Office of Congressional and Legislative Affairs, agreed with our results. VA also provided technical comments, which have been incorporated as appropriate.

BACKGROUND

The VA data breach coupled with recent reports of other federal data breach incidents have heightened awareness of the need for agencies to be prepared to effectively respond to a breach that poses privacy risks.

While existing laws generally do not require agencies to notify affected individuals of data breaches, such notification appears to be consistent with agencies' responsibilities under the Privacy Act of 1974 and promotes accountability for privacy protection [3].

When data breaches occur, notification has clear benefits such as allowing the affected individuals the opportunity to take steps to protect themselves from identify theft or other misuse of their personal information.

As we noted in June 2006, public notification of data breaches presents challenges as well as benefits [4].

Determining the specific criteria for incidents that merit notification involves these important considerations:

- Notification of a breach when there is little or no risk of harm might create unnecessary concern and confusion.

- Sending too many notices, based on overly strict criteria, could render all such notices less effective, because consumers could become desensitized to them and fail to act when risks are truly significant.
- The costs associated with notification are not insignificant for either agencies or individuals.

While care needs to be taken to avoid requiring organizations to notify the public of trivial incidents, setting criteria that are too open- ended or that rely too heavily on the discretion of the affected organization could lead to inadequate notification.

To mitigate such a risk, we suggested that a two-tiered approach could be adopted, by which agencies are required to notify an entity such as OMB of alldata breach incidents while notifying affected individuals only of incidents where there is a risk of identity theft.

Guidance subsequently issued by OMB conforms to this approach; it requires agencies to report all incidents involving PII to the Department of Homeland Security's Computer Emergency Readiness Team (US-CERT) within one hour of discovering the incident and recommending that senior agency officials make risk- based determinations of whether to inform the affected individuals.

In addition, OMB responded to the VA data breach incident by issuing several other guidance documents in late May and June 2006 to all federal agencies. These documents directed agencies to:

- review their practices to ensure they had adequate safeguards to prevent misuse of or unauthorized access to PII; and
- use security measures, such as data encryption for mobile computers and devices, to protect data removed from an agency location.

In a separate action, the Identity Theft Task Force was chartered by the President in early May 2006 to strengthen efforts to protect against identity theft. The task force is composed of senior officials from major federal agencies.

In September 2006, OMB issued interim guidance on data breach notification based on recommendations made by the task force. It included these recommended practices:

- • Each agency should establish a core management group to respond to the loss of personal information. In the event of a loss, that group should convene to conduct a risk analysis to determine whether the incident might pose problems related to identity theft. If such a risk exists, the agency should tailor its response to the nature and scope of the risk.

- The core management group is to include the chief information officer, chief privacy officer, chief legal officer, a senior management official, and the agency's inspector general.
- According to the interim guidance, in tailoring its response, the group should consider:
  - procuring commercial services to monitor whether a breach results in identity theft—an option that may be useful for incidents involving data gathered on large numbers of individuals,
  - offering credit monitoring services to affected individuals—a potentially expensive option—and
  - coordinating the agency's response with law enforcement through the agency's inspector general.

- Should agencies decide to notify affected individuals, they are encouraged by the interim guidance to incorporate the following elements into the notification process:
  - Provide the notice in a timely manner, but not based on incomplete facts or in a manner likely to make identity theft more likely to occur.
  - Have a responsible official of the agency be the official source of the notice.
  - Deliver notices primarily through first class mail to the last known mailing addresses of the affected individuals.
  - Prepare for follow-on inquiries from affected individuals with Web site postings by establishing call centers and by alerting other entities, such as credit-reporting agencies.
- Further, agencies are encouraged to include the following content in their notification letters:
  - a brief description of what happened;
  - to the extent possible, a description of the types of personal information that were involved in the data security breach (e.g., full name, Social Security number, date of birth, etc.);
  - a brief description of agency actions to investigate the breach, to mitigate losses, and to protect against any further breaches;
  - contact procedures for those wishing to ask questions or learn additional information, including a toll-free telephone number, Web site, and/or postal address; and

- steps individuals should take to protect themselves from the risk of identity theft, including steps to take advantage of any credit monitoring or other service the agency intends to offer and contact information for the Federal Trade Commission Web site.

In December 2006, the Veterans Benefits, *Health Care, and Information Technology Act of 2006* (Public Law 109-461) became law. Among other things, the law specifies circumstances under which VA is required to provide credit protection services. Specifically, the law provides that:

- In the event of a data breach, an independent assessment is to be conducted by the Inspector General or another independent entity to determine the risk that the breached information may be misused;
- VA is to provide credit protection services, if the Secretary determines that a reasonable risk of misuse exists, based on the independent assessment;
- VA is to develop regulations regarding notification, data mining, fraud alerts, data breach analysis, credit monitoring, identity theft insurance, and credit protection services;
- VA is to provide reports to Congress on data breaches, including the required independent assessments, the Secretary's determinations based on the assessments, and the services offered in response.

Like VA, many other federal agencies have experienced security breaches. According to the House Government Reform Committee, since January 2003 all 19 departments and numerous federal agencies have reported at least one loss of PII that could expose individuals to identify theft [5].

Compromised information included individual Social Security numbers, names, addresses, dates of birth, medical information, fingerprint cards, taxpayer records, and financial information.

Agencies have taken a variety of actions to notify government officials as well as the affected individuals and the public.

Attachment 1 provides case examples of recent data breaches and the responses to them at the five federal agencies we reviewed.

DATA BREACH NOTIFICATION LESSONS LEARNED

Based on the experience of VA and other federal agencies in responding to data breaches, the following are lessons learned regarding how and when to notify government officials, affected individuals, and the public:

- Rapid internal notification of key government officials is critical.
- Because incidents vary, a committee of key officials should make decisions regarding an agency's response.
- Mechanisms must be in place to obtain contact information for affected individuals.
- Determining whether, or not, to offer the credit monitoring to affected individuals requires risk-based management decisions.
- Interaction with the public requires careful coordination and can be resource-intensive.
- Internal training and awareness are critical.
- Contractor responsibilities for data breaches should be clearly defined.

Rapid Internal Notification

Rapid internal notification of key government officials is critical.

Internal delays prevented key VA officials, including the Secretary, from being aware of the data breach until as long as two weeks after it occurred.

- The VA employee whose computer equipment was stolen on May 3, 2006, notified VA's Deputy Assistant Secretary for Policy about the incident on the same day.
- Two days later (May 5), the Acting Assistant Secretary for Policy and Planning was notified.
- In turn, the Acting Assistant Secretary informed the VA's Chief of Staff on May 9.
- Finally, the Chief of Staff informed the Secretary on May 16—almost two weeks after the theft.
- On May 22, almost three weeks after the incident, VA publicly announced the data theft. Contractors did not begin mailing initial notification letters to affected individuals on VA's behalf until June 9—more than 1 month after the incident.

Because of these delays, the department's decisions about how to respond were also delayed, and, as a result, affected individuals were denied the opportunity to take prompt steps to protect themselves against the dangers of identify theft.

In addition, the public's trust and confidence in VA may have been diminished because of the slow response.

VA has taken steps to develop a uniform response policy and standard operating procedures to improve its data breach response capabilities. As part of these procedures, VA has established key organizational responsibilities for various aspects of breach response—such as roles for information security officers, the chief privacy officer, and the chief information officer—and is in the process of identifying criteria to conduct timely and uniform risk assessments and determine appropriate levels of VA response.

On July 12, 2006, OMB issued guidance [6] requiring agencies to report "all incidents involving personally identifiable information in electronic or physical form" to US-CERT within one hour of becoming aware of the occurrence. The OMB guidance requires all incidents—whether suspected or confirmed—to be reported.

Other agencies have taken steps to improve the timeliness of their responses and have implemented the OMB guidance.

For example:

- In October 2006, the Department of Transportation issued updated procedures for implementing protection of sensitive PII. It calls for all incidents involving a possible or confirmed compromise of such information to be reported to the appropriate unit's chief information officer and computer incident response team within one hour of discovery.
- In November 2006, the Department of Health and Human Services (HHS) issued procedures requiring the chief information security officer to report PII breaches within one hour of detection to the department's PII Breach Response Team and US-CERT.

If followed, these procedures should help ensure that future data breaches are addressed promptly, maximizing the opportunity for affected individuals to effectively take precautions.

Core Decision-Making Group

Because incidents vary, a core group of senior officials should be designated to make decisions regarding an agency's response.

In the VA incident, a variety of key decisions needed to be made including:

- how to work with law enforcement to recover the stolen equipment,
- what information had been compromised and what risks the theft posed,
- how affected individuals should be notified, and
- what services should be provided to assist affected individuals.

Cognizant officials at VA were initially unsure about who should be involved in decision making about the incident.

Since the VA incident, the Identity Theft Task Force and OMB have recommended that agencies identify a core response group that can be convened in the event of a breach to evaluate the situation and help guide further response. Among other things, the core group should:

- consist of the chief information officer, chief privacy officer, chief legal officer, a senior management official, and the agency's inspector general; and
- ensure that the agency has brought together employees who have expertise in the basic competencies needed to respond, including information technology and legal considerations (e.g., the Privacy Act).

Since the data breach, VA has established an Incident Resolution Core Team consisting of key management officials including the chief information officer, chief technology officer, privacy officer, and other senior officials from VA's offices of Information Technology, General Counsel, Cyber and Information Security, Congressional Relations, Public Affairs, and Human Resources.

Officials from each of the five agencies said that they had or were in the process of establishing core management groups to respond to the loss of personal information. For example, HHS has established a PII Breach Response Team consisting of senior officials with expertise in information technology, legal requirements, privacy, law enforcement, and information security. This group is chartered to analyze incidents, evaluate the risk of identify theft, and provide guidance for further response.

Within individual agencies, establishment of a core management group should help ensure that future data breaches are addressed consistently.

Obtaining Contact Information

Mechanisms must be in place to obtain contact information for affected individuals.

VA mailed two notifications to individuals affected by the May 2006 breach: an initial notice in June and a follow-up notice in August after the stolen equipment had been recovered.

The VA did not have contact information on hand for all affected individuals. To obtain addresses for mailing the first notification letter, VA sought assistance from the Social Security Administration (SSA) and the Internal Revenue Service (IRS). SSA agreed to verify the names and Social Security numbers of the approximately 26.5 million affected individuals against data contained in its systems and delete the names and Social Security numbers of individuals that did not match SSA's records or were identified as deceased. SSA then forwarded the verified names and Social Security numbers to the IRS. IRS agreed to forward the first round of letters on VA's behalf to individuals verified by SSA.

According to VA officials, IRS made specific legal determinations before participating in the notification process. Disclosure of personal information associated with tax returns is protected by Internal Revenue Code provisions as well as the Privacy Act of 1974. Regarding the first letter, VA officials reported that IRS had determined that the potential compromise of personal information from the VA breach could result in an impact on tax administration and thus it was appropriate to disclose address information for the purpose of notifying affected individuals.

After the first notice was issued, the stolen equipment was recovered and, based on forensic analysis, the Federal Bureau of Investigation made a determination that the data had not been compromised. As a result, VA decided to issue a second notice informing affected individuals of the status of the data breach and services that the department was continuing to offer.

However, IRS denied VA's request for addresses for the second notification because IRS concluded that, since the data had not been compromised, there was no longer any potential impact on tax administration and thus the address information could not be disclosed a second time.

To carry out the notification, VA obtained the addresses it needed from a commercial information reseller [7].

Other agencies also faced challenges in identifying addresses for all individuals affected by data breaches. For example:

- Although Education identified addresses for most of the individuals affected by its data breach, it was not able to contact all of them. Specifically, Education's contractor was unable to identify addresses for 60 of the 13,756 affected individuals. Of the letters it sent to the other 13,696 affected individuals, 619 were returned as undeliverable, and the contractor then identified 560 alternative addresses from parents of survey participants, school records, or public database searches and mailed the letters again with the updated address information to those addresses. This left 119 affected individuals that the department was unable to contact through these means.
- Faced with the challenge of attempting to identify all affected individuals and their addresses, Agriculture decided instead to mail notification letters to all individuals included on their Tobacco Transition Payment Program mailing list. While this approach likely resulted in contact with most affected individuals, it did not provide a guarantee that all affected individuals had been reached.
- Likewise, Navy took broad action to notify affected persons of their data breach rather than attempt to identify specific affected individuals and their addresses. Navy issued an e-mail to notify all current active and reserve Marines, published a notification in a Marine quarterly newsletter issued to retired Marines, and posted two news announcements (Washington DateLine on 4/4/06 and Marine Corps Times on 4/10/06).

To improve federal agencies' ability to obtain contact information to respond to a data breach, the Identity Theft Task Force proposed directing federal agencies to publish a "routine use" for their systems of records under the Privacy Act [8] that would allow for the disclosure of information such as addresses to assist in the response to a breach of federal data.

If the disclosure of contact information in the event of data breaches is specified as a routine use, a major obstacle would be removed from other agencies providing addresses or other contact information to affected agencies.

OMB has drafted guidance that incorporates the task force's recommendation, which it plans to issue when the task force publishes its final report.

Credit Monitoring

Determining when to offer credit monitoring to affected individuals requires risk-based management decisions.

VA initially decided to provide affected individuals with credit monitoring for one year. The department estimated that this would cost about $160 million. Despite the substantial cost, VA officials believed this service was an important element in protecting the personal information of veterans and their beneficiaries.

Due to the substantial anticipated cost, VA initially requested a supplemental appropriation of $131.5 million in fiscal year 2006. However, VA subsequently decided not to offer credit monitoring services after the stolen equipment was recovered and it was determined that there was little risk of misuse.

In deciding when to provide credit monitoring services, other agencies we reviewed primarily considered two key factors— the cost of the service and the risk of identity theft. Because of the high anticipated cost, these agencies decided not to offer credit monitoring services or to limit the availability of such services.

- For example, after considering credit monitoring services, Transportation Inspector General officials stated that their office could not afford the estimated $500,000 per month cost.
- Contractors representing Education and HHS provided credit monitoring services only to those individuals who contacted them and specifically requested the service. The notification letters sent to the affected individuals did not mention that the service was available.

Other types of monitoring have been used in place of credit monitoring. For example, commercial data breach analysis services are available to analyze whether a particular data loss can be linked to reported cases of identify theft.

According to the Identity Theft Task Force, data breach analysis can assist an agency in determining whether the particular incident is the source of identity theft, or whether reported cases of identity theft are due to other causes. VA and Transportation both used data breach analysis to help monitor whether there was evidence of identity theft as a result of their data breaches.

The result of variations in approaches to credit monitoring and data breach monitoring on the part of federal agencies is that individuals who are exposed to the risk of identity theft may receive inconsistent protection depending on the varying decisions made by the agencies that suffered the data breaches.

The Identity Theft Task Force has noted that agencies may wish to consider offering credit monitoring services and has advised that they consider the seriousness of the risk of identity theft in doing so.

However, the task force did not develop specific guidance for making such risk-based determinations. Such guidance would characterize the risk levels of typical categories of breach incidents and recommend the type of privacy protection services that would be most appropriate for each category.

OMB has directed that agencies choosing to offer credit monitoring services use blanket purchase agreements managed by GSA. However, it also has not developed guidance for agencies on making risk-based determinations on when to offer credit monitoring or when to contract for data breach monitoring.

As seen in the varying decisions that federal agencies have made in how and when to offer credit monitoring, affected individuals may not always receive a consistent level of support from the federal government when their personal information is compromised. As a result, some may be more vulnerable to the adverse effects of identity theft than others. Until guidance is available to promote consistent decision-making by federal agencies, protections offered to affected individuals are likely to remain inconsistent.

Interaction with the Public

Interaction with the public requires careful coordination and can be resource-intensive. VA invested substantially in facilities to help address follow-on inquiries and provide information to support affected individuals.

- With the support of the General Services Administration (GSA), VA established a call center with the capacity to handle up to 260,000 calls a day. VA reprogrammed about $25 million to pay for this center. (The volume of calls received was less than VA expected; according to a GSA official, the call center received a total of about 250,000 calls.)
- VA developed a citizen telephone response plan and assigned "response approvers" to work with call center personnel who were interacting with the public.
- VA also developed an expedited approval process for updates to information regarding the data breach to ensure that complete and consistent information was made available to the public.

Other agencies have taken a variety of actions to establish call centers to interact with the public. For example:

- The contractor for Education set up a call center and logged each call, e-mail, or letter received from an affected individual. Through November 28, 2006, the center had logged 235 entries.

- Transportation established a hotline for affected individuals to contact if they suspected fraud. The hotline was staffed 24 hours a day, seven days a week.
- The contractor for HHS set up several call centers. From July 27 through July 31, 2006, a total of 1,406 individuals had contacted these call centers.

The ID Theft Task Force addressed the use of call center support in its September 2006 recommendations, which were subsequently promulgated by OMB. Specifically, the task force recommended that agencies

- Consider implementing an announcement strategy in preparing for follow-on inquiries about an incident. Such a strategy could include public statements and Web site postings.
- Prepare for follow-on inquiries from affected individuals by establishing call centers staffed with individuals prepared to answer the most frequently asked questions and by alerting other entities such as credit reporting agencies.

Internal Training and Awareness

Internal training and awareness are critical to timely breach response, including notification.

The slow response to the May 2006 VA incident highlighted the need for personnel to be more aware of the agency's privacy and security procedures, including incident response and reporting procedures.

Effective training and awareness of agency privacy and security practices are essential for ensuring that staff are qualified to effectively carry out agency policy. Because a prompt response is critical, agency personnel must be prepared in advance with an understanding of their roles and responsibilities in responding to a data breach.

Federal guidance requires agencies to train staff at least annually on their privacy and security responsibilities before permitting access to information and information systems.

Recognizing the importance of privacy training and awareness, VA took steps to reinforce its training of staff and contractors.

For example,

- On May 26, 2006, VA has issued a directive to all of its leadership to reinforce, in each one of the VA managers, supervisors, or team leader, his or her duties and full responsibilities in the protecting of sensitive and confidential information.
- VA directed all employees and contractors to complete its annual Cyber Security Awareness Training and Privacy Awareness Training by June 30, 2006. This training was designed to make VA employees aware of their responsibilities to protect sensitive information.
- VA required all employees and contractors to sign a statement of commitment and understanding subsequent to completion of the security and privacy training to confirm their understanding of the training and their commitment to protecting sensitive and confidential VA data.
- During Security Awareness Week in June 2006, managers throughout VA were tasked with reviewing information security and reinforcing privacy obligations and responsibilities with their staff.
- Privacy officers were tasked with ensuring that new employees complete the agency's privacy awareness training within 30 days. They were also tasked with identifying staff who use PII and observing their adherence to privacy protection procedures.

Other agencies we reviewed have also taken steps to ensure that their staff are effectively trained and aware of their privacy procedures.

For example:

- Transportation launched a course to raise awareness of the proper techniques for handling and protecting personal information. The department required all employees to take this training by August 30, 2006.
- Navy took steps to have its personnel sensitized to privacy by requiring "stand down" Privacy Act training, issuing training aids, and posting new policy guidance on the department's Web site.

In its May 2006 guidance, OMB directed agencies to remind their employees of their responsibilities in safeguarding PII as well as the rules for acquiring and using it and the penalties for violating those rules.

Contractor Responsibilities

Contractor responsibilities for data breaches should be clearly defined.

While the VA data breach did not involve contractors, the issue of contractor responsibilities has figured prominently in three other recent incidents (at Agriculture, Education, and HHS).

Under the Privacy Act, a contractor operating a system of records on behalf of a federal agency is responsible for complying with the act. However, as already discussed, existing laws (including the Privacy Act) generally do not specifically address agency or contractor responses to data breaches. Contractor obligations for taking steps such as notifying affected individuals or providing credit monitoring may be unclear unless specified in the contract.

- Notifications were issued to affected individuals for each of the three data breaches involving contractors. In two of the three incidents, the contractor issued the notification.
- Two of the three contractors established call centers and provided credit monitoring services on request.

In response to the uncertainty regarding contractor responsibilities, officials from VA and HHS suggested that the Federal Acquisition Regulation address breach response requirements.

VA is in the process of establishing a VA-wide policy that ensures contractor personnel are held to the same standards as VA employees.

HHS officials said they were in the process of developing guidance requiring contractors to adhere to the department's privacy policies and for new contracts to include requirements for contractors to follow agency privacy policies.

Identity Theft Task Force noted, when a data security breach involves a federal contractor, responsibility for complying notification procedures should be established with contractor, partner prior to entering business relationship.

OMB has drafted guidance that incorporates the task force's recommendation, which it plans to issue when the task force publishes its final report.

CONCLUSIONS

VA's data breach of May 2006 and other recent federal data breaches provide valuable lessons learned for agencies about responding to such incidents. Key government officials need to be informed promptly, and a designated group of agency officials must be ready to make prompt decisions about notification, which can be challenging if address information is not readily available. Careful planning is needed to be able to interact effectively with the public, training and awareness are critical, and contractor roles and responsibilities must be defined.

To its credit, OMB responded to the VA data breach by issuing guidance and forwarding recommendations by the ID Theft Task Force that largely address these lessons. However, the issue of how to make risk-based determinations on when to offer credit monitoring and when to contract for an alternative form of monitoring, such as data breach monitoring, has not been addressed in guidance. Without such guidance, agencies are likely to continue to make inconsistent decisions about what protections to offer affected individuals.

AGENCY COMMENTS

An OMB Policy Analyst in the Information Policy and Technology Branch provided an e-mail message stating that OMB concurred with our recommendation. OMB noted that while it is important that individuals receive consistent responses and levels of support from federal agencies, the same response or type of support will not be appropriate in every situation. We agree that appropriate responses must be tailored to address the circumstances of the breach and believe additional guidance from OMB can facilitate consistent agency decision making about such responses.

In oral comments on a draft of this briefing, VA officials, including the VA/GAO Liaison, Office of Congressional and Legislative Affairs, agreed with our results. VA also provided technical comments, which we have incorporated into the briefing as appropriate.

RECOMMENDATION

We recommend that the Director of OMB develop guidance for federal agencies on conducting risk analyses to determine when to offer credit monitoring and when to contract for an alternative form of monitoring, such as data breach monitoring, to assist individuals at risk of identity theft as a result of a federal data breach.

ATTACHMENT I: SUMMARY OF DATA BREACHES AT FIVE AGENCIES

Agriculture (USDA)

Date: January 19, 2006

Summary of incident:

- A Freedom of Information Act (FOIA) contractor for the Farm Services Agency inadvertently released informational CDs that contained Social Security numbers and tax identification data on tobacco producers/contract holders under the agency's Tobacco Transition Payment Program.
- On January 27, 2006, the contractor reviewed the data files that had been released and determined that they contained PII. The contractor contacted all nine individuals who had received the data and all agreed to return the unauthorized CDs and destroy any derived or copied information.

Number of affected individuals: approximately 350,000

Actions taken:

- The contractor reported that it had contacted a FOIA official on January 27, 2006, to inform him of the inadvertent release of PII to nine external requesters. The contractor stated that the FOIA official instructed the contractor to continue to work to recover the data and not to notify USDA management of the data breach.
- On February 9, 2006, the contractor met with the USDA's chief Freedom of Information Act officer, and he then informed the officer of the data breach.
- Between February 9 and 16, 2006, USDA officials assessed the nature and magnitude of the data breach to determine how to best respond.
- On February 17, 2006, the department mailed notices to all individuals on its Tobacco Transition Payment Program mailing list.

Department of Defense (Navy)

Date: March 14, 2006

Summary of incident:

- The Marine Corps reported the loss of a thumb drive containing PII— names, Social Security numbers, and other information— for enlisted Marines serving on active duty from the years, 2001 through 2005. The information was being used for a research project on retention of service personnel.
- Navy officials considered the risk from the breach to be greatly diminished since the thumb drive was lost on a government installation and the drive's data were readable only through software that was password protected and "considered in limited distribution."
- Navy reported that there has been no evidence that the information was compromised.

Number of affected individuals: 207,570

Actions taken:

- Navy officials contacted the three credit bureaus and they agreed to offer free fraud alert on credit files of the affected individuals for up to 24 months.
- The Marine Corps took a number of actions to notify affected individuals, including:
    - issuing an electronic notice to all current active and reserve Marines on March 24, 2006;
    - publishing notification in the April-June issue of a quarterly newsletter (Semper Fidelis) issued to retired Marines; and
    - publishing news announcements in the Washington DateLine (April 4, 2006) and Marine Corps Times (April 10, 2006).
- The notifications, among other things, encouraged affected individuals to visit the Federal Trade Commission's Web site for identity theft guidance, informed them of free fraud alert services, and suggested that they review their credit reports for suspicious activities.

Education

Date: June 19, 2006

Summary of incident: A contractor for the department's National Center for Education Statistics sent a compact disc (CD) containing PII, including names and Social Security numbers via Federal Express to department officials for file-matching to the National Student Loan Data System. The CD, which was password protected, was lost in transit.

Number of affected individuals: 13,756

Actions taken:

- On Friday, June 23, 2006, Education officials contacted the contractor because they had not yet received the CD. Both the contractor and Education contacted Fed Ex on that day. Fed Ex had a record of the CD being picked up but no further information.
- On Monday, June 26th, the contractor called Fed Ex to let them know that the package contained a CD and to determine whether it had been located. The contractor continued to monitor the status of the lost package.
- On July 12, 2006, the contractor filed an incident report with its Institutional Review Board (IRB). The commissioner of the department's National Center for Education Statistics was made aware of the data loss on the same day that the contractor filed the incident report with its IRB. The commissioner decided that transfer of PII should cease and that a secure server should be established for the transfer of PII. Such a secure server went into use on August 1, 2006, and the restriction on data transfer was lifted.
- The IRB monitored the efforts, ultimately unsuccessful, to recover the lost CD. On August 15, 2006, even though the search was not finally completed, the IRB directed the contractor to draft a notification letter. At its meeting on September 19, 2006, the IRB approved the draft letter for mailing.
- On October 2, 2006, notification letters were mailed to individuals for whom address information was available (13,696 of the 13,756 affected individuals). The notice included an attached list of recommended actions in the event the affected individual noticed any suspicious activities concerning their financial accounts.

- Of the 13,696 letters that were mailed, 619 had been returned as undeliverable by November 27, 2006. Of these, the department was able to identify 560 alternative addresses and the contractor mailed the 560 letters again.

Health and Human Services (HHS)

Date: June 22, 2006

Summary of incident: An HHS Centers for Medicare & Medicaid Services (CMS) contractor reported the theft of a contractor employee's laptop computer from his office. The computer contained PII including names, telephone numbers, medical record numbers, and dates of birth.

Number of affected individuals: 49,572 Medicare beneficiaries

Actions taken:

- On June 22, 2006, the CMS contractor notified regional security of the incident and filed a police report.
- On July 10, 2006, the contractor notified CMS of the incident.
- Between July 26 and July 31, 2006, a CMS-approved notification letter was sent to the affected individuals. The letter included the CMS contractor's Notice of Privacy Practices and also provided guidance on placing fraud alerts on credit accounts by contacting the appropriate credit agencies. The CMS contractor set up call centers.

From July 27 through July 31, 2006, a total of 1,406 members contacted the call centers. Although not offered in the notification letter, the CMS contractor offered one-year free credit monitoring to those who made telephone inquiries. A total of 141 members accepted the credit monitoring service

Transportation

Date: July 27, 2006

Summary of incident: A laptop computer containing PII including names, addresses, Social Security numbers, and dates of birth on Florida drivers and others was stolen from a parked car.

Number of affected individuals: Approximately 133,000 persons: 81,160 persons issued commercial drivers licenses in Miami-Dade County; 42,800 persons in Florida with Federal Aviation Administration pilot certificates; and 9,000 persons with Florida driver's licenses.

Actions taken:

- On August 5, 2006, after learning that the stolen laptop contained PII, the acting Inspector General (IG) immediately ordered an investigation to recover the stolen laptop. The Office of Inspector General (OIG) also established a $10,000 reward for information leading to the recovery of the laptop and/or arrest of the perpetrator.
- On August 9, 2006, the acting IG posted open letters on the OIG Web site to the Florida governor, Florida Congressional delegation and Chairs and Ranking Members of Department of Transportation Oversight Committees and Subcommittees discussing the incident.
- On August 14, 2006, the OIG began mailing letters to affected individuals, notifying them of the incident and providing information on actions that they could take to prevent identify theft.
- The OIG established a hotline for affected individuals to contact if they suspected fraud. The hotline was staffed 24 hours a day, seven days a week.
- The OIG also awarded a contract to a risk management company (ID Analytics, Inc.) to provide data breach analysis services to determine whether any PII of the affected individuals was being exploited. The company is to provide the IG with quarterly reports over a two-year period.

Appendix II: Comments from the Office of Management and Budget

EXECUTIVE OFFICE OF THE PRESIDENT
OFFICE OF MANAGEMENT AND BUDGET
WASHINGTON, D.C. 20503

April 23, 2007

Ms. Linda D. Koontz
Director
Information Management Issues
Government Accountability Office
441 G Street, SW
Washington, DC 20548

Dear Ms. Koontz:

Thank you for the opportunity to comment on the draft Government Accountability Office (GAO) report, "Lessons Learned about Data Breach Notification" (code 310875), addressing the privacy implications resulting from data breaches.

In this report, GAO recommends that the Office of Management and Budget (OMB) develop guidance on conducting risk analyses to determine when to offer credit monitoring and when to contract for an alternative form of monitoring, such as data breach monitoring, to assist individuals at risk of identity theft as a result of a federal data breach. The report also includes a definition for the term "personally identifiable information."

OMB concurs with GAO's recommendation. Consistent responses to data breaches can be achieved through consistent application of a risk-based analysis of the relevant circumstances. Providing further guidance and a risk-based framework will enable federal agencies to determine the appropriate response which is focused on treating citizens fairly, founded on the type of information lost, and commensurate with the level of risk of identity theft.

It is important for individuals affected when their personal information, including personally identifiable information, has been compromised to receive consistent responses and levels of support from the federal agency involved in the breach; however, it is important to note the same particular response and/or type of support will not be appropriate, or even necessary, for every situation.

For example, a few of the many factors considered when deciding whether to provide services following a breach, such as credit monitoring or data breach monitoring services, include the type of information lost, cost of the service being considered, risk of identity theft for the affected individuals, and likelihood the service will reduce this risk. These and other factors differ in each situation. As such, the appropriate response must be tailored to address each particular set of circumstances.

EXECUTIVE OFFICE OF THE PRESIDENT
OFFICE OF MANAGEMENT AND BUDGET
WASHINGTON, D.C. 20503

Additionally, the report includes a definition for the term "personally identifiable information" (PII) which is the same as one included in the draft policy memorandum, "Safeguarding Against and Responding to the Breach of Personally Identifiable Information," OMB recently circulated for interagency comment. OMB notes the definition of this term will likely be revised in the final policy based on comments received. As such, OMB suggests the language of the definition for PII should be clarified in the report as tentative language.

Thank you for the opportunity to review and comment on the draft report on this important issue. Protection of personal information, both generally and our response to data breaches, is vital to ensuring the trust of the American people in the federal government.

Sincerely,

Karen Evans
Administrator
Office of E-Government and
Information Technology
Office of Management and Budget

APPENDIX III: COMMENTS FROM THE DEPARTMENT OF VETERANS AFFAIRS

THE SECRETARY OF VETERANS AFFAIRS
WASHINGTON

April 19, 2007

Ms. Linda D. Koontz
Director
Information Management Issues
U. S. Government Accountability Office
441 G Street, NW
Washington, DC 20548

Dear Ms. Koontz:

The Department of Veterans Affairs (VA) has reviewed the Government Accountability Office's (GAO) draft report: ***Privacy: Lessons Learned about Data Breach Notification*** (GAO-07-657) and agrees with its findings. VA also agrees with GAO's recommendations that the Director of the Office of Management and Budget develop guidance for Federal agencies on conducting risk analyses to determine when to offer credit monitoring and when to contract for an alternative form of monitoring, such as data breach monitoring, to assist individuals at risk of identity theft as a result of a Federal data breach.

The Department is finalizing its new data breach regulation that implements the Veterans Benefits, Health Care, and Information Technology Act of 2006, Public Law 109-461. The new Part 75 will follow the statutory framework of 38 U.S.C. 5724. Under this authority, upon the discovery of a data breach, VA must ensure that a non-VA entity or VA's Office of Inspector General conducts an independent risk analysis to determine the level of risk associated with the data breach for the potential misuse of any sensitive personal information. If the Secretary determines, based on the findings of the risk analysis, that a reasonable risk exists for the potential misuse of sensitive personal information, the statute requires that the Secretary provide notification to the affected individuals and may provide one or more of the following: credit monitoring, fraud resolution services, and identity theft insurance.

Sincerely yours,

R. James Nicholson

References

[1] "Personally identifiable information" refers to any information about an individual maintained by an agency, including any information that can be used to distinguish or trace an individual's identity, such as their name, Social Security Number, date and place of birth, mother's maiden name, biometric records, etc., and any other personal information which is linked or linkable to an individual.

[2] The recently enacted Department of Veterans Affairs Information Security Enhancement Act of 2006, Pub. L. No. 109-461 requires VA to issue interim regulations for the provision of certain services, including notification, in the event a data breach of veterans' sensitive personal information results in a determination that a reasonable risk exists for the potential misuse of the information.

[3] GAO, *Privacy: Preventing and Responding to Improper Disclosures of Personal Information, GAO-06-833T* (Washington, D.C.: June 8, 2006).

[4] Title IX of this statute contains the Department of Veterans Affairs Information Security Enhancement Act of 2006 referred to on page 1.

Appendixes

[1] Personally Identifiable Information refers to any information about an individual maintained by an agency, including any information that can be used to distinguish or trace an individual's identity, such as their name, social security number, date and place of birth, mother's maiden name, biometric records, etc., and any other personal information which is linked or linkable to an individual.

[2] For detailed information about the facts and circumstances surrounding the VA data breach incident, see Department of Veterans Affairs Office of Inspector General, *Review of Issues Related to the Loss of VA Information Involving the Identity of Millions of Veterans,* Report No. 06-02238-163 (Washington, D.C.: July 11, 2006).

[3] The recently enacted Department of Veterans Affairs Information Security Enhancement Act of 2006, Pub. L. No. 109-461, requires VA to issue interim regulations for the provision of certain services, including notification, in the event a data breach of veterans' sensitive personal information results in a determination that a reasonable risk exists for the potential misuse of the information.

[4] GAO, *Privacy: Preventing and Responding to Improper Disclosures of Personal Information*, GAO-06-833T (Washington, D.C.: June 8, 2006).

[5] Committee on Government Reform, Staff Report: Agency Data Breaches Since January 1, 2003 (Washington, D.C.; Oct. 13, 2006).

[6] OMB, Reporting Incidents Involving Personally Identifiable Information and Incorporating the Cost for Security in Agency Information Technology Investments, *Memorandum M-06-19* (Washington, D.C.; July 12, 2006).

[7] Information resellers are companies that amass and sell data, including personal data, from many sources.

[8] A "system of records" is defined by the Privacy Act as a group of records from which information is retrieved by personal identifier. The act requires that agencies issue public notices that define, among other things, "routine uses" of the information in these systems—uses that are compatible with the purpose for which the information was originally collected.

Chapter 2

USE OF DATA FROM INFORMATION RESELLERS*

WHAT GAO FOUND

In fiscal year 2005, the Departments of Justice, Homeland Security, and State and the Social Security Administration reported that they used personal information obtained from resellers for a variety of purposes, including performing criminal investigations, locating witnesses and fugitives, researching assets held by individuals of interest, and detecting prescription drug fraud. The agencies planned spending approximately $30 million on contractual arrangements with resellers that enabled the acquisition and use of such information. About 91 percent of the planned fiscal year 2005 spending was for law enforcement (69 percent) or counterterrorism (22 percent).

Agency practices for handling personal information acquired from information resellers did not always fully reflect the Fair Information Practices. That is, for some of these principles, agency practices were uneven. For example, although agencies issued public notices when they systematically collected personal information, these notices did not always notify the public that information resellers were among the sources to be used. This practice is not consistent with the principle that individuals should be informed about privacy policies and the collection of information. Contributing to the uneven application of the Fair Information Practices are ambiguities in guidance from the Office of Management and Budget (OMB) regarding the applicability of privacy

* Excerpted from GAO Report 08-543T, dated March 11, 2008.

requirements to federal agency uses of reseller information. In addition, agencies generally lacked policies that specifically address these uses.

GAO made recommendations to OMB to revise privacy guidance and to the four agencies to develop specific policies for the use of personal information from resellers. The five agencies generally agreed with the report and described actions initiated to address the recommendations. Since GAO issued its report, agencies have taken steps to address the recommendations. For example, the Department of Homeland Security Privacy Office incorporated specific questions in its May 2007 Privacy Impact Assessment guidance concerning use of commercial data. In addition, the Department of Justice took steps to update its public notices to specify their use of data from information resellers. OMB, however, has not implemented GAO's recommendation to clarify guidance on use of commercial data.

The Federal Agency Data Protection Act was introduced on December 18, 2007. The legislation, among other things would require that agencies (1) conduct privacy impact assessments for their uses of commercial data, and (2) promulgate regulations concerning the use of commercial data brokers. GAO considers these requirements to be consistent with the results and the recommendations made to the agencies in its 2006 report.

Why GAO Did This Study

Federal agencies collect and use personal information for various purposes from information resellers—companies that amass and sell data from many sources. GAO was asked to testify on its April 2006 report on agency use of reseller data. For that report, GAO was asked to determine how the Departments of Justice, Homeland Security, and State and the Social Security Administration used personal data from resellers and to review the extent to which agencies' policies and practices for handling this information reflected the Fair Information Practices, a set of widely accepted principles for protecting the privacy and security of personal data. GAO was also asked to provide an update on the implementation status of its recommendations and to comment on provisions of the proposed Federal Agency Data Protection Act. In preparing this testimony, GAO relied primarily on its April 2006 report.

WHAT GAO RECOMMENDS

GAO is not making additional recommendations at this time. However, in its 2006 report, GAO made recommendations to the Office of Management and Budget and the four agencies to address agency use of personal information from commercial sources. Agency officials generally agreed with the content of the report. Since then, 2 of the 4 agencies have taken steps to address its recommendations; however, OMB has not issued clarified guidance.

ABBREVIATIONS

DEA	Drug Enforcement Administration
DHS	Department of Homeland Security
DOJ	Department of Justice
FBI	Federal Bureau of Investigation
OECD	Organization for Economic Cooperation and Development
OIG	Office of the Inspector General
OMB	Office of Management and Budget
PIA	privacy impact assessments
SSA	Social Security Administration
State	Department of State
TSA	Transportation Security Administration

Mr. Chairman and Members of the Subcommittee:

I appreciate the opportunity to discuss critical issues surrounding the federal government's purchase of personal information [1] from businesses known as information resellers. As you are aware, the ease and speed with which people's personal information can be collected by information resellers from a wide variety of sources and made available to government and other customers has accelerated with technological advances. In recent years, security breaches at large information resellers such as ChoicePoint and LexisNexis have raised questions about how resellers and their federal customers handle people's personal information—and especially whether their practices are fully consistent with widely accepted practices for protecting the privacy and security of personal information.

Federal agency use of personal information is governed primarily by the E-Government Act of 2002 and the Privacy Act of 1974. The E- Government Act of 2002 strives to enhance protection for personal information in government information systems by requiring that agencies conduct privacy impact assessments (PIA). A PIA is an analysis of how personal information is collected, stored, shared, and managed in a federal system. The Privacy Act of 1974 [2] requires that the use of personal information be limited to predefined purposes and involve only information germane to those purposes. The provisions of the Privacy Act, in turn, are largely based on a set of principles for protecting the privacy and security of personal information, known as the Fair Information Practices, which were first proposed in 1973 by a U.S. government advisory committee [3]. These principles, now widely accepted, include:

1. collection limitation,
2. data quality,
3. purpose specification,
4. use limitation,
5. security safeguards,
6. openness,
7. individual participation, and
8. accountability [4]

These principles, with some variation, are used by organizations to address privacy considerations in their business practices and are also the basis of privacy laws and related policies in many countries, including the United States, Germany, Sweden, Australia, and New Zealand, as well as the European Union.

As agreed, my testimony today will be based primarily on the agency information contained in a report we issued in April 2006 [5]. For that report, we analyzed fiscal year 2005 contracts and other vehicles for the acquisition of personal information from information resellers by the Departments of Justice (DOJ), Homeland Security (DHS), and State (State) and the Social Security Administration (SSA). We compared relevant agency guidelines and management policies and procedures to the Fair Information Practices. We also updated the implementation status of recommendations contained in our 2006 report and analyzed provisions of the proposed Federal Agency Data Protection Act [6]. Our work was performed in accordance with generally accepted government auditing standards. Those standards require that we plan and perform the audit to obtain sufficient, appropriate evidence to provide a reasonable basis for our findings and conclusions based on our audit objectives. We believe that the evidence obtained provides a reasonable basis for our findings and conclusions based on our audit objectives.

Today, after a brief summary of the laws that govern agency use of personal information, I will summarize the information contained in our 2006 report on how the selected agencies used the personal information that they purchased from resellers and the extent to which the agencies had policies and practices that reflected the Fair Information Practices. I will also provide an update on steps taken by the agencies to address the recommendations contained in our 2006 report. Finally, I will comment on specific privacy related provisions of the proposed Federal Agency Data Protection Act.

RESULTS IN BRIEF

In fiscal year 2005, DOJ, DHS, State, and SSA reported that they planned to spend a combined total of approximately $30 million [7] to purchase personal information from resellers. The vast majority— approximately 91 percent—of the planned spending was for purposes of law enforcement (69 percent) or counterterrorism (22 percent). For example, components of DOJ (the largest user of resellers) used the information for criminal investigations, locating witnesses and fugitives, researching assets held by individuals of interest, and detecting fraud in prescription drug transactions. DHS acquired personal information to aid its immigration fraud detection and border screening programs. SSA and State purchased personal information from information resellers to detect and investigate fraud, verify identities, and determine benefits eligibility.

Agency practices for handling personal information acquired from information resellers reflected four of eight principles established by the Fair Information Practices. Agency practices generally reflected the collection limitation, data quality, use limitation, and security safeguards principles. For example, law enforcement agencies (including the Federal Bureau of Investigation and the U.S. Secret Service) generally reported that they corroborate information obtained from resellers to ensure that it is accurate when it is used as part of an investigation, reflecting the data quality principle that data should be accurate, current, and complete, as needed for the defined purpose. However, agencies did not always have practices for handling reseller information to fully address the purpose specification, individual participation, openness, and accountability principles. For example:

- Although agencies notified the public through Federal Register notices and published PIAs that they collected personal information from various sources, they did not always indicate specifically that information resellers were among those sources.
- Some agencies lacked robust audit mechanisms to ensure that use of personal information from information resellers was for permissible purposes, reflecting an uneven application of the accountability principle.

Contributing to agencies' uneven application of the Fair Information Practices were ambiguities in guidance from the Office of Management and Budget (OMB) on how privacy requirements apply to federal agency uses of reseller information. In addition, agencies generally lacked policies that specifically address these uses.

We made recommendations to OMB to revise privacy guidance and to the four agencies to develop specific policies for the use of personal information from resellers. The agencies generally agreed with the report and described actions initiated to address our recommendations. Since we issued our report, two of the four agencies have taken steps to address our recommendations. For example, the DHS Privacy Office incorporated specific questions in its May 2007 PIA guidance concerning use of commercial data. In addition, DOJ took steps to ensure that their system-of-records notices specifically reference their use of data from information resellers. OMB, however, has not implemented our recommendation to clarify guidance on use of commercial data.

On December 18, 2007, the Federal Agency Data Protection Act was introduced. This legislation, among other things would require that agencies (1) conduct PIAs for their uses of commercial data and (2) promulgate regulations concerning the use of commercial data brokers. We believe that these requirements are consistent with the results of our 2006 report and the recommendations we made to the agencies.

BACKGROUND

Before advanced computerized techniques, obtaining people's personal information usually required visiting courthouses or other government facilities to inspect paper-based public records, and information contained in product registrations and other business records was not generally available at all. Automation of the collection and aggregation of multiple-source data, combined with the ease and speed of its retrieval, have dramatically reduced the time and effort needed to obtain such information. Information resellers provide services based on these technological advances.

We use the term "information resellers" to refer to businesses that vary in many ways but have in common collecting and aggregating personal information from multiple sources and making it available to their customers. These businesses do not all focus exclusively on aggregating and reselling personal information. For example, Dun & Bradstreet primarily provides information on commercial enterprises for the purpose of contributing to decision making regarding those enterprises. In doing so, it may supply personal information about individuals associated with those commercial enterprises.

To a certain extent, the activities of information resellers may also overlap with the functions of consumer reporting agencies, also known as credit bureaus—entities that collect and sell information about individuals' creditworthiness, among other things.

To the extent that information resellers perform the functions of consumer reporting agencies, they are subject to legislation specifically addressing that industry, particularly the Fair Credit Reporting Act.

Information resellers have now amassed extensive amounts of personal information about large numbers of Americans. They supply it to customers in both government and the private sector, typically via a centralized online resource. Generally, three types of information are collected:

- Public records such as birth and death records, property records, motor vehicle and voter registrations, criminal records, and civil case files.
- Publicly available information not found in public records but nevertheless publicly available through other sources, such as telephone directories, business directories, classified ads or magazines, Internet sites, and other sources accessible by the general public.
- Nonpublic information derived from proprietary or nonpublic sources, such as credit header data, [8] product warranty registrations, and other application information provided to private businesses directly by consumers.

Figure 1 illustrates how these types of information are collected and aggregated into reports that are ultimately accessed by customers, including government agencies.

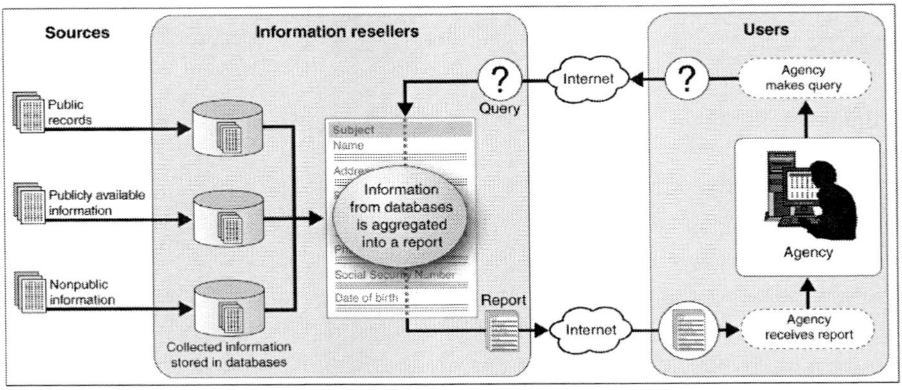

Source: GAO analysis of information reseller and agency-provided data.

Figure 1. Typical Information Flow through Resellers to Government Customers.

Federal Laws and Guidance Govern Use of Personal Information in Federal Agencies

No single federal law governs all use or disclosure of personal information. The major requirements for the protection of personal privacy by federal agencies come from the Privacy Act of 1974 and the privacy provisions of the E-Government Act of 2002.

Federal use of personal information is governed primarily by the Privacy Act of 1974, [9] which places limitations on agencies' collection, disclosure, and use of personal information maintained in systems of records. The act describes a "record" as any item, collection, or grouping of information about an individual that is maintained by an agency and contains his or her name or another personal identifier. It also defines "system of records" as a group of records under the control of any agency from which information is retrieved by the name of the individual or by an individual identifier. The Privacy Act requires that when agencies establish or make changes to a system of records, they must notify the public by placing a notice in the Federal Register identifying, among other things, the type of data collected, the types of individuals about whom the information is collected, the routine uses [10] of the data, and procedures that individuals can use to review and correct their personal information. Additional provisions of the Privacy Act are discussed in the 2006 report.

The E-Government Act of 2002 requires that agencies conduct PIAs. A PIA is an analysis of how personal information is collected, stored, shared, and managed in a federal system. Under the E- Government Act and related OMB guidance, agencies must conduct.

PIAs (1) before developing or procuring information technology that collects, maintains, or disseminates information that is in a personally identifiable form; (2) before initiating any new data collections involving personal information that will be collected, maintained, or disseminated using information technology if the same questions are asked of 10 or more people; or (3) when a system change creates new privacy risks, for example, by changing the way in which personal information is being used.

OMB is tasked with providing guidance to agencies on how to implement the provisions of the Privacy Act and the E-Government Act and has done so, beginning with guidance on the Privacy Act, issued in 1975 [11] OMB's guidance on implementing the privacy provisions of the E-Government Act of 2002 identifies circumstances under which agencies must conduct PIAs and explains how to conduct them.

The PIA mandate in the E-Government Act of 2002 provided a mechanism by which agencies can consider privacy in the earliest stages of system development. PIAs can be an important tool to help agencies to address openness and purpose specification principles early in the process of developing new information systems. To the extent that PIAs are made publicly available, [12] they provide explanations to the public about such things as the information that will be collected, why it is being collected, how it is to be used, and how the system and data will be maintained and protected.

The Fair Information Practices Are Widely Agreed to Be Key Principles for Privacy Protection

The Privacy Act of 1974 is largely based on a set of internationally recognized principles for protecting the privacy and security of personal information known as the Fair Information Practices. A U.S. government advisory committee first proposed the practices in 1973 to address what it termed a poor level of protection afforded to privacy under contemporary law [13].

The Organization for Economic Cooperation and Development (OECD) [14] developed a revised version of the Fair Information Practices in 1980. This version of the principles was reaffirmed by OECD ministers in a 1998 declaration and further endorsed in a 2006 OECD report [15]. The Fair Information Practices, have, with some variation, formed the basis of privacy laws and related policies in many countries, including the United States, Germany, Sweden, Australia, and New Zealand, as well as the European Union [16].

In addition, in its 2007 report, Engaging Privacy and Information Technology in a Digital Age, the National Research Council [17] found that the principles of fair information practice for the protection of personal information are as relevant today as they were in 1973. Accordingly, the committee recommended that the Fair Information Practices should be extended as far as reasonably feasible to apply to private sector organizations that collect and use personal information. The eight principles of the OECD Fair Information Practices are shown in table 1.

Table 1. The OECD Fair Information Practices

Principle	Description
Collection limitation	The collection of personal information should be limited, should be obtained by lawful and fair means, and, where appropriate, with the knowledge or consent of the individual.
Data quality	Personal information should be relevant to the purpose for which it is collected, and should be accurate, complete, and current as needed for that purpose.
Purpose specification	The purposes for the collection of personal information should be disclosed before collection and upon any change to that purpose, and its use should be limited to those purposes and compatible purposes.
Use limitation	Personal information should not be disclosed or otherwise usedfor other than a specified purpose without consent of the individual or legal authority.

The Fair Information Practices are not precise legal requirements. Rather, they provide a framework of principles for balancing the need for privacy with other public policy interests, such as national security, law enforcement, and administrative efficiency. Ways to strike that balance vary among countries and according to the type of information under consideration.

Agencies Used Governmentwide Contracts to Obtain Personal Information from Information Resellers for a Variety of Purposes

DOJ, DHS, State, and SSA reported approximately $30 million through contracts with information resellers in fiscal year 2005 [18]. The agencies reported using personal information obtained from resellers for a variety of purposes including law enforcement, counterterrorism, fraud detection/prevention, and debt collection. In all, approximately 91 percent of agency uses of reseller data were in the categories of law enforcement (69 percent) or counterterrorism (22 percent). Figure 2 details contract values categorized by their reported use.

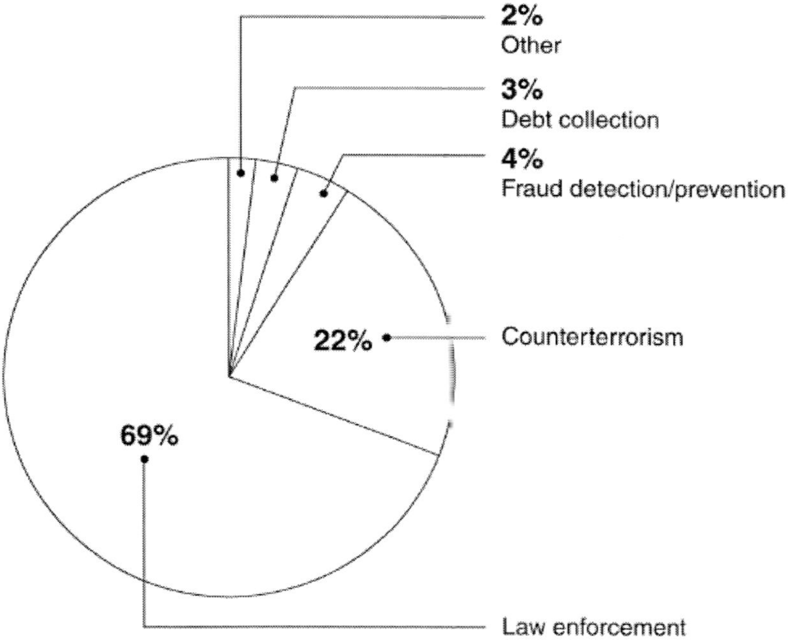

Source: GAO analysis of agency-provided data.

Figure 2. Fiscal Year 2005 Contractual Vehicles Enabling the Use of Personal Information from Information Resellers, Categorized by Reported Use.

DOJ, which accounted for about 63 percent of the funding, mostly used the data for law enforcement and counterterrorism. DHS also used reseller information primarily for law enforcement and counterterrorism. State and SSA reported acquiring personal information from information resellers for fraud prevention and detection, identity verification, and benefits eligibility determination.

DOJ and DHS Used Information Resellers Primarily for Law Enforcement and Counterterrorism

In fiscal year 2005, DOJ and its components reported approximately $19 million through contracts with a wide variety of information resellers, primarily for purposes related to law enforcement (75 percent) and counterterrorism (18 percent). The Federal Bureau of Investigation (FBI), which is DOJ's largest user of information resellers, used reseller information to, among other things, analyze intelligence and detect terrorist activities in support of ongoing investigations by law enforcement agencies and the intelligence community. In this capacity, resellers provided the FBI's Foreign Terrorist Tracking Task Force with names, addresses, telephone numbers, and other biographical and demographical information as well as legal briefs, vehicle and boat registrations, and business ownership records [19]. The Drug Enforcement Administration (DEA), the second largest DOJ user of information resellers in fiscal year 2005, obtained reseller data primarily to detect fraud in prescription drug transactions [20]. Agents used reseller data to detect irregular prescription patterns for specific drugs and trace this information to the pharmacy and prescribing doctor [21].

DHS and its components reported that they used information reseller data in fiscal year 2005 primarily for law enforcement purposes, such as developing leads on subjects in criminal investigations and detecting fraud in immigration benefit applications (part of enforcing immigration laws). DHS's largest investigative component, the U.S. Immigration and Customs Enforcement, is also its largest user of personal information from resellers. It collected data such as address and vehicle information for criminal investigations and background security checks. Another DHS component, U.S. Customs and Border Protection, conducts queries on people, businesses, property. The Federal Emergency Management Agency, an additional component, used an information reseller to detect fraud in disaster assistance applications.

DHS also reported using information resellers in its counterterrorism efforts. For example, the Transportation Security Administration (TSA), a DHS component, used data obtained from information resellers as part of a test associated with the development of its domestic passenger prescreening program, called Secure Flight [22]. TSA planned for Secure Flight to compare domestic flight reservation information submitted to TSA by aircraft operators with federal watch lists of individuals known or suspected of activities related to terrorism [23].

SSA and State Used Information Resellers Primarily for Fraud Prevention and Detection

In an effort to ensure the accuracy of Social Security benefit payments, the SSA and its components reported approximately $1.3 million in contracts with information resellers in fiscal year 2005 for purposes relating to fraud prevention (such as skiptracing), [24] confirming suspected fraud related to workers' compensation payments, obtaining information on criminal suspects for follow-up investigations, and collecting debts. For example, the Office of the Inspector General (OIG), the largest user of information reseller data at SSA, used several information resellers to assist investigative agents in detecting benefits abuse by Social Security claimants and to assist agents in locating claimants. Regional office agents may also use reseller data in investigating persons suspected of claiming disability fraudulently.

State and its components reported approximately $569,000 in contracts with information resellers for fiscal year 2005, mainly to support investigations of passport-related activities. For example, several components accessed personal information to validate familial relationships, birth and identity data, and other information submitted on immigrant and nonimmigrant visa petitions. State also used reseller data to investigate passport and visa fraud cases.

Agencies Lacked Policies on Use of Reseller Data, and Practices Do Not Consistently Reflect the Fair Information Practices

Agencies generally lacked policies that specifically addressed their use of personal information from commercial sources (although DHS Privacy Office officials reported in 2006 that they were drafting such a policy [25]), and agency practices for handling personal information acquired from information resellers did not always fully reflect the Fair Information Practices. Specifically, agency practices generally reflected four of the eight Fair Information Practices.

As table 2 shows, the collection limitation, data quality, use limitation, and security safeguards principles were generally reflected in agency practices.

Table 2. Application of Fair Information Practices to the Reported Handling of Personal Information from Data Resellers at Four Agencies

Principle	Agency application of principle	Agency practices
Collection limitation. The collection of personal information should be limited, should be obtained by lawful and fair means, and, where appropriate, with the knowledge or consent of the individual.	General	Agencies limited personal data collection to individuals under investigation or their associates.
Data quality. Personal information should be relevant to the purpose for which it is collected, and should be accurate, complete, and current as needed for that purpose.	General	Agencies corroborated information from resellers and did not take actions based exclusively on such information.
Purpose specification. The purpose for the collection of personal information should be disclosed before collection and upon any change to that purpose, and its use should be limited to that purpose and compatible purposes.	Uneven	Agency system-of-records notices did not generally reveal thatagency systems could incorporate information from data resellers. Agencies also generally did not conduct privacy impact assessments for their systems or programs that involveuse of reseller data.
Use limitation. Personal information should not be disclosed or otherwise used for other than a specified purpose without consent of the individual or legal authority.	General	Agencies generally limited their use of personal information to specific investigations (including law enforcement, counterterrorism, fraud detection, and debt collection).
Security safeguards. Personal information should be protected with reasonable security safeguards against risks such as loss or unauthorized access, destruction, use, modification, or disclosure.	General	Agencies had security safeguards such as requiring passwords to access databases, basing access rights on need to know, and logging search activities (including "cloaked logging," which prevents the vendor from monitoring search content).

Principle	Agency application of principle	Agency practices
Security safeguards. Personal information should be protected with reasonable security safeguards against risks such as loss or unauthorized access, destruction, use, modification, or disclosure.	General	Agencies had security safeguards such as requiring passwords to access databases, basing access rights on need to know, and logging search activities (including "cloaked logging," which prevents the vendor from monitoring search content).
Openness. The public should be informed about privacy policies and practices, and individuals should have ready means of learning about the use of personal information.	Uneven	See Purpose specificationabove. Agencies did not have established policies specifically addressing the use of personal information obtained from resellers.
Individual participation. Individuals should have the following rights: to know about the collection of personal information, to access that information, to request correction, and to challenge the denial of those rights.	Uneven	See Purpose specificationabove. Because agencies generallydid not disclose their collections of personal information from resellers, individuals were often unable to exercise these rights.
Accountability. Individuals controlling the collection or use of personal information should be accountable for taking steps to ensure the implementation of these principles.	Uneven	Agencies did not generally monitor usage of personal information from information resellers to hold users accountable for appropriate use; instead, they relied on users to be responsible for their behavior. For example, agencies may instruct users in their responsibilities to use personal information appropriately, have them sign statements of responsibility, and have them indicate what permissible purpose a given search fulfills.

Legend: *General* = policies or procedures to address all major aspects of a particular principle. *Uneven* = policies or procedures addressed some, but not all, aspects of a particular principle or some but not all agencies and components had policies or practices in place addressing the principle.

Note: We did not independently assess the effectiveness of agency information security programs. Our assessment of overall agency application of the Fair Information Practices was based on the policies and management practices described by the Department of State and SSA as a whole and by major components of DOJ and DHS. We did not obtain information on smaller components of DOJ and DHS.

For example, several agency components (specifically, law enforcement agencies such as the FBI and the U.S. Secret Service) reported that in practice, they generally corroborate information obtained from resellers when it is used as part of an investigation. This practice is consistent with the principle of data quality.

Agency policies and practices with regard to the other four principles were uneven. Specifically, agencies did not always have policies or practices in place to address the purpose specification, openness, and individual participation principles with respect to reseller data. The inconsistencies in applying these principles as well as the lack of specific agency policies can be attributed in part to ambiguities in OMB guidance regarding the applicability of the Privacy Act to information obtained from resellers. Further, privacy impact assessments, a valuable tool that could address important aspects of the Fair Information Practices, were often not conducted. Finally, components within each of the four agencies did not consistently hold staff accountable by monitoring usage of personal information from information resellers and ensuring that it was appropriate; thus, their application of the fourth principle, accountability, was uneven.

Agency procedures generally reflected the collection limitation, data quality, use limitation, and security safeguards principles. Regarding collection limitation, for most law-enforcement and counterterrorism purposes (which accounted for 90 percent of usage in fiscal year 2005), agencies generally limited their personal data collection in that they reported obtaining information only on specific individuals under investigation or associates of those individuals. Regarding data quality, agencies reported taking steps to mitigate the risk of inaccurate information reseller data by corroborating information obtained from resellers. Agency officials described the practice of corroborating information as a standard element of conducting investigations. Likewise, for non-lawenforcement use, such as debt collection and fraud detection and prevention, agency components reported that they mitigated potential problems with the accuracy of data provided by resellers by obtaining additional information from other sources when necessary.

As for use limitation, agency officials said their use of reseller information was limited to distinct purposes that were generally related to law enforcement or counterterrorism. Finally, while we did not assess the effectiveness of information security at any of these agencies, we found that all four had measures in place intended to safeguard the security of personal information obtained from resellers [26].

Limitations in the Applicability of the Privacy Act and Ambiguities in OMB Guidance Contributed to an Uneven Adherence to the *Purpose Specification, Openness, and Individual Participation* Principles

The purpose specification, openness, and individual participation principles stipulate that individuals should be made aware of the purpose and intended uses of the personal information being collected about them, and, if necessary, have the ability to access and correct their information. These principles are reflected in the Privacy Act requirement for agencies to publish in the Federal Register, "upon establishment or revision, a notice of the existence and character of a system of records." This notice is to include, among other things, the categories of records in the system as well as the categories of sources of records [27].

In a number of cases, agencies using reseller information did not adhere to the purpose specification or openness principles in that they did not notify the public that they were using such information and did not specify the purpose for their data collections. Agency officials said that they generally did not prepare system-of-records notices that would address these principles because they were not required to do so by the Privacy Act. The act's vehicle for public notification—the system-of-records notice—is required of an agency only when the agency collects, maintains, and retrieves personal data in the way defined by the act or when a contractor does the same thing explicitly on behalf of the government. Agencies generally did not issue system-of-records notices specifically for their use of information resellers largely because information reseller databases were not considered "systems of records operated by or on behalf of a government agency" and thus were not considered subject to the provisions of the Privacy Act [28]. OMB guidance on implementing the Privacy Act does not specifically refer to the use of reseller data or how it should be treated. According to OMB and other agency officials, information resellers operate their databases for multiple customers, and federal agency use of these databases does not amount to the operation of a system of records on behalf of the government. Further, agency officials stated that merely querying information reseller databases did not amount to agency "maintenance" of the personal information being queried and thus also did not trigger the provisions of the Privacy Act. In many cases, agency officials considered their use of resellers to be of this type—essentially "ad hoc" querying or "pinging" of reseller databases for personal information about specific individuals, which they believed they were not doing in connection with a formal system of records.

In other cases, however, agencies maintained information reseller data in systems for which system-of-records notices had been previously published. For example, law enforcement agency officials stated that, to the extent they retain the results of reseller data queries, this collection and use is covered by the system-of-records notices for their case file systems. However, in preparing such notices, agencies generally did not specify that they were obtaining information from resellers.

Among system-of-records notices that were identified by agency officials as applying to the use of reseller data, only one—TSA's system-of-records notice for the test phase of its Secure Flight program—specifically identified the use of information reseller data [29].

In several of these cases, agency sources for personal information were described only in vague terms, such as "private organizations," "other public sources," or "public source material," when information was being obtained from information resellers.

The inconsistency with which agencies specify resellers as a source of information in system-of-records notices is due in part to ambiguity in OMB guidance, which states that "for systems of records which contain information obtained from sources other than the individual to whom the records pertain, the notice should list the types of sources used" [30].

Although the guidance is unclear as to what would constitute adequate disclosure of "types of sources," OMB and DHS Privacy Office officials agreed that to the extent that reseller data is subject to the Privacy Act, agencies should specifically identify information resellers as a source and that merely citing public records information does not sufficiently describe the source.

Aside from certain law enforcement exemptions 31 to the Privacy Act, adherence to the purpose specification and openness principles is critical to preserving a measure of individual control over the use of personal information. Without clear guidance from OMB or specific policies in place, agencies have not consistently reflected these principles in their collection and use of reseller information.

As a result, without being notified of the existence of an agency's information collection activities, individuals have no ability to know that their personal information could be obtained from commercial sources and potentially used as a basis, or partial basis, for taking action that could have consequences for their welfare.

Privacy Impact Assessments Could Address Openness and Purpose Specification Principles but Often Were Not Conducted

PIAs can be an important tool to help agencies to address openness and purpose specification principles early in the process of developing new information systems. To the extent that PIAs are made publicly available, [32] they provide explanations to the public about things such as the information that will be collected, why it is being collected how it is to be used, and how the system and data will be maintained and protected.

However, few agency components reported developing PIAs for their systems or programs that make use of information reseller data. As with system-of-records notices, agencies often did not conduct PIAs because officials did not believe they were required. Current OMB guidance on conducting PIAs is not always clear about when they should be conducted. According to guidance from OMB, a PIA is required by the E-Government Act when agencies "systematically incorporate into existing information systems databases of information in identifiable form purchased or obtained from commercial or public sources." [33] However, the same guidance also instructs agencies that "merely querying a database on an ad hoc basis does not trigger the PIA requirement." Reported uses of reseller data were generally not described as a "systematic" incorporation of data into existing information systems; rather, most involved querying a database and, in some cases, retaining the results of these queries. OMB officials stated that agencies would need to make their own judgments on whether retaining the results of searches of information reseller databases constituted a "systematic incorporation" of information.

Until PIAs are conducted more thoroughly and consistently, the public is likely to remain incompletely informed about agency purposes and uses for obtaining reseller information.

Agencies Often Did Not Have Practices in Place to Ensure Accountability for Proper Handling of Information Reseller Data

According to the accountability principle, individuals controlling the collection or use of personal information should be accountable for ensuring the implementation of the Fair Information Practices. This means that agencies should take steps to ensure that they use personal information from information resellers appropriately.

Agencies described using activities to oversee their use of reseller information that were largely based on trust in the individual user to use the information appropriately, rather than on management oversight of usage details. For example, in describing controls placed on the use of commercial data, officials from component agencies identified measures such as instructing users that reseller data are for official use only and requiring users to sign statements attesting 1) to their need to access information reseller databases and 2) that their use will be limited to official business. Additionally, agency officials reported that their users are required to select from a list of vendor-defined "permissible purposes" (for example, law enforcement, transactions authorized by the consumer) before conducting a search on reseller databases.

While these practices appear consistent with the accountability principle, they are focused on individual user responsibility instead of monitoring and oversight. Agencies did not have practices in place to obtain reports from resellers that would allow them to monitor usage of reseller databases at a detailed level. Although agencies generally receive usage reports from the information resellers, these reports are designed primarily for monitoring costs. Further, these reports generally contained only high-level statistics on the number of searches and databases accessed, not the contents of what was actually searched, thus limiting their utility in monitoring usage.

To the extent that federal agencies do not implement methods such as user monitoring or auditing of usage records, they provide limited accountability for their usage of information reseller data and have limited assurance that the information is being used appropriately.

Not All Agencies Have Taken Steps to Address our Recommendations

In our report, we recommended that the agencies develop specific policies for the collection, maintenance, and use of personal information obtained from resellers. We also recommended that OMB revise its privacy guidance to clarify the applicability of requirements for public notices and privacy impact assessments to agency use of personal information from resellers and direct agencies to review their uses of such information to ensure it is explicitly referenced in privacy notices and assessments. The agencies generally agreed with our findings and described actions initiated to address our recommendations.

Since the issuance of our 2006 report, two of the four agencies have taken action to address our recommendation. For example, the DHS Privacy Office incorporated specific questions in its May 2007 PIA guidance concerning use of commercial data. The guidance requires programs that use commercial or publicly available data to explain why and how such data are used. Further, the guidance for systems that use or rely on commercial data requires an explanation of how data accuracy and integrity are preserved and the reliability of the data assessed with regard to its value to the purpose of the system. According to DHS Privacy Office officials, after identifying use of commercial data through the PIA process, the Privacy Office works with the relevant DHS component to review uses of commercial data to ensure appropriate controls are in place and that the planned uses are appropriately disclosed in privacy notices. In addition, officials at DOJ informed us that the Privacy and Civil Liberties Office has in place a verbal agreement with agency components that there are to be no bulk acquisitions of commercial data and that when the agency takes in data from commercial sources, there should be a valid system-of-records notice that specifically identifies commercial data as a source. Further, DOJ has updated several of its system-of-records notices to reflect their use of data from information resellers. SSA and State have not yet addressed our recommendation.

However, OMB has not addressed our recommendations. In an August 2006 letter to congressional committees in response to the recommendations contained in our April 2006 report, OMB noted that work on the protection of personal information through the Identity Theft Task Force was ongoing and that following the completion of this work, they would consider issuing appropriate clarifying guidance concerning reseller data. Since then, OMB's efforts on the Identity Theft Task Force have been completed and on May 22, 2007 OMB issued M-07-16, "Safeguarding Against the Breach of Personally Identifiable Information." To date, OMB has not issued additional clarifying guidance concerning reseller data.

Privacy Provisions of the Proposed Federal Agency Data Protection Act are Consistent with Our Recommendations

The Federal Agency Data Protection Act was introduced on December 18, 2007. Among other things, the legislation contains privacy provisions that would require agencies to conduct PIAs when "purchasing or subscribing for a fee to information in identifiable form from a data broker." We believe that such a requirement is consistent with the recommendations contained in our report, particularly given the debate concerning whether or not agencies "systematically incorporate" information or are "merely pinging or querying the information." Our report found that PIAs could serve to address certain Fair Information

Practice principles such as purpose specification and openness, but often were not conducted. Such a requirement could more readily ensure agencies perform these assessments. Further, since OMB has not clarified its guidance on this issue, a requirement in law could provide needed direction to agencies.

The proposed Federal Agency Data Protection Act would also require each agency to prescribe regulations that specify, among other things, the personnel permitted to access, analyze, or otherwise use commercial reseller databases. This legislation is consistent with our recommendation that agencies develop policies concerning their use of personal information from information resellers.

In summary, services provided by information resellers are important to federal agency functions such as law enforcement and fraud protection and identification. While agencies have taken steps to adhere to some Fair Information Practices such as the collection limitation, data quality, use limitation, and security safeguards principles, they have not taken all the steps they could to reflect others—or to use the specific processes of the Privacy Act and E-Government Act requirements—in their handling of reseller data. Because OMB privacy guidance does not clearly address information reseller data, agencies are left largely on their own to determine how to satisfy legal requirements and protect privacy when acquiring and using reseller data. Since we issued our report in 2006, two of the four agencies have taken steps to address our recommendations. However, OMB has not modified its guidance. Without current and specific guidance, the government risks continued uneven adherence to important, well-established privacy principles and lacks assurance that the privacy rights of individuals are being adequately protected. Absent action from OMB to revise guidance, privacy provisions contained in the proposed Federal Agency Data Protection Act could clarify the need to conduct privacy impact assessments wherever reseller data are involved and promote the development of agency policies and procedures concerning the use of such data. We believe these provisions are consistent with the results and recommendations contained in our 2006 report.

Mr. Chairman, this concludes my testimony today. I would be happy to answer any questions you or other members of the subcommittee may have.

References

[1] For purposes of this report, the term personal information is defined as any information about an individual maintained by an agency, including (1) any information that can be used to distinguish or trace an individual's identity,

such as name, Social Security number, date and place of birth, mother's maiden name, or biometric records, and (2) any other information that is linked or linkable to an individual, such as medical, educational, financial, and employment information.

[2] The Privacy Act of 1974, Pub. L. No. 93-579, 88 Stat. 1896 (codified as amended at 5 U.S.C. § 552a) provides safeguards against an invasion of privacy through the misuse of records by federal agencies and allows citizens to learn how their personal information is collected, maintained, used, and disseminated by the federal government.

[3] Congress used the committee's final report as a basis for crafting the Privacy Act of 1974. See U.S. Department of Health, Education, and *Welfare, Records, Computers, and the Rights of Citizens: Report of the Secretary's Advisory Committee on Automated Personal Data Systems* (Washington, D.C.; July 1973).

[4] Descriptions of these principles are shown in table 1.

[5] GAO, *Personal Information: Agency and Reseller Adherence to Key Privacy Principles*, GAO-06-421 (Washington, D.C.: Apr. 4, 2006).

[6] H.R. 4791, Federal Agency Data Protection Act, 110th Cong., introduced by Representative Wm. Lacy Clay, December 18, 2007.

[7] This figure may include uses that do not involve personal information. Except for instances where the reported use was primarily for legal research, agency officials were unable to separate the dollar values associated with use of personal information from uses for other purposes (for example, LexisNexis and West provide news and legal research in addition to public records). The four agencies obtained personal information from resellers primarily through two general-purpose governmentwide contract vehicles—the Federal Supply Schedule of the General Services Administration and the Library of Congress's Federal Library and Information Network.

[8] Credit header data are the nonfinancial identifying information located at the top of a credit report, such as name, current and prior addresses, telephone number, and Social Security number.

[9] The Privacy Act of 1974, Pub. L. No. 93-579, 88 Stat. 1896 (codified as amended at 5 U.S.C. § 552a) provides safeguards against an invasion of privacy through the misuse of records by federal agencies and allows citizens to learn how their personal information is collected, maintained, used, and disseminated by the federal government.

[10] Under the Privacy Act of 1974, the term "routine use" means (with respect to the disclosure of a record) the use of such a record for a purpose that is

compatible with the purpose for which it was collected. 5 U.S.C. § 552a (a(7))

[11] OMB, "Privacy Act Implementation: Guidelines and Responsibilities," Federal Register, Volume 40, Number 132, Part III, pages 28948-28978 (Washington, D.C.; July 9, 1975). Since the initial Privacy Act guidance of 1975, OMB has periodically published additional guidance. Further information regarding OMB Privacy Act guidance can be found on the OMB Web site at http://www.whitehouse.gov/omb/inforeg/info poltech.html.

[12] The E-Government Act requires agencies, if practicable, to make PIAs publicly available through agency Web sites, publication in the Federal Register or by other means. Pub. L. No. 107-347, § 208 (b)(1)(B)(iii).

[13] U.S. Department of Health, Education, and Welfare, *Records, Computers and the Rights of Citizens*.

[14] OECD, *Guidelines on the Protection of Privacy and Transborder Flow of Personal Data* (Sept. 23, 1980). The OECD plays a prominent role in fostering good governance in the public service and in corporate activity among its 30 member countries. It produces internationally agreed-upon instruments, decisions, and recommendations to promote rules in areas where multilateral agreement is necessary for individual countries to make progress in the global economy.

[15] OECD, *Making Privacy Notices Simple: An OECD Report and Recommendations* (July 24, 2006).

[16] European Union Data Protection Directive ("Directive 95/46/EC of the European Parliament and of the Council of 24 October 1995 on the Protection of Individuals with Regard to the Processing of Personal Data and the Free Movement of Such Data") (1995).

[17] National Research Council of the National Academies, *Engaging Privacy and Information Technology in a Digital Age* (Washington, D.C.; 2007)

[18] This figure comprises contracts and task orders with information resellers that included the acquisition and use of personal information. However, some of these funds may have been for uses that do not involve personal information; we could not omit all such uses because agency officials were not always able to separate the amounts associated with the use of personal information from those for other uses (for example, LexisNexis and West provide news and legal research in addition to public records). In some instances, where the reported use was primarily for legal research, we omitted these funds from the total.

[19] GAO, *Data Mining: Agencies Have Taken Key Steps to Protect Privacy in Selected Efforts, but Significant Compliance Issues Remain*, GAO-05-866 (Washington, D.C.: Aug. 15, 2005).

[20] DEA's mission includes enforcing laws pertaining to the manufacture, distribution, and dispensing of legally produced controlled substances.

[21] The personal information contained in this information reseller database is limited to the prescribing doctor and does not contain personal patient information.

[22] For an assessment of privacy issues associated with the Secure Flight commercial data test, see GAO, *Aviation Security: Transportation Security Administration Did Not Fully Disclose Uses of Personal Information during Secure Flight Program Testing in Initial Privacy Notices, but Has Recently Taken Steps to More Fully Inform the Public*, GAO-05- 864R (Washington, D.C.: July 22, 2005).

[23] TSA's current plans for Secure Flight do not include the use of reseller information.

[24] Skiptracing is the process of locating people who have fled in order to avoid paying debts.

[25] Subsequent to the 2006 report, the DHS Privacy Office took steps to develop guidance on the use of personal information from information resellers in its PIA guidance.

[26] Although we did not assess the effectiveness of information security at any agency as part of this review, we have previously reported on weaknesses in almost all areas of information security controls at 24 major agencies, including DOJ, DHS, State, and SSA. For additional information see GAO, *Information Security: Weaknesses Persist at Federal Agencies Despite Progress Made in Implementing Related Statutory Requirements*, GAO- 05-552 (Washington, D.C.: July 15, 2005) and *Information Security: Department of Homeland Security Needs to Fully Implement Its Security Program*, GAO-05-700 (Washington, D.C.: June 17, 2005).

[27] 5 U.S.C. § 552a(e)(4)(C) & (I). The Privacy Act allows agencies to claim an exemption from identifying the categories of sources of records for records compiled for criminal law enforcement purposes, as well as for a broader category of uses, including investigative records compiled for criminal or civil law enforcement purposes.

[28] The act provides for its requirements to apply to government contractors when agencies contract for the operation by or on behalf of the agency, a system of records to accomplish an agency function. 5 U.S.C. § 552a(m).

[29] As we have previously reported, this notice did not fully disclose the scope of the use of reseller data during the test phase. See GAO, *Aviation Security: Transportation Security Administration Did Not Fully Disclose Uses of Personal Information during Secure Flight Program Testing in Initial Privacy Notices, but Has Recently Taken Steps to More Fully Inform the Public*, GAO-05-864R (Washington, D.C.: July 22, 2005).

[30] OMB, "Privacy Act Implementation: Guidelines and Responsibilities," *Federal Register*, Volume 40, Number 132, Part III, p. 28964 (Washington, D.C.: July 9, 1975).

[31] The Privacy Act allows agencies to claim exemptions if the records are used for certain purposes. 5 U.S.C. § 552a (j) and (k). For example, records compiled for criminal law enforcement purposes can be exempt from the access and correction provisions. In general, the exemptions for law enforcement purposes are intended to prevent the disclosure of information collected as part of an ongoing investigation that could impair the investigation or allow those under investigation to change their behavior or take other actions to escape prosecution. In most cases where officials identified system-of-record notices associated with reseller data collection for law enforcement purposes, agencies claimed this exemption.

[32] The E-Government Act requires agencies, if practicable, to make privacy impact assessments publicly available through agency Web sites, publication in the *Federal Register*, or by other means. Pub. L. No. 107-347, § 208 (b)(1)(B)(iii).

[33] OMB, *Guidance for Implementing the Privacy Provisions of the E-Government Act of 2002*, Memorandum M-03-22 (Washington, D.C.: Sept. 26, 2003).

Chapter 3

ENHANCING PROTECTION OF PERSONALLY IDENTIFIABLE INFORMATION*

WHAT GAO FOUND

Increasingly sophisticated ways of obtaining and using personally identifiable information have raised concerns about the adequacy of the legal framework for privacy protection. Although the Privacy Act, the E-Government Act, and related guidance from the Office of Management and Budget set minimum privacy requirements for agencies, they may not consistently protect personally identifiable information in all circumstances of its collection and use throughout the federal government and may not fully adhere to key privacy principles. Based on discussions with privacy experts, agency officials, and analysis of laws and related guidance, GAO identified issues in three major areas:

Applying privacy protections consistently to all federal collection and use of personal information. The Privacy Act's definition of a "system of records" (any grouping of records containing personal information retrieved by individual identifier), which sets the scope of the act's protections, does not always apply whenever personal information is obtained and processed by federal agencies. One alternative to address this concern would be revising the system-of-records definition to cover all personally identifiable information collected, used, and maintained systematically by the federal government.

Ensuring that collection and use of personally identifiable information is limited to a stated purpose. According to generally accepted privacy principles of

---

* Excerpted from GAO Report 08-536, dated May 2007.

purpose specification, collection limitation, and use limitation, the collection of personal information should be limited, and its use should be limited to a specified purpose. Yet, current laws and guidance impose only the modest requirements in these areas. While, in the post-9/11 environment, the federal government needs better analysis and sharing of certain personal information, there is general agreement that this need must be balanced with individual privacy rights. Alternatives to address this area of concern include requiring agencies to justify the collection and use of key elements of personally identifiable information and to establish agreements before sharing such information with other agencies.

Establishing effective mechanisms for informing the public about privacy protections. Another key privacy principle, the principle of openness, suggests that the public should be informed about privacy policies and practices. Yet, Privacy Act notices may not effectively inform the public about government uses of personal information. For example, system-ofrecords notices published in the Federal Register (the government's official vehicle for issuing public notices) may be difficult for the general public to fully understand. Layered notices, which provide only the most important summary facts up front, have been used as a solution in the private sector. In addition, publishing such notices at a central location on the Web would help make them more accessible.

WHY GAO DID THIS STUDY

The centerpiece of the federal government's legal framework for privacy protection, the Privacy Act of 1974, provides safeguards for information maintained by federal agencies. In addition, the E-Government Act of 2002 requires federal agencies to conduct privacy impact assessments for systems or collections containing personal information.

GAO was asked to determine whether laws and guidance consistently cover the federal government's collection and use of personal information and incorporate key privacy principles. GAO was also asked, in doing so, to identify options for addressing these issues.

To achieve these objectives, GAO analyzed the laws and related guidance, obtained an operational perspective from federal agencies, and consulted an expert panel convened by the National Academy of Sciences.

WHAT GAO RECOMMENDS

To address the issues identified by GAO, Congress should consider revising privacy laws in accordance with the alternatives outlined in the report. While OMB could address some of these issues in its guidance to federal agencies, Congress is ultimately responsible for balancing the needs of government and individual privacy rights. OMB commented that the Congress should consider these alternatives in the broader context of all privacy and related statutes.

ABBREVIATIONS

ADVISE	Analysis Dissemination Visualization Insight and Semantic Enhancement
CBP	Customs and Border Protection
CIPSEA	Confidential Information Protection and Statistical Efficiency Act
DHS	Department of Homeland Security
DOJ	Department of Justice
DOT	Department of Transportation
FBI	Federal Bureau of Investigation
FISMA	Federal Information Security Management Act
HHS	Department of Health and Human Services
HIPAA	Health Insurance Portability and Accountability Act of 1996
IRS	Internal Revenue Service
ISPAB	Information Security and Privacy Advisory Board
NAS	National Academy of Sciences
NIST	National Institute of Standards and Technology
NRC	National Research Council
OCED	Organization for Economic Cooperation and Development
OMB	Office of Management and Budget
PIA	privacy impact assessment
PPSC	Privacy Protection Study Commission
PRA	Paperwork Reduction Act
SSA	Social Security Administration
TSA	Transportation Security Administration

May 19, 2008 Congressional Requesters

The increasingly sophisticated ways in which personally identifiable information [1] is obtained and used by the federal government has the potential to assist in performing critical functions, such as preventing terrorism, but also can pose challenges in ensuring the protection of citizens' privacy. In this regard, concerns have been raised that the framework of legal mechanisms for protecting personal privacy that has been developed over the years may no longer be sufficient, given current practices.

Federal agency use of personal information is governed primarily by the Privacy Act of 1974 and the E-Government Act of 2002 [2]. The Privacy Act of 1974 serves as the major mechanism for controlling the collection, use, and disclosure of personally identifiable information within the federal government. The act provides safeguards for information in a system of records (any grouping of records containing personal information retrieved by individual identifier) maintained by a federal agency. The act also allows citizens to learn how their personal information is collected, maintained, used, and disseminated by the federal government. As a result of the act's requirements, the public has benefited from privacy protections applied to countless government systems of records.

The E-Government Act of 2002 strives to enhance protection of personal information in government information systems by requiring that agencies conduct privacy impact assessments (PIA) [3]. This provision has led to the preparation of many PIAs that provide in-depth discussions of protections for personally identifiable information maintained in automated systems.

The Office of Management and Budget (OMB) is charged with ensuring implementation of the PIA requirement and the Privacy Act by federal agencies and is also responsible for providing guidance to agencies. In 1975, OMB issued Privacy Act Implementation Guidelines. Since that time, it has provided periodic supplemental guidance related to privacy on specific subjects.

The provisions of the Privacy Act are largely based on a set of principles for protecting the privacy and security of personal information, known as the Fair Information Practices, which were first proposed in 1973 by a U.S. government advisory committee.4 These principles, now widely accepted, include:

- collection limitation,
- data quality,
- purpose specification,
- use limitation,
- security safeguards,

- openness,
- individual participation, and
- accountability [5]

These principles, with some variation, are used by organizations to address privacy considerations in their business practices and are also the basis of privacy laws and related policies in many countries, including the United States, Germany, Sweden, Australia, and New Zealand, as well as the European Union.

Since enactment of the Privacy Act nearly 35 years ago, both the techniques employed by the federal government to obtain and process personally identifiable information and the technology used to support its collection, maintenance, dissemination, and use have changed dramatically. Advances in information technology have enabled agencies to more easily acquire, analyze, and share personally identifiable information from a variety of sources in increasingly diverse ways and for increasingly sophisticated purposes.

Given the advances in technology used to process, store, share, and manipulate personal information, you asked us to identify major issues regarding whether the Privacy Act of 1974, the E-Government Act of 2002, and related guidance consistently cover the federal government's collection and use of personal information and incorporate key privacy principles. Our objective was not focused on evaluating compliance with these laws; rather, it was to identify major issues concerning their sufficiency in light of current uses of personal information by the federal government. You also asked us to identify options for addressing these issues.

To address our objective, we analyzed the Privacy Act of 1974, section 208 of the E-Government Act, and related guidance to identify any inconsistencies or gaps in the coverage of these laws as they apply to uses of personal information by federal agencies. We also compared these laws and related guidance with the fair information practices to identify any significant gaps, including assessing the role of the Paperwork Reduction Act (PRA) in protecting privacy by limiting collection of information. We obtained an operational perspective on the sufficiency of these laws from six departments and agencies with large inventories of information collections, prominent privacy issues, and varied missions: the Departments of Health and Human Services (HHS), Homeland Security (DHS), Justice (DOJ), and Transportation (DOT); the Internal Revenue Service (IRS); and the Social Security Administration (SSA). We also obtained expert perspective on key issues through use of an expert panel, convened for us by the National Academy of Sciences (NAS). A full description of our objective, scope, and methodology can be found in appendix I. In addition, the names of privacy experts participating in the NAS expert forum can be found in appendix II.

We conducted this performance audit from March 2007 to May 2008 in accordance with generally accepted government auditing standards. Those standards require that we plan and perform the audit to obtain sufficient, appropriate evidence to provide a reasonable basis for our findings and conclusions based on our audit objectives. We believe that the evidence obtained provides a reasonable basis for our findings and conclusions based on our audit objectives.

RESULTS IN BRIEF

Although the Privacy Act, the E-Government Act, and related OMB guidance set minimum requirements for agencies, they may not consistently protect personally identifiable information in all circumstances of its collection and use throughout the federal government and may not fully adhere to key privacy principles. Based on discussions with privacy experts, agency officials, and analysis of laws and related guidance, we identified issues in three major areas:

Applying privacy protections consistently to all federal collection and use of personal information. The Privacy Act's definition of a "system of records" (any grouping of records containing personal information retrieved by individual identifier), which sets the scope of the act's protections, does not always apply whenever personal information is obtained and processed by federal agencies. For example, if agencies do not retrieve personal information by identifier, the act's protections do not apply. Our 2003 report concerning compliance with the Privacy Act found that among the agencies surveyed, the most frequently cited reason for systems not being considered Privacy Act systems of records was that the agency did not use a personal identifier to retrieve the information [6]. Further, recent OMB guidance reflects an acknowledgement that, although personally identifiable information does not always reside in Privacy Act systems of records, it should nevertheless be protected. In addition, as we previously reported, [7]federal agencies have not always implemented Privacy Act requirements because they did not clearly apply to their use of personal information from information resellers. Factors such as these have led experts to agree that the Privacy Act's system-of-records construct is too narrowly defined. The E-Government Act's privacy provisions, in contrast, apply more broadly; however, the E-Government Act does not include the specific constraints on how information is to be collected, maintained, and shared that are included in the Privacy Act nor does it address federal rulemaking, in which federal agencies can influence how other entities, including state and local government agencies, collect and use personal information. Alternatives for addressing these issues could include revising the system-of-records definition to cover all personally identifiable information collected, used, and maintained systematically by the federal government, and revising the E-Government Act's scope to cover federal rulemaking.

Ensuring that collection and use of personally identifiable information is limited to a stated purpose. According to the purpose specification, collection limitation, and use limitation principles, the collection of personal information should be limited, and its use should be limited to a specified purpose. Yet, current laws and guidance impose only modest requirements for describing the purposes for collecting and using personal information and limiting how that information is collected and used. For example, agencies are not required to be specific in formulating purpose descriptions in their public notices. While purpose statements for certain law enforcement and anti-terrorism systems might need to be phrased broadly enough so as not to reveal investigative techniques or the details of ongoing cases, overly broadly defined purposes could allow for unnecessarily broad collections of information and ranges of subsequent uses, thus calling into question whether meaningful limitations had been imposed.

Laws and guidance also may not effectively limit the collection of personal information. For example, the Privacy Act's requirement that information be "relevant and necessary" gives broad latitude to agencies in determining the amount of information to collect. Under these criteria, agency officials do not have specific requirements for justifying how much information to collect. Without establishing more specific requirements for justifying information collections, it may difficult to ensure that agencies limit collection of personal information to what is relevant and necessary.

In addition, mechanisms to limit use to a specified purpose may be weak. For example, the Privacy Act does not limit agency internal use of information, as long as it is needed for an official purpose. Recognizing that information sharing is critically important to certain government functions such as homeland security and anti-terrorism, it has also been established that protecting privacy in these functions is an equally important goal. However, the Privacy Act does not include provisions addressing external sharing with other entities to ensure that the information's new custodians preserve the act's protections.

Examples of alternatives for addressing these issues include setting specific limits on routine uses and use of information within agencies to include more specific limits, requiring agencies to limit collection of personally identifiable information and to explain how such collection has been limited in privacy notices, and requiring agencies to establish formal agreements with external governmental entities before sharing personally identifiable information with them.

Establishing effective mechanisms for informing the public about privacy protections. According to the openness principle, the public should be informed about privacy polices and practices, and the accountability principle calls for those who control the collection or use of personal information to be held accountable for taking steps to ensure privacy protection. Public notices are a primary means of establishing accountability for privacy protections and giving individuals a measure of control over the use of their personal information. Yet concerns have been raised that Privacy Act notices may not serve this function well. Although the Federal Register is the government's official vehicle for issuing public notices, critics have questioned whether system-of-records notices published in the Federal Register effectively inform the public about government uses of personal information. Among others, options for addressing concerns about public notice could include setting requirements to ensure that purpose, collection limitations, and use limitations are better addressed in the content of privacy notices, and revising the Privacy Act to require that all notices be published on a standard Web site, such as www.privacy.gov.

Some of these issues—particularly those dealing with limitations on collection and use as well as mechanisms for informing the public—could be addressed by OMB through revisions or supplements to guidance. However, unilateral actions by OMB would not have the benefit of public deliberations regarding how best to achieve an appropriate balance between the government's need to collect, process, and share personally identifiable information and the rights of individuals to know about such collections and be assured that they are only for limited purposes and uses. In assessing such a balance, Congress should consider amending applicable laws, such as the Privacy Act and the E-Government Act, according to the alternatives outlined in this report, including

- revising the scope of the laws to cover all personally identifiable information collected, used, and maintained by the federal government;
- setting requirements to ensure that the collection and use of personally identifiable information is limited to a stated purpose; and
- establishing additional mechanisms for informing the public about privacy protections by revising requirements for the structure and publication of public notices.

We received written comments on a draft of this report from the Deputy Administrator of the Office of E-Government and Information Technology and the Deputy Administrator of the Office of Information and Regulatory Affairs of OMB. The letter is reprinted in appendix V. In their comments, the officials noted that they shared our concerns about privacy and stated they believe it would be important for Congress to consider potential amendments to the Privacy Act and the E-Government Act in the broader context of the several privacy statutes that Congress has enacted.

Though we did not make specific recommendations to OMB, the agency provided comments on the alternatives identified in conjunction with our matter for congressional consideration. Regarding alternatives for revising the scope of laws to cover all personally identifiable information collected, used, and maintained by the federal government, OMB stated that it would be important for Congress to evaluate fully the potential implications of revisions such as amending the Privacy Act's system-of-records definition. We agree with OMB that such consideration should be thorough and include further public debate.

Regarding alternatives for setting requirements to ensure that the collection and use of personally identifiable information is limited to a stated purpose, OMB stated that agencies are working to implement a requirement in a recent OMB memorandum to review and reduce the volume of personally identifiable information they handle "to the minimum necessary." The draft report notes that this requirement is in place; however, because significant concerns have been raised in this area by our previous work and by experts at our forum, we believe Congress should consider additional alternatives for ensuring that the collection and use of personally identifiable information is limited to a stated purpose Finally, regarding effective mechanisms for informing the public, OMB stated that it supports ensuring that the public is appropriately informed of how agencies are using their information. OMB stated that they will review agency practices in informing the public and review the alternatives outlined in our report.

OMB provided additional technical comments, which are addressed in appendix V. We also received technical comments from DHS, DOJ, DOT, and IRS. We have addressed these comments in the final report as appropriate.

BACKGROUND

In response to growing concern about the harmful consequences that computerized data systems could have on the privacy of personal information, the Secretary of Health, Education, and Welfare commissioned an advisory committee in 1972 to examine to what extent limitations should be placed on the application of computer technology to record keeping about people. The committee's final report [8] proposed a set of principles for protecting the privacy and security of personal information, known as the Fair Information Practices. These practices were intended to address what the committee termed a poor level of protection afforded to privacy under existing law, and they underlie the major provisions of the Privacy Act, which was enacted the following year. A revised version of the Fair Information Practices, developed by the Organization for Economic Cooperation and Development (OECD) in 1980, has been widely adopted [9]. This version of the principles was reaffirmed by OECD ministers in a 1998 declaration and further endorsed in a 2006 OECD report [10]. The OECD version of the principles is shown table 1.

Table 1. The Fair Information Practices

Principle	Description
Collection limitation	The collection of personal information should be limited, should be obtained by lawful and fair means, and, where appropriate, with the knowledge or consent of the individual.
Data quality	Personal information should be relevant to the purpose for which it is collected, and should be accurate, complete, and current as needed for that purpose.
Purpose specification	The purposes for the collection of personal information should be disclosed before collection and upon any change to that purpose, and its use should be limited to those purposes and compatible purposes.
Use limitation	Personal information should not be disclosed or otherwise usedfor other than a specified purpose without consent of the individual or legal authority.
Security safeguards	Personal information should be protected with reasonable security safeguards against risks such as loss or unauthorized access, destruction, use, modification, or disclosure.
Openness	The public should be informed about privacy policies and practices, and individuals should have ready means of learning about the use of personal information.
Individual participation	Individuals should have the following rights: to know about the collection of personal information, to access that information, to request correction, and to challenge the denial of those rights.
Accountability	Individuals controlling the collection or use of personal information should be accountable for taking steps to ensure the implementation of these principles.

The Fair Information Practices are, with some variation, the basis of privacy laws and related policies in many countries, including the United States, Germany, Sweden, Australia, and New Zealand, as well as the European Union [11]. They are also reflected in a variety of federal agency policy statements, beginning with an endorsement of the OECD principles by the Department of Commerce in 198 1, [12] and including policy statements from DHS, DOJ, and the Department of Housing and Urban Development [13]. In 2004, the Chief Information Officers Council issued a coordinating draft of its Security and Privacy Profile for the Federal Enterprise Architecture [14] that links privacy protection with a set of acceptable privacy principles corresponding to the OECD's version of the Fair Information Practices.

In addition, in a 2007 report on "Engaging Privacy and Information Technology in a Digital Age," the National Research Council found that the principles of fair information practice for the protection of personal information are as relevant today as they were in 1973 [15]. Accordingly, the committee recommended that the fair information practices should be extended as far as reasonably feasible to apply to private-sector organizations that collect and use personal information.

The Fair Information Practices are not precise legal requirements. Rather, they provide a framework of principles for balancing the need for privacy with other public policy interests, such as national security, law enforcement, and administrative efficiency. Striking that balance varies among countries and among types of information (e.g., medical, employment information).

Federal Laws and Guidance Govern Use of Personal Information in Federal Agencies

There is no single federal law that governs all use or disclosure of personal information. Instead, U.S. law includes a number of separate statutes that provide privacy protections for information used for specific purposes or maintained by specific entities. The major requirements for the protection of personal privacy by federal agencies come from two laws, the Privacy Act of 1974 and the privacy provisions of the E-Government Act of 2002.

The Privacy Act places limitations on agencies' collection, disclosure, and use of personal information maintained in systems of records. The act describes a "record" as any item, collection, or grouping of information about an individual that is maintained by an agency and contains his or her name or another personal identifier. It also defines "system of records" as a group of records under the control of any agency from which information is retrieved by the name of the individual or by an individual identifier. The Privacy Act requires that when agencies establish or make changes to a system of records, they must notify the public through a system-of-records notice in the Federal Register that identifies, among other things, the categories of data collected, the categories of individuals about whom information is collected, the intended "routine" uses of data, and procedures that individuals can use to review and correct personally identifiable information [16].

The act's requirements also apply to government contractors when agencies contract for the operation of a system of records to accomplish an agency function. According to OMB guidance, in these situations the contractual instrument between the agency and the contractor must specify that such records are to be maintained in accordance with the act. As explained by OMB, this requirement was not intended to cover private- sector record-keeping systems, but only those systems actually taking the place of a federal system that, but for the contract, would have been performed by an agency and covered by the Privacy Act.

Several provisions of the act require agencies to define and limit collection and use to predefined purposes. For example, the act requires that to the greatest extent practicable, personal information should be collected directly from the subject individual when it may affect an individual's rights or benefits under a federal program. The act also requires that an agency inform individuals whom it asks to supply information of (1) the authority for soliciting the information and whether disclosure of such information is mandatory or voluntary; (2) the principal purposes for which the information is intended to be used; (3) the routine uses that may be made of the information; and (4) the effects on the individual, if any, of not providing the information. According to OMB, this requirement is based on the assumption that individuals should be provided with sufficient information about the request to make a decision about whether to respond.

In handling collected information, agencies are generally required by the Privacy Act to, among other things, allow individuals to (1) review their records (meaning any information pertaining to them that is contained in the system of records), (2) request a copy of their record or information from the system of records, and (3) request corrections to their information.

Agencies are allowed to claim exemptions from some of the provisions of the Privacy Act if the records are used for certain purposes. For example, records compiled by criminal law enforcement agencies for criminal law enforcement purposes can be exempt from a number of provisions, including (1) the requirement to notify individuals of the purposes and uses of the information at the time of collection and (2) the requirement to ensure the accuracy, relevance, timeliness, and completeness of records. A broader category of investigative records compiled for criminal or civil law enforcement purposes can also be exempted from a somewhat smaller number of Privacy Act provisions, including the requirement to provide individuals with access to their records and to inform the public of the categories of sources of records. In general, the exemptions for law enforcement purposes are intended to prevent the disclosure of information collected as part of an ongoing investigation that could impair the investigation or allow those under investigation to change their behavior or take other actions to escape prosecution. Statutory exemptions under the Privacy Act are summarized in appendix III.

In 1988, Congress passed the Computer Matching and Privacy Protection Act as an amendment to the Privacy Act, to establish procedural safeguards that affect agencies' use of Privacy Act records from benefit programs in performing certain types of computerized matching programs. For example, the 1988 act requires agencies to create written agreements specifying the terms under which matches are to be done More recently, in 2002, Congress enacted the E-Government Act to, among other things, enhance protection for personal information in government information systems or information collections by requiring that agencies conduct PIAs. A PIA is an analysis of how personal information is collected, stored, shared, and managed in a federal system. More specifically, according to OMB guidance, [17] a PIA is an analysis of how ...

> information is handled: (i) to ensure handling conforms to applicable legal, regulatory, and policy requirements regarding privacy; (ii) to determine the risks and effects of collecting, maintaining, and disseminating information in identifiable form in an electronic information system; and (iii) to examine and evaluate protections and alternative processes for handling information to mitigate potential privacy risks.

Agencies must conduct PIAs (1) before developing or procuring information technology that collects, maintains, or disseminates information that is in identifiable form or (2) before initiating any new data collections of information in an identifiable form that will be collected, maintained, or disseminated using information technology if the same questions are asked of 10 or more people. OMB guidance also requires agencies to conduct PIAs when a system change creates new privacy risks, for example, changing the way in which personal information is being used. According to OMB, no assessment is required when the information relates to internal government operations, the information has been previously assessed under an evaluation similar to a PIA, or when privacy issues are unchanged.

The PRA applies to federal information collections and was designed to help ensure that when the government asks the public for information, the burden of providing this information is as small as possible and the information itself is used effectively [18]. Such collections may have a range of purposes, which may or may not involve the collection of personal information, including applications for government benefits, program evaluation, general purpose statistics, research and regulation or compliance; all of these information collections may occur in a variety of forms, including questionnaires and telephone surveys. To achieve the goal of minimizing paperwork burden while maximizing the public benefit and utility of the information collected, the act includes provisions that establish standards and procedures for effective implementation and oversight of information collections. Among these provisions is the requirement that agencies not establish information collections without having them approved by OMB, and that before submitting them for approval, agencies' chief information officers certify that the collections meet 10 specified standards, including that the collection is necessary for the proper performance of agency functions and avoids unnecessary duplication. The law also requires agencies both to publish notices in the Federal Register and to otherwise consult with the public about their planned collections.

Privacy is also addressed in the legal framework for the emerging information sharing environment. As directed by the Intelligence Reform and Terrorism Prevention Act of 2004, [19] the administration has taken steps, beginning in 2005, to establish an information sharing environment to facilitate the sharing of terrorism-related information with protections for privacy and civil liberties. The move was driven by the recognition that before the attacks of September 11, 2001, federal agencies had been unable to effectively share information about suspected terrorists and their activities. In addressing this problem, the National Commission on Terrorist Attacks Upon the United States (9/11 Commission) recommended that the sharing and uses of information be guided by a set of practical policy guidelines that would simultaneously empower and constrain officials, closely circumscribing what types of information they would be permitted to share as well as the types of information they would need to protect. Exchanging terrorism-related information continues to be a significant challenge for federal, state, and local governments—one that we recognize is not easily addressed. Accordingly, since January 2005, we have designated information sharing for homeland security a high-risk area [20].

OMB Has Primary Responsibility for Oversight of the Privacy, E-Government, and Paperwork Reduction Acts

The Privacy Act gives OMB responsibility for developing guidelines and providing "continuing assistance to and oversight of" agencies' implementation of the Privacy Act. The E-Government Act of 2002 also assigns OMB responsibility for developing PIA guidance and ensuring agency implementation of the privacy impact assessment requirement.

In July 1975, OMB published guidance for implementing the provisions of the Privacy Act. Since then, OMB has periodically issued additional guidance. For example, in 1991, OMB provided guidance to assist agencies in complying with the Computer Matching and Privacy Protection Act.

In September 2003, consistent with its responsibility under section 208 of the E-Government Act, OMB issued guidance to agencies on conducting privacy impact assessments.

Enacted in 1980, the PRA made virtually all federal agency information collection activities subject to OMB review and established broad objectives for OMB oversight of the management of federal information resources.

The act established the Office of Information and Regulatory Affairs within OMB and gave this office a variety of oversight responsibilities over federal information functions, including general information policy, reduction of paperwork burden, and information privacy.

To assist agencies in fulfilling their responsibilities under the act, OMB took various steps. It issued a regulation [21] and provided agencies with instructions on filling out a standard form for submissions and providing supporting statements.

OMB has also periodically issued guidance on other privacy-related issues, including:

- federal agency Web site privacy policies;
- interagency sharing of personal information;
- designation of senior staff responsible for privacy; and
- data breach notification.

A list of privacy guidance from OMB can be found in appendix IV.

Previous Studies Have Raised Concerns about the Sufficiency of Privacy Laws

Concerns about the Privacy Act have arisen periodically since its passage. The Privacy Act established a temporary national study commission to conduct a comprehensive assessment of privacy policy and to make recommendations for better protecting the privacy of individuals. This commission, called the Privacy Protection Study Commission (PPSC), was to study privacy issues and recommend future legislation.

In its final report, [22] the PPSC concluded that, as transactions involving personal information have proliferated, there has been no compensating tendency to give the individual the kind of control over the collection, use, and disclosure of personal information that natural, or face-to-face, encounters normally entail. The PPSC found that if informational privacy is to be protected, public policy must focus on certain systemic features such as the proliferating use of information for a different purpose than for what it was originally collected, and the greater use of third-party reporting.

The commission concluded that it would be beneficial to create a federal body to oversee, regulate, and enforce compliance with the commission's recommendations. The PPSC formally recommended that the President and Congress create an independent entity to participate in any federal proceeding that would affect personal privacy, including the issuance of rules that must be followed by federal agencies in interpreting the Privacy Act.

As another example, in a 1983 report summarizing 9 years (1975 to 1983) of congressional oversight of the Privacy Act, the House Committee on Government Operations concluded that OMB had not pursued its responsibility to revise and update its original guidance from 1975 and had not actively monitored agency compliance with its guidance. It stated "Interest in the Privacy Act at [OMB] has diminished steadily since 1975. Each successive Administration has shown less concern about Privacy Act oversight" [23].

More recently, in 2002, the Information Security and Privacy Advisory Board (ISPAB), a federal advisory committee originally established by the Computer Security Act of 1987, [24] issued a report on government privacy policy setting and management. In its report, the ISPAB raised a number of concerns about advances in technology and its impact on privacy. Specifically, ISPAB observed that "with the migration toward e- government services, greater demands will be placed on the government's privacy policies and systems." ISPAB further observed that the public's willingness to use such services will depend "in large measure on their confidence that the information that they disclose will be safeguarded "[25].

The ISPAB report further stated that, "changes in technology, the privacy management challenges stemming from expanded e-government services, the accelerated interaction of networked information systems within and across critical infrastructure boundaries, and the extended, routine exchange of data among Federal and non-Federal government and non- government systems - all mandate immediate and serious attention to Federal government's data privacy policies and operational controls." Among the issues identified was a need for a review of the sufficiency and relevance of the Privacy Act to determine whether modifications were required, given the numerous changes affecting privacy that had occurred since the act was passed.

Following up on its 2002 report, in 2005 ISPAB issued a "Privacy Act White Paper" raising the question of whether the existing legal and policy framework governing the information practices of federal agencies was sufficient to protect the privacy of individuals about whom the federal government maintained or used personal information. The paper postulated that "laws and policies have not kept pace with changes in technology and information and handling processes and suggests the need for an open dialogue on what changes in law and policy are needed and how to best make those changes." Accordingly, in 2006 ISPAB initiated a partnership with the DHS Data Privacy and Integrity Advisory Committee [26] to develop recommendations on a 21st century framework for revisions to the Privacy Act and other federal privacy statutes. Work on this initiative was ongoing at the time of our review.

In 2007, the National Research Council [27] issued a report entitled Engaging Privacy and Information Technology in a Digital Age [28]. The report identified a number of issues related to the implications of advances in technology on privacy. With regard to government use of personal information, the committee found that the government has important roles to play in protecting the privacy of individuals and groups and in ensuring that decisions concerning privacy are made in an informed fashion. However, the report characterized the U.S. legal and regulatory framework as "a patchwork that lacks consistent principles or unifying themes." The committee concluded that a less decentralized and more integrated approach to privacy policy in the United States could bring a greater degree of coherence to the subject of privacy. The committee recommended that the U.S. government undertake a broad systematic review of national privacy laws and regulations.

Further, with regard specifically to government use of personal information, the committee found that "because the benefits of privacy often are less tangible and immediate than the perceived benefits of other interests, such as public security and economic efficiency, privacy is at an inherent disadvantage when decision makers weigh privacy against these other interests." The committee concluded that, to reduce this inherent disadvantage, governments at federal, state, and local levels should establish mechanisms for the institutional advocacy of privacy within government. Much as the PPSC had recommended in 1977, the NRC recommended that a national privacy commissioner or standing privacy commission be established to provide ongoing and periodic assessments of privacy developments.

We have previously reported on a number of agency-specific and governmentwide privacy-related issues at federal agencies. For example, in 2003, [29] we reported that agencies generally did well with certain aspects of the Privacy Act's requirements—such as issuing systems-of-records notices when required—but did less well at other requirements, such as ensuring that information is complete, accurate, relevant, and timely before it is disclosed to a nonfederal organization. In discussing this uneven compliance agency officials reported the need for additional OMB leadership and guidance to assist in difficult implementation issues in a rapidly changing environment. For example, officials had questions about the act's applicability to electronic records. We have also reported on key privacy challenges facing federal agencies, federal Web site privacy, notification of individuals in the event of a data breach, and government data-mining initiatives. A list of our privacy-related products can be found in appendix V.

Additional Laws Provide Protections for Federal Agency Use of Personal Information

Other federal laws address privacy protection for personal information with respect to information security requirements as well as for certain types of information, such as when taxpayer, statistical, or health information is involved.

The Federal Information Security Management Act (FISMA) addresses the protection of personal information by defining federal requirements for securing information and information systems that support federal agency operations and assets; it requires agencies to develop agencywide information security programs that extend to contractors and other providers of federal data and systems [30]. Under FISMA, information security means protecting information and information systems from unauthorized access, use, disclosure, disruption, modification, or destruction, including controls necessary to preserve authorized restrictions on access and disclosure to protect personal privacy, among other things [31].

Other laws address protection of personal information by federal agencies in specific circumstances and are described in Table 2.

Table 2. Major Federal Laws That Address Federal Agency Use of Personal Information

Information covered	Applicable law
Patient health information	To the extent a federal agency is a covered entity under the Health Insurance Portability and Accountability Act of 1996 (HIPAA), e.g., a provider of health care programs or services, it may not use or disclose an individual's health information without the individual's authorization, except for certain reasons, and is required to inform individuals of its privacy practices. 42 U.S.C. §§1320d – d-7; 45 C.F.R. Part 164.
Statistical information	The Confidential Information Protection and Statistical Efficiency Act (CIPSEA) requires that information acquired by an agency under a pledge of confidentiality and for exclusively statistical purposes shall be used by the agency only for such purposes and shall not be disclosed in identifiable form for any other use, except withthe informed consent of the respondent. Sec. 512, Title V, Pub. L. No. 107-347, Dec. 17, 2002; 44 U.S.C. §3501 note.
Census data	Except as specifically authorized by law, the Census Bureau may not disclose identifiable census data. Penalties of up to $5,000 and 5 years in prison apply for violating the law. 13 U.S.C. §§ 9 & 214.
Taxpayer data	The IRS must keep taxpayer information confidential and may only disclose it under limited circumstances, e.g., for federal or state tax administration, to assist in the enforcement of child support programs to verify eligibility for public assistance programs, and for use in a criminal investigation. Individuals or agencies receiving taxpayer data must, as a condition of receiving such data, have safeguards for the protection of, and for accounting for, the use of such data. 26 U.S.C. § 6103.
Social Security information	Social Security numbers and related records must be treated as confidential and maynot be disclosed, except as authorized. 42 U.S.C. §§405 & 1306. Such other authorized uses include disclosures for bankruptcy proceedings (11 U.S.C. 342(c)), enforcement of child support programs (42 U.S.C. §§653, 653a, & 666(a)(13)), and enforcement of immigration laws (8 U.S.C. §§1304 & 1360).

THE PRIVACY ACT AND E-GOVERNMENT ACT DO NOT ALWAYS PROVIDE PROTECTIONS FOR FEDERAL USES OF PERSONAL INFORMATION

The Privacy Act's controls on the collection, use, and disclosure of personally identifiable information do not consistently protect such information in all circumstances of its collection and use throughout the federal government. Issues have largely centered on the Privacy Act's definition of a "system of records" (any grouping of records containing personal information retrieved by individual identifier), which triggers the act's protections. Personal information is not always obtained and processed by federal agencies in ways that conform to the definition of a system of records, and in cases where such information falls outside this definition, it may not receive the full privacy protections established by the act. In contrast, the E-Government Act of 2002 sets broader terms for its requirement to conduct PIAs—namely, (1) before an agency develops or procures information technology that collects, maintains, or disseminates information that is in identifiable form, or (2) before an agency collects information in identifiable form using information technology. Although the E-Government Act's broader definition is more inclusive than the system-of-records concept, its requirements are more limited because it imposes no restrictions on agency collection and use of personally identifiable information. Alternatives for addressing these issues could include revising the system-of-records definition to cover all personally identifiable information collected, used, and maintained systematically by the federal government, and revising the E-Government Act's scope to cover federal rulemaking.

Key Terms in the Privacy Act May Be Defined Too Narrowly

The Privacy Act's controls on the collection, use, and disclosure of personally identifiable information only apply when such information is covered by the act's key terms, especially the "system-of-records" construct. There are several different ways in which federal collection and use of personally identifiable information could be outside of such a construct and thus not receive the Privacy Act's protections:

- Personally identifiable information held by the government is not always retrieved by identifier. The Privacy Act defines a system of records as "a

> group of records [32] under the control of any agency from which information is retrieved by the name of the individual or by some identifying number, symbol, or other identifying particular assigned to the individual." If personally identifiable information (records) is not retrieved by identifier but instead accessed through some other method or criteria— for example, by searching for all individuals who have a certain medical condition or who applied for benefits on a certain date—the system would not meet the Privacy Act's system-of-records definition and therefore would not be governed by the act's protections. OMB's 1975 Privacy Act implementation guidance reflects an acknowledgement that agencies could potentially evade the act's requirements by organizing personal information in ways that may not be considered to be retrieved by identifier [33].

This scope of the system-of-records definition has been an issue since the Privacy Act became law in 1974. In its 1977 report, the PPSC pointed out that retrieval by name or identifier reflected a manual rather than a computer-based model of information processing and did not take into account emerging computing technology. As the study explained, while manual record-keeping systems are likely to store and retrieve information by reference to a unique identifier, this is unnecessary in computer-based systems that permit attribute searches [34]. The PPSC noted that retrieval of individually identifiable information by scanning (or searching) large volumes of computer records was not only possible but an ever-increasing agency practice.

Our 2003 report concerning compliance with the Privacy Act found that the PPSC's observations had been borne out across federal agencies. A key characteristic of agencies' systems of records at the time was that a large proportion of them were electronic, reflecting the government's significant use of computers and the Internet to collect and share personal information. Based on survey responses from 25 agencies in 2002, we estimated that 70 percent of the agencies' systems of records contained electronic records and that 11 percent of information systems in use at those agencies contained personal information that was outside a Privacy Act system of records. We also reported that among the agencies we surveyed, the most frequently cited reason for systems not being considered Privacy Act systems of records was that the agency did not use a personal identifier to retrieve the personal information [35].

Recent OMB guidance reflects an acknowledgement that, although personally identifiable information does not always reside in Privacy Act systems of records, it should nevertheless be protected. Following a number of highly publicized data breaches at government agencies, OMB issued guidance instructing agencies to take action to safeguard "personally identifiable information." Beginning in May 2006, OMB required senior agency privacy officials to "conduct a review of policies and processes and take corrective action as appropriate to ensure adequate safeguards to prevent the intentional or negligent misuse of, or unauthorized access to personally identifiable information." Most recently, in May 2007, OMB required agencies to review and reduce "all current holding of personally identifiable information." This guidance is not limited to information that is "retrieved by identifier" or contained within systems of records.

- The Privacy Act's protections may not apply to contemporary data processing technologies and applications. In today's highly interconnected environment, information can be gathered from many different sources, analyzed, and redistributed in very dynamic, unstructured ways that may have little to do with the file-oriented concept of a Privacy Act system of records. For example, data mining, a prevalent technique used by federal agencies [36] for extracting useful information from large volumes of data, may escape the purview of the Privacy Act's protections. Specifically, a data-mining system that performs analysis by looking for patterns in personal information located in other systems of records or that performs subject-based queries across multiple data sources may not constitute a system of records under the act.

In recent years, reports required by law on data mining have described activities that had not been identified as systems of records covered by the Privacy Act. In one example, DHS reported that all the data sources for the planned Analysis Dissemination Visualization Insight and Semantic Enhancement (ADVISE) data mining program were covered by existing system-of-records notices; however, the system itself was not covered, and no system of records notice was created specifically to document protections under the Privacy Act governing the specific activities of the system [37]. ADVISE was a data-mining tool intended to allow an analyst to search for patterns in data—such as relationships among people, organizations, and events—and to produce visual representations of those patterns.

This was also the case with other data mining programs reported by DHS and DOJ [38]. For example, DHS reported on a data mining system known as Intelligence and Information Fusion—which provides intelligence analysts with an ability to view, query, and analyze multiple data sources from within the government—that is not considered a Privacy Act system of records. While DHS reported that the system was "covered" by the systemof-records notice for the Homeland Security Operations Center Database, [39] that notice does not specifically describe the uses of the Intelligence and Information Fusion system. Thus, while the underlying data sources are subject to the protections of the act, the uses of the Intelligence and Information Fusion system have not been specifically addressed.

Likewise, DOJ reported that its Foreign Terrorist Tracking Task Force [40] was developing a data mining system, known as the System to Assess Risk, to assist analysts in prioritizing persons of possible investigative interest in support of a specified terrorist threat. DOJ reported that the system's data sources were covered by the system-of-records notice for the Federal Bureau of Investigation's (FBI) Central Records System [41] However, the Central Records System notice does not specifically describe the uses of the System to Assess Risk and thus provides no evidence that the Privacy Act's protections are being applied to the system. The fact that these notices do not specifically describe data-mining systems that they are said to include reflects the limitations of the system-of-records construct as a way to identify, assess, and report on the protections being applied to these types of analytical uses. As a result, personally identifiable information collected and processed by such systems may be less well protected than if it were more specifically addressed by the Privacy Act.

- Use of personal information from third party sources is not consistently covered by the Privacy Act. The Privacy Act requires agencies to collect information to the greatest extent practicable directly from the subject individual when the information may result in adverse determinations about an individual's rights, benefits, and privileges under federal programs. Yet agencies have increasingly turned to other sources to collect personal information, particularly third-party sources such as information resellers—companies that amass and sell personal information from many sources. Concerns were raised in our expert forum that government agencies may be using such third-party sources as a way to avoid the constraints of the Privacy Act.

In our 2006 report on federal agency use of personal information from information resellers, [42] we noted that agency officials said they generally did not prepare system-of-records notices for the use of information resellers because they were not required to do so by the Privacy Act. The Privacy Act makes its provisions applicable to third-party systems when "an agency provides by a contract for the operation by or on behalf of the agency a system of records to accomplish an agency function." According to agency officials, information reseller databases were not considered systems of records operated "by or on behalf of a government agency" because resellers develop their databases for multiple customers, not the federal government exclusively. Further, agency officials stated that merely querying information reseller databases did not amount to maintaining the information that was obtained, and thus the provisions of the Privacy Act did not apply. In many cases, agency officials considered their use of reseller data to be of this type—essentially "ad hoc" querying or "pinging" of databases for personal information about specific individuals, which they were not doing in connection with a designated system of records. Thus, these sources, which agencies use for many purposes, have not been considered subject to the provisions of the Privacy Act. As a result, individuals may be limited in their ability to learn that information is being collected about them, because the information is being obtained from other sources and the activity is not publicly described in a system-of-records notice. Further, the Privacy Act's constraints on collection, use, and disclosure would not apply.

In our 2006 report, we made recommendations to OMB to revise its guidance to clarify the applicability of requirements for public notices and privacy impact assessments with respect to agency use of personal information from resellers. We also recommended that OMB direct agencies to review their uses of such information to ensure it is explicitly referenced in privacy notices and assessments. However, OMB has not addressed our recommendations. OMB stated that following the completion of work on the protection of personal information through the Identity Theft Task Force, it would consider issuing appropriate guidance concerning reseller data. OMB issued guidance based on the work of the Identity Theft Task Force in May 2007; however, it did not include clarifying guidance concerning reseller data. Without clarifying guidance, agencies may continue to consider use of reseller data as not covered by the Privacy Act and thus may not apply the Privacy Act's protections to this use.

The E-Government Act Applies More Broadly Than the Privacy Act but Lacks Explicit Constraints on Agency Actions

The E-Government Act's requirements for the conduct of PIAs apply to a broader range of government activities than are currently covered by the Privacy Act's definition of a system of records. Specifically, the E- Government Act requires agencies to conduct PIAs before (1) developing or procuring information technology that collects, maintains, or disseminates information that is in individually identifiable form or (2) initiating data collections involving personal information that will be collected, maintained or disseminated using information technology if the same questions are asked of 10 or more people.

The PIA requirement has provided a mechanism for agencies to consider privacy protections during the earliest stages of development of their systems, when it may be relatively easy to make critical adjustments. Senior agency privacy officials at several agencies reported that their PIA processes are incorporated into key stages in systems development. For example, senior agency privacy officials at the IRS reported that PIAs are required at every stage of the systems development life cycle for new systems or systems undergoing major modifications. In addition, five of the six agencies we interviewed reported that they use a privacy threshold analysis, a brief assessment that requires system owners to answer basic questions on the nature of their systems and whether the systems contain personally identifiable information, to identify systems that require a PIA; this approach enables agencies to ensure that systems undergo the PIA process at the earliest stages of development.

Privacy experts and senior agency privacy officials we interviewed also noted that the E-Government Act provides a mechanism to address certain uses of personal information that might not have been covered by the Privacy Act. According to OMB guidance, PIAs are required to be performed and updated whenever a system change creates new privacy risks. Among the types of changes identified in OMB guidance that might require conducting a PIA are when converting from paper to electronic records, when applying new technologies that significantly change how information in identifiable form is managed in the system, and when merging databases to create one central source of information. Typically, under the Privacy Act changes of this nature could result in limited modifications to a system-of-records notice to reflect additional categories of records and/or routine uses. It would not result in a reassessment of privacy risks, as is required for a PIA.

Because the E-Government Act's PIA requirement applies more broadly than the Privacy Act, it may help in part to address concerns about the narrow definition of terms in the Privacy Act. Specifically, a well-written PIA can inform the public about such things as what information is being collected, why it is being collected, and how it is to be used. However, the E-Government Act does not include the specific constraints on how information is to be collected, maintained, and shared that are included in the Privacy Act—such as restrictions on disclosure of personal information and requirements to allow for access to and correction of records by individuals, among other things. Further, the E-

Government Act only applies to information technology systems and therefore does not address personal information contained in paper records.

In addition, the E-Government Act may not be broad enough to cover all cases in which the federal government makes determinations about what personal information is to be collected and how it is to be protected. A major function that is not covered is rulemaking that involves the collection of personally identifiable information. Rulemaking is the process by which federal agencies establish regulations that can govern individual behavior as well as commercial and other activities. For example, DHS is required by the Homeland Security Act to conduct PIAs for all of its proposed rules, [43] and, as a result, PIAs have been conducted for major initiatives, including the REAL ID Act, which required DHS to establish minimum standards for state-issued drivers' licenses and identification cards that federal agencies would accept for official purposes, and the Western Hemisphere Travel Initiative, aimed at strengthening border security and facilitating entry into the United States for U.S. citizens and certain foreign visitors through a standardized identification card. These PIAs have provided for the evaluation of privacy considerations before final decisions are made concerning specific technologies to be used in drivers' licenses and border-crossing identification cards issued by state governments. However, DHS, DOT, Treasury, and a number of smaller agencies are currently the only agencies required to conduct PIAs on proposed rules. Other agencies may be issuing rules that have privacy implications without conducting privacy assessments of them.

Alternatives for Broadening the Coverage of Privacy Laws

A number of alternatives exist to address the issues associated with the coverage of existing privacy laws governing federal use of personal information. These alternatives involve revisions to the Privacy Act and E- Government Act, as follows:

- Revise the system of records definition to cover all personally identifiable information collected, used, and maintained by the federal government. Like the Privacy Protection Study Commission, which believed in 1977 that the act's definition of a system of records should be revised, experts at our forum were in agreement that the system-ofrecords definition is outdated and flawed. The experts agreed that the act's protections should be applied whenever agencies obtain, process, store, or share personally identifiable information—not just when records are retrieved by personal identifier. Such an approach could address concerns that certain activities, such as data mining or retrieving information from commercial information resellers could avoid the protections of the act.

As shown in table 3, several recent OMB memoranda providing direction to federal agencies on privacy protection reflects this approach.

Table 3. Recent OMB Guidance on the Protection of Personally Identifiable Information

Memorandum	Major requirement
OMB M-06-15: Safeguarding Personally Identifiable Information	Requires the Senior Official for Privacy at each agency to conduct a review ofagency policies and processes, and take corrective action as appropriate, to ensure adequate safeguards to prevent the intentional or negligent misuse of,or unauthorized access to, personally identifiable information.
OMB M-06-19: Reporting Incidents Involving Personally Identifiable Information and Incorporating the Cost for Security in Agency Information Technology Investments	Requires agencies to report all incidents involving personally identifiable information to the federal incident response center at DHS within 1 hour of discovering the incident. The guidance defines personally identifiable information as "any information about an individual maintained by an agency, including, but not limited to, education, financial transactions, medical history, and criminal or employment history and information which can be used to distinguish or trace an individual's identity, such as their name, social securitynumber, date and place of birth, mother's maiden name, biometric records, etc., including any other personal information which is linked or linkable to an individual."
OMB M-07-16: Safeguarding against and Responding to the Breach of Personally Identifiable Information	Requires agencies to develop a policy for handling breaches of personally identifiable information as well as policies concerning the responsibilities of individuals authorized to access such information. Agencies are urged to reduce the volume of collected and retained information to the minimum necessary, limit access to only those individuals who must have such access,and use encryption, strong authentication procedures, and other security controls to make information unusable by unauthorized individuals.

The Privacy Act's narrowly scoped system-of-records definition does not match OMB's broadened approach to protecting personally identifiable information. Changing the system-of-records definition is an option that could help ensure that the act's protections are consistently applied to all personally identifiable information.

- Revise the E-Government Act's scope to cover federal rulemaking. The E- Government Act's privacy provisions could be broadened to apply to all federal rulemaking involving the collection of personally identifiable information, as the Homeland Security Act currently requires of DHS and the Transportation, Treasury, Independent Agencies and General Government Appropriations Act of 2005 requires of Transportation, Treasury, and certain other agencies. This change would ensure that privacy concerns are addressed as the federal government proposes and adopts rules that affect how other entities, including state and local government agencies, collect and use personally identifying information.

Laws and Guidance May Not Effectively Limit Agency Collection and Use of Personal Information to Specific Purposes

Current laws and guidance impose only modest requirements for describing the purposes for collecting and using personal information and limiting how that information is collected and used. For example, agencies are not required to be specific in formulating purpose descriptions in their public notices. Laws and guidance also may not effectively limit the collection of personal information. For example, the Privacy Act's requirement that information be "relevant and necessary" gives broad latitude to agencies in determining the amount of information to collect. In addition, mechanisms to limit use to a specified purpose may be weak. For example, the Privacy Act does not limit agency internal use of information, as long as it is needed for an official purpose or include provisions addressing external sharing with other entities to ensure that the information's new custodians preserve the act's protections. Examples of alternatives for addressing these issues include setting specific limits on routine uses and use of information within agencies to include more specific limits, requiring agencies to justify how collection has been limited in privacy notices, and requiring agencies to establish formal agreements with external governmental entities before sharing personally identifiable information with them.

Fair Information Practices Call for Purpose Specification and Limitations on Collection and Use of Personal Information

A key area of concern about personal information maintained by government agencies is to ensure that limits are placed on what the government acquires and how it uses the information—thus giving individuals a measure of control over their own personal information. Two of the fair information practices relate specifically to limiting the way the government collects and uses personal information: collection limitation and use limitation. A third principle—purpose specification—is critical to ensuring that the other two are applied effectively.

The purpose specification principle states that the purpose for the collection of personal information should be disclosed before the collection is made and upon any change to that purpose, and its use should be limited to that purpose and compatible purposes. Clearly specifying the purpose of a given activity establishes the measure for determining whether the collection of information has been sufficiently limited to what is relevant for the purpose and whether the ways in which the information is used have also been limited to what is appropriate for the same purpose.

The collection limitation principle states that the collection of personal information should be limited, should be obtained by lawful and fair means, and, where appropriate, with the knowledge or consent of the individual. When the collection limitation principle is applied, individuals can gain assurance that the information about them that is being collected is only what is needed to perform a specific, predisclosed function. In the government arena, this mitigates the risk that an over-collection of personal information could facilitate the improper use of that information to make adverse determinations. For example, the Transportation Security Administration (TSA) received criticism about its now-cancelled Computer-Assisted Passenger Pre-screening System II because it proposed to collect information from third-party sources in addition to airline passengers themselves. Concerns were raised that individuals could be delayed or denied boarding their airline flights based on third-party information that was potentially inaccurate. In developing a successor project, called Secure Flight, TSA responded to privacy concerns by planning to collect far less information and to focus on information collected directly from individuals [44].

A closely related principle—the use limitation principle—provides that personal information, once collected, should not be disclosed or used for other than a specified purpose without consent of the individual or legal authority. The use limitation principle is arguably of heightened importance in the government arena because the government has many functions that affect numerous aspects of an individual's well-being. Hence, it is important to ensure that information the government collects for one function is not used indiscriminately for other unrelated functions. By requiring the government to define a specific purpose for the collection of personal information and limit its use to that specified purpose, individuals gain assurance that their privacy will be protected and their information will not be used in ways that could jeopardize their rights or otherwise unfairly affect them.

The Privacy Act Does Not Ensure That Purposes Are Always Stated and Are Specific

The Privacy Act includes requirements that agencies (1) inform individuals from whom information is being collected of the principal purpose or purposes for which the information is intended to be used and (2) publish a system-of-records notice in the Federal Register of the existence and character of the system of records, including planned routine uses of the records and the purpose of each of these routine uses. Concerns have been raised that the act's requirements do not go far enough in ensuring that the government's planned purposes are sufficiently specified:

- *Statements of overall purpose are not always required.* The Privacy Act requires agencies to inform individuals on forms used to collect information from them of the principal purpose or purposes for which the information is intended to be used. This is an important provision that protects individuals when the government is collecting information directly from them. However, in many cases, agencies obtain information about individuals from other sources, such as commercial entities (including information resellers) and other governmental entities. In those cases, no overall declaration of purpose is required in the system-of-records notice. For each of the stated routine uses a description is required of the potential purposes for which the records may be used; however, there is no requirement for a declaration of the purpose or purposes for the system of records as a whole. Given that individuals may be especially concerned about how their information is collected from different government and commercial entities, not having an overall purpose associated with this information raises concerns.
- *Purpose descriptions in public notices are not required to be specific.* As mentioned above, while there is no requirement for an overall statement

of purpose, Privacy Act notices may contain multiple descriptions of purposes associated with routine uses, and agencies are not required to be specific in formulating these purposes. OMB guidance on the act gives agencies discretion to determine how to define the range of appropriate uses and associated purposes that it intends for a given system of records. For example, purpose statements for certain law enforcement and anti-terrorism systems might need to be phrased broadly enough so as not to reveal investigative techniques or the details of ongoing cases. However, overly broadly-defined purposes could allow for unnecessarily broad collections of information and ranges of subsequent uses, thus calling into question whether meaningful limitations had been imposed.

For example, in previous work on international passenger prescreening by DHS's Customs and Border Protection (CBP), [45] we reported that CBP's public notices and reports regarding its international prescreening process did not fully or accurately describe CBP's use of personal data throughout the passenger prescreening process. In that case, CBP relied on a systemof-records notice for the Treasury Enforcement Communications System—one of several data sources used in the prescreening process—to notify the public about the purpose of the international prescreening program. The notice, however, did not mention CBP's passenger prescreening purpose but simply included a broad statement about its law enforcement purpose, namely that "every possible type of information from a variety of Federal, state and local sources, which contributes to effective law enforcement may be maintained in this system of records" [46]. Use of such a sweeping purpose statement obscured its use in international passenger prescreening and did not establish a basis for limiting use of the information in the system. Its use shows that the act does not require the government to clearly state its purposes for collecting and using personal information.

Another example can be found in the system-of-records notice for the FBI's Central Records System. The FBI relies on this notice to inform the public about a broad range of files it maintains and uses for a variety of different purposes. According to the notice, the Central Records System contains investigative, personnel, applicant, administrative, and "general" files [47]. In addition to information within 281 different categories of legal violations over which the FBI has investigative jurisdiction, the files also include information pertaining to personnel, applicant, and administrative matters. As a result, it is unclear from the notice how any given record in this system is to be used. While law enforcement agencies are often concerned about revealing their methods to criminals, descriptions of the specific purposes of FBI systems could be crafted to avoid revealing what information had been collected about any specific individual or how it was being used by the agency. DOJ officials acknowledged that there has been frequent criticism of the broad scope of the Central Records System notice but said the notice had been structured that way because all the records covered by the notice are organized according to that same indexing hierarchy. More significantly, the Privacy Act does not require that systems of records be defined and described more specifically. Like the CBP notice, the FBI notice demonstrates that the act does not require the government to clearly state its purposes for collecting and using personal information.

Laws and Guidance May Not Effectively Limit Collection of Personal Information

Regarding collection limitation, the Privacy Act states that each agency should maintain only such information about individuals in its systems of records that is "relevant and necessary" to accomplish a purpose the agency is required to accomplish by statute or executive order of the President. The act further states that agencies generally cannot disclose records about an individual without his or her consent, except under a number of specific conditions [48].

Collection limitation may also be addressed indirectly as part of agency procedures under the E-Government Act for conducting PIAs. Based on OMB guidance, PIAs are required to include explanations regarding what information is being collected, why it is being collected, and what the intended uses are. According to agency privacy officials, they often question agency program officials about whether planned collections are really necessary or could be reduced during the process of reviewing draft PIAs.

The Paperwork Reduction Act also addresses collection limitation when information is to be collected individually from 10 or more people. It requires agency chief information officers to determine whether the information has practical utility and is necessary for the proper performance of agency functions. Once a chief information officer has certified that a planned information collection meets 10 standards set forth in the act, the collection is submitted to OMB for review. The agency may not collect the information without OMB's approval.

Finally, OMB also has issued guidance instructing agencies to limit the collection of personally identifiable information. In early 2007, OMB issued Memorandum M-07-16, which required agencies to review and reduce the volume of their holdings of personally identifiable information to the minimum necessary for the proper performance of documented agency functions. The memorandum noted that "by collecting only the information necessary and managing it properly, agencies can often reduce the volume of information they possess, the risk to the information, and the burden of safeguarding it." The memorandum also required agencies to develop a plan to reduce their use of Social Security numbers and to make public a schedule by which they would periodically update the review of their overall holdings of personally identifiable information.

Nothwithstanding these various provisions in law and guidance, the government's collection of personal information may not be effectively limited:

- *The Privacy Act's "relevant and necessary" provision gives broad latitude to agencies in determining the amount of information to collect.* The Privacy Act states that each agency shall "maintain in its records only such information about an individual as is relevant and necessary to accomplish a purpose of the agency required to be accomplished by statute or by Executive order of the President." Under these criteria, agency officials do not have specific requirements for justifying how much information to collect; instead, it is a matter of judgment whether any specific piece of information is relevant and necessary. OMB's implementation guidance advises agencies to identify the specific provisions in law that authorize a collection before it is implemented and provides questions that agencies should consider in determining what information to collect but concludes that a final decision on what is relevant and necessary is a matter of judgment. For certain functions, such as homeland security, new and varied collections of personal information may be relevant and necessary. However, several experts at our forum expressed concern about what they view as an increasing trend in the post-9/11 era for federal agencies to collect as much information as possible in the event that such information might be needed at a future date. Without establishing more specific requirements for justifying information collections, it may be difficult to ensure that agencies collect only relevant and necessary personal information.
- *The Paperwork Reduction Act information collection review process has not always been effective at limiting collection.* In addition to provisions in the Privacy Act, the PRA has the potential to serve as a useful control

for ensuring that agencies make reasoned judgments about what personal information to collect. However, it has not always achieved this objective. As we reported in 2005, the PRA's constraints on information collection are not always completely followed [49] For our previous report, we examined a sample of 12 approved information collections to assess the effectiveness of the PRA review process. We found that while chief information officers reviewed information collections regularly, support for a particular collection was often partial. For example, of the 12 approved data collections we reviewed, 6 provided only partial support for determining whether the collection was necessary for the proper performance of agency functions and 8 had only partial support for determining whether a collection provided the information it was intended to provide. Despite these shortcomings, all 12 data collections were certified by agency chief information officers, and all 12 were also approved by OMB. The fact that agencies are able to have information collections approved despite incomplete justification contributes to concern that the PRA information collection review process may not be effective at limiting collection of personally identifiable information by the government. We recommended that OMB take steps to improve the review process, and OMB responded that it was considering changing its instructions to align them more closely with 10 standards specified in the act. However, OMB has not yet addressed our recommendation.

- *OMB guidance does not provide specific measures for limiting information collections.* Although agency privacy officials believe the PIA process gives them the opportunity to address collection limitation, the requirements of the E-Government Act do not specifically address collection limitation, and OMB PIA guidance accordingly does not include requirements for limiting information collection, and the process does not include criteria for making determinations as to whether specific planned data elements are necessary. The lack of specific control mechanisms contributes to concerns by privacy experts that collection of personally identifiable information is not being effectively limited. Similarly, OMB's recent guidance to limit collection of personally identifiable information did not include plans to monitor agency actions or take other proactive steps to ensure that agencies are effectively limiting their collections of personally identifiable information. OMB has not reported publicly on agencies' progress in responding to its guidance, and thus it remains unclear what steps agencies have taken. Finally, like previous guidance, M07-16 did not provide any criteria for making determinations about whether specific data elements are needed. Without a legal requirement to limit collection of personally identifiable information, it is unclear the extent to which agencies will follow OMB's guidance.

Mechanisms to Limit Use of Personally Identifiable Information to a Specified Purpose May Be Ineffective

The Privacy Act generally prevents agencies from sharing personal information in systems of records, except pursuant to a written request by, or with prior written consent of, the affected individual. There are, however, a number of specific conditions defined by the Privacy Act under which federal agencies may share information from systems of records with other government agencies without the affected individuals' consent.

For example, agencies may share information with another agency for civil or criminal law enforcement activity [50]. Sharing is also allowed if it is for a purpose that is "compatible" with the purpose for which the information was collected, referred to as a "routine use." Agencies are required to enumerate these routine uses in their system-of-records notices [51] and publish the notice in the Federal Register for public comment. According to OMB's 1975 implementation guidance, the routine use provisions were intended to "serve as a caution to agencies to think out in advance what uses it will make of information" and was intended "to discourage the unnecessary exchange of information to other persons or to agencies who may not be as sensitive to the collecting agency's reasons for using and interpreting the material." Section 208 of the E-Government Act of 2002 and related OMB guidance also have provisions that implement the use limitation principle, chiefly by requiring that PIAs include the intended uses of the information and with whom the information will be shared.

Although the Privacy Act and E-Government Act have provisions for limiting the use of personally identifiable information to a specified purpose, these mechanisms may not always be effective for the following reasons:

- *Unconstrained application of pre-defined "routine" uses may weaken use limitations.* A number of concerns have been raised about the impact on privacy of potentially unnecessary routine uses for agency systems of records, particularly through the application of "standard" routine uses that are developed for general use on multiple systems of records. This practice is not prohibited by the Privacy Act.

Table 4. Sample Descriptions from Five Agencies of a Standard Routine Use for Hiring or Retention of an Individual or the Issuance of a Security Clearance, Contract, Grant, or Other Benefit

Agency	Standard routine use
DHS	To appropriate federal, state, local, tribal, territorial, foreign, or international agency, if the information is relevant and necessary to a requesting agency's decision concerning the hiring or retention of an individual, or issuance of a securityclearance, license, contract, grant or other benefit, or if the information is relevant and necessary to a DHS decision concerning the hiring or retention of an employee, the issuance of a security clearance, the reporting of an investigation of an employee, the letting of a contract, or the issuance of a license, grant, or other benefit and when disclosure is appropriate to the proper performance of the official duties of the person making the request.
DOT	A record from this system of records may be disclosed, as a routine use, to a federal agency, in response to its request,in connection with the hiring or retention of an employee, the issuance of a security clearance, the reporting of an investigation of an employee, the letting of a contract, or the issuance of a license, grant, or other benefit by the requesting agency, to the extent that the information is relevant and necessary to the requesting agency's decision on the matter.
HHS	Disclosure may be made to a federal, state, local, foreign, or tribal or other public authority of the fact that this system ofrecords contains information relevant to the retention of an employee, the retention of a security clearance, the letting ofa contract, or the issuance or retention of a license, grant, or other benefit. The other agency or licensing organization may then make a request supported by the written consent of the individual for the entire record if it so chooses. No disclosure will be made unless the information has been determined to be sufficiently reliable to support a referral to another office within the agency or to another federal agency for criminal, civil, administrative personnel, or regulatory action.
IRS	Disclose to a federal, state, local, or tribal agency, or other public authority, which has requested information relevant or necessary to hiring or retaining an employee, or issuing or continuing a contract, security clearance, license, grant, or other benefit. This is compatible with the purpose for which the records were collected because the disclosure permits the IRS to assist another agency or authority in ensuring that it only hires or issues benefits to eligible individuals.
DOJ	To appropriate officials and employees of a federal agency or entity that requires information relevant to a decision concerning the hiring, appointment, or retention of an employee; the issuance, renewal, suspension, or revocation of a security clearance; the execution of a security or suitability investigation; the letting of a contract; or the issuance of a grant or benefit.

All six agencies we reviewed had lists of standard routine uses for application to their systems of records. However, the language of these standard routine uses varies from agency to agency. For example, as shown in table 4, several agencies have a routine use allowing them to share information about individuals with other governmental entities for purposes of decision-making about hiring or retention of an individual, issuance of a security clearance, license, contract, grant, or other benefit.

As shown in the table, one agency (HHS) includes a provision that sharing of this information will occur only after the requesting agency has submitted a request supported by written consent of the affected individual. In contrast, similar routine uses at other agencies (DHS, DOJ, IRS, and DOT) have no requirement for the written consent of the individual. Still another agency (SSA) has no comparable standard routine use at all. Experts expressed concern that "standard" routine uses such as these vary so much from agency to agency, with no specific legal requirement that they be formulated consistently.

Further, agencies do not apply these uses consistently. DHS, for example, has a "library" of routine uses that are applied selectively to systems of records on a case-by-case basis. In contrast, DOT applies its list of general routine uses to all of its systems of records, unless explicitly disavowed in the system's public notice. Similarly, the FBI applies its "blanket" routine uses to "every existing FBI Privacy Act system of records and to all FBI systems of records created or modified in the future." As a result, use may not always be limited as the Privacy Act intended.

- *The Privacy Act sets only modest limits on the use of personal information for multiple purposes within an agency.* Recognizing the need for agency personnel to access records to carry out their duties, the Privacy Act permits disclosures from agency systems of records "to those officers and employees of the agency which maintains the record who have a need for the record in the performance of their duties." However, without additional limits, internal uses could go beyond uses that are related to the purpose of the original collection. In our interviews with senior agency privacy officials, we asked what, if any, limits were placed on internal agency uses of information. Several agencies responded that, consistent with the Privacy Act and OMB guidance, internal agency usage of personal information was limited to those personnel with a "need to know." [52]. Because the Privacy Act and related guidance do not require it, none of these agencies took steps to determine whether internal uses were consistent with the purposes originally stated for the collection of information. Reliance on the "need to know" criteria for sharing information does not require a determination regarding compatibility with the original collection.

The potential that personal information could be used for multiple, unspecified purposes is especially heightened in large agencies with multiple components that may collect personal information in many different ways for disparate purposes. For example, the establishment of DHS in March 2003 brought 22 agencies with varied missions and 180,000 employees into a single agency. These agencies collect personal information for a range of purposes, including administering citizenship, enforcing immigration laws, protecting land and sea ports of entry, and protecting against threats to aviation security. The Privacy Act does not constrain DHS or other agencies from using information obtained for one of these specific missions for another agency mission. As a result, individuals do not have assurance that their information will be used only for the purpose for which it was collected.

- The Privacy Act's provisions may not apply when data are shared for use by another agency. In addition to concerns about limiting use to a specified purpose within an agency, more extensive issues have been raised when data are shared outside an agency, even when such sharing is pursuant to a predefined "routine" use. Although the Privacy Act provides assurance that the information in systems of records cannot be disclosed unless it is pursuant to either a routine use or another statutorily allowed condition, the act does not attach its protections to data after they have been disclosed [53]. Despite the lack of requirements, agencies we reviewed reported taking measures to ensure the data are used appropriately by recipients. For example, agencies reported using mechanisms such as computer matching agreements under the matching provisions of the Privacy Act or other types of data-sharing agreements to impose privacy protections on recipients of shared data. However, absent these measures taken by agencies, data shared outside federal agencies would not always have sufficient protections.

Data sharing among agencies is central to the emerging information sharing environment intended to facilitate the sharing of terrorism information. If the information sharing environment is to be effective, it will require policies, procedures, and technologies that link people, systems, and information among all appropriate federal, state, local, and tribal entities and the private sector. In the recent development of guidelines for the information-sharing environment, there has been general agreement that privacy considerations must also be addressed alongside measures for enhancing the exchange of information among agencies. The Intelligence Reform and Terrorism Prevention Act of 2004 called for the issuance of guidelines to protect privacy and civil liberties in the development of the information sharing environment, and the President reiterated that requirement in an October 2005 directive to federal departments and agencies. Based on the President's directive, a committee within the Office of the Director of National Intelligence was established to develop such guidelines, and they were approved by the President in November 2006 [54] However, as we previously testified, [55] the guidelines as issued provide only a high-level framework for addressing privacy protection and do not include all of the Fair Information Practices.

More recently, in September 2007, the Program Manager for the Information Sharing Environment released a Privacy and Civil Liberties Implementation Guide for the Information Sharing Environment [56]. The guide describes the processes for information-sharing environment participants to follow when integrating privacy and civil liberties safeguards into their information sharing efforts, including an assessment of whether current activities comply with the privacy guidelines. However, as noted by our expert panel, these guidelines do not address the application of protections to Privacy Act data as they are shared within the information sharing environment, mentioning the act only in passing. In the absence of the adoption of more specific implementation guidelines or more explicit protections in the Privacy Act for data that are disclosed, agency information-sharing activities may not ensure that the use of personal information is sufficiently limited.

Alternatives for Better Ensuring That Purpose Is Specified and That Collection and Use of Personal Information Are Limited

A number of options exist for addressing the issues associated with specifying the purpose for obtaining personal information, limiting the collection of such information, and limiting its use to specified purposes. Alternatives in each of these categories are as follows

Purpose Specification

- *Require agencies to state the principal purpose for each system of records.* Having a specific stated purpose for each system of records would make it easier to determine whether planned uses were consistent with that purpose

Collection Limitation

- *Require* agencies to limit collection of personally identifiable information and to explain how such collection has been limited in system-of-records notices. This requirement would more directly require agencies to limit their collection of personally identifiable information than the current requirement, which is simply to maintain only such information as is relevant and necessary to accomplish a purpose of the agency.
- *Revise the Paperwork Reduction Act to include specific requirements for limiting the collection of personally identifiable information.* The Paperwork Reduction Act currently does not specifically address limiting the collection of personally identifiable information but could serve as an established mechanism for incorporating such limits.

Use Limitation

- *Require agencies to justify the use of key elements of personally identifiable information.* Agencies could be required to state their reasons for collecting specific personally identifiable information, such as Social Security numbers and dates of birth. The Secure Flight program within DHS, for example, recently went through a process of analyzing specific data elements to be collected from airline passengers for prescreening purposes and was able as a result to limit its requirements to only a few key elements for most passengers. Given concerns about data collection, it is likely that other government data collections could also be reduced based on such an analysis.
- *Set specific limits on routine uses and internal uses of information within agencies.* Sharing of information within an agency could be limited to purposes clearly compatible with the original purpose of a system of

records. Agencies could also be required to be specific in describing purposes associated with routine uses.

- *Require agencies to establish formal agreements with external governmental entities before sharing personally identifiable information with them, as is already done at certain agencies.* These formal agreements would be a means to carry forward to external entities the privacy controls that applied to the information when it was in an agency system of records.

These requirements could be set explicitly in law or a legal requirement could be set for another agency, such as OMB, to develop specific implementation guidelines for agencies. Setting such requirements could help ensure that a proper balance exists in allowing government agencies to collect and use personally identifiable information while also limiting that collection and use to what is necessary and relevant.

The Privacy Act May Not Include Effective Mechanisms for Informing the Public

Transparency about government programs and systems that collect and use personal information is a key element in maintaining public trust and support for programs that use such information. A primary method for providing transparency is through public written notices. A clear and effective notice can provide individuals with critical information about what personal data are to be collected, how they are to be used, and the circumstances under which they may be shared. An effective notice can also provide individuals with information they need to determine whether to provide their personal information (if voluntary), or who to contact to correct any errors that could result in an adverse determination about them.

In formal terms, the openness principle states that the public should be informed about privacy policies and practices and that individuals should have a ready means of learning about the use of personal information. The openness principle underlies the public notice provisions of the Privacy Act. Specifically, the Privacy Act requires agencies to publish in the Federal Register, "upon establishment or revision, a notice of the existence and character of a system of records." This notice is to include, among other things, the categories of records in the system as well as the categories of sources of records. The notice is also required to explain agency procedures whereby an individual can gain access to any record pertaining to him or her contained in the system of records and contest its content. Agencies are further required to publish notice of any new use or intended use of the information in the system and provide an opportunity for interested persons to submit written data, views, or arguments to the agency [57].

In addition, when collection of personal information is received directly from the affected individual, agencies are required to notify the individual of the primary purposes for the collection and the planned routine uses of the information. The act encourages agencies, to the extent practicable, to collect information directly from the subject individual when the information may result in adverse determinations about the individual's rights, benefits, and privileges under federal programs.

It is critical that Privacy Act notices effectively communicate to the public the nature of agency collection and use of personal information because such notices are the fundamental mechanisms by which agencies are held accountable for specifying purpose, limiting collection and use, and providing a means to access and correct records. These notices can be seen as agreements between agencies and the public to provide protections for the data in the custody of the government.

System-of-records notices are especially important in cases where information is not obtained directly from individuals because there is no opportunity for them to be informed directly. As experts noted, collection from individuals may be less prevalent in an environment where agencies are encouraged to participate in cross agency e-government initiatives that promote a "collect once, use many" approach. Experts also noted that since the terrorist attacks on 9/11, agencies are charged with sharing information more readily, one of the major goals of the information sharing environment. In situations such as these, the system-of-records notice may be one of the only ways for individuals to learn about the collection of their personal information.

However, experts at our forum as well as agency privacy officials questioned the value of system-of-records notices as vehicles for providing information to the general public. Specifically, concerns were raised that the content of these notices and their publication in the Federal Register may not fully inform the public about planned government uses of personal information, for the following reasons:

- *System of record notices may be difficult to understand.* As with other legally-required privacy notices, such as the annual privacy notices provided to consumers by banks and other financial institutions, system-of-records notices have been criticized as hard to read and understand.

For example, lay readers may have difficulty understanding the extent to which lists of "routine" uses actually explain how the government intends to collect and use personal information. Likewise, for an uninformed reader, a list of exemptions claimed for the system—cited only by the corresponding paragraph number in the Privacy Act—could raise more questions than it answers. Agency senior privacy officials we interviewed frequently cited legal compliance as the primary function of a system-of-records notice, thus leading to legalistic descriptions of the controls on collection and use of personal information. These officials acknowledged that these descriptions of privacy protections may not be very useful to the general public. Privacy experts at our forum likewise viewed system-ofrecords notices as having limited value as a vehicle for public notification.

- *System-of-records notices do not always contain complete and useful information about privacy protections.* As discussed earlier in this report, system-of-records notices can be written to describe purposes and uses of information in such broad terms that it becomes questionable whether those purposes and uses have been significantly limited. Likewise, broad purpose statements contained in system-of-records notices may not contain enough information to usefully inform the public of the government's intended purposes, and the citation of multiple routine uses does little to aid individuals in learning about how the government is using their personal information. The Privacy Act does not require agencies to be specific in describing the purposes associated with routine uses. Further, individuals are limited in their ability to know how extensively their information may be used within an agency, since there are no requirements to publish all expected internal agency uses of personal information.

Several agency privacy officials as well as experts at our forum noted that privacy impact assessments, when properly prepared, can lead to more meaningful discussions about privacy protections and may serve as a better vehicle to convey purposes and uses of information to the public. OMB guidance requires agency PIAs to identify what choices were made regarding an IT system or information collection as a result of performing a PIA, while a system-of-records notice contains no comparable requirement. As a result, a well-crafted PIA may provide more meaningful notice to the public not only about the planned purposes and uses of personal information, but also about how an agency's assessment was used to drive decisions about the system.

- *Publication in the Federal Register May Reach Only a Limited Audience.* Agency privacy officials questioned whether the required publication of system-of-records notices in the Federal Register would be useful to a broader audience than federal agency officials and public interest groups, such as privacy advocacy groups. Notices published in the Federal Register may not be very accessible and readable. The Federal Register Web site does not provide a ready means of determining what system-of records notices are current, when they were last updated, or which ones apply to any specific governmental function. Officials agreed that it can be difficult to locate a system-of-records notice on the Federal Register Web site, even when the name of the relevant system of records is known in advance. Privacy experts at our forum likewise agreed that the Federal Register is probably not effective with the general public and that a more effective technique for reaching a wide audience in today's environment is via consolidated publication on a governmentwide Web site devoted to privacy. Both agency officials and privacy experts also agreed, however, that the Federal Register serves a separate but important role as the official public record of federal agencies, and thus it would not be advisable to cease publishing system-of-records notices in the Federal Register. Notice in the Federal Register also serves an important role as the official basis for soliciting comments from the public on proposed systems of records.

Alternatives for Improving Notice to the Public

Based on discussions with privacy experts, agency officials, and analysis of laws and related guidance, a number of options exist for addressing the issues associated with improving public notice regarding federal collection and use of personal information. As with the alternatives previously discussed, these could be addressed explicitly in law or a legal requirement could be set for another agency, such as OMB, to develop specific implementation guidelines for agencies. These alternatives are as follows:

- *Require layered public notices in conjunction with system-of-records notices.* Given the difficulty that a lay audience may face in trying to understand the content of notices, experts at our forum agreed that a new approach ought to be taken to designing notices for the public about use of personal information. Specifically, the use of layered notices, an approach that is actively being pursued in the private sector for consumer privacy notices, could also be effective for Privacy Act notices. Layering involves providing only the most important summary facts up front—often in a graphically oriented format—followed by one or more lengthier, more narrative versions. By offering both types of notices, the benefits of each can be realized: long notices have the advantage of being complete, but may not be as easy to understand, while brief notices may be easier to understand but may not capture all the detail that needs to be conveyed.

A recent interagency research project on the design of easy-to-understand consumer financial privacy notices found, among other things, that providing context to the notice (explaining to consumers why they are receiving the notice and what to do with it) was key to comprehension, and that comprehension was aided by incorporating key visual design elements, such as use of a tabular format, large and legible fonts, and appropriate use of white space and simple headings [58].

The multilayered approach discussed and lessons learned could be applied to government privacy notices. For example, a multilayered government privacy notice could provide a brief description of the information required, the primary purpose for the collection, and associated uses and sharing of such data at one layer. The notice could also provide additional details about the system or program's uses and the circumstances under which data could be shared at a second layer. This would accomplish the purpose of communicating the key details in a brief format, while still providing complete information to those who require it. Aiming to improve comprehension of notices by citizens through clearer descriptions could better achieve the Privacy Act's objective of publishing a public notice of the "existence and character" of systems of records.

- *Set requirements to ensure that purpose, collection limitations, and use limitations are better addressed in the content of privacy notices.* Additional requirements could be established for the content and preparation of system-of-records notices, to include a specific description of the planned purpose of a system as well as what data needs to be collected to serve that purpose and how its use will be limited to that purpose, including descriptions of primary and secondary uses of information. Agencies may be able to use material developed for PIAs to help meet these requirements. Setting these requirements could spur agencies to prepare notices that include more meaningful descriptions of the intents and purposes of their systems of records.

- *Make all notices available on a governmentwide privacy Web site.* Experts at our forum and agency officials also agreed that the most effective and practical method for sharing information with the public is through the Web. Relevant privacy notices could be published at a central governmentwide location, such as www.privacy.gov, and at corresponding standard locations on agency Web sites, such as www.agency.gov/privacy. Given that adequate attention is paid to making the information searchable as well as easy to locate and peruse, such a Web site has the potential to reach a far broader spectrum of users than the Federal Register.

CONCLUSIONS

Current laws and guidance governing the federal government's collection, use, and disclosure of personal information have gaps and other potential shortcomings in three broad categories: (1) the Privacy Act and E-Government Act do not always provide protections for federal uses of personal information, (2) laws and guidance may not effectively limit agency collection and use of personal information to specific purposes, and (3) the Privacy Act may not include effective mechanisms for informing the public.

MATTER FOR CONGRESSIONAL CONSIDERATION

In assessing the appropriate balance between the needs of the federal government to collect personally identifiable information for programmatic purposes and the assurances that individuals should have that their information is being sufficiently protected and properly used, Congress should consider amending applicable laws, such as the Privacy Act and the E-Government Act, according to the alternatives outlined in this report, including:

- revising the scope of the laws to cover all personally identifiable information collected, used, and maintained by the federal government;
- setting requirements to ensure that the collection and use of personally identifiable information is limited to a stated purpose; and

- establishing additional mechanisms for informing the public about privacy protections by revising requirements for the structure and publication of public notices.

AGENCY COMMENTS AND OUR EVALUATION

We received written comments on a draft of this report from the Deputy Administrator of the Office of E-Government and Information Technology and the Deputy Administrator of the Office of Information and Regulatory Affairs of OMB. The letter is reprinted in appendix V. In their comments, the officials noted that they shared our concerns about privacy and listed guidance the agency has issued in the areas of privacy and information security. The officials stated they believe it would be important for Congress to consider potential amendments to the Privacy Act and the E-Government Act in the broader context of the several privacy statutes that Congress has enacted.

Though we did not make specific recommendations to OMB, the agency provided comments on the alternatives identified in conjunction with our matter for congressional consideration. Regarding alternatives for revising the scope of laws to cover all personally identifiable information collected, used, and maintained by the federal government, OMB stated that it would be important for Congress to evaluate fully the potential implications of revisions such as amending the Privacy Act's system-of-records definition. We believe that, given the Privacy Act's controls on the collection, use, and disclosure of personally identifiable information do not consistently protect such information in all circumstances of its collection and use throughout the federal government, amending the act's definition of a system of records is an important alternative for Congress to consider. However, we agree with OMB that such consideration should be thorough and include further public debate on all relevant issues.

Regarding alternatives for setting requirements to ensure that the collection and use of personally identifiable information is limited to a stated purpose, OMB stated that agencies are working to implement a requirement in a recent OMB memorandum to review and reduce the volume of personally identifiable information they handle "to the minimum necessary." The draft report notes that this requirement is in place; however, because significant concerns were raised about this issue by our previous work and by experts at our forum, we believe Congress should consider additional alternatives for ensuring that the collection and use of personally identifiable information is limited to a stated purpose.

Finally, regarding effective mechanisms for informing the public, OMB stated that it supports ensuring that the public is appropriately informed of how agencies are using their information. OMB stated that they will review agency practices in informing the public and review the alternatives outlined in our report.

OMB provided additional technical comments, which are addressed in appendix V. We also received technical comments from DHS, DOJ, DOT, and IRS. We have addressed these comments in the final report as appropriate.

Unless you publicly announce the content of this report earlier, we plan no further distribution until 30 days from the report date. At that time, we will send copies of this report to the Attorney General, the Secretaries of Homeland Security, Health and Human Services, and Transportation; the Commissioners of the Internal Revenue Service and the Social Security Administration; the Director, Office of Management and Budget; and other interested congressional committees. Copies will be made available at no charge on our Web site, www.gao.gov.

If you have any questions concerning this report, please call me at (202) 512-6240 or send e-mail to koontzl@gao.gov. Contact points for our office of Congressional Relations and Public Affairs may be found on the last page of this report. Key contributors to this report are listed in appendix VI.

Linda D. Koontz
Director, Information Management Issues

List of Congressional Requesters

The Honorable Harry Reid
Senate Majority Leader
United States Senate

The Honorable Daniel K. Akaka
Chairman
Committee on Veterans' Affairs
United States Senate

The Honorable Joseph I. Lieberman
Chairman
Committee on Homeland Security and Governmental Affairs
United States Senate

The Honorable Bob Filner
Chairman
Committee on Veterans' Affairs
House of Representatives

The Honorable Hillary Rodham Clinton
United States Senate

The Honorable Byron L. Dorgan
United States Senate

The Honorable Patty Murray
United States Senate

The Honorable Barack Obama
United States Senate

The Honorable John D. Rockefeller, IV
United States Senate

The Honorable Ken Salazar
United States Senate

The Honorable Charles E. Schumer
United States Senate

APPENDIX I: OBJECTIVE, SCOPE, AND METHODOLOGY

Our objective was to identify major issues regarding whether the Privacy Act of 1974, the E-Government Act of 2002, and related guidance consistently cover the federal government's collection and use of personal information and incorporate key privacy principles, and in doing so, to identify options for addressing these issues. Our objective was not focused on evaluating compliance with these laws; rather, it was to identify major issues concerning their sufficiency in light of current uses of personal information by the federal government.

To address our objective, we reviewed and analyzed the Privacy Act, section 208 of the E-Government Act, and related Office of Management and Budget (OMB) guidance to determine the types of activities and information they apply to and to identify federal agency privacy responsibilities. We compared privacy protection requirements of these laws and related OMB guidance with the Fair Information Practices to identify any issues or gaps in privacy protections for personal information controlled by the federal government. In this regard, we also assessed the role of the Paperwork Reduction Act in protecting privacy by limiting collection of information. We also drew upon our prior work to identify examples of potential gaps in addressing the Fair Information Practices. A list of related GAO products can be found at the end of this report.

We also obtained an operational perspective on these issues by analyzing agency privacy-related polices and procedures and through discussion sessions on the sufficiency of these laws with senior agency privacy officials at six federal agencies. These agencies were the Departments of Health and Human Services, Homeland Security, Justice, and Transportation; the Internal Revenue Service; and the Social Security Administration. We selected these agencies because they have large inventories of information collections, prominent privacy issues, and varied missions. Additionally, our colleagues at the National Academy of Sciences (NAS) agreed that this selection was appropriate for obtaining an operational perspective on these issues. The perspective obtained from the six agencies is not representative governmentwide. However, because we selected these agencies based on a rigorous set of selection criteria, the information we gathered during this discussion session provided us with an overview and operational perspective of key privacy-related policies and procedures. The design of our discussion session was informed by a small group meeting held with several agency privacy officials in June 2007.

To obtain a citizen-centered perspective on the impact of gaps in privacy laws and guidance, we contracted with NAS to convene an expert panel The panel, which was held in October 2007, consisted of 12 privacy experts, who were selected by NAS and were from varying backgrounds, such as academic, commercial, advocacy, and other private-sector communities. A list of the individuals participating in the expert forum can be found in appendix II. We developed an agenda and facilitated a detailed discussion concerning major issues with the existing framework of privacy laws. In addition, we met separately with

Franklin Reeder, an expert involved in development of the Privacy Act and OMB guidance on the act, who was unable to participate in the expert forum.

To identify options for addressing major issues identified, we drew from our own analysis, our interviews with senior agency privacy officials, as well as feedback and suggestions brought forth during the expert forum.

We conducted this performance audit from March 2007 to May 2008, in Washington, D.C., in accordance with generally accepted government auditing standards. Those standards require that we plan and perform the audit to obtain sufficient, appropriate evidence to provide a reasonable basis for our findings and conclusions based on our audit objectives. We believe that the evidence obtained provides a reasonable basis for our findings and conclusions based on our audit objectives.

APPENDIX II: NATIONAL ACADEMY OF SCIENCES EXPERT PANEL PARTICIPANTS

We contracted with NAS to convene a panel of privacy experts outside government to obtain a citizen-centered perspective on the impact of gaps in privacy laws and guidance. Below is a listing of panel participants and their current affiliations:

Jennifer Barrett, Privacy Leader, Acxiom Corporation

Fred Cate, Distinguished Professor, Indiana University School of Law-Bloomington

Daniel Chenok, Senior Vice President, Pragmatics

Robert Gellman, Privacy and Information Policy Consultant Jim Harper, Director, Cato Institute, Information Policy Studies

Nuala O'Connor Kelly, Chief Privacy Leader, General Electric Company

Priscilla M. Regan, Professor of Government and Politics, George Mason University, Department of Public and International Affairs

Leslie Ann Reis, Director & Adjunct Professor of Law, The John Marshall Law School Center for Information Technology and Privacy Law

David Sobel, Senior Counsel, Electronic Frontier Foundation

John T. Sabo, Director, Global Government Relations, Computer Associates, Inc.

Barry Steinhardt, American Civil Liberties Union, Technology and Liberty Program

Peter Swire, C. William O'Neill Professor of Law, Ohio State University, Moritz College of Law

NAS staff assisting in coordinating the selection of experts and organizing the forum included, Joan Winston, Program Officer; Kristen Batch, Associate Program Officer; and Margaret Huynh, Senior Program Assistant

Forum Facilitators:

John de Ferrari, Assistant Director
David Plocher, Senior Attorney
Andrew Stavisky, Methodologist

Appendix III: Privacy Act Exemptions and Exceptions to the Prohibition Against Disclosure without Consent of the Individual

Agencies are allowed to claim exemptions from some of the provisions of the Privacy Act if the records are used for certain purposes such as law enforcement. The Privacy Act also provides that agencies not disclose information from a system of records without prior written consent of the individual to whom the record pertains, unless the disclosure falls under 1 of 12 exceptions defined by the act.

The Privacy Act Provides Exemptions for Certain Sensitive Activities

Subsections (j) and (k) of the Privacy Act prescribe the circumstances under which exemptions can be claimed and identify the provisions of the act from which agencies can claim exemptions. When an agency uses the authority in the act to exempt a system of records from certain provisions, it is to issue a rule explaining the reasons for the exemption.

Subsection (k) of the Privacy Act permits agencies to claim specific exemptions from seven provisions of the act that relate to notice to an individual concerning the use of personal information, requirements that agencies maintain only relevant and necessary information, and procedures for permitting access to and correction of an individual's records, when the records are:

1. subject to the exemption for classified information in b(1) of the Freedom of Information Act;
2. certain investigatory material compiled for law enforcement purposes other than material within the scope of a broader category of investigative records compiled for civil or criminal law enforcement purposes addressed in subsection (j);
3. maintained in connection with providing protective services to the President of the United States;
4. required by statute to be maintained and used solely as statistical records;
5. certain investigatory material compiled solely for the purpose of determining suitability, eligibility, or qualifications for federal civilian employment, military service, federal contracts, or access to classified information;
6. certain testing or examination material used solely to determine individual qualifications for appointment or promotion in the federal service; and 7. certain evaluation material used to determine potential promotion in the armed services
7. certain evaluation material used to determine potential promotion in the armed services

Under these circumstances, agencies may claim exemptions from the provisions of the act, described in table 5

Table 5. Privacy Act Provisions Agencies May Claim an Exemption under Subsection (k)

Citation	Description of provision
5 U.S. C. §552a(c)(3)	Agencies must make an accounting of disclosures available to the individual named in the record at his request.
5 U.S.C. § 552a(d)	Agencies must permit an individual to have access to his record, request amendment, if necessary, and if the agency refuses to amend the record, permit the individual to request,review of such refusal. If a contested record is disclosed, agencies must note any portion of the record that is disputed prior making a disclosure.
5 U.S.C. § 552a(e)(1)	Agencies must maintain in their records only such information about an individual as is relevant and necessary to accomplish a purpose of the agency required to be accomplished by statute or by executive order of the President.

Table 5. (Continued)

Citation	Description of provision
5 U.S.C. § 552a(e)(4)(G),(H), and (I)	Agencies must publish a system-of-records notice including the procedures by which an individual can be notified at his request if the system of records contains a record pertaining to him; the procedures by which an individual can be notified at his request how he can gain access to any record pertaining to him and how he can contest its content; and the categories of sources in the system.
5 U.S.C. §552a(f)	Agencies must issue rules to establish,among other things, procedures whereby an individual can gain access to his records and request amendment.

Source: The Privacy Act of 1974.

Subsection (j) provides a broader set of general exemptions, which permits records maintained by the Central Intelligence Agency or certain records maintained by an agency which has enforcement of criminal laws as its principal function to be exempted from any provision of the act, except those described in table 6.

Table 6. Privacy Act Provisions from Which Agencies May Not Claim Exemptions

Citation	Description of provision
5 U.S.C. § 552a(b)	Agencies cannot disclose records without prior written consent of the individual to whom the record pertains unless disclosure of the records falls under 1 of 12 exceptions.
5 U.S.C. § 552a(c)(1) and (2),	Agencies must account for certain disclosures including the date, nature, and purpose of each disclosure and the name and address of the person or agency to whom the disclosure is made. Agencies must retain the accounting for at least five years or the life of the record, whichever is longer.
5 U.S.C. § 552a(e)(4)(A) through (F)	Agencies must publish a systems of records notice in the Federal Registerincluding; the name and location of the system; the categories of individuals on whom records are maintained in the system; the categories of records maintained in the system; each routine use of the records contained in the system, including the categories of users and the purpose of such use; the policies and practices of the agency regarding storage, retrievability, access controls, retention, and disposal of the records; and the title and business address of the agency official who is responsible for the system of records.

Citation	Description of provision
U.S.C. §552a(e)(6),(7), (9), (10) and (11)	*Agencies:* • must make reasonable efforts to assure that records are accurate, complete, timely, andrelevant for agency purposes prior to disseminating any record to any person other than an agency; • may not maintain records describing how an individual exercises rights guaranteed by the First Amendment; • must establish rules of conduct for persons involved in the design, development, operation or maintenance of any system of records; • must establish appropriate administrative, technical, and physical safeguards to insure the security and confidentiality of records; and • must publish a notice of any new or intended routine use or intended use of the information in the system in the Federal Registerand provide an opportunity for interested persons to comment at least 30 days before publication of the final notice.
U.S.C. §552a(i)	*Criminal penalties shall be imposed when:* • an employee of the agency knowingly and willfully discloses individually identifiable information from agency records in any manner to any person or agency not entitled to receive it; • an employee of any agency willfully maintains a system of records without meeting the notice requirements of the act; and • any person who knowingly and willfully requests or obtains any record concerning an individual from an agency under false pretenses.

Source: The Privacy Act of 1974, 5.U.S.C. §552a.

In general, the exemptions for law enforcement purposes are intended to prevent the disclosure of information collected as part of an ongoing investigation that could impair the investigation or allow those under investigation to change their behavior or take other actions to escape prosecution.

Exceptions to the Prohibition against Disclosure without Prior Written Consent of the Individual

Subsection (b) of the Privacy Act provides that "No agency shall disclose any record which is contained in a system of records by any means of communication to any person, or to another agency, except pursuant to a written request by, or with the prior written consent of, the individual to whom the record pertains, unless disclosure of the record would be

1. to those officers and employees of the agency which maintains the record who have a need for the record in the performance of their duties;
2. required under the Freedom of Information Act;
3. for a routine use as defined in the act;
4. to the Bureau of the Census for planning or carrying out a census or survey or related activity;
5. for statistical research, provided the information is not individually identifiable;
6. to the National Archives and Records Administration for historical preservation purposes;
7. to any government agency (e.g., federal, state, or local) for a civil or criminal law enforcement activity if the head of the agency has made a written request specifying the information desired and the law enforcement activity for which the record is sought;
8. to a person upon showing compelling circumstances affecting the health or safety of an individual if notice is transmitted to the last known address of such individual;
9. to either House of Congress or any committee or subcommittee with related jurisdiction;
10. to the Government Accountability Office;
11. pursuant to a court order; or
12. to a consumer reporting agency for the purpose of collecting a claim of the government."

APPENDIX IV: OMB PRIVACY GUIDANCE

Since its 1975 Privacy Act Implementation Guidelines, OMB has periodically issued guidance related to privacy addressing specific issues as they have arisen. Nearly all of this guidance can be found on the OMB Web site, www.whitehouse.gov/omb, by searching in the "Agency Information" and "Information and Regulatory Affairs" sections of the Web site.

Memorandum M-08-09 — New FISMA Privacy Reporting Requirements for FY 2008. January 18, 2008.

Top Ten Risks Impeding the Adequate Protection of Government Information. July 2007.

Memorandum M-07-19 — FY 2007 Reporting Instructions for the Federal Information Security Management Act and Agency Privacy Management. July 25, 2007.

Guidance on Protecting Federal Employee Social Security Numbers and Combating Identity Theft. June 18, 2007.

OMB Implementation Guidance for Title V of the E-Government Act of 2002. June 15, 2007.

Memorandum M-07-16 — Safeguarding Against and Responding to the Breach of Personally Identifiable Information. May 22, 2007.

Use of Commercial Credit Monitoring Services Blanket Purchase Agreements (BPA). December 22, 2006.

Recommendations for Identity Theft Related Data Breach Notification. September 20, 2006.

Memorandum M-06-20 — FY 2006 Reporting Instructions for FISMA. July 17, 2006.

Memorandum M-06-19 — Reporting Incidents Involving Personally Identifiable Information and Incorporating the Cost for Security in Agency Information Technology Investments. July 12, 2006.

Memorandum M-06-1 6 — Protection of Sensitive Agency Information. June 23, 2006.

Memorandum M-06-15 — Safeguarding Personally Identifiable Information. May 22, 2006.

Memorandum M-06-06 — Sample Privacy Documents for Agency Implementation of HSPD-12 Common Identification Standard. February 17, 2006.

Memorandum M-05-15 — FY 2005 Reporting Instructions for the Federal Information Security Management Act and Agency Privacy Management. June 13, 2005.

Memorandum M-05-08 — Designation of Senior Agency Officials for Privacy. February 11, 2005.

Memorandum M-03-22 — Guidance for Implementing the Privacy Provisions of the E-Government Act. September 26, 2003.

Memorandum M-03-18 — Implementation Guidance for the E- Government Act of 2002. August 1, 2003.

Guidance on Inter-Agency Sharing of Personal Data—Protection Personal Privacy. December 20, 2000.

Baker/Spotila Letters and Memorandum M-00-13 – Privacy Policies and Date Collection on Federal Websites. June 22, July 28, and September 5, 2000.

Status of Biennial Reporting Requirements Under the Privacy Act and the Computer Matching and Privacy Protection Act. June 21, 2000.

Memorandum M-99-18 — Privacy Policies on Federal Web Sites. June 2, 1999.

Memorandum M-99-05 — Instructions on Complying with "Privacy and Personal Information in Federal Records." January 7, 1999.

Biennial Privacy Act and Computer Matching Reports. June 1998. Privacy in Personal Information in Federal Records. May 4, 1998.

Privacy Act Responsibilities for Implementing the Personal Responsibility and Work Opportunity Reconciliation Act (PRWORA) of 1996. November 3, 1997. Office of Management and Budget Order Providing for the

Confidentiality of Statistical Information and Extending the Coverage of Energy Statistical Programs Under the Federal Statistical Confidentiality Order. June 27, 1997.

Report of the Privacy Working Group: Principles for Providing and Using Personal Information. June 1995.

OMB Guidance on Computer Matching and Privacy Protection Amendments of 1990 and Privacy Act of 1974. April 23, 1991.

Office of Management and Budget Final Guidance Interpreting the Provisions of the Computer Matching and Privacy Protection Act of 1988. June 19, 1989.

OMB Guidance on the Privacy Act Implications of "Call Detail" Programs. April 20, 1987.

OMB Circular A-130, Management of Federal Information Resources, including Federal Agency Responsibilities for Maintaining Records About Individuals, and Implementation of the Paperwork Elimination Act. November 28, 2000.

Updates to Original OMB Privacy Act Guidance. May 24, 1985.

Revised Supplemental Guidance on Implementation of the Privacy Act of 1974. March 29, 1984.

Guidelines on the Relationship of the Debt Collection Act of 1982 to the Privacy Act of 1974. April 11, 1983.

OMB Supplemental Guidance for Conducting Matching Programs. May 14, 1982.

Supplementary Guidance for Implementation of the Privacy Act of 1974. November 21, 1975.

Congressional Inquiries Which Entail Access to Personal Information Subject to the Privacy Act. October 3, 1975.

Privacy Act Implementation Guidelines and Responsibilities. July 9, 1975.

APPENDIX V: COMMENTS FROM THE OFFICE OF MANAGEMENT AND BUDGET*

EXECUTIVE OFFICE OF THE PRESIDENT
OFFICE OF MANAGEMENT AND BUDGET
WASHINGTON, D.C. 20503

May 2, 2008

Ms. Linda D. Koontz
Director
Information Management Issues
U.S. Government Accountability Office
441 G Street, NW
Washington, DC 20548

Dear Ms. Koontz:

Thank you for the opportunity to comment on the draft GAO report "Privacy: Alternatives Exist for Enhancing Protection of Personally Identifiable Information" (GAO-08-536). The Office of Management and Budget (OMB) welcomes GAO's review of alternatives for better safeguarding individuals' personally identifiable information (PII).

OMB shares your concerns about privacy and information security, and we take seriously our responsibilities under the Privacy Act of 1974, the E-Government Act of 2002, and the Federal Information Security Management Act of 2002. In recent years, OMB has issued several memoranda addressing privacy and information security, including:

- M-08-16 of April 4, 2008, *Guidance for Trusted Internet Connection Statement of Capability Form (SOC)*,
- M-08-10 of February 4, 2008, *Use of Commercial Independent Risk Analysis Services Blanket Purchase Agreements (BPA)*,
- M-08-09 of January 18, 2008, *New FISMA Privacy Reporting Requirements for FY 2008*,
- M-08-05 of November 20, 2007, *Implementation of Trusted Internet Connections (TIC)*,
- M-07-20 of August 14, 2007, *FY 2007 E-Government Act Reporting Instructions*,
- M-07-19 of July 25, 2007, *FY 2007 Reporting Instructions for the Federal Information Security Management Act and Agency Privacy Management*,
- M-07-18 of June 1, 2007, *Ensuring New Acquisitions Include Common Security Configurations*,
- M-07-16 of May 22, 2007, *Safeguarding Against and Responding to the Breach of Personally Identifiable Information*,
- M-07-11 of March 22, 2007, *Implementation of Commonly Accepted Security Configurations for Windows Operating Systems*,

* Note: GAO comments supplementing those in the report text appear at the end of this appendix.

- M-07-04 of December 22, 2006, *Use of Commercial Credit Monitoring Services Blanket Purchase Agreements (BPA)*,
- Memorandum for the Heads of Departments and Agencies of September 20, 2006, *Recommendations for Identity Theft Related Data Breach Notification*,
- M-06-25 of August 25, 2006, *FY 2006 E-Government Act Reporting Instructions*,
- M-06-20 of July 17, 2006, *FY 2006 Reporting Instructions for the Federal Information Security Management Act and Agency Privacy Management*,
- M-06-19 of July 12, 2006, *Reporting Incidents Involving Personally Identifiable Information Incorporating the Cost for Security in Agency Information Technology Investments*,
- M-06-16 of June 23, 2006, *Protection of Sensitive Agency Information*,
- M-06-15 of May 22, 2006, *Safeguarding Personally Identifiable Information*,
- M-05-15 of June 13, 2005, *FY 2005 Reporting Instructions for the Federal Information Security Management Act and Agency Privacy Management*, and
- M-05-08 of February 11, 2005, *Designation of Senior Agency Officials for Privacy*.

We appreciate the careful consideration of privacy issues in the draft report. The draft report provides several matters for congressional consideration regarding privacy, specifically, suggesting Congress should consider revising the Privacy Act and the E-Government Act. Among the alternatives the draft report discusses would be for Congress to amend the Privacy Act so that it would apply to all PII collected, maintained, and used by Federal agencies.

During the course of a legislative consideration of possible amendments to the Privacy Act and the E-Government Act, along the lines of the alternatives in the draft report, we believe it would be important for Congress to consider these issues in the broader context of the several privacy statutes that Congress has enacted. In addition to such government-wide statutes as the Privacy Act, the Privacy Impact Assessment requirements of the E-Government Act, and the Federal Information Security Management Act (FISMA), Congress has also enacted privacy laws covering such areas as health-related information (the Health Insurance Portability and Accountability Act of 1996), statistical information about individuals (the Confidential Information Protection and Statistical Efficiency Act of 2002), and intelligence, law enforcement, and homeland security (the Intelligence Reform and Terrorism Prevention Act of 2004 and the Implementing Recommendations of the 9/11 Commission Act of 2007), as well as statutes that apply specifically to information about individuals that is collected by particular agencies, such as the Census Bureau, the Internal Revenue Service, and the Social Security Administration.

In addition, during legislative consideration of possible revisions to privacy laws, we believe that it would be important for Congress to evaluate fully the potential implications of such revisions. For example, one of the alternatives that the draft report discusses would have Congress amend the Privacy Act in a very fundamental way. This alternative would involve abandoning the Act's framework that has been in place for over 30 years, which has been to safeguard information about individuals that is found in a "system of records," and instead to have the Act apply to all PII, however maintained by an agency. We believe it would be important for Congress, in considering such a fundamental change to the Privacy Act, to consider the full range of implications flowing from that change. It may be that, based on this consideration, other legislative alternatives might be identified that would be more desirable in terms of strengthening privacy protections in the most effective and efficient manner.

The draft report also offers alternatives for ensuring that the purpose of agency use of PII is specified and agency collection and use of personal information is limited. As OMB stated in recent guidance in response to recommendations from the President's Identity Theft Task Force, agencies must review and reduce the volume of PII they handle "to the minimum necessary for the proper performance of a documented agency function." (Please see OMB Memorandum M-07-16 of May 22, 2007, *Safeguarding Against and Responding to the Breach of Personally Identifiable Information.*) Agencies are currently working to implement this guidance and the recommendations of the Task Force. In our annual reporting instructions last year to agencies on FISMA and privacy management, OMB required agencies to submit copies of policies and plans required by M-07-16, including an agency breach notification policy, an implementation plan to eliminate unnecessary use of social security numbers, an implementation plan and progress update on the review and reduction of agency holdings of PII, and an agency policy outlining rules of behavior for safeguarding PII. (Please see OMB Memorandum M-07-19 of July 25, 2007, *FY 2007 Reporting Instructions for the Federal Information Security Management Act and Agency Privacy Management.*)

We also support ensuring the public is appropriately informed of how agencies are using their information. The publication of System of Records Notices and Privacy Impact Assessments is a crucial piece of the Federal privacy framework. We will review agency practices in informing the public and review the alternatives the draft report provides.

Finally, we would like to respond to several statements in the draft report.

On page 19, the draft report discusses draft guidance on the Paperwork Reduction Act (PRA) that OMB had prepared in 1999: "Further, [OMB] developed guidance, which while remaining in draft, is widely used as a handbook for agencies on compliance with the law, according to OMB officials." The draft report continues by stating in footnote 23 that "[a]lthough this guidance is draft, OMB officials stated that agencies are generally aware of the guidance and are expected to follow it."

The draft report is incorrect when it states that agencies "are expected to follow" the draft 1999 guidance. The draft guidance has not been finalized, and thus remains a draft. GAO made this exact same (incorrect) statement in its draft of a 2005 report on the Paperwork Reduction Act, and OMB pointed out its disagreement with this statement in OMB comments to GAO on the draft report. (See "Paperwork Reduction Act: New Approach May Be Needed to Reduce Government Burden on Public," GAO 05-424 (May 2005), Appendix III (OMB letter of April 20, 2005), pages 53-54.) However, GAO did not correct this statement in the final version of the 2005 report (see page 22 footnote 34), and the current draft report repeats this incorrect statement. To be clear, agencies are expected to follow the Paperwork Reduction Act, OMB's implementing PRA regulations at 5 C.F.R. Part 1320, and OMB's January 2006 guidance to agencies on surveys conducted under the PRA.

On page 23, the draft report refers to a prior GAO conclusion from a 2003 GAO report: "In discussing this uneven compliance, agency officials reported the need for additional OMB leadership and guidance to assist in difficult implementation issues in a rapidly changing environment." We would note here that, in the comment letter that OMB submitted to GAO on the draft of the referenced 2003 report, OMB expressed concerns with the report's methodology and conclusions. (OMB's comment letter of June 20, 2003, is enclosed as Appendix VII of the final report.)

On page 48, the draft report states that "OMB guidance does not provide specific measures for limiting information collections . . . OMB's recent guidance to limit collection of personally identifiable information did not include plans to monitor agency actions or take other proactive steps to ensure that agencies are effectively limiting their collections of personally identifiable information. Without a legal requirement to limit collection of personally identifiable information, it is unclear the extent to which agencies will follow OMB's guidance."

As noted earlier in our letter, Federal agencies are working diligently to implement the OMB Memorandum M-07-16 requirement to review and reduce the volume of PII they handle "to the minimum necessary for the proper performance of a documented agency function." In the aftermath of major data breaches in 2006 and the findings of the President's Identity Theft Task Force, agencies have become sensitized to limiting collections of personally identifiable information. Limiting the collection of personally identifiable information to what is authorized and necessary will require on-going attention by departments and oversight by OMB, as part of its Paperwork Reduction Act and Privacy Act responsibilities.

In closing, thank you again for the opportunity to comment on the draft report.

Sincerely,

Kevin F. Neyland
Deputy Administrator
Office of Information
and Regulatory Affairs

Tim K. Young
Deputy Administrator
Office of E-Government and
Information Technology

4

GAO Comments

1. Statements in the 2005 report regarding the draft OMB Paperwork Reduction Act guidance were accurate for that review and supported by the evidence gathered. For that report, among other things, we selected detailed case reviews of 12 OMB-approved collections and compared the agencies' processes and practices in these case studies with the (1) act's requirements, (2) OMB's regulation and draft guidance to agencies, and (3) agencies' written directives and orders. Nevertheless, in its written response to the 2005 report, OMB officials stated that OMB's draft PRA guidance to agencies had become outmoded. Further, in its response, OMB stated that the report had convinced them that its draft PRA guidance did not serve its intended purpose and that it would explore alternative approaches to advising agencies on their PRA responsibilities. Accordingly, because the draft guidance has not been in effect since the 2005 report was issued, we have removed statements from our current draft regarding this guidance.
2. As we stated in our response to OMB's comments on our 2003 report[#], we consider this report to be a comprehensive and accurate source of information on agencies' implementation of the Privacy Act. Our conclusions were based on the results of a comprehensive analysis of agency compliance with a broad range of requirements.
3. We agree that the responsibility for limiting the collection of personally identifiable information to what is authorized and necessary will require ongoing attention by agencies and oversight by OMB. We also believe that Congress should consider alternatives, as identified in our report, to improve controls on the collection and use of personally identifiable information.

References

[1] For purposes of this report, the terms personal information and personally identifiable information are used interchangeably to refer to any information about an individual maintained by an agency, including (1) any information that can be used to distinguish or trace an individual's identity, such as

[#] GAO, Privacy Act: OMB Leadership Needed to Improve Agency Compliance, GAO-03-304 (Washington, D.C.: June 30, 2003).

name, Social Security number, date and place of birth, mother's maiden name, or biometric records; and (2) any other information that is linked or linkable to an individual, such as medical, educational, financial, and employment information.

[2] In addition, the Paperwork Reduction Act, enacted in 1980 and significantly revised in 1995, also has provisions affecting privacy protection in that it sets requirements for limiting the collection of information from individuals, including personal information. While the act's requirements are aimed at reducing the paperwork burden on individuals rather than specifically protecting personally identifiable information, the act nevertheless serves an important role in protecting privacy by setting these controls.

[3] A privacy impact assessment is an analysis of how personal information is collected, stored, shared, and managed in an information system.

[4] Congress used the committee's final report as a basis for crafting the Privacy Act of 1974. See U.S. Department of Health, Education, and Welfare, *Records, Computers, and the Rights of Citizens: Report of the Secretary's Advisory Committee on Automated Personal Data Systems* (Washington, D.C.: July 1973).

[5] These principles are described in table 1.

[6] GAO, *Privacy Act: OMB Leadership Needed to Improve Agency Compliance,* GAO-03-304 (Washington, D.C.: June 30, 2003).

[7] GAO, *Personal Information: Agency and Reseller Adherence to Key Privacy Principles,* GAO-06-421 (Washington, D.C.: Apr. 4, 2006).

[8] Department of Health, Education & Welfare, *Records, Computers, and the Rights of Citizens: Report of the Secretary's Advisory Committee on Automated Personal Data Systems* (Washington, D.C.: 1973).

[9] OECD, *Guidelines on the Protection of Privacy and Transborder Flow of Personal Data* (Sept. 23, 1980). The OECD plays a prominent role in fostering good governance in the public service and in corporate activity among its 30 member countries. It produces internationally agreed-upon instruments, decisions, and recommendations to promote rules in areas where multilateral agreement is necessary for individual countries to make progress in the global economy.

[10] OECD, *Making Privacy Notices Simple: An OECD Report and Recommendations* (July 24, 2006)

[11] European Union Data Protection Directive ("Directive 95/46/EC of the European Parliament and of the Council of 24 October 1995 on the

Protection of Individuals with Regard to the Processing of Personal Data and the Free Movement of Such Data'') (1995).

[12] "Report on OECD Guidelines Program, Memorandum from Bernard Wunder, Jr., Assistant Secretary for Communications and Information, Department of Commerce (Oct. 30, 1981).

[13] Privacy Office Mission Statement, U.S. Department of Homeland Security, "Privacy Policy Development Guide," Global Information Sharing Initiative, U.S. Department of Justice, www.it.ojp.gov/global (September 2005); "Homeless Management Information Systems, U.S. Department of Housing and Urban Development (*69 Federal Register* 45888, July 30, 2004). See also "Options for Promoting Privacy on the National Information Infrastructure," Information Policy Committee of the National Information Infrastructure Task Force, Office of Information and Regulatory Affairs, Office of Management and Budget (April 1997).

[14] The Federal Enterprise Architecture is intended to provide a common frame of reference or taxonomy for agencies' individual enterprise architecture efforts and their planned and ongoing information technology investment activities. An enterprise architecture is a blueprint, defined largely by interrelated models, that describes (in both business and technology terms) an entity's "as is" or current environment, its "to be" or future environment, and its investment plan for transitioning from the current to the future environment.

[15] National Research Council of the National Academies, *Engaging Privacy and Information Technology in a Digital Age* (Washington, D.C.: 2007).

[16] Under the Privacy Act of 1974, the term "routine use" means (with respect to the disclosure of a record) the use of such a record for a purpose that is compatible with the purpose for which it was collected. 5 U.S.C. § 552a(a)(7).

[17] OMB, *OMB Guidance for Implementing the Privacy Provisions of the E-Government Act of 2002*, M-03-22 (Sept. 26, 2003).

[18] The Paperwork Reduction Act was originally enacted into law in 1980 (Pub. L. No. 96-5 11, Dec. 11, 1980). It was reauthorized with minor amendments in 1986 (Pub. L. No. 99-591, Oct. 30, 1986) and was reauthorized a second time with more significant amendments in 1995 (Pub. L. No. 104-13, May 22, 1995)

[19] Pub. L. No. 108-458 (Dec. 17, 2004).

[20] For more information, see *GAO, High-Risk Series: An Update,* GAO-07-310 (Washington, D.C. January 2007), p.47, and *Information Sharing: The Federal Government Needs to Establish Policies and Processes for Sharing*

Terrorism-Related and Sensitive but Unclassified Information, GAO-06-385 (Washington, D.C.: Mar. 17, 2006).

[21] 5 C.F.R. Part 1320.

[22] Privacy Protection Study Commission, *Personal Privacy in an Information Society* (Washington, D.C.: July 1977).

[23] U.S. Congress, House of Representatives, *Who Cares About Privacy? Oversight of the Privacy Act of 1974 by the Office of Management and Budget and by the Congress,* House Report No. 98-455 (Washington, D.C.:1983)

[24] The Information Security and Privacy Advisory Board's duties include identifying emerging managerial, technical, administrative, and physical safeguard issues relative to information security and privacy; and advising the National Institute of Standards and Technology (NIST), the Secretary of Commerce, and the Director of the OMB on information security and privacy issues pertaining to federal government information systems. Until December 2002, the ISPAB was named the Computer System Security and Privacy Advisory Board.

[25] Computer System Security and Privacy Advisory Board, *Findings and Recommendations on Government Privacy Policy Setting and Management* (September 2002)

[26] The DHS Data Privacy and Integrity Advisory Committee is a federal advisory committee that advises the Secretary of DHS and the DHS Chief Privacy Officer on programmatic, policy, operational, administrative, and technological issues within DHS that affect individual privacy, as well as data integrity and data interoperability and other privacy related issues.

[27] The National Research Council (NRC) functions under the auspices of the National Academy of Sciences (NAS), the National Academy of Engineering, and the Institute of Medicine. The mission of the NRC is to improve government decision making and public policy, increase public education and understanding, and promote the acquisition and dissemination of knowledge in matters involving science, engineering, technology, and health.

[28] National Research Council of the National Academies, *Engaging Privacy and Information Technology in a Digital Age* (Washington, D.C.: 2007)

[29] GAO, *Privacy Act: OMB Leadership Needed to Improve Agency Compliance*, GAO-03-304 (Washington, D.C.: June 30, 2003).

[30] FISMA, Title III, E-Government Act of 2002, Pub. L. No. 107-347 (Dec. 17, 2002).

[31] Although we did not assess the effectiveness of information security or compliance with FISMA at any agency as part of this review, we have previously reported on weaknesses in almost all areas of information security controls at 24 major agencies. For additional information see, GAO, *Information Security: Progress Reported, but Weaknesses at Federal Agencies Persist,* GAO-08-571 (Washington, D.C.: Mar. 12, 2008); *Information Security: Despite Reported Progress, Federal Agencies Need to Address Persistent Weaknesses*, GAO-07-837 (Washington, D.C.: July 27, 2007); and *Information Security: Weaknesses Persist at Federal Agencies Despite Progress Made in Implementing Related Statutory Requirements*, GAO-05-552 (Washington, D.C.: July 15, 2005).

[32] A record is defined as "any item, collection, or grouping of information about an individual that is maintained by an agency, including, but not limited to, his education, financial transactions, medical history, and criminal or employment history and that contains his name, or the identifying number, symbol, or other identifying particular assigned to the individual, such as a finger or voice print or a photograph."

[33] According to OMB, "systems should not be subdivided or reorganized so that information which would otherwise have been subject to the act is no longer subject to the act. For example, if an agency maintains a series of records not arranged by name or personal identifier but uses a separate index file to retrieve records by name or personal identifier it should not treat these files as separate systems." 40 Federal Register 28963 (July 9, 1975).

[34] An attribute search, in contrast to the conventional "name search" or "index search," starts with a collection of data about many individuals and seeks to identify those particular individuals in the system who meet a set of prescribed conditions or who have a set of prescribed attributes or combination of attributes.

[35] GAO, Privacy Act: OMB *Leadership Needed to Improve Agency Compliance,* GAO-03-304 (Washington, D.C.: June 30, 2003).

[36] GAO, *Data Mining: Federal Efforts Cover a Wide Range of Uses*, GAO-04-548 (Washington, D.C.: May 4, 2004)

[37] The DHS Privacy Office determined that because the data mining applications did not involve retrieval by individual identifier, a separate system of records notice describing the data mining application was not required. DHS Privacy Office, *ADVISE Report: DHS Privacy Office Review of the Analysis, Dissemination, Visualization, Insight, and Semantic Enhancement (ADVISE) Program* (Washington, D.C.: July 11, 2007).

[38] DHS Privacy Office, *2007 Report to Congress on the Impact of Data Mining Technologies on Privacy and Civil Liberties (Washington, D.C.: July 6, 2007); Justice, Report on "Data-Mining" Activities Pursuant to Section 126 of the USA PATRIOT Improvement and Reauthorization Act of 2005* (Washington, D.C.: July 9, 2007).

[39] Homeland Security Operations Center Database, 70 *Federal Register* 20156 (Apr. 18, 2005).

[40] The task force's mission is to assist federal law enforcement and intelligence agencies in locating foreign terrorists and their supporters who are in or have visited the United States, and to provide information to other law enforcement and intelligence community agencies that can lead to their surveillance, prosecution, or removal.

[41] 63 *Federal Register* 8671 (Feb. 20, 1998).

[42] GAO-06-421.

[43] Section 222(4) of the Homeland Security Act of 2002 requires the DHS Privacy Officer to conduct "a privacy impact assessment of proposed rules of the Department or that of the Department on the privacy of personal information, including the type of personal information collected and the number of people affected."

[44] TSA's current plans for Secure Flight do not include the use of reseller information.

[45] GAO, *Aviation Security: Efforts to Strengthen International Passenger Prescreening Security Are Under Way, but Planning and Implementation Issues Remain*, GAO-07-346 (Washington, D.C.: May 16, 2007).

[46] 66 *Federal Register* 53029 (Oct. 18, 2001).

[47] 63 *Federal Register* 8671 (Feb. 20, 1998).

[48] See appendix III for a list of the specific exceptions where agencies do not need the consent of individuals to share their information.

[49] GAO, *Paperwork Reduction Act: New Approach May Be Needed to Reduce Government Burden on Public*, GAO-05-424 (Washington, D.C.: May 20, 2005).

[50] 5 U.S.C. § 552a(b)(7): "to another agency or to an instrumentality of any governmental jurisdiction within or under the control of the United States for a civil or criminal law enforcement activity if the activity is authorized by law, and if the head of the agency or instrumentality has made a written request to the agency which maintains the record specifying the particular portion desired and the law enforcement activity for which the record is sought."

[51] In cases where the collection occurs directly from the individual, an agency is required to include the routine uses on the form which it uses to collect the information.

[52] OMB's 1975 guidance states that "Minimally, the recipient officer or employee must have an official 'need to know.' [The legislative history] would also seem to imply that the use should be generally related to the purpose for which the record is maintained."

[53] If personal data are disclosed to another federal agency, the recipient agency may maintain this data in a system of records, and thus protections for this data would be defined by the recipient agency's system-of-records notice. However, these protections may not be consistent with statements originally made in the contributing agency's system- of records notice. For example, the recipient agency may state different routine uses and purposes. Further, if data are disclosed to an agency and are not maintained in a system of records, the Privacy Act no longer provides protections for that information.

[54] Program Manager, Information Sharing Environment, *Guidelines to Ensure That the Information Privacy and Other Legal Rights of Americans Are Protected in the Development and Use of the Information Sharing Environment* (Nov. 22, 2006).

[55] GAO, *Homeland Security: Continuing Attention to Privacy Is Needed as Programs Are Developed,* GAO-07-630T (Washington, D.C.: Mar. 21, 2007).

[56] Program Manager, Information Sharing Environment, *Privacy and Civil Liberties Implementation Guide for the Information Sharing Environment* (Sept. 10, 2007).

[57] The Privacy Act allows agencies to claim exemptions if the records are used for certain purposes. 5 U.S.C. § 552a (j) and (k). For example, records compiled by criminal law enforcement agencies for criminal law enforcement purposes can be exempt from the access and correction provisions. In general, the exemptions for law enforcement purposes are intended to prevent the disclosure of information collected as part of an ongoing investigation that could impair the investigation or allow those under investigation to change their behavior or take other actions to escape prosecution. See appendix III for a complete description of these exemptions.

[58] Kleimann Communication Group, Inc., *Evolution of a Prototype Financial Privacy Notice: A Report on the Form Development Project* (Feb. 28, 2006)

Chapter 4

STRENGTHENING PROTECTION OF PERSONALLY IDENTIFIABLE INFORMATION*

WHAT GAO FOUND

Although privacy laws and guidance set minimum requirements for agencies, they may not consistently protect personally identifiable information in all circumstances of its collection and use throughout the federal government and may not fully adhere to key privacy principles. Based on discussions with privacy experts and agency officials, as well as analysis of laws and related guidance, GAO identified issues in three major areas:

Applying privacy protections consistently to all federal collection and use of personal information. The Privacy Act's definition of a "system of records," which sets the scope of the act's protections, does not always apply whenever personal information is obtained and processed by federal agencies. For example, if agencies do not retrieve personal information by identifier, the act's protections do not apply. This has led experts to agree that the Privacy Act's system-of-records construct is too narrowly defined. An alternative for addressing these issues could include revising the system-ofrecords definition to cover all personally identifiable information collected, used, and maintained systematically by the federal government.

Ensuring that use of personally identifiable information is limited to a stated purpose. According to the Fair Information Practices, the use of personal

---

* Excerpted from GAO Report 08-795T, dated June 18, 2008.

information should be limited to a specified purpose. Yet current laws and guidance impose only modest requirements for describing the purposes for personal information and limiting how it is used. For example, agencies are not required to be specific in formulating purpose descriptions in their public notices. Overly broad specifications of purpose could allow for unnecessarily broad ranges of uses, thus calling into question whether meaningful limitations had been imposed. Alternatives for addressing these issues include setting specific limits on use of information within agencies and requiring agencies to establish formal agreements with external governmental entities before sharing personally identifiable information with them.

Establishing effective mechanisms for informing the public about privacy protections. Public notices are a primary means of establishing accountability for privacy protections and giving individuals a measure of control over the use of their personal information. Although the Federal Register is the government's official vehicle for issuing public notices, critics have questioned whether system-of-records notices published in the Federal Register effectively inform the public about government uses of personal information. Options for addressing concerns about public notices include requiring that purpose, collection limitations, and use limitations are better addressed in the content of privacy notices, and revising the Privacy Act to require that all notices be published on a standard Web site, with an address such as www.privacy.gov.

WHY GAO DID THIS STUDY

Concerns have been raised about the privacy and security of personal information in light of advances in information technology and the increasingly sophisticated ways in which the government obtains and uses information. Federal agencies' use of personal information is governed by the Privacy Act of 1974 and the E-Government Act of 2002, while the Office of Management and Budget (OMB) provides implementation guidance and oversight. These laws and guidance are based on the Fair Information Practices , a set of widely accepted principles for protecting privacy.

GAO was asked to testify on its report, being released today, concerning the sufficiency of privacy protections afforded by existing laws and guidance. To do this, GAO analyzed privacy laws and guidance, compared them with the Fair Information Practices, and obtained perspectives from federal agencies as well as an expert forum.

WHAT GAO RECOMMENDS

In its report GAO identified alternatives that the Congress should consider, including revising the scope of privacy laws to cover all personal information, requiring that the use of such information be limited to a specific purpose, and revising the structure and publication of privacy notices.

OMB commented that the Congress should consider these alternatives in the broader context of existing privacy and related statutes.

June 18, 2008

Mr. Chairman and Members of the Committee:

I appreciate the opportunity to discuss today the critical protections afforded to individual privacy by laws and guidance governing the federal government's use of personally identifiable information [1]. The increasingly sophisticated ways in which personal information is obtained and used by the federal government has the potential to assist in performing critical functions, such as preventing terrorism, but also can pose challenges in ensuring the protection of citizens' privacy. In this regard, concerns have been raised that the framework of legal mechanisms for protecting personal privacy that has been developed over the years may no longer be sufficient, given current practices.

Federal agency use of personal information is governed primarily by the Privacy Act of 1974 and the E-Government Act of 2002 [2]. The Privacy Act of 1974 serves as the major mechanism for controlling the collection, use, and disclosure of personally identifiable information within the federal government. The E-Government Act of 2002 strives to enhance the protection of personal information in government information systems by requiring that agencies conduct privacy impact assessments [3]. The Office of Management and Budget (OMB) is charged with ensuring implementation of the privacy impact assessment requirement and the Privacy Act by federal agencies and is also responsible for providing guidance to agencies.

The provisions of the Privacy Act are largely based on a set of principles for protecting the privacy and security of personal information known as the Fair Information Practices, which were first proposed in 1973 by a U.S. government advisory committee [4]. These principles, with some variation, are used by organizations to address privacy considerations in their business practices and are also the basis of privacy laws and related policies in many countries, including the

United States, Germany, Sweden, Australia, and New Zealand, as well as the European Union.

My testimony today will highlight key findings from a report that we are releasing today [5]. In the report, we assess the sufficiency of laws and guidance covering the federal government's collection and use of personal information. We also identify alternatives for addressing issues raised by our review. In conducting our work, we analyzed the Privacy Act of 1974, section 208 of the E-Government Act, and related guidance to identify any inconsistencies or gaps in the coverage of these laws as they apply to uses of personal information by federal agencies. We also compared these laws and related guidance with the Fair Information Practices to identify any significant gaps, including assessing the role of the Paperwork Reduction Act (PRA) in protecting privacy by limiting collection of information. We obtained an operational perspective on the sufficiency of these laws from six federal departments and agencies with large inventories of information collections, prominent privacy issues, and varied missions. We also obtained expert perspective through the use of an expert panel convened for us by the National Academy of Sciences. We conducted our work for this performance audit in accordance with generally accepted government auditing standards. Those standards require that we plan and perform the audit to obtain sufficient, appropriate evidence to provide a reasonable basis for our findings and conclusions based on our audit objectives. We believe that the evidence obtained provides a reasonable basis for our findings and conclusions based on our audit objectives.

Today, after a brief summary of the laws and guidance currently in place, my remarks will focus on key results of our review of their sufficiency in governing the government's collection and use of personal information.

RESULTS IN BRIEF

Although the Privacy Act, the E-Government Act, and related OMB guidance set minimum requirements for agencies, they may not consistently protect personally identifiable information in all circumstances of its collection and use throughout the federal government and may not fully adhere to key privacy principles. Based on discussions with privacy experts and agency officials, as well as analysis of laws and related guidance, we identified issues in three major areas:

Applying privacy protections consistently to all federal collection and use of personal information. The Privacy Act's definition of a "system of records" (any grouping of records containing personal information retrieved by individual identifier), which sets the scope of the act's protections, does not always apply whenever personal information is obtained and processed by federal agencies. For example, if agencies do not retrieve personal information by identifier, the act's protections do not apply. Our 2003 report concerning compliance with the Privacy Act found that among the agencies surveyed, the most frequently cited reason for systems not being considered Privacy Act systems of records was that the agency did not use a personal identifier to retrieve the information [6]. Factors such as these have led experts to agree that the Privacy Act's system-of-records construct is too narrowly defined. An alternative for addressing these issues could include revising the system-of-records definition to cover all personally identifiable information collected, used, and maintained systematically by the federal government.

Ensuring that use of personally identifiable information is limited to a stated purpose. According to the purpose specification and use limitation principles, the use of personal information should be limited to a specified purpose. Yet current laws and guidance impose only modest requirements for describing the purposes for personal information and limiting how it is used. For example, agencies are not required to be specific in formulating purpose descriptions in their public notices. While purpose statements for certain law enforcement and antiterrorism systems might need to be phrased broadly enough so as not to reveal investigative techniques or the details of ongoing cases, very broadly defined purposes could allow for unnecessarily broad ranges of uses, thus calling into question whether meaningful limitations had been imposed. Examples of alternatives for addressing these issues include setting specific limits on the use of information within agencies and requiring agencies to establish formal agreements with external governmental entities before sharing personally identifiable information with them.

Establishing effective mechanisms for informing the public about privacy protections. According to the openness principle, the public should be informed about privacy policies and practices, and the accountability principle calls for those who control the collection or use of personal information to be held accountable for taking steps to ensure privacy protection. Public notices are a primary means of establishing accountability for privacy protections and giving individuals a measure of control over the use of their personal information. Yet concerns have been raised that Privacy Act notices may not serve this function well. Although the Federal Register is the government's official vehicle for issuing public notices, critics have questioned whether system-of-records notices published in the Federal Register effectively inform the public about government uses of personal information. Among others, options for addressing concerns about public notices could include setting requirements to ensure that purpose, collection limitations, and use limitations are better addressed in the content of privacy notices, and revising the Privacy Act to require that all notices be published on a standard Web site, with an address such as www.privacy.gov.

Some of these issues—particularly those dealing with limitations on use and mechanisms for informing the public—could be addressed by OMB through revisions or supplements to guidance. However, unilateral actions by OMB would not have the benefit of public deliberations regarding how best to achieve an appropriate balance between the government's need to collect, process, and share personally identifiable information and the rights of individuals to know about such collections and be assured that they are only for limited purposes and uses. In assessing such a balance, we suggested that Congress consider amending applicable laws, such as the Privacy Act and the E-Government Act, according to the alternatives outlined in the report, including:

- revising the scope of the laws to cover all personally identifiable information collected, used, and maintained by the federal government;
- setting requirements to ensure that the collection and use of personally identifiable information is limited to a stated purpose; and
- establishing additional mechanisms for informing the public about privacy protections by revising requirements for the structure and publication of public notices.

In commenting on a draft of our report OMB officials noted that they shared our concerns about privacy and listed guidance that the agency has issued in the areas of privacy and information security. The officials stated that they believe it would be important for Congress to consider potential amendments to the Privacy Act and the E-Government Act in the broader context of the several privacy statutes that Congress has enacted.

Though we did not make specific recommendations to OMB, the agency provided comments on the alternatives identified in conjunction with our matter for congressional consideration. Regarding alternatives for revising the scope of laws to cover all personally identifiable information collected, used, and maintained by the federal government, OMB stated that it would be important for Congress to evaluate fully the potential implications of revisions such as amending the Privacy Act's system-of-records definition. We believe that, given that the Privacy Act's controls on the collection, use, and disclosure of personally identifiable information do not consistently protect such information in all circumstances of its collection and use throughout the federal government, amending the act's definition of a system of records is an important alternative for Congress to consider. However, we agree with OMB that such consideration should be thorough and include further public debate on all relevant issues.

BACKGROUND

In response to growing concern about the harmful consequences that computerized data systems could have on the privacy of personal information, in 1972 the Secretary of Health, Education, and Welfare commissioned an advisory committee to examine to what extent limitations should be placed on the application of computer technology to record keeping about people. The committee's final report proposed a set of principles for protecting the privacy and security of personal information, known as the Fair Information Practices [7]. These practices were intended to address what the committee termed a poor level of protection afforded to privacy under then-existing law, and they underlie the major provisions of the Privacy Act, which was enacted the following year. A revised version of the Fair Information Practices was developed in 1980 by the Organization for Economic Cooperation and Development (OECD) and has been widely adopted [8]. This version of the principles was reaffirmed by OECD ministers in a 1998 declaration and further endorsed in a 2006 OECD report [9]. The OECD version of the principles is shown in table 1.

Table 1. The Fair Information Practices

Principle	Description
Collection limitation	The collection of personal information should be limited, should be obtained by lawful and fair means, and, where appropriate, with the knowledge or consent of the individual.
Data quality	Personal information should be relevant to the purpose for which it is collected, and should be accurate, complete, and current as needed for that purpose.
Purpose specification	The purposes for the collection of personal information should be disclosed before collection and upon any change to that purpose, and its use should be limited to those purposes and compatible purposes.
Use limitation	Personal information should not be disclosed or otherwise used for other than a specified purpose without consent of the individual or legal authority.

Table 1. (Continued)

Principle	Description
Security safeguards	Personal information should be protected with reasonable security safeguards against risks such as loss or unauthorized access, destruction, use, modification, or disclosure.
Openness	The public should be informed about privacy policies and practices, and individuals should have ready means of learning about the use of personal information.
Individual participation	Individuals should have the following rights: to know about the collection of personal information, to access that information, to request correction, and to challenge the denial of those rights.
Accountability	Individuals controlling the collection or use of personal information should be accountable for taking steps to ensure theimplementation of these principles.

Source: Organization for Economic Cooperation and Development.

The Fair Information Practices are, with some variation, the basis of privacy laws and related policies in many countries, including the United States, Germany, Sweden, Australia, and New Zealand, as well as the European Union [10]. They are also reflected in a variety of federal agency policy statements, beginning with an endorsement of the OECD principles by the Department of Commerce in 1981 [11].

The Fair Information Practices are not legal requirements but provide a framework of principles for balancing the need for privacy with other public policy interests, such as national security, law enforcement, and administrative efficiency. Striking that balance varies among countries and among types of information.

Federal Laws and Guidance Govern Use of Personal Information in Federal Agencies

There is no single federal law that governs all use or disclosure of personal information. Instead, U.S. law includes a number of separate statutes that provide privacy protections for information used for specific purposes or maintained by specific entities. The major requirements for the protection of personal information by federal agencies come from two laws: the Privacy Act of 1974 and the privacy provisions of the E-Government Act of 2002.

The Privacy Act places limitations on agencies' collection, disclosure, and use of personal information maintained in systems of records. The act describes a "record" as any item, collection, or grouping of information about an individual that is maintained by an agency and contains his or her name or another personal identifier. It also defines a "system of records" as a group of records under the control of any agency from which information is retrieved by the name of the individual or by an individual identifier. The Privacy Act requires that when agencies establish or make changes to a system of records, they must notify the public through a system-of-records notice in the Federal Register that identifies, among other things, the categories of data collected, the categories of individuals about whom information is collected, the intended "routine" uses of data, and procedures that individuals can use to review and correct personally identifiable information [12].

Several provisions of the act require agencies to define and limit collection and use to predefined purposes. For example, the act requires that, to the greatest extent practicable, personal information should be collected directly from the subject individual when it may affect that individual's rights or benefits under a federal program. The act also requires that an agency inform individuals whom it asks to supply information of (1) the authority for soliciting the information and whether disclosure of such information is mandatory or voluntary; (2) the principal purposes for which the information is intended to be used; (3) the routine uses that may be made of the information; and (4) the effects on the individual, if any, of not providing the information. According to OMB, this requirement is based on the assumption that individuals should be provided with sufficient information about the request to make a decision about whether to respond.

In handling collected information, agencies are generally required by the Privacy Act to, among other things, allow individuals to (1) review their records (meaning any information pertaining to them that is contained in the system of records), (2) request a copy of their record or information from the system of records, and (3) request corrections to their information.

Agencies are allowed to claim exemptions from some of the provisions of the Privacy Act if the records are used for certain purposes. For example, records compiled by law enforcement agencies for criminal law enforcement purposes can be exempt from a number of provisions, including (1) the requirement to notify individuals of the purposes and uses of the information at the time of collection and (2) the requirement to ensure the accuracy, relevance, timeliness, and completeness of records. A broader category of investigative records compiled for criminal or civil law enforcement purposes can also be exempted from a somewhat smaller number of Privacy Act provisions, including the requirement to provide individuals with access to their records and to inform the public of the categories of sources of records. In general, the exemptions for law enforcement purposes are intended to prevent the disclosure of information collected as part of an ongoing investigation that could impair the investigation or allow those under investigation to change their behavior or take other actions to escape prosecution.

In 2002, Congress enacted the E-Government Act to, among other things, enhance protection for personal information in government information systems or information collections by requiring that agencies conduct privacy impact assessments, which are analyses of how personal information is collected, stored, shared, and managed in a federal system.

In addition, the Paperwork Reduction Act applies to federal information collections and was designed to help ensure that when the government asks the public for information, the burden of providing this information is as small as possible and the information itself is used effectively [13]. Among the act's provisions is the requirement that agencies not establish information collections without having them approved by OMB, and that before submitting them for approval, agencies' chief information officers certify that the collections meet 10 specified standards. The law also requires agencies both to publish notices in the Federal Register and to otherwise consult with the public about their planned collections.

Privacy is also addressed in the legal framework for the emerging information sharing environment. As directed by the Intelligence Reform and Terrorism Prevention Act of 2004, the administration has taken steps, beginning in 2005, to establish an information sharing environment to facilitate the sharing of terrorism-related information [14]. The move was driven by the recognition that before the attacks of September 11, 2001, federal agencies had been unable to effectively share information about suspected terrorists and their activities. In addressing this problem, the National Commission on Terrorist Attacks Upon the United States (9/11 Commission) recommended that the sharing and uses of information be guided by a set of practical policy guidelines that would simultaneously empower and constrain officials, closely circumscribing what types of information they would be permitted to share as well as the types of information they would need to protect. Exchanging terrorism- related information continues to be a significant challenge for federal, state, and local governments—one that we recognize is not easily addressed. Accordingly, since January 2005, we have designated information sharing for homeland security a high-risk area [15].

Other federal laws address privacy protection for personal information with respect to information security requirements, as well as for certain types of information, such as when taxpayer, statistical, or health information is involved. This includes the Federal Information Security Management Act (FISMA), which addresses the protection of personal information by defining federal requirements for securing information and information systems that support federal agency operations and assets; the Health Insurance Portability and Accountability Act of 1996, which addresses the use and disclosure of individual health information; the Confidential Information Protection and Statistical Efficiency Act, which limits the use of information gathered for statistical purposes; and laws governing the disclosure of taxpayer data collected by the Internal Revenue Service.

OMB Has Primary Responsibility for Oversight of the Privacy, E-Government, and Paperwork Reduction Acts

The Privacy Act gives OMB responsibility for developing guidelines and providing "continuing assistance to and oversight of" agencies' implementation of the Privacy Act. The E-Government Act of 2002 also assigns OMB responsibility for developing privacy impact assessment guidance and ensuring agency implementation of the privacy impact assessment requirement. In July 1975, OMB published guidance for implementing the provisions of the Privacy Act. Since then, OMB has periodically issued additional guidance, including guidance to assist agencies in complying with the Computer Matching and Privacy Protection Act [16] and guidance to agencies on conducting privacy impact assessments.

In 1980, the enactment of the Paperwork Reduction Act made virtually all federal agency information collection activities subject to OMB review and established broad objectives for OMB oversight of the management of federal information resources. The act established the Office of Information and Regulatory Affairs within OMB and gave this office a variety of oversight responsibilities over federal information functions, including general information policy, reduction of paperwork burden, and information privacy. To assist agencies in fulfilling their responsibilities under the act, OMB took various steps. It issued a regulation [17] and provided agencies with instructions on filling out a standard form for submissions and providing supporting statements.

OMB has also periodically issued guidance on other privacy-related issues, including:

- federal agency Web site privacy policies;
- interagency sharing of personal information;
- designation of senior staff responsible for privacy; and
- data breach notification.

Prior GAO Reports Have Identified Privacy Challenges at Federal Agencies

We have previously reported on a number of agency-specific and governmentwide privacy-related issues at federal agencies. For example, in 2003, we reported that agencies generally did well with certain aspects of the Privacy Act's requirements—such as issuing systems-of-records notices when required—but did less well at other requirements, such as ensuring that information is complete, accurate, relevant, and timely before it is disclosed to a nonfederal organization [18]. In discussing this uneven compliance, agency officials reported the need for additional OMB leadership and guidance to assist in difficult implementation issues in a rapidly changing environment. For example, officials had questions about the act's applicability to electronic records. We have also reported on key privacy challenges facing federal agencies, federal Web site privacy, notification of individuals in the event of a data breach, and government data-mining initiatives.

Key Terms in the Privacy Act May Be Defined Too Narrowly

Because the Privacy Act's controls on the collection, use, and disclosure of personally identifiable information only apply when such information is covered by the act's key terms, especially the "system-of-records" construct, they do not consistently protect such information in all circumstances of its collection and use throughout the federal government. There are several different ways in which federal collection and use of personally identifiable information could be outside of such a construct and thus not receive the Privacy Act's protections, as shown by the following examples:

- *Personally identifiable information held by the government is not always retrieved by identifier.* The Privacy Act defines a system of records as "a group of records"19 that is "under the control of any agency from which information is retrieved by the name of the individual or by some identifying number, symbol, or other identifying particular assigned to the individual." If personally identifiable information (records) is not retrieved by identifier but instead accessed through some other method or criteria—for example, by searching for all individuals who have a certain medical condition or who applied for benefits on a certain date—the system would not meet the Privacy Act's system-of-records definition and therefore would not be governed by the act's protections. OMB's 1975 Privacy Act implementation guidance reflects an acknowledgement that agencies could potentially evade the act's requirements by organizing personal information in ways that may not be considered to be retrieved by identifier.

In our 2003 report concerning compliance with the Privacy Act, we found that the increasing use of electronic records by federal agencies resulted in personal information falling outside the scope of Privacy Act protections. A key characteristic of agencies' systems of records at the time was that a large proportion of them were electronic, reflecting the government's significant use of computers and the Internet to collect and share personal information. Based on survey responses from 25 agencies in 2002, we estimated that 70 percent of the agencies' systems of records contained electronic records and that 11 percent of information systems in use at those agencies contained personal information that was outside a Privacy Act system of records. We also reported that among the agencies we surveyed, the most frequently cited reason for systems not being considered Privacy Act systems of records was that the agency did not use a personal identifier to retrieve the personal information [20]

- *The Privacy Act's protections may not apply to contemporary data processing technologies and applications.* In today's highly interconnected environment, information can be gathered from many different sources, analyzed, and redistributed in very dynamic, unstructured ways that may have little to do with the file-oriente d concept of a Privacy Act system of records. For example, data mining, a prevalent technique used by federal agencies for extracting useful information from large volumes of data, may escape the purview of the Privacy Act's protections [21] Specifically, a data-mining system that performs analysis by looking for patterns in personal information located in other systems of records or that performs subject-based queries across multiple data sources may not constitute a system of records under the act.

In recent years, reports required by law on data mining have described activities that had not been identified as systems of records covered by the Privacy Act. In one example, DHS rep orted that all the data sources for the planned Analysis Disseminatio n Visualization Insight and Semantic Enhancement (ADVISE) data mining program were covered by existing system-of-records noti ces; however, the system itself was not covered, and no system of records notice was created specifically to document protections under the Privacy Act governing the specific activities of the system [22]. ADVISE was a data-mining tool intended to allow an analyst to search for patterns in data—such as relationships among people, organizations, and events—and to produce visual representations of those patterns.

As a result, personally identifiable information collected and processed by such systems may be less well protected than if it were more specifically addressed by the Privacy Act.

The issues associated with the coverage of the Privacy Act's protections could be addressed by revising the system-of-records definition to cover all personally identifiable information collected, used, and maintained by the federal government. Experts at o ur forum were in agreement that the system-of-records definition is outdated and flawed and that the act's protections should be applied whenever agencies obtain, process, store, or share personally identifiable information—not just when records are retrieved by personal identifier. Changing the system-of-records definition is an option that could help ensure that the act's protections are consistently applied to all personally identifiable information.

THE PRIVACY ACT DOES N OT ENSURE THAT THE USE OF PERSONAL INFORMATION IS LIMITED TO CLEARLY STATED PURPOSES

The fair information practices' purpose specification p rinciple states that the purpose for the collection o f personal information should be disclosed before the collection is made and upon any change to that purpose, while the use limitation principle provides that personal information, once collected, should not be disclosed or used for other than its specified purpose without consent of the individual or legal authority. When the government is required to define a specific purpose for the collection of personal information and limit its use to that purpose, individuals gain assurance that their privacy will be protected and their information will not be us ed in ways that could jeopardize their rights or otherwise unfairly affect them.

The Privacy Act requires agencies to (1) inform individuals from whom inform ation is being collected of the principal purpose or purposes for which the information is intended to be used and (2) publish a system-of-records notice in the Federal Register of t he existence and character of the system of records, including plann ed routine uses of the records and the purpose of each of these routine uses. Concerns have been raised, however, that these requirements do not go far enough in ensuring that the government's planned purposes are sufficiently specified and that the use of information is limited to these purposes:

- *Purpose descriptions in public notices are not required to be specific.* While there is no r equirement for an overall statement of purpose, Privacy Act notices may contain multiple descriptions of purposes associated with routine uses, and agencies are not required to be specific in formulating these purposes. OMB guidanc e on the act gives agencies discretion to determine how to define the range of appropriate uses and associated purposes that it intends for a given system of records. While purpose statements for certain law enforcement and anti-terrorism systems might need to be phrased broadly enough so as not to reveal investigative techniques or the details of ongoing cases, very broadly defined purposes could allow for unnecessarily broad ranges of uses, thus calling into question whether meaningful limitations had been imposed.
- *Unconstrained application of predefined "routine" uses may weaken use limitations.* A number of concerns have been raised about the impact on privacy of potentially unnecess ary routine uses for agency systems of records, particularly through the application of "standard" routine uses that are developed for general use on multiple systems of records. This practice is not prohibited by the Privacy Act. All six agencies we reviewed had lists of standard routine uses for application to their systems of records. However, the language of these standard routine uses varies from agency to agency. For example, several agencies have a routine use allowing them to share information about individuals with other governmental entities for purposes of decision-making about hiring or retention of an individual, issuance of a security clearance, license, contract, grant, or other benefit. Experts expressed concern that

"standard" routine uses such as these vary to such a great extent from agency to agency, with no specific legal requirement that they be formulated consistently.

- *The Privacy Act sets only modest limits on the use of personal information for multiple purposes within an agency.* The Privacy Act permits disclosures from agency systems of records "to those officers and employees of the agency which maintains the record who have a need for the record in the performance of their duties." However, without additional limits, internal uses could go beyond uses related to the purpose of the original collection. In our interviews with senior agency privacy officials, we asked what, if any, limits were placed on internal agency uses of information. Several agencies responded that, consistent with the Privacy Act and OMB guidance, internal agency usage of personal information was limited to those personnel with a "need to know." However, because the Privacy Act and related guidance do not require it, none of these agencies took steps to determine whether internal uses were consistent with the purposes originally stated for the collection of information. The potential that personal information could be used for multiple, unspecified purposes is especially heightened in large agencies with multiple components that may collect personal information in many different ways for disparate purposes.
- *The Privacy Act's provisions may not apply when data are shared for use by another agency.* In addition to concerns about limiting use to a spe cified purpose within an agency, more extensive issues have been raised when data are shared outside an agency. Although the Privacy Act provides assurance that the information in systems of records cannot be disclosed unless it is pursuant to either a routine use or another statutorily allowed condition, the act does not attach its protections to data after they have been disclosed. As data sharing among agencies becomes central to the sharing of terrorism-related information, measures to ensure that data are being used appropriately will become more important. Despite not being required to do so, agencies we reviewed reported taking measures to ensure the data are used appropriately by recipients . However, in the absence of such measures, data shared outside federal agencies would not always have sufficient protections.

To better confine agencies' use of personal information to its specified purposes, laws or guidance could be revised to (1) require agencies to justify the use of key elements of personal information, (2) set specific limits on routine uses and internal agency uses of personal information, and (3) require agencies to establish formal agreements with external entities before sharing personal information with them.

THE PRIVACY ACT MAY NOT INCLUDE EFFECTIVE MECHANISMS FOR INFORMING THE PUBLIC

A primary method for providing transparency about government programs and systems that collect and use personal information is through public written notices. A clear and effective notice can provide individuals with critical information about what personal data are to be collected, how they are to be used, and the circumstances under which they may be shared. An effective notice can also provide individuals with information they need to determine whether to provide their personal information (if voluntary), or who to contact to correct any errors that could result in an adverse determination about them.

In formal terms, the openness principle states that the public should be informed about privacy policies and practices and that individuals should have a ready means of learning about the use of personal information. The openness principle underlies the public notice provisions of the Privacy Act. Specifically, the Privacy Act requires agencies to publish in the Federal Register, "upon establishment or revision, a notice of the existence and character of a system of records." This notice is to include, among other things , the categories of records in the system as well as the catego ries of sources of records. The notice is also required to explain agency procedures whereby an individual can gain access to any record pertaining to him or her contained in the system of records and contest its content. Agencies are further required to publish notice of any new use or intended use of the information in the system and provide an opportunity for interested persons to submit written data, views, or arguments to the agency [23].

However, experts at our forum as well as agency privacy officials questioned the value of system-of-records notices as vehicles for providing information to the general public for several reasons:

- *System-of-records notices may be difficult to understand.* As with other legally required privacy notices, system-of-records notices have been criticized as hard to read and understand. To the lay reader, the meaning of "routine" uses may be unclear, or a list of exemptions could raise more questions than it answers. Agency privacy officials and privacy experts at our forum both agreed that system-of-records notices have limited value as vehicles for public notification.

- *System-of-records notices do not always contain complete and useful information about privacy protections.* They often describe purposes and use in such broad terms that it becomes questionable whether those purposes and uses have been significantly limited. Likewise, broad purpose statements may not usefully inform the public of the government's intended purposes, and the citation of multiple routine uses does little to aid individuals' understanding of how the government is using their personal information. The Privacy Act does not require agencies to be specific in describing the purposes associated with routine uses of personal information or to publish all expected internal agency uses of that information.
- *Publication in the Federal Register may reach only a limited audience.* Agency privacy officials questioned whether the required publication of system-of-records notices in the Federal Register would be useful to a broader audience than federal agency officials and public interest groups, such as privacy advocacy groups. Notices published in the Federal Register may not be very accessible and readable. The Federal Register Web site does not provide a ready means of determining what system-of-records notices are current, when they were last updated, or which ones apply to any specific governmental function. Officials agreed that it can be difficult to locate a system-of-records notice on the Federal Register Web site, even when the name of the relevant system of records is known in advance. Privacy experts at our forum likewise agreed that the Federal Register is probably not effective with the general public and that a more effective technique for reaching a wide audience in today's environment is via consolidated publication on a governmentwide Web site devoted to privacy. Both agency officials and privacy experts also agreed, however, that the Federal Register serves a separate but important role as the official public record of federal agencies and as the official basis for soliciting comments from the public on proposed systems of records.

Based on discussions with privacy experts, agency officials, and analysis of laws and related guidance, a number of options exist for improving public notice regarding federal collection and use o f personal information:

- *Require layered public notices in conjunction with system-ofrecords notices.* Layering involves providing only the most important summary facts up front—often in a graphically oriented format—followed by one or more lengthier, more narrative versions.

By offering both types of notices, the benefits of each can be realized: long notices offer completeness, while brief notice s offer ease of understanding.

- *Set requirements to ensure that purpose, collection limitations, and use limitations are better addressed in the content of privacy notices.* These could include requirements for a specific description of the planned purpose of a system, what data needs to be collected to serve that purpose, and how its use will be limited to that purpose, including descriptions of primary and secondary uses of information. Setting these requirements could spur agencies to prepare notices that include more meaningful descriptions of the intents and purposes of their systems of records.
- *Make all notices available on a governmentwide privacy Web site.* Relevant privacy notices could be published at a central governmentwide location, with an address such as www.privacy.gov, and at corresponding standard locations on agency Web sites with addresses of the form www.agency.gov/privacy. These sites have the potential to reach a far broader spectrum of users than the Federal Register.

Amending Privacy Laws Could Address Gaps and Shortcomings in Privacy Protections

In summary, current laws and guidance governing the federal government's collection, use, and disclosure of personal information have gaps and other potential shortcomings in three broad categories: (1) the Privacy Act and E-Government Act do not always provide protections for federal uses of personal information, (2) laws and guidance may not effectively limit agency collection and use of personal information to specific purposes, and (3) the Privacy Act may not include effective mechanisms for informing the public.

In assessing the appropriate balance between the needs of the federal government to collect personally identifiable information for programm atic purposes and the assurances that individuals should have that their information is being sufficiently protected and properly used, Congress should consider amending applicable laws, such as the Privacy Act and the E-Government Act, according to the alternatives outlined in our report, including:

- revising the scope of the laws to cover all personally identifiable information collected, used, and maintained by the federal government;
- setting requirements to ensure that the collection and use of personally identifiable information is limited to a stated purpose; and
- establishing additional mechanisms for informing the public about privacy protections by revising requirements for the structure and publication of public notices.

In commenting on a draft of our report, OMB officials noted that they shared our concerns about privacy and stated they believe it would be important for Congre ss to consider potential amendments to the Privacy Act and the E-Government Act in the broader context of all existing privacy and related laws that Congress has enacted.

Though we did not make specific recommendations to OMB, the agency provided comments on the alternatives identified in conjunction with our matter for Congressional consideration. Regarding alternatives for revising the scope of laws to cover all personally identifiable information collected, used, and maintained by the federal government, OMB stated that it would be important for Congress to evaluate fully the potential implications of revisions such as amending the Privacy Act's system-of-records definition. We believe that, given that the Privacy Act's controls on the collection, use, and disclosure of personally identifiable information do not consistently protect such information in all circumstances of its collection and use throughout the federal government, amending the act's definition of a system of records is an important alternative for Congress to consider.

We agree with OMB, however, that any consideration of amendments to the Privacy Act and E-Government Act should be considered thoroughly and within the context of all existing laws. Further, the challenge of how best to balance the federal government's need to collect and use information with individuals ' privacy rights in the current technological and political environment merits a national public debate on all relevant issues, including the alternatives I have highlighted today.

Mr. Chairman, this concludes my testimony today. I would be happy to answer any questions you or other m embers of the committee may have.

REFERENCES

[1] For purposes of this testimony, the terms personal *information and personally identifiable information are used interchangeably to refer to any information about an individual maintained by an agency*, including (1) any information that can be used to distinguish or trace an individual's identity, such as name, Social Security number, date and place of birth, mother's maiden name, or biometric records; and (2) any other information that is linked or linkable to an individual, such as medical, educational, financial, and employment information.

[2] In addition, the Paperwork Reduction Act, enacted in 1980 and significantly revised in 1995, also has provisions affecting privacy protection in that it sets requirements for limiting the collection of information from individuals, including personal information. While the act's requirements are aimed at reducing the paperwork burden on individuals rather than specifically protecting personally identifiable information, the act nevertheless serves an important role in protecting privacy by setting these controls.

[3] A privacy impact assessment is an analysis of how personal information is collected, stored, shared, and managed in an information system.

[4] Congress used the committee's final report as a basis for crafting the Privacy Act of 1974. See U.S. Department of Health, Education, and Welfare, *Records, Computers, and the Rights of Citizens: Report of the Secretary's Advisory Committee on Automated Personal Data Systems* (Washington, D.C.: July 1973).

[5] GAO, *Privacy: Alternatives Exist for Enhancing Protection of Personally Identifiable Information,* GAO-08-536 (Washington, D.C.: May 19, 2008).

[6] GAO, *Privacy Act: OMB Leadership Needed to Improve Agency Compliance,* GAO-03-304 (Washington, D.C.: June 30, 2003)

[7] Department of Health, Education & Welfare, Records, Computers, and the Rights of Citizens: Report of the Secretary's Advisory Committee on Automated Personal Data Systems (Washington, D.C.: 1973).

[8] OECD, Guidelines on the Protection of Privacy and Transborder Flow of Personal Data (Sept. 23, 1980) The OECD plays a prominent role in fostering good governance in the public service and in corporate activity among its 30 member countries. It produces internationally agreed-upon instruments, decisions, and recommendations to promote rules in areas where multilateral agreement is necessary for individual countries to make progress in the global economy.

[9] OECD, *Making Privacy Notices Simple: An OECD Report and Recommendations* (July 24, 2006).

[10] European Union Data Protection Directive ("Directive 95/46/EC of the European Parliament and of the Council of 24 October 1995 on the Protection of Individuals with Regard to the Processing of Personal Data and the Free Movement of Such Data") (1995).

[11] "Report on OECD Guidelines Program," Memorandum from Bernard Wunder, Jr., Assistant Secretary for Communications and Information, Department of Commerce (Oct. 30, 1981).

[12] Under the Privacy Act of 1974, the term "routine use" means (with respect to the disclosure of a record) the use of such a record for a purpose that is compatible with the purpose for which it was collected. 5 U.S.C. § 552a (a)(7).

[13] The Paperwork Reduction Act was originally enacted into law in 1980 (Pub. L. No. 96-5 11, Dec. 11, 1980). It was reauthorized with minor amendments in 1986 (Pub. L. No. 99-591, Oct. 30, 1986) and was reauthorized a second time with more significant amendments in 1995 (Pub. L. No. 104-13, May 22, 1995)

[14] Pub. L. No. 108-458 (Dec. 17, 2004).

[15] For more information, see GAO, *High-Risk Series: An Update*, GAO-07-310 (Washington, D.C.: January 2007), p. 47, *and Information Sharing: The Federal Government Needs to Establish Policies and Processes for Sharing Terrorism-Related and Sensitive but Unclassified Information*, GAO-06-385 (Washington, D.C.: Mar. 17, 2006).

[16] In 1988, Congress passed the Computer Matching and Privacy Protection Act as an amendment to the Privacy Act, to establish procedural safeguards that affect agencies' use of Privacy Act records from benefit programs in performing certain types of computerized matching programs. For example, the 1988 act requires agencies to create written agreements specifying the terms under which matches are to be done.

[17] 5 C.F.R. Part 1320.

[18] GAO, *Privacy Act: OMB Leadership Needed to Improve Agency Compliance*, GAO-03-304 (Washington, D.C.: June 30, 2003)

[19] A record is defined as "any item, collection, or grouping of information about an individual that is maintained by an agency, including, but not limited to, his education, financial transactions, medical history, and criminal or employment history and that contains his name, or the identifying number, symbol, or other identifying particular assigned to the individual, such as a finger or voice print or a photograph."

[20] GAO, *Privacy Act: OMB Leadership Needed to Improve Agency Compliance*, GAO-03-304 (Washington, D.C.: June 30, 2003)

[21] GAO, *Data Mining: Federal Efforts Cover a Wide Range of Uses*, GAO-04-548 (Washington, D.C.: May 4, 2004).

[22] The DHS Privacy Office determined that because the data mining applications did not involve retrieval by individual identifier, a separate system of records notice describing the data mining application was not required. DHS Privacy Office, *ADVISE Report: DHS Privacy Office Review of the Analysis, Dissemination, Visualization, Insight, and Semantic Enhancement* (ADVISE) Program (Washington, D.C., July 11, 2007)

[23] The Privacy Act allows agencies to claim exemptions if the records are used for certain purposes, such as criminal law enforcement. See the earlier discussion on pp. 9-10.

Chapter 5

OVERSIGHT OF PRIVACY ACTIVITIES*

WHAT GAO FOUND

Federal laws set varying roles and responsibilities for senior agency privacy officials. Despite much variation, all of these laws require covered agencies to assign overall responsibility for privacy protection and compliance to a senior agency official. In addition, Office of Management and Budget guidance directs agencies to designate a senior agency official for privacy with specific responsibilities. The specific privacy responsibilities defined in these laws and guidance can be grouped into six broad categories: (1) conducting privacy impact assessments (which are intended to ensure that privacy requirements are addressed when personal information is collected, stored, shared, and managed in a federal system), (2) complying with the Privacy Act, (3) reviewing and evaluating the privacy implications of agency policies, (4) producing reports on the status of privacy protections, (5) ensuring that redress procedures to handle privacy inquiries and complaints are in place, and (6) ensuring that employees and contractors receive appropriate training. The laws and guidance vary in how they frame requirements in these categories and which agencies must adhere to them.

Agencies also have varying organizational structures to address privacy responsibilities. For example, of the 12 agencies we reviewed, 2 had statutorily designated chief privacy officers who also served as senior agency officials for privacy, 5 designated their agency chief information officers as their senior privacy officials, and the others designated a variety of other officials, such as the general counsel or assistant secretary for management. Further, not all of the

---

* Excerpted from GAO Report 08-603, dated May 2008.

agencies we reviewed had given their designated senior officials full oversight over all privacy-related functions. While 6 agencies had these officials overseeing all key privacy functions, 6 others relied on other organizational units not overseen by the designated senior official to perform certain key privacy functions. The fragmented way in which privacy functions were assigned to organizational units in these agencies is at least partly the result of evolving requirements in law and guidance. However, without oversight of all key privacy functions, designated senior officials may be unable to effectively serve as agency central focal points for information privacy.

WHY GAO DID THIS STUDY

Government agencies have a longstanding obligation under the Privacy Act of 1974 to protect the privacy of individuals about whom they collect personal information. A number of additional laws have been enacted in recent years directing agency heads to designate senior officials as focal points with overall responsibility for privacy.

GAO was asked to (1) describe laws and guidance that set requirements for senior privacy officials within federal agencies, and (2) describe the organizational structures used by agencies to address privacy requirements and assess whether senior officials have oversight over key functions. To achieve these objectives, GAO analyzed the laws and related guidance and analyzed policies and procedures relating to key privacy functions at 12 agencies.

WHAT GAO RECOMMENDS

GAO is recommending that certain agencies it reviewed take steps to ensure that their senior agency officials for privacy have oversight of all key privacy functions. Seven of the 12 agencies had no comment or concurred with GAO's assessment. Commerce and Defense did not state whether they agreed, but said that their current structures were adequate. Justice, Labor, and Treasury disagreed with GAO's characterization of their senior privacy officials as not having oversight of all key privacy functions. However, these agencies' policies do not assign oversight of such functions to their senior privacy officials.

Abbreviations

CIO	chief information officer
CPO	chief privacy officer
CISO	chief information security officer
DHS	Department of Homeland Security
E-Gov Act	E-Government Act
FISMA	Federal Information Security Management Act
OMB	Office of Management and Budget
PIA	privacy impact assessment
SAOP	senior agency official for privacy

May 30, 2008
The Honorable Daniel K. Akaka
Chairman
Subcommittee on Oversight of Government Management,
the Federal Workforce, and the District of Columbia
Committee on Homeland Security and Governmental Affairs
United States Senate
Dear Senator Akaka:

As you know, government agencies have long-standing obligations to protect the privacy of individuals about whom they collect personal information. Based on concerns about privacy, a number of laws have been enacted in recent years directing agency heads to designate chief privacy officers (CPO) as focal points with overall responsibility for privacy. For example, the Homeland Security Act of 2002 created the first statutorily required senior privacy official at the Department of Homeland Security (DHS). Several other laws followed with similar direction to other agencies Furthermore, the Office of Management and Budget (OMB) issued guidance in 2005 directing each agency to designate a senior agency official for privacy (SAOP).

Agency responsibilities for protecting privacy are based primarily on two laws, the Privacy Act of 1974 and the E-Government Act (E-Gov Act) of 2002. Under the Privacy Act, federal agencies must issue public notices that identify, among other things, the type of data collected, the types of individuals about whom information is collected, the intended "routine" uses of the data, and procedures that individuals can use to review and correct personal information. The E-Gov Act requires agencies to conduct privacy impact assessments (PIA) of privacy risks associated with information technology used to process personal information [1]. In addition, the Paperwork Reduction Act sets conditions for collecting information from individuals and designates agency chief information officers (CIO) as responsible for privacy protection. Recent laws and guidance have also designated specific agency officials with responsibilities for ensuring agency compliance with privacy protection requirements.

Our objectives were to (1) describe laws and guidance that set requirements for senior privacy officials within federal agencies, and (2) describe the organizational structures used by agencies to address privacy requirements and assess whether senior officials have oversight over key functions.

To address our first objective, we reviewed and analyzed laws and OMB guidance that assign agencywide privacy responsibilities to senior officials within federal agencies. To address our second objective, we analyzed policies and procedures at these agencies, and interviewed senior agency privacy officials to identify the privacy management structures used at each of these agencies and the roles and responsibilities of senior privacy officials. The agencies included in this review (Departments of Commerce, Defense, Health and Human Services, Homeland Security, Justice, Labor, State, Treasury, Transportation, and Veterans Affairs, as well as the Social Security Administration and the U.S. Agency for International Development) are major agencies with statutorily designated privacy officers, have a central mission for which the collection of personally identifiable information is a critical component, or have implemented a unique organizational privacy structure. We examined and compared agency management structures for fulfilling privacy responsibilities and assessed the differences in roles and responsibilities of privacy officers based on the differences in agencies' organizational structures. We conducted this performance audit from September 2007 to May 2008 in accordance with generally accepted government auditing standards. Those standards require that we plan and perform the audit to obtain sufficient, appropriate evidence to provide a reasonable basis for our findings and conclusions based on our audit objectives. We believe that the evidence obtained provides a reasonable basis for our findings and conclusions based on our audit objectives.

RESULTS IN BRIEF

Laws and guidance set a variety of requirements for senior privacy officials at federal agencies. For example, agencies have had a long standing requirement under the Paperwork Reduction Act to assign agency CIOs overall responsibility for privacy policy and compliance with the Privacy Act. In recent years, additional laws have also set roles and responsibilities for senior agency privacy officials. Despite much variation, all of these laws require agencies to assign overall responsibility for privacy protection and compliance to a senior official. In addition, OMB guidance directs agencies to designate an SAOP with specific responsibilities. These laws and guidance define specific privacy responsibilities that can be grouped into six broad categories: (1) conducting PIAs; (2) complying with the Privacy Act; (3) reviewing and evaluating the privacy implications of agency policies, regulations, and initiatives; (4) producing reports on the status of privacy protections; (5) ensuring that redress procedures are in place; and (6) ensuring that employees and contractors receive appropriate training. The laws and guidance vary in how they frame requirements in these categories and which agencies must adhere to them.

Agencies have varying organizational structures to address privacy responsibilities. For example, of the 12 agencies we reviewed, 2 had statutorily designated CPOs who also served as SAOPs, 5 designated their agency CIOs as their senior officials, and the others designated a variety of other officials, such as the general counsel or assistant secretary for management. Further, not all of the agencies we reviewed had given their designated senior officials full oversight over all privacy-related functions. While 6 agencies had these officials overseeing all key privacy functions, 6 others relied on other organizational units not overseen by the designated senior official to perform certain key privacy functions. The fragmented way in which privacy functions have been assigned to organizational units in these agencies is at least partly the result of evolving requirements in law and guidance. As requirements have evolved, organizational responsibilities have been established incrementally to meet them. However, without oversight and involvement in all key privacy functions, SAOPs may be unable to effectively serve as agency central focal points for information privacy.

We are recommending that the heads of certain agencies we reviewed take steps to ensure that their SAOPs have oversight over all key privacy functions.

We provided a draft of this report to OMB and to the Departments of Commerce, Defense, Health and Human Services, Homeland Security, Justice, Labor, State, Treasury, Transportation, and Veterans Affairs, as well as the Social Security Administration and the U.S. Agency for International Development, for review and comment. Five agencies provided no comments on this review [2]. In comments provided via Email, the Veterans Affairs and the Social Security Administration concurred with our assessment and recommendations and provided technical comments, which we incorporated in the final report as appropriate. In oral comments, OMB also concurred with our assessment and recommendations and provided technical comments, which we incorporated in the final report as appropriate. Commerce and Defense provided written comments that did not state whether they agreed or disagreed with the content of the report; however, both agencies stated that their privacy management structures were adequate. In contrast, we believe that clearly establishing the role of the SAOP as a focal point for departmental privacy functions would help ensure that these agencies provide consistent privacy protections and would align with OMB direction. Justice, Labor, and Treasury provided written comments and disagreed with our characterization of their agency SAOPs as not having oversight of all key privacy functions. However, our review of agency policies and procedures relating to privacy management showed that SAOPs at these agencies had not been assigned oversight of all key functions.

BACKGROUND

In recent years, a number of factors have led to growing concern about the protection of privacy when personally identifiable information is collected and maintained by the federal government [3]. Recent data breaches of personal information at government agencies, such as the data breach at the Department of Veterans Affairs, which exposed the personal information of 26.5 million veterans and active duty members of the military in May 2006, have raised concerns about identity theft [4]. In addition, increasingly sophisticated analytical techniques employed by federal agencies, such as data mining, also raise concerns about how personally identifiable information is used and what controls are placed on its use. Concerns such as these have focused attention on the structures agencies have instituted to ensure privacy protections are in place.

The major requirements for privacy protection by federal agencies come from two laws, the Privacy Act of 1974 and the E-Gov Act of 2002.

The Privacy Act places limitations on agencies' collection, disclosure, and use of personal information maintained in systems of records. The act describes a "record" as any item, collection, or grouping of information about an individual that is maintained by an agency and contains his or her name or another personal identifier. It also defines "system of records" as a group of records under the control of any agency from which information is retrieved by the name of the individual or by an individual identifier. The Privacy Act requires that when agencies maintain a system of records, they must notify the public by a system-of-records notice: that is, a notice in the Federal Register identifying, among other things, the type of data collected, the types of individuals about whom information is collected, the intended "routine" use of the data, and procedures that individuals can use to review and correct personal information. The act also requires agencies to define and limit their use of covered personal information. In addition, the act requires that to the greatest extent practicable, personal information should be collected directly from the subject individual when it may affect an individual's rights or benefits under a federal program.

The E-Gov Act of 2002 also assigns agencies significant responsibilities relating to privacy. The E-Gov Act strives to enhance protection for personal information in government information systems or information collections by requiring that agencies conduct PIAs. A PIA is an analysis of how personal information is collected, stored, shared, and managed in a federal system. Furthermore, according to OMB guidance, a PIA is an analysis of how information is handled. Specifically, a PIA is to (1) ensure that handling conforms to applicable legal, regulatory, and policy requirements regarding privacy; (2) determine the risks and effects of collecting, maintaining, and disseminating information in identifiable form in an electronic information system; and (3) examine and evaluate protections and alternative processes for handling information to mitigate potential privacy risks.

Agencies must conduct PIAs (1) before developing or procuring information technology that collects, maintains, or disseminates information that is in a personally identifiable form or (2) before initiating any new data collections involving personal information that will be collected, maintained, or disseminated using information technology if the same questions are asked of 10 or more people. To the extent that PIAs are made publicly available, they provide explanations to the public about such things as the information that will be collected, why it is being collected, how it is to be used, and how the system and data will be maintained and protected.

OMB is tasked with providing guidance to agencies on how to implement the provisions of these two acts and has done so, beginning with guidance on the Privacy Act, issued in 1975. The guidance provides explanations for the various provisions of the law as well as detailed instructions on how to comply. OMB's guidance on implementing the privacy provisions of the E- Gov Act of 2002 identifies circumstances under which agencies must conduct PIAs and explains how to conduct them.

We have previously reported on the role of senior privacy officials in the federal government. In 2006, we testified that the elevation of privacy officers to senior positions reflected the growing demands that these individuals faced in addressing privacy challenges on a day-to-day basis [5]. The challenges we identified included ensuring compliance with relevant privacy laws, such as the

Privacy Act and the E-Gov Act, and controlling the collection and use of personal information obtained from commercial sources. Additionally, in 2007 we reported that the DHS Privacy Office had made significant progress in carrying out its statutory responsibilities under the Homeland Security Act and its related role in ensuring E-Gov Act compliance, but noted that more work remained to be accomplished [6]. We recommended that DHS designate privacy officers at key DHS components, implement a department wide process for reviewing Privacy Act notices, establish a schedule for the timely issuance of privacy reports, and ensure that the Privacy Office's annual reports to Congress contain a specific discussion of complaints of privacy violations. In response, DHS included a discussion of privacy complaints in its most recent annual report; however, the other recommendations have not yet been implemented.

Laws and Guidance Set Varying Requirements for Senior Privacy Officials

Laws and guidance set a variety of requirements for senior privacy officials at federal agencies. For example, agencies have had a long standing requirement under the Paperwork Reduction Act to assign agency CIOs overall responsibility for privacy policy and compliance with the Privacy Act.

In recent years, additional laws have been enacted that also address the roles and responsibilities of senior officials with regard to privacy.

Despite much variation, all of these laws require agencies to assign overall responsibility for privacy protection and compliance to a senior agency official. In addition, OMB guidance has directed agencies to designate senior officials with overall responsibility for privacy.

These laws and guidance set specific privacy responsibilities for these agency officials. These responsibilities can be grouped into six broad categories: (1) conducting PIAs; (2) Privacy Act compliance; (3) reviewing and evaluating the privacy implications of agency policies, regulations, and initiatives; (4) producing reports on the status of privacy protections; (5) ensuring that redress procedures are in place; and (6) ensuring that employees and contractors receive appropriate training.

The laws and guidance vary in how they frame requirements in these categories and which agencies must adhere to them.

Laws and Guidance Address the Roles and Responsibilities of Privacy Officials

Numerous laws assign privacy responsibility to senior agency officials. The earliest of these laws is the Paperwork Reduction Act of 1980, which, as amended, directs agency heads to assign a CIO with responsibility for carrying out the agency's information resources management activities to improve agency productivity, efficiency, and effectiveness [7]. The act directs agency CIOs to undertake responsibility for implementing and enforcing applicable privacy policies, procedures, standards, and guidelines, and to assume responsibility and accountability for compliance with and coordinated management of the Privacy Act of 1974 and related information management laws [8].

As concerns about privacy have increased in recent years, Congress has enacted additional laws that include provisions addressing the roles and responsibilities of senior officials with regard to privacy. Despite variations, a common thread among these laws, as well as relevant OMB guidance, is that they all require agencies to assign overall responsibility for privacy protection and compliance to a senior agency official. Relevant laws include the following:

- The Homeland Security Act of 2002 directed the secretary of DHS to designate a senior official with primary responsibility for privacy policy.
- The Intelligence Reform and Terrorism Prevention Act of 2004 required the Director of National Intelligence to appoint a Civil Liberties Protection Officer and assigned this individual specific privacy responsibilities.
- The Violence Against Women and Department of Justice Reauthorization Act of 2005 instructed the Attorney General to designate a senior official with primary responsibility for privacy policy.
- The Transportation, Treasury, Independent Agencies and General Government Appropriations Act of 2005 directed each agency whose appropriations were provided by the act, including the Departments of Transportation and Treasury, to designate a CPO with primary responsibility for privacy and data protection policy [9].

The Implementing Recommendations of the 9/11 Commission Act of 2007 instructed the heads of Defense, DHS, Justice, Treasury, Health and Human Services, and State, as well as the Office of the Director of National Intelligence and the Central Intelligence Agency to designate no less than one senior officer to serve as a privacy and civil liberties officer [10]. Specific privacy provisions of these laws are summarized in appendix II.

A number of OMB memorandums have also addressed the roles and responsibilities of senior privacy officials. In 1999, OMB required agencies to designate a senior official to assume primary responsibility for privacy policy [11] OMB later reiterated this requirement in its guidance on compliance with the E-Gov Act, in which it directed agency heads to designate an appropriate senior official with responsibility for the coordination and implementation of OMB Web and privacy policy and to serve as the agency's principal contact for privacy policies [12]. Most recently, in 2005, OMB directed agencies to designate an SAOP with agency wide responsibility for information privacy issues and with responsibility for specific privacy functions, including ensuring agency compliance with all federal privacy laws, playing a central policy-making role in the development of policy proposals that implicate privacy issues, and ensuring that contractors and employees are provided with adequate privacy training [13]

Beginning in 2005, OMB has also issued guidance significantly enhancing longstanding requirements for agencies to report on their compliance with privacy laws [14]. OMB's 2005 guidance directed agencies to add a new section addressing privacy to their annual reports under the Federal Information Security Management Act (FISMA) [15]. SAOPs were assigned responsibility for completion of this section, in which they were to report on such things as agency policies and procedures for the conduct of PIAs, agency policies for ensuring adequate privacy training, as well as their own involvement in agency regulatory and policy decisions. In 2006, OMB issued further guidance requiring agencies to include as part of their FISMA reports a section addressing measures for protecting personally identifiable information. This guidance also required that agencies provide OMB with quarterly privacy updates and report all incidents relating to the loss of or unauthorized access to personally identifiable information [16]. Most recently, OMB directed agencies in 2007 to include in their FISMA reports additional items, such as their breach notification policies, plans to eliminate unnecessary use of Social Security numbers, and plans for reviewing and reducing their holdings of personally identifiable information [17].

These laws and guidance set a variety of requirements for senior officials to carry out specific privacy responsibilities. These responsibilities can be grouped into the following six key functions:

- *Conduct of PIAs:* A PIA is an analysis of how personal information is collected, stored, shared, and managed in a federal system, and is required before developing or procuring information technology that collects, maintains, or disseminates information that is in a personally identifiable form. Several laws assign privacy officials at covered agencies responsibilities that are met in part by performing PIAs on systems that collect, process, or store personally identifiable information. This includes the requirements for several agencies to ensure that "technologies sustain and do not erode privacy protections." Furthermore, OMB guidance requires agency SAOPs to ensure compliance with federal laws, regulations, and policies relating to information privacy, such as the E-Gov Act, which spells out agency PIA requirements.

- *Privacy Act compliance*: As previously discussed, the Privacy Act sets a variety of requirements for all federal agencies regarding privacy protection. For example, the act requires that when agencies establish or make changes to a system of records, they must notify the public by a notice in the Federal Register , identifying, among other things, the type of data collected, the types of individuals about whom information is collected, the intended "routine" use of the data, and procedures that individuals can use to review and correct personal information. Several other laws explicitly direct agency privacy officials to ensure that the personal information contained in their Privacy Act systems of records is handled in compliance with fair information practices as set out in the act. Further, OMB guidance assigns agency SAOPs with responsibility for ensuring Privacy Act compliance.
- *Policy consultation*: Relevant laws direct senior privacy officials to actively participate in the development and evaluation of privacy-sensitive agency policy decisions. Several specifically task the SAOP with evaluating legislative and regulatory proposals or periodically reviewing agency actions affecting privacy. As agencies develop new policies, senior officials responsible for privacy issues play a key role in identifying and mitigating potential privacy risks prior to finalizing a particular policy decision. Moreover, OMB directed agency SAOPs to undertake a central role in the development of policy proposals that implicate privacy issues.
- *Privacy reporting:* Agency senior privacy officials are often required to prepare periodic reports to ensure transparency about their activities and compliance with the law. Many laws reviewed required agencies to produce periodic privacy reports to agency stakeholders and Congress. OMB also requires agency SAOPs to report on their privacy activities as part of their annual FISMA reports, including such measures as their total numbers of systems of records, the number of written privacy complaints

they have received, and whether a senior official has responsibility for all privacy-related activities.

- *Redress*: With regard to federal agencies, the term "redress" generally refers to an agency's complaint resolution process, whereby individuals may seek resolution of their concerns about an agency action. Specifically, in the privacy context, redress refers to processes for handling privacy inquiries and complaints as well as for allowing citizens who believe that agencies are storing and using incorrect information about them to gain access to and correct that information. The Privacy Act requires that all agencies, with certain exceptions, allow individuals access to their records and the ability to have inaccurate information corrected. Several recent laws also direct senior privacy officials at specific agencies to provide redress by ensuring that they have adequate procedures for investigating and addressing privacy complaints by individuals. Several laws also provide for attention to privacy in a broader context of civil liberties protection.
- *Privacy training*: Privacy training is critical to ensuring that agency employees and contractor personnel follow appropriate procedures and take proper precautions when handling personally identifiable information. For example, The Transportation, Treasury, Independent Agencies and General Appropriations Act of 2005 requires senior privacy officials at covered agencies to ensure that employees have adequate privacy training. OMB also requires agency SAOPs to ensure that employees and contractors receive privacy training.

In addition to performing key privacy functions, requirements in laws include responsibilities to ensure adequate security safeguards to protect against unauthorized access, use, disclosure, and destruction of sensitive personal information. Generally, this is provided through agency information security programs established under FISMA, and overseen by agency CIOs and chief information security officers (CISO) [18]. Moreover, OMB has issued guidance instructing agency heads to establish appropriate administrative, technical, and physical safeguards to ensure the security and confidentiality of records.

Figure 1 shows the extent to which laws have requirements that specifically address each privacy function and to which agencies these requirements apply [19].

Laws and guidance	Apply to	Privacy functions: PIA	Privacy Act compliance	Policy consultation	Reporting	Redress	Training
Homeland Security Act of 2002	DHS	●	●	●	●		
Intelligence Reform and Terrorism Prevention Act of 2004	Office of the Director of National Intelligence	●	●	●		●	
Violence Against Women and Department of Justice Reauthorization Act of 2005	Department of Justice	●	●	●	●	●	●
Transportation, Treasury, Independent Agencies and General Government Appropriations Act of 2005	All entities whose appropriations are provided by this act. This includes Transportation, Treasury and many other entities.	●	●	●	●		●
Implementing Recommendations of the 9/11 Commission Act of 2007[a]	Department of Defense, DHS, Justice, Treasury, Health and Human Services, State, Office of the Director of National Intelligence, and the Central Intelligence Agency			●	●	●	
OMB memo M-05-08: *Designation of Senior Agency Officials for Privacy*	All executive branch agencies	●	●	●			●
OMB memos M-06-20, M-07-19, M-08-09	All executive branch agencies				●		

● Provision relating to key function

☐ No provision

Source: GAO analysis.

[a]This act also contains more specific requirements for DHS regarding PIAs, Privacy Act compliance, and training.

Figure 1. Laws with Provisions That Specifically Address Key Privacy Functions.

AGENCIES HAVE VARYING PRIVACY MANAGEMENT STRUCTURES, AND SENIOR AGENCY OFFICIALS FOR PRIVACY DO NOT CONSISTENTLY HAVE OVERSIGHT OF ALL KEY FUNCTIONS

Agencies have varying organizational structures to address privacy responsibilities. For example, of the 12 agencies we reviewed, 2 had statutorily designated CPOs who also served as SAOPs, 5 designated their agency CIOs as their senior officials, and the others designated a variety of other officials, such as the general counsel or assistant secretary for management. Further, not all of the agencies we reviewed had given their designated senior officials full oversight over all privacy-related functions. While 6 agencies had these officials overseeing all key privacy functions, 6 others relied on other organizational units not overseen by the designated senior official to perform certain key privacy functions. The fragmented way in which privacy functions have been assigned to organizational units in these agencies is at least partly the result of evolving requirements in law and guidance. As requirements have evolved, organizational responsibilities have been established incrementally to meet them.

However, without oversight and involvement in all key privacy functions, SAOPs may be unable to effectively serve as agency central focal points for privacy.

Agencies Varied in Their Designation of Senior Privacy Officials and in Their Organizational Placement of Key Privacy Functions

Agencies have taken varied approaches to designating senior agency officials with privacy responsibilities. Two of the 12 agencies we reviewed had separate CPOs that were also designated as the senior officials for privacy. Five agencies assigned their agency CIOs as SAOPs, and 1 agency assigned its CISO. Lastly, 4 agencies assigned another high-level official, such as a general counsel or assistant secretary for management, as the SAOP.

In addition to varying in how they designated senior officials for privacy, agencies also varied in the way they assigned privacy responsibilities to organizational units. Four of the 12 agencies we reviewed (Transportation, DHS, State, and U.S. Agency for International Development) had one organization primarily responsible for all of the six key privacy functions outlined in the previous section. The remaining 8 agencies (Social Security Administration, Veterans Affairs, Defense, Commerce, Labor, Justice, Treasury, and Health and Human Services) relied on more than one organizational unit to perform privacy functions. Figure 2 summarizes the organizational structures in place at agencies to address the six key privacy functions, including the specific organizational units responsible for carrying out each of the key privacy functions.

Six of the agencies (DHS, State, Social Security Administration, Transportation, U.S. Agency for International Development, and Veterans Affairs) established privacy structures in which the SAOP oversaw all key privacy functions. For example, DHS's Privacy Office performed these functions under the direction of the CPO, who was also the department's SAOP. Similarly, U.S. Agency for International Development's CISO (also the SAOP) oversaw the agency's privacy office, which was responsible for all key functions. While more than one organizational unit carried out privacy functions in two cases (Veterans Affairs and the Social Security Administration), all such units were overseen by the senior agency official for privacy.

Agency	SAOP	Privacy functions					
		PIA	Privacy Act compliance	Policy Consultation	Redress	Reporting	Training
Department of Transportaion	CIO	Office of the CIO / Office of the General Counsel	Office of the CIO / Office of the General Counsel	Office of the CIO	Office of the CIO	Office of the CIO	Office of the CIO
DHS	Chief Privacy Officer	Privacy Office	Privacy Office	Privacy Office	Privacy Office	Privacy Office	Privacy Office
Social Security Administration	General Counsel	Office of Public Disclosure	Office of Public Disclosure	Office of Public Disclosure	Office of General Law / Office of Public Disclosure	Office of Public Disclosure	Office of Public Disclosure
State	Assistant Secretary for Administration	Office of Information Programs and Services	Office of Information Programs and Services	Office of Information Programs and Services	Office of Information Programs and Services	Office of Information Programs and Services	Office of Information Programs and Services
U. S. Agency for International Development	Chief Privacy Officer	Privacy Office	Privacy Office	Privacy Office	Privacy Office	Privacy Office	Privacy Office
Veterans Affairs	CIO	Privacy Service	Records Management Service	Privacy Service	Privacy Service / Components	Privacy Service	Privacy Service
Department of Justice	Chief Privacy and Civil Liberties Officer	Privacy and Civil Liberties Office	Privacy and Civil Liberties Office	Privacy and Civil Liberties Office	Components	Privacy and Civil Liberties Office	Privacy and Civil Liberties Office
Treasury	Assistant Secretary for Management	Office of the CIO / Components	Office of the Deputy Assistant Secretary for Headquarters Operations	Office of the Deputy Assistant Secretary for Headquarters Operations / Office of the CIO	Components	Office of the Deputy Assistant Secretary for Headquarters Operations / Office of the CIO	Office of the Deputy Assistant Secretary for Headquarters Operations / Components
Department of Commerce	CIO	Office of the CIO	Privacy Act Office	Office of the CIO/ Office of the General Counsel	Privacy Act Office	Office of the CIO/ Privacy Act Office	Office of the CIO
Department of Defense	Director for Administration and Management	Office of the CIO	Defense Privacy Office	Defense Privacy Office	Components	Defense Privacy Office	Defense Privacy Office
Department of Labor	CIO	Office of the CIO	Office of the Solicitor	Office of the CIO	Office of the Solicitor	Office of the CIO	Office of the Solicitor
Health and Human Services	CIO	Office of the CIO	Privacy Act Officer	Senior Advisor, Privacy Policy	Privacy Act Officer	Office of the CIO / Components	Office of the CIO

Overseen by the agency SAOP

Not overseen by the agency SAOP

Source: GAO analysis of agency data.

Figure 2. Responsibility for Key Privacy Functions at 12 Agencies.

However, six other agencies (Commerce, Health and Human Services, Labor, Transportation, Defense, and Treasury) had privacy management structures in which the SAOP did not oversee all key privacy functions. For two agencies—Justice and Treasury—the SAOP had oversight over all key functions except for redress, which was handled by individual component organizations. For the other four agencies, key functions were divided among two or more organizations, and the senior privacy official did not have oversight of all of them. For example, key privacy functions at Labor were being performed not only by the office of the CIO (who is also the SAOP) but also by the Office of the Solicitor, who is independent of the CIO. Likewise, the senior official at Commerce was responsible for overseeing conduct of PIAs, policy consultation, and privacy training, while a separate Privacy Act Officer was responsible for Privacy Act compliance. Without full oversight of key privacy functions, SAOPs may be limited in their ability to ensure that privacy protections are administered consistently across the organization.

g Requirements in Laws and Related Guidance Have Led to Fragmented Assignment of Privacy Functions

The fragmented way in which privacy functions have been assigned to organizational units in several agencies is at least partly the result of evolving requirements in law and guidance. As requirements have evolved, organizational responsibilities have been established incrementally to meet them.

For example, although the Privacy Act does not specify organizational structures for carrying out its provisions, many agencies established Privacy Act officers to address the requirements of that act and have had such positions in place for many years. In some cases, agencies designated their general counsels to be in charge of ensuring that the Privacy Act's requirements were met.

More recently, the responsibility to conduct PIAs under the E-Gov Act frequently has been given to another office, such as the Office of the CIO, because the E-Gov Act's requirements apply to information technology, which is generally the purview of the CIO. If an SAOP was designated in such agencies without reassigning these responsibilities, that official may not have oversight and involvement in all key privacy activities.

Uneven implementation of the Paperwork Reduction Act also may have contributed to fragmentation of privacy functions. As previously discussed, the Paperwork Reduction Act requires agency CIOs to take responsibility for privacy policy and compliance with the Privacy Act, and thus agencies could ensure they are in compliance with the Paperwork Reduction Act by designating their CIOs as SAOPs [20]. However, 7 out of the 12 agencies we reviewed did not designate their CIOs as SAOPs. Further, if CIOs were designated as agency SAOPs but did not have responsibility for compliance with the Privacy Act—as was the case at Commerce, Labor, and Health and Human Services—the SAOPs would be left without full oversight of key privacy functions.

Agencies that have more than one internal organization carrying out privacy functions run the risk that those organizations may not always provide the same protections for personal information if they are not overseen by a central authority.

Thus, unless steps are taken to ensure that key privacy functions are under the oversight of the SAOP, agencies may be limited in their ability to ensure that information privacy protections are implemented consistently across their organizations.

CONCLUSIONS

While agencies have had the responsibility for many years to establish management structures to ensure coordinated implementation of privacy policy and compliance with the Privacy Act, recent laws and guidance have significantly changed requirements for privacy oversight and management. These laws and guidance vary in scope and specificity, but they all require the designation of a senior agency official with overall responsibility for privacy protection and compliance with statutory requirements.

In adopting varied assignments for key privacy functions, not all agencies gave their SAOPs responsibility for all key privacy functions. As a result, agencies may not be implementing privacy protections consistently. While the particulars of privacy management may vary according to the size of the agency and the sensitivity of its mission, agencies generally would likely benefit from having SAOPs that serve as central focal points for privacy matters and have oversight of all key functions, as required by law and guidance. Such focal points can help ensure that agency activities provide consistent privacy protections.

RECOMMENDATION FOR EXECUTIVE ACTION

In order to ensure that their SAOPs function effectively as central focal points for privacy management, we recommend that the Attorney General and the Secretaries of Commerce, Defense, Health and Human Services, Labor, and Treasury take steps to ensure that their SAOPs have oversight over all key privacy functions.

AGENCY COMMENTS AND OUR EVALUATION

We provided a draft of this report to OMB and to the departments and agencies we reviewed: the Departments of Commerce, Defense, Health and

Human Services, Homeland Security, Justice, Labor, State, Treasury, Transportation, and Veterans Affairs, as well as the Social Security Administration and the U.S. Agency for International Development, for review and comment. Five agencies provided no comments on this draft [21]. In comments provided via email, the Associate Deputy Assistant Secretary for Privacy and Records Management at Veterans Affairs and the Audit Management Liaison at the Social Security Administration concurred with our assessment and recommendations and provided technical comments, which we incorporated in the final report as appropriate. In oral comments, the Acting Branch Chief of the Information Policy and Technology Branch at OMB also concurred with our assessment and recommendations and provided technical comments, which we incorporated in the final report as appropriate. Commerce and Defense provided written comments that did not state whether they agreed or disagreed with our recommendations; however, both agencies stated that their privacy management structures were adequate. Their comments are reprinted in appendixes II and III respectively. Justice, Labor, and Treasury provided written comments and disagreed with our characterization of their agency SAOPs as not having oversight of all key privacy functions. Their comments are reprinted in appendixes IV, V, and VI respectively.

The Chief Information Officer of the Department of Commerce stated that the department agreed with our characterization of the fragmentation that has resulted from recent laws and guidance that have significantly changed requirements for privacy oversight and management. However, she stated that applicable law does not require that the administration of the Privacy Act be consolidated with other privacy functions under the Office of the Chief Information Officer. Law and OMB guidance direct agencies to have a senior agency official, the CIO in the case of the Paperwork Reduction Act, serving as a focal point for privacy and ensuring compliance with the Privacy Act. Clearly establishing a senior official as a focal point for departmental privacy functions aligns with direction provided by law and OMB and would help ensure that the agency provides consistent privacy protections.

The Senior Agency Official for Privacy at the Department of Defense stated that, while privacy responsibilities are divided among the Defense Privacy Office, the CIO, and agency components, the current privacy management structure at Defense has proven to be successful over time. We did not assess the effectiveness of the privacy management structures we reviewed. However, establishing an agency official that serves as a central focal point for departmental privacy functions aligns with direction provided by law and OMB and would help ensure that the agency provides consistent privacy protections.

The Acting Chief Privacy and Civil Liberties Officer at Justice disagreed with our assessment that the department's SAOP did not have oversight of redress procedures. He stated that the Chief Privacy and Civil Liberties Officer has statutory authority under the Violence Against Women and Department of Justice Reauthorization Act to assume primary responsibility for privacy policy and to ensure appropriate notifications regarding the department's privacy policies and privacy-related inquiry and complaint procedures. We agree that the Chief Privacy and Civil Liberties officer has the statutory authority and responsibility for the oversight of privacy functions at Justice, including redress. However, our analysis of agency policies and procedures showed that the Chief Privacy and Civil Liberties Officer did not have an established role in oversight of redress procedures. Clearly defining the role of the Chief Privacy and Civil Liberties Officer in the departmental redress procedures would help ensure that the SAOP has oversight of this key privacy function. In its comments, the department noted that the Office of Privacy and Civil Liberties was undertaking a review of its orders and guidance to clarify and, as appropriate, strengthen existing authorities to ensure that the department implements thoroughly the Chief Privacy and Civil Liberties Officer authorities.

The Chief Information Officer at Labor disagreed with our assessment that the SAOP did not have full oversight of all key privacy functions. He stated that Privacy Act compliance, redress, and training were addressed jointly by his office and the Office of the Solicitor. However, our review of Labor's policies and procedures relating to privacy management showed that a joint oversight management structure had not been established. Rather, we found that while the CIO was responsible for three key privacy functions, the Office of the Solicitor was responsible for the remaining three functions. Clearly defining the role of the SAOP in Privacy Act compliance, redress, and training would help ensure that the SAOP has oversight of all key privacy functions.

The Assistant Secretary for Management at Treasury agreed that the SAOP should have overall responsibility for privacy protection and compliance with statutory requirements and that agencies generally would likely benefit from having SAOPs that serve as central focal points for privacy matters and have oversight of all key functions. The Assistant Secretary noted that as of March 2008, the department had implemented a new privacy management structure to emphasize the importance of protecting privacy at its highest levels. However, Treasury disagreed with a statement in our draft report that it had realigned its organization in order to ensure that the SAOP had oversight of privacy functions. We recognize that privacy functions, with the exception of redress, were under the oversight of the SAOP prior to the reorganization and accordingly have deleted this statement from the final report. Treasury also disagreed that its SAOP did not have full oversight of agency redress processes, stating that the department has longstanding regulations that provide departmentwide and bureau-specific policies and procedures relating to redress. While we agree that such redress policies are in place, they do not establish a role for the SAOP. Clearly defining the role of the SAOP in the departmental redress procedures would help ensure that the SAOP has oversight of this key privacy function. Lastly, Treasury stated it submits quarterly reports to Congress on privacy complaint and redress activities. We agree that reporting is an important privacy function; however, it is separate from redress and does not constitute oversight of Treasury redress activities.

As agreed with your office, unless you publicly announce the contents of this report earlier, we plan no further distribution until 30 days from the report date. At that time, we will send copies of this report to the Attorney General; the Secretaries of Commerce, Defense, Health and Human Services, Homeland Security, State, Treasury, Labor, Transportation, and Veterans Affairs; the Commissioner of the Social Security Administration; and the Administrator of the U.S. Agency for International Development as well as other interested congressional committees. Copies will be made available at no charge on our Web site, www.gao.gov.

If you have any questions concerning this report, please call me at (202) 512-6240 or send e-mail to koontzl@gao.gov. Contact points for our Offices of Congressional Relations and Public Affairs may be found on the last page of this report. Key contributors to this report are listed in appendix III.

Sincerely,

Linda D. Koontz
Director, Information Management Issues

Appendix I: Objectives, Scope, and Methodology

Our objectives were to (1) describe laws and guidance that set requirements for senior privacy officials within federal agencies, and (2) describe the organizational structures used by agencies to address privacy requirements and assess whether senior officials have oversight over key functions. We did not evaluate agency compliance with these laws and guidance.

To address our first objective, we reviewed and analyzed relevant laws and guidance to determine privacy responsibilities for privacy officials at agencies. We reviewed relevant laws, including the Implementing Recommendations of the 9/11 Commission Act of 2007, the Homeland Security Act of 2002, and others (see app. II for a full listing), which designate senior privacy officials and assign them privacy responsibilities. We also analyzed the Paperwork Reduction Act, which has long-standing privacy requirements assigned to agency chief information officers (CIO), and the Office of Management and Budget (OMB) guidance relating to the designation of senior agency officials with privacy responsibilities, such as Memorandum M-05-08. We also analyzed the specific privacy responsibilities identified in these laws and guidance and categorized the key privacy functions they represented.

To address our second objective, we identified 12 agencies (Departments of Commerce, Defense, Health and Human Services, Homeland Security, Justice, Labor, State, Treasury, Transportation, and Veterans Affairs; the Social Security Administration, and the U.S. Agency for International Development) that either have a statutorily designated privacy officer, have a central mission for which privacy protection is a critical component, or have implemented a unique organizational privacy structure. We analyzed policies and procedures at these agencies, and interviewed senior agency privacy officials to identify the privacy management structures used at each of these agencies and the roles and responsibilities of senior privacy officials. We also compared the varying management structures at these agencies to identify the differences and similarities across agencies in their implementation of these structures. Further, we analyzed agency management structures to determine whether senior privacy officials at each of these agencies had full oversight over all key functions.

We conducted our work from September 2007 to May 2008, in Washington, D.C., in accordance with generally accepted government auditing standards. Those standards require that we plan and perform the audit to obtain sufficient, appropriate evidence to provide a reasonable basis for our findings and conclusions based on our audit objectives. We believe that the evidence obtained provides a reasonable basis for our findings and conclusions based on our audit objectives.

APPENDIX II: COMMENTS FROM THE DEPARTMENT OF COMMERCE

UNITED STATES DEPARTMENT OF COMMERCE
Chief Information Officer
Washington, D.C. 20230

MAY 1 2 2008

Ms. Linda Koontz
Director, Information Management Issues
Government Accountability Office
441 G. Street, N.W.
Washington, D.C. 20548

Dear Ms. Koontz:

Thank you for the opportunity to review the draft of GAO 310794 – *Agencies Should Ensure that Designated Senior Officials Have Oversight of Key Functions.*

The report is useful in illustrating the diverse ways agencies carry out their privacy responsibilities and the fragmentation that exists as a result of recent laws and guidance that have significantly changed requirements for privacy oversight and management. The laws and guidance vary in scope and specificity, but as the report indicates, require the designation of a Senior Agency Official for Privacy with overall responsibility for privacy protection and compliance with statutory requirements.

However, the report appears to indicate that existing laws and guidance require that agencies organize their internal privacy functions, including the administration of the Privacy Act, so that, for example, at the Department of Commerce they would be consolidated under the direct supervision of, and report to, the Commerce Chief Information Officer, who is the designated Senior Agency Official for Privacy and the Chief Privacy Officer. It is our view that applicable law does not require that administration of the Privacy Act be consolidated with other privacy functions under the Office of the Chief Information Officer. In fact, at Commerce, the Privacy Act is administered under the Chief Financial Officer and Assistant Secretary for Administration, who coordinates with the Office of the Chief Information Officer on Privacy Act issues. The Chief Privacy Officer provides oversight and guidance on privacy issues, but does not handle Privacy Act requests or appeals.

Indeed, agencies are accorded some flexibility precisely to provide the opportunity to organize their privacy functions in the way that works best for each of them. Since its enactment in 1974, administration of the Privacy Act has at Commerce been the responsibility of the Chief Financial Officer and Assistant Secretary for Administration. The Commerce Privacy Act program is well regarded, and cooperates fully with the Chief Privacy Officer with regard to all privacy functions within the Office of the Chief Information Officer.

-2-

We see no reason to upset this well-coordinated well-functioning institutional arrangement absent specific and explicit requirements to do so. We would expect that other agencies would have similar interests in maintaining existing organizational arrangements that they have found effective in providing privacy oversight, coordination, and protection.

Sincerely,

Suzanne Hilding
Chief Information Officer

APPENDIX III: COMMENTS FROM THE DEPARTMENT OF DEFENSE

OFFICE OF THE SECRETARY OF DEFENSE
1950 DEFENSE PENTAGON
WASHINGTON, DC 20301-1950

ADMINISTRATION & MANAGEMENT

MAY 1 3 2008

MEMORANDUM FOR UNITED STATES GOVERNMENT ACCOUNTIBILITY OFFICE

SUBJECT: Conclusions and recommendations from Draft GAO Report titled: PRIVACY: Agencies Should Ensure that Designated Senior Officials Have Oversight of Key Functions (GAO-08-603)

The DoD appreciates the opportunity to comment on the subject report. The report concluded that "not all agencies gave their Senior Agency Official for Privacy (SAOP) responsibility for all key privacy functions. The single recommendation made was "In order to ensure that their SAOPs function effectively as central focal points for privacy management, we recommend that the Attorney General and the Secretaries of Commerce, Defense, Health and Human Services, Labor, and Treasury take steps to ensure that their SAOPs have oversight over all key privacy functions.

The Director, Administration and Management for the DoD is assigned as the SAOP. In this role, he has direct oversight of the core privacy functions and executes these through the Defense Privacy Office. This office administers the Privacy Act of 1974 and the other privacy functions required by various laws. The area of redress of complaints and inquiries has been further delegated to the DoD Components who are the liaison organizations between DoD and the various systems owners located within the components. The process to address these issues has been found to be most effective when resolved at this level in the organization.

The DoD CIO serves as the DoD principal point of contact for Information Technology (IT) matters, oversees the PIAs and the protection of information in IT. The Office of the DoD CIO works closely with the Defense Privacy Office on all matters involving IT privacy policy and implementation. Per our DoD PIA guidance, the DoD SAOP serves as the DoD principal point of contact for the privacy policies and provides assistance on privacy matters impacting PIAs. The review of completed PIAs and annual reporting of the completion of these assessments is conducted with the Defense Privacy Office and other DoD Components as required. This arrangement has proven to be successful over time.

The DoD CIO concurs in this response. Questions regarding this response should be directed to Samuel Jenkins, Director, Defense Privacy Office at (703) 607-2943 or via email at DPO.Correspondence@osd.mil.

Michael B. Donley
Senior Agency Official for Privacy

APPENDIX IV: COMMENTS FROM THE DEPARTMENT OF JUSTICE

U.S. Department of Justice

Office of the Deputy Attorney General

Chief Privacy and Civil Liberties Officer

Washington, D.C. 20530

May 12, 2008

Linda D. Koontz
Director
Information Management
Government Accountability Office
441 G. Street, NW
Washington, DC 20548

Dear Ms. Koontz:

Thank you for the opportunity to review and comment on the Government Accountability Office's (GAO) draft report entitled, "Privacy: Agencies Should Ensure that Designated Senior Officials Have Oversight of Key Functions" (GAO-08-603). The Department of Justice is pleased that this report acknowledges that the Department of Justice has taken important and significant steps in ensuring the effectiveness of its privacy official and embedding the protection of privacy and civil liberties into the fabric of the Department.

We would like to address GAO's statement that the Department of Justice's Chief Privacy and Civil Liberties Officer (CPCLO), the Department's Senior Agency Official for Privacy (SAOP), does not have oversight concerning the redress mechanisms associated with the Department's handling of personally identifiable information (PII).

We disagree that this oversight function does not already lie with the CPCLO. At the core of the statutorily mandated activities of the CPCLO is section 1174 of the Violence Against Women and Department of Justice Reauthorization Act of 2005, Pub. L. No. 109-162, January 5, 2006. Specifically, subsection (a) provides that "[t]he Attorney General shall designate a senior official in the Department of Justice to assume primary responsibility for privacy policy." Subsequently, on March 10, 2006, Deputy Attorney General Paul McNulty issued a memorandum, which designated this senior official, stating that "[a]s the CPCLO, the official will oversee and administer the Department's privacy functions, in accordance with [section 1174]."

As such, the CPCLO does already have full responsibility for the oversight and management of all the privacy functions associated with the Department and its constituent components. Although it is true that the various components deal with day-to-day aspects of the operations concerning privacy functions, the CPCLO administers such functions through the promulgation of appropriate policies, the leadership of Departmental privacy officers, and the provision of specific guidance as required.

Further, section 1174(b) notes specific responsibilities of the CPCLO, including under subsection (5), "appropriate notifications regarding the Department's privacy policies and privacy-related inquiry and complaint procedures," which deal with the redress processes at the

Linda D. Koontz (GAO) Page 2
GAO-08-603, Privacy: Senior Agency Officials May 12, 2008

Department. In addition, section 1162 of the Intelligence Reform and Terrorism Prevention Act of 2004, Pub. L. 108-458, December 17, 2005, was amended by section 805 of the Implementing Recommendations of the 9/11 Commission Act of 2007, Pub. L. 110-53, August 3, 2007, to provide, in part, that agency privacy officials "ensure that such department, agency, or element has adequate procedures to receive, investigate, respond to, and *redress* complaints from individuals who allege such department, agency, or element has violated their privacy or civil liberties." [Emphasis added] As such, even if the general requirement for the CPCLO to oversee all the privacy functions of the Department were not enough authority to exercise leadership over the Department's redress processes, these additional two statutory authorities create a specific mandate for the CPCLO to fulfill.

Nonetheless, the Department, through its Office of Privacy and Civil Liberties is undertaking a review of the existing orders and guidance issued by the Department to clarify and, as appropriate, strengthen these existing authorities. The goal of this endeavor is to ensure that the Department implements thoroughly the CPCLO's authorities and to increase awareness of these authorities by all parts of the Department.

Again, we appreciate the opportunity to comment on GAO's draft report, and we look forward to additional collaboration to ensure full application of privacy protective authorities government wide. If you have any questions regarding our comments, please contact Richard P. Theis, Department of Justice Audit Liaison, Audit Liaison Group at (202) 514-0469.

Respectfully submitted,

Kenneth P. Mortensen
Acting Chief Privacy and Civil Liberties Officer

APPENDIX V: COMMENTS FROM THE DEPARTMENT OF LABOR

U.S. Department of Labor

Office of the Assistant Secretary
for Administration and Management
Washington, D.C. 20210

[illegible] 12 [illegible]

Linda D. Koontz
Director, Information Management Issues
Government Accountability Office
441 G Street, N.W.
Washington, DC 20548

Dear Ms. Koontz:

This letter responds to draft report GAO 08-603, *Agencies Should Ensure that Designated Senior Officials Have Oversight of Key Functions*, dated May 2008. We take seriously our responsibility to ensure the protection of our computer systems, web-based resources and collection points for Personally Identifiable Information (PII) and appreciate the opportunity to comment on the draft report.

Overall, the draft report provides a fair depiction of the Department of Labor's (DOL) management and operating environment for the protection of PII. However, I ask that the representation of how responsibilities for the key privacy functions are overseen at DOL be revised. As the Chief Information Officer (CIO) and Senior Agency Official for Privacy (SAOP), I have responsibility for *all* key privacy functions. In addition, three of the key privacy functions—namely, Privacy Act compliance, Redress, and Training—are jointly addressed by my office and the Department's Office of the Solicitor. This process has worked well for the Department in meeting our privacy protection related responsibilities.

With this in mind, to accurately reflect DOL's management structure for meeting its privacy protection responsibilities, the draft report should be revised in two areas:

- On page 20, Figure 2 should show for the Department of Labor that the SAOP is the CIO who has primary responsibility for all key privacy functions, including joint responsibility with the Office of the Solicitor for the three privacy functions of Privacy Act compliance, Redress, and Training. This management structure appears very similar to that portrayed in Figure 2 for the Department of Transportation.
- Correspondingly, the draft report Recommendation on page 24 should be amended to remove reference to the Department of Labor in addition to other conforming revisions throughout the draft report.

Thank you again for the opportunity to comment on the draft report. If there are questions or further discussion about our comments is needed, please have your staff contact Ms. Tonya Manning, Chief Information Security Officer, at Manning.Tonya@dol.gov or 202-693-4431.

Sincerely,

Patrick Pizzella
Assistant Secretary for Administration and Management,
Chief Information Officer

APPENDIX VI: COMMENTS FROM THE DEPARTMENT OF THE TREASURY

DEPARTMENT OF THE TREASURY
WASHINGTON, D.C.

ASSISTANT SECRETARY

MAY 1 5 2008

Mr. Idris Adjerid
Analyst-in-Charge
Government Accountability Office
441 G Street, NW
Washington, D.C. 20548

Dear Mr. Adjerid:

Thank you for the opportunity to review and comment on your draft report entitled "PRIVACY: Agencies Should Ensure that Designated Senior Officials Have Oversight of Key Functions", GAO-08-603. The Treasury Department concurs with your conclusions that the Senior Agency Official for Privacy (SAOP) should have overall responsibility for privacy protection and compliance with statutory requirements and that agencies generally would likely benefit from having SAOPs that serve as central focal points for privacy matters and have oversight of all key functions, because such focal points can help ensure that agency activities provide consistent privacy protections.

The policy of the Department of the Treasury is to protect the privacy of individuals by ensuring that due consideration and regard for information privacy is addressed in the execution of Departmental programs and policies. To emphasize the importance of protecting privacy at the highest levels of the Department, and to assign accountability, the Department has designated the Assistant Secretary for Management and Chief Financial Officer (ASM/CFO) as the SAOP pursuant to Office of Management and Budget Memorandum OMB M-05-08. The ASM/CFO has also been designated as the Chief Privacy Officer, pursuant to Section 522 of Division H of the Consolidated Appropriations Act of 2005, and the Chief Privacy and Civil Liberties Officer, pursuant to Section 803 of the Implementing Recommendations of the 9/11 Commission Act of 2007.

The ASM/CFO has historically had overall responsibility for key privacy functions. Nonetheless, in order to strengthen oversight of this important area, the Department realigned components of the Office of the ASM/CFO on March 24, 2008, to create a new Office of the Deputy Assistant Secretary for Privacy and Treasury Records. The realignment combined the Privacy Act and E-Government Act privacy functions and programs into one office and elevated the importance of the privacy office by creating a new Deputy Assistant Secretary for Privacy and Treasury Records, who is a direct report to the ASM/CFO. The Department continues to review a wide variety of activities and procedures within the Department to find opportunities to enhance protections of the privacy of individuals.

In that light, we respectfully request that your statement on page 22, that Treasury was reorganizing in order to ensure that the SAOP had overall responsibility for key privacy functions, be amended to reflect that the Treasury SAOP has historically had overall responsibility for key privacy functions, and has also now realigned its privacy functions from two offices into one office and has elevated the position of that office within the organization. In conjunction, we also request that your statement on page 23, that Treasury is currently considering consolidating privacy functions under a central office reporting directly to the SAOP, be amended to reflect that Treasury has, as of March 2008, consolidated its privacy functions from two Management divisions into one Management office reporting directly to the SAOP.

On page 15, the draft report defines redress in the privacy context as an agency's complaint-resolution process that allows individuals access to their records and the ability to correct inaccurate information, pursuant to the Privacy Act of 1974. On pages 6 and 15, the draft report presents federal agency redress responsibilities as ensuring that redress procedures are in place; that is, ensuring adequate procedures for investigating and addressing privacy complaints by individuals. Regarding the chart on page 20 and your statement on page 21, that the SAOP does not have oversight over the Treasury privacy redress function, we point out that Treasury has long-standing regulations at 31 C.F.R. §§ 1.26 and 1.27, that provide Treasury-wide procedures for redress in the privacy context. In addition, each Treasury bureau has specific, additional procedures published in Appendix A to Subpart C of 31 C.F.R. Part 1, tailored to the mission and functions of the particular bureau. These bureau-specific procedures have been fully approved and authorized by the Department. Moreover, Treasury has developed and implemented binding Department-wide policy and procedures in Treasury Directive 25-04 and The Privacy Handbook, TD Publication 25-04. In fact, Treasury Directive 25-04 stipulates that the ASM/CFO is responsible for ensuring Treasury's compliance with the Privacy Act of 1974.

Finally, the SAOP submits to Congress quarterly reports of Department-wide privacy complaint and redress activities, pursuant to Section 803 of the Implementing Recommendations of the 9/11 Commission Act of 2007. In addition to these procedures for providing redress, we continue to look for improvements that can be made to the Treasury redress process. In light of existing redress procedures as spelled out above, we respectfully request that the chart on page 20 and the statement on page 21of the draft report be amended to reflect that the Treasury SAOP does have oversight responsibilities over Treasury redress functions in the privacy context.

Again, we appreciate the opportunity to comment on GAO's draft report. If you have any questions regarding our comments, please contact me, or Elizabeth Cuffe of my staff, at 202-622-1682 or by email at Elizabeth.Cuffe@do.treas.gov.

Sincerely,

Peter B. McCarthy
Assistant Secretary for Management
and Chief Financial Officer

APPENDIX VII: RECENT LAWS ESTABLISHING PRIVACY PROTECTION RESPONSIBILITIES AT FEDERAL AGENCIES

The following are recent laws and their major provisions regarding privacy protection responsibilities at federal agencies.

Homeland Security Act of 2002

Section 222 of the Homeland Security Act of 2002, [1] as amended, instructed the secretary of DHS to appoint a senior official with primary responsibility for privacy policy, including the following:

- ensuring that technologies sustain, and do not erode, privacy protections;
- ensuring that personal information contained in Privacy Act systems of records is handled in full compliance with fair information practices as set out in the act;
- evaluating legislative and regulatory proposals and conducting privacy impact assessments of proposed rules;
- coordinating functions with the Officer for Civil Rights and Civil Liberties;
- preparing an annual report to Congress (without prior comment or amendment by agency heads or OMB); and
- having authority to investigate and having access to privacy-related records, including through subpoena in certain circumstances.

Intelligence Reform and Terrorism Prevention Act of 2004

Section 1011 of this act required the Director of National Intelligence to appoint a Civil Liberties Protection Officer and gave this officer the following functions: [2]

- ensuring that the protection of civil liberties and privacy is appropriately incorporated into the policies and procedures of the Office of the Director of National Intelligence and the elements of the intelligence community within the National Intelligence Program;

- overseeing compliance by the Office of the Director of National Intelligence with all laws, regulations, and guidelines relating to civil liberties and privacy;
- reviewing complaints about abuses of civil liberties and privacy in Office of the Director of National Intelligence programs and operations;
- ensuring that technologies sustain, and do not erode, privacy protections;
- ensuring that personal information contained in a system of records subject to the Privacy Act is handled in full compliance with fair information practices as set out in that act;
- conducting privacy impact assessments when appropriate or as required by law; and
- performing such other duties as may be prescribed by the Director of National Intelligence or specified by law.

Violence Against Women and Department of Justice Reauthorization Act of 2005

Section 1174 of the Violence Against Women and Department of Justice Reauthorization Act of 2005 [3] instructed the Attorney General to designate a senior official to assume primary responsibility for privacy policy, which included responsibility for advising the Attorney General in the following areas:

- appropriate privacy protections for the department's existing or proposed information technology and systems;
- privacy implications of legislative and regulatory proposals;
- implementation of policies and procedures, including training and auditing, to ensure compliance with privacy-related laws and policies;
- that adequate resources and staff are devoted to meeting the department's privacy-related functions and obligations;
- appropriate notifications regarding privacy policies and inquiry and complaint procedures; and
- privacy-related reports from the department to Congress and the President, including an annual report to Congress on activities affecting privacy.

Transportation, Treasury, Independent Agencies and General Government Appropriations Act of 2005

Section 522 of this act [4] directed each agency with appropriations provided by the act to designate a chief privacy officer with primary responsibility for privacy and data protection policy, including:

- ensuring that technology sustains, and does not erode, privacy and that technology used to collect or process personal information allows for continuous auditing of compliance with stated privacy policies and practices;
- ensuring that personal information contained in Privacy Act systems of records is handled in full compliance with fair information practices as defined in the Privacy Act;
- evaluating legislative and regulatory proposals and conducting privacy impact assessments of proposed rules;
- preparing an annual report to Congress on activities affecting privacy;
- ensuring the protection of personal information and information systems from unauthorized access, use, disclosure, or destruction, providing employees with privacy training; and
- ensuring compliance with privacy and data protection policies.

Implementing Recommendations of the 9/11 Commission Act of 2007

This law [5] amended the National Intelligence Reform Act of 2004 to require the heads of covered agencies to designate no less than one senior officer to serve as a privacy and civil liberties officer. This act applies to the Departments of Defense, Homeland Security, Justice, Treasury, Health and Human Services, and State, as well as the Office of the Director of National Intelligence, and the Central Intelligence Agency. The act requires the senior privacy official to perform the following functions:

- assisting the agency head in considering privacy and civil liberties issues with regard to anti-terrorism efforts;
- investigating and reviewing agency actions to ensure adequate consideration of privacy and civil liberties;

- ensuring that the agency has adequate redress procedures, considering privacy and civil liberties when deciding to retain or enhance a governmental power;
- coordinating activities, when relevant, with the agency Inspector General; and
- preparing periodic reports, not less than quarterly, to the agency head, Congress, and the Privacy and Civil Liberties Oversight Board [6].

Agencies covered under this act are also required to establish a direct reporting relationship between the senior privacy official and the agency head.

REFERENCES

[1] A PIA is an analysis of how personal information is collected, stored, shared, and managed in a federal system to ensure that privacy requirements are addressed.

[2] These agencies are Health and Human Services, Homeland Security, State, Transportation, and the U.S. Agency for International Development.

[3] For purposes of this report, the terms *personal information* and *personally identifiable information* are used interchangeably to refer to any information about an individual maintained by an agency, including (1) any information that can be used to distinguish or trace an individual's identity, such as name, Social Security number, date and place of birth, mother's maiden name, or biometric records, and (2) any other information that is linked or linkable to an individual, such as medical, educational, financial, and employment information.

[4] For analysis of issues associated with the Veterans Affairs data breach, see GAO, *Privacy: Preventing and Responding to Improper Disclosures of Personal Information,* GAO-06-833T (Washington, D.C.: June 8, 2006) *and Veterans Affairs: Leadership Needed to Address Information Security Weaknesses and Privacy Issues, GAO-06-866T* (Washington, D.C.: June 14, 2006).

[5] GAO, *Privacy: Key Challenges Facing Federal Agencies*, GAO-06-777T (Washington, D.C.: May 17, 2006).

[6] GAO, *DHS Privacy Office: Progress Made but Challenges Remain in Notifying and Reporting to the Public*, GAO-07-522 (Washington, D.C.: Apr 27, 2007).

[7] While the Privacy Act of 1974 established privacy responsibilities for agencies, it did not specify a senior agency official to be responsible for meeting these requirements.

[8] OMB issued guidance for agencies on the implementation of the Paperwork Reduction Act, including the responsibility of CIOs for privacy. See OMB Circular A-130, Management of Federal Information Resources (Washington D.C.: November 28, 2000). For an analysis of CIO roles and responsibilities, see GAO, *Federal Chief Information Officers: Responsibilities, Reporting Relationships, Tenure, and Challenges,* GAO-04-823 (Washington, D.C.: July 21, 2004).

[9] The Transportation, Treasury, Independent Agencies and General Government Appropriations Act of 2005 applies to the Department of Transportation, Department of Treasury, Executive Office of the President, Architectural and Transportation Barriers Compliance Board, Election Assistance Commission, Federal Election Commission, Federal Labor Relations Authority, Federal Maritime Commission, General Services Administration, Merit Systems Protection Board, Morris K. Udall Scholarship and Excellence in National Environmental Policy Foundation, National Archives and Records Administration, National Historical Publications and Records Commission, National Transportation Safety Board, Office of Government Ethics, Office of Personnel Management, Office of Special Counsel, U.S. Postal Service, and U.S. Tax Court.

[10] This law grants the Privacy and Civil Liberties Oversight Board authority to require any other agency or element of the executive branch to establish a privacy and civil liberties officer. Further, this law specifies that if covered agencies have another statutorily designated privacy officer, this officer must also undertake the responsibilities described in the act.

[11] Office of Management and Budget, *OMB Instructions on complying with President's Memorandum of May 14, 1998, "Privacy and Personal Information in Federal Records",* M-99-05 (Washington, D.C.: Jan. 7, 1999).

[12] Office of Management and Budget, *OMB Guidance for Implementing the Privacy Provisions of the E-Government Act of 2002,* M-03-22 (Washington, D.C.: Sept. 26, 2003).

[13] Office of Management and Budget, *Designation of Senior Agency Officials for Privacy*, M-05-08 (Feb. 11, 2005).

[14] Office of Management and Budget, *FY 2005 Reporting Instructions for the Federal Information Security Management Act and Agency Privacy Management,* M-05-15 (Washington, D.C.: June 13, 2005).

[15] FISMA, Title III, E-Government Act of 2002, Pub. L. No. 107-347 (Dec. 17, 2002).

[16] Office of Management and Budget, *FY 2006 Reporting Instructions for the Federal Information Security Management Act and Agency Privacy Management,* M-06-20 (Washington, D.C.: July 17, 2006).

[17] Office of Management and Budget, *FY 2007 Reporting Instructions for the Federal Information Security Management Act and Agency Privacy Management,* ,M-07-19 (Washington, D.C.: July 25, 2007)

[18] For purposes of this report, we did not address information security assurance as a privacy function. Prior GAO reports have examined information security at federal agencies. For example, in March 2008, we testified that agencies continue to experience significant information security control deficiencies and that most agencies did not implement controls to sufficiently prevent, limit, or detect access to computer networks, systems, or information. As a result, federal systems and information were at increased risk of unauthorized access to and disclosure, modification, or destruction of sensitive information. See GAO, Information Security: Progress Reported, but Weaknesses at Federal Agencies Persist, GAO-08-571T (Washington, D.C.: Mar. 12, 2008).

[19] These laws may make designated agency officials responsible for additional privacy functions that are not specifically mentioned. For example, by designating agency officials as responsible for Privacy Act compliance, these laws would implicitly make such officials responsible for meeting all requirements specified in the Privacy Act, including such things as providing a means to access and correct information, which is a component of the redress function.

[20] In 2004, GAO reported that 17 of 27 CIOs were responsible for privacy, See GAO-04-823. OMB guidance also acknowledged the Paperwork Reduction Act's CIO requirement, but stated that the CIO "may perform" the privacy role, and that "if the CIO, for some reason, is not designated, the agency may have designated another senior official (at the Assistant Secretary or equivalent level) with agency-wide responsibility for information privacy issues. In any case, the senior agency official should have authority within the agency to consider information privacy policy issues at a national and agency-wide level." M-05-08 (Feb 11, 2005).

[21] These agencies are Health and Human Services, Homeland Security, State, Transportation, and the U.S. Agency for International Development.

Appendix VII

[1] Pub. L. No. 107-296, November 25, 2002, as amended by the Intelligence Reform and Terrorism Prevention Act of 2004, Sec. 8305, and the Implementing Recommendations of the 9/11 Commission Act of 2007, Sec. 802.

[2] Pub. L. No. 108-458, December 17, 2004.

[3] Pub. L. No. 109-162, January 5, 2005

[4] Div H, Pub. L. No. 108-447, December 8, 2004.

[5] Pub. L. No. 110-53 August 3, 2007.

[6] This board was created by the Intelligence Reform and Terrorism Prevention Act of 2004 to review executive branch anti-terrorism activities and to ensure that privacy and civil liberties are adequately protected.

INDEX

B

C

D

E

F

G

H

I

Q

R

S

T

U

Economic Time Series

Modeling and Seasonality

Economic Time Series
Modeling and Seasonality

Edited by

William R. Bell
Scott H. Holan
Tucker S. McElroy

CRC Press
Taylor & Francis Group
Boca Raton London New York

CRC Press is an imprint of the
Taylor & Francis Group, an informa business
A CHAPMAN & HALL BOOK

CRC Press
Taylor & Francis Group
6000 Broken Sound Parkway NW, Suite 300
Boca Raton, FL 33487-2742

First issued in hardback 2019

ISBN: 978-1-4398-4657-5 (hbk)

Library of Congress Cataloging-in-Publication Data

Economic time series : modeling and seasonality / [edited by] William R. Bell, Scott H. Holan, and Tucker S. McElroy.
p. cm.
Includes bibliographical references and index.
ISBN 978-1-4398-4657-5 (alk. paper)
1. Seasonal variations (Economics)--Mathematical models. 2. Time-series analysis--Mathematical models. 3. Econometrics. 4. Economics, Mathematical. I. Bell, William R., 1943- II. Holan, Scott H. III. McElroy, Tucker.

HB141.E255 2012
330.01'51955--dc23 2011041494

Visit the Taylor & Francis Web site at
http://www.taylorandfrancis.com

and the CRC Press Web site at
http://www.crcpress.com

Contents

Preface

A major topic of methodological research in time series analysis and econometrics over the past five decades has been the modeling and seasonal adjustment of economic time series. The reason for this is simple: tens of thousands of economic time series are seasonally adjusted and published every month or quarter by dozens of statistical agencies around the world, and these data provide much of the empirical foundation for macroeconomic policymaking. The sheer bulk of these data warrants continual improvements to methodology.

Research on time series modeling, and particularly on seasonal time series modeling, exploded with the publication of the book, *Time Series Analysis: Forecasting and Control*, by Box and Jenkins in 1970. Also of considerable importance was the not unrelated appearance around that time of computer software for fitting seasonal time series models. First, computer programs written for this specific purpose appeared, and then time series modeling capabilities began to appear in various statistical software packages, making these modeling capabilities widely available.

Parallel developments in seasonal adjustment methodology occurred separately and even slightly earlier. In 1953, Julius Shiskin introduced the first computerized method of seasonal adjustment on the U.S. Census Bureau's UNIVAC I computer. This approach, called Method I, was quickly replaced by Method II, X-1 variant, with successive improvements culminating in the mid-1960s with the famous X-11 program. Further developments saw seasonal adjustment start borrowing recently developed techniques from time series modeling, as in the X-11-ARIMA method and program of Estela Dagum and Statistics Canada, and in the development of time series model-based methods of seasonal adjustment. Additionally, problems faced in seasonal adjustment inspired further developments in seasonal time series modeling methodology. To facilitate this cross-fertilization, in 1976 and 1981 the Census Bureau organized conferences on the modeling and seasonal adjustment of economic time series. These conferences brought academic statisticians and econometricians doing research on time series modeling together with government statisticians working on the enhancement of seasonal adjustment methods.

In the midst of much of this exciting activity was David Findley, who arrived at the U.S. Census Bureau in the early 1980s to supervise a small staff focused on research and computer software development to improve the techniques of modeling and seasonal adjustment of economic time series. In his own research, David made important contributions to time series model selection (especially in studying the properties of Akaike's information criterion [AIC]), in the diagnostics for time series modeling and seasonal adjustment, in the calendar adjustments of seasonal time series, and in the study of properties of linear filters used for seasonal adjustment and trend estimation. He also supervised the software development leading to the introduction of the now widely used X-12-ARIMA seasonal adjustment program. Additionally, through his many professional contacts, he helped foster continued interaction on the problems of time series modeling and seasonal adjustment between academic researchers and government statisticians, and between statisticians working on seasonal adjustment at different government statistical agencies.

Now that David Findley has recently retired, it seems fitting to honor his career and contributions with a volume of articles that reflect the general topics of his own work. The result is this compilation of 21 chapters that appropriately show the cross-fertilization between the fields of time series modeling and seasonal adjustment. This is reflected both in the contents of the chapters and in their authorship, with contributors coming from both academia and government statistical agencies.

For easier perusal and absorption of the contents, the chapters have been grouped into seven topical sections. Section I deals with periodic modeling of time series. Chapter 1 by Koopman, Ooms, and Hindrayanto introduces a seasonal vector time series model that allows for periodic variability in the cyclical component, and applies the model in a detailed analysis of employment in various U.S. economic sectors. Chapter 2 by Trimbur and Bell considers seasonally periodic heteroskedasticity that can be described, or at least approximated, by two groups (high and low variance months); develops an algorithm for empirically assigning months to the two groups; and studies, for three alternative models, the performance of likelihood ratio tests for detecting the presence of this form of seasonal heteroskedasticity. Chapter 3 by Lund proposes a test to assess whether a periodic autoregressive moving-average (PARMA) model is to be preferred to a simpler seasonal autoregressive moving-average (SARMA) model.

Section II examines the estimation of time series components when the models for series have been misspecified in some sense. In particular, Chapter 4 by Delle Monache and Harvey examines the effects that misspecification of component models has upon the efficiency of signal extraction estimates of the components, and the broader implications this has for seasonal adjustment. Chapter 5 by McElroy and Holan examines the true signal extraction error that results in business cycle estimates obtained from seasonally adjusted data when the cycle is not explicitly accounted for by the seasonal adjustment. Chapter 6 by Tiller shows how the presence of sampling error in time series obtained from repeated sample surveys, particularly autocorrelated sampling error that results when samples overlap across time, can significantly compromise trend estimates and, to a lesser extent, seasonal adjustments, when these are obtained from conventional methods (such as X-11 or SEATS) that make no allowance for sampling error. This chapter also shows how prefiltering the data via signal extraction to remove sampling error can substantially improve the results (echoing related results on cycle estimation given in Chapter 5.)

Section III provides two chapters that examine the quantification of error in X-11 seasonal adjustments. Chapter 7 by Bell, Chu, and Tiao examines the mean squared error (MSE) of X-12-ARIMA seasonal adjustments relative to that of model-based adjustments in the idealized setting where the latter provide optimal estimates from a known time series model. The chapter shows that, for the popular "airline model," if the "best" (lowest MSE) of the available X-12 filters is chosen, the X-12 MSE is typically only slightly larger than that of the optimal adjustment. Chapter 8 by Scott, Pfeffermann, and Sverchkov provides an overview of methods proposed for producing variances of X-11 seasonal adjustments, examining their general characteristics, and studying these methods in applications to simulated series and to real-time series of U.S. labor force characteristics.

Section IV features four chapters discussing practical problems that arise in seasonal adjustment. Chapter 9 by Dagum and Luati studies nonparametric trend-cycle filters via frequency domain tools, providing an objective means of comparing contending trend-cycle estimation methods. Chapter 10 by Quenneville and Fortier provides an overview of the general benchmarking problem faced by statistical agencies and reviews several current methodologies for addressing this problem. Chapter 11 by Ladiray investigates what are the most important spectrum frequencies reflecting trading-day effects in monthly and quarterly time series, and uses a simulation study to compare the performances of alternative methods for detecting trading-day effects. Chapter 12 by Maravall and Pérez provides a careful case study illustrating the use of diagnostics in conjunction with model-based seasonal adjustment. The series analyzed is the Euro-area industrial production index, and the chapter works through the analysis of this series step-by-step to develop an appropriate model and corresponding seasonal adjustment that successfully deals with the effects of the 2008 financial crisis and following recession.

Section V has three chapters that explore outlier detection and the modeling of time series containing extreme values. Chapter 13 by Galeano and Peña develops a new procedure for detecting additive outliers in seasonal ARIMA time series models that is based on model selection strategies and uses a modification of BIC. Chapter 14 by Hotta and Tsay examines two types of outliers that can arise in financial data modeled with an ARCH (autoregressive-conditionally-heteroskedastic) process, and shows how these outliers may be estimated and removed. Chapter 15 by Tanokura, Tsuda, Sato, and Kitagawa presents a statistical method of constructing a price index for financial assets having skewed and heavy-tailed price distributions.

Alternative models and approaches to inference for seasonal and other time series components are considered in Section VI. Chapter 16 by Dickey extends previous work that showed how a test statistic for seasonal unit roots approaches a normal distribution under the unit root null hypothesis as the seasonal period becomes large. Specifically, the chapter extends the results by making mean and variance adjustments to the test statistics that make the normal approximation very good for the practically important seasonal periods of 4 and 12, even for relatively short time series. Chapter 17 by Holan and McElroy introduces a novel seasonal long memory model for unobserved components, and provides finite sample minimum mean squared error (MMSE) seasonal adjustments from this model utilizing fully Bayesian methodology. In Chapter 18, Proietti and Grassi apply a recently proposed Bayesian model selection technique, known as stochastic model specification search, to the problem of determining whether seasonality and calendar effects in macroeconomic time series are fixed over time or are stochastically time-varying.

Section VII presents three chapters dealing with the aspects of modeling and estimation for nonseasonal economic time series. Chapter 19 by Kohli and Pourahmadi reviews various nonparametric estimators of the innovation variance, σ^2, obtained in the spectral domain using raw, smoothed, tapered, and multitapered periodograms for complete and incomplete time series data. Chapter 20 by Tu, Song, Breidt, Berger, and Wang proposes a class of dynamic generalized linear models for functional input and output signals, with a time-varying event probability modeled through a known link function (such as logit or probit) as a linear combination of the recent pasts of the multiple input signals. Finally, to close the volume, Chapter 21 by Tunnicliffe Wilson and Haywood illustrates the application of a recently introduced class of nonseasonal time series models (ZAR models) that generalize conventional autoregressive models by extending their dependence to high lags in order to improve long-range prediction of time series.

Some of the chapters in the volume develop new methodology, whereas others provide pertinent empirical analyses and reviews of established methods. We are confident that a serious researcher and analyst of economic time series will find much that is stimulating and practically useful here.

William R. Bell, Scott H. Holan, and
Tucker S. McElroy*

* Any views expressed in this preface on statistical or operational issues are those of the authors and not necessarily those of the U.S. Census Bureau.

Editors

William R. Bell, Ph.D., is the Senior Mathematical Statistician for Small Area Estimation at the U.S. Census Bureau. He is a recognized researcher in the area of modeling and adjustment of seasonal economic time series. He has also worked on the development of related computer software, including software for RegARIMA modeling of seasonal economic time series (this was incorporated into the X-12-ARIMA seasonal adjustment program), and the REGCMPNT program for time series models with regression effects and ARIMA component errors.

Scott H. Holan, Ph.D., is an associate professor of statistics at the University of Missouri. He is the author of over 30 articles on topics of time series, spatio-temporal methodology, Bayesian methods, and hierarchical models. His research is largely motivated by problems in federal statistics, econometrics, ecology, and environmental science.

Tucker S. McElroy, Ph.D., is a Principal Researcher for Time Series Analysis at the U.S. Census Bureau. His research is focused primarily upon developing novel methodology for time series problems, such as model selection and signal extraction. He has contributed to the model diagnostic and seasonal adjustment routines in the X-12-ARIMA seasonal adjustment program, and has taught seasonal adjustment to both domestic and international students.

Contributors

William R. Bell
Research and Methodology Directorate
U.S. Census Bureau
Washington, DC

Theodore W. Berger
Department of Biomedical Engineering
University of Southern California
Los Angeles, California

F. Jay Breidt
Department of Statistics
Colorado State University
Fort Collins, Colorado

Yea-Jane Chu
IBM
Chicago, Illinois

Estela Bee Dagum
Department of Statistics
University of Bologna
Bologna, Italy

David A. Dickey
Department of Statistics
North Carolina State University
Raleigh, North Carolina

Susie Fortier
Statistics Canada
Ottawa, Canada

Pedro Galeano
Department of Statistics
Universidad Carlos III de Madrid
Madrid, Spain

Stefano Grassi
Center for Research in Econometric Analysis of Time Series
University of Aarhus
Aarhus, Denmark

Andrew Harvey
Faculty of Economics
Cambridge University
Cambridge, England

John Haywood
School of Mathematics, Statistics and Operations Research
Victoria University
Wellington, New Zealand

Irma Hindrayanto
De Nederlandsche Bank
Amsterdam, The Netherlands

Scott H. Holan
Department of Statistics
University of Missouri
Columbia, Missouri

Luiz K. Hotta
Departamento de Estatistica
Universidade Estadual de Campinas
São Paulo, Brazil

Genshiro Kitagawa
Research Organization of Information and Systems
Tokyo, Japan

Priya Kohli
Department of Statistics
Texas A&M University
College Station, Texas

Siem Jan Koopman
Department of Econometrics
VU University Amsterdam
Amsterdam, The Netherlands

Dominique Ladiray
Short Term Statistics Department
Institut National de la Statistique et des Etudes Economiques (INSEE)
Paris, France

Alessandra Luati
Department of Statistics
University of Bologna
Bologna, Italy

Robert Lund
Department of Mathematical Sciences
Clemson University
Clemson, South Carolina

Agustín Maravall
Bank of Spain
Madrid, Spain

Tucker S. McElroy
Time Series Group
Center for Statistical Research and Methodology
U.S. Census Bureau
Washington, DC

Davide Delle Monache
University of Rome "Tor Vergata"
Rome, Italy

Marius Ooms
Department of Econometrics
VU University Amsterdam
Amsterdam, The Netherlands

Daniel Peña
Department of Statistics
Universidad Carlos III de Madrid
Madrid, Spain

Domingo Pérez-Cañete
Indra Sistemas and Bank of Spain
Madrid, Spain

Danny Pfeffermann
Hebrew University of Jerusalem
Jerusalem, Israel
and
University of Southampton
Southampton, England

Mohsen Pourahmadi
Department of Statistics
Texas A&M University
College Station, Texas

Tommaso Proietti
Discipline of Operations Management and Econometrics
University of Sydney Business School
New South Wales, Australia

Benoît Quenneville
Statistics Canada
Ottawa, Canada

Seisho Sato
Department of Data Science
The Institute of Statistical Mathematics
Tokyo, Japan

Stuart Scott
U.S. Bureau of Labor Statistics (retired)
Arlington, Virginia

Dong Song
Department of Biomedical Engineering
University of Southern California
Los Angeles, California

Michail Sverchkov
U.S. Bureau of Labor Statistics
Washington, DC

Yoko Tanokura
Department of Data Science
The Institute of Statistical Mathematics
Tokyo, Japan

George C. Tiao
University of Chicago
Chicago, Illinois

Richard B. Tiller
U.S. Bureau of Labor Statistics
Washington, DC

Thomas M. Trimbur
Federal Reserve Board
Washington, DC

Ruey S. Tsay
Booth School of Business
University of Chicago
Chicago, Illinois

Hiroshi Tsuda
Faculty of Science and Engineering
Doshisha University
Kyoto, Japan

Catherine Y. Tu
Department of Statistics
Colorado State University
Fort Collins, Colorado

Granville Tunnicliffe Wilson
Department of Mathematics and Statistics
Lancaster University
Lancaster, England

Haonan Wang
Department of Statistics
Colorado State University
Fort Collins, Colorado

Part I

Periodic Modeling of Economic Time Series

1

A Multivariate Periodic Unobserved Components Time Series Analysis for Sectoral U.S. Employment

Siem Jan Koopman*, **Marius Ooms**, **and Irma Hindrayanto**

CONTENTS

1.1 Introduction

An unobserved components time series (UC) model is built of a number of stochastic linear processes that typically capture trend, seasonal, cycle, and remaining stationary dynamic features in an observed time series. The basic theory and methodology are laid out in Harvey (1989). Each stochastic component can be represented as an autoregressive integrated moving average (ARIMA) process. We can therefore consider the UC model as a special

* We would like to thank the three editors and three referees for their excellent comments on earlier drafts of this chapter. All opinions and possible errors in this chapter are those of the authors only.

case of the RegComponents framework of Bell (2004). The typical parameters that need to be estimated in a UC model are the variances of the innovations driving the components and a selection of other coefficients associated with the ARIMA processes. For a seasonal time series, the UC model usually contains a stochastic seasonal component that is able to capture the time-varying seasonal effects. However, other dynamic features in the time series may also be subject to seasonal effects. For example, in the case of an economic time series, cyclical effects may be relatively more apparent or have a bigger impact in a particular season (winter) compared to another season (summer). In such cases, we can let the coefficients associated with a particular component be dependent on the season. We define this extension of the UC model as a periodic UC (PUC) model, which is explored in Koopman and Ooms (2002, 2006). In this chapter, we extend the PUC approach into a multivariate framework where several observed time series are modeled simultaneously.

An early multivariate periodic analysis based on a multivariate UC model with a stochastic cycle component was carried out by Krane and Wascher (1999). They analyzed the time series of U.S. quarterly employment data for nine different industrial sectors, including construction, motor vehicle manufacturing, durable and nondurable goods, retail trade, government, and mining. The sum of these sectors equals the total nonfarm employment numbers published by the U.S. Bureau of Labor Statistics (BLS). Sectoral employment time series are key in tracking economic activity (recessions and expansions); therefore they are intensively analyzed by policy decision makers. The motivation for the analysis was to study whether coefficients associated with the economic cycle component are subject to periodic variations. The study of Krane and Wascher (1999) found significant evidence of periodic variations in the cycle coefficients for more than half of the sectors. The Krane and Wascher (KW) study is taken as one of the motivations for our empirical study. Although our modeling framework is also based on a multivariate unobserved components (MUC) time series model, there are differences between our frameworks. Krane and Wascher modeled the time series in first differences, while in our study we consider the time series in levels. Our model is also more elaborate because we include more stochastic components and a wider variety of periodic coefficients. The extensions are considered with the aim to avoid model misspecification that may lead to inaccurate conclusions about the periodic nature of the dynamic features in the multiple time series.

In our study, we analyze seven sectoral time series from the Current Employment Statistics (CES) survey, which is conducted by the BLS. These time series are in accordance with the North American Industry Classification System (NAICS), originally established in 1997. We notice that although the NAICS started in 1997, the CES only started to use this classification from June 2003 onward. Since June 2003, the CES survey converted all their national employment series to the 2002 NAICS version from the 1987 Standard Industrial Classification (SIC) system. The CES conversion process resulted in the sectoral employment series that we use in our analysis, of which have a long reconstruction history starting in 1939, the year the SIC database was established. At a lower aggregation level, the employment series have a history going back to at least 1990. The length of the series depends on the degree of interchangeability between the SIC and NAICS series. For more background information about recent changes in the national CES survey, we refer to Morisi (2003). At the start of our study on sectoral employment, the CES has already updated the 2002 NAICS to its 2007 version. The NAICS will be updated every 5 years. The dataset for U.S. sectoral employment from the BLS is well documented and is easily available.

We specifically examine whether our main findings hold for different sample selections in our quarterly dataset, which ranges from 1950 until 2009 and includes past and more recent economic recession periods. In other words, how robust are the findings when different subsamples of the dataset are considered? This study also shows that we are able to fit multivariate PUC models simultaneously without any univariate preanalyses of the data. The general model includes trend, seasonal, cycle, and irregular components with variance matrices that can have different values for different quarters and different values for different subsamples of the data. In this general setup, we can allow for periodicity and for the Great Moderation, which refers to a reduction of overall volatility in economic time series after the early 1980s. We also formally test for each component whether the additional parameters for periodicity and the Great Moderation are statistically significant. In summary, our empirical study is motivated by Krane and Wascher (1999), but we analyze the data in levels rather than in differences, our multivariate class of PUC time series models under study is comprehensive, and the parameters are estimated simultaneously for all equations and all components.

An observed seasonal time series with a sample autocorrelation function that changes with the season is referred to as a periodic time series. To enable the identification of these dynamic characteristics in a time series, Gladysev (1961) and Tiao and Grupe (1980) have formally defined periodic autocorrelations using a stationary vector representation of the periodic univariate time series. Once periodic properties of a time series are detected, the time series analyst can consider time series models that allow for these periodic correlations. Periodic time series models were originated by Hannan (1955) in the context of geophysics and environmental empirical studies. However, periodic dynamic regression models for economic time series have been applied since the 1930s; see the review in Mendershausen (1937). A range of periodic analyses for environmental and economic time series have appeared ever since with the classical references given by Wallis (1978), Plosser (1979), Ghysels (1988, 1991), Barsky and Miron (1989), and Canova and Ghysels (1994). More specifically, Osborn and Smith (1989) introduced the periodic time series framework in dynamic macroeconomic models. A model-based periodic time series analysis becomes effective when appropriate methods and algorithms are developed for estimation and diagnostic checking. For this purpose, Ghysels and Osborn (2001) and Franses and Paap (2004) have discussed a wide spectrum of periodic models with a focus on their econometric implications. Maximum likelihood estimation methods for periodic autoregressive moving average models have been discussed by Vecchia (1985), Li and Hui (1988), Jimenez et al. (1989), and Lund and Basawa (2000), while Anderson and Meerschaert (2005) have provided asymptotic theory for efficient moment-based estimation. Furthermore, many environmental and economic studies have given empirical evidence that time series models require periodically changing parameters; see, e.g., Osborn (1988), Osborn and Smith (1989), Bloomfield et al. (1994), Ghysels and Osborn (2001), and Franses and Paap (2004).

Periodic extensions of the UC class of time series models have been explored in a variety of studies. Proietti (2004) considered a UC model with the trend component modeled as a weighted average of separate independent random walks for each season. Penzer and Tripodis (2007) studied the seasonal component with a periodic variance. Koopman and Ooms (2002, 2006) explored different periodic specifications of the UC model. In the context of RegComponent UC models, Bell (2004) considered the effect of seasonal heteroskedasticity in the irregular component on seasonal adjustment, see also Findley (2005). Different types of periodicity in a UC model imply different optimal seasonal adjustment filters. It is of general interest to investigate how we can identify different types of periodicity, both in theory and in practice.

The remaining part of this chapter is organized as follows. Section 1.2 introduces a general class of multivariate periodic unobserved components (MPUC) time series models. In the Appendix, we provide some details of how the models can be formulated in state-space form. Section 1.3 provides the details of our dataset of sectoral U.S. employment quarterly time series. We present our results of an extensive empirical analysis of U.S. sectoral employment in Section 1.4. The estimates of coefficients and of unobserved components (trend, seasonal, and cycle) are presented together with test statistics for hypotheses where coefficients are not periodic under the null. Section 1.5 provides a detailed comparison of the results and conclusions from a similar empirical study by Krane and Wascher (1999). Section 1.6 concludes this chapter.

1.2 Multivariate Periodic Unobserved Components Model

We define y_t as the $N \times 1$ vector of quarterly time series observations, which are modeled by an MUC time series model consisting of $N \times 1$ vectors μ_t for trend, γ_t for seasonal, Ψ_t for cycle, and ε_t for irregular. The resulting MUC model can simply be represented by

$$y_t = \mu_t + \gamma_t + \Psi_t + \varepsilon_t, \tag{1.2.1}$$

and we have n quarterly observations for y_t, i.e., $t = 1, \ldots, n$. The trend component is specified as in a multivariate local linear trend model, i.e.,

$$\mu_{t+1} = \mu_t + \beta_t + \eta_t, \qquad \eta_t \sim \text{NID}(0, \Sigma_{\eta,t}), \tag{1.2.2}$$

$$\beta_{t+1} = \beta_t + \zeta_t, \qquad \zeta_t \sim \text{NID}(0, \Sigma_{\zeta,t}), \tag{1.2.3}$$

where β_t represents the $N \times 1$ vector of growth or slope components for the trend vector μ_t. The normally distributed disturbances, η_t and ζ_t, drive the trend and slope components. These disturbances are serially and mutually uncorrelated at all times, have zero means, and have time-varying variance matrices, $\Sigma_{\eta,t}$ and $\Sigma_{\zeta,t}$, which are fixed functions of the time index t. In our study, we have adopted this trend specification, but alternative formulations for the trend can also be considered. We should mention that different combinations of values for the variances $\Sigma_{\eta,t}$ and $\Sigma_{\zeta,t}$ will also lead to different dynamic properties; see the discussion in Harvey (1989, Chapter 2). For example, the conditions $\Sigma_{\eta,t} = \Sigma_{\zeta,t} = 0$ imply the trend $\mu_t = \mu_1 + \beta_1 t$, a vector of fixed linear trends with constant μ_1 and gradient β_1, while the single condition $\Sigma_{\eta,t} = 0$ leads to a trend component μ_t that is smoothly evolving through time.

The stochastic seasonal component vector γ_t can be specified in different ways. For this study, we opt for the elementary time-varying dummy seasonal specification as given by

$$S(B)\gamma_{t+1} = \omega_t, \qquad \omega_t \sim \text{NID}(0, \Sigma_{\omega,t}), \tag{1.2.4}$$

where $S(B) = 1 + B + B^2 + B^3$ is the seasonal sum operator for quarterly time series and B is the lag operator, i.e., $B^k y_t = y_{t-k}$. The normally distributed disturbance, ω_t, drives the changes in the seasonal effect over time and is serially and mutually uncorrelated (with all other disturbances and for all time periods). In the limiting case $\Sigma_{\omega,t} = 0$, the quarterly effects are fixed over time and are specified as a set of unknown fixed dummy coefficients that sum up to zero.

The cycle component is common to all time series in y_t; therefore, we specify

$$\Psi_t = \Theta_t \psi_t, \tag{1.2.5}$$

where Θ_t is an $N \times 1$ vector of fixed and unknown coefficients that are deterministic functions of the time index t. The autoregressive process for the cycle component ψ_t is modeled as

$$\begin{pmatrix} \psi_{t+1} \\ \psi^*_{t+1} \end{pmatrix} = \rho_t \begin{pmatrix} \cos\lambda & \sin\lambda \\ -\sin\lambda & \cos\lambda \end{pmatrix} \begin{pmatrix} \psi_t \\ \psi^*_t \end{pmatrix} + \begin{pmatrix} \kappa_t \\ \kappa^*_t \end{pmatrix}, \quad \begin{pmatrix} \kappa_t \\ \kappa^*_t \end{pmatrix} \sim \text{NID}\left(\begin{pmatrix} 0 \\ 0 \end{pmatrix}, \sigma^2_{\kappa,t} I_2\right), \tag{1.2.6}$$

with autoregressive coefficient $0 < \rho_t < 1$ and cycle frequency λ. The normally distributed disturbances, κ_t and κ^*_t, drive the autoregressive cyclical process. These disturbances have the variance $\sigma^2_{\kappa,t}$ as a deterministic function of the time index t. The parameters Θ_t and $\sigma^2_{\kappa,t}$ are not jointly identified because they both affect the scaling of the elements in Ψ_t. The identification problem can be solved in different ways, e.g., by restricting the first element in Θ_t to be equal to unity. We therefore have

$$\Theta_t = (1\,,\, \theta_{2,t}\,, \ldots, \, \theta_{N,t})', \tag{1.2.7}$$

where the element $\theta_{i,t}$ is treated as unknown for $i = 2, \ldots, N$. The coefficients $\theta_{2t}, \ldots, \theta_{N,t}$, ρ_t, and $\sigma^2_{\kappa,t}$ are time varying as fixed functions of the time index t.

Finally, the irregular component is given by

$$\varepsilon_t \sim \text{NID}(0, \Sigma_{\varepsilon,t}), \tag{1.2.8}$$

where the variance matrix $\Sigma_{\varepsilon,t}$ can also be time-varying as a fixed function of time. All disturbances η_t, ζ_t, ω_t, κ_t, κ^*_t, and ε_t are serially and mutually uncorrelated at all times t and s and at all lags.

We have introduced a general class of MUC time series models where the variance matrices and some key coefficients of the model are time-varying. Even when we consider time-invariant versions of such models, the modeling framework is still of a general nature. More detailed discussions on properties, estimation, and testing are provided in Harvey and Koopman (1997). A particularly interesting feature is the notion that the variance matrices associated with the components may be of a lower rank. This implies that particular components can be common to all time series in y_t. In our cycle specification for Ψ_t, we have a limiting case where a single stationary process (with cyclical properties) is common to all individual time series in the vector y_t.

1.2.1 Periodic Specification

Assume that ϑ_t is a particular time-varying coefficient of the MUC model introduced here. The MPUC model is the MUC model where the coefficient ϑ_t obtains different values only for different seasonal periods. For quarterly time series, ϑ_t would take four different values, one for each season. The four different values can be restricted such that, for example, ϑ_t is different for one season while it has the same value for the other seasons. In all these settings, we refer to this specification as a periodic model and effectively we have

$$\vartheta_t \equiv \vartheta^{(j)}, \qquad j = J(s,t), \qquad j \in \{1, \ldots, s\}, \tag{1.2.9}$$

for fixed coefficients $\vartheta^{(1)}, \ldots, \vartheta^{(s)}$, where s is the seasonal length (for a quarterly time series, $s = 4$) and the seasonal index function $J(s,t)$ is typically given by

$$J(s,t) = 1 + (t - 1 \bmod s).$$

In the MPUC model, all coefficients will be specified as ϑ_t in Equation 1.2.9 and therefore are treated as periodic, except for the cycle frequency λ in Equation 1.2.6.

The number of coefficients in the MPUC model is high. The maximum number of coefficients p for our MPUC model with the number of seasons s and the number of series N is given by

$$p = c_{np} + sc_p + s(N-1) + \frac{N}{2}(N+1)s(q-1),$$

where c_{np} and c_p are the number of nonperiodic and periodic coefficients in the cycle component, respectively, i.e., $c_{np} = 1$ and $c_p = 2$, and q is the number of variances in the univariate version of the model, i.e., $q = 5$. Some examples for the number of coefficients are given by

s	N	q	p
2	2	5	31
12	2	5	181
4	7	5	481

In the last example, we require a bit more than 17 years of quarterly observations to identify all parameters ($7 \times 4 \times 17 = 476$). In our empirical study, we have 60 years of observations and therefore a sufficient number of degrees of freedom remain.

The number of coefficients in our MPUC model is large nevertheless. To enable a feasible empirical analysis, we will simplify the MPUC model specification considerably in the main study of this chapter. We consider the following restrictions on the coefficients. First, we restrict the three variance matrices associated with the trend, seasonal, and irregular components to be diagonal. In this way, the number of coefficients reduces to

$$p = c_{np} + s\,(c_p - 1) + Nsq.$$

The consequence of assuming diagonal variance matrices is that the individual time series in y_t depend on idiosyncratic factors for trend, seasonal, and irregular. If the common cycle component is not present in the model, the individual time series can be analyzed separately by a univariate UC model. The presence of the common cycle component in the model requires the simultaneous, multivariate analysis that we pursue in our empirical study. Secondly, we can take the trend component (1.2.2) as a smooth stochastic function of time by restricting $\Sigma_{\eta,t} = 0$ for all t and $\Sigma_{\zeta,t}$ diagonal. The number of coefficients reduces since q becomes 4 instead of 5.

In our periodic modeling framework, other options are also available to reduce the number of coefficients. For example, in a particular case, we may consider only a different coefficient value for quarter 4, while we have another coefficient value for the other three quarters. Such considerations are discussed in our empirical study of Section 1.4.

1.2.2 Estimation, Testing, and Signal Extraction

The unknown periodic coefficients will be estimated by the method of maximum likelihood. The MPUC model can be represented in state-space form. Details of the MPUC state-space form are given in the Appendix. Once the model is in state-space form, we adopt the Kalman filter to evaluate the loglikelihood function of the model; see Durbin and Koopman (2001) for a complete treatment of a state-space time series analysis. A quasi-Newton method is used for the numerical optimization of the loglikelihood function with respect to the coefficients; see, e.g., Fletcher (1987). In this way, we are able to estimate all coefficients by the method of maximum likelihood. An important factor in our successful implementation is the ability to compute the exact score analytically for each coefficient; see Koopman and Shephard (1992).

In an empirical study, it is not likely that all coefficients in our MPUC model are periodic. We aim to find the appropriate periodic model specification via likelihood-based hypothesis tests. We will test the null hypothesis of "no periodicity" for individual coefficients and for groups of coefficients using tests such as the likelihood ratio, Lagrange multiplier, and Wald. For the single periodic coefficient, ϑ_t, in Equation 1.2.9, the null and alternative hypotheses are given by

$$H_0 : \vartheta^{(1)} = \vartheta^{(2)} = \cdots = \vartheta^{(s)}, \qquad H_1 : \vartheta^{(1)} \neq \vartheta^{(2)} \neq \cdots \neq \vartheta^{(s)}, \tag{1.2.10}$$

where we have $s - 1$ restrictions under the null. The likelihood-based test statistics have an asymptotic χ^2 distribution with $s - 1$ degrees of freedom. The likelihood functions of the models under the null and under the alternative hypotheses are properly defined. We emphasize that the test under the null does not concern the parameters on the boundary of the parameter space. Taniguchi and Kakizawa (2000) discuss test statistics for null hypotheses of zero variances for which standard distribution theory breaks down. However, we do not consider such hypotheses. Our hypothesis (1.2.10) aims at testing whether different nonzero variances have equal values.

In the case of joint hypotheses involving variance matrix coefficients, we assume that the associated variance matrices have full rank or have at least the same rank under the null and the alternative hypotheses. Furthermore, all variances are strictly positive. We prefer to adopt the general-to-specific strategy in the process of finding the appropriate periodic model specification.

Once an appropriate model specification is determined, we may want to visually inspect estimates of the trend, seasonal, and cycle components to gain further insights into the dynamic properties of the time series. We obtain the component estimates at each time t recursively via signal extraction methods that are typically carried out by the Kalman filter and the associated smoothing algorithms in a model-based state-space time series analysis; see Durbin and Koopman (2001, Chapter 4) for a comprehensive treatment. These component estimates have optimal statistical properties under appropriate assumptions; see Bell and Hillmer (1991) for a complete discussion. Applications of signal extraction are detrending and seasonal adjustment of time series. All necessary computations for our empirical study are carried out by SsfPack 3.0 using the programming environment Ox; see Koopman et al. (1999, 2008) and Doornik (2009).

An alternative and appropriate treatment for estimating a large number of parameters simultaneously is a Bayesian analysis. We can carry out a Markov chain Monte Carlo analysis for estimating large sets of parameters simultaneously by means of a Gibbs sampler; see, e.g., Fruhwirth-Schnatter (1994a, b). The MPUC model lends itself naturally to such a Bayesian inference approach. We will explore this option for future research. In the analyses below, we only present the results from a classical perspective.

1.3 Data Description: U.S. Employment Series

Our empirical analysis of Section 1.4 is based on the CES national nonfarm payroll database of the BLS. The database consists of monthly observations on employment, hours, and earnings. The payroll employment data measure the number of employees in nonfarm sectors. The survey includes about 140,000 businesses and government agencies, which cover approximately 440,000 individual worksites that are drawn from a sampling frame of roughly 9 million unemployment insurance tax accounts. The active CES sample frame includes approximately one-third of all nonfarm payroll workers. The complete description of historical employment statistics is available at the CES and BLS webpages.* We have collected several monthly sectoral U.S. nonfarm payroll employment time series. The aggregated employment series (from the aggregation level of sectoral employment and higher) are available from January 1939 onward. The aggregated employment series at a lower level typically start at a later time. Some of these series only start in January 1990.

The basic structure of the nonfarm employment time series is given by

$$\text{total nonfarm} = \text{goods production} + \text{private service providing} \\ + \text{government}.$$

The goods production employment consists of four sectors: durable (e.g., woods, metals, electronics, and cars) and nondurable (e.g., food, textile, paper, and plastics) goods manufacturing, construction businesses (related to building, e.g., houses, offices, bridges, and roads), and natural resources exploitation businesses (e.g., logging, mining, oil, and gas). The private service-providing sector has the largest number of employees. This sector includes trade, transport, utility, publishing, entertainment, financial, legal, education, health, leisure, and maintenance industries, and many nonprofit organizations. The government sector consists of federal, state, and local government employment. With slightly less than 3 million civilian employees (as of 2011), the federal government (including the U.S. Postal Service) is the largest single employer in the U.S. State and local governments account for the remaining 19 million or so government employees, about half of whom are teachers and other educational workers at state universities and public schools.

* CES website http://www.bls.gov/ces/, BLS website http://www.bls.gov/webapps/legacy/cesbtab1.htm.

For our empirical study, we have selected seven sectors of employees on nonfarm payrolls, which we refer to as:

D	durable goods manufacturing	
ND	nondurable goods manufacturing	
NR	natural resources	
C	construction businesses	(1.3.1)
TTU	trade, transport, and utility industries	
OS	other service-providing industries	
G	all government workers	

These seven sectors add up to total nonfarm employment.

In the related study of Krane and Wascher (1999), nine "sectors" are selected, based on the 1987 SIC system. The differences are twofold. First, Krane and Wascher excluded the subsector motor vehicles from sector D. We have not been able to do this since the BLS database has not included motor vehicle employment for the months before January 1990. The degree of interchangeability between the SIC and NAICS for motor vehicle series is too low. The CES has not been able to reconstruct this particular time series for the months before 1990. Therefore, we have not excluded the subsector motor vehicles from sector D in our analysis. Second, we have pooled all government-related employment together into a single sector G instead of using the subsectors federal, state, and local governments. The original series are provided by the BLS in a monthly frequency from 1950 onward. We follow Krane and Wascher in transforming the monthly series into quarterly series by taking the average of the three months in each quarter.

Figure 1.1 presents our resulting seven time series after the employment totals are transformed into logarithms. All series start in 1950, quarter 1, and finish in 2009, quarter 4, which includes the first two years of the most recent financial crisis. When we take a look at the data, the historical employment series are clearly upward trending. The employment sectors D and ND show declines after the 1990s. The NR sector appears to have a different trend behavior. Cyclical behavior in the time series is most pronounced for the D and C sectors. The study of Krane and Wascher (1999) was based on nine quarterly employment series spanning from 1953 until 1989. It will be interesting to see how the results and conclusions have changed due to analyses that consider the more recent sample.

1.4 Empirical Results for U.S. Employment Sectors

The seven quarterly employment series introduced in Section 1.3 are analyzed using the MPUC time series model of Section 1.2. In particular, we consider model (1.2.1) for which

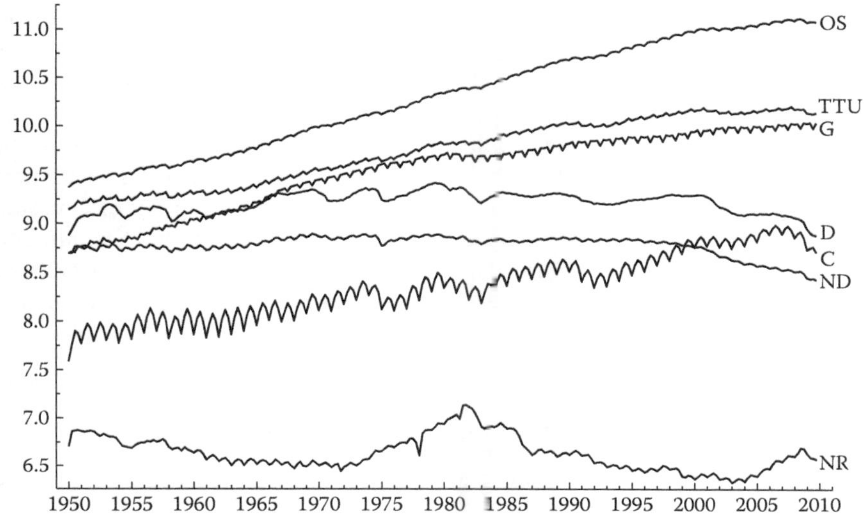

FIGURE 1.1
Log of quarterly U.S. nonfarm employment subseries from 1950, quarter 1 to 2009, quarter 4. (From U.S. Bureau of Labor Statistics.) Seven series of log employment: D = durable goods manufacturing; ND = nondurable goods manufacturing; NR = natural resources industries; C = construction businesses; TTU = trade/transport/utility industries; OS = other service-providing industries; G = aggregated government sector.

- The trend μ_t in Equation 1.2.2 is modeled as a smooth process with $\Sigma_{\eta,t} = 0$, and individual trends that are idiosyncratic, i.e., $\Sigma_{\zeta,t}$ is diagonal.
- The seasonal component in Equation 1.2.4 and the irregular in Equation 1.2.8 are also idiosyncratic; therefore their corresponding variance matrices $\Sigma_{\omega,t}$ and $\Sigma_{\varepsilon,t}$ are diagonal.
- The common cycle component is given by Equation 1.2.6 and its loading factors are given by Equation 1.2.7.
- Each time-varying periodic coefficient is specified as in Equation 1.2.9.

Since we have $N = 7$ and $s = 4$, it follows that for this periodic model specification we have 117 coefficients to estimate from a total of 1680 quarterly observations (60 years of data).

In addition to this model specification, we also take account of the Great Moderation in the business cycle dynamics, which is well documented in the empirical macroeconomic literature; see, e.g., McConnell and Perez-Quiros (2000), Stock and Watson (2002), and Sensier and van Dijk (2004). To account for the Great Moderation of the business cycle, we let the cycle variance $\sigma^2_{\kappa,t}$

in Equation 1.2.6 have different values before 1983 and another value from quarter 1 of 1983 onward. We refer to this model with a break in the cycle variance as the "single switch in cycle variance." The financial crisis may have stopped the Great Moderation period, therefore we also consider models where the cycle variance from 2008 onward returns to its value of the one before 1983. We refer to this model as the "two switches in cycle variance," and we notice that it does not require additional coefficients. The introduction of new values for the periodic cycle variance after 2007 may be desirable, but the number of observations after 2007 is limited. The estimation of new cycle variances for a period as short as eight quarters may not lead to reliable results. The cycle variance with two switches is therefore specified as

$$\sigma^2_{\kappa,t} = \begin{cases} \sigma^{2(j)}_{\kappa,I} & \text{for } t \text{ in the years from 1950 up to 1982 and 2008 up to 2009;} \\ \sigma^{2(j)}_{\kappa,II} & \text{for } t \text{ in the years from 1983 up to 2007,} \end{cases}$$

for $j = 1, \ldots, 4$. It follows that 1983, quarter 1, and 2008, quarter 1, are the break points.

Table 1.1 presents the maximum likelihood estimates of the cycle standard deviations in the MPUC model with periodic coefficients for all components. The results are presented for the model without and with cycle moderation (single or two switches). The number of coefficients are reported together with the log-likelihood value at the maximum likelihood parameter estimates. The associated information criteria of Akaike and Schwartz's Bayesian are also presented in Table 1.1. All results indicate that we prefer to adopt the model that accounts for the Great Moderation between 1983 and 2007. In all models considered below, we have included the cycle moderation with two switches.

1.4.1 Model Specification Within the Class of Multivariate Periodic Unobserved Component Models

Next, we investigate whether all coefficients require a periodic specification in our MPUC model. In most cases, we do not consider individual coefficients, but we concentrate on groups of coefficients. For example, we investigate whether the 7×7 diagonal variance matrix $\Sigma_{\omega,t}$ for the seasonal component is periodic (28 coefficients) or not (7 coefficients). We formulate a joint null hypothesis for a group of coefficients, similar to Equation 1.2.10 for an individual coefficient. The likelihood ratio statistic is used to test the hypothesis. In addition, we compute Akaike and Bayesian information criteria to decide the final model selection. We pursue a general-to-specific approach of finding the appropriate model specification. The number of combinations of periodic and nonperiodic coefficients is large. Therefore, we have limited ourselves to the models reported in Table 1.2. In our considered models, the common cycle is associated with the employment time series for durable goods manufacturing (D), since the first loading in Θ_t in Equation 1.2.6 is restricted to one and the order of the series in the 7×1 vector y_t is given in Equation 1.3.1; the first series in y_t is D.

TABLE 1.1
Estimated Cycle Standard Deviations from the Full Periodic Models, with and without the Great Moderation

	No Switch	Single Switch	Two Switches
Cycle std.dev $\sigma_{\kappa,I}^{(1)}$	0.0112	0.0121	0.0116
$\sigma_{\kappa,I}^{(2)}$	0.0079	0.0101	0.0098
$\sigma_{\kappa,I}^{(3)}$	0.0128	0.0165	0.0173
$\sigma_{\kappa,I}^{(4)}$	0.0146	0.0158	0.0167
Moderation $\sigma_{\kappa,II}^{(1)}$	–	0.0052	0.0028
$\sigma_{\kappa,II}^{(2)}$	–	0.0033	0.0027
$\sigma_{\kappa,II}^{(3)}$	–	0.0040	0.0038
$\sigma_{\kappa,II}^{(4)}$	–	0.0096	0.0027
Estimated log-likelihood value	5678.69	5702.84	**5722.22**
Akaike information (AIC)	−11123.38	−11163.68	**−11202.44**
Akaike corrected (AICc)	−11105.70	−11144.73	**−11183.49**
Schwartz Bayesian (BIC)	−10488.47	−10507.07	**−10545.83**
Number of coefficients	117	121	121

Note: These results are estimates of our multivariate periodic unobserved components time series model. No switch = periodic cycle standard deviations $\sigma_{\kappa,t}$ are the same for the full sample; single switch = periodic cycle standard deviations change after 1982; two switches = periodic cycle standard deviations are different after 1982 and before 2008. Number of observations is 1680 (60 years). The values in bold signal the preferred values.

The estimation results for our range of models are presented in Table 1.2. We have been able to estimate the full periodic Model 1 with 121 coefficients, and the resulting log-likelihood value is reported. Since the estimated irregular variances in the diagonal matrix $\Sigma_{\varepsilon,t}$ are the smallest estimated variances in Model 1, and they are not very different for the four quarters, we have imposed the necessary restrictions for the nonperiodic hypothesis $H_0 : \Sigma_\varepsilon^{(1)} = \cdots = \Sigma_\varepsilon^{(4)}$ and have labeled it as Model 2. The number of coefficients in Model 2 reduces from 121 to 100. The maximum likelihood procedure is repeated successfully and we obtain a slightly lower log-likelihood value. The p-value of the corresponding χ^2 likelihood ratio test with 21 degrees of freedom is 0.123, which indicates that the drop in log-likelihood is not significant and that the null hypothesis of equal variances in the irregular component cannot be rejected. The information criteria confirm our preference for Model 2 over Model 1.

TABLE 1.2
Estimation Results for MPUC Model with Two Switches: General to Specific

	Model 1	**Model 2**	**Model 3**	**Model 4**	**Model 5**	**Model 6**	**Model 7a**	**Model 7b**	**Model 8**
Trend $\sigma^2_{\zeta,t}$	P	P	P	P	P	P	P	NP	NP
Seasonal $\sigma^2_{\omega,t}$	P	P	P	P	P	P	NP	P	NP
Irregular $\sigma^2_{\varepsilon,t}$	P	NP	NP	NP	NP	NP	NP	NP	NP
Cycle $\sigma^2_{\kappa,I}$	P	P	P	P	NP	NP	NP	NP	NP
Moderation $\sigma^2_{\kappa,II}$	P	P	P	P	P	NP	NP	NP	NP
Loadings Θ_t	P	P	NP	NP	NP	NP	NP	NP	NP
Discounting ρ_t	P	P	P	NP	NP	NP	NP	NP	NP
Frequency λ	NP	NP	NP	NP	NP	NP	NP	NP	NP
Number of coefficients	121	100	82	79	76	73	55	55	31
Log-likelihood	5722.22	5707.9	5696.01	5694.01	5691.18	5691.13	5662.61	5666.19	5636.58
Akaike criterion	−11202.44	−11215.80	−11228.02	−11230.02	−11230.36	**−11236.26**	−11221.22	−11228.38	−11211.16
Akaike corrected	−11183.49	−11203.01	−11219.50	−11222.12	−11223.06	**−11229.53**	−11217.83	−11224.99	−11209.96
Schwartz' criterion	−10545.83	−10673.15	−10783.04	−10801.32	−10817.94	−10840.12	−10939.04	−10946.20	**−11042.94**

Note: Table presents estimation results for a selection of MPUC models for which a selection of coefficients is periodic: P = periodic coefficients; NP = not periodic coefficients. The estimation sample is from 1950 to 2009 and contains 1680 quarterly observations.

TABLE 1.3
Estimation Results for the Cycle Coefficients of MPUC Model 2 together with Their Standard Errors in Parentheses

	Q1	Q2	Q3	Q4	χ^2 test	p-value
ρ	0.9431	0.9517	0.9387	0.9976	4.34	0.227
	(0.0314)	(0.0333)	(0.0384)	(0.0375)		
θ_D	1	1	1	1	–	–
	–	–	–	–		
θ_{ND}	0.4120	0.4057	0.3864	0.3787	5.88	0.118
	(0.0294)	(0.0285)	(0.0294)	(0.0277)		
θ_{NR}	0.5495	0.5866	0.6381	0.5520	4.24	0.237
	(0.0976)	(0.1080)	(0.0942)	(0.1007)		
θ_C	0.5290	0.5787	0.5504	0.5003	4.26	0.235
	(0.0740)	(0.0676)	(0.0672)	(0.0675)		
θ_{TTU}	0.2834	0.2749	0.2671	0.2724	2.92	0.404
	(0.0173)	(0.0167)	(0.0166)	(0.0183)		
θ_{OS}	0.2308	0.2248	0.2119	0.2197	6.14	0.105
	(0.0139)	(0.0131)	(0.0141)	(0.0133)		
θ_G	−0.0432	−0.0261	−0.0265	−0.0576	5.94	0.115
	(0.0210)	(0.0223)	(0.0200)	(0.0227)		
$\sigma_{\kappa,I}$	0.0114	0.0101	0.0134	0.0167	5.50	0.139
	(0.0019)	(0.0018)	(0.0028)	(0.0026)		
$\sigma_{\kappa,II}$	0.0028	0.0031	0.0036	0.0024	0.62	0.892
	(0.0011)	(0.0012)	(0.0012)	(0.0014)		
Period in years	4.9087					
	(0.2442)					

Note: The null hypotheses for the reported χ^2 tests are given by H_0: $\rho^{(1)} = \cdots = \rho^{(4)}$; H_0: $\Theta_j^{(1)} = \cdots = \Theta_j^{(4)}$; and H_0: $\sigma_\kappa^{(1)} = \cdots = \sigma_\kappa^{(4)}$ for $j = 2, \ldots, 7$. The reported p-values correspond to the 5% significance level.

In Table 1.3, we present the estimated coefficients related to the common cycle component in Model 2 together with the estimated standard errors in parentheses. We also present the likelihood ratio tests for the individual coefficient hypothesis (1.2.10) and their associated p-values. The persistence of the cycle component is measured by the discounting factor ρ and we find that its estimate is high for all quarters. The corresponding p-value suggests that the different ρ values are insignificantly different and therefore not periodic. The estimated cycle loadings for the different sectors all have positive values except those for the government sector (G). The cycle has the highest impact on D, but is also strongly present in the sectors NR, C, and ND. The government employment appears to be anticyclical (negative loadings). However, the loadings are not significantly different from zero except for quarter 4. Furthermore, the likelihood ratio test indicates that the estimated loadings for G are not significantly different for different quarters. From these results, we may conclude that during a recession period, the number of available jobs in the private sectors decreases while employment increases somewhat in the government, and vice versa. We can also conclude that no evidence is found for periodic coefficients related to the business cycle dynamics of the time series.

We have learned from Table 1.3 that all cycle coefficients are individually not periodic. To investigate whether the cycle coefficients are jointly periodic, we have included the estimation results for Models 3, 4, 5, and 6 in Table 1.2. In comparison with Model 2, Model 3 has no periodic loading coefficients for the cycle; in comparison with Model 3, Model 4 has no periodic discounting factor ρ; in comparison with Model 4, Model 5 has no periodic cycle variance; and in comparison with Model 5, Model 6 has no periodic cycle moderation. In effect, Model 6 has only periodic coefficients for the trend and seasonal variances with a total of 73 coefficients. When we track the log-likelihood values of the subsequent models, and implicitly the likelihood ratio test statistics, we find no evidence of periodic coefficients related to the cycle component. After maximum likelihood estimation of parameters, the log-likelihood value is 5691.13, which is not significantly different at the 5% level from the log-likelihood values for the Models 2, 3, 4, and 5. Also, the information criteria AIC, AICc, and BIC all point to the more parsimonious Model 6.

Finally, we take a closer look at the periodic coefficients for the trend and seasonal components. Model 7a is Model 6 with the seasonal variances kept constant for different quarters, while Model 7b is Model 6 with the trend variances kept constant. The log-likelihood values for both Models 7a and 7b, after estimation, reduce significantly according to the 5% critical value of χ^2 distribution with 21 degrees of freedom. It indicates that both the trend and seasonal components have periodic coefficients. To confirm this finding further, we have also considered the MUC model without any periodic coefficient, Model 8. For this model, the log-likelihood value, after parameter estimation, has also clearly and significantly reduced. Therefore, we prefer to work with Model 6. This MPUC model has also the lowest AIC and AICc values, as reported in Table 1.2. However, the Schwartz Bayesian information criterion points to Model 8. Therefore, we investigate the estimation results for Model 6 more closely.

Table 1.4 presents the estimated periodic variances for the trend and seasonal components of Model 6. We find that for certain sectors in the economy, trend and seasonal variances are significantly different for different quarters. The likelihood ratio test statistic for the hypothesis (1.2.10) points to significant trend periodicity for the sectors ND, NR, and G; significant seasonal periodicity is found for the ND, C, and TTU sectors. The other sectors have variances that are not significantly different for different quarters. The nondurable production sector appears to be subject to periodic coefficients most strongly. We expect that it is caused by the presence of processed food and agricultural industries in the sector ND. The reason for periodic trend variances for the government sector may be partly due to the popular scheme of "9-month-job" contracts that are granted by the state and local governments for the employment of public school teachers and faculty members of state universities. For completeness, we report in Table 1.5 the coefficient

TABLE 1.4
Estimated Standard Deviations for the Trend and Seasonal Variances in MPUC Model 6

Trend	**Q1**	**Q2**	**Q3**	**Q4**	**χ^2 test**
$\sigma_{\zeta,D}$	0.0028	0.0059	0.0028	0.0061	4.38
	(0.0019)	(0.0010)	(0.0018)	(0.0011)	
$\sigma_{\zeta,ND}$	0.0039	0.0035	0.0030	0.0054	**12.06**
	(0.0006)	(0.0006)	(0.0007)	(0.0007)	
$\sigma_{\zeta,NR}$	0.0166	0.0000	0.0145	0.0086	**8.22**
	(0.0027)	(0.0156)	(0.0023)	(0.0037)	
$\sigma_{\zeta,C}$	0.0091	0.0079	0.0046	0.0102	4.58
	(0.0017)	(0.0014)	(0.0021)	(0.0017)	
$\sigma_{\zeta,TTU}$	0.0018	0.0000	0.0018	0.0012	5.86
	(0.0003)	(0.0009)	(0.0003)	(0.0006)	
$\sigma_{\zeta,OS}$	0.0010	0.0014	0.0007	0.0015	0.04
	(0.0004)	(0.0003)	(0.0005)	(0.0003)	
$\sigma_{\zeta,G}$	0.0037	0.0000	0.0031	0.0019	**11.08**
	(0.0005)	(0.0015)	(0.0005)	(0.0008)	
Seasonal	**Q1**	**Q2**	**Q3**	**Q4**	**χ^2 test**
$\sigma_{\omega,D}$	0.0000	0.0003	0.0000	0.0000	1.32
	(0.0003)	(0.0002)	(0.0003)	(0.0002)	
$\sigma_{\omega,ND}$	0.0009	0.0000	0.0006	0.0004	**12.64**
	(0.0002)	(0.0002)	(0.0002)	(0.0002)	
$\sigma_{\omega,NR}$	0.0020	0.0012	0.0009	0.0060	5.04
	(0.0009)	(0.0009)	(0.0014)	(0.0023)	
$\sigma_{\omega,C}$	0.0000	0.0047	0.0048	0.0039	**13.52**
	(0.0016)	(0.0006)	(0.0006)	(0.0008)	
$\sigma_{\omega,TTU}$	0.0000	0.0010	0.0008	0.0008	**13.24**
	(0.0004)	(0.0002)	(0.0002)	(0.0001)	
$\sigma_{\omega,OS}$	0.0003	0.0007	0.0005	0.0003	5.38
	(0.0001)	(0.0001)	(0.0001)	(0.0001)	
$\sigma_{\omega,G}$	0.0013	0.0013	0.0008	0.0003	6.67
	(0.0003)	(0.0003)	(0.0002)	(0.0008)	

Note: The estimated standard deviations are reported with their asymptotic standard errors in parentheses below. The critical value for the χ^2 tests with three degrees of freedom is 7.81 at the 5% significance level and 6.25 at the 10% significance level. Significant test statistics at 5% are given in bold.

estimates for the common cycle and the irregular component. These results confirm our earlier findings: positive cycle loading estimates for all series except for the government sector and small estimates for the irregular variances. As we have presented coefficient estimates that are very similar under different model specifications, we regard our findings as robust to possible model misspecification.

Given the results presented in Table 1.4, we can reduce the number of coefficients in Model 6 by enforcing periodic coefficients for a selection of sectors

TABLE 1.5
Estimates of Nonperiodic Components from MPUC Model 6: Cycle and Irregular

	Cycle			**Irregular**	
	est.par	s.e.		est.par	s.e.
ρ	0.9526	0.0139	$\sigma_{\epsilon,D}$	0.0025	0.0004
θ_{ND}	0.3988	0.0286	$\sigma_{\epsilon,ND}$	0.0005	0.0007
θ_{NR}	0.6063	0.0944	$\sigma_{\epsilon,NR}$	0.0079	0.0010
θ_{C}	0.5449	0.0677	$\sigma_{\epsilon,C}$	0.0000	0.0022
θ_{TTU}	0.2773	0.0161	$\sigma_{\epsilon,TTU}$	0.0007	0.0002
θ_{OS}	0.2269	0.0129	$\sigma_{\epsilon,OS}$	0.0005	0.0002
θ_{G}	−0.0336	0.0202	$\sigma_{\epsilon,G}$	0.0014	0.0004
$\sigma_{\kappa,\text{regime I}}$	0.0135	0.0010			
$\sigma_{\kappa,\text{regime II}}$	0.0029	0.0005			
Period in years	4.8115	0.2234			

only. However, we prefer to keep the main structure of our model simple. Therefore, we take Model 6 as our preferred model. It implies that the multiple time series of employment figures for seven sectors in the U.S. economy are decomposed by an MUCS time series model with idiosyncratic trend, seasonal, and irregular effects, a single common cycle with its variance adjusted for the Great Moderation, and periodic variances for the disturbances driving the trend and seasonal components.

1.4.2 Decomposition of the Unobserved Components in the Final Model

The main motivation of this study is to investigate the dynamic properties of U.S. employment and the common cyclical behavior in the time series. We have concluded that Model 6 is the most appropriate specification within the general class of MPUC models introduced in Section 1.2. To gain further insights into the dynamic properties of the series, we present graphs of the estimated components. These estimates and their confidence intervals can be constructed from Kalman filter and smoother methods.

1.4.2.1 Trend Extraction

Figure 1.2 presents the estimated trend level ($\mu_{i,t}$) from Model 6. Since the trend component is specified without the level disturbance, the slope represents the growth rate of the trend function, i.e., $\beta_{i,t} = \Delta\mu_{i,t}$. Also, it leads to smooth trend estimates as is apparent from Figure 1.2. None of the estimated trends in Figure 1.2 are exactly the same or appear to be common. The estimated trends of TTU, OS, and G appear to have similar upward

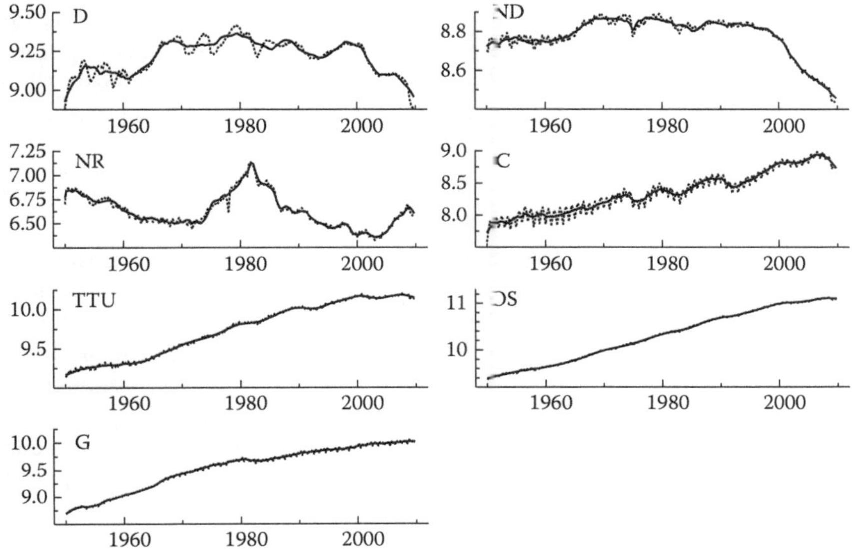

FIGURE 1.2
Data (···) and trend (—) estimates computed by the Kalman filter and smoother based on Model 6. The decompositions are given for each employment series: D = durable goods manufacturing; ND = nondurable goods manufacturing; NR = natural resources industries; C = construction businesses; TTU = trade/transport/utility industries; OS = other service-providing industries; G = aggregated government sector.

sloping trends, although differences are visible. The trends in the manufacturing sectors (D and ND) have been moving downward since the late 1990s after a more stable development since the 1970s. The ND trend has been affected by the low employment numbers during the recession period of the mid-1970s. The pattern of the NR trend is somewhat atypical compared to the trends for the other sectors. Since employment in the energy sector is highly dependent on the oil market and the oil price, its trend seems more dictated by specific energy market conditions rather than general economic conditions. The NR trend appears to follow smoothly the main movements in oil prices. The estimated trend in the construction sector appears to pick up various business cycle features. It may indicate that the business cycle component in C is neither similar to the imposed common business cycle nor is it coincidental. The cycle in construction may be leading other sectors in the economy as it is partly associated with investments (a leading indicator) in the economy. From the data and estimated trend plots, we further learn that the C series is the most seasonal.

For private services series (TTU and OS), the estimated trend is slowly increasing while a cycle component is not clearly present; service sector employers appear to be only weakly affected by recessions. Similarly, the employment in the government sector (G) has shown a steadily increasing trend without much cyclical variation in the time series.

1.4.2.2 Seasonal Effects

Figure 1.3 presents the estimated seasonal components for each time series. The seasonal patterns and their impacts are different for each series. It is interesting to view the changes in the seasonal patterns over the years. The seasonal effects for the employment series ND and C diminish in the more recent years, while for the NR, TTU, OS, and G series, the seasonal effects become somewhat stronger. A structural break in the seasonality of the TTU and OS series appears at the beginning of the 1990s. The estimated seasonality in the D series is stable in general; the pattern changes mostly for quarter 3,

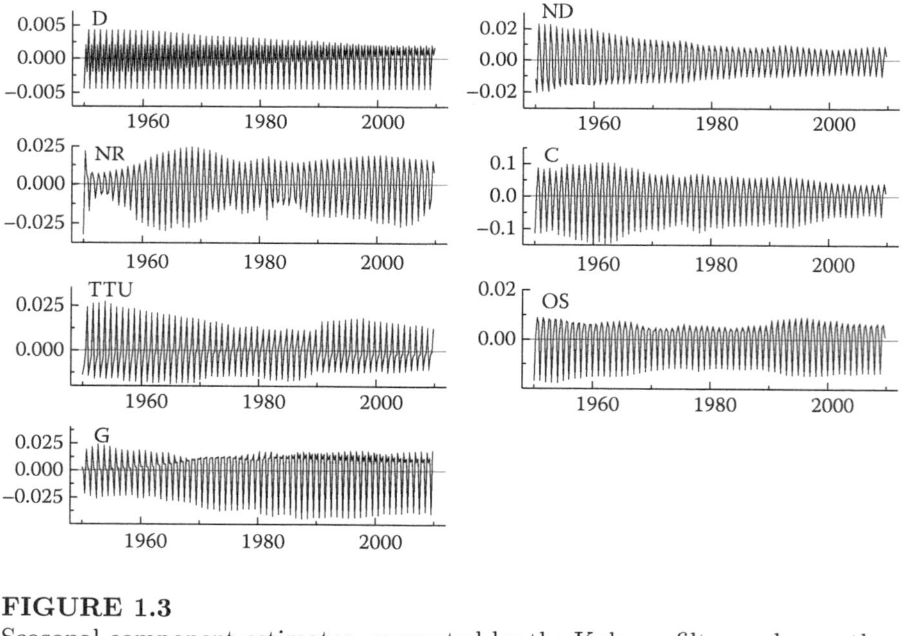

FIGURE 1.3
Seasonal component estimates, computed by the Kalman filter and smoother based on Model 6, for each employment series: D = durable goods manufacturing; ND = nondurable goods manufacturing; NR = natural resources industries; C = construction businesses; TTU = trade/transport/utility industries; OS = other service-providing industries; G = aggregated government sector.

the summer holiday months. The seasonal component has its highest impact for employment in the construction sector (C) and the second largest impact is for the government sector (G).

1.4.2.3 Common Cycle Estimate

The estimated common cycle for the seven series analyzed by MPUC Model 6 is presented in Figure 1.4a; the gray shaded areas indicate the official NBER U.S. recession periods. The estimated unemployment cycle coincides with the recession periods of the U.S. economy. However, it is noteworthy to observe that the depths of the unemployment cycle occur in almost all cases at the end of the NBER recession periods. The effect of the Great Moderation is clearly visible, while the depth during the recent financial recession in 2008

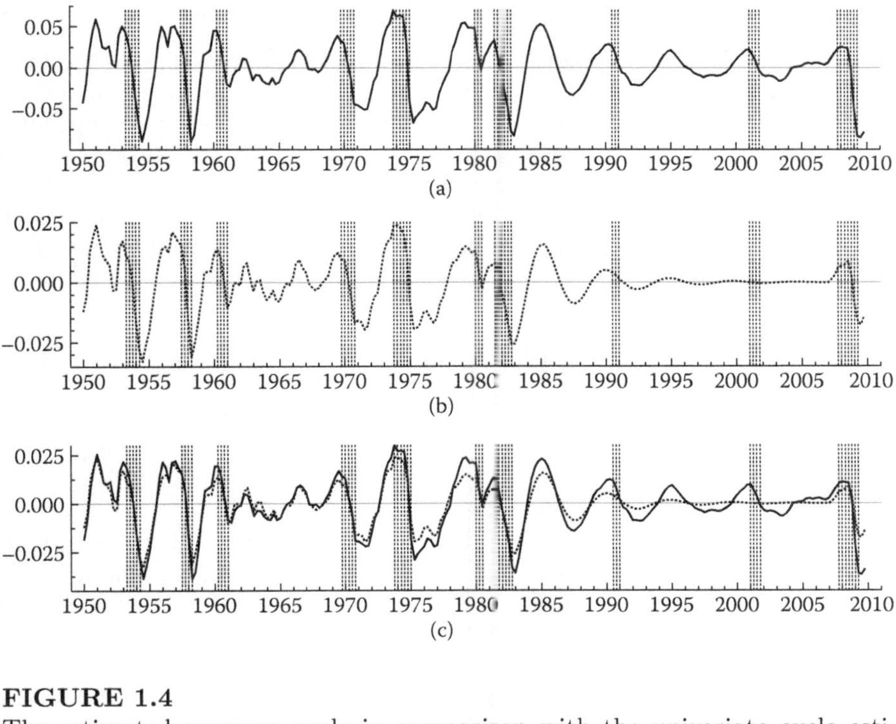

FIGURE 1.4
The estimated common cycle in comparison with the univariate cycle estimate for total U.S. employment: (a) the estimated common cycle from MPUC Model 6; (b) the estimated cycle from a univariate UC model for total U.S. employment and (c) both estimated cycles but with the common cycle from MPUC Model 6 scaled by $\bar{\theta}$ (solid line). The gray shaded areas indicate the official NBER U.S. recession periods.

is pronounced. The depth of the employment cycle during the financial crisis reaches the lowest levels (in logs) of the recessions in 1954, 1958, and 1983. The estimated values of changes in the cycle can be interpreted as the percentage cyclical change in employment. We can therefore learn that at the depth of the 2008 recession, the impact of the business cycle on employment was a reduction of almost 9%. The estimated frequency of the cycle is 0.326, which corresponds to a cycle period of 4.8 years with a standard deviation of around one quarter. This length is typical for economic cyclical changes. The cycle is represented as the component for the logged series durable goods manufacturing (D) for which the loading, θ_D, is set equal to unity. To obtain the cycle effect for the other logged series, we multiply the cycle component by its estimated loading in θ, see Table 1.5.

We compare the estimated common cycle with an estimate of the cycle from a univariate UC model with the same trend, seasonal, cycle, and irregular components, and with a cycle variance adjustment for the Great Moderation; see the discussion in Section 1.2. The univariate model is adopted to extract the cycle component from total U.S. employment (in logs). The estimated univariate cycle is presented in Figure 1.4b. Since all sectoral cycle effects rely on a single common cycle, it seems natural to compare the common cycle in sectoral employment with the univariate cycle from the total employment series. Given that we have analyzed the multivariate and univariate series in logs, we need to take care in comparing the extracted cycles. The cycle effect for the logged total employment is denoted as ψ_t^{total} and it relates approximately to the common cycle of the logged sectoral employment series as follows:

$$\begin{aligned}\psi_t^{total} &\approx \log\left(\sum_{i=1}^{N} \exp \Psi_{it}\right)\\ &\approx \log\left(N + \sum_{i=1}^{N} \Psi_{it}\right) = \log(N[1+\bar{\theta}\psi_t]) \approx \log N + \bar{\theta}\psi_t,\end{aligned}$$

where $\bar{\theta} = N^{-1}\sum_{i=1}^{N}\theta_i$ and $\Psi_{it} = \theta_i\psi_t$ is the ith element of the cycle vector Ψ_t that is used in our model (1.2.1) and is specified in Equation 1.2.5. We notice that we have dropped the t index from $\theta_{i,t}$ since the cycle loadings are not periodic in MPUC Model 6. The term $\log N$ is assigned to the trend component of the univariate model. Hence, the cycle effect in the logged total employment is approximately equal to the common cycle from the sectoral model but scaled by $\bar{\theta}$. From the loading estimates reported in Table 1.5 of our MPUC Model 6, we obtain $\bar{\theta} = 0.4315$. In Figure 1.4c, we present the cycle $\hat{\psi}_t^{total}$ for total employment and compare it with the estimate of the common cycle from our MPUC Model 6 $\hat{\psi}_t$, but scaled with $\bar{\theta}$. The two estimated cycles are very similar to each other. However, the peaks and troughs of the scaled common cycle are clearly more pronounced than the estimated cycle for logged U.S. total employment. In particular, the depth at the end of 2008 in $\hat{\psi}_t^{total}$ is estimated as not quite -2%, while it is close to -3.5% according to its counterpart from the MPUC Model 6, $\bar{\theta}\psi_t$. The depth of the common cycle from the sectoral employment model appears to be somewhat more realistic, given the impact of the 2008 financial crisis on employment.

1.4.3 Residual Diagnostics

The one-step ahead prediction residuals from MPUC Model 6 after estimation should be serially uncorrelated when the model is correctly specified. We measure the serial correlation in the seven (standardized) residual series by the sample autocorrelation function, which is presented in Figure 1.5 for each residual series. We observe weak residual cyclicality in all seven series, but their presence is not significant according to the asymptotic error bands based on 95% confidence levels. However, the weak but persistent appearance of cyclicality in the residuals may indicate that an idiosyncratic cyclical dynamic may be present in the time series. For example, in the employment for durable goods manufacturing (D), we may extend the analysis with an idiosyncratic cycle component.

The first-order serial correlation appears significant in the residuals for D, while the second-order serial correlation appears significant for the residual series in ND and G. Thus, we may need to investigate the dynamic properties

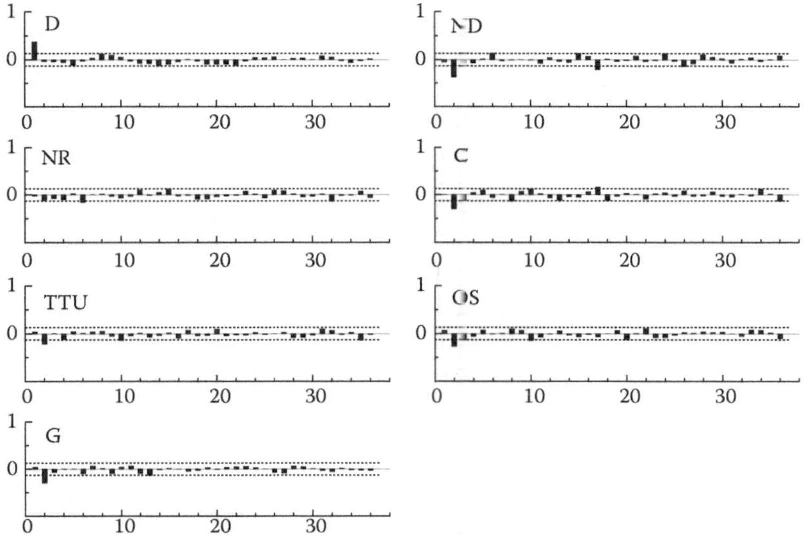

FIGURE 1.5
The sample autocorrelation functions for the seven standardized residual series from MPUC Model 6 with asymptotic error bands based on 95% confidence levels ($\pm 2/\sqrt{240}$).

for these series in more detail. However, for the purpose of this study, we are pleased with the results. We would like to emphasize that our current model has a basic time series decompostion structure.

Residual diagnostic statistics for tests against normality and heteroskedasticity are also computed and investigated. These statistics are computed for all seven residual series. Overall, these statistics are satisfactory, although the normality assumption for the ND, C, and TTU sectors can be rejected based on their skewness and kurtosis. Such rejections are most likely caused by the existence of outlying observations in the original time series.

1.5 Comparison with the Krane and Wascher Study

One of the motivations of our empirical study in Section 1.4 is to study the empirical findings of Krane and Wascher (1999) in more detail and for a new and extended dataset of sectoral U.S. employment time series. The Krane and Wascher (KW) study is based on an MUC time series model with periodic coefficients, similar to the model used in our study. However, the KW results are obtained by adopting a clearly different model specification (not discussed in Section 1.2), using different time series (in log-differences, employment growth) for a different set of sectors (nine sectors instead of our seven sectors) and for a different sample (quarterly time series from 1953 to 1989). Although the structure of their decomposition model is similar, the details of their study are different. For example, in comparison with the KW study, we have considered a larger set of periodic coefficients in the study of Section 1.4 and we have estimated the coefficients simultaneously without relying on *ad-hoc* preanalyses.

In this section, we reconsider the KW analysis and compare our main findings with those of KW. For this purpose, we adopt an MPUC model specification that is close to the model used in KW, namely, it contains idiosyncratic trend, seasonal, and irregular components, without periodic coefficients, and a common cycle component with periodic coefficients. This model specification is labeled MPUC Model KW and has not been considered in Section 1.4.

In our analysis, we consider seven sectors instead of the nine sectors that are used by KW. This difference can be explained for the following reasons. First, employment in the sector of "motor vehicle manufacturing industry" is considered by KW but is not provided as a complete time series by the BLS. The NAICS has included the "motor vehicle" sector in the overall sector of "total durable goods manufacturing industry." We, therefore, have not considered this sector separately in our analysis. Second, we have pooled the government employment data into one sector instead of three separate sectors. After a separate preanalysis of the three government employment series (federal, state, and local), we have concluded that the dynamic features of the three series have been very close to each other. Therefore, we have taken this group of employment series together and have analyzed this sector jointly with the other six sectors.

Our main findings, as reported and discussed in Section 1.4, differ from those of KW. The most pronounced difference is that KW found significant statistical evidence of periodic coefficients for the common cycle component implying an interaction between seasonal and cyclical features in the data. In our study, we have not found such interactions. By starting with MPUC Model 1, where all coefficients in the model are periodic (except the cycle length), we have not found statistical evidence of periodic coefficients that are related with the common cycle component. We have only found that the trend and the seasonal variances are periodic for employment in five sectors of the economy.

The possible reasons for the different findings are as follows. First, the MPUC Model 1 has allowed for periodicity in the trend and seasonal components, while KW has no periodicity in these components. The only periodic component in the KW model is the cycle component. In our specification, the cycle component turns out to be nonperiodic since all the periodic properties in the time series appear to be sufficiently captured by the periodic trend and seasonal components. The periodic properties in the data can only be captured by the KW model through the cycle component. Secondly, the Great Moderation for the cycle variance was not taken into account in KW. Empirical studies on the statistical evidence of the Great Moderation, such as those in Kim and Nelson (1999), McConnell and Perez-Quiros (2000), Stock and Watson (2002), Sensier and van Dijk (2004), and Kim et al. (2004), have appeared in the economic literature some years after the research of KW. We have shown in Table 1.1 that the cycle variance moderation has a major impact on the estimation of coefficients.

When we consider the MPUC Model KW, we do not find statistical evidence of periodic coefficients for the cycle component using the dataset from Section 1.3. Before making a conclusion on this difference between KW and our findings, we reestimate the coefficients for MPUC Model KW using the data sample used in the KW study. This sample is between 1953, quarter 1, and 1989, quarter 4. The estimation results for this sample appear to indicate that the periodic cycle coefficients are distinct from each other. In Table 1.6, we present the values of the χ^2 tests, with three degrees of freedom, related to the null hypothesis (1.2.10) for the individual cycle coefficients. The test values from the KW study, as reported by Krane and Wascher (1999), and those from our MPUC Model KW are presented. Although the values of the test statistics from the two studies are different, similar conclusions can be taken. The cycle loadings for the sectors TTU and G are not periodic, but all other estimated cycle coefficients are significantly periodic at a 10% significance level. Therefore, we cannot reject the findings of KW. However, our

TABLE 1.6
Periodic Tests for the Cycle Coefficients

	KW	**MPUC Model KW**
	χ^2 test	χ^2 test
ρ	15.86	7.71
θ_{ND}	22.13	10.62
θ_{NR}	16.35	9.36
θ_{C}	8.67	7.66
θ_{TTU}	2.92	0.58
θ_{OS}	8.88	6.82
θ_{G}	2.58	3.22

Note: Table presents test statistics for the null hypothesis (1.2.10) that coefficients are not periodic. The KW test statistics in the middle column are taken from Krane and Wascher (1999), while MPUC Model KW test statistics are computed using the data sample as considered by Krane and Wascher (1999), i.e., from 1953 quarter 1 to 1989 quarter 4. The critical value for the χ^2 tests with three degrees of freedom is 7.81 at the 5% significance level and 6.25 at the 10% significance level.

earlier conclusion remains because when we consider a more elaborate periodic model, such as our preferred MPUC Model 6, the cycle coefficients are not estimated as being significantly periodic, even in this specific data sample.

As our empirical findings appear to be sensitive to different samples of our dataset, we repeat our analyses for the MPUC Model 6 and MPUC Model KW for different samples. We reestimate all coefficients for each model using data samples that all start in 1950, quarter 1, but end in 1989, quarter 4, for the first sample, in 1990, quarter 4, for the second sample, etc., up to the 21st sample that ends in 2009, quarter 4. We first consider MPUC Model 6 and investigate whether the trend variances are periodic in all samples. For each sample, we compute the combined test statistic for the null hypothesis that all trend variances in the MPUC Model 6 are not periodic. This χ^2 test has 21 degrees of freedom since we have seven trend variances. Figure 1.6a presents the values of these test statistics for each sample that is indicated by the year in which the sample ends. The critical value for the χ^2 tests with 21 degrees of freedom is 33.0 at the 5% significance level and is indicated by the vertical line. The results show clearly that the null hypothesis of the nonperiodic trend component is clearly rejected for all samples except the first two. We therefore prefer to have periodic trend variances in our MPUC model specification. The computations are repeated for the null hypothesis where the seasonal component is nonperiodic. These test statistics are reported in Figure 1.6b and the rejection is even stronger. In each sample, we prefer to have seasonal variances that are different for different quarters in the MPUC Model 6.

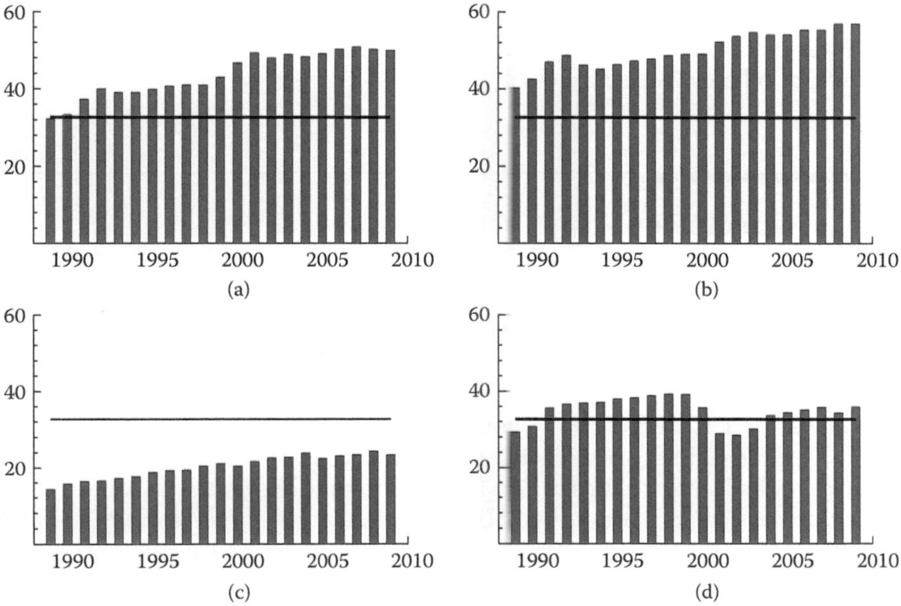

FIGURE 1.6
The joint χ^2 tests for different sets of coefficients, for different MPUC models, and for different samples. In all panels, the tests are presented as series of bars for samples starting in 1950, quarter 1, and ending in the year as indicated on the x-axis, quarter 4. Panel (a) presents the test values for the joint hypothesis with a null in which the trend variances are not periodic in MPUC Model 6; panel (b) is for a null where the seasonal variances are not periodic in MPUC Model 6; panel (c) is for a null where the cycle coefficients are not periodic in MPUC Model 2; panel (d) is for a null where the cycle coefficients are not periodic in MPUC Model KW.

We also compute the joint periodic χ^2 test for the cycle coefficients in MPUC Model 2, which is equivalent to MPUC Model 6 but with the cycle coefficients periodic. Here, we only take the seven coefficients in Table 1.6 to be periodic and compute the joint χ^2 test that has 21 degrees of freedom. The computations are repeated for all subsamples and the results are presented in Figure 1.6c. It is clear that in all samples we cannot reject the null hypothesis of nonperiodic cycle coefficients in MPUC Model 2.

We repeat the above computations for MPUC Model KW where only the cycle coefficients are periodic. The joint χ^2 tests for this case are presented in Figure 1.6d. Here the test statistics are closer to the critical value of rejecting the null hypothesis that cycle coefficients are not periodic with a 5% significance level. However, the evidence is much less convincing when we compare them to the periodic tests for the trend and seasonal variances in MPUC

Model 6. Also, in terms of information criteria, such as those of Akaike and Schwartz, the preference is clearly for MPUC Model 6 in which we do not have periodic cycle coefficients.

1.6 Conclusion

We have discussed a multivariate extension of a class of PUC time series models and have shown that the parameters driving the stochastic components of the model can be estimated by the method of maximum likelihood. The empirical study concerns a dataset of seven U.S. sectoral employment time series. We have shown that the seven time series of employment can be effectively modeled by an MPUC model with idiosyncratic components for trend, seasonal, and irregular together with a common cyclical component. The common cycle can be interpreted as the business cycle that affects the U.S. macroeconomy. A particular feature of the U.S. business cycle is the Great Moderation in which the shocks that drive the cycle have moderated in the period from the early 1980s in comparison with the earlier period. We have allowed for this phenomenon by having a different (smaller) cycle variance for the moderation period. We have decided to end the Great Moderation period at the beginning of the financial crisis in 2007, quarter 4.

By adopting this MPUC modeling framework, we have looked for a more sophisticated model specification by adopting the general-to-specific modeling strategy. It means that we started by having an MPUC model with all coefficients being periodic. Such a specification contains many coefficients in a multivariate model context, but we have shown that we are able to estimate all coefficients by the method of maximum likelihood. A crucial ingredient of this successful implementation is the ability to compute the exact score function analytically for each coefficient.

The general-to-specific modeling strategy has led us to conclude that an appropriate model specification for this important dataset is the MPUC model with only periodic variances for the disturbances that drive the seven idiosyncratic trend and seasonal components. We have not found significant evidence of periodic coefficients for the cycle component. This finding is in contrast with the thorough study of Krane and Wascher (1999); since we allowed for periodic variances in the trend and seasonal components, the cycle coefficients do not appear to be significantly periodic. We have established periodic effects in the cycle coefficients when the trend and seasonal variances are not specified as periodic. The statistical evidence is, however, weak. A model with periodicity only in the cycle is close to the model specification considered by Krane and Wascher (1999). However, the model with periodic trend and seasonal components finds more support in the data.

Although we have revisited the study of Krane and Wascher (1999) and presented this as a main motivation of this study, we also regard our study as an illustration that an MPUC model can be considered as a viable model for analyzing multiple seasonal time series. The advances in computer technology and the efficient software implementation of state-space time series methods have enabled us to use extensive model-based frameworks in the practice of economic time series analysis.

Appendix: MPUC Model in State-Space Form

In this Appendix, we show how the MPUC model of Section 1.2 can be formulated as a state-space model. We adopt the state-space formulation of De Jong (1991), i.e.,

$$\alpha_{t+1} = T_t \alpha_t + H_t \epsilon_t, \qquad \alpha_1 \sim N(a, P), \tag{A.1}$$

$$y_t = Z_t \alpha_t + G_t \epsilon_t, \qquad \epsilon_t \sim NID(0, I), \tag{A.2}$$

where, for $t = 1, \ldots, n$, y_t is the $N \times 1$ observation vector, α_t is the $m \times 1$ state vector, and the system matrices, T_t, H_t, Z_t, and G_t, can be time-varying to allow for periodicity. The initial state vector is α_1 with mean vector a and variance matrix P. The transition matrix T_t is given by

$$T_t = \begin{pmatrix} T_{\text{level}} & 0_{2N\times 3N} & 0_{2N\times 2} \\ 0_{3N\times 2N} & T_{\text{season}} & 0_{3N\times 2} \\ 0_{2\times 2N} & 0_{2\times 3N} & T_{\text{cycle}} \end{pmatrix} \tag{A.3}$$

where the submatrices are structured as follows:

$$T_{\text{level}} = \begin{pmatrix} I_N & I_N \\ 0_{N\times N} & I_N \end{pmatrix}$$

$$T_{\text{season}} = \begin{pmatrix} -I_N & -I_N & -I_N \\ I_N & 0_{N\times N} & 0_{N\times N} \\ 0_{N\times N} & I_N & 0_{N\times N} \end{pmatrix}$$

$$T_{\text{cycle}} = \rho_t \begin{pmatrix} \cos\lambda & \sin\lambda \\ -\sin\lambda & \cos\lambda \end{pmatrix}. \tag{A.4}$$

The measurement matrix Z_t is given by

$$Z_t = \begin{pmatrix} I_N & 0_{N\times N} & I_N & 0_{N\times N} & 0_{N\times N} & \Theta_t \end{pmatrix} \tag{A.5}$$

with vector Θ_t defined in Equation 1.2.7, and the state vector is given by

$$\alpha_t = \left(\mu_t',\ \beta_t',\ \gamma_t',\ \gamma_{t-1}',\ \gamma_{t-2}',\ \psi_t,\ \psi_t^*\right)'.$$

The initialization of the state vector is diffuse for the nonstationary component. For the periodic cycle component, we use the initialization as explained in Koopman et al. (2009). The variance matrix of the state disturbances, $H_t H_t' = \mathbb{V}\text{ar}(H_t \epsilon_t)$, is given by

$$H_t H_t' = \text{diagonal}\left(\Sigma_{\eta,t}, \Sigma_{\zeta,t}, \Sigma_{\omega,t}, 0_{N \times N}, 0_{N \times N}, \sigma_\kappa^2 I_2\right), \tag{A.6}$$

and the variance matrix of the measurement disturbances is given by $G_t G_t' = \Sigma_{\varepsilon,t}$. Note that the unknown coefficients Θ_t, ρ_t, $\sigma_{\kappa,t}^2$, $\Sigma_{\eta,t}$, $\Sigma_{\zeta,t}$, $\Sigma_{\omega,t}$, and $\Sigma_{\varepsilon,t}$ are time-varying as fixed functions of time index t.

References

Anderson, P. and Meerschaert, M. M. (2005). Parameter estimation for periodically stationary time series. *Journal of Time Series Analysis* 26:489–518.

Barsky, R. B. and Miron, J. A. (1989). The seasonal cycle and the business cycle. *Journal of Political Economy* 97:503–34.

Bell, W. and Hillmer, S. (1991). Initializing the Kalman filter for nonstationary time series models (Corr: V13 p281–282). *Journal of Time Series Analysis* 12:283–300.

Bell, W. R. (2004). On RegComponent time series models and their applications. In *State Space and Unobserved Component Models*, eds. A. Harvey, S. J. Koopman, and N. Shephard, 248–83. Cambridge: Cambridge University Press.

Bloomfield, P., Hurd, H. L., and Lund, R. B. (1994). Periodic correlation in stratospheric ozone data. *Journal of Time Series Analysis* 15:127–50.

Canova, F. and Ghysels, E. (1994). Changes in seasonal patterns: Are they cyclical? *Journal of Economic Dynamics & Control* 18:1143–72.

De Jong, P. (1991). The diffuse Kalman filter. *Annals of Statistics* 19:1073–83.

Doornik, J. A. (2009). *Ox: An Object-Oriented Matrix Language, Version 6.* London: Timberlake Consultants Press.

Durbin, J. and Koopman, S. J. (2001). *Time Series Analysis by State Space Methods.* Oxford: Oxford University Press.

Findley, D. F. (2005). Some recent developments and directions in seasonal adjustment. *Journal of Official Statistics* 21:343–65.

Fletcher, R. (1987). *Practical Methods of Optimisation.* 2nd edition. New York: John Wiley.

Franses, P. H. and Paap, R. (2004). *Periodic Time Series Models.* Oxford: Oxford University Press.

Fruhwirth-Schnatter, S. (1994a). Bayesian model discrimination and Bayes factors for state space models. *Journal of the Royal Statistical Society, Series B* 56:237–46.

Fruhwirth-Schnatter, S. (1994b). Data augmentation and dynamic linear models. *Journal of Time Series Analysis* 15:183–202.

Ghysels, E. (1988). A study toward a dynamic theory of seasonality for economic time series. *Journal of the American Statistical Association* 83(401): 168–72.

Ghysels, E. (1991). Are business cycle turning points uniformly distributed throughout the year?, Cahiers de recherche 9135, Centre interuniversitaire de recherche en conomie quantitative, CIREQ.

Ghysels, E. and Osborn, D. R. (2001). *The Econometric Analysis of Seasonal Time Series.* Cambridge: Cambridge University Press.

Gladysev, E. G. (1961). Periodically correlated random sequences. *Soviet Mathematics* 2:385–8.

Hannan, E. J. (1955). A test for singularities in Sydney rainfall. *Australian Journal of Physics* 8:289–97.

Harvey, A. C. (1989). *Forecasting, Structural Time Series Models and the Kalman Filter.* Cambridge: Cambridge University Press.

Harvey, A. C. and Koopman, S. J. (1997). Multivariate structural time series models. In *Systematic Dynamics in Economic and Financial Models,* eds. C. Heij, H. Schumacher, B. Hanzon, and C. Praagman, 269–298. Chichester: John Wiley.

Jimenez, C., McLeod, A. I., and Hipel, K. W. (1989). Kalman filter estimation for periodic autoregressive-moving average models. *Stochastic Hydrology and Hydraulics* 3:227–40.

Kim, C. and Nelson, C. (1999). Has the U.S. economy become more stable? A Bayesian approach based on a Markov-switching model of the business cycle. *Review of Economics and Statistics* 81:608–16.

Kim, C. J., Nelson, C., and Piger, J. (2004). The less volatile U.S. economy: A Bayesian investigation of timing breadth, and potential explanations. *Journal of Business & Economic Statistics* 22:80–93.

Koopman, S. J. and Ooms, M. (2002). Periodic structural time series models: Estimation and forecasting with application. In *Proceedings of the 3rd International Symposium on Frontiers of Time Series Modeling:*

Modeling Seasonality and Periodicity, Institute of Statistical Mathematics, Tokyo, Japan, January 2002, ed, Y. Kawasaki, 151–72. Tokyo, Japan: Institute of Statistical Mathematics.

Koopman, S. J. and Ooms, M. (2006). Forecasting daily time series using periodic unobserved components time series models. *Computational Statistics & Data Analysis* 51:885–903.

Koopman, S. J., Ooms, M., and Hindrayanto, I. (2009). Periodic unobserved cycles in seasonal time series with an application to U.S. unemployment. *Oxford Bulletin of Economics and Statistics* 71(5):683–713.

Koopman, S. J. and Shephard, N. (1992). Exact score for time series models in state space form. *Biometrika* 79:823–6.

Koopman, S. J., Shephard, N., and Doornik, J. A. (1999). Statistical algorithms for models in state space using SsfPack 2.2. *The Econometrics Journal* 2:107–60, www.ssfpack.com.

Koopman, S. J., Shephard, N., and Doornik, J. A. (2008). *Statistical Algorithms for Models in State Space Form – SsfPack 3.0.* London: Timberlake Consultants Ltd.

Krane, S. and Wascher, W. (1999). The cyclical sensitivity of seasonality in U.S. unemployment. *Journal of Monetary Economics* 44:523–53.

Li, W. K. and Hui, Y. V. (1988). An algorithm for the exact likelihood of periodic autoregressive moving average models. *Communications in Statistics, Simulations and Computation* 17:1483–94.

Lund, R. and Basawa, I. (2000). Recursive prediction and likelihood evaluation for periodic ARMA models. *Journal of Time Series Analysis* 21:75–93.

McConnell, M. and Perez-Quiros, G. (2000). Output fluctuations in the United States: What has changed since the early 1980s? *American Economic Review* 90:1464–76.

Mendershausen, H. (1937). Annual survey of statistical technique: Method of computing and eliminating changing seasonal fluctuations. *Econometrica* 5:234–62.

Morisi, T. (2003). Recent changes in the national Current Employment Statistics survey. *Monthly Labor Review* pp. 3–13, June, http://www. bls.gov/opub/mlr/2003/06/art1full.pdf.

Osborn, D. R. (1988). Seasonality and habit persistence in a life cycle model of consumption. *Journal of Applied Econometrics* 3:255–66.

Osborn, D. R. and Smith, J. P. (1989). The performance of periodic autoregressive models in forecasting seasonal UK consumption. *Journal of Business & Economic Statistics* 7:117–27.

Penzer, J. and Tripodis, Y. (2007). Single-season heteroscedasticity in time series. *Journal of Forecasting* 26:189–202.

Plosser, C. I. (1979): The analysis of seasonal economic models. *Journal of Econometrics* 10(2):147–63.

Proietti, T. (2004). Seasonal specific structural time series. *Studies in Nonlinear Dynamics & Econometrics* 8 (2), Article 16, http://www.epress.com/snde/vol8/iss2/art16.

Sensier, M. and van Dijk, D. (2004). Testing for volatility changes in U.S. macroeconomic time series. *The Review of Economics and Statistics* 86:833–39.

Stock, J. H. and Watson, M. W. (2002). Has the Business Cycle Changed and Why? *NBER Macroeconomics Annual 2002*, 17:159–218. Cambridge: MIT Press.

Taniguchi, M. and Kakizawa, Y. (2000). *Asymptotic Theory of Statistical Inference for Time Series*. New York: Springer-Verlag.

Tiao, G. C. and Grupe, M. R. (1980). Hidden periodic autoregressive-moving average models in time series data. *Biometrika* 67:365–73.

Vecchia, A. V. (1985). Maximum likelihood estimation for periodic autoregressive moving average models. *Technometrics* 27:375–84.

Wallis, K. F. (1978). Seasonal adjustment and multiple time series analysis (with discussion). In *Seasonal Analysis of Economic Time Series*, ed. Arnold Zellner. pp. 347–364. U.S. Department of Commerce, U.S. Census Bureau. Available from National Bureau of Economic Research at http://www.nber.org/chapters/c4330.pdf.

2

Seasonal Heteroskedasticity in Time Series Data: Modeling, Estimation, and Testing

Thomas M. Trimbur and William R. Bell*

CONTENTS

2.1 Introduction

Seasonal heteroskedasticity refers to variation in uncertainty or volatility that occurs in a seasonal pattern across calendar years. In this chapter, we examine and compare two different approaches to modeling seasonal

---

* Disclaimer: This report is released to inform interested parties of ongoing research and to encourage discussion of work in progress. The views expressed on statistical, methodological, technical, or operational issues are those of the authors and not necessarily those of the Federal Reserve Board or the U.S. Census Bureau.

heteroskedasticity: the seasonal specific models introduced by Proietti (2004) and an extension of the airline model proposed by Bell (2004). We examine the use of likelihood ratio tests with the models to test for the presence of seasonal heteroskedasticity, and the use of model comparison statistics (AIC) to compare the models and to search among alternative patterns of seasonal heteroskedasticity. We apply the models and tests to the U.S. Census Bureau monthly time series of regional housing starts and building permits. For some of these series, there is a clear reason to expect seasonal heteroskedasticity—the variable effects of winter weather on the activity surrounding new construction.

Seasonal heteroskedasticity is a particular form of periodic behavior. Two general types of periodic models are the periodic autoregressive-moving average models studied in Tiao and Grupe (1980) and the form-free seasonal effects models of West and Harrison (1989). A key feature of the latter is the use of a multivariate model for a complete set of processes, one for each month, which is defined at all time points, although only the process corresponding to the calendar month of observation is observed at each time point. The required hidden components are then easily handled in the state-space form of the model. Proietti's model is of this type. Bell's model is more related to those of Tiao and Grupe, in that it starts with the popular "airline model" of Box and Jenkins (1976), but augments it with an additional white noise component with seasonally heteroskedastic variance. While Bell's model differs fundamentally from Proietti's model, it suggests a variant of Proietti's model with seasonal heteroskedasticity only in the irregular component, and we consider this third model as well. Proietti (2004, 2) noted this possibility, but did not pursue it.

Proietti (1998) discussed some earlier models for seasonal heteroskedasticity and developed an extension to Harvey's (1989) basic structural model (BSM) using a heteroskedastic seasonal component, which generalizes the seasonal component of Harrison and Stevens (1976). Proietti (2004, 5) notes how his seasonal specific trends model reduces to a variant of his earlier model when certain constraints are imposed on the parameters. Tripodis and Penzer (2007) also used this heteroskedastic extension of the BSM, as well as a variant with a seasonally heteroskedastic irregular (analogous to our third model). For both these models, Tripodis and Penzer considered the case where only one month (or, for quarterly series, one quarter) has a different variance from the others, a particular case of the form of seasonal heteroskedasticity that we consider here.

In fact, in this chapter, we focus on the case where "seasonal heteroskedasticity" takes the simplified form of there being just two distinct variances, leading to what we call "high variance months" and "low variance months." This simplified form makes sense for our application to monthly time series of regional housing starts and issuance of building permits, where the concern is about the varying effects of winter weather on new construction. This simplified form could also provide a useful approximation for other economic applications for which the limited length of available time series would raise concerns about modeling a fully general pattern of seasonal heteroskedasticity—different variances for each of the 12 months. For other types of applications, other simplified patterns could be considered to reduce the number of variance parameters to be estimated. For example, Jones and Brelsford (1967) considered periodic models for meteorological time series and used a Fourier series parameterization of heteroskedasticity. However, such smooth patterns of seasonal heteroskedasticity seem less appropriate for monthly economic time series.

Simplifying the pattern of heteroskedasticity to two groups of months still leaves unanswered the question of precisely which months should comprise the high and low variance groups. We address this here by developing an algorithm analogous to forward selection stepwise regression for selecting the high and low variance months. In our application, we split the time series, apply this algorithm to the first part to determine the groups, and then use the last part to estimate the resulting model and to test for the presence of seasonal heteroskedasticity.

The chapter proceeds as follows. Section 2.2 presents the three models for seasonal heteroskedasticity: the seasonal specific trends model of Proietti (2004), the autoregressive integrated moving average (ARIMA) plus seasonal noise model of Bell (2004), and the variant of Proietti's model with a seasonally heteroskedastic irregular component. Section 2.3 presents our algorithm for determining which months should be regarded as high variance and which as low variance, and applies it to time series of regional housing starts and building permits from the U.S. Census Bureau. Section 2.4 examines, through simulations, the behavior of likelihood ratio tests for the presence of seasonal heteroskedasticity in the contexts of the three models. Section 2.5 then applies these likelihood ratio tests to the time series of regional housing starts and building permits. Finally, Section 2.6 discusses the conclusions.

2.2 Models for Seasonal Heteroskedasticity

2.2.1 Seasonal Specific Trends Model (Proietti 2004)

Here we review the model proposed in Proietti (2004), where heteroskedastic movements are specified in a set of trend equations that involve separate processes for the different calendar months. We refer to this as the seasonal specific trends model. Since the applications we consider involve monthly data, "month" and "season" are used interchangeably in what follows.

Given a seasonal time series, y_t, observed at time points $t = 1, \ldots, T$, the model is

$$y_t = z_t' \mu_t + \varepsilon_t, \qquad \varepsilon_t \sim i.i.d.(0\ \sigma_\varepsilon^2), \quad t = 1, \ldots, T, \tag{2.2.1}$$

$$\mu_{t+1} = \mu_t + 1\beta_t + 1\eta_t + \eta_t^*, \qquad \mu_t = (\mu_{1t}, \ldots, \mu_{st})', \tag{2.2.2}$$

$$\eta_t \sim i.i.d.(0, \sigma_\eta^2), \qquad \eta_t^* = (\eta_{1t}^*, \ldots, \eta_{st}^*)', \qquad \eta_{jt}^* \sim i.i.d.(0, \sigma_{\eta*,j}^2),$$
$$\beta_{t+1} = \beta_t + \zeta_t, \qquad \zeta_t \sim i.i.d.(0, \sigma_\zeta^2),$$

where $\imath$ is an $s \times 1$ vector of ones, with s denoting the number of seasons in a year, i.e., $s = 12$ for monthly data. In the observation equation (2.2.1), z_t is an $s \times 1$ selection vector that has a 1 in the position $j = 1 + (t-1)(\text{mod}\, s)$ and zeroes elsewhere. Thus, $z_t'\mu_t$ picks off the element of μ_t corresponding to the month of time point t, and this is the only part of μ_t that directly affects the observation y_t. The observation at time t is then the sum of the appropriate μ_{jt} and the noise term ε_t.

The state equation (2.2.2) specifies the evolution of the vector of monthly trends, μ_t. At time t, each of the s elements of μ_t is subject to a shared level disturbance, η_t, and to an idiosyncratic level disturbance, η_{jt}^*, that is uncorrelated with η_t and with η_{kt}^* for $k \neq j$. The η_{jt}^* have variances $\sigma_{\eta*,j}^2$ that depend, in general, on the season j, and so are the source of seasonal heteroskedasticity in the model. If, however, $\sigma_{\eta*,j}^2$ is constant over $j = 1, \ldots, 12$, then the model becomes homoskedastic. The elements of μ_t are incremented at time t by a common slope β_t, whose disturbance, ζ_t, is assumed uncorrelated with the other disturbances in the model.

Proietti (2004) considers various alternative versions of the structure given in Equation 2.2.2. These include a restricted version that sets $\beta_t = 0$, a more general version that allows seasonal heteroskedasticity in β_t, a version with a circular correlation structure between the η_{jt}^* and a multivariate extension. However, he appears to suggest the model given by Equation 2.2.2 as the most common variant.

We estimate the model given by Equations 2.2.1 and 2.2.2, and the models of the next two sections, via Gaussian maximum likelihood (ML), by assuming normality of the disturbance terms. We implement Gaussian ML estimation using state-space methods. Given a feasible parameter vector, the likelihood function is evaluated from the prediction error decomposition generated by the Kalman filter; see Harvey (1989). The Kalman filter is assigned diffuse initial conditions to deal with the differencing in the models, as described in Durbin and Koopman (2001, Chapter 5). The ML parameter estimates are then computed by optimizing over the likelihood surface in each case. To do these calculations, we used programs written in the Ox language (Doornik 1999), which includes the SsfPack library of state-space functions (Koopman et al. 1999).

Another point worth noting is that, while not immediately obvious, the differencing required to remove unit root nonstationarities in Equations 2.2.1 and 2.2.2 is $(1-B)(1-B^{12})$, where B is the backshift operator ($By_t = y_{t-1}$). As the same differencing is used in the next two models, the likelihoods (and AICs, defined later) can be compared across the three models.

2.2.2 Airline Model with Seasonal Noise (Bell 2004)

Bell (2004) starts with a standard seasonal time series model, but extends it to include seasonally heteroskedastic noise. Specifically, he extends the airline model (Box and Jenkins 1976) as follows:

$$y_t = Y_t + h_t\varepsilon_t \tag{2.2.3}$$

$$(1-B)(1-B^{12})Y_t = (1-\theta_1 B)(1-\theta_{12}B^{12})a_t \tag{2.2.4}$$

$$a_t \sim i.i.d.(0,\sigma_a^2), \qquad \varepsilon_t \sim i.i.d.(0,\sigma_\varepsilon^2),$$

where Y_t and ε_t are independent. For the most general model of seasonal heteroskedasticity, we could set $\sigma_\varepsilon^2 = 1$, thereby making h_t the standard deviations of the additive noise, which would follow some seasonal pattern. Bell (2004), however, considers just the simpler case of high and low variance months by letting h_t be 1 for the high variance months and zero otherwise. Thus, σ_ε^2 becomes an additional irregular variance added in only for the high variance months. One can then think of base irregular variation as embedded in the Y_t component, say via the canonical seasonal plus trend plus irregular decomposition of Hillmer and Tiao (1982).

2.2.3 Seasonal Specific Irregular Model

Bell's model suggests an easy modification to Proietti's model to use a heteroskedastic irregular rather than heteroskedastic monthly trends. To do this, we set $\sigma_{\eta*,j}^2 = \sigma_{\eta*}^2$, a constant value for all j, and make the irregular in Equation 2.2.1 heteroskedastic. The model then becomes

$$y_t = z_t'\mu_t + \varepsilon_{jt}^*, \qquad \varepsilon_{jt}^* \sim i.i.d.(0,\sigma_{\varepsilon*,j}^2), \qquad t = 1,\ldots,T. \tag{2.2.5}$$

The random shocks ε_{jt}^* are still assumed uncorrelated across seasons, and their variance depends only on the season index $j = 1 + (t-1)(\text{mod}\, s)$. Equation 2.2.2 still applies for μ_t, but with the homoskedasticity constraint on the variances of η_{jt}^*.

For heteroskedastic seasonal variation linked to weather or other factors with seasonal, but otherwise temporary, effects, models (2.2.3) and (2.2.5) have some appeal since the heteroskedasticity comes from the irregular component.

2.3 Determining the Pattern of Seasonal Heteroskedasticity

We will consider the heteroskedastic models of Section 2.2 in the case for which months are classified into two groups with different variances. For Proietti's model (2.2.1), we can label the variances for the two groups $\sigma_{\eta*I}^2$ and $\sigma_{\eta*II}^2$ with no constraint about which of these two is the larger. Similarly for the variant given by Equation 2.2.5, we can write $\sigma_{\varepsilon*I}^2$ and $\sigma_{\varepsilon*II}^2$ for the irregular variances of the two groups. For these two models, reversing the assignment of the months between groups I and II does not change the model. For example, the model for which January is assigned to group I and the remaining months are all assigned to group II is equivalent to the model with January assigned to group II and the remaining months all assigned to group I. Thus, there are $2^{11} = 2048$ possible groupings of the months for these models. The labels "high variance months" and "low variance months" can be assigned to the two groups according to the estimated variances, e.g., for the model (2.2.2), according to whether $\hat{\sigma}^2_{\eta*I} > \hat{\sigma}^2_{\eta*II}$ or $\hat{\sigma}^2_{\eta*I} < \hat{\sigma}^2_{\eta*II}$.

For the airline plus seasonal noise model (2.2.3), the months with $h_t = 1$ are necessarily the "high variance months" since $\sigma^2_\varepsilon \geq 0$. For example, if $h_t = 1$ only for January, then January is the only high variance month, and the remaining months are low variance. Note that this model is not equivalent to the model where $h_t = 1$ for all months except January. Thus, there are $2^{12} = 4096$ possible groupings of the months for this model, although for half of these groupings the estimated model is likely to reduce to the homoskedastic model. For example, if the model for which $h_t = 1$ only for January yields $\hat{\sigma}^2_\varepsilon > 0$, then it seems likely (although we have no mathematical proof that this is always true) that the model for which $h_t = 1$ for all months except January will yield $\hat{\sigma}^2_\varepsilon = 0$.

For all three models, we first need to specify the grouping of the months. In some cases, the grouping may be suggested by prior knowledge or previous analyses, but in other cases it may need to be determined empirically. Even if prior knowledge suggests a possible grouping, an empirical search over alternative groupings may help refine or confirm the prior grouping. Therefore, in Section 2.3.1, we present an algorithm for empirically selecting the best fitting grouping of months. As it is computationally demanding to search over the full set of 2048 possible groupings for models (2.2.1) and (2.2.5), or 4096 for model (2.2.3), we develop a search strategy to approximate the best fitting grouping without checking all possibilities. The search strategy is somewhat analogous to forward selection stepwise regression with built-in checks. In Section 2.3.2, we apply the algorithm to the time series of building permits and housing starts.

Previous papers (Proietti 1998, 2004; Tripodis and Penzer 2007) have determined reduced parameterizations of seasonal heteroskedasticity in less formal ways, although in most of their applications the months with potentially different variances were fairly obvious.

2.3.1 Algorithm for Grouping Months

We now describe a simple search algorithm that attempts to approximate the best fitting grouping of months as measured by the AIC criterion (Akaike 1974), defined as $\text{AIC} = -2 \log \hat{L} + 2k$, where $\log \hat{L}$ is the maximized Gaussian log-likelihood and k is the number of model parameters. However, for any of our three model forms, k will be constant over all models being compared that actually involve two groups, i.e., k will be different only for the homoskedastic model. So, except for comparisons with the homoskedastic model, the AIC comparisons reduce to comparisons of differences in $2 \log \hat{L}$.

The search algorithm proceeds as follows. First, the homoskedastic model is estimated and the AIC recorded. Then, the algorithm runs a number of iterations. At each iteration, the algorithm starts with January, switches its grouping, fits the resulting model, and stores the AIC resulting from the switch. The algorithm then resets January to its original group, switches the grouping of February, fits this model, and records the AIC generated by this switch. The algorithm moves through each calendar month in the same way until December is reached, which ends the iteration. If the lowest AIC among all the models coming from these single month switches is lower than the AIC for the model at the beginning of the iteration, i.e., before any switches were made, then the corresponding model is adopted, resulting in one month having its grouping switched, and another iteration begins, starting with switching January. If, on the other hand, no switch has improved the AIC, then the algorithm stops.

After the algorithm stops with a particular grouping, we check for the possibility that "double switches," i.e., simultaneous switches of two months, could improve the AIC. To make this operational, we start with the grouping obtained by the single switch algorithm, and determine which month, when switched, would give the second best AIC. Following this, the algorithm determines which additional month, when also switched, would give the best AIC. Switching this pair of months provides another candidate grouping. We have found that this simultaneous switch of two months may, on infrequent occasions, give a better AIC than that for the grouping determined by testing just the single switches. This occurs when switching a particular pair of months leads to a better AIC, but switching each of the months individually fails to improve the AIC.

When a double switch improves the AIC, we update the starting grouping and rerun the single switch search from this point. After this, we again check for double switches. We ultimately stop the search when neither the single nor double switches improve the AIC. We expect this algorithm to be robust at finding the grouping with the best or nearly best AIC.

Using this algorithm saves a substantial amount of computing time versus searching over all possible combinations. For example, for Midwest total housing starts (one of the series analyzed here), the search algorithm applied with the seasonal specific irregular model required just 60 model estimations to determine the month grouping (which assigned January and February to the high variance group), compared with the total number of 2048 potential groupings. For the case of building permits in the South region and the seasonal specific irregular model, the number of model estimations within the search algorithm (which assigned five months to the high variance group—see Table 2.1) was 96. These results are typical. While more model estimations are required to determine a grouping that switches more months from the homoskedastic model, there is still a dramatic reduction in the number of model estimations compared with fitting all possible models.

TABLE 2.1
Calendar Month Groups for the Building Permits Time Series (Using Data from the "Prior" Period, 1959:1 to 1988:12)

Series	High Variance Months	$[\Delta\text{AIC}]_1$	Second Best	$[\Delta\text{AIC}]_2$
	Seasonal Specific Trends Model			
Permits, NE	Jan, Feb, Apr, Sep	−6.6	+Nov	0.9
Permits, MW	Jan, Feb, Dec	−40.6	+Mar	7.4
Permits, SO	Jan, Mar, May, Jun, Sep, Dec	−7.5	−May	0.9
Permits, WE	Dec	−8.0	+Jan, +Jun	5.8
	Airline Plus Seasonal Noise Model			
Permits, NE	Jan, Feb, Mar	−19.9	+Dec	0.6
Permits, MW	Jan, Feb, Mar, Dec	−57.7	−Mar	1.2
Permits, SO	Jan, Mar, Jun, Sep, Dec	−4.7	−Jan	0.4
Permits, WE	Dec	−16.1	+Nov	3.6
	Seasonal Specific Irregular Model			
Permits, NE	Jan, Feb, Mar	−19.5	+Dec	0.4
Permits, MW	Jan, Feb, Dec	−57.4	+Mar	0.7
Permits, SO	Jan, Mar, Jun, Sep, Dec	−4.6	−Jan	0.1
Permits, WE	Dec	−16.5	+Nov	3.3

Note: The second column shows, for each series, the months assigned higher variability in the selected model, and the third column shows the AIC difference from the homoskedastic model. The fourth column shows the change in grouping from the best to the second best model, with the associated change in AIC given in the fifth column.

2.3.2 Application

The set of time series we consider, listed in Tables 2.1 and 2.2, are monthly estimates of the numbers of building permits issued, as well as estimates of the numbers of total housing starts, for the four regions of the United States: Northeast (NE), Midwest (MW), South (SO), and West (WE). The data are from the U.S. Census Bureau.* Changes in housing starts signal the performance of the construction sector, and they have broader relevance, as the cyclical variation in this series tends to lead residential investment and personal consumption expenditures, which make up most of real GDP. Because of the geographic patterns in weather, the role of seasonal heteroskedasticity in starts and permits becomes clearer by examining the data at the level of the regions. Note that the Census Bureau seasonally adjusts the permits and

* See the Census Bureau web site at www.census.gov/const/regionmap.pdf for a map showing the regions, and www.census.gov/const/www/newresconstdoc.html for source and reliability information for these series.

TABLE 2.2
Calendar Month Groups for the Housing Starts Time Series (Using Data from the "Prior" Period, 1964:1 to 1988:12)

Series	**High Variance Months**	**[ΔAIC]₁**	**Second Best**	**[ΔAIC]₂**
	Seasonal Specific Trends Model			
Starts, NE	Jan, Feb	−49.7	+Apr	8.0
Starts, MW	Jan, Feb	−62.2	+Dec	7.6
Starts, SO	Jan	−4.9	+Feb	1.8
Starts, WE	Jan, Dec	−10.7	−Dec	0.5
	Airline Plus Seasonal Noise Model			
Starts, NE	Jan, Feb	−47.9	+Sep	4.4
Starts, MW	Jan, Feb	−63.2	+Dec	5.2
Starts, SO	Jan, Feb	−15.6	+Dec	2.3
Starts, WE	Jan, Feb, Apr, Aug, Oct, Dec	−24.0	−Oct, +Nov	1.9
	Seasonal Specific Irregular Model			
Starts, NE	Jan, Feb	−47.8	+Sep	4.2
Starts, MW	Jan, Feb	−64.6	+Dec	5.6
Starts, SO	Jan, Feb	−15.6	+Dec	2.3
Starts, WE	Jan, Feb, Apr, Aug, Oct, Dec	−23.8	+Nov	2.2

Note: The definitions of entries are the same as in Table 2.1.

starts data at the regional level, and then aggregates the results. Due to differences in seasonal components across the census regions, it is believed that this gives a cleaner estimate of the underlying total for the seasonally adjusted series than would seasonally adjusting the U.S. totals directly.

The observation period for our series of building permits is from January 1959 to April 2009, while for housing starts it is from January 1964 to April 2009. However, because we are interested later (Section 2.4) in testing for the presence of seasonal heteroskedasticity, for each series the sample period is divided into prior and testing periods. In making this division, our aim is to have a long enough series for testing, while leaving enough observations at the beginning to give a representative prior selection. The permits series are thus split into two samples, 1959:1–1988:12 (prior, 360 observations) and 1989:1–2009:4 (testing, 244 observations); and the housing starts series are split into the two samples, 1964:1–1988:12 (prior, 300 observations) and 1989:1–2009:4 (testing, 244 observations).

An alternative strategy, possibly necessary for shorter-length time series, would be to apply the grouping algorithm and the test of heteroskedasticity to the full series. However, searching for the month grouping with the same data used for testing would clearly affect the properties of the test, complicating inference. Thus, we do not pursue this strategy here.

Prior to applying the three models, each series was logged and then adjusted for trading-day effects via a fitted RegARIMA model (Bell and Hillmer 1983), using the X-12-ARIMA program (Findley et al. 1998). Further, we adjusted for one additive outlier in both starts and permits in the Northeast region in June 2008 when spikes occurred in anticipation of stricter building regulations taking effect in New York. It is this set of logged, trading-day (and, in two cases, outlier) adjusted series to which we apply the three models of Section 2.2.

Tables 2.1 and 2.2 show the results of applying the grouping algorithm to the permits and housing starts series (for their "prior" periods) with our three models. The second column in each table shows the group of months determined by the algorithm to have higher variance. The third column shows $[\Delta\text{AIC}]_1$, the difference in AIC between the selected heteroskedastic model and the homoskedastic model. This indicates evidence of heteroskedasticity (larger AIC differences imply stronger evidence of heteroskedasticity), but since the specific patterns of heteroskedasticity were determined by searching over the various month groupings to find the best fitting model, these results can be misleading. (A more objective decision on whether heteroskedasticity is truly present comes in Section 2.5 from application of the likelihood ratio tests to the models selected here for the series, but fitted over their testing samples.) Some indication of how definitive the groupings are is given by the fourth and fifth columns of the tables. These show the changes from the best fitting groupings that yield the second best fitting groupings, and the corresponding changes in AIC, $[\Delta\text{AIC}]_2$. As noted earlier, all these comparisons involve models with the same number of parameters, hence the $[\Delta\text{AIC}]_2$ are just differences in $2\log\hat{L}$.

We first consider the results for the Northeast and Midwest series. In all cases, $[\Delta\text{AIC}]_1$ is negative, and in nearly all cases (Northeast permits for the seasonal specific trends model being perhaps the sole exception), it is large in magnitude, so the heteroskedastic model is strongly preferred over the homoskedastic model. For starts, the $[\Delta\text{AIC}]_2$ values are somewhat large so that the groupings appear decisive. For permits, most of the values of $[\Delta\text{AIC}]_2$ are small in magnitude, so in these cases the model with the alternative grouping fits about as well. For example, for Northeast permits with either the airline plus seasonal noise model or the seasonal specific irregular model, January, February, and March are selected as the months with high variance, but the fits are not much worse if December is added to this group.

Notice that the grouping results for the Northeast and Midwest series generally suggest a simple pattern of higher variance in winter, with the definition of the "winter group" including more months for permits than for starts. The general pattern of higher variance in winter is plausibly due to the effects of unusually bad or unusually good winter weather on construction activity.

For the South and West series, $[\Delta\text{AIC}]_1$, while always negative, is smaller in magnitude than for the Northeast and Midwest series (with one exception in Table 2.1). Also, in some of these cases, notably for South permits and West starts (except for the seasonal specific trends model of West starts), the month groupings do not suggest a simple explanation, as the groupings appear somewhat random. Given that the month groupings were selected to minimize the AICs for the heteroskedastic models, there is some doubt about whether these results suggest that heteroskedasticity is really present. (As noted earlier, we shall revisit this issue in Section 2.5.) The $[\Delta\text{AIC}]_2$ values for the South and West series are mostly small, suggesting that their month groupings are not very precisely determined.

Also note that there is considerable consistency between the groupings chosen for the airline plus seasonal noise and the seasonal specific irregular models (for a given series), with the grouping from the seasonal specific trends model showing more differences.

We checked the performance of the search algorithm by estimating the models for all possible groupings for each of the 24 cases. The optimal grouping (lowest AIC) was found with just single month switches for seven out of eight series for the seasonal specific trends and seasonal specific irregular models, and for six out of eight series for the airline plus seasonal noise model. In each of the remaining cases, the optimal grouping was found after just one double switch check.

As a consistency check, we applied the search algorithm to the data for the testing period, and got very similar results for the decisive groups, i.e., the winter months were again selected as high variance for the Midwest and Northeast. The results changed somewhat for some of the South and West series. This is not surprising, because for some of these series the heteroskedastic models did not improve the fits so dramatically over the homoskedastic models.

2.4 Finite Sample Behavior of Likelihood Ratio Tests for Seasonal Heteroskedasticity

Given a grouping of months, likelihood ratio tests can be applied for the three models under consideration to test for the presence of seasonal heteroskedasticity. For the seasonal specific trends model (2.2.1), the hypothesis to be tested is H_0: $\sigma^2_{\eta*I} = \sigma^2_{\eta*II}$, and the corresponding hypothesis for the seasonal specific irregular model (2.2.5) is H_0: $\sigma^2_{\varepsilon*I} = \sigma^2_{\varepsilon*II}$. For the airline plus seasonal noise model (2.2.3), the hypothesis to be tested is H_0: $\sigma^2_{\varepsilon} = 0$. For any of these models, denoting the maximized likelihood from estimation of the model under the null hypothesis (homoskedastic model) as $\hat{L}_0$, and that from the unrestricted model as $\hat{L}$, the likelihood ratio test statistic is $LR = -2(\log \hat{L}_0 - \log \hat{L})$. For all three models, the hypotheses to be tested imply one restriction on the model parameters, so that standard asymptotic results for ML estimates would suggest comparing LR with a critical value from a chi-squared distribution with one degree of freedom. In this section, we use simulation to examine the finite sample null distributions of these LR tests in time series with specified lengths (10 or 20 years), month groupings, and values of the model parameters.

One issue with the finite sample performance of the LR tests is that there may be positive probability of the ML estimates satisfying the homoskedasticity constraint, thus yielding zero for the LR test statistic and potentially affecting its finite sample distribution. For the two versions of Proietti's model, homoskedastic fitted models can arise in practice from obtaining $\hat{\sigma}^2_{\eta*I} = \hat{\sigma}^2_{\eta*II} = 0$ or $\hat{\sigma}^2_{\varepsilon*I} = \hat{\sigma}^2_{\varepsilon*II} = 0$, respectively, since estimates of zero for variance components are fairly common in component models—see Tanaka (1996, section 8.7) and Shephard (1993). Assuming that the true values of these variances are positive, this problem should disappear as $T \to \infty$, but it may affect the finite sample distribution of LR.

The situation for Bell's model (2.2.3) is somewhat different. The null hypothesis of homoskedasticity for this model constrains σ^2_ε to be on the boundary of the parameter space ($\sigma^2_\varepsilon = 0$). For the case of independent observations, Self and Liang (1987), extending the results of Chernoff (1954), provide general results on the asymptotic distribution of ML estimates and LR statistics when the parameters are on the boundary. For testing whether a single parameter is on the boundary with other (nuisance) parameters away from the boundary (Self and Liang's Case 5), they show that the asymptotic distribution of LR is $\frac{1}{2}\chi^2_0 + \frac{1}{2}\chi^2_1$, where $\chi^2_0 = 0$ with probability 1. Harvey (1989, 236–37) discusses application of such results to time series component models related to those considered here. Following this prescription, for Bell's model (2.2.3), we assume that the null distribution of LR can be approximated by the $\frac{1}{2}\chi^2_0 + \frac{1}{2}\chi^2_1$ distribution. Thus, to perform a 5% test with model (2.2.3), we would compare LR with the 10% critical value from the χ^2_1 distribution, which is 2.71.*

We used simulation to assess the finite sample null distribution of LR for each of the models. For all three models, we considered four cases of the group of high variance months: January only, January and February, January to April (first four), and January to June (first six). For each given model, we simulated a large number J of series from the null (homoskedastic) model, estimated both the null and heteroskedastic models by ML, and computed LR. We then examined the distribution of LR across the simulations. In simulating the series, the disturbance terms in the models were assumed to be normally distributed. The iterations to maximize the likelihood of a model started with initial values of parameters set to the true values—those used to generate the simulated series. To help ensure that we had reached the global, and not a local, maximum of the likelihood, for each model the maximization was repeated with two alternative sets of initial values different from the true values, and the fit with the largest likelihood value was used. Occasionally, use of the alternative starting values led to an improvement in log-likelihood,

* For Proietti's models, homoskedasticity (from $\sigma^2_{\eta*I} = \sigma^2_{\eta*II}$ or $\sigma^2_{\varepsilon*I} = \sigma^2_{\varepsilon*II}$) does not require the variances to be zero, so the null hypothesis does not constrain parameters to be on the boundary of the parameter space, and this issue does not arise.

and although the difference was usually relatively small, this strategy helped guarantee that the strict global optimum was computed in each case.

Tripodis and Penzer (2007) used simulations to study the size and power of likelihood ratio tests of seasonal heteroskedasticity for Proietti's (1998)'s basic structural model with the heteroskedastic extension of Harrison and Stevens (1976) seasonal, and for the corresponding model with a seasonally heteroskedastic irregular. They restricted consideration to the case of quarterly series with the first quarter having a variance different from the rest. For both models, they found reasonable sizes for the likelihood ratio tests with the asymptotic χ_1^2 approximation. The tests had good power in most cases when the variance differences were large and the series were of moderate length (20 years) or longer, but not surprisingly had low power when the variation in the heteroskedastic component was low relative to the total variation in the other components. Their simulation results are difficult to compare to ours below, because of differences in the model forms and their use of quarterly series.

2.4.1 Finite Sample Size of the LR Test for the Seasonal Specific Trends Model

To focus on the scale invariant dynamics of the model, we look at the variance parameters relative to the irregular variance, and so use the signal–noise ratio for the trend, $q_\eta = \sigma_\eta^2/\sigma_\varepsilon^2$, and for the seasonal, $q_{\eta*} = \sigma_{\eta*}^2/\sigma_\varepsilon^2$, by setting $\sigma_\varepsilon^2 = 1$. We set $\sigma_\zeta^2 = 0$ (so $\beta_t = 0$) for simplicity. We considered homoskedastic model estimation results for the permits and starts series to determine a range of parameter values to use in the simulations, settling on the values $q_\eta = \{0.1, 1\}$ and $q_{\eta*} = \{0.0002, 0.002, 0.02\}$. We simulated 20,000 time series for each of the six possible combinations of $(q_\eta, q_{\eta*})$ and for two series lengths: $T = 120$ (10 years of monthly data) and $T = 240$ (20 years of monthly data). We applied the model and performed the LR tests for the four patterns of high variance month groupings noted earlier. The simulation results are presented in Table A.1 of the Appendix.

Table A.1 is divided into two parts—one for $T = 120$ and one for $T = 240$. The first two columns in each part show the $(q_\eta, q_{\eta*})$ values, while the remaining columns show the results of the simulations for each pattern of the month groupings. The results shown are: $\Pr(LR = 0)$ (denoted $Pr(0)$ in the column headings); $X_{0.05}$, the actual 5% critical value (which can be compared to $\chi_1^2(0.05) = 3.84$); and $\Pr(Reject)$, the actual size of the test when using the χ_1^2 critical value. Monte Carlo uncertainty in the estimates of $\Pr(LR = 0)$ and $\Pr(Reject)$ is reflected in standard errors computed from the binomial distribution of the number of "successes," which gives $\sqrt{p(1-p)/20,000}$ where p is the probability in question. For reference, these standard errors are approximately 0.001, 0.0015, 0.002, 0.003, and 0.0035 for p values of 0.02, 0.05, 0.1, 0.2, and 0.5, respectively.

Examining Table A.1, we see that the lowest value of $q_{\eta*}$, corresponding to the least amount of monthly idiosyncratic variation in μ_{jt}, often leads

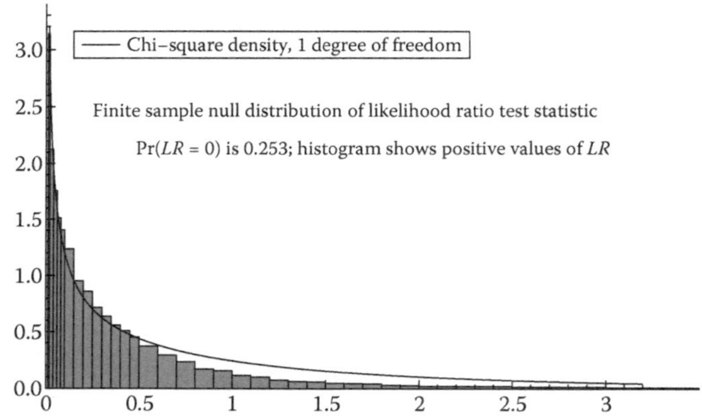

FIGURE 2.1
Null distribution of the LR test statistic from Proietti's seasonal specific trends model (2.2.1) with the January-only high variance month grouping, for the case of $(q_\eta, q_{\eta*}) = (0.1, 0.002)$ with $T = 120$ observations.

to substantial values of $\Pr(LR = 0)$. These values decrease as $q_{\eta*}$ increases and also as the length of the series, T, increases. Examining the values of $\Pr(Reject)$, we see that the LR test is often undersized, and by substantial amounts for the cases where $\Pr(LR = 0)$ is especially large. The corresponding actual 5% critical values are thus often considerably lower than the χ_1^2 5% critical value of 3.84. The results are somewhat better overall for the first four and first six month groupings than they are for the January-only and January- and February-only groupings, although these differences are smaller than that across different values of $q_{\eta*}$. In fact, the magnitude of the latter differences makes it difficult to specify approximate size-adjusted critical values, since the appropriate critical value obviously depends strongly on $q_{\eta*}$, which in practice will be unknown. This suggests that proper application of the LR test in finite samples for the seasonal specific trends model is difficult.*

More detail can be seen in Figure 2.1, which shows a histogram of simulations from the null distribution of LR for the January-only case when $q_\eta = 0.1, q_{\eta*} = 0.002$, and $T = 120$, along with an approximating χ_1^2 density. The actual 5% critical value of 1.60 (from Table A.1) is well below the standard value of 3.84 and, in the graph, the steeper decline of the density compared to the χ_1^2 is easily seen. (The bin widths of the histogram are narrower for

* An anonymous reviewer pointed out that fitting the full model (2.2.1) to simulated series for which the true slope disturbance variance was set to zero might adversely affect the properties of the LR test. We checked this possibility explicitly with some addtional simulations for which the fitted model also constrained the slope disturbance variance to zero, and found that this change had little effect on the results.

values of LR closer to zero to provide more visual detail; thus, the heights of the rectangles are set so that the areas of the rectangles all represent the relative frequencies from the simulations.)

2.4.2 Finite Sample Size of the LR Test for the Airline Plus Seasonal Noise Model

Estimates of the nonseasonal and seasonal moving average coefficients (θ_1, θ_{12}) for the standard airline model are nearly always positive (e.g., Depoutot and Planas 1998). Considering this, and considering estimation results for model (2.2.3) for the building permits and housing starts series, we chose the following parameter values for the simulations: $\theta_1 = \{0.3, 0.6\}$ and $\theta_{12} = \{0.5, 0.7, 0.9\}$. We set $\sigma_a^2 = 1$. For each of the six combinations of (θ_1, θ_{12}), and for each of the four different month groupings and two series lengths considered above, we simulated 20,000 time series from the airline model, this being the homoskedastic version of Equation 2.2.3, i.e., the model with $\sigma_\varepsilon^2 = 0$. We then computed the LR statistics for the simulated series, along with $\Pr(LR = 0)$; $X_{0.05}$, the actual 5% critical values; and the actual test sizes, $\Pr(Reject)$. For reasons discussed above, the latter were computed by checking if $LR > 2.71$, where 2.71 is the $\chi_1^2(0.10)$ value. Results of this exercise are reported in Table A.2 of the Appendix, which is structured similarly to Table A.1.

Examining first the values of $\Pr(LR = 0)$, we notice that, for the models with the first three patterns of heteroskedasticity, these probabilities slightly exceed 0.5, but for the fourth pattern (January–June modeled as high variance), they are not significantly different from 0.5. (Note that twice the standard error of these entries is about 0.007.) So the result from Self and Liang (1987) does appear to hold when there are six months in both the high and low variance groups, although it appears slightly off in finite samples when the high and low variance groups are of unequal size. Turning to $\Pr(Reject)$, we see that the LR test appears to be very slightly undersized for the January-only and the January and February only month groupings, about right for the first four grouping, and possibly slightly oversized in some cases for the first six groupings. (Twice the standard error of these entries is about 0.003.) But the deviations from the nominal 5% value are slight, and it appears that applying the test as suggested (using the $\chi_1^2(0.10)$ critical value for an overall 5% test) will yield reasonable results. If desired, the critical value used could be refined by making reference to the $X_{0.05}$ entries in the tables, say, by taking as critical values something like 2.4 for the January-only grouping, 2.55 for the January and February only grouping, 2.71 (the standard value) for the first four groupings, and 2.8 for the first six groupings. This inference is aided by the fact that, in contrast to the seasonal specific trends model, for the airline plus seasonal noise model there is not much variation in the critical values across different values of the model parameters—there is just some slight variation across the different month groupings.

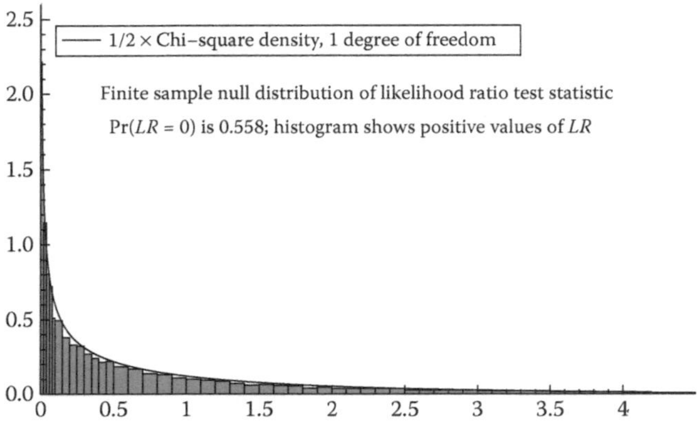

FIGURE 2.2
Null distribution of the LR test statistic from the airline plus seasonal noise model (2.2.3) with the January-only high variance month grouping for the case of $(\theta_1, \theta_{12}) = (0.6, 0.7)$ and $T = 120$ observations.

Figure 2.2 shows an example of an estimated density for the LR test with this model. This result is typical across different parameter values. Thus, with $T = 120, (\theta_1, \theta_{12}) = (0.6, 0.7)$, and for a single high variance month, the probability of getting zero for LR is slightly greater than one-half, and the density for values of $LR > 0$ appears well approximated by half a chi-squared density with one degree of freedom.

We also found that, for the parameter values used in our simulations, the null distribution of the LR test for the model (2.2.3) could be well approximated by the null distribution of the corresponding LR test statistic for the case of independent observations. If there are T independent observations of which n_1 are $N(0, \sigma_1^2)$ and n_2 are $N(0, \sigma_2^2)$, then this LR statistic can be written as

$$LR_I = T[\log(\alpha F + 1 - \alpha) - \alpha \log(F)],$$

where $\alpha = n_1/T$, $F = \hat{\sigma}_1^2/\hat{\sigma}_2^2$, and $\hat{\sigma}_1^2$ and $\hat{\sigma}_2^2$ are the usual ML estimators of σ_1^2 and σ_2^2. Under the null hypothesis $\sigma_1^2 = \sigma_2^2$, F follows an F-distribution with (n_1, n_2) degrees of freedom, so the null distribution of LR_I is easily simulated. Comparing the results from 10 million such simulations of LR_I with the results in our tables, we noted that, for the January-only and January and February only month groupings, the distribution of LR_I offered some improvement over the $\frac{1}{2}\chi_0^2 + \frac{1}{2}\chi_1^2$ approximation. Results for the first four and first six month groupings did not yield an appreciable improvement. Further study may establish that using the distribution of LR_I could also yield some improvement for the first three month groupings and for shorter series lengths or parameter values not covered by our tables.

2.4.3 Finite Sample Size of the LR Test for the Seasonal Specific Irregular Model

The null model for this case, Equation 2.2.5, is the same as that for the seasonal specific trends model, thus, the same simulated series were used. The simulation results are reported in Table A.3 of the Appendix. We first note that in all cases, $\Pr(LR = 0)$ is quite small Next, we note that the actual test sizes are mostly close to 5%, although for $T = 120$ they are not quite as close to 5% as are those for the airline plus seasonal noise model. Size distortions are largest for the January-only pattern and, while these are fairly small, they are not so readily corrected since they depend somewhat on the parameter values. Overall, though, use of the χ_1^2 distribution to approximate the null distribution of LR seems reasonable.

2.5 Application of LR Tests and Model Comparisons

This section applies the LR tests developed in the previous section to the set of monthly regional building permit and housing starts time series under investigation. We also use AIC to compare, for each given series, the fits of the three models. (As noted in Section 2.3.2, each series was logged and then adjusted for trading-day effects before applying the models used here.) The heteroskedastic models were specified using the month groupings given in Tables 2.1 and 2.2 that were obtained from the search algorithm applied to the "prior samples" (1959:1–1988:12 for permits and 1964:1–1988:12 for starts). The testing sample used here is 1989:1–2009:4 for both permits and starts.

2.5.1 LR Test Results

Table 2.3 shows the LR test statistics for the eight series under study, for each of the three models. For the seasonal specific trends model and the seasonal specific irregular model, these can be compared with the 5% χ_1^2 value of 3.84, although for the former model the size distortions shown in Table A.1 of the Appendix imply that the null distribution of LR is not well approximated by a χ_1^2. Nonetheless, Table 2.3 presents the LR values. For the airline plus seasonal noise model, the LR test statistics for a 5% test can be compared with the 10% χ_1^2 value of 2.71, as discussed in Section 2.4.

There is a good deal of agreement in the implications of the tests. For both permits and starts, nearly all of the test statistics are large and highly significant for both the Northeast and Midwest regions, the two regions for which we expect that unusually bad or unusually good winter weather could have significant effects on construction activity, leading to higher variance in the winter months. (The one insignificant LR test, for Northeast starts for the seasonal specific trends model, could be due to the tendency noted

TABLE 2.3
LR Test Statistics for Seasonal Heteroskedasticity for the Building Permits and Housing Starts Time Series

Series	Trend	Airline	Irregular
Permits, NE	**12.4**	**45.1**	**50.8**
Permits, MW	**81.0**	**84.6**	**95.6**
Permits, SO	0.0	**7.4**	**7.0**
Permits, WE	1.5	0.5	0.7
Starts, NE	2.6	**9.8**	**9.9**
Starts, MW	**17.5**	**42.3**	**33.9**
Starts, SO	**11.5**	**4.2**	**6.2**
Starts, WE	0.1	0.2	1.4

Note: The "Trend" column refers to the seasonal specific trends model (2.2.1), "Airline" to the airline plus seasonal noise model (2.2.3), and "Irregular" to the seasonal specific irregular model (2.2.5). Test statistics significant at the nominal 5% level are shown in bold.

in Section 2.4.1 of the LR test to be undersized for this model.) For the South region, all but one of the LR test statistics is significant, although the statistics are, with one exception, much smaller than those for the Northeast and Midwest. For both building permits and housing starts in the West region, none of the test statistics is significant.

Another interesting result in the table is that the values of the test statistics for the airline plus seasonal noise and for the seasonal specific irregular model are quite similar. Given that both these models allow for seasonal heteroskedasticity in the irregular, although the model forms differ in other ways, it is reassuring that inferences about seasonal heteroskedasticity do not seem to differ greatly according to the choice between these two different models. This is also consistent with the result noted in Section 2.3.2 that the selection of the month groupings was fairly similar for these two models. The test statistics for the seasonal specific trends model are more different.

2.5.2 Heteroskedastic Model Comparisons

Table 2.4 gives AIC values for comparing the fit of the three heteroskedastic models being investigated when applied to our eight time series. For the South and West regional series, we also include AICs for the three homoskedastic models, since the results of Table 2.3 show that the LR test statistics for these regions are smaller and, in many cases, insignificant.

Note that the validity of the AIC comparisons in Table 2.4 depends on the fact (noted in Section 2.2.1) that all three models apply the same differencing to the series, which here is $(1 - B)(1 - B^{12})y_t$. For the component models,

TABLE 2.4
AIC Values for the Three Seasonal Heteroskedastic Models for the Building Permits and Housing Starts Time Series

Series	Trend	Airline	Irregular
Permits, NE	−365.5	**−403.8**	**−403.8**
Permits, MW	−470.6	−480.5	**−485.1**
Permits, SO (heteroskedastic)	−553.8	−556.5	**−560.8**
Permits, SO (homoskedastic)	−555.8	−551.2	−555.8
Permits, WE (heteroskedastic)	−484.3	−480.3	−483.4
Permits, WE (homoskedastic)	**−484.8**	−481.8	**−484.8**
Starts, NE	−121.0	**−134.1**	−128.4
Starts, MW	−241.1	**−266.6**	−257.5
Starts, SO (heteroskedastic)	**−432.7**	−412.3	−427.4
Starts, SO (homoskedastic)	−423.2	−410.1	−423.2
Starts, WE (heteroskedastic)	−322.9	−314.2	−324.2
Starts, WE (homoskedastic)	**−324.8**	−316.0	**−324.8**

Note: The model with the minimum AIC value for a given series—the AIC preferred model—is indicated by its AIC value being in bold. The "Trend" column refers to the seasonal specific trends model (2.2.1), "Airline" to the airline plus seasonal noise model (2.2.3), and "Irregular" to the seasonal specific irregular model (2.2.5).

if $\sigma_\zeta^2 = 0$, we could actually reduce the differencing to $1 - B^{12}$ (and add a trend constant), while for the airline plus seasonal noise model, if $\theta_{12} = 1$, we could reduce the differencing to $1 - B$ (and add a trend constant and fixed seasonal regression effects). These situations do occur with the estimated models for a few of the cases considered here. In such cases, our application of $(1 - B)(1 - B^{12})$ will "overdifference" the series, although since this does not invalidate the model, we include AIC comparisons for these cases. It is also worth noting that the seasonal specific trends and irregular models both involve five parameters, so that AIC comparisons between them reduce to log-likelihood comparisons. The airline plus seasonal noise model contains four parameters, so its AIC "penalty term" is two less than those for the other two models.

In Table 2.4, the minimum AIC value for each series, indicating the preferred model, is shown in bold. For the Northeast and Midwest series, which appear to have strong seasonal heteroskedasticity, the models with heteroskedasticity in the irregular are preferred: the seasonal specific irregular model for Midwest permits, the airline plus seasonal noise model for Northeast and Midwest starts, and effectively a tie between the two models for Northeast permits. For these series, AICs for the seasonal specific trends model are substantially worse. For South permits, the heteroskedastic seasonal specific irregular model is preferred, while for South starts the heteroskedastic seasonal specific trends model is preferred. For West permits and starts, the homoskedastic models have better AICs than the corresponding heteroskedastic models, with the seasonal specific irregular and trends model being preferred. (Recall that their homoskedastic versions are the same.)

2.6 Conclusions

This chapter considered alternative time series models for seasonal heteroskedasticity: the seasonal specific trends model of Proietti (2004), the airline plus seasonal noise model of Bell (2004), and a variant of Proietti's model that moves the seasonal heteroskedasticity to the irregular component. We restricted the form of heteroskedasticity in the models to there being two groups of months with different levels of variability. We presented an algorithm analogous to forward selection stepwise regression that uses AIC comparisons to determine, for a given series, which months to assign to each of the two groups. We also examined, for given groupings of the months, the performance of likelihood ratio tests for the presence of seasonal heteroskedasticity. We used simulations to examine the finite sample distributions of such tests under the null hypothesis of homoskedasticity, finding appreciable size distortions for the seasonal specific trends model, but much better performance of the tests for the other two models. We also noted some differences in the distribution of the test statistics according to differences in the month grouping (e.g., a grouping with January alone distinct from the other months versus a grouping with January through June in one group and July through December in the other).

We applied our month grouping algorithm and the likelihood ratio tests for seasonal heteroskedasticity to a set of U.S. Census Bureau regional construction series (building permits and housing starts). For these series, we expect any seasonal increase in variance to be concentrated in the winter months. Results from the grouping algorithm were consistent with this expectation for the series for the Northeast and Midwest regions, the two regions most likely to show seasonal heteroskedasticity due to winter weather effects. The likelihood ratio tests then strongly confirmed the presence of seasonal heteroskedasticity in these series. While the tests also detected some evidence for seasonal heteroskedasticity in the South region, the evidence for the West region was more in favor of a homoskedastic pattern.

Acknowledgments

Special thanks go to David Findley for extensive discussion on this project. Tomasso Proietti is acknowledged for providing Ox code where the seasonal specific trends model was implemented for the Italian industrial production series; we developed programs to handle the seasonal specific model applications in this chapter by extending and modifying this code as needed. We also thank Tucker McElroy for his comments and for providing Ox code for the estimation of seasonal ARIMA models, and John Hisnanick for his comments on an earlier draft. Richard Gagnon is acknowledged for his assistance in using the REGCMPNT program, and we are grateful to Brian Monsell for discussion and information on using X-12-ARIMA. We also thank Kathleen McDonald-Johnson, who provided the construction time series used in the empirical analysis and gave important practical information on characteristics of the series and details of their seasonal adjustment. Thomas Trimbur is grateful to the Statistical Research Division of the Census Bureau for hospitality and financial support during his residence there as a postdoctoral researcher.

Appendix: Simulation Results

The following tables contain estimates of critical values and size for the LR test for the three different models when testing for the four different monthly patterns of heteroskedasticity. The estimates are based on 20,000 simulated series for each case.

TABLE A.1
Seasonal Specific Trends Model: LR Test for Heteroskedasticity, Simulations From Null (Homoskedastic) Model

		Months Specified in the Model as the "High Variance" Group											
		January Only			January and February			January–April			January–June		
q_η	$q_{\eta*}$	$Pr(0)$	$X_{0.05}$	$Pr(Reject)$	$Pr(0)$	$X_{0.05}$	$Pr(Reject)$	$Pr(0)$	$X_{0.05}$	$Pr(Reject)$	$Pr(0)$	$X_{0.05}$	$Pr(Reject)$
$T = 120$ Observations													
0.100	0.0002	0.373	1.35	0.007	0.340	1.61	0.007	0.320	1.90	0.007	0.312	1.95	0.008
0.100	0.002	0.253	1.60	0.009	0.245	1.83	0.010	0.210	2.35	0.013	0.203	2.44	0.014
0.100	0.020	0.016	2.38	0.014	0.014	3.17	0.029	0.011	3.70	0.045	0.011	3.82	0.049
1.000	0.0002	0.360	1.64	0.010	0.334	1.75	0.010	0.316	1.95	0.009	0.308	2.07	0.009
1.000	0.002	0.284	1.70	0.012	0.261	1.91	0.011	0.242	2.20	0.013	0.235	2.29	0.012
1.000	0.020	0.037	2.27	0.017	0.030	2.87	0.022	0.027	3.42	0.038	0.025	3.74	0.047
$T = 240$ Observations													
0.100	0.0002	0.324	1.44	0.008	0.298	1.61	0.008	0.282	1.89	0.007	0.278	1.98	0.006
0.100	0.002	0.066	1.97	0.013	0.062	2.46	0.016	0.051	3.03	0.025	0.049	3.17	0.028
0.100	0.020	0.002	3.28	0.028	0.001	4.00	0.057	0.002	4.21	0.061	0.002	4.08	0.058
1.000	0.0002	0.336	1.58	0.009	0.410	1.50	0.007	0.384	1.72	0.005	0.383	1.86	0.005
1.000	0.002	0.117	1.93	0.013	0.106	2.28	0.015	0.096	2.72	0.018	0.095	2.86	0.021
1.000	0.020	0.002	2.89	0.020	0.001	3.78	0.048	0.001	4.09	0.058	0.001	4.19	0.060

Notes: $q_\eta = \sigma_\eta^2/\sigma_\varepsilon^2$ and $q_{\eta*} = \sigma_{\eta*}^2/\sigma_\varepsilon^2$ are the variance ratios for the homoskedastic seasonal specific trends model with $\sigma_\varsigma^2 = 0$. The other entries give results from values of the LR test statistic for heteroskedasticity obtained from 20,000 simulated series: $Pr(0)$ gives the estimated probability that LR is zero, $X_{0.05}$ gives the empirically determined 5% critical value, and $Pr(Reject)$ gives the actual size of the test when the asymptotic χ_1^2 5% critical value (3.84) is used.

TABLE A.2
Airline Plus Seasonal Noise Model: LR Test for Heteroskedasticity, Simulations From Null (Homoskedastic) Model

		Months Specified in the Model as the "High Variance" Group											
		January Only			January and February			January–April			January–June		
θ_1	θ_{12}	$Pr(0)$	$X_{0.05}$	$Pr(Reject)$	$Pr(0)$	$X_{0.05}$	$Pr(Reject)$	$Pr(0)$	$X_{0.05}$	$Pr(Reject)$	$Pr(0)$	$X_{0.05}$	$Pr(Reject)$
$T = 120$ Observations													
0.3	0.5	0.562	2.36	0.040	0.547	2.54	0.045	0.520	2.71	0.050	0.505	2.77	0.052
0.3	0.7	0.555	2.39	0.041	0.539	2.53	0.045	0.513	2.80	0.053	0.501	2.91	0.057
0.3	0.9	0.553	2.45	0.043	0.532	2.63	0.047	0.514	2.88	0.055	0.501	3.02	0.059
0.6	0.5	0.560	2.41	0.041	0.537	2.55	0.046	0.517	2.65	0.049	0.504	2.93	0.057
0.6	0.7	0.558	2.33	0.040	0.533	2.57	0.046	0.514	2.68	0.049	0.503	2.77	0.052
0.6	0.9	0.554	2.49	0.043	0.533	2.59	0.045	0.515	2.65	0.048	0.503	2.76	0.052
$T = 240$ Observations													
0.3	0.5	0.540	2.50	0.044	0.527	2.59	0.046	0.518	2.72	0.050	0.503	2.74	0.051
0.3	0.7	0.538	2.47	0.043	0.525	2.52	0.045	0.512	2.62	0.048	0.503	2.78	0.052
0.3	0.9	0.542	2.37	0.040	0.529	2.52	0.045	0.518	2.60	0.046	0.502	2.72	0.050
0.6	0.5	0.541	2.46	0.042	0.525	2.56	0.046	0.510	2.64	0.048	0.500	2.83	0.055
0.6	0.7	0.544	2.38	0.041	0.524	2.50	0.044	0.515	2.63	0.048	0.504	2.67	0.049
0.6	0.9	0.533	2.58	0.046	0.520	2.55	0.046	0.507	2.71	0.050	0.496	2.71	0.050

Notes: θ_1 and θ_{12} are the nonseasonal and seasonal moving average parameters for the homoskedastic airline model (without seasonal noise, i.e., $\sigma_\varepsilon^2 = 0$). The other entries give results from values of the LR test statistic for heteroskedasticity obtained from 20,000 simulated series: $Pr(0)$ gives the estimated probability that LR is zero, $X_{0.05}$ gives the empirically determined 5% critical value, and $Pr(Reject)$ gives the actual size of the test when the asymptotic 5% critical value (2.71, obtained from the $1/2\chi_0^2 + 1/2\chi_1^2$ distribution) is used.

TABLE A.3

Seasonal Specific Irregular Model: LR Test for Heteroskedasticity, Simulations From Null (Homoskedastic) Model

		Months Specified in the Model as the "High Variance" Group											
		January Only			**January and February**			**January–April**			**January–June**		
q_η	$q_{\eta*}$	$Pr(0)$	$X_{0.05}$	$Pr(Reject)$	$Pr(0)$	$X_{0.05}$	$Pr(Reject)$	$Pr(0)$	$X_{0.05}$	$Pr(Reject)$	$Pr(0)$	$X_{0.05}$	$Pr(Reject)$
$T = 120$ Observations													
0.100	0.0002	0.003	4.44	0.068	0.003	4.18	0.060	0.003	4.11	0.058	0.003	4.03	0.056
0.100	0.002	0.002	4.39	0.068	0.003	4.28	0.063	0.003	4.16	0.060	0.003	4.04	0.056
0.100	0.020	0.003	4.30	0.065	0.003	4.23	0.061	0.003	4.12	0.059	0.003	3.95	0.053
1.000	0.0002	0.001	3.71	0.045	0.001	4.14	0.060	0.001	4.06	0.057	0.001	4.03	0.056
1.000	0.002	0.002	3.66	0.043	0.001	4.10	0.059	0.001	4.11	0.058	0.001	4.09	0.057
1.000	0.020	0.002	3.52	0.039	0.001	4.02	0.055	0.002	4.06	0.056	0.001	4.09	0.057
$T = 240$ Observations													
0.100	0.0002	0.001	4.11	0.058	0.002	4.04	0.055	0.001	3.97	0.054	0.001	3.97	0.054
0.100	0.002	0.002	4.00	0.055	0.002	4.04	0.056	0.002	3.95	0.053	0.002	3.92	0.052
0.100	0.020	0.002	4.03	0.056	0.002	3.90	0.052	0.001	3.85	0.050	0.002	3.93	0.053
1.000	0.0002	0.001	3.93	0.053	0.001	3.98	0.054	0.001	3.86	0.051	0.001	3.91	0.052
1.000	0.002	0.001	4.01	0.056	0.001	3.97	0.054	0.001	3.97	0.054	0.001	3.94	0.053
1.000	0.020	0.002	3.83	0.050	0.001	4.01	0.055	0.001	3.91	0.052	0.001	3.96	0.053

Notes: $q_\eta = \sigma_\eta^2/\sigma_\varepsilon^2$ and $q_{\eta*} = \sigma_{\eta*}^2/\sigma_\varepsilon^2$ are the variance ratios for the homoskedastic seasonal specific irregular model with $\sigma_\varsigma^2 = 0$. The other entries give results from values of the LR test statistic for heteroskedasticity obtained from 20,000 simulated series: $Pr(0)$ gives the estimated probability that LR is zero, $X_{0.05}$ gives the empirically determined 5% critical value, and $Pr(Reject)$ gives the actual size of the test when the asymptotic χ_1^2 5% critical value (3.84) is used.

References

Akaike, H. (1974). A new look at the statistical model identification. *IEEE Transactions on Automatic Control* 19:716–23.

Bell, W. R. (2004). On regcomponent time series models and their applications. In *State Space and Unobserved Components Models: Theory and Applications*, eds. A. C. Harvey, S. J. Koopman, and N. Shephard, 248–83. Cambridge: Cambridge University Press.

Bell, W. R. and Hillmer, S. C. (1983). Modeling time series with calendar variation. *Journal of the American Statistical Association* 78:526–34.

Box, G. E. P. and Jenkins, G. M. (1976). *Time Series Analysis: Forecasting and Control.* 2nd edition. San Francisco: Holden Day.

Chernoff, H. (1954). On the distribution of the likelihood ratio. *Annals of Mathematical Statistics* 25:573–8.

Depoutot, R. and Planas, C. (1998). Comparing seasonal adjustment and trend extraction filters with application to a model-based selection of X11 linear filters. Eurostat working papers, Eurostat, Luxembourg. No. 9/1998/A/9.

Doornik, J. A. (1999). *Ox: An Object-Oriented Matrix Programming Language.* London: Timberlake Consultants.

Durbin, J. and Koopman, S. J. (2001). *Time Series Analysis by State Space Methods.* Oxford: Oxford University Press.

Findley, D. F., Monsell, B. C., Bell, W. R., Otto, M. C., and Chen, B. C. (1998). New capabilities and methods of the X-12-ARIMA seasonal adjustment program (with discussion) *Journal of Business and Economic Statistics* 16:127–77.

Harrison, P. and Stevens, C. (1976). Bayesian forecasting (with discussion). *Journal of the Royal Statistical Society, B* 38:205–47.

Harvey, A. (1989). *Forecasting, Structural Time Series Models and the Kalman Filter.* Cambridge: Cambridge University Press.

Hillmer, S. C. and Tiao, G. C. (1982). An ARIMA-model-based approach to seasonal adjustment. *Journal of the American Statistical Association* 77:63–70.

Jones, R. H. and Brelsford, W. M. (1967). Time series with periodic structure. *Biometrika* 54:403–8.

Koopman, S. J., Shephard, N., and Doornik, J. (1999). Statistical algorithms for models in state space using SsfPack 2.2. *Econometrics Journal* 2:113–66.

Proietti, T. (1998). Seasonal heteroscedasticity and trends. *Journal of Forecasting* 17:1–17.

Proietti, T. (2004). Seasonal specific structural time series. *Studies in Nonlinear Dynamics and Econometrics* Vol. 8: No. 2, Art. 16, available online at www.bepress.com/snde/vol8/iss2/.

Self, S. G. and Liang, K. Y. (1987). Asymptotic properties of maximum likelihood estimators and likelihood ratio tests under nonstandard conditions. *Journal of the American Statistical Association* 82:605–10.

Shephard, N. (1993). Maximum likelihood estimation of regression models with stochastic trend components. *Journal of the American Statistical Association* 88:590–5.

Tanaka, K. (1996). *Time Series Analysis: Nonstationary and Noninvertible Distribution Theory.* New York: John Wiley.

Tiao, G. C. and Grupe, M. (1980). Hidden periodic autoregressive-moving average models in time series data. *Biometrika* 67:365–73.

Tripodis, Y. and Penzer, J. (2007). Single season heteroscedasticity in time series. *Journal of Forecasting* 26:189–202.

West, M. and Harrison, J. (1989). *Bayesian Forecasting and Dynamic Models.* New York: Springer-Verlag.

3

Choosing Seasonal Autocovariance Structures: PARMA or SARMA?

Robert Lund

CONTENTS

3.1 Introduction

Many time series have some type of seasonality (periodicity) in their first two moments. While seasonality in the first moment is typically removed by differencing at the seasonal lag (or estimated and removed by subtracting periodic sample means), selecting the appropriate type of seasonal model for the autocovariances is a more involved issue. Here, we present a simple test to assess whether a periodic autoregressive moving-average (PARMA) model is preferred to a seasonal autoregressive moving-average (SARMA) model. The test can be used to check for periodic variances (periodic heteroskedasticity) or periodic autocorrelations. The methods are developed in the frequency domain, where the discrete Fourier transform (DFT) is used to check estimates of the series' frequency increments for periodic correlation. Asymptotic results are proven and the methods are illustrated with applications to two economic series.

Autoregressive moving-average (ARMA) models are stationary short-memory time series modeling staples (Brockwell and Davis 1991; Shumway and Stoffer 2006). A zero-mean ARMA(p, q) series $\{X_t\}_{t=-\infty}^{\infty}$ satisfies

$$X_t - \phi_1 X_{t-1} - \cdots - \phi_p X_{t-p} = Z_t + \theta_1 Z_{t-1} + \cdots + \theta_q Z_{t-q}, \qquad (3.1.1)$$

where $\{Z_t\}$ is zero-mean white noise with $\text{Var}(Z_t) \equiv \sigma^2$. Here, p and q are the autoregressive and moving-average orders, respectively; $\phi_1, \ldots, \phi_p$ are the autoregressive coefficients; and $\theta_1, \ldots, \theta_q$ are the moving-average coefficients. We assume that the autoregressive and moving-average polynomials, $\Phi(z) = 1 - \phi_1 z - \cdots - \phi_p z^p$ and $\Theta(z) = 1 + \theta_1 z + \cdots + \theta_q z^q$, have no common roots and that the model is causal and invertible. One can write causal ARMA solutions in the form

$$X_t = \sum_{k=0}^{\infty} \psi_k Z_{t-k}, \tag{3.1.2}$$

for some weight sequence $\{\psi_k\}_{k=0}^{\infty}$ satisfying $\psi_0 = 1$ and $\sum_{k=0}^{\infty} |\psi_k| < \infty$. Chapter 3 of Brockwell and Davis (1991) discusses these and other ARMA properties.

All nonunit-root ARMA series $\{X_t\}_{t=-\infty}^{\infty}$ are stationary in that $\text{Cov}(X_t, X_{t+h})$ depends only on h. The purpose of this chapter is to statistically investigate whether (or not) a stationary model is appropriate for the series in the first place. The alternative here is that the autocovariance structure of the series is periodic with period P:

$$\text{Cov}(X_{n+P}, X_{m+P}) = \text{Cov}(X_n, X_m), \tag{3.1.3}$$

for all integers n and m. Before we test this hypothesis, we need to review two variants of ARMA series, SARMA and PARMA, which have been used to describe seasonal time series.

3.2 SARMA and PARMA Models

Our goal is to test whether or not a zero-mean series has a periodic autocovariance structure with known period P. We assume that $\{X_t\}$ has short memory (this means that $\sum_{h=-\infty}^{\infty} |\text{Cov}(X_t, X_{t+h})| < \infty$ for all t). Constructing zero-mean short-memory data may require some preprocessing of the original series, such as subtraction of a periodic mean or trend, and/or differencing. Section 3.4 rehashes this point with applications.

SARMA models, which stem from Harrison (1965) and Chatfield and Prothero (1973) and were popularized in Chapter 9 of Box et al. (1994), drive a stationary ARMA equation at lags that are multiples of the period P in an attempt to accommodate seasonality. Specifically, a SARMA(p, q) series $\{X_t\}_{t=-\infty}^{\infty}$ satisfies

$$X_t - \phi_1 X_{t-P} - \cdots - \phi_p X_{t-pP} = Z_t + \theta_1 Z_{t-P} + \cdots + \theta_q Z_{t-qP}. \tag{3.2.1}$$

Written in terms of the backshift operator B, Equation 3.2.1 is $\Phi(B^P)X_t = \Theta(B^P)Z_t$.

Contrary to the seasonality implied in its acronym, SARMA sequences are actually stationary. Specifically, a SARMA(p, q) model is an ARMA(pP, qP)

model with most coefficients equal to zero. Hence, by ARMA theory, SARMA models must have unique stationary solutions. Another property of solutions to Equation 3.2.1 is that their autocovariances are zero unless the lag h is a whole multiple of the period P. This is easily inferred from the SARMA expansion (assuming causality)

$$X_t = \sum_{k=0}^{\infty} \psi_k Z_{t-kP}, \tag{3.2.2}$$

and the fact that $\{Z_t\}$ is white noise. As such structure is not frequently encountered in practice, many authors have modified the assumption that $\{Z_t\}$ is white noise to that of $\{Z_t\}$ satisfying an additional ARMA(p^*, q^*) recursion of form

$$\phi^*(B)Z_t = \theta^*(B)\epsilon_t, \tag{3.2.3}$$

where now $\{\epsilon_t\}$ is zero-mean white noise with variance σ_ϵ^2. Combining Equations 3.2.1 and 3.2.3 produces a single difference equation of ARMA form:

$$\Phi(B^P)\phi^*(B)X_t = \Theta(B^P)\theta^*(B)\epsilon_t. \tag{3.2.4}$$

Assuming no common roots in any of the AR and MA polynomials involved, one sees that $\{X_t\}$ is actually an ARMA series with autoregressive order $pP + p^*$ and moving-average order $qP + q^*$. While solutions to Equation 3.2.4 can have nonzero covariances at each and every lag, they are still stationary in structure. It follows that true periodic covariances satisfying Equation 3.1.3 cannot be produced from the SARMA model class.

A model type that does have periodic covariances is the PARMA class. PARMA models were introduced in Hannan (1955) to describe the seasonality in rainfall data and were further developed in Jones and Brelsford (1967), Pagano (1978), and Troutman (1979). Parzen and Pagano (1979) were the first to pursue PARMA economic applications. A series $\{X_t\}_{t=-\infty}^{\infty}$ is called a PARMA(p, q) series if it obeys the periodic linear difference equation

$$X_{nP+\nu} - \sum_{k=1}^{p} \phi_k(\nu)X_{nP+\nu-k} = Z_{nP+\nu} + \sum_{k=1}^{q} \theta_k(\nu)Z_{nP+\nu-k}, \tag{3.2.5}$$

where $\{Z_t\}$ is zero-mean periodic white noise. The notation adopted above emphasizes periodicity in that $X_{nP+\nu}$ denotes the observation from season ν of the nth cycle. The seasonal index ν runs from season 1 to season P. Periodic white noise refers to white noise with periodic variances—say, $\text{Var}(Z_{nP+\nu}) = \sigma^2(\nu)$. The PARMA equation is simply an ARMA equation with periodically varying parameters

$$X_t - \sum_{k=1}^{p} \phi_k(t)X_{t-k} = Z_t + \sum_{k=1}^{q} \theta_k(t)Z_{t-k},$$

where $\phi_k(\cdot)$, $1 \le k \le p$, and $\theta_k(\cdot), 1 \le k \le q$ are periodic sequences with period P.

Lund and Basawa (1999) show that solutions to Equation 3.2.5 are truly periodic in that they obey Equation 3.1.3 and have short memory whenever the model does not have a unit root. Notions of unit roots and causality in PARMA models are quantified through the P-variate ARMA representations of Equation 3.2.5 and are discussed in Vecchia (1985) and Lund and Basawa (1999). When the PARMA model is causal, one can express its solution in the form

$$X_{nP+\nu} = \sum_{k=0}^{\infty} \psi_k(\nu) Z_{nP+\nu-k}, \tag{3.2.6}$$

where $\psi_0(\nu) \equiv 1$ and $\sum_{k=0}^{\infty} |\psi_k(\nu)| < \infty$ for every season ν. Notice that X_t in Equation 3.2.6 depends on all prior Z_ts $(Z_t, Z_{t-1}, \ldots)$ and not only on $Z_t, Z_{t-P}, Z_{t-2P}, \ldots$. One should compare Equations 3.2.2 with 3.2.6.

Viewed collectively, SARMA and PARMA models are two ARMA-like models that are used to describe time series with periodic characteristics. Holan et al. (2010) discuss SARMA and PARMA models in more detail along with other ARMA model modifications. Often, the application or physical reasoning suggests which model type the practitioner should adopt. For example, in forecasting daily high temperatures (take $P = 365$) beyond a simple seasonal mean, physical reasoning would prefer the PARMA paradigm. In fact, if one tried to forecast, say, an April 5th temperature, then the most important predictands would be the most recent April 4 temperature (yesterday), April 3 temperature (2 days ago), etc., and not temperatures from April 5 of last year, April 5 of two years ago, etc. Indeed, daily weather forecasts have little predictive power beyond about 10 days. But what about a situation in economics, say, monthly housing starts ($P = 12$), where it is generally accepted that this November's observation is more heavily correlated with last November's observation than the latest October and September observations? This seems to suggest the SARMA paradigm. In the next section, a test for such situations is constructed based on the work in Lund et al. (1995). Section 3.4 applies the test to several simulated and real economic series.

3.3 Average Squared Coherences

Suppose that $X_0, \ldots, X_{N-1}$ is sampled from a zero-mean short-memory series with possibly periodic covariances with known period P. To avoid trite work, N is assumed as a whole multiple of P; i.e., $d = N/P$ is a whole number. Our objective is to test whether or not the series is best modeled by a SARMA model (our null hypothesis) or whether a PARMA structure is needed (our alternative hypothesis). The test statistics we devise is based on the DFT of the series, which is defined by

$$I_j = \frac{1}{\sqrt{2\pi N}} \sum_{t=0}^{N-1} X_t e^{-it\lambda_j},$$

where $\lambda_j = 2\pi j/N$ is the jth Fourier frequency and $i = \sqrt{-1}$.

Our test is based on the spectral representation for stationary and periodic series. Specifically, all zero-mean stationary and periodic series can be written with the harmonic (spectral) representation

$$X_t = \int_{[0,2\pi)} e^{-t\lambda} dZ(\lambda)$$

for some complex-valued process $\{Z(\lambda), 0 \leq \lambda < 2\pi\}$ (Loéve 1978). The frequency increments of $\{X_t\}$ are estimated by the DFT: $\widehat{dZ(\lambda_j)} = \sqrt{N/(2\pi)} I_j$.

It is well known that a series is stationary if and only if its frequency increments are uncorrelated (see Chapter 4 of Brockwell and Davis [1991] or Shumway and Stoffer [2006]). It is also known that a series has the periodic structure in Equation 3.1.3 if and only if its frequency increments are uncorrelated except "every periodic now and again." Specifically, series obeying Equation 3.1.3 have $E[dZ(\lambda_1)\overline{dZ(\lambda_2)}] = 0$ unless $\lambda_2 = \lambda_1 + 2\pi P/T$ for some $k = 0, \pm 1, \ldots, \pm(P-1)$ (Hurd 1991). Here, an overline denotes complex conjugation.

Phrasing the above concept in another way, if $\{X_t\}$ is SARMA, then its frequency increments should always be uncorrelated; however, if $\{X_t\}$ is in truth PARMA, then the frequency increments should be uncorrelated except for every periodic now and again. It follows that to test for a PARMA presence, one should check $\widehat{dZ(\lambda_j)}$ for nonzero correlations that occur every periodic now and again.

We now make this idea precise. Define the squared sample correlation of the estimated frequency increments as

$$\begin{aligned} \rho_h^2(j) &= \frac{\left| \sum_{m=0}^{M-1} I_{j+m} \overline{I_{j+h+m}} \right|^2}{\sum_{m=0}^{M-1} |I_{j+m}|^2 \sum_{m=0}^{M-1} |I_{j+h+m}|^2} \\ &= \text{Corr}\left\{ \begin{pmatrix} I_j \\ I_{j-1} \\ \vdots \\ I_{j+M-1} \end{pmatrix}, \begin{pmatrix} I_{j+h} \\ I_{j+h+1} \\ \vdots \\ I_{j+h+M-1} \end{pmatrix} \right\}^2, \end{aligned} \qquad (3.3.1)$$

where $M \geq 1$ is a smoothing parameter to be selected later. We take $I_j = I_{j-N}$ should an index $j \geq N$ be encountered. The above discussion translates into the following: if $\{X_t\}$ is SARMA, then $|\rho_h^2(j)|$ should be statistically small (approximately zero) for all $h \geq 1$ and j; however, if $\{X_t\}$ is PARMA, then

$|\rho_h^2(j)|$ may be significantly positive for some h that are whole multiples of $d = N/P$. Again, d is the number of complete cycles of observed data.

There are redundancies in the values of $\rho_h^2(j)$. In fact, N^2 values of $\rho_h^2(j)$ were made from N series observations. To summarize the squared coherences, we define the average squared coherence as

$$\bar{\rho}_h^2 = \frac{1}{N} \sum_{j=0}^{N-1} \rho_h^2(j). \tag{3.3.2}$$

The PARMA diagnostic test that we propose is now simply stated: plot the values of $\bar{\rho}_h^2$ for varying h. If one encounters large average squared coherences at *any* of the hs that are multiples of N/P, then the SARMA null hypothesis should be rejected. The next result quantifies how large an average squared coherence should be to be declared statistically large.

Theorem 3.1 *If $\{X_t\}$ is a causal SARMA series where the error components are independent and identically distributed with finite fourth moments, then the asymptotic normality*

$$\bar{\rho}_h^2 \sim AN\left(\frac{1}{M}, \frac{\eta_M^2}{N}\right) \tag{3.3.3}$$

holds as $N \to \infty$, $M \to \infty$, and $M/N \to 0$. The value of η_M is determined solely on the smoothing parameter M and not on any properties of the time series model or the distribution of time series errors.

Proof. We present an outline only because a full proof is technical, lengthy, and somewhat out of spirit with an expository book chapter. We build the result up, first establishing what happens in the case of Gaussian noise. Then, spectral density transfer results are used to handle the general null hypothesis SARMA case.

First, suppose that $\{X_t\}$ is Gaussian white noise. Then the DFT $\{I_j\}_{j=1}^{N/2-1}$ is an IID sequence of complex-valued Gaussian random variables (there is a qualifier to this below). In this case, $\rho_h^2(j)$ is known to have (exactly) the beta-type density

$$P[|\rho_h^2(j)| > x] = (1-x)^{M-1}, \quad 0 < x < 1, \tag{3.3.4}$$

for each fixed $h \geq 1$ and j (Enochson and Goodman 1965). Koopmans (1995, Chapter 8) lists the elementary properties of correlation statistics. Because each I_j has the same complex Gaussian distribution and I_j and I_k are independent when $j \neq k$, one sees that for a fixed h, $\{\rho_h^2(j)\}$ is a stationary sequence in j. In fact, if j_1 and j_2 are indices such that $|j_1 - j_2| \geq h + M$, then no DFT value used in calculation of $\rho_h^2(j_1)$ in Equation 3.3.1 is also used in computing $\rho_h^2(j_2)$. It follows that for a fixed h, $\{\rho_h^2(j)\}$ is an $(h+M)$-dependent strictly stationary sequence. Hence, the asymptotic normality in Equation 3.3.3 follows from an application of the central limit theorem for K-dependent strictly stationary sequences (Theorem 6.4.2 in Brockwell and Davis 1991). Observe that the mean of the distribution in Equation 3.3.4 is M^{-1}.

Now suppose that $\{X_t\}$ is IID but not Gaussian and that $E[X_t^4] < \infty$. Under these conditions, the DFT is asymptotically complex Gaussian. To see this, use Proposition 10.3.2 in Brockwell and Davis (1991) or alternatively verify the classical Lindeberg conditions of asymptotic normality. Hence, in this case, the asymptotic normality quoted in Equation 3.3.3 is again seen to hold.

Finally, suppose that $\{X_t\}$ can be written as $X_t = \sum_{k=0}^{\infty} \psi_k Z_{t-k}$, where $\sum_{k=0}^{\infty} k|\psi_k| < \infty$ and $\{Z_t\}$ is IID with finite fourth moments. The summability $\sum_{k=0}^{\infty} k|\psi_k| < \infty$ holds under the causal SARMA null hypothesis. Equation 10.3.12 in Brockwell and Davis (1991) relates the DFT of $\{X_t\}$ and $\{Z_t\}$ via

$$I_{X,j} = \psi(e^{-i\lambda_j})I_{Z,j} + D(\lambda_j), \tag{3.3.5}$$

where $\{D(\lambda_k)\}$ are error terms and the notation has used

$$I_{X,k} = \sum_{t=0}^{N-1} X_t e^{-it\lambda_k}, \quad I_{Z,k} = \sum_{t=0}^{N-1} Z_t e^{-it\lambda_k},$$

with $\psi(z) = \sum_{k=0}^{\infty} \psi_k z^k$. The error term in Equation 3.3.5 is known to be uniform in that

$$\max_{0 \le j \le N-1} E[|D(\lambda_j)|^2] = O(N^{-1}). \tag{3.3.6}$$

Under the null hypothesis of a causal SARMA structure, $\psi(z)$ is continuous in z (in fact, it is infinitely differentiable) and is bounded away from zero inside and on the complex unit circle. Hence,

$$\begin{aligned}
&\text{Corr}\left\{\begin{pmatrix} I_{X,j} \\ I_{X,j+1} \\ \vdots \\ I_{X,j+M-1} \end{pmatrix}, \begin{pmatrix} I_{X,j-h} \\ I_{X,j+h+1} \\ \vdots \\ I_{X,j-h+M-1} \end{pmatrix}\right\}^2 \\
&\approx \text{Corr}\left\{\begin{pmatrix} \psi(e^{-i\lambda_j})I_{Z,j} \\ \psi(e^{-i\lambda_{j+1}})I_{Z,j+1} \\ \vdots \\ \psi(e^{-i\lambda_{j+M-1}})I_{Z,j+M-1} \end{pmatrix}, \begin{pmatrix} \psi(e^{i\lambda_{j+h}})I_{Z,j+h} \\ \psi(e^{-i\lambda_{j+h+1}})I_{Z,j+h+1} \\ \vdots \\ \psi(e^{i\lambda_{j+h+M-1}})I_{Z,j+h+M-1} \end{pmatrix}\right\}^2 \\
&\approx \text{Corr}\left\{\begin{pmatrix} I_{Z,j} \\ I_{Z,j+1} \\ \vdots \\ I_{Z,j+M-1} \end{pmatrix}, \begin{pmatrix} I_{Z,j+h} \\ I_{Z,j+h+1} \\ \vdots \\ I_{Z,j+h+M-1} \end{pmatrix}\right\}^2 .
\end{aligned} \tag{3.3.7}$$

The last approximation above follows from the continuity of $\psi(\cdot)$ and the fact that as $N \to \infty$, $M/N \to 0$, meaning that the middle correlation in

Equation 3.3.7 is essentially a squared sample correlation between aX and bY for some positive constants a and b and some random variables X and Y—and this of course equals the square of $\text{Corr}(X, Y)$.

While the general idea is clear, there are issues that merit precise bookkeeping. First, the DFT $\{I_j\}$ over the full range $j = 0, 1, \ldots, N-1$ is not truly IID, even when the series is Gaussian noise. This is due to the conjugate symmetry $\overline{I}_{N-h} = I_h$, which implies that $\bar{\rho}^2_{N-h} = \bar{\rho}^2_h$. Also, the DFT ordinates at $j = 0$ and $j = N/2$ do not behave as the other DFT ordinates (Brockwell and Davis 1991, Chapter 10). However, since $M \to \infty$ as $N \to \infty$, these two edge terms are asymptotically negligible in a squared correlation. The conjugate symmetry structure is easily dealt with in a sample average—the effective sample size is merely $N/2$. Also, the approximations made should be justified in rigor. For example, the error induced by the first approximation in Equation 3.3.7 can be bounded with the Cauchy–Schwarz inequality, the fact that $\psi(z)$ is bounded away from zero inside and on the complex unit circle, and the bound in Equation 3.3.6. The error in the second approximation in Equation 3.3.7 involves the fact that the squared correlation is continuous in its arguments. Another issue for rigorization lies with how non-Gaussian the DFT is for IID non-Gaussian series when $E[X_t^4] < \infty$. □

Table 3.1 lists values of η_M for varying M and were obtained by simulating Gaussian white noise akin to Lund et al. (1995).

In spirit, Theorem 3.1 shows how to distinguish SARMA and PARMA dynamics: look for large values of $\bar{\rho}^2_h$ at hs that are multiples of d. While such a graphical procedure does not give a formal level-α test, one could attempt to construct a conservative test from a Bonferroni procedure involving $\bar{\rho}^2_h$ at all hs that are multiples of d. Another approach for constructing a definitive level-α test lies with deriving the joint asymptotic distribution of the $\bar{\rho}^2_h$s at all hs that are whole multiples of d. Unfortunately, quantifying the asymptotic correlation between $\bar{\rho}^2_{h_1}$ and $\bar{\rho}^2_{h_2}$ when $h_1 \neq h_2$ does not appear easy at this time.

TABLE 3.1
Simulated Values of η_M

M	η_M
2	0.4310
4	0.4193
6	0.3971
8	0.3574
10	0.3369
12	0.3128
16	0.2728
20	0.2443
24	0.2276
32	0.1962

3.4 Applications

We first investigate how the test of the last section works on simulated series where ultimate truth is known. Figure 3.1 shows a realization of length $N = 240$ of a Gaussian SARMA series with $P = 12$. The model is Equation 3.2.4, where the chosen polynomials are

$$\Phi(B^P) = 1 - \frac{1}{2}B^P, \quad \Theta(B^P) = 1 + \frac{1}{4}B^P,$$
$$\phi^*(B) = 1 - \frac{1}{2}B + \frac{1}{18}B^2, \quad \theta^*(B) = 1 + \frac{3}{28}B - \frac{1}{28}B^2,$$

and $\sigma^2 = 1$. Here, the roots of Φ are $2^{1/12}$ (all 12 complex values of $2^{1/12}$), the roots of Θ are $(-4)^{1/12}$ (again all 12 complex values), the roots of ϕ^* are 3 and 6, and the roots of θ^* are -4 and 7. The second graphic in Figure 3.1 shows an average squared coherence plot with $M = 2$ for this data. The dotted line is a pointwise 99% confidence threshold for the average squared coherences constructed under a null hypothesis of a stationary SARMA model. As no large $\bar{\rho}_h^2$s are seen, one could have concluded that this series is SARMA without having known this *a priori*.

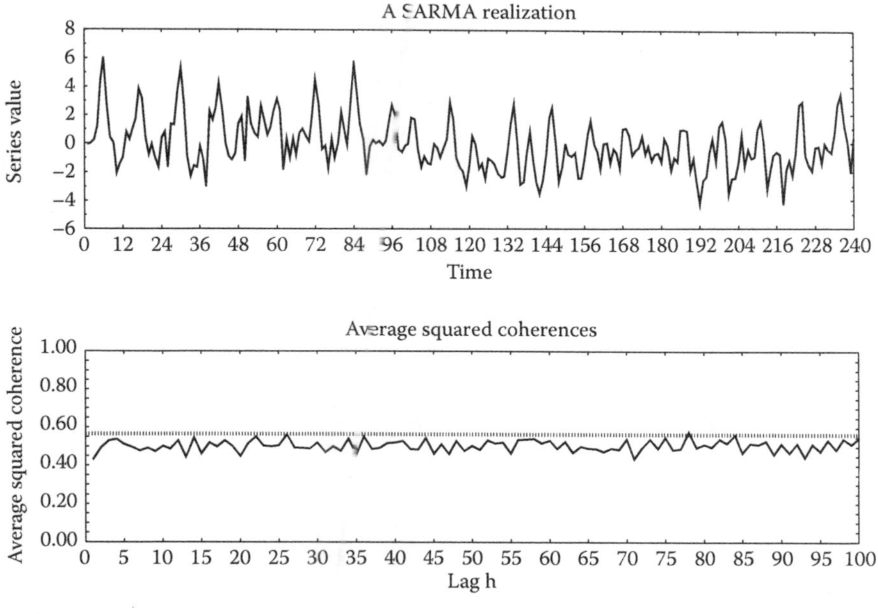

FIGURE 3.1
A SARMA realization and its averaged squared coherences. The dashed line in the bottom graphic is a pointwise 99% threshold for SARMA (stationary) dynamics.

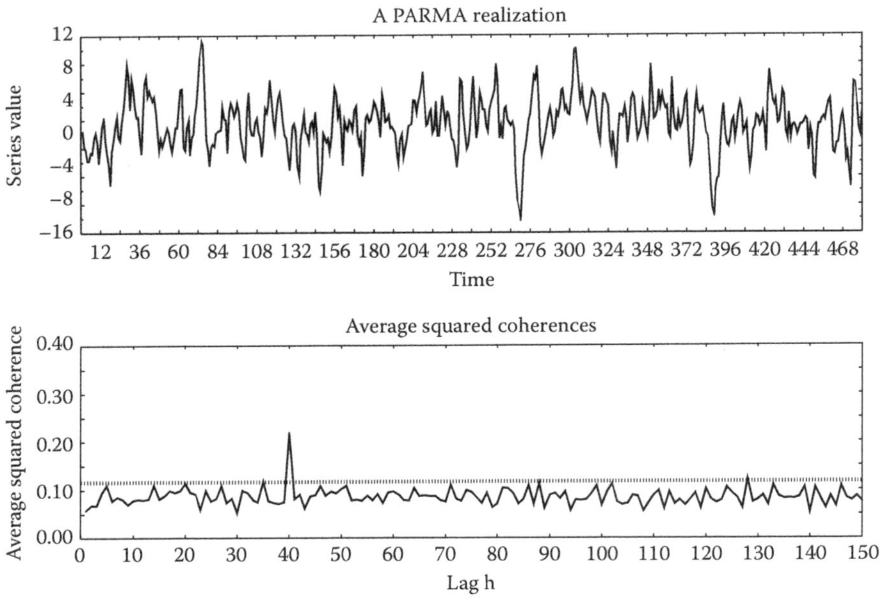

FIGURE 3.2
A PARMA realization and its averaged squared coherences. The dashed line in the bottom graphic is a pointwise 99% threshold for PARMA dynamics. The large exceedence at $d = 40$ suggests a PARMA model.

Figure 3.2 shows a realization of a Gaussian PARMA series of length $N = 480$ with $P = 12$ ($d = 40$), $p = 1$, $q = 1$, and model coefficients selected as

$$\phi_1(\nu) = \frac{1}{2} + \frac{1}{4}\cos\left\{\frac{2\pi(\nu-5)}{P}\right\}; \quad \theta_1(\nu) = \frac{1}{2} - \frac{1}{3}\cos\left\{\frac{2\pi(\nu-7)}{P}\right\}.$$

The white noise variances were chosen as

$$\sigma^2(\nu) = 5 + 4\cos\left\{\frac{2\pi(\nu+8)}{P}\right\}.$$

This model can be verified as causal. The averaged squared coherences in Figure 3.2 for $M = 12$ show a large value at $h = 40$, which is a multiple of the number of observed cycles of data. Clearly, the conclusion is that a PARMA model is appropriate for this series. One can ask why large averaged squared coherences did not appear at lags 80, 120, etc. When a series is PARMA, our results do not mandate that there should be large average squared coherences at all lags that are multiples of d; however, at least one multiple of d should have a large averaged squared coherence. A more detailed explanation lies with the location of the nonzero coefficients in the Fourier expansion of the

PARMA model's seasonal autocovariance structure, but we will not discuss this here.

Now consider a causal PAR(1) series with $P = 8$ and the parameters

$$\phi_1(\nu) = \frac{1}{2} + \kappa \cos\left\{\frac{2\pi(\nu - 5)}{P}\right\}; \quad \sigma^2(\nu) = 5 + \Delta \cos\left(\frac{2\pi\nu}{P}\right).$$

Unless $\kappa = 0$ and $\Delta = 0$, the model has PARMA-type dynamics. To study the power of the above methods in detecting PARMA-type structure when $d = 32$, we simply compare the average squared coherence $\bar{\rho}_d^2$ against its asymptotic distribution in Theorem 3.1 at level 95% with $M = 16$. As mentioned above, a more detailed test would consider $\bar{\rho}_h^2$ at $h = 2d$, $h = 3d$, etc. Here, we have selected an M that is arguably too big. Our motivation for this choice lies with demonstrating that the methods still work well when M is not chosen optimally. Table 3.2 shows empirical powers of PARMA detection aggregated from 1000 independent simulations for each pair of κ and Δ values. For example, when $\kappa = 0.2$ and $\Delta = 3$, the test rejects a SARMA structure (in favor of PARMA dynamics) 98% of the time. In general, the powers appear reasonable. When $\kappa = 0$ and $\Delta = 0$, the test erroneously rejects SARMA dynamics 7.6% of the time, which is reasonably close to the true asymptotic 5% type-one error. The powers increase with increasing Δ. This is because the seasonality in the series' variances increases with increasing Δ, which makes PARMA detection easier. Also, the powers increase with increasing κ. This is because the PAR(1) autocovariance structure varies more from one season to another when $\phi_1(\nu)$ varies more over ν. Lund and Basawa (1999) give expressions for the PAR(1) autocovariances in terms of the PAR(1) model parameters.

As the above methods have worked well on simulated series, we now move to data applications. In particular, we are curious whether or not the PARMA structure surfaces in economic series.

Figure 3.3 shows 14 years of monthly housing-start data for the United States during 1992–2005. Data for 2006 is also available but is not included because a major mean shift in the series is visible at this time, which is presumably due to the subprime mortgage crisis. The top panel of this graphic shows the raw data and the middle panel shows the data after removal of a linear trend and a seasonal mean (we refer to these as mean-adjusted residuals). One can, of course, use other tactics to preprocess the series to a zero-mean state.

TABLE 3.2
Empirical PAR(1) Detection Powers

	$\kappa = 0.0$	$\kappa = 0.1$	$\kappa = 0.2$	$\kappa = 0.3$	$\kappa = 0.4$
$\Delta = 0$	0.076	0.189	0.425	0.793	0.963
$\Delta = 1$	0.223	0.329	0.574	0.849	0.977
$\Delta = 2$	0.645	0.710	0.837	0.946	0.998
$\Delta = 3$	0.970	0.975	0.980	0.996	1.000
$\Delta = 4$	1.000	1.000	1.000	1.000	1.000

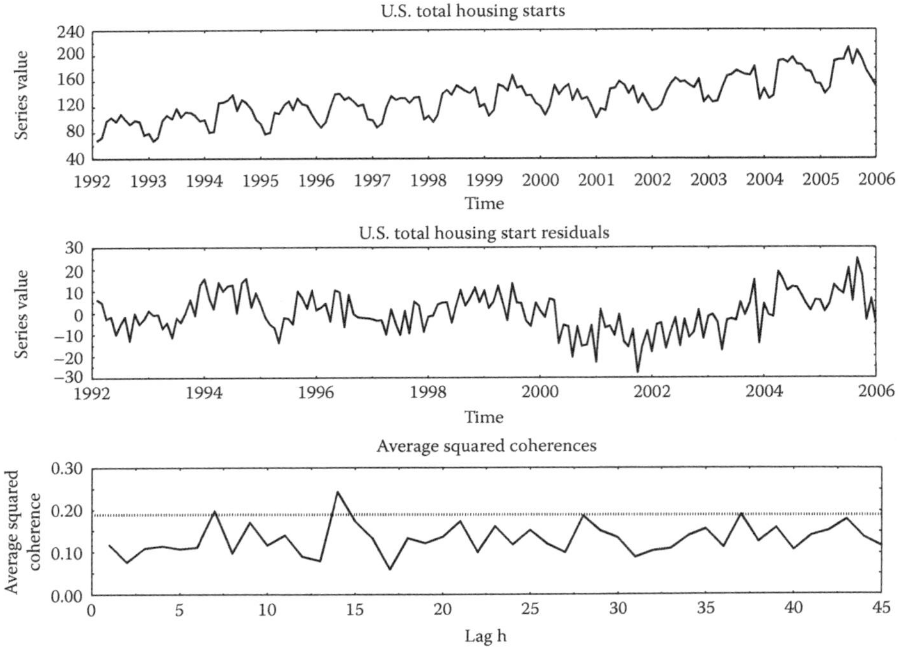

FIGURE 3.3
U.S. monthly housing starts, their detrended values, and average squared coherences. The exceedence of the 99% threshold at $d = 14$ gives evidence for PARMA dynamics.

The lower panel plots the average squared coherences of the mean-adjusted residuals and reveals a large value at $d = 14$. In fact, the average squared coherence at lag $h = 14$ was 0.2208 and has a p-value of 0.000274 exceeding $1/M$, where we have used $M = 8$. For comparison's sake, $\bar{\rho}_d^2 = 0.3592$ when $M = 4$ (p-value of 0.000366) and $\bar{\rho}_d^2 = 0.1610$ when $M = 12$ (p-value of 0.000641). The average squared coherence in Figure 3.3 with $M = 8$ also slightly exceeds the 99% threshold at $h = 37$. It is not clear why this is the case, but it could be due to the almost periodic structure of our Julian calendar (our calendar is not periodic in a strict mathematical sense) and the varying number of trading days per month. We refer to Hurd (1991) for a related topic called almost periodic time series. Overall, it appears that this U.S. housing starts segment has periodic covariances and that a PARMA model is preferable to a SARMA model.

One may ask in what manner the mean-adjusted residuals are periodic. We contend, akin to the conclusions in Trimbur and Bell (2008) for other related series, that our series has heteroskedastic variances. Parzen and Pagano (1979) suggest fitting ARMA models to seasonally standardized versions of

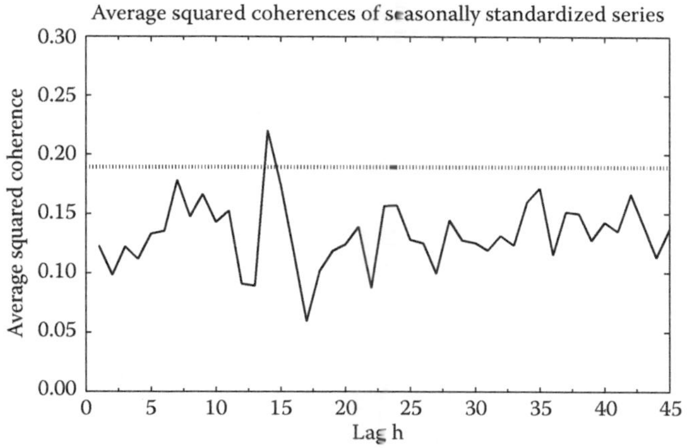

FIGURE 3.4
Average squared coherence of seasonally standardized monthly housing starts. The exceedence of the 99% threshold at $d = 14$ suggests periodic autocorrelations.

the residuals in financial series. However the U.S. housing start residuals are not well described by a SARMA model when scaled by a monthly standard deviation. To see this, the mean-adjusted residuals were divided by an estimate of their monthly standard deviation. Figure 3.4 shows the average squared coherences of this sequence. Observe that the large average squared coherence at $h = 14$ is still present. The implication is that the entire autocorrelation structure of this series is periodic and that a PARMA model is needed. As a tangential issue, one sees that our methods can be used to check for seasonal variances.

As a final example, we examine the $d = 15$ years of monthly U.S. inventories plotted in the top graph in Figure 3.5. These data are recorded from January 1992 to December 2006. Data for 2007–2009 were discarded due to an obvious changepoint presumably induced by the economic crisis. To obtain zero-mean short-memory data, we have fitted and removed a linear trend and monthly seasonal means. The middle graphic in Figure 3.5 shows residuals adjusted for this mean structure. The bottom graphic in Figure 3.5 plots the average squared coherences of the mean-adjusted residuals with $M = 8$. Apparent are large averaged squared coherences at lags 15 and 45, which are both multiples of d. In fact, the average squared coherence at $h = 15$ is 0.2272, which has a one-sided p-value of 0.0000623 of being larger than M^{-1}, and the average squared coherence at $h = 45$ is 0.2115 (a p-value of 0.000277 of being larger than M^{-1}). For comparison's sake, $\bar{\rho}_d^2 = 0.3681$ when $M = 4$ (p-value of 0.0000793) and $\bar{\rho}_d^2 = 0.1741$ when $M = 12$ (p-value of 0.0000491). Again, the series seems best described by PARMA dynamics. There is also a "small exceedence" of the 99% confidence threshold for the averaged squared coherence

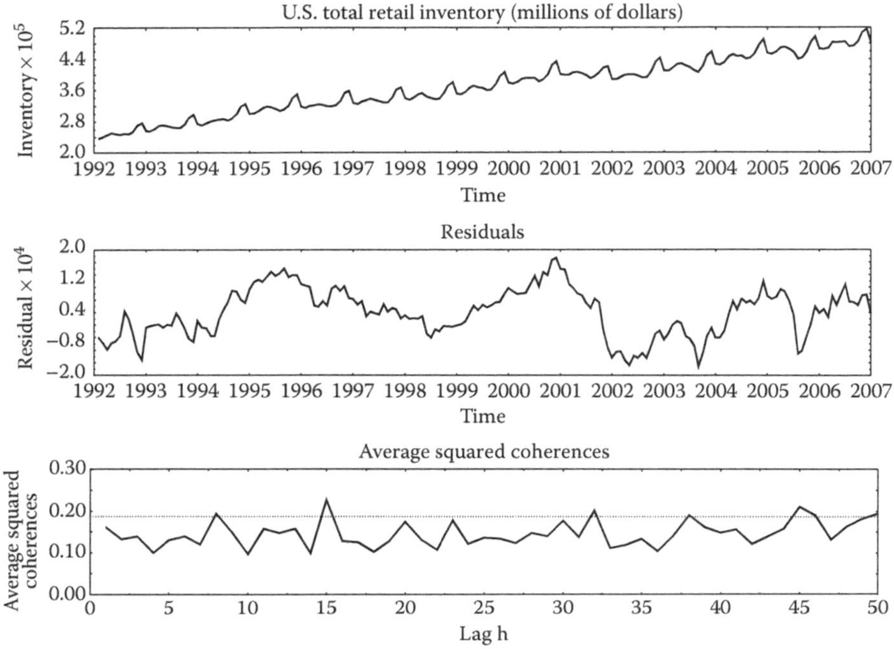

FIGURE 3.5
U.S. monthly inventories, their detrended values, and average squared coherences. The exceedence of the 99% threshold at $d = 15$ gives evidence for PARMA dynamics.

at $h = 32$. It is not known what to attribute this to—if anything—but it is conceivable that cycles exist in economic data other than that at the fundamental period $P = 12$. Figure 3.6 shows the average squared coherences of the mean-adjusted residuals after division by an estimated monthly standard deviation and reveals several exceedences of the 99% threshold. As with the housing start series above, it appears that the autocorrelation structure of this series is seasonal and that a PARMA model is truly needed.

3.5 Summary and Comments

The methods presented here allow one to infer whether a SARMA or PARMA model is preferable for a zero-mean economic series. From a modeling standpoint, SARMA models are advantageous in that they have fewer parameters than PARMA models, especially for large to moderate P. While parsimonious

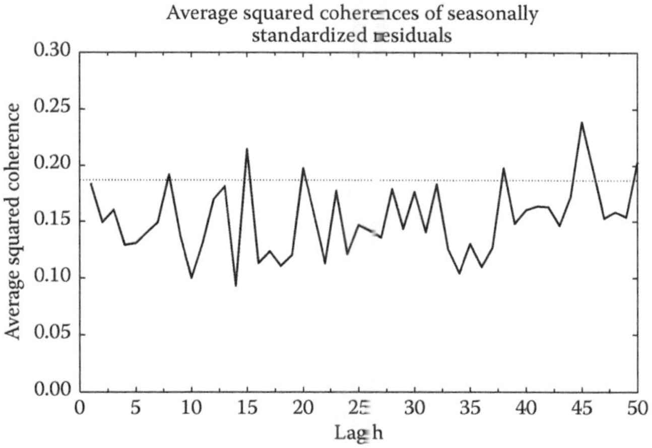

FIGURE 3.6
Average squared coherence of seasonally standardized monthly inventories. The exceedences of the 99% threshold at $d = 15$ and $d = 45$ suggest periodic autocorrelations.

PARMA models can be fitted (Lund et al. 2006), software for such a task has not been automated to date and the parsimonizing task remains somewhat laborious.

With economic series, one might want to test seasonal autoregressive integrated moving-average (SARIMA) versus periodic autoregressive integrated moving-average (PARIMA) models; i.e., repeat the above analysis allowing for a random walk component in each model class. Unfortunately, the limit theory presented in Theorem 3.1 breaks down in such settings. This problem seems considerably more involved.

We have not delved into selection of the smoothing parameter M. Indeed, there are smoothing reasons why one should not choose M too big or too small. While optimal asymptotic quantification of M (in terms of N) likely depends on curvatures and other structure of the P-variate spectral densities of $\{X_t\}$, practical selection of M is not difficult and reasonable advice is akin to histogram bandwidth selection: try a few values of M and see which ones work best (visually). As demonstrated in the last section, conclusions generally do not depend greatly on M.

Finally, while the mean-adjusted monthly housing starts and inventory series examined here showed PARMA seasonality with $P = 12$, other series examined—such as monthly unemployment and manufacturing indices—were far more complex and could not be adequately described by either PARMA or SARMA series. In some cases, long-memory components appeared; other cases involved spectrums where periodicities beyond the annual one were present.

Acknowledgments

The author acknowledges support from National Science Foundation Grant DMS-0905570. Comments from two referees and the editors helped improve this manuscript.

References

Box, G. E. P., Jenkins, G. M., and Reinsel, G. C. (1994). *Time Series. Forecasting and Control.* 3rd edition. Englewood Cliffs, New Jersey: Prentice Hall.

Brockwell, P. J. and Davis, R. A. (1991). *Time Series: Theory and Methods.* 2nd edition. New York: Springer-Verlag.

Chatfield, C. and Prothero, D. L. (1973). Box-Jenkins seasonal forecasting: Problems in a case-study. *Journal of the Royal Statistical Society, Series A* 136:295–336.

Enochson, L. D. and Goodman, N. R. (1965). Gaussian Approximation to the Distribution of the Sample Coherence. Online at http://handle.dtic.mil/100.2/AD620987.

Hannan, E. J. (1955). A test for singularities in Sydney rainfall. *Australian Journal of Physics* 8:289–97.

Harrison, P. J. (1965). Short-term sales forecasting. *Journal of the Royal Statistical Society, Series C* 14:102–39.

Holan, S., Lund, R. B., and Davis, G. (2010). The ARMA alphabet soup: A tour of ARMA model variants. *Statistics Surveys* 4:232–74.

Hurd, H. L. (1991). Correlation theory of almost periodically correlated processes. *Journal of Multivariate Analysis* 37:24–45.

Jones, R. H. and Brelsford, W. M. (1967). Time series with periodic structure. *Biometrika* 54:403–8.

Koopmans, L. H. (1995). *The Spectral Analysis of Time Series.* 2nd edition. New York: Academic Press.

Lo'eve, M. M. (1978). *Probability Theory II.* New York: Springer.

Lund, R. B. and Basawa, I. V. (1999). Modeling for periodically correlated time series. In *Asymptotics, Nonparametrics, and Time Series*, ed. S. Ghosh, 37–62. New York: Marcel Dekker.

Lund, R. B., Hurd, H., Bloomfield, P., and Smith, R. L. (1995). Climatological time series with periodic correlation. *Journal of Climate* 11:2787–2809.

Lund, R. B., Shao, Q., and Basawa, I. V. (2006). Parsimonious periodic time series modeling. *Australian & New Zealand Journal of Statistics* 48:33–47.

Parzen, E. and Pagano, M. (1979). An approach to modelling seasonally stationary time series. *Journal of Econometrics* 9:137–153.

Shumway, R. H. and Stoffer, D. S. (2006). *Time Series Analysis and its Applications: With R Examples.* 2nd edition. New York: Springer.

Trimbur, T. M. and Bell, W. R. (2008). Seasonal heteroskedasticity in time series data: Modeling, estimation, and testing. Research Report # 2008–11, U.S. Census Bureau.

Troutman, B. M. (1979). Some results in periodic autoregressions. *Biometrika* 66:219–28.

Vecchia, A. V. (1985). Periodic autoregressive moving-average (PARMA) modeling with applications to water resources. *Water Resources Bulletin* 21:721–30.

Part II

Estimating Time Series Components with Misspecified Models

4

Specification and Misspecification of Unobserved Components Models

Davide Delle Monache and Andrew Harvey

CONTENTS

4.1 Introduction

Time series model selection methodology is based on the premise that a model can be identified by analyzing the data and applying diagnostic tests to competing models. However, many tests, such as those for unit roots, can have high type I and type II errors in small samples, so the risk of choosing an inappropriate model can be high.

The specification of unobserved components (UC), or structural time series (STS), models is not heavily dependent on correlograms and unit root/ stationarity tests. For example, the basic structural model (BSM), which is widely used for forecasting and seasonal adjustment, consists of a stochastic trend, a stochastic seasonal, and an irregular component. A cyclical component, as in Harvey and Trimbur (2003), can be added and such a specification can usually be fitted more easily if the stochastic trend is constrained to be an integrated random walk (IRW). The fitted trend then tends to be relatively smooth. In fact, the continuous time version of the simple integrated random walk plus noise (IRWN) model yields a cubic spline; see, Kohn et al. (1992). In some situations it can be argued that the IRW trend is a more natural way of introducing flexibility into a deterministic linear trend than a random walk plus drift (RWD), so there may be strong reasons for wishing to use it.

If IRW trends are to be fitted on *a priori* grounds, questions arise about robustness to misspecification. In particular, there are concerns regarding how much is lost in terms of mean squared error (MSE) when components are estimated by filtering and smoothing, and how much is lost in forecasting accuracy. The first aim of this chapter is to provide answers to these questions for a range of STS models. Thus, having reviewed the statistical foundations of such models in Section 4.2, we move on, in Section 4.3, to investigate the effect of incorrectly fitting the wrong model. The main proposition in Section 4.3.1 extends David Findley's work recently published in McElroy and Findley (2010). Specifically, we analyze the effect of fitting a misspecified model of an order of integration different from that of the true data generating process (DGP). Then, we investigate the effect of incorrectly fitting an IRW trend. We also investigate the robustness of imposing a different constraint, namely, one derived from double exponential smoothing (DES). We also consider a different criterion to estimate the parameter values, namely, the cross-validation criterion.

Models consisting of trend, seasonal, and irregular components are a natural vehicle for seasonal adjustment. Section 4.4 analyzes the implications of misspecifications in the trend component for the estimation of the seasonal and hence for seasonal adjustment. It is also shown that, when the true model is of the UC form, the effect of fitting a seasonal autoregressive integrated moving average (ARIMA) model and using it for seasonal adjustment can be determined. Conversely, the effect of fitting UC model when the true DGP is a seasonal ARIMA can also be analyzed. The conclusions are presented in Section 4.5.

4.2 Stochastic Trends

The Gaussian *local level* model consists of an RWN model,

$$y_t = \mu_t + \varepsilon_t, \quad \varepsilon_t \sim N(0, \sigma_\varepsilon^2), \quad t = 1, \ldots, T \tag{4.2.1}$$

$$\mu_t = \mu_{t-1} + \eta_t, \quad \eta_t \sim N(0, \sigma_\eta^2), \tag{4.2.2}$$

where the irregular and level disturbances, ε_t and η_t, respectively, are mutually independent and the notation $N(0, \sigma^2)$ denotes normally and independently distributed with mean zero and variance σ^2. When σ_η^2 is zero, the level is constant. The signal–noise ratio, $q = \sigma_\eta^2/\sigma_\varepsilon^2$, plays the key role in determining how observations should be weighted for prediction and signal extraction. As is well-known, the weighting scheme is an exponentially weighted moving average (MA).

The local linear trend (LLT) model generalizes the local level model by introducing into Equation 4.2.2 a stochastic slope, β_t, which itself follows a random walk (RW). Thus, the trend follows

$$\begin{aligned} \mu_t &= \mu_{t-1} + \beta_{t-1} + \eta_t, \quad \eta_t \sim N(0, \sigma_\eta^2), \\ \beta_t &= \beta_{t-1} + \zeta_t, \quad \zeta_t \sim N(0, \sigma_\zeta^2), \end{aligned} \tag{4.2.3}$$

where the irregular, level, and slope disturbances, ε_t, η_t, and ζ_t, respectively, are mutually independent. Now the signal–noise ratios are $q_\eta = \sigma_\eta^2/\sigma_\varepsilon^2$ and $q_\zeta = \sigma_\zeta^2/\sigma_\varepsilon^2$. If both variances σ_η^2 and σ_ζ^2 are zero, the trend is deterministic. When only σ_ζ^2 is zero, the slope is deterministic and the trend reduces to a RWD, i.e.,

$$\mu_t = \mu_{t-1} + \beta + \eta_t, \quad \eta_t \sim N(0, \sigma_\eta^2). \tag{4.2.4}$$

Allowing σ_ζ^2 to be positive, but setting σ_η^2 to zero gives an IRW trend, which when estimated tends to be relatively smooth. The Hodrick–Prescott (HP) filter, which is widely used for detrending macroeconomic time series, can be computed as the smoothed estimates of the irregular of the IRWN model with smoothing parameter equal to $1/q_\zeta$.

It is also possible to restrict the parameters of the LLT model by setting $q_\zeta = (q_\eta/2)^2$. This yields the DES recursions and it can be rationalized as a discounted least squares estimation of a linear trend; see Harvey (1989, 27–8, 177). As with the IRW trend, the DES specification ensures that the slope is stochastic, unless the signal–noise ratio q_η is estimated to be zero.

UC models can be handled by putting them in state-space form (SSF). The general algorithms of the Kalman filter (KF) and the associated Kalman smoother (KS) can then be used to estimate components and make predictions. Furthermore, the KF yields the one-step ahead predictive distribution of each observation, thereby enabling a likelihood function to be constructed. Once the parameters have been estimated by numerically maximizing the likelihood function, the innovations (prediction errors) can be used for diagnostic checking. Standard models can be easily handled by the menu-driven STAMP package of Koopman et al. (2007). Intervention variables can easily be added to allow for outliers and breaks in the trend. The weights used to extract unobserved components are implicitly defined by the KF and KS. They can be displayed using an option in STAMP that is based on the algorithm in Harvey and Koopman (2003).

4.2.1 Specification

The LLT model is very flexible, with allowance made for changes in the level and the slope. Possible simplifications may be apparent when this general model is fitted. For example, if the estimate of the slope variance is zero and the slope itself is statistically insignificant, the trend may be reduced to an RW. However, matters may not always be so clear cut and there are a number of testing procedures that might be considered. Of course, choices can also be made on the basis of information criteria.

If the specification of the trend is to be simplified, careful consideration needs to be given to the following issues.

1. Should the forecasts contain a slope? If not, the RW is appropriate. With no clear prior guidance, the test of Busetti and Harvey (2008) can be carried out to see whether a slope needs to be included. The test does not discriminate between deterministic and stochastic slopes, but it is usually best to estimate the more general model, with a stochastic slope, at the outset. Further support for this strategy is provided by the results in Section 4.3. A unit root test of the hypothesis that the slope is stochastic, i.e., that the series is integrated of order two, is not recommended as the size can be seriously distorted; see, e.g., Harvey and Jaeger (1993). A stationarity test of the null hypothesis that the series is integrated of order one, that is the slope is deterministic, is not recommended either since, as will be argued later, making the assumption that the slope is deterministic when it should be stochastic typically leads to more serious consequences than making the opposite assumption.

2. Setting σ_η^2 to zero may be quite reasonable if it is felt that the extracted trend should be smooth. A likelihood ratio test can be carried out, but with the modification that the one-sided nature of the alternative requires that the 2α significance value be used for a test of size α; see Harvey (1989, 236–37).

The IRW includes a deterministic trend as a special case but, unlike the unrestricted LLT, it does not encompass models that are stationary in the first differences. As an illustration, Figure 4.1 shows an IRW trend extracted from seasonally adjusted quarterly data on U.S. inflation, as measured by the first difference of logarithms of the consumer price index from 1947(1) to 2007(2). Fitting the LLT results in σ_ζ^2 being estimated as zero. The level is plotted in Figure 4.2 and it is much more variable* than the level in Figure 4.1.

3. In small samples, it is not unusual for the maximum likelihood estimator (MLE) of the unrestricted LLT model to yield estimates of either σ_ζ^2 or σ_η^2, or indeed both, that are zero when there are no compelling arguments for this to be the case. There are technical reasons why this might happen. Shephard and Harvey (1990) analyze the RWN model and derive formulae for the probability that the MLE of σ_η^2 is zero. To our knowledge, a similar analysis for the IRWN model has not been carried out and we leave it for future research.

* Actually, a random walk trend is usually considered to be a more plausible model for inflation and a less volatile estimate can, in fact, be obtained by including a cyclical component in the model, as in Harvey (2011).

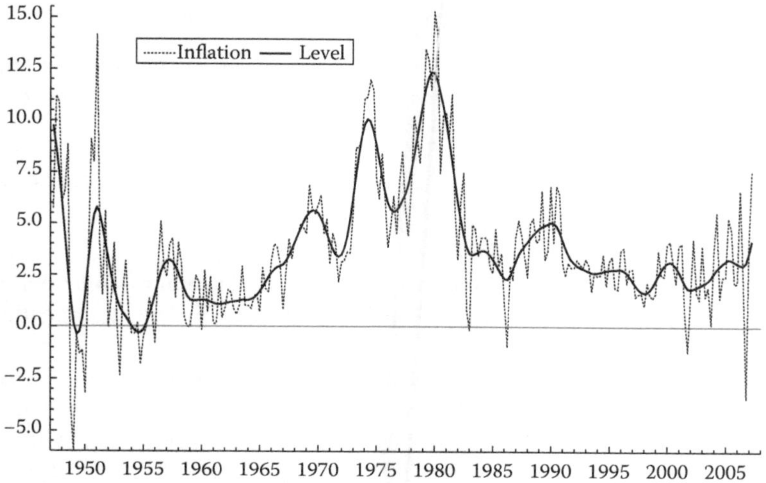

FIGURE 4.1
The IRW plus noise model is fitted to the inflation rate.

The constraint imposed by the DES specification seems effective in preventing the signal–noise ratios attaining zero. A standard likelihood ratio test of the validity of the constraint is possible; see Harvey (1989, 249–50).

One of the themes of this chapter is that robustness is a key consideration in model specification. Sections 4.3.2 and 4.3.3 investigate robustness issues surrounding the use of IRW trend and DES.

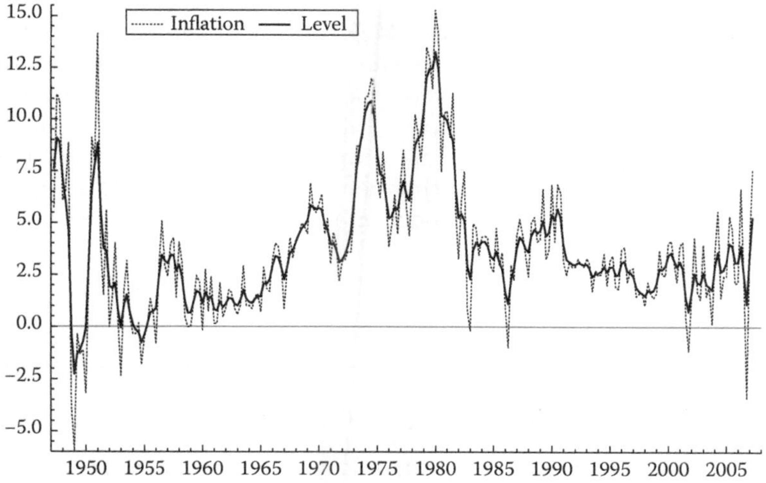

FIGURE 4.2
The RW plus noise model is fitted to the inflation rate.

4.2.2 ARIMA Models and the Reduced Form

An ARIMA(p, d, q) model is one in which the observations follow a stationary and invertible ARMA(p, q) process after they have been differenced d times. If a constant term, θ_0, is included, we may write

$$\Delta^d y_t = \theta_0 + \phi_1 \Delta^d y_{t-1} + \cdots + \phi_p \Delta^d y_{t-p} + \xi_t + \theta_1 \xi_{t-1} + \cdots + \theta_q \xi_{t-q},$$
$$\xi_t \sim N(0, \sigma_\xi^2),$$

where $\Delta = (1 - B)$ is the difference operator, B is the backshift operator, and the autoregressive (AR) and MA parameters are $\phi_1, \ldots, \phi_p$ and $\theta_1, \ldots, \theta_q$, respectively.

An STS model normally contains several disturbance terms. Provided the model is linear, the components driven by these disturbances can be combined to give a model with a single disturbance. This reduced form is an ARIMA model, and the fact that it is derived from a structural form will typically imply restrictions on the parameter space. For example, the reduced form of the RWN model is an ARIMA(0,1,1) model and by equating the autocorrelations of first differences at lag one, it can be shown that $\theta_1 = (\sqrt{q^2 + 4q} - 2 - q)/2$, where $q = \sigma_\eta^2/\sigma_\varepsilon^2$. Since $0 \le q \le \infty$ corresponds to $-1 \le \theta_1 \le 0$, the MA parameter in the reduced form covers only half the usual parameter space. On the other hand, the reduced form of the LLT model is an ARIMA(0,2,2) with MA parameters covering only a portion of the usual space; see Harvey (1989, 68). It can be shown that the reduced form models of the IRWN and DES are restricted ARIMA(0,2,2) with

$$0 \le \theta_2 \le 1, \quad \theta_1 = -4\theta_2/(1 + \theta_2) \text{ and } 0 \le \theta_2 \le 1, \quad \theta_1 = -2\sqrt{\theta_2}, \qquad (4.2.5)$$

respectively. For the IRWN model, McElroy (2008) derived an exact relationship between the reduced form parameter θ_2 and the signal–noise ratio q_ζ.

Models constructed from several components may have quite complex reduced forms, but with strong restrictions on the parameter space. For example, the reduced form of the model made up of trend plus cycle and irregular is ARIMA(2,2,4). Unrestricted estimation of high order ARIMA models may not be possible. Indeed, such models are unlikely to be selected by the usual ARIMA methodology.

4.3 Misspecification and Robustness

When a model is correctly specified, or is more general than the true DGP, the MLE $\widehat{\psi}$ is, in general, a consistent estimator of the true parameters, denoted as ψ. On the other hand, when the model is misspecified, and the true model is not nested within it, the MLE $\widehat{\psi}^*$, of the parameters ψ^*, may or may not converge as the sample size increases. If $\widehat{\psi}^*$ does converge to a value, denoted as $\overline{\psi}^*$, the algorithms developed in Harvey and Delle Monache (2009; HDM henceforth) can be used to compute the true MSEs of the estimated state and predicted observations at $\overline{\psi}^*$.

Let $\widehat{y}_{t|t-1}$ denote the predicted value of the tth observation, y_t, from fitting a misspecified univariate model. If variances, such as those in Equation 4.2.3, are expressed as signal–noise ratios, relative to the noise variance, σ_ε^2, then ψ^* may be redefined without including σ_ε^2. Following Harvey (1989, 126–27), the concentrated loglikelihood function for the misspecified (univariate) model is

$$\ln \ell_c(\psi^*; Y) = constant - \frac{T}{2} \ln \widehat{\sigma}_\varepsilon^{*2} - \frac{1}{2} \sum_{t=d^*+1}^{T} \ln f_t^*, \tag{4.3.1}$$

with

$$\widehat{\sigma}_\varepsilon^{*2} = \frac{1}{T} \sum_{t=d^*+1}^{T} \frac{v_t^2}{f_t^*},$$

where $Y = \{y_1, \ldots, y_T\}$ denotes the sample observations and $v_t = y_t - \widehat{y}_{t|t-1}$ is the one-step ahead prediction error, or *pseudo-innovation*, at time t, with $t = d^* + 1, \ldots, T$. The integer d^* denotes the number of observations required to get a proper initial distribution for the state. In the present context, d^* is the order of integration of the stochastic trend. The estimated variance of the pseudo-innovation, at time t, is $\widehat{\sigma}_\varepsilon^{*2} f_t^*$, where f_t^* is computed by the KF. For a given value of ψ^* in the misspecified model, the true prediction error variance at time t, denoted as f_t, may be computed by the algorithm in HDM.

The concentrated loglikelihood function must be maximized with respect to ψ^* to obtain $\widehat{\psi}^*$. Alternatively, dropping the constant, the following expression can be minimized

$$-2 \ln \ell_c(\psi^*; Y) = T \ln \widehat{\sigma}_\varepsilon^{*2} + \sum_{t=d^*+1}^{T} \ln f_t^*. \tag{4.3.2}$$

In large samples, f_t^* converges to a steady-state f^* (assuming that the misspecified model has an SSF that, in engineering terminology, is observable and controllable) and, following Harvey (1989, 129), it can be seen that the misspecified MLE effectively minimizes

$$S_T(\psi^*; Y) = \sum_{t=d^*+1}^{T} v_t^2,$$

which is the sum of squares of the true prediction errors.

In large samples, if $p \lim T^{-1} \sum_{t=d^*+1}^{T} v_t^2 = f(\psi^*; \psi)$, where $f(\psi^*; \psi)$ is the unconditional (steady-state) true prediction error variance* in the misspecified

---

* The asymptotic prediction error variance no longer depends on the sample observations, which are replaced by the parameter ψ of the true DGP.

model at ψ^*, then

$$\overline{\psi}^* = p\lim \widehat{\psi}^* = \arg\min_{\psi^*} f(\psi^*;\psi).$$

Following the terminology in Taniguchi and Kakizawa (2000, Section 3.2.5) and McElroy and Findley (2010), we call $\overline{\psi}^*$ the *pseudo-true value*. The following subsection explores the conditions under which $\overline{\psi}^*$ exists, with special emphasis on the situation where the orders of integration of the misspecified and true models are different. The remaining subsections study the consequences of trend misspecification.

4.3.1 Convergence of Misspecified Models

Proposition 4.1 *Let an $I(d^*)$ misspecified model be fitted to an $I(d)$ series, the ARIMA representation of which is $\Delta^d y_t = \beta + \{\theta(B)/\phi(B)\}\xi_t$, where $\xi_t \sim N(0,\sigma_\xi^2)$ and β is a constant. Assuming stable initial conditions, so that f_t^* is time invariant, the pseudo-innovation follows a stationary process with finite steady-state variance $f(\psi^*;\psi)$, if $d \le d^*$, namely,*

$$v_t(\psi^*;\psi) = \frac{\phi^*(B)}{\theta^*(B)}\frac{\theta(B)}{\phi(B)}\Delta^{d^*-d}\xi_t, \qquad (4.3.3)$$

where $\theta^*(B)$ and $\phi^*(B)$ are the AR and MA polynomials associated with the ARIMA representation (reduced form) of the misspecified model. It is assumed that these polynomials have roots outside the unit circle, as do $\theta(B)$ and $\phi(B)$.

Proof. Suppose that $d = 1$ and $d^* = 2$. Then, $\beta = E(\Delta y_t)$ is the drift. The misspecified model is $I(2)$, so has an autoregressive representation in second differences. Let the AR coefficients in this representation be denoted as φ_j^*, with $i = 1, 2, \ldots$, the one-step ahead forecast is

$$\widehat{y}_{t|t-1} = 2y_{t-1} - y_{t-2} + \sum_{j=1}^{\infty} \varphi_j^* \Delta^2 y_{t-j},$$

and the pseudo-innovation is

$$\begin{aligned} v_t(\varphi_j^*;\psi) &= y_t - \widehat{y}_{t|t-1} = y_t - 2y_{t-1} + y_{t-2} - \sum_{j=1}^{\infty} \varphi_j^* \Delta^2 y_{t-j} \\ &= \left(1 - \sum_{j=1}^{\infty} \varphi_j^* L^j\right) \Delta^2 y_t, \end{aligned}$$

from which Equation 4.3.3 follows. The proof may be easily extended to deal with other cases. □

Remark 4.1 If the misspecified model is an ARIMA(p^*, d^*, q^*) and the true DGP is ARIMA(p, d, q) with $d \leq d^*$, the pseudo-innovation follows a stationary ARMA$(p + q^*, q + p^* + d^* - d)$ process with variance $f(\psi^*; \psi) \geq \sigma_\xi^2$. In the case of correct specification, v_t is a white noise process with minimum variance σ_ξ^2. When $d = d^*$, then the process (4.3.3) is equal to the one-step ahead prediction error of McElroy and Findley (2010, 3657).

Proposition 4.2 *When $v_t(\psi^*; \psi)$ is a stationary process, as in Equation 4.3.3, with $E|\varepsilon_t|^r < \infty$ for some $r > 2$, then $p\lim T^{-1} \sum_{t=d^*+1}^{T} v_t^2(\psi^*; Y) = f(\psi^*; \psi)$, where $f(\psi^*; \psi) = E\{v_t^2(\psi^*; \psi)\}$.*

Proof. Hamilton (1994, 192). □

When $d < d^*$, the prediction error $v_t(\psi^*; \psi)$ is strictly noninvertible, as illustrated by the following example.

Example 4.1 Suppose an ARIMA(1,1,0) model is fitted to an ARIMA(2,0,0) process, such that $\psi^* = \phi^*$ and $\psi = (\phi_1, \phi_2)'$. The pseudo-innovation follows the (noninvertible) ARMA(2,2) process

$$v_t(\phi^*; \psi) = \frac{(1 - \phi^* B)(1 - B)}{(1 - \phi_1 B - \phi_2 B^2)} \xi_t,$$

and the pseudo-true value is $\overline{\phi}^* = p\lim \widehat{\phi}^* = \arg\min_{\phi^*} f(\phi^*; \psi)$. However, there is a closed form expression for $\overline{\phi}^*$,

$$\overline{\phi}^* = p\lim \widehat{\phi}^* = \frac{p\lim T^{-1} \sum_{t=2}^{T} \Delta y_t \Delta y_{t-1}}{p\lim T^{-1} \sum_{t=2}^{T} (\Delta y_{t-1})^2}.$$

Since $\mathrm{Var}(\Delta y_t) = 2\gamma_0(1 - \rho_1)$ and $E(\Delta y_t \Delta y_{t-1}) = \gamma_0(2\rho_1 - 1 - \rho_2)$, where γ_0 is the variance and ρ_1 and ρ_2 are the the first- and second-order autocorrelation of the true DGP, the pseudo-true value is

$$\overline{\phi}^* = \frac{2\rho_1 - 1 - \rho_2}{2(1 - \rho_1)} = \frac{2\phi_1/(1 - \phi_2) - 1 - \phi_1^2/(1 - \phi_2) - \phi_2}{2\{1 - \phi_1/(1 - \phi_2)\}} = \frac{\phi_1 - \phi_2 - 1}{2}.$$

After a bit of algebra, we obtain the prediction error variance at $\overline{\phi}^*$,

$$f(\overline{\phi}^*; \psi) = \frac{3 + \phi_2 - \phi_1}{2(1 + \phi_2)} \sigma_\xi^2.$$

In the simple case when $\phi_2 = 0$, so the true DGP is ARIMA(1,0,0), the pseudo-true value is $\overline{\phi}^* = (\phi_1 - 1)/2$ and the pseudo-innovation follows an ARMA(1,2) process with variance

$$f(\overline{\phi}^*; \psi) = \frac{3 - \phi_1}{2} \sigma_\xi^2.$$

Hence, when the true GDP is white noise, i.e., $\phi_1 = \phi_2 = 0$, the pseudo-true value is $\overline{\phi}^* = -1/2$ and the pseudo-innovation follows an MA(2) process with variance $f(\overline{\phi}^*, \psi) = (3/2)\sigma_\xi^2$. Finally, when the true GDP is a pure RW, i.e., $\phi_1 = 1$ and $\phi_2 = 0$, there is no misspecification and $\overline{\phi}^* = 0$.

McElroy and Findley (2010, 3661) showed that when an ARMA$(p^*, 0)$ is fitted to an ARMA(p, q), the Yule–Walker formulae give closed form expressions for the pseudo-true value $\overline{\phi}^* = (\overline{\phi}_1^*, \ldots, \overline{\phi}_p^*)' = \Gamma_y^{-1}\gamma_y$, where $\gamma_y = (\gamma_1, \ldots, \gamma_p)'$, with γ_k being the autocovariances of the true DGP and Γ_y is a $p \times p$ matrix with ijth element equal to γ_{i-j} for $i, j = 1, \ldots, p$. The corresponding prediction error variance, at $\overline{\phi}^*$, is $f(\overline{\phi}^*; \psi) = \gamma_0 - \gamma_y'\Gamma_y^{-1}\gamma_y$. The misspecified model and the true GDP are both stationary (or have the same order of integration), while our result includes cases in which the misspecified model and the true GDP have different order of integration. In the example above, the expression for the pseudo-true value, $\overline{\phi}^*$, is equal to the the Yule–Walker formulae computed for the differenced observations. In general, when we fit an ARIMA$(p^*, d^*, 0)$ to an ARIMA(p, d, q) with $d \leq d^*$, the Yule–Walker formulae still give closed form expressions for the pseudo-true values and the corresponding prediction error variance, computed from $\Delta^{(d^*-d)}y_t$.

Remark 4.2 McElroy and Findley (2010, 3662) consider the case of fitting an ARIMA(0,0,1) model when the true GDP is an ARIMA(0,0,2). Hence, $\psi^* = \theta^*$, $\psi = (\theta_1, \theta_2)'$ and pseudo-innovation follows an ARMA(1,2), namely,

$$v_t(\theta^*; \psi) = \frac{(1 + \theta_1 B + \theta_2 B^2)}{(1 + \theta^* B)}\xi_t.$$

It is straightforward to obtain an algebraic expression for prediction error variance $f(\theta^*; \psi)$; from this expression, McElroy and Findley (2010) are able to derive a formula for the pseudo-true value as $\overline{\theta}^* = \arg\min_{\theta^*} f(\theta^*; \psi)$.

The Appendix provides the analysis of misspecified models in the frequency domain. The consequences of having $d > d^*$ are illustrated by the following example.

Example 4.2 Let b be the MLE of the drift, β, in a random walk plus drift that is,

$$b = \frac{1}{T}\sum_{t=2}^{T} \Delta y_t = \frac{1}{T}(y_T - y_1).$$

When the true model is a Gaussian IRW, so $d > d^*$, b does not converge. More specifically, $\frac{1}{\sqrt{T}}b$ has a limiting $N(0, \sigma^2/3)$ distribution (and b diverges); see Hamilton (1994).

In Example 4.1, there is a closed form expression for the estimator of the parameter in the misspecified model together with the corresponding prediction error variance. This is not usually possible and the analysis of the following subsections is based on finding numerically the pseudo-true value $\overline{\psi}^*$. These values are then used to determine the asymptotic MSEs and the corresponding efficiencies of the misspecified model using the algorithm in HDM. The performance is based on an efficiency measure, which is the ratio between the MSE when the model is correctly specified and the MSE of the misspecified model. For UC models, we refer to different MSEs, associated with the prediction (one-step ahead), the filter, and the smoother of the state vector. Given a general SSF model with state vector α_t, the prediction, the filter, and the smoother are $a_{t+1|t} = E(\alpha_{t+1}|Y_t)$, $a_{t|t} = E(\alpha_t|Y_t)$, and $a_{t|T} = E(\alpha_t|Y_T)$, respectively, with $Y_t = \{y_1, \ldots, y_t\}$ being the information set for $t = 1, \ldots, T$. The corresponding MSEs are $P_{t+1|t} = E\{(\alpha_{t+1} - a_{t+1|t})(\alpha_{t+1} - a_{t+1|t})'\}$, $P_{t|t} = E\{(\alpha_t - a_{t|t})(\alpha_t - a_{t|t})'\}$, and $P_{t|T} = E\{(\alpha_t - a_{t|T})(\alpha_t - a_{t|T})'\}$. For large samples, the MSEs converge to their steady-state value; see HDM for a discussion on the convergence of the MSEs in case of misspecification.

4.3.2 Integrated Random Walk Plus Noise Model Fitted to a Local Level Model

Suppose that the true DGP is an RWN, as in Equations 4.2.1 and 4.2.2. The RW may contain a drift, as in Equation 4.2.4, but this makes no difference to the analysis. The misspecified model has an IRW trend. Hence $\psi^* = q_\zeta^*$ and $\psi = q$, where the signal–noise ratios have been defined in Section 4.2. The pseudo-innovation follows ARMA(2,2)

$$v_t(q_\zeta^*; q) = \frac{(1+\theta B)(1-B)}{1 - \{4\theta_2^*/(1+\theta_2^*)\}B + \theta_2^* B^2}\xi_t,$$

where ξ_t are the one-step ahead prediction errors of the true DGP, θ is the parameter of the restricted ARIMA(0,1,1) implied by the true DGP, and θ_2^* is the parameter of the restricted ARIMA(0,2,2) implied by misspecified model as in Equation 4.2.5. In all cases, it was found that the criterion function $f(q_\zeta^*; q)$ was concave with a global minimum* at $\bar{q}_\zeta^*$.

The first and second columns of Table 4.1 give the signal–noise ratios, q and $\bar{q}_\zeta^*$. In the third, fourth, and fifth columns, we report the relative efficiency of the trend for the misspecified model. The prediction has a stable efficiency of around 0.8. Since in this simple trend plus noise model, the prediction of the observation is the same as the one-step ahead prediction of the level, the efficiency of the prediction is then maximized (because the MSE of the true model is fixed).

The efficiency of the filter is greater than that of the prediction for small signal–noise ratios, q, but it deteriorates as q increases. This deterioration is

* The computations were programmed in Ox language and the function $f(\psi^*; \psi)$ was minimized by BFGS; see Doornik (1999).

TABLE 4.1
IRWN Fitted to RWN

q	$\bar{q}_\zeta^*$	Pred	Filter	Smoothed
0.01	0.00001	0.86	0.86	0.80
0.1	0.0008	0.82	0.83	0.77
0.2	0.0026	0.81	0.81	0.75
0.5	0.0117	0.80	0.79	0.69
1	0.0318	0.80	0.76	0.62
5	0.1653	0.79	0.55	0.36
10	0.2436	0.78	0.41	0.24

also a feature of the smoother efficiency. As $q \to \infty$, the efficiencies of the contemporaneous filter and the smoother at $\bar{q}_\zeta^*$ tend to zero as the true series tends to an RW (so its level is known exactly).

Figure 4.3 shows plots of efficiency against q_ζ^* for four values of q. As can be seen, the maximum efficiencies of the filter are reached for values of q_ζ^*, which are bigger than the ones that maximize the efficiency of the prediction. The efficiency of the smoother is maximized at even bigger values of q_ζ^*.

Figure 4.4 shows the efficiency of the IRW trend model with signal–noise ratio, q_ζ^*, when forecasting the level of the trend for lead times from 1 to 50. The loss from forecasting the observations is slightly smaller as the variance of the irregular is common to both the true and misspecified models.

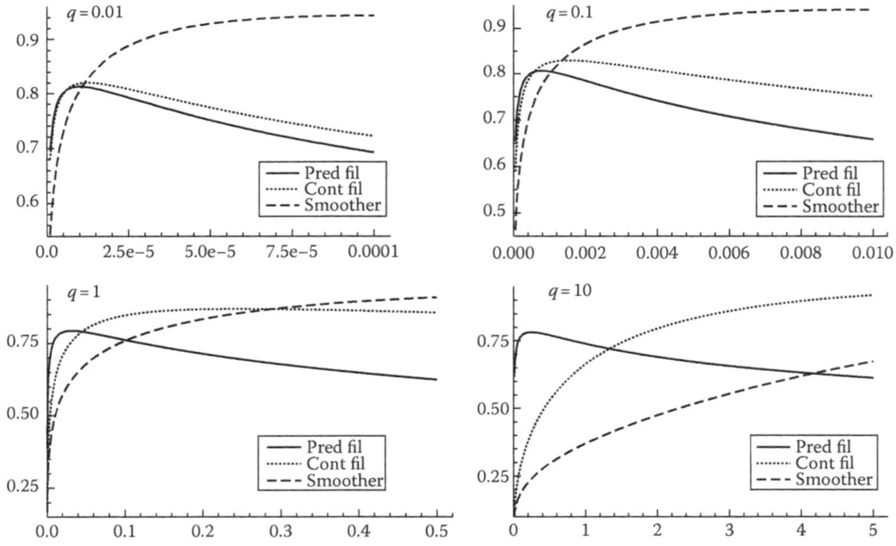

FIGURE 4.3
Efficiency for misspecified IRWN model plotted against q_ζ^*, the true DGP is an RWN with different values of q.

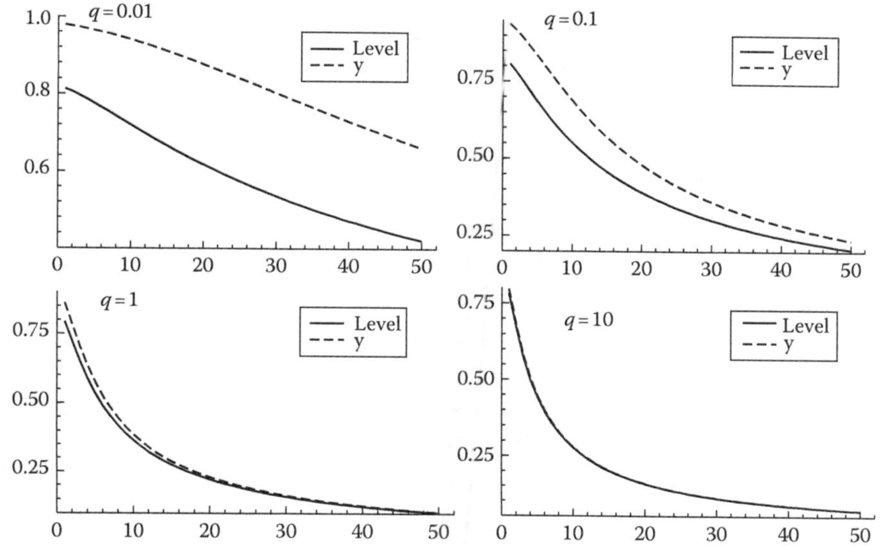

FIGURE 4.4
Forecast efficiency plotted against the forecast horizon, the misspecified model is an IRWN with $\bar{q}_\zeta^*$ and the true DGP is an RWN with different values of q.

4.3.3 Double Exponential Smoothing Fitted to a Local Level Model

Here the true DGP is still an RWN and the misspecified model is an LLT subject to the DES constraint, i.e., $q_\zeta^* = (q_\eta^*/2)^2$. The pseudo-innovation is still an ARMA(2,2) process, namely,

$$v_t(q_\eta^*; q) = \frac{(1+\theta B)(1-B)}{(1-\omega^* B)^2}\xi_t,$$

where θ is the parameter of the reduced form ARIMA(0,1,1), associated with the true DGP, while both MA parameters of the reduced form ARIMA(0,2,2), associated with the misspecified model, are functions of ω^*, as in Equation 4.2.5, i.e., $\theta_2^* = \omega^{*2}$ and $\theta_1^* = -2\omega^*$. Table 4.2 shows the pseudo-true values $\bar{q}_\eta^*$ that minimize $f(q_\eta^*; q)$ with respect to q_η^*, together with efficiencies. As might be expected, the efficiencies are higher than those in the IRW case, but the relationship between the prediction, the filter, and the smoother is similar. As before, the numerical algorithm finds the minima very rapidly and is robust to random initialization. Figure 4.5 shows efficiencies plotted against q_η^*. Forecasting efficiencies are a little higher than those shown for the IRW trend in Figure 4.4, but the general pattern with respect to the lead time is similar.

TABLE 4.2
DES Fitted to RWN

q	$\bar{q}^*_\eta$	Pred	Filter	Smoothed
0.01	0.0038	0.81	0.89	0.94
0.1	0.0352	0.88	0.89	0.92
0.2	0.0663	0.88	0.90	0.90
0.5	0.1452	0.87	0.89	0.87
1	0.2471	0.87	0.87	0.82
5	0.6060	0.85	0.71	0.56
10	0.7517	0.85	0.56	0.39
1,000	0.9960	0.84	0.01	0.01

4.3.4 Double Exponential Smoothing Fitted to an Integrated Random Walk Plus Noise Model

Table 4.3 reports the estimated pseudo-true values and the efficiencies when a DES is fitted to an IRWN model. The prediction error follows an ARMA(2,2)

$$v_t(q^*_\eta; q_\zeta) = \frac{1 - 4\{\theta_2/(1+\theta_2)\}B + \theta_2 B^2}{(1-\omega^* B)^2}\xi_t.$$

The parameter values, q_ζ, in the IRWN are chosen so as to be similar to the values implied by typical values of the smoothing constant in the HP

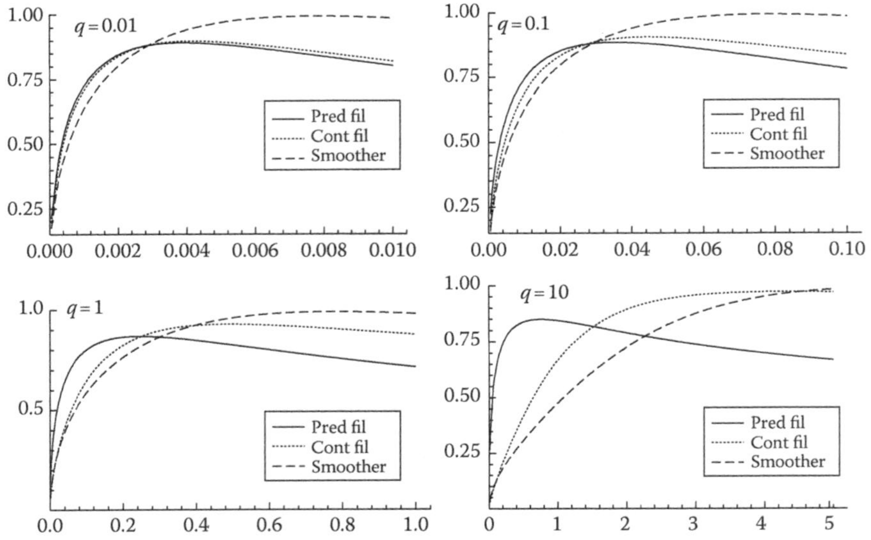

FIGURE 4.5
Efficiency for the misspecified DES plotted against q^*_η, the true DGP is an RWN with different values of q.

TABLE 4.3
DES Fitted to IRWN

$1/q$	$1/\bar{q}_\zeta^*$	Pred	Filter	Smoothed
32,000	51,546	0.96	0.96	0.87
1,600	2,451	0.96	0.96	0.86
400	588.2	0.97	0.96	0.86
100	138.9	0.97	0.96	0.85
10	11.5	0.97	0.95	0.81

filter. For example, $1/q_\zeta = 1600$ is the standard value for quarterly observations and it is known to give a good fit to U.S. GDP; see Harvey and Trimbur (2008). As can be seen, the loss in efficiency is quite small for filtering. The values of $\bar{q}_\zeta^*$, implied by $\bar{q}_\eta^*$, are slightly smaller than the corresponding values of q_ζ.

Figure 4.6 shows the efficiencies of filtering and smoothing plotted against q_η^*. The loss in forecasting efficiency was computed for the same values of q_ζ as in Figure 4.6 and plotted against lead time, as was done in Figure 4.4. The losses turned out to be very small, with the efficiency never falling below 0.94.

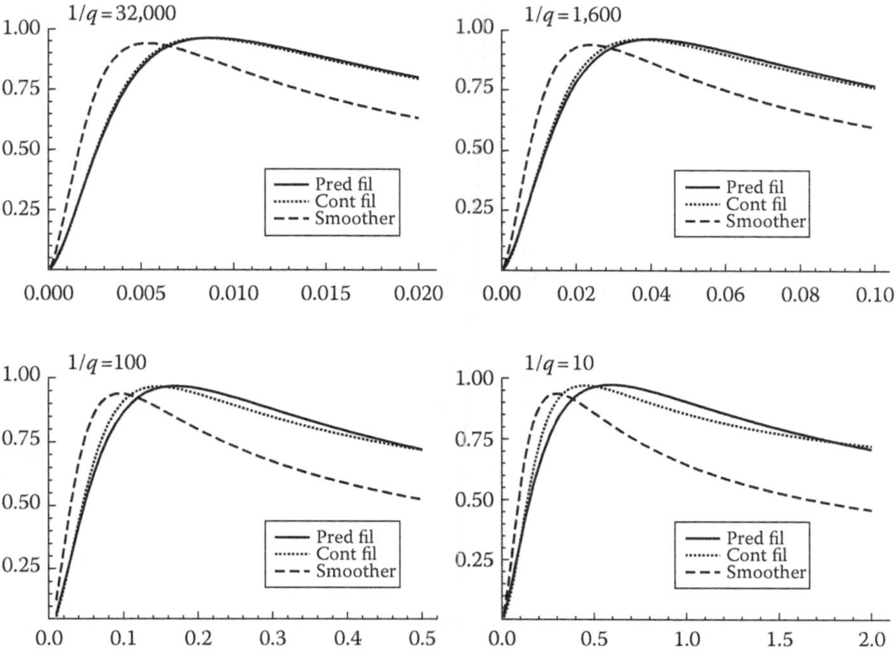

FIGURE 4.6
Efficiency for the misspecified DES plotted against q_η^*, the true DGP is an IRWN with different values of $1/q_\zeta$.

TABLE 4.4
Monte Carlo; IRWN Fitted to RWN Using Cross-Validation

q	$\widehat{q}_\zeta^*$		Efficiency			
	Mean (s.d.)	Median	Pred	Filter	Smoothed	Max sm ($\widehat{q}_\zeta^*$)
0.01	0.0003 (0.01)	0.0001	0.61	0.65	0.92	0.94 (0.0001)
0.1	0.009 (0.02)	0.007	0.67	0.76	0.94	0.94 (0.01)
0.2	0.027 (0.02)	0.024	0.68	0.79	0.93	0.94 (0.04)
0.5	0.14 (0.15)	0.11	0.66	0.83	0.92	0.93 (0.28)
1	0.31 (0.13)	0.29	0.68	0.87	0.87	0.93 (1.19)
5	1.64 (0.66)	1.56	0.67	0.88	0.66	0.97 (13.9)
10	2.57 (0.98)	2.37	0.67	0.83	0.52	0.98 (30.5)
1000	4.62 (1.90)	4.25	0.67	0.05	0.01	0.99 (3331)

4.3.5 Smoothing and Cross-Validation

It is clear from Figure 4.3 that the signal–noise ratio at which the efficiency of the misspecified smoother is maximized is much bigger than the one that maximizes the efficiency of the predictions and the filters. For example, when $q_\eta = 0.1$, $\bar{q}_\zeta^* = 0.0008$, but the efficiency of the smoother is maximized at $\bar{q}_\zeta^* = 0.01$. If the main interest is in smoothing, it may therefore be appropriate to consider the estimation by cross-validation rather than maximum likelihood. The cross-validation criterion function is

$$CV(\psi^*; Y) = \sum_{t=1}^{T} (y_t - \widehat{y}_t^{(-t)})^2,$$

where $\widehat{y}_t^{(-t)}$ denotes the value estimated for the tth observations using all the other observations. As shown by De Jong (1988), it may be computed from the smoothing errors obtained from the backward smoothing recursions; see also Durbin and Koopman (2001, 74). A Monte Carlo experiment for $T = 1000$ was carried out by generating 10,000 samples from the RWD model used in Section 4.3.2. The IRW model was then fitted and the parameter was estimated using the cross-validation criterion. Table 4.4 shows the mean, the standard deviation (in brackets), and the median of the estimated parameter $\widehat{q}_\zeta^*$. As can be seen, the mean of each $\widehat{q}_\zeta^*$ is much bigger than the corresponding $\bar{q}_\zeta^*$ in Table 4.1, and, at least for small values of q_η, is not far from the $\widehat{q}_\zeta^*$, shown in the last column, that maximizes the efficiency of the smoother.*

It was shown earlier that the MSE of the filtered estimator from a misspecified model will only be finite (has a steady-state value) iff $d \leq d^*$. On the other hand, HDM (Appendix B) showed that if the order of integration

* Note that we did perform a Monte Carlo experiment, so the estimated parameters $\widehat{q}_\zeta^*$ are sample estimates, and they eventually converge to the pseudo-true value $\bar{q}_\zeta^*$.

TABLE 4.5
RWN Fitted to IRWN

$1/q_\zeta$	$1/\bar{q}^*$	**Smoothed**
32,000	103.1	0.806
10,000	57.8	0.805
1,600	23.2	0.804
400	11.7	0.803
100	5.9	0.800
10	1.9	0.796

of a misspecified model is d^*, then the MSE of the smoothed estimator of the trend in a doubly infinite sample will be finite so long as $d \leq 2d^*$.

Now we assume that the true DGP follows an IRWN and we fit an RWN model. The pseudo-true value, $\bar{q}^*$, maximizing the smoother efficiency is shown in Table 4.5. This corresponds to minimizing the true MSE of the smoothing estimator; namely, $\bar{q}^* = \arg\min_{q^*} f_s(q^*; q_\zeta)$, where $f_s(\bullet) = p\lim E(y_t - \widehat{y}_{t|T})^2$ is the steady-state MSE of the smoothed estimator, i.e., $\widehat{y}_{t|T} = \widehat{m}_{t|T} = E(\mu_t|Y_T)$. As can be seen, the efficiencies are reasonably high, being close to 0.8 for a wide range of values of q_ζ. Figure 4.7 plots the smoother efficiency against q^* and shows how the function has a unique maximum at $\bar{q}^*$.

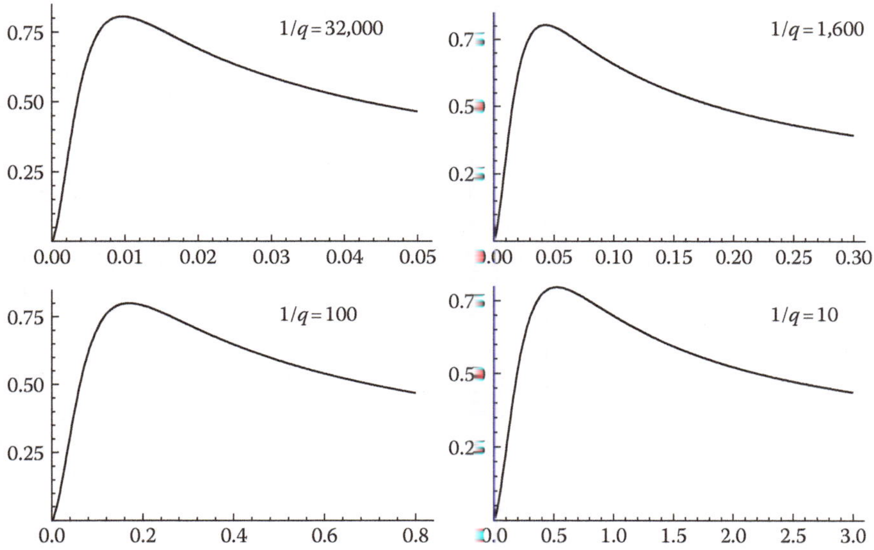

FIGURE 4.7
Efficiency of the smoother for the misspecified RWN model plotted against q^*, the true DGP is IRWN with different values of $1/q_\zeta$.

4.4 Seasonality

A seasonal component, γ_t, may be added to a model consisting of a trend, as in Equation 4.2.3, and irregular to give

$$y_t = \mu_t + \gamma_t + \varepsilon_t, \quad t = 1, \ldots, T. \tag{4.4.1}$$

A fixed seasonal pattern may be modeled as

$$\gamma_t = \sum_{j=1}^{s} \gamma_j z_{jt},$$

where s is the number of seasons and the dummy variable, z_{jt}, is one in season j and zero otherwise. In order not to confound trend with seasonality, the coefficients, γ_j, $j = 1, \ldots, s$, are constrained to sum to zero. The seasonal pattern may evolve over time and hence a stochastic seasonal component is needed. Let γ_{jt} denote the effect of season j at time t and let the vector $\gamma_t = (\gamma_{1t}, \ldots, \gamma_{st})'$ be a multivariate RW,

$$\gamma_t = \gamma_{t-1} + \omega_t, \quad t = 1, \ldots, T,$$

where $\omega_t = (\omega_{1t}, \ldots, \omega_{st})'$ is a zero-mean disturbance with

$$\operatorname{Var}(\omega_t) = \sigma_\omega^2 (I - s^{-1} ii'), \tag{4.4.2}$$

where σ_ω^2 is a nonnegative parameter and i is a vector of ones. Although all s seasonal components are continually changing, only one affects the observations at any particular time, i.e., $\gamma_t = \gamma_{jt}$, when season j prevails at time t. The requirement that the seasonal components always sum to zero is enforced by the restriction that the disturbances sum to zero at each t. This restriction is implemented by the correlation structure in Equation 4.4.2, where $\operatorname{Var}(i'\omega_t) = 0$, coupled with initial conditions constraining the seasonal components to sum to zero at $t = 0$. Specifically, γ_0 has mean zero and a covariance matrix proportional to Equation 4.4.2. Hence, $E(i'\gamma_0) = \operatorname{Var}(i'\gamma_0) = 0$, and thereafter $i'\omega_t = 0$ ensures $i'\gamma_t = 0$.

In the BSM, μ_t in Equation 4.4.1 is a stochastic trend, the irregular component, ε_t, is assumed to be random, and the disturbances in all three components are taken to be mutually uncorrelated. The signal–noise ratio associated with the seasonal, i.e., $q_\omega = \sigma_\omega^2/\sigma_\varepsilon^2$, determines how rapidly the seasonal changes relative to the irregular.

The reduced form of the dummy variable stochastic seasonal model is

$$\gamma_t = -\sum_{j=1}^{s-1} \gamma_{t-j} + \omega_t, \tag{4.4.3}$$

with ω_t following an MA$(s-2)$ process. Thus, the expected value of the seasonal effects over the previous year is zero. The simplicity of a *single shock* model, which is formulated directly as in Equation 4.4.3 with ω_t white noise, can be useful for pedagogic purposes, but it is usually preferable to work with the *balanced dummy variable* model based on Equation 4.4.2. Given Equation 4.4.3, which can be written as $S(B)\gamma_t = \omega_t$, where $S(B) = 1 + B + \cdots + B^{s-1}$ is the seasonal summation operator, it can be seen that $\Delta^2 S(B)y_t$ is stationary and that the reduced form of the BSM is $\Delta\Delta_s y_t \sim MA(s+1)$, where $\Delta_s = 1 - B^s$ is the seasonal difference operator.

4.4.1 Weights for Signal Extraction

Seasonal adjustment procedures, such as the Bureau of the Census X-11 or X-12, are explicitly based on sets of weights. The weighting patterns change toward the end of the sample and become one-sided at the end. In an STM the observations are implicitly weighted when the KF and smoother are run and the weights automatically adapt in order to be optimal at and near the end of the sample. The weighting patterns for the extraction of any component at any point in the sample can be obtained when using the STAMP8 package of Koopman et al. (2007).

Although the classic Wiener–Kolmogorov formulae are not used in STAMP8—the state-space approach is more efficient and more general—they can be helpful in providing insight into the structure of the weighting procedures used for signal extraction. Consider a BSM with a single shock seasonal component. The Wiener–Kolmogorov formula for the seasonal adjustment filter in the middle of a doubly infinite sample is

$$\begin{aligned} w(B) &= \frac{\sigma_\eta^2/|1-B|^2 + \sigma_\zeta^2/|1-B|^4 + \sigma_\varepsilon^2}{\sigma_\omega^2/|S(B)|^2 + \sigma_\eta^2/|1-B|^2 + \sigma_\zeta^2/|1-B|^4 + \sigma_\varepsilon^2} \\ &= \frac{|S(B)|^2\sigma_\zeta^2 + |1-B^s|^2\sigma_\eta^2 + |1-B^s|^2|1-B|^2\sigma_\varepsilon^2}{|1-B|^4\sigma_\omega^2 + |S(B)|^2\sigma_\zeta^2 + |1-B^s|^2\sigma_\eta^2 + |1-B^s|^2|1-B|^2\sigma_\varepsilon^2}. \end{aligned}$$

A seasonal adjustment filter should normally contain the $S(B)$ polynomial as a factor in order to cancel out seasonal unit roots in the raw series. A symmetric filter, like the one above, will usually contain $S(B)S(B^{-1}) = |S(B)|^2$. The weights in the above formula sum to 1, but this is because of the integrated trend, rather than the seasonally integrated seasonal. (Correspondingly, the weights for extracting the seasonal sum to zero.) Exact formulae for weights for the IRWN model are also available in McElroy (2008).

Figure 4.8 shows the weights implicitly used for extracting the components from an RW plus seasonal plus noise model fitted to quarterly data on the U.S. rate of inflation. The output is from STAMP, with the point at which the smoothing weights are computed being 2 years from the end of the series.

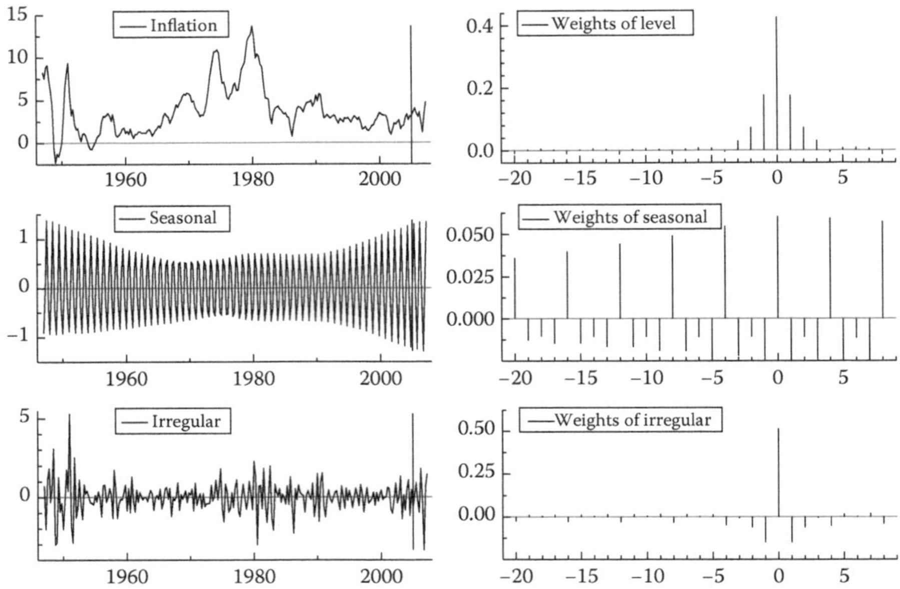

FIGURE 4.8
Smoothed components for U.S. inflation together with weights implicitly used by STAMP.

4.4.2 Specification and Misspecification

For monthly or quarterly data, the default seasonality model is the (balanced dummy) stochastic seasonal. If there is some doubt as to whether a seasonal component should be included, the seasonal stationarity test proposed by Busetti and Harvey (2003) may be applied. This test may be implemented nonparametrically, outside a UC framework. An alternative test, which can be done in STAMP, is a simple F-test (or chi-square test) on the seasonal factors in a model estimated with a fixed seasonal. Note that these tests can be used for checking the effectiveness of seasonal adjustment procedures.

The Canova–Hansen stationarity test can be used to test the null hypothesis of a deterministic seasonal against the alternative of a stochastic seasonal; see Canova and Hansen (1995). The seasonal unit root test of Hylleberg et al. (1990) can be used to test the opposite hypothesis. However, the seasonal unit root test is based on autoregressive models and such models may be poor approximations when the seasonal component changes relatively slowly; see the discussion in Harvey (2006, Section 5.5).

It was shown in Section 4.3 that the trend component is reasonably robust to misspecification. Here, the implications for seasonal adjustment (or equivalently the estimation of the seasonal component) are investigated by first fitting the BSM, Equations 4.4.1 through 4.4.3, to the (logarithm of the)

TABLE 4.6
IRW Plus Seasonal Fitted to BSM

Series	True Parameters			Pseudo-True Values		Efficiency of Seasonal		
	q_η	q_ζ	q_ω	$\bar{q}_\zeta^*$	$\bar{q}_\omega^*$	Pred	Filter	Smoothed
Price	1	0.81	0.0004	3.890	0.002	0.96	0.96	0.96
Infl	0.87	0	0.0013	0.052	0.001	0.99	0.98	0.99
OfuGASl	0.49	0	0.92	0.005	0.520	0.99	0.98	0.99
OiGASL	8.30	0	0.14	0.095	0.030	0.98	0.97	0.99

U.S. price level, the corresponding rate of inflation (first differences), and two UK energy series provided with STAMP. All the series are quarterly. For the price level, the preferred model has a stochastic slope, but no irregular, but for all the other series the trend is an RW (with drift). The signal–noise ratios in Tables 4.6 and 4.7 are expressed with respect to σ_ε^2, except for the price level, which has $\sigma_\varepsilon^2 = 0$ and the signal–noise ratios expressed with respect to σ_η^2. Assuming these models to be the true ones, the implied parameters for the IRW and DES trend specifications are obtained and the efficiencies for the seasonal components computed. Tables 4.6 and 4.7 show clearly that there is almost no loss of efficiency for either filtering or smoothing.

4.4.3 Seasonal ARIMA Models

For modeling seasonal data, Box and Jenkins (1976, chapter 9) proposed a class of multiplicative seasonal ARIMA models; see the review in Ghysels et al. (2006). The most important model within this class has subsequently become known as the *airline* model since it was originally fitted to a monthly series on UK airline passengers. The model is written as

$$\Delta\Delta_s y_t = (1+\theta B)(1+\Theta B^s)\xi_t, \quad \xi_t \sim N(0,\sigma_\xi^2), \tag{4.4.4}$$

TABLE 4.7
DES Plus Seasonal Fitted to BSM

Series	True Parameters			Pseudo-True Values		Efficiency of Seasonal		
	q_η	q_ζ	q_ω	$\bar{q}_\zeta^*$	$\bar{q}_\omega^*$	Pred	Filter	Smoothed
Price	1	0.81	0.0004	6.110	0.005	0.99	0.99	0.99
Infl	0.87	0	0.0013	0.304	0.001	0.99	0.99	0.99
OfuGASl	0.49	0	0.92	0.134	0.870	0.99	0.98	0.99
OiGASl	8.30	0	0.14	0.557	0.043	0.99	0.98	0.99

where θ and Θ are the MA parameters that, if the model is to be invertible, must have a modulus less than 1.

Maravall (1985), compares the autocorrelation functions of the $\Delta\Delta_s y_t$ for the BSM and the airline model, for some typical values of the parameters; he finds them to be quite similar, particularly when the seasonal MA parameter, Θ, is close to -1. In fact, in the limiting case when Θ is equal to -1, the airline model is equivalent to a BSM in which σ_ζ^2 and σ_ω^2 are both zero. The airline model provides a good approximation to the reduced form when the slope and seasonal are close to being deterministic. If this is not the case, the implicit link between the variability of the slope and that of the seasonal component may be limiting.

An STM model-based seasonal adjustment is straightforward as the seasonal component is modeled explicitly and can be removed by smoothing. For some seasonal ARIMA model, a UC form may be derived, assuming that the model satisfies certain constraints. It is sufficient that $\Theta < 0$ for the airline model (4.4.4) to have an admissible *canonical decomposition*; see Hillmer and Tiao (1982, 67). The canonical decomposition leads to an IMA(2,2) trend and a seasonal component in which $S(B)\gamma_t$ is an MA$(s-1)$.

The BSM and the airline model-based decomposition can be nested in the composite SSF so as to compute the asymptotic efficiency of the extracted components in one model, given that the other is true. Maravall (1985) matches the BSM and the airline model by equating the autocovariance functions; see Harvey (1989, 72–3). Here, we match them by minimizing the prediction errors variance when we fit the airline model to the BSM. The resulting parameters are close to those obtained by Maravall. Table 4.8 shows the BSM parameters, the implied airline model parameters, $\overline{\theta}^*$ and $\overline{\Theta}^*$, and the efficiency of the prediction error, together with the efficiencies for the trend component and, in brackets, the seasonal component based on the canonical decomposition. As might be expected, the efficiencies are very high for these parameter configurations. The same exercise could be carried out by taking the airline model to be the true DGP and computing the loss in efficiency from fitting the BSM with the IRW and DES restrictions.

TABLE 4.8
Airline Fitted to BSM

True Parameters			**Pseudo-True Values**		**Pred Error**	**Efficiency of Trend (Seasonal)**		
σ_η^2	σ_ε^2	σ_ω^2	$\overline{\theta}^*$	$\overline{\Theta}^*$		Pred	Filter	Smoothed
1	20	0.25	−0.82	−0.86	0.98	0.98 (0.96)	0.99 (0.96)	0.98 (0.96)
1	3	0.75	−0.68	−0.54	0.94	0.92 (0.98)	0.92 (0.98)	0.89 (0.97)
1	1.13	0.01	−0.42	−0.89	0.98	0.99 (0.99)	0.97 (0.99)	0.95 (0.99)
1	0.70	0.25	−0.48	−0.55	0.94	0.90 (0.98)	0.90 (0.97)	0.86 (0.96)

4.5 Conclusions

If the aim of the analysis is signal extraction, including detrending and seasonal adjustment, then a model-based approach using unobserved components is a relatively straightforward and transparent way to proceed. Concerns about the slope variance parameter being estimated as zero can be mitigated by imposing a constraint so that there is only one signal–noise ratio rather than two. The contribution of this chapter is to show that imposing the IRW or DES constraint generally entails only a small loss in efficiency, with the DES being particularly robust. However, in a reasonably large sample, model selection techniques may be effectively employed to specify an unconstrained LLT.

Misspecification of the trend in a BSM has little effect on the efficiency of seasonal adjustment. Again, a reduction in the number of parameters in the trend may be appealing and the DES restriction has much to commend it.

Appendix: Estimation of a Misspecified Model in the Frequency Domain

Following Dahlhaus and Wefelmeyer (1996) and Taniguchi and Kakizawa (2000, Section 3.1.1), an equivalent approach to the minimization of prediction error variance is to look at the Kullback–Leibler (KL) discrepancy.

Assuming that the true DGP follows the ARIMA(p, d, q), i.e., $y_t = \Psi(B)\sigma^2$, with $\Psi(B) = \theta(B)/\{\phi(B)\Delta^d\}$. We denote its pseudo autocovariance generating function (ACGF) by $g(B) = |\Psi(B)|^2\sigma^2$, where $|\Psi(B)|^2 = \Psi(B)\Psi(B^{-1})$. Replacing the backshift operator by the complex exponential, $\exp(-\iota\lambda)$, we obtain the spectral generating function (SGF), denoted as $g(\lambda) = |\Psi(\lambda)|^2$, and its spectral density is equal to $\sigma^2/2\pi g(\lambda)$. The spectral density of the pseudo-innovation (4.3.3) is then equal to

$$\frac{\sigma^2}{2\pi}|\Psi^*(\lambda)|^{-2}g(\lambda),$$

where $|\Psi^*(\lambda)|^2 = g^*(\lambda)$ is the SGF of the misspecified model. Now if $d \leq d^*$, the pseudo-innovation has a bounded spectrum with finite variance

$$\frac{\sigma^2}{2\pi}\int_{-\pi}^{\pi}|\Psi^*(\lambda)|^{-2}g(\lambda)d\lambda,$$

and the pseudo-true value is the minimizer of the KL discrepancy

$$D(g^*; g) = \frac{1}{2\pi}\int_{-\pi}^{\pi}\left\{\log g^*(\lambda) + \frac{g(\lambda)}{g^*(\lambda)}\right\}d\lambda,$$

which is the distance between the spectrum of the misspecified model and the spectrum of the true DGP. If we replace $g(\lambda)$ with the sample periodogram, i.e., $I(\lambda) = T^{-1}|\sum_{t=1}^{T} y_t \exp(-\iota t\lambda)|^2$, the KL discrepancy leads to $D(g^*; I)$, known as the Whittle likelihood. The Whittle estimator is the minimizer of $D(g^*; I)$ and it is equivalent to the MLE. Dahlhaus and Wefelmeyer (1996, Theorems 3.2 and 3.3) show that in case of misspecification, the Whittle estimator and the MLE are both consistent estimators of the pseudo-true value.

Acknowledgments

We are grateful to two referees and the associate editor for their very helpful comments. Any errors are our responsibility. We acknowledge financial support from Eurostat. Davide Delle Monache thanks the CiDE for the "C. Giannini" Postdoctoral Fellowship.

References

Box, G. E. P. and Jenkins, G. M. (1976). *Time Series Analysis: Forecasting and Control* (revised ed.). San Francisco: Holden-Day.

Busetti, F. and Harvey, A. C. (2003). Seasonality tests. *Journal of Business and Economic Statistics* 21:420–36.

Busetti, F. and Harvey, A. C. (2008). Testing for trend. *Econometric Theory* 24:72–87.

Canova, F. and Hansen, B. E. (1995). Are seasonal patterns constant over time? A test for seasonal stability. *Journal of Business and Economic Statistics* 13:237–52.

Dahlhaus, R. and Wefelmeyer, W. (1996). Asymptotically optimal estimation in misspecified times series models. *The Annals of Statistics* 24(3):952–74.

De Jong, P. (1988). A cross validation filter for time series models. *Biometrika* 75:594–600.

Doornik, J. A. (1999). *Ox: An Object-Oriented Matrix Programming Language.* London: Timberlake Consultants.

Durbin, J. and Koopman, S. J. (2001). *Time Series Analysis by State Space Methods.* Oxford: Oxford University Press.

Ghysels, E., Osborn, D. R. and Rodrigues, P. M. M. (2006). *Forecasting Seasonal Time Series. Handbook of Economic Forecasting*, eds. G. Elliot, C. Granger, and A. Timmermann, 659–711. Amsterdam: North Holland.

Hamilton, J. D. (1994). *Time Series Analysis*. Princeton: Princeton University Press.

Harvey, A. C. (1989). *Forecasting, Structural Time Series Models and the Kalman Filter*. Cambridge: Cambridge University Press.

Harvey, A. C. (2006). Forecasting with Unobserved Components Time Series Models. In *Handbook of Economic Forecasting*, eds. G. Elliot, C. Granger, and A. Timmermann, 327–412. Amsterdam: North Holland.

Harvey, A. C. (2011). Modelling the Phillips curve with unobserved components. *Applied Financial Economics (special issue in honour of Clive Granger)* 21:7–17.

Harvey, A. C. and Delle Monache, D. (2009). Computing the mean square error of unobserved components extracted by misspecified time series models. *Journal of Economic Dynamics and Control* 33:283–95.

Harvey, A. C. and Jaeger, A. (1993). Detrending, stylised facts and the business cycle. *Journal of Applied Econometrics* 8:231–47.

Harvey, A. C. and Koopman, S. J. (1992). Diagnostic checking of unobserved components time series models. *Journal of Business and Economic Statistics* 10:377–89.

Harvey, A. C. and Koopman, S. J. (2003). Computing observation weights for signal extraction and filtering. *Journal of Economic Dynamics and Control* 27:1317–33.

Harvey, A. C. and Trimbur, T. (2003). General model-based filters for extracting cycles and trends in economic time series. *Review of Economics and Statistics* 85:244–55.

Harvey, A. C. and Trimbur, T. (2008). Trend estimation and the Hodrick-Prescott filter. *Journal of the Japanese Statistical Society (volume in honor of H. Akaike)* 38:41–9.

Hillmer, S. C. and Tiao, G. C. (1982). An ARIMA-model-based approach to seasonal adjustment. *Journal of the American Statistical Association* 77:63–70.

Hodrick, R. J. and Prescott, E. C. (1997). Postwar US business cycles: An empirical investigation. *Journal of Money, Credit and Banking* 24:1–16.

Hylleberg, S., Engle, R., Granger, C. W. J., and Yoo, B. S. (1990). Seasonal integration and co-integration. *Journal of Econometrics* 44:215–38.

Kohn, R., Ansley, C. F., and Wong, C-H. (1992). Nonparametric spline regression with autoregressive moving average errors. *Biometrika* 79:335–46.

Koopman, S. J., Harvey, A. C., Doornik, J. A., and Shephard, N. (2007). *STAMP 8: Structural Time Series Analysis Modeller and Predictor.* London: Timberlake Consultants.

Maravall, A. (1985). On structural time series models and the characterization of components. *Journal of Business and Economic Statistics* 3:350–5.

McElroy, T. S. (2008). Exact formulas for the Hodrick-Prescott filter. *Econometrics Journal* 11:209–217.

McElroy, T. S. and Findley, D. (2010). Selection between models through multistep-ahead forecasting. *Journal of Statistical Planning and Inference* 140:3655–75.

Shephard, N. G. and Harvey, A. C. (1990). On the probability of estimating a deterministic component in the local level model. *Journal of Time Series Analysis* 11:339–47.

Taniguchi, M. and Kakizawa, Y. (2000). *Asymptotic Theory of Statistical Inference for Time Series.* New York: Springer.

Whittle, P. (1983). *Prediction and Regulation.* 2nd edition. Oxford: Blackwell.

5

Error in Business Cycle Estimates Obtained from Seasonally Adjusted Data

Tucker S. McElroy* **and Scott H. Holan**

CONTENTS

5.1 Introduction

Economists have great interest in measuring the business cycle inherent to economic time series; see Baxter and King (1999), Kaiser and Maravall (2001), Stock and Watson (1999), and references therein. A popular method for estimating the cycle is the Hodrick–Prescott (HP) filter (Hodrick and Prescott 1997). Since the HP is designed for nonseasonal series, it can only be sensibly applied to seasonally adjusted data. This serves as the context of this chapter: cycle estimation for univariate time series. Given that it is not uncommon for economists to start with seasonally adjusted data, which is typically produced without taking cyclical effects into account, it is natural to ask the

* This chapter is released to inform interested parties of research and to encourage discussion. The views expressed on statistical issues are those of the authors and not necessarily those of the U.S. Census Bureau.

question: how is the estimation of the cycle affected? If there is additional signal extraction error due to the prior activity of seasonal adjustment, can this error be quantified? We set out to provide answers to these important questions.

In general, economic time series undergo several distinct patterns of stochastic variation. Apart from trading-day and holiday effects (Bell and Hillmer 1983; Roberts et al. 2010; Soukup and Findley 2001), the major stochastic components are the trend, seasonal, cycle, and irregular (see Peña et al. [2001], Harvey and Proietti [2005], Durbin and Koopman [2001], and references therein). In this chapter, we focus on an observed series Y that can be viewed, after suitable transformations and removal of fixed regression effects, as a sum of four unobserved components: cycle C, trend T, seasonal S, and irregular I. In particular, we assume

$$Y_t = C_t + T_t + S_t + I_t \tag{5.1.1}$$

for times $t = 1, 2, \ldots, n$. This basic model of economic time series plays a prominent role in autoregressive integrated moving average (ARIMA) model-based signal extraction methods, such as structural time series models (Harvey 1989) and SEATS (Maravall and Caporello 2004).

Define the "two-stage approach" to cycle estimation via first obtaining an estimate of $T + I$ given Y (typically ignoring the putative presence of C), followed by estimation of C from the seasonally adjusted data. This is clearly not an ideal approach; ignoring C may corrupt the estimation of S when these components share common spectral power. However, it arises in practice due to two principal considerations: (1) some of the most popular cycle estimation filters (e.g., the HP) do not achieve suppression of seasonal frequencies; (2) it is difficult to estimate cyclical models from unadjusted data (see the discussion in Kaiser and Maravall [2005]). However, were this point resolved, then one could proceed with direct estimation of the cycle for the unadjusted series, and the result would be less prone to error. Recognizing this difficulty, Kaiser and Maravall (2005) developed the so-called "recast" approach, which can be viewed as generating a HP-hybrid filter that suppresses seasonality. This technique utilizes the information about the seasonal, trend, and irregular models from the seasonal adjustment stage. More dubious is the approach that models the seasonally adjusted data as $C + T + I$, resulting in a misstatement of the cycle mean squared error (MSE).*

This chapter first provides an in-depth discussion of the above techniques in Section 5.2. One can give a precise theoretical description of the approximate values of maximum likelihood estimates (MLEs) obtained by fitting misspecified models via the machinery of "pseudo-true" values, and this will help us see exactly what is happening in the two-stage approach. Knowing the pseudo-true parameter values, we can then precisely quantify the asymptotic

* Misstated MSE refers to a reported MSE quantity that is calculated based on erroneous assumptions.

MSE of cycle estimates, using signal extraction formulas derived in Sections 5.3 and 5.4; these are derived in generality for possible application to other scenarios. Having written computer programs to compute both pseudo-true values and MSEs for each method, given an initial specification of the data generating process (DGP), we display some of the most interesting results and provide a discussion in Section 5.5. A full illustration is provided on an employment series in Section 5.6, and Section 5.7 concludes this chapter. All proofs are provided in the Appendix.

5.2 Methods of Cycle Estimation

As alluded to in the Introduction, there are several methods of model-based cycle estimation that are utilized in practice. The best method, from a theoretical standpoint, models all the dynamics present in Equation 5.1.1 and constructs the cycle extraction filter in an MSE optimal fashion. This will be called the *direct* method, and will serve as a benchmark for other techniques. In particular, one obtains models for the cycle process C_t and the data Y_t, and computes the conditional expectation $\mathbb{E}[C_t|Y]$ as a linear transformation of the data vector Y, utilizing estimated parameter values.

The *two-stage* method begins with a seasonal–trend–irregular model that does not explicitly account for cyclical behavior. In practice (as is subsequently demonstrated), the cyclical dynamics, when actually present, become incorporated in the models for seasonal and trend, in the sense that the parameter estimates for these models are somewhat different than they would be if no cyclicality were present. Mathematically, the situation is described through the behavior of the pseudo-true values of the parameters, which are by definition the limit of MLEs when a misspecified model is fitted to the data (Taniguchi and Kakizawa 2000). Although this material has existed in the time series literature for many decades, we review it in the Appendix. Seasonal adjustment filters can then be computed by using the fitted model (either using model-based filters or a fixed forecast-extended filter as in X-11-ARIMA), and the resulting seasonal adjustment is the input for the second stage: one can model this as cycle–trend–irregular. The idea is that any cyclical effects initially present in the data are carried through into the seasonal adjustment. One then computes the MSE optimal cycle estimate from the seasonally adjusted data.

The actual MSE for this two-stage procedure can be somewhat different from what would be derived from the cycle signal extraction formulas, which assume that the given data have no seasonality. However, some seasonality remains to distort the error formulas, so that ignoring this contribution results in a misstatement of the MSE; this is demonstrated theoretically and empirically next.

If instead of applying a cycle extraction filter in the second stage, we use a nonparametric filter, such as the HP, we obtain the *recast* method of Kaiser and Maravall (2005). Using the presumed dynamics of the seasonally adjusted output as given, one can know the exact dynamics of a putative cycle implied by using such a filter. However, the actual cycle (if one exists) may differ in its dynamics from those suggested by the recast approach, which can result in a misstatement of the MSE.

This defines the three techniques considered here: direct, two-stage, and the recast. In Sections 5.3 and 5.4, we present the mathematical formulas to correctly compute, in finite sample, the MSE of the cycle. These formulas do not take parameter uncertainty into account. Instead, the MSEs are computed as if the signal extraction filters are given, whereas in practice they actually depend on the data through the parameter estimates.* We also present a method for computing the MSE for a bi-infinite sample, when the MLEs have converged to their pseudo-true values. For large samples, the MLEs for the parameters will be close to the pseudo-true values, so the method for the bi-infinite sample can provide us with an asymptotic picture of the true MSE, including the misspecified case. Results for both the finite sample and bi-infinite sample MSEs are presented in Section 5.5.

The work of this chapter is predicated on a model-based approach to signal extraction; see McElroy (2008a) for a discussion of model estimation and optimal signal extraction in the context of finite sample econometric time series data. We remind the reader that the two most popular approaches to modeling are the decomposition and structural techniques. The decomposition method (Burman 1980; Hillmer and Tiao 1982) starts with a seasonal autoregressive integrated moving average (SARIMA) model for the time series, identified according to standard unit root tests and diagnostics such as Ljung-Box. Then, component models for seasonal, trend, cycle, and irregular can be deduced using a partial fraction decomposition. By contrast, the structural method (Gersch and Kitagawa 1983; Harvey 1989) begins with putative SARIMA models for each component in Equation 5.1.1 (the so-called structural models are parameter-restricted SARIMA models) and derives a model for the data, called the reduced form, and uses the resulting likelihood as the objective function. We will have recourse to both approaches in this chapter.

5.3 Basic Results on Two-Stage Signal Extraction

This section presents formulas for signal extraction MSE from a fairly generic perspective. We begin by writing the decomposition (5.1.1) in vector form:

$$Y = C + S + T + I.$$

* It is quite difficult to determine analytically the impact of parameter uncertainty on MSE, although this could be done numerically by conducting Monte Carlo studies.

So $Y = \{Y_1, Y_2, \ldots, Y_n\}'$, and similarly for the components. For most applications, the seasonal and trend components are difference stationary, with associated differencing polynomials $\delta^S(z)$ and $\delta^T(z)$, respectively, whereas the cycle and irregular are stationary. However, Theorems 5.1 and 5.2 are proved generally, in that any of the components may be stationary or nonstationary (i.e., integrated); the one assumption is that their differencing polynomials are relatively prime, i.e., share no common zeroes. The differencing polynomial for Y_t is $\delta(z) = \delta^S(z)\delta^T(z)$, and $\partial Y_t = \delta(B)Y_t$ is stationary, where B is the backshift operator. These polynomials, δ, δ^S, and δ^T, all have their zeroes located on the unit circle of the complex plane, and their leading coefficient is 1 by convention. We let the differenced components be defined as $\partial S_t = \delta^S(B)S_t$ and $\partial T_t = \delta^T(B)T_t$, which are mean zero weakly stationary time series. This introduces a general notation: if X_t consists of any combination of stationary or integrated components, then $\partial X_t = \delta^X(B)X_t$, where δ^X is the polynomial containing all necessary differencing factors, with coefficients* δ_j^X. Let d be the order of δ, and let d_S and d_T be the orders of δ^S and δ^T, respectively. Clearly, $d = d_S + d_T$. For example, the seasonal operator δ^S for monthly data would be $U(z) = 1 + z + z^2 + \cdots + z^{11}$, and $\delta^T(z) = (1-z)^2$ is appropriate for a second-order trend.

We assume that Assumption A of Bell (1984) holds on the component decomposition, appropriately generalized to four components. Assumption A states that the initial values, i.e., the variables $Y_* = (Y_1, Y_2, \ldots, Y_d)'$, are uncorrelated with the differenced component series $\{\partial S_t\}$, $\{\partial T_t\}$, $\{C_t\}$, and $\{I_t\}$. Bell (1984), Bell and Hilmer (1988), McElroy and Sutcliffe (2006), and McElroy (2008a) all discuss the implications of this assumption. Note that MSE optimal signal extraction filters derived under Assumption A agree exactly with the filters implicitly used by a properly initialized state-space smoother (Bell and Hillmer 1991). We will also assume that the differenced components $\{\partial S_t\}$, $\{\partial T_t\}$, $\{C_t\}$, and $\{I_t\}$ are uncorrelated with one another.

Next, we formulate these notations in matrix form. Let Δ be an $n-d \times n$ matrix with entries given by $\Delta_{ij} = \delta_{i-j+d}$ (the convention being that $\delta_k = 0$ if $k < 0$ or $k > d$). The matrices Δ_S and Δ_T have entries given by the coefficients of $\delta^S(z)$ and $\delta^T(z)$, but are $n - d_S \times n$ and $n - d_T \times n$ dimensional, respectively. This means that each row of these matrices consists of the coefficients of the corresponding differencing polynomial, horizontally shifted in an appropriate fashion. Hence, we can write $\partial Y = \Delta Y$, $\partial S = \Delta_S S$, and $\partial T = \Delta_T T$. Now to relate these quantities, we need to define further differencing matrices $\underline{\Delta}_T$ and $\underline{\Delta}_S$, which have row entries given by the coefficients of $\delta^T(z)$ and $\delta^S(z)$, respectively, but are $n - d \times n - d_S$ and $n - d \times n - d_T$ dimensional. Then, the equation that relates the differenced components is

$$\partial Y = \underline{\Delta}_T \partial S + \underline{\Delta}_S \partial T + \Delta C + \Delta I,$$

* The sign convention is $\delta^X(z) = 1 + \delta_1^X z + \cdots + \delta_d^X z^d$, which differs from Bell (1984).

which uses the relationship

$$\Delta = \underline{\Delta}_T \Delta_S = \underline{\Delta}_S \Delta_T \tag{5.3.1}$$

proved in McElroy and Sutcliffe (2006). We are principally interested in making estimates of C. For each $1 \leq t \leq n$, the minimum MSE signal extraction estimate is $\widehat{C}_t = \mathrm{E}[C_t|Y]$. This can be expressed as a certain linear function of the data vector Y when the data are Gaussian. This estimate is also the minimum MSE *linear* estimate when the data are non-Gaussian. For the remainder of the chapter, we do not assume Gaussianity, and by optimality we always refer to the minimum MSE linear estimate. Writing $\widehat{C} = (\widehat{C}_1, \widehat{C}_2, \ldots, \widehat{C}_n)'$, the coefficients of these linear functions form the rows of a matrix F, namely, $\widehat{C} = FY$. Letting Σ_X denote the covariance matrix of any random vector X, the formula for F is

$$F = \Sigma_C \Delta' \Sigma_{\partial Y}^{-1} \Delta; \tag{5.3.2}$$

see, e.g., McElroy (2008a). From this formula, it is clear that we only need a model for C and a model for the differenced data ∂Y; it is not necessary to compute models for S, T, and I, but only for their aggregate.

Now since we will be analyzing two-stage filtering procedures, we require a more flexible notation, which generalizes ideas in McElroy and Sutcliffe (2006). Since we wish to state our results more generally, we will consider a scenario with three components $\{\alpha_t\}$, $\{\beta_t\}$, and $\{\gamma_t\}$ that are possibly integrated, with relatively prime differencing polynomials δ^α, δ^β, and δ^γ; let $\{\partial\alpha_t\}$, $\{\partial\beta_t\}$, and $\{\partial\gamma_t\}$ be the differenced components. We denote by F^X_{XZ} the signal extraction filter matrix for signal X and noise Z derived under the appropriate analog of Assumption A. In this fashion, we define $F^\alpha_{\alpha\beta}$, $F^\alpha_{\alpha\beta\gamma}$, $F^{\alpha\beta}_{\alpha\beta\gamma}$, etc., the formulas for these being given explicitly in Theorem 1 of McElroy (2008a)—although the initial value assumptions under which they are derived are inconsistent.* The following theorem shows how the filter matrices are related.

Theorem 5.1 *The filter matrices are algebraically related via* $F^\alpha_{\alpha\beta\gamma} = F^\alpha_{\alpha\beta} F^{\alpha\beta}_{\alpha\beta\gamma}$.

Letting α, β, and γ denote trend, cycle, seasonal, irregular, or combinations thereof as appropriate, we have the following corollary:

Corollary 5.1 *The following relations hold:* $F^C_{CSTI} = F^C_{CT} F^{CT}_{CSTI} = F^C_{CTI} F^{CTI}_{CSTI} = F^C_{CSI} F^{CSI}_{CSTI}$.

Now F^C_{CSTI} is the optimal cycle filter in the direct approach, while the other three expressions in Corollary 5.1 all represent different two-step approaches, where the parameter values used in the first and second stages are assumed to be those of the true DGP. $F^C_{CT} F^{CT}_{CSTI}$ corresponds to the recast approach,

---

* That is, we assume that Assumption A holds for the decomposition $\alpha + \beta + \gamma$, while also assuming that Assumption A holds for the decomposition $\alpha + \beta$, etc.

since the trend and cycle are initially lumped together in the trend–cycle component CT, and this is followed by a "high-pass" filter for cycle estimation. $F^C_{CTI} F^{CTI}_{CSTI}$ corresponds to a two-step approach to cycle estimation; the two-stage approach used in practice—and studied further in this chapter—is $F^C_{CTI} F^{TI}_{STI}$, but this does not appear in Corollary 5.1 since it does not yield the optimal filter. The fourth expression is not pursued further in this chapter, but illustrates yet another way of viewing cycle estimation. The Appendix contains some related results that do not directly enter into the main trajectory of the chapter, but are of independent interest.

5.4 Errors in Cycle Estimation

In this section, we consider the various cycle estimation methods discussed in the Introduction and provide formulas for the cycle estimation filter F and error covariance matrix M. In general, the MSEs are the diagonal entries of the error covariance matrix M. We employ the following notation. The true covariance matrix of a random vector X is denoted as Σ_X, while a proxy for this quantity, perhaps based on some fitted model for $\{X_t\}$, is denoted as $\dot{\Sigma}_X$. If there is a second proxy, it is denoted as $\ddot{\Sigma}_X$. Next, we will consider proxies $\dot{\Sigma}_X$ for Σ_X used in the first stage, of the filtering, obtained perhaps by fitting a model to the data; in the second stage, we have different proxies $\ddot{\Sigma}_X$ that arise from different models. Note that even though the MLEs that enter into these proxies are data dependent, and hence random, we treat them as deterministic in the variance formulas developed next. Finally, $\dot{F}$ and $\ddot{F}$ will denote filter matrices utilized in the first and second stages, respectively. Derivations are provided in the Appendix.

5.4.1 Direct Approach

The direct method was discussed in Section 5.3, and from Equation 5.3.2 it follows that

$$\begin{aligned} \dot{F}^C_{CSTI} &= \dot{\Sigma}_C \Delta' \dot{\Sigma}^{-1}_{\partial Y} \Delta \\ M &= \left(\dot{\Sigma}_C^{-1} + \Delta' \dot{\Sigma}^{-1}_{\partial STI} \Delta\right)^{-1} \left(\dot{\Sigma}_C^{-1} \Sigma_C \dot{\Sigma}_C^{-1} + \Delta' \dot{\Sigma}^{-1}_{\partial STI} \Sigma_{\partial STI} \dot{\Sigma}^{-1}_{\partial STI} \Delta\right) \\ &\quad \times \left(\dot{\Sigma}_C^{-1} + \Delta' \dot{\Sigma}^{-1}_{\partial STI} \Delta\right)^{-1}, \end{aligned} \tag{5.4.1}$$

where $\partial STI = \Delta(S + T + I)$. Typically, the proxies $\dot{\Sigma}_C$ and $\dot{\Sigma}_{\partial STI}$ are substituted for Σ_C and $\Sigma_{\partial STI}$ in Equation 5.4.1, resulting in the stated error covariance of

$$\left(\dot{\Sigma}_C^{-1} + \Delta' \dot{\Sigma}^{-1}_{\partial STI} \Delta\right)^{-1} = \dot{\Sigma}_C - \dot{\Sigma}_C \Delta' \dot{\Sigma}^{-1}_{\partial Y} \Delta \dot{\Sigma}_C.$$

5.4.2 Two-Stage Approach

As mentioned in Section 5.2, the two-stage method corresponds to using the filter $\dot{F}^{TI}_{STI}$ followed by $\ddot{F}^{C}_{CTI}$. Note that, typically, no accounting of the cycle is made in the first stage, so cyclical behavior gets incorporated into the other three components. In the second stage, it is now assumed that a cycle is present in the seasonally adjusted data, so that a $C+T+I$ type model is fitted. The filter and error covariance matrices are

$$\begin{aligned}
\ddot{F}^{C}_{CTI}\dot{F}^{TI}_{STI} &= \ddot{\Sigma}_C \Delta_T' \ddot{\Sigma}^{-1}_{\partial CTI} \dot{\Sigma}_{\partial TI} \underline{\Delta}_S' \dot{\Sigma}^{-1}_{\partial STI} \Delta, \\
M &= \Sigma_C + \ddot{\Sigma}_C \Delta_T' \ddot{\Sigma}^{-1}_{\partial CTI} \dot{\Sigma}_{\partial TI} \underline{\Delta}_S' \dot{\Sigma}^{-1}_{\partial STI} \Sigma_{\partial Y} \\
&\quad \times \dot{\Sigma}^{-1}_{\partial STI} \underline{\Delta}_S \dot{\Sigma}_{\partial TI} \ddot{\Sigma}^{-1}_{\partial CTI} \Delta_T \ddot{\Sigma}_C - \ddot{\Sigma}_C \Delta_T' \ddot{\Sigma}^{-1}_{\partial CTI} \\
&\quad \times \dot{\Sigma}_{\partial TI} \underline{\Delta}_S' \dot{\Sigma}^{-1}_{\partial STI} \Delta \Sigma_C - \Sigma_C \Delta' \dot{\Sigma}^{-1}_{\partial STI} \underline{\Delta}_S \dot{\Sigma}_{\partial TI} \ddot{\Sigma}^{-1}_{\partial CTI} \Delta_T \ddot{\Sigma}_C.
\end{aligned}$$

This presumes that the order of trend differencing used in the first and second stage models is the same. This M is problematic to approximate via proxies, since it requires a knowledge of both the first and second stage models. In practice it is misstated via $\ddot{\Sigma}_C - \ddot{\Sigma}_C \Delta' \ddot{\Sigma}^{-1}_{\partial CTI} \Delta \ddot{\Sigma}_C$, which is the error covariance for extracting C from a $C+T+I$ process, with proxies substituted.

5.4.3 Recast Approach

As alluded to in Section 5.2, the recast method is given by $\ddot{F}^{C}_{CT}\dot{F}^{CT}_{CSTI}$, where $\ddot{F}$ denotes a filter matrix chosen in some *ad hoc* fashion; e.g., using model-based HP filters with predetermined parameter values. The filter and error covariance matrices are

$$\begin{aligned}
\ddot{F}^{C}_{CT}\dot{F}^{CT}_{CSTI} &= \ddot{\Sigma}_C \Delta' \dot{\Sigma}^{-1}_{\partial STI} \Delta, \\
M &= \Sigma_C + \ddot{\Sigma}_C \Delta' \dot{\Sigma}^{-1}_{\partial STI} \Sigma_{\partial Y} \dot{\Sigma}^{-1}_{\partial STI} \Delta \ddot{\Sigma}_C - \ddot{\Sigma}_C \Delta' \dot{\Sigma}^{-1}_{\partial STI} \Delta \Sigma_C \\
&\quad - \Sigma_C \Delta' \dot{\Sigma}^{-1}_{\partial STI} \Delta \ddot{\Sigma}_C.
\end{aligned}$$

Here $\dot{\Sigma}_{\partial STI}$ refers to the covariance matrix of a noncyclical model $\Delta(S+T+I)$, which is misspecified when a cycle is truly present. The recasting method of SEATS assumes that $\Sigma_C = \ddot{\Sigma}_C$, essentially taking this as a definition of the cyclical model. Using the proxy $\dot{\Sigma}_{\partial STI}$ for $\Sigma_{\partial Y}$, the error covariance would then be stated as $\ddot{\Sigma}_C - \ddot{\Sigma}_C \Delta' \dot{\Sigma}^{-1}_{\partial STI} \Delta \ddot{\Sigma}_C$; this is optimal when the true cycle process is defined as the HP high-pass filter applied to the trend.

5.5 Simulation Results

We now make an assessment of the cycle MSE for the methods discussed above. For each of the three methods, there is a true MSE and a misstated

MSE based on using certain proxies or other dubious assumptions. In this section, we simulate time series of various sample sizes, apply each of the three procedures, and generate both cycle estimates and MSE curves. By repeating the simulations, we obtain a picture of the overall effect. We also look at the bi-infinite sample situation, by computing the pseudo-true values and generating the asymptotic MSEs for all three methods via the techniques described in the Appendix. In both approaches (finite and infinite), we ignore the contribution of MLE variability to the stated MSEs.

In particular, we begin by simulating a process with both a cycle $\{C_t\}$ and seasonal–trend–irregular $\{X_t\}$, the latter being given by an airline process, i.e.,

$$(1-B)^2 U(B) X_t = (1-\theta_X B)(1-\Theta_X B^{12})\epsilon_t^X.$$

We take the parameters $\theta_X = 0.6$, $\Theta_X = 0.6$, and $\sigma_X^2 = 1$ for our initial simulation. The cyclical component is given by an AR(2) model:

$$(1-2\rho\cos(\omega)B + \rho^2 B^2)C_t = \epsilon_t^C. \tag{5.5.1}$$

Our DGP has $\rho = 0.9$, $\omega = \pi/12$, and $\sigma_C^2 = \kappa\sigma_X^2$; we set $\kappa = 1$ corresponding to a strong cycle. So our DGP is $Y_t = C_t + X_t$, although it is only required to simulate $\partial Y_t = (1-B)^2 U(B) Y_t$, since all cycle estimates can be written in terms of the differenced data. Note carefully that from inception this exercise favors the direct and two-stage methods; to fairly evaluate the recast technique, we should set $\kappa = 0$ and define $C_t = (1 - H(B))T_t$ in the DGP, where $H(B)$ is the HP filter and $\{T_t\}$ is the trend process (from the canonical decomposition of $\{X_t\}$).

The next step is to estimate the correctly specified model by fitting the $C + X$ model to the DGP; this is done using a likelihood based on structural ARIMA models. We can immediately compute direct cycle estimates and the true MSE via Equation 5.4.1, as well as the misstated MSE. The diagonal entries of these MSE matrices are of principal interest. For both the recast and two-stage methods, we next fit an airline model to the DGP, which of course is a misspecified model when $\kappa > 0$. From these estimates, we obtain the canonical decomposition, and hence the signal extraction filters $\dot{F}_{STI}^{T}$ and $\dot{F}_{STI}^{TI}$. In the recast method, the cycle covariances $\ddot{\Sigma}_C$ are obtained as described in the Appendix, utilizing the HP filter with $q = 1/130{,}000$ (the value appropriate for monthly series—Hodrick and Prescott [1997]) and the spectral representation described in McElroy (2008b). Then, we obtain at once the cycle estimates, the true cycle MSE, and the misstated cycle MSE.

Finally, the seasonally adjusted data from the previous step are taken as input to the two-stage method, and we fit a cycle–trend–irregular model with components C, T, and I. The cycle follows (5.5.1) as before, the irregular I is white noise, and the trend follows a smooth trend structural model, i.e., $(1-B)^2 T_t$ is white noise. These model choices were made to mimic structural models popular with econometricians (although our cycle model (5.5.1) differs from that of Harvey [1989]). Once we have the parameter

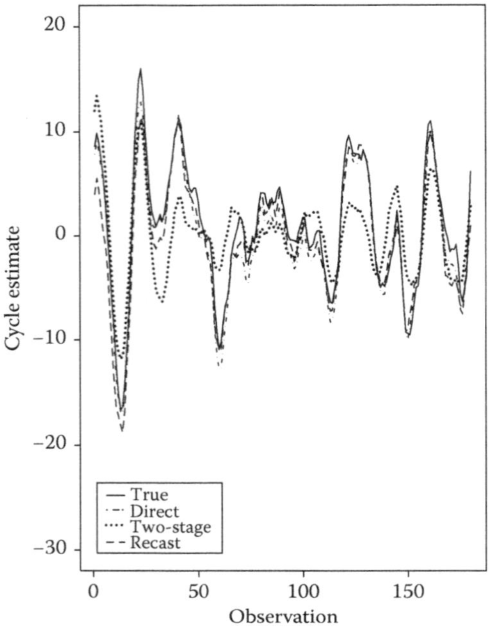

FIGURE 5.1
Representative cycle estimate in the finite sample simulation discussed in Section 5.5. Note that all three approaches are considered.

estimates, again obtained via a structural likelihood, we can compute $\ddot{\Sigma}_C$ and $\ddot{\Sigma}_{\partial CTI}$, thereby obtaining the cycle estimate, true cycle MSE, and misstated cycle MSE.*

Our numerical studies examine several specifications of the basic DGP outlined above for three sample sizes, computing for each of the three methods the cycle estimate, the true MSE curve (i.e., the diagonal of the M matrices described in Section 5.4), and the misstated MSE curve. We simulated 200 realizations of each DGP with $n = 120, 180, 240$ and $\kappa = 1$, and the other parameter choices mentioned above. These sample sizes were chosen to reflect lengths typical of series being seasonally adjusted at statistical agencies. The MLEs tended to be accurate for the direct method for $n = 180, 240$: the root MSE over the 200 simulations for ρ and ω is 0.0382 and 0.0497 at sample size 180, and 0.0297 and 0.0303 at sample size 240. The results of this simulation study are extensive and, as a result, we only provide a summary of the most salient aspects along with a plot from a representative realization (with $n = 180$), presented in Figures 5.1 through 5.3.

* The same procedure can be followed for real data, except for the construction of true MSE (for any of the three techniques), since the DGP is unknown.

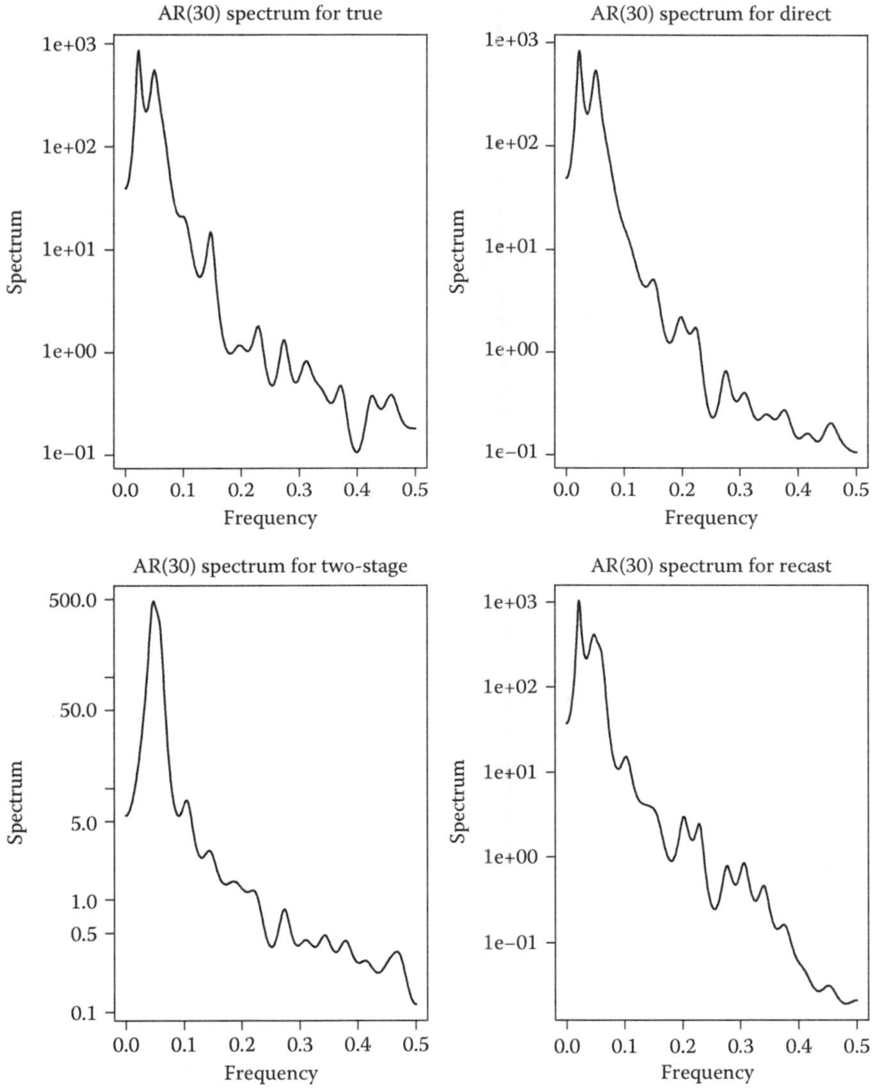

FIGURE 5.2
AR(30) spectral density estimates from a representative cycle estimate in the finite sample simulation discussed in Section 5.5. Note that all three approaches are considered.

Figure 5.1 displays the various cycle estimates along with the true generating process for a particular simulation. The direct estimate is closest to the true cycle, with the recast approach doing an excellent job as well, and the two-stage method performing worst. The temporal averages of squared

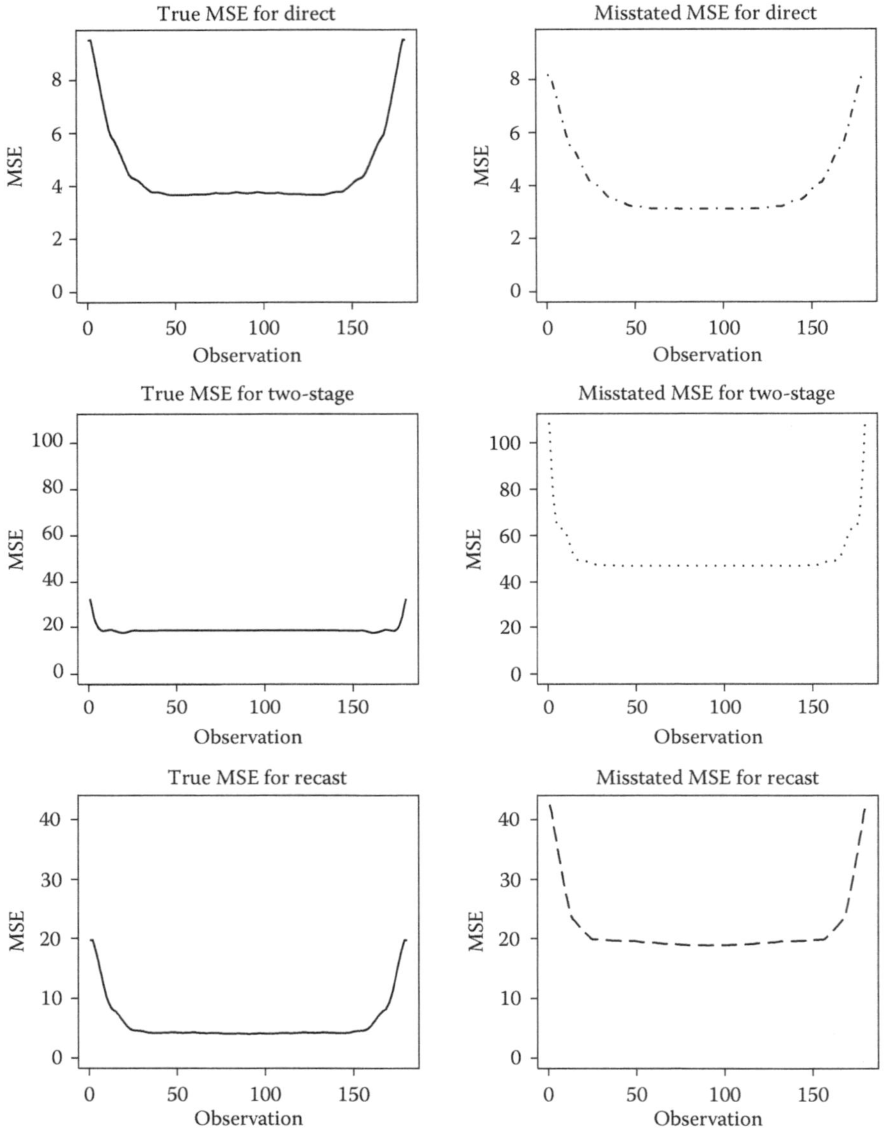

FIGURE 5.3
True and misstated MSEs for a representative cycle estimate in the finite sample simulation discussed in Section 5.5. Note that all three approaches are considered. Also the scales on the y-axes differ according to the method considered.

differences—for the direct, two-stage, and recast methods versus the truth—for this particular simulation were 2.19, 15.98, and 3.90, respectively. In the spectral domain (Figure 5.2), it is apparent that the direct method captures the underlying second-order dynamics more closely than either the two-stage or the recast approach, although it should be noted that even the MSE optimal direct estimate will always have different spectral characteristics from the true cycle, as is well-known in the signal extraction literature. In addition, Figure 5.3 illustrates that the direct method has the lowest MSE, followed by the recast approach and finally the two-stage method. Also, misstated MSEs tend to be higher than the true MSEs for these latter two methods. One key conclusion from the empirical studies is that the misstated MSEs and true MSEs for the direct method tend to be very close indeed.

The situation can be more easily digested by considering the limiting case of a bi-infinite sample size. We next present MSEs for all three methods, using pseudo-true values for parameters and frequency domain calculations described in the Appendix. This is equivalent to examining the center values of the matrix-based finite-sample MSEs when the sample size n is extremely large, so that the MLEs have converged. Of course, this calculation is intractable for large n; hence, we adopt the frequency domain methodology outlined in the Appendix, to obtain the exact asymptotic quantities. Note that the MSE is no longer time-varying. Tables 5.1 and 5.2 display pseudo-true values and asymptotic MSEs for the three methods and for a variety of DGPs.

The results indicate that the two-stage approach has slightly higher MSE than the optimal direct estimate. The recast method fares poorly for large values of κ, which is to be expected, given the parametric form of our DGP, but improves somewhat as κ shrinks. It is interesting to see which pseudo-true values are produced from the fitting of the generally misspecified airline model to the DGP and which cycle parameters arise from the two-stage method. In this latter case, fairly accurate cycle parameters can be obtained even when seasonal adjustment is first done (Table 5.1), so long as ρ is large. Most interesting, perhaps, are the results when $\kappa = 0$, i.e., no cycle actually exists in the DGP. In this case, the cycle parameter values obtained for the direct method are meaningless, but the airline model parameters match those of the DGP.

5.6 Illustration

The preceding results highlight the dangers of the two-stage method. We next provide a further illustration on the time series of unemployment level (job losers in thousands, 16 years and over) published by the Bureau of Labor Statistics (http://data.bls.gov). This has the series identification

TABLE 5.1
Pseudo-True Values for the Bi-Infinite Sample under the Three Approaches Discussed in Section 5.5

	Estimation: $\theta_X = 0.6$; $\Theta_X = 0.6$; $\omega = \pi/12$							
DGP	Airline			Two-Stage				
$\rho = 0.7$	θ_X	Θ_X	σ_X^2	ρ	ω	σ_C^2	σ_T^2	σ_I^2
$\kappa = 1$	−0.017	0.731	3.009	0.674	0.084	0.900	0.0002	0.373
$\kappa = 0.25$	0.253	0.674	1.680	0.686	0.000	0.230	0.0003	0.361
$\kappa = 0.1$	0.408	0.646	1.321	0.247	0.000	0.636	0.0022	0.000
$\kappa = 0$	0.600	0.600	1.000	0.832	0.000	0.011	0.0003	0.343
$\rho = 0.8$	θ_X	Θ_X	σ_X^2	ρ	ω	σ_C^2	σ_T^2	σ_I^2
$\kappa = 1$	−0.134	0.736	3.379	0.799	0.221	0.850	0.0002	0.394
$\kappa = 0.25$	0.132	0.683	1.868	0.791	0.190	0.225	0.0002	0.366
$\kappa = 0.1$	0.302	0.657	1.440	0.781	0.147	0.104	0.0002	0.356
$\kappa = 0$	0.600	0.600	1.000	0.832	0.000	0.011	0.0003	0.343
$\rho = 0.9$	Θ_X	θ_X	σ_X^2	ρ	ω	σ_C^2	σ_T^2	σ_I^2
$\kappa = 1$	−0.287	0.763	4.402	0.907	0.251	0.851	0.0002	0.417
$\kappa = 0.25$	−0.035	0.710	2.316	0.906	0.246	0.214	0.0002	0.386
$\kappa = 0.1$	0.140	0.681	1.713	0.903	0.241	0.091	0.0003	0.374
$\kappa = 0$	0.600	0.600	1.000	0.832	0.000	0.011	0.0003	0.343

Note: The left column gives the DGP parameter values of ρ and κ. Other columns give pseudo-true values for various parameters, for the fitted airline model and the fitted cycle–trend–irregular model of the two-stage approach. For the direct approach, pseudo-true values equal the DGP values.

LBU03023621, denoted hereafter as LBU. We examine the period from January 1967 through December 2007, purposefully excluding the current economic crisis. Figure 5.4 displays a plot of the logged series, along with its seasonal adjustment in the upper panel.

No calendar effects were found to be significant. The data were fitted with the cycle-plus-airline model of the previous section, as well as the airline model and the model of the two-stage approach. The cycle-plus-airline model had MLEs of $\widehat{\rho} = 0.973$, $\widehat{\omega} = 0.09$ (a period of 69.69 months), $\widehat{\kappa} = 0.016$, $\widehat{\theta}_X = 0$, $\widehat{\Theta}_X = 0.817$, and $\widehat{\sigma}_X^2 = 0.0028$. Fitting the airline model to the same data yields $\widehat{\theta}_X = -0.080$, $\widehat{\Theta}_X = 0.612$, and $\widehat{\sigma}_X^2 = 0.2092$. Unfortunately, the two-stage approach yields MLEs of $\widehat{\rho} = 0.471$, $\widehat{\omega} = 0.366$ (a period of 17.16 months), $\widehat{\sigma}_C^2 = 0.0516$, $\widehat{\sigma}_T^2 = 0.0218$, and $\widehat{\sigma}_I^2 = 0.0370$. The signal-to-noise ratio is adequate to capture a component, but the values of ρ and ω cannot be associated with a business cycle.

The direct estimate successfully captures the cycle of given parametric form, and this is remarkably corroborated by the result of the recast method, as seen in the second panel of Figure 5.4. The failure of the two-stage method on LBU is disappointing, but highlights the difficulty of fitting cyclical models

TABLE 5.2
MSE Values Associated with the Psuedo-True Values for a Bi-Infinite Sample under the Three Approaches Discussed in Section 5.5

	MSEs: $\theta_X = 0.6$; $\Theta_X = 0.6$								
	$\rho = 0.7$			$\rho = 0.8$			$\rho = 0.9$		
$\omega = \pi/12$	Direct	Two-Stage	Recast	Direct	Two-Stage	Recast	Direct	Two-Stage	Recast
$\kappa = 1$	1.660	1.846	1.775	2.426	2.639	2.672	3.306	3.492	3.940
$\kappa = 0.25$	0.743	0.879	0.942	1.079	1.220	1.183	1.453	1.540	1.526
$\kappa = 0.1$	0.418	0.705	0.725	0.627	0.785	0.838	0.861	0.940	0.996
$\kappa = 0$	0.000	0.297	0.502	0.000	0.297	0.502	0.000	0.297	0.502
$\omega = \pi/60$	Direct	Two-Stage	Recast	Direct	Two-Stage	Recast	Direct	Two-Stage	Recast
$\kappa = 1$	2.449	2.587	2.642	6.055	6.211	8.641	31.495	31.765	84.301
$\kappa = 0.25$	1.061	1.177	1.156	2.471	2.598	2.670	11.801	11.838	21.608
$\kappa = 0.1$	0.593	0.737	0.812	1.378	1.526	1.431	6.261	6.323	9.026
$\kappa = 0$	0.000	0.297	0.502	0.000	0.297	0.502	0.000	0.297	0.502

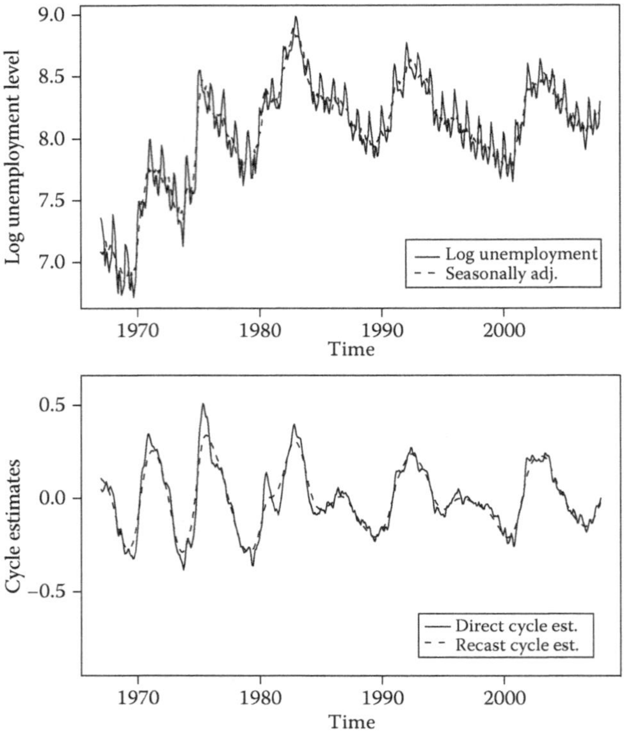

FIGURE 5.4
The top panel plots the LBU series in logs with its seasonal adjustment arising from a fitted airline model. The bottom panel provides cycle estimates from the direct and recast methods.

in practice.* One is tempted to conclude that the estimation of the cycle has been impacted by the seasonal adjustment procedure. However, it must be acknowledged that our results are contingent on a certain parametric specification of the cycle. In practice, an economist encountering such a result with the two-stage method would have recourse to fixing the value of ρ and/or ω *a priori* and reestimating the other parameters—or utilizing the HP filter on the estimated trend. The analysis would not end here.

This example does advocate the direct approach, although it must be acknowledged that the cycle-plus-airline model is rarely successful, in our experience, in the sense that many series viewed by economists as having a business cycle (e.g., housing starts and permits series) result in infeasible estimates of ρ and/or ω. However, when it works correctly, a key advantage of

* In our experience with dozens of economic series, rarely does the direct method produce viable cycle estimates, even while the two-stage approach is sometimes successful.

the direct estimation method is a fairly accurate statement of the MSE, as borne out by our simulation studies. The central values (which also happen to be the minimum values) of the MSE curves are 0.015 and 0.759 for the direct and recast methods, respectively. We know that the latter value tends to severely overestimate the true MSE in practice. Particularly as the two cyclical estimates are so close (their empirical mean square difference is 0.0022), it seems reasonable to conclude that both are providing decent estimates of an underlying cycle, but the direct method does a much better job of quantifying the MSE.

5.7 Conclusion

This chapter examines the problem of cycle estimation in the presence of seasonality. Under the rubric of a model-based univariate approach to cyclical dynamics, we quantify the real MSE of cycle estimation arising from three approaches: direct estimation, the recast approach of SEATS, and a two-stage approach involving cyclical analysis of seasonally adjusted data. The mathematical formulas are useful for demonstrating that, in finite samples, the real MSE can be quite different from the quantity that is typically stated. This discrepancy arises for two reasons: cyclical dynamics are ignored in the seasonal adjustment procedure, and the error in seasonal adjustment itself is ignored. The first problem may afflict the recast method (depending on the form of the true cycle), while both problems certainly afflict the two-stage approach. Another tool we introduce for the study of the problem is the actual limiting MSE based on a bi-infinite sample, where parameter estimates have been assumed to converge to their limiting pseudo-true values. This is informative for showing how model misspecification and the signal-to-noise ratio of cycle to seasonal–trend dynamics impact the MSE for the three methods; the pseudo-true values themselves are also helpful for understanding how spurious cycles can arise from seasonal adjustment procedures.

The scope of our numerical study is necessarily limited. We have chosen a particular form of the true cycle that biases the outcomes against the recast method; all results are based on certain choices of models (e.g., airline models and basic structural models), which we elected in an effort to mimic economic practice. It would be interesting to consider the impact of seasonal adjustment by X-11 filters, or by a model that encompasses autoregressive effects to allow for cyclical dynamics. To any of these further questions, the formulas and tools of this chapter can be readily applied with some additional effort. The issue of spurious cycles certainly merits further study.

Although the direct approach can be difficult in practice—due to the challenge of getting reasonable MLEs—it is quite appealing when it works, because we know empirically that the stated MSE is a decent approximation to the true MSE. Moreover, cycle estimates arising from this approach are likely to be most accurate when the model is correctly specified. If we wish to remain agnostic about the parametric form of the cycle, the recast method can be utilized. The caution here is that the stated MSE can be quite inaccurate if a parametric cycle is indeed present; it can also perform optimally when the cycle takes the form of a HP high-pass of the trend. The performance of the two-stage approach can be adequate in some cases, but, in general, the quantification of the MSE is highly problematic, leading to false inferences about turning points.

5.8 Appendix

5.8.1 Further Results Related to Theorem 5.1

The following theorem provides an explicit formula for the filter $F^{\alpha}_{\alpha\beta\gamma}$ in terms of "two-component" filters $F^{\alpha}_{\alpha\beta}$, $F^{\beta}_{\beta\gamma}$, etc. It is a generalization of Theorem 1 of McElroy and Sutcliffe (2006) to the case where all three unobserved components are difference stationary. We let 1 denote a shorthand for the $n \times n$ identity matrix.

Theorem 5.2 *The matrices* $1 - F^{\alpha}_{\alpha\gamma}F^{\beta}_{\beta\gamma}$ *and* $1 - F^{\alpha}_{\alpha\beta}F^{\gamma}_{\beta\gamma}$ *are invertible, and*

$$F^{\alpha}_{\alpha\beta\gamma} = \left(1 - F^{\alpha}_{\alpha\gamma}F^{\beta}_{\beta\gamma}\right)^{-1} F^{\alpha}_{\alpha\gamma}\left(1 - F^{\beta}_{\beta\gamma}\right) = \left(1 - F^{\alpha}_{\alpha\beta}F^{\gamma}_{\beta\gamma}\right)^{-1} F^{\alpha}_{\alpha\beta}\left(1 - F^{\gamma}_{\beta\gamma}\right).$$

The invertibility claimed in Theorem 5.2 depends upon the assumption that the differencing operators are relatively prime. This result can be applied to cycle estimation via the following corollary:

Corollary 5.2 *We have the following expressions:*

$$\begin{aligned} F^{C}_{CSTI} &= \left(1 - F^{C}_{CTI}F^{S}_{STI}\right)^{-1} F^{C}_{CTI}\left(1 - F^{S}_{STI}\right) \\ &= \left(1 - F^{C}_{CT}F^{SI}_{STI}\right)^{-1} F^{C}_{CT}\left(1 - F^{SI}_{STI}\right). \end{aligned}$$

The second expression in this result is interesting, because the filter $F^{C}_{CTI}(1 - F^{S}_{STI})$ corresponds to seasonal adjustment that ignores cyclical dynamics followed by cycle estimation from a nonseasonal specification. The result indicates that this matrix fails to equal the correct filter F^{C}_{CSTI}, but requires further application of $\left(1 - F^{C}_{CTI}F^{S}_{STI}\right)^{-1}$. The third expression likewise shows that trend filtering without utilizing cyclical dynamics, followed by F^{C}_{CT} for cycle estimation, does not equal the optimal cycle filter, but the additional application of $\left(1 - F^{C}_{CT}F^{SI}_{STI}\right)^{-1}$ is required.

5.8.2 Proofs

Proof of Theorem 5.1

First we note that $F^{\alpha}_{\alpha\beta\gamma} + F^{\beta}_{\alpha\beta\gamma} + F^{\gamma}_{\alpha\beta\gamma} = 1$ implies that $F^{\alpha}_{\alpha\beta\gamma} + F^{\beta}_{\alpha\beta\gamma} = 1 - F^{\gamma}_{\alpha\beta\gamma} = F^{\alpha\beta}_{\alpha\beta\gamma}$. Now the theorem results from a commutativity property of the extraction matrices:

$$F^{\alpha}_{\alpha\beta} F^{\alpha\beta}_{\alpha\beta\gamma} = \left(1 - F^{\beta}_{\alpha\beta}\right) F^{\alpha}_{\alpha\beta\gamma} + F^{\alpha}_{\alpha\beta} F^{\beta}_{\alpha\beta\gamma} = F^{\alpha}_{\alpha\beta\gamma} + \left(F^{\alpha}_{\alpha\beta} F^{\beta}_{\alpha\beta\gamma} - F^{\beta}_{\alpha\beta} F^{\alpha}_{\alpha\beta\gamma}\right),$$

which uses $F^{\alpha}_{\alpha\beta} + F^{\beta}_{\alpha\beta} = 1$. The expression in parentheses is similar to a commutator for the matrices; next we show that it is zero, which will prove the theorem. Let the matrices $\underline{\Delta}_{\alpha\beta}$, $\underline{\Delta}_{\alpha\gamma}$, and $\underline{\Delta}_{\beta\gamma}$ be defined similarly to $\underline{\Delta}_T$ and $\underline{\Delta}_S$, but with coefficients of $\delta^{\alpha}\delta^{\beta}$, $\delta^{\alpha}\delta^{\gamma}$, and $\delta^{\beta}\delta^{\gamma}$, respectively, and with appropriate dimensions such that, similar to Equation 5.3.1, $\underline{\Delta}_{\alpha\beta}\Delta_{\gamma} = \underline{\Delta}_{\alpha\gamma}\Delta_{\beta} = \underline{\Delta}_{\beta\gamma}\Delta_{\alpha} = \Delta$ is satisfied. Following McElroy (2008a), the filter formulas are given by

$$F^{\alpha}_{\alpha\beta} = \left(\Delta'_{\alpha}\Sigma^{-1}_{\partial\alpha}\Delta_{\alpha} + \Delta'_{\beta}\Sigma^{-1}_{\partial\beta}\Delta_{\beta}\right)^{-1} \Delta'_{\beta}\Sigma^{-1}_{\partial\beta}\Delta_{\beta}, \quad \Delta_{\beta}F^{\beta}_{\alpha\beta\gamma} = \Sigma_{\partial\beta}\underline{\Delta}'_{\alpha\gamma}\Sigma^{-1}_{W}\Delta.$$

Therefore, $F^{\alpha}_{\alpha\beta}F^{\beta}_{\alpha\beta\gamma} = \left(\Delta'_{\alpha}\Sigma^{-1}_{\partial\alpha}\Delta_{\alpha} + \Delta'_{\beta}\Sigma^{-1}_{\partial\beta}\Delta_{\beta}\right)^{-1} \Delta'\Sigma^{-1}_{W}\Delta$. Similarly,

$$F^{\beta}_{\alpha\beta} = \left(\Delta'_{\alpha}\Sigma^{-1}_{\partial\alpha}\Delta_{\alpha} + \Delta'_{\beta}\Sigma^{-1}_{\partial\beta}\Delta_{\beta}\right)^{-1} \Delta'_{\alpha}\Sigma^{-1}_{\partial\alpha}\Delta_{\alpha}, \quad \Delta_{\alpha}F^{\alpha}_{\alpha\beta\gamma} = \Sigma_{\partial\alpha}\underline{\Delta}'_{\beta\gamma}\Sigma^{-1}_{W}\Delta,$$

which produces $F^{\beta}_{\alpha\beta}F^{\alpha}_{\alpha\beta\gamma} = \left(\Delta'_{\alpha}\Sigma^{-1}_{\partial\alpha}\Delta_{\alpha} + \Delta'_{\beta}\Sigma^{-1}_{\partial\beta}\Delta_{\beta}\right)^{-1} \Delta'\Sigma^{-1}_{W}\Delta$. This concludes the proof. □

Proof of Theorem 5.2

We prove the first line of the theorem. To show the invertibility of $1 - F^{\alpha}_{\alpha\gamma}F^{\beta}_{\beta\gamma}$, we compute

$$1 - F^{\alpha}_{\alpha\gamma}F^{\beta}_{\beta\gamma} = 1 - F^{\alpha}_{\alpha\gamma}(1 - F^{\gamma}_{\beta\gamma}) = F^{\gamma}_{\alpha\gamma} + F^{\alpha}_{\alpha\gamma}F^{\gamma}_{\beta\gamma}.$$

We need to define some additional differencing matrices. Let $\underline{\Delta}_{\beta}$ and $\underline{\Delta}_{\gamma}$ be defined similarly to the matrices in the proof of Theorem 5.1. Also, the matrix $\Delta_{\beta\gamma}$ does $\delta^{\beta}\delta^{\gamma}$ differencing, but is $n - (d_{\beta} + d_{\gamma}) \times n$ dimensional. Then we have the relation $\Delta_{\beta\gamma} = \underline{\Delta}_{\beta}\Delta_{\gamma} = \underline{\Delta}_{\gamma}\Delta_{\beta}$ as in Equation 5.3.1. Let $\partial\beta\gamma$ denote the differenced $\beta + \gamma$ component: $\partial\beta\gamma = \Delta_{\beta\gamma}(\beta + \gamma) = \underline{\Delta}_{\gamma}\partial\beta + \underline{\Delta}_{\beta}\partial\gamma$. Then the following formulas hold:

$$\begin{aligned}
F_{\alpha\gamma}^{\alpha} &= \left(\Delta_\alpha' \Sigma_{\partial\alpha}^{-1} \Delta_\alpha + \Delta_\gamma' \Sigma_{\partial\gamma}^{-1} \Delta_\gamma\right)^{-1} \Delta_\gamma' \Sigma_{\partial\gamma}^{-1} \Delta_\gamma, \\
F_{\alpha\gamma}^{\gamma} &= \left(\Delta_\alpha' \Sigma_{\partial\alpha}^{-1} \Delta_\alpha + \Delta_\gamma' \Sigma_{\partial\gamma}^{-1} \Delta_\gamma\right)^{-1} \Delta_\alpha' \Sigma_{\partial\alpha}^{-1} \Delta_\alpha, \\
\Delta_\gamma F_{\beta\gamma}^{\gamma} &= \Sigma_{\partial\gamma} \underline{\Delta}_\beta' \Sigma_{\partial\beta\gamma}^{-1} \Delta_{\beta\gamma}, \\
F_{\alpha\gamma}^{\alpha} F_{\beta\gamma}^{\gamma} &= \left(\Delta_\alpha' \Sigma_{\partial\alpha}^{-1} \Delta_\alpha + \Delta_\gamma' \Sigma_{\partial\gamma}^{-1} \Delta_\gamma\right)^{-1} \Delta_{\beta\gamma}' \Sigma_{\partial\beta\gamma}^{-1} \Delta_{\beta\gamma}, \\
F_{\alpha\gamma}^{\gamma} + F_{\alpha\gamma}^{\alpha} F_{\beta\gamma}^{\gamma} &= \left(\Delta_\alpha' \Sigma_{\partial\alpha}^{-1} \Delta_\alpha + \Delta_\gamma' \Sigma_{\partial\gamma}^{-1} \Delta_\gamma\right)^{-1} \left[\Delta_\alpha' \Sigma_{\partial\alpha}^{-1} \Delta_\alpha + \Delta_{\beta\gamma}' \Sigma_{\partial\beta\gamma}^{-1} \Delta_{\beta\gamma}\right].
\end{aligned}$$

The expression in square brackets is invertible, since it is the sum of two nonnegative definite matrices whose null spaces' intersection is the zero vector because δ^α and $\delta^\beta\delta^\gamma$ are relatively prime; see Lemma 2 of McElroy and Sutcliffe (2006). This establishes the invertibility of $1 - F_{\alpha\gamma}^{\alpha} F_{\beta\gamma}^{\beta}$ and gives an expression for its inverse. Finally, we compute the result:

$$\begin{aligned}
&\left(1 - F_{\alpha\gamma}^{\alpha} F_{\beta\gamma}^{\beta}\right)^{-1} F_{\alpha\gamma}^{\alpha} \left(1 - F_{\beta\gamma}^{\beta}\right) \\
&= \left[\Delta_\alpha' \Sigma_{\partial\alpha}^{-1} \Delta_\alpha + \Delta_{\beta\gamma}' \Sigma_{\partial\beta\gamma}^{-1} \Delta_{\beta\gamma}\right]^{-1} \Delta_\gamma' \Sigma_{\partial\gamma}^{-1} \Delta_\gamma F_{\beta\gamma}^{\gamma}, \\
&= \left[\Delta_\alpha' \Sigma_{\partial\alpha}^{-1} \Delta_\alpha + \Delta_{\beta\gamma}' \Sigma_{\partial\beta\gamma}^{-1} \Delta_{\beta\gamma}\right]^{-1} \Delta_\gamma' \underline{\Delta}_\beta' \Sigma_{\partial\beta\gamma}^{-1} \Delta_{\beta\gamma} = F_{\alpha\beta\gamma}^{\alpha}.
\end{aligned}$$

□

5.8.3 Derivations for Section 5.4

Direct Approach

The formula for the filter matrix is (5.3.2); the corresponding error is

$$\begin{aligned}
\dot{F}_{CSTI}^{C} Y - C = &-\left(\dot{\Sigma}_C^{-1} + \Delta' \dot{\Sigma}_{\partial STI}^{-1} \Delta\right)^{-1} \dot{\Sigma}_C^{-1} C \\
&+ \left(\dot{\Sigma}_C^{-1} + \Delta' \dot{\Sigma}_{\partial STI}^{-1} \Delta\right)^{-1} \Delta' \dot{\Sigma}_{\partial STI}^{-1} \partial STI,
\end{aligned}$$

from which Equation 5.4.1 easily follows.

Two-Stage Approach

We use the fact that $\Delta_T \dot{F}_{STI}^{TI} = \dot{\Sigma}_{\partial TI} \underline{\Delta}_S' \dot{\Sigma}_{\partial STI}^{-1} \Delta$ and $\ddot{F}_{CTI}^{C} = \ddot{\Sigma}_C \Delta_T' \ddot{\Sigma}_{\partial CTI}^{-1} \Delta_T$ to derive the filter formula. The error process and error covariance formula then follow by standard calculations.

Recast Approach

We begin with the definition of the implied cycle model, utilizing both the fitted model for ∂Y and the HP filter, as described in Kaiser and Maravall (2005); also see McElroy (2008b). We begin with a fitted pseudo-spectral density $\dot{f}_Y$

from which we obtain, via canonical decomposition, the trend component spectrum $\dot{f}_T$. However, we take the viewpoint that this actually corresponds to a trend cycle, not just a trend, so we will write $\dot{f}_{CT}$. Utilize the following notation: the covariance matrix associated with a spectral density g has jkth entry $\Sigma_{jk}(g) = 1/2\pi \int_{-\pi}^{\pi} g(\lambda)e^{i\lambda(j-k)}\,d\lambda$, i.e., the autocovariance at lag $j-k$ corresponding to the spectral density g. Let the frequency response function of the HP filter $H(B)$ be denoted as $H(e^{-i\lambda})$ (which is given by the formula $q/\{(2-2\cos\lambda)^2+q\}$ for signal-to-noise ratio q); then we define implied spectra for the cycle and trend as follows:

$$\ddot{f}_T(\lambda) := H(e^{-i\lambda})\dot{f}_{CT}(\lambda) \quad \ddot{f}_C(\lambda) := (1-H(e^{-i\lambda}))\,\dot{f}_{CT}(\lambda).$$

Since the HP high-pass accomplishes second differencing, we have $1-H(e^{-i\lambda})$ equal to $|1-e^{-i\lambda}|^2$ times a bounded function, see McElroy (2008b). This differencing factor cancels with the poles in $\dot{f}_{CT}$, resulting in a bounded function for $\ddot{f}_C$. Trivially, $\ddot{f}_{CT} := \ddot{f}_C + \ddot{f}_T = \dot{f}_{CT}$. With these definitions, we can define $\ddot{F}^C_{CT}$ as follows: $\ddot{\Sigma}_C := \Sigma(\ddot{f}_C)$ and $\ddot{F}^C_{CT} = \ddot{\Sigma}_C\Delta_T'\ddot{\Sigma}^{-1}_{\partial CT}\Delta_T$. Of course, $\ddot{f}_{\partial CT} = \dot{f}_{\partial CT}$, which shows how to compute the matrix $\ddot{\Sigma}_{\partial CT} = \dot{\Sigma}_{\partial CT}$. Next, note that the estimate of the differenced trend cycle would be $\dot{\Sigma}_{\partial CT}\underline{\Delta}_S'\dot{\Sigma}^{-1}_{\partial Y}\partial Y$, which should correspond to the action of $\Delta_T\dot{F}^{CT}_{CSTI}$ on Y; therefore,

$$\ddot{F}^C_{CT}\dot{F}^{CT}_{CSTI} = \ddot{\Sigma}_C\Delta_T'\ddot{\Sigma}^{-1}_{\partial CT}\Delta_T\dot{F}^{CT}_{CSTI} = \ddot{\Sigma}_C\Delta_T'\underline{\Delta}_S'\dot{\Sigma}^{-1}_{\partial Y}\Delta = \ddot{\Sigma}_C\Delta'\dot{\Sigma}^{-1}_{\partial Y}\Delta,$$

using Equation 5.3.1. This demonstrates the stated filter formula, and the error process is $\ddot{\Sigma}_C\Delta'\dot{\Sigma}^{-1}_{\partial Y}\partial Y - C$, from which the stated error covariance formula follows using the fact that the covariance of ∂Y and C is $\Delta\Sigma_C$.

5.8.4 Frequency Domain Calculations for Asymptotic MSE

We begin by reviewing elementary material on pseudo-true values. Letting $f_{\partial Y}(\cdot;\psi)$ denote the spectral density of a model for the stationary process $\{\partial Y_t\}$, and $\widetilde{f}_{\partial Y}$ its true spectral density, the Kullback–Leibler discrepancy between these spectra is

$$D(\psi) = \frac{1}{2\pi}\int_{-\pi}^{\pi}\log f_{\partial Y}(\lambda;\psi)\,d\lambda + \frac{1}{2\pi}\int_{-\pi}^{\pi}\frac{\widetilde{f}_{\partial Y}(\lambda)}{f_{\partial Y}(\lambda;\psi)}\,d\lambda,$$

expressed as a function of the parameter vector ψ (Taniguchi and Kakizawa 2000). This is essentially the Whittle likelihood. The minimizers of D are called the pseudo-true values of ψ, and are denoted as $\dot{\psi}$ when they are unique. When the model is correctly specified, $\widetilde{f}_{\partial Y} = f_{\partial Y}(\cdot;\widetilde{\psi})$ and the pseudo-true values are equal to the true parameter values; but when the model is misspecified, the pseudo-true values are the limit in probability of the MLEs. As a numerical exercise, given the knowledge of a process and a misspecified model, one can compute $D(\psi)$ and calculate its minimizers. Analytical solutions can be found in the case of an AR(p), in which $\dot{\psi}$ solves the Yule–Walker equations (with innovation variance given by concentration), but, in general, the minimization must be computed numerically, similar to the MLE calculations.

When we compute quantities (such as MSEs) using the pseudo-true values, we are accounting for a type of distortion that arises from model misspecification. In viewing a pseudo-true value as an approximation to an MLE, we ignore statistical variation in the MLE. We next derive the asymptotic MSE quantities. First, consider fitting a correctly specified cycle-plus-airline model to the DGP. We have the following pseudo-spectra, where $z = e^{-i\lambda}$:

$$
\begin{aligned}
f_C(\lambda) &= \frac{\sigma_C^2}{|1 - 2\rho\cos(\omega)z + \rho^2 z^2|^2},\\
f_X(\lambda) &= \frac{|(1-\theta_X z)(1-\Theta_X z^{12})|^2 \sigma_X^2}{|(1-z)(1-z^{12})|^2},\\
f_C(\lambda) + f_X(\lambda) &= \frac{|\Theta_{CX}(z)|^2 \sigma_{CX}^2}{|1 - 2\rho\cos(\omega)z + \rho^2 z^2|^2 |(1-z)(1-z^{12})|^2}.
\end{aligned}
$$

The third spectral density is expressed in reduced form, where $\Theta_{CX}(B)$ has degree 15 and is obtained via spectral factorization. Then, the WK MSE is the integral of $f_C f_X/(f_C + f_X)$ evaluated at the true parameter values:

$$
\frac{1}{2\pi}\int_{-\pi}^{\pi} \frac{|(1-\theta_X z)(1-\Theta_X z^{12})|^2 \, \sigma_C^2 \sigma_X^2}{|\Theta_{CX}(z)|^2 \, \sigma_{CX}^2} \, d\lambda.
$$

In the two-stage method, the final cycle filter is given by the composition of the seasonal adjustment filter and the cycle filter, i.e., $\ddot{f}_C \dot{f}_{TI}/(\ddot{f}_{CTI}\dot{f}_{STI})$, and the MSE simplifies to

$$
\begin{aligned}
&\frac{1}{2\pi}\int_{-\pi}^{\pi} \frac{|\dot{\Theta}_{TI}(z)|^4 |\tilde{\Theta}_{STI}(z)|^2 |1-z|^4 |U(z)|^2 \ddot{\sigma}_C^4 \dot{\sigma}_{TI}^4 \tilde{\sigma}_{STI}^2}{|\ddot{\Theta}_{CTI}(z)|^4 |\dot{\Theta}_{STI}(z)|^4 \ddot{\sigma}_{CTI}^4 \dot{\sigma}_{STI}^4} \, d\lambda\\
&+ \frac{1}{2\pi}\int_{-\pi}^{\pi} \frac{|\dot{\Theta}_{TI}(z)|^4 |1-z|^8 |U(z)|^4 \ddot{\sigma}_C^4 \dot{\sigma}_{TI}^4 \tilde{\sigma}_C^2}{|\ddot{\Theta}_{CTI}(z)|^4 |\dot{\Theta}_{STI}(z)|^4 |1-2\tilde{\rho}\cos(\tilde{\omega})z + \tilde{\rho}^2 z^2|^2 \ddot{\sigma}_{CTI}^4 \dot{\sigma}_{STI}^4} \, d\lambda\\
&- \frac{2}{2\pi}\int_{-\pi}^{\pi} \frac{|\dot{\Theta}_{TI}(z)|^2 |1-z|^4 |U(z)|^2 \ddot{\sigma}_C^2 \dot{\sigma}_{TI}^2 \tilde{\sigma}_C^2}{|\ddot{\Theta}_{CTI}(z)|^2 |\dot{\Theta}_{STI}(z)|^2 |1-2\tilde{\rho}\cos(\tilde{\omega})z + \tilde{\rho}^2 z^2|^2 \ddot{\sigma}_{CTI}^2 \dot{\sigma}_{STI}^2} \, d\lambda\\
&+ \frac{1}{2\pi}\int_{-\pi}^{\pi} \frac{\tilde{\sigma}_C^2}{|1-2\tilde{\rho}\cos(\tilde{\omega})z + \tilde{\rho}^2 z^2|^2} \, d\lambda.
\end{aligned}
$$

Here, the second dot denotes pseudo-true parameter values for the cycle-trend-irregular model fitted to the limiting estimated seasonal adjustment process with spectrum $\dot{f}_{TI}^2 \tilde{f}_{CSTI}/\dot{f}_{STI}^2$, which is given by

$$
\frac{\dot{f}_{TI}^2 \tilde{f}_{CSTI}}{\dot{f}_{STI}^2} = \frac{|\dot{\Theta}_{TI}(z)|^4 |\tilde{\Theta}_{CSTI}(z)|^2 |U(z)|^2}{|\dot{\Theta}_{STI}(z)|^4 |1-2\tilde{\rho}\cos(\tilde{\omega})z + \tilde{\rho}^2 z^2|^2 |1-z|^4} \, \frac{\dot{\sigma}_{TI}^4 \tilde{\sigma}_{CSTI}^2}{\dot{\sigma}_{STI}^4}.
$$

Next, for the recast method, we fit an airline model to the DGP and produce the WK trend estimate—the corresponding pseudo-true values are denoted with a dot. In this case, the cycle estimate is $\widehat{C}_t = (1 - H(B))\Psi(B)Y_t$, where $H(B)$ is the HP filter and $\Psi(B)$ is the WK trend extraction filter. The ARMA form of $1 - H(z)$ is useful for computing MSE: $1 - H(z) = |1 - z|^4 / |\phi(z)|^2 \, c/q$ with q the given signal-to-noise ratio of the HP filter, and c and $\phi(B) = 1 + \phi_1 B + \phi_2 B^2$ given by (2.10) through (2.12) of McElroy (2008b); also see (3.2). The error process can then be written as

$$\begin{aligned}\widehat{C}_t - C_t = {} & \frac{c\dot{\sigma}_T^2}{q\dot{\sigma}_X^2} \frac{\dot{\Theta}_T(B)\dot{\Theta}_T(F)(1-F)^2 U(F)}{\phi(B)\phi(F)\dot{\Theta}_X(B)\dot{\Theta}_X(F)} \partial X_t \\ & + \left(\frac{c\dot{\sigma}_T^2}{q\dot{\sigma}_X^2} \frac{\dot{\Theta}_T(B)\dot{\Theta}_T(F)(1-F)^2(1-B)^2 U(F)U(B)}{\phi(B)\phi(F)\dot{\Theta}_X(B)\dot{\Theta}_X(F)} - 1 \right) C_t.\end{aligned}$$

Hence (with the tilde on parameters denoting the true values), the recast MSE can be written as

$$\begin{aligned}& \frac{1}{2\pi}\int_{-\pi}^{\pi} \frac{|\dot{\Theta}_T(z)|^4 |1-z|^4 |U(z)|^2 |\tilde{\Theta}_X(z)|^2}{|\phi(z)|^4 |\dot{\Theta}_X(z)|^4} \frac{c^2\dot{\sigma}_T^4}{q^2\dot{\sigma}_X^4} \tilde{\sigma}_X^2 \, d\lambda \\ & + \frac{1}{2\pi}\int_{-\pi}^{\pi} \left(\frac{c\dot{\sigma}_T^2}{q\dot{\sigma}_X^2} \frac{|\dot{\Theta}_T(z)|^2 |1-z|^4 |U(z)|^2}{|\phi(z)|^2 |\dot{\Theta}_X(z)|^2} - 1 \right)^2 \frac{\tilde{\sigma}_C^2}{|1 - 2\tilde{\rho}\cos(\tilde{\omega})z + \tilde{\rho}^2 z^2|^2} \, d\lambda.\end{aligned}$$

References

Baxter, M. and King, R. (1999). Measuring business cycles: Approximate band-pass filters for economic time series. *The Review of Economics and Statistics* 81:575–93.

Bell, W. (1984). Signal extraction for nonstationary time series. *The Annals of Statistics* 12:646–64.

Bell, W. and Hilmer, S. (1988). A matrix approach to likelihood evaluation and signal extraction for ARIMA component time series models. Technical Report, U.S. Census Bureau.

Bell, W. and Hilmer, S. (1991). Initializing the Kalman filter for nonstationary time series models (Corr: V13 P281-282). *Journal of Time Series Analysis* 12:283–300.

Bell, W. R. and Hillmer, S. C. (1983). Modeling time series with calendar variation. *Journal of the American Statistical Association* 78:526–34.

Burman, J. P. (1980). Seasonal adjustment by signal extraction. *Journal of the Royal Statistical Society, Series A: General* 143:321–37.

Durbin, J. and Koopman, S. J. (2001). *Time Series Analysis by State Space Methods.* Oxford: Oxford University Press.

Gersch, W. and Kitagawa, G. (1983). The prediction of time series with trends and seasonalities. *Journal of Business and Economic Statistics* 1:253–64.

Harvey, A. and Proietti, T. (2005). *Readings in Unobserved Component Models.* Oxford: Oxford University Press.

Harvey, A. C. (1989). *Forecasting, Structural Time Series Models, and the Kalman Filter.* Cambridge: Cambridge University Press.

Hillmer, S. C. and Tiao, G. C. (1982). An ARIMA Model-Based Approach to Seasonal Adjustment. *Journal of the American Statistical Association* 77:63–70.

Hodrick, R. and Prescott, E. (1997). Postwar U.S. business cycles: An empirical investigation. *Journal of Money, Credit, and Banking* 29:1–16.

Kaiser, R. and Maravall, A. (2001). *Measuring Business Cycles in Economic Time Series.* New York: Springer-Verlag.

Kaiser, R. and Maravall, A. (2005). Combining filter design with model-based filtering (with an application to business-cycle estimation) (Pkg: P691-715). *International Journal of Forecasting* 21(4):691–710.

Maravall, A. and Caporello, G. (2004). Program TSW: Revised reference manual. Technical Report, Research Department, Bank of Spain.

McElroy, T. (2008a). Matrix formulas for nonstationary ARIMA signal extraction. *Econometric Theory* 24:1–22.

McElroy, T. (2008b). NOTES: Exact formulas for the Hodrick-Prescott filter. *The Econometrics Journal Online* 11(1):209–17.

McElroy, T. and Sutcliffe, A. (2006). An iterated parametric approach to nonstationary signal extraction. *Computational Statistics and Data Analysis* 50:2206–231.

Peña, D., Tiao, G. C., and Tsay, R. S. (2001). *A Course in Time Series Analysis.* New York: John Wiley.

Roberts, C., Holan, S., and Monsell, B. (2010). Comparison of X-12 ARIMA trading day regressors to country specific regressors. *Journal of Official Statistics* 26:371–94.

Soukup, R. and Findley, D. (2001). Detection and modeling of trading day effects. In *ICES II: Proceedings of the Second International Conference on Establishment Surveys*, 743–753. Alexandria: American Statistical Association.

Stock, J. and Watson, M. (1999). Business cycle fluctuations in U.S. macroeconomic time series. In *Handbook of Macroeconomics*, eds. J. Taylor and M. Woodford, Vol. 1a, 3–64. North-Holland: Elsevier.

Taniguchi, M. and Kakizawa, Y. (2000). *Asymptotic Theory of Statistical Inference for Time Series.* New York: Springer-Verlag.

6

Frequency Domain Analysis of Seasonal Adjustment Filters Applied to Periodic Labor Force Survey Series

Richard B. Tiller

CONTENTS

6.1 Introduction

Statistical agencies routinely seasonally adjust large numbers of time series generated from periodic labor force surveys. While these surveys produce highly reliable estimates for national aggregates, the national samples are spread too thin geographically to produce reliable subnational estimates. Moreover, these surveys often use a rotating panel design in which a portion of the sample is retained each period. As a result, survey error (SE) with complex autocorrelation patterns can be a major source of variation in the observed series. The purpose of this paper is to examine the effects of seasonally adjusting a labor force survey series with two widely used methods that ignore SE, X-11/X-12-ARIMA (Dagum 1980; Findley et al. 1998) and SEATS (Gómez and Maravall 1994), and to show how adjustments produced by these methods can be modified to account for SE. The two methods differ in how signal extraction filters are obtained. SEATS filters are more tailored to the specific properties of the series than the X-11 filters. A question to explore is whether this difference in filter selection makes SEATS more effective in handling the effects of SE than X-11. Where SE is small, the seasonal adjustments ignoring SE differ little from those that account for it.

Labor force estimates from the Current Population Series (CPS) are used as examples. Following Findley and Martin (2006), we use frequency domain diagnostics in a nonparametric way as a principal tool for analyzing the properties of alternative filters for both historical and real-time application.

There has been considerable research on expanding time series models to account for SE. These models originated in the "small area" estimation literature where the focus is on reducing high variability due to small sample size by estimating the "true series," i.e., the survey series that would be produced from a complete census of the population (Scott, Smith, and Jones 1977; Bell and Hillmer 1990; Pfeffermann 1991; and Tiller 1992). Hausman and Watson (1985) were among the first to recognize the importance of accounting for SE when seasonally adjusting a survey series. Pfeffermann, Feder, and Signorelli (1998) demonstrated that trend estimation can be seriously distorted by SE. Bell (2004) also presents an example of model-based seasonal adjustment accounting for SE. These studies concentrated on time domain analysis and some only on historical filters where, except for the end points, signal extraction is done with two-sided filters that are symmetric in the middle of the series. In this paper, we go beyond these studies to provide special insights available from frequency domain analysis and to study both historical filters and real-time performance of one-sided filters designed to account for SE.

To produce SEATS and X-11 type time series decompositions and filter weights, we use the X-13-ARIMA-SEATS (X-13A-S) program currently in beta release from the Bureau of Census in collaboration with the Bank of Spain (Findley 2005). This software integrates SEATS into the X-12-ARIMA program as an alternative option to X-11 seasonal adjustment. Special software was written in SAS Interactive Matrix Language (IML) to directly account for SE in estimating time series models.

The plan of the rest of this chapter is as follows. Section 6.2 discusses the characteristics of the CPS that are important for time series decomposition. Section 6.3 analyzes the effects that SE has on the outputs of conventional nonseasonal and trend filters, which ignore SE, referred to as ISE filters, and how these filters can be modified to account for SE, referred to as ASE filters. Section 6.4 presents a numerical example based on the results of Section 6.3. In Section 6.5, we study a specific state employment series from the CPS where the SE is not only autocorrelated but also heteroskedastic. Section 6.6 presents the conclusions.

6.2 Time Series Properties of Current Population Survey Sampling Errors

We use employment series at the state level from the CPS as an example. The CPS is a nationwide monthly sample of households that produces estimates of employment and unemployment and other labor force characteristics of the population. The CPS design raises two types of problems for seasonal adjustment at the state level. The first, and most obvious, is the variability in the data due to large sampling errors. Moreover, this variability changes over time with changes in the sample size or design and in the true levels. Secondly, its overlapping sample induces autocorrelations in the SE, giving it trend-like properties.

In the classical decomposition, the aggregate time series, Y_t, is assumed to be observed without error (true series) and to be decomposable into mutually independent nonseasonal, N_t, and seasonal, S_t, components. We consider an additive decomposition (possibly after a log transformation),

$$Y_t = N_t + S_t, \quad N_t = T_t + I_t,$$

where N_t is further decomposed into mutually independent trend (T_t) and irregular (I_t) components. When the observed series is generated by a periodic survey, a fourth unobserved component, the SE (e_t), independent of Y_t, is added to the classical decomposition,

$$y_t = Y_t + e_t; \quad e_t \sim (0, \sigma^2_{e,t}), \quad \mathrm{Cov}(e_\tau, e_t) = \rho_{e,|t-\tau|}(\sigma_{e,t}\sigma_{e,\tau}),$$

where the SE variance is time-varying and the SE autocorrelations, $\rho_{e,|t-\tau|}$, are fixed for a given lag length since, in the case of the CPS, the survey panel rotation (discussed below) is fixed.

The source of SE autocorrelation is the CPS rotating panel design that generates major overlaps in the monthly samples. The sample is divided into 8 panels, which are introduced into the sample, once a month for 8 months, using a 4-8-4 scheme; i.e., each panel is interviewed for 4 months, dropped for 8 months, interviewed for 4 additional months, and then permanently dropped from the sample. Replacement household units are selected from nearby addresses.

Figure 6.1 shows the employment autocorrelations, averaged over the states, along with the proportion of the sample consisting of identical units in the current sample that were also in sample k months ago (sample overlap). Samples 1 month apart have 75% of their units in common and over 12 months have 50% of their units in common. As can be seen in Figure 6.1, the autocorrelation pattern is directly related to the size of the overlap. Note, however, that samples from 4 to 8 months and over 15 months apart have no units in common but nevertheless, there is still some correlation since units that permanently leave the sample are replaced with nearby addresses. These autocorrelations were computed based on a method discussed by Zimmerman and Robison (1995).

We develop and analyze results for two types of models of the CPS. In Section 6.3, we assume the SE is stationary with a known variance–covariance matrix and the true series is generated by a known model, and show how to adjust conventional filters for SE and how to compute gains from the adjustment. In Section 6.4, an Airline model with parameter values selected to be broadly representative of the state CPS series is used to provide a numerical example

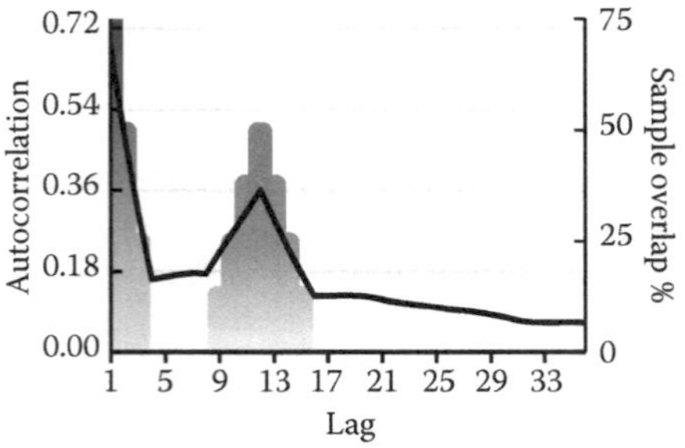

FIGURE 6.1
CPS employment SE autocorrelations (line) and sample overlap (shaded bars).

to illustrate the results of Section 6.3. In our second example, presented in Section 6.5, we fit a model to the CPS series for the State of Maryland where the SE is heteroskedastic as well as autocorrelated. This model is used to produce estimates of the true series, which are seasonally adjusted and compared to direct seasonal adjustment of the CPS series.

6.3 Time-Invariant Filtering with Stationary Survey Error

Conventional seasonal adjustment methods ignore SE. These ISE filters produce a decomposition of only the survey series, whereas a method that does account for survey error (ASE) produces, in addition, a decomposition of the true series. How different these two decompositions are depends on the properties of the SE. To illustrate this point, we begin with a hypothetical case where we assume knowledge of the ISE filters applicable to series without SE, and also consider the ASE filters appropriate for series with SE. In practice, both filters are unknown and have to be estimated with a model that accounts for SE. Although hypothetical, the results of this section and the following numerical example closely correspond to what happens in real empirical applications, as will be demonstrated in Section 6.5.

Let the decomposition of the observed series be expressed in general form as the sum of $k-1$ mutually independent components, generated by difference stationary or stationary processes, plus SE

$$y_t = \sum_{j=1}^{k-1} Y_{j,t} + e_t.$$

The seasonal adjustment methods we consider are implemented by taking linear combinations of the observed series. Let the unobserved component of interest, $Y_{j,t}$, be estimated by applying a filter of the form,

$$\hat{Y}_{j,t} = w_j(B)y_t, \quad w_j(B) = \sum_m w_{j,m}B^m,$$

where the signal extraction filter, $w_j(B)$, is a polynomial in powers of the backshift operator ($B^l y_t = y_{t-l}$) with the limits of summation left unspecified to allow for time-invariant filters with either symmetric two-sided or asymmetric one-sided weights corresponding to a doubly infinite or semi-infinite number of observations. These are the appropriate filters for this study since the span of data for our example covers over 20 years, which is of sufficient length to allow application of time-invariant symmetric filters in the center of the series and time-invariant concurrent filters at the end of the series.

In the analysis that follows, we will convert to the frequency domain where filter properties are most easily understood. The Fourier transform of the linear filter weights, $w_j(B)$, yields the frequency response function (FRF) of the filter,

$$w_j(e^{-i\lambda}) = \sum_m w_{j,m}e^{-i\lambda m} = W_j(\lambda)e^{i\phi_j(\lambda)},$$

where λ is angular frequency in radians, $e^{-i\lambda m}$ is the complex exponential, $W_j(\lambda)$ is the gain of the filter, and $\phi_j(\lambda)$ is the phase shift. The gain and phase shift completely describe the actions of a linear filter on the input series. For symmetric filters, the phase shift is zero.

It is useful to view a decomposition accounting for SE as a two-step process where we first apply a true series extraction filter to the direct survey data to suppress the effects of SE and then decompose the true series into trend, seasonal, and irregular components using conventional ISE filters.

This two-step process may be represented as the convolution of two linear filters where a filter, $w_1(B)$, is applied to a series and then the output is input to a second filter, $w_2(B)$. The FRF of the combined filter is the product of each filter's FRF,

$$w(e^{-i\lambda}) = w_1(e^{-i\lambda})w_2(e^{-i\lambda}) = W_1(\lambda)W_2(\lambda)e^{i\phi_1(\lambda)+i\phi_2(\lambda)}. \quad (6.3.1)$$

Thus, the gain of the combined filter is the product of the two individual filter gains, and the phase angle is the sum of the phase angles.

Given a model of the true series, Y_t, combined with information on the SE covariances, a signal extraction filter is derived that suppresses SE variation along with noise in the true series. The Wiener–Kolmogorov filter, generalized to nonstationary series, provides the minimum mean square error estimator of the unobserved components with a bi-infinite number of observations (Bell 1984). In the rest of this section, we will use N_t as an example, but the same basic results hold for the trend and other components.

First consider the case where SE is not present. Given the nonstationary components of Y_t can be made stationary through differencing, the gain of the optimal filter for extracting N_t from Y_t is given by the ratio of their pseudo-spectrums $f_N(\lambda)$ and $f_Y(\lambda)$

$$W_N^*(\lambda) = f_N(\lambda)/f_Y(\lambda), \tag{6.3.2}$$

where $f_Y(\lambda) = f_T(\lambda) + f_S(\lambda) + f_I(\lambda)$, and the asterisk for W_N^* signifies an ISE filter. The term "pseudo-spectrum" refers to the spectrum of a nonstationary series that has discontinuities at frequencies corresponding to unit roots (Harvey 1989). From Equation 6.3.2 we see that the gain of the optimal linear filter for estimating N_t has an intuitive interpretation as the proportion of the total variance in Y_t due to N_t for a given frequency. The optimum filter, therefore, is nonzero only at the frequencies where N_t has power and suppress the frequencies of Y_t where N_t contributes little to the total variation in Y_t. The pseudo-spectrum for estimated N_t is given by

$$f_{\hat{N}}^*(\lambda) = [W_N^*(\lambda)]^2 f_Y(\lambda). \tag{6.3.3}$$

When SE is present, a filter for this component is constructed in a manner completely analogous to other types of filters, with a gain given by,

$$W_e(\lambda) = f_e(\lambda)/f_y(\lambda) \tag{6.3.4}$$

where $f_y(\lambda) = f_Y(\lambda) + f_e(\lambda)$ is the pseudo-spectrum for the observed survey series, and f_e is the SE spectrum, which is the Fourier transform of the SE autocovariance function given as

$$f_e(\lambda) = 1/2\pi \left(1 + 2\sum_l \gamma_{e,l}\cos(\lambda l)\right), \tag{6.3.5}$$

where $\gamma_{e,l}$ is the SE autocovariance at lag l. Since the SE variance is the area under the spectral density, $\sigma_e^2 = \int_{-\pi}^{\pi} f_e(\lambda)d(\lambda)$, $f_e(\lambda)$ gives the contribution to variance of the individual frequency components. Thus, the gain of the SE filter is equal to the proportion of the variability of y_t due to SE at a given frequency.

The signal extraction filter for the true series is given by the complement of the SE filter

$$W_Y(\lambda) = 1 - W_e(\lambda) = f_Y(\lambda)/f_y(\lambda), \tag{6.3.6}$$

the pseudo-spectrum for the estimated true series is given by

$$f_{\hat{Y}}(\lambda) = [W_Y(\lambda)]^2 f_y(\lambda), \tag{6.3.7}$$

and the optimum filter for extracting N_t from y_t is given by

$$W_N(\lambda) = f_N(\lambda)/f_y(\lambda). \tag{6.3.8}$$

From Equations 6.3.2, 6.3.6, and 6.3.8, the two-step procedure may now be illustrated for the FRF of the nonseasonal ASE extraction filter as follows:

$$W_N(\lambda) = \frac{f_N(\lambda)}{f_y(\lambda)} = \frac{f_Y(\lambda)}{f_y(\lambda)}\frac{f_N(\lambda)}{f_Y(\lambda)} = W_Y(\lambda)W_N^*(\lambda). \tag{6.3.9}$$

Thus, the ASE filter is the convolution of the true series extraction filter, denoted as $W_Y(B)$, with the conventional nonseasonal ISE filter, denoted as $W_N^*(B)$, which is equivalent to the two-step approach of first removing SE from y_t with the $W_Y(B)$ filter and then applying the ISE filter $W_N^*(B)$ to the first step filtered series to remove seasonality. The final result is a filtered series that accounts for both the true series characteristics and the SE structure. Note that from Equations 6.3.8 and 6.3.9, $f_{\hat{N}}(\lambda) = [W_N(\lambda)]^2 f_y(\lambda) = W_N(\lambda) f_N(\lambda) \leq f_N(\lambda)$, i.e., the optimal estimator will always be smoother than its corresponding true series component as long as SE is present in the observed series.

The two-step approach of Equation 6.3.9 is based on filters derived from explicit models of the components and thus applies directly to SEATS filters. X-11 filters lack an explicit model-based structure but have an approximate linear filter form (Wallis 1982) that can be adjusted for SE in an analogous way. Accordingly, Equation 6.3.9 holds when the ISE model-based filter, W_N^*, is replaced by the X-11 filter, $W_{N_{X-11}}^*$. To ensure finite mean squared error (MSE) measures, as discussed later, special restrictions are required that are not necessarily satisfied by some of the X-11 asymmetric filters.

Next we derive some expressions for the signal extraction errors to be used to quantify the effects of SE for either SEATS or X-11 (ISE) filters. Let the signal extraction error for N_t be given by $\xi_{N,t}^*$, which is decomposed into a part due to the unobserved true component, $\xi_{N_t|Y_t}^*$, and a part due to SE, $\xi_{N_t|e_t}^*$

$$\xi_{N,t}^* = N_t - \hat{N}_t^* = \xi_{N_t|Y_t}^* - \xi_{N_t|e_t}^*,$$

where

$$\begin{aligned} \hat{N}_t^* &= W_N^*(B) y_t, \\ \xi_{N_t|Y_t}^* &= [1 - W_N^*(B)] N_t - W_N^*(B)(Y_t - N_t), \\ \xi_{N_t|e_t}^* &= W_N^*(B) e_t. \end{aligned}$$

The spectrum of the signal extraction error is given by

$$f_{\xi_N^*}(\lambda) = f_{\xi_N^*|Y}(\lambda) + f_{\xi_N^*|e}(\lambda),$$

where

$$\begin{aligned} f_{\xi_N^*|Y}(\lambda) &= [1 - W_N^*(\lambda)]^2 f_N(\lambda) + W_N^{*2}(\lambda)[f_Y(\lambda) - f_N(\lambda)]. \\ f_{\xi_N^*|e}(\lambda) &= W_N^{*2}(\lambda) f_e(\lambda) \end{aligned} \tag{6.3.10}$$

Assuming $W_N^*(\lambda)$ and $1 - W_N^*(\lambda)$ contain factors that cancel out the nonstationary roots of the component processes, the signal extraction error will be stationary with MSE given by (Bell 1984)

$$\begin{aligned} E(N_t - \hat{N}_t^*)^2 &= \int_{-\pi}^{\pi} f_{\xi_N^*|Y}(\lambda) d\lambda + \int_{-\pi}^{\pi} f_{\xi_N^*|e}(\lambda) d\lambda \\ &= \sigma_{\xi_N^*|Y}^2 + \sigma_{\xi_N^*|e}^2. \end{aligned} \tag{6.3.11}$$

These conditions obviously hold for the model-based SEATS filters and can be shown to hold for X-11 symmetric filters. The X-11 asymmetric filters may not always satisfy these conditions unless they are derived from the symmetric ones with full forecast extension. The default for X-11 is one-year forecast extension, which is not sufficient to produce stationary signal extraction errors if both ordinary and seasonal differencing are used in the model (Bell 2010). Given the required conditions, Equation 6.3.11 partitions the MSE for estimating N_t from the survey series into a component due to stochastic variation in the true series, $\sigma^2_{\xi^*_N|Y}$, and a component due to the SE, $\sigma^2_{\xi^*_N|e}$.

To fully evaluate the MSE models for the unobserved true series components are required. However, the contribution of SE to MSE can be evaluated from just the ISE filter gain and SE covariances as follows from Equation 6.3.11

$$\sigma^2_{\xi^*_N|e} = \int_{-\pi}^{\pi} f_{\xi^*_N|e}(\lambda)d\lambda = \int_{-\pi}^{\pi} W_N^{*2}(\lambda)f_e(\lambda)d\lambda, \tag{6.3.12}$$

where $f_{\xi^*_N|e}(\lambda)$ is the contribution of SE to the MSE of the ISE extraction filter at a given frequency. As discussed later, Equation 6.3.12 is also equivalent to the increase in MSE due to SE for the ISE filter but not for the ASE filter. An important result follows from Equation 6.3.12; the increase in MSE depends on how similar the properties of e_t are to those of N_t. When the two are similar, $W_N^*(\lambda)$ and $f_e(\lambda)$ will be high over the same frequencies and the contribution of SE to MSE will be large.

For the ASE filter, the contribution of SE to MSE, from Equations 6.3.6, 6.3.9, and 6.3.10, is given by

$$\sigma^2_{\xi_N|e} = \int_{-\pi}^{\pi} [1 - W_e(\lambda)]^2 f_{\xi^*_N|e}(\lambda)d\lambda. \tag{6.3.13}$$

Thus, accounting for SE reduces its contribution to MSE of the ASE filter relative to the ISE filter in proportion to the relative power of SE at that frequency. When the magnitude of the SE is high and e_t and N_t have similar properties, the gain from accounting for SE will be large.

The purpose of Equation 6.3.13 is to provide a measure of the extent to which the ASE filter suppresses the effects of SE when it is present in the series. This measure should not be confused with the increase in MSE due to SE defined as the difference between the MSE of the ASE filter when SE is present and when it is not present in the series. As noted above, this distinction does not have to be made for an ISE filter since the two measures are identical because the filter does not adapt to the presence of SE.

6.4 Numerical Example

This section presents a numerical example using results from the previous section. For this example, we make specific assumptions about the SE and the model for the true series. For the SE, we specify a fixed coefficient of variation (CV) of 1.3%, about 10 times the National CV. The survey autocorrelations used are the ones shown in Figure 6.1.

State CPS labor force series are characterized by variable trends and stable seasonality. We represent this behavior by an airline model of the true series

$$(1-B)(1-B^{12})Y_t = (1-\theta B)(1-\Theta B^{12})\nu_t, \quad E(\nu_t^2) = \sigma_\nu^2, \tag{6.4.1}$$

with parameter values $\theta = 0.4$ and $\Theta = 0.8$. We use the SEATS algorithm (Gómez and Maravall 1994) as implemented in X-13A-S to decompose this model into nonstationary ARMA component models for trend and seasonality and a stationary irregular, where the variances of the respective white noise disturbances, $\nu_{j,t}$, are expressed as proportions of the reduced form white noise variance, σ_ν^2. For the given set of reduced form MA parameters, the decomposition yields an unstable trend, a stable seasonal, and a relatively, large irregular component. The component models are shown as follows:

$$T_t = \frac{(1+B)(1-0.98B)}{(1-B)^2}\nu_{T,t}, \quad \sigma_{\nu_T}^2 = 0.07\sigma_\nu^2$$

$$S_t = \frac{\begin{pmatrix} 1.0 + 1.42B + 1.49B^2 + 1.42B^3 + 1.22B^4 + 0.98B^5 \\ +0.71B^6 + 0.44B^7 + 0.22B^8 + 0.01B^9 - 0.12B^{10} - 0.41B^{11} \end{pmatrix}}{(1 + B + B^2 + \cdots + B^{11})}\nu_{S,t},$$

$$\sigma_{\nu_S}^2 = 0.01\sigma_\nu^2$$

$$I_t = \nu_{I,t}, \quad \sigma_{\nu_I}^2 = 0.40\sigma_\nu^2$$

6.4.1 Symmetric Filters

Assuming a sufficiently long observation period, both SEATS and X-11/X-12-ARIMA produce time-invariant symmetric two-sided filters for the central observations, and one-sided concurrent filters for the last observation. Given stationary SE, the ASE filters will also be time-invariant.

To compute filter weights for X-11/X-12-ARIMA, we use the well-known linear approximation approach, which ignores corrections for outliers and calendar effects (Wallis 1982). X-11 is then a convolution of several finite moving averages, which is itself a moving average. The properties of the central weights depend on specifying the trend and seasonal moving averages. We select the option consisting of the Henderson 13-term trend moving average and the 3×5 seasonal filter. This option is not the one that most closely corresponds to the SEATS filter, but is the one most often selected for the CPS series when using the automated features of the software.

There are a number of alternative ways to generate filter weights. For this study, the impulse response method is most convenient for producing weights for both symmetric and concurrent filters. Application of this method to X-11 is described by Ladiray and Quenneville (2001). We use this method to generate filter weights for X-11/X-12-ARIMA with full forecast extension. The X-11

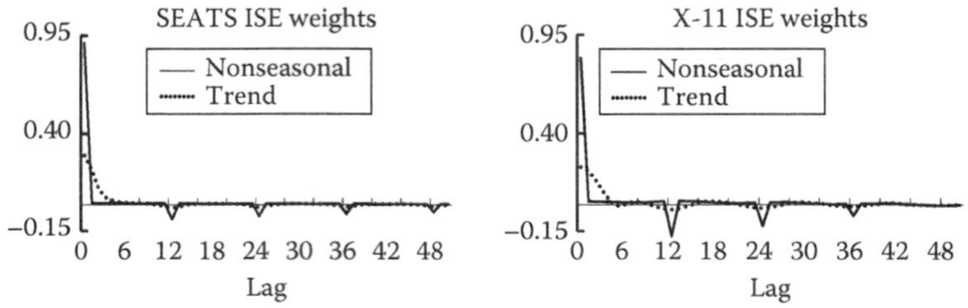

FIGURE 6.2
SEATS and X-11 symmetric ISE filter weights (only one side shown).

option of X-13A-S is run on artificial series taken from columns of a $T \times T$ identity matrix where T is of sufficient length to produce the time-invariant symmetric and concurrent weights. The same approach is used to generate filter weights for SEATS (Findley and Martin 2006). For the true series extraction filter, to be described in more detail, the airline model (6.4.1) and the corresponding SE model are put into state-space form, then the impulse response method is executed by running the Kalman filter and smoother on the identity matrix. Once the filter weights are computed, the FRF is computed by taking the Fourier transform of the weights.

The ISE nonseasonal and trend filter weights for SEATS based on Equation 6.4.1, and X-11/X-12-ARIMA based on this same ARIMA model and the default options previously mentioned, are shown in Figure 6.2. The nonseasonal central weights are around 0.95 and the other weights are near zero except for negative values at lags/leads of multiples of 12. The central trend weight is much lower at 0.25 with successive weights on both sides of the center declining smoothly over the first four lags/leads.

The ASE filters are derived from convoluting the ISE filters with the true series extraction filter as in Equation 6.3.9. Accounting for SE can radically alter the decomposition filters. To illustrate, the left side of Figure 6.3 shows the filter weights for extracting the true series from the CPS series, which,

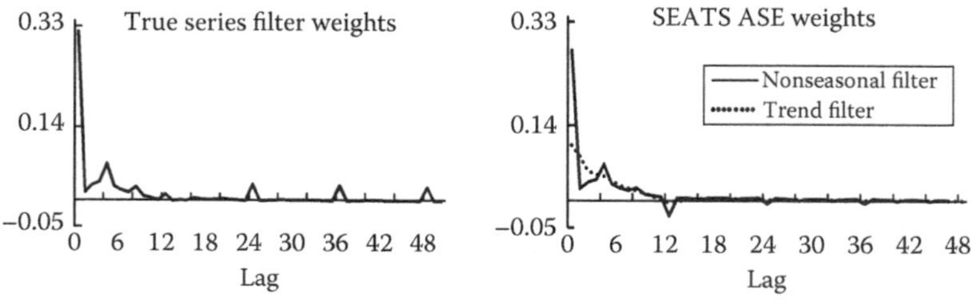

FIGURE 6.3
Symmetric ASE filter weights (only one side shown).

when convoluted with the ISE filters for N_t and T_t in Figure 6.2, give the ASE filters for N_t and T_t shown on the right side of Figure 6.3. Compared to SEATS and X-11/X-12-ARIMA ISE filters, the central weights for the ASE filters are much smaller in magnitude.

6.4.1.1 Decompositions Ignoring Survey Error

We use frequency domain analysis to investigate how the SE properties affect the outputs of various types of filters. The spectrum of the SE (6.3.5) gives the contribution to variance of the individual frequency components. We normalize by dividing by the SE variance

$$f'_e(\lambda) = f_e(\lambda)/\sigma_e^2, \tag{6.4.2}$$

which is simply the Fourier transform of the SE autocorrelation function. Since the area under this function is 1, $100 \times f'_e(\lambda)$ gives the percent contribution of the individual frequency components to the total SE variance.

We compare the autocorrelated SE under the CPS design with the SE from a simple random sample (SRS) where the sample units are independently replaced each period. This comparison is of interest for several reasons. First, the SRS design produces SE with white noise properties identical to the classical irregular component and thus conforms to the assumption implicit in the application of SEATS and X-11 to a survey series. The SE then has a pure variance effect in the sense that it is equivalent to increasing the variance of the irregular component. Secondly, as discussed below, the SRS design provides insight into understanding why autocorrelated SE matters apart from a pure variance increase.

Compared to the frequency distribution of the CPS SE, e_t, the SE for a SRS design, $e_{\mathrm{SRS},t}$, has a spectrum that is constant across frequency

$$f'_{e_{\mathrm{SRS}}}(\lambda) = 1/2\pi, \text{ since } \rho_{e_{\mathrm{SRS}},l} = 0 \quad \text{for } l \neq 0. \tag{6.4.3}$$

The normalized SE spectral densities for the CPS and SRS design are shown in Figure 6.4. Relative to SRS, the CPS SE is much more concentrated in the

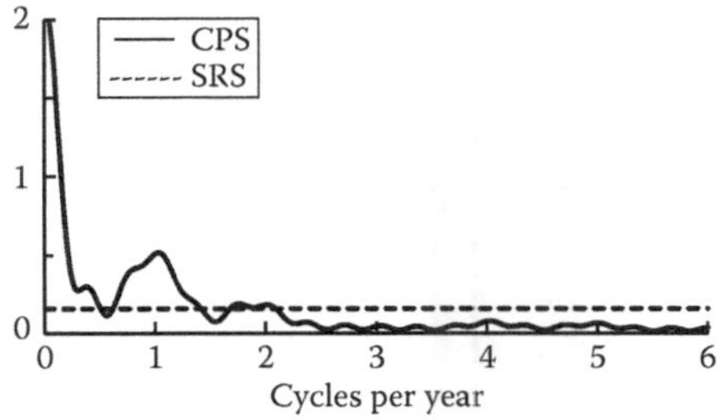

FIGURE 6.4
Normalized SE spectrums.

TABLE 6.1
Distribution of SE Variance (%)

Survey Series	Trend	Irregular (Residual)	Nonseasonal	Seasonal (Cycles/Year)						
				1	2	3	4	5	6	Total
CPS Employment	43	33.7	76.7	13.4	4.7	1.0	1.9	1.6	0.7	23.3
SRS	11.1	62.3	73.4	4.4	4.4	4.4	4.4	4.4	4.4	26.6

Note: Irregular (residual) frequencies that fall between the seasonal frequency bands.

trend frequencies. There is also a broad peak around the one cycle per year frequency resulting from the 50% year-to-year overlap in the CPS sample (Figure 6.1). These results are summarized in Table 6.1, which shows the percent distribution of the SE variance for frequencies associated with the trend (periodicities of 18 months or longer), seasonal (6 seasonal frequencies ± 4 degrees), and irregular (residual band of frequencies that fall between the seasonal frequency bands) frequencies. Table 6.1 quantifies the extra power generated by the CPS design for key components of the decomposition. For example, 43% of the CPS SE variance is concentrated in the trend frequencies compared to only 11% for SRS. For the seasonal frequencies, overall, both the CPS and SRS account for about one fourth of the total variance but for the annual cycle, the CPS accounts for three times as much of the variance as SRS.

To quantify the effect of SE on ISE filters, we compute the contribution of SE to the MSE of the estimator of the jth unobserved component as a percent of the total SE variance by replacing f_e with f_e' in Equation 6.3.12. The SE contribution for an SRS design is computed by using the SRS spectral density (Equation 6.4.3) in Equation 6.3.12. Taking the ratio of the variance of the complex sample (CPS) to the SRS variance gives a type of design effect (DE) for the SEATS and X-11 estimators. This DE holds SE variance constant, where the conventional DE holds sample size constant.

While the presence of SE increases the error in the estimator, not all of the SE variance is absorbed into the estimation error since the gain of the symmetric filter generally varies between zero and one over frequency (this constraint is exact for model-based filters but not strictly satisfied by X-11 filters). Thus, the total increase in MSE will be less than the SE variance (Hausman and Watson 1985). As noted in Section 6.3, the increase in MSE and the contribution of SE to MSE are the same for the ISE filters. Also, as previously mentioned, the exact amount of the increase depends on the degree to which the spectra of the signal and SE overlap. Figure 6.5 illustrates the degree of overlap by plotting the squared gains of the symmetric SEATS and X11-ARIMA trend and nonseasonal filters with the normalized SE spectra for the CPS and SRS design. Using Equation 6.3.12 we quantify this overlap in part A of Table 6.2 in terms of the contribution of SE to MSE for the various estimators.

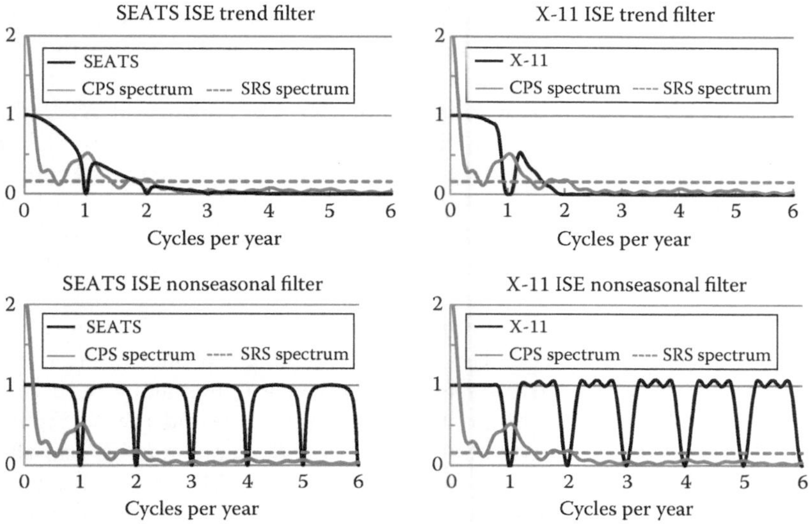

FIGURE 6.5
Squared gains of SEATS and X-11-ARIMA symmetric ISE filters with CPS and SRS SE spectra.

The properties of the nonseasonal, trend, seasonal, and irregular filters for SEATS and X-11 are generally similar. The top row of Figure 6.5 shows the symmetric trend filters for both SEATS and X-11 that suppress the high frequency part of the SE (two or more cycles per year) but pass much of the extra SE power in the low frequency range (cycles less than one per year). Overall, the trend filters absorb about 74% of the CPS SE variance (Table 6.2, part A, column labeled % of SE variance). By contrast, with an SRS design,

TABLE 6.2
Contribution of SE to MSE, Symmetric Time-Invariant Filters

	Ignoring Survey Error						Accounting for Survey Error	
	SEATS			X11			SEATS	X11
Component	% of SE Variance CPS	% of SE Variance SRS	DE	% of SE Variance CPS	% of SE Variance SRS	DE	% of SE Variance (% Reduction from ISE)	% of SE Variance (% Reduction from ISE)
Trend	73.8	42.1	1.7	74.5	42.0	1.8	52.2 (29.2)	52.7 (29.2)
Irregular	40.1	71.3	0.6	40.5	74.3	0.5	10.2 (74.6)	10.5 (0.7)
Nonseasonal	93.3	93.0	1.0	89.1	88.6	1.0	54.2 (42.0)	53.9 (39.5)
Seasonal total	22.7	5.1	1.0	36.8	38.3	1.0	13.7 (0.4)	15.5 (0.6)
1-year cycle	17.1	1.0	18.6	27.2	2.4	11.6	9.7 (43.1)	10.6 (30.3)

the trend filters work relatively well in suppressing SE; only 42% of the SE variance is absorbed. The DE for the trend filter is 1.7, indicating that the information loss due to autocorrelated SE is high.

For the seasonal component as a whole, the DE for both SEATS and X-11 is approximately 1. The seasonal filters, however, pick up the extra SE variance at the annual cycle. The irregular filters pick up none of the low frequency SE noise, which mostly goes to the trend component. The DE for the irregular is much lower than 1 over the high frequency irregular bands, a reflection of the much lower concentration of the CPS error variance relative to SRS in these frequencies.

The nonseasonal (seasonal adjustment) filters have a DE equal to about 1. Since a nonseasonal filter is the complement of a seasonal filter, it removes only the power in the narrow seasonal frequency bands along with the extra power in the CPS at the 12-month frequency (see second row of Figure 6.5). These filters, however, absorb both low and high frequency SE, and thus will produce highly variable estimates under both the CPS and SRS design. Thus, it is the size of the SE variance and not its autocorrelation properties that matters in estimating the nonseasonal component where no attempt is made to separate the trend from the irregular. This is in contrast to trend estimation where the autocorrelation properties are important.

The problem of SE variability is illustrated in Figure 6.6, which compares the theoretical pseudo-spectra for the trend and nonseasonal series (dotted black line) with the SEATS ISE pseudo-spectra of the trend and nonseasonal estimates (dashed gray line). We see a pair of spurious peaks in the SEATS ISE pseudo-spectrum of the estimated trend on either side of the 1 cycle per year frequency corresponding to approximately 16 and 11 month cycles, respectively, and another pair in the spectrum of the estimated nonseasonal around the 2 cycle per year frequency but with much less power. This pattern is reflected in the spectrum for the estimated nonseasonal component. The X-11 nonseasonal and trend estimators (not shown) are very similar to

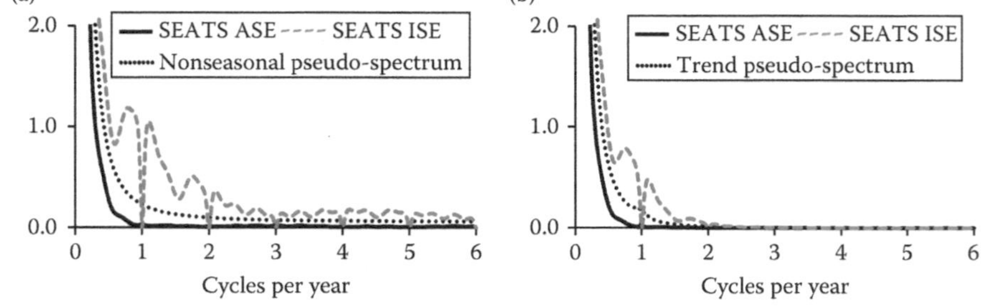

FIGURE 6.6
Theoretical nonseasonal pseudo-spectrum (a), trend pseudo-spectrum (b), and respective SEATS ASE and ISE estimators.

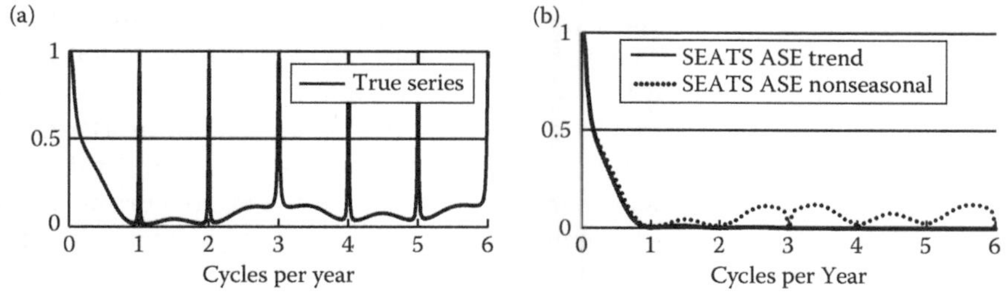

FIGURE 6.7
Squared gain of symmetric true series filters (a) and squared gain of symmetric SEATS trend and nonseasonal filters adjusted for SE (b).

the SEATS results. Thus, when SE is ignored not only is there increased overall variability, but also spurious cycle-like behavior appears in the trend and nonseasonal estimates.

6.4.1.2 Decompositions Accounting for Survey Error

The first step in constructing an ASE decomposition is to suppress SE with a signal extraction filter. The gain of the filter for extracting the true series from the survey series gives the proportion of the variability in the survey series accounted for by the true series (6.3.6). It is, thus, a direct measure of the amount of information in the sample about the behavior of the true series over frequency. Figure 6.7 presents the squared gain for the true series filter. For samples with large SE, there is little information (squared gain near zero) outside of seasonal and long run trend variation.

The right side of Figure 6.7 shows the effects that accounting for SE has on the SEATS trend and seasonal adjustment filters. These filters are strongly attenuated in the low frequency range. Since the data provide little information about the true series in the nonseasonal high frequency range, the adjusted trend and nonseasonal filters are also strongly attenuated in that range, and so are much more similar there than are the corresponding ISE filters shown in Figure 6.5. The same result holds for the X-11 filters. Part B of Table 6.2 shows the contribution of SE to MSE for the ASE filters and the percent reduction in the contribution of SE from the ISE filters.

Once SE is accounted for the pseudo-spectra for the SEATS estimated components (SEATS ASE, Figure 6.6) more closely conform to their respective theoretical true series pseudo-spectrum. Note also that the estimated spectrum lies inside the theoretical one (dotted line), since the optimal filter suppresses power over frequencies where SE is strong (6.3.6).

6.4.2 Concurrent Filters

At the end of the observation period, filtering has to adapt to a reduced information set and this can introduce major distortions. Concurrent filters place heavier weight on the current and more recent observations than do symmetric filters. This increases the variability of the output of the filter, and the lack of future observations also tends to shift the timing of the output relative to the input series. Accordingly, to completely describe the actions of a concurrent filter on a time series requires not only the squared gain of the FRF but also the associated phase shift function. The concurrent weights were computed in the same manner as discussed in the previous section for the symmetric weights.

For both the SEATS and X-11/X-12-ARIMA ISE concurrent trend filters, the squared gains (Figure 6.8) are much higher relative to those of the symmetric filters (Figure 6.5) and therefore pass more noise. For the nonseasonal SEATS and X-11/X-12 ARIMA ISE filters, the gains for the concurrent filters compared with the symmetric ones are lower over the irregular frequencies and the seasonal troughs are narrower.

For the concurrent true series extraction filter, the weight on the current observation is much higher than the symmetric weight (left part of Figure 6.9), and the squared gain is higher over the trend and irregular frequencies compared with the symmetric filter (right part of Figure 6.9). When this filter is convoluted with each of the ISE filters in Figure 6.8, the result is a corresponding concurrent ASE filter (not shown). Like their symmetric counterparts, these ASE filters attenuate power at frequencies where SE is large, but not as effectively.

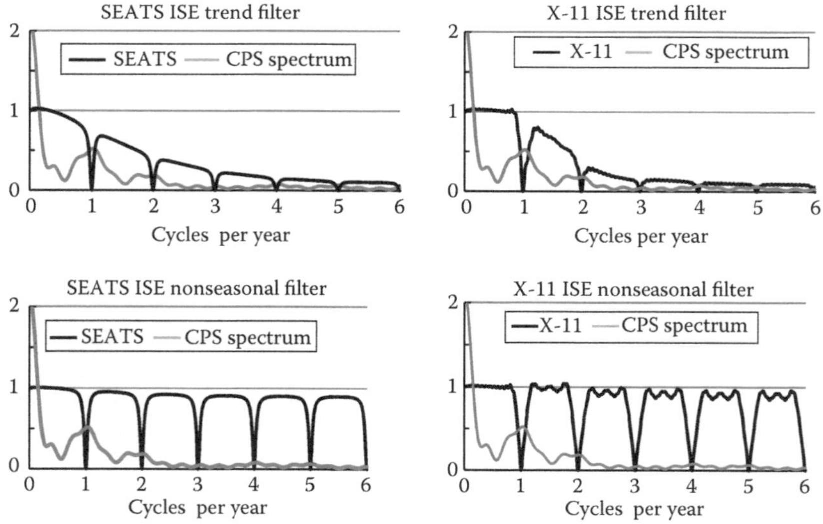

FIGURE 6.8
Squared gains of SEATS and X-11-ARIMA ISE concurrent filters.

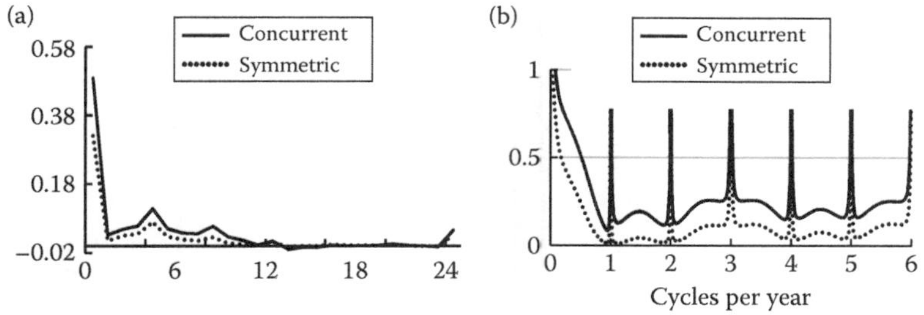

FIGURE 6.9
Concurrent and symmetric true series filter weights (a) and squared gains (b).

Part A of Table 6.3 shows how much of the SE variance is absorbed by each concurrent ISE filter. The concurrent trend filter, as a result of its higher gain, absorbs considerably more SE variance than the symmetric filter. Adjusting the SEATS and X11 concurrent filters for SE (part B of Table 6.3) results in smaller reductions in the contributions of SE to MSE than for the symmetric filters (Table 6.2), but the reductions are still substantial.

Next we investigate the phase shift functions shown in Figure 6.10 over the trend cycle range of frequencies. For the nonseasonal component, the phase lags for both SEATS and X11-ARIMA, ignoring SE, are less than 1 month. (See Figure 2 in Findley and Martin 2006, for an example of a similar phase lag for the SEATS filter.) For the trend, SEATS lags 1 month while X-11/X-12-ARIMA generally shows less than 1 month lag. By contrast, the true series extraction filter for the autocorrelated CPS SE shows a 4 month lag for cycle lengths between 11 and 22 years and a 2 month lag for shorter cycles. When convoluting the ISE filters with the true series filters to form the ASE

TABLE 6.3
Contribution of SE to MSE, Concurrent Time Invariant Filters

	Ignoring Survey Error		Accounting for Survey Error	
	% of SE Variance		% of SE Variance (% Reduction from ISE)	
Component	**SEATS**	**X11-ARIMA**	**SEATS**	**X11-ARIMA**
Trend	83.3	84.1	64.8 (22.2)	65.1 (22.6)
Irregular	32.3	34.1	14.4 (55.5)	14.8 (56.5)
Nonseasonal	94.3	92.6	67.4 (28.6)	67.0 (27.7)
Seasonal				
total	30.3	38.2	18.4 (39.4)	20.7 (45.8)
1-year cycle	22.0	26.6	12.8 (41.9)	13.9 (47.7)

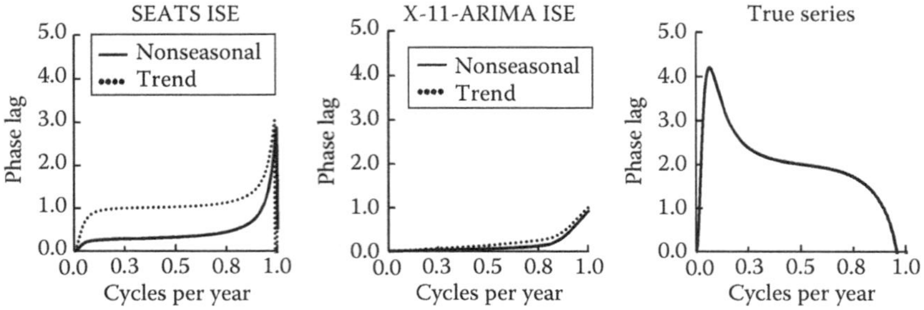

FIGURE 6.10
Phase lag in months for concurrent filters.

filters, the phase lag functions add (6.3.1), which therefore increases the lags in the nonseasonal and trend filters after accounting for SE.

While the SEATS and X11 ISE filters do not generate as large phase shifts as the ASE filters, this does not mean that they are more effective in identifying real turning points. As we have seen, the absorption of SE into the trend and nonseasonal components is high and induces spurious cycles when using the symmetric filters (Figure 6.6). The asymmetric filters absorb even more SE and produce more variable estimates, which may generate false turning points that mask the real ones. This issue is further explored with a specific example in the next section.

6.5 Filtering with Nonstationary Survey Error

When considering an actual empirical application of conventional methods to survey series, the actual mechanism for constructing a model-based filter that ignores SE differs from our hypothetical case. The reduced form ARIMA model is estimated directly from y_t, and so differs from the population model for Y_t used to derive the ISE filters in Section 6.3. Ignoring SE, however, results in a model of a highly variable trend and an irregular component with an inflated variance. As a result, the empirical ISE SEATS filters have properties very similar to the hypothetical ones since SE is absorbed into the estimated trend and irregular model components. The ISE approach of Section 6.3 is also relevant to X-11/X-12, which selects from a fixed set of filters.

Our empirical example uses the CPS employment series for the State of Maryland for the period 1990–2009. As is common for periodic surveys that have been in operation for a long time, there have been redesigns, sample size changes, and fluctuations in population proportions that result in heteroskedastic SE. We formulate a model that accounts for these SE characteristics. Our estimator of the true series is design consistent in the sense that if the sample size for the survey series gets large, the estimator of the signal converges to the survey estimator (Bell and Hillmer 1990).

The data are logged, which implies a multiplicative model

$$y_t = Y_t(1 + r_t), \quad r_t = e_t / Y_t,$$

where r_t is the relative SE with variance approximated by the relvariance of e_t (for fixed Y_t), $\sigma^2_{r,t} = \sigma^2_{e,t}/Y_t^2$. The time-varying CPS variances are estimated by the method of generalized variance functions. To account for both autocorrelation and heteroscedasticity, the SE is modeled as follows:

$$r_t = \sigma_{r,t} r'_t, \quad r'_t = \sum_{i=1}^{15} \phi_i r'_{t-i} + \nu_t, \quad E(\nu_t^2) = \left(\sum_i \psi_i^2 \right)^{-1}, \quad \psi(B) = \phi(B)^{-1},$$

where $\phi(B) = 1 - \sum_{i=1}^{15} \phi_i B^i$ and the AR(15) model for r'_t is fit to the autocorrelations shown in Figure 6.1. The model of the true series with estimated parameter values is given by

$$\nabla\nabla^{12} \log(Y)_t = (1 - 0.33B)(1 - 0.94B^{12})\nu_{Y,t}, \quad \sigma^2_{\nu_Y} = 4.0 \times 10^{-5}.$$

To estimate the parameters, the SE and true series models are put into state-space form, the SE model parameters held fixed, and the unknown parameters estimated by maximizing the innovation form of the likelihood. The program was written in SAS IML. A value of 25.7 for the Lung-Box test for autocorrelated one-step ahead prediction errors over the first 24 lags indicates a satisfactory fit.

Even though the true series model cannot be represented by a time-invariant linear filter when the SE is heteroscedastic, the estimation accounting for SE parallels the two-step process for time-invariant linear filters discussed previously. Given the estimated parameters, the Kalman filter and smoother are used to produce the minimum mean squared error estimates of the true series. To produce the ASE estimates, we use the X-13A-S program to decompose the estimated true series with the SEATS option where the ARIMA model is fixed to correspond to the estimated model of the true series. To produce the ISE estimates, we use the SEATS and X-11 options to directly decompose the CPS series, where the ARIMA model is not fixed but estimated directly from the CPS using the automodel option. A (212)(011) model was fit with satisfactory diagnostics and used for the X-11 decomposition. But because it was nondecomposable, SEATS substituted a (112)(011) model (Gómez and Maravall 1994) with higher residual autocorrelations from which it derived trend, seasonal, and irregular models for decomposition where the trend is modeled as an unstable trend and the irregular as white noise with a variance much larger than the corresponding ASE estimate. The signal extraction estimates closely parallel the ones generated by applying the SEATS ISE filters for N_t and T_t directly to the CPS series rather than to the estimated true series (following the approach of Sections 6.3 and 6.4). The X-11 decomposition was run using automatic selection of the seasonal and trend filters. The 3 × 5 seasonal and 13-term Henderson filters were selected, which correspond to our specification used in Section 6.4.

The employment series for Maryland is divided by the corresponding civilian noninstitutional population aged 16 and over to more clearly reveal the cyclical fluctuations. The left part of Figure 6.11 plots the CPS employment to population ratio (E/P) in percentage form on the left-hand vertical scale, and the CPS CV on the right-hand vertical scale. Up to 2001, there are very large fluctuations in the CPS that induce CV fluctuations in the opposite direction. As a result, the model fit follows the peaks more closely than the troughs in the CPS. After a large sample expansion in 2001, the CPS fluctuations are much reduced, and as a consequence of accounting for the SE heteroscedasticity, there is a much tighter fit of the estimated true series to the CPS. This is a reflection of the design consistency of our estimator.

Direct seasonal adjustments of the historical CPS series by either SEATS or X-11 are produced by finite sample filters that are symmetric two-sided filters in the middle of the series and become increasingly asymmetric toward either end of the series where they converge to the one-sided concurrent filter. The right side of Figure 6.11 compares the historical SEATS nonseasonal estimates with and without accounting for SE. While SEATS adequately removed seasonality from the CPS series (no evidence of residual seasonality in the adjusted series), the resulting ISE seasonally adjusted series is very rough compared with the ASE series. Just removing seasonality from the CPS series has surprisingly little effect on the overall variability of the series. The same results occur for the X-11/X-12-ARIMA ASE and ISE series (not shown). Comparisons of trend estimates are shown in Figure 6.12, where it is demonstrated that the ISE trend estimates, while an improvement over the seasonally adjusted results, still do not effectively suppress autocorrelated SE.

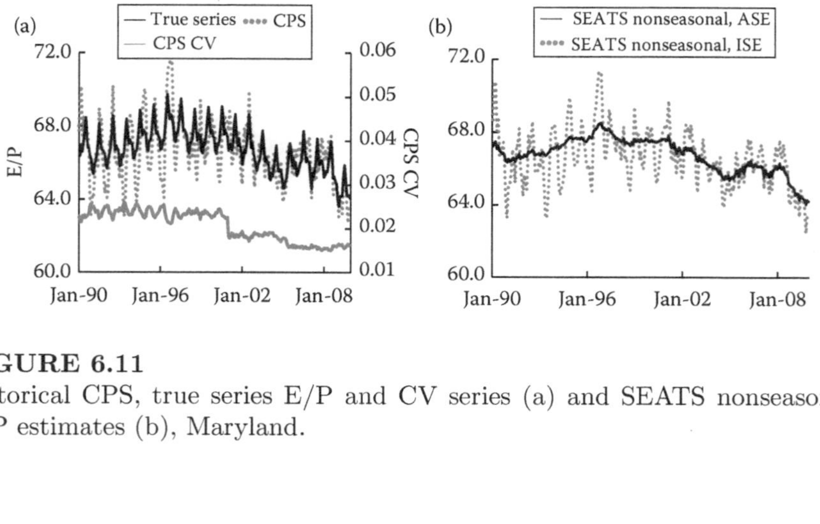

FIGURE 6.11
Historical CPS, true series E/P and CV series (a) and SEATS nonseasonal E/P estimates (b), Maryland.

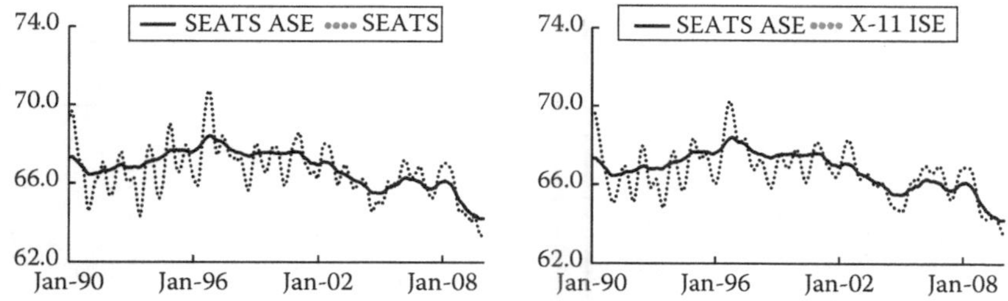

FIGURE 6.12
Historical SEATS and X-11 ISE trend compared with ASE SEATS trend, E/P ratio for Maryland.

To compare the performance in real time, all adjustments are produced concurrently, one observation at a time without updating the previous estimates. Data from 1980 to 1989 are used as a base period to initialize concurrent estimates for January 1990. The concurrent ASE estimates are less smooth relative to the historical estimates (left part of Figure 6.13), but the ISE estimates are still much more variable (right part of Figure 6.13).

While the concurrent ISE estimates have smaller phase lags than the ASE estimates (Section 6.4.2), this advantage appears more apparent than real in this empirical example. It is difficult to identify turning points with any precision in the concurrent nonseasonal SEATS ISE series (right-hand side of Figure 6.13. We also compare in Figure 6.14 the SEATS ASE trend with the X-11/X-12-ARIMA trend estimates where the phase lags for the latter are less than 1 month (Figure 6.10). Again, the variability in the ISE estimates appears to mask any phase differences. Finally, we compare the concurrent SEATS ASE trend estimates with its historical trend estimates on the right-hand side of Figure 6.14. Here we do see evidence of a phase lag in the concurrent estimates. Four 'x' markers have been placed on the historical SEATS ASE series that identify where a major change in direction preceded a

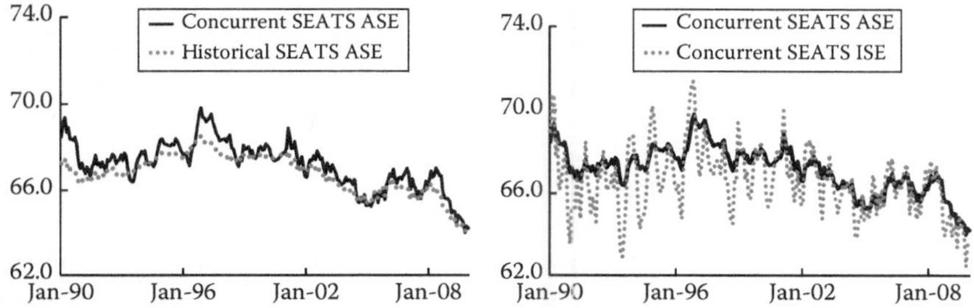

FIGURE 6.13
Concurrent SEATS nonseasonal, E/P ratio for Maryland.

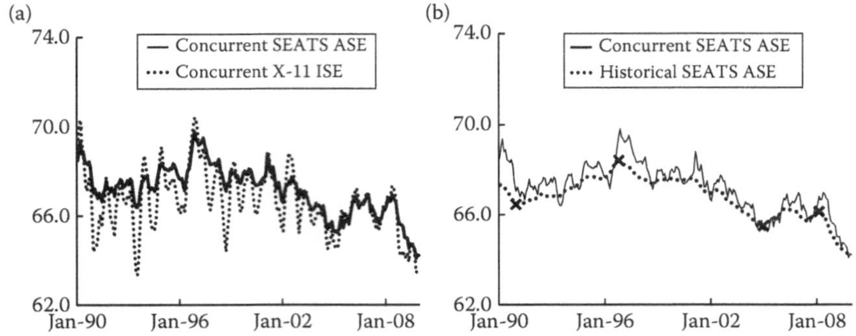

FIGURE 6.14
Concurrent SEATS ASE trend compared with concurrent X-11-ARIMA ISE trend (a) and with historical SEATS ASE trends (b), E/P ratio for Maryland.

seemingly similar change in the direction of the concurrent series. The historical ISE estimates, however, are too variable to detect these delays. Ironically, identification of peaks and troughs requires historical ASE trend estimates to smooth out high frequency fluctuations.

6.6 Conclusions

Without information on the variance–covariance structure of the SE, it is not, in general, possible to identify key unobserved components of the true series. Even though SEATS filters are more tailored to the characteristics of the observable series, without additional identifying information on SE properties, SEATS is no more effective in supressing SE than the less flexible X-11 filters. How badly ISE filters perform depends on the properties of the SE. Where SE variance is relatively small, as in key national aggregates, ignoring SE makes little difference. When SE is white noise, ignoring SE confounds it with the irregular component, which actually benefits the ISE trend estimates, but the ISE nonseasonal estimates will suffer. When SE is autocorrelated, the ISE filters will not be able to effectively separate the trend from the SE.

Where SE is large, there will be substantial smoothing of the survey series by the ASE filters. From a signal processing perspective, ASE filters have a drawback in real time since strong smoothing introduces phase lags. From the "small area estimation perspective," mentioned in Section 6.1, conventional filters ignoring sampling error may have shorter phase lags, but they pass too much low frequency SE and, as a result, are prone to generating many false turning points. In samples with large SEs, it appears to be unrealistic to expect a high degree of accuracy in identifying the timing of turning points in real time.

Acknowledgments

I am grateful to the referees and the editors for their careful review and constructive criticisms that substantially improved this paper. Also, thanks to Jennifer Oh for her computational assistance.

References

Bell, W. R. (1984). Signal extraction for nonstationary time series. *Annals of Statistics* 12:646–664.

Bell, W. R. and Hillmer, S. C. (1990). The time series approach to estimation for repeated surveys. *Survey Methodology* 16:195–215.

Bell, W. R. (2004). On RegComponent time series models and their applications. In *State Space and Unobserved Component Models: Theory and Applications*, eds. A. C. Harvey, S. J. Koopman, and N. Shephard, 248–283. Cambridge: Cambridge University Press.

Bell, W. R. (2010). Unit root properties of seasonal adjustment and related filters, Research Report RRS2010-08, Center for Statistical Research and Methods, U.S. Census Bureau.

Dagum, E. B. (1980). *The X-11-ARIMA Seasonal Adjustment Method.* Catalogue No. 12-564E. Ottawa: Statistics Canada.

Findley, D. F., Monsell, B. C., Bell, W. R., Otto, M. C., and Chen, B.-C. (1998). New capabilities and methods of the X-12-ARIMA seasonal-adjustment program. *Journal of Business and Economic Statistics* 16:127–177.

Findley, D. F. and Martin, D. E. K. (2006). Frequency domain diagnostics of SEATS and X-11/12-ARIMA seasonal adjustment filters for short and moderate-length time series. *Journal of Official Statistics* 22(1):1–34.

Findley, D. F. (2005). Some recent developments and directions in seasonal adjustment. *Journal of Official Statistics* 21(2):343–365.

Gómez, V. and Maravall, A. (1994). Program SEATS signal extraction in ARIMA timeseries: Instructions for the user. *Working Paper* ECO 94/28, European University Institute, Florence.

Harvey, A. C. (1989). *Forecasting, Structural Time Series Models and the Kalman Filter.* Cambridge: Cambridge University Press.

Hausman, J. and Watson, M. (1985). Errors in variables and seasonal adjustment procedures. *Journal of the American Statistical Association* 80(391):531–540.

Ladiray, D. and Quenneville, B. (2001). *Seasonal adjustment with the X-11 method.* Lecture Notes in Statistics, No. 158, New York: Springer.

Pfeffermann, D., Feder, M., and Signorelli, D. (1998). Estimation of autocorrelations of survey errors with application to trend estimation in small areas. *Journal of Business and Economic Statistics* 16:339–348.

Pfeffermann, D. (1991). Estimation and seasonal adjustment of population means using data from repeated surveys. *Journal of Business & Economic Statistics* 9:163–175.

Scott, A. J., Smith, T. M. F., and Jones, R. G. (1997). The application of time series methods to the analysis of repeated surveys. *International Statistical Review* 45:13–28.

Tiller, R. B. (1992). Time series modeling of sample survey data from the U.S. Current Population Survey. *Journal of Official Statistics* 8:149–166.

Wallis, K. F. (1982). Seasonal adjustment and revision of current data: Linear filters for the X-11 method. *Journal of the Royal Statistical Society, Series A* 145:74–85.

Zimmerman, T. S. and Robison, E. (1995). Estimation of autocorrelations for current population survey labor force characteristics, Presented at ASA Survey Research Methods Section.

Part III

Quantifying Error in X-11 Seasonal Adjustments

7

Comparing Mean Squared Errors of X-12-ARIMA and Canonical ARIMA Model-Based Seasonal Adjustments

William R. Bell, Yea-Jane Chu, and George C. Tiao*

CONTENTS

7.1 Introduction

The fixed filtering approach to seasonal adjustment, as implemented in the original Census X-11 program (Shiskin et al. 1967) and its successors, X-11-ARIMA (Dagum 1975) and X-12-ARIMA (Findley et al. 1998; U.S. Census Bureau 2009), has been widely used by government and industry.

* Disclaimer: This chapter is released to inform interested parties of ongoing research and to encourage discussion. The views expressed on statistical, methodological, technical, or operational issues are those of the authors and not necessarily those of the U.S. Census Bureau, IBM, or the University of Chicago.

This approach relies on a finite set of empirically developed moving averages (MAs). The user can either specify the particular MAs used for a time series or let the program choose them automatically according to some empirical criteria. By contrast, a model-based approach to seasonal adjustment specifies stochastic models for the observed series and underlying components, and derives seasonal adjustment filters from optimal signal extraction theory. The filters used are thus determined by the model form specified, by assumptions made about the component decomposition, and by estimates of the model parameters. (See Bell and Hillmer (1984) for discussion.) The fixed filtering approach is often seen as easier to use, particularly for people with limited statistical backgrounds. The model-based approach, by contrast, offers more flexibility in determining filters and determines its filters according to standard statistical principles.

To relate these two approaches, Cleveland and Tiao (1976) and Burridge and Wallis (1984) proposed stochastic models leading to seasonal adjustment filters close to filters in the Census X-11 program. This line of work was further extended in Chu et al. (2011a) to provide models for 24 X-12 symmetric filters.* However, these models developed to approximate the X-12 filters are rather complicated, making it hard to see the implications of these results for the simpler models actually used in practice. Depoutot and Planas (1998), and Planas and Depoutot (2002), avoided complex approximating models by restricting consideration to the popular "airline" ARIMA model (Box and Jenkins 1976), using the canonical ARIMA model-based seasonal decomposition approach of Hillmer and Tiao (1982), hereafter HT, and Burman (1980). Still, while these papers showed how signal extraction filters obtained from models could approximate X-12 filters, and vice versa, they provided no statistical measure of how important or unimportant the differences between the X-12 and model-based filters may be.

Chu et al. (2011b), hereafter CTB, took a different approach to comparing symmetric X-12 and model-based filters. More specifically, for a given ARIMA model, CTB proposed computation of the mean squared error (MSE) when a specific X-12 symmetric filter is used to estimate the underlying seasonal component from the ARIMA model-based decomposition. This approach provides results on how much accuracy is lost (in terms of increased MSE) by using an X-12 filter rather than the optimal model-based filter. CTB did such calculations for the airline model with various values of the model parameters, finding in each case the X-12 symmetric filter that provided the lowest MSE for estimating the seasonal. Examining the MSEs of these "best" X-12 filters, CTB found that, for the canonical decomposition, the relative loss of accuracy (increase in MSE relative to the optimal model-based symmetric filter) was

---

* We use the term "X-12 filter" to refer to the filters available in the X-12-ARIMA program, though we could equally use the term "X-11 filter." This is because the basic filtering approach of X-12-ARIMA is that of the original X-11 program, although X-12 does provide some additional filter choices based on a few seasonal and trend moving averages not available in X-11.

generally small, except for large (0.9) or small (0.1 or 0.2) values of the seasonal MA parameter. Use of X-12 filters other than the best did substantially worse in some cases, but when the other X-12 filter was at least close to the best, the additional increase in MSE tended to be small.

CTB developed results for both the canonical decomposition of HT and an alternative approach that effectively put a uniform prior on the proportion of white noise variance allocated to the seasonal component. The canonical decomposition is defined by setting this proportion to zero. Results for this alternative approach were much less favorable to the X-12 filters—the best X-12 filters often had much higher MSEs than the optimal model-based filters for estimating this alternative seasonal. Here, however, we shall be concerned only with the canonical decomposition, the version of ARIMA model-based adjustment actually used in practice (as in the SEATS part of the TSW (TRAMO-SEATS for Windows) program (Caporello and Maravall 2004)).

CTB considered only the case of symmetric filters (X-12 and model-based) that, in practice, would apply only in the middle of a sufficiently long time series. Here we extend these results to concurrent (one-sided) filters applied to a series long enough so that backcasting of data prior to the observed series is unnecessary. We consider, as in CTB, airline models with various parameter values, and find the X-12 seasonal filters that best approximate the concurrent model-based filters, i.e., that have the lowest MSE among concurrent X-12 filters when estimating the canonical seasonal component. These X-12 concurrent filter choices turn out to be essentially the concurrent versions of the symmetric X-12 filter choices of CTB (i.e., they are defined by the asymmetric seasonal and trend MAs that correspond to the symmetric seasonal and trend MAs used in the symmetric filter choices of CTB). For these particular X-12 filter choices, we further extend the MSE results by computing MSEs when the analogous finite filters are applied to time series of various lengths. We examine how these finite sample results vary over different sets of airline model parameters and the different series lengths.

The concurrent and finite "X-12" filters used here are implicitly obtained by the application of a given symmetric X-12 filter to a time series extended with sufficient forecasts and backcasts (obtained from the true airline model) so that symmetric X-12 filters can be applied to the extended series. This can be called "full forecast and backcast extension."* This differs from standard practice—the default option in the X-12-ARIMA program is 1 year of forecast extension and no backcast extension—but this difference is necessary here for a technical reason discussed in Section 7.3.

* X-12 filters have many small weights at their extreme tails; see the plots in Bell and Monsell (1992). For practical purposes, applying X-12 filters with somewhat less than full forecast extension produces results very close to those obtained with full forecast extension. For example, for the "x11default" filter of X-12 (S3335-H13, defined shortly), 7 years of forecasts and backcasts would represent full extension, but extension with 3 years of forecasts and backcasts is practically the same.

The remainder of the chapter is organized as follows. Section 7.2 reviews the canonical ARIMA model-based approach to seasonal adjustment, and Section 7.3 the calculation of MSEs for estimates of seasonal (or, equivalently, nonseasonal) components. Section 7.4 describes our framework for comparing MSEs of X-12 and optimal model-based filters, and reviews the MSE results of CTB for symmetric filters applied to time series following airline models. Section 7.5 then develops the analogous results for concurrent filters applied to a series with data extending into the infinite past, and Section 7.6 the analogous results for finite series. Finally, Section 7.7 offers some conclusions.

7.2 The Canonical ARIMA Model-Based Approach to Seasonal Adjustment

Suppose that an observable time series, Z_t, where in this chapter t indexes months, follows the seasonal ARIMA model (Box and Jenkins 1976)

$$\phi(B)(1-B)^d(1-B^{12})Z_t = \theta(B)a_t. \tag{7.2.1}$$

In Equation 7.2.1, B is the backshift operator such that $BZ_t = Z_{t-1}$, $\phi(B)$ and $\theta(B)$ are polynomials in B of degrees p and $q \leq p+d+12$, respectively, with zeros lying outside the unit circle, and a_t is Gaussian white noise with variance σ_a^2. HT and Burman (1980) show that, subject to mild restrictions on the model (7.2.1), Z_t can be viewed as the sum of independent seasonal (S_t) and nonseasonal (N_t) components

$$Z_t = S_t + N_t, \tag{7.2.2}$$

where S_t and N_t follow the ARIMA models

$$U(B)S_t = \eta_S(B)b_t, \tag{7.2.3}$$

and

$$(1-B)^{d+1}\phi(B)N_t = \eta_N(B)c_t, \tag{7.2.4}$$

respectively. In Equations 7.2.3 and 7.2.4, $U(B) = (1 + B + \cdots + B^{11})$, while $\eta_S(B)$ and $\eta_N(B)$ are polynomials of degrees at most 11 and $p+d+1$, respectively, with zeros lying on or outside the unit circle. They also assume that $U(B)$ and $\eta_S(B)$ have no common zeros, and that $(1-B)^{d+1}\phi(B)$ and $\eta_N(B)$ have no common zeros. The innovation series b_t and c_t are mutually independent Gaussian white noises with variances σ_b^2 and σ_c^2, respectively. Obvious modifications apply to Equations 7.2.1 through 7.2.4 in the case of quarterly time series. (HT and Burman actually considered a three-component decomposition where N_t is further decomposed into trend and irregular components.

For discussion specifically of the two component decomposition (Equation 7.2.2), see Bell and Hillmer (1984).)

A fundamental requirement of the models (7.2.3) and (7.2.4) is that their corresponding "pseudo" autocovariance generating functions (ACGFs), $A_S(z)$ and $A_N(z)$, respectively, satisfy the relation

$$A_Z(z) = A_S(z) + A_N(z), \tag{7.2.5}$$

where

$$A_S(z) = \frac{\eta_S(z)\eta_S(z^{-1})}{U(z)U(z^{-1})}\sigma_b^2, \tag{7.2.6}$$

$$A_N(z) = \frac{\eta_N(z)\eta_N(z^{-1})}{(1-z)^{d+1}(1-z^{-1})^{d+1}\phi(z)\phi(z^{-1})}\sigma_c^2, \tag{7.2.7}$$

and

$$A_Z(z) = \frac{\theta(z)\theta(z^{-1})}{(1-z)^d(1-z^{-1})^d(1-z^{12})(1-z^{-12})\phi(z)\phi(z^{-1})}\sigma_a^2, \tag{7.2.8}$$

the last of these being the pseudo ACGF of Z_t. The resulting pseudo-spectral densities must be nonnegative for all values of the frequency $\lambda \in [0, \pi]$. For N_t, for example, this means that $A_N(e^{-i\lambda}) \geq 0$ for all λ. From this we see that an alternative to Equation 7.2.5 would have component ACGFs of $A_S(z) + \tau$ and $A_N(z) - \tau$, where τ is a constant, provided that $A_S(e^{-i\lambda}) + \tau$ and $A_N(e^{-i\lambda}) - \tau$ remain nonnegative for all $\lambda \in [0, \pi]$. Thus, in general, there are an infinite number of ways one can decompose $A_Z(z)$, and hence decompose a series Z_t as in Equation 7.2.2, corresponding to a given overall model (7.2.1). HT suggested considering the decomposition that corresponds to the smallest possible value of τ, and termed this the "canonical decomposition." The canonical decomposition provides the most stable seasonal component, i.e., the one that shows the least variation over time from a fixed seasonal pattern.

Given the models (7.2.1) through (7.2.4) corresponding to the canonical decomposition, one can perform seasonal adjustment by computing the conditional expectation of the components given the data, i.e., $E(S_t|\{Z_t\})$ and $E(N_t|\{Z_t\}) = Z_t - E(S_t|\{Z_t\})$. These can be expressed as linear functions of the observed data, e.g., $E(S_t|\{Z_t\}) = \sum_k \omega_{S,k} Z_{t-k} = \omega_S(B)Z_t$, where $\omega_S(B) = \sum_k \omega_{S,k} B^k$. MSEs are equal to the associated conditional variances, $\text{Var}(S_t|\{Z_t\}) = \text{Var}(N_t|\{Z_t\})$, which can also be computed. Bell (1984) discusses signal extraction calculations for the case of a doubly infinite series ($\{Z_t; t = 0, \pm1, \pm2, \ldots\}$), and Bell and Martin (2004) discuss the case of a semi-infinite series ($\{Z_t; t = n, n-1, n-2, \ldots\}$). Such calculations are implemented in the SEATS part of the TSW program for canonical ARIMA model-based seasonal adjustment (Caporello and Maravall 2004). For finite series ($\{Z_t; t = 1, \ldots, n\}$), Bell and Hillmer (1988), Bell (2004), and McElroy (2008) discuss a matrix approach to signal extraction that is implemented in the X-13 seasonal adjustment program (Monsell 2007). Alternatively, one can do such calculations using the Kalman filter and a suitable smoother (see, e.g., Harvey (1989) or Durbin and Koopman (2001)), coupled with a suitable initialization to deal with the differencing in the model (Ansley and Kohn 1985; Bell and Hillmer 1991). Finite sample signal extraction calculations were done here using the REGCMPNT program (Bell 2004, 2011), which uses the Kalman filter with the initialization of Bell and Hillmer and a fixed point smoother of reduced dimension (Anderson and Moore 1979).

7.3 Computing Mean Squared Errors of Seasonal Component Estimates

Let $\omega_S(B)$ be a linear filter to be used for estimating the seasonal component S_t of Equation 7.2.2, i.e., $\hat{S}_t = \omega_S(B)Z_t$. Note that we do not assume here that $\omega_S(B)$ is an optimal model-based filter—it can be any linear seasonal filter. Let $\omega_N(B) = 1 - \omega_S(B)$ be the corresponding linear filter for estimating N_t. The error in estimating S_t by $\hat{S}_t$, which we shall denote as $g_t = S_t - \hat{S}_t$, is

$$g_t = \omega_N(B)S_t - \omega_S(B)N_t. \tag{7.3.1}$$

Given that S_t and N_t are assumed to follow models of the form of Equations 7.2.3 and 7.2.4, it is easy to see from Equation 7.3.1 that the error series g_t will be stationary if $\omega_N(B)$ contains $U(B)$ as a factor and $\omega_S(B)$ contains $(1 - B)^{d+1}$ as a factor. When this is true, the ACGF of g_t is

$$A_g(z) = \omega_N(z)\omega_N(z^{-1})A_S(z) + \omega_S(z)\omega_S(z^{-1})A_N(z), \tag{7.3.2}$$

and the corresponding MSE is

$$MS(g_t) = (2\pi)^{-1} \int_{-\pi}^{\pi} A_g(e^{-i\lambda})d\lambda. \tag{7.3.3}$$

Note that the error in estimating $N_t = Z_t - S_t$ is $-g_t$, so Equation 7.3.3 also gives $MS(N_t - \hat{N}_t)$.

The above results were given by Pierce (1979). Since Equation 7.3.2 shows $A_g(z)$ to be symmetric (coefficients of z^k and z^{-k} are equal for all k), we can compute $MS(g_t)$ by expanding Equation 7.3.2 and taking the constant term (coefficient of z^0 in the expansion). Before doing so, however, we must cancel the unit root factors $U(z)U(z^{-1})$ that appear in $\omega_N(z)\omega_N(z^{-1})$ and in the denominator of $A_S(z)$, and similarly cancel $(1 - z)^{d+1}(1 - z^{-1})^{d+1}$ that appears in $\omega_S(z)\omega_S(z^{-1})$ and in the denominator of $A_N(z)$.

When $\omega_S(B)$ is the (symmetric or asymmetric) filter obtained from signal extraction theory with the true models (7.2.1) through (7.2.4), we get the optimal (MMSE) signal extraction estimate, which we shall denote as $\tilde{S}_t$. The unit root conditions on the filters then hold, so the resulting error

g_t is stationary. The MSE can be calculated from Equation 7.3.3 and is equal to $\text{Var}(S_t|\{Z_t\}) = \text{Var}(S_t - \tilde{S}_t)$. In the symmetric doubly infinite case, under suitable assumptions about initial conditions, the optimal signal extraction filter is $\omega_S(B) = A_S(B)/A_Z(B)$, and Equation 7.3.2 simplifies to $A_g(z) = A_S(z)A_N(z)/A_Z(z)$ (Bell 1984). Calculation of MSEs of optimal model-based filters in the other cases (semi-infinite or finite data) is discussed by the references cited in Section 7.2.

For X-12 filters, Bell (2010) observes that (*i*) all X-12 seasonal adjustment filters $\omega_N(B)$, symmetric and asymmetric, contain $U(B)$, (*ii*) all X-12 symmetric seasonal filters contain $(1-B)^6$, and (*iii*) X-12 asymmetric seasonal filters obtained with full forecast and backcast extension from the model (7.2.1) contain $(1-B)^{d+1}$ (or $(1-B)^6$ if $d \geq 6$). Since, in practice, d should rarely exceed 1, the conditions required for stationarity of g_t should always hold for the X-12 filters as considered here. Without full forecast extension, however, X-12 concurrent seasonal filters will include only $1-B$, and the resulting g_t in Equation 7.3.1 will be stationary only when $d=0$ in Equation 7.2.1. For $d>0$, such a g_t will be nonstationary, and so its MSE cannot be calculated. This is the case with the airline model considered in this chapter (for which $d=1$), and is the reason we must assume full forecast extension when calculating MSEs for X-12 filters. These observations apply not just to concurrent X-12 filters, but to any X-12 seasonal filter applied without full forecast and backcast extension.

While one could use the results (7.3.2) through (7.3.3) to calculate the MSE for an X-12 filter applied to a finite time series with full forecast and backcast extension, this would require figuring out the linear filter implied by this procedure, and factoring out of this filter, and respectively its complement, the $(1-B)^{d+1}$ and $U(B)$ factors. Rather than do this, to calculate MSEs in the finite sample case, we use a matrix approach given in the appendix. This approach provides the entire MSE matrix, $[\text{Cov}(S_t - \hat{S}_t, S_j - \hat{S}_j)]_{t,j=1,\ldots,n}$.

7.4 Framework for Comparing Mean Squared Errors for X-12 and Model-Based Filters, and Results for Symmetric Filters

We use the approach of CTB for comparing MSEs. As in CTB, we restrict consideration to the popular airline model (Box and Jenkins 1976), which is written as

$$(1-B)(1-B^{12})Z_t = (1-\theta_1 B)(1-\theta_{12}B^{12})a_t, \tag{7.4.1}$$

with $|\theta_1| \leq 1$ and $|\theta_{12}| \leq 1$. For the canonical decomposition of the airline model, the model (7.2.3) for S_t has $\eta_S(B)$ of degree 11, and the model (7.2.4) for N_t becomes $(1-B)^2 = \eta_N(B)c_t$, with $\eta_N(B)$ of degree 2.

The various X-12 symmetric filters considered here are determined by the choices of seasonal and trend MAs that are applied in the iterative filtering calculations of X-12. (See Ladiray and Quenneville (2001) for discussion.) As notation for these X-12 filters we write, for example, S3335-H13 to denote the X-12 seasonal filter that results when the first seasonal MA is the 3×3 $((1/9)(F^{12}+1+B^{12})(F^{12}+1+B^{12}))$, the second seasonal MA is the 3×5 $((1/15)(F^{12}+1+B^{12})(F^{24}+F^{12}+1+B^{12}+B^{24}))$, and the trend MA is the 13-term symmetric Henderson MA. (Note: $F = B^{-1}$ is the forward shift operator.) Findley et al. (1998, pp. 149–151) and Dagum (1985, 634) discuss the Henderson trend MAs. Here, as in CTB, we use the set of 20 X-12 filters generated from the combinations of five different seasonal MAs (S3131, S3333, S3335, S3339, and S315315) and four Henderson trend MAs (H9, H13, H17, and H23). The S3333, S3335, and S3339 seasonal MAs, as well as the H9, H13, and H23 Henderson trend MAs, are possibilities that can arise from the X-12-ARIMA automatic filter selection scheme, while the S3131 and S315315 seasonal MAs, and the H17 Henderson trend MA, are available as user-specified options.

Now let j index the filters within the set J of X-12 filters to be considered. We write $x_S^j(B)$ for a particular X-12 seasonal filter, with corresponding seasonal component estimate $\hat{S}_t^j = x_S^j(B)Z_t$. Letting $g_t^j = S_t - \hat{S}_t^j$ be the error series for each $j \in J$, we can compute $MS[g_t^j]$ as discussed in Section 7.3 and the Appendix. We can then examine the results over j to find, for a given airline model, the best X-12 filter, denoted as $x_S^{j*}(B)$, for estimating S_t, i.e., the filter in the set J that yields the lowest MSE. Let $g_t^{j*} = S_t - x_S^{j*}(B)Z_t$, so that

$$MS[g_t^{j*}] = \min_{j \in J}\{MS[S_t - \hat{S}_t^j]\}. \tag{7.4.2}$$

As in CTB, we compare these best X-12 MSEs with the optimal model-based MSEs in terms of percentage differences defined as:

$$100 \times \left\{ \frac{MS[g_t^{j*}] - MS[S_t - \tilde{S}_t]}{MS[S_t - \tilde{S}_t]} \right\}. \tag{7.4.3}$$

We can simplify the numerator of Equation 7.4.3 by writing

$$g_t^{j*} = S_t - x_S^{j*}(B)Z_t = [S_t - \tilde{S}_t] + [(\omega_S(B) - x_S^{j*}(B))Z_t], \tag{7.4.4}$$

where $\tilde{S}_t = \omega_S(B)Z_t$ is the optimal model-based estimator. The first term on the right-hand side of Equation 7.4.4, the error in the optimal estimate $\tilde{S}_t$, is orthogonal to all linear functions of Z_t. Thus, the two terms in Equation 7.4.4 are orthogonal and the numerator of Equation 7.4.3 immediately reduces to $MS[(\omega_S(B) - x_S^{j*}(B))Z_t]$, the MS of the difference of the two estimators $\tilde{S}_t$ and $x_S^{j*}(B)Z_t$. For the airline model, $\omega_S(B) - x_S^{j*}(B)$ always contains $U(B)(1-B)^2 = (1-B)(1-B^{12})$, so that $(\omega_S(B) - x_S^{j*}(B))Z_t$ is stationary. Thus, the ACGF of $(\omega_S(B) - x_S^{j*}(B))Z_t$, and hence its MS, could be calculated directly, as well as through the numerator of Equation 7.4.3.

Note that Equation 7.4.3 compares the accuracy of the X-12 estimator of S_t against that of the model-based estimator for the ideal situation where the latter is optimal. This assumes that the true model is used and the true parameter values are known. Uncertainty about the model or its parameters would tend to increase $MS(S_t - \tilde{S}_t)$; e.g., (with a Bayesian treatment), see Bell and Otto (1992). Such uncertainty would also tend to increase $MS(g_t^{j*})$ near the end of the series due to increased forecast extension error.

For symmetric filters, CTB present results (their Table 1) showing, for the airline model with various values of (θ_1, θ_{12}), the best X-12 symmetric filter, the minimum MSE in Equation 7.4.2, and the best X-12 symmetric filter's MSE percentage difference (Equation 7.4.3). The sets of parameter values used included all combinations with $\theta_1 \in \{0.9, 0.7, 0.5, 0.3, 0.1\}$ and $\theta_{12} \in \{0.9, 0.8, 0.7, 0.6, 0.5, 0.4, 0.3, 0.2, 0.1\}$. The results show that the percentage increase in MSE from using the best X-12 symmetric filter, rather than the optimal model-based filter, is generally small (less than or equal to about 12%), except for large values of θ_{12} (0.9) or small values of θ_{12} (0.1, 0.2). The largest MSE increase was 59% for $(\theta_1, \theta_{12}) = (0.9, 0.1)$. For combinations with $\theta_{12} = 0.9$, the MSE increases ranged from 25% to 37%; and for $\theta_{12} = 0.1$ or 0.2, they ranged from 14% to the noted 59%.

CTB noted substantially more variation in the MSE increases across the different values of θ_{12} than across the different values of θ_1, and across different choices of X-12 seasonal MAs than across different choices of Henderson trend MAs. Thus, CTB provided a table showing, roughly, the best seasonal MA choices for given values of θ_{12}. This is repeated here as Table 7.1.

CTB performed a simulation experiment examining the performance of the X-12-ARIMA program's automatic selection of seasonal and Henderson trend MAs in relation to the MSEs of the filters. When simulating series from the airline model with various parameters, CTB observed that, for $\theta_{12} \geq 0.7$, the automatic filter selection procedure tends to pick seasonal MAs shorter than the best for estimating the canonical seasonal, while it tends to make better choices when $\theta_{12} \leq 0.5$. In some cases, the next shorter seasonal MA was chosen, resulting in a small increase in MSE, but sometimes the seasonal MA chosen could be still shorter, resulting in a more substantial MSE increase. As these results were for symmetric filters used with sufficiently long time series, they leave open questions about the performance of the algorithm when concurrent adjustment is of interest. This would depend on what are the best X-12 filter choices for concurrent adjustment, a question examined in the next section.

TABLE 7.1
Best Choices of X-12 Seasonal MAs for Estimating the Canonical Seasonal from the Airline Model (from CTB)

Value of θ_{12}	0.1–0.2	0.3–0.4	0.5–0.6	0.7	0.8–0.9
Best seasonal MA	S3131	S3333	S3335	S3339	S315315

7.5 Comparing Mean Squared Errors of X-12 and Model-Based Concurrent Filters

In this section, we provide analogous results to those given in CTB, for comparing MSEs of X-12 and model-based *concurrent* filters for estimating the canonical seasonal of the airline model. These filters are used to estimate S_n based on data $\{Z_t; t = n, n-1, n-2, \ldots\}$, i.e., estimating the seasonal for the most recent time point. In practice, this assumes that the observed series is sufficiently long so that the filter weights die out before reaching the start of the time series. We do the calculations as discussed in Section 7.3, and, as in CTB, use all combinations of the parameter values from $\theta_1 \in \{0.9, 0.7, 0.5, 0.3, 0.1\}$ and $\theta_{12} \in \{0.9, 0.8, 0.7, 0.6, 0.5, 0.4, 0.3, 0.2, 0.1\}$. We restrict our consideration to positive values of θ_1 and θ_{12} since (*i*) this is nearly always the case for estimated values in practice (see, e.g., Depoutot and Planas (1998)), and (*ii*) the condition $\theta_{12} \geq 0$ is needed for the model-based decomposition to exist (HT, p. 67). Since our interest is in relative comparisons of MSEs via Equation 7.4.3, without loss of generality, we set $\sigma_a^2 = 1$. Table 7.2 gives the results showing, for each set of parameter values, the best X-12 concurrent filter, its MSE, and the percentage difference (from Equation 7.4.3) between this best X-12 concurrent estimator's MSE and the MSE of the optimal model-based concurrent estimator.

Examining the results presented in Table 7.2, we see that the increases in MSE from using the best X-12 concurrent filters are small (around 10% or less)* with one exception $((\theta_1, \theta_{12}) = (0.9, 0.1))$. In fact, these percentage increases are substantially smaller than those given by CTB for the symmetric filters. This is due to the facts that (*i*) the MSEs for both the model-based and X-12 filters are substantially larger for concurrent than for symmetric filter adjustment, due to substantial contribution from forecast extension error, while (*ii*) the differences between the MSEs of the model-based and X-12 filters are smaller for the concurrent than for the symmetric filters. In any case, except for perhaps $(\theta_1, \theta_{12}) = (0.9, 0.1)$, it appears that the percent increases in MSE by using the best X-12 concurrent seasonal filters rather than the best model-based concurrent seasonal filters are small enough to be ignored.

Table 7.2 shows that, as was the case with symmetric X-12 filters, longer seasonal MAs are best for larger values of θ_{12}. In fact, most of the chosen X-12 filters in Table 7.2 for given (θ_1, θ_{12}) values are the same as those given by CTB for the symmetric filters. (CTB also note that these choices are substantially in agreement with those found by Depoutot and Planas (1998) using a criterion measuring closeness of filter weights.) The lone exceptions occur for $\theta_{12} = 0.5$ with θ_1 equal to 0.7, 0.3, and 0.1. In these cases, the choice for the symmetric

* Note that corresponding increases in root mean squared errors (RMSEs) are roughly half the increases in the MSEs so, with the one noted exception, the RMSE increases are about 5% or less, a very small amount.

TABLE 7.2
Concurrent Filter Estimation of the Canonical Seasonal for the Airline Model (Choices of the Best Concurrent X-12 Filters, Their MSE Values, and the Percentage Increases in MSE over Those of the Optimal Model-Based Filters)

	$\boldsymbol{\theta_{12} = 0.9}$	**0.8**	**0.7**	**0.6**	**0.5**	**0.4**	**0.3**	**0.2**	**0.1**
$\boldsymbol{\theta_1 = 0.9}$	S315315-H9	S315315-H9	S3339-H9	S3335-H9	S3333-H9	S3333-H23	S3333-H23	S3333-H23	S3131-H23
	0.082786	0.138064	0.182530	0.210536	0.224784	0.224975	0.219123	0.208031	0.186888
	10.44%	3.18%	3.09%	2.39%	2.04%	1.42%	3.87%	10.38%	20.52%
0.7	S315315-H9	S315315-H9	S3339-H9	S3335-H9	S3333-H9	S3333-H23	S3333-H23	S3333-H23	S3131-H23
	0.072343	0.121951	0.162764	0.190721	0.208636	0.214769	0.216230	0.214057	0.203812
	9.90%	2.93%	2.72%	2.07%	1.93%	0.93%	1.94%	5.21%	8.61%
0.5	S315315-H9	S315315-H9	S3339-H9	S3335-H9	S3335-H23	S3333-H23	S3333-H23	S3131-H23	S3131-H23
	0.069984	0.119986	0.162464	0.194115	0.217026	0.231001	0.240300	0.246507	0.245520
	9.17%	2.59%	2.35%	1.77%	1.44%	0.78%	1.19%	2.92%	3.97%
0.3	S315315-H9	S315315-H9	S3339-H9	S3335-H9	S3333-H9	S3333-H23	S3333-H23	S3131-H23	S3131-H23
	0.075999	0.133932	0.185155	0.225895	0.258629	0.281711	0.301301	0.316547	0.325150
	8.15%	2.32%	2.15%	1.57%	1.45%	0.81%	1.63%	3.25%	4.79%
0.1	S315315-H9	S315315-H9	S3339-H9	S3335-H9	S3333-H17	S3333-H23	S3333-H23	S3131-H23	S3131-H23
	0.089834	0.161806	0.227141	0.281296	0.326676	0.362381	0.394746	0.421064	0.440916
	7.25%	2.10%	2.00%	1.43%	1.23%	0.89%	1.99%	3.56%	5.45%

Note: In each cell, 1st row: the chosen X-12 filter, i.e., j^* as defined by Equation 7.4.2; 2nd row: the MMSE value from Equation 7.4.2 when t is at the end of a sufficiently long series; 3rd row: the percentage increase in MSE (X-12 filter compared to optimal model-based filter) from Equation 7.4.3.

X-12 filter is S3335-H23, whereas for concurrent filters it is S3333-H9 for $\theta_1 = 0.7, 0.3$ and S3333-H17 for $\theta_1 = 0.1$ (Table 7.2). For these cases where the best X-12 filter choice for symmetric adjustment differs from that for concurrent adjustment, this difference has little effect on the MSE. That is, when the best X-12 filter for concurrent seasonal adjustment is applied to symmetric adjustment, or vice versa, the MSE increases only slightly. Thus, for a given airline model, for the comparisons being made here, we believe we can get by with a single choice of X-12 filter as the basis for both symmetric and concurrent seasonal adjustment (and presumably for everything in between). Note that if we use a single X-12 filter for concurrent through symmetric adjustment, then doing full forecast extension (with the correct model) will minimize the mean squared revisions (Geweke 1978; Pierce 1980).

Figure 7.1 shows how the MSEs of the estimated seasonals vary across different X-12 filters. The figure consists of two columns with three plots each. The first column of plots shows, for comparison purposes, results from the corresponding graph of CTB for symmetric filters. The second column of plots shows corresponding results obtained here for the concurrent filters. The three rows of plots in each column correspond to the values $\theta_{12} = 0.8$, 0.5, and 0.2, respectively. We use these three values to generically represent high, medium, and low values of θ_{12}. Within each plot are sets of results for θ_1 values 0.8, 0.5, and 0.2, as noted on the plots. For each θ_1 value, the MSEs as plotted are seen to fall into five groups of four values, each group corresponding to a particular choice of X-12 seasonal MA (S3131, S3333, S3335, S3339, and S315315). The four values within each group correspond to the four choices of Henderson trend MAs considered (9-term, 13-term, 17-term, and 23-term, in that order).

Several results are evident from the plots of Figure 7.1:

- For both symmetric and concurrent X-12 filters, choice of the best seasonal MA is not crucial. For $\theta_{12} = 0.8$, the S3339 seasonal MA does about as well as the best choice of S315315; for $\theta_{12} = 0.5$, the S3333 and S3335 are best and perform similarly; and for $\theta_{12} = 0.2$, the S3333 does about as well as the best choice of S3131. Straying further than this from the best choice of seasonal MA entails a more substantial increase in MSE.

- For both symmetric and concurrent X-12 filters, MSEs are generally insensitive to the choice of Henderson trend MA. Some exceptions occur when a very poor choice is made for the seasonal MA (e.g., in the symmetric case with the S3131 seasonal MA when $\theta_{12} = 0.8$). In contrast to these results, we would expect more sensitivity to the choice of Henderson trend MAs in MSEs for X-12 trend estimates.

- For concurrent X-12 filters, MSEs for $\theta_1 = 0.2$ are, in most cases, notably larger than those for $\theta_1 = 0.5$ and $= 0.8$. (Exceptions occur with $\theta_{12} = 0.8$ when using the S3131 and S3333 seasonal MAs.) This is generally not the case with the symmetric X-12 filters.

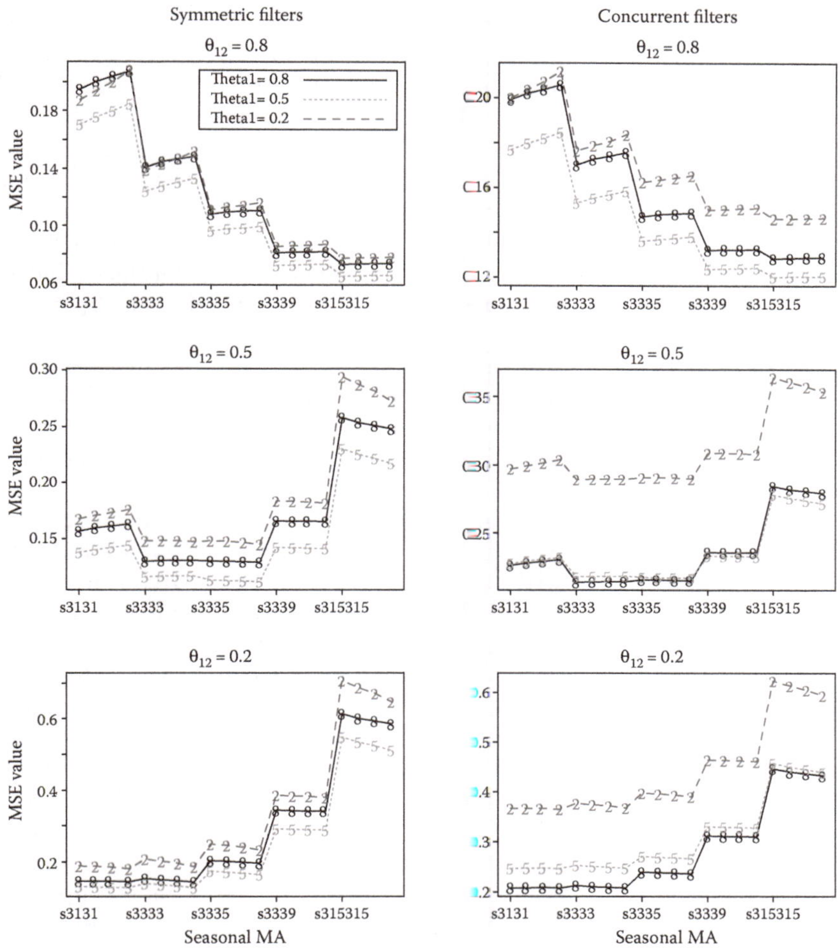

FIGURE 7.1
The MSEs when using various X-12 seasonal filters to estimate the canonical seasonal component of the airline model with various parameter values (left column – symmetric filters, right column – concurrent filters).

7.6 Comparing Mean Squared Errors of X-12 and Model-Based Finite Filters

The results of the previous section, and those of CTB, show that when the best X-12 filter (symmetric or concurrent) is chosen for estimating the canonical seasonal of the airline model, there is generally little increase in MSE relative to the use of the corresponding optimal model-based filter. There are exceptions, however, where the MSE difference is not so small; these occur more for symmetric filters than for concurrent filters. On the other hand, both these situations are somewhat artificial in that they assume that the filters apply to a series sufficiently long that the symmetric filter weights effectively die out before reaching the start or end of the series, and the concurrent filter weights die out before reaching the start of the series. In this section, we make MSE comparisons for the more realistic setting of filters applied to a finite sample of data, $\{Z_t; t = 1, \ldots, n\}$, assumed to arise from the airline model (7.4.1). We restrict our consideration to parameter values of $\theta_1 = 0.5$ and $\theta_{12} = 0.9, 0.8, 0.5, 0.2$. With these parameter values, the best X-12 symmetric filters show increases in MSEs of about 33%, 10%, 6%, and 14%, respectively (from results of CTB), over those for the optimal model-based filters, while the best X-12 concurrent filters showed MSE increases of about 9%, 2.6%, 1.4%, and 2.9%, respectively (from Table 7.2). We can compare these figures to the results computed here for finite series.

For the X-12 filters, we compute MSEs here for only the best X-12 filter choices. For the four values of θ_{12} considered here, these are S315315-H9 (for $\theta_{12} = 0.9, 0.8$), S3335-H23 (for $\theta_{12} = 0.5$), and S3131-H23 (for $\theta_{12} = 0.2$). These choices are the best X-12 filters for both the symmetric case (from results of CTB) and the concurrent case (from results of Section 7.5).

The results, in terms of the percent differences in MSE (from Equation 7.4.3), are plotted in Figure 7.2. The graphs in the left column refer to the use of symmetric finite filters (for estimating S_t at the midpoint of the series), and the graphs in the right column to the use of concurrent finite filters (for estimating S_t at the end of the series). Each row corresponds to a different value of θ_{12} $(0.9, 0.8, 0.5, 0.2)$. The points plotted in each graph show the MSE percent differences for various lengths of series: k years plus 1 month for $k = 8$, 12, 16, 20, and 40. The additional 1 month provides an odd number of observations so that the series have a central observation at which symmetric (finite) filters would apply.

For symmetric filters, we see a substantial MSE difference (about 30%) for a 40-year (plus one month) series with $\theta_{12} = 0.9$. For a 20-year series with $\theta_{12} = 0.9$, the MSE difference is only about 9%. For $\theta_{12} = 0.8$, all the MSE differences are less than 10%, and for $\theta_{12} = 0.5$, less than 6%. For $\theta_{12} = 0.2$, the MSE differences are somewhat higher, around 15%. We also note that, for $\theta_{12} = 0.5$ and $\theta_{12} = 0.2$, the series length (at least for 8 years and more) hardly affects these results, which are essentially the same as those given by CTB for a doubly infinite series. Apparently, for $\theta_{12} \leq 0.5$, 8 years of data is enough for the symmetric filter weights to effectively die out before the start and end of the series. For $\theta_{12} = 0.8$ or 0.9, the shorter series do yield results different from those of CTB—the MSE percent differences are smaller.

For the concurrent finite filters, the MSE percent differences are even smaller than those for the symmetric finite filters. For $\theta_{12} = 0.9$, the MSE difference is about 9% with a 40-year series, and smaller with shorter series. For the other values of θ_{12}, the MSE percent differences are quite small. Only

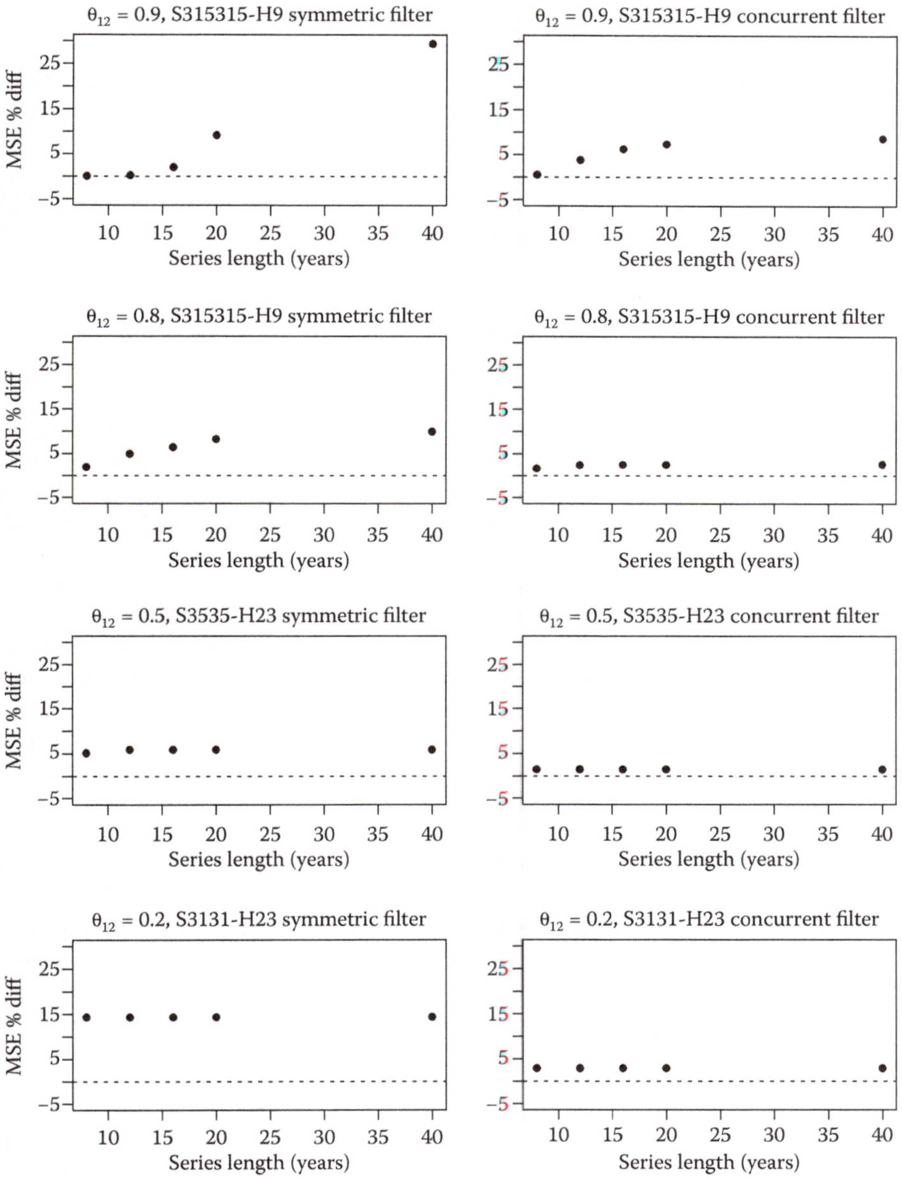

FIGURE 7.2
Percent differences in MSE, X-12 versus ARIMA model-based seasonal adjustment. Airline model with $\theta_1 = 0.5$, various θ_{12}, applied to time series of lengths k years +1 month for $k = 8, 12, 16, 20$, and 40.

for $\theta_{12} = 0.9$ and series shorter than 20 years do the results show any noticeable difference from those of Table 7.2.

In general, we see that with finite series, the MSE percent differences between using the best X-12 filter and the optimal model-based filter are either smaller or about the same as those for infinite series. Only for a very high value of θ_{12} and a very long series (represented here by the case of $\theta_{12} = 0.9$ and a 40-year series), and for estimation with symmetric filters, does the MSE percent difference appear nonnegligible.

7.7 Conclusions and Topics for Future Research

In this chapter, we examined the performance of X-12 symmetric and concurrent filters, with infinite and finite data, for estimating the seasonal component of the canonical model-based decomposition of a time series following the airline model. (Symmetric infinite filter results were presented in CTB, but were reviewed here.) We noted that, in most cases, the best among a set of X-12 filters produced an estimated seasonal with MSE not much larger (in relative terms) than the estimate obtained from the model-based filter optimal for the given airline model. In fact, in most cases, the MSE percent differences could be judged to be negligible. Some exceptions of higher MSE differences were noted, but these occurred only for limited cases, namely, for symmetric filters applied to very long (or infinite) series from airline models with a large value of the seasonal moving average parameter θ_{12}, such as 0.9. For finite series of realistic lengths, and especially for concurrent filters, the MSE percent differences all appeared negligible.

Overall, then, we can conclude that, in real situations that are something like those considered here—series of reasonable length approximately following an airline model—if a suitable choice is made of an X-12 filter, the difference in statistical accuracy between its use versus using model-based seasonal adjustment may well be negligible. Since the difference in MSE of the two estimators depends on the mean squared difference of the estimators themselves, clearly this result is at least partly due to the fact that the estimator using the suitable X-12 filter can well approximate the model-based estimator (and vice versa), at least in terms of the magnitude of the MSE.

Several questions remain for future research. One concerns whether similar results to those shown here would be obtained with different models than the airline model? The results here suggest that for other seasonal ARIMA models the value of the seasonal moving average parameter θ_{12} would be an important determining factor in the results. Another question concerns the accuracy of X-12 trend estimates. The approach presented here extends in a straightforward fashion to the estimation of the trend component. Results of Depoutot and Planas (1998) suggest that MSEs for X-12 trend filters would depend on the choices of Henderson trend MAs as well as on the choices of seasonal MAs.

Acknowledgments

We thank two anonymous reviewers for helpful comments that have improved the chapter.

Appendix: Calculating the Mean Squared Error for Finite Filters with Full Forecast and Backcast Extension

To calculate the MSE of seasonal estimates from X-12 filters with full forecast and backcast extension, we adapt an approach of Bell and Kramer (1999), hereafter BK (see note at end). Let $\omega_S(B) = \sum_{-m}^{m} \omega_{S,k} B^k$ be a symmetric seasonal filter of length $2m+1$, and let $\omega_N(B) = 1 - \omega_S(B)$ be the corresponding symmetric seasonal adjustment filter. As in Section 7.3, we assume that $\omega_S(B)$ contains $(1-B)^{d+1}$ and $\omega_N(B)$ contains $U(B)$. Let $Z_{obs} = (Z_1, \ldots, Z_n)'$ be the vector of observed data. To apply $\omega_N(B)$ for seasonal adjustment with full forecast and backcast extension, we need to append m forecasts and m backcasts to Z_{obs}. Let $Z_f = (Z_{n+1}, \ldots, Z_{n+m})'$ and $Z_b = (Z_{1-m}, \ldots, Z_0)'$ be the m Z_t values in the forecast and backcast periods, respectively, and let $\hat{Z}_f$ and $\hat{Z}_b$ be the vectors of optimal forecasts and backcasts from the model (7.2.1). Explicit expressions for $\hat{Z}_f$ and $\hat{Z}_b$ are given later. Define the extended vectors

$$Z = \begin{bmatrix} Z_b \\ Z_{obs} \\ Z_f \end{bmatrix} \qquad \hat{Z} = \begin{bmatrix} \hat{Z}_b \\ Z_{obs} \\ \hat{Z}_f \end{bmatrix} \qquad Z - \hat{Z} = \begin{bmatrix} b \\ 0 \\ f \end{bmatrix}, \tag{7.8.1}$$

where b and f are the vectors of backcast and forecast errors, respectively. To save space and simplify notation, we shall write $[b|0|f]'$ to mean the column vector in Equation 7.8.1, i.e., when we actually mean $[b'|0'|f']'$. Let $\hat{S}_{obs}$ be the vector of estimated seasonals for $t = 1, \ldots, n$ obtained with full forecast and backcast extension. We can write this as

$$\hat{S}_{obs} = \Omega_S \hat{Z}$$

where

$$\Omega_S = \begin{bmatrix} \omega_{S,-m} & \cdots & \omega_{S,0} & \cdots & \omega_{S,m} & & & & \\ & \ddots & & \ddots & & \ddots & & & \\ & & & & \omega_{S,-m} & \cdots & \omega_{S,0} & \cdots & \omega_{S,m} \end{bmatrix}.$$

Note that Ω_S is an $n \times (n+2m)$ matrix. The corresponding matrix for producing the seasonally adjusted series is $\Omega_N = [0_{n\times m}|I_n|0_{n\times m}] - \Omega_S$, where I_n is the $n \times n$ identity matrix and $0_{n\times m}$ is an $n \times m$ matrix of zeros.

The error in estimating the true seasonals, S_{obs}, by $\hat{S}_{obs}$, can be written

$$S_{obs} - \hat{S}_{obs} = (S_{obs} - \Omega_S Z) + \Omega_S (Z - \hat{Z}).$$

From Equation 7.8.1, the covariance matrix of this error is then

$$\begin{aligned} \text{Var}(S_{obs} - \hat{S}_{obs}) = & \text{ Var}(S_{obs} - \Omega_S Z) + \Omega_S \text{Var}([b|0|f]')\Omega_S' \\ & + \text{ Cov}(S_{obs} - \Omega_S Z, [b|0|f]')\Omega_S' \\ & + \Omega_S \text{Cov}([b|0|f]', S_{obs} - \Omega_S Z). \end{aligned} \tag{7.8.2}$$

Thus, to compute $\text{Var}(S_{obs} - \hat{S}_{obs})$, we need to compute the variance and covariance matrices on the right-hand side of Equation 7.8.2.

Computing $\text{Var}(S_{obs} - \Omega_S Z)$

Since we assume that $\omega_S(B)$ contains $(1-B)^{d+1}$ and $\omega_N(B)$ contains $U(B)$, we can write

$$\omega_S(B) = \lambda_S(B)(1-B)^{d+1}$$

and

$$\omega_N(B) = \lambda_N(B)U(B),$$

where $\lambda_S(B) = \sum_{k=-m}^{m-d-1} \lambda_{S,k} B^k$ and $\lambda_N(B) = \sum_{k=-m}^{m-11} \lambda_{N,k} B^k$ can be obtained by polynomial division. (Doing this for $\lambda_S(B)$ amounts to cumulatively summing the coefficients of $\omega_S(B)$ $d+1$ times.) Then, $g_t = S_t - \hat{S}_t = S_t - \omega_S(B)Z_t$ can be written using Equation 7.3.1 as

$$\begin{aligned} g_t &= \lambda_N(B)U(B)S_t - \lambda_S(B)(1-B)^{d+1}N_t \\ &= \lambda_N(B)U_t - \lambda_S(B)V_t, \end{aligned} \tag{7.8.3}$$

where, from Equations 7.2.3 and 7.2.4, $U_t = U(B)S_t = \eta_S(B)b_t$ and $V_t = (1-B)^{d+1}N_t = \{\eta_N(B)/\phi(B)\}c_t$. Using Equation 7.8.3, we can compute the ACGF of g_t to obtain its variances and autocovariances. These are the elements of $\text{Var}(S_{obs} - \Omega_S Z)$. Alternatively, the matrix-vector analog to Equation 7.8.3 is

$$S_{obs} - \Omega_S Z = \Lambda_N U - \Lambda_S V, \tag{7.8.4}$$

where $U = (U_{12-m}, \ldots, U_{n+m})'$ and $V = (V_{d+2-m}, \ldots, V_{n+m})'$, and the rows of Λ_N ($n \times (n+2m-11)$) and Λ_S ($n \times (n+2m-d-1)$) contain the coefficients of $\lambda_N(B)$ and $\lambda_S(B)$, i.e.,

$$\Lambda_N = \begin{bmatrix} \lambda_{N,-m} & \cdots & \lambda_{N,m-11} & & \\ & \ddots & & \ddots & \\ & & \lambda_{N,-m} & \cdots & \lambda_{N,m-11} \end{bmatrix},$$

with Λ_S defined similarly. One could then compute $\text{Var}(S_{obs} - \Omega_S Z) = \Lambda_N \text{Var}(U)\Lambda_N' + \Lambda_S \text{Var}(V)\Lambda_S'$, though this is less efficient than computing the ACGF of g_t. We will need the matrices Λ_N and Λ_S later though.

Computing $\text{Var}([b|0|f]')$

We could compute the variances of the forecast and backcast errors using classical results (Box and Jenkins 1976), which provide only approximations, or we could compute exact results using the Kalman filter. However, we need the entire covariance matrices of b and f, as well as $\text{Cov}(b, f)$, something not readily provided by either of these approaches. We thus use a matrix approach instead.

Let the differenced time series be $W_t = (1 - B)^d(1 - B^{12})Z_t$, and define $W = [W_b', W_{obs}', W_f']'$, where $W_b = (W_{-m+d+13}, \dots, W_{d+12})'$, $W_{obs} = (W_{d+13}, \dots, W_n)'$, and $W_f = (W_{n+1}, \dots, W_{n+m})'$ are the vectors of the differenced series in the backcast, observation, and forecast periods. Also define

$$\text{Var}(W) = \begin{bmatrix} \Sigma_{bb} & \Sigma_{b,obs} & \Sigma_{bf} \\ \Sigma_{obs,b} & \Sigma_{obs} & \Sigma_{obs,f} \\ \Sigma_{fb} & \Sigma_{f,obs} & \Sigma_{ff} \end{bmatrix},$$

which is partitioned conformably to W, e.g., $\Sigma_{bf} = \text{Cov}(W_b, W_f)$. (Note that, to avoid overly complicated notation, we write Σ_{obs} rather than $\Sigma_{obs,obs}$ for $\text{Var}(W_{obs})$.) The elements of $\text{Var}(W)$ can be computed given the ARMA model $\phi(B)W_t = \theta(B)a_t$ (Tunnicliffe Wilson 1979). From standard results on conditional expectations in multivariate normal distributions, the optimal forecasts and backcasts of W_t (note that W_t is assumed here to have mean zero) are $\hat{W}_f = \Sigma_{f,obs}\Sigma_{obs}^{-1}W_{obs}$ and $\hat{W}_b = \Sigma_{b,obs}\Sigma_{obs}^{-1}W_{obs}$, respectively. BK note that the forecast and backcast errors for Z_t can be expressed as

$$f = Z_f - \hat{Z}_f = C(W_f - \hat{W}_f) \qquad b = Z_b - \hat{Z}_b = (-1)^{d+1}C'(W_b - \hat{W}_b), \tag{7.8.5}$$

where

$$C = \begin{bmatrix} 1 & & & \\ \xi_1 & 1 & & \\ \vdots & \ddots & \ddots & \\ \xi_{m-1} & \cdots & \xi_1 & 1 \end{bmatrix},$$

and $\xi(B) = 1 + \xi_1 B + \xi_1 B^2 + \cdots$ is the expansion of $[(1 - B)^d(1 - B^{12})]^{-1}$. From Equation 7.8.5 and standard results on conditional variances in multivariate normal distributions,

$$\begin{aligned} \text{Var}(f) &= C \ \text{Var}(W_f - \hat{W}_f) \ C' = C[\Sigma_{ff} - \Sigma_{f,obs}\Sigma_{obs}^{-1}\Sigma_{obs,f}]C' \\ \text{Var}(b) &= C' \ \text{Var}(W_b - \hat{W}_b) \ C = C'[\Sigma_{bb} - \Sigma_{b,obs}\Sigma_{obs}^{-1}\Sigma_{obs,b}]C \\ \text{Cov}(f, b) &= C[\text{Cov}(W_f - \hat{W}_f, W_b - \hat{W}_b)]C \\ &= (-1)^{d+1}C[\Sigma_{fb} - \Sigma_{f,obs}\Sigma_{obs}^{-1}\Sigma_{obs,b}]C. \end{aligned} \tag{7.8.6}$$

BK outline an approach to computing the results in Equation 7.8.6 by using the Cholesky decomposition of Σ_{obs} rather than its inverse.

Computing $\mathrm{Cov}(S_{obs} - \Omega_S Z, [b|0|f]')$

From the results in Equation 7.8.5 and the expressions for $\hat{W}_f$ and $\hat{W}_b$, we can express f and b as

$$f = K_f W \quad \text{and} \quad b = K_b W$$

where $K_f = C[0| - \Sigma_{f,obs}\Sigma_{obs}^{-1}|I_m]$ and $K_b = (-1)^{d+1}C'[I_m| - \Sigma_{b,obs}\Sigma_{obs}^{-1}|0]$. Then, using Equation 7.8.4,

$$\begin{aligned}
\mathrm{Cov}(S_{obs} - \Omega_S Z, f) &= \mathrm{Cov}(\Lambda_N U - \Lambda_S V, K_f W) \\
&= [\Lambda_N \mathrm{Cov}(U, W) - \Lambda_S \mathrm{Cov}(V, W)]K_f' \\
\mathrm{Cov}(S_{obs} - \Omega_S Z, b) &= \mathrm{Cov}(\Lambda_N U - \Lambda_S V, K_b W) \\
&= [\Lambda_N \mathrm{Cov}(U, W) - \Lambda_S \mathrm{Cov}(V, W)]K_b'.
\end{aligned}$$

We can readily compute these expressions given $\mathrm{Cov}(U, W)$ and $\mathrm{Cov}(V, W)$. The elements of these matrices are easily computed using the expression $W_t = (1 - B)^{d+1}U(B)[S_t + N_t] = (1 - B)^{d+1}U_t + U(B)V_t$, and recalling that U_t and V_t are independent of one another. For example, for the airline model $d = 1$ so $(1 - B)^{d+1} = 1 - 2B + B^2$, and then

$$\begin{aligned}
\mathrm{Cov}(U_t, W_{t+k}) &= \mathrm{Cov}(U_t, U_{t+k} - 2U_{t+k-1} + U_{t+k-2}) \\
&= \gamma_U(k) - 2\gamma_U(k-1) + \gamma_U(k-2) \\
\mathrm{Cov}(V_t, W_{t+k}) &= \mathrm{Cov}(V_t, V_{t+k} + \cdots + V_{t+k-11}) \\
&= \gamma_V(k) + \cdots + \gamma_V(k-11),
\end{aligned}$$

where $\gamma_U(k) = \mathrm{Cov}(U_t, U_{t+k})$ and $\gamma_V(k) = \mathrm{Cov}(V_t, V_{t+k})$.

Note: The difference between the above MSE calculation and the calculation of “X-11 variances” in BK is that BK defined a certain restricted “target” for X-11 seasonal adjustment that was different from the nonseasonal component of a model-based decomposition. This had the consequence that the calculated variances effectively ignored the variation contributed to the error by some of the components. An essentially similar comment applies to the method proposed for X-11 variances by Pfeffermann (1994); see Bell (2005) and Scott et al. (2011) for general discussion. (Both BK and Pfeffermann allow for a sampling error component in the decomposition, but that is easily added to Equation 7.2.2 with minor changes to the above calculations.) By accounting for contributions to error from all the components, the above approach to MSE calculation for X-12 estimates provides a more complete measure of error than do the approaches of BK and of Pfeffermann.

References

Anderson, B. D. O. and Moore, J. B. (1979). *Optimal Filtering.* Englewood Cliffs: Prentice-Hall.

Ansley, C. F. and Kohn, R. (1985). Estimation, filtering, and smoothing in state space models with incompletely specified initial conditions. *Annals of Statistics*, 13:1286–1316.

Bell, W. R. (1984). Signal extraction for nonstationary time series. *Annals of Statistics*, 12:646–664.

Bell, W. R. (2004). On RegComponent time series models and their applications. In *State Space and Unobserved Component Models: Theory and Applications*, Chapter 12, eds. A. C. Harvey, S. J. Koopman, and N. Shephard, Cambridge, UK: Cambridge University Press.

Bell, W. R. (2005). Some consideration of seasonal adjustment variances. In *ASA Proceedings of the Joint Statistical Meetings.* 2747–2758. American Statistical Association.

Bell, W. R. (2010). Unit root properties of seasonal adjustment and related filters. Research Report RRS2010-08, Center for Statistical Research and Methods, U.S. Census Bureau, available online at www.census.gov/srd/papers/pdf/rrs2010-08.pdf.

Bell, W. R. (2011). REGCMPNT – A Fortran program for regression models with ARIMA component errors. *Journal of Statistical Software*, 41(7), available online at www.jstatsoft.org/v41/i07.

Bell, W. R. and Hillmer, S. C. (1984). Issues involved with the seasonal adjustment of economic time series. *Journal of Business & Economic Statistics*, 2:291–320.

Bell, W. R. and Hillmer, S. C. (1988). A matrix approach to signal extraction and likelihood evaluation for ARIMA component time series models. Research Report 88/22, Statistical Research Division, U.S. Census Bureau, available online at www.census.gov/srd/papers/pdf/rr88-22.pdf.

Bell, W. R. and Hillmer, S. C. (1991). Initializing the Kalman filter for nonstationary time series models. *Journal of Time Series Analysis*, 12:283–300.

Bell, W. R. and Kramer, M. (1999). Toward variances for X-11 seasonal adjustments. *Survey Methodology*, 25:13–29.

Bell, W. R. and Martin, D. E. K. (2004). Computation of asymmetric signal extraction filters and mean squared error for ARIMA component models. *Journal of Time Series Analysis*, 25(4):603–623.

Bell, W. R. and Monsell, B. C. (1992). X-11 symmetric linear filters and their transfer functions. Research Report 92/15, Statistical Research Division, U.S. Census Bureau, available online at www.census.gov/srd/papers/pdf/rr92-15.pdf.

Bell, W. R. and Otto, M. C. (1992). Bayesian assessment of uncertainty in seasonal adjustment with sampling error present. Research Report 92/12, Statistical Research Division, U.S. Census Bureau, available online at www.census.gov/srd/papers/pdf/rr92-12.pdf.

Box, G. E. P. and Jenkins, G. M. (1976). *Time Series Analysis: Forecasting and Control*. 2nd edition. San Francisco: Holden Day.

Burman, J. P. (1980). Seasonal adjustment by signal extraction. *Journal of the Royal Statistical Society, Series A: General*, 143:321–337.

Burridge, P. and Wallis, K. F. (1984). Unobserved-components models for seasonal adjustment filters. *Journal of Business & Economic Statistics*, 2:350–359.

Caporello, G. and Maravall, A. (2004). *Program TSW Revised Manual, Version May 2004*. Working Paper Number 0408, Bank of Spain, Servicio de Estudios, Madrid, Spain, available online at www.bde.es/webbde/SES/Secciones/Publicaciones/PublicacionesSeriadas/DocumentosOcasionales/04/Fic/do0408e.pdf.

Chu, Y.-J., Tiao, G. C., and Bell, W. R. (2011a). ARIMA component models to approximate X-12-ARIMA trend and seasonal adjustment filters. Research Report, Center for Statistical Research and Methods, U.S. Census Bureau. To appear.

Chu, Y.-J., Tiao, G. C., and Bell, W. R. (2011b). A mean squared error criterion for comparing X-12-ARIMA and model-based seasonal adjustment filters. Submitted for publication.

Cleveland, W. P. and Tiao, G. C. (1976). Decomposition of seasonal time series: A model for the Census X-11 Program. *Journal of the American Statistical Association*, 71:581–587.

Dagum, E. B. (1975). Seasonal factor forecasts from ARIMA models. In *Proceedings of the 40th Session of the International Statistical Institute*, 203–216. Voorburg, The Netherlands: International Statistical Institute.

Dagum, E. B. (1985). Moving averages. In *Encyclopedia of Statistical Sciences* (9 vols. plus Supplement), eds. D. L. Banks, C. B. Read, and S. Kotz, 5, 630–634. New York: Wiley-Blackwell.

Depoutot, R. and Planas, C. (1998). Comparing seasonal adjustment and trend extraction filters with application to a model-based selection of

X11 linear filters. *Eurostat Working Papers*, No. 9/1998/A/9, Eurostat, Luxembourg.

Durbin, J. and Koopman, S. J. (2001). *Time Series Analysis by State Space Methods.* Number 24 in Oxford statistical science series. Oxford: Oxford University Press.

Findley, D. F., Monsell, B. C., Bell, W. R., Otto, M. C., and Chen, B.-C. (1998). New capabilities and methods of the X-12-ARIMA seasonal adjustment program (with discussion). *Journal of Business and Economic Statistics*, 16:127–177.

Geweke, J. (1978). Revision of seasonally adjusted time series. Technical Report, Department of Economics, University of Wisconsin.

Harvey, A. C. (1989). *Forecasting, Structural Time Series Models and the Kalman Filter.* Cambridge: Cambridge University Press.

Hillmer, S. C. and Tiao, G. C. (1982). An ARIMA-model-based approach to seasonal adjustment. *Journal of the American Statistical Association*, 77:63–70.

Ladiray, D. and Quenneville, B. (2001). *Seasonal Adjustment with the X-11 Method.* New York: Springer-Verlag Inc.

McElroy, T. S. (2008). Matrix formulas for nonstationary ARIMA signal extraction. *Econometric Theory*, 24:988–1009. Earlier version available at www.census.gov/srd/papers/pdf/rrs2005-04.pdf

Monsell, B. C. (2007). The X-13A-S seasonal adjustment program. In *Proceedings of the 2007 Federal Committee On Statistical Methodology Research Conference*, available online at www.fcsm.gov/07papers/Monsell.II-B.pdf.

Pfeffermann, D. (1994). A general method for estimating the variances of X-11 seasonally adjusted estimators. *Journal of Time Series Analysis*, 15:85–116.

Pierce, D. A. (1979). Signal extraction error in nonstationary time series. *Annals of Statistics*, 7:1303–1320.

Pierce, D. A. (1980). Data revisions with moving average seasonal adjustment procedures. *Journal of Econometrics*, 14:95–114.

Planas, C. and Depoutot, R. (2002). Controlling revisions in ARIMA-model-based seasonal adjustment. *Journal of Time Series Analysis*, 23(2):193–213.

Scott, S., Pfeffermann, D., and Sverchkov, M. (2011). Estimating variance in X-11 seasonal adjustment. In *Economic Time Series: Modeling and Seasonality*, eds. W. R. Bell, S. H. Holan, and T. S. McElroy, London, UK: Chapman and Hall. Included in this volume.

Shiskin, J., Young, A. H., and Musgrave, J. C. (1967). The X-11 variant of the Census Method II seasonal adjustment program. Technical Paper No. 15, U.S. Department of Commerce, Bureau of Economic Analysis, available online at www.census.gov/ts/papers/ShiskinYoungMusgrave1967.pdf.

Tunnicliffe Wilson, G. (1979). Some efficient computational procedures for high order ARMA models. *Journal of Statistical Computation and Simulation*, 8:301–310.

U.S. Census Bureau (2009). *X-12-ARIMA Reference Manual, Version 0.3.* Time Series Staff, Statistical Research Division, Washington, DC, available online at www.census.gov/srd/www/x12a/.

8

Estimating Variance in X-11 Seasonal Adjustment

Stuart Scott, Danny Pfeffermann, and Michail Sverchkov

CONTENTS

8.1 Introduction

Obtaining measures of uncertainty for seasonal adjustment is a long-standing problem (President's Committee to Appraise Employment and Unemployment statistics, 1962). Wolter and Monsour (1981) propose two variance measures for X-11 seasonal adjustment that account for sampling error (SE), one better suited for the typical case of nonstationary time series. Pfeffermann (1994) and Bell and Kramer (1999) develop measures capturing additional uncertainty. Pfeffermann, Morry, and Wong (1995) apply the Pfeffermann method with ARIMA (autoregressive-integrated-moving average) extrapolation and the multiplicative mode of adjustment. Pfeffermann and Scott (1997) further extend the method by proposing modifications that use all the X-11 irregular terms, not just the central ones, and simplify the equations for estimating the error variances when SE autocovariances are available. Scott, Sverchkov, and Pfeffermann (2005) treat month-to-month change where the series are similar to many index series.

Bell (2005) discusses issues in variance measures both for X-11 and model-based seasonal adjustment. Bell emphasizes that variance for seasonal adjustment *error* is appropriate, discusses alternative choices for error, and especially for the X-11 case, indicates which components of error are, or are not, accounted for by proposed variances. The present chapter studies these measures and applies them to employment and unemployment series from the U.S. Bureau of Labor Statistics (BLS). TRAMO-SEATS and X-13ARIMA-SEATS are seasonal adjustment programs that compute variance measures for ARIMA model-based adjustment, but neither program explicitly accounts for the contribution of SE to the variance, a serious drawback.

Section 8.2 discusses the variance measures and their estimation, and presents results of a simulation experiment in a setting applicable to important U.S. labor force series. Section 8.3 reviews alternative plausible choices for a seasonal adjustment error measure. Section 8.4 contains results for monthly change from a large-scale empirical study involving important industry employment series. A summary is given in Section 8.5.

8.2 Review and Illustration of Basic Methods

8.2.1 Variance Measures and Estimation Methods

Consider the conventional decomposition of an economic time series Y_t into a trend or trend-cycle, a seasonal effect, and an irregular or noise term, or, alternatively, into a seasonally adjusted series and a seasonal component,

$$Y_t = T_t + S_t + I_t = A_t + S_t.$$

Typically, the population or signal values Y_t are unknown and the data are obtained from a sample survey, so that the observed series is

$$y_t = Y_t + \varepsilon_t,$$

ε_t representing the SE. X-11 seasonal adjustment is usually carried out by augmenting the series with ARIMA model extrapolations. Let

$$\hat{y} = [\hat{y}_{-m+1}, \ldots, \hat{y}_0, y_1, \ldots, y_n, \hat{y}_{n+1}, \ldots, \hat{y}_{n+m}]' = [\hat{y}_b', y_o', \hat{y}_f']'$$

define the $(n + 2m) \times 1$ vector consisting of m backcasts, n observed values, and m forecasts. The vector of estimated seasonally adjusted values is

$$\hat{A} = \Omega \hat{y},$$

where Ω is the $n \times (n + 2m)$ matrix of the X-11 seasonal adjustment filters. Similarly, we consider the SE, the signal, and its components to be vectors across backcast, observed, and forecast time spans, e.g., $Y = [Y_{-m+1}, \ldots, Y_0, Y_1, \ldots, Y_n, Y_{n+1}, \ldots, Y_{n+m}]'$. Bell and Kramer (1999) define the target seasonally adjusted series to be $A^* = \Omega Y$ (the seasonally adjusted series that would be obtained from X-11 if Y were observed for all $n + 2m$ time points), and hence the variance measure as

$$\text{Var}(A^* - \hat{A}) = \text{Var}(\Omega Y - \Omega \hat{y}) = \Omega \text{Var}(Y - \hat{y})\Omega'. \tag{8.2.1}$$

Note that $\hat{A}$ and A^* have dimension $n \times 1$, i.e., values are defined only for $t = 1, \ldots, n$. Application of the method requires models for the signal series Y and the SE ε. In this chapter, we employ ARIMA models for Y and ARMA models for ε. Certain time-varying SE models can also be accommodated. The measure (Equation 8.2.1) accounts for the variability of the SEs and the backcast and forecast error. The authors provide all the necessary details for calculating $\text{Var}(Y - \hat{y})$. We refer to this as the Bell–Kramer (BK) method.

Pfeffermann (1994) proposes another method (hereafter DP) for variance estimation. We evaluate it with respect to the target $\tilde{A} = Y_o - \tilde{S}$, where $\tilde{S} = \Omega_S(Y - I) = \Omega_S(T + S)$ and Ω_S is the X-11 seasonal filter matrix consistent with Ω defined above. (See Sverchkov, Scott, and Pfeffermann 2009.) Notice that this $n \times 1$ target vector is different both from $A_o = Y_o - S_o$, considered in Pfeffermann's original paper and, unless $I \equiv 0$, from the target vector with the BK method. We elaborate on this issue below and in Section 8.3.

Pfeffermann (1994) assumes that the irregular component and the SE are stationary and mutually independent, implying that for the combined error, $e_t = \varepsilon_t + I_t$,

$$\gamma_k = \text{Cov}(e_t, e_{t+k}) = \text{Cov}(\varepsilon_t, \varepsilon_{t+k}) + \text{Cov}(I_t, I_{t+k}) \equiv \lambda_k + \nu_k, \quad k = 1, 2, \ldots. \tag{8.2.2}$$

Let $\hat{A}^{(DP)} = y_o - \hat{\Omega}_S y_o$, where $\hat{\Omega}_S, n \times n$, contains the weights $\{w_{tk}^S\}$ of an X-11 seasonal filter for time t, possibly accounting for ARIMA extrapolation. We consider Pfeffermann's approximation with respect to the target $\tilde{A}$,

$$\text{Var}(\tilde{A}_t - \hat{A}_t^{(DP)}) \approx \text{Var}\left(\sum_{k=1}^{n} w_{tk}^{(S)} e_k\right) + \lambda_0(1 - 2w_{tt}^{(S)}) - 2\sum_{k \neq t} w_{tk}^{(S)} \lambda_{t-k}. \tag{8.2.3}$$

This approximation accounts in part for the variability of the SE and the irregular component. It does not account for the differences

$$\tilde{A} - (Y_o - \hat{\Omega}_S(T_o + S_o)) = \hat{\Omega}_S(T_o + S_o) - \Omega_S(T + S). \tag{8.2.4}$$

(These last differences are nonzero only toward the ends of the series; see Sverchkov, Scott, and Pfeffermann (2009) for details.) Computing the approximation (Equation 8.2.3) requires estimating the vector γ of autocovariances γ_k in Equation 8.2.2. To this end, Pfeffermann (1994) and Pfeffermann and Scott (1997) consider the irregular estimator $\hat{I}_t$ produced by X-11, and derive the approximation

$$\hat{I}_t \approx \sum_{k=1}^{n} w_{tk}^{(I)} e_k, \tag{8.2.5}$$

where $\{w_{tk}^{(I)}\}$ represent a set of irregular filter weights for time t consistent with the weights in $\hat{\Omega}_S$. With or without extrapolation, the X-11 irregular series is nonstationary because of the use of asymmetric, time-dependent weights when moving away from the center of the series. Evaluating autocovariances on both sides of Equation 8.2.5 permits expressing an autocovariance $U_{tl} = \mathrm{Cov}(\hat{I}_t, \hat{I}_{t+l})$ as a function of autocovariances γ_k,

$$U_{tl} = \sum_{j=0}^{C} d_{lj}^{(t)} \gamma_j.$$

It is assumed that the autocovariances are negligible beyond some cutoff log C. Estimating U_{tl} by $(\hat{I}_t \times \hat{I}_{t+l})$ and averaging over t yield a system of linear equations for $\hat{\gamma}$,

$$\hat{U} = D\hat{\gamma} = D(\hat{\lambda} + \hat{\nu}). \tag{8.2.6}$$

The matrix D is a known matrix built from the irregular weights. When SE autocovariance estimates $\hat{\lambda}$ are available externally, we can solve the system $\hat{U} - D\hat{\lambda} = D\hat{\nu}$ for $\hat{\nu}$ to get $\hat{\gamma} = \hat{\lambda} + \hat{\nu}$. We typically model the irregular component as a low-order MA(q) process (including $q = 0$, white noise [WN]), say, $q \leq 3$, in which case Equation 8.2.6 reduces to a low-order system. See Pfeffermann and Scott (1997) for details.

The DP method is flexible in that it can be applied with or without ARIMA extrapolation. Pfeffermann, Morry, and Wong (1995) and Pfeffermann, Scott, and Tiller (2000) treat the extrapolation case. Given the coefficients of the ARIMA model for the series, we may express each forecast and backcast as a linear combination of the observed values, so that, again, we may approximate each seasonally adjusted value as a linear combination of the observed values. With "full" forecasting and backcasting, i.e., choosing m so that the symmetric filter is used for $t = 1, \ldots, n$, we have $\hat{A}^{(DP)} = \hat{A}$, since $\hat{S}^{(DP)} = \hat{\Omega}_S^{(DP)} y_o = \Omega_S \hat{y}$. In what follows, we assume that the DP method is applied with full forecasting. This is consistent with common practice to use at least some extrapolation in X-11 seasonal adjustment.

Remarks

1. X-11 includes nonlinear operations such as the identification and estimation of ARIMA models and the identification and partial

replacement of extreme observations. We assume that the time series under consideration is already corrected for outliers. The effects of the identification and nonlinear estimation of ARIMA models are generally minor and are ignored in the application of both methods. See, e.g., Pfeffermann, Morry, and Wong (1995) and Pfeffermann, Scott, and Tiller (2000).

2. If X-11 is applied without ARIMA extrapolation, Ω_S is a combination of symmetric and internal asymmetric filters of X-11; clearly, the set of seasonally adjusted values will be different.

The X-11 procedure is subject to possible bias in estimating the seasonal effects and the seasonally adjusted series toward the endpoints of the observed series. These effects are not captured by the BK and DP methods. Sverchkov, Scott, and Pfeffermann (2009) therefore consider mean squared error (MSE) estimation. Expressed in terms of the BK target, the paper shows that the conditional bias and variance, given the signal values, can be written as

$$\mathrm{Bias}(\hat{S}_t|Y) = E[(\hat{S}_t - S_t^*)|Y] = \sum_{k=1}^{n} w_{tk}^{(S)} Y_k - \sum_{k=1}^{n} w_k^{(S)} Y_{k+t-[n/2]}$$

$$\mathrm{Var}(\hat{S}_t|Y) = E\left\{\left[\sum_{k=1}^{n} w_{tk}^{(S)} y_k - E\left(\sum_{k=1}^{n} w_{tk}^{(S)} y_k|Y\right)\right]^2 \middle| Y\right\} = E\left(\sum_{k=1}^{n} w_{tk}^{(S)} \varepsilon_k\right)^2.$$

The coefficients $\{w_k^{(S)}\} = \{w_{[n/2],k}^{(S)}\}$ in the bias formula are the (symmetric) weights of the X-11 seasonal filter in the center of the series, where the estimator of the seasonal effect is unbiased. (Implicitly, we assume $n > 2m + 1$.) The bias is only a function of the signal. The variance is computed over the distribution of the SEs. Sverchkov, Scott, and Pfeffermann (2009) suggest alternative estimators of the squared bias, which when added to the estimator of the variance yields an estimator for the MSE. Results so far show that the MSE estimators are approximately unbiased but with larger variability than the variability of the BK variance estimators. Similar expressions and empirical results are found when the method is applied along with the DP method, in which case the bias is a function of the seasonal component and the trend, and the variance is taken over the distribution of the SEs and the irregulars.

8.2.2 Labor Force Application—Simulation Results

In this section, we report the results of a simulation study to get a first impression of the performance of the BK and DP methods in estimating variances for seasonally adjusted series. Series are simulated from models suggested by the series Teenage Male Unemployment (TMU). This is one of eight series used to compute the seasonally adjusted civilian unemployment rate, the key household figure reported in the monthly BLS *Employment Situation* press release. The data come from the U.S. Census Bureau's Current Population Survey

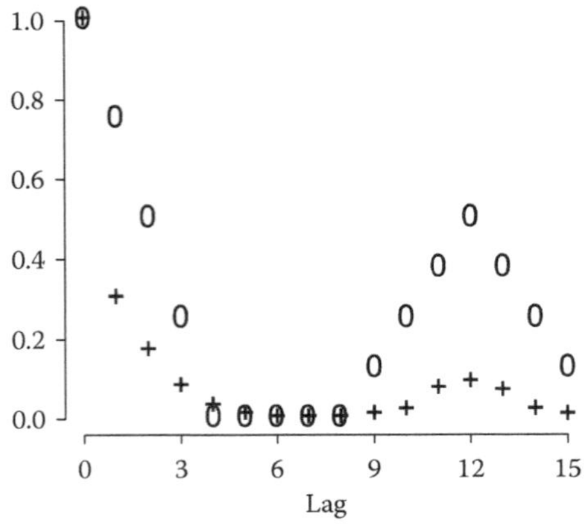

FIGURE 8.1
Teenage Male Unemployment (TMU). Sampling error autocorrelations (+). Percentage sample overlap (O).

(CPS). Estimates of SE variance and autocorrelations of this and other series have been developed in various studies, such as Pfeffermann, Tiller, and Zimmerman (2000). The CPS sampling design produces sample overlaps for most lags up to 15 months. This results from the household rotation pattern of 4 months in the sample, 8 months out of the sample, and 4 months in the sample again. Figure 8.1 shows the percentage sample overlap and the autocorrelations of an AR(12) model selected to represent the SE. Autocorrelations for lags 1, 2, 3, 11, and 12 are 0.30, 0.17, 0.08, 0.07, and 0.09, respectively, with the other autocorrelations smaller in magnitude. The AR model has been fit to autocorrelations with the same shape as estimates for the TMU series, but increased somewhat to test the impact of sizable autocorrelations at high lags. Autocorrelations for other CPS unemployment series can be higher, and for employment series they are typically much higher. The general conclusion from Figure 8.1 is that one needs to account for high-order autocorrelations when estimating the error variances. The simulations are based on $\sigma_\varepsilon = 2.8$. The estimated value for the TMU series is 4.3, but Scott and Sverchkov (2010) find deficiencies in applying the methods with that level of SE variance.

Application of the BK method for variance estimation requires modeling the signal and its components. Figure 8.2 shows the observed series for the years 1991–2002. The series is dominated by seasonal effects. Given the models for the signal Y and the SE ε, the REGCMPNT program developed by Bell (2004) estimates the model parameters and computes a goodness-of-fit test. In this application of the software, the SE model is entirely fixed; only the signal model parameters are estimated. Bell suggests the form of the model fitted to the observed series as a candidate for the signal model.

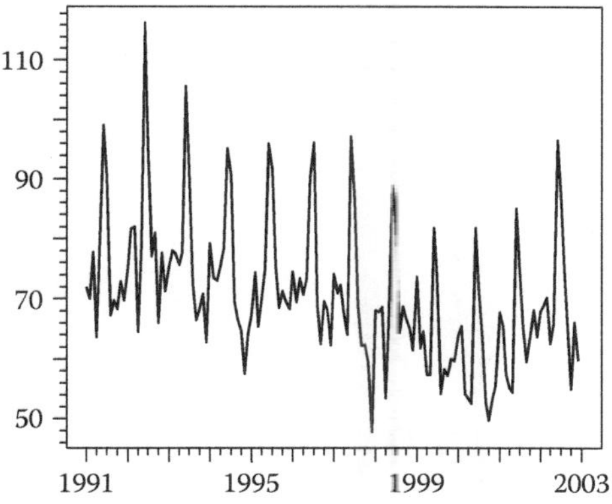

FIGURE 8.2
Observed series, TMU, 1/91–12/02.

The familiar airline model (0,1,1) $(0,1,1)_{12}$ gives an acceptable, parsimonious fit, both for the observed series and for the signal. The parameter estimates of 0.61 and 0.63 for the signal have been rounded to 0.60 for the simulation experiment. This airline model is decomposed into a (0,2,2) trend model, an (11,0,11) seasonal model, and a WN irregular by the Census Bureau's X-13ARIMA-SEATS program. The AR operator for the seasonal model is $1 + B + \cdots + B^{11}$.

We generate 3000 series for each component of length 312 (26 years), labeled 1981 to 2006, and add them up to produce the observed series. The years 1988–1999 form the time span for which observations are considered available, and the additional years allow us to compute the target values for the two methods. We apply the BK and DP methods to each of the 3000 series and average the results. In both cases, the ARIMA model form is fixed, but parameter values are estimated for each individual series. Estimates with the DP method are computed for each MA(q) model, $q = 0$ to 3. For each time point and replicate, we compute the error, i.e., the difference between the target seasonally adjusted value and its estimate. Fixing the time point, we then compute the mean square of these errors across replicates,

$$\mathrm{MSE}_{\mathrm{BK}} = \frac{1}{3000}\sum_{j=1}^{3000}(A^*_{jt} - \hat{A}_{jt})^2, \quad \mathrm{MSE}_{\mathrm{DP}} = \frac{1}{3000}\sum_{j=1}^{3000}(\tilde{A}_{jt} - \hat{A}_{jt})^2$$

for the BK method and the DP method, respectively. The MSEs reflect the total error in seasonal adjustment by accounting for the variances defined by Equations 8.2.1 and 8.2.3, the biases that can arise away from the center of the series, and the effect of model parameter estimation.

Figure 8.3 displays, for each time point, the mean estimate of the standard deviation of the seasonal adjustment error ($\mathrm{SDA}_{\mathrm{BK}}$ and $\mathrm{SDA}_{\mathrm{DP}}$) from the two

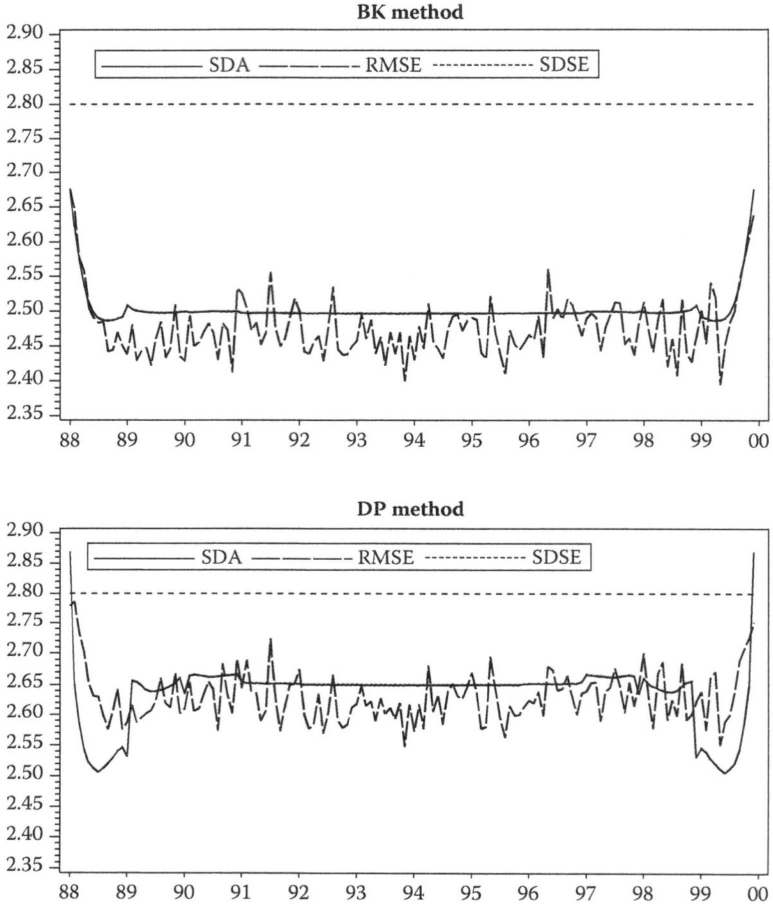

FIGURE 8.3
TMU experiment. Mean estimated SDA and empirical RMSE.

methods across the 3000 series, as well as the corresponding empirical "true" root mean squared errors $\text{RMSE}_{\text{BK}} = \sqrt{\text{MSE}_{\text{BK}}}$ and $\text{RMSE}_{\text{DP}} = \sqrt{\text{MSE}_{\text{DP}}}$. There is considerable variability across time in the RMSE values, even in the central part of the series, where they should be constant. Table 8.1 contains mean SDA estimates and mean RMSE values for the two methods in the central part of the series and at the ends. The central part is taken to be the central 48 time points, which smooths somewhat the roughness of the empirical values. Note that the mean estimates should be and are virtually constant there. Performance at the ends is based on the first and last four time points. With the BK method, mean estimates are extremely close to the empirical truth: a 1.1% overestimate in the center and a 0.4% underestimate

TABLE 8.1
Teenage Male Unemployment Experiment

	# Points	BK Method			DP Method		
		SDA Est.	RMSE "True"	Diff (%)	SDA Est.	RMSE "True"	Diff (%)
Center	48	2.49	2.46	0.03 (1.1%)	2.65	2.61	0.04 (1.4%)
End	8	2.59	2.60	−0.01 (−0.4%)	2.66	2.73	−0.07 (−2.7%)
End-Center (SDA)	2, 48			0.18 (7.1%)			0.22 (8.2%)

Note: True root mean square errors and means of estimated standard deviations under the BK and DP approaches (with number of points included in mean estimates).

at the ends. With the DP method, the mean estimate in the center is also a slight overestimate (1.4%); underestimation at the ends is a little larger in magnitude, 2.7% below the empirical truth. A second notable feature is that both the true values and the estimates from the DP method are larger than the corresponding values from the BK method, by about 6%. This reflects the fact that the DP method captures an error contribution from the irregular. Note also that $\mathrm{SDA}_{\mathrm{BK}}$ lies entirely below SDSE, which denotes the (constant) standard deviation of the SE; $\mathrm{SDA}_{\mathrm{DP}}$ is below SDSE until it exceeds it by 1.7% at the end points.

Both graphs show a dip occurring at 12 months from the ends. It is quite substantial with DP, 5.4% below the central value at $t = 7$ and $t = 138$. With the BK method, the dip is mild, always less than 0.4% in magnitude. Also, the estimates under both methods rise sharply at the end. Estimates at the two end points are 7.1% and 8.2% above the central values under BK and DP, respectively. It is important to emphasize, however, that the present simulation and others we have carried out show that the dip is a property of the measure (the true variance) and not a problem of estimation. The character of the dips is examined in detail in Scott and Sverchkov (2010).

8.3 Choice of Measure of Error in Seasonal Adjustment

8.3.1 Plausible Measures

This section studies the choice of target for measuring the error in seasonal adjustment. We continue to assume that X-11 is applied with full forecasting and backcasting. This discussion is influenced by Bell (2005). See in particular his Section 4, but note that A_t in the current chapter is the same as Bell's N_t, not his A_t. Based on the definitions in Section 8.2, the following are three potential error measures and their relationships:

$$\mathcal{E}_1 = A^* - \hat{A} = \Omega(Y - \hat{y}) \tag{8.3.1a}$$

$$\mathcal{E}_2 = \tilde{A} - \hat{A} = \mathcal{E}_1 + \Omega_S I \tag{8.3.1b}$$

$$\mathcal{E}_3 = A_o - \hat{A} = \mathcal{E}_2 + \Omega_S T - \Omega S \tag{8.3.1c}$$

We have defined $\text{Var}(\mathcal{E}_1)$ as the BK measure and $\text{Var}(\mathcal{E}_2)$ as the DP measure. Note, however, that the approximation in Equation 8.2.3 does not capture the differences (Equation 8.2.4), which occur even with full forecasting. What about $\mathcal{E}_3$ as a measure of error? It represents the difference between the population and estimated seasonally adjusted value. From the alternative expression $\mathcal{E}_3 = (\hat{S} - S_o) - \varepsilon_o$,

$$\text{Var}(\mathcal{E}_3) = \text{Var}(\varepsilon_o) + \text{Var}(\hat{S} - S_o) - \text{Cov}(\varepsilon_o, \hat{S} - S_o) - \text{Cov}(\hat{S} - S_o, \varepsilon_o). \tag{8.3.2}$$

Expanding the second term, we have

$$\text{Var}(\hat{S} - S_o) = \text{Var}(\Omega_S T) + \text{Var}(\Omega S) + \text{Var}(\Omega_S e). \tag{8.3.3}$$

The approximation in Equation 8.2.3 covers the last term in Equation 8.3.3 and the first and third terms in Equation 8.3.2. So, the approximation misses the contributions of the first two terms of Equation 8.3.3. Since these correspond to the "extra" terms in going from $\mathcal{E}_2$ to $\mathcal{E}_3 = \mathcal{E}_2 + \Omega_S T - \Omega S$, we see that Equation 8.2.3 is reasonable for estimating $\text{Var}(\mathcal{E}_2)$ but not necessarily $\text{Var}(\mathcal{E}_3)$. These extra terms correspond to the seasonal component derived from the trend and the remainder from seasonally adjusting the seasonal using X-11, both of which "should be" small. This is addressed in the simulation experiment next.

8.3.2 Simulation Experiment that Distinguishes $\mathcal{E}_3$ from $\mathcal{E}_2$

Simulations based on the labor force series Adult Male Employment (AME) give evidence to support the use of $\mathcal{E}_1$ or $\mathcal{E}_2$, rather than $\mathcal{E}_3$. We present this experiment in detail, since it illuminates several points. This experiment follows the same steps as that for TMU. We begin by determining the models for time series components in the usual framework for an observed series, $y = T + S + I + \varepsilon$. Figure 8.4 shows the AME series for the period 1994–2002. This span includes the 6 years from which SE autocovariances have been estimated. Like most employment series, AME exhibits strong autocorrelations, shown partially in Table 8.2, which are nonzero to lag 15 and beyond. An AR(15) model with constant variance represents the SE series.

The AICC criterion in X-13ARIMA-SEATS prefers that no transformation be used when modeling the series, which fits with the additive mode of seasonal adjustment. While the airline model is competitive, the simpler ARIMA model $(0,1,0)(0,1,1)_{12}$, that is, $(1 - B)(1 - B^{12})Y_t = (1 - \theta_{12}B^{12})\, a_t$ where B is the backshift operator ($BY_t = Y_{t-1}$) and a_t is white noise, proves to be adequate and is adopted for the signal. The REGCMPNT program estimates

FIGURE 8.4
AME observed (dashed) and seasonally adjusted series (solid), 1994–2002.

the parameters for the signal model, taking into account the SE component. Then, the decomposition procedure in X-13ARIMA-SEATS determines the signal component models. Models and values of the disturbance variances for the components are given in Table 8.3a.

For each component, 3000 replicate series of length 144 are generated. Additive X-11 seasonal adjustment is carried out on the observed series formed from these components. ARIMA extrapolation is employed using the ARIMA model $(0,1,0)(0,1,1)_{12}$, with MA and variance parameters estimated for each replicate. When we apply the DP method, we consider alternative MA(q) models for the time series irregular and compute the estimates of the standard deviation of the error by the use of Equation 8.2.3. Figure 8.5a plots for each time point (1) mean estimates SDA_{DP} under the (correct) assumption of a WN irregular; (2) the "true" empirical values RMSE($\mathcal{E}_3$), defined as the root mean square of errors $A_{jt} - \hat{A}_{jt}$ across replicates; and (3) SDSE, which is constant. The shapes of the mean SDA estimates and the empirical values are similar, except that the SDA estimates have a much stronger dip in the end years. The DP method estimates are on average 5.4% lower than the empirical estimates in the central portion of the series and 10.8% lower in the end years. These biases are much larger than those in the TMU simulation experiment in

TABLE 8.2
Estimates of Sampling Error Autocorrelations at Selected Lags for AME Series

1	2	3	4	···	10	11	12	13	14
0.67	0.52	0.41	0.32		0.23	0.26	0.27	0.23	0.21

TABLE 8.3
Models and Results for AME Initial and Test Simulations

	Component Models			
	Trend	**Seasonal**	**Irregular**	**SE**
Model	0,2,2	11,0,11	WN	15,0,0
Disturbance variance				
Initial	29.0	17.3	29.5	159.0
Test	1.0	1.0	29.5	159.0

% Contribution to Var($\hat{S} - S_o$) of Three Components in Equation 8.3.3

	Center			Ends		
	Var($\Omega_S T$)	Var(ΩS)	Var($\Omega_S e$)	Var($\Omega_S T$)	Var(ΩS)	Var($\Omega_S e$)
Initial	18	33	49	17	42	41
Test	1	4	95	1	6	93

Section 8.2 and in other experiments we have conducted, e.g., in Pfeffermann, Scott, and Tiller (2000).

The disturbance variances of the trend and seasonal components in Table 8.3 are relatively large compared to those in the TMU simulation and in other earlier experiments. Clearly, the larger the disturbance variance for trend and seasonal, the larger the potential for sizable contributions from Var($\Omega_S T$) and Var(ΩS) in Equation 8.3.3. A simulation labeled "Test" uses the same models as the initial simulation experiment described above, except that the trend and seasonal disturbance variances have been arbitrarily reduced to 1. A new set of 3000 replicates is generated and SDA calculations made. Figure 8.5b plots the empirical RMSE($\mathcal{E}_3$) and estimated SDA values for this simulation. Underestimation is now much smaller; it is cut to 0.5% at the center of the series and 4.9% at the ends.

These results are further clarified by computing empirically the separate components of Var($\hat{S} - S_o$) in Equation 8.3.3 and their contribution to the total. Table 8.3b shows that for the initial simulation, Var($\Omega_S T$) and Var(ΩS) account for roughly half Var($\hat{S} - S_o$) at the center of the series and nearly 60% at the ends, with the larger portion coming from Var(ΩS) in each case. This is highly surprising: our sense is that very little should remain after applying the seasonal adjustment filter to the seasonal component. With the "Test" simulation, Var($\Omega_S e$) dominates; the other terms account for only 5%–6% of the total variance. These simulation results therefore indicate that in certain cases the two error components not estimated by the DP method can be fairly sizable and cause substantial underestimation with respect to the error $\mathcal{E}_3$.

We claim further that there are positive reasons for not using $\mathcal{E}_3$. The simulation involves a highly noisy seasonal component. Figure 8.6 contains monthplots of the two target series S_o and S^* for one of the replicates from the initial simulation. The monthplot for S_o in Figure 8.6a shows that it is

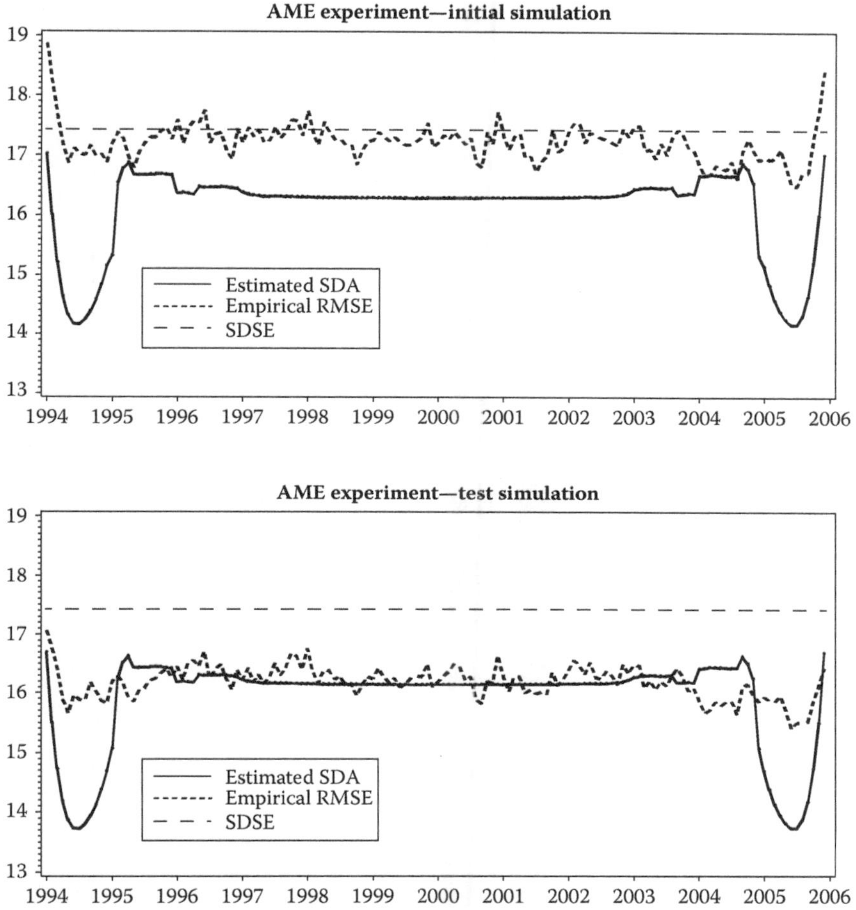

FIGURE 8.5
Mean estimated SDA and RMSE with target A_t for error in seasonal adjustment.

undesirable as a seasonal component. The within-month movement is sizable and too abrupt. The monthplot for S^* in Figure 8.6b exhibits smooth within-month movements; these movements also tend to be less variable. Thus, $A^* = Y_o - S^*$ makes more sense as a target than $A_o = Y_o - S_o$. The monthplot for $\tilde{S}$ is similar to that for S^*, so $\tilde{A} = Y_o - \tilde{S}$ also merits consideration. Finally, it could be argued that if the estimated seasonally adjusted value is a function of the X-11 filters, then it makes sense that the target value should be, too, as is the case with A^* and $\tilde{A}$.

In fact, with the available measures, we could consider four options, rather than two. The BK method can be extended to measure error with respect

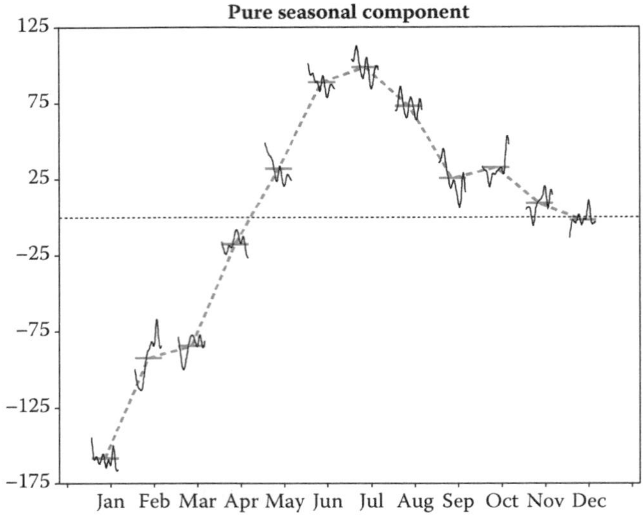

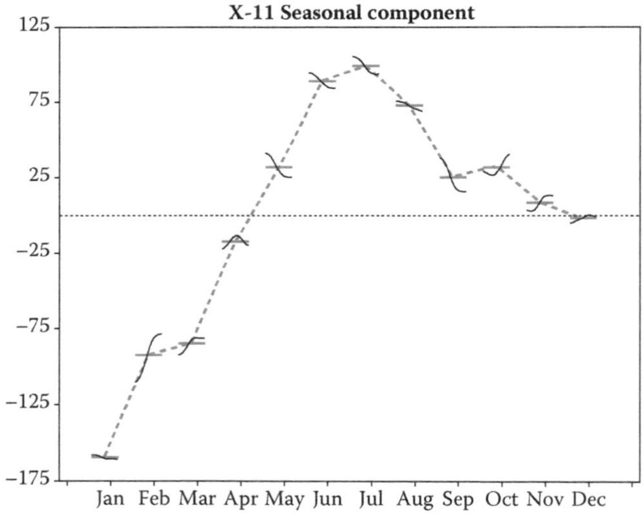

FIGURE 8.6
Monthplots for a simulated series, AME experiment.

to $\tilde{A} = Y_o - \tilde{S}$, and the DP method can be applied with $A^* = Y_o - S^*$ as target. However, in the latter case, the DP method essentially reduces to estimating the variance accounting only for the SE, as under the Wolter and Monsour method. Empirical work in Scott and Sverchkov (2010) contains some additional evidence supporting the use of A^*, so in this chapter we do not pursue extending the BK method. As a whole, the AME simulations justify the use of either $A^* = Y_o - S^*$ or $\tilde{A} = Y_o - \tilde{S}$, in preference to A_o, as the target value for the variance measures we seek.

8.4 Empirical Results for Monthly Seasonally Adjusted Change

8.4.1 Adapting the Methods for Monthly Change

"Total nonfarm payroll employment declined by 131,000 in July.... Private-sector payroll employment edged up by 71,000," stated the lead paragraph in BLS's *Employment Situation* press release for July 2010. Word choices such as "declined," "edged up," and "was essentially unchanged" depend on an assessment of whether the movement is significant. For a statistical agency, analyzing change is regularly one of the most important parts in the release of new data. This section derives variance measures for seasonally adjusted monthly change with the BK and DP methods and applies them to a large number of employment series.

These industry employment statistics come from the BLS Current Employment Statistics (CES) program, a monthly survey of over 300,000 establishments. Variance and covariance estimates for the unadjusted series are computed monthly using the balanced repeated replication (BRR) method. Fay's version is applied with a factor 0.5 to reflect the survey design (cf. http://www.bls.gov/web/empsit/cestn2.htm# 4). The survey has the further advantage of having population figures from an external source, the Unemployment Insurance program. Quarterly business tax forms collected in this program include monthly employment data, which are assembled first at the state and then at the national level. Benchmark population values for March become available with a 10-month lag and are incorporated annually into estimation. If t is the current month, the employment estimate is computed from a "link-relative" estimator,

$$\hat{E}_t = E_0 \cdot r_1 \cdot r_2 \cdots r_t,$$

where E_0 is the latest available benchmark, subsequent subscripts denote months after the benchmark month, and

$$r_j = \sum_{i \in M_j} h_{ij} x_{ij} \Big/ \sum_{i \in M_j} h_{i,j-1} x_{i,j-1}$$

is the ratio of weighted employment in adjacent months. For establishment i in month j, x_{ij} represents the number of employees and h_{ij} the survey weight; M_j is the set of establishments reporting in both months j and $j-1$.

Traditionally, CES national employment series have been seasonally adjusted multiplicatively. This leads us to consider monthly change on the log scale.

$$y_t = \log(\hat{E}_t) - \log(\hat{E}_{t-1}) = \log(\hat{E}_t/\hat{E}_{t-1}) = \log(r_t).$$

This simple form looks promising for deriving an SE model. We may write

$$\log(\hat{E}_t) - \log(\hat{E}_{t-1}) = (\log(E_t) - \log(E_{t-1})) + \log(\varepsilon_t/\varepsilon_{t-1}),$$

to express monthly change in terms of a signal part and an SE part. If we can find an ARIMA model for the logarithm of the series with at least one regular difference, then we will have an ARIMA model for applying X-11 with extrapolation to $y_t = (1 - B)\log(\hat{E}_t) = \log(r_t)$. Our approach is to compute variance estimates with the BK and DP methods for this variable. We claim that seasonally adjusted values for $y_t = \log(r_t)$ are approximately equal to seasonally adjusted percentage change in employment. This is based on the approximation near $r_t = 1$

$$\log(r_t) \approx r_t - 1 = (\hat{E}_t - \hat{E}_{t-1})/\hat{E}_{t-1},$$

and similarly for the seasonally adjusted values. In the next subsection, we examine the properties of the SE and adopt a simple but reasonable model for use in computing our variance measures.

Remarks

1. The link-relative estimator capitalizes on the high correlation between an establishment's employment in adjacent months.
2. Current month estimates are 10 to 21 months away from the most recent benchmark. For example, for December 2003, the last available benchmark is March 2002, 21 months away; a month later, January 2004 estimates are derived using the March 2003 benchmark, 10 months away. Benchmarking may be regarded as a bias correction for employment estimates. This effect is not considered in the chapter.
3. The official estimates of seasonally adjusted change are regularly computed from X-11 adjustment of employment levels with ARIMA extrapolation. Currently, 2 years of extrapolation are used, while variance measures considered here assume "full" extrapolation. The impact of this difference on variance measures is likely to be small. A further difference, harder to assess, is that most higher-level industry series are adjusted indirectly from several component series.

8.4.2 Results for Press Release Employment Series

We now report the results of a large-scale assessment of the performance of the BK and DP methods on most of the industry employment series that appear in the *Employment Situation* press release. Industry definitions come from the North America Industry Classification System (NAICS). Overall, the empirical analysis shows certain advantages of the BK method over the DP method. The results confirm the claim in Bell (2005) that BK captures uncertainty at the ends of the series more fully than DP. The methods have been applied to 10- and 17-year series with time spans 1997–2006 and 1990–2006, respectively. The pre-2000 estimates are reconstructions based on data obtained under the older Standard Industrial Classification (SIC) system, some of which are not so successful. Because of this and other limitations, the number of series included in the comparisons varies from about 125 to 140 of the 145 series in all. In what follows, we discuss SE modeling, present in detail the results for three series, and analyze the overall results.

8.4.2.1 Models for Sampling Error

Using the BRR method, SE standard deviations and autocorrelations are computed each month for various statistics, including the log ratios. Figure 8.7 is a scatterplot of a set of absolute log ratios (multiplied by 10^4) and the corresponding SE standard deviations for the Durable Manufacturing series (MD00). The two largest standard deviations occur for large log ratios, but, overall, there is very little pattern. This holds for most of the series examined,

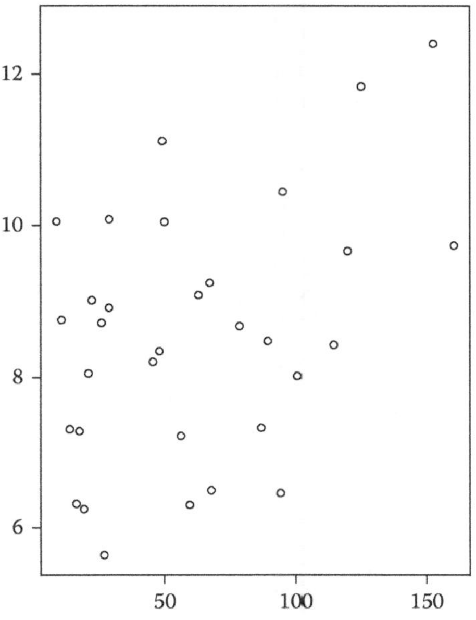

FIGURE 8.7
Plot of MD00 absolute values vs. SE standard deviations.

which has led us to assume a constant variance for the SE. Another common feature to these series is that lag 1 SE autocorrelation estimates tend to be negative and lag 12 estimates positive. It is noteworthy that both sets of autocorrelations are quite variable, with sizable positive and negative values. Autocorrelations at other lags are also variable, with medians close to 0. This leads us to adopt a WN or MA(1) model for all series, given the modest magnitudes of median values and the large variability at other lags (including lag 12). We compute median lag 1 autocorrelation and round to the nearest 0.05, except for rounding all magnitudes below 0.075 to 0 and allowing a maximum magnitude of 0.20. For example, for a recent set of estimates for MD00, we find median ρ_1 and ρ_{12} autocorrelation estimates to be -0.11 and -0.02, which we round to -0.10 and 0, respectively.

8.4.2.2 Results for Manufacturing, Durable Goods (MD00)

Figure 8.8 graphs the observed and seasonally adjusted series for the span 1994–2003. As a change series, it is fairly volatile, but clearly seasonal. Table 8.4a displays the estimates for the SE model, $\hat{\rho}_1 = -0.10$ and $\hat{\sigma}_\varepsilon^2 = 71.5$. Application of Equation 8.2.6 for the DP method, assuming a WN irregular component, yields a variance estimate $\hat{\nu}_0 = \hat{\sigma}_I^2 = 126.1$. A $(1,0,1)(0,1,1)_{12}$ model is adopted for the signal. REGCMPNT estimates the signal model parameters as

$$\hat{\phi}_1 = 0.95, \quad \hat{\theta}_1 = 0.30, \quad \hat{\theta}_{12} = 0.98, \quad \hat{\sigma}_a^2 = 294.7.$$

Figure 8.9a shows the SDA values obtained from the BK and DP methods. The SDA_{BK} estimates rise monotonically from 7.47 at the center (11.6% below

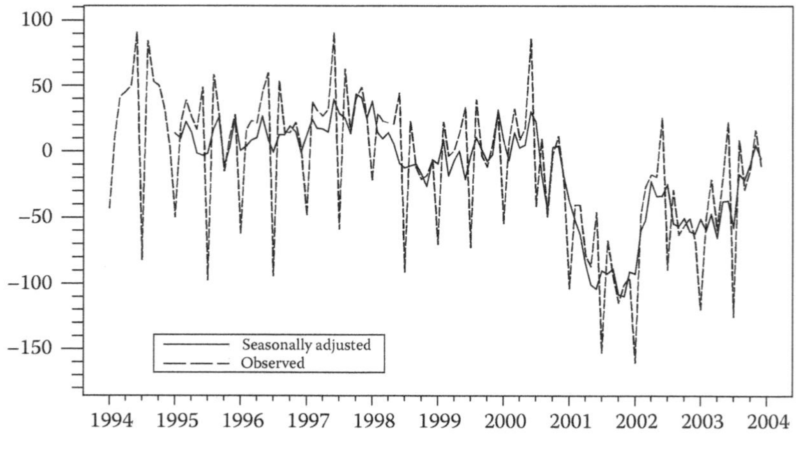

FIGURE 8.8
MD00 log ratios, 1994–2003.

TABLE 8.4
Results for MD00, MN00, and MN10 Series

Model Information					
Series	**Sampling Error**		**Irregular**	**Signal**	
	$\hat{\rho}_1$	$\hat{\sigma}_\varepsilon^2$	$\hat{\sigma}_I^2$	$\hat{\sigma}_a^2$	Model
MD00	−0.10	71.5	126.1	294.7	$(1,0,1)(0,1,1)_{12}$
MN00	−0.10	123.1	3.6	180.7	$(1,0,1)(0,1,1)_{12}$
MN10	0	2807.7	0	145.9	$(1,0,1)(0,1,1)_{12}$

Key SDA Statistics under the BK and DP Methods							
Series	**SDSE**	**SDA (BK)**	**Diff from SDSE (%)**	**SDA (DP)**	**Diff from SDSE (%)**	**End-Ctr (%) BK**	**DP**
MD00							
Center	8.46	7.47	−11.6	8.53	+0.8	19.4	0.7
End	8.46	8.92	+5.5	8.58	+1.5		
MN00							
Center	11.09	9.80	−11.6	10.06	−9.3	6.7	−11.7
End	11.09	10.46	−5.8	8.89	−19.9		
MN10							
Center	52.99	46.94	−11.4	46.94	−11.4	−4.4	−5.6
End	52.99	44.86	−15.3	44.30	−16.4		

SDSE) to 8.92 at the ends (5.5% above SDSE). Except for a modest dip during the last year, SDA_{DP} values exceed SDSE, by 1.7% at the center and 2.4% at the ends. This figure illustrates well that the DP method captures an extra error term, the irregular component, seen in Table 8.4a to be quite large, while the BK method captures more uncertainty due to forecast–backcast error. The fact that both end values exceed SDSE reflects the relatively small amount of SE for this highly aggregated series. Finally, Table 8.4b shows that both methods satisfy the desirable property SDA(end) > SDA(center), DP by 0.7%, and BK by 19.4%.

8.4.2.3 Manufacturing, Nondurable Goods (MN00)

From Table 8.4, SE for MN00 has first-order autocorrelation −0.10; its variance $\hat{\sigma}_\varepsilon^2 = 123.1$ dominates the estimated irregular variance $\hat{\sigma}_I^2 = 3.6$. Signal parameter estimates for the $(1,0,1)(0,1,1)_{12}$ model are $\hat{\phi}_1 = 0.87$, $\hat{\theta}_1 = 0.41$, $\hat{\theta}_{12} = 0.16$, $\hat{\sigma}_a^2 = 180.7$. In contrast to MD00, MN00 has rapidly changing seasonal effects.

The SDA_{BK} estimates in Figure 8.9b are relatively flat, with value of 0.97, less than 10% of its mean across time. Moving toward the ends, the estimates rise for the most part until dropping to a minimum 12 time points from the end and then rising again to the maximum value of 10.46 at the end. The

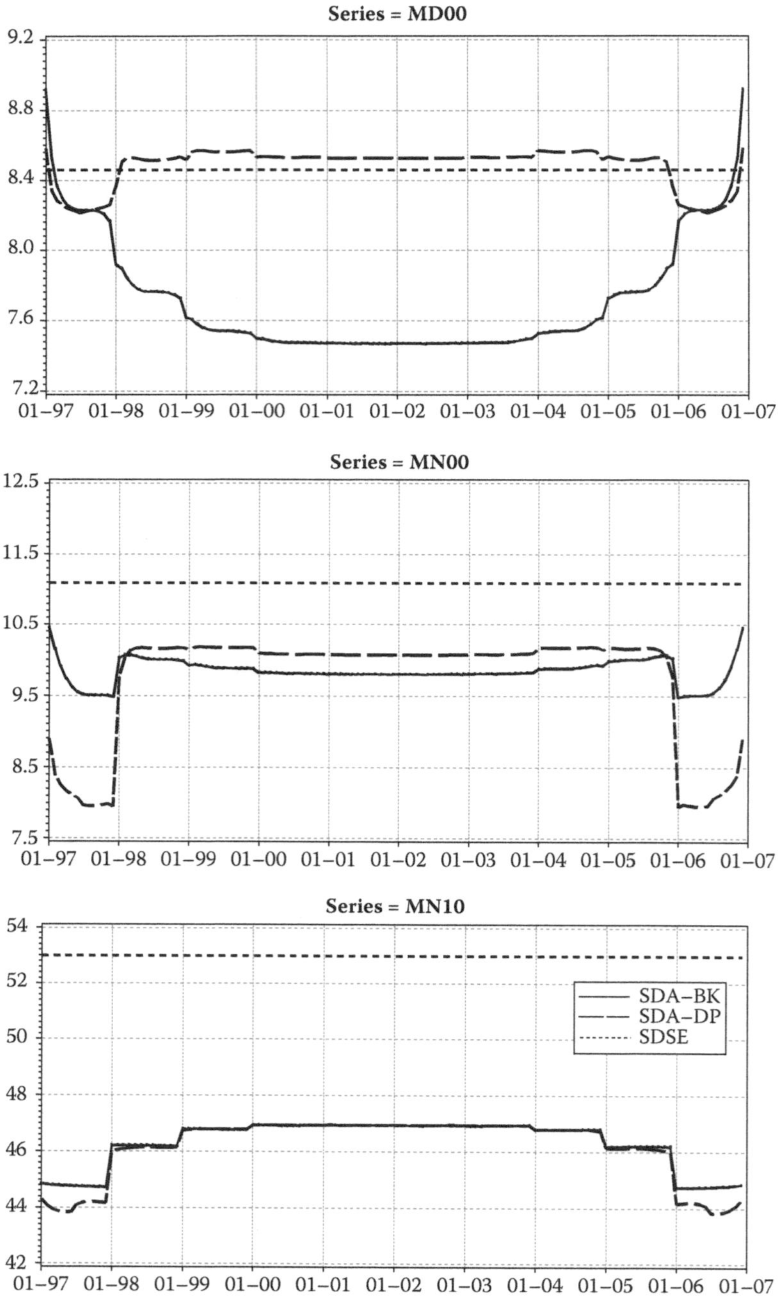

FIGURE 8.9
BK and DP standard deviations of seasonal adjustment error.

SDA_{DP} estimates are slightly larger than SDA_{BK} at the center, but then drop sharply, also 12 points from the end, and only partially recover. They lie below SDA_{BK} throughout the last year. For both methods, SDA estimates lie entirely below SDSE, indicating a larger amount of SE than for MD00. Strikingly, the end value under the DP method is 11.7% below the value at the center, while that for BK is 6.7% higher. Summarizing, SDA_{BK} has more pleasing characteristics. Unlike SDA_{DP}, it is higher at the end time points than at the center. At the ends, its difference from SDSE is −5.9%, compared to −24.6% with SDA_{DP}. Table 8.4b contains the key statistics.

8.4.2.4 Petroleum and Coal Products (MN10)

MN10 has an extreme SE variance. REGCMPNT initially finds the signal disturbance variance to be almost vanishingly small, $\hat{\sigma}_a^2 = 7.0$. Not surprisingly, applying Equation 8.2.6, no irregular component is found for this series. Unlike the two previous series, some of the parameter estimates for MN10's $(1,0,1)(0,1,1)_{12}$ signal model differ greatly from the estimates for the observed series. The AR parameter is about the same, 0.79 vs. 0.75, but the MA parameters move from sizable positive values to $\hat{\theta}_1 = -0.92$ and $\hat{\theta}_{12} = -0.60$. Models with $\theta_{12} < 0$ are likely to lack valid decompositions. We regard such values as implausible and introduce constraints, leading to the results in Table 8.4. Changes to the ARMA parameters are limited to 0.20. Disturbance variances for the signal and SE are adjusted for consistency with that for the observed series. In particular, for MN10, the adjusted signal disturbance variance is $\hat{\sigma}_a^2 = 145.9$. Scott and Sverchkov (2010) provide a detailed description of the constraints.

The SDA measures in Figure 8.9c are quite close, with SDA_{BK} slightly higher at the ends. Both are far below $\hat{\sigma}_\varepsilon = 53.0$, by 11.4% at the center and by 15.3% (SDA_{BK}) and 16.4% (SDA_{DP}) at the ends. Both shapes are unsatisfying, since the end values lie well below the center values, by 4.4% with BK and 5.6% with DP.

8.4.2.5 Overall Results for Press Release Series, Based on 17-Year Spans

For the three examples considered so far, moving from small to medium to large relative amounts of SE worsens the performance of the SDA measures. Seasonally adjusted values are most fully determined at the center of the series and least determined at the end. Thus, a monotonic increase in the SDA estimates could be expected in moving from the center to the ends of the series, as seen for SDA_{BK} in Figure 8.9a. Yet we see dips in the SDA graphs near the ends of the series in Figures 8.9b and c and even in Figure 8.3. Scott and Sverchkov (2010) address these dips in some detail. Here, using all the press release series, we examine empirically a simple, desirable property for SDA measures,

$$\text{SDA(end)} > \text{SDA(center)}. \qquad (8.4.1)$$

This intuitive property fails when the SE is substantial. Results are similar for the 10- and 17-year series. Here we report results for the 17-year series, since work in Scott and Pfeffermann (2009) suggests that longer series should be preferred.

Let $\delta(B)$ be the differencing operator in the ARIMA model for the signal. Then,

$$w_t = \delta(B)y_t = \psi(B)a_t + \delta(B)\varepsilon_t,$$

where $\psi(B)$ represents the ARMA model for the differenced signal. An important property in the derivations of Bell and Kramer (1999) is that the error in forecasting the series is a linear function of error in forecasting the differenced series,

$$y_f - \hat{y}_f = C(w_f - \hat{w}_f),$$

C a lower triangular matrix with rows defined by the coefficients in the expansion of $\delta(B)^{-1}$. The differenced series is stationary and we can justifiably consider variances. A natural measure of the SE contribution to the total variance is the "differenced variance ratio,"

$$\text{DVR} = \text{Var}[\delta(B)\varepsilon_t]/\text{Var}(w_t).$$

Table 8.5 shows results on fulfillment of property (8.4.1) for 128 series. Overall, only 31% of the series satisfy Equation 8.4.1 with the BK method and a scant 9% with DP. However, with $\text{DVR} \leq 1/2$, the condition is satisfied for 100% of the series with BK and 32% with DP. With $\text{DVR} > 1/2$, only two series satisfy the condition and only with the BK method; both these series have $\text{DVR} = 0.51$. Significantly, SDA_{BK} exceeds SDA_{DP} at the ends 68% of the time when $\text{DVR} \leq 1/2$ and 81% overall. The exceptions are cases where a large irregular component is estimated.

The series for which the end value exceeds SDSE are the same for the two methods. They occur only when $\text{DVR} \leq 1/2$ and then for about one-third of the series. Variability in the signal is evident when the SE is not dominant.

TABLE 8.5
Frequency Table for End Behavior by Relative Size of Sampling Error

		SDA(End)> SDA(Center)		**SDA(End)> SDSE**		**SDA(End)**
	Total	BK	DP	BK	DP	BK > DP
DVR						
≤1/2	38 (30%)	38 (100%)	12 (32%)	12 (32%)	12 (32%)	26 (68%)
>1/2	90 (70%)	2 (2%)	0 (0%)	0 (0%)	0 (0%)	78 (87%)
Total	128	40 (31%)	12 (9%)	12 (9%)	12 (9%)	104 (81%)

Having SDA smaller than SDSE most of the time seems a natural property, since seasonal adjustment is a smoothing operation. The main finding reflected in Table 8.5 is disappointing. Property (8.4.1) fails most of the time. For the DP method, this stems in part from the differences (8.2.4) not captured in the approximation in Equation 8.2.3. Yet the breakdown by DVR size suggests that when the SE is not too large, one or both measures may indeed satisfy Equation 8.4.1. Empirically at least, the BK method is likely to satisfy this intuitive property, as long as the SE contribution is less than half.

Among the 128 series are 17 highly aggregated series, including 13 "supersectors" defined under the current industry classification system and Total Private (Sector) Employment, the most highly aggregated series for which SE information is available. Eleven of the seventeen series satisfy property (8.4.1) with the BK method and five with DP. The property is not satisfied with either method for the following six series: Mining, Utilities, Wholesale Trade, Information, Education and Health Services, and Other Services.

So far, our analysis has focused on *indicators*, counting how many times *end–center* differences are positive. Table 8.6 presents the *magnitude* of the differences. For the case DVR $\leq 1/2$, the median difference is 7.2% with the BK method and slightly negative at -1.7% with DP. Simple sample correlations between DVR values and *end–center* differences are roughly -0.70 for both methods, another demonstration that these differences take larger negative values as the SE contribution to the total variance grows. The table also contains statistics for the difference between SDA at the ends of the series and SDSE. With DVR $\leq 1/2$, the medians are -5.3% and -6.4% under the BK and DP methods, respectively. In two of three recent simulation experiments (not otherwise covered in this chapter), SDA is lower at the ends, by 5.6% for Professional & Business Services and by 3.1% for Construction. For Total Private Employment, SDA is 3.3% higher.

Summarizing, end behavior is better with the BK method, since it captures more uncertainty at the ends of the series than the DP method. Even with the BK method, the end value exceeds the central value only when the SE contribution is limited to roughly half the variance of the differenced series. This property holds for a majority of the highly aggregated series, 11 of 17 so-called supersectors, but only for about 30% of all press release series.

TABLE 8.6
Medians for % Difference by Size and Overall

	SDA(End) – SDA(Center)		**SDA(End) – SDSE**	
	BK	**DP**	**BK**	**DP**
DVR $\leq 1/2$	7.2	−1.7	−5.3	−6.4
DVR $> 1/2$	−4.3	−8.4	−15.5	−18.6
Total	−3.4	−6.6	−14.7	−16.6

8.5 Conclusions

The Bell–Kramer (BK) and Pfeffermann (DP) methods both provide conceptually reasonable variance measures for error in seasonal adjustment that account for SE. The extensive empirical results in this chapter confirm earlier characterizations of the methods:

1. The BK method captures more fully the contribution of forecast–backcast error.
2. The DP method accounts for the contribution of the time series irregular component, since this method separates it from the signal, unlike the BK method.

An issue arising in our empirical work on the CES series is that signal model parameter estimation in the BK method often yields implausible estimates (cf. the MN10 example in Section 8.4.2). We believe this stems from SE variance estimates that are too large. Simulations in Scott and Sverchkov (2010) confirm that, given an SE variance above the true value, estimation of the signal model is unstable and often gives poor or implausible signal parameter estimates. Underestimates of the SE variance also bias the signal parameter estimates, but, unlike the overestimation case, signal parameter estimation tends to be stable. The occurrence of variance estimates substantially above and below the true value is not surprising, since the variance of a variance estimator involves the fourth moment of the underlying distribution and can be quite large. Scott and Sverchkov (2010) discuss this issue and introduce constraints in order to ensure reasonable signal models. With the DP method, incorrect estimates of the SE variance impact identification of the irregular component autocovariances. Overestimation of the SE variance causes underestimation of the irregular variance and vice versa.

The main advantage of the BK method over the DP method is that it captures more fully the uncertainty at the end of the series, which is the most important point in time. Both methods can have unnatural dips in the first and last years of the series. These dips may be due to (1) ignoring some contributions to uncertainty and (2) inherent properties of the X-11 filters. They are particularly pronounced when the SE is dominant. Results are more likely to be satisfactory when the relative contribution of the SE is less than half the variance of the differenced series, as measured by the "DVR" statistic in Section 8.4. Behavior near the ends of the series is explored further in Scott and Sverchkov (2010).

SDA estimates with the BK method are always lower than SE standard deviations at the center of the series. They also tend to be lower at the ends, by 5%, for series with relatively low SE.

For the employment change application in Section 8.4, we feel that we have established that the BK method is tenable for use in assessing the significance of monthly change, as long as the SE contribution is not too large. Section 8.4 shows that this holds for a majority of the highly aggregated series.

Acknowledgments

The authors wish to thank the editors and two referees for suggestions leading to substantial improvements; William Bell and Brian Monsell for helpful discussions and support for use of the REGCMPNT program; Julie Gershunskaya for advice and SE autocovariances for the CES series; and Richard Tiller and Tamara Zimmerman for advice and SE autocovariances for the CPS series.

References

Bell, W. R. (2004). On RegComponent time series models and their applications. In *State Space and Unobserved Component Models: Theory and Application.* eds. A. C. Harvey, S. J. Koopman, and N. Shephard, 248–283. Cambridge: Cambridge University Press.

Bell, W. R. (2005). Some consideration of seasonal adjustment variances. In *ASA Proceedings of the Joint Statistical Meetings*, 2747–2758. American Statistical Association.

Bell, W. R. and Kramer, M. (1999). Toward variances for X-11 seasonal adjustments. *Survey Methodology*, 25:13–29.

Pfeffermann, D. (1994). A general method for estimating the variances of X-11 seasonally adjusted estimators. *Journal of Time Series Analysis*, 15:85–116.

Pfeffermann, D., Morry, M., and Wong, P. (1995). Estimation of the variances of X-11 ARIMA seasonally adjusted estimators for a multiplicative decomposition and heteroscedastic variances. *International Journal of Forecasting*, 11:271–283.

Pfeffermann, D. and Scott, S. (1997). Variance measures for X-11 seasonally adjusted estimators; some new developments with application to labor force series. In *ASA Proceedings of the Joint Statistical Meetings*, 211–216. American Statistical Association.

Pfeffermann, D., Scott, S., and Tiller, R. (2000). Comparison of variance measures for seasonally adjusted and trend series. In *Proceedings of the*

2nd International Conference on Establishment Surveys, 755–764. American Statistical Association.

Pfeffermann, D., Tiller, R., and Zimmerman, T. (2000). Accounting for sampling error autocorrelations: Towards signal extraction from models with sampling error. In *ASA Proceedings of the Joint Statistical Meetings*, 108–113. American Statistical Association.

President's Committee to Appraise Employment and Unemployment Statistics (1962). *Measuring Employment and Unemployment.* U.S. Government Printing Office, Washington, DC.

Scott, S. and Pfeffermann, D. (2009). On the impact of sampling error on modeling seasonal time series. In *ASA Proceedings of the Joint Statistical Meetings*, 2349–2363. American Statistical Association.

Scott, S. and Sverchkov, M. (2010). Measuring uncertainty in X-11 seasonal adjustment: Methods and empirical results. BLS Internal Report.

Scott, S., Sverchkov, M., and Pfeffermann, D. (2005). Variance measures for X-11 seasonal adjustment: A summing up of empirical work. In *ASA Proceedings of the Joint Statistical Meetings*, 3534–3545. American Statistical Association.

Sverchkov, M., Scott, S., and Pfeffermann, D. (2009). On X11 seasonal adjustment and estimation of its MSE. In *ASA Proceedings of the Joint Statistical Meetings*, 2456–2467. American Statistical Association.

Wolter, K. M. and Monsour, N. J. (1981), On the problem of variance estimation for a deseasonalized series. In *Current Topics in Survey Sampling.* eds. D. Krewski, R. Platek, and J. N. K. Rao, 367–403. New York: Academic Press.

Part IV

Practical Problems in Seasonal Adjustment

9

Asymmetric Filters for Trend-Cycle Estimation

Estela Bee Dagum and Alessandra Luati

CONTENTS

9.1 Introduction

The estimation of the nonstationary mean of a seasonally adjusted time series, defined as trend-cycle, has attracted the attention of many statisticians and actuaries for a long time. Two major approaches have been followed, one parametric, or model-based, and the other nonparametric, or based on linear digital filtering. The most common assumption in the parametric approach is that the nonstationary mean can be represented by a stochastic model belonging to the ARIMA Box and Jenkins (1976) class or a random walk with or without a random drift. Major significant contributions have been made by Akaike (1980), Gersch and Kitagawa (1983), Harvey and Jaeger (1993), King and Rebelo (1993), Gómez and Maravall (1994), Maravall (1993), Harvey (1997), Gómez (1999), and Kaiser and Maravall (1999) among others.

Concerning the nonparametric approach, the literature is very vast and includes estimators built according to different procedures, such as local polynomial regression, cubic smoothing splines, probability distribution kernels, graduation theory, and finite weighted moving averages. The earliest classical references are Henderson (1916), Whittaker and Robinson (1924), and Macaulay (1931). These authors were mainly interested in the smoothing properties of finite filters and their kernel shapes. More recent contributions have concentrated on the asymptotic statistical properties of optimally estimated smoothing parameters, e.g., Cleveland (1979), Cleveland and Devlin (1988), Hardle (1990), Fan (1992, 1993), Green and Silverman (1994), Simonoff (1995), Fan and Gijbels (1996), Wand and Jones (1996), and Eubank (1999).

Within the context of current economic analysis, significant contributions have been made, among several others, by Cholette (1981), Kenny and Durbin (1982), Bell (1984), Laniel (1986), Cleveland et al. (1990), Faliva (1994), Gray and Thomson (1997, 2002), Doherty (2001), Hodrick and Prescott (1997), Baxter and King (1999), and Quenneville et al. (2003).

In many time series decomposition softwares, such as Census X-11 and X-11/X-12 ARIMA (see Findley et al. (1998) and Ladiray and Quenneville (2001)), the nonstationary mean for central observations is estimated with the linear Henderson symmetric filters. For monthly data, which is the periodicity we shall be concerned with throughout this chapter, the 13-term Henderson filter (H13) is widely applied. It is a symmetric filter that reproduces a third-order polynomial trend without bias. In practice, it possesses the property of fast turning point detection but has the limitations of producing a large number of short cycles of 10 months, which can be falsely interpreted as true turning points, as well as large revisions to most recent estimates with new data. To obtain estimates for the trend at the beginning and end of the series, the asymmetric filters developed by Musgrave (1964) are used; see also Doherty (2001), Gray and Thomson (2002), and Proietti and Luati (2008). Although developed by Musgrave, the latter are often called asymmetric Henderson filters, and so will be referred to herein. In recent studies, Dagum and Luati (2002) found that two symmetric filters, the locally weighted regression smoother (loess) of degree 2 (L2) and the Gaussian kernel (GK), if constrained to be of 13 terms, are very similar to H13 with the advantage of GK of producing a smaller number of false turning points without a deterioration of signal passing.

In this chapter, we study the asymmetric filters of GK and L2 from the viewpoints of revision and false turning points. Hence, we derive the asymmetric filters of each of them and analyze their time path, i.e., their behavior in time, by starting with the one applied to the last data point up to the central, symmetric filter. Since the asymmetric filters are time-varying and applied in a moving manner, the estimates based on the most recent observations are subject to revisions as new observations are added. Thus, the real-time estimate based on the current and past available observations will be revised six times before the symmetric time-invariant filter can be applied. It should be noted that the revisions are due to both filter changes and the innovations introduced by new observations. We shall discuss only the revision due to filter changes. From this viewpoint, we define as "optimal" the smoother with asymmetric filters that satisfy the property of producing revisions that are small in size and monotonically converge to zero. Hence, the time path of the nonsymmetric filters is here studied in terms of: (1) consecutive filter distances, and (2) convergence pattern to the central one.

Another important aspect investigated in the chapter concerns the short cycles of 10 months present in the estimated trend, which can lead to the wrong identification of turning points. In this regard, we analyze the power of each asymmetric filter at the frequency $\lambda = 0.10$ corresponding to cycles of periods equal to 10 months, $2\pi\lambda \in (0, \pi)$. Furthermore, we investigate if one of the nonsymmetric filters can be used as a substitute for the central one to avoid unnecessary revisions.

The sequence of the chapter is organized as follows: Section 9.2 introduces the basic assumptions of GK, L2, and H13, and derives the symmetric and asymmetric weights of the two former while for H13 we use those already available in the X-11/X-12 ARIMA seasonal adjustment software. Section 9.3 gives the definitions of total and consecutive filter distances using a frequency domain approach. Section 9.4 shows the time path of the nonsymmetric filters of GK, L2, and H13 based on the total and consecutive distances, and discusses their implications for revisions and false turning points. Section 9.5 illustrates the trend-cycle estimates produced by the symmetric GK, L2, and H13 smoothers and by corresponding asymmetric filters that can be applied as substitutes for the symmetric ones, using three U.S. leading indicators. Finally, Section 9.6 gives the conclusion.

9.2 Symmetric and Asymmetric Linear Filters

In time series analysis, it is often assumed that a time series $\{y_t\}_{t=1,\ldots,T}$, $T < \infty$, is decomposed as the sum of a signal, g_t, plus an erratic component, u_t, i.e., $y_t = g_t + u_t$, where g_t can be either deterministic or stochastic and u_t usually follows a stationary stochastic process with zero mean and constant variance σ_u^2. The most common assumption for u_t is that of a white noise but, more generally, it can be assumed that it follows an autoregressive moving average (ARMA) process.

We assume that the signal g_t is generated by a smooth function $g(t)$ that can be locally approximated by a polynomial of degree d of the time distance between each y_t and neighboring observations. In this local polynomial regression model, the estimates for the signal $\widehat{g}_\eta(t)$ are obtained with the method of weighted least squares and depend on a smoothing parameter, η, which determines the degree of smoothness of the estimated values. It follows that, for fixed values of the smoothing parameter, $\eta = \eta_0$, any estimator $\widehat{g}_{\eta_0}(t)$ becomes a linear function of the data, and estimation of g_t results from applying, in a moving manner, a number of weights to the observations, such that, for $m < t \leq T - m$, $\widehat{g}_{\eta_0}(t) = \sum_{j=-m}^{m} w_j y_{t+j}$, where the length of the symmetric filter, $2m + 1$, is determined by η_0. Hence, $\widehat{g}_{\eta_0}(t)$ can be interpreted equivalently as: (a) a nonparametric estimator of g_t, and (b) using a shorthand notation, a smooth estimate $\widehat{g}_t$ resulting from a $(2m + 1)$-term symmetric moving average centered at y_t. Only asymmetric filters can be applied to the first and last m observations, such that, e.g., the real-time estimate is $\hat{g}_T = \sum_{j=-m}^{0} w_j y_{T+j}$.

The nonparametric estimators studied here are based on different criteria of smoothing. The locally weighted regression smoother fits local polynomials of a degree d where the parameters are estimated either by ordinary or weighted least squares. Thus, it satisfies the property of best fit to the data. On the other hand, the Gaussian kernel is a locally weighted average with a weighting function that follows the Gaussian standard distribution. The Henderson smoothing filters are derived from the graduation theory, known to be unbiased and to maximize smoothness of the estimate subject to the constraints of reproducing a third-degree polynomial within the span of the filter. Recently, it has been shown that they are best linear unbiased estimators for the trend, when the error process follows a noninvertible moving average of order 3 (Luati and Proietti 2011).

Next, we discuss briefly how the symmetric and asymmetric filters are derived for each smoother (for more details see Dagum and Luati (2000, 2001, 2002)). We then calculate the symmetric and asymmetric weights of the constrained smoothers.

The symmetric locally weighted regression smoother that we use in this study, known as *loess* in the current literature, is the one developed by Cleveland et al. (1990). At the boundaries of the series, we approximate the nearest neighbor weights produced by loess by fixed-length time-varying filters, by discarding the last term and proportionally adjusting the approximated filters such that they add up to one. This operation is against the principles loess is built upon, but it is necessary to compare loess with the Henderson filter in real time according to the criteria of this chapter. Furthermore, since the last weights of the asymmetric loess filter are very close to zero, the approximated fixed-length weights are almost indistinguishable from the original nearest neighbor weights. For the loess of degree d (in our study $d = 2$), the vector of weights to be applied to the 13 neighboring observations and including each y_j, $j = 1, \ldots, n$, in order to produce the estimated $\hat{y}_j$ is calculated by

$$\hat{g}_j = \mathrm{t}_j' \boldsymbol{\beta}_j$$

where $\mathrm{t}_j' = [1 t_j \cdots t_j^d]$ and $\boldsymbol{\beta}_j$ is the $(d+1)$-dimensional least square estimate of a weighted regression computed over a neighborhood of t_j,

$$\boldsymbol{\beta}_j = (T_j' W_j T_j)^{-1} T_j' W_j$$

where T_j is a $13 \times (d+1)$ matrix of t_ks belonging to each 13-term neighborhood $N(t_j)$ of t_j, and W_j is the 13×13 diagonal matrix of weights

$$w_k(t_j) = W\left(\frac{|t_j - t_k|}{\max\limits_{t_k \in N(t_j)} |t_j - t_k|} \right)$$

based on the tricube weighting function $W(x) = (1 - |x|^3)^3 I_{\{[0,1]\}}(x)$.

TABLE 9.1
Symmetric (First Row) and Asymmetric Weights of GK Constrained to 13-Terms

w_{-6}	w_{-5}	w_{-4}	w_{-3}	w_{-2}	w_{-1}	w_0	w_1	w_2	w_3	w_4	w_5	w_6
0.001	0.007	0.023	0.060	0.121	0.183	0.210	0.183	0.121	0.060	0.023	0.007	0.001
0.001	0.007	0.023	0.060	0.121	0.183	0.210	0.183	0.121	0.060	0.023	0.007	0
0.001	0.007	0.023	0.061	0.122	0.184	0.212	0.184	0.122	0.061	0.023	0	0
0.001	0.007	0.024	0.062	0.125	0.189	0.217	0.189	0.125	0.062	0	0	0
0.002	0.007	0.025	0.066	0.133	0.201	0.231	0.201	0.133	0	0	0	0
0.002	0.008	0.029	0.077	0.153	0.232	0.267	0.232	0	0	0	0	0
0.002	0.011	0.038	0.100	0.199	0.302	0.347	0	0	0	0	0	0

The weights of the Gaussian kernel are obtained by

$$w_{hj} = \frac{K\left(\frac{t_h^* - t_j}{b}\right)}{\sum_{i=1}^{T} K\left(\frac{t_h^* - t_i}{b}\right)}$$

where

$$K\left(\frac{t_h^* - t_j}{b}\right) = \frac{1}{\sqrt{2\pi}} \exp\left\{-\frac{1}{2}\left(\frac{t_h^* - t_j}{b}\right)^2\right\}$$

and b is the smoothing parameter, which determines the filter span and denotes the standard deviation of the Gaussian distribution function. For an approximation of the weights to three decimal points, the span is equal to $6b + 1$ or equivalent to $6\sigma + 1$ and therefore, we have chosen $b = 2$.

The Henderson symmetric weights are obtained from the general formula for a filter of length $2k - 3$,

$$w_j = \frac{315\{(k-1)^2 - j^2\}(k^2 - j^2)\{(k+1)^2 - j^2\}(3k^2 - 16 - 11j^2)}{8k(k^2-1)(4k^2-1)(4k^2-9)(4k^2-25)}$$

by making $k = 8$ for $j = -6, \ldots, 6$.

The Henderson asymmetric weights developed by Musgrave (1964) do not follow the assumptions of the symmetric H13. They are based on the minimization of the mean squared revision between the final estimates (obtained by the

TABLE 9.2
Symmetric (First Row) and Asymmetric Weights of L2 Constrained to 13-Terms

w_{-6}	w_{-5}	w_{-4}	w_{-3}	w_{-2}	w_{-1}	w_0	w_1	w_2	w_3	w_4	w_5	w_6
−0.015	−0.036	−0.004	0.074	0.157	0.210	0.227	0.210	0.157	0.074	−0.004	−0.036	−0.015
−0.038	−0.006	0.050	0.111	0.159	0.184	0.188	0.172	0.134	0.077	0.012	−0.042	0
−0.028	0.015	0.070	0.121	0.157	0.170	0.173	0.151	0.113	0.060	−0.002	0	0
−0.009	0.032	0.076	0.114	0.141	0.153	0.154	0.142	0.117	0.081	0	0	0
0.027	0.058	0.089	0.119	0.145	0.168	0.205	0.189	0	0	0	0	0
−0.025	−0.012	0.017	0.061	0.120	0.192	0.371	0.275	0	0	0	0	0
−0.099	−0.084	−0.029	0.067	0.201	0.371	0.574	0	0	0	0	0	0

TABLE 9.3
Symmetric (First Row) and Asymmetric Weights of H13

w_{-6}	w_{-5}	w_{-4}	w_{-3}	w_{-2}	w_{-1}	w_0	w_1	w_2	w_3	w_4	w_5	w_6
−0.019	−0.028	0	0.066	0.147	0.214	0.240	0.214	0.147	0.066	0	−0.028	−0.019
−0.017	−0.025	0.001	0.066	0.147	0.213	0.238	0.212	0.144	0.061	−0.006	−0.034	0
−0.011	−0.022	0.003	0.067	0.145	0.210	0.235	0.205	0.136	0.050	−0.018	0	0
−0.009	−0.022	0.004	0.066	0.145	0.208	0.230	0.201	0.131	0.046	0	0	0
−0.016	−0.025	0.003	0.068	0.149	0.216	0.241	0.216	0.148	0	0	0	0
−0.043	−0.038	0.002	0.080	0.174	0.254	0.292	0.279	0	0	0	0	0
−0.092	−0.058	0.012	0.120	0.244	0.353	0.421	0	0	0	0	0	0

application of the symmetric filter) and the preliminary estimates (obtained by the application of an asymmetric filter) subject to the constraint that the trend outside the boundary follows a first-degree polynomial and that the filter is capable of reproducing a constant; see Laniel (1986) and Doherty (2001).

It should be noted that the symmetric filter of GK is that of a second-order kernel for it satisfies the conditions $\sum_{j=-m}^{m} w_j = 1, \sum_{j=-m}^{m} jw_j = 0$ and $\sum_{j=-m}^{m} j^2 w_j \neq 0$, whereas those of L2 and H13 are higher order estimators. In fact, besides the conditions of adding up to unity and of symmetry, these latter satisfy $\sum_{j=-m}^{m} j^p w_j = 0$ for even $p \geq 2$. On the contrary, the asymmetric weights of the three smoothers are first- or second-order kernel depending on their length.

The symmetric and asymmetric weights of each smoother, shown up to three decimals (for space reasons), are given in Tables 9.1 through 9.3.

9.3 Total and Consecutive Asymmetric Filter Distances

As discussed in Priestley (1981), the properties of a linear filter are best studied in terms of its frequency response function $H(\lambda) = G(\lambda)e^{-i\phi(\lambda)}$. The gain function is defined as $G(\lambda) = \sqrt{A^2(\lambda) + B^2(\lambda)}$, where $A(\lambda) = \sum_j w_j \cos(2\pi\lambda j)$ and $B(\lambda) = \sum_j w_j \sin(2\pi\lambda j)$, $0 \leq \lambda \leq 1/2$. The phase shift is given in time units as

$$\phi^*(\lambda) = \frac{\phi(\lambda)}{2\pi\lambda} = \frac{1}{2\pi\lambda} \arctan\left\{\frac{B(\lambda)}{A(\lambda)}\right\}.$$

In the context of smoothing monthly time series, we divide the total range of λ, i.e., $\Lambda = \{0 \leq \lambda \leq 0.50\}$ in two major intervals: (1) $\Lambda_S = \{0 \leq \lambda \leq 0.06\}$ associated with cycles of 16 months or longer, attributed to the "signal" (nonstationary mean or trend-cycle); and (2) the frequency band $\overline{\Lambda_S} = \{0.06 < \lambda \leq 0.50\}$ corresponding to short cyclical fluctuations attributed to the "noise." In this latter interval, it is of great interest to see how much of the power is not suppressed at $\lambda = 0.10$ corresponding to a short cycle of 10 months sometimes called an "unwanted ripple," for it can lead to the misidentification of a false turning point as a true one. In the sequel, we shall denote as signal gain the integral of $G(\lambda)$ over Λ_S, and as noise gain the integral of $G(\lambda)$ over $\Lambda_N = \overline{\Lambda_S} \setminus \Lambda_f$, where Λ_f contains bands around the seasonal frequencies and is formally defined next.

From the viewpoint of signal passing and noise suppression, an optimal smoothing filter should have a gain as close as possible to 1 for $0 \leq \lambda \leq 0.06$, and near to 0 for $0.10 \leq \lambda \leq 0.50$. Monthly time series data are often affected by seasonal variations but they are removed before the estimation of the non-stationary mean. In general, seasonal adjustment methods suppress practically all the power present in the bands around the fundamental seasonal frequency $\lambda_f = 1/12 = 0.0833$ and its five harmonics defined by the set

$$\Lambda_f = \{\lambda \in \Lambda : 0.077j \leq \lambda_f j \leq 0.091j, j = 1, 2, \ldots, 6, \lambda_f = 0.0833\}.$$

Therefore, the amount of noise passed by the asymmetric and symmetric filters has been calculated without taking into consideration the gain power at all these frequency bands, which should be almost 0 when the input series is seasonally adjusted.

Following an approach similar to that in Dagum (1982), the total distance is measured in terms of the frequency response functions of each asymmetric filter and the symmetric one.

The total signal distance is defined by

$$D_S^{(s,k)} = \left[\int_{\Lambda_S} \|H_s(\lambda) - H_k(\lambda)\|^2 \, d\lambda \right]^{1/2} \quad \text{for } k = 0, 1, \ldots, 5, \qquad (9.3.1)$$

where $H_s(\lambda)$ and $H_k(\lambda)$ denote the transfer functions of the symmetric and asymmetric filters, respectively. It should be noted that the index s refers to the symmetric filters, $s = 6$, while the index S refers to the signal frequency λ_S. These total distances provide a measure of the amount of total revision of an estimated value, due to filter changes. In effect, they measure the square root mean square error of the revision of the filters, when applied to a white noise sequence (with unit variance) and when $\Lambda_S = [-\pi, \pi]$. For current analysis, the most important are those for $k = 0, 1$ corresponding to the last and penultimate data point asymmetric filters, respectively.

Similarly, the total noise distance is defined by

$$D_N^{(s,k)} = \left[\int_{\Lambda_N} \|H_s(\lambda) - H_k(\lambda)\|^2 \, d\lambda \right]^{1/2} \quad \text{for } k = 0, 1, 2, \ldots, 5. \qquad (9.3.2)$$

The noise frequency band excludes the λs associated to the signal plus those corresponding to the seasonal frequency bands.

These signal and noise measures can also be used to identify if the revision process of the most recent estimates can be stopped before the symmetric filter can be applied. In fact, a k-th asymmetric filter can be used as a substitute of the symmetric one if $D_S^{(s,k)}$ and $D_N^{(s,k)}$ are very small and its phase shift is close to 0. Therefore, the revisions to estimated values can be stopped earlier in time without jeopardizing accuracy.

It should be noted that the end point will be estimated and reestimated six times before the symmetric filter can be applied. The first estimate will be done by the end point asymmetric filter (7-term filter, $k = 0$), the second estimate (when one more observation is added to the series) by the penultimate point filter (8-term filter, $k = 1$), the third estimate (when two more observations are added to the series) by the second previous to the end point filter (9-term filter, $k = 2$), and so on, till the symmetric filter is applied (after six more observations are added). This means that the last estimate will be revised once, twice, three times, and so on, up to six times.

Another crucial distance measure is that between consecutive asymmetric filters. These distances provide information on the size of the revisions due to filter changes, as more data are added to a series.

The consecutive asymmetric filter distance for the signal is defined by

$$D_S^{(k+1,k)} = \left[\int_{\Lambda_S} \|H_{k+1}(\lambda) - H_k(\lambda)\|^2 \, d\lambda\right]^{1/2} \quad \text{for } k = 0, 1, \ldots, 5. \tag{9.3.3}$$

Similarly, the consecutive asymmetric filter distance for the noise is defined by

$$D_N^{(k+1,k)} = \left[\int_{\Lambda_N} \|H_{k+1}(\lambda) - H_k(\lambda)\|^2 \, d\lambda\right]^{1/2} \quad \text{for } k = 0, 1, \ldots, 5. \tag{9.3.4}$$

The convergence pattern of the asymmetric filters to the central one is monotone if $D_S^{(k+1,k)}$ and $D_N^{(k+1,k)}$ are strictly decreasing for $k = 0, 1, \ldots, 5$.

Lack of monotonicity clearly indicates that the revision process should be stopped earlier for the asymmetric filters are departing from the central one.

The study of the asymmetric filters properties is not complete if we do not analyze their phase shift functions. Hence, we define the average phase shift for the signal by

$$\overline{\phi}_S^* = \frac{1}{0.06} \int_{\Lambda_S} \phi_S^*(\lambda) d\lambda$$

where $\phi^*(\lambda) = (\phi(\lambda))/(2\pi\lambda)$ is the phase shift in months.

9.4 Time Path of the Asymmetric Filters of GK, L2, and H13

We use the definitions of total and consecutive asymmetric filter distances to study the time path of GK, L2, and H13.

First, we calculate the signal and noise gains for the asymmetric and central filters of each smoother.

For GK, Table 9.4 shows the signal and noise gain values of the symmetric and nonsymmetric filters, $G(\lambda = 0.10)$ for the false turning points, and the

TABLE 9.4
Signal and Noise Gain Integrals of the Symmetric and Asymmetric Filters of the Gaussian Kernel

GK	**Central**	**7-Term**	**8-Term**	**9-Term**	**10-Term**	**11-Term**	**12-Term**
Signal (S)	56.17	58.88	58.20	57.36	56.84	56.39	56.15
Noise (N)	35.95	98.35	73.45	52.85	40.75	36.88	36.08
$S+N$	92.12	157.23	131.65	110.21	97.59	93.26	92.22
$G(\lambda = 0.10)$	0.49	0.75	0.68	0.59	0.54	0.50	0.49
Standardized Values	**Central**	**7-Term**	**8-Term**	**9-Term**	**10-Term**	**11-Term**	**12-Term**
$S/(S+N)$	0.61	0.37	0.44	0.52	0.58	0.60	0.61
$N/(S+N)$	0.39	0.63	0.56	0.48	0.42	0.40	0.39

standardized values with respect to the total gain. The latter represent the proportional distribution of the total variance between the signal and the noise. In this regard, the central GK filter will produce an output where 61% of its total variance will be due to the signal and 39% to the noise. For the last point filter, the proportional distribution is reversed, being 37% and 63% for the signal and the noise, respectively.

On the other hand, we can observe that already the signal and noise proportional distributions of the 10-term filter are very close to those of the central, and similarly $G(\lambda = 0.10)$. The 10-term filter reveals to be a good substitute of the central one when one aims at stopping the filter revision process.

Table 9.5 gives the total and consecutive distances for the asymmetric filters together with the phase shift in months.

The total distances approach monotonically to 0 as the asymmetric filters converge to the central one (k taking values from 0 to 5). This good property of monotonicity is observed for both signal and noise.

The total filter distance is a measure of the total revision of each point estimate due to filter changes. The largest total distance is between the last point and the central filters and becomes smaller as the other asymmetric filters approach to the central one. It should also be noted that, concerning the consecutive filter distances, these are quite large for $k = 0, 1, 2$, implying

TABLE 9.5
Total and Consecutive Signal and Noise Distances, and Average Phase Shift of the Asymmetric Gaussian Kernel Filters

GK	$k=0$ **7-Term**	$k=1$ **8-Term**	$k=2$ **9-Term**	$k=3$ **10-Term**	$k=4$ **11-Term**	$k=5$ **12-Term**
$D_S^{(s,k)}$	1.88	1.08	0.52	0.21	0.06	0.00
$D_S^{(k+1,k)}$	0.83	0.57	0.32	0.15	0.06	0.01
ϕ_S^*	−1.21	0.69	−0.33	−0.13	−0.04	0.00
$D_N^{(s,k)}$	5.06	2.77	1.22	0.43	0.12	0.01
$D_N^{(s,k)}$	3.74	2.15	1.00	0.38	0.11	0.01

TABLE 9.6
Signal and Noise Gain Integrals of the Symmetric and Asymmetric Filters of Loess of Degree 2

L2	**Central**	**7-Term**	**8-Term**	**9-Term**	**10-Term**	**11-Term**	**12-Term**
Signal (S)	60.36	65.46	60.67	58.71	58.56	59.26	59.71
Noise (N)	35.95	98.35	101.56	55.20	30.20	32.68	41.78
$S+N$	111.79	231.62	162.36	113.91	88.76	91.94	101.49
$G(\lambda = 0.10)$	0.72	1.35	0.79	0.41	0.35	0.47	0.56
Standardized Values	**Central**	**7-Term**	**8-Term**	**9-Term**	**10-Term**	**11-Term**	**12-Term**
$S/(S+N)$	0.54	0.28	0.37	0.52	0.66	0.64	0.59
$N/(S+N)$	0.46	0.72	0.63	0.48	0.34	0.36	0.41

that filter changes will have a major role in the revision process when one, two, and three more observations are added. This is true for the signal as well as for the noise. The phase shift turns out to be small in absolute value and negative (the shift is toward the left) for almost all the weights.

The L2 (approximate) asymmetric filter time path differs very much from those of the Gaussian kernel. Table 9.6 shows that the L2 central filter standardized gain values are equal to 54% for the signal and 46% for the noise, whereas those of GK have more smoothing. It can also be seen that the monotonic filter distance convergence stops at the 10-term filter for which $G(\lambda = 0.10)$ equals to 0.35, whereas for the central filter it is 0.72.

Table 9.7 shows the total and consecutive distances for the asymmetric filters and their average phase shift in month. Similar to the results observed in Table 9.6, neither the total nor the consecutive distances decrease monotonically as k increases from 0 to 5. Monotonicity of the total distance stops for the 9-term filter ($k = 2$) and, furthermore, the distance of this filter with respect to the final is still very large.

The consecutive revisions also give contradictory results as the length of the asymmetric filters increases from 7 to 12 terms. From this viewpoint, revising the last point estimates until $k = 3$ (corresponding to the 10-term filter)

TABLE 9.7
Total and Consecutive Signal and Noise Distances, and Average Phase Shift of the Asymmetric Loess of Degree 2

L2	$k=0$ **7-Term**	$k=1$ **8-Term**	$k=2$ **9-Term**	$k=3$ **10-Term**	$k=4$ **11-Term**	$k=5$ **12-Term**
$D_S^{(s,k)}$	1.00	0.18	0.56	0.70	0.57	0.30
$D_S^{(k+1,k)}$	0.95	0.49	0.15	0.15	0.27	0.30
ϕ_S^*	0.05	−0.05	−0.16	−0.21	−0.18	−0.10
$D_N^{(s,k)}$	8.43	3.87	2.90	3.45	3.08	2.04
$D_N^{(s,k)}$	8.03	4.63	2.15	0.99	1.23	2.04

TABLE 9.8
Signal and Noise Gain Integrals of the Symmetric and Asymmetric Filters of the Asymmetric 13-Term Henderson Filter

H13	**Central**	**7-Term**	**8-Term**	**9-Term**	**10-Term**	**11-Term**	**12-Term**
Signal (S)	60.33	63.45	61.20	59.21	58.42	58.80	59.76
Noise (N)	49.41	128.03	88.30	59.12	45.66	49.96	51.50
$S+N$	109.74	191.49	149.50	118.33	104.08	108.75	111.27
$G(\lambda = 0.10)$	0.72	1.06	0.86	0.70	0.64	0.67	0.71
Standardized Values	**Central**	**7-Term**	**8-Term**	**9-Term**	**10-Term**	**11-Term**	**12-Term**
$S/(S+N)$	0.55	0.33	0.41	0.50	0.56	0.54	0.54
$N/(S+N)$	0.45	0.67	0.59	0.40	0.44	0.46	0.46

would be preferable since the noise is substantially reduced but it has the limitation of an increase in the average phase shift in month.

The above observations indicate that there is no optimal k-th asymmetric L2 filter that can be used as a substitute for its central one. From the viewpoint of standardized gains and total distance, the 10-term filter is to be preferred.

Table 9.7 also gives the average phase shifts in month for the signal for each asymmetric filter. They are much smaller with respect to GK for $k = 0, 1, 2$ but larger for $k = 3, 4, 5$.

In summary, the time path of the approximate asymmetric filters of L2 behaves in an erratic manner as we move from the last point filter to the symmetric one.

The time path of the H13 asymmetric filters lies between L2 and GK. Table 9.8 shows that as for L2, the signal and noise gains for H13 do not approach monotonically to the central filter. The gain standardized values for H13 and L2 central filters are almost identical, and so are their gain functions (not plotted here). This implies that for a given input, the estimated nonstationary means will almost be identical. On the other hand, the 10-term filter seems to be a good approximation of the central one since the signal and noise total distances (see Table 9.9) are rather small; furthermore, it offers the

TABLE 9.9
Total and Consecutive Signal and Noise Distances, and Average Phase Shift of the Asymmetric 13-Term Henderson Filter

H13	$k=0$ **7-Term**	$k=1$ **8-Term**	$k=2$ **9-Term**	$k=3$ **10-Term**	$k=4$ **11-Term**	$k=5$ **12-Term**
$D_S^{(s,k)}$	1.20	0.44	0.21	0.31	0.26	0.10
$D_S^{(k+1,k)}$	0.75	0.46	0.16	0.08	0.16	0.10
ϕ_S^*	−0.53	−0.19	−0.03	0.03	0.00	−0.01
$D_N^{(s,k)}$	6.53	3.21	1.18	0.82	0.74	0.31
$D_N^{(s,k)}$	4.93	2.63	0.80	0.31	0.59	0.31

advantage of a significant reduction of power at $\lambda = 0.10$. Table 9.9 also shows that the monotonic behavior of the total and consecutive distances stops for $k = 3$, and that the phase shift is small.

It is a widely followed practice, among users of this filter, to stop revising the last point estimate after three more observations are added to the series, implying that the chosen substitute for the central one is the 10-term asymmetric filter ($k = 3$). Our theoretical measures confirm this to be an optimal revision policy from the viewpoint of its asymmetric filters.

9.5 Illustrations

The results given above refer to the asymmetric linear filter theoretical properties. Applied to real-time series, the empirical results will also depend on the input power along with frequency and the presence of outlying observations.

We shall illustrate to which extent the 10-term filter can be used as a substitute for the central one, by applying the symmetric and the 10-term

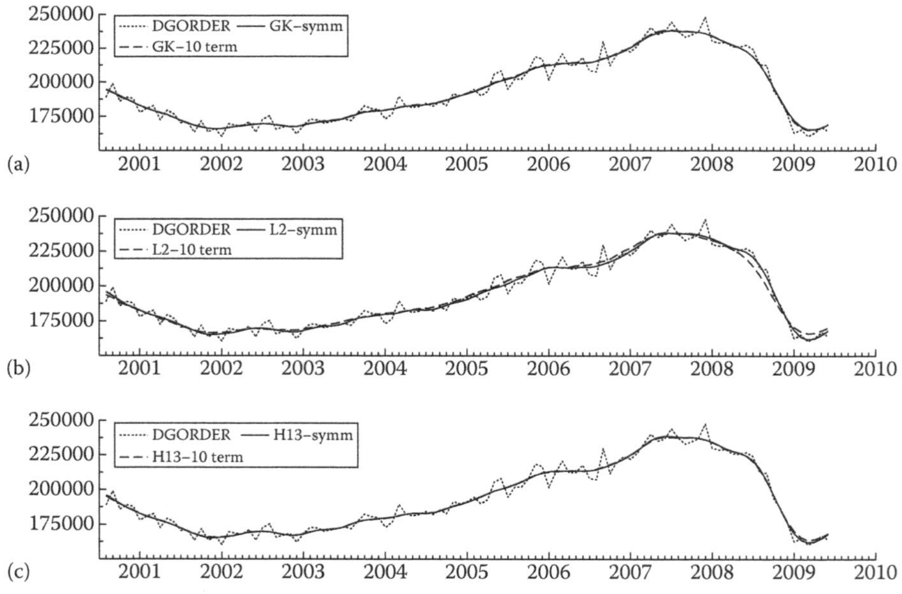

FIGURE 9.1
Trend estimates of series New Order of Durable Goods in Manufacturing with 13-term (line) and 10-term (dashed line) GK (a), L2 (b), and H13 (c).

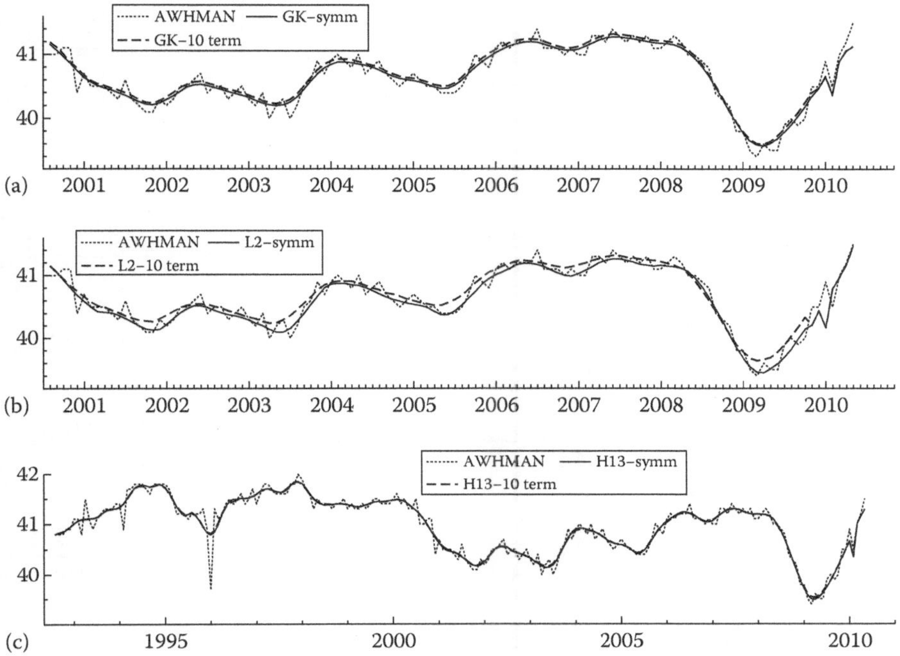

FIGURE 9.2
Trend estimates of series Average Weekly Hours in Manufacturing with 13-term (line) and 10-term (dashed line) GK (a), L2 (b), and H13 (c).

asymmetric filters of GK, L2, and H13 to three U.S. monthly seasonally adjusted leading indicators. The series are: Manufacturers' New Orders for Durable Goods (DGORDER) in millions of dollars, ranging from February 1992 to June 2009; Average Weekly Hours of Production and Nonsupervisory Employees in Manufacturing (AWHMAN) in hours, ranging from February 1992 to May 2010; Housing Starts, total of new privately owned housing units started (HOUST) in thousands of units, ranging from February 1992 to May 2010. Source: the FRED (Federal Reserve Economic Data) archive of the Federal Reserve Bank of St. Louis (http://research.stlouisfed.org/fred2/).

These series are characterized, respectively, by different signal-to-noise ratios. The results for DGORDER, AWHMAN, and HOUST are illustrated for the period 2000–2010 in Figures 9.1 through 9.3, respectively. The case of L2 (central panel) is the one where a discrepancy between the 13-term and the 10-term estimator is evident, as expected from our previous analysis. The 10-term trend estimates obtained by GK (top panel) and H13 (bottom panel) are almost indistinguishable from the corresponding 13-term estimates.

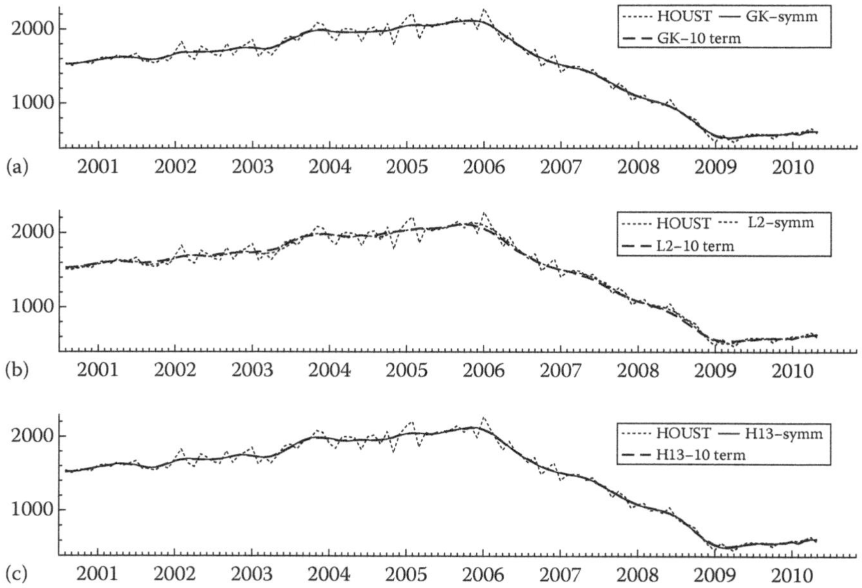

FIGURE 9.3
Trend estimates of series of Housing starts with 13-term (line) and 10-term (dashed line) GK (a), L2 (b), and H13 (c).

9.6 Conclusions

We analyzed the asymmetric filters for current estimation of the trend-cycle in seasonally adjusted time series. These filters belong to loess of degree 2 (L2), Gaussian kernel (GK), and 13-term Henderson (H13) smoothers. The former two have been restricted to 13 terms in agreement with the Henderson filter length most often applied to monthly data, by nonparametric time series decomposition softwares.

The nonsymmetric filters were analyzed in terms of: (1) total distance to the central one, i.e., a measure of the total revision of the last data point due to filter changes; (2) consecutive filter distances, which give the convergence pattern to the central filter; and (3) the power of each filter at frequency $\lambda = 0.10$.

We were also interested in finding if one of the nonsymmetric filters can be used as a substitute for the central one. The stopping asymmetric filter must satisfy the properties of: (1) significant suppression of power at the 10-month cycle frequency, (2) total power distribution between the signal and the noise close to that of the central filter, and (3) small phase shift. The distances have been calculated by means of gain functions decomposed into signal and noise frequency bands. The nonsymmetric filters studied range from a 7-term ($k = 0$) applied to the last data point up to a 12-term ($k = 5$) applied to the data point immediately before the central one.

Our results showed that only the GK asymmetric filters converge monotonically to the central, whereas those of L2 and H13 reverse direction after the 10-term filter. This is due to the fact that the Gaussian kernel underlies a probability distribution, whereas the other two do not. The reversal of direction implies that for the latter two, successive revisions will not necessarily improve the accuracy of the estimates. In fact, our theoretical results confirmed the widely applied practice by H13 users of stopping trend revisions after three more observations are added to the series. We found that there is no L2 approximate asymmetric filter that can be used as a good substitute for the central one, whereas the 10-term GK and H12 filters can be so. These conclusions were corroborated by an empirical analysis based on three U.S. leading indicators characterized by low, medium, and large signal-to-noise ratios.

Acknowledgments

We would like to thank the editors and two referees for their useful comments.

References

Akaike, H. (1980). Seasonal adjustment by a bayesian modelling. *Journal of Time Series Analysis*, 1:1–13.

Baxter, M. and King, R. (1999). Measuring business cycles: Approximate band-pass filters for economic time series. *Review of Economics and Statistics*, 81:575–593.

Bell, W. R. (1984). Signal extraction for nonstationary time series. *Annals of Statistics*, 12:646–664.

Box, G. and Jenkins, G. (1976). *Time Series Analysis: Forecasting and Control.* San Francisco: Holden Day.

Cholette, P. (1981). Comparison of various trend-cycle estimators. In *Time Series Analysis*, eds. O. D. Anderson and M. R. Perryman, 77–87. Amsterdam: North Holland.

Cleveland, R., Cleveland, W., McRae, J., and Terpenning, I. (1990). Stl a seasonal trend decomposition procedure based on loess. *Journal of Official Statistic*, 6(1):3–73.

Cleveland, W. (1979). Robust locally weighted regression and smoothing scatterplots. *Journal of the American Statistical Association*, 74:829–836.

Cleveland, W. and Devlin, S. (1988). Locally weighted regression: An approach to regression analysis by local fitting. *Journal of the American Statistical Association*, 83:596–610.

Dagum, E. (1982). The effects of asymmetric filters of seasonal factor revisions. *Journal of the American Statistical Association*, 77:732–738.

Dagum, E. and Luati, A. (2000). Predictive performance of some linear and nonlinear smoothers for noisy data. *Statistica*, LX(4):635–654.

Dagum, E. and Luati, A. (2001). A study of the asymmetric and symmetric weights of kernel smoothers and their spectral properties. *Estadistica*, 1(3):215–258.

Dagum, E. and Luati, A. (2002). Global and local statistical properties of fixed-length nonparametric smoothers. *Statistical Methods and Applications*, 11(3):313–333.

Doherty, M. (2001). Surrogate henderson filters in x-11. *Australian and New Zealand Journal of Statistics*, 43:385–392.

Eubank, R. (1999). *Nonparametric Regression and Spline Smoothing.* New York: Marcel Dekker.

Faliva, M. (1994). Trend-cycle detection as a filtering problem. *Statistica*, XLIV:601–617.

Fan, J. (1992). Design-adaptive nonparametric regression. *Journal of the American Statistical Association*, 87:998–1004.

Fan, J. (1993). Local linear regression smoothers and their minimax efficiencies. *Annals of Statistics*, 21:196–216.

Fan, J. and Gijbels, I. (1996). *Local Polynomial Modeling and its Applications.* New York: Chapman and Hall.

Findley, D., Monsell, B., Bell, W., Otto, M., and Chen, B. (1998). New capabilities and methods of the X12-ARIMA seasonal adjustment program. *Journal of Business and Economic Statistics*, 16:127–176.

Gersch, W. and Kitagawa, G. (1983). The prediction on time series with trend and seasonality. *Journal of Business and Economic Statistics*, 1:253–263.

Gómez, V. (1999). Three equivalent methods for filtering finite nonstationary time series. *Journal of Business and Economic Statistics*, 17:109–116.

Gómez, V. and Maravall, A. (1994). Estimation, prediction and interpolation for nonstationary series with the Kalman filter. *Journal of the American Statistical Association*, 89:611–624.

Gray, A. and Thomson, P. (1997). Design of moving average trend filters using fidelity, smoothness and minimum revisions criteria. *Research Paper*, Victoria University of Wellington.

Gray, A. and Thomson, P. (2002). On a family of finite moving average trend filters for the ends of sseries. *Journal of Forecasting*, 21:125–149.

Green, P. and Silverman, B. (1994). *Nonparametric Regression and Generalized Linear Models: A Roughness Penalty Approach.* London: Chapman and Hall.

Hardle, W. (1990). *Applied Nonparametric Regression.* Cambridge University Press.

Harvey, A. and Jaeger, A. (1993). Detrending, stylized facts and the business cycle. *Journal of Applied Econometrics*, 8:231–247.

Harvey, A. C. (1997). Trends, cycles and autoregressions. *Economic Journal*, 107:192–201.

Henderson, R. (1916). Note on graduation by adjusted average. *Transaction of the Actuarial Society of America*, 17:43–48.

Hodrick, J. and Prescott, E. (1997). Post-war U.S. business cycles: An empirical investigation. *Journal of Money, Credit and Banking*, 29:1–16.

Kaiser, M. and Maravall, A. (1999). Estimation of the business-cycle: A modified hodrick-prescott filter. *Spanish Economic Review*, 1:175–206.

Kenny, P. and Durbin, J. (1982). Local trend estimation and seasonal adjustment of economic and social time series. *Journal of the Royal Statistical Society A*, 145:1–81.

King, R. and Rebelo, S. (1993). Low frequency filtering and real business cycles. *Journal of Economic Dynamics and Control*, 17:207–233.

Ladiray, D. and Quenneville, B. (2001). Seasonal adjustment with the X-11 method. *Lecture Notes in Statistics.* New York: Springer-Verlag.

Laniel, N. (1986). Design criteria for the 13-term henderson end-weights. *Techincal Report Working Paper*, Statistics Canada.

Luati, A. and Proietti, T. (2011). On the equivalence of the weighted least squares and the generalised least squares estimators, with application to kernel smoothing. *Annals of the Institute of Statistical Mathematics*, forthcoming 63:851–871.

Macaulay, F. (1931). The smoothing of time series. *National Bureau of Economic Research*, New York.

Maravall, A. (1993). Stochastic and linear trends: Models and estimators. *Journal of Econometrics*, 56:5–37.

Musgrave, J. (1964). A set of end weights to end all end weights. *Working Paper*, U.S. Bureau of Census.

Priestley, M. B. (1981). *Spectral Analysis and Time Series.* London: Academic Press.

Proietti, T. and Luati, A. (2008). Real time estimation in local polynomial regression, with application to trend-cycle analysis. *Annals of Applied Statistics*, 2(4):1523–1553.

Quenneville, B., Ladiray, D., and Lefrancois, B. (2003). A note on musgrave asymmetrical trend-cycle filters. *International Journal of Forecasting*, 19:727–734.

Simonoff, J. (1995). *Smoothing Methods in Statistics.* New York: Springer-Verlag.

Wand, M. and Jones, M. (1996). *Kernel Smoothing.* New York: Chapman and Hall.

Whittaker, E. and Robinson, G. (1924). *Calculus of Observations: A Treasure on Numerical Calculations.* London: Blackie and Son.

10

Restoring Accounting Constraints in Time Series—Methods and Software for a Statistical Agency

Benoît Quenneville and Susie Fortier

CONTENTS

10.1 Introduction

The vast majority of time series data produced by a statistical agency are part of a system of time series classified by attributes. The series of such systems must satisfy cross-sectional (contemporaneous) aggregation constraints. This requires that the values of the component elementary series add up to marginal totals for each period of time. In some cases, each series must also add up to temporal benchmarks and therefore, must satisfy temporal aggregation constraints. Many time series processes such as seasonal adjustment are nonlinear and will destroy the linear relationships of the system.* Other processes such as those related to the combination of various sources of data and forecasting can also produce series that will fail to meet the aggregation constraints. To restore the coherence of the set of series, temporal benchmarking, reconciliation, or balancing processes must be applied.

The benchmarking and reconciliation problems and some of their solutions are presented and discussed in great detail in Dagum and Cholette (2006). The book also contains relevant historical references on the subject with appropriate discussions and includes an extensive literature review on benchmarking and reconciliation methods.

Over the years, a practical two-step method to restore the coherence in a set of series has been developed (Quenneville and Rancourt 2005; Quenneville and Fortier 2006; Fortier and Quenneville 2009) and incorporated into appropriate software. The first step is a univariate treatment for the temporal constraints; and the second step is a multivariate treatment for the contemporaneous constraints, given the temporal constraints from the first step. The corresponding software are two in-house `SAS`® procedures developed at Statistics Canada called `PROC BENCHMARKING` (Latendresse et al. 2007) and `PROC TSRAKING` (Bérubé and Fortier 2009). The methodology to restore univariate temporal constraints has also been adapted to the seasonal adjustment context with the `X-12-ARIMA FORCE` spec (Census Bureau 2009).

The benchmarking methods available with `PROC BENCHMARKING` are: the method of Denton (1971) as modified by Cholette (1984); the regression method of Cholette and Dagum (1994); and a few extensions described in Bloem et al. (2001, Chapter 6). The reconciliation or balancing method available with `PROC TSRAKING` is the plain old least squares solution with origin as far back as Stone et al. (1942) (Dagum and Cholette 2006, in p. 11).

Our contribution is to have parameterized both the benchmarking and reconciliation methods for easy implementation into computer software. We also simplified the multivariate reconciliation by first dealing with the movement preservation issue with univariate benchmarking and then breaking the remaining overall reconciliation problem into smaller ones. Using a result from Hyndman et al. (2007), we show that the simple application of weighted least squares in each of these smaller problems provides an overall optimal solution of the reconciliation problem, both in terms of statistical interpretation and computer performance. This permits an easy implementation of the methods into software programs, which facilitate large-scale applications. Our methods are also parameterized to accept external information on the reliability of the input values if available; otherwise, default values are used and justifications for using them are provided.

Di Fonzo and Marini (2011) is the only multivariate method against which our two-step method is compared. Alternative univariate or multivariate

* Unless the same combined seasonal/trading-day/holiday factors are applied uniformly to all the series.

methods that require additional parametric model assumptions were not considered because they are impractical in the context of the large-scale application problems for which our two-step method was developed.

This chapter is organized as follows. Section 10.2 discusses the need to go beyond direct and indirect seasonal adjustment and sets the context for reconciliation. It provides a typical seasonal adjustment example where the methods need to be applied. Section 10.3 discusses concepts related to the constraints and provides the basic ideas behind the methodologies for restoring the contemporaneous or the temporal constraints. It also provides the methodology implemented in `PROC BENCHMARKING` and in the `FORCE` spec of `X-12-ARIMA`. Section 10.4 addresses the theoretical basis for simultaneous benchmarking and reconciliation. The movement preservation issue is discussed in the context of a least squares approach with a detailed proof on how we go from generalized least squares to simple weighted least squares. This permits the efficient implementation of the proposed two-step method such as in Statistics Canada's `PROC TSRAKING`. References to illustrative examples are provided throughout the chapter. Guidelines for interpreting various summary quality statistics on movement preservation are also provided. Section 10.5 provides a brief conclusion.

10.2 Beyond Direct and Indirect Seasonal Adjustment

Consider a set of $M+1$ time series consisting of M component series and their total $X_{\bullet,\bullet} = X_{1,\bullet} + \cdots + X_{M,\bullet}$. A *direct* or *indirect* adjustment can be used to seasonally adjust the total $X_{\bullet,\bullet}$ with `X-12-ARIMA` (Census Bureau 2009; Findley et al. 1998) or `X-11-ARIMA` (Dagum 1988).

The *direct* adjustment is obtained when the total series is seasonally adjusted on its own using the total of the raw series: $SA(X_{\bullet,\bullet}) = SA(X_{1,\bullet} + \cdots + X_{M,\bullet})$, where $SA(X)$ denotes seasonal adjustment of X. The *indirect* adjustment of the total series is obtained by summing the seasonal adjustment of the components or the breakdown series: $ISA(X_{\bullet,\bullet}) = \sum_{m=1}^{M} SA(X_{m,\bullet})$, where $ISA(X)$ denotes the indirect seasonal adjustment of X.

The advantages of the direct approach are that $SA(X_{\bullet,\bullet})$ does not usually contain residual seasonality and can be easily reproduced by external users with publicly available seasonal adjustment options; however, the disadvantage is that the sum of the M seasonally adjusted components does not add to the directly seasonally adjusted total because, in general, seasonal adjustment is a nonlinear process, i.e., $ISA(X_{\bullet,\bullet}) = \sum_{m=1}^{M} SA(X_{m,\bullet}) \neq SA\left(\sum_{m=1}^{M} X_{m,\bullet}\right) = SA(X_{\bullet,\bullet})$.

The advantages of the indirect approach are that the additivity is respected; moreover, the growth rate in $ISA(X_{\bullet,\bullet})$ could be explained by the growth rates in some of the major components. The disadvantage is that the indirect seasonally adjusted series may contain residual seasonality.

The direct approach $SA(X_{\bullet,\bullet})$ should be selected when the seasonally adjusted aggregate is the major release and its seasonal adjustment is of high quality, when there is a need to easily reproduce $SA(X_{\bullet,\bullet})$ or when there is residual seasonality in the indirect seasonally adjusted total $ISA(X_{\bullet,\bullet})$. The indirect approach should be selected when there is more emphasis on the component series in the publication, e.g., when a few of the components dominate the aggregate, or when the seasonal patterns between the component series are very different.

There are, however, situations where the direct approach is preferred and the additivity constraint has to be respected. In such a case, reconciliation must be used, i.e., the seasonally adjusted components and the total series must be corrected to satisfy the constraint. In other cases, such as the Canadian Monthly Wholesale Trade Survey (MWTS), even an indirect approach does not guarantee the coherence of the additivity constraints. MWTS seasonally adjusted series are published by both industry (15 trade groups)* and region (10 provinces and 3 territories). The seasonally adjusted national total can be obtained indirectly as either the sum of the 15 industries or the sum of the 13 regions, and since seasonal adjustment is a nonlinear process, the two *indirect* seasonally adjusted national totals will not be equal. Nothing is available in `X-12-ARIMA` to solve this problem.

Notationwise, the problem is that there are two classifications for the national total, i.e., $X_{\bullet,\bullet} = \sum_{m=1}^{M} X_{m,\bullet} = \sum_{n=1}^{N} X_{\bullet,n}$, where the summation over the index m may refer to the regional breakdown and the summation over the index n to the industrial breakdown. Consequently, it is very likely that $\sum_{m=1}^{M} SA(X_{m,\bullet}) \neq \sum_{n=1}^{N} SA(X_{\bullet,n})$. Reconciliation is thus the process that starts with the seasonally adjusted series and ensures that $RSA(X_{\bullet,\bullet}) = \sum_{m=1}^{M} RSA(X_{m,\bullet}) = \sum_{n=1}^{N} RSA(X_{\bullet,n})$, where $RSA(X)$ denotes reconciled seasonal adjustment of X.

Obviously, one simple solution to the reconciliation problem is to seasonally adjust at the lowest level of the cross-classification such as the industry–region level, say, $SA(X_{m,n})$, and to obtain all the marginal totals indirectly; however, the industry–region level may be too detailed and the impact of the irregular components at that level may be too dominant for proper seasonal adjustment.

In MWTS, the indirect approach from the industrial breakdown is used to obtain the national total because it is easier to identify breaks, outliers, calendar effects, the seasonal effects, and so on at the industrial level. Moreover, there is an emphasis on the seasonally adjusted industrial totals in the publication. Hence, by choice, subject matter specialists decide to set $RSA(X_{\bullet,n}) = SA(X_{\bullet,n})$ so that the seasonally adjusted industrial totals are not modified by the reconciliation procedure. As a consequence, only the

* As of April 2010, MWTS data is published with a new breakdown of 25 industrial aggregations.

regional series $SA(X_{m,\bullet}), m = 1, \ldots, M$, need to be corrected to add up to the national total $\sum_{n=1}^{N} SA(X_{\bullet,n})$, which becomes a binding constraint for all time points. As publishing and accepting the discrepancies is ruled out, reconciliation is performed after seasonal adjustment to restore the accounting relationships that exist between the series.

The simplest way to reconcile the 13 regional MWTS seasonally adjusted series is by prorating, i.e., to distribute the discrepancy proportionally among the 13 series; however, for the MWTS, as well as for many Statistics Canada surveys, the seasonally adjusted series must preserve the annual total of their unadjusted counterparts; hence, reconciliation must preserve those constraints.

The proposed two-step procedure to solve this problem is illustrated with a numerical example and graphs from MWTS in Quenneville and Fortier (2006) and can be summarily described as follows: In the first step, each individual seasonally adjusted series is benchmarked to satisfy its temporal constraints, using, e.g., the `FORCE` spec of `X-12-ARIMA` (Census Bureau 2009) to force annual totals on the seasonally adjusted series. When the annual benchmarks are external and therefore not available through `X-12-ARIMA`, appropriate software such as `PROC BENCHMARKING` (Latendresse et al. 2007) may be used on the raw series prior to seasonal adjustment or on the seasonally adjusted data directly. The benchmarking step is designed to preserve the period-to-period movement as much as possible.

In the second step, we reconcile all the series so that the contemporaneous aggregation constraints between the series are satisfied, making sure that the temporal benchmarking constraints from the first step remain satisfied. For each time point $t = 1, \ldots, T$, with T the total number of observations, $\sum_{m=1}^{M} RSA(X_{m,\bullet,t}) = \sum_{n=1}^{N} RSA(X_{\bullet,n,t})$ so that the reconciled series satisfy the contemporaneous aggregation constraints. Moreover, when there are temporal benchmarks in a given year, then for the P observations in that given year (i.e., $P = 4$ for quarterly and $P = 12$ for monthly), $\sum_{t=1}^{P} RSA(X_{m,\bullet,t}) = \sum_{t=1}^{P} BSA(X_{m,\bullet,t})$, $m = 1, \ldots, M$, and $\sum_{t=1}^{P} RSA(X_{\bullet,n,t}) = \sum_{t=1}^{P} BSA(X_{\bullet,n,t})$, $n = 1, \ldots, N$, where $BSA(X_{m,\bullet,t})$ and $BSA(X_{\bullet,n,t})$ are the benchmarked seasonally adjusted series from the first step. In other words, the reconciled series also satisfy the temporal benchmarking constraints. This second step is performed with `PROC TSRAKING` (Bérubé and Fortier 2009).

The advantage of our two-step approach is that it is not necessary to account for movement preservation in the second step when temporal benchmarking is done in the first step (see Section 10.4.4); hence, the second step can be divided into smaller numerical problems that consider either one month at a time, or a year at a time, when an annual benchmark is involved. Numerically, this translates into using simple weighted least squares instead of generalized least squares.

The overall approach splits the computations between the seasonal adjustment program, the temporal benchmarking program, and a simple reconciliation method on only the years and months that need to be reconciled for publication purposes. For each of these steps, the corresponding software with suitable options can be used in a modular approach; see Ferland and Fortier (2009).

10.3 Constraints

Systems of time series classified by attributes must usually satisfy aggregation constraints. Two types of constraints are distinguished: *contemporaneous* and *temporal* constraints.

10.3.1 Contemporaneous Constraints

10.3.1.1 One-Way Classification

The simplest case of contemporaneous constraints is in a one-way classification system where, say, geographic estimates s_m for $m = 1, \ldots, M$, where M is the number of geographical regions, must add up to a national estimate g. To link with the previous section, s_m could be the regional seasonally adjusted estimates at time t, labeled $SA(X_{m,\bullet,t})$, and g the national seasonally adjusted estimate at time t obtained indirectly from the industrial breakdown, labeled $RSA(X_{\bullet,\bullet,t}) = \sum_{n=1}^{N} SA(X_{\bullet,n,t})$ for a time period t where an annual benchmark is not yet available.

The natural and almost trivial solution for such a problem comes from prorating where a reconciled estimate $\hat{\theta}_m$, labeled $RSA(X_{m,\bullet,t})$ in the previous section, may be obtained as the solution to the following constrained minimization problem:* $\min \sum_{m=1}^{M} (s_m - \theta_m)^2 / s_m$ subject to $\sum_{m=1}^{M} \theta_m = g$. The solution is simply $\widehat{\theta}_m = g s_m / \sum_l s_l$, which can be written as

$$\widehat{\theta}_m = s_m + \left(g - \sum_l s_l \right) \frac{s_m}{\sum_l s_l}, \tag{10.3.1}$$

showing that the discrepancy $(g - \sum_l s_l)$ is allocated to the components s_m in proportion to their contribution to the total $\sum_l s_l$; obviously, $\sum_m \widehat{\theta}_m = g$.

Using Equation 10.3.1, it is possible to think of alternative ways to allocate the discrepancy $(g - \sum_l s_l)$. For example, it can be allocated uniformly to the m components, i.e., by replacing $s_m / \sum_l s_l$ in Equation 10.3.1 by $1/m$; or in proportion to s_m^2, i.e., $s_m^2 / \sum_l s_l^2$; or in general, by specifying prior alterability coefficients c_m and by allocating the discrepancy in proportion to $c_m s_m$, i.e., $c_m s_m / \sum_l c_l s_l$. Specifying $c_m = 1, 1/s_m$ or s_m gives the above cases.

If measurement errors from survey data are available, the alterability coefficient can be set to the coefficient of variation (cv); consequently, the

* Assuming positive values of s_m for simplicity.

discrepancy is allocated in proportion of the standard errors since $\text{cv}(s_m)s_m = \sqrt{\text{Var}(s_m)}$. For an allocation proportional to the variances, c_m has to be set to $\text{cv}^2(s_m)s_m$ so that $c_m s_m = \text{Var}(s_m)$.

The alterability coefficients could also be subjectively assigned by the analysts based on their objectives. That is, the analysts determine M numbers r_m and set $c_m = r_m/s_m$; since, $c_m s_m = r_m$, the allocation will be proportional to $r_m/\sum_l r_l$.

With the alterability coefficient notation, the reconciled estimates may be defined as the solution of: $\min \sum_{m=1}^{M}(s_m - \theta_m)^2/|c_m s_m| + (g - \sum_{m=1}^{M}\theta_m)^2/|c_g g|$, where $c_m > 0$ and $c_g > 0$ are the alterability coefficients associated with each estimate. This solution may be written as:

$$\widehat{\theta}_m = s_m + \left(g - \sum_l s_l\right)\frac{|c_m s_m|}{|c_g g| + \sum_l |c_l s_l|}, \tag{10.3.2}$$

which also permits $c_m \geq 0$ and $c_g \geq 0$ as long as they are not all equal to 0. Obviously, in Equation 10.3.2, the reconciled estimates $\hat{\theta}_m$ will only fully satisfy the constraint g when the alterability coefficient associated with g is set to $c_g = 0$;* otherwise, part of the discrepancy is also allocated to g, which must then be revised to $\hat{g} = g - (g - \sum_l s_l)|c_g g|/(|c_g g| + \sum_l |c_l s_l|) = \sum_m \hat{\theta}_m$.

For a National Statistical Agency, the interest of solution (Equation 10.3.2) lies in its interpretation—the numerical optimization approach uses the least assumptions—and in its easy link to prorating obtained with the default setting $c_g = 0$ and $c_m = 1$. Prorating is often seen as an acceptable setting in absence of other information on the reliability of the estimates. The flexibility of the alterability coefficients is also an added value as they allow varying degree of reliability in s_m and g.

In a Bayesian context, the alterability coefficients permit specifying a prior distribution for the variance associated with s_m or g. As far as statistical inference is concerned, the resulting estimates $\hat{\theta}_m$ can be studied either in a frequentist or a Bayesian school of thought.

For the numerical, frequentist, and Bayesian approaches, we can write the linear model $y = (s', g)' = X\theta + \mu$. The components of the observation vector y are $s = (s_1, \ldots, s_M)'$ and g. The design matrix is $X = [I_M, G']'$ with I_M the identity matrix of order M and $G = 1'_M$ the unit row vector of length M. The error vector $\mu = (e', \epsilon)'$ has mean 0 with diagonal covariance matrix V_μ with $(|c_1 s_1|, \ldots, |c_M s_M|, |c_g g|)$ on the main diagonal. Let $V_\mu = \text{block}(V_e, V_\epsilon)$ be partitioned according to s and g. The resulting least squares estimate of θ is then

$$\begin{aligned}\hat{\theta} &= (X'V_\mu^{-1}X)^{-1}X'V_\mu^{-1}y \\ &= (V_e^{-1} + G'V_\epsilon^{-1}G)^{-1}(V_e^{-1}s + G'V_\epsilon^{-1}g) \\ &= s + V_e G'(GV_e G' + V_\epsilon)^{-1}(g - Gs),\end{aligned} \tag{10.3.3}$$

* In this case, the second term of the minimization function may be interpreted as the strict constraint $\sum_{m=1}^{M}\theta_m = g$.

where $GV_eG' + V_\epsilon$ is a real number in this case. This solution can be further generalized to handle redundant constraints using the Moore–Penrose inverse. Equation 10.3.3 is a vectorized version of Equation 10.3.2 with a notation that will be used throughout this chapter.

10.3.1.2 Two-Way Classification

In a two-way classification system, the estimates have two sets of aggregation constraints, one for each classification. Let s_{mn} be the estimate for region $m = 1, \ldots, M$, and for industry $n = 1, \ldots, N$. Let $g_{.n}$ be the desired national total for industry n and $g_{m.}$ be the desired industrial total for region m. Prorating can easily be extended to this two-dimensional setting and reconciled estimates θ_{mn} may be obtained as the solution to the following constrained minimization problem:

$$\min \sum_{m=1}^{M} \sum_{n=1}^{N} \frac{(s_{mn} - \theta_{mn})^2}{s_{mn}} \tag{10.3.4}$$

subject to

$$\sum_{m=1}^{M} \theta_{mn} = g_{.n} \text{ for } n = 1, \ldots, N \quad \text{and} \quad \sum_{n=1}^{N} \theta_{mn} = g_{m.} \text{ for } m = 1, \ldots, M. \tag{10.3.5}$$

Historically, the proportional iterative raking method was one way to reach a solution: each dimension was balanced with simple prorating, and this was iterated between the two dimensions until constraints (10.3.5) were satisfied. Nowadays, a direct solution is feasible via generalized least squares. The methodology implemented in `PROC TSRAKING` uses alterability coefficients (see Section 10.4.5).

The advantage of the least squares solution is that, when it is positive, it is the solution to which proportional iterative raking converges. The disadvantage is that it can give negative reconciled estimates for nonnegative values s_m. However, this usually occurs when proportional iterative raking does not converge.

The following example illustrates the situation. Table 10.1 displays a 2×3 table to be reconciled to the given marginal totals, and the least squares results are provided in Table 10.2. Iterative prorating gives essentially the same numerical results with a difference in the second decimal after rounding.

However, if the initial Table 10.1 is modified to Table 10.3, the generalized least squares balanced table will result in Table 10.4 with one negative number; the iterative prorating will not converge but will alternate between Tables 10.5 and 10.6.

TABLE 10.1
Example of a 2 × 3 Table to Be Balanced

	Alb	Sas	Man	Total
Cars	12	14	13	40
Other	20	20	24	53
Total	30	31	32	93

TABLE 10.2
Data from Table 10.1 Balanced by GLS or Iterative Prorating

	Alb	Sas	Man	Total
Cars	12.72	14.38	12.90	40
Other	17.28	16.62	19.10	53
Total	30	31	32	93

TABLE 10.3
Example of a 2 × 3 Table to Be Balanced

	Alb	Sas	Man	Total
Cars	0	0	13	40
Other	30	20	24	53
Total	30	31	32	93

TABLE 10.4
Data from Table 10.3 Balanced by GLS

	Alb	Sas	Man	Total
Cars	0	0	40	40
Other	30	31	−8	53
Total	30	31	32	93

TABLE 10.5
Data from Table 10.3 Balanced by Iterative Prorating with Convergence to the Column-Totals

	Alb	Sas	Man	Total
Cars	0	0	$32 - \epsilon$	40
Other	30	31	ϵ	53
Total	30	31	32	93

TABLE 10.6
Data from Table 10.3 Balanced by Iterative Prorating with Convergence to the Row-Totals

	Alb	**Sas**	**Man**	**Total**
Cars	0	0	40	40
Other	$26 - \epsilon_1$	$27 - \epsilon_2$	$\epsilon_1 + \epsilon_2$	53
Total	30	31	32	93

10.3.2 Temporal Constraints

Temporal constraints are the second type of aggregation constraints. For a given classification domain $m \times n$, a time series s_{mnt} ($= s_t$ when the domain is specified) may also be required to match temporal benchmark a_{mnl} ($= a_l$ when the domain is specified), $l = 1, \ldots, L$. For example, monthly estimates of the given domain may need to add up to corresponding annual estimates.

A widely used solution to the univariate benchmarking problem is the Denton (1971) method modified by Cholette (1984), also presented in Dagum and Cholette (2006). A specific variant of the solution is implemented at Statistics Canada as an in-house `SAS`® procedure called `PROC BENCHMARKING` (see Latendresse et al. 2007), which also includes the regression method of Cholette and Dagum (1994) and a few extensions described in Bloem et al. (2001, Chap. 6). The method and its links to the Denton method are discussed in Fortier and Quenneville (2007). The numerical optimization justification for `PROC BENCHMARKING` is now provided to permit reprogramming.

Assuming that the domain (m, n) is specified, let $s = (s_t)$, $t = 1, \ldots, T$ represent the component (usually subannual) series. Let $a = (a_l)$, $l = 1, \ldots, L$ represent the (usually annual) benchmarks. Both series are associated with dates. The calendar dates of s are assumed to be mapped onto the set of integers $t = 1, \ldots, T$. Each benchmark a_l is associated with its coverage period defined by its starting date $t_{1,l}$ and its ending date $t_{2,l}$. Dates for the benchmarks must be such that $1 \leq t_{1,l} \leq t_{2,l} \leq T$. To simplify the notation, let $t \in l$ mean that $t_{1,l} \leq t \leq t_{2,l}$.

The relation between the subannual series and the benchmarks is formalized by the *temporal sum operator*, the matrix J of dimensions $L \times T$ where, for $l = 1, \ldots, L$ and $t = 1, \ldots, T$, $j_{l,t} = 1$ when $t_{1,l} \leq t \leq t_{2,l}$ and 0 otherwise.

When considering only the temporal constraints, the benchmarked series $\hat{\theta} = (\hat{\theta}_1, \ldots, \hat{\theta}_T)'$ can be obtained as the solution of the following minimization problem: given the parameters ρ and λ, find the values $\hat{\theta}_t$ that minimize the following function of θ_t, $t = 1, \ldots, T$:

$$f(\theta_1, \ldots, \theta_T) = (1 - \rho^2)\left(\frac{s_1^\dagger - \theta_1}{\left|s_1^\dagger\right|^\lambda}\right)^2 + \sum_{t=2}^{T}\left\{\left(\frac{s_t^\dagger - \theta_t}{\left|s_t^\dagger\right|^\lambda}\right) - \rho\left(\frac{s_{t-1}^\dagger - \theta_{t-1}}{\left|s_{t-1}^\dagger\right|^\lambda}\right)\right\}^2 \quad (10.3.6)$$

under the constraints $\sum_{t \in l} \theta_t = a_l$, $l = 1, \ldots, L$.

In Equation 10.3.6, $s_t^\dagger, t = 1, \ldots, T$ refers to a *bias corrected* indicator series in which a constant adjustment may initially be applied to the component series s_t. This constant adjustment, also called the *bias*, is the expected discrepancy between a benchmark and its related subannual values. A consistent* estimate of the bias is the average discrepancy:

$$b = \frac{\sum_{l=1}^{L} a_l - \sum_{l=1}^{L} \sum_{t=t_{1,l}}^{t_{2,l}} s_t}{\sum_{l=1}^{L} \sum_{t=t_{1,l}}^{t_{2,l}} 1} = \frac{1_L'(a - Js)}{1_L' J 1_T}, \tag{10.3.7}$$

where $1_L = (1, \ldots, 1)'$ and $1_T = (1, \ldots, 1)'$ are respectively $L \times 1$ and $T \times 1$ vectors of 1; $a = (a_1, \ldots, a_L)'$ and $s = (s_1, \ldots, s_T)'$.

An alternative is to estimate the bias in terms of a ratio instead of a difference in levels:

$$b = \frac{\sum_{l=1}^{L} a_l}{\sum_{l=1}^{L} \sum_{t=t_{1,l}}^{t_{2,l}} s_t} = \frac{1_L' a}{1_L' J s}. \tag{10.3.8}$$

The bias-corrected series is either $s_t^\dagger = b + s_t$ when the bias correction factor is expressed in the term of a difference in the levels such as in Equation 10.3.7, or $s_t^\dagger = b \cdot s_t$ when the bias is expressed as a ratio such as in Equation 10.3.8. In both cases, it may be advantageous to estimate the bias from the last few years with benchmarks in order to achieve better timeliness. In periods not covered by a benchmark, the benchmarked series will converge to the bias-corrected subannual series when the parameter ρ is less than 1.†

The rationale for estimating a bias parameter with either Equation 10.3.7 or 10.3.8 is that these are simple methods that permit external users to recompute the constant bias adjustment. Moreover, under some additional assumptions, it would be possible to test if the bias is significant. Optimal estimators are provided in Dagum and Cholette (2006), but they require additional parametric assumptions.

Parameter $0 \leq \rho \leq 1$ controls movement preservation as it links one observation to its preceding value. Parameter λ quantifies how the discrepancies between the original series s and the desired series θ contribute to the objective function, and is used to select specific variants. The modified Denton's proportional first difference method (Cholette 1984) uses $\rho = 1$ and $\lambda = 1$; the nonproportional method uses $\lambda = 0$. Simple temporal prorating uses $\rho = 0$ and $\lambda = 0.5$.

Parameter λ implicitly defines global alterability coefficients for the observations s_t. Setting $\lambda = 0$ implies equal reliability for each observation; $\lambda = 0.5$ implies reliability proportional to the standard error, and finally, $\lambda = 1$ to the variance.

A future version of `PROC BENCHMARKING` will have the option of specifying alterability coefficients for each observation s_t and for each benchmark a_l to

---

* The sample mean of a sample from a stationary time series is a consistent but not optimal estimator of the theoretical mean.

† This is because the forecasts from a stationary AR(1) process converge geometrically to the mean.

account for their specific reliability as described in Bloem et al. (2001, Chap. 6) or to incorporate information on the measurement errors.

10.3.3 Temporal Constraints: `X-12-ARIMA FORCE` Specification

In `X-12-ARIMA` (Census Bureau 2009), the seasonally adjusted series s_t may be benchmarked to control totals derived from the corresponding raw series using the `FORCE` specification (spec). The spec comes with various arguments to parameterize the benchmarking method. A bias option does not exist, so $s_t^\dagger = s_t$. However, the **`target`** argument specifies which series is used as the target for forcing the totals of the seasonally adjusted series. The choices of target are the original series; the calendar adjusted series; the original series adjusted for permanent prior adjustment factors; and, the original series adjusted for calendar and permanent prior adjustment factors. For each of them, the option **`usefcst`** determines if forecasts are appended to the target series in order to achieve better timeliness for the observations in the current year with annual benchmark not yet available.

By default, the `FORCE` spec implies that the calendar year totals in the seasonally adjusted series will be made equal to the calendar year totals of the target series. An alternative starting period for the annual total can be specified with the **`start`** argument; consequently, annual totals between the benchmarked seasonally adjusted series and the target series that start at any period other than that specified by the **`start`** argument may not be equal.

Notationwise, the benchmarks a_l are derived from the **`target`** series, say, $x_t, t = 1, \ldots, T$. Let $x = (x_1, \ldots, x_T)'$. If we write $P = 4$ for quarterly series and $P = 12$ for monthly series, then a typical row of the temporal sum operator J will take the form $(0, \ldots, 0, 1'_P, 0, \ldots, 0)$. The vector of benchmarks is $a = Jx$.

The arguments **`rho`** and **`lambda`** are used to specify the parameters ρ and λ. Other arguments are described in the reference manual (Census Bureau 2009).

10.3.4 Temporal Constraints: Benchmarking Formulae

Define C as the $T \times T$ diagonal matrix with $|s_t^\dagger|^\lambda$ as the t-th element of the main diagonal.* If information on the measurement errors is available, C is replaced by the diagonal matrix with the standard errors of the measurement errors.

For $\rho < 1$, let Ω_e be the $T \times T$ matrix† defined by $\Omega_e = ((\rho^{|i-j|})), i, j = 1, \ldots, T$. Let $V_e = C\Omega_e C$ and $V_d = JV_eJ'$. The minimization of Equation 10.3.6 under its constraints entails minimizing the function $(s^\dagger - \theta)' (C\Omega_e C)^{-1}(s^\dagger - \theta) + 2\nu'(J\theta - a)$ with respect to the elements of θ and ν, where

* The diagonal elements of the matrix C can be rescaled to avoid numerical problems. For example, they can be divided by their overall mean.

† Define $\rho^0 = 1$. Also, for $\rho = 0$, the matrix Ω_e is the identity matrix.

2ν is the vector of Lagrange multipliers. Differentiation with respect to these elements leads to the equations $(C\Omega_e C)^{-1}(s^\dagger - \theta) = J'\nu$ and $J\theta = a$. The first equation gives $\theta = s^\dagger - C\Omega_e CJ'\nu$ and using $J\theta = Js^\dagger - JC\Omega_e CJ'\nu = a$ permits one to solve for $\nu = -(JC\Omega_e CJ')^{-1}(a - Js^\dagger)$; consequently, the benchmarked series is $\hat{\theta} = s^\dagger + V_e J'V_d^{-1}(a - Js^\dagger)$.

This notation permits a direct generalization of benchmarking with optimal estimation of θ using the information on the measurement errors instead of using a movement preservation criteria. It suffices to replace the matrix C by the diagonal matrix with the standard deviation of the measurement errors of the series s_t and Ω_e by the correlation matrix of the measurement errors so that $V_e = C\Omega_e C$ becomes the covariance matrix of the measurement error vector. Furthermore, if the benchmarks are subjected to measurement errors uncorrelated with those in s_t, then let $V_d = JV_e J' + V_\epsilon$, where V_ϵ is the covariance matrix of the measurement errors in the benchmarks. $\hat{\theta}$ is then the optimal estimator of θ when the bias is also estimated optimally using C, V_e, and V_ϵ. It is optimal in the sense that $\mathrm{E}(\hat{\theta} - \theta)^2$ is minimized. When $V_\epsilon > 0$, the benchmarks are not satisfied since $\hat{a} = J\hat{\theta} \neq a$; however, the estimator $\tilde{\theta} = s^\dagger + V_e J'(JV_e J')^{-1}(a - Js^\dagger)$ will be such that $J\tilde{\theta} = a$.

Calculation of the benchmarking prediction error covariance matrices is a little outside the scope of this chapter; nevertheless, assuming there is no bias, the measurement error model $s = \theta + e$ and $a = J\theta + \epsilon$ with e and ϵ uncorrelated will hold. Hence, $\hat{\theta} - \theta = s - \theta + V_e J'V_d^{-1}(a - Js) = e + V_e J'V_d^{-1}(\epsilon - Je)$ permits deriving the benchmarking prediction error covariance matrix of $\hat{\theta}$ easily since e and ϵ are uncorrelated. `PROC BENCHMARKING` does not in its current development stage calculate prediction error covariance matrices because this requires exact knowledge of the true V_e and V_ϵ matrices, which are design-dependent and usually partially unknown.

For $\rho = 1$, the original derivation can be found in Cholette (1984); however, we show it here to permit reprograming. Let Δ be the $T - 1 \times T$ first difference matrix with -1 at index (i, i), 1 at index $(i, i + 1)$, $i = 1, \ldots, T - 1$, and 0 elsewhere and let I_L be the $L \times L$ Identity matrix.

Minimization of Equation 10.3.6 entails minimizing the function $(s^\dagger - \theta)' C^{-1}\Delta'\Delta C^{-1}(s^\dagger - \theta) + 2\nu'(J\theta - a)$ with respect to the elements of θ and ν, where 2ν is the vector of Lagrange multipliers. Differentiation with respect to these elements leads to $C^{-1}\Delta'\Delta C^{-1}(s^\dagger - \theta) = J'\nu$ and $J\theta = a$. Rewriting these equations in terms of the unknown vectors θ and ν gives $C^{-1}\Delta'\Delta C^{-1}\theta + J'\nu = C^{-1}\Delta'\Delta C^{-1}s^\dagger$ and $J\theta = Js^\dagger + (a - Js^\dagger)$. This requires solving

$$\begin{bmatrix} C^{-1}\Delta'\Delta C^{-1} & J' \\ J & 0 \end{bmatrix} \begin{bmatrix} \theta \\ \nu \end{bmatrix} = \begin{bmatrix} C^{-1}\Delta'\Delta C^{-1} & 0 \\ J & I_L \end{bmatrix} \begin{bmatrix} s^\dagger \\ a - Js^\dagger \end{bmatrix}; \qquad (10.3.9)$$

hence

$$\begin{bmatrix} \hat{\theta} \\ \hat{\nu} \end{bmatrix} = \begin{bmatrix} C^{-1}\Delta'\Delta C^{-1} & J' \\ J & 0 \end{bmatrix}^{-1} \begin{bmatrix} C^{-1}\Delta'\Delta C^{-1} & 0 \\ J & I_L \end{bmatrix} \begin{bmatrix} s^\dagger \\ a - Js^\dagger \end{bmatrix}. \qquad (10.3.10)$$

The benchmarked series $\hat{\theta}$ and the Lagrange multipliers $\hat{\nu}$ from Equation 10.3.10 are linear combination of the vectors $s^\dagger$ and $(a - Js^\dagger)$; so, write $\hat{\theta} = s^\dagger + W(a -$
$Js^\dagger)$ and $\hat{\nu} = W_\nu(a - Js^\dagger)$ as the corresponding linear combinations since $\hat{\theta}$ is of dimension $T \times 1$ and $\hat{\nu}$ is of dimension $L \times 1$. In matrix notation:

$$\begin{bmatrix} \hat{\theta} \\ \hat{\nu} \end{bmatrix} = \begin{bmatrix} I_T & W \\ 0 & W_\nu \end{bmatrix} \begin{bmatrix} s^\dagger \\ a - Js^\dagger \end{bmatrix} \tag{10.3.11}$$

It follows from Equations 10.3.11 and 10.3.10 that

$$\begin{bmatrix} I_T & W \\ 0 & W_\nu \end{bmatrix} = \begin{bmatrix} C^{-1}\Delta'\Delta C^{-1} & J' \\ J & 0 \end{bmatrix}^{-1} \begin{bmatrix} C^{-1}\Delta'\Delta C^{-1} & 0 \\ J & I_L \end{bmatrix}; \tag{10.3.12}$$

so, W is the $T \times L$ upper-right corner matrix and W_ν is the $L \times L$ lower-right corner matrix of the product of matrices on the right-hand side of Equation 10.3.12.

10.4 Temporal and Contemporaneous Reconciliation Approaches

When considered independently, restoring temporal or cross-sectional constraints each has simple and well-known solutions, but in a joint reconciliation problem both sets of constraints have to be *simultaneously* met. How can this be done?

10.4.1 Simultaneous Approach

From a numerical point of view, the objective function (10.3.6) can be extended as

$$f(\theta) = \sum_{n=1}^{N}\sum_{m=1}^{M}\left[(1-\rho^2)\left(\frac{s^\dagger_{mn1} - \theta_{mn1}}{\left|s^\dagger_{mn1}\right|^\lambda}\right)^2 \right.$$
$$\left. + \sum_{t=2}^{T}\left\{\left(\frac{s^\dagger_{mnt} - \theta_{mnt}}{\left|s^\dagger_{mnt}\right|^\lambda}\right) - \rho\left(\frac{s^\dagger_{mn(t-1)} - \theta_{mn(t-1)}}{\left|s^\dagger_{mn(t-1)}\right|^\lambda}\right)\right\}^2\right] \tag{10.4.1}$$

subject to $\sum_{m=1}^{M}\theta_{mnt} = g_{.nt}$ for $n = 1, \ldots, N$ and $t = 1, \ldots, T$; $\sum_{n=1}^{N}\theta_{mnt} = g_{m.t}$ for $m = 1, \ldots, M$ and $t = 1, \ldots, T$; and $\sum_{t \in l}\theta_{mnt} = a_{mnl}$ for $m = 1, \ldots, M$, $n = 1, \ldots, N$ and $l = 1, \ldots, L$.

With a simultaneous approach, the goal can be to incorporate either the *contemporaneous* constraints (represented by the sums of m and n) to single benchmarking (Equation 10.3.6) or the movement preservation (represented by the ρ parameter) in prorating (Equation 10.3.4). The two approaches would yield different results as the "natural" selection of the weight parameter λ differs: $\lambda = 1$ for proportional Denton and $\lambda = 0.5$ for simple prorating.

As shown below, Equation 10.4.1 can also be extended to use alterability coefficients c_{mnt} in the denominator of each term in the equation. Even there, the natural selection for the reliability of s_{mnt} is to use the variance for proportional Denton and the standard error for prorating.

10.4.2 Least Squares Approach

Generalizing the least squares solution of the one-way classification as described by Equation 10.3.3, the joint benchmarking and reconciliation problem can also be written as a linear model and the solution computed from least squares.

Assume a mapping of the indices $(m, n, t), m = 1, \ldots, M,\ n = 1, \ldots, N,$ $t = 1, \ldots, T$ into the integers $1, \ldots, K$ and let $k = k(m, n, t) = (m_k, n_k, t_k)$. Let $\theta = (\theta_k)$ be the vector of the "true" value of interest (those that would meet the constraints), $s = (s_k)$ be the vector of the observed component values and $g = (g_h)$ be the vector of the constraints' values, where $h = 1, \ldots, H$ and H is the total number of contemporaneous and temporal constraints. Define G as a $H \times K$ constraint coverage matrix, i.e., a design matrix of 0 and 1 used to link the constraints with their components.

Like in Dagum and Cholette (2006), the model can be written as:

$$y = X\theta + \mu, \quad \mathrm{E}(\mu) = 0, \quad \mathrm{E}(\mu\mu') = V_\mu \tag{10.4.2}$$

where

$$y = \begin{bmatrix} s \\ g \end{bmatrix}, X = \begin{bmatrix} I_K \\ G \end{bmatrix}, \mu = \begin{bmatrix} e \\ \epsilon \end{bmatrix}, V_\mu = \begin{bmatrix} V_e & \mathrm{Cov}(e, \epsilon) \\ \mathrm{Cov}(\epsilon, e) & V_\epsilon \end{bmatrix}, \tag{10.4.3}$$

and I_K is the $K \times K$ identity matrix. For a reconciliation model, one has to properly describe the constraints coverage matrix G and most importantly, the variance matrix V_μ made of the variance matrix of e, of the variance matrix of ϵ, and of the covariance matrix between e and ϵ. Assuming that they are given, results from generalized least squares apply and the solution may be expressed as

$$\hat{\theta} = \left(X'V_\mu^{-1}X\right)^{-1} X'V_\mu^{-1}y. \tag{10.4.4}$$

When the required inverses do not exist—which is likely to happen given the structure of the data—the Moore–Penrose generalized inverse is used. In general, the size of the matrices involved in Equation 10.4.4 can become quite large when cross-correlation is allowed between the components series. Dagum and Cholette (2006, Section 11.2) provides a convenient expression of the solution (10.4.4) when $\mathrm{Cov}(e, \epsilon) = 0$, i.e., $\hat{\theta} = s + V_e G'(G V_e G' + V_\epsilon)^{-1}$ $(g - Gs)$.

The numerical minimization and the least squares approaches are related since, for given ρ and λ, one can identify a covariance matrix V_μ that would yield the same solutions. Conversely, this also means that the linear model-based approach has the same drawback as the pure numerical one: the implied covariance matrices will be different for solving temporal constraints than for solving contemporaneous constraints. As proposed in Dagum and Cholette (2006), one solution is to use a *two-step approach.*

10.4.3 Two-Step Approach

The two-step approach proposed by Dagum and Cholette (2006) can be summarized as follows. First, assume $\text{Cov}(e, \epsilon) = 0$, then for *Step 1*: benchmark each component series to its temporal constraints and compute the resulting error covariance matrices for each benchmarked series; and for *Step 2*: reconcile the contemporaneous constraints using the error covariance matrices computed in Step 1. With this solution, the matrix V_e in the second step becomes a block diagonal matrix where each diagonal subblock is itself the error covariance matrix associated with one series from Step 1. That is, the cross-correlation matrices between the benchmarking prediction error component series are assumed to be the null matrix. Even with this simplification, the size of the matrices involved in Step 2 can be large, and this usually leads to an extremely computer intensive solution like the simultaneous approach.

Quenneville and Rancourt (2005) presented an even more simplified two-step approach. For *Step 1*: benchmark each component series to its temporal constraints without computing any kind of error covariance matrices; and for *Step 2*: reconcile the contemporaneous constraints with a simple *weighted* (and not generalized) least squares approach; in other words, the covariance matrix V_μ in Step 2 may have terms on the diagonal but no covariance terms: neither between nor within the benchmarking prediction error vectors of the component series. When there is an annual benchmark, Step 2 only requires the joint use of the observations and constraints within the range of an annual benchmark; hence, the method is applied year by year. For contemporaneous constraints alone, processing for Step 2 is done by period.

The main advantage of this last approach is its simplicity. The univariate benchmarking of Step 1 may be achieved with any software package that implements temporal benchmarking, e.g., `PROC BENCHMARKING` or the `FORCE` spec of `X-12-ARIMA`. As Step 2 is only using a weighted least squares regression, it can be implemented with many types of software. Statistics Canada originally used `SAS`® `PROC REG` (see Quenneville and Rancourt 2005), but has been moving to the in-house procedure `PROC TSRAKING` to facilitate large-scale applications (see Quenneville and Fortier 2006; Bérubé and Fortier 2009). The year-by-year application also significantly reduces the size of the matrices involved and decreases the processing time.

10.4.4 Movement Preservation Issue

The simplified two-step approach of Quenneville and Rancourt (2005) is operationally interesting but seems very counterintuitive from a theoretical point of view. The full reconciliation problem requires that the contemporaneous and the temporal constraints be respected and ideally, this should be done without undue impact on the basic characteristics of the original component series. One of these characteristics is the period-to-period movement, which is usually associated with some covariance terms, at least in the V_e matrix. The two-step approach of Dagum and Cholette (2006) deletes $\mathrm{Cov}(e, \epsilon)$ and the covariance matrices between the benchmarking prediction errors of the component series; the two-step approach of Quenneville and Rancourt (2005) further deletes the covariances within the benchmarking prediction errors of each component series. How can the method by Quenneville and Rancourt (2005) "preserve" this movement if no covariance terms are used in Step 2?

The result comes from similar issues in the context of forecasts for hierarchical time series. Theorem 1 of Hyndman et al. (2007) states that the generalized least squares estimates of a linear regression model obtained using the Moore–Penrose can be independent of the covariance matrix (and thus be obtained from ordinary least squares) under some conditions. The main ideas are reproduced here for convenience.

Let the model and notation be as in Equation 10.4.2 with the added condition $\epsilon = Ge$, which implies $V_\mu = XV_eX' = V_e(I_K + GG')$.

With appropriately sized and ranked matrices, the Moore–Penrose inverse of the matrix product $A = BC$ can be written as $A^+ = C'(CC')^{-1}(B'B)^{-1}B'$.

Writing $V_\mu = BC$ with $B = XV_e$ and $C = X'$, the Moore–Penrose inverse of V_μ is $V_\mu^+ = X(X'X)^{-1}(V_eX'XV_e)^{-1}V_eX'$.

Using the Moore–Penrose inverse of $V_\mu = XV_eX'$ in Equation 10.4.4, the solution of the regression model can be written as

$$\begin{aligned}
\hat{\theta} &= (X'V_\mu^+X)^{-1}X'V_\mu^+y \\
&= [X'\{X(X'X)^{-1}(V_eX'XV_e)^{-1}V_eX'\}X]^{-1}(V_eX'XV_e)^{-1}V_eX'y \\
&= \{(V_eX'XV_e)^{-1}V_eX'X\}^{-1}(V_eX'XV_e)^{-1}V_eX'y \\
&= (V_eX'X)^{-1}(V_eX'XV_e)(V_eX'XV_e)^{-1}V_eX'y \\
&= (X'X)^{-1}V_e^{-1}V_eX'y \\
&= (X'X)^{-1}X'y \\
&= (I_K + G'G)^{-1}(s + G'g) \\
&= s + G'(I_H + GG')^{-1}(g - Gs).
\end{aligned}$$

To use this result in the context of the two-step method, let $Gs = G\theta + Ge$ and $g = G\theta + \epsilon$ so that $Gs - g = Ge - \epsilon$. Suppose the discrepancies $Gs - g$ are very small, i.e., $Gs \approx g$, then $\epsilon \approx Ge$. From this last approximation, the error vector μ in Equation 10.4.3 becomes $\mu \approx Xe$ and consequently, $V_\mu \approx XV_eX'$. How accurate is the $Gs \approx g$ approximation? For the temporal constraints, after Step 1, the discrepancies are exactly 0. So in Step 2, the only nonzero elements of the vector $(g - Gs)$ are those related to the contemporaneous constraints.

Various examples of reconciled series computed with and without covariance terms (i.e., with or without explicit movement preservation) are available in Fortier and Quenneville (2009), and they confirm that the covariances can be ignored with the two-step method. However, different alterability coefficients related to the variance (diagonal terms) make a significant difference to the results. In the Fortier and Quenneville (2009) paper, four methods in three sets of examples are compared: *SimL1*: simultaneous method where the movement is explicitly preserved ($\rho = 1$) and the "errors" are proportional to s^2 (i.e., $\lambda = 1$); *SimLh*: simultaneous method where the movement is explicitly preserved ($\rho = 1$) and the "errors" are proportional to s (i.e., $\lambda = 0.5$); *2StepL1*: two-step method where the movement is explicitly preserved in the first step only ($\lambda_1 = 1$ and $\rho_1 = 1$) and the "errors" in Step 2 are proportional to s^2 (i.e., $\lambda_2 = 1$ and $\rho_2 = 0$); *2StepLh*: two-step method where the movement is explicitly preserved in Step 1 only ($\lambda_1 = 1$ and $\rho_1 = 1$) and the "errors" in Step 2 are proportional to s (i.e., $\lambda_2 = 0.5$ and $\rho_2 = 0$); λ and ρ refer to Equation 10.4.1, λ_1 and ρ_1 refer to Equation 10.3.6, and λ_2 and ρ_2 refer to Equation 10.4.1.

Two conclusions emerged from that paper. First, given the temporally benchmarked series, setting $\rho_2 = 0$ in the reconciliation step of the two-step method gives results similar to those of the simultaneous approach. Hence, the two-step approach that uses weighted least squares in the reconciliation step is more appropriate for implementation purposes and practical convenience. Second, it is necessary to use $\lambda = 0.5$ to preserve the relative contribution of the components series to the total, before and after Step 2 (reconciliation).

When the relative contributions of the components series vary significantly, the discrepancies allocated to the largest components with method *SimL1* are large and often comparable in size to the overall discrepancies, leaving the smallest components almost unmodified. Method *2StepLh*, on the other hand, allocates a share of the overall discrepancies approximately equivalent to the contribution of each components.

To compare the four methods, a movement preservation measure was also used. The measure—also used in Di Fonzo and Marini (2011)—is a root mean squared adjustment (RMSA) to the percentage growth rate:

$$\mathrm{RMSA}_m = 100 * \sqrt{\frac{1}{T-1}\left\{\sum_{t=2}^{T}\left(\frac{s_{mt}}{s_{m(t-1)}} - \frac{\theta_{mt}}{\theta_{m(t-1)}}\right)^2\right\}} \text{ for } m = 1, \ldots, M.$$

The two methods with the errors proportional to s^2 (*SimL1* and *2StepL1* with $\lambda = 1$) give very similar results. The two other methods with errors proportional to s (*SimLh* and *2StepLh* with $\lambda = 0.5$) also show strong similarities. In other words, for a given value of λ, the methodological difference between the *Sim* methods and the *2Step* methods is related to the movement preservation issues; however, even without trying to explicitly preserve the movement in Step 2, the *2Step* methods give results almost identical to those from the *Sim* methods. As the *2Step* methods are applied year by year (see below in Section 10.4.5) and the size of the problem is considerably reduced, they also yield results much faster that their simultaneous counterpart.

A simple summary statistic such as the average of the RMSA_m, i.e., $\sum_{m=1}^{M} w_m \text{RMSA}_m$ with $w_m = 1/M$, could lead to the conclusion that the *L1* methods are "better" than the *Lh* methods; however, when weighted with w_m set to the % share, the weighted RMSA_m average are almost identical for all methods. Overall, similar conclusions were acknowledged in Di Fonzo and Marini (2011).

The *Lh* methods allocate the discrepancies proportionally to the level, which translates into evenhanded adjustments to the movements. Without external information on the quality of the initially measured series (level and movement), this seems a reasonable and rational guideline to provide as a default weighting scheme in the reconciliation step. The reader should consult Di Fonzo and Marini (2011) for an interpretation in favor of the *L1* methods.

If external information on the reliability of initial estimates is available, they can be used to specify the alterability coefficients in both Step 1 and 2. One could ask if the benchmarking prediction error covariance matrix $\text{E}(\hat{\theta} - \theta)^2$ from the benchmarking step should not be used as input into Step 2. The answer is that it is not necessary. This is because conditional on Step 1, using $\rho = 0$ or $\rho > 0$, does not produce significant differences in the Step 2; so, this means that the covariance terms from the benchmarking prediction error covariance matrix are not necessary but only the variance terms from the diagonal are required. Hence, in the two-step method of Dagum and Cholette (2006), after Step 1 and prior to Step 2, the benchmarking prediction error covariance matrix is recomputed with $\rho = 0$ to simplify the input to Step 2 and to speed up the computations; consequently, under suitable assumptions, this error covariance matrix reduces to a matrix proportional to C^2. Assuming standard errors are used for C, then C^2 is the initial variance of the measurement errors; however, as discussed above and in Dagum and Cholette (2006) (Chapter 11.3), it is more appropriate to use the standard errors instead of the variances to spread out the discrepancy among the alterable series more evenly.

The methodological details for `PROC TSRAKING` are provided to enable the reader to independently program them.

10.4.5 `PROC TSRAKING`

To implement the solution of Step 2, Statistics Canada developed an inhouse `SAS`® procedure called `PROC TSRAKING` using the `SAS`®`/TOOLKIT` software. The procedure and its functionalities are fully described in Bérubé and Fortier (2009). The implemented solution is conceptually in the form of Equation 10.4.4 with $V_\mu = block(V_e, V_\epsilon)$, $V_e = diag(c_s * s)$, $V_\epsilon = diag(c_g * g)$.

Here $*$ represents the elementwise product and *diag* refers to the diagonal matrix obtained with the corresponding vector of the main diagonal and 0 elsewhere. Using the block structure of the matrices involved, the matrix inversion lemma (also referred to as the Woodbury matrix identity)*, and matrix manipulation, the solution simplifies to

$$\begin{aligned}\hat{\theta} &= (X'V_{\mu}^{-1}X)^{-1}X'V_{\mu}^{-1}y \\ &= (V_e^{-1} + G'V_{\epsilon}^{-1}G)^{-1}(V_e^{-1}s + G'V_{\epsilon}^{-1}g) \\ &= s + V_eG'(GV_eG' + V_{\epsilon})^{-1}(g - Gs), \end{aligned} \tag{10.4.5}$$

PROC TSRAKING uses the Moore–Penrose inverse when required. In the definition of the variance matrices, the terms $c_s = (c_{s_k}), k = 1, \ldots, K$ and $c_{g_h}, h = 1, \ldots, H$ are vectors of *alterability coefficients* and lend much flexibility to the procedure. When $c_{g_h} = 0$, the corresponding constraint is considered as binding (i.e., the total g_h is nonalterable). Similarly in c_s, when $c_{s_k} = 0$, the component s_k would be nonalterable. When $c_{s_k} = 1$ for $k = 1, \ldots, K$, the problem is equivalent to its numerical version (10.4.1) with parameter $\lambda = 0.5$ and $\rho = 0$. When $c_{s_k} = s_k$ for $k = 1, \ldots, K$, the problem is equivalent to its numerical version (10.4.1) with parameter $\lambda = 1$ and $\rho = 0$. As no covariance terms are used in the solution, there is no *explicit* movement preservation that translates into $\rho = 0$ in the numerical setting of Equation 10.4.1. In general, alterability coefficients are used to input a prior knowledge about how much the values can be modified or altered by the reconciliation procedure.

Further exploitation of the structure reduces the calculations to the year-by-year application of Equation 10.4.5 when a temporal benchmark is present or to the period-by-period application when there is no such temporal constraints.

Examples of balancing such as one-way, two-way, both with or without known annual totals, and multiple calls of PROC TSRAKING are provided in Bérubé and Fortier (2009).

An alternative to explicitly program (10.4.5) is to specify the minimization problem and to solve it with an optimization software package, see Chen (2007), where the reliability of the initial values is also considered. One advantage of using a modern commercial solver is that it is often possible to also add the nonnegativity constraint of the resulting estimates if required.

10.5 Conclusions

In this chapter, we presented a typical example with seasonal adjustment of the Canadian MWTS to motivate the need for a benchmarking and reconciliation

* The identity states that for properly sized and defined matrices, $(A + UCV)^{-1} = A^{-1} - A^{-1}U(C^{-1} + VA^{-1}U)^{-1}VA^{-1}$, known as the Sherman–Woodbury formula.

methodology. The proposed solution uses simple methods that can be parameterized and easily interpreted using least squares fitting. It also employs the concept of alterability coefficients to account for the reliability of the values or to input prior information on which values can be modified and their extent. The approach is reproducible and purely numerical but can be justified in the frequentist or Bayesian contexts.

We provided references to direct the reader to examples that illustrate the application of the proposed methods or that confirm the theoretical justification of our proposed two-step method for simultaneous benchmarking and reconciliation. The examples also give some guidelines on specifying alterability coefficients and on interpreting summary statistics on movement preservation.

Finally, our proposed methods were described with enough details for a statistical agency to reprogram them into any computing environment. Statistics Canada's in-house `SAS`® procedures (`PROC BENCHMARKING` and `PROC TSRAKING`) may also be obtained for evaluation purposes (Forillon@statcan.gc.ca).

Acknowledgments

The authors would like to thank the editors for their invitation to present a chapter summarizing the time series methodology for official statistics, which we have developed to complement that developed at the U.S. Census Bureau. Over the years, we had a very good collaboration with Dr. David Findley, who was always very supportive of our work. Thanks are due to an associate editor and two referees for their valuable comments.

References

Bérubé, J. and Fortier, S. (2009). `PROC TSRAKING`: An in-house `SAS`® procedure for balancing time series. In *ASA Proceedings of the Business and Economic Section.* American Statistical Association.

Bloem, A. M., Dippelsman, R. J., and Mæhle, N. Ø. (2001). *Quarterly National Accounts Manual, Concepts, Data Sources and Compilation.* International Monetary Fund, Washington, DC.

Census Bureau, U. S. (2009). *X-12-ARIMA Reference Manuel.* Version 0.3. U.S. Census Bureau, Washington, DC.

Chen, B. (2007). A balanced system fo industry accounts for the US and estimated distribution of statistical discrepancy by industry. Technical Report, Bureau of Economic Analysis, Washington, DC. baoline.chen@bea.gov.

Cholette, P. A. (1984). Adjusting sub-annual series to yearly benchmarks. *Survey Methodology*, 10:35–49.

Cholette, P. A. and Dagum, E. B. (1994). Benchmarking time series with autocorrelated sampling errors. *International Statistical Review*, 62:365–377.

Dagum, E. B. (1988). *The `X-11-ARIMA/88` Seasonal Adjustment Method.* Statistics Canada, Ottawa, ON.

Dagum, E. B. and Cholette, P. A. (2006). *Benchmarking, Temporal Distribution and Reconciliation Methods for Time Series Data.* Springer-Verlag, New York. Lecture Notes in Statistics #186.

Denton, F. (1971). Adjustment of monthly or quarterly series to annual totals: An approach based on quadratic minimization. *Journal of the American Statistical Association*, 82:99–102.

Di Fonzo, T. and Marini, M. (2011). Simultaneous and two-step reconciliation of systems of time series: Methodological and practical issues. *Journal of the Royal Statistical Society – Series C (Applied Statistics)*, 60–2.

Ferland, M. and Fortier, S. (2009). Recent developments in Statistics Canada's time series processing system: Transition to `SAS®` `PROC X12`. In *ASA Proceedings of the Business and Economic Section.* American Statistical Association.

Findley, D. F., Monsell, B. C., Bell, W. R., Otto, M. C., and Chen, B. C. (1998). New capabilities and methods of the `X-12-ARIMA` seasonal-adjustment program. *Journal of Business and Economic Statistics*, 16:127–177.

Fortier, S. and Quenneville, B. (2007). Theory and application of benchmarking in business surveys. In *Proceedings of the International Conference on Establishment Surveys III.* American Statistical Association.

Fortier, S. and Quenneville, B. (2009). Reconciliation and balancing of accounts and time series: From concepts to a `SAS®` procedure. In *ASA Proceedings of the Business and Economic Section.* American Statistical Association.

Hyndman, R. J., Ahmed, R. A., and Athanasopoulos, G. (2007). Optimal combination forecasts for hierarchical time series. Technical Report, Monash University, Australia. Working paper ISSN 1440–771X.

Latendresse, E., Djona, M., and Fortier, S. (2007). Benchmarking sub-annual series to annual totals – from concepts to `SAS®` procedure and `SAS®`

enterprise guide custom task. In *Proceedings of the SAS Global Forum 2007 Conference*. SAS Institute Inc.

Quenneville, B. and Fortier, S. (2006). Balancing seasonally adjusted series as a complement to the direct and indirect approaches to seasonal adjustment. In *ASA Proceedings of the Business and Economic Section*. American Statistical Association.

Quenneville, B. and Rancourt, E. (2005). Simple methods to restore the additivity of a system of time series. In *2005 Eurostat Workshop on Frontiers in Benchmarking Techniques and Their Application to Official Statistics*.

Stone, J. N. R., Champernowne, D. G., and Meade, J. E. (1942). The precision of national income estimates. *Review of Economic Studies*, 9:111–125.

11

Theoretical and Real Trading-Day Frequencies

Dominique Ladiray

CONTENTS

11.1 Introduction

Practically, all economic time series are computed and published according to the Gregorian calendar, a calendar based on the motion of the earth around the sun. This solar calendar also brings rhythm to our lives and usually has a deep impact on the economy. The most well-known and important calendar effect is seasonality, often defined as fluctuations observed during the year (each month, each quarter) that appear to repeat themselves with a more or less regular magnitude from one year to the other. But most economic indicators are also linked, directly or indirectly, to a daily activity, which is usually summed up and reported each month or each quarter. In this case, the number of working days, which varies from one month to another in a quasi-predetermined way, can explain some short-term movements in the time series. One more Saturday in a month, for example drastically impacts the retail trade turnover in European countries. Apart from the day composition of the month, other calendar effects such as public holidays or religious events may also affect the series. Religious events are often closely linked to other calendars and their dates, expressed in the Gregorian calendar, may not be fixed. This is the case for Easter whose date, linked to the full moon, is usually expressed in the Gregorian calendar for Western Christian countries and in the Julian calendar for Eastern Orthodox countries.

These periodic fluctuations, as well as seasonality, are usually detected and eliminated in order to exhibit the irregular and nonperiodic movements, which are probably of most interest and importance. In this paper, we focus on the trading-day effect caused by the day composition of the month (or quarter) that changes across time. In Section 11.2, we construct the periodograms corresponding to the seven days of the week and we derive the main theoretical trading-day frequencies for monthly and quarterly data. In Section 11.3, we exhibit the most common real trading-day frequencies from a large set of economic indicators. Finally, in Section 11.4, we check the accuracy of the "visual spectral test" implemented in X-12-ARIMA (U.S. Census Bureau 2009). We use simulated series to determine the significance level of this diagnostic and to assess its power. The results permit us to propose some improvements to the test, especially for quarterly data but, as far as the detection of constant trading day is concerned, it is shown that the F-test and approximate equivalents will almost always perform better.

11.2 Theoretical Trading-Day Frequencies

The Gregorian calendar* is the one commonly used today. In this calendar, the concept of a year, and its length (the tropical year), are based on the earth's motion around the sun. A usual year is made of 12 months—January, February, March, April, May, June, July, August, September, October, November, and December—with respective numbers of days 31, 28, 31, 30, 31, 30, 31, 31, 30, 31, 30, and 31. A usual year, therefore, contains 365 days, which is unfortunately a bit too short, and the approximation of the tropical year is achieved by having in the Gregorian calendar 97 special years every 400 years (the leap years) in which February has 29 days. A leap year is a year divisible by 4 but not by 100, unless the year is also divisible by 400. So 1900 was not a leap year, 2000 was a leap year, and 2100 will not be a leap year.

Each period of 400 years thus contains $400 \times 365 + 97 = 146{,}097$ days, which is exactly 20,871 weeks. The Gregorian calendar is thus periodic with period 400 years. The average length of a year over this cycle is $146{,}097/400 = 365.2425$ days. The average length of a month is $365.2425/12 = 30.436875$ days.

* See Tøndering (2008) for more details.

11.2.1 Distributions of the Numbers of Each Day of the Week

Given the 400 year cycle of the calendar, it is easy to compute, over one complete cycle, the seven monthly (or quarterly) distributions of the numbers of each day of the week. Basic statistics and correlations have been computed on the seven distributions and on the weekday series (# Mondays + # Tuesdays + ··· + # Fridays). The results are displayed in Table 11.1 for monthly data and in Table 11.2 for quarterly data. It clearly appears that the day distributions have the same basic characteristics but that, especially in the monthly case, they are not independent: e.g., the correlation coefficient may rise up to −0.53 between Sunday and Wednesday.

11.2.2 Periodograms of the Various Days

Using a 400-year cycle permits one to get very good estimates of the periodograms and it appears that the seven days have very similar periodograms.* Figures 11.1 and 11.2 (upper panels) show the periodograms of the series number of Sundays per month or quarter.

The periodograms computed on the raw data present some seasonality mainly due to a length-of-month, or length-of-quarter, effect. For example, the second quarter of the year has always 13 weeks and does not induce any trading-day effect. This seasonality is even more evident on the weekday periodograms (see Figures 11.1 and 11.2 lower left panels, where the vertical dash lines indicate the main seasonal frequency harmonics). The raw data can be easily seasonally adjusted by removing from each day its long-term average observed for each month (or quarter). Then the periodograms computed on the centered distributions show the main trading-day frequencies (see Figures 11.1 and 11.2, right panels). The main theoretical trading-day frequencies ordered by their magnitude for monthly and quarterly data are presented in Tables 11.3 and 11.4. If the seven day-of-week distributions have roughly the same important frequencies, sometimes with a slightly different order, the situation is quite different for monthly and quarterly data.

Monthly periodograms are characterized by two important frequencies only: 0.348125, the highest one, and 0.431458, as all other frequencies seem negligible. On the contrary for quarterly data, after removing the very important seasonal frequency, several trading-day frequencies appear. The frequency 0.294375 is the most important followed by 0.338750 and 0.205625. But they are immediately followed by other frequencies that could also be considered: 0.044375, 0.383125, 0.455625, and 0.411250.

It is difficult to find a rational explanation for these frequencies, even the most important. One can notice that the main monthly frequency (0.348125) is an alias of the average number of weeks per month, since dividing the average month length (30.436875) by 7 gives 4.348125. The same computation done for

---

* McNulty and Huffman (1989) reached a quite different conclusion but they only used a 28-year cycle, which is a very crude approximation of the real periodicity of the calendar.

TABLE 11.1
Basic Statistics on the Distributions of the Numbers of Each Day of the Week (Monthly Data)

		Sunday	**Monday**	**Tuesday**	**Wednesday**	**Thursday**	**Friday**	**Saturday**	**Weekdays**
Mean		4.3481	4.3481	4.3481	4.3481	4.3481	4.3481	4.3481	21.7406
STD		0.4764	0.4764	0.4764	0.4764	0.4764	0.4764	0.4764	0.9614
N		33600	33600	33600	33600	33600	33600	33600	33600
Corr	Sunday	1	0.4115	−0.1659	−0.5340	−0.5340	−0.1668	0.4088	−0.4902
Corr	Monday	0.4115	1	0.4088	−0.1687	−0.5340	−0.5340	−0.1677	0.0853
Corr	Tuesday	−0.1659	0.4088	1	0.4106	−0.1650	−0.5340	−0.5340	0.5552
Corr	Wednesday	−0.5340	−0.1687	0.4106	1	0.4106	−0.1677	−0.5340	0.7358
Corr	Thursday	−0.5340	−0.5340	−0.1650	0.4106	1	0.4097	−0.1659	0.5556
Corr	Friday	−0.1668	−0.5340	−0.5340	−0.1677	0.4097	1	0.4115	0.0862
Corr	Saturday	0.4088	−0.1677	−0.5340	−0.5340	−0.1659	0.4115	1	−0.4907
Corr	Weekdays	−0.4902	0.0853	0.5552	0.7358	0.5556	0.0862	−0.4907	1

TABLE 11.2
Basic Statistics on the Distributions of the Numbers of Each Day of the Week (Quarterly Data)

		Sunday	**Monday**	**Tuesday**	**Wednesday**	**Thursday**	**Friday**	**Saturday**	**Weekdays**
Mean		13.0444	13.0444	13.0444	13.0444	13.0444	13.0444	13.0444	65.2219
STD		0.3101	0.3121	0.3101	0.3121	0.3101	0.3101	0.3101	0.6663
N		11200	11200	11200	11200	11200	11200	11200	11200
Corr	Sunday	1	−0.0203	−0.0205	−0.0203	−0.0205	−0.0205	−0.0205	−0.0477
Corr	Monday	−0.0203	1	−0.0203	−0.0202	−0.0203	−0.0203	−0.0203	0.4306
Corr	Tuesday	−0.0205	−0.0203	1	−0.0203	−0.0205	−0.0205	−0.0205	0.4273
Corr	Wednesday	−0.0203	−0.0202	−0.0203	1	−0.0203	−0.0203	−0.0203	0.4306
Corr	Thursday	−0.0205	−0.0203	−0.0205	−0.0203	1	−0.0205	−0.0205	0.4273
Corr	Friday	−0.0205	−0.0203	−0.0205	−0.0203	−0.0205	1	−0.0205	0.4273
Corr	Saturday	−0.0205	−0.0203	−0.0205	−0.0203	−0.0205	−0.0205	1	−0.0477
Corr	Weekdays	−0.0477	0.4306	0.4273	0.4306	0.4273	0.4273	−0.0477	1

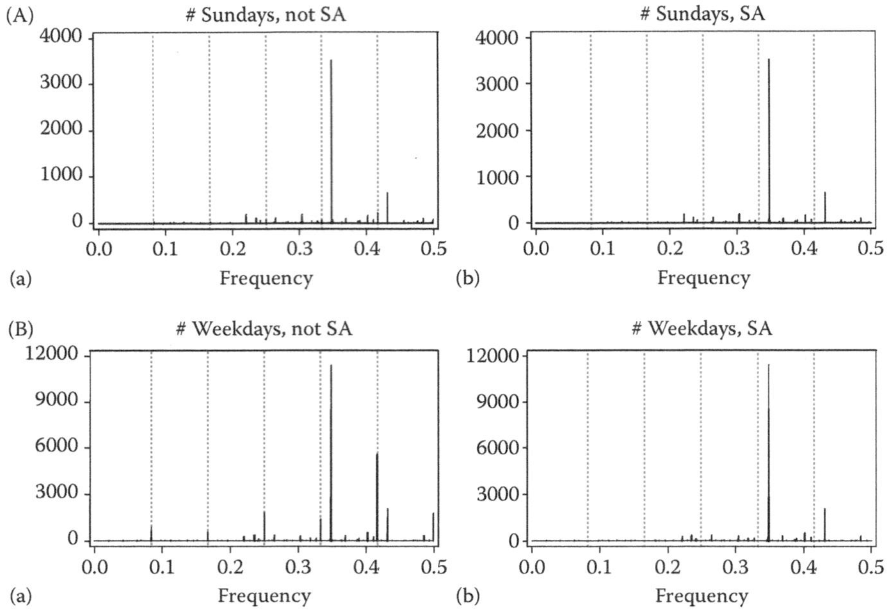

FIGURE 11.1
Day-of-the-week and weekday periodograms for monthly data. Periodograms are computed for the # of Sundays (A) and the weekday series (# Mondays + # Tuesdays $+ \cdots +$ # Fridays, (B)); and on raw (not SA) data (Aa and Ba) or seasonally adjusted (SA) data (Ab and Bb).

quarterly series comes to an average number of weeks per quarter of 13.044375, which aliases to 0.044375, a frequency that only ranks sixth in the quarterly day-of-week periodograms.

11.3 Real Trading-Day Frequencies

The real trading-day effect is in fact a linear combination of the basic day effects. As the day-of-the-week distributions are not independent, the frequencies attached to a real trading-day effect may be different from the theoretical ones. For example, if we consider the weekday series, we can notice in Tables 11.3 and 11.4 that the frequency ranked sixth in the monthly and quarterly day periodograms is ranked fourth in the weekday periodograms. In consequence, the theoretical trading-day frequencies may not be the ones that are observed in real time series. A large scale study was conducted on the series from both the Organization for Economic Cooperation and Development (OECD) Main Economic Indicators database and the Eurostat Euro-Indicators database on real time series to validate the previous results.

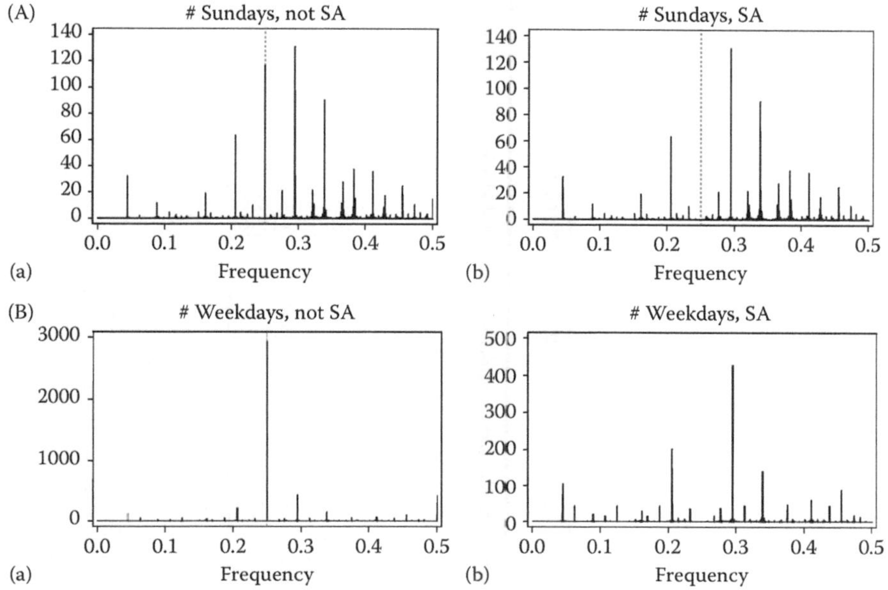

FIGURE 11.2
Day-of-the-week and weekday periodograms for quarterly data. Periodograms are computed for the # of Sundays (A) and the weekday series (# Mondays + # Tuesdays + ⋯ + # Fridays, (B)); and on raw (not SA) data (Aa and Ba) or seasonally adjusted (SA) data (Ab and Bb).

The complete set of raw data contains 13683 monthly series and 9665 quarterly series. A first adjustment with X-12-ARIMA, using all default parameters, selected 4173 monthly series and 1880 quarterly series with a significant trading-day effect (with 1 or 6 trading-day regressors). These 6053 series are then adjusted without any trading-day estimation. In this case, we expect the trading-day effect to be part of the irregular component. Then, for each series, we compute the values of the irregular periodogram on a set of frequencies including the main theoretical frequencies. These frequencies are then ranked according to their magnitude in the periodogram, and the results for the 6053 series are pooled.

The results are displayed in Table 11.5. For the monthly series, the results are quite clear: the same two frequencies (0.348125 and 0.431458) rank first and second for both sets of regressors. But it is difficult to distinguish between the other main frequencies as their importance changes according to the number of regressors used in the regression. Note that these two frequencies are those used for monthly series by X-12-ARIMA version 0.3 in its "visual spectral test" and exhibited by Cleveland and Devlin (1980).

The situation is less clear with the quarterly series, as the scores obtained by the main frequencies are not as high. It is therefore quite difficult to

TABLE 11.3
The 10 Main Theoretical Frequencies Associated with a Monthly Trading-Day Effect

	Sunday	**Monday**	**Tuesday**	**Wednesday**	**Thursday**	**Friday**	**Saturday**	**Weekdays**
1	0.348125	0.348125	0.348125	0.348125	0.348125	0.348125	0.348125	0.348125
2	0.431458	0.431458	0.431458	0.431458	0.431458	0.431458	0.431458	0.431458
3	0.220417	0.303750	0.303750	0.303750	0.303750	0.303750	0.303750	0.401875
4	0.303750	0.220417	0.220417	0.220417	0.220417	0.220417	0.220417	0.264792
5	0.401875	0.401875	0.401875	0.401875	0.401875	0.401875	0.401875	0.235208
6	0.264792	0.264792	0.235208	0.264792	0.235208	0.264792	0.235208	0.485208
7	0.235208	0.235208	0.264792	0.235208	0.264792	0.235208	0.264792	0.368958
8	0.485208	0.368958	0.485208	0.368958	0.485208	0.485208	0.485208	0.303750
9	0.368958	0.485208	0.368958	0.485208	0.368958	0.368958	0.368958	0.220417
10	0.347917	0.347917	0.347917	0.347917	0.410625	0.347917	0.347917	0.347917

TABLE 11.4
The 10 Main Theoretical Frequencies Associated with a Quarterly Trading-Day Effect

	Sunday	**Monday**	**Tuesday**	**Wednesday**	**Thursday**	**Friday**	**Saturday**	**Weekdays**
1	0.294375	0.294375	0.294375	0.294375	0.294375	0.294375	0.294375	0.294375
2	0.338750	0.338750	0.338750	0.338750	0.338750	0.338750	0.338750	0.205625
3	0.205625	0.205625	0.205625	0.205625	0.205625	0.205625	0.205625	0.338750
4	0.383125	0.411250	0.383125	0.411250	0.411250	0.383125	0.411250	0.044375
5	0.411250	0.383125	0.411250	0.383125	0.383125	0.411250	0.383125	0.455625
6	0.044375	0.044375	0.044375	0.044375	0.044375	0.044375	0.044375	0.411250
7	0.366875	0.455625	0.366875	0.455625	0.366875	0.366875	0.366875	0.375000
8	0.455625	0.366875	0.455625	0.366875	0.455625	0.455625	0.455625	0.125000
9	0.320625	0.276250	0.276250	0.276250	0.320625	0.320625	0.320625	0.062500
10	0.276250	0.320625	0.161250	0.320625	0.276250	0.276250	0.276250	0.187500

TABLE 11.5
The Main Real Frequencies Associated with a Trading-Day Effect

	Monthly Series				
		1 Regressor		**6 Regressors**	**Total**
Frequency	**%**	**Theoretical Rank**	**%**	**Theoretical Rank**	**%**
0.348125	32.89	1	27.50	1	30.29
0.431458	31.92	2	21.53	2	26.90
0.401875	10.28	3	6.78	5	8.59
0.391667	10.10	>10	2.38	>10	6.37
0.395833	7.30	>10	1.81	>10	4.65
0.303750	0.96	8	7.97	4	4.34
0.479167	1.45	>10	7.08	>10	4.17
0.475000	0.11	>10	6.21	>10	3.05
0.470833	0.08	>10	4.18	>10	2.06
0.454167	.	>10	4.03	>10	1.95

	Quarterly Series				
		1 Regressor		**6 Regressors**	**Total**
Frequency	**%**	**Theoretical Rank**	**%**	**Theoretical Rank**	**%**
0.294375	7.66	1	14.08	1	10.59
0.338750	9.80	3	11.2	2	10.44
0.383125	13.43	>10	0.55	5	7.54
0.429375	8.79	>10	0.17	>10	4.85
0.437500	1.12	>10	8.77	>10	4.62
0.341667	2.33	>10	7.33	>10	4.62
0.375000	1.93	7	7.74	>10	4.59
0.320625	6.31	>10	0.14	9	3.49
0.291667	1.70	>10	5.1	>10	3.26
0.475000	3.46	>10	2.88	>10	3.19

Note: For quarterly series, the frequency 0.383125 ranks third in 7.5% of the cases. But it ranks first (13.4%) when a weekday regressor was used even if in the theoretical weekday periodogram this frequency does not belong to the 10 most important.

distinguish between the four following frequencies: 0.294375, 0.338750, 0.383125, and 0.429375. Note that for quarterly series, X-12-ARIMA version 0.3 only uses 0.044375 and 0.088750 in its "visual spectral test." These trading-day frequencies do not appear in the results of the experiment.

11.4 X-12-ARIMA "Visual Spectral Test"

X-12-ARIMA version 0.3 (U.S. Census Bureau, 2009) provides spectral plots and associated interpretative messages to alert the user to the presence of seasonal and trading-day effects in the original series, and to the presence of residual effects in the residuals of the RegARIMA model, the seasonally adjusted series, and the irregular component. Warning messages are based on an empirically obtained criterion of "visual significance." X-12-ARIMA calculates values of the spectrum (or periodogram) at 61 frequencies, including the seasonal and trading-day frequencies, and graphs the results in the output file using line printer plots (see Figure 11.3). Both seasonal and trading-day frequencies are marked on the graph. When larger than the median of the spectral estimates, a "6-star" peak at one of the seasonal or trading-day frequencies is considered "visually significant" with one star corresponding to 1/52nd of the range between the maximum and minimum spectral values (Soukup and Findley, 1999). By default, X-12-ARIMA uses the last 96 observations (8 years for a monthly series and 24 years for a quarterly series) in its calculations of the spectrum. The "6-star" peak is examined for visual significance in relation to the values of the spectral estimate at the two (respectively six) adjacent frequencies plotted for monthly (respectively quarterly) data. In the case of trading-day, a peak in the spectrum at one of the trading-day frequencies shows the need for trading-day estimation.

11.4.1 An Important Remark

When checking for the presence of seasonal and trading-day effects in the original and seasonally adjusted series, the "visual spectral test" is applied to the spectrum of the first differenced series. The first difference operator $(X_t - X_{t-1})$ is an asymmetric linear filter, which is used here to remove the trend part of the series. The gain of the transfer function of the first difference filter is equal to $|G(\lambda)| = \sqrt{2 - 2\cos\lambda}$.

Table 11.6 shows the effect of the first difference operator on the trading-day frequencies. As noted by Zhang et al. (2005), a large part of the main spectral power of the trading-day variation in quarterly series is also a part of the trend-cycle and is therefore filtered out: more than 70% of frequency 0.044375 and 45% of frequency 0.088750 are removed by the high-pass filter. It turns out that the detection of trading-day frequencies by means of the spectrum will be more difficult for quarterly series than for monthly series for which trading-day frequencies are, on the contrary, amplified by the filter.

11.4.2 Various Parameters of the Simulation

The methodology used here to determine the significance level of the "visual spectral test" and to assess its power is based on simulations and is very similar to the methodology used in Lytras et al. (2007). We simulated a series from 22 different nonseasonal and seasonal ARIMA (autoregressive-integrated-moving average) models with various parameters. All of them have a zero mean and an innovation variance equal to 1. These models illustrate the various cases when the "visual spectral test" is used: to check for residual trading-day effects

```
++++++++++I+++++++++++++++++++++++++++++++++++++++++++++++++++++++++++++I
    -14.92I                              S                              I   -14.92
          I                    S         S         S         S          I
          I                    S         S         S         S          I
          I                    S         S         S         S          I
    -18.70I                    S         S         S         S          I   -18.70
          I                    S         S         S         S         SI
          I                    S         S         S         S         SI
          I          S         S         S         S         S         SI
    -22.47I          S         S         S         S         S*        SI   -22.47
          I          S         S         S         S*        S*        SI
          I          S         S         S         S*        S*        SI
          I          S         S         S         S*T       S*        SI
    -26.25I          S         S        *S         S*T       S*        SI   -26.25
          I          S         S        *S         S*T       S*T       SI
          I          S        *S        *S*        S*T       S*T       SI
          I          S        *S*       *S*        S*T       S*T       SI
    -30.03I          S       **S*       *S**      *S*T      *S*T       SI   -30.03
          I        * S       **S*       *S**      *S*T      *S*T*   *  SI
          I        **S       **S*      **S**     **S*T      *S*T*   *  SI
          I       ***S      ***S**     **S***    **S*T     **S*T*   * *SI
    -33.81I       ***S      ***S**     **S***    **S*T     **S*T*  ****SI   -33.81
          I*      ***S      ***S**    ***S***    **S*T*   ***S*T** ****SI
          I*  *   ***S      ***S**    ***S***    **S*T*   ***S*T** ****SI
          I* **   ***S*    ****S**    ***S***  * **S*T*   ***S*T** ****SI
    -37.59I* **   ***S*    ****S**    ***S***  * **S*T*   ***S*T** ****SI   -37.59
          I* *** ****S*    ****S**    ***S***  ****S*T*   ***S*T** ****SI
          I* *** ****S*    ****S***   ***S***  ****S*T** ****S*T** ****SI
          I***** ****S*  * ****S***   ***S***  ****S*T** ****S*T** ****SI
    -41.36I***** ****S*  * ****S***   ***S***  ****S*T** ****S*T** ****SI   -41.36
          I***** ****S* ** ****S***   ***S**** ****S*T*******S*T** ****SI
          I***** ****S* ** ****S***   ***S**** ****S*T*******S*T** ****SI
          I***** ****S* ** ****S***   ***S**** ****S*T*******S*T** ****SI
    -45.14I***** ****S* ** ****S***   ***S**** ****S*T*******S*T** ****SI   -45.14
          I***** ****S* ** ****S***   ***S**** ****S*T*******S*T** ****SI
          I***** ****S* ** ****S***   ***S**** ****S*T*******S*T*******SI
          I***** ****S**** ****S***  ****S**** ****S*T*******S*T*******SI
    -48.92I***** ****S**** ****S***  ****S**** ****S*T*******S*T*******SI   -48.92
          I***** ****S**** ****S***  ****S**** ****S*T*******S*T*******SI
          I**********S**** ****S***  ****S**** ****S*T*******S*T*******SI
          I**********S*********S**** ****S**** ****S*T*******S*T*******SI
    -52.70I**********S*********S**** ****S**** ****S*T*******S*T*******SI   -52.70
          I**********S*********S**** ****S*********S*T*******S*T*******SI
          I**********S*********S**** ****S*********S*T*******S*T*******SI
          I**********S*********S**** ****S*********S*T*******S*T*******SI
    -56.48I**********S*********S**** ****S*********S*T*******S*T*******SI   -56.48
          I**********S*********S**** ****S*********S*T*******S*T*******SI
          I**********S*********S**** ****S*********S*T*******S*T*******SI
          I**********S*********S**** ****S*********S*T*******S*T*******SI
    -60.25I**********S*********S**** ****S*********S*T*******S*T*******SI   -60.25
          I**********S*********S**** ****S*********S*T*******S*T*******SI
          I**********S*********S**** ****S*********S*T*******S*T*******SI
          I**********S*********S**** ****S*********S*T*******S*T*******SI
    -64.03I**********S*********S*********S*********S*T*******S*T*******SI   -64.03
++++++++++I+++++++++++++++++++++++++++++++++++++++++++++++++++++++++++++I
                S = Seasonal frequencies, T = Trading-day frequencies
```

FIGURE 11.3
A spectrum ouput by X-12-ARIMA. The seasonal frequencies are represented with an S; the trading-day frequencies with a T.

TABLE 11.6
Impact of the First-Difference Operator on the Trading-Day Frequencies (Values of the Gain Function)

Monthly Series		Quarterly Series	
Frequency	**Gain**	**Frequency**	**Gain**
0.348125	1.777	0.044375	0.278
0.431458	1.954	0.088750	0.550
		0.294375	1.597
		0.338750	1.749
		0.383125	1.867
		0.429375	1.951

in the RegARIMA residuals and the irregular component (white noise), in the seasonally adjusted series (nonseasonal models), and in the original series (seasonal models). The models used are:

- ARIMA (0 0 0)
- ARIMA (0 1 0)
- ARIMA (0 1 1), with $\theta = 0.3$, 0.5, and 0.8
- ARIMA (1 1 0), with $\phi = 0.3$, 0.5, and 0.8
- ARIMA (0 1 0)(0 1 1), with $\Theta = 0.5$ and 0.8
- ARIMA (0 1 1)(0 1 1), with $\theta = 0.3$, 0.5, 0.8 and $\Theta = 0.5$ and 0.8
- ARIMA (1 1 0)(0 1 1), with $\phi = 0.3$, 0.5, 0.8 and $\Theta = 0.5$ and 0.8

In these models, θ, ϕ, and Θ are the nonseasonal moving average (MA) and autoregressive (AR), and seasonal MA parameters.

We simulate monthly and quarterly series of different lengths: 8, 14, 20 and 26 years.

Three different trading-day components are used to model the trading-day effect. These components (see Figure 11.4) have been selected from a hierarchical cluster analysis performed on the previous 6053 indicators presenting a trading-day effect. One of the selected effects is common in production indicators, another in export series, and the last one in European retail trade series. These three trading-day components have been standardized: the sum of the seven coefficients is equal to zero and their variance is equal to 1.

A series presenting a trading-day effect is simulated as $X_t = \text{ARIMA}_t + \alpha TD_t$, where the α scale factors have been selected from the observed size

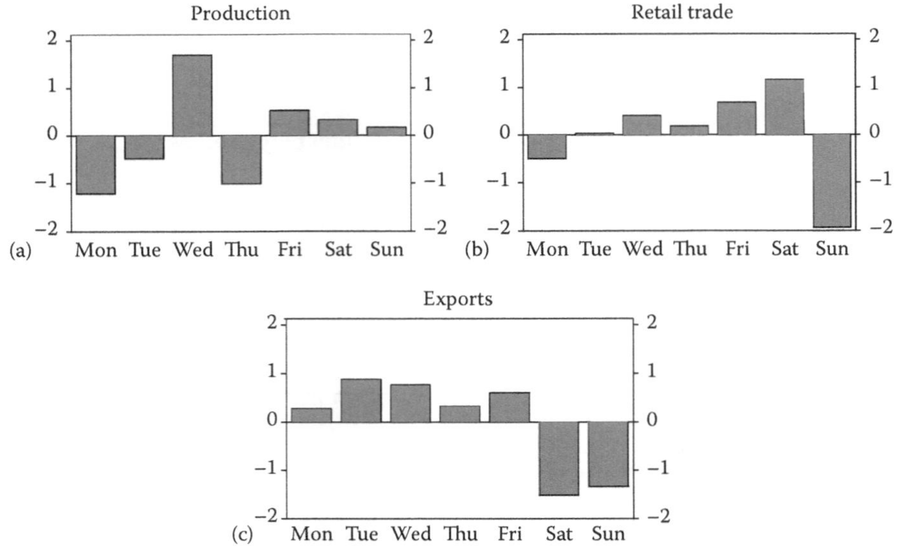

FIGURE 11.4
Trading-day coefficients. The first trading-day effect (a) refers to a production series, the second one (b) to a retail trade index, and the last one (c) to an export series.

of the trading-day components of our 6053 real time series. The scale factors used for the experiment are 0.1, 0.3, and 0.5.

11.4.3 The "Visual Tests"

An *SAS*© macro has been developed to compute some "visual tests." This routine offers more flexibility for the simulations than the X-12-ARIMA program itself. The main macro parameters are:

- The type of spectral estimate used in the spectral plots output by the program: the periodogram and an autoregressive model spectrum.
- The width of the band used to determine spectral peaks (the `peakwidth` parameter in X-12-ARIMA). The values 1, 2, 3, 4 and 5 are used in the simulations.*
- The trading-day frequencies for monthly series are those already used in X-12-ARIMA, 0.348125 and 0.431458, and another important frequency exhibited in Section 11.3, 0.401875.

* In X-12-ARIMA, the `peakwidth` parameter is by default set to 1 for monthly series and to 3 for quarterly series, but integer values from 1 to 5 are permitted.

- The trading-day frequencies for quarterly series are those used in X-12-ARIMA, 0.044375 and 0.088750, and three important frequencies exhibited in Section 11.3: 0.294375, 0.338750 and 0.383125.

The "visual tests" are computed on the raw series for the (0 0 0) model, which simulates an irregular or residual component, and on the first-differenced series for the other models, which simulate either a seasonally adjusted series (nonseasonal models) or an original series (seasonal models).

11.4.4 Methodology

We therefore have 22 different ARIMA models, 2 periodicities, and 4 different series lengths, which comes to 176 different kinds of series with no trading-day effect. We also have 3 different trading-day components and 3 scale factors and this comes to 1584 kinds of series with a trading-day effect. For each of these cases, 1000 time series are simulated. Two "visual tests" and two tests based on the maximum likelihood (ML) estimation of the RegARIMA model are considered to detect a trading-day effect:

- The "X-12 test" based on frequencies 0.348125 and 0.431458 for monthly data, and frequencies 0.044375 and 0.088750 for quarterly data.

- A "New test" based on the previous frequencies plus some important frequencies exhibited in Section 11.3: 0.401875 for monthly data and 0.294375, 0.338750, and 0.383125 for quarterly data.

  A trading-day effect is considered significant if the spectrum estimate at a trading-day frequency satisfies the "6-star" criterion. On each series, the visual tests are computed for both the periodogram and the AR spectrum and for the five possible values of the `peakwidth` parameter.

- The "Chi-squared test" based on the regression done by X-12-ARIMA to estimate the trading-day coefficients (U.S. Census Bureau, 2009). It also calculates t-statistics to determine if the individual parameter estimates are different from zero, and conducts a chi-squared test to see if the parameters are collectively zero, using the test statistic $\hat{\chi}^2 = \hat{\beta}'[\text{Var}(\hat{\beta})^{-1}]\hat{\beta}$. When X-12-ARIMA calculates this statistic, it must estimate the innovation variance. We can correct the chi-squared test to account for error in the estimation of the innovation variance by using the test statistic F^M, calculated as follows: $F^M = [\hat{\chi}^2/k] \times [(n-d-k)/(n-d)]$. Here n is the number of observations in the series, d is the degree of differencing, and k is the number of elements estimated in β, six in our case (the six trading-day contrasts). F^M approximately follows an $F_{k,n-d-k}$ distribution under the null hypothesis of no trading-day effect.

The various tests are computed on the complete length of the series. The global performance of each test is then summarized by the percentage of the 1000 series that show a significant trading-day effect.

Several model-based alternatives for testing for trading-day should perform similarly to the F^M test in moderate to large samples. This includes the $\hat{\chi}^2$ test just mentioned, along with the likelihood ratio (LR) test, and model comparisons made using Akaike's information criterion (AIC, Akaike, 1974), or the bias corrected AIC (AICC) criterion (Hurvich and Tsay, 1989). Note that X-12-ARIMA's "aictest" of trading-day is based on AICC comparisons (Soukup and Findley, 2000). The F^M, $\hat{\chi}^2$, and LR tests are asymptotically equivalent (Silvey, 1975), though one would expect the F^M test to somewhat better maintain its nominal significance level in moderate length series, as was found by Lytras et al. (2007) for the corresponding F^M and $\hat{\chi}^2$ tests of fixed seasonality. Use of AIC or AICC compares the LR trading-day test statistic against certain criterion values determined from their overfitting "penalty terms." The similarity of using AIC and AICC comparisons for trading-day to the hypothesis tests at a 5% level of significance is facilitated by a somewhat coincidental closeness of the criteria for testing the significance of six parameters.*

Table 11.7 summarizes the results† when there is no trading-day effect in the simulated series. In this case, the significance level of the test can be interpreted as a "false alarm rate": a trading-day effect is detected when no trading-day effect is present. Due to the random aspect of the simulations, a rate close to 5% seems *a priori* acceptable.

Table 11.8 summarizes the results when a trading-day effect is present in the simulated series. In this case, the power of the test can be interpreted as a "detection rate." In these simulations, the higher the rate, the more efficient the test. Due to the random aspect of the simulations, a rate close to 95% would be good at least if the size of the test is close to 5%. Unfortunately, as Table 11.7 shows substantial variations in the sizes of the diagnostics, the power results of the original tests would be difficult to interpret. This is why Table 11.8 presents results obtained using size-adjusted critical values, which are critical values determined from the simulations so that the rejection probability under the null is approximately 5%.

As the performances of the tests depend on many parameters—tested frequencies, spectral estimate, model of the series, kind of trading-day effect, length and periodicity of the series, etc.—the choice of the right test is therefore a trade-off between its size and power and between the "false alarm rate" and the "detection rate."

---

* To test for trading-day, AIC compares the LR statistic against $2 \times 6 = 12$, while the χ^2_6 5% critical value used for $\hat{\chi}^2$ and the LR test is 12.6. The criterion values derived from AICC's penalty terms for six parameters depend on the series length n and the model being used. With a series following an airline model with no regression variables other than for trading day, the AICC criteria are 14.2 for $n = 96$ (8 years) and 13.0 for $n = 180$ (15 years). The corresponding F-distribution critical values used by F^M are 13.3 and 12.9, respectively.

† As the amount of data generated by the simulations is huge, we focus in the following on the main results. Thus, the results given in Tables 11.7 and 11.8 for a particular model pool simulations for the different parameter values and series lengths. Most of the cross effects are trivial and so are not discussed. However, all results are available from the author.

TABLE 11.7
Significance Level ("False Alarm Rates") of the Various Tests according to the Characteristics of the Series and the Parameters of the Spectral Estimate

		Quarterly Series					Monthly Series				
		AR-Spectrum		Periodogram		Regression	AR-Spectrum		Periodogram		Regression
		X-12	New	X-12	New	F^M	X-12	New	X-12	New	F^M
PeakW	1	0.001	0.001	0.093	0.225	0.035	0.028	0.041	0.149	0.212	0.037
	2	0.021	0.038	0.122	0.307	0.035	0.091	0.127	0.084	0.119	0.037
	3	0.070	0.132	0.126	0.317	0.035	0.098	0.138	0.164	0.231	0.037
	4	0.122	0.231	0.123	0.304	0.035	0.136	0.193	0.212	0.311	0.037
	5	0.151	0.291	0.123	0.304	0.035	0.186	0.281	0.248	0.354	0.037
Model	(0,0,0)	0.176	0.355	0.233	0.470	0.030	0.299	0.425	0.263	0.373	0.041
	(0,1,0)	0.176	0.355	0.236	0.474	0.049	0.295	0.424	0.261	0.369	0.035
	(0,1,1)	0.033	0.195	0.108	0.379	0.037	0.217	0.314	0.244	0.348	0.035
	(1,1,0)	0.193	0.278	0.217	0.401	0.045	0.135	0.193	0.181	0.258	0.038
	(0,1,0)(0,1,1)	0.038	0.076	0.110	0.267	0.030	0.084	0.124	0.165	0.237	0.037
	(0,1,1)(0,1,1)	0.006	0.038	0.046	0.226	0.029	0.059	0.088	0.155	0.227	0.035
	(1,1,0)(0,1,1)	0.076	0.089	0.107	0.207	0.034	0.034	0.048	0.118	0.167	0.039
Length	8	0.108	0.181	0.095	0.229	0.024	0.145	0.214	0.174	0.250	0.041
	14	0.077	0.145	0.118	0.292	0.040	0.108	0.160	0.183	0.267	0.036
	20	0.058	0.121	0.127	0.316	0.038	0.093	0.133	0.164	0.229	0.033
	26	0.048	0.107	0.129	0.328	0.037	0.085	0.118	0.165	0.236	0.036
	All	0.073	0.139	0.117	0.291	0.035	0.108	0.156	0.171	0.245	0.037

Note: No trading-day effect in the series.

TABLE 11.8
Power ("Detection Rate") of the Various Tests according to the Characteristics of the Series and the Parameters of the Spectral Estimate

		Quarterly Series					Monthly Series				
		AR-Spectrum		Periodogram		Regression	AR-Spectrum		Periodogram		Regression
		X-12	New	X-12	New	F^M	X-12	New	X-12	New	F^M
PeakW	1	0.001	0.001	0.092	0.369	0.541	0.235	0.240	0.634	0.660	0.766
	2	0.020	0.045	0.119	0.474	0.541	0.350	0.363	0.344	0.356	0.766
	3	0.066	0.151	0.123	0.463	0.541	0.413	0.427	0.676	0.701	0.766
	4	0.113	0.263	0.120	0.478	0.541	0.588	0.611	0.733	0.764	0.766
	5	0.140	0.332	0.120	0.388	0.541	0.603	0.640	0.724	0.766	0.766
Model	(0,0,0)	0.167	0.367	0.262	0.573	0.345	0.619	0.676	0.645	0.694	0.600
	(0,1,0)	0.138	0.352	0.218	0.619	0.563	0.767	0.801	0.787	0.816	0.752
	(0,1,1)	0.022	0.197	0.099	0.492	0.440	0.612	0.649	0.677	0.717	0.675
	(1,1,0)	0.193	0.335	0.216	0.614	0.651	0.774	0.787	0.825	0.841	0.829
	(0,1,0)(0,1,1)	0.030	0.090	0.104	0.405	0.568	0.340	0.357	0.580	0.607	0.786
	(0,1,1)(0,1,1)	0.005	0.045	0.042	0.325	0.461	0.236	0.251	0.483	0.517	0.704
	(1,1,0)(0,1,1)	0.076	0.119	0.108	0.381	0.635	0.331	0.337	0.615	0.631	0.863
Length	8	0.100	0.197	0.089	0.257	0.271	0.426	0.458	0.486	0.524	0.658
	14	0.072	0.164	0.114	0.387	0.549	0.455	0.474	0.624	0.657	0.754
	20	0.054	0.142	0.127	0.511	0.647	0.439	0.452	0.671	0.690	0.808
	26	0.046	0.130	0.130	0.582	0.696	0.430	0.439	0.708	0.727	0.843
TD effect	Exports	0.068	0.149	0.114	0.435	0.535	0.506	0.520	0.677	0.698	0.760
	Production	0.068	0.173	0.117	0.438	0.531	0.314	0.339	0.523	0.558	0.768
	Retail Trade	0.068	0.153	0.114	0.431	0.556	0.493	0.509	0.667	0.692	0.768
Scale	1	0.070	0.138	0.114	0.312	0.118	0.181	0.219	0.337	0.393	0.361
	3	0.070	0.163	0.115	0.451	0.635	0.494	0.506	0.704	0.723	0.939
	5	0.064	0.174	0.116	0.541	0.869	0.638	0.642	0.825	0.833	0.997
	All	0.068	0.158	0.115	0.434	0.541	0.438	0.456	0.622	0.649	0.766

Note: A trading-day effect is present in the series. Size-adjusted critical values are used to assess the power of the "visual tests."

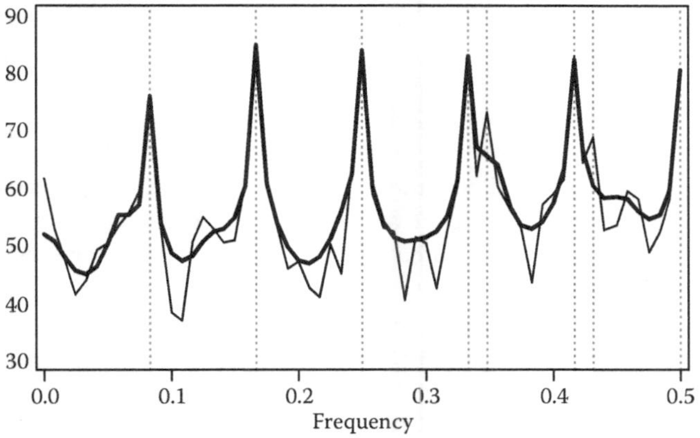

FIGURE 11.5
Periodogram (thin line) and AR-spectrum (bold line) of the Canadian Retail Trade Turnover Index.

11.4.5 Testing for a Trading-Day Effect in Monthly Series

Even if the results vary according to the characteristics of the series, the "X-12 visual test"* applied to the periodogram, with a `peakwidth` parameter equal to 1, appears to be the best of the four visual spectral tests for detecting a trading-day effect in a monthly time series.

Figure 11.5 illustrates the main fault of the AR-spectrum in trading-day effect detection. The monthly Canadian Retail Trade Index presents a trading-day effect that clearly appears in the periodogram, but not in the AR-spectrum, which is too smooth in this case. This explains the large difference between the two average "detection rates:" 62% when the test is applied to the periodogram against 44% when applied to the AR-spectrum. As a consequence of the AR-spectrum smoothness, the "false alarm rate" is much smaller when the test is applied to the AR-spectrum: 11% against 17%. The simulation results reported here for the X-12 visual test are broadly similar to the results reported by Soukup and Findley (1999), who determined the 6-star criterion to achieve a 10%–15% false alarm rate in a simulation study. The simulations were done quite differently from those reported here. Soukup and Findley simulated series by taking X-12-ARIMA seasonal plus trend plus irregular decompositions of 42 time series (all of which had trading-day detected by an AIC comparison) and "bootstrapping" the irregular components (drawing irregulars with replacement from the 42 estimated irregulars and combining these with the estimated seasonal and trend components to form simulated series.). The X-12 spectral diagnostic with the 6-star criterion detected trading-day effects in about 80% of the simulated series.

* Applying the "6-star" rule to the two main trading-day frequencies (0.348125 and 0.431458).

Testing one more frequency (0.401875) does not really improve the test: the average "detection rate" gains three points only (62% to 65%) while the "false alarm rate" jumps from 17% to 24%.

The length of the series does not have a big effect on the "false alarm rate," but impacts the "detection rate," which goes from 52% for an 8-year series to 73% for a 26-year series. The simulations also show that a length of at least 14 years is recommended to expect a "detection rate" equal or superior to 66%.

The kind of trading-day effect (exports, production, or retail trade) does not have a big effect on the test performance. But the magnitude of the trading-day effect has, as expected, a huge effect on the "detection rate" that increases from 39%, for a scale factor equal to 0.1, to 83% for a scale factor of 0.5.

Finally, the performances of the "X-12 visual tests" vary according to the complexity of ARIMA model. A trading-day effect seems to be easier to detect in nonseasonal models. Table 11.9 shows the link between the performance of the tests, the length of the series, and the model. The "false alarm" rates are also given for the complete set of 22 models. It clearly appears that the "detection rate" for seasonal series strongly increases with the length of the series and the span used to compute the periodogram. The test does not behave well with airline series, the most common model in economic time series, as the trading-day effect is detected only for 53% of 20-year long time series.

It is clear from the simulations that the F-test outperforms the "visual tests" for seasonal models: their "false alarm rates" are stable and remain under 5% while their "detection rates" reach an average of 77% and are almost always superior to those of the "visual tests." In particular, they are close to 1 when the trading-day effect is large enough (scale equal to 0.3 and up).

11.4.6 Testing for a Trading-Day Effect in Quarterly Series

The performance of the current "X-12 visual test" for quarterly series is indeed very poor: both the "false alarm rate" and the "detection rate" are on average small, close to 7%. Because of the calendar, a quarterly trading-day effect is often smaller than a monthly trading-day effect*, and more difficult to detect as it is not concentrated on a small number of frequencies. Moreover, as we already noticed, the first difference operator tends to eliminate a part of the quarterly trading-day effect. Consequently, the AR-spectrum is likely too smooth to show this effect.

To detect a trading-day effect in a quarterly series, it appears from the simulations that the best test is definitely the F-test. Its "false alarm rate" is stable and remains under 5% while its "detection rate" reaches a quite low average of 54% but is always superior to those of the "visual tests." The "New visual test" based on the periodogram presents by construction a much higher

---

* A quarter contains always 13 weeks + 0 or 1 day, while a month contains always 4 weeks + 0, 1, 2, or 3 days.

TABLE 11.9
Performances of the Tests for Monthly Series according to the Model and the Length of the Series

		8 Years			14 Years			20 Years			26 Years		
Model	**Params**	**X-12**	**New**	F^M	**X-12**	**New**	F^M	**X-12**	**New**	F^M	**X-12**	**New**	F^M
No TD effect													
(0,0,0)		0.262	0.364	0.043	0.254	0.364	0.039	0.271	0.373	0.038	0.260	0.356	0.046
(0,1,0)		0.262	0.352	0.032	0.264	0.361	0.036	0.293	0.398	0.039	0.258	0.356	0.034
(0,1,1)	0.3	0.267	0.372	0.037	0.274	0.373	0.035	0.302	0.412	0.040	0.263	0.368	0.042
(0,1,1)	0.5	0.252	0.348	0.033	0.260	0.361	0.033	0.294	0.395	0.035	0.247	0.349	0.037
(0,1,1)	0.8	0.223	0.316	0.034	0.225	0.317	0.026	0.252	0.346	0.027	0.209	0.298	0.037
(1,1,0)	0.3	0.225	0.309	0.040	0.217	0.306	0.040	0.253	0.344	0.037	0.216	0.308	0.046
(1,1,0)	0.5	0.186	0.263	0.032	0.184	0.263	0.039	0.220	0.289	0.031	0.180	0.255	0.043
(1,1,0)	0.8	0.138	0.203	0.033	0.143	0.200	0.033	0.163	0.223	0.031	0.135	0.195	0.048
(0,1,0)(0,1,1)	0.5	0.032	0.054	0.046	0.182	0.256	0.049	0.055	0.082	0.036	0.122	0.163	0.026
(0,1,0)(0,1,1)	0.8	0.092	0.154	0.044	0.202	0.298	0.037	0.113	0.163	0.035	0.186	0.267	0.026
(0,1,1)(0,1,1)	0.3, 0.5	0.031	0.055	0.044	0.178	0.254	0.035	0.053	0.073	0.038	0.113	0.159	0.037
(0,1,1)(0,1,1)	0.3, 0.8	0.096	0.147	0.044	0.197	0.296	0.035	0.117	0.175	0.037	0.183	0.264	0.037
(0,1,1)(0,1,1)	0.5, 0.5	0.034	0.056	0.040	0.178	0.255	0.032	0.051	0.071	0.032	0.107	0.150	0.039
(0,1,1)(0,1,1)	0.5, 0.8	0.090	0.140	0.035	0.192	0.287	0.031	0.114	0.168	0.032	0.174	0.249	0.036
(0,1,1)(0,1,1)	0.8, 0.5	0.027	0.045	0.033	0.159	0.227	0.031	0.038	0.055	0.030	0.098	0.131	0.036
(0,1,1)(0,1,1)	0.8, 0.8	0.079	0.123	0.032	0.176	0.259	0.026	0.093	0.140	0.031	0.147	0.215	0.038
(1,1,0)(0,1,1)	0.3, 0.5	0.028	0.047	0.054	0.166	0.236	0.048	0.038	0.053	0.032	0.105	0.144	0.034
(1,1,0)(0,1,1)	0.3, 0.8	0.077	0.125	0.050	0.184	0.274	0.042	0.082	0.117	0.031	0.166	0.233	0.034
(1,1,0)(0,1,1)	0.5, 0.5	0.019	0.029	0.060	0.135	0.203	0.044	0.032	0.047	0.035	0.087	0.122	0.032
(1,1,0)(0,1,1)	0.5, 0.8	0.063	0.101	0.059	0.140	0.209	0.045	0.069	0.097	0.031	0.132	0.184	0.031
(1,1,0)(0,1,1)	0.8, 0.5	0.014	0.019	0.048	0.080	0.121	0.031	0.022	0.031	0.032	0.062	0.084	0.037
(1,1,0)(0,1,1)	0.8, 0.8	0.039	0.065	0.037	0.095	0.140	0.029	0.035	0.056	0.025	0.106	0.150	0.030

(continued)

TABLE 11.9 (Continued)

	8 Years			14 Years			20 Years			26 Years		
Model	**X-12**	**New**	F^M	**X-12**	**New**	F^M	**X-12**	**New**	F^M	**X-12**	**New**	F^M
With TD effect												
(0,0,0)	0.511	0.581	0.445	0.629	0.690	0.593	0.705	0.745	0.663	0.731	0.771	0.697
(0,1,0)	0.680	0.723	0.670	0.779	0.810	0.738	0.843	0.867	0.783	0.862	0.881	0.818
(0,1,1)	0.538	0.595	0.558	0.651	0.689	0.672	0.736	0.771	0.720	0.757	0.787	0.748
(1,1,0)	0.723	0.748	0.736	0.815	0.833	0.808	0.880	0.893	0.867	0.898	0.908	0.908
(0,1,0)(0,1,1)	0.323	0.352	0.696	0.670	0.705	0.767	0.636	0.653	0.819	0.765	0.787	0.863
(0,1,1)(0,1,1)	0.223	0.251	0.593	0.546	0.589	0.703	0.506	0.528	0.744	0.652	0.678	0.777
(1,1,0)(0,1,1)	0.374	0.393	0.754	0.720	0.741	0.844	0.702	0.712	0.909	0.817	0.829	0.947
All	0.418	0.450	0.658	0.670	0.702	0.754	0.678	0.698	0.808	0.768	0.789	0.843

Note: The "visual tests" are computed on the periodogram of the complete series. When a trading-day effect is present, size-adjusted critical values are used to assess the power of the "visual tests." The power results given in this second part of the table pool simulations across different parameter values for a given model, and across all models for the "All" row.

"false alarm rate" than the current "X-12 visual test" (29.1% on average) but also a better "detection rate" (43.4% on average).

As in the monthly case, the length of the series does not have a big effect on the "false alarm rate" but impacts the "detection rate," which goes for the F-test (respectively the "New visual test") from 27% for an 8-year series (respectively 26%) to 70% for a 28-year series (respectively 58%). The simulations show also that a length of at least 20 years is recommended to have a "detection rate" superior to 64% (respectively 51%).

The kind of trading-day effect (exports, production, or retail trade) does not have a big effect on the test performance. But the magnitude of the trading-day effect has, as expected, a huge effect on the "detection rate" that increases for the F-test from 12%, for a scale factor equal to 0.1, to 87% for a scale factor of 0.5.

Finally, as in the monthly case, the performances of the tests vary according to the ARIMA model. A trading-day effect seems to be easier to detect in nonseasonal series; among seasonal models, the airline model presents the lowest "detection rate."

11.5 Conclusions

The identification of the main theoretical trading-day frequencies from the calendar periodogram gives some ways to slightly improve the "visual test" currently proposed in X-12-ARIMA. This test can certainly be enhanced by using the periodogram instead of the AR-spectrum that appears to be too smooth, especially for quarterly series. If the set of trading-day frequencies used in the test is correct in the monthly case, it should be extended for quarterly series to three other frequencies (0.294375, 0.338750 and 0.383125). These modifications will improve the "detection rate" while, unfortunately, increasing the "false alarm rate."

The performance of the test could perhaps be improved by considering another spectral estimate, a smoothed version of the periodogram using various kernels (Tukey, Bartlett, Parzen, etc.) or a different cutoff (an "n-star" test). But this "visual test" will always lack a proper statistical background. As the test performance also depends on the underlying model, a promising alternative could be the nonparametric test recently proposed by McElroy and Holan (2009).

The F-test obtained from a fitted RegARIMA model gives better results for trading-day detection in all the cases considered and it, or one of its rough equivalents (LR test or AIC test), should probably be preferred. Its size is close to the nominal 5%, so it performed much better as a hypothesis test than did the trading-day spectral diagnostics.*

* Lytras et al. (2007) reached a similar conclusion for seasonality diagnostics.

Soukup and Findley (1999) suggested that one can view the spectral diagnostics as a tool for flagging series that may contain the trading day, with these results to be followed up by a formal test from fitting a RegARIMA model. But it has to be remembered that this test is related to fixed trading-day effects and the "spectral visual tests" could be used to detect stochastic time-varying trading day effects.* This possibility opens the field for future research.

Acknowledgments

This work was part of a research program supported by Eurostat, the statistical office of the European Community. The author would like to thank William Bell and Demetra Lytras, both from the U.S. Census Bureau, and to two anonymous referees for their kind help and their very useful comments.

References

Akaike, H. (1974). A new look at the statistical model identification. *IEEE Transactions on Automatic Control*, 19:716–723.

Bell, W. R. (2004). On RegComponent time series models and their applications. In *State Space and Unobserved Component Models: Theory and Applications*, eds. A. C. Harvey, S. J. Koopman, and N. Shephard, 248–283. Cambridge, UK: Cambridge University Press.

Cleveland, W. and Devlin, S. (1980). Calendar effects in monthly time series: Detection by spectrum analysis and graphical methods. *Journal of the American Statistical Association*, 75:487–496.

Harvey, A. C. (1989). *Forecasting, Structural Time Series Models and the Kalman Filter*. Cambridge: Cambridge University Press.

Hurvich, C. M. and Tsai, C. (1989). Regression and time series model selection in small samples, *Biometrika*, 76:297–307.

Lytras, D., Feldpausch, R. and Bell, W. R. (2007). Determining seasonality: A comparison of diagnostics from X-12-ARIMA. In *Proceedings of the Third International Conference on Establishment Surveys (ICES-III)*, Montréal, Canada.

* Models for stochastic time-varying trading-day effects have been proposed by Harvey (1989) and Bell (2004).

McElroy, T. and Holan, S. (2009). A nonparametric test for residual seasonality. *Survey Methodology*, 35:67–83.

McNulty, M. S. and Huffman, W. E. (1989). The sample spectrum of time series with trading day variation. *Economics Letters*, 31:367–370.

Silvey, S. D. (1975). *Statistical Inference.* London: Chapman and Hall.

Soukup, R. J. and Findley, D. F. (1999). On the spectrum diagnostics used by X-12-ARIMA to indicate the presence of trading day effects after modeling or adjustment. In *Proceedings of the American Statistical Association, Business and Economic Statistics Section*, 144–149. Alexandria, VA: American Statistical Association.

Soukup, R. J. and Findley, D. F. (2000). Detection and modeling of trading-day effects. In *Proceedings of the 2nd International Conference on Establishment Surveys.*

Tøndering, C. (2008). Frequently asked questions about calendars, version 2.9. Technical Report. URL: http://www.tondering.dk/claus/cal/calendar29.pdf.

U.S. Census Bureau (2009). X-12-ARIMA reference manual, Version 0.3. Time Series Staff Statistical Research Division U.S. Census Bureau, Washington, DC. URL: http://www.census.gov/ts/x12a/v03/x12adocV03.pdf.

Zhang, M., Apted, L., Hudson, J. and Outteridge, T. (2005). Trading-day effect estimation for quarterly time series. In *Proceedings of the International Statistical Institute.*

12

Applying and Interpreting Model-Based Seasonal Adjustment—The Euro-Area Industrial Production Series

Agustín Maravall and Domingo Pérez

CONTENTS

12.1 Introduction

The economic crisis of the last 3 years has had an impact on the behavior of economic series, and models and methods used by statisticians and economists have had a difficult time dealing with it. The *European Statistical System (ESS) Guidelines for Seasonal Adjustment* (Eurostat 2009), aimed at harmonizing and providing guidelines for seasonal adjustment within the ESS, was completed as the crisis unfolded. The Guidelines did not specifically deal with a crisis like the present one, and seasonal adjusters have felt disoriented. In July 2010, a workshop was held at the European Central Bank (ECB) on implementation of the Guidelines and on ways to treat the crisis; 15 central banks and 20 statistical offices were present. One of the sessions centered on seasonal adjustment of the Euro-Area Industrial Production (EIP) series, and this chapter expands on the comment we contributed.

One point under discussion was the behavior of the monthly, seasonally adjusted (SA) EIP series in recent periods. The official adjustment carried out by Eurostat for the period January 1990–March 2010 (243 observations) is displayed in Figure 12.1. Because the economic recession has introduced significant uncertainties, some ECB statisticians conducted alternative test calculations, which led them to suspect that official SA monthly rates of growth for the past few months were too high (Eiglsperger and Haine 2010). Figure 12.2 compares the SA monthly growth rates of Eurostat with those of the Eiglsperger and Haine (EH) procedure for the last few years of the period considered. The slope of the recovery in the last few months of the sample is clearly higher for the Eurostat SA series.

While Eurostat uses the TRAMO–SEATS (TS) method*, EH tests were performed with X-12-ARIMA (X12A). TS and X12A are widely used procedures and are the two methods considered in the ESS Guidelines. The programs and documentation can be downloaded from the U.S. Census Bureau and Bank of Spain web sites (www.census.gov/srd/www/x12a, and www.bde.es/webbde/en/secciones/servicio/software/econom.html, respectively). Overviews of the two methodologies can be found in Findley et al. (1998), Gómez and Maravall (2001a,b) and Findley (2005). Both methods consist of two steps. First, the series is preadjusted; second, it is seasonally

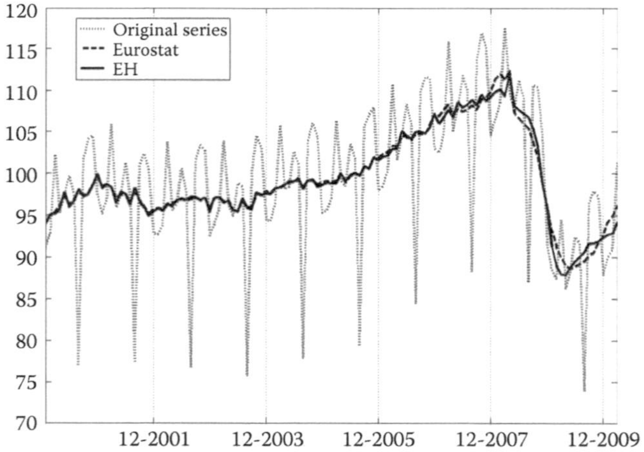

FIGURE 12.1
The official SA series (Eurostat) and the alternative (EH) proposal.

* TRAMO stands for "Time Series Regression with ARIMA noise, Missing observations, and Outliers." SEATS stands for "Signal Extraction in ARIMA Time Series."

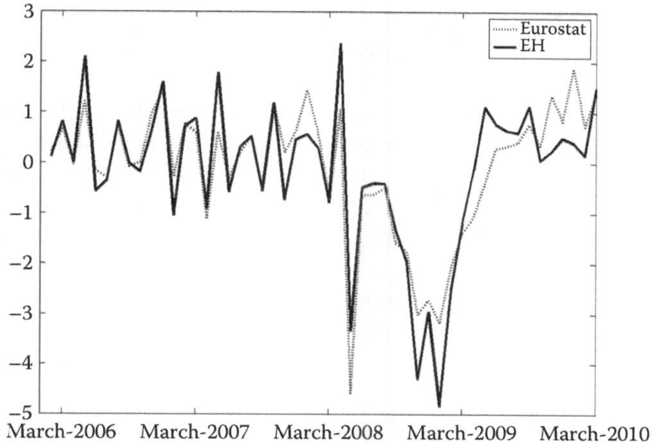

FIGURE 12.2
Rates of growth of the SA series (last four years).

adjusted. The preadjustment step determines a possible transformation of the data, and identifies (often automatically) a regression(reg)-ARIMA model. This model is used to extend the series with forecasts, and to identify and estimate outliers, calendar, and other effects captured through regression variables. In the second step, a filter is applied to the extended series—net of outliers and regression effects—to obtain estimators of the (stochastic) SA series, as well as of the seasonal, trend-cycle, and irregular components. Combining them with the outliers and regression effects, the final estimators of the components are obtained.

The previous general structure is common to both methods. The similarities in the preadjustment step are many (e.g., the "*automdl*" option of X12A is based on the automatic model identification procedure in TRAMO). The adjustment step, on the contrary, follows different methodologies. The filter of X12A is selected from a set of *a priori* designed filters (X11 in essence). SEATS follows the so-called ARIMA-model-based (AMB) approach (see Burman (1980), Hillmer and Tiao (1982), and Bell and Hillmer (1984)). The filter in SEATS yields the minimum-mean-squared-error (MMSE) estimator of a theoretically specified component. This filter is often referred to as the Wiener–Kolmogorov (WK) filter. The component model is derived from the ARIMA model identified and fitted to the observed series. The two approaches represent different philosophies, and this has repercussions in terms of analysis, diagnostics, and interpretation of results. Due to the continuity in the X11-X12A family, 50 years of use have made users familiar with its output. This is not quite the case for TS and for how its output can be used to evaluate seasonal adjustment.

Because a seasonal component is never observed and no universal definition is available, it is difficult to compare the results from different adjustment methods in a systematic manner. Within the model-based approach, however, a framework for systematic analysis is indeed present. In this chapter, the EPI series is analyzed under the TS model-based framework. No comparison of different methods is made; our aim is to show how the results can be exploited at the identification, diagnostic, and inference stages of modeling.

For the rest of the chapter, unless otherwise specified, model-based diagnostics and inference are derived and computed under the assumption that the model is correct. The results should be interpreted thus as a "best case" approximation in which model parameters are "known." (Some improvements that take into account parameter estimation error are presented in Blakely and McElroy (2011) and Bell (2005).)

12.2 The Series and the "Alternative" Procedure

The seasonal adjustment method suggested by EH is X12A with the following specifications: log transformation, two level shift outliers (November 2008 and January 2009), no correction for calendar effects, and $(0,1,1)(0,1,1)_{12}$ ARIMA model orders (i.e., those of an Airline model). As shown in Figure 12.3, the seasonal factors obtained are reasonably stable and, as seen in the first row of Table 12.1, the residuals pass the Bera–Jarque test for normality.

But the output of X12A flags some problems: (a) the residuals are autocorrelated; (b) the in-sample forecast errors are large; (c) a peak at the TD frequency is detected in the spectra of the residuals, differenced log SA series, and irregular component; (d) the autocorrelation function (ACF) of the squared residuals indicates some nonlinearity. Direct inspection of Figure 12.4 shows, for the last 2 years, an accumulation of large negative residuals followed by a sequence of mostly positive ones. This abnormal behavior coincides with the crisis period.

To understand the model choice, X12A was run automatically with the automdl option and all pretests included. The series is modeled in levels, five outliers are detected (one is the November 2008 level shift outlier), significant calendar effects are found, and the identified ARIMA is a $(1,1,2)(0,1,1)_{12}$ model. The EH regARIMA model and the one automatically detected by X12A are considerably different, and the automatic result provides a better fit. The residuals show no evidence of autocorrelation and all normality tests, as well as the Q2 test on the squared residuals, are comfortably passed. However, a few problems remain: the in-sample forecast errors are still large, a peak in the residual spectrum is found at the TD frequency, and the M4 X12A statistic signals too much autocorrelation in the irregular component. The problems, however, do not seem major. The forecast problem is mostly associated with the recent crisis, the TD peak is moderate, and the M4 statistic is of little interest (MMSE estimators of a white noise irregular in an ARIMA series ought to be autocorrelated; see Maravall (1987)).

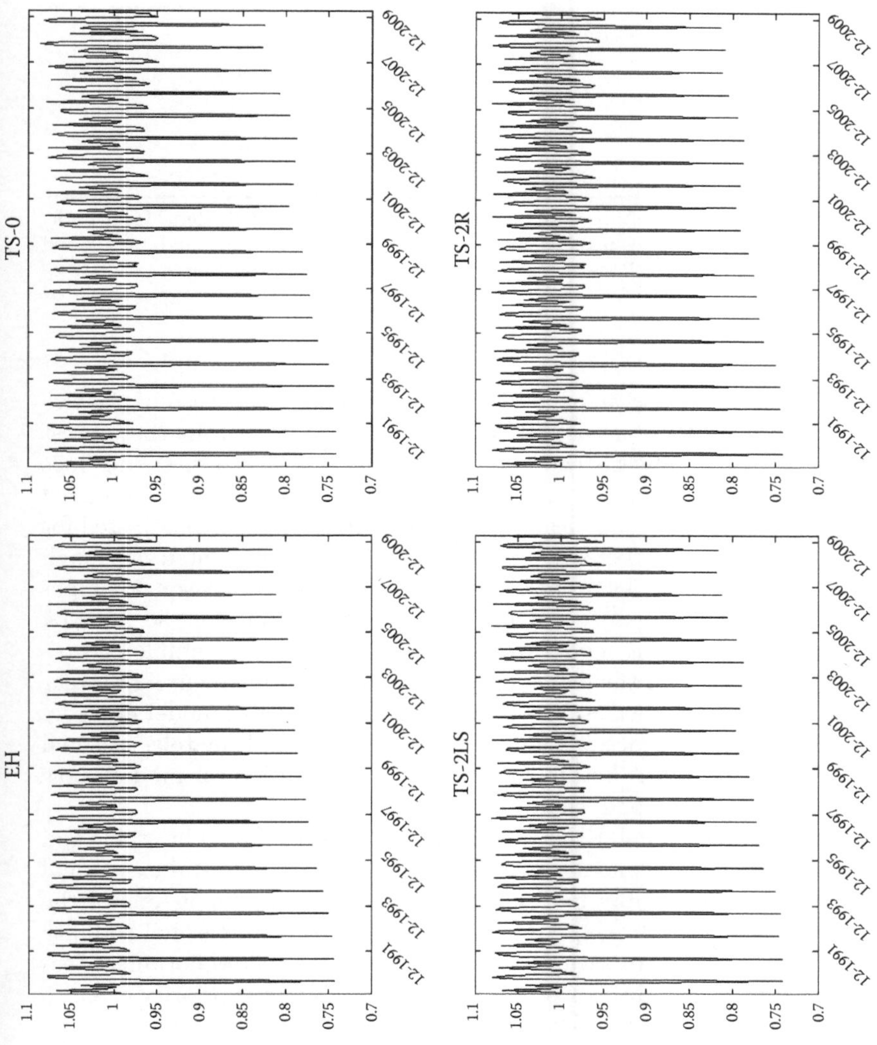

FIGURE 12.3
Seasonal factors: Four alternative estimates. (EH = Eiglsperger and Haine, TS-0 = TRAMO-SEATS automatic with no outliers, TS-2LS = TRAMO-SEATS automatic with two level shifts, TS-2R = TRAMO-SEATS automatic with two ramps).

TABLE 12.1
Model Diagnostics

	Residual SE (in 10^{-2})	Residual Diagnostics							OS Forecast RMSE (in 10^{-2})
		Q	**N**	**Sk**	**K**	**Q2**	**Runs**	**QS**	
EH	1.31	54.3	1.5	−0.8	−0.9	46.6	0.9	0.0	1.8
TS-0	1.28	20.0	2.3	−0.9	1.2	42.7	2.4	0.2	1.7
TS-2LS	1.21	29.1	2.1	−1.0	1.0	36.6	2.2	0.0	1.6
TS-2R	1.11	27.6	1.0	0.6	−0.8	15.2	1.6	0.3	0.9
Approx. 95% Critical Value	—	32	6	2	2	37	2	6	—

Note: SE: Standard Error; Q: Ljung-Box test for 24 autocorrelations; N: Bera–Jarque normality test; Sk: t-test for skewness; K: t-test for kurtosis; Q2: McLeod and Li squared residuals test for nonlinearity; Runs: t-test for randomness in signs; QS: Pierce test for seasonality; RMSE (OS Forecast): Out-of-Sample one-period-ahead forecast root mean squared error (last 12 observations).

The EH choice of logs versus levels seems acceptable: the ratio of the two likelihoods (appropriately adjusted) is extremely close to 1, thus the pretest cannot discriminate between the two transformations; besides, taking logs improves normality. As for TD and Easter effects, the EIP series is obtained from aggregation of country series supposed to have already been adjusted for calendar effects. Indirect TD adjustment is thus taken for granted, although it does not correct the series properly. Still, compared to the seasonal component, calendar effects are of secondary importance. Concerning the ARIMA model, possibly the Airline model was motivated because it is simple and robust. Given that in X12A the model is only used for preadjustment and 1-year forecast extension of the series, it is thought that the effect of model misspecification on the seasonal factors is likely to be small and, ultimately, seasonal factors are all that matter. Yet, in the absence of a definition (or model), how do we know how the seasonal component should be?

In justifying their model, EH stressed that seasonality should be stable and uncontaminated by the economic crisis. Considering that more stable seasonal components will likely imply more unstable SA series, insofar as one of the main uses of SA series is to help cyclical assessment, forcing seasonal stability would not help. Further, to assume that a profound crisis does not affect seasonality of industrial production seems unrealistic. Thus, the priority given to seasonal stability has fuzzy grounds. Some series will have more moving seasonality than others, and the seasonal component should adapt accordingly. In TS, this adaptation is achieved through the width of the spectral peaks at seasonal frequencies in the model for the seasonal component and by the size of its innovation. (The dilemma "stability versus optimality" is discussed in Maravall (1998).)

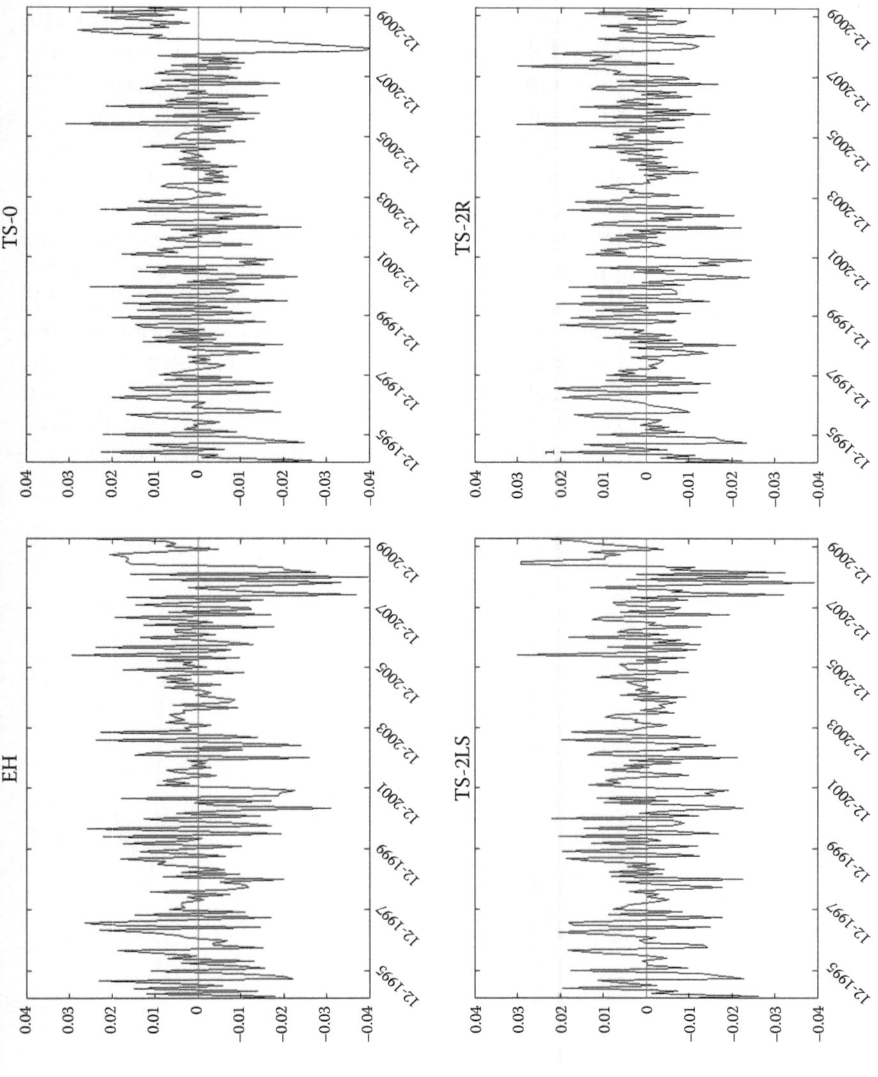

FIGURE 12.4
RegARIMA model residuals: The four models.

In summary, the EH proposal presents problems. (Both the EH and Eurostat procedures have been improved after the workshop and are now closer.) The automatic run suggests that the problems could be properly dealt with working with X12A. We will not pursue this issue and will look instead at the approach of TS. The aim will not be to find the best possible model, but to show how one can proceed within the model-based framework, and how the quality of the seasonal adjustment can be addressed. (The analysis will also use results of a new version of TS not yet released. Some of them, such as the phase delay function and the autoregressive spectrum used in Section 12.5, have benefited from the X12A developers' help.)

Although the X12A and TS filters represent different methodologies, it has often been pointed out that, for many series, they yield similar results. Running TS with the EH specifications, as seen in Figure 12.5, the difference between the X12A and TS SA series is negligible even for the crisis years. Thus, the EH SA series can be approximately seen as the MMSE estimator of the SA series implied by the fitted airline model, and the output of TS could provide inference such as the standard error (SE) of the X12A SA series (interpreted as a model-based estimator) and of its rates of growth or forecasts. In our case, however, the presence of autocorrelation in the ARIMA residuals would invalidate the model and the inference. (Be that as it may, given that the X11 filter is not model based, model-based inferences need not be relevant.)

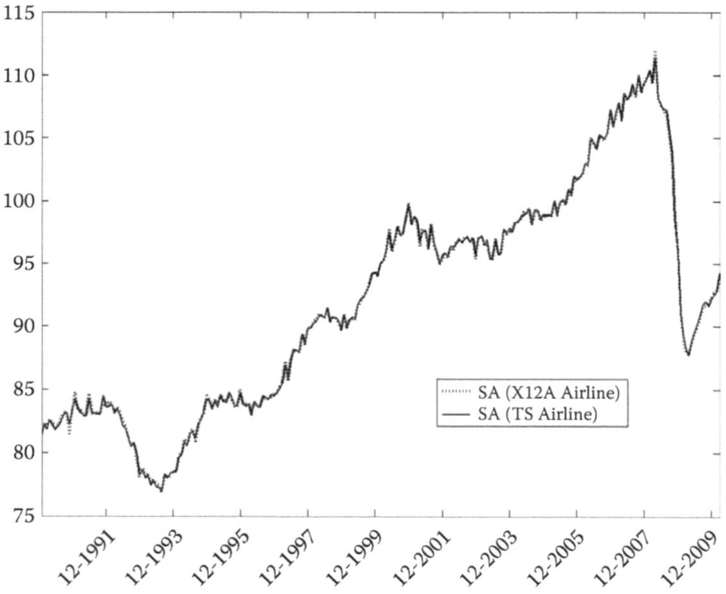

FIGURE 12.5
X12A and TS-0 SA series: Airline model.

12.3 TRAMO–SEATS Automatic (Model-Based) Procedure

12.3.1 Summary of the Procedure

We use program TSW (a Windows version of TS, also available at the Bank of Spain website), and start with the automatic option that pretests for a six parameter TD variable. This option estimates a general model of the type

$$y(t) = \sum_{i=1}^{n_O} \alpha_i D_i(B) d_i(t) + \sum_{i=1}^{n_c} \beta_i cal_i(t) + x(t), \tag{12.3.1}$$

where B denotes the lag operator, $d_i(t)$ is a dummy variable that indicates the position of the ith outlier, and $D_i(B)$ is a polynomial in B reflecting the type of outlier. For an additive outlier (AO), $D_i(B) = 1$; for a transitory change (TC), $D_i(B) = 1/(1 - 0.7B)$; and for a level shift (LS), $D_i(B) = 1/(1 - B)$. "*cal*" denotes a calendar effect variable, such as for TD or Easter effects, β_i is its associated coefficient, and $x(t)$ is an invertible ARIMA model, say,

$$\varphi(B)x(t) = \theta(B)a(t), \quad \varphi(B) = \phi(B)\delta(B), \tag{12.3.2}$$

where $a(t)$ is a zero-mean, white-noise innovation with variance $\mathrm{Var}(a)$, and $\phi(B), \theta(B)$, and $\delta(B)$ are finite polynomials in B, the last one containing the unit AR roots. Thus,

$$\delta(B) = \nabla^d \nabla_s^{d_s}, \quad \nabla = 1 - B, \quad \nabla_s = 1 - B^s = \nabla S, \tag{12.3.3}$$

where $S = 1 + B + \cdots + B^{s-1}$, s denotes the number of observations per year, and $d = 0, 1, 2, 3$, and $d_s = 0, 1$ are the possible choices for the differencing orders. (The TSW procedure also allows for missing observations in $y(t)$.) In TS, after testing for a log transformation, possible outliers and calendar effects, as well as the ARIMA model for $x(t)$, are automatically identified. The resulting model is estimated by exact maximum likelihood.

When used for seasonal adjustment, first, removal of the regression effects from $y(t)$ yields an estimate of the stochastic component $x(t)$. In what follows, it is assumed that the stochastic component is equal to this estimate, which is then split into an uncorrelated stochastic seasonal component, $s(t)$, and a stochastic SA series, $n(t)$, as in

$$x(t) = s(t) + n(t). \tag{12.3.4}$$

The roots of $\phi(B)$ and $\delta(B)$ are assigned to either the seasonal component or to the SA series. This yields the factorizations $\phi(B) = \phi_s(B)\phi_n(B)$ and $\delta(B) = \delta_s(B)\delta_n(B)$, where the subindex indicates the allocation of roots to the components. For example, when $d_s = 1$, Equation 12.3.3 implies $\delta_s(B) = S$ and $\delta_n(B) = \nabla^{d+1}$.

Letting $\varphi_s(B) = \phi_s(B)\delta_s(B)$ and $\varphi_n(B) = \phi_n(B)\delta_n(B)$, a partial fraction expansion eventually yields the decomposition

$$\frac{\theta(B)}{\varphi(B)}a(t) = \frac{\theta_s(B)}{\varphi_s(B)}a_s(t) + \frac{\theta_n(B)}{\varphi_n(B)}a_n(t), \tag{12.3.5}$$

where a_s and a_n are the (uncorrelated) innovations in the seasonal component and SA series. The partial fractions decomposition is done in the frequency domain; the pseudo-spectrum of $x(t)$ is partitioned into additive spectra associated with the terms on the right-hand side of Equation 12.3.5. Identification of a unique decomposition is achieved by imposing the canonical condition that the minimum of the seasonal component pseudo-spectrum be zero (see Burman 1980). The WK filter for estimating $s(t)$ is given by the ratio of the $s(t)$ and $x(t)$ pseudo-spectra, and yields the MMSE estimator – also the conditional mean – of $s(t)$ given $x(t)$. The filter is centered, symmetric, and convergent; its derivation requires an infinite realization of $x(t)$ in the direction of the past and of the future. To apply the filter to a finite realization, model (12.3.2) is used to extend $x(t)$ with forecasts and backcasts; the full effect of the infinite filter can be captured with a moderate number of them. As new observations become available, forecasts will be updated and eventually replaced by observations. As a consequence, the estimator of $s(t)$ near the end of the series is preliminary and will be revised. For long enough series, the filter for periods in the central years would have converged and the estimator would be final (or "historical"). This estimator can be assumed to have been obtained with the complete WK filter applied to the observed series. The duration of the revision process of a preliminary estimator depends on the ARIMA model identified for the series. (For the EIP case, the revision of a concurrent estimator is completed in 2 years, and hence historical estimators can be assumed for the central 16 years.)

Spectral factorization provides the time-domain expression of the component models, say,

$$\varphi_s(B)s(t) = \theta_s(B)a_s(t), \tag{12.3.6a}$$

$$\varphi_n(B)n(t) = \theta_n(B)a_n(t). \tag{12.3.6b}$$

Letting F denote the forward shift operator (i.e., $F = B^{-1}$) and replacing the ratio of pseudo-spectra by the ratio of autocovariance generating functions (ACGFs), the time domain expression of the WK filter becomes (after simplification)

$$\nu_s(B, F) = k_s \frac{\theta_s(B)\theta_s(F)\varphi_n(B)\varphi_n(F)}{\theta(B)\theta(F)}, \tag{12.3.7}$$

where $k_s = \text{Var}(a_s)/\text{Var}(a)$, so that the final estimator is given by

$$\hat{s}(t) = \nu_s(B, F)x(t), \tag{12.3.8}$$

where $\nu_s(B, F)$ is the ACGF of the stationary autoregressive moving average (ARMA) model

$$\theta(B)z_t = \theta_s(B)\varphi_n(B)b(t), \quad \text{Var}(b) = k_s. \tag{12.3.9}$$

From Equations 12.3.2, 12.3.7, and 12.3.8, $\hat{s}(t)$ can be expressed in terms of the innovations in $x(t)$,

$$\varphi_s(B)\theta(F)\hat{s}(t) = k_s\theta_s(B)\theta_s(F)\varphi_n(F)a(t), \tag{12.3.10}$$

so that the ACGFs and spectra of $s(t)$ and $\hat{s}(t)$ will be different. In particular, if $n(t)$ is nonstationary, the model for $\hat{s}(t)$ will be noninvertible, displaying spectral zeros associated with the unit roots in $\varphi_n(B)$. (Changing the subscript s for n in Equations 12.3.7 and 12.3.8, the previous derivation yields $\nu_n(B, F)$ and $\hat{n}(t)$.)

When the series $x(t)$ is split into more components (as in: trend-cycle + seasonal + stochastic TD + irregular component), the procedure is a straightforward extension, with all components made canonical.

12.3.2 Application

The automatic TS procedure yields the SA series of Figure 12.6. The regARIMA model obtained selects the logs, finds significant calendar effects, and identifies the (3,1,0) $(0,1,1)_{12}$ ARIMA model

$$(1 + 0.04B - 0.20B^2 - 0.35B^3)\nabla\nabla_{12}x(t) = (1 - 0.41B^{12})a(t),$$

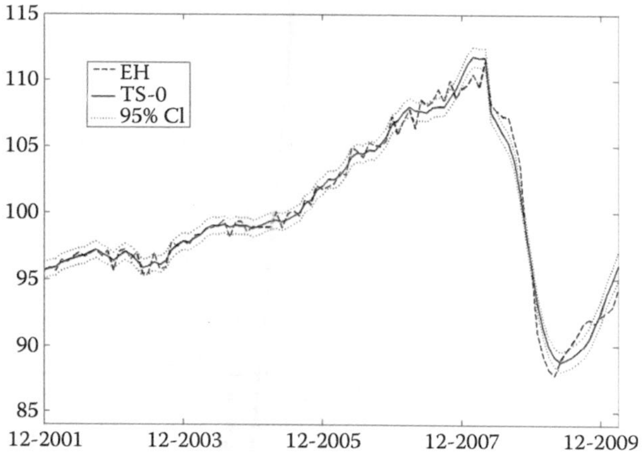

FIGURE 12.6
EH and TS-0 SA series (with confidence interval for the latter).

with $\text{Var}(a) = 0.013^2$. We shall refer to this model as the "TS-0 model." (In previous versions of TS that had lower critical values for outlier detection, a moderate LS was detected for May 2008.)

The difference between the result of the automatic modeling of X12A and TS is perhaps puzzling because the *automdl* procedure of X12A is based on TRAMO. When adapting the code to X12A, modifications were made in the default sequence of estimation algorithms, in the critical value for outlier detection, in the main information criterion for model comparison, in some model restrictions, etc. (see Monsell 2009). These modifications may induce differences in results. In our example, these differences are: (a) TS selects logs, X12A levels. As mentioned before, the likelihood ratio is very close to 1, so that trivial differences might tip the coin. (b) TS detects no outlier, X12A detects five, mostly due to the fact that the use of levels tends to increase the number of outliers detected (when logs are imposed, the automatic X12A procedure detects no outlier). (c) X12A selects a (1,1,2) $(0,1,1)_{12}$ model, while TS chooses a (3,1,0) $(0,1,1)_{12}$ one. Thus, the stationary regular part of the model for X12A has an ARMA(1,2) structure, with a real AR root (0.75) and a pair of complex conjugate MA roots; the AR(3) model of TRAMO factors into a real root (0.80) and a pair of complex conjugate ones. Figure 12.7 compares the pseudo-spectra for the two models. The most relevant difference is a small amount of variance centered between the fourth and fifth harmonics, near the TD frequency, associated with the complex roots of the AR(3) polynomial in TS-0.

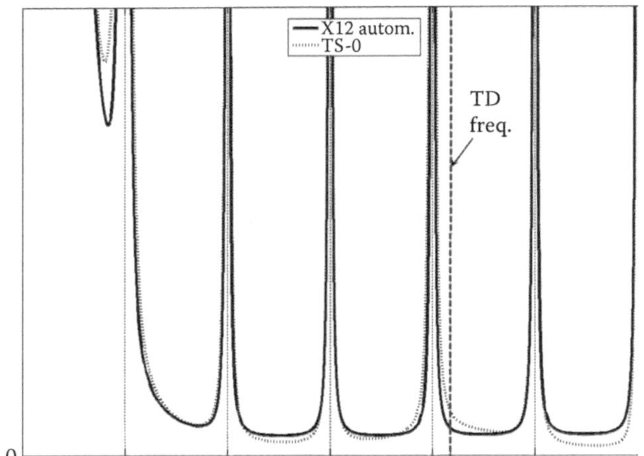

FIGURE 12.7
Pseudo-spectra of automatically identified models.

12.4 Calendar Effects

12.4.1 Stochastic Trading Day

There is evidence that calendar effects are still present in the aggregate of the working-day adjusted series provided by the individual countries. Given that the quality of calendar adjustment varies considerably across countries, the result may be understandable. More intriguing is that, after the automatic run of X12A has removed the calendar effects remaining in the indirectly adjusted series, the spectrum of the residuals still presents a peak for the TD frequency. This is not the case with TS. The pair of complex conjugate roots in the AR(3) polynomial have frequency = 2.22 radians, not far from 2.19 (or 4.2 cycles per year), which is the main frequency used in the TS and X12A spectral TD checks (frequency will always be expressed in radians). These roots may suggest a stochastic TD effect not removed by the deterministic specification. TS models this effect as a stationary ARMA(2,2), where the AR contains the roots close to the TD frequency, and the MA(2) is obtained from the model decomposition. Because of the canonical condition, the MA(2) will have two real roots (at the 0 and π frequencies), and the first one will be a unit root (i.e., a spectral zero). For the EIP series, the stochastic TD effect, $c(t)$, follows the stationary model

$$(1 + 0.84B + 0.47B^2)c(t) = (1 - B)(1 + 0.58B)a_c(t), \qquad (12.4.1)$$

with $a_c(t)$ white noise with $\mathrm{Var}(a_c) = 0.0018^2$. Its spectrum is shown in Figure 12.8. Figures 12.9 and 12.10 compare the deterministic and stochastic TD component estimators: broadly, both look noisy, especially the stochastic trading-day component.

Our TD adjustment consists, first, of the removal of a deterministic TD through regression and, second, when the resulting series still exhibits a spectral peak at the TD frequency, removal of this peak through MMSE estimation of an ARMA(2,2) component. Purely stochastic TD components, whereby random walk models on the TD regression coefficients are specified, have been used by Harvey (1989) and Bell (2004). In our approach, the stochastic TD is captured with a single stochastic component plus the deterministic TD effects, while in the random walk approach, the mean of each TD coefficient evolves over time subject to the constraint that, at any point in time, the seven stochastic TD coefficients sum to zero.

12.4.2 A Comment on Trading-Day Spectral Diagnostics

Spectral peaks in the residuals or in the SA series are useful diagnostic tools for TD effects. However, TD detection by looking at the spectrum of the unadjusted series is trickier: because of the proximity between the main TD frequency and the fourth seasonal harmonic, the TD effect may well pass

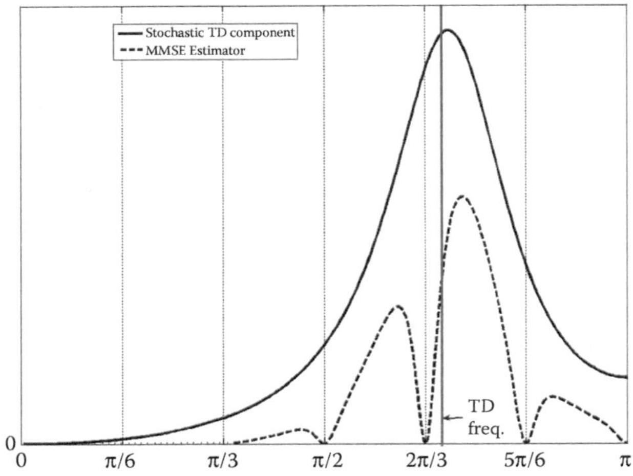

FIGURE 12.8
Spectra of the stochastic trading-day component model and of its theoretical estimator.

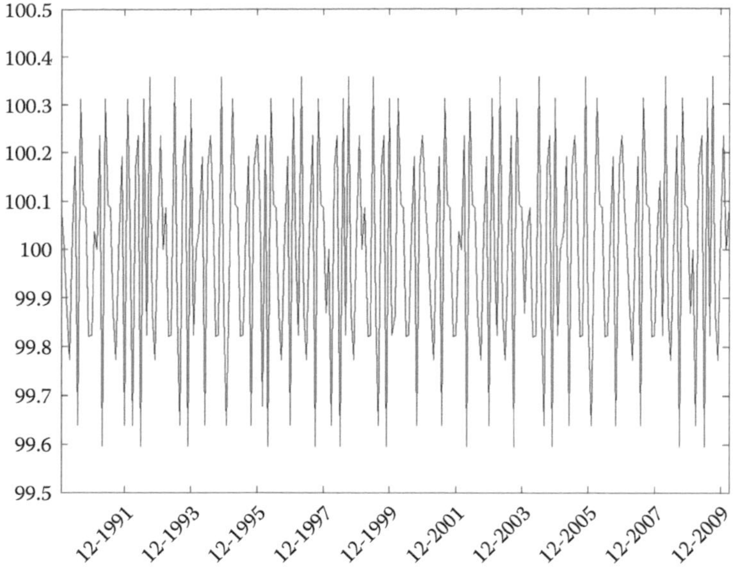

FIGURE 12.9
Deterministic trading-day effect.

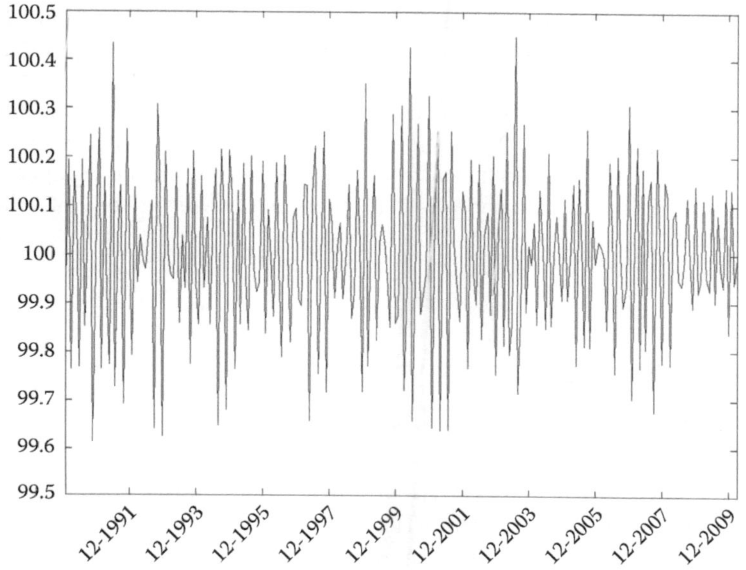

FIGURE 12.10
Stochastic trading-day effect.

unnoticed. In TS, a stochastic TD can also be detected through the presence of a pair of AR roots associated with the main TD frequency. This complex root will typically be stationary and an ambiguity emerges. First, the frequency of the AR roots is not the same as the frequency of the spectral peak they induce (Jenkins and Watts 1968). Consider, e.g., an AR(2) model with polynomial $(1 + \phi_1 B + \phi_2 B^2)$ that contains a pair of complex conjugate roots. The frequency of the root is $\lambda_r = \arccos|\phi_1|/2\sqrt{\phi_2}$, while the maximum of the model spectrum is achieved at the frequency $\lambda_s = \arccos[-\phi_1(1+\phi_2)/4\phi_2]$. The two frequencies are different and the difference $(\lambda_r - \lambda_s)$ depends only on the modulus of the root or, equivalently, on ϕ_2. As the root approaches nonstationarity, the difference goes to zero. This "frequency displacement" effect is aggravated because, when $c(t)$ follows the stationary model (12.4.1) and its estimator $\hat{c}(t)$ follows a model similar to Equation 12.3.10 (with s replaced by c), it is easily checked that the frequencies of the spectral peaks in $c(t)$ and $\hat{c}(t)$ are not the same.

As a consequence, for a stationary stochastic TD, there are three relevant frequencies. One is the frequency of the AR root, λ_r, that will also be driving the "eventual" ACF and forecast function (i.e., the ACF and forecast function for lags and horizon beyond the model MA order). The others are the frequencies associated with the spectral peaks of the model for the component, λ_s, and of the model for its MMSE estimator, $\hat{\lambda}_s$. In the model-based approach, the three frequencies can be derived from the ARIMA model for the series. For the EIP series and the stochastic TD component given by Equation 12.4.1, it is found that $\lambda_r = 2.22$, $\lambda_s = 2.23$, and $\hat{\lambda}_s = 2.29$. As seen in Figure 12.8, these frequencies are slightly above the TD frequency used in the spectral diagnostics. Thus, if a fixed frequency is used in the checks, the associated interval (in SEATS at present, 2.15–2.30) should allow for the previous distortions. The discussion applies in an identical way to stationary seasonal components, but given that highly stationary seasonal components are unlikely, it will seldom be relevant.

12.5 Some Frequency Domain Results

Model TS-0 contains 11 parameters; their estimators, however, have small correlations, never exceeding 0.17 (in absolute value). As seen in Table 12.1, the TS-0 model improves upon the EH model in that no residual autocorrelation is detected. Still, the runs test for randomness in the residual's signs flags a problem, evidenced by direct inspection of Figure 12.4. The last 12 residuals are positive, which seems unacceptable and implies underestimation of the series for the last months.

From the point of view of seasonal adjustment, a consequence of not having introduced LS outliers to capture the spectacular plunge at the turn of the year 2008 is a more moving estimate of seasonality. As seen by comparing the E-H and TS-0 plots in Figure 12.3, the increased variability is nevertheless moderate. Spectra of the differenced SA series (in logs) are displayed in Figure 12.11. The first plot shows a parametric AR(30) spectrum, similar to the one in X12A. The second plot shows a nonparametric Tukey spectrum. The AR spectrum is appropriate for detecting peaks at the seasonal and TD frequencies (see Childers 1976). The Tukey spectrum, on the other hand, is more informative in what concerns spectral minima. In the AMB approach, the right-hand side of the equation for the historical estimator of the SA series (i.e., Equation 12.3.10 exchanging s and n) contains the polynomial $\varphi_s(F)$. Hence, nonstationary seasonal components induce zeros at seasonal frequencies in the spectrum of the SA historical estimator. Given that seasonal ARIMA models typically contain a seasonal difference, all seasonal frequencies will present that feature. For preliminary estimators, the spectral minima (at the seasonal frequencies) are close to (but not quite) zero. Thus, the spectrum of an estimated SA series that includes preliminary estimators at both ends will be close to (though not strictly) noninvertible. Given that AR models are always invertible, the spectral minima will be poorly captured (and pushed away from zero—see Maravall 1995). The spectral dips (or near-zeros) at the seasonal frequencies are likely to be better captured with the Tukey spectrum. The EH SA series shows a slight distortion in the frequency of the local minimum near some seasonal frequencies (e.g., third and fifth harmonics in

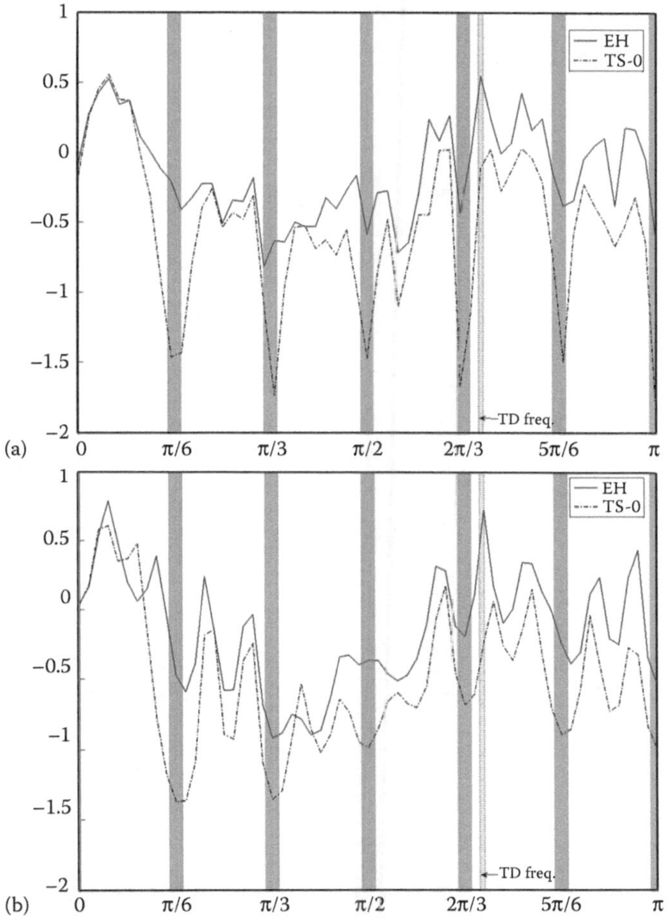

FIGURE 12.11
Estimates of the spectrum of the SA series (differenced and mean corrected). (a) Nonparametric Tukey (log) spectrum. (b) AR (log) spectrum.

the AR(30) spectrum) and the two spectra show that more variance has been removed at the seasonal frequencies with the TS-0 model, in accordance with its more moving seasonal component. Accordingly, as shown in Figure 12.6, the EH SA series is more erratic.

Using the AMB SEATS decomposition of the EH model (as shown in Figure 12.5, very close to the X12A one), Figure 12.12 plots the finite-filter phase delay functions (adapted from the one provided to us by the X12A developers) of the EH and TS-0 concurrent estimators of the SA series. Although, as shown in Findley and Martin (2006), smoother SA series tend to imply larger phase delays, in our case, the opposite result is obtained. Within the

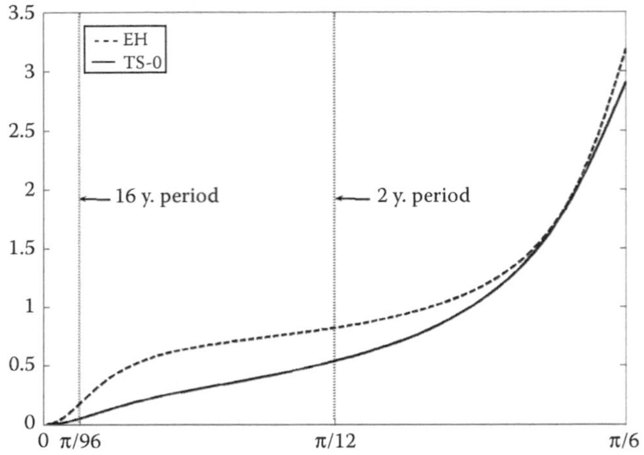

FIGURE 12.12
Phase delay (in months) of the SA series concurrent estimation filter (finite filter).

range of frequencies of cyclical interest, the TS-0 estimator induces a smaller phase delay that extends from a few days (long-term cycles) to half-a-month (2-year cycle).

12.6 Seasonal Adjustment Errors and Revisions

It is difficult to assess the significance of the difference between two SA figures without having information on their estimation errors. TS provides SE of the SA series for the semi-infinite filter realization. (McElroy (2008a) presents a matrix extension for the finite filter case; Bell (2005) considers the effect of adding sampling and parameter estimation errors.) The SA series estimation error is the sum of two types of orthogonal errors. One is the error in the historical estimator, which typically characterizes the central years of the period considered. For months at both ends of the series, preliminary estimators will suffer revisions as they converge to the historical estimator. The difference between the preliminary and historical estimators is the revision error. Let $x(t)$ follow model (12.3.2), and consider the decomposition of $x(t)$ as in Equation 12.3.4. Assume $s(t)$ and $n(t)$ follow the models (12.3.6a) and (12.3.6b). The error in the historical estimator, $s(t) - \hat{s}(t)$, has the ACGF of the model

$$\theta(B)z(t) = \theta_n(B)\theta_s(B)b(t), \tag{12.6.1}$$

with $\text{Var}(b) = \text{Var}(a_n)\text{Var}(a_s)/\text{Var}(a)$; see Pierce (1979). As for the revision error, let $s(t|t+k)$ denote the estimator of $s(t)$ when $x(t+k)$ is the last available observation. (When $k < 0$, $s(t|t+k)$ yields a forecast.) Model (12.3.10) can be expressed as the partial fractions decomposition

$$\hat{s}(t) = k_s \frac{\theta_s(B)\theta_s(F)\varphi_n(F)}{\varphi_s(B)\theta(F)} a(t) = \left[\frac{M(B)}{\varphi_s(B)} + F\frac{N(F)}{\theta(F)}\right] a(t)$$

(see Maravall 1994, Bell and Martin 2004). The series expansion of the fraction in F is convergent; the one in B is not. Thus, $\hat{s}(t)$ can be expressed as

$$\hat{s}(t) = \psi_B(B)a(t) + \psi_F(F)a(t+1), \tag{12.6.2}$$

where $\psi_B(B)$ contains the effect of the starting conditions and of the innovations up to period t, and $\psi_F(B) = N(F)/\theta(F)$ is a convergent filter of innovations posterior to t. Because the expectation at time t of $a(t+k)$ when $k > 0$ is zero, the concurrent estimator is $\hat{s}(t|t) = \psi_B(B)a(t)$, and its associated revision is $r(t|t) = \hat{s}(t) - \hat{s}(t|t) = \psi_F(F)a(t+1)$. Therefore, $r(t|t)$ follows the model

$$\theta(F)r(t|t) = N(F)a(t+1), \tag{12.6.3}$$

from which its variance and autocorrelations can be computed.

The derivation extends easily to any preliminary estimator, including forecasts. In particular, and taking conditional expectations at times t_1 and t_2 $(t_2 > t_1 \geq t)$ in Equation 12.6.3, the revision in the preliminary estimator $\hat{s}(t|t_1)$ caused by the new observations $x(t_1+1), \ldots, x(t_2)$, is an MA$(t_2 - t_1)$ process (Pierce 1980). (Finite sample extensions are considered in McElroy and Gagnon 2008, and a model-based diagnostic based on them is developed in McElroy and Wildi 2010.) The ACGF of the total estimation error is the sum of the ACGFs of the historical and revision errors. All three ACGFs correspond to stationary ARMA models with the AR polynomial equal to $\theta(B)$. From the models, inferences can be drawn having to do with the precision of the estimators and their rates of growth. Further, some general properties can be derived. For example, under the standardization $\text{Var}(a) = 1$, when the model for $x(t)$ contains the seasonal difference $(1 - B^{12})$, if $\theta(B)$ contains the factor $(1 + \theta_{12}B^{12})$ with θ_{12} close to -1, the model will present a stable seasonal component that will require small revision. But due to the close-to-unit root in $\theta(B)$, these revisions will be slow to converge to zero. On the contrary, when $\theta_{12} \approx 0$, the revision will tend to be large but converge fast.

For the TS-0 model, it is found that the concurrent estimator of the SA series follows the model

$$(1 - 0.78B)\nabla^2\hat{n}(t|t) = 0.72(1 - 0.53B + 0.58B^2 - 0.02B^3)a(t), \tag{12.6.4}$$

where the MA(3) polynomial has three real roots (0.92, 0.57, and 0.03). The model is close to (though not quite) noninvertible. The revision this estimator will suffer follows the model

$$(1 - 0.41F^{12})r(t|t) = 0.37\theta_r(F)a(t+1),$$

with $\theta_r(F)$ a polynomial of degree 15, with three real roots (0.92, 0.55, and 0.14) and five pairs of complex conjugate roots. The SD of the total estimation error of the concurrent SA series estimator is equal to 0.69 percent points (p.p.) and a 95% confidence interval for its month-to-month rate of growth is given by ± 1.16 p.p. Given that the historical estimation error is never observed, of more practical interest is the error with respect to the best measure that can eventually be achieved, i.e., the revision error. For the concurrent estimator, the SD of the revision is 0.60 p.p.; after 1 year, 78% of its variance has been removed, and the concurrent estimator has practically converged to the historical estimator in 2 years. The revision error is relatively large, but converges to zero reasonably fast. Figure 12.6 plots the 95% confidence interval of the TS-0 estimator of the SA series. The months with a significant disagreement between the EH and TS-0 estimators are numerous, more noticeably since the year 2007. The two adjustments seem "significantly different."

12.7 Distribution of Minimum Mean Squared Error Estimators

The M4 diagnostic, failed by the automatic option of X12A in Section 12.2, serves to illustrate model-based translation of X12A quality assessment statistics. The M4 statistic indicates too much autocorrelation in the estimator of the irregular component. Not knowing what the proper autocorrelation should be, the diagnostic indicates that an estimator with autocorrelation beyond a certain amount would indicate poor quality. A similar diagnostic can be made in the model-based framework, but a more complete analysis of the irregular is now possible.

In general, TS decomposes $x(t)$ into the sum of orthogonal components all of which follow ARIMA-type models. Denoting by $u(t)$ the irregular component and by $s(t)$ the sum of all other components, the decomposition can be expressed as $x(t) = s(t) + u(t)$, and a derivation similar to the one in Section 12.3.1 shows that the final estimator of $u(t)$ can be expressed as

$$\theta(F)\hat{u}(t) = k_u\varphi(F)a(t), \tag{12.7.1}$$

with $k_u = \text{Var}(u)/\text{Var}(a)$ and the ACF of $\hat{u}(t)$ is that of the "inverse" model of Equation 12.3.2 (Bell and Hillmer 1984). For close to noninvertible models, the autocorrelations can be remarkably high, although they will not be associated with trend or seasonal frequencies due to the spectral zeros induced by the unit roots in $\varphi(F)$.

SEATS estimates $u(t)$ as the residual after all other components have been removed. Let this estimator be $\tilde{u}(t)$. If the model is correct, the sample variance and ACF of $\tilde{u}(t)$ should be in agreement with the theoretical ones implied by Equation 12.7.1, and this agreement can be assessed by means of the SE of the estimated autocorrelations. In this way, simple tests are obtained, which are, in essence, misspecification tests (see Maravall 1987, 2003).

The comparison between theoretical and empirical second-order moments of the estimator extends to other components. Thus, e.g., using TS to decompose the EH model, it is obtained that the variance of the stationary transformation of the estimated trend-cycle is 0.016, with SE = 0.003, while according to Equation 12.3.10—with s standing now for the trend—it should be 0.026. This discrepancy may indicate underestimation of the trend-cycle component. Findley, McElroy, and Wills (2004), and McElroy (2008b) show that the SEATS test—based on final estimators—are biased toward underestimation, and provide a finite sample improvement (not incorporated into SEATS yet). For the TS-0 case, Table 12.2 compares the sample variance and autocorrelations of the irregular component estimator with those implied by model (12.7.1), together with the associated SE. No discrepancy is found.

As already mentioned, the frequency domain expression of the WK filter that provides the final estimator of $s(t)$ is the ratio of the pseudo-spectrum of $s(t)$ to that of $x(t)$. Letting $f_*(\lambda)$ denote a pseudo-spectrum, it follows from Equation 12.3.8 that

$$f_{\hat{n}}(\lambda) = \left[\frac{f_n(\lambda)}{f_x(\lambda)}\right]^2 f_x(\lambda) = \left(\frac{f_n(\lambda)}{f_x(\lambda)}\right) f_n(\lambda) < f_n(\lambda),$$

$$f_{\hat{s}}(\lambda) = \left(\frac{f_s(\lambda)}{f_x(\lambda)}\right) f_s(\lambda) < f_s(\lambda).$$

The difference $f_x(\lambda) - [f_{\hat{n}}(\lambda) + f_{\hat{s}}(\lambda)]$ (>0) is the cross-spectrum or, in the time domain, the cross-covariance function. Thus, although the components are assumed uncorrelated, MMSE yields correlated estimators. For the two component decomposition of Equation 12.3.4, the cross-covariance generating function between $\hat{s}(t)$ and $\hat{n}(t)$ is the ACGF of the stationary ARMA model given by Equation 12.6.1. An implication is that the error in the historical estimator of $n(t)$ (and of $s(t)$) is equal to the lag-0 cross-covariance between $\hat{n}(t)$ and $\hat{s}(t)$. (Thus, in the absence of explicit models for the series and components, the sample lag-0 cross-covariance could provide a rough estimate of

TABLE 12.2
Irregular Component: Autocorrelations and Variance

Autocorrelation	Model for Estimator	Sample Estimate	SE
Lag-1	−0.35	−0.36	0.07
Lag-2	−0.08	−0.06	0.09
Lag-3	−0.23	−0.24	0.07
Lag-4	0.17	0.10	0.07
Variance	0.008	0.007	0.001

the SA series historical estimation error variance. For the EIP case, the theoretical value of the lag-0 cross-covariance is 0.0034 while the sample estimate is 0.0040.)

The appearance of cross-covariances between the estimators of components assumed uncorrelated has often been signaled as an inconvenience of the standard unobserved components MMSE model-based approach. (Although the result would apply, in general, to any components estimated as linear functions of the same observations.) In the TS approach, given that the cross-covariances between component estimators are always finite, when at least one of the components is nonstationary, the corresponding cross-correlations would tend to zero and hence their sample estimates will be small. If $d + d_s > 1$—a condition satisfied by the vast majority of series that are SA—the convergence to zero will also be true for the cross-correlations between the component rates of growth. Thus, in practice, the inconvenience will likely be of little relevance.

Given that typically the SA series and seasonal component are nonstationary, cross-correlations have to be computed for their stationary transformations. Proceeding as with the autocorrelations, the theoretical cross-correlations between the component estimators should be close to their sample estimates. Table 12.3 exhibits the lag-0 theoretical and sample cross-correlations for the TS-0 procedure. Except for the stochastic TD-irregular case, correlations are small and the comparison shows no anomalies. The relatively high correlation between the stochastic TD and irregular component may cause instability in the detection of the former.

Remark: The role of the moving average polynomial in the observed series model.

In the model-based approach, while the models for the series and the components are models in B (i.e., the past explains the present), those of the revision error and irregular estimator are models in F (the future explains the present). As expressions (12.6.1), (12.6.3), and (12.7.1) indicate, the historical estimation error, the revision, and the irregular component estimator (the residual of the decomposition) are stationary and autocorrelated (although

TABLE 12.3
Cross-Correlations between Stationary Transformations of Estimators

	Model for Estimator	**Sample Estimate**	**SE**
Trend-cycle/Seasonal	−0.09	−0.15	0.05
Seasonal/Irregular	0.06	0.06	0.02
Trend-cycle/Irregular	−0.17	−0.16	0.03
Seasonal/Stoch. TD	0.07	0.08	0.01
Trend-cycle/ Stoch. TD	0.05	0.05	0.01
Stoch. TD/Irregular	0.79	0.78	0.02

their forecast will always be 0). In the three cases, the ACF is that of an ARMA model with AR polynomial equal to $\theta(B)$, the MA polynomial of the original series model. The ACFs of the "errors" will have different starting conditions, as a result of the different MA parts of models (12.6.1), (12.6.3), and (12.7.1), after which they will follow the same difference equation. Therefore, a slow converging revision error, e.g., will be associated with a highly autocorrelated irregular component estimator. The $\theta(B)$ polynomial is also the AR polynomial in Equation 12.3.9, the model whose ACF is the WK filter; its roots will determine the speed of convergence of the filter, i.e., how many terms are needed for a finite truncation.

12.8 Diagnostics and Quality Assessment

The diagnostics of the previous section are based on statistics that, if the regARIMA model is correctly specified, should be close to some theoretical values. Ultimately, these comparisons are misspecification tests. Obviously, they have implications for seasonal adjustment. For example, a high value of the seasonal autocorrelation QS statistics in the model residuals indicates that the model has not captured seasonality properly. Or, if the sample and theoretical variances of the SA estimator are in clear disagreement, one may suspect some adjustment failure.

It may happen, however, that with no evidence of misspecification, the decomposition may be questionable. As a simple example, the model $(1 + \phi_{12}B^{12})x_t = a_t$ with $\phi_{12} = -0.3$ has peaks in the spectrum at all seasonal frequencies, but the seasonal correlation is small and, in practice, only lasts 1 year. The AMB estimator would imply (as it should) a very erratic seasonality, unrecognizable as such through direct inspection. Would it make sense to seasonally adjust the series? Possibly not, because the concept of seasonality would seem to be associated with longer lasting inertia. In other words, there are criteria that should be satisfied on *a priori* grounds by a seasonal component or an SA series for the adjustment to be justified. Some important criteria are the following:

1. The seasonal correlation should last for several years. In TSW, this criterion would be satisfied if $d_s = 1$ or $\phi_{12} < k$ ($k = -0.5$ by default).

2. The seasonal component should not move too fast. Given that the moving features are caused by the seasonal innovation, this could translate into $\text{Var}(a_s) < k\text{Var}(a)$.

3. Historical estimation of seasonality should be reliable and revisions in preliminary estimators should not be excessive. In TSW, these

requirements could also set a limit to the variance of the final and preliminary estimators.

4. The delay induced by the phase shift in the concurrent SA series estimator in the frequency range of cyclical interest should not be too large.

One could easily introduce additional criteria (e.g., on the autocorrelation of the irregular estimator, on the cross-correlation between trend-cycle and seasonal component, on the speed of convergence of the revision, etc.). These quality measures, however, are judgmental. In the seasonal AR(1) example, most people would agree with not adjusting when $\phi_{12} = -0.3$, but what if $\phi_{12} = -0.8$? The cutting point is unclear.

In the model-based approach, the variances of the component innovations, estimation errors, and revisions, as well as the revision speed of convergence, depend on the proper model for the series. Thus, e.g., some series will require large revisions, others will require small ones, and the vague criterion of minimizing revisions is replaced by the criterion of "optimal revisions," tailored to the stochastic properties of the series. The characteristics of the adjustment, however, can be of help at the model selection stage. If seasonal adjustment is the application of interest and several models seem to provide acceptable fits, looking for smaller estimation error and smaller revision of the SA series would be sensible. An example is provided in the next section.

12.9 Outliers and Intervention Variables

12.9.1 TRAMO–SEATS Automatic with Level Shifts

The EH and TS-0 models do not provide a satisfactory adjustment. The TS-0 model overcomes some of the problems but does a poor job with the last 12 months of observations. The large negative residuals at the beginning of the recent recession and the large positive ones during the recovery period suggest introducing outliers to capture the big drop at the turn of the year 2008. Thus, the two LS outliers of the EH model are specified and automatic model identification is performed. The resulting model will be referred to as the "TS-2LS model." The ARIMA model obtained is very similar to the TS-0 case. The model orders are (3,1,0) $(0,1,1)_{12}$ and calendar effects are significant. The regular AR(3) polynomial presents the same pair of complex conjugate roots, with similar moduli, and frequency close to the TD one. Table 12.1 indicates that the residuals are not autocorrelated and can be accepted as normally distributed with zero skewness and no excess kurtosis. However, the randomness in the signs of residuals test is again failed, and Figure 12.4 shows that the residuals for the last 2 years exhibit the unpleasant pattern of the EH and TS-0 residuals. Still, a slight improvement is detected in the out-of-sample performance for the last year of observations in Table 12.1.

The EIP series provides a good example of the limitations of the automatic outlier detection procedure (based on AO, TC, and LS outliers) when the series experiences explosive behavior and increased uncertainty in the recent year(s). The TS automatic procedure was applied to the first $(243 - j, j = 0, 1, \ldots, 100)$ observations of the series. For the series that end before November 2008, only two marginally significant outliers are detected. Both last for a few periods and eventually disappear. Then, the outlier for November 2008 is concurrently detected as an AO and becomes an LS 1 month later. But, after November 2008, outlier detection becomes unstable, with LS outliers for October, November, and December 2008, and for January 2009, appearing and disappearing in several combinations. These outliers disappear throughout 2009, possibly as a result of the accumulation of abnormally large values at the end of the series. The three types of outliers considered have a difficult time capturing the crisis in a parsimonious way. In the example, to model the recent crisis as sudden drops in two particular months seems somewhat inadequate.

12.9.2 TRAMO–SEATS Automatic with Ramps

Direct inspection of the trend-cycle component obtained with the TS-0 model shows a spectacular drop in the series that starts at about March 2008 and lasts for about 1 year. Moreover, the rate of decrease is different for the first and last months within that period. These considerations suggest that ramps may be more appropriate than LS to capture the recession. In TS, inclusion of outliers in the model is seen as a price paid for maintaining the normality assumption that underlies the likelihood function (also needed for testing and inference). Intervention variables are intended to capture some known special effect. Outliers should be kept to a minimum and do not require an ex-post explanation. Often, however, an explanation is found, in which case it makes sense to replace the outlier with an intervention variable. Thus, two ramps are entered as intervention variables, to capture the drop at the beginning of the crisis.

From a first guess provided by the trend-cycle inspection, a comparison of Bayesian Information Criteria (BICs), or likelihoods, for various ramp specifications leads to the choice of March and September 2008 as the starting dates, and of five and seven months for the lengths. TS was run in automatic mode (RSA $= 5$) with the two ramps. As before, the ARIMA model obtained is a $(3,1,0)\ (0,1,1)_{12}$ for the logs, with a six-variable TD, Easter Effect, and the two specified ramps. The AR(3) polynomial contains a pair of complex conjugate roots with modulus 0.70 and frequency 2.22 that produce again a stochastic TD with an ARMA(2,2) model. The complete model will be referred to as the "TS-2R model." Table 12.1 shows that, of the four models considered, the TS-2R case produces the best results, and the RMSE of the out-of-sample forecasts for the last 12 months shows a remarkable improvement. Figure 12.4

plots the TS-2R model residuals; the abnormal behavior at the end of the series is no longer present.

The model for the SA series is found to be

$$(1 - 0.53B)\nabla^2 n(t) = (1 - 1.49B + 0.62B^2 - 0.09B^3)a_n(t),$$

with innovation standard deviation $\sigma_n = 0.0057$. Noticing that one of the roots of the MA polynomial is $(1 - 0.92B)$, the model for the SA series is close to a (1,1,2) ARIMA model plus mean. (Interestingly enough, these are the same orders as those of the regular part of the model identified by X12A in Section 12.2.)

Some relevant features of the seasonal adjustment for the three TS cases considered are contained in Table 12.4. First, given that the standard deviation of the innovation in a component measures stability (close to zero innovation variances imply close to deterministic components), the TS-2R model provides the most stable SA series and seasonal component. The innovation standard deviation also provides a measure of the size of the one-period-ahead forecast error of the component.

Second, estimation precision of the SA series can be measured by the SE of its concurrent estimator. Table 12.4 shows that the TS-2R model yields the most precise estimator. For the month-to-month rate of growth, the width of a 95% confidence interval is about ±1p.p. Third, an additional desirable feature of the SA series is that they require small revisions. TS measures the SE of the revisions in preliminary estimators of the SA series. Table 12.4 shows that the TS-2R model has the smallest revisions in the concurrent estimator; its variance, nevertheless, is three times the variance of the historical estimation error. Convergence is practically unaffected: for the three TS models, close to 80% of the revision is completed in the first year; 100% during the second.

Concerning seasonal adjustment of the EIP series, what the previous analysis has shown is that improvements in the regARIMA model improve the adjustment, that some intervention is needed to deal with the recent crisis, and that ramps do a better job than LS outliers. Judging from the results

TABLE 12.4
Features of the Decomposition

Model	SE of Innovation (in 10^{-2})			Concurrent Estimator (in p.p.)		% Convergence of Revision in One Year	SE of m-to-m SA Rog (in 10^{-2})
	Seasonal	Stoch. TD	SA Series	SE of Estimator	SE of Revision		
TS-0	0.44	0.18	0.68	0.69	0.60	76	0.58
TS-2LS	0.43	0.18	0.63	0.61	0.52	78	0.56
TS-2R	0.41	0.17	0.57	0.54	0.44	78	0.55

TABLE 12.5
Month-to-Month SA Series Rates of Growth (in p.p.) for October 2009–February 2010

(March Estimate)	October	November	December	January	February
EH	0.0	0.2	0.5	0.4	0.2
Eurostat	0.3	1.3	0.8	1.9	0.7
TS-2R	0.3	0.7	0.6	0.9	0.4

obtained with the TS-2R model for the original period of concern (October 2009–February 2010), Table 12.5 indicates that Eurostat overestimated the SA rates of growth, while the EH model underestimated them.

Besides seasonal adjustment, other components can be of help in forecasting and cyclical assessment. Information similar to that having to do with the SA series is provided in TSW for the trend-cycle component, thus, the relative merits of both components can be compared. In our example, the trend-cycle component is the SA series without a relatively small white-noise irregular component. Except for a mild improvement in the SE of the monthly rate of growth, and a mild increase in the phase delay (see Figure 12.13), the trend-cycle yields very similar results. Further, the trend-cycle component (or the SA series) can be decomposed in turn into long-term trend and cycle by means of a model-based adaptation of the Hodrick–Prescott filter (Kaiser and Maravall 2005). This decomposition is shown in Figure 12.14.

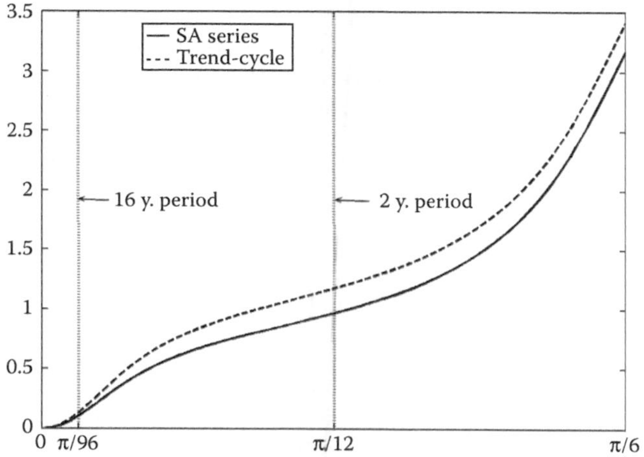

FIGURE 12.13
Phase delay (in months) of the SA series and trend-cycle concurrent finite estimation filters: TS-2R model.

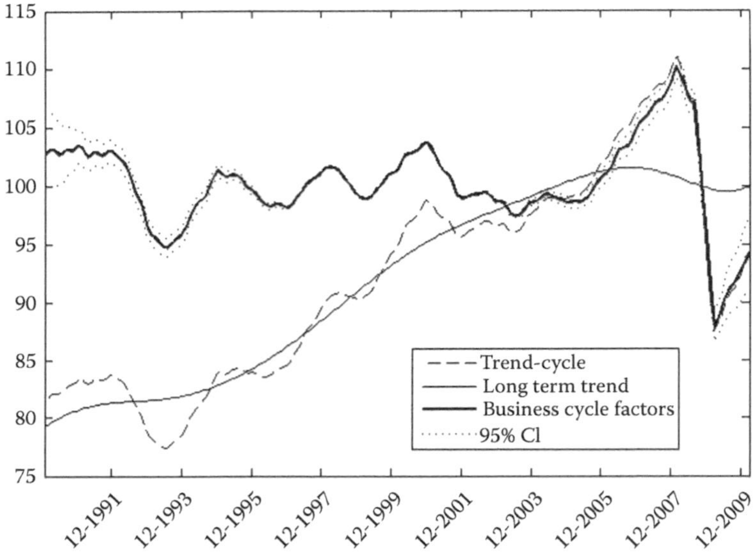

FIGURE 12.14
Long-term trend component and business-cycle factors.

Models for these new components—compatible with the overall model for the series—are also derived and, e.g., the model for the cycle is

$$(1 - 1.92B + 0.93B^2)(1 - 0.53B)z(t) = (1 - 0.26B - 0.95B^2 + 0.32B^3)a_z(t),$$

with $\mathrm{Var}(z) = 0.04\mathrm{Var}(a)$. These models permit the analyst to extend the analysis of the previous sections (e.g., distribution of estimators, estimation and revision errors, and forecasting) to the long-term trend and cycle components.

12.10 Stability of the Model-Based Method

An objection often made to model-based adjustment is that changes in the model as new observations are added may produce instability in the results. To maintain a balance between instability and misspecification, it is often recommended that, as a rule, the model be reidentified perhaps once a year and, for the periods before the next reidentification, parameters be reestimated every month, keeping fixed the general model specifications. Since work in this chapter was started, nine new observations have become available (period April–December 2010) and we use them to analyze out-of-sample stability

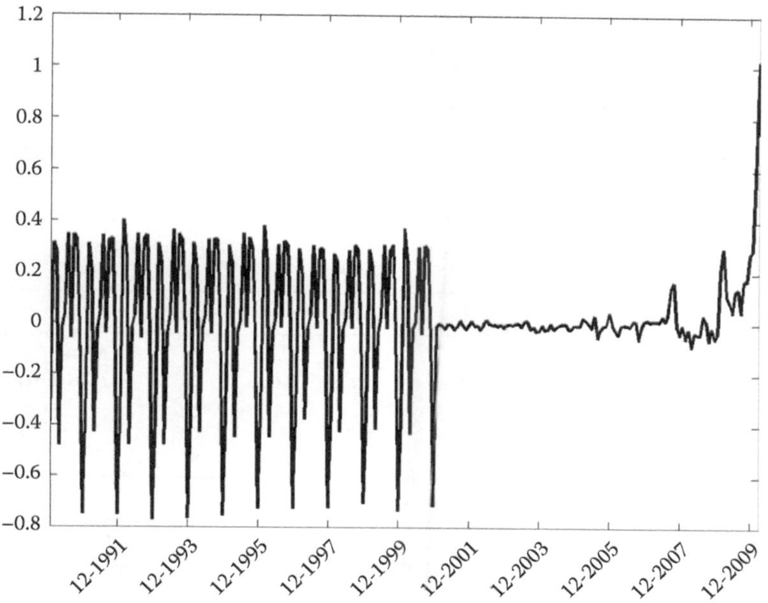

FIGURE 12.15
Revisions in the unadjusted series (percent points) made in the period April–December 2010.

of the results. Unfortunately, each new release includes revisions of the unadjusted series for previous periods. Typically, the revision affects the most recent months, although in May 2010 it affected the entire series and exhibited a strongly seasonal pattern for the first half (see Figure 12.15).

Adding the two ramps of the previous section, the automatic procedure was applied to the series finishing in each of the 10 months for March–December 2010. (The sequence of concurrent releases of the series were used, thus revisions in unadjusted data were ignored.) The 10 series produce the same model (for the logs), namely, the ARIMA (3,1,0) $(0,1,1)_{12}$ model with 6 TD variables, Easter effect, and no outlier. A summary of results is presented in Table 12.6.

The model fit, parameter estimates, residual diagnostics, and basic features of the decomposition barely change. Figure 12.16 plots the one-period-ahead forecast errors of the (log) series for the nine new months; they are small and random, with SE $= 0.0130$, in line with the in-sample residual SE. Despite the uncertainty created by the crisis and despite the revisions in the unadjusted data, automatic reestimation every month provides stable and acceptable results. The results are identical to those that would have been obtained with the rule mentioned above to balance stability versus misspecification.

TABLE 12.6
Results of Monthly Automatic Model Reidentification

Model Fit

	SE (res)	BIC	Real AR Root	Complex AR Roots Mod	Complex AR Roots Period	Seasonal MA Parameter	Ramp Coeff (t-val) 1st Ramp	Ramp Coeff (t-val) 2nd Ramp
Min	0.0110	−8.75	0.52	0.70	2.83	−0.37	−3.8	−11.1
Max	0.0111	−8.77	0.54	0.73	2.85	−0.39	−4.0	−11.4

Residual Diagnostics

	Q	N	Sk	Kur	Q2	Runs	QS	RMSE (in 10^{-2}) (OS Forecast)
Min	26.0	1.0	0.6	0.8	15	1.2	0.2	0.7
Max	27.6	1.8	0.7	1.2	16.7	1.8	0.3	1.0
CV	31.4	6	2	2	34	2	6	1.8

Features of the Adjustment

	SE of Innov (in 10^{-2}) Seasonal	SE of Innov (in 10^{-2}) Stoch TD	SE of Innov (in 10^{-2}) SA Series	SE of Concurrent Estimator (pp)	SE of Revision (pp)	% Convergence of Revision in One Year	SE of m-to-m SA Rog (in 10^{-2})
Min	0.39	0.17	0.56	0.53	0.43	75	0.54
Max	0.41	0.18	0.58	0.54	0.44	78	0.56

Note: Interval of variation for period March–November 2010.

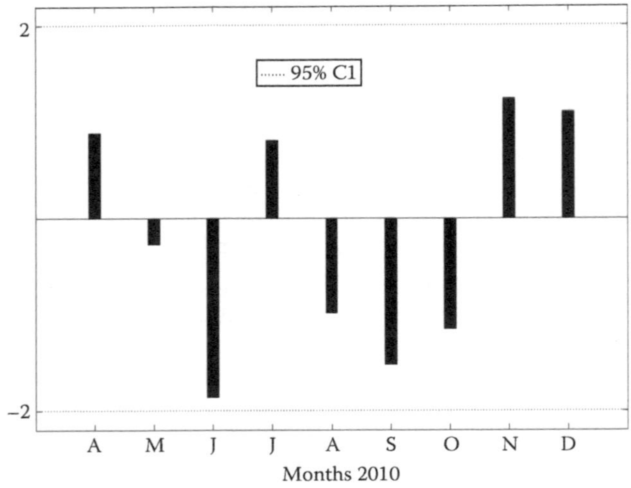

FIGURE 12.16
Out-of-sample forecast errors (t-values): period April–December 2010.

12.11 Conclusions

In the context of a recent debate among some European statisticians having to do with seasonal adjustment of the EIP Index, it is shown how the regARIMA model-based method of programs TRAMO–SEATS can be efficiently used, the results can be analyzed, and the quality of the adjustment—as well as the information the adjustment provides—can be improved.

In particular, it is seen how, by adding two ramps to deal with the abnormal drop at the beginning of the recent crisis, automatic use of the programs (that includes automatic model identification) provides excellent and stable results (despite nontrivial revisions in the unadjusted data).

References

Bell, W. R. (2004). On RegComponent time series models and their applications. In *State Space and Unobserved Component Models: Theory and Applications*, eds. A. C. Harvey, S. J. Koopman, and N. Shepard, 248–283. Cambridge: Cambridge University Press.

Bell, W. R. (2005). Some consideration of seasonal adjustment variances. *2005 Proceedings of the American Statistical Association*: Alexandria, VA.

Bell, W. R. and Hillmer, S. C. (1984). Issues involved with the seasonal adjustment of economic time series. *Journal of Business and Economic Statistics*, 2:291–320.

Bell, W. R. and Martin, D. E. K. (2004). Computation of asymmetric signal extraction filters and mean squared error for ARIMA component models. *Journal of Time Series Analysis*, 25:603–623.

Blakely, C. and McElroy, T. (2010). An empirical evaluation of signal extraction goodness-of-fit diagnostic tests. Mimeo. Statistical Research Division. U.S. Census Bureau.

Burman, J. P. (1980). Seasonal adjustment by signal extraction. *Journal of the Royal Statistical Society A*, 143:321–337.

Childers, D. G. (ed.) (1976). *Modern Spectrum Analysis.* New York: IEEE Press.

Eiglsperger, M. and Haine, W. (2010). Seasonal adjustment of Euro Area GDP and industrial production and the statistical treatment of the crisis.

Workshop on the Implementation of ESS Guidelines on Seasonal Adjustment. Mimeo. European Central Bank. May 2010.

Eurostat (2009). *ESS Guidelines on Seasonal Adjustment.* Luxembourg: Office for Official Publications of the European Communities.

Findley, D. F. (2005). Some recent developments and directions in seasonal adjustment. *Journal of Official Statistics*, 21(2):343–365.

Findley, D. F. and Martin, D. E. K. (2006). Frequency domain analyses of SEATS and X-11/12-ARIMA seasonal adjustment filters for short and moderate-length time series. *Journal of Official Statistics*, 22(1):1–34.

Findley, D. F., McElroy, T. S., and Wills, K. C. (2004). Modifications of SEAT's diagnostic for detecting over – or underestimation – of seasonal adjustment decomposition components. *2004 Proceedings of the American Statistical Association.* Alexandria, VA.

Findley, D. F., Monsell, B. C., Bell, W. R., Otto, M. C., and Chen, B. C. (1998). New capabilities and methods of the X-12-ARIMA seasonal adjustment program (with discussion). *Journal of Business and Economic Statistics*, 12:127–177.

Gómez, V. and Maravall, A. (2001a). Automatic modeling methods for univariate series. In *A Course in Time Series Analysis*, Chapter 7, eds. D. Peña, G. C. Tiao, and R. S. Tsay. New York: John Wiley.

Gómez, V. and Maravall, A. (2001b). Seasonal adjustment and signal extraction in economic time series. In *A Course in Time Series Analysis*, Chapter 8, eds. D. Peña, G. C. Tiao, and R. S. Tsay. New York: John Wiley.

Harvey, A. C. (1989). *Forecasting, Structural Time Series Models and the Kalman Filter.* Cambridge: Cambridge University Press.

Hillmer, S. C. and Tiao, G. C. (1982). An ARIMA model based approach to seasonal adjustment. *Journal of the American Statistical Association*, 77:63–70.

Jenkins, G. M. and Watts, D. G. (1968). *Spectral Analysis and Its Applications.* San Francisco: Holden Day.

Kaiser, R. and Maravall, A. (2005). Combining filter design with model-based filtering: An application to business-cycle estimation. *International Journal of Forecasting*, 21:691–710.

Maravall, A. (2003). A class of diagnostics in the ARIMA-model-based decomposition of a time series. *Seasonal Adjustment.* European Central Bank. November 2003.

Maravall, A. (1998). Comment on the X-12-ARIMA seasonal adjustment method. *Journal of Business and Economic Statistics*, 16:155–160.

Maravall, A. (1995). Unobserved components in economic time series. In *The Handbook of Applied Econometrics*, Chapter 1, eds. H. Pesaran and M. Wickens, 12–72. Oxford: Basil Blackwell.

Maravall, A. (1987). On minimum mean squared error estimation of the noise in unobserved component models. *Journal of Business and Economic Statistics*, 5:115–120.

McElroy, T. S. (2008a). Matrix formulas for non-stationary signal extraction. *Econometric Theory*, 24:1–22.

McElroy, T. S. (2008b). Statistical properties of model-based signal extraction diagnostic tests. *Communications in Statistics, Theory and Methods*, 37:591–616.

McElroy, T. S. and Wildi, M. (2010). Signal extraction revision variances as a goodness-of-fit measure. Statistical Research Division Research Report #2010-06. U.S. Census Bureau.

McElroy, T. S. and Gagnon, R. (2008). Finite sample revision variances for ARIMA model-based signal extraction. *Journal of Official Statistics*, 24:451–467.

Monsell, B. C. (2009). Update on the development of X-13ARIMA-SEATS. *Joint Statistical Meetings Proceedings*. Alexandria: VA.

Pierce, D. A. (1980). Data revisions in moving average seasonal adjustment procedures. *Journal of Econometrics*, 14:95–114.

Pierce, D. A. (1979). Signal extraction error in non-stationary time series. *Annals of Statistics*, 7:1303–1320.

Part V

Outlier Detection and Modeling Time Series with Extreme Values

13

Additive Outlier Detection in Seasonal ARIMA Models by a Modified Bayesian Information Criterion

Pedro Galeano and Daniel Peña

CONTENTS

13.1 Introduction

The detection of outliers in a time series is an important issue because their presence may have serious effects on the analysis in many different ways. For instance, even if the time series model is well specified, outliers can lead to biased parameter estimation, which may result in poor forecasts. Several outlier detection procedures have been proposed for detecting different outlier types in autoregressive-integrated-moving average (ARIMA) time series models, including those proposed in Fox (1972), Tsay (1986, 1988), Chang et al. (1988), Chen and Liu (1993), McCulloch and Tsay (1994), Luceño (1998), Justel et al. (2001), Bianco et al. (2001), and Sánchez and Peña (2003), among others. Most of these methods are based on sequential detection procedures that first search for the presence of an outlier. When the first outlier is found, its size is estimated, its effect is cleaned from the series, and a new search for outliers is carried out. However, as Sánchez and Peña (2003) pointed out, sequential detection procedures have three main drawbacks. First, a biased estimation of the initial parameter values may strongly affect the power to detect the outliers. Second, in many situations, the distributions of the test statistics are unknown and critical values needed to apply the tests should be estimated via simulation for different sample sizes and models. Indeed, iterative procedures sequentially test for the presence of outliers, which usually leads to overdetection of their number as a consequence of the inability to control the size of the outlier tests. Third, they suffer from both the masking effect, which means that outliers are undetected because of the presence of others, and the swamping effect, which means that outliers affect the data in such a way that good observations appear to be outliers as well.

The main purpose of this chapter is to develop a procedure for detecting additive outliers in seasonal ARIMA time series models based on model selection strategies. The proposed procedure is designed to try to mitigate the drawbacks of sequential detection methods. In order to achieve this goal, it is shown that the problem of detecting additive outliers in seasonal ARIMA models can be formulated as a model selection problem in which the candidate models explicitly assume the presence of additive outliers at given time points. Therefore, the problem of detecting additive outliers reduces to the problem of selecting the best model, which is the one that contains the true outliers in the series. It is important to note that this chapter is focused on the detection of additive outliers, which are especially pernicious, for instance, in unit root testing; see Perron and Rodriguez (2003). Although the proposed methodology can be extended to additional types of outliers, this requires more elaboration and is beyond the scope of this chapter. Therefore, this chapter can be seen as a first attempt at outlier detection in time series based on model selection strategies.

Model selection is one of the most important problems in statistics and consists in selecting, from a set of candidate models, the one that best fits the data under some specific criteria. Two main strategies have been developed: the goal of the efficient criteria is to select the model that it is expected to best predict new observations, while the goal of the consistent criteria is to select the model that actually has generated the data. These strategies lead to different model selection criteria. The efficient criteria include, among others, the Final Prediction Error (FPE), proposed by Akaike (1969), which is an estimator of the one-step-ahead prediction variance; the Akaike Information Criterion (AIC), proposed by Akaike (1973), which is an estimator of the expected Kullback–Leibler divergence between the true and the fitted model; and the corrected Akaike Information Criterion (AICc), derived by Hurvich and Tsai (1989), which is a bias-corrected form of the AIC that appears to work better in small samples. These criteria have the property that, under the main assumption that the data come from a model with an infinite number of parameters, they asymptotically select the model producing the least mean squared prediction error. The consistent criteria include, among others, the Bayesian information criterion (BIC), derived by Schwarz (1978), which approaches the posterior probabilities of the models; and the Hannan and Quinn

Criterion (HQC), derived by Hannan and Quinn (1979), which was designed to have the fastest convergence rate to the true model. These criteria have the property that, assuming that the data come from a model with a finite number of parameters, the criteria will asymptotically select the true model.

This chapter proposes a new model selection criterion for selecting the model for a time series that follows a seasonal ARIMA model and is contaminated by additive outliers. The proposed model selection criterion avoids the use of multiple hypothesis testing, iterative procedures, and the simulation of critical values. As the objective is to incorporate in the final model the true number of additive outliers in a time series, the model selection criterion considered in this chapter falls more naturally into the category of consistent criteria. Therefore, we explore some modification of the Bayesian information criterion including an additional term useful for outlier detection. However, computation of the values of the criterion for all the possible candidate models, including all the possible configurations of outliers, may be impossible even for small sample sizes. Therefore, this chapter also proposes a procedure for selecting the most promising models.

The remainder of this chapter is organized as follows. In Section 13.2, the additive outlier detection problem for seasonal ARIMA models is formulated as a model selection problem. Section 13.3 presents the modified Bayesian information criterion for these models. Section 13.4 proposes a procedure for selecting the most promising models. Finally, Section 13.5 is devoted to showing the performance of the procedure by means of simulated and real data examples.

13.2 Formulation of the Outlier Detection Problem

A time series x_t follows a seasonal ARIMA$(p,d,q) \times (P,D,Q)_s$ model if,

$$\Phi_P(B^s)\phi_p(B)(1-B^s)^D(1-B)^d x_t = \Theta_Q(B^s)\theta_q(B)\epsilon_t, \qquad (13.2.1)$$

where B is the backshift operator such that $Bx_t = x_{t-1}$; $\phi_p(B) = 1 - \phi_1 B - \cdots - \phi_p B^p$ and $\theta_q(B) = 1 - \theta_1 B - \cdots - \theta_q B^q$ are regular backshift operator polynomials of finite degrees p and q, respectively; $\Phi_P(B^s) = 1 - \Phi_1 B^s - \cdots - \Phi_P B^{sP}$ and $\Theta_Q(B^s) = 1 - \Theta_1 B^s - \cdots - \Theta_Q B^{sQ}$ are seasonal backshift operator polynomials with seasonal period s of finite degrees P and Q, respectively; d is the number of regular differences; D is the number of seasonal differences; and ϵ_t is a sequence of independent and identically distributed Gaussian random variables with zero mean and standard deviation σ. It is assumed that the roots of $\phi_p(B)$, $\theta_q(B)$, $\Theta_Q(B^s)$, and $\Phi_P(B^s)$ are all outside the unit circle and that neither the polynomials $\phi_p(B)$ and $\theta_q(B)$ nor $\Phi_P(B^s)$ and $\Theta_Q(B^s)$ have common factors. In the case of $D = P = Q = 0$, the model in Equation 13.2.1 reduces to the nonseasonal ARIMA model.

Suppose now that the observed time series $(y_1, \ldots, y_T)$ contains m additive outliers. Therefore,

$$y_t = x_t + w_{t_1} I_t^{(t_1)} + \cdots + w_{t_m} I_t^{(t_m)},$$

where x_t follows the seasonal ARIMA$(p, d, q) \times (P, D, Q)_s$ model in Equation 13.2.1, $\tau_m = (t_1, \ldots, t_m)'$ is the $m \times 1$ vector containing the locations of the outliers, for each $h \in \tau_m$, $I_t^{(h)}$ is a dummy variable such that $I_t^{(h)} = 1$ if $t = h$ and is zero otherwise, and $w_{t_1}, \ldots, w_{t_m}$ are the outlier sizes at the corresponding locations. Consequently, the time series y_t follows the regression model with seasonal ARIMA errors given by

$$\begin{aligned} \Phi_P(B^s)\phi_p(B)(1-B^s)^D(1-B)^d(y_t - w_{t_1} I_t^{(t_1)} - \cdots - w_{t_m} I_t^{(t_m)}) \\ = \Theta_Q(B^s)\theta_q(B)\epsilon_t, \qquad (13.2.2) \end{aligned}$$

in which the regressors are the dummy variables and the parameters linked with the regressors are the outlier sizes. This model is denoted as M_{τ_m}. Note that this notation suppresses whichever combination $t_1, \ldots, t_m$ and seasonal ARIMA model are being considered, but this will be clear in the context. The parameters of the model M_{τ_m} can be summarized in the $p_m \times 1$ vector given by

$$\rho_{\tau_m} = (\phi_1, \ldots, \phi_p, \theta_1, \ldots, \theta_q, \Phi_1, \ldots, \Phi_P, \Theta_1, \ldots, \Theta_Q, w_{t_1}, \ldots, w_{t_m}, \sigma)',$$

where $p_m = p + q + P + Q + m + 1$.

Let $\mathcal{L}(\rho_{\tau_m} | y, M_{\tau_m})$ be the likelihood function of the time series $y = (y_1, \ldots, y_T)'$, given the model M_{τ_m} and its parameters ρ_{τ_m}. Exact maximum likelihood estimates (MLEs) of the model parameters, denoted as $\widehat{\rho}_{\tau_m}$, are obtained after maximizing the likelihood $\mathcal{L}(\rho_{\tau_m} | y, M_{\tau_m})$ with respect to the parameters ρ_{τ_m}. Several methods for maximizing the likelihood of seasonal ARIMA regression models such as the one in Equation 13.2.2 are available. See, for instance, the methods proposed by Harvey and Phillips (1979), Kohn and Ansley (1985), and Gómez and Maravall (1994), among others. In particular, in the simulated and real data examples in Section 13.5, the `arima` function implemented in the statistical software R (http://www.r-project.org/) is used. This function computes the exact likelihood via a state-space representation of the ARIMA process, and the innovations and their variances are found by a Kalman filter.

In summary, given the time series y, the number and location of the additive outliers, m and τ_m, respectively, and the parameter vector, ρ_{τ_m}, are unknown and have to be estimated from the observed time series. Determining the number and location of outliers in y is now equivalent to selecting the model M_{τ_m} with the true outliers from among the set of candidate models. Once this is done, inference on the vector of parameters, ρ_{τ_m}, can be carried out by means of the MLEs, $\widehat{\rho}_{\tau_m}$. However, note that such inferences are conditional on the assumption that the true outliers have been selected.

13.3 Modified Bayesian Information Criterion for Outlier Detection

Once the outlier detection problem has been written as a model selection problem, the aim of this section is to propose a criterion to select the model M_{τ_m} that contains the true additive outliers in the series. Note that the candidate models include the one without outliers, M_{τ_0}, the T models with one outlier, M_{τ_1}, and so on. In total, there are $\binom{T}{m}$ candidate models with m outliers covering all the possible outlier locations. Thus, assuming that the number of outliers has an upper bound, $m_{\max} < T$, the total number of candidate models is given by

$$\binom{T}{0} + \binom{T}{1} + \cdots + \binom{T}{m_{\max}}. \tag{13.3.1}$$

This section proposes a model selection criterion for selecting the model M_{τ_m} by a modification of the BIC that includes an additional term that may be useful for outlier detection.

The BIC is derived after approximating the posterior distributions of the candidate models, denoted as $p(M_{\tau_m}|y)$. This is given by (see Claeskens and Hjort (2008)),

$$p(M_{\tau_m}|y) = \frac{p(M_{\tau_m})\mathcal{L}(M_{\tau_m}|y)}{f(y)}, \tag{13.3.2}$$

where $p(M_{\tau_m})$ is the prior probability of model M_{τ_m}, $\mathcal{L}(M_{\tau_m}|y)$ is the marginal likelihood for model M_{τ_m} given by

$$\mathcal{L}(M_{\tau_m}|y) = \int \mathcal{L}\left(\rho_{\tau_m}|y, M_{\tau_m}\right) p\left(\rho_{\tau_m}|M_{\tau_m}\right) d\rho_{\tau_m}, \tag{13.3.3}$$

with $p(\rho_{\tau_m}|M_{\tau_m})$, the prior probability of the parameters given the model M_{τ_m}, and $f(y)$ is the unconditional likelihood of y given by

$$f(y) = \sum_{j=0}^{m_{\max}} \sum_{\tau_j} p(M_{\tau_j})\mathcal{L}(M_{\tau_j}|y).$$

From a Bayesian point of view, and taking into account that $f(y)$ is constant for all the models, in order to compute $p(M_{\tau_m}|y)$, it is required to give prior probabilities to the models M_{τ_m} and to compute the marginal likelihood for each model M_{τ_m}, $\mathcal{L}(M_{\tau_m}|y)$. Therefore, calculation of the posterior probabilities in Equation 13.3.2 requires specification of the priors of the models and parameters, and integration over the parameter space. However, obtaining an analytical expression for $\mathcal{L}(M_{\tau_m}|y)$ is infeasible. Alternatively, a second-order expansion of the log-likelihood function, $\ell_{\tau_m}(\rho_{\tau_m}) = \log \mathcal{L}(\rho_{\tau_m}|y, M_{\tau_m})$, around the MLEs, $\widehat{\rho}_{\tau_m}$, leads to the following Laplace approximation to the integral in Equation 13.3.3; see Claeskens and Hjort (2008),

$$\mathcal{L}(M_{\tau_m}|y) = \left(\frac{2\pi}{T}\right)^{\frac{p_m}{2}} \exp\left(\ell_{\tau_m}(\widehat{\rho}_{\tau_m})\right) p\left(\widehat{\rho}_{\tau_m}|M_{\tau_m}\right) \left|H_{\tau_m}\left(\widehat{\rho}_{\tau_m}\right)\right|^{-\frac{1}{2}} + O\left(T^{-\frac{p_m}{2}-1}\right),$$

where $p\left(\widehat{\rho}_{\tau_m}|M_{\tau_m}\right)$ is the prior of the parameters given the model, and $\ell_{\tau_m}(\widehat{\rho}_{\tau_m})$ and $H_{\tau_m}(\widehat{\rho}_{\tau_m})$ are, respectively, the log-likelihood and the Hessian matrix of $T^{-1}\ell_{\tau_m}(\rho_{\tau_m})$, all evaluated at $\widehat{\rho}_{\tau_m}$. Therefore, Equation 13.3.2 can be written as follows:

$$p(M_{\tau_m}|y) = \frac{p(M_{\tau_m})}{f(y)}\left[\left(\frac{2\pi}{T}\right)^{\frac{p_m}{2}} \exp\left(\ell_{\tau_m}(\widehat{\rho}_{\tau_m})\right) p\left(\widehat{\rho}_{\tau_m}|M_{\tau_m}\right) \left|H_{\tau_m}\left(\widehat{\rho}_{\tau_m}\right)\right|^{-\frac{1}{2}} + O\left(T^{-\frac{p_m}{2}-1}\right)\right], \tag{13.3.4}$$

which also depends on the prior probabilities of the models, $p(M_{\tau_m})$, and on the unconditional likelihood, $f(y)$. Taking logarithms, Equation 13.3.4 leads to,

$$\log p(M_{\tau_m}|y) = \ell_{\tau_m}(\widehat{\rho}_{\tau_m}) + \frac{p_m}{2}\log\frac{2\pi}{T} - \frac{1}{2}\log\left|H_{\tau_m}(\widehat{\rho}_{\tau_m})\right| + \log p(\widehat{\rho}_{\tau_m}|M_{\tau_m}) + \log p(M_{\tau_m}) - \log f(y) + O(T^{-1}). \tag{13.3.5}$$

Following Claeskens and Hjort (2008), the dominant terms in Equation 13.3.5 are the first two, which are of sizes $O_P(T)$ and $\log T$, respectively, while the others are $O_P(1)$. The usual BIC approximation of the posterior probability in Equation 13.3.5 is based on assuming uniform prior probabilities for all the candidate models. Thus, the prior probability of model M_{τ_m} under the BIC approximation is given by

$$p_{\text{BIC}}(M_{\tau_m}) = \frac{1}{\binom{T}{0} + \binom{T}{1} + \cdots + \binom{T}{m_{\max}}},$$

which is independent of the number of outliers, m. Now, taking uniform prior probabilities for the parameters of the models and ignoring all the lower order terms, minus two times Equation 13.3.5 leads to the BIC, which selects the model M_{τ_m} that minimizes

$$\text{BIC}(M_{\tau_m}) = -2\ell_{\tau_m}(\widehat{\rho}_{\tau_m}) + p_m \log T. \tag{13.3.6}$$

However, note that the prior probability of the number of outliers used by the BIC approximation is given by

$$p_{\text{BIC}}(m) = \sum_{\tau_m,\ m \text{ fixed}} p_{\text{BIC}}(M_{\tau_m}) = \frac{\binom{T}{m}}{\binom{T}{0} + \binom{T}{1} + \cdots + \binom{T}{m_{\max}}}. \tag{13.3.7}$$

As a consequence, when $m_{\max} \ll T/2$, i.e., when the maximum possible number of outliers is small compared with $T/2$, as is expected in most real time series applications, the model with the largest prior probability is the model with the largest possible number of outliers. Indeed, the prior probabilities assigned by the BIC in Equation 13.3.7 are an increasing function of the number of outliers m, which may be unreasonable. For instance, note that $p_{\mathrm{BIC}}(1)$ and $p_{\mathrm{BIC}}(2)$ are T and $T(T-1)/2$ times larger than $p_{\mathrm{BIC}}(0)$.

Next, an alternative criterion to the BIC in Equation 13.3.6 is proposed. This is called *BICUP* (for BIC with uniform prior), and it is based on penalizing for the possible number of outliers. This leads to a uniform prior distribution over the number of outliers. Then, taking equal prior probabilities for all the models with the same number of outliers, the prior probability of the model M_{τ_m} under the *BICUP* approximation is given by

$$p_{BICUP}(M_{\tau_m}) = \frac{1}{1+m_{\max}} \frac{1}{\binom{T}{m}}.$$

Now, taking uniform prior probabilities for the parameters of the models, and after deleting constants and low order terms, minus two times Equation 13.3.5 leads to the *BICUP* for outlier detection, which selects the model M_{τ_m} that minimizes

$$BICUP(M_{\tau_m}) = -2\ell_{\tau_m}(\widehat{\rho}_{\tau_m}) + p_m \log T + 2\log\binom{T}{m}. \qquad (13.3.8)$$

Note that the expression of the *BICUP* in Equation 13.3.8 is similar to the expression of the BIC in Equation 13.3.6 except for the last term, which shows an additional penalization for models that increases with m. Consequently, the *BICUP* naturally incorporates the information about the number of models for different numbers of outliers. The prior probability of the number of outliers taken by the *BICUP* approximation is given by

$$p_{BICUP}(m) = \sum_{\tau_m,\ m \text{ fixed}} p_{BICUP}(M_{\tau_m}) = \frac{1}{1+m_{\max}},$$

which has the attractive property that the probability of having an additional additive outlier does not depend on the global number of outliers, since the prior ratio,

$$\frac{p_{BICUP}(M_{\tau_{m+1}})}{p_{BICUP}(M_{\tau_m})} = 1,$$

is independent of m. Then, all the possible numbers of outliers are equally probable *a priori*. Figure 13.1 shows the last term in Equation 13.3.8 as a function of m and T. In particular, the additional term increases with m and/or T, so that the penalization is larger than the BIC penalization for large values of m and T.

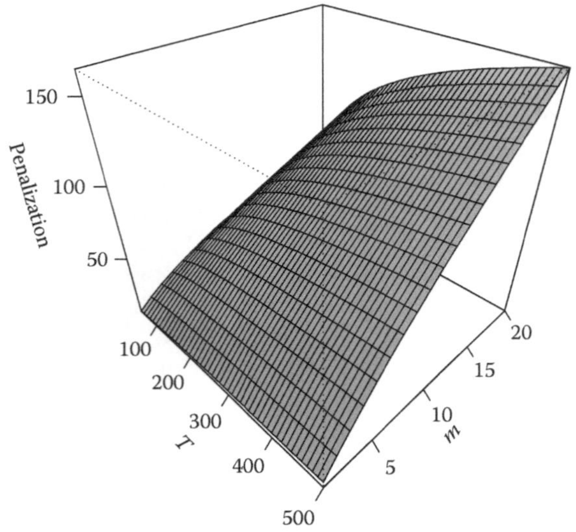

FIGURE 13.1
Last term of *BICUP* as a function of T and m.

In summary, the model M_{τ_m} is selected as the one that provides the minimum value of the proposed *BICUP*. Note that the model selection determines the number of outliers, m, their locations, τ_m, and the MLEs, $\widehat{\rho}_{\tau_m}$, of the model parameters. Additionally, the model selection criterion for outlier detection in Equation 13.3.8 provides approximations of the posterior probabilities $p(M_{\tau_m}|y)$. More precisely, the approximated value of $p(M_{\tau_m}|y)$ is given by

$$p_{BICUP}(M_{\tau_m}|y) = \frac{\exp\left(-\frac{BICUP(M_{\tau_m})}{2}\right)}{\sum_{j=0}^{m_{\max}} \sum_{\tau_j} \exp\left(-\frac{BICUP(M_{\tau_j})}{2}\right)}.$$

Also, pairwise comparison of two models can be done using the *BICUP* approximation of the posterior odds for model M_{τ_m} against M_{τ_n}, which is given by

$$\begin{aligned} o_{BICUP}(M_{\tau_m}, M_{\tau_n}|y) &= \frac{p_{BICUP}(M_{\tau_m}|y)}{p_{BICUP}(M_{\tau_n}|y)} \\ &= \exp\left(\frac{BICUP(M_{\tau_n}) - BICUP(M_{\tau_m})}{2}\right), \end{aligned} \quad (13.3.9)$$

which only requires computation of the values of the *BICUP* for models M_{τ_m} and M_{τ_n}.

13.4 Procedure for Detecting Potential Outliers

There is an additional problem in computing the value of the *BICUP*. As noted in Section 13.2, the number of candidate models, given in Equation 13.3.1, may be huge even for small values of T and $m_{\max}$. Consequently, getting the values of the proposed criterion for all the possible candidate models is a computationally expensive problem. This section proposes a procedure for reducing the number of models for which the criterion should be computed. The procedure is based on that proposed by Peña and Tiao (1992) for defining Bayesian robustness functions in linear models. The idea is to split the time series observations into two groups: the first would include observations that have high potential of being outliers, while the second includes the observations that should be discarded as outliers beyond any reasonable doubt. If T_1 is the number of observations in the first group, then, instead of computing the value of the proposed criterion for all the candidate models, it is possible to compute it for all the models, which include as outliers all the combinations of the T_1 observations in the first group. Thus, the number of candidate models reduces to,

$$\binom{T_1}{0} + \binom{T_1}{1} + \cdots + \binom{T_1}{T_1},$$

which is a much smaller number than the one in Equation 13.3.1.

Obviously, the key point in the procedure is to split the time series observations into these two groups. Due to the masking and swamping effects, the groups cannot be made by simply computing the value of the proposed criterion for the T models M_{τ_1}. Alternatively, the following approach is considered. Let A_r be the event "the observation y_r is an outlier given the y." Then, the probability of two observations, y_r and y_s, being outliers can be written as follows:

$$P(A_r \cap A_s) = P(A_r|A_s)P(A_s). \tag{13.4.1}$$

If y_r and y_s are nonoutlying time points, the probability in Equation 13.4.1 is approximately given by $P(A_r)P(A_s)$ because $P(A_r|A_s) \simeq P(A_r)$. However, if y_s is an outlier, $P(A_r|A_s)$ will be very different than $P(A_r)$ because the correct detection of an outlier will affect the value of $P(A_r)$, and $P(A_r \cap A_s)$ will be quite different from $P(A_r)P(A_s)$. As a consequence, a way to distinguish potential outliers is to examine the values of the differences, $P(A_r \cap A_s) - P(A_r)P(A_s)$.

However, computation of these probabilities is also a difficult task because they involve a large number of probabilities. As an alternative, it is possible to use the approximated posterior odds given in Equation 13.3.9. The idea is to build the interactions matrix with elements,

$$\begin{aligned} &d_{BICUP}(r,s) \\ &\quad = |o_{BICUP}(M_{\tau_2}^{r,s}, M_{\tau_0}|y) - o_{BICUP}(M_{\tau_1}^{r}, M_{\tau_0}|y)o_{BICUP}(M_{\tau_1}^{s}, M_{\tau_0}|y)|, \end{aligned}$$

for $r, s = 1, \ldots, T$, where $o_{BICUP}(M_{\tau_2}^{r,s}, M_{\tau_0}|y)$ is the *BICUP* approximation of the posterior odds of the model that assumes that y_r and y_s are outliers against M_{τ_0}, and $o_{BICUP}(M_{\tau_1}^{r}, M_{\tau_0}|y)$ and $o_{BICUP}(M_{\tau_1}^{s}, M_{\tau_0}|y)$ are the *BICUP* approximations of the posterior odds of the model that assumes that, on the one hand, y_r and, on the other hand, y_s, are outliers, against M_{τ_0}. If y_r is an outlier, the values $d_{BICUP}(r, \cdot)$ are expected to have relatively large values. Indeed, if there are other outliers masked by y_r, these will show up as large values in the distribution of $d_{BICUP}(r, \cdot)$. Thus, large values of $d_{BICUP}(r, \cdot)$ will indicate outliers, and relatively large values in a column, possible masking between these points. Therefore, a procedure for pointing out potential outliers is the following:

1. Compute the values of $o_{BICUP}(M_{\tau_1}^{r}, M_{\tau_0}|y)$ for all the models with an outlier at time point $r = 1, \ldots, T$. Let $m(o_{BICUP})$ and $sd(o_{BICUP})$ be the mean and the standard deviation of the values of $o_{BICUP}(M_{\tau_1}^{r}, M_{\tau_0}|y)$. Then, include in the set of potential outliers those points that satisfy

$$o_{BICUP}\left(M_{\tau_1}^{r}, M_{\tau_0}|y\right) \geq m(o_{BICUP}) + 3 \times sd(o_{BICUP}). \quad (13.4.2)$$

2. Compute the values of $d_{BICUP}(r, s)$ for all the models with two outliers at the time points $r, s = 1, \ldots, T$. Let $m(d_{BICUP})$ and $sd(d_{BICUP})$ be the mean and the standard deviation of the values of $d_{BICUP}(r, \cdot)$. Then, include in the set of potential outliers those points y_s that satisfy

$$d_{BICUP}(r, s) \geq m(d_{BICUP}) + 5 \times sd(d_{BICUP}). \quad (13.4.3)$$

Several comments on this procedure are in order. First, once the procedure provides the set of potential outliers, the values of the *BICUP* for all the models included in this set are computed and the model that gives the minimum value of the *BICUP* is the selected model. Then, estimation of the model parameters and outlier sizes is made jointly through the MLEs. Second, note that the use of the procedure avoids the problem of choosing the value of $m_{\max}$, i.e., the maximum number of outliers allowed, because it is only required to compute the value of the criterion for those models that include potential outliers. Therefore, the number of potential outliers can be seen as the value of $m_{\max}$. Third, the values 3 and 5 have been chosen following the suggestions in Peña and Tiao (1992). Indeed, in our experience with simulated time series, these values provide a number of potential outliers equal to or slightly larger than the true number of outliers. Therefore, these values contribute in an appropriate way to establishing the observations that are suspected to be outliers and to give an accurate estimate of the maximum number of possible outliers m_{max}. This is important because taking smaller values may lead to a large group of potential outliers that includes false outliers, which may lead to estimation problems, while taking larger values may lead to a small group of potential outliers not including all the true outliers. In those unexpected situations in which the number of candidate outliers given by the procedure is large, we can use the median and MAD (median of the absolute deviations from the sample median) instead of the mean and standard deviation. In this situation, following Peña (2005), we can consider as heterogeneous observations those that deviate from the median by more than 4.5 times the MAD. Fourth, it may appear that the *BICUP* interactions matrix is only able to point out the presence of two outliers and that higher order interactions should be analyzed. However, our simulation experiments showed us that this not the case. An example of this can be seen in Section 13.5.

13.5 Examples

This section illustrates the performance of the proposed outlier detection methodology for a simulated series and for the time series of logarithms of the monthly total retail sales in the United States.

13.5.1 Outlier Detection for a Simulated Time Series

A simulated time series contaminated with three additive outliers is built as follows. First, a series with sample size $T = 100$ is simulated from the seasonal ARIMA$(0,1,1) \times (0,1,1)_{12}$ model given by

$$(1 - B^{12})(1 - B)x_t = (1 + 0.5B^{12})(1 + 0.4B)\epsilon_t,$$

where ϵ_t follows a Gaussian distribution with zero mean and standard deviation $\sigma = 0.7071$. Then, the series $(x_1, \ldots, x_T)$ is contaminated with three additive outliers at time points $t_1 = 50$, $t_2 = 51$, and $t_3 = 52$ and outlier sizes $w_{50} = 3$, $w_{51} = -3$, and $w_{52} = 3$, respectively. Thus, the outlier magnitudes are around 4.25 times the error standard deviation. The contaminated time series is, then, given by

$$y_t = x_t + 3I_t^{(50)} - 3I_t^{(51)} + 3I_t^{(52)},$$

for $t = 1, \ldots, T$. Both the outlier-free and the contaminated time series are shown in Figure 13.2. Note that the outlier effects are almost imperceptible in the plot. However, the additive outliers produce large effects in parameter estimation. This is illustrated in Table 13.1, which includes the estimates of the parameters of two seasonal ARIMA$(0,1,1) \times (0,1,1)_{12}$ models fitted to the contaminated series y_t. The table shows that the parameter estimates ignoring the presence of the additive outliers are very different than the true model parameters, whereas when the model includes the three outliers the estimation is accurate.

Next, we apply the procedure described in Section 13.4 for selecting potential outliers to the contaminated series $(y_1, \ldots, y_T)$. The first step of the

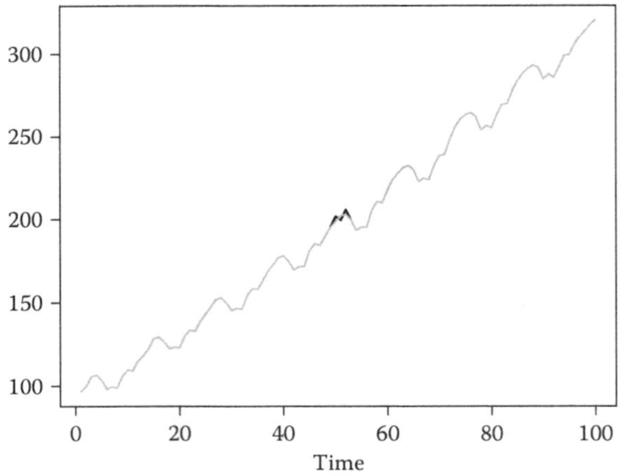

FIGURE 13.2
Simulated time series with (in black) and without (in gray) outliers.

procedure consists of computing the values of the *BICUP* approximated posterior odds for models with one outlier, i.e., $M_{\tau_1}^t$ for $t = 1, \ldots, T$, against M_{τ_0}. Figure 13.3 shows these values. The straight horizontal line in the plot is the height of the threshold in Equation 13.4.2. The plot in Figure 13.3 shows that the observation at time point $t = 51$ is labeled as a potential outlier because the value of its *BICUP* approximated posterior odds is much larger than the threshold. Importantly, note that the observations at time points $t = 50$ and

TABLE 13.1
Estimated Parameters and Standard Errors in the Simulated Series Contaminated by Three Outliers

True Parameter Values	Estimated Parameter Values: Model without the Outliers	Model with the Outliers
$\theta_1 = -0.4$	0.378	−0.456
	(0.092)	(0.125)
$\Theta_1 = -0.5$	0.220	−0.408
	(0.135)	(0.153)
$w_{50} = 3$	—	2.814
		(0.58)
$w_{51} = -3$	—	−2.973
		(0.785)
$w_{52} = 3$	—	2.84
		(0.568)
$\sigma = 0.707$	1.373	0.722

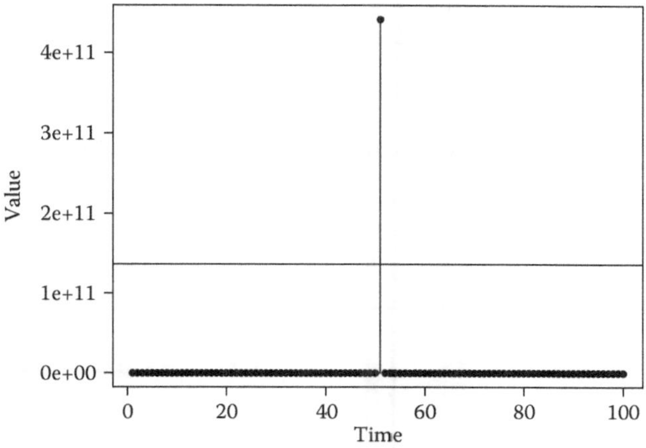

FIGURE 13.3
BICUP approximated posterior odds for models with one outlier in the simulated series contaminated with three outliers.

$t = 52$ are not labeled as potential outliers in this first step, maybe because they are masked by the outlier at $t = 51$. This example shows the need for the second step in the algorithm described in Section 13.4.

The second step of the procedure starts by computing the *BICUP* interactions matrix and the corresponding thresholds for the 100 rows of the matrix given in Equation 13.4.3. The three observations at $t = 50$, $t = 51$, and $t = 52$ are labeled as potential outliers by the procedure. More precisely, on the one hand, the rows 1 to 49 and 53 to 100 of the interactions matrix point out that the observation at $t = 51$ is a potential outlier. On the other hand, the rows 50 and 51, and then 51 and 52, point out that the observations at $t = 52$ and $t = 50$ are also potential outliers, respectively. Figure 13.4 shows the row numbers 50, 51, and 52 of the *BICUP* interactions matrix. The straight horizontal lines in the plots are the height of the corresponding thresholds given in Equation 13.4.3. Note that there are no nonoutlier observations pointed out as potential outliers.

The last step of the proposed methodology is to compute the values of the *BICUP* for only those models that incorporate the potential outliers at time points $t = 50$, $t = 51$, and $t = 52$. Table 13.2 shows these values for all the models considered. As can be seen, the *BICUP* selects the model with the true outliers. Once the outliers have been detected, inference on the model parameters can be performed through the MLEs. The second column in Table 13.1 shows the parameter estimates of the model that incorporates the true outliers. Note that the parameter estimates of the seasonal ARIMA$(0,1,1) \times (0,1,1)_{12}$ fitted to the contaminated series y_t and the outlier size estimates are very close to their real values.

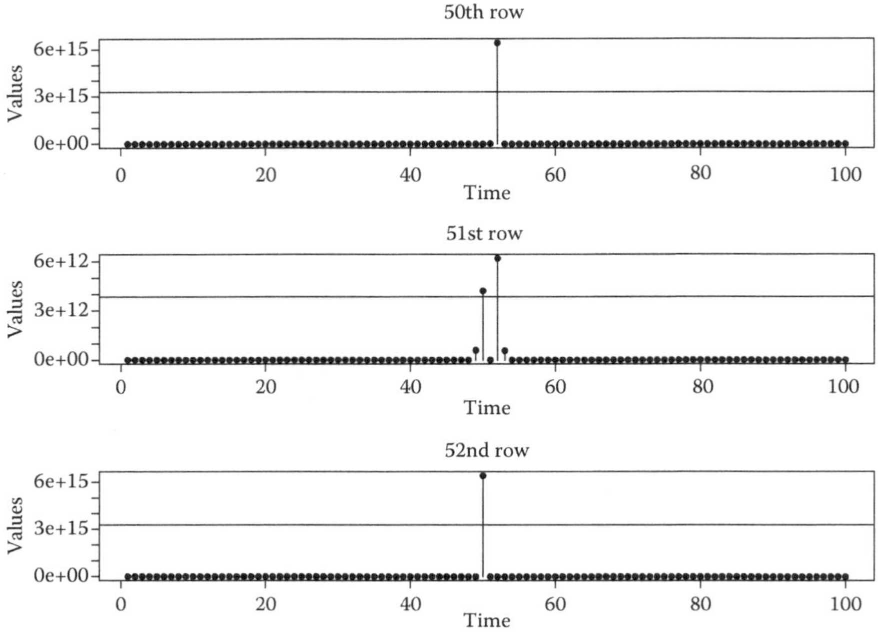

FIGURE 13.4
Rows of the *BICUP* interactions matrix in the simulated series contaminated with three outliers.

Finally, although the proposed procedure is only suited for series with additive outliers, we compare the previous results with the results obtained with the seasonal adjustment software X-12-ARIMA developed by the U.S. Census Bureau. The X-12-ARIMA software, besides fitting the seasonal ARIMA model, searches for three outlier types—additive outliers, level changes and transitory changes—using a sequential detection procedure. In this case, the X-12-ARIMA software detects a level shift at $t = 50$ with estimated size 3.0391, an additive outlier at $t = 51$ with estimated size -5.8669, and a level shift at $t = 53$ with estimated size -2.8975. Note that the estimated size of the second level shift is very close to the estimated size of the first level shift but with negative sign. Therefore, the second level shift somehow cancels the effect of the first level shift.

TABLE 13.2
Values of the Criteria for Candidate Models in the Simulated Series Contaminated with Three Outliers

τ_m	(−)	(50)	(51)	(52)	(50, 51)	(50, 52)	(51, 52)	(50, 51, 52)
BICUP	321.3	316.6	267.6	315.9	268.5	248.5	269	**246.8**

13.5.2 Outlier Detection for the Logarithms of the Monthly Total Retail Sales in the United States

The performance of the proposed methodology is illustrated by analyzing the logarithms of the monthly total retail sales in the United States. The time series, which starts in January 1992 and ends in December 2007, so that it consists of $T = 192$ data points, is plotted in Figure 13.5. The series has clearly seasonal behavior. In order to account for trading-day effects, we include seven regressor variables in the model. The first six variables are defined as $r_{1t} = (no.\ of\ Mondays) - (no.\ of\ Sundays)$ in month $t, \ldots, r_{6t} = (no.\ of\ Saturdays) - (no.\ of\ Sundays)$ in month t, along with a variable defined as $r_{7t} = length\ of\ month\ t$. Then, a seasonal ARIMA$(0,1,1) \times (0,1,1)_{12}$ model plus the seven regressors is fitted to the time series. The autocorrelation function of the residual series does not show serial dependence, so that the fit appears to be appropriate. Table 13.3 includes the estimates of the parameters of two seasonal ARIMA$(0,1,1) \times (0,1,1)_{12}$ models with trading-day effects fitted to the time series. In particular, the second column in Table 13.3 shows the MLEs of the parameters of this model along with their standard errors.

Next, we apply the procedure described in Section 13.4 for selecting potential outliers in the logarithm of the monthly total retail sales series. The first step of the procedure consists of computing the values of the *BICUP* approximated posterior odds for models with one outlier. Figure 13.6 shows these values. The straight horizontal line in the plot is the height of the threshold in Equation 13.4.2. The plot in Figure 13.6 shows that the observation at October 2001 is labeled as a potential outlier because the value of its *BICUP*

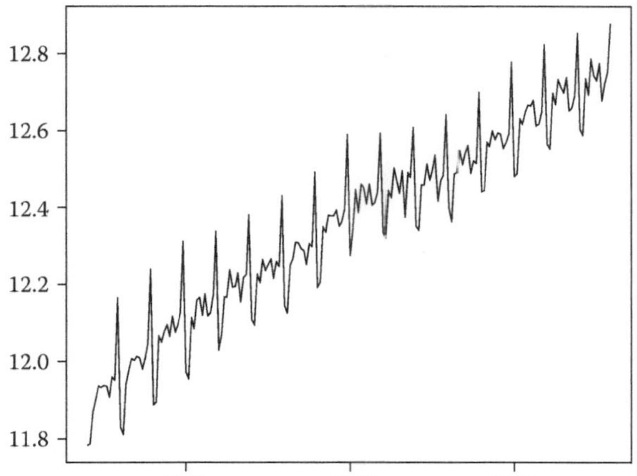

FIGURE 13.5
Logarithm of the monthly total retail sales in the United States.

TABLE 13.3
Estimated Parameters and Standard Errors in the Monthly Total Retail Sales Series

	Estimated Parameter Values	
Parameter	**Seasonal ARIMA**	**Outliers at October 2001 and May 2005**
θ_1	0.570	0.426
	(6.73×10^{-2})	(9.38×10^{-2})
Θ_1	0.602	0.547
	(5.83×10^{-2})	(5.84×10^{-2})
β_1	0.5×10^{-3}	-0.6×10^{-3}
	(1.8×10^{-3})	(1.5×10^{-3})
β_2	1.9×10^{-3}	1.8×10^{-3}
	(1.8×10^{-3})	(1.4×10^{-3})
β_3	1.1×10^{-3}	0.5×10^{-3}
	(1.9×10^{-3})	(1.5×10^{-3})
β_4	5.7×10^{-3}	6.7×10^{-3}
	(1.8×10^{-3})	(1.5×10^{-3})
β_5	6.7×10^{-3}	6.6×10^{-3}
	(1.8×10^{-3})	(1.4×10^{-3})
β_6	-1.2×10^{-3}	-1.2×10^{-3}
	(1.8×10^{-3})	(1.5×10^{-3})
β_7	4.11×10^{-2}	4.02×10^{-2}
	(5.8×10^{-3})	(0.47×10^{-3})
w_{118}	—	5.38×10^{-2}
		(8.8×10^{-3})
w_{161}	—	-4.4×10^{-2}
		(8.7×10^{-3})
σ	1.33×10^{-2}	1.15×10^{-2}

approximated posterior odds is larger than the threshold. None of the values of the *BICUP* approximated posterior odds for the rest of observations is close to the corresponding threshold.

Then, the second step of the procedure starts by computing the *BICUP* interactions matrix. Figure 13.7 shows the row numbers 118 and 161 of this matrix. The straight horizontal lines in the plots are the height of the corresponding threshold given in Equation 13.4.3. These plots show that the observations in October 2001 and May 2005 are labeled as potential outliers. Indeed, these two observations are labeled as potential outliers in many of the rows of the interaction matrix that are not shown here. No more observations are labeled as potential outliers.

The final step of the proposed methodology is to compute the values of the *BICUP* for only those models that incorporate the potential outliers at October 2001 and May 2005. Table 13.4 shows these values for all the models considered. The *BICUP* selects the model with outliers in October 2001 and

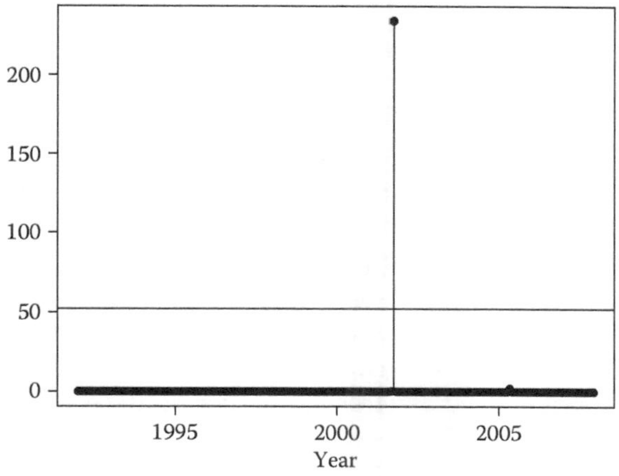

FIGURE 13.6
BICUP approximated posterior odds for models with one outlier in the logarithm of the monthly total retail sales series in the United States.

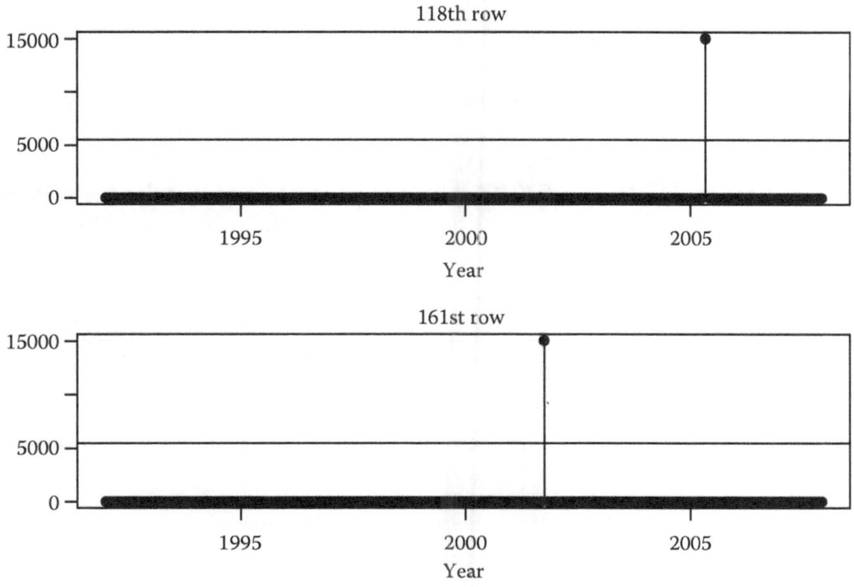

FIGURE 13.7
118th and 161st rows of *BICUP* interactions matrix in the logarithm of the monthly total retail sales series in the United States.

TABLE 13.4
Values of the Criteria for Candidate Models in the Logarithm of the Monthly Total Retail Sales Series

τ_m	(−)	(118)	(161)	(118, 161)
BICUP	−1015.2	−1026.2	−1016.7	**−1034.5**

May 2005. Thus, the proposed criterion provides a model for the logarithm of the monthly total retail sales in the United States that incorporates two outliers. The third column in Table 13.3 shows the MLEs of the parameters of this model. This includes the outlier size estimates of the two outliers, $\widehat{w}_{118}$ and $\widehat{w}_{161}$. Apparently, the first/second outlier produced an increase/decrease in the monthly total retail sales series.

Finally, as in the simulated example, we compare the previous results with the results produced by X-12-ARIMA. For that, we include regressor variables to model trading-day and Easter effects. For this series, the X-12-ARIMA software only detects an additive outlier in October 2001 with estimated size 0.0527, which is very close to the estimated value in our final model with two outliers. X-12-ARIMA does not detect the observation in May 2005 as an outlier.

Acknowledgments

The authors would like to thank the excellent comments made by the editors and two referees, which have led to a much improved chapter. The first author acknowledges the financial support by Ministerio de Ciencia e Innovación project MTM2008-03010. The second author acknowledges the financial support by Ministerio de Educación y Ciencia project SEJ2007/64500/ECON4438.

References

Akaike, H. (1969). Fitting autoregressive models for prediction. *Annals of the Institute of Statistical Mathematics*, 21(1):243–247.

Akaike, H. (1973). Information theory and an extension of the maximum likelihood principle. In *Proceedings of the 2nd International Symposium on Information Theory*, 267–281. Akademiai Kiadó, Budapest.

Bianco, A. M., Garcia Ben, M., Martínez, E. J., and Yohai, V. J. (2001). Outlier detection in regression models with ARIMA errors using robust estimates. *Journal of Forecasting*, 20(8):565–579.

Chang, I., Tiao, G. C., and Chen, C. (1988). Estimation of time series parameters in the presence of outliers. *Technometrics*, 30(2):193–204.

Chen, C. and Liu, L. (1993). Joint estimation of model parameters and outlier effects in time series. *Journal of the American Statistical Association*, 88(421):284–297.

Claeskens, G. and Hjort, N. L. (2008). *Model Selection and Model Averaging*. New York: North-Holland.

Fox, A. J. (1972). Outliers in time series. *Journal of the Royal Statistical Society Series B*, 34(3):350–363.

Gómez, V. and Maravall, A. (1994). Estimation, prediction, and interpolation for nonstationary series with the Kalman filter. *Journal of the American Statistical Association*, 89(426):611–624.

Hannan, E. J. and Quinn, B. G. (1979). The determination of the order of an autoregression. *Journal of the Royal Statistical Society Series B*, 41(2):190–195.

Harvey, A. C. and Phillips, G. D. A. (1979). Maximum likelihood estimation of regression models with autoregressive-moving average disturbances. *Biometrika*, 66(1):49–58.

Hurvich, C. M. and Tsai, C. (1989). Regression and time series model selection in small samples. *Biometrika*, 76(2):297–307.

Justel, A., Peña, D., and Tsay, R. S. (2001). Detection of outlier patches in autoregressive time series. *Statistica Sinica*, 11(3):651–673.

Kohn, R. and Ansley, C. F. (1985). Efficient estimation and prediction in time series regression models. *Biometrika*, 72(3):694–697.

Luceño, A. (1998). Detecting possibly non-consecutive outliers in industrial time series. *Journal of the Royal Statistical Society Series B*, 60(2):295–310.

McCulloch, R. E. and Tsay, R. S. (1994). Bayesian analysis of autoregressive time series via the Gibbs sampler. *Journal of Time Series Analysis*, 15(2):235–250.

Peña, D. (2005). A new statistic for influence in linear regression. *Technometrics*, 47(1):1–12.

Peña, D. and Tiao, G. C. (1992). Bayesian robustness functions for linear models. In *Bayesian Statistics 4*, 365–388. Oxford University Press.

Perron, P. and Rodriguez, G. (2003). Searching for additive outliers in nonstationary time series. *Journal of Time Series Analysis*, 24(2):193–220.

Sánchez, M. J. and Peña, D. (2003). The identification of multiple outliers in ARIMA models. *Communications in Statistics, Theory and Methods*, 32(6):1265–1287.

Schwarz, G. (1978). Estimating the dimension of a model. *Annals of Statistics*, 6(2):461–464.

Tsay, R. S. (1986). Time series model specification in the presence of outliers. *Journal of the American Statistical Association*, 81(393):132–141.

Tsay, R. S. (1988). Outliers, level shifts and variance changes in time series. *Journal of Forecasting*, 7(1):1–20.

14

Outliers in GARCH Processes

Luiz K. Hotta and Ruey S. Tsay

CONTENTS

14.1 Introduction

Many models have been proposed in the literature to describe some stylized facts of empirical financial time series. The autoregressive conditional heteroscedastic (ARCH) model of Engle (1982) is capable of modeling volatility clustering and large kurtosis. Several extensions of the model have also been developed to fit specific features of empirical series, e.g., the generalized ARCH (GARCH) and exponential GARCH models. See Bollerslev et al. (1992) for a survey. These models enjoy much success in studying the volatility evolution of a financial time series, but they are unable to explain the frequency and sizes of extreme jumps commonly occurring in practice. A natural way to deal with these big jumps is to treat them as outliers and handle them accordingly. The goal of this chapter is to provide a rigorous investigation in the modeling and detection of outliers in a GARCH process.

Classical time series analysis entertains two types of outlier: additive and innovational outliers. An additive outlier only affects a single observation such as a typo or a recording error. On the other hand, an innovational outlier affects many observations, and it often signifies an external disturbance to the series that has a gradually decaying impact. In this chapter, we generalize the basic concept of outliers to ARCH and GARCH models. Our objectives are to present simple outlier models and to derive appropriate tests to detect outliers in volatility modeling.

The goal of a GARCH model is to study the volatility evolution of the underlying process over time. Outlier study in GARCH processes therefore encounters two rather different scenarios. First, there exist situations in which an outlier does not have any impact on volatility. Consider the monthly excess returns of S&P 500 index. Typos and recording errors may occur, but these abnormal observations have no relation whatsoever to the volatility of the series. Overlooking these observations may have adverse consequences in studying the volatility of the index returns. See, for instance, van Dijk et al. (1999). Another example is that the Federal Reserve Board might raise the short-term interest rates in the middle of a month. This could result in a substantial drop in stock prices that could not be quickly recovered at the end of the month. If the Federal Resource Board action was expected, it would only have some minor impact on the stock volatility. Consequently, we would observe a "big drop" in the return series, but would fail to see any noticeable change in volatility. In the above two examples, external events affected the level of the financial time series under study, but they had no measurable impact on its volatility. We refer to this type of disturbance as a level outlier (LO).

The second scenario is that the external disturbances affect the volatility of the series of interest. For example, consider the 1997 financial crisis in Southeast Asia and South Korea. The uncertainty and fear remained high for a period of time, creating uneasiness among investors around the world. The financial markets thus showed some big drops and big gains, resulting in substantial increases in volatility. Events like this introduce unusual shocks (and observations) to financial time series and, hence, affect the volatility of the data. These shocks cannot be adequately described by the usual GARCH model. In this chapter, we refer to these types of aberrant observations as volatility outliers (VO). We study LO and VO in a GARCH process and derive test statistics to detect them. In the traditional time series analysis, an LO is called an additive outlier and a VO an innovational outlier.

This chapter is organized as follows: Section 14.2 presents some simple outlier models and proposes test statistics to detect outliers in an ARCH process. We focus on the ARCH(1) model, but generalization to ARCH(p) models is straightforward. Section 14.3 presents results for a GARCH(1,1) series, and Section 14.4 provides some applications.

14.2 Outliers in an ARCH Process

In this section, we focus on ARCH models. Let us start with an outlier-free ARCH(1) model:

$$z_t = \sqrt{h_t}\epsilon_t, \quad h_t = \alpha_0 + \alpha_1 z_{t-1}^2, \quad \alpha_0 > 0 \tag{14.2.1}$$

where $\{\epsilon_t\}$ is an independent and identically distributed standard Gaussian process and $\alpha_1 > 0$. The latter condition ensures the ARCH behavior; otherwise, the model reduces to the usual white noise series and the traditional techniques of outlier detection apply. The two equations in Equation 14.2.1 are referred to as the mean and volatility equations, respectively. An outlier can affect the level of z_t or the volatility h_t in Equation 14.2.1. In this chapter, we adopt a similar approach as those of ARMA models in Chen and Liu (1993a,b) to study the effect. For simplicity, we only consider a single outlier that directly affects Equation 14.2.1.

Consider the data $z_1, \ldots, z_n$ of the ARCH(1) model in Equation 14.2.1. If there exists no outlier, the log-likelihood function of the data, ignoring the constant and conditions on the initial value z_0, is given by

$$\log f(z_1, \ldots, z_n | z_0, \alpha_0, \alpha_1) = -\frac{1}{2}\sum_{t=1}^{n} \log(h_t) - \frac{1}{2}\sum_{t=1}^{n} \frac{z_t^2}{h_t}. \tag{14.2.2}$$

In the presence of outliers, what we observe is a contaminated series denoted by y_t. Suppose that there is a single outlier at the kth observation. In this case, the observation equation in Equation 14.2.1 becomes $y_t = z_t + \delta_t^k\beta = \sqrt{h_t}\epsilon_t + \delta_t^k\beta$, where δ_t^k is an indicator for the time index k, i.e., $\delta_t^k = 1$ if $t = k$ and $\delta_t^k = 0$, otherwise, and β is the size of the outlier. The form of the volatility equation in Equation 14.2.1 depends on the type of the outlier. For a VO, it remains the same except z_{t-1}^2 in Equation 14.2.1 is replaced by the observed y_{t-1}^2, because the outlier affects the innovation variance at time $t = k$ with impact carrying over to subsequent observations. For an ARCH model, a VO may represent an extraordinary shock whose impact cannot be adequately described by the usual innovation ϵ_t of the system. For an LO at time $t = k$, the volatility equation becomes $h_{t+1} = \alpha_0 + \alpha_1(y_t - \delta_t^k\beta)^2$. A typo in the data illustrates this effect clearly. While the typo is present in the observed series, it does not have any impact on the evolution of the volatility of the series. The volatility depends on the true, but unobserved, value $z_k = y_k - \beta$.

More complicated outlier configurations can be introduced for an ARCH(1) model, including using a hierarchical model under which occurrence of outliers is governed by a probability law. Here we shall keep the problem simple by assuming that outliers occur randomly without any pattern. This enables us to make use of the simple likelihood structure of an ARCH model. Our discussion focuses on a single outlier; multiple outliers can be handled by an iterative procedure. However, the locations of all outliers are unknown.

14.2.1 Volatility Outlier

The effect of a VO is carried into the future observations via the volatility equation in Equation 14.2.1 that holds for every observation. Thus, the parameter β enters the log-likelihood only in the kth term, which ignoring the constant and noting that $y_t = z_t$ when $t \neq k$ is given by

$$l(\beta) = -\frac{1}{2}\log(\alpha_0 + \alpha_1 y_{k-1}^2) - \frac{(y_k - \beta)^2}{2(\alpha_0 + \alpha_1 y_{k-1}^2)}.$$

Maximum likelihood estimator (MLE): The score and the second-order derivatives of the log-likelihood are

$$\frac{\partial l}{\partial \beta} = \frac{y_k - \beta}{\alpha_0 + \alpha_1 y_{k-1}^2}, \quad I_{\beta\beta} = -\frac{\partial^2 l}{\partial^2 \beta} = \frac{1}{\alpha_0 + \alpha_1 y_{k-1}^2},$$

$$I_{\beta\alpha_0} = -\frac{\partial^2 l}{\partial \beta \partial \alpha_0} = \frac{y_k - \beta}{(\alpha_0 + \alpha_1 y_{k-1}^2)^2}, \quad I_{\beta\alpha_1} = -\frac{\partial^2 l}{\partial \beta \partial \alpha_1} = \frac{y_{k-1}^2 (y_k - \beta)}{(\alpha_0 + \alpha_1 y_{k-1}^2)^2}.$$

It is immediate that y_k is the MLE of the size of the outlier. The other parameters are estimated by maximizing the log-likelihood after plugging in β, i.e., by maximizing

$$\begin{aligned} L(\alpha) &= \log f(y_1, \ldots, y_n | y_0, \alpha) \\ &= -\frac{1}{2} \log(\alpha_0 + \alpha_1 y_{k-1}^2) - \frac{1}{2} \sum_{t \neq k} \log(h_t) - \frac{1}{2} \sum_{t \neq k} \frac{y_t^2}{h_t}. \end{aligned}$$

Lagrange multiplier (LM) test: The LM test statistic is defined as $\text{LM} = (\partial l / \partial \beta)^2 I^{\beta\beta}$, where $I^{\beta\beta}$ is from the inverse of the information matrix and the derivative and the information matrix are evaluated using parameters estimated under the null hypothesis ($\beta = 0$). See Engle (1984) for Wald and LM tests in the econometric literature. In many practical problems, the observed information matrix is used to estimate the information matrix and a χ^2 distribution is employed to approximate the LM distribution under the null hypothesis. Here we cannot use the χ^2 approximation because the central limit theorem is not applicable to the score function for the gradient having only one term that is affected by the outlier.

It is easily seen that under the null hypothesis $E[I_{\beta\alpha_0}] = E[I_{\beta\alpha_1}] = 0$ when α_0 and α_1 are known, and the two expectations are approximately equal to zero when the parameters are replaced by their estimates. Using this approximation and the fact that the estimated information matrix is diagonal, the LM test statistic simplifies to $\text{LM} = (\partial l / \partial \beta)^2 I^{\beta\beta}$. Using the observed value, $I_{\beta\beta}^*$, we obtain one form of the LM test statistic given by $\text{LM}_k^{vo} = y_k^2 / (\hat{\alpha}_0 + \hat{\alpha}_1 y_{k-1}^2)$, where $\hat{\alpha}_0$ and $\hat{\alpha}_1$ are the maximum likelihood estimates under the null hypothesis, and we reject the null hypothesis when the value of LM_k^{vo} is large. In practice, the position of the outlier is unknown and we employ the test statistic $\text{LM}_{\max}^{vo} = \max_{2 \le k \le n} \text{LM}_k^{vo}$ to detect a VO. Conditions on α_0 and α_1 being known, the statistic LM_k^{vo} has a χ_1^2 distribution and, hence, $\text{LM}_{\max}^{vo}$ is distributed as the maximum of $n-1$ independent χ_1^2 random variates. However, the parameters α_0 and α_1 are unknown, and we use simulation to obtain the critical values of $\text{LM}_{\max}^{vo}$. For a sufficiently large n, the estimates $\hat{\alpha}_0$ and $\hat{\alpha}_1$ are consistent and one may use the maximum of $n-1$ independent χ_1^2 to obtain approximate p-values for $\text{LM}_{\max}^{vo}$. Specifically, $p \approx 1 - P(\chi_1^2 < \text{LM}_{\max}^{vo})^{n-1}$. Results of our limited simulation support such an approximation. We estimated the cumulative distribution function (CDF) of $\text{LM}_{\max}^{vo}$ using 1000 replications for $(\alpha_0, \alpha_1) = (0.1, 0.7)$ and $(0.05, 0.90)$ and sample size 500. We chose these values based on empricial findings of high persistence in asset volatility.

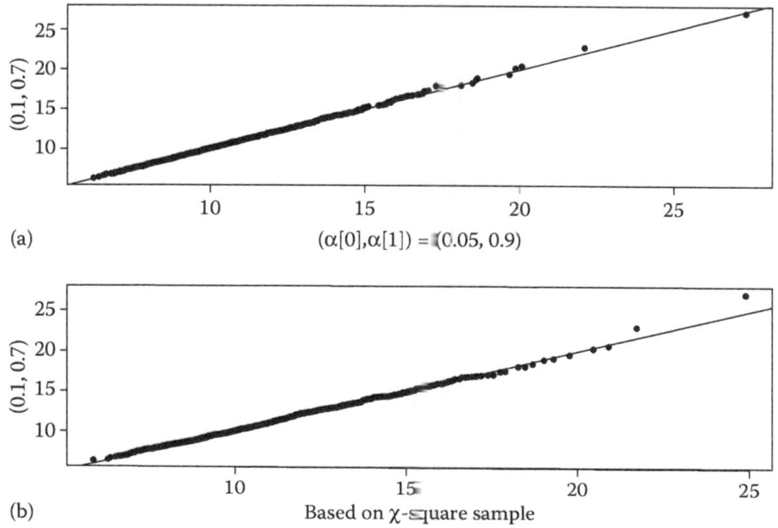

FIGURE 14.1
Scatterplots of empirical percentiles of LM tests for a volatility outlier in an ARCH(1) model with $h_t = \alpha_0 + \alpha_1 y_{t-1}^2$ based on sample size 500 and 1000 replications. (a) $(\alpha_0, \alpha_1) = (0.1, 0.7)$ versus $(0.05, 0.9)$. (b) $(\alpha_0, \alpha_1) = (0.1, 0.7)$: empirical percentiles versus the percentiles of the maximum of a random sample of size 499 from a χ_1^2 distribution.

In each replication a series was generated, the parameters were estimated, and $\mathrm{LM}_{\max}^{vo}$ was evaluated. The top graph of Figure 14.1 shows the scatterplot of estimated percentiles of the test statistic for the two models. From the plot, the parameter values have little influence on the distribution function of the test statistic. This result indicates that one can use the χ^2 approximation mentioned before to perform the test. To demonstrate, we compare the empirical CDF of the test statistic with that of the maximum of a random sample of size $n-1$ of a χ_1^2 distribution. The comparison between both CDFs is given in the bottom graph of Figure 14.1. The plot shows that the distributions are very close. Table 14.1 presents the empirical sizes of the test when the critical values were obtained from the maximum of a random sample of size $n-1$ of a χ_1^2 distribution. The results show that we can use the approximation based on the maximum of a χ_1^2 distribution to conduct the proposed VO test. Finally, it is easy to see that, for a VO, the Wald test statistic is equal to the LM test statistic LM_k^{vo}.

14.2.2 Level Outlier

When the outlier is in the level, it only affects the series at the observation where it occurs. The effect is carried neither into the subsequent observations,

TABLE 14.1
Estimated Sizes of the LM Test Statistic When the Critical Values Were Obtained by Using the Maximum of a Random Sample from a χ_1^2 Distribution

Parameters		Nominal Size	
α_0	α_1	5%	10%
0.10	0.70	4.2	9.3
0.05	0.90	4.6	9.8
Critical values based on χ_1^2 distribution		15.08	13.73

Note: The length of the series is 500. The critical values are based on 5000 replications and the sizes of the test are based on 1000 replications.

nor into the volatility. In practice, this means that one needs to adjust the volatility equation in Equation 14.2.1, because the volatility depends on the absolute value of $z_k = y_k - \beta$. This also means that $z_k = y_k$ and $z_k = y_k - 2y_k = -y_k$ will produce the same likelihood, i.e, no outlier and an outlier of size $2y_k$ give the same likelihood. Similarly, outliers with sizes β and $(2y_k - \beta)$ will give the same likelihood. Thus, in order to solve this identification problem we will always consider the outlier with the smallest absolute value. This is equivalent to considering no outlier when it is in doubt about no outlier or an outlier of size $2y_k$, or considering β with the same sign as ϵ_k. For an ARCH(1) model, the outlier parameter enters the model in the following equations:

$$y_k = \sqrt{h_k}\epsilon_k + \beta \quad \text{and} \quad h_{k+1} = \alpha_0 + \alpha_1(y_k - \beta)^2.$$

That is, the outlier parameter appears in the log-likelihood in the kth and the $(k+1)$th terms. For a general ARCH(p) model, the outlier parameter appears from the kth to the $(k+p)$-term of the likelihood function.

Maximum likelihood estimator: Ignoring the constant, the log-likelihood of the affected terms becomes

$$l(\beta) = -\frac{(y_k - \beta)^2}{2(\alpha_0 + \alpha_1 y_{k-1}^2)} - \frac{1}{2}\log\{\alpha_0 + \alpha_1(y_k - \beta)^2\} - \frac{y_{k+1}^2}{2\{\alpha_0 + \alpha_1(y_k - \beta)^2\}}.$$

This is a function of y_k only through $z_k = |y_k - \beta|$, which denotes the true, but unobserved, value of the series at time index k. Thus, estimating β is equivalent to estimating z_k, i.e., treating y_k as a missing value. For a given estimate of z_k, we have two estimates of β.

The score of β is given by

$$\frac{\partial l}{\partial \beta} = \frac{y_k - \beta}{\alpha_0 + \alpha_1 y_{k-1}^2} + \frac{\alpha_1(y_k - \beta)}{\alpha_0 + \alpha_1(y_k - \beta)^2} - \frac{\alpha_1 y_{k+1}^2 (y_k - \beta)}{\{\alpha_0 + \alpha_1(y_k - \beta)^2\}^2},$$

from which the MLE of $z_k = (y_k - \beta)$ has the following possible values: (1) $\hat{z}_k = 0$, i.e., $\hat{\beta} = y_k$; and (2) $\hat{z}_k$ is the square root of the positive solution of the second-order equation

$$g(x) = \alpha_1^2 x^2 + (2\alpha_0\alpha_1 + \alpha_1^2 D)x + (\alpha_0^2 + \alpha_0\alpha_1 D - \alpha_1 y_{k+1}^2 D), \qquad (14.2.3)$$

where $D = \alpha_0 + \alpha_1 y_{k-1}^2$, provided that such a solution exists. Here we are only concerned with $x > 0$ because $x = z_k^2$ in our application.

Consider Equation 14.2.3. A positive solution of $g(x) = 0$ exists if the following inequality holds

$$y_{k+1}^2 \geq \alpha_0 + \frac{\alpha_0^2}{\alpha_1(\alpha_0 + \alpha_1 y_{k-1}^2)}, \qquad (14.2.4)$$

because in this case $g(x)$ is an increasing function of $x \geq 0$ with $g(0) < 0$ but $g(x) \to \infty$ as $x \to \infty$. Furthermore, by computing the second derivative of the likelihood function, we see that $\hat{z}_k = 0$ is a minimum solution of the score function when the inequality (14.2.4) holds. Therefore, the MLE of z_k is given by: (1) $\hat{z}_k = 0$ when the inequality (14.2.4) fails, and (2) $\hat{z}_k = \sqrt{x}$, where x satisfies $g(x) = 0$, when the inequality (14.2.4) holds. Note that for the ARCH(1) model in Equation 14.2.1, $g(x) > 0$ for all $x \geq 0$ if the inequality (14.2.4) fails. We shall make use of this property to simplify the computation later. Also, for simplicity, we shall only focus on the LM test in the rest of this chapter.

Lagrange multiplier test: The score and the information matrix under the null hypothesis can be derived; see Hotta and Tsay (2010). These formulas are not simple algebraically, but they can be easily evaluated. It is also shown that the LM test statistic is given by

$$\mathrm{LM}_{\max}^{lo} = \max_{2 \leq k \leq n-1} \mathrm{LM}_k^{lo} \qquad (14.2.5)$$

where

$$\mathrm{LM}_k^{lo} = \mathrm{LM}_k^{vo} \left\{ 1 + \hat{\alpha}_1 \hat{h}_k \left(\frac{1}{\hat{h}_{k+1}} - \frac{y_{k+1}^2}{\hat{h}_{k+1}^2} \right) \right\}^2 \left(1 + 2\hat{\alpha}_1^2 \hat{h}_k \frac{y_k^2}{\hat{h}_{k+1}^2} \right)^{-1},$$

where $\hat{h}_t$ is the estimate of the conditional volatility at time t, i.e., $\hat{h}_t = \hat{\alpha}_0 + \hat{\alpha}_1 y_{t-1}^2$. Thus, in contrast to the LM test for VO, LM_k^{lo} for a fixed k does not have a χ^2 distribution even when the parameters are known. As expected, the test statistic LM_k^{lo} is equivalent to LM_k^{vo} when $\hat{\alpha}_1 = 0$. Therefore, the two test statistics should not differ substantially when $\hat{\alpha}_1$ is close to zero.

The test statistic $\mathrm{LM}_{\max}^{lo}$ in Equation 14.2.5 may require intensive computation and encounter the difficulty of masking (an outlier is undetected because of the presence of another adjacent outlying observation) or swamping (a good observation is incorrectly identified as an outlier because of the presence of another adjacent outlying observation) effects that are common to outlier detection in statistical analyses when multiple outliers exist. See, for instance, Peña (1990) and Lawrence (1995). Some modifications are needed to simplify the computation involved and to make the test statistics robust to the influence of multiple outliers. Writing

$$1 + \hat{\alpha}_1 \hat{h}_k \left(\frac{1}{\hat{h}_{k+1}} - \frac{y_{k+1}^2}{\hat{h}_{k+1}^2} \right) = \frac{1}{\hat{h}_{k+1}^2} g(y_k^2),$$

we can make use of the properties of $g(y_k^2)$ to simplify the computation of $\mathrm{LM}_{\max}^{lo}$. First, if $\hat{z}_k = 0$ is the solution of the score function, then $\hat{\beta} = y_k$, implying that y_k is a possible outlier, and the inequality in Equation 14.2.4 fails. In this case, we have $g(y_k^2) > 0$. Secondly, if $\hat{z}_k = 0$ is not a solution, then inequality (14.2.4) holds. If $|\hat{z}_k| > |y_k|$, then the magnitude of the observed value is smaller than that of the underlying true value. In this case, we have an "inlier," rather than an outlier, and $g(y_k^2) < 0$. On the other hand, if $|\hat{z}_k| \leq |y_k|$, then y_k is a possible outlier and $g(y_k^2) \geq g(\hat{z}_k^2) = 0$. Consequently, for outlier detection, we can focus on the case of $g(y_k^2) > 0$ to simplify the computation.

A possible swamping effect is as follows: When a large LO occurs at time index k, it will inflate the estimate of $\hat{h}_{k+1} = \hat{\alpha}_0 + \hat{\alpha}_1 y_k^2$, which leads to an underestimation of the test statistic at time $k+1$ and, hence, reduces the power of the test. To minimize such a swamping effect, we replace $\hat{h}_{k+1}$ by its predicted value at time k, namely $\hat{h}_{k+1} = \hat{\alpha}_0 + \hat{\alpha}_1 \hat{h}_k$. However, a possible complication arises because $\hat{h}_{k+1}$ appears three times in LM_k^{lo}. Our limited simulation experiment shows that replacing the second term of $\hat{h}_{k+1}$ works well. Further research is needed to better understand the masking effects of multiple outliers.

The above discussions lead us to propose the following score statistic for LO at the time index k:

$$\mathrm{LM}_k^{lo} = \mathrm{LM}_k^{vo} \left[\max \left\{ 1 + \hat{\alpha}_1 \hat{h}_k \left(\frac{1}{\hat{h}_{k+1}} - \frac{y_{k+1}^2}{(\hat{\alpha}_0 + \hat{\alpha}_1 \hat{h}_k)^2} \right) ; 0 \right\} \right]^2 \times \left(1 + 2\hat{\alpha}_1^2 \hat{h}_k \frac{y_k^2}{\hat{h}_{k+1}^2} \right)^{-1} . \quad (14.2.6)$$

Using the modified LM_k^{lo} in Equation 14.2.6, we estimate the empirical CDF of the test statistic $\mathrm{LM}_{\max}^{lo}$ with $(\alpha_0, \alpha_1) = (0.05, 0.90)$ and $(0.10, 0.70)$. The sample size used is 500 and the number of replications is 1000. For each replication, we estimate the parameters, i.e., obtain $(\hat{\alpha}_0, \hat{\alpha}_1)$, and use the estimates to evaluate Equation 14.2.6. The results provide an empirical CDF of $\mathrm{LM}_{\max}^{lo}$ for the given (α_0, α_1) value. The CDF appears to be stable when the simulation is repeated, especially for critical values not too close to the extreme tails. The 5% and 10% critical values are $(10.4625, 9.3640)$ and $(10.8027, 9.5309)$, respectively, for the two sets of (α_0, α_1) values. If smaller

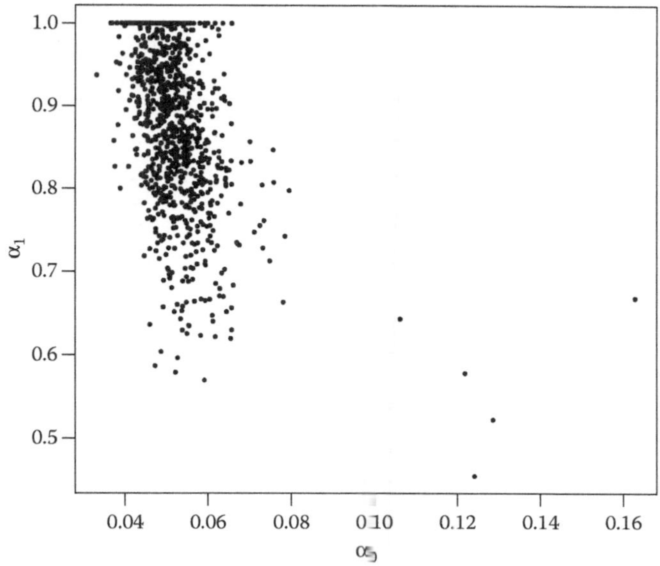

FIGURE 14.2
Parameter estimates of an ARCH(1) model based on sample size 500 and 1000 replications. The true parameter values are $(\alpha_0, \alpha_1) = (0.05, 0.9)$.

significance levels are needed, one needs to increase the number of replications to obtain more accurate empirical percentiles. For ease in reference, we treat the above empirical CDF as the "true" CDF of LM_{max}^{lo} for the given parameter values.

Figure 14.2 shows the scatterplot of $\hat{\alpha}_1$ versus $\hat{\alpha}_0$ for 1000 replications used in our simulation for $(\alpha_0, \alpha_1) = (0.05, 0.9)$. The empirical ranges of $\hat{\alpha}_0$ and $\hat{\alpha}_1$ are $(0.033, 0.163)$ (only 16 cases larger than 0.071) and $(0.454, 1]$, respectively. The estimates of α_0 seem more stable than those of α_1. Among the 1000 replications, 162 of them give $\hat{\alpha}_1 = 1$. This is not surprising because the true value is $\alpha_1 = 0.9$. However, the variabilities in $\hat{\alpha}_0$ and $\hat{\alpha}_1$ suggest that it is important to study the effect of parameter estimation on the empirical CDF of LM_{max}^{lo}. To this end, we conduct a further simulation study.

Because α_0 is a scale parameter of y_t, its estimate has a smaller impact on LM_{max}^{lo} than that of α_1, and we shall focus on $\hat{\alpha}_1$. Based on the empirical ranges shown in Figure 14.2, we selected certain values of $\hat{\alpha}_0$ and $\hat{\alpha}_1$. For each selected pair of $\hat{\alpha}_0$ and $\hat{\alpha}_1$, we generate 1000 realizations of y_t with sample size 500. For each realization, we evaluate the test statistic LM_{max}^{lo} in Equation 14.2.6 using the selected $\hat{\alpha}_0$ and $\hat{\alpha}_1$ without re-estimating the parameters. This step substantially reduces the computational burden. Table 14.2 shows (a) the 5% and 10% critical values of the resulting empirical CDFs of LM_{max}^{lo}, (b) the sizes of these critical values with respect to the "true" empirical CDF

TABLE 14.2
Estimated Critical Values for the LM Test for LO for the ARCH(1) Model: $h(t) = 0.05 + 0.90y_t^2$, $t = 1, \ldots, 500$

$\hat{\alpha}_1$	Critical Values 5%	Critical Values 10%	Size of the Test 5%	Size of the Test 10%	% Estimates $\leq$ or $\geq \hat{\alpha}_1$
0.70	10.930	9.839	3.8	7.2	4.2 ($\leq$)
0.75	10.829	9.712	4.0	7.4	10.6 ($\leq$)
0.80	10.700	9.575	4.6	8.1	21.9 ($\leq$)
0.85	10.692	9.566	4.6	8.1	21.9 ($\leq$)
0.90	10.567	9.535	4.8	8.4	47.0 ($\geq$)
0.95	10.532	9.476	4.9	8.9	29.0 ($\geq$)
1.00	10.492	9.440	4.9	9.2	16.2 (=)

Note: The parameters are not re-estimated. All results are based on 1000 replications, except for the case of $\hat{\alpha}_1 = 1$, which uses 5000 replications.

of $LM_{\max}^{lo}$ with $(\alpha_0, \alpha_1) = (0.05, 0.9)$, and (c) the location of the selected $\hat{\alpha}_1$ with respect to the empirical distribution of $\hat{\alpha}_1$ obtained from our original simulation study. From Table 14.2, we see that the variabilities in $\hat{\alpha}_0$ and $\hat{\alpha}_1$ do not have serious impacts on the empirical distribution of $LM_{\max}^{lo}$. Consequently, to obtain the empirical CDF of $LM_{\max}^{lo}$ in an application, we can reduce the computational burden by fixing $(\hat{\alpha}_0, \hat{\alpha}_1)$ at their estimates obtained from the data.

The above discussions lead us to propose a simulation procedure to estimate the empirical CDF of $LM_{\max}^{lo}$ and to obtain its critical values. For a given set of data of an ARCH(1) model, we obtain the maximum likelihood estimates of α_0 and α_1, assuming no outliers. The estimates are denoted by $\hat{\alpha}_0$ and $\hat{\alpha}_1$. The procedure is as follows: (a) generate a series of size n using the model with the estimated parameters $\hat{\alpha}_0$ and $\hat{\alpha}_1$, where n is the sample size; (b) evaluate LM_k^{lo} using Equation 14.2.6 without parameter estimation; and (c) find $LM_{\max}^{lo}$. Repeating the procedure over many iterations, we obtain an empirical CDF of $LM_{\max}^{lo}$ for the given data set. Finally, in an application, if both $LM_{\max}^{vo}$ and $LM_{\max}^{lo}$ are significant, we recommend that one chooses the test that gives the smaller p-value, where p-values are estimated by the procedures described in this chapter. If both p-values are close to zero, then one may entertain both possibilities in further analysis. Examples of multiple outliers are given in Section 14.4.

An ARCH(p) model: One can easily extend the results to higher-order ARCH(p) models for which the proposed test statistics at the time index k are as follows:

$$LM_k^{vo} = \frac{y_k^2}{\hat{h}_k} = \frac{y_k^2}{\hat{\alpha}_0 + \hat{\alpha}_1 y_{k-1}^2 + \cdots + \hat{\alpha}_p y_{k-p}^2},$$

$$\mathrm{LM}_k^{lo} = \mathrm{LM}_k^{vo} \left[\max\left\{ 1 + \sum_{j=1}^{p} \hat{\alpha}_j \hat{h}_k \left(\frac{1}{\hat{h}_{k+j}} - \frac{y_{k+j}^2}{h_{k+j}^{*2}} \right); 0 \right\} \right]^2$$
$$\times \left(1 + 2\hat{h}_k^2 \sum_{j=1}^{p} \frac{\hat{\alpha}_j^2}{\hat{h}_{k+j}^2} \right)^{-1},$$

where $h_{k+j}^* = \hat{h}_{k+j} + \hat{\alpha}_j(\hat{h}_{k+j} - y_{k+j}^2)$, i.e., replacing y_k^2 in $\hat{h}_{k+j}$ by $\hat{h}_k$.

14.3 Outliers in a GARCH Process

Consider a GARCH(1,1) model with volatility equation

$$h_t = \alpha_0 + \alpha_1 y_{t-1}^2 + \alpha_2 h_{t-1}.$$

See Bollerslev (2009) and Taylor (1986). The parameters satisfy $\alpha_0 > 0$, $\alpha_i \geq 0$ for $i = 1$, 2, and $\alpha_1 + \alpha_2 \leq 1$. The process y_t is covariance stationary with unconditional variance $\alpha_0/(1 - \alpha_1 - \alpha_2)$ if $\alpha_1 + \alpha_2 < 1$ (see Nelson 1990). The log-likelihood of $\{y_t\}$ is given by Equation 14.2.2.

14.3.1 Volatility Outlier

Consider a single VO of size β at time k. The outlier parameter enters the log-likelihood only through the equation:

$$l(\beta) = -\frac{1}{2} \frac{(y_k - \beta)^2}{\alpha_0 + \alpha_1 y_{k-1}^2 + \alpha_2 h_{k-1}},$$

and the MLE of β is y_k. Using a similar argument as that for an ARCH(1) model, we obtain an LM test statistic

$$\mathrm{LM}_{\max}^{vo} = \max_{21 \leq k \leq n} \frac{y_k^2}{\hat{\alpha}_0 + \hat{\alpha}_1 y_{k-1}^2 + \hat{\alpha}_2 \hat{h}_{k-1}} \tag{14.3.1}$$

to detect a VO. The test statistic starts at $t = 21$ because we used the first 20 observations to compute the initial value h_{20} of the volatility in evaluating the likelihood function. In addition, we can use critical values derived from the maximum of a random sample of size $(n - 20)$ from a χ_1^2 density to perform the test. For illustration, we conduct a simulation study. We generated 1000 series of size 520 from a GARCH(1,1) model with parameters $(\alpha_0, \alpha_1, \alpha_2) = (0.05, 0.05, 0.90)$, obtained the maximum likelihood estimates of the parameters, evaluated the test statistic in Equation 14.3.1, and compared the resulting empirical critical values with those found using χ_1^2 random samples. The empirical sizes of the χ_1^2-based 5% and 10% critical values are 3.2% and 9.1%, respectively, indicating that the χ_1^2-based critical values work reasonably well.

In the above simulation, we use the first 20 observations of each replication to compute the starting value $\hat{h}_{20}$ of the conditional volatility. Therefore, the likelihood estimation we used is conditioned on this starting value and the actual maximization is carried out using $\{y_t\}_{t=21}^{520}$. The effective sample size in estimation is kept at 500. Furthermore, the parameters α_i are only constrained to be in the interval [0,1]. The inequality constraint $\alpha_1 + \alpha_2 \leq 1$ is not enforced. This seems not to be a serious problem, because the difficulty of $\alpha_1 + \alpha_2 \geq 1$ is encountered in only 3 out of 1000 replications. Among these three violations, the maximum of $\hat{\alpha}_1 + \hat{\alpha}_2$ is 1.00175 and all three cases show $\hat{\alpha}_2 \approx 1.0$. Thus, we do not expect any significant changes in the simulation results when the inequality constraint is used.

14.3.2 Level Outlier

Similarly to the case of an ARCH(1) model, the maximum likelihood estimate of the true underlying series $z_k = (y_k - \beta)$ is equal to zero if the following inequality holds

$$1 + \hat{\alpha}_1 \hat{h}_k \sum_{j=1}^{n-k} \hat{\alpha}_2^{j-1} \left(\frac{1}{\hat{h}_{k+j}} - \frac{y_{k+j}^2}{\hat{h}_{k+j}^2} \right) > 0, \tag{14.3.2}$$

where $\hat{h}_{k+1} = \hat{\alpha}_0 + \hat{\alpha}_2 \hat{h}_k$, and the estimate is the positive solution of

$$1 + \hat{h}_k + \hat{\alpha}_1 \hat{h}_k \sum_{j=1}^{n-k} \hat{\alpha}_2^{j-1} \left(\frac{1}{\hat{h}_{k+j}} - \frac{y_{k+j}^2}{\hat{h}_{k+j}^2} \right) = 0,$$

where $\hat{h}_{k+1} = \hat{\alpha}_0 + \hat{\alpha}_1 z_k^2 - \hat{\alpha}_2 \hat{h}_k$, if the inequality in Equation 14.3.2 fails. However, the above equation is relatively hard to solve because for a GARCH(1,1) model an LO at the kth observation can affect all conditional volatilities h_t for $t \geq k$ in evaluating the likelihood function. Consequently, the LM test statistic for an LO in a GARCH(1,1) model is much more complicated than that in an ARCH(1) model. Details of the derivation are also given in Hotta and Tsay (2010). Here we only give the result. The LM test statistic for an LO at the kth observation is

$$\mathrm{LM}_k^{lo} = \mathrm{LM}_k^{vo} \left\{ 1 + \hat{\alpha}_1 \hat{h}_k \sum_{j=1}^{n-k} \hat{\alpha}_2^{j-1} \left(\frac{1}{\hat{h}_{k+j}} - \frac{y_{k+j}^2}{\hat{h}_{k+j}^2} \right) \right\}^2$$
$$\times \left(1 + 2\hat{\alpha}_1^2 \hat{h}_k^2 \sum_{j=1}^{n-k} \frac{\hat{\alpha}_2^{2j-2}}{\hat{h}_{k+j}^2} \right)^{-1}. \tag{14.3.3}$$

If $\hat{\alpha}_2$ is smaller than 1.0, then $\hat{\alpha}_2^{j-1}$ converges to zero quickly and the summations in Equation 14.3.3 can be truncated to simplify the computation. In any case, further simplification of the test statistic in Equation 14.3.3 is in order.

We propose to simplify the test statistic (14.3.3) in two ways. First, using the same rationale from ARCH(1) models we now substitute all h_{k+j} with h^*_{k+j} defined similarly as that for ARCH(p) models. For the GARCH (1,1) model, we have $h^*_{k+1} = \hat{\alpha}_0 + \hat{\alpha}_1 \hat{h}_k + \hat{\alpha}_2 \hat{h}_k$ and $h^*_{k+j} = \hat{\alpha}_0 + \hat{\alpha}_1 y^2_{k+j-1} + \hat{\alpha}_2 \hat{h}_{k+j-1}, j \geq 2$. Secondly, we truncate the upper limit of the summations from $(n-k)$ to J, where $J \ll n-k$. This truncation has an added value because it can reduce the masking or swamping effects when there are multiple outliers in the data. Note that when $J = 1$, the test statistic in Equation 14.3.3 reduces to that for a VO. For simplicity, we continue to use the notation $\mathrm{LM}^{lo}_{\max}$ after the simplifications. However, the number J used will be given.

The empirical CDF of the modified LM test statistic $\mathrm{LM}^{lo}_{\max}$ for a GARCH(1,1) model can be evaluated as before via simulation. For illustration, consider the model with $(\alpha_0, \alpha_1, \alpha_2) = (0.05, 0.15, 0.80)$ and a random sample of size 500. Because the starting conditional volatility h_0 is unknown, we use a burn-in procedure to generate the data. Specifically, for each realization of the model, we use $h_0 = 0$, $y_0 = 0$, and generate 620 observations. The first 100 observations are then discarded, resulting in a random sample of 520 observations. We then use the sample variance of the data $\{y_t\}^{120}_{t=101}$ as the starting conditional volatility $\hat{h}_{120}$. Conditional on $\hat{h}_{120}$ and y_{120}, we perform the maximum likelihood estimation using the remaining 500 observations, i.e., $\{y_t\}^{600}_{t=121}$. Figure 14.3 shows the scatterplot of $\hat{\alpha}_2$ versus $\hat{\alpha}_1$ for 1000 realizations. For this particular model, 75.5% of $\hat{\alpha}_0$ are in the

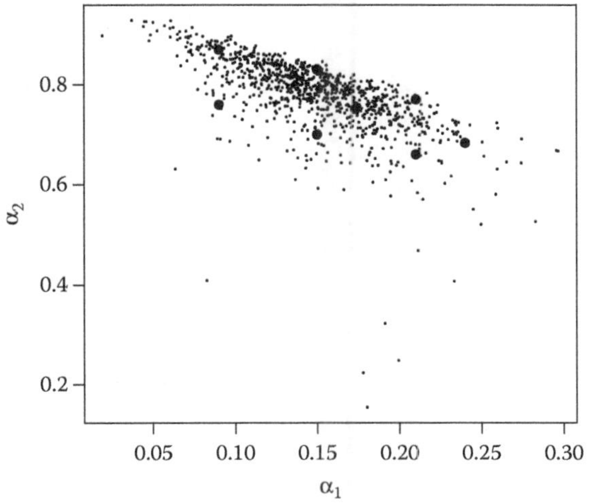

FIGURE 14.3
Maximum likelihood estimates of the GARCH(1,1) model: $h_t = \alpha_0 + \alpha_1 y^2_{t-1} + \alpha_2 h_{t-1}$. The sample size is 500 and the true parameters are $(\alpha_0, \alpha_1, \alpha_2) = (0.05, 0.15, 0.80)$. The results are based on 1000 replications. Marked points are used in further simulation.

TABLE 14.3
Empirical Sizes (in Percent) of the LO Test LM^{lo}_{max} for a GARCH(1,1) Model with Respect to the "True" Distribution Using Critical Values Obtained via Simulation for Selected Parameter Values

$\hat{\alpha}_1$	0.09	0.09	0.15	0.15	0.21	0.21	0.173	0.240
$\hat{\alpha}_2$	0.76	0.87	0.70	0.83	0.66	0.77	0.751	0.683
			5% Critical Values Used					
$J = 3$	7.8	5.7	4.0	3.8	4.0	3.1	4.0	3.6
$J = 9$	6.4	6.0	5.6	3.6	4.8	4.3	4.8	4.7
			10% Critical Values Used					
$J = 3$	11.7	11.5	9.1	9.5	8.2	7.6	8.6	8.1
$J = 9$	11.3	10.1	9.9	7.9	9.1	7.9	8.6	8.3

Note: The value of J of Equation 14.3.3 is fixed to 3 or 9. The GARCH model used is $h_t = 0.05 + 0.15y_{t-1}^2 + 0.8h_{t-1}$, where y_t is a serially uncorrelated process. The results are based on 1000 realizations of sample size 500.

interval $(0.03, 0.10)$ and 94.6% of them are in $(0.02, 0.15)$; 77.5% of $\hat{\alpha}_1$ are in $(0.10, 0.20)$ and 95.0% in $(0.07, 0.23)$; 77.2% of $\hat{\alpha}_2$ are in $(0.71, 0.85)$ and 94.0% in $(0.65, 0.90)$.

Since the true parameters are unknown in an application, we adapt a procedure similar to that of the LM test and use $J = 3$ and $J = 9$ for $(n - k)$ in Equation 14.3.3 to further reduce the computational burden. Table 14.3 presents the sizes of the test with respect to the "true" reference distribution when critical values obtained via simulation for some selected parameter values are used. The sizes are not far away from their expected values, indicating that the simplification of the test statistic is worthwhile. In selecting the parameter values, we chose some values that are far from the true ones used to generate the data. These selections illustrate that the simplified test statistic works reasonably well even in some unfavorable situations. For instance, only 7.4% of $\hat{\alpha}_1$ were as small as 0.09 and only 7.5% as large as 0.21; only 5.2% of $\hat{\alpha}_2$ were as small as 0.66 and only 6.2% as large as 0.87; and only 6.4% of $(\hat{\alpha}_1 + \hat{\alpha}_2)$ were as large as 0.98 and only 6.8% were smaller than 0.85. The extension of the test statistics to general GARCH models is also straightforward.

14.4 Applications

In this section, we illustrate the proposed outlier detection statistics by analyzing simulated and real examples. The simulated example has four outliers and is used to demonstrate the performance of the proposed tests when the true answer is known. We then apply the tests to the widely used series of monthly S&P 500 log returns from 1950 to 2009 and an exchange rate series between the Deutsche Mark and the U.S. Dollar in 1989. When multiple outliers exist, we iterate the testing procedure after adjusting the effects of detected outliers to reduce the masking and swamping effects.

Example 14.1 The top graph of Figure 14.4 shows the time plot of an ARCH(1) series with four outliers. The data are generated from the model $h_t = 0.05 + 0.90z_{t-1}^2$, $t = 1, \ldots, 500$. The four outliers are: (1) an LO of size $-3\sigma_z$ at $t = 150$, (2) a VO of size $5\sigma_z$ at $t = 200$, (3) a VO of size $3\sigma_z$ at $t = 300$, and (4) an LO of size $-3\sigma_z$ at $t = 350$, where $\sigma_z = 0.707$ which is the unconditional standard error of the outlier-free series z_t. The sizes of these outliers are not excessive because z_t has a heavy-tailed unconditional distribution.

The partial autocorrelation function of the data easily suggests that the series follow an ARCH(1) model. Assuming no outliers, the estimated model is $h_t = 0.0878 + 0.8053y_{t-1}^2$, where y_t denotes the observed series, i.e., $y_t = z_t +$ outlier. Using this model, we compute the test statistics LM_k^{vo} and LM_k^{lo}

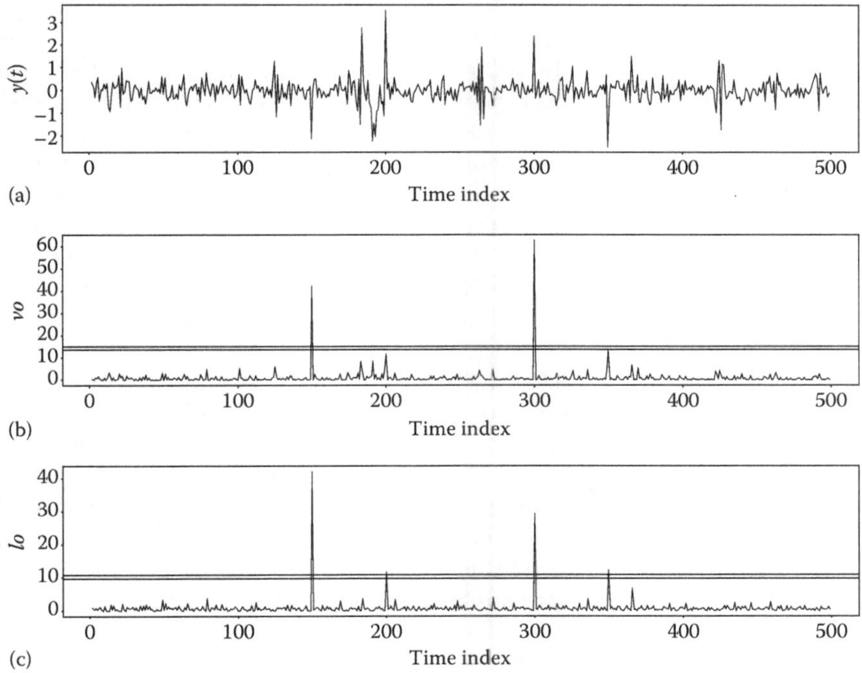

FIGURE 14.4
Results of Example 14.1 with $h_t = 0,05 + 0,90z_{t-1}^2$. The outliers are level outliers at $t = 150$, 350 and volatility outliers at $t = 200$ and 300. (a) Observed series, (b) LM test for VO, (c) LM test for LO. The horizontal lines in the middle and bottom graphs are 5% and 10% critical values, respectively.

TABLE 14.4
Summary of Outlier Tests for Example 14.1

	LM_k^{vo}		LM_k^{lo}		
Time Index	**Test**	***p*-value**	**Test**	***p*-value**	**Inference**
150	42.32	≈ 0	42.08	≈ 0	LO
200	11.56	0.29	11.56	0.026	LO
300	62.89	≈ 0	29.24	≈ 0	VO
350	13.62	0.11	12.10	0.019	LO
191	8.50	0.83	0.00	≈ 1	
366	6.63	0.99	6.67	0.53	

Note: The outlier-free series z_t follows the ARCH(1) model: $h_t = 0.05 + 0.9z_{t-1}^2$. The observed series is y_t obtained from z_t by adding 2 LOs and 2 VOs.

to detect outliers. The middle and bottom graphs of Figure 14.4 show the time plots of LM_k^{vo} and LM_k^{lo}, respectively. The horizontal lines in the plots denote the 5% and 10% critical values of the test statistics $\mathrm{LM}_{\max}^{vo}$ and $\mathrm{LM}_{\max}^{lo}$. For LOs, the critical values are 10.73 and 9.66 for 5% and 10% significance levels, respectively. For VOs, the critical values are 15.08 and 13.73. The existence of outliers is clearly shown. Table 14.4 summarizes the results of the tests, where p-values are based on respective reference distributions that are generated by the proposed procedures with 5000 replications. The table also includes the next largest value of each test statistic and its p-value. These two p-values are large, indicating that no additional outlier exists in the data. The last column of Table 14.4 gives our classification of the detected outliers. When both test statistics are significant at the 5% level, we classify a detected outlier based on the smaller p-value. The classification of outliers at $t = 150$ and $t = 300$ is based on this decision rule. For this particular example, the VO at $t = 200$ is misclassified as an LO.

Because the test statistics $\mathrm{LM}_{\max}^{lo}$ and $\mathrm{LM}_{\max}^{vo}$ are derived from a single outlier, one can use an iterative detection procedure, which only detects a single outlier in an iteration, to handle multiple outliers. Such an iterative procedure may require several iterations and become inefficient in practice. For simplicity, in this simulated example, we adjust all four detected outliers simultaneously based on their classification in Table 14.4. This results in a revised model $h_t = 0.052 + 0.813y_{t-1}^2$, which is closer to the generating model. Using this revised model, we apply the proposed test statistics to detect any additional outlier and obtain $\mathrm{LM}_{\max}^{vo} = 9.58$ (at $t = 183$) and $\mathrm{LM}_{\max}^{lo} = 7.31$ (at $t = 366$). The p-values of these two statistics are 0.62 and 0.38, respectively, indicating that indeed there exists no other outlier in the data.

Example 14.2 Consider the monthly log returns of the S&P 500 index from February 1950 to December 2009 with 719 observations. Denoting the return series by r_t, we entertain the commonly used GARCH(1,1) model for the data: $r_t = \mu + y_t$, $h_t = \alpha_0 + \alpha_1 y_{t-1}^2 + \alpha_2 h_{t-1}$, where as usual h_t is the conditional

TABLE 14.5
Outlier Detection for Monthly S&P 500 Log Returns from 1951 to 2009, Using the Test Statistics LM_k^{vo} and LM_k^{lo}

Time Index	Date Month/Year	LM_k^{vo} Test	LM_k^{vo} p-value	LM_k^{lo} Test	LM_k^{lo} p-value	Inference
		Initial Detection Using Model (14.4.1)				
275	11/73	13.60	0.15	20.34	0.013	LO
442	10/87	34.23	≈ 0	10.17	0.68	VO
524	8/94	6.89	≈ 1	10.26	0.63	
572	8/98	18.33	0.013	8.78	0.90	VO

Note: A GARCH(1,1) model is used. The time indexes shown either have a p-value ≤ 0.1 or have the maximum test statistic among the remaining data points. The p-values for LM_k^{lo} are based on simulations with 5000 replications under the null hypothesis of no outliers. There is no outlier detected in the second iteration.

variance of y_t, given the past information. In this exercise, we used only the 11 returns of 1950 to estimate the initial volatility so that test statistics are evaluated from January 1951. Without considering outliers, the fitted model is

$$r_t = 0.00618 + y_t, \quad h_t = 0.000089 + 0.114y_{t-1}^2 + 0.844h_{t-1}. \tag{14.4.1}$$

Usual model checking statistics fail to suggest any model inadequacy, e.g., the Ljung–Box statistics of the standardized residuals and its squared series give $Q(15) = 17.71$ and 7.04, respectively, with p-values 0.28 and 0.96. Using this model and $J = 3$ for the LM_k^{lo} statistic, we apply the proposed test statistics to detect outliers in the data. Table 14.5 summarizes the results of outlier detection using the proposed test statistics LM_k^{vo} and LM_k^{lo}. The time indexes shown either have a significant statistic at the 10% level or have the maximum test statistic among the remaining data points. The p-values for $\text{LM}_{\max}^{vo}$ are based on the distribution of the maximum of a random sample of size 708 from a χ_1^2 distribution, whereas those of $\text{LM}_{\max}^{lo}$ are based on a simulation of 5000 realizations of size 719 using the fitted GARCH(1,1) model in Equation 14.4.1. From the table, two VOs (October 1987 and August 1998) and one LO (September 1973) are detected at the 5% significance level. The next smallest p-values are approximately equal to 15% for VO and larger than 40% for LO. Adjusting for detected outliers, we obtain a refined model $r_t = 0.00750 + y_t$, $h_t = 0.00014 + 0.138y_{t-1}^2 + 0.769h_{t-1}$. We then iterate the detecting procedure. The smallest p-value for the VO was 23.0% (October 2008) and that for LO was about 38.8% (October 1978). Thus, no additional outlier is detected and the detection process is terminated.

In summary, using the commonly used GARCH(1,1) model, we detected three outliers in the monthly log returns of the S&P 500 index. These outliers are LO in November 1973 and VO in October 1987 and August 1998. The detected outliers might be due to the 1973–1974 oil crisis, the 1987 stock market crash, and the Russian/Long-Term Capital Management crisis, respectively. It is interesting to see that the model specifies the crash in October 1987 and August 1998 crisis as a VO, supporting that these crises increased volatility in the U.S. stock markets. It is also interesting to note that the subprime crisis was not classified as an outlier. The result could be different if daily data were used.

Example 14.3 Next, we study a 20-minute return series of the Deutsche Mark/Dollar exchange rate from 5 June, 1989 to 19 June, 1989. Let $R_t = 100r_t$, where r_t is the 20-minute log returns of the exchange rate. Figure 14.5 shows the time plot of R_t with 1243 observations. We employed an ARCH(5) and a GARCH(1,1) model in our study. The proposed test statistics detect similar outliers for both models. Therefore, we shall only report the results for the GARCH(1,1) model.

Following the same procedure as that of Example 14.2, we start with no outliers. The fitted GARCH(1,1) model is

$$R_t = 0.052 + y_t, \quad h_t = 0.197 + 0.274y_{t-1}^2 + 0.521h_{t-1}, \tag{14.4.2}$$

where h_t is the conditional variance of y_t at time $t-1$. Using model (14.4.2), we apply the test statistics LM_k^{vo} and LM_k^{lo} with $J = 3$ to detect outliers. Table 14.6(a) gives the test results for time indexes where an outlier is detected at the 10% significance level or a test statistic assumes its maximum among the remaining data points. The p-values are obtained by using the same methods

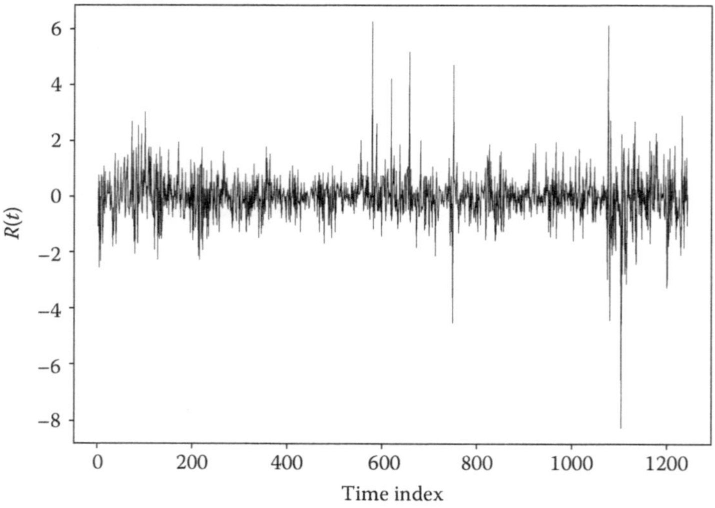

FIGURE 14.5
Time plot of 20-minute returns (r_t) of the exchange rate between the Deutsche Mark and U.S. Dollar from 5 June to 19 June, 1989. The Y-axis is $R_t = 100r_t$.

TABLE 14.6
Results of Outlier Detection for the 20-Minute Return Series of the Deutsche Mark/Dollar Exchange Rate from 5 June to 19 June, 1989

Time Index	LM_k^{vo} Test	LM_k^{vo} p-value	LM_k^{io} Test	LM_k^{io} p-value	Inference
(a) Initial Detection Using Model (14.4.2)					
100	12.81	0.34	20.02	0.039	LO
579	77.32	≈ 0	84.47	≈ 0	VO or LO
619	29.14	0.0001	20.71	0.028	VO
657	37.43	≈ 0	30.89	0.001	VO or LO
712	11.16	0.64	15.95	0.18	
748	28.32	0.0001	0.00	≈ 1	VO
1075	17.81	0.029	0.00	≈ 1	VO
1104	52.37	≈ 0	0.04	≈ 1	VO
1200	17.76	0.030	0.00	≈ 1	VO
(b1) Second Iteration Using Model (14.4.3)					
72	18.65	0.019	16.94	0.097	VO
588	12.63	0.37	16.88	0.10	
1076	23.42	0.0016	25.04	0.0032	VO or LO
(b2) Third Iteration Using Model (14.4.4)					
588	13.75	0.22	17.56	0.066	LO
672	11.95	0.48	14.62	0.22	
1080	20.62	0.007	0.59	≈ 1	VO
(b3) Fourth Iteration Using Model (14.4.5)					
555	13.52	0.25	13.64	0.30	
750	10.69	0.73	15.17	0.16	
(c1) Second Iteration Using Model (14.4.6)					
72	18.67	0.019	17.13	0.082	VO
575	12.87	0.33	13.44	0.36	
750	8.69	0.98	13.77	0.32	
1076	25.73	0.0005	26.59	0.0018	VO
(c2) Third Iteration Using Model (14.4.7)					
555	13.67	0.23	13.80	0.27	
750	11.25	0.62	15.63	0.12	

Note: The model used is GARCH(1,1) and the time indexes shown either have a significant test statistic at the 10% level or have the maximum test statistic among the remaining data points. The p-values are obtained based on simulations with 5000 replications.

as those in Example 14.2. It is clear that the tests detect one LO at $t = 100$, five VOs, and two additional outliers that can be classified in either way because p-values of the test statistics are very close for these two observations.

As before, we consider two situations in further analysis. The first situation is to classify a detected outlier as LO whenever both p-values of the test statistics are close to zero. For the exchange rate series, this means that the two outliers at $t = 579$ and $t = 657$ are classified as LO, resulting in three LOs and five VOs in the initial detection. Incorporating these detected outliers, we refine the model to

$$R_t = 0.026 + y_t, \quad h_t = 0.058 + 0.143y_{t-1}^2 + 0.753h_{t-1}. \tag{14.4.3}$$

Again, the test statistics are applied to obtain the results shown in Table 14.6(b1). This second iteration identified a VO at $t = 72$ and an outlier at $t = 1076$, which can be classified as VO or LO. Following the adopted strategy, we classify the outlier at $t = 1076$ as LO, resulting in six VOs and four LOs for the data. With the newly identified outliers, the model becomes

$$R_t = 0.022 + y_t, \quad h_t = 0.042 + 0.115y_{t-1}^2 + 0.804h_{t-1}. \tag{14.4.4}$$

Table 14.6(b2) gives the results of outlier detection based on this model. We detect an additional LO at $t = 588$ and an additional VO at $t = 1080$. The model becomes

$$R_t = 0.019 + y_t, \quad h_t = 0.034 + 0.092y_{t-1}^2 + 0.835h_{t-1}. \tag{14.4.5}$$

Table 14.6(b3) shows that no more outliers are detected by the proposed test statistics. Consequently, if we adopt the policy that classifies outliers as LO whenever the p-values of both test statistics are close to zero, then the proposed test statistics detect seven VOs and five LOs in the data.

In the second situation, we classify a detected outlier as VO when both p-values of the test statistics are close to zero. Under this strategy, the initial detection identified a single LO at $t = 100$ and seven VOs (see Table 14.6(a)). Incorporating these outliers, we obtain

$$R_t = 0.030 + y_t, \quad h_t = 0.051 + 0.128y_{t-1}^2 + 0.775h_{t-1}. \tag{14.4.6}$$

Table 14.6(c1) gives the results of outlier detection based on this refined model. Two additional VOs are detected at $t = 72$ and 1076, and we further refine the model to

$$R_t = 0.024 + y_t, \quad h_t = 0.033 + 0.086y_{t-1}^2 + 0.840h_{t-1}. \tag{14.4.7}$$

Table 14.6(c2) shows that no new outliers exist. Consequently, if we adopt the strategy that classifies a detected outlier as VO when the p-values of both test statistics are close to zero, then there are nine VOs and a single LO in the data. Again, the final models shown in Equations 14.4.5 and 14.4.7 are very close to each other, indicating that outlier classification has little effects on parameter estimation when p-values of both test statistics are close to zero.

Finally, it is interesting to compare the estimated GARCH(1,1) models before and after outlier adjustment. (a) The outlier adjustment substantially reduces the estimate of the mean return of the exchange rate series R_t, changing from 0.052 before adjustment to 0.024 after adjustment (see models (14.4.2) and (14.4.7)). (b) The outliers also have a marked effect on the unconditional variance of the return series R_t. The unconditional standard errors of y_t in models (14.4.2), (14.4.5), and (14.4.7) are 0.98, 0.67, and 0.68, respectively. Thus, there is a 30% reduction in the estimated unconditional standard error of R_t. Such a reduction is rather remarkable because there are only 10 to 12 outliers in 1243 observations. This particular example shows that overlooking a few outliers may result in substantial overestimation of the mean and volatility of a financial time series.

In summary, the applications show that the proposed test statistics can detect outliers in volatility modeling and that overlooking outliers may lead to substantial overestimation of asset volatility. The two types of outliers considered are relatively simple. Other types of outliers such as a level shift in volatility can also be entertained. Finally, further research on the limitng distributions of the proposed test statistics is needed.

References

Bollerslev, T. (2009). Generalized autoregressive conditional heteroskedasticity. *Journal of Econometrics*, 51:307–327.

Bollerslev, T., Chou, R. Y., and Kroner, K. F. (1992). ARCH modeling in finance: A review of the theory and empirical evidence. *Journal of Econometrics*, 52:5–60.

Chen, C. and Liu, L. M. (1993a). Forecasting time series with outliers. *Journal of Forecasting*, 12:13–35.

Chen, C. and Liu, L. M. (1993b). Joint estimation of model parameters and outlier effects in time series. *Journal of American Statistical Association*, 88:284–297.

Engle, R. F. (1982). Autoregressive conditional heteroscedasticity with estimates of the variance of the united kingdom inflation. *Econometrica*, 50:987–1007.

Engle, R. F. (1984). Wald, likelihood ratio, and Lagrange multiplier tests in econometrics. In *Handbook of Econometrics, Volume II*, eds. Z. Griliches and M. Lntriligator, 775–826. Amsterdam: Elsevier Science Publishers.

Hotta, L. and Tsay, R. S. (2010). Outliers in GARCH processes. Technical Report, Booth School of Business, University of Chicago, Chicago, IL.

Lawrence, A. (1995). Deletion influence and masking in regression. *Journal of the Royal Statistical Society. Series B*, 57:181–189.

Nelson, D. (1990). Stationary and persistence in the GARCH(1,1) model. *Econometric Theory*, 6:318–334.

Peña, D. (1990). Influential observations in time series. *Journal of Business and Economic Statistics*, 8:235–241.

Taylor, S. (1986). *Modelling Financial Time Series*. New York: John Wiley.

van Dijk, D., Franses, P. H., and Lucas, A. (1999). Testing for ARCH in the presence of additive outliers. *Journal of Applied Econometrics*, 14:539–562.

15

Constructing a Credit Default Swap Index and Detecting the Impact of the Financial Crisis

Yoko Tanokura, Hiroshi Tsuda, Seisho Sato, and Genshiro Kitagawa

CONTENTS

15.1 Introduction

The behavior of prices or returns on financial assets has been investigated since the 1960s, and it has been reported that the distribution is often heavy-tailed and possibly skewed. In particular, modeling of the return distributions has been discussed in many studies. Mandelbrot (1963) and Fama (1965) found that the asset return distribution has heavier tails than a normal distribution and can better be described as a stable Paretian distribution. McDonald (1996) reviewed various specifications of return distribution alternatives fit to empirical data, and Praetz (1972), Madan and Seneta (1990), and Linden

(2001) used a mixture of distributions for modeling the return distributions. Modeling of price or return distributions of financial assets remains an open question. Recently, derivative products dealing with credit risk, which measures the exposure to loss resulting from failure of a company or even a government to fulfill the debt obligation, have been highlighted. As their price fluctuations can be influential on the economy, in spite of being immature markets, fully exploiting insufficient information on them to capture their long-term price trends becomes essential.

This chapter presents a statistical method of constructing a price index of a financial asset where the price distributions are skewed and heavy-tailed. To fully reflect the price movements of the market, the distribution should be taken into account. Simply taking the average price as an index may cause bias and unevenly reflect the extreme prices in the tails. To cope with both skewed and heavy-tailed distributions, we first apply the Box–Cox transformation (Box and Cox, 1964). Then, the long-term trend of the distributions is estimated by fitting a trend model with Cauchy or Gaussian observation noise to the transformed prices. The estimation is performed by applying state space modeling. Considering the case of an asset where the number of price observations rises, falls, and even vanishes at certain times, we suppose that the dispersion of the noise distribution depends on the number of observations. Missing observations are interpolated by a smoothing algorithm for the state space model (Kitagawa, 2010; Kitagawa and Gersch, 1996). For each parameter λ of the Box–Cox transformation, we calculate the AIC (Akaike Information Criterion, see Akaike (1973); Konishi and Kitagawa (2008)) of the trend model fitted to the transformed prices. To select the optimal λ, each AIC is modified for the transformation back to the original price scale (Kitagawa, 2010). Finally, an index is defined by taking the inverse Box–Cox transformation of the long-term trend of the optimal transformed prices. To our knowledge, there have been few studies on estimating a non-Gaussian time series model by using a variable transformation and AIC.

Investigating the relationship between price fluctuations of the new index and other market indices can be an effective way to verify the usefulness of the new index. We apply the generalized power contribution (Tanokura and Kitagawa, 2004), a generalized version of Akaike's power contribution (Akaike, 1968), as a tool to detect causal relations between indices in terms of frequency domain properties of the noises in a multivariate dynamic system with feedback. The correlated noise sources of fluctuations between indices can be detected. In order to visualize the analysis effectively, we define the influence distance (ID) to represent the strength of the relationship between two indices. The entire picture of price fluctuations between indices can thus be observed.

As an example, we apply our method to the Japanese Credit Default Swap (CDS) market of which the price distributions are skewed and heavy-tailed. As the market is immature, the number of observations is often up-and-down and even vanishes at certain times. A CDS is an insurance contract where the buyer periodically pays a premium (quoted as an annual rate called the CDS price) to the seller for credit protection of a corporate debt, and the seller will make a payment on the occurrence of a credit event of the reference entity. For the practical reason that the prices of CDS issues with the same credit rating often comove, we suppose that a CDS price follows the price distribution specific to its rating. By categorizing the CDS entities into four ratings, CDS rating indices were constructed by our method. Then, we constructed a new CDS index for the entire CDS market in a rating-weighted form. It was found that the higher the credit risk, the higher is the rating index. It is noteworthy that the new CDS index reflects the price movements of the rating indices in a balanced manner.

By investigating the relationship between the new CDS index and other Japanese market indices, the influence of the financial crisis on these indices is examined. By power contribution analysis, we find that there were drastic price fluctuations across the Japanese markets and that the CDS market behavior increased its impact on the other markets due to the crisis. Moreover, the Japanese markets became significantly sensitive to the CDS market and the behavior of the indices became tightly coupled after the crisis. Several prior studies investigated the relationship between bond yields, stock returns, and CDS price changes. For example, Norden and Weber (2009) showed that stock returns lead both CDS price changes and bond spread changes. However, the analyses were mostly performed on U.S. and European firms, and not on the market index level.

The organization of this chapter is as follows. Section 15.2 presents a method of constructing a price index where the price distribution is non-Gaussian. Section 15.3 briefly reviews the generalized power contribution as a tool to detect causal relations between market indices, and defines the ID to effectively visualize the analysis. In Section 15.4, we apply our method to the Japanese CDS market and construct the CDS rating indices and the new CDS index. The relationship between price fluctuations of the Japanese markets before and after the occurrence of the U.S. subprime crisis is examined by the power contribution analysis. Finally, we present our conclusions in Section 15.5.

15.2 Construction of a Price Index by Time Series Modeling

It is not easy to construct a price index of a financial asset to reflect the entire price behavior of the market when the price distribution is heavily skewed or non-Gaussian, because simply taking average prices as an index may cause bias. In this section, we present a method of constructing a price index based on time series modeling. First, we perform the Box–Cox transformation (Box and Cox, 1964) to make the identification of the distribution easy. Then, we estimate the long-term trend of the distributions by fitting a trend model to the transformed prices. The optimal parameter of the Box–Cox transformation is selected by AIC (Akaike, 1973; Konishi and Kitagawa, 2008). Finally, the index is defined by the inverse Box–Cox transformation of the estimated long-term trend.

15.2.1 Box–Cox Transformation and Estimation of the Long-Term Trend of Distributions Where the Number of Observations Varies

Consider a financial asset market of which the price distributions are non-Gaussian or skewed. Let $p_{i,n}$ $(i = 1, \ldots, k_n)$ denote prices of the comprising issues of the market at time n, where the number of observations is denoted as k_n. It should be noted that k_n varies over time and can be zero at certain times, and that $p_{i,n}$ is a positive value. In order to make the identification of the distribution easy, we consider the Box–Cox transformation (Box and Cox, 1964) of the prices

$$q_{i,n} = h_\lambda(p_{i,n}) = \begin{cases} \lambda^{-1}(p_{i,n}^\lambda - 1) & \lambda \neq 0 \\ \log p_{i,n} & \lambda = 0, \end{cases} \tag{15.2.1}$$

which has been applied in various areas of finance. For each λ, the time series of the mean y_n^λ $(n = 1, \ldots, t)$ of the transformed prices $q_{i,n}$ $(i = 1, \ldots, k_n)$ is obtained, and it can be nonstationary.

Then, we estimate the long-term trend of y_n^λ for each λ by fitting the following first-order trend model

$$t_n^\lambda = t_{n-1}^\lambda + v_n^\lambda, \quad v_n^\lambda \sim N(0, \tau_\lambda^2), \tag{15.2.2}$$

$$y_n^\lambda = t_n^\lambda + w_n^\lambda, \quad w_n^\lambda \sim D(0, \sigma_\lambda^2), \tag{15.2.3}$$

where t_n^λ represents a nonstationary mean value function. The noise v_n^λ follows a normal distribution with mean 0 and unknown variance τ_λ^2, and the observation noise w_n^λ follows a possibly non-Gaussian distribution D with location parameter 0 and unknown scale parameter σ_λ (Kitagawa, 2010; Kitagawa and Gersch, 1996).

In Equation 15.2.3, the scale parameter σ_λ of the observation noise is assumed to be a constant. However, we deal with the case of a financial market where the number of price observations changes and even vanishes at certain times due to insufficient information. Taking such cases into account, we instead assume that σ_λ^2 is inversely proportional to the number of observations. Therefore, we replace the observation model (15.2.3) with the following expression

$$y_n^\lambda = t_n^\lambda + w_n^\lambda, \quad w_n^\lambda \sim D(0, \sigma_\lambda^2/k_n). \tag{15.2.4}$$

Now, the trend model consisting of Equations 15.2.2 and 15.2.4 can be expressed as the following state space model

$$x_n^\lambda = Fx_{n-1}^\lambda + Gv_n^\lambda, \tag{15.2.5}$$

$$y_n^\lambda = Hx_n^\lambda + w_n^\lambda. \tag{15.2.6}$$

With this state space representation, we can flexibly and effectively address parameter estimation and interpolation for the model, as discussed in the next section. The state vector x_n^λ, and F, G, and H, are defined by $x_n^\lambda = t_n^\lambda$,

$F = G = H = 1$, respectively. For each λ, we will estimate x_n^λ as stated in the following section.

15.2.2 State Estimation by Kalman Filtering and Sequential Monte Carlo Filtering

The estimation of the state x_n^λ at time n corresponds to evaluating the conditional distribution $p(x_n^\lambda|Y_t^\lambda)$, where $Y_t^\lambda \equiv \{y_1^\lambda, \ldots, y_t^\lambda\}$ denotes the set of observations up to time t. For the three cases $n > t$, $n = t$, and $n < t$, evaluating $p(x_n^\lambda|Y_t^\lambda)$ is called prediction, filtering, and smoothing, respectively. For the case that the observation noise distribution D in Equation 15.2.4 is Gaussian, the conditional distributions for $n \geq t$ can be estimated using the Kalman filter. For $n < t$, and to interpolate missing observations, one also uses a smoothing algorithm (Anderson and Moore 1979; Kitagawa 2010; Kitagawa and Gersch 1996). On the other hand, for the case that the distribution D is non-Gaussian such as a Cauchy distribution, we apply a sequential Monte Carlo filter, which approximates a distribution by many (say, 10,000) particles that can be regarded as independent realizations from the distribution (Gordon et al. 1993; Kitagawa 1996; Doucet et al. 2001; Kitagawa 2010). We will briefly outline the procedure of the sequential Monte Carlo filter as follows.

We assume that the initial state x_0^λ follows the density $p_0(x^\lambda)$ and that each distribution in the above three cases is expressed using m particles as follows: $\{p_n^{(1)}, \ldots, p_n^{(m)}\} \sim p(x_n^\lambda|Y_{n-1}^\lambda)$ for prediction, $\{f_n^{(1)}, \ldots, f_n^{(m)}\} \sim p(x_n^\lambda|Y_n^\lambda)$ for filtering, and $\{s_{n|t}^{(1)}, \ldots, s_{n|t}^{(m)}\} \sim p(x_n^\lambda|Y_t^\lambda)$ for smoothing. When m particles $\{p_n^{(1)}, \ldots, p_n^{(m)}\}$ from $p(x_n^\lambda|Y_{n-1}^\lambda)$ are given, the distribution is approximated by the empirical distribution determined by the m particles. That is, it is approximated by the probability function $\Pr(x_n^\lambda = p_n^{(j)}|Y_{n-1}^\lambda) = 1/m$ for $j = 1, \ldots, m$. As stated below, a set of realizations expressing the one-step-ahead predictor $p(x_n^\lambda|Y_{n-1}^\lambda)$ and the filter $p(x_n^\lambda|Y_n^\lambda)$ can be obtained recursively.

1. Generate a random number $f_0^{(j)} \sim p_0(x^\lambda)$ for $j = 1, \ldots, m$.
2. Repeat the following steps for $n = 1, \ldots, t$.
   (a) Generate random numbers $v_n^{(j)} \sim N(0, \tau_\lambda^2)$ for $j = 1, \ldots, m$, to obtain independent realizations of the system noise v_n^λ in Equation 15.2.2.
   (b) Compute $p_n^{(j)} = Ff_{n-1}^{(j)} + Gv_n^{(j)}$ for $j = 1, \ldots, m$.
   (c) Compute $\alpha_n^{(j)} = d(y_n^\lambda - Hp_n^{(j)})$ for $j = 1, \ldots, m$, where $d(w^\lambda)$ is the density function of the observation noise w_n^λ in Equation 15.2.4.
   (d) Generate $f_n^{(j)}$ for $j = 1, \ldots, m$, by resampling $p_n^{(1)}, \ldots, p_n^{(m)}$ with weights proportional to $\alpha_n^{(1)}, \ldots, \alpha_n^{(m)}$.

Let θ denote a set of the unknown parameters of the state space model such as the variances or scale parameters of the noises. Then, the likelihood of the model is given by $L(\theta) = p(y_1^\lambda, \ldots, y_t^\lambda|\theta) = \prod_{n=1}^{t} p(y_n^\lambda|Y_{n-1}^\lambda)$, where

$p(y_1^\lambda|Y_0^\lambda) = p_0(y_1^\lambda)$. For applying the sequential Monte Carlo filter, we use the approximation

$$p(y_n^\lambda|Y_{n-1}^\lambda) = \int p(y_n^\lambda|x_n^\lambda)p(x_n^\lambda|Y_{n-1}^\lambda)dx_n^\lambda \cong \frac{1}{m}\sum_{j=1}^{m} p(y_n^\lambda|p_n^{(j)}) = \frac{1}{m}\sum_{j=1}^{m} \alpha_n^{(j)}.$$

The maximum likelihood estimate can be obtained by maximizing the log-likelihood: $\log L(\theta) = \sum_{j=1}^{m} \log p(y_n^\lambda|Y_{n-1}^\lambda)$.

For the case of non-Gaussian observation noise in the trend model, this chapter uses the Cauchy distribution as a viable non-Gaussian alternative to a normal distribution. The Cauchy distribution is often used in modeling nonstationary time series including extreme values and level shifts, such as in Kitagawa and Gersch (1996). In finance, large (in magnitude) values of the noise may correspond to the occurrence of the crisis.

15.2.3 Selection of the Box–Cox Transformation by the Akaike Information Criterion and Constructing a Price Index

For each λ of the Box–Cox transformation (15.2.1), the long-term trend t_n^λ was estimated as described in the previous section. Now, we search for an optimal λ for constructing a price index by using AIC in the following way.

Let AIC^λ denote the AIC value of the trend model fitted to the mean value y_n^λ of the Box–Cox transformed prices. For selecting the optimal parameter λ, AIC^λ should be modified to AIC_0^λ, that is, the AIC value of the model for the original prices obtained by the inverse Box–Cox transformation of y_n^λ:

$$z_n^\lambda = h_\lambda^{-1}(y_n^\lambda) = \begin{cases} (1 + \lambda\, y_n^\lambda)^{1/\lambda} & \lambda \neq 0 \\ \exp\, y_n^\lambda & \lambda = 0. \end{cases}$$

Then, AIC_0^λ is expressed as

$$\text{AIC}_0^\lambda = \text{AIC}^\lambda - 2\sum_{n=1}^{t} \log \left|\frac{dh_\lambda}{dz}\right|_{z=z_n^\lambda}, \tag{15.2.7}$$

where dh_λ/dz is the Jacobian of the Box–Cox transformation (Kitagawa, 2010). Therefore, the optimal λ is selected by minimizing AIC_0^λ values. Finally, the price index is defined by the inverse Box–Cox transformation of the long-term trend.

15.3 Detection of Causal Relations by Power Contribution Analysis

Once a price index is established, capturing the behavior of the short-term cyclical component around the index trend is important, and analyzing causal relations between those of financial markets is indispensable for investment management. We conduct a power contribution analysis through multivariate autoregressive (AR) modeling, as a tool for detecting causal relations between detrended index series. In this section, we briefly review the concept of the generalized power contribution (Tanokura and Kitagawa, 2004), a generalized version of Akaike's power contribution (Akaike 1968; Akaike and Nakagawa 1988). Then, to effectively visualize the analysis, we define the ID to represent the strength of the relationship between two indices.

15.3.1 Brief Review of the Generalized Power Contribution

Let x_n denote an l-dimensional detrended index series. We fit the following multivariate AR model with order M to x_n

$$x_n = \sum_{m=1}^{M} A_m x_{n-m} + v_n, \tag{15.3.1}$$

where $A_m = (a_m(j,k))$ is an $l \times l$ AR coefficient matrix, and the l-dimensional white noise v_n satisfies: $\mathrm{E}(v_n) = [0,\ldots,0]'$, $\mathrm{E}(v_n v_n') = W$, $\mathrm{E}(v_n v_r') = \mathrm{O}$ for $n \neq r$, and $\mathrm{E}(v_n x_r') = \mathrm{O}$ for $n > r$. Here W is the $l \times l$ variance matrix of the noise v_n, and O denotes the $l \times l$ matrix with zero elements.

It is well-known that the cross-spectrum matrix at a frequency f can be obtained by $P(f) = (P_{jk}(f)) = A(f)^{-1}W(A(f)^{-1})^*$, where $A(f) = (A_{jk}(f))$ is an $l \times l$ complex matrix such that $A_{jk}(f) = \sum_{m=0}^{M} a_m(j,k)e^{-2\pi imf}$, $a_0(j,j) = -1$, $a_0(j,k) = 0$ for $j \neq k$ (Akaike and Nakagawa, 1988). The symbol * denotes the complex conjugate of a matrix. For simplicity, hereafter $A(f)^{-1}$ is denoted as $B(f) = (b_{jk}(f))$. By assuming that the noises are mutually uncorrelated, i.e., $W = \mathrm{diag}\{\sigma_{11},\ldots,\sigma_{ll}\}$, the power spectrum $P_{jj}(f)$ for each index j can be simply expressed as

$$P_{jj}(f) = \sum_{i=1}^{l} b_{ji}(f)\sigma_{ii}b_{ji}(f)^* \equiv \sum_{i=1}^{l} |b_{ji}(f)|^2\sigma_{ii}. \tag{15.3.2}$$

This implies that the power spectrum can be expressed as the sum of l influences of the noises, where $|b_{ji}(f)|^2\sigma_{ii}$ $(i = 1,\ldots,l)$ expresses the degree of its influence. Therefore, Akaike's power contribution is defined as $r_{ij}(f) = |b_{ij}(f)|^2/\sigma_{jj}P_{ii}(f)$, which expresses the proportion of the fluctuation of $x_n(j)$ at a frequency f caused by $v_n(i)$ (Akaike, 1968; Akaike and Nakagawa, 1988). This concept of power contribution is very useful and has been applied to the analysis of feedback control systems.

Unfortunately, financial time series are usually highly correlated, and the assumption of the independence of the noise inputs does not hold. We can mitigate this problem by modeling multivariate correlations among the noise terms, and then, by decomposing the variance matrix, we can define a generalized power contribution (Tanokura and Kitagawa, 2004). Then, the power spectrum $P_{ii}(f)$ is generally decomposed into $l(l+1)/2$ contributions of influences from various noises: $l(l-1)/2$ contributions from multivariate noises, and l contributions from single noises. Similarly, the generalized power contribution can be defined. The details can be found in Tanokura and Kitagawa (2004).

For example, in the system of three time series of A, B, and C, the power spectrum at a frequency for A is expressed as the sum of six contributions: the contribution of the influence from A itself, that from B, that from C, that of the simultaneous influence from A and B (expressed as A + B), and that from A, B, and C (likewise ALL or A + B + C). Therefore, the multidimensional sources of fluctuations such as simultaneous influential components of various combinations of noises are detected. It is noted that the index combinations of the influential components depend on the variance matrix of the noises.

15.3.2 Definition of the Influence Distance

To effectively visualize the power contribution analysis, which provides information on the multidimensional causal relations between indices, we define the ID to measure the strength of the relationship between the price fluctuations of two indices. This is done in the following way.

By generalizing Equation 15.3.2, the power spectrum of an index I_j at a frequency f is expressed as $P_{jj}(f) = \Sigma_i^{l(l+1)/2} C_f(K_i, I_j)$, where K_i expresses the combination of contributing indices, say, I_1, I_2, $I_2 + I_3$, and so on. For example, the contribution from I_1 to I_j, $C_f(I_1, I_j)$, is assigned to the contributing index I_1, and a half of the simultaneous contribution from I_2 and I_3 to I_j, $C_f(I_2 + I_3, I_j)$, is assigned to I_2 and I_3 as $C_f(I_2, I_j)$ and $C_f(I_3, I_j)$, respectively. The remainder is the same as above. Then, the assigned contributions $C_f(I_i, I_j)$ are aggregated over all frequencies to give the total contribution, $C(I_i, I_j)$. As a result, the two total contributions between I_i and I_j, $C(I_i, I_j)$ and $C(I_j, I_i)$, which measure the degrees of contributions from I_i to I_j and vice versa, can be obtained. In an opposite manner, to express the closeness between two indices in terms of fluctuations, we define the ID between I_i and I_j to be the reciprocal value of the average between $C(I_i, I_j)$ and $C(I_j, I_i)$. The smaller the value of the ID, the stronger is the relationship between two indices.

15.4 Application to the Japanese Credit Default Swap Market

We apply our method to the Japanese CDS market. As shown in Figure 15.1, the time series of price distributions of the Japanese standard CDS contracts denominated in Japanese Yen are skewed and significantly heavy-tailed, with most of the CDS prices concentrated at the lowest levels of the price range. For this reason, only the leftmost 10% or so of the price range is shown along the x-axis.

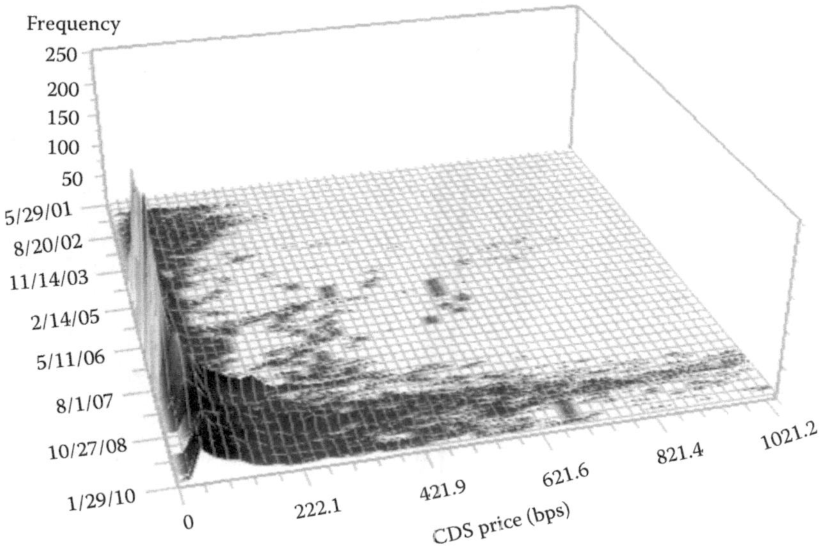

FIGURE 15.1
Histogram transition of the CDS prices (only the leftmost 10% or so of the price range is shown) (From Bloomberg LP).

From 29 May, 2001 to 29 January, 2010 (from the back to the front) in Figure 15.1, the number of observations varies even though an increasing trend can be seen, and certain trading days with no price observations are found. There are at most 327 CDS issues in any one day during the observation period. For the purpose of constructing an index to express the whole CDS market, it is found that simply taking an average of CDS prices at each point in time seems to be inappropriate because the average values may cause bias and unevenly reflect the extreme prices.

For the price comovements of CDS issues having the same credit rating, we suppose that the CDS prices follow the price distribution specific to their ratings. Among the major rating agencies in Japan (R&I, JCR, Moody's and Standard & Poor's), we regard ratings across agencies in similar categories such as AAA and Aaa as practically the same. The price and ratings data are provided by Bloomberg LP. By determining the rating prioritization for the agencies, which is usually recognized in the Japanese market, we uniquely define the four rating categories: [AAA + AA], [A], [BBB], and [Lower than BBB]. Then, one available rating category including that of the parent company is assigned to each CDS entity. It is noted that some contracts may have periods of no ratings and that ratings vary over time.

We first construct four CDS rating indices, and then construct a new CDS index in a rating-weighted form. Finally, focusing on the 5-year period

TABLE 15.1
Top Five λ and AIC_0^λ by Rating Category—Model (15.2.4) with Cauchy Observation Noise

	[AAA+AA]		[A]		[BBB]		[Lower than BBB]	
Rank	λ	AIC_0^λ	λ	AIC_0^λ	λ	AIC_0^λ	λ	AIC_0^λ
1	−0.5	4,447	−0.6	6,734	−0.7	8,095	−0.4	13,927
2	−0.6	4,465	−0.4	6,740	−1	8,110	−0.5	13,935
3	−0.4	4,477	−0.2	6,785	−0.6	8,126	−0.8	14,039
4	−0.7	4,487	−0.5	6,797	−0.5	8,157	−0.2	14,171
5	−0.3	4,492	−0.7	6,807	−0.4	8,217	−0.3	14,829

surrounding the occurrence of the U.S. subprime crisis, the relationship between price fluctuations of the new CDS index and the other Japanese market indices is examined.

15.4.1 Construction of a Japanese Credit Default Swap Index

In order to construct a CDS rating index, we search for an optimal λ of the Box–Cox transformation (15.2.1) in Section 15.2.1 for each rating category. We also examine whether the observation noise in Equation 15.2.4 of the trend model follows a Gaussian or a Cauchy distribution.

In Table 15.1, the top five λ between −1 and 1, in terms of the AIC_0^λ defined by Equation 15.2.7 for each rating category, are listed for models whose observation noise follows a Cauchy distribution. In fact, for each λ, AIC_0^λ of the model with Cauchy observation noise is significantly better than that with Gaussian observation noise for all rating categories. As an example, Table 15.2 compares AIC_0^λ of the model with Gaussian observation

TABLE 15.2
AIC_0^λ Comparison between Observation Noise Distributions for λ of Major Transformations in the Case of [AAA + AA]

	Observation Noise Distribution	
λ	**Gaussian**	**Cauchy**
1.0	12,657	9,976
0.5	9,512	6,584
0.0	8,179	4,908
−0.5	7,853	4,447
−1.0	8,226	4,725

noise with that with Cauchy observation noise for major λ in the case of [AAA + AA].

Considering the estimation results, for all rating categories we select the model with Cauchy observation noise and with the parameter λ of the Box–Cox transformation as -0.5. This value of λ gives the reciprocal square root transformation when the constant terms are ignored. It is noteworthy that, for both observation noise distributions, AIC_0^λ for $\lambda = -0.5$ is better than that for $\lambda = 0.0$, the logarithmic transformation, which is often used in finance. Searching for an optimal parameter λ is necessary because the AIC_0^λ is the worst for $\lambda = 1.0$ (original prices) for the models with either Cauchy or Gaussian observation noises.

The estimated long-term trends of the transformed prices for the four rating categories are illustrated in Figure 15.2. From top to bottom, the same information for each rating category is shown: the estimated long-term trend with $\pm\hat{\sigma}_\lambda$ (where $\hat{\sigma}_\lambda$ is the estimated scale parameter of the observation noise for $\lambda = -0.5$); the residual term, which is the difference between the mean of the observations and the smoothed value at each point in time; and the number of observations.

Due to the long interval without observations at the beginning of the period, divergent $\hat{\sigma}_\lambda$ are seen for all rating categories as shown in the left hand parts of the plots. Although residual terms large in magnitude can occasionally be found when a sharp short-term rise or fall of the observations occurs, the long-term trend is generally estimated well. In particular, the long-term trend for [Lower than BBB] is fitted well in spite of the relatively small number of observations.

Each CDS rating index is obtained from the inverse Box–Cox transformation of the estimated trend as shown in Figure 15.3. From top to bottom, the overall and closeup graphs of the rating index and the empirical price distributions (the minimum, the 20th, 50th, and 80th percentiles, and the maximum) are shown for [AAA + AA], [A], [BBB], and [Lower than BBB], respectively. For simplicity, the data based on month-end are shown.

It is noteworthy that, for all rating categories, the rating index is located mostly close to the 50th percentile. However, this is not the case when the number of observations is insufficient or significantly heavy tails of the distribution occur. For example, the [Lower than BBB] index has generally been close to the 20th percentile since the shock caused from the bankruptcy of Lehman Brothers in the fall of 2008. Considering the back and forth movements of the indices, it can be found that they are positioned at appropriate places for each rating category. That is, there are no extreme transitions of the indices, and they seem to be natural considering a historical view of the market. Comparing the levels of the rating indices, it is clearly found that the higher the credit risk, the higher is the rating index. For all rating indices, the upside tails of the distributions have significantly been distorted since the revelation of the U.S. subprime problem. As a whole, we conclude that our rating indices are well-balanced to reflect the market views on the credit risk of the CDS entities concerned.

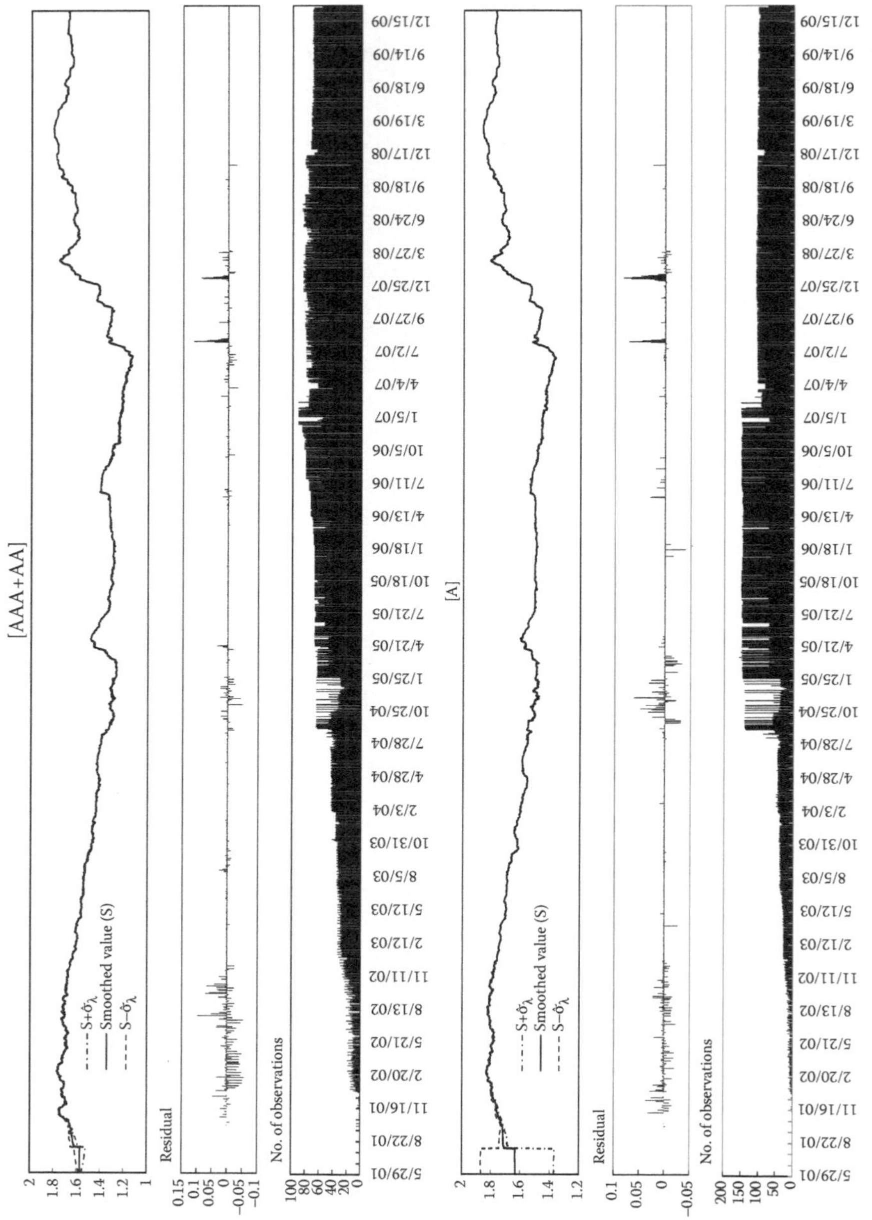

FIGURE 15.2
Estimated long-term trend with $\pm\hat{\sigma}_\lambda$, the residual term, and the number of observations for [AAA + AA], [A], [BBB], and [lower than BBB] (from top to bottom).

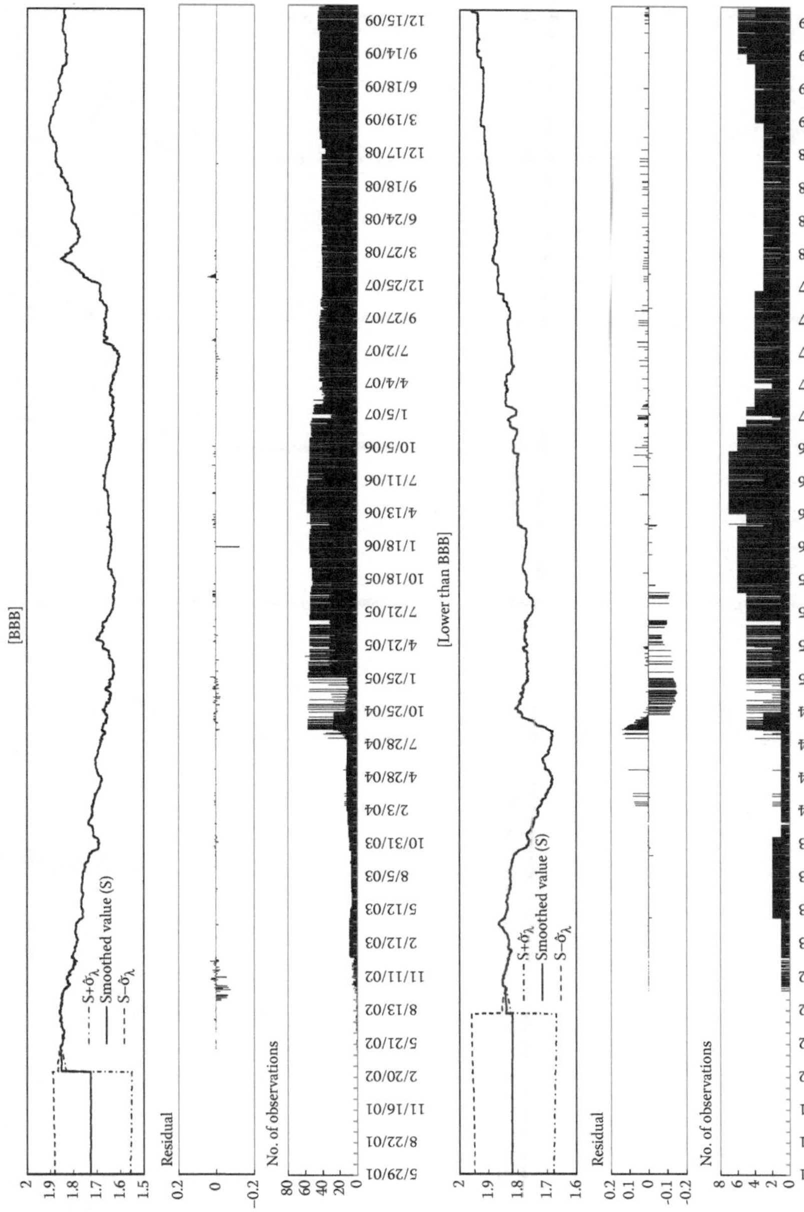

FIGURE 15.2
(continued)

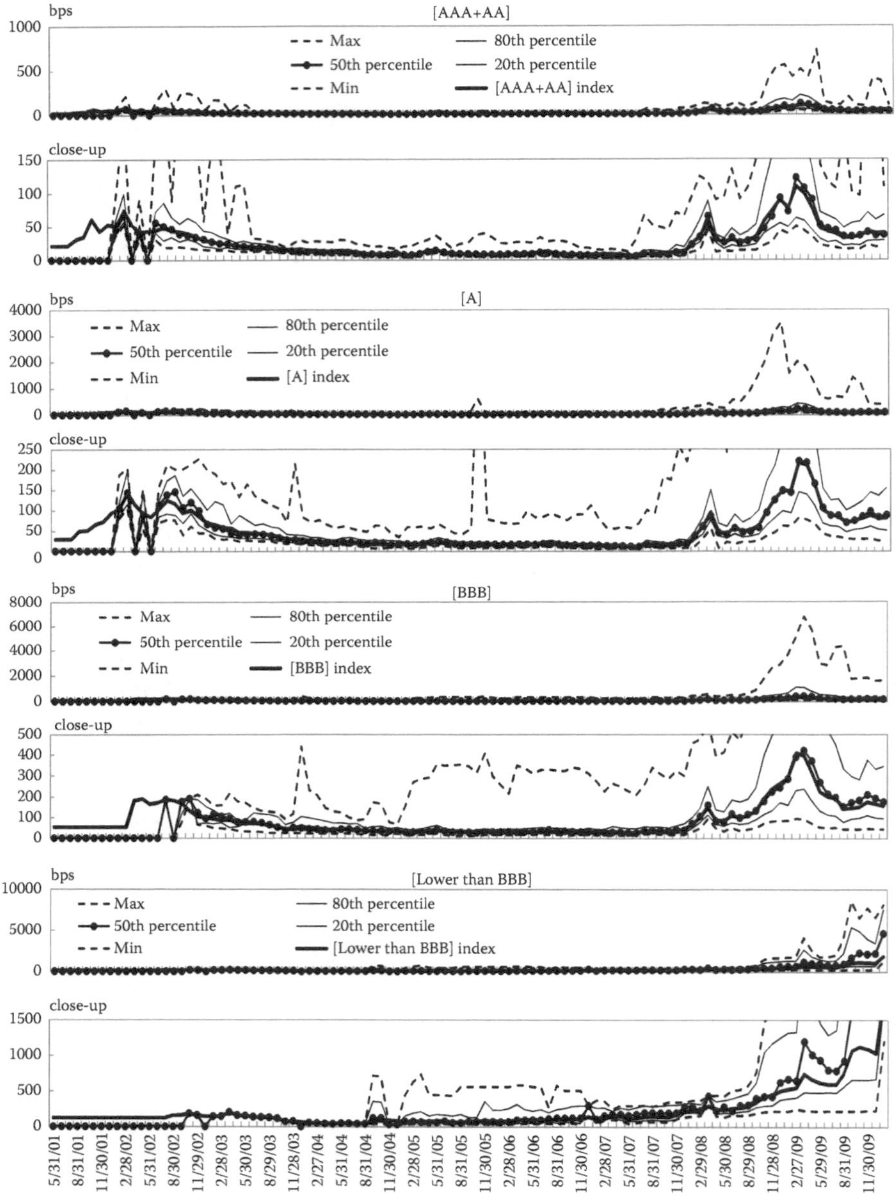

FIGURE 15.3
Overall and closeup graphs of the CDS rating index and the price distributions showing the minimum, the 20th, 50th, and 80th percentiles, and the maximum for [AAA + AA], [A], [BBB], and [lower than BBB] (from top to bottom).

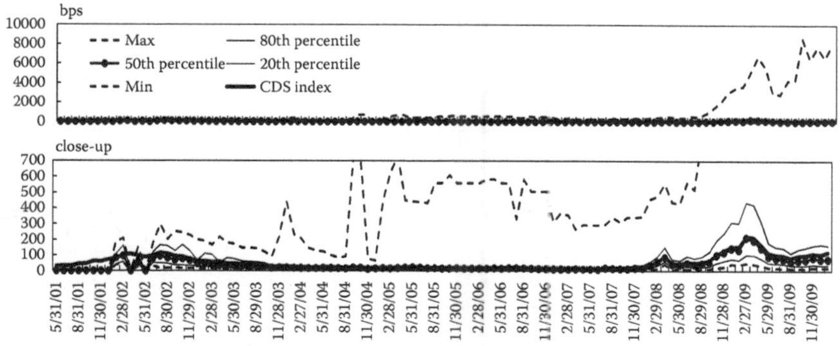

FIGURE 15.4
Overall and closeup graphs of the new CDS index and the price distributions such as the minimum, the 20th, 50th, and 80th percentiles, and the maximum of the CDS market.

A new CDS index is constructed in a rating-weighted form, summing values of the rating indices multiplied by rating weights proportional to the numbers of entities included. It is noted that the rating weights are based on the rating information on the reference entities of the CDS issues, even though no prices exist on some trading-days. As in the cases of the four rating indices, Figure 15.4 shows the overall and closeup graphs of the new CDS index and the empirical price distributions (the minimum, the 20th, 50th, and 80th percentiles, and the maximum) of the whole CDS market.

Similarly, it is found that the CDS index is located mostly close to the 50th percentile, and that it is positioned at an appropriate place even when the number of observations is not enough. Comparing the level of the CDS index with those of the rating indices in Figure 15.3, the CDS index is generally located near the [A] index. It is recognized that the CDS index reflects the four rating indices in a balanced manner. We will verify the usefulness of our new CDS index in the next section.

15.4.2 Detection of the Influence of the Financial Crisis on the Japanese Financial Markets

By investigating the relationship between price fluctuations of the four Japanese domestic markets: TPX (TOPIX: the stock market index), BPI (Nomura-BPI overall index: the fixed income market index), JPUS (JPY/USD: the foreign exchange rate), and CDS (our CDS index as a measure of credit risk), the impact of the financial crisis on the four markets is examined. The analysis is conducted for the following two periods: the pre-subprime period (from 1 February, 2005 to 29 June, 2007: 595 trading days) and the post-subprime period (from 2 July, 2007 to 29 January 2010: 630 trading days). We use the detrended index series, which are estimated by the program package

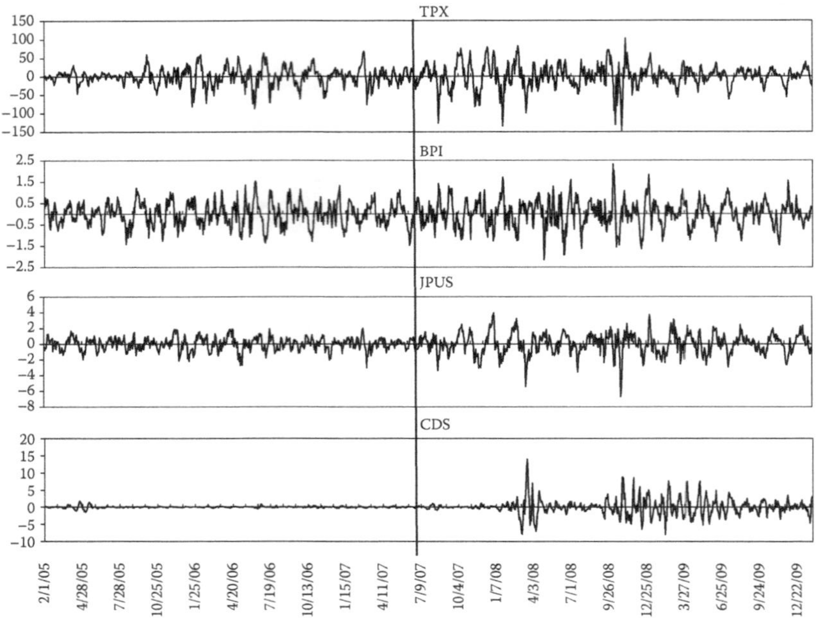

FIGURE 15.5
Detrended index series of TPX (TOPIX), BPI (Nomura-BPI overall), JPUS (JPY/USD), and CDS (new CDS index) and the occurrence of the subprime crisis (vertical line).

Web DECOMP (http://alpha1.ism.ac.jp/inets2/title.html: developed by the Institute of Statistical Mathematics). The package is based on the seasonal adjustment model presented in Gersch and Kitagawa (1983) and Kitagawa and Gersch (1984). The detrended index is not affected by the feature of the asset (i.e., the price units in which the asset values are expressed). Alternatively, rates of return and daily price changes are often used in finance. However, they strongly depend on the previous prices of the asset. It should be noted that the detrended index series are separately estimated for each period. As shown in Figure 15.5, all four detrended index series became volatile after the crisis.

Now we fit the multivariate AR model (15.3.1) to the four detrended index series for the pre- and the post-subprime periods, respectively. The AR orders selected by using AIC for the pre- and the post-subprime periods are 9 and 14, respectively, setting the upper limit of the AR order to 20. Table 15.3 displays the variances, covariances, and correlations of the noises for both periods. It is found that the values of all elements became significantly larger, or strengthened their tendencies, after the occurrence of the crisis. In particular, the correlation coefficients of CDS with the other three indices, which were almost negligible for the pre-subprime period, increased in magnitude for the post-subprime period.

TABLE 15.3
Variances, Covariances, and Correlations of the Noises for the Pre-Subprime (Top) and Post-Subprime (Bottom) Periods

Pre-Subprime	**TPX**	**BPI**	**JPUS**	**CDS**
TPX	213.2400	−1.8910	1.0095	0.0421
BPI	−0.368	0.1241	−0.0273	−0.0028
JPUS	0.125	−0.139	0.3083	0.0006
CDS	0.021	−0.056	0.008	0.0194
Post-Subprime	**TPX**	**BPI**	**JPUS**	**CDS**
TPX	367.6600	−3.9471	9.2850	−8.5279
BPI	−0.480	0.1837	−0.1367	0.0916
JPUS	0.575	−0.379	0.7093	−0.2154
CDS	−0.320	0.154	−0.184	1.9374

As shown in Figure 15.6, the power spectrum for each index, especially for CDS, significantly changed after the crisis. The peaks of the power spectrum became sharpened and stronger at the low frequencies for each index.

Next, by using the generalized power contribution in Section 15.3.1, the influential components of the power spectrum for each index are investigated. As shown in Figure 15.7, we calculate the generalized power contributions (%)

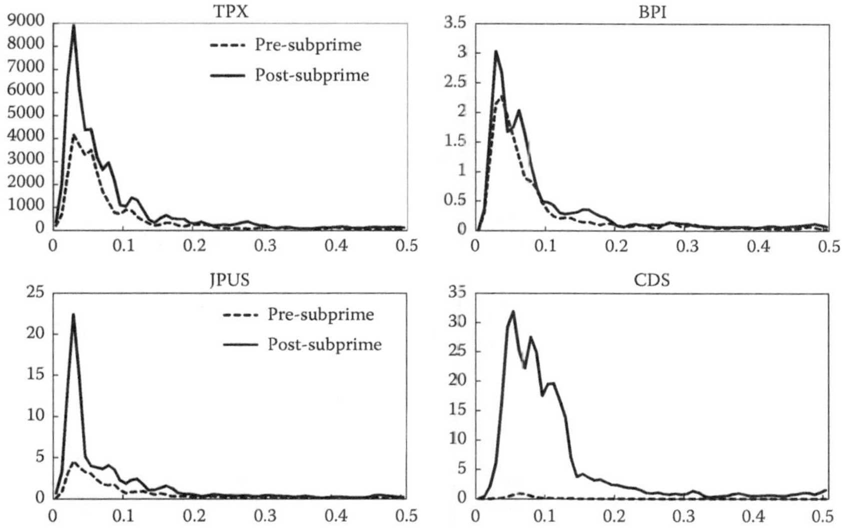

FIGURE 15.6
Power spectrum of each index for the pre-subprime (dashed curve) and post-subprime (solid curve) periods.

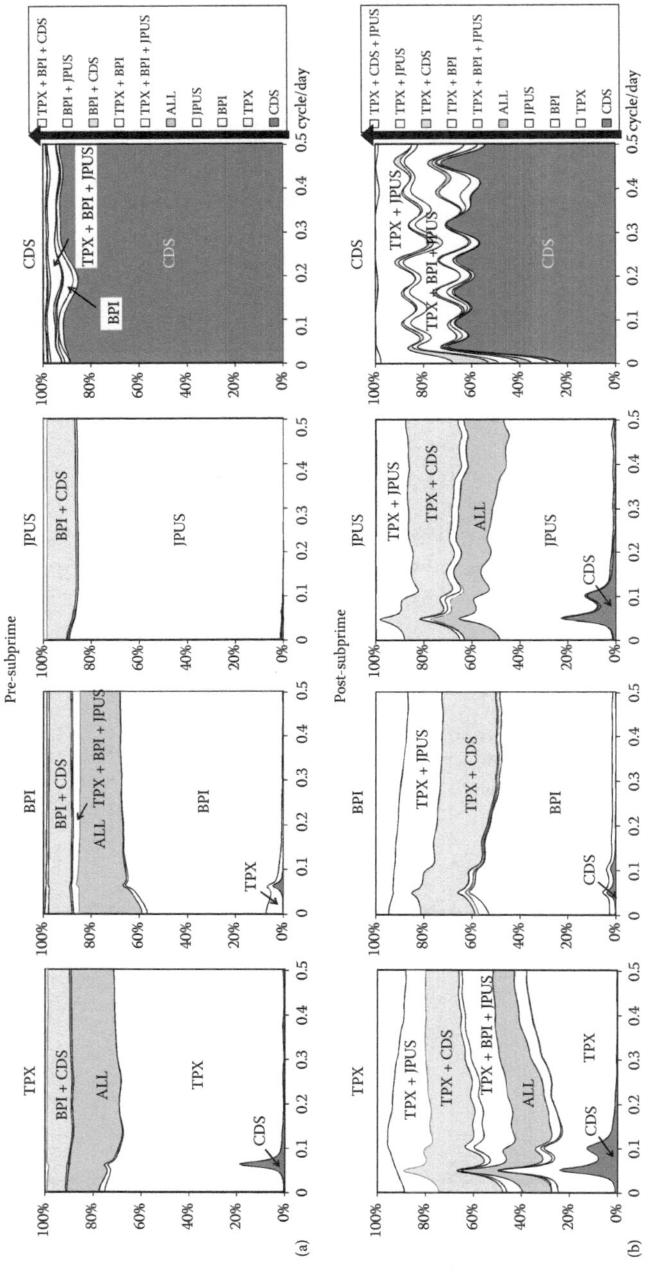

FIGURE 15.7
Generalized power contributions (%) for the pre-subprime (a) and post-subprime (b) periods.

of the four indices for the pre-subprime (a) and post-subprime (b) periods, respectively.

In our method, each power spectrum is decomposed into 10 terms consisting of four contributions of influences from single indices and six contributions of simultaneous influences from the combinations of plural indices (e.g., TPX + CDS) to an index, as shown in the rightmost legends. It is noted that the index combinations for the pre-subprime period are not always consistent with those for the post-subprime period as the index combinations depend on the variance matrix of the noises. In our analysis, the seven components from the bottom in the rightmost legend box are common to both periods. For the pre-subprime period as a whole, the contribution of each index to the index itself largely dominates. For example, the TPX contribution to the TPX index was more

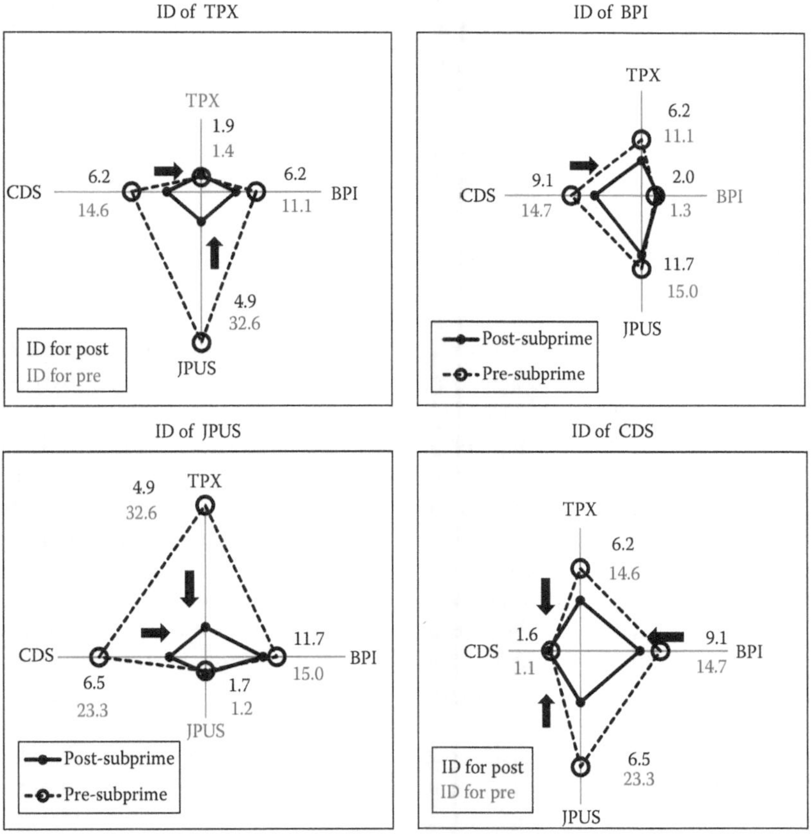

FIGURE 15.8
Influence distance (ID) of each index from the four indices for the pre-subprime (dashed line with round dots) and post-subprime (straight line with small round dots).

than 60% at all frequencies, as shown in the top left graph. However, for the post-subprime period, this self-contribution decreased for all indices, and the contributions of CDS to the other indices increased, especially in the specific frequency domain around 0.05 (a 20-day cycle). Several common components to both periods such as CDS, ALL, and TPX + BPI + JPUS are found.

Finally, to visualize the analysis effectively, the radar charts of the ID by index for both periods are shown in Figure 15.8. Each chart shows the IDs of the index from the four indices including the index itself for overall frequencies, and the arrow highlights the outstanding change of ID. For example, in the bottom right chart showing the IDs of CDS from the four indices, the ID from JPUS became significantly less, from 23.3 to 6.5, after the occurrence of the crisis. Similarly, the IDs of CDS from the other two indices sharply decreased. The smaller the ID area connecting the IDs, the tighter the mutual relationship between the four markets. Therefore, for all indices, the ID area for the post-subprime period became much smaller than that for the pre-subprime period. This implies that the Japanese markets became significantly sensitive to credit risk, and that comovements between the indices were strengthened. We found that the influence of the financial crisis on the Japanese markets cannot be ignored.

15.5 Conclusions

We presented a method of constructing a price index of a financial asset with a non-Gaussian price distribution through time series modeling. An optimal transformation among the Box–Cox transformations was found in order to estimate the appropriate long-term trend of the transformed prices. Considering the case of an asset with a varying number of price observations, a trend model with Cauchy observation noise depending on the number of observations was developed. The optimal transformation was selected using the AIC modified for the original prices, and the price index was defined by the inverse Box–Cox transformation of the long-term trend.

Our method was applied to the Japanese market of CDS, which has been recently highlighted during the financial crisis. Using our method, the four CDS rating indices were constructed. It was found that each rating index was well-balanced, reflecting the market view on the rating credit risk. Then, the new CDS index was constructed in a rating-weighted form. We also confirmed that it reflected the rating indices in a balanced manner. To detect the influence of the financial crisis on the Japanese financial markets, the relationship between price fluctuations of the new index and other Japanese market indices was investigated by the generalized power contribution analysis. Significant changes in price fluctuations between the detrended index series were detected after the occurrence of the U.S. subprime crisis. The Japanese markets became significantly sensitive to credit risk, and the behavior of their indices became tightly coupled after the occurrence of the crisis.

Applying our method to other financial markets such as fast-growing and immature markets can be effective. In particular, constructing the U.S. and European CDS indices in a similar way will be useful to examine the international spillover effects of the financial crisis.

References

Akaike, H. (1968). On the use of a linear model for the identification of feedback systems. *Annals of the Institute of Statistical Mathematics*, 20:425–439.

Akaike, H. (1973). Information theory as an extension of the maximum likelihood principle. In *Second International Symposium on Information Theory*, eds. B. N. Petrov and F. Csaki, 267–281. Budapest: Academiai Kiado.

Akaike, H. and Nakagawa, T. (1988). *Statistical Analysis and Control of Dynamic Systems.* Dordrecht: Kluwer Academic Publishers.

Anderson, B. D. O. and Moore, J. B. (1979). *Optimal Filtering.* New Jersey: Prentice-Hall.

Box, G. E. P. and Cox, D. R. (1964). An analysis of transformations. *Journal of the Royal Statistical Society. Series B*, 26(2):211–252.

Doucet, A., de Freitasm N., and Gordon, N. (2001). *Sequential Monte Carlo Methods in Practice.* New York: Springer-Verlag.

Fama, E. F. (1965). The behavior of stock market prices. *Journal of Business*, 38(1):34–105.

Gersch, W. and Kitagawa, G. (1983). The prediction of time series with trends and seasonalities. *Journal of Business and Economic Statistics*, 1:253–264.

Gordon, N. J., Salmond, D. J., and Smith, A. F. M. (1993). Novel approach to nonlinear/non-Gaussian Bayesian state estimation. *IEE Proceedings–F*, 140:107–113.

Kitagawa, G. (1996). Monte Carlo filter and smoother for non-Gaussian nonlinear state space model. *Journal of Computational and Graphical Statistics*, 5:1–25.

Kitagawa, G. (2010). *Introduction to Time Series Modeling.* Monographs on Statistics and Applied Probability. Boca Raton: Chapman and Hall/CRC.

Kitagawa, G. and Gersch, W. (1984). A smoothness priors-state space modeling of time series with trend and seasonality. *Journal of the American Statistical Association*, 79:378–389.

Kitagawa, G. and Gersch, W. (1996). *Smoothness Priors Analysis of Time Series*. Number 116 in Lecture Notes in Statistics. New York: Springer-Verlag.

Konishi, S. and Kitagawa, G. (2008). *Information Criteria and Statistical Modeling*. New York: Springer Science+Business Media.

Linden, M. (2001). A model for stock return distribution. *International Journal of Finance and Economics*, 6:159–169.

Madan, D. B. and Seneta, E. (1990). The variance gamma (V.G.) model for share market returns. *Journal of Business*, 63(4):511–524.

Mandelbrot, B. (1963). The variation of certain speculative prices. *Journal of Business*, 36(4):394–419.

McDonald, J. B. (1996). Probability distributions for financial models. In *Handbook of Statistics. Statistical Methods in Finance*, eds. G. S. Maddala and C. R. Rao, 427–461. Amsterdam: Elsevier Science.

Norden, L. and Weber, M. (2009). The co-movement of credit default swap, bond and stock markets: An empirical analysis. *European Financial Management*, 15(3):529–562.

Praetz, P. D. (1972). The distribution of share price changes. *Journal of Business*, 45(1):49–55.

Tanokura, Y. and Kitagawa, G. (2004). Modeling influential correlated noise sources in multi-variate dynamic systems. In *The 15th IASTED International Conference on Modelling and Simulation*, ed. M. H. Hamza, 19–24. Marina del Rey, CA: ACTA Press.

Part VI

Alternative Models for Seasonal and Other Time Series Components

16

Normally Distributed Seasonal Unit Root Tests

David A. Dickey

CONTENTS

16.1 Introduction

Dickey and Zhang (2010) developed a central limit theorem for seasonal unit root tests based on the studentized coefficient in the regression of $Y_t - Y_{t-d}$ on Y_{t-d} when the seasonal period d gets large. They give an easily computable order $d^{-1/2}$ bias adjustment whose inclusion brings the statistic's distribution quite close to its $N(0, 1)$ limit for d as small as 4. Their results extend to allow for a fixed number of deterministic regressors, low degree polynomials or sinusoids, e.g., whose inclusion introduces an additional order $d^{-1/2}$ bias. In the case of such deterministic trend adjustments, their simulations suggest that the number of regressors k must be small relative to d. Cases in which the number of regressors is proportional to d, such as the addition of seasonal dummy variables to the model, are not covered by their theory. This chapter extends the results to include the use of such dummy variables. From existing unit root tests for seasonal series, Dickey, Hasza, and Fuller (1984), e.g., it is clear that without some adjustment the student t-test for a unit root will not have a standard normal limit. A model for a series that displays regular seasonal behavior should contain some deterministic periodic functions in order for the test to have a chance of concluding that the residuals from the deterministic function are stationary.

In this chapter, we extend the results of Dickey and Zhang (2010) to include cases with dummy variable regressors. Following their Taylor series expansion approach reveals that a different bias adjustment is required for these cases. Simulations are performed to investigate whether the large d asymptotics give reasonable approximations for such small d values as 4 and 12 as happened in the absence of seasonal dummy variables. While the example used will be monthly data, a case for which many tools are already available, a contribution of the chapter is that the normal approximation developed here holds for any reasonably large seasonal period, such as 52 weeks in a year, for which unit root tests have thus far not been developed.

16.2 Models and Test Statistics

We start here with a basic model that will allow investigation of the essential large sample features of the cases of interest. This will be extended to more practical situations in later sections.

In this section, the basic autocorrelation model will be $Z_t = \rho Z_{t-d} + e_t$, where $e_t \sim N(0,1)$; and the observed data will be assumed to satisfy $Y_t = \sum_{j=1}^{d} \beta_j D_j(t) + Z_t$, where $D_j(t) = 1$ if time t is in season j (e.g., month j) and 0 otherwise. The d coefficients β_j are the d seasonal effects. Because these repeat with period $d, Y_t - Y_{t-d}$ will not involve them at all and in fact $Y_t - Y_{t-d}$ will be just e_t when $\rho = 1$. On the other hand, $Y_t - \rho Y_{t-d}$ will involve these dummy variables when $|\rho| < 1$ (the stationarity region for Z) and so, if we are to give the hypothesis H_1: $|\rho| < 1$ a chance of being chosen, it is important to include some kind of periodic regressors to adjust for seasonality in the data. After all, a test like this would only be used when seasonality is apparent or suspected in the data.

Before we begin, a couple of well-known facts from existing unit root literature are recalled. First, the coefficient in the regression of the differences $Y_t - Y_{t-d}$, on the seasonal lagged level Y_{t-d} is a ratio of quadratic forms and hence is independent of σ^2. Setting $\sigma^2 = 1$ for simplicity, then, can be done without loss of generality. For the case with d fixed, the error mean square converges, with increasing sample size $n = md$, to the true error variance, and this fact applied to the studentized statistics ensures that they too are invariant to the value of σ^2. This invariance holds for fixed m and increasing d, where we will see that the error mean square converges to a multiple of σ^2. Second, the inclusion of regressors in the model gives behavior that is the same for any values of their parameters, including 0. Thus for studying the behavior of the estimators, data generated with those parameters set to 0 will contribute to the analysis and simulations relevant for all values of the parameters. As long as we include the appropriate regressors in the analysis, our test statistic for ρ is invariant to the actual values of those other parameters.

We now use a simple model, one without additional regressors, to introduce notation. For this paragraph, consider the case where $d = 1$ and $\rho = 1$, i.e., $Y_t = \rho Y_{t-1} + e_t$ becomes $Y_t = Y_{t-1} + e_t$, a random walk. We typically regress $Y_t - Y_{t-1}$ on Y_{t-1} motivated by the algebraic rearrangement of the model as $Y_t - Y_{t-1} = (\rho - 1)Y_{t-1} + e_t$ and compare the studentized coefficient, the t-test on the lagged Y from regression output, with a special distribution appropriate for such unit root tests. Because this statistic, under the null hypothesis, is nonnormal even in the limit, it is often renamed τ. The lag Y coefficient, multiplied by n, is sometimes called the "normalized bias" statistic and is given by $n(\hat{\rho} - 1) = n(\rho - 1) + (n\sigma^2)^{-1} \sum_{t=2}^{n} Y_{t-1}e_t/(n\sigma)^{-2} \sum_{t=2}^{n} Y_{t-1}^2 = N/D$, where N and D are defined by the numerator and denominator quadratic forms on the left. Note that $\hat{\rho} - 1$ is an estimate of 0 under the null hypothesis that $\rho = 1$. Both N and D are functions of n and it is reasonably well-known that they converge jointly to functionals of a Wiener Process $W(t)$ on the interval $[0, 1]$.

16.2.1 Notation, Simplest Model, and Test Statistics

Throughout, let e_t and $e_{i,j}$ denote white noise and for simplicity, assume a normal distribution. Donsker's invariance principle (Fuller 1996, 237, or Billingsley 1968, 68) will then allow the results to extend to a broader class of distributions. The presented statistics are invariant to the variance of e_t, as is well-known in the unit root literature. As we progress, a close link between these seasonal cases and panel data with d panels will be seen. Let $Y_{i,j} = Y_{i,j-1} + e_{i,j}$ define independent random walks $i = 1, 2, \ldots, d$. Here i will represent the season, e.g., month with $i = 1, 2, \ldots, 12$ or hour with $i = 1, 2, \ldots, 24$. We will use md as the series length so $m = 5$ and $n = md = 60$ for 5 years of monthly data. In this section, we will review the results from the regression of $Y_t - Y_{t-d}$ on Y_{t-d} for the model $Y_t = \rho Y_{t-d} + e_t$ under the null hypothesis $\rho = 1$ (seasonal random walk) as discussed in Dickey and Zhang (2010) and then extend the results to data with seasonal means removed, a case not covered by those authors.

In general, as in the $d = 1$ case, the regression of $Y_t - Y_{t-d}$ on Y_{t-d} gives $\hat{\rho} - 1$ and the associated studentized statistic τ for testing H_0: $\rho = 1$. Following Dickey and Zhang (2010), henceforth D&Z, we map time t into a two-variable index (i, j) using $t = d(j - 1) + i$. With this, Y_t maps into $Y_{d(j-1)+i}$, which we denote as $Y_{i,j}$, and the relationship $Y_t = \rho Y_{t-d} + e_t$ into $Y_{i,j} = \rho Y_{i,j-1} + e_{i,j}, i = 1, 2, \ldots, d$. The series is thus partitioned into d independent channels (or panels) $i = 1, 2, \ldots, d$. The coefficient $\hat{\rho} - 1$ in the regression of $Y_t - Y_{t-d}$ on Y_{t-d} is a ratio of quadratic forms. When $\rho = 1$, as we henceforth assume, $Y_t - Y_{t-d} = e_t$, and we have $\tilde{N}_i = (m - 1)^{-1} \sum_{j=2}^{m} Y_{i,j-1}e_{i,j}/\sigma^2 = O_p(1)$ and $\tilde{D}_i = (m - 1)^{-2} \sum_{j=2}^{m} Y_{i,j-1}^2/\sigma^2 = O_p(1)$ from which the regression coefficient satisfies $(\hat{\rho} - 1) = (\sum_{i=1}^{d} \tilde{N}_i)/((m-1)\sum_{i=1}^{d} \tilde{D}_i)$. We begin our study by replacing the error mean square s^2 in the estimator's standard error, $\sqrt{s^2/(\sum_{i=1}^{d}\sum_{j=2}^{m} Y_{i,j-1}^2)}$ by the true variance σ^2. The effect of this is nontrivial for finite m and is discussed later. Dividing $\hat{\rho} - 1$ by this expression, gives $\tau^* = (\sum_{i=1}^{d} \tilde{N}_i)/\sqrt{\sum_{i=1}^{d} \tilde{D}_i}$, a modified studentized test statistic for this simple model. Recall that there is no loss of generality in assuming that $\sigma^2 = 1$. It is well-known in the unit root literature (Chan and Wei 1988 or Fuller 1996) that when $\sigma^2 = 1$, $(\tilde{N}_i, \tilde{D}_i) \xrightarrow{L} (\frac{1}{2}[W_i^2(1) - 1], \int_0^1 W_i^2(t)dt)$ with the $W_i(t)$ independent Wiener processes on $[0, 1]$.

D&Z discuss the distribution of τ^*, showing that for large d and m, its distribution is approximately $N(0, 1)$. They give a finite d adjustment and a further adjustment for the case in which the data are initially detrended by a fixed number k of regressors, such as linear trends or sine waves, where the number of these regressors is small relative to d. The theory looked at d increasing and k fixed. Empirically, the approximation seems to hold well even for d as small as 4, as long as the number of regressors is 0 or small compared with d. The theory extends to all cases with $k/d \to 0$ as d increases. Clearly, seasonal dummy variables do not share that property and are hence not covered.

16.3 Removing Seasonal Means

While the results of D&Z are helpful for long period seasonality, such as 168 hours in a week or 52 weeks in a year, where a few sinusoids rather than 167 or 51 dummy variables would likely be used to model seasonal behavior, they do not cover the case in which seasonal means are modeled when testing $\rho = 1$. Herein we follow the Taylor series approach in D&Z to see if, as happened there, a limit (in d) normal distribution provides a good approximation even for relatively small d when seasonal means are modeled. When limits are discussed without qualification, we assume the d limit. The number of observations is md, e.g., m years of $d = 12$ monthly data values.

We now define seasonally adjusted versions N_i and D_i of $\tilde{N}_i$ and $\tilde{D}_i$, removing the tildes to indicate the adjusted versions. We have

$$N_i = (m-1)^{-1}\left(\sum_{j=2}^{m} Y_{i,j-1}e_{i,j} - (m-1)\bar{Y}_{i\cdot}\bar{e}_{i\cdot}\right)/\sigma^2 = \tilde{N}_i - \bar{Y}_{i\cdot}\bar{e}_{i\cdot}/\sigma^2 = O_p(1).$$

The regression contains $md - d$ terms, $m - 1$ from each of the d channels. The seasonal means are $\bar{Y}_{i\cdot} = (m-1)^{-1}\sum_{j=2}^{m} Y_{i,j-1}$ and $\bar{e}_{i\cdot} = (m-1)^{-1}\sum_{j=2}^{m} e_{i,j}$. If $\rho = 1$, these are $O_p(\sqrt{m})$ and $O_p(1/\sqrt{m})$ as shown in Fuller (1996). One of the main differences in this chapter and that of D&Z will come from the fact (Dickey 1976) that

$$N_0 \overset{def.}{\equiv} E\{N_i\} = E\{\tilde{N}_i\} - E\{\bar{Y}_{i\cdot}\bar{e}_{i\cdot}/\sigma^2\}$$
$$= -E\{\bar{Y}_{i\cdot}\bar{e}_{i\cdot}/\sigma^2\} = -(m-2)/(2(m-1)),$$

so the expected value of each numerator term is about $-1/2$ instead of 0 as it is in the case without adjustments. In the upcoming Taylor series expansion, then, terms that dropped out in D&Z will remain in the expansion, producing rather dramatic differences between this seasonal mean adjusted case and that of k fixed regression adjustments. I am grateful to David Findley for pointing out, during my year's visit to the Census Bureau's Statistical Research Division in the early 1980s, the importance of considering such regression adjustments.

The denominator likewise changes in an appreciable way. We have

$$D_i = (m-1)^{-2}\left(\sum_{j=2}^{m} Y_{i,j-1}^2 - (m-1)\left(\bar{Y}_{i\cdot}^2\right)\right)/\sigma^2 = \tilde{D}_i - \left(\bar{Y}_{i\cdot}/\left(\sigma\sqrt{(m-1)}\right)\right)^2.$$

From Dickey (1976), the expectation of D_i is $D_0 = m(m-2)/(6(m-1)^2)$, approximately 1/6.

We have $\tau^* = \sum_{i=1}^{d} N_i/\sqrt{\sum_{i=1}^{d} D_i} = \sqrt{d}\bar{N}./\sqrt{\bar{D}.}$, where the usual dot and bar denote means of d items. The $*$ superscript is used to distinguish the studentized statistic that uses the true error variance. We reserve τ with no superscript for the usual least squares studentized statistic that uses the error mean square. Using N_0 and D_0 as the expected values of N_i and D_i the leading (constant) term in the Taylor series expansion of $\tau^*/\sqrt{d}$ around (N_0, D_0) is $N_0/\sqrt{D_0} = -\sqrt{3/2}\sqrt{(m-2)/m}$, suggesting that a bias adjustment might involve the addition of $\sqrt{3d(m-2)/(2m)} \approx \sqrt{3d/2}$ to τ^*. These adjustments $\sqrt{3d(m-2)/(2m)}$ are plotted against m in Figure 16.1 along with asymptotes at $\sqrt{3d/2}$. For $d = 2$, 4, 6, and 12, these asymptotes are 1.732, 2.449, 3.000 and 4.243, respectively.

The existing (Dickey, Hasza, and Fuller (1984)) tables of τ have medians -2.00, -2.65, and -4.36 for $d = 2$, 4, and 12, respectively, in large (m) samples. The first-order adjustment $\sqrt{3d/2}$ will bring the (large m) medians to -0.27, -0.20, and -0.12, quite a bit closer to 0. Investigating the behavior of the error mean square and further terms in the Taylor series may suggest further adjustments.

16.3.1 Taylor's Series for Mean Adjusted Tests

In this section, known moments of $(N_i - N_0, D_i - D_0)$ from Dickey (1976) will be used. The mean vector is a vector of zeros and the variance matrix is

$$\frac{m(m-2)}{6(m-1)^2}\begin{pmatrix} \dfrac{(m+6)}{2m} & \dfrac{-1}{(m-1)} \\ \dfrac{-1}{(m-1)} & \dfrac{2m^2-4m+9}{15(m-1)^2} \end{pmatrix} = D_0 \begin{pmatrix} \dfrac{(m+6)}{2m} & \dfrac{-1}{(m-1)} \\ \dfrac{-1}{(m-1)} & \dfrac{2m^2-4m+9}{15(m-1)^2} \end{pmatrix}.$$

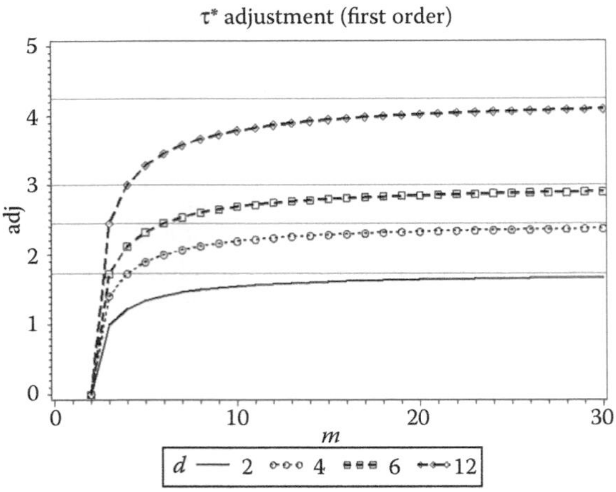

FIGURE 16.1
Bias of τ^* in terms of d and m.

With increasing m, the variance matrix approaches a diagonal matrix with entries 1/12 and 1/45. Note the common factor $D_0 = m(m-2)/(6(m-1)^2)$ in the variance matrix. Expanding $\tau^*/\sqrt{d}$ further in Taylor's series with remainder R of order $O_p(d^{-3/2})$ gives

$$\begin{aligned}\tau^*/\sqrt{d} = N_0/\sqrt{D_0} + \left[(\bar{N}-N_0)/\sqrt{D_0} - \left(N_0/(2\sqrt{D_0}^3)\right)(\bar{D}-D_0)\right] \\ + \frac{1}{2}\left[0(\bar{N}-N_0)^2 + \left(3N_0/(4\sqrt{D_0}^5)\right)(\bar{D}-D_0)^2\right. \\ \left. -(\bar{N}-N_0)(\bar{D}-D_0)/\sqrt{D_0}^3\right] + O_p(d^{-3/2}).\end{aligned}$$

The 0 coefficient is the second derivative, with respect to N, of $N/\sqrt{D}$. Looking at the linear term in square brackets, we have mean $E\{[(\bar{N}-N_0)/\sqrt{D_0} - (N_0/2)(\bar{D}-D_0)/\sqrt{D_0}^3]\} = 0$ and variance

$$\left(\frac{1}{d}\right)(1 - N_0/(2D_0))\begin{pmatrix} \dfrac{(m+6)}{2m} & \dfrac{-1}{(m-1)} \\ \dfrac{-1}{(m-1)} & \dfrac{2m^2-4m+9}{15(m-1)^2} \end{pmatrix}\begin{pmatrix} 1 \\ -N_0/(2D_0) \end{pmatrix}.$$

Using $N_0/(2D_0) = -3(m-1)/(2m)$, this product becomes

$$\frac{(m+6)}{2dm} - \frac{6}{2dm} + \frac{3(2m^2-4m+9)}{20dm^2} = \frac{16m^2-12m+27}{20dm^2} \approx 0.8/d.$$

This is the variance associated with $\tau^*/\sqrt{d} - N_0/\sqrt{D_0} = \tau^*/\sqrt{d} + \sqrt{3(m-2)/(2m)}$ so that, approximately, $\tau^* + \sqrt{d}\sqrt{3(m-2)/(2m)} \sim N(0, 0.8)$.

There is a mean of order $d^{1/2}$ instead of 0, and a variance approximately 0.8 instead of 1 associated with τ^*.

In the work of D&Z, the covariance term in the quadratic portion of the Taylor series expansion gave a quite helpful $O(d^{-1/2})$ adjustment without which the use of $N(0,1)$ to approximate the distribution of τ^* would require rather large d in practice. It is relevant here that in the $d = 1$ (nonseasonal) unit root case, the numerator and denominator, N and D, of $(m-1)(\hat{\rho}-1)$ are fairly strongly correlated even when m approaches infinity as long as there are no deterministic terms in the data or model. Adjusting for the mean and/or a linear trend produces asymptotically (as m increases) uncorrelated numerator and denominator quadratic forms. The quadratic portion of the expansion of $\tau^*/\sqrt{d}$ in our case is

$$\frac{1}{2}\left[\left(3N_0/(4\sqrt{D_0}^5)\right)(\bar{D}-D_0)^2 - (\bar{N}-N_0)(\bar{D}-D_0)/\sqrt{D_0}^3\right)\right]$$
$$= \frac{1}{2}\left\{\frac{-27\sqrt{6}(m-1)^4}{2m^2(m-2)\sqrt{m(m-2)}}(\bar{D}-D_0)^2 - \frac{6\sqrt{6}(m-1)^3}{m(m-2)\sqrt{m(m-2)}}(\bar{N}-N_0)(\bar{D}-D_0)\right\}.$$

Using the variances and covariances above, we find that the expectation of this term is

$$\frac{1}{2d}\left[\left(\frac{-3\sqrt{6}(2m^2-4m+9)}{20m\sqrt{m(m-2)}}\right) + \left(\frac{20m\sqrt{6}}{20m\sqrt{m(m-2)}}\right)\right]$$
$$= \left(\frac{\sqrt{6}(-6m^2+32m-27)}{40md\sqrt{m(m-2)}}\right),$$

which for large m indicates an additional bias term for τ^* of $-0.15\sqrt{6/d} \sim -0.37/\sqrt{d}$.

16.3.2 Simulation, Known Variance

To check on the finite sample performance of these corrections, using the complete expressions in m and d for the bias and variance, 500,000 series and τ^* statistics were generated for all combinations of $m = 5, 10, 15$, and 20 and $d = 4, 6, 8, 10$, and 12. The top graph of Figure 16.2 shows the histogram for $m = 5$ and $d = 4$. Also shown are a kernel density estimator, a normal distribution with parameters estimated, and a $N(0,1)$ distribution. These distributions are almost indistinguishable from each other and the histogram outline. The fit appears to be excellent even for this case with only 20 quarterly observations. At the bottom is the same kind of graph for $m = 20$, $d = 12$. It appears that the $N(0,1)$ provides an excellent approximation for the appropriately centered and scaled τ^* statistic.

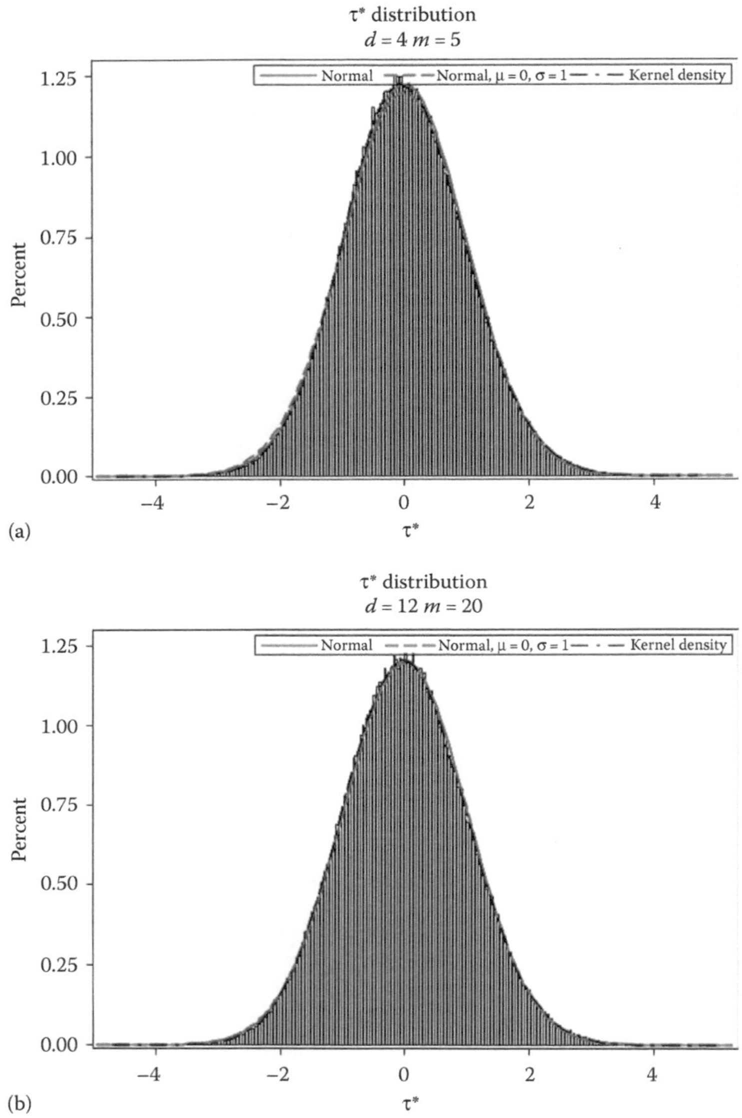

FIGURE 16.2
Normalized τ^* distributions: $(d, m) = (4, 5)$ (a) and $(12, 20)$ (b).

Further evidence of the degree of approximation is given by the empirical percentiles of the 500,000 τ^* statistics after the mean and variance adjustments. Appendix A gives the empirical percentiles of this study, and shows that in this unrealistic case of a known error variance, the nominal 5% level is pretty well preserved if the normal approximation is used. The mean is within 0.01 of 0 in all cases. In the case of a close call, the percentiles in the table can be used.

Thus far we have dealt with τ^*, the modified statistic substituting the true error variance σ^2 for the sample variance s^2. The relationship $\tau/\sqrt{d} = (\tau^*/\sqrt{d})\sqrt{\sigma^2/s^2}$ combined with Slutzky's theorem suggests the computation of the probability limit (in d) of s^2/σ^2. In most developments of this sort, s^2/σ^2 converges in probability to 1 and this is easy to show and has little effect on the results. Such is not the case here.

16.4 Behavior of the Error Mean Square

The error sum of squares can be computed from the simple linear regression of the mean corrected seasonal differences on the mean corrected lagged levels. Using this idea, the error sum of squares is

$$SSE = \sum_{j=2}^{m}(e_{i,j} - \bar{e}_{i\cdot})^2$$
$$- \left[\sum_{i=1}^{d}\sum_{j=2}^{m}(e_{i,j} - \bar{e}_{i\cdot})(Y_{i,j-1} - \bar{Y}_{i\cdot})\right]^2 \Bigg/ \sum_{i=1}^{d}\sum_{j=2}^{m}(Y_{i,j-1} - \bar{Y}_{i\cdot})^2,$$

so that

$$SSE/(d(m-2)\sigma^2) = \sum_{j=2}^{m}\sum_{i=1}^{d}(e_{i,j} - \bar{e}_{i\cdot})^2/(d(m-2)\sigma^2) - (d\bar{N})^2/(d^2\bar{D}(m-2)),$$

which is the approximate ratio of the error mean square to the true error variance. It is approximate because the degrees of freedom should be $d(m-2)-1$. Substituting 1 (its limit) for the first term, we have $1 - \bar{N}^2/(\bar{D}(m-2))$ and we thus have the approximation

$$\tau \approx \sqrt{d}\bar{N}/\sqrt{\bar{D} - \bar{N}^2/(m-2)} = -\sqrt{d}/\sqrt{(D_0/N_0^2) - (1/(m-2))} + O_p(1),$$

indicating that the dominant location term is $-\sqrt{d}/\sqrt{(2m-3)/3(m-2)} = -\sqrt{3d(m-2)/(2m-3)}$ as compared with $-\sqrt{3d(m-2)/2m}$ in the τ^* case. The $O_p(1)$ remainder term in the Taylor series above consists of a linear term with mean 0 and an order $1/\sqrt{d}$ term so that adding $\sqrt{3d(m-2)/(2m-3)}$ will center its Taylor series out to the order $1/\sqrt{d}$ term. The order 1 term will then give the leading term of the variance of this appropriately centered τ statistic. The linear term in the Taylor series expansion has mean 0 and uses partial derivatives. Each partial derivative begins with $-\sqrt{d}/2((D_0/N_0^2) - (1/(m-2)))^{-3/2}$ so that, associated with this common factor, there is an overall multiplier $27d/4((m-2)/(2m-3))^3$ in the variance of the linear term. The rest of the linear term comes from the two partial derivatives of D_0/N_0^2 and we have $(\sqrt{D_0}/N_0^2)(\bar{D}-D_0)/\sqrt{D_0}$ $-(2D_0\sqrt{D_0}/N_0^3)(\bar{N}-N_0)/\sqrt{D_0}$ with variance

$$\frac{D_0}{N_0^4}V_{DD}+\frac{4D_0^3}{N_0^6}V_{NN}-4\frac{D_0^2}{N_0^5}V_{ND}=\frac{8m(m-1)^2}{3(m-2)^3}V_{DD}+\frac{32m^3}{27(m-2)^3}V_{NN}$$
$$+\frac{32m^2(m-1)}{9(m-2)^3}V_{ND},$$

where the V factors are variance and covariance terms distinguished by their subscripts. Inserting the overall multiplier and those $O(1/d)$ variance terms, we have

$$\left(\frac{27(m-2)^3}{4(2m-3)^3}\right)\left(\frac{4}{27(m-2)^3}\right)(18m(m-1)^2V_{DD}+8m^3V_{NN}$$
$$+24m^2(m-1)V_{ND})$$
$$=\frac{1}{(2m-3)^3}\left\{18m(m-1)^2\left(\frac{2m^2-4m+9}{15(m-1)^2}\right)+8m^3\left(\frac{m+6}{2m}\right)\right.$$
$$\left.+24m^2(m-1)\left(\frac{-1}{m-1}\right)\right\}$$
$$=\frac{m}{(2m-3)^3}\left\{\frac{6}{5}(2m^2-4m+9)+4m^2\right\}$$
$$=\frac{m(16m^2-12m+27)}{20(m-1.5)^3},$$

as compared with $(16m^2-12m+27)/20dm^2$ in the case of τ^*. Note that as m increases, this approaches 0.80 as we would expect from the τ^* results.

16.4.1 Simulation, Unknown Variance

A rather large simulation of various d and m combinations gave percentiles as shown in Appendix B. The simulations included all combinations of $d=4,6,8,10,12$ and $m=5,6,7,8,9,10,12,15,20,30,35$ so as to investigate the finite sample behavior. Also included, as a check on the asymptotics, were some combinations with $d=100$ and some with $m=100$. For each combination used in the study, 500,000 replicates were generated. Notice that the replacement of $\sum_{j=2}^{m}\sum_{i=2}^{d}(e_{ij}-\bar{e}_{i\cdot})^2/(d(m-2)\sigma^2)$ by its expected value (and probability limit) 1 adds an $O_p(1/\sqrt{md})$ term to the expression for τ so that for small m values, additional adjustments might be possible and of course adjustments to the moments for small d values may help as well.

Because the simulations are so large, the empirical moments will be very close to the true ones so the strategy here is to subtract the Taylor series based mean and variance estimates derived above from the empirical ones then, motivated by the terms in the Taylor series, fit polynomials in $1/\sqrt{(2m-3)}$

and $1/\sqrt{d}$ to fine-tune the results. The smallest values of m and d in the simulations were $m = 5$ and $d = 4$, representing 20 quarterly observations over 5 years, a regression with only 16 observations, and 11 error degrees of freedom. The adjustment from the Taylor series approximation in that case moved the mean of the 500,000 τs from -2.47 to -0.20, much closer to 0, the mean of the standard normal, but still not close enough. Based on the polynomial regression adding $0.3704/\sqrt{d} + 0.4235/((2m-3)\sqrt{d}) - 0.0505/d$ brings all of the means within 0.004 of 0 except for the above $m = 5$ $d = 4$ case where the mean is -0.0080. These are not displayed in Appendix B as they are so close to 0. The centering operation, then, for τ is to add $\sqrt{3d(m-2)/2m-3} + 0.3704/\sqrt{d} + 0.4235/((2m-3)\sqrt{d}) - 0.0505/d$.

Turning to the variance, similar polynomial inputs were used for the fine-tuning. A slightly more involved adjustment results here. Using the quantity

$$\left(\frac{m(0.8m^2 - 0.6m + 1.35)}{(m-1.5)^3}\right) - \frac{0.0852}{\sqrt{d}} - \frac{1.7554}{2m-3} + \frac{4.4429}{(2m-3)\sqrt{d}} - \frac{12.6444}{\sqrt{(2m-3)^3}},$$

as a variance approximation gives numbers within 0.02 of the empirical variances across the m and d combinations except $d = 4$ $m = 5$ where the error is 0.033.

16.4.2 Empirical Performance

The extreme values of m were 5 and 100 and for d were 4 and 100 in the simulations. Normal probability plots seem to indicate excellent approximations by $N(0,1)$ to the true distribution for most of the cases. Plots for $(d, m) = (4, 5)$ and $(12, 10)$ are shown in Figure 16.3. On the vertical axis is Z, the normalized τ statistic, and on the horizontal axis is the normal score as usual. The horizontal axis extends from -6 to 6 and between -2.5 and 2.5 the fit is reasonable, indicating that even the extremely small 16-point regression statistic is reasonably close to $N(0,1)$ until the extreme left tail is reached. For $d = 12$ and $m = 10$, the fit is remarkably close to $N(0,1)$.

As further evidence of a good approximation, the four panels in Figure 16.4 show normal *p–p* plots consisting of the empirical cumulative probabilities for the simulated (centered and scaled) t-statistics versus the cumulative probabilities of a standard normal variate. It is, after all, these probabilities that are critical to using the results in testing. A reference 45 degree dashed line is included in each plot. Note that, despite the disappointing normal probability plot for $d = 4$, $m = 5$ in the extreme tails, the probabilities involved are so close to those of the normal (i.e., nearly 0) that the probabilities seem reasonable even for this very small sample size.

The worst deviation of the normal cumulative distribution function (CDF) from the true CDF is about 0.03 near the middle of the $d = 4$, $m = 5$ plot.

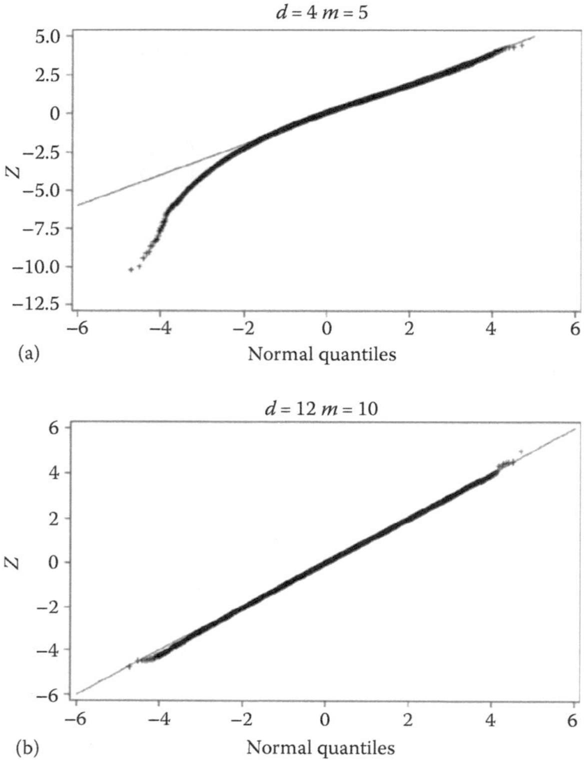

FIGURE 16.3
Normal probability plots. (a) $(d, m) = (4, 5)$ and (b) $(d, m) = (12, 10)$.

The more important probabilities, in terms of testing, are those in the tails. Further investigation reveals that the normal approximation probabilities are within 0.01 of the empirically approximated true probabilities in the 15% right and 15% left tails. Note that the nonlinearity in the normal probability plot in Figure 16.3 is so far in the left tail as to be associated with probabilities near 0. With monthly data over 5 or more years, p-values less than 0.10 appear to be accurate to within 0.005. Overall, the approximation seems adequate for approximate tests. Furthermore, in close calls, the appendix tables can be used for added accuracy.

16.5 Example

It is worth reemphasizing that the purpose of this research is to provide tests in cases for which existing distributions are not available. The example used

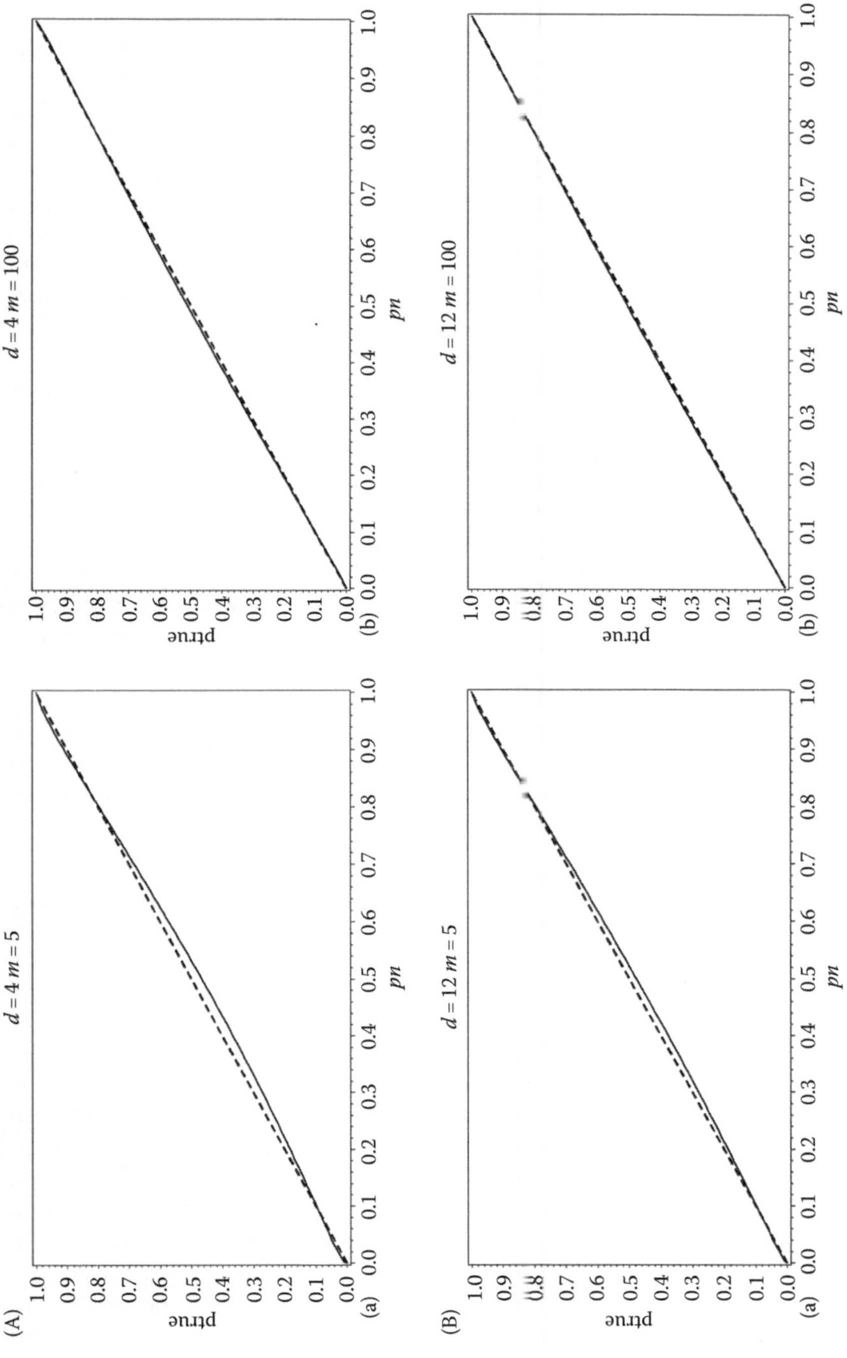

FIGURE 16.4
p-p plots. (Aa and Ba) $m = 5$; (Ab and Bb) $m = 100$; (A) $d = 4$; (B) $d = 12$.

here will be monthly. With quarterly or monthly data, existing tables and alternative analyses, as shown in the next section, are available.

Monthly oil imports from 1973 through 2008 were downloaded from the Census Bureau's Web page ($d = 12, m = 36$). Differences were taken initially in light of obvious trending in the data. A more rigorous justification for differencing is in the next section. Correction for additional lags was done as suggested in Dickey, Hasza, and Fuller (1984). As they suggest, initial estimates appropriate under the null hypothesis are computed as follows. The data are differenced at a span of 12 and an autoregressive model fit to the differenced data, thus providing a prefilter for the mean adjusted data. A seasonal multiplicative model with eight nonseasonal lags ($(1 - \Phi_1 \mathrm{B} \cdots - \Phi_8 \mathrm{B}^8)(1 - \mathrm{B}^{12})Y_t = e_t$) gave good Box–Ljung fit statistics (all displayed p-values through lag 42 exceeded 0.11) while all p-values for the fitted coefficients were less than 0.01. As this suggests, a prefilter of eight lags was chosen. Sensitivity to filter length will be discussed later.

The preliminary autoregression with eight lags, performed on the span 12 differences of the data has residuals that would be appropriate if the data did have a seasonal unit root. That is, $(1 - \mathrm{B}^{12})$ is assumed to be a factor in the seasonal multiplicative model. A one-step adjustment based on the Taylor series regresses these residuals on lag 12 of the filtered mean adjusted series and span 12 differences of the data, one for each of the filter's eight lags. These terms provide a test for unit roots as well as one-step adjustments to each of the filter's coefficients. A more detailed description of the procedure is available in Dickey, Hasza, and Fuller (1984), henceforth DHF.

The printed t-test statistic for the lag 12 filtered term was -16.19, which needs to be centered by adding $\sqrt{3d(m-2)/(2m-3)} = 4.21$ plus the additional fine-tuning adjustments $0.3704/\sqrt{12} + 0.4235/((72-3)\sqrt{12}) - 0.0505/12 = 0.10$. The variance associated with this statistic is

$$\frac{m(0.8m^2 - 0.6m + 1.35)}{(m-1.5)^3} - \frac{0.0852}{\sqrt{d}} - \frac{1.7554}{(2m-3)} + \frac{4.4429}{(2m-3)\sqrt{d}} - \frac{12.6444}{\sqrt{(2m-3)^3}}$$
$$= 0.8377.$$

The first term, the linear term in the Taylor series, is the major contributor to the variance. Computing $(-16.19 + 4.31)/0.9152 = -12.98$ and comparing with a $N(0,1)$ distribution, the evidence strongly rejects the unit roots. It seems that the seasonal means were sufficient for handling the seasonality so we conclude that the first differences, adjusted for seasonal means, are stationary. An additional span 12 difference seems unnecessary. The same conclusion is reached by comparing the unadjusted t-statistic -16.19 with Table 7 of DHF. As a check on sensitivity to filter length, prefiltering using lags of 2, 4, 6, and 10 all gave unadjusted t-values within 0.1 of -16.19, suggesting minor effects of the filter length, provided it is less than the seasonal period. When filters of length 12 and 24 were used, however, the printed t's changed to -13.48 and -10.24.

16.5.1 An Alternative Model

For monthly or quarterly data, additional approaches are available. Hylleberg et al. (1990, henceforth HEGY), in a seminal paper, show a way to test individually the 4 roots of $(1 - B^4)$ to see if all are on the unit circle. Beaulieu and Miron (1993, henceforth B&M) extend this to monthly data where $(1 - B^{12}) = (1 - B)(1 + B + B^2 + \cdots + B^{11})$ implying a real root 1, and 11 others around the unit circle. The DHF approach above is restrictive in that it assumes that all 12 roots have the same magnitude. The HEGY and B&M approaches allow different magnitudes for the roots with the restriction that those associated with complex conjugates have the same magnitude.

The span 12 differences are regressed on variables described by B&M along with seasonal dummy variables and t-test statistics obtained for the 12 individual roots around the unit circle. The first B&M variable produces a test for the $(1 - B)$ factor, which does not reject, indicating an ordinary unit root (first differencing). The test associated with the Nyquist frequency rejects, leaving 10 other t-tests, some of which are significant and some not. It is logical to consider these in five pairs, associated with the complex conjugate roots. B&M give the 5% critical value of the F ratios for each of these pairs as 6.42. The data give least squares F tests ranging between 18.72 and 31.64, indicating, as did the previous tests, that the first difference and seasonal dummy variables have rendered the series stationary.

B&M do not give the F test that all but the positive real root are on the unit circle versus the alternative that some are in the stationarity region. A Monte Carlo study was therefore run (200,000 replicates each with 420 observations as in the example) producing 5.54, 4.74, and 4.33 as the 1%, 5%, and 10% empirical critical values, respectively. The F test statistic for the oil data had a value of 31.05, again providing significant evidence against more than first differencing in the presence of seasonal dummy variables.

We chose a data range of complete years; however, if an incomplete year is encountered, then some of the d sums of squares or cross-products will be sums of $m - 1$ terms rather than m. For large m the effect will be small, but for smaller m, replacing m by an interpolated value between m and $m - 1$ in the adjustment formulas should improve the approximation. As d increases, normality will still result even if the terms come from two different distributions.

16.6 Conclusions

In testing for unit roots in seasonal data, normality is approached as the number of observations d within a cycle increases. The studentized statistic involves sums of d independent quadratic forms with known moments depending on the number of cycles m. The constant term in the Taylor series provides a mean adjustment that is an increasing function of d while the linear term provides an expression that, with the central limit theorem for independent variables, provides the limit normality and variance. Additional fine-tuning adjustments are provided by regression on empirical means and variances from a large (500,000 replications) simulation for several (d, m) values. The resulting mean adjustment for τ is to add

$$\sqrt{\frac{3d(m-2)}{2m-3}} + 0.3704/\sqrt{d} + 0.4235/((2m-3)\sqrt{d}) - 0.0505/d,$$

and for the approximating variance, the results suggest the use of

$$\left(\frac{m(0.8m^2 - 0.6m + 1.35)}{(m-1.5)^3}\right) - \frac{0.852}{\sqrt{d}} - \frac{1.7554}{(2m-3)} + \frac{4.4429}{(2m-3)\sqrt{d}} - \frac{12.6444}{\sqrt{(2m-3)^3}}.$$

Doing so provides an approximation that appears to be quite reasonable for testing purposes. An appendix giving percentiles from the large simulation is provided. The tables use full mean and variance adjustments.

Appendix A

Simulation results using 500,000 replicates of τ^* for varying d and m combinations. The column of means is followed by empirical percentile estimates for the percentiles commonly used in practice. Inserted after the 5th percentile is a boldface column labeled $N(0, 1)$ giving the probability of being below the 5th percentile in a normal distribution. The nominal 5% level is pretty well preserved if the normal approximation is used. The mean is within 0.01 of 0 in all cases.

d	*m*	mean	0.01	0.025	0.05	***N*(0,1)**	0.10	0.50	0.90	0.95	0.975	0.99
4	5	0.01	−2.21	−1.87	−1.57	**0.06**	−1.23	−0.01	1.27	1.64	1.97	2.35
4	10	0.01	−2.18	−1.84	−1.55	**0.06**	−1.22	−0.01	1.28	1.66	1.99	2.37
4	15	0.01	−2.18	−1.85	−1.56	**0.06**	−1.22	−0.01	1.28	1.66	1.99	2.38
4	20	0.01	−2.18	−1.85	−1.56	**0.06**	−1.22	−0.01	1.29	1.67	2.00	2.39
6	5	0.01	−2.24	−1.89	−1.59	**0.06**	−1.25	−0.01	1.27	1.65	1.97	2.35
6	10	0.01	−2.22	−1.88	−1.58	**0.06**	−1.24	−0.01	1.28	1.65	1.99	2.37
6	15	0.00	−2.22	−1.88	−1.59	**0.06**	−1.24	−0.01	1.28	1.66	1.98	2.37
6	20	0.01	−2.23	−1.88	−1.58	**0.06**	−1.24	−0.01	1.28	1.66	1.99	2.39
8	5	0.00	−2.26	−1.91	−1.61	**0.05**	−1.26	−0.01	1.28	1.65	1.97	2.35
8	10	0.01	−2.23	−1.89	−1.59	**0.06**	−1.25	−0.01	1.28	1.66	1.98	2.37
8	15	0.00	−2.24	−1.90	−1.60	**0.05**	−1.25	−0.01	1.28	1.66	1.99	2.38
8	20	0.00	−2.25	−1.90	−1.60	**0.05**	−1.25	−0.01	1.28	1.66	1.98	2.37
10	5	0.00	−2.27	−1.92	−1.62	**0.05**	−1.26	−0.01	1.28	1.65	1.97	2.34
10	10	0.00	−2.26	−1.91	−1.61	**0.05**	−1.26	−0.01	1.28	1.65	1.98	2.36

(*continued*)

d	*m*	mean	0.01	0.025	0.05	**N(0,1)**	0.10	0.50	0.90	0.95	0.975	0.99
10	15	0.00	−2.25	−1.90	−1.60	**0.05**	−1.26	−0.01	1.28	1.66	1.98	2.36
10	20	0.00	−2.24	−1.91	−1.61	**0.05**	−1.26	−0.01	1.28	1.65	1.98	2.36
12	5	0.00	−2.28	−1.92	−1.62	**0.05**	−1.27	−0.01	1.28	1.65	1.97	2.34
12	10	0.00	−2.26	−1.91	−1.61	**0.05**	−1.26	−0.01	1.28	1.65	1.98	2.36
12	15	0.00	−2.26	−1.91	−1.61	**0.05**	−1.26	−0.01	1.28	1.66	1.98	2.36
12	20	0.00	−2.25	−1.91	−1.61	**0.05**	−1.27	−0.01	1.28	1.65	1.98	2.36

Appendix B

Simulation results using 500,000 replicates of τ for varying d and m combinations. The d and m columns are followed by empirical percentile estimates for the percentiles commonly used in practice. Inserted after the 5th percentile is a boldface column labeled $N(0,1)$ giving the probability of being below the 5th percentile in a normal distribution. The nominal 5% level is pretty well preserved if the normal approximation is used.

d	*m*	0.01	0.025	0.05	**N(0,1)**	0.10	0.50	0.90	0.95	0.975	0.99
4	5	−2.74	−2.17	−1.73	**0.042**	−1.27	0.08	1.23	1.55	1.82	2.15
4	6	−2.62	−2.10	−1.69	**0.046**	−1.26	0.07	1.26	1.58	1.87	2.21
4	7	−2.54	−2.05	−1.67	**0.047**	−1.26	0.05	1.27	1.61	1.90	2.24
4	8	−2.48	−2.02	−1.65	**0.050**	−1.25	0.04	1.27	1.61	1.91	2.27
4	9	−2.44	−2.01	−1.65	**0.050**	−1.26	0.04	1.27	1.62	1.92	2.28
4	10	−2.42	−1.99	−1.64	**0.051**	−1.25	0.04	1.28	1.63	1.93	2.29
4	12	−2.38	−1.97	−1.63	**0.052**	−1.25	0.02	1.28	1.64	1.95	2.32
4	15	−2.35	−1.95	−1.62	**0.053**	−1.25	0.01	1.28	1.65	1.96	2.33
4	20	−2.32	−1.94	−1.62	**0.053**	−1.26	0.01	1.29	1.66	1.98	2.36
4	30	−2.31	−1.94	−1.62	**0.053**	−1.26	−0.01	1.29	1.67	2.00	2.38
4	35	−2.31	−1.93	−1.62	**0.053**	−1.27	−0.01	1.29	1.67	2.00	2.38
4	100	−2.29	−1.93	−1.63	**0.052**	−1.28	−0.03	1.30	1.69	2.03	2.42
6	5	−2.61	−2.10	−1.70	**0.044**	−1.27	0.07	1.24	1.56	1.83	2.15
6	6	−2.54	−2.06	−1.69	**0.046**	−1.27	0.06	1.26	1.59	1.88	2.21
6	7	−2.49	−2.04	−1.68	**0.047**	−1.27	0.04	1.27	1.61	1.90	2.25
6	8	−2.44	−2.02	−1.66	**0.049**	−1.26	0.04	1.27	1.62	1.92	2.27
6	9	−2.41	−1.99	−1.65	**0.050**	−1.27	0.03	1.27	1.62	1.93	2.28
6	10	−2.40	−1.99	−1.65	**0.050**	−1.27	0.03	1.28	1.63	1.94	2.30
6	12	−2.37	−1.97	−1.64	**0.050**	−1.27	0.02	1.28	1.64	1.95	2.32
6	15	−2.34	−1.96	−1.64	**0.051**	−1.27	0.01	1.28	1.64	1.96	2.32
6	20	−2.33	−1.95	−1.63	**0.052**	−1.27	−0.00	1.29	1.65	1.97	2.35
6	30	−2.32	−1.95	−1.64	**0.051**	−1.28	−0.01	1.29	1.66	1.98	2.35
6	35	−2.31	−1.95	−1.64	**0.051**	−1.28	−0.01	1.29	1.66	1.99	2.37
8	5	−2.55	−2.08	−1.69	**0.045**	−1.27	0.06	1.25	1.57	1.84	2.16
8	6	−2.50	−2.05	−1.69	**0.046**	−1.28	0.05	1.27	1.60	1.89	2.22
8	7	−2.46	−2.03	−1.68	**0.047**	−1.28	0.04	1.28	1.62	1.91	2.26
8	8	−2.43	−2.01	−1.67	**0.048**	−1.28	0.03	1.28	1.62	1.92	2.28
8	9	−2.40	−1.99	−1.66	**0.049**	−1.28	0.02	1.28	1.63	1.94	2.29
8	10	−2.39	−1.99	−1.65	**0.049**	−1.28	0.02	1.28	1.64	1.94	2.30
8	12	−2.37	−1.98	−1.65	**0.049**	−1.28	0.01	1.28	1.64	1.94	2.30
8	15	−2.35	−1.97	−1.65	**0.050**	−1.28	0.01	1.28	1.64	1.96	2.33
8	20	−2.34	−1.96	−1.64	**0.050**	−1.28	−0.00	1.28	1.65	1.96	2.33

(*continued*)

d	m	0.01	0.025	0.05	**N(0,1)**	0.10	0.50	0.90	0.95	0.975	0.99
8	30	−2.32	−1.96	−1.64	**0.050**	−1.28	−0.01	1.29	1.66	1.98	2.36
8	35	−2.32	−1.95	−1.64	**0.051**	−1.28	−0.01	1.28	1.65	1.98	2.35
10	5	−2.52	−2.06	−1.68	**0.046**	−1.27	0.06	1.25	1.58	1.85	2.17
10	6	−2.49	−2.05	−1.69	**0.046**	−1.28	0.05	1.27	1.61	1.89	2.23
10	7	−2.45	−2.03	−1.68	**0.047**	−1.28	0.03	1.28	1.61	1.91	2.26
10	8	−2.42	−2.01	−1.67	**0.047**	−1.28	0.02	1.28	1.63	1.94	2.28
10	9	−2.41	−2.01	−1.67	**0.048**	−1.28	0.02	1.28	1.63	1.93	2.29
10	10	−2.39	−2.00	−1.66	**0.049**	−1.28	0.02	1.28	1.63	1.94	2.30
10	12	−2.37	−1.98	−1.66	**0.049**	−1.28	0.01	1.28	1.64	1.95	2.31
10	15	−2.35	−1.97	−1.64	**0.050**	−1.28	0.00	1.28	1.64	1.96	2.32
10	20	−2.33	−1.97	−1.65	**0.050**	−1.28	−0.00	1.28	1.64	1.96	2.34
10	30	−2.32	−1.95	−1.64	**0.050**	−1.28	−0.01	1.28	1.66	1.98	2.35
10	35	−2.32	−1.96	−1.65	**0.050**	−1.29	−0.01	1.29	1.66	1.98	2.35
12	5	−2.50	−2.05	−1.68	**0.046**	−1.27	0.06	1.26	1.58	1.86	2.18
12	6	−2.47	−2.04	−1.68	**0.047**	−1.28	0.04	1.27	1.61	1.89	2.23
12	7	−2.44	−2.03	−1.68	**0.047**	−1.29	0.03	1.28	1.62	1.92	2.27
12	8	−2.42	−2.01	−1.67	**0.048**	−1.28	0.02	1.28	1.63	1.94	2.28
12	9	−2.40	−2.00	−1.67	**0.048**	−1.29	0.02	1.28	1.64	1.94	2.29
12	10	−2.39	−1.99	−1.66	**0.048**	−1.29	0.01	1.28	1.63	1.94	2.30
12	12	−2.38	−1.99	−1.66	**0.048**	−1.29	0.01	1.28	1.64	1.95	2.32
12	15	−2.35	−1.97	−1.65	**0.049**	−1.28	0.00	1.28	1.65	1.95	2.32
12	20	−2.33	−1.97	−1.65	**0.050**	−1.28	−0.01	1.28	1.64	1.96	2.33
12	30	−2.33	−1.96	−1.65	**0.050**	−1.29	−0.01	1.28	1.65	1.97	2.35
12	35	−2.32	−1.96	−1.64	**0.050**	−1.29	−0.01	1.29	1.65	1.98	2.36
12	100	−2.31	−1.96	−1.65	**0.049**	−1.29	−0.02	1.29	1.66	1.98	2.37
35	100	−2.33	−1.96	−1.65	**0.049**	−1.29	−0.01	1.28	1.65	1.98	2.35
100	5	−2.36	−1.97	−1.64	**0.051**	−1.25	0.06	1.33	1.68	1.99	2.34
100	35	−2.35	−1.98	−1.67	**0.048**	−1.31	−0.02	1.26	1.63	1.94	2.31
100	100	−2.33	−1.97	−1.65	**0.049**	−1.29	−0.01	1.28	1.64	1.96	2.33

References

Beaulieu, J. Joseph and Miron, Jeffrey A. (1993). Seasonal unit roots in aggregate U.S. data (Disc: p329–331). *Journal of Econometrics*, 55:305–328.

Chan, N. H. and Wei, C. Z. (1988). Limiting distributions of least squares estimates of unstable autoregressive processes. *Annals of Statistics*, 15:1050–1063.

Dickey, D. A. (1976). Estimation and Hypothesis Testing in Nonstationary Time Series, PhD thesis, Iowa State University.

Dickey, D. A., Hasza, D. P., and Fuller, W. A. (1984). Testing for unit roots in seasonal time series. *Journal of the American Statistical Association*, 79:355–367.

Dickey, D. A. and Zhang, Y. (2010). Seasonal unit root tests in long periodicity cases. *Journal of Korean Statistical Society*, 39:271–279.

Fuller, W. A. (1996). *Introduction to Statistical Time Series*. New York: Wiley.

Hylleberg, S., Engle, R. F., Granger, C. W. J., and Yoo, B. S. (1990). Seasonal integration and cointegration. *Journal of Econometrics*, 44:215–238.

Osborne, D. (2002). Unit root versus deterministic representations of seasonality for forecasting. In *A Companion to Forecasting*, eds. M. P. Clements and D. F. Hendry, Malden, MA: Blackwell Publishers.

17

Bayesian Seasonal Adjustment of Long Memory Time Series

Scott H. Holan and Tucker S. McElroy*

CONTENTS

17.1 Introduction

Existing approaches to the seasonal adjustment of economic time series are typically either nonparametric or model-based. In both cases, the goal is to remove seasonal variation from the time series. In each of the two paradigms, both the seasonally adjusted series and the seasonal component are latent processes. As such, seasonal adjustment can be viewed as an unobserved components (UC) problem and specifically that of UC estimation. Though the nonparametric approach has a rich history going back to the development of X-11 and X-11 ARIMA (Dagum 1980; Shiskin et al. 1967), our focus centers on model-based methodology.

* Disclaimer: This chapter is released to inform interested parties of research and to encourage discussion. The views expressed on statistical issues are those of the authors and not necessarily those of the U.S. Census Bureau.

Within the model-based framework, two directions have emerged. The first direction, or the direction pursued here, directly specifies models for the components and is known as the structural time series approach (Harvey 1990). Alternatively, one could start with a model for the observed time series and derive appropriate models for each component (Hillmer and Tiao 1982). This latter approach is often referred to as "canonical decomposition."

In the seasonal adjustment of economic time series, it is common to "preadjust" the series. This preadjustment often includes interpolation of missing values, outlier adjustment, and adjustment for trading-day (TD) and holiday effects. In addition to the customary preadjustments, many model-based approaches require that the observed series be differenced (and/or seasonally differenced) to handle nonstationarity. One question that naturally arises when implementing such an approach is whether or not the correct number of differencing operations have been imposed. In practice, typically, only integer orders of integration are considered. Nevertheless, it is possible that differencing the data once results in a series that still exhibits nonstationary behavior, whereas, imposing a second difference may result in a series that is "over-differenced" and thus noninvertible. In these cases, a natural alternative is to difference the observed series and then model the residual series as a fractionally differenced process.

The models and signal extraction methodology we propose are applied to nonstationary data. However, the approach we develop assumes that, after suitable differencing, the residual series is stationary but allows for long-range dependence (in the seasonal and/or trend component) or antipersistance (sometimes referred to as intermediate or negative memory). Long-memory time series modeling has experienced tremendous growth during the past three decades. Beginning with the seminal papers on fractional differencing by Granger and Joyeux (1980) and Hosking (1981), many methods have been proposed for modeling long-memory and seasonal long-memory processes with many of these efforts focused on estimation of the fractional differencing parameter, also known as the memory parameter.

Although some research on long-memory has taken a Bayesian viewpoint, the literature is still very heavily frequentist (see Robinson (2003) for a discussion). In general, the literature on long-memory time series is extensive. Excellent references for long-memory time series that include discussion of seasonal long-memory can be found in Palma (2007), Bisognin and Lopes (2009), and the references therein. General discussion regarding long-memory from a Bayesian perspective can be found in Palma (2007), Holan et al. (2009), and the references therein. Together, these references, along with Holan et al. (2010), provide a detailed survey of the existing literature in long-memory time series.

Even though there exists a substantial body of research on modeling seasonal long-range dependent processes, relatively few efforts have been made toward the seasonal adjustment of economic time series exhibiting such behavior. Further, methods for seasonally adjusting economic time series using

Bayesian methodology are also rather limited. The work of Carlin and Dempster (1989) provides one exception.

Carlin and Dempster (1989) developed a Bayesian approach to seasonal adjustment that considers long-memory behavior. However, due to computational limitations, the method they propose is necessarily empirical Bayes and estimates the models using a *plug-in* approach on the fractional differencing parameter from a grid of values. One of the principal differences between our approach and that of Carlin and Dempster (1989) is that our approach is fully Bayesian. Specifically, our method assumes noninformative priors for the fractional differencing parameters and estimates them as part of the model. Additionally, our method uses finite sample minimum mean squared error (MMSE) signal extraction formulas (McElroy 2008) to facilitate seasonal adjustment. This relies on a matrix representation of the signal extraction filters that is necessary due to the long-memory behavior; these formulas were unavailable to Carlin and Dempster (1989). In addition, the fully Bayesian framework we propose for conducting finite sample MMSE seasonal adjustment extends the current methodology even when the differenced data does not present long-range dependence. Finally, using the matrix approach requires efficient computation of autocovariances for models with multiple memory parameters (McElroy and Holan 2011).

Our approach relies on the seasonal fractionally differenced exponential model (SFEXP) (McElroy and Holan 2011) and more generally the Gegenbauer exponential (GEXP) model (Hsu and Tsai 2009; McElroy and Holan 2011). Additionally, our approach allows for versatile models on the seasonal component as well as easy inclusion of extra components that can be modeled rather flexibly. For example, our model allows for straightforward specification of a cycle component of unknown frequency (with or without long-range dependence) and/or a sampling error component using GEXP and exponential (EXP) models, respectively.

Finally, we pose our model from a Bayesian hierarchical perspective and, as a result, it is straightforward to include regression effects (e.g., holiday and TD effects) and to quantify uncertainty. In this context, there are several advantages to proceeding from a Bayesian hierarchical perspective, rather than taking a maximum likelihood approach to estimation. In particular, the likelihood surface is complex and so convergence of numerical optimization algorithms must be carefully monitored. In addition, in the case of maximum likelihood, standard errors for the parameter estimates are typically obtained through asymptotic arguments (using the estimated inverse Hessian matrix) and the final signal extraction estimates are conditioned on the estimated UC model parameters instead of directly accounting for this extra source of uncertainty. By contrast, we design a block Metropolis–Hastings algorithm for efficient model estimation and explicitly propagate uncertainty from the model fitting stage to the signal extraction. Although, our primary focus is on Bayesian methodology, for comparison, we also present results from maximum likelihood estimation (based on the *exact* likelihood rather than the so-called

Whittle approximation), which is also novel in this context. Also, maximum likelihood is useful in cases where rapid estimation is desired and/or as starting values for Bayesian estimation.

The remainder of this chapter proceeds as follows. Section 17.2 introduces the SFEXP model and describes an efficient approach to calculating the necessary model autocovariances. Section 17.3 describes long-memory unobserved component models and their application to seasonal adjustment. The methodology is illustrated in Section 17.4 through two real data examples. Finally, Section 17.5 provides a brief conclusion. Details surrounding our Markov Chain Monte Carlo (MCMC) algorithm and Bayesian signal extraction estimator are provided in the Appendix.

17.2 Seasonal Fractionally Differenced Exponential Model

The structural models of Section 17.3 depend, in large part, on the SFEXP spectral representation and efficient autocovariance computation. The necessary background material is provided here. In particular, we consider a process $\{Y_t\}$ that has long memory at both trend and seasonal frequencies. We focus on the case of monthly data, so that the seasonal frequencies are $\pi j/6$ for $j = 1, 2, \ldots, 6$; the trend frequency ($j = 0$) is treated separately. Now to each of the seasonal frequencies and the trend frequency, we may associate a pole in the pseudo-spectral density with rate of explosion governed by the seasonal and nonseasonal memory parameter δ_S and δ_N, respectively. These may be numbers greater than 0.5, indicating nonstationarity. Letting $\mu_t = \mathrm{E}(Y_t)$, our basic assumption is that

$$(1 - B)^{\delta_N} U(B)^{\delta_S} (Y_t - \mu_t) \qquad (17.2.1)$$

is a mean zero stationary process modeled by an exponential model (Bloomfield 1973) of order m, where B is the backshift operator and $U(z) = 1 + z + z^2 + \cdots + z^{11}$. The parameters δ_N and δ_S broadly define the dependence structure.

Specifically, when $\delta_N \in (0, 0.5)$, the process has (stationary) long memory at frequency zero, whereas if $\delta_N = 0$ the process has short memory. If $\delta_N \in (-0.5, 0)$, the process has intermediate memory at frequency zero, which is also stationary. Similar statements apply to the range of δ_S, except we substitute seasonal frequencies for frequency zero. It will be convenient to separate out the integer portion of δ_N and δ_S so that we can focus on the stationary aspects of the model. Since the process Y_t is stationary if and only if $|\delta_N| < 0.5$ and $|\delta_S| < 0.5$, it makes sense to define the integer portion of δ_N and δ_S to be given by rounding to the nearest integer (with fractional values of 0.5 being rounded upward), which will be denoted by the symbol $[\cdot]$. Hence $\delta_N = [\delta_N] + d$ and $\delta_S = [\delta_S] + D$, where the Latin letters d and D denote the remainders, which are guaranteed to lie in $(-0.5, 0.5)$. If we let Z_t denote the suitably differenced $(Y_t - \mu_t)$, such that the result is stationary, we have

$$Z_t = (1-B)^{[\delta_N]}U(B)^{[\delta_S]}(Y_t - \mu_t) = (1-B)^{[\delta_N]}U(B)^{[\delta_S]}Y_t - \zeta_t.$$

We use the notation $W_t = (1-B)^{[\delta_N]}U(B)^{[\delta_S]}Y_t$ for the differenced observed process and $\zeta_t = (1-B)^{[\delta_N]}U(B)^{[\delta_S]}\mu_t$ for the differenced time-varying mean. Thus $W_t = \zeta_t + Z_t$, with $\{Z_t\}$ stationary and mean zero. It follows that $\{Z_t\}$ has an integrable spectral density function f, which given our basic assumption (17.2.1) means that

$$f(\lambda) = |1-z|^{-2d}|U(z)|^{-2D} \exp\left\{ \sum_{j=-m}^{m} g_j z^j \right\}, \qquad (17.2.2)$$

where we use the convenient abbreviation $z = e^{-i\lambda}$. This defines the SFEXP model (McElroy and Holan 2011), where $g_j = g_{-j}$ by assumption.

Example. If $\delta_N = 1.33$ and $\delta_S = 1.15$, then the nonstationary integer differencing order is $[\delta_N] = 1$ for trend and $[\delta_S] = 1$ for seasonal (fairly typical values), and $d = 0.33$ and $D = 0.15$ are the resulting memory parameters. The values of these memory parameters indicate fairly strong memory for the trend, but weaker long-range dependence for the seasonal frequencies.

The fitting of the SFEXP model to seasonal data involves first the identification of integer differencing orders, which are the numbers $[\delta_N]$ and $[\delta_S]$. These are applied to the observed time series, resulting in the differenced series $\{W_t\}$. Subsequently, a short-memory model order m is selected and, conditional on m, values for d and D and the $\{g_j\}_{j=0}^{m}$ are determined using Bayesian (or maximum likelihood) estimation. Alternatively, in principal, taking a Bayesian approach similar to Holan et al. (2009), the choice of m (order selection) can be directly incorporated into the modeling procedure using reversible jump MCMC.

Whether a Bayesian or a maximum likelihood procedure is carried out, it is convenient to use the Gaussian likelihood function corresponding to Equation 17.2.2, since, conditional on ζ_t, this only depends on autocovariances that can be computed directly and accurately via algorithms described in McElroy and Holan (2011). Note, as demonstrated below, that the main determinants of the seasonal adjustment filters are the parameters d and D, whereas the short memory parameters have little effect. The key to estimation of a Gaussian SFEXP model is efficient, accurate computation of the autocovariances. The method of McElroy and Holan (2011) is extremely general; nonetheless, improvements to speed and precision of parameter estimates can be achieved in the special case of Equation 17.2.2 when only one pole is present and is useful in the case of UC models. We provide the details for relevant cases of this situation as follows.

Suppose first that $D = 0$ in Equation 17.2.2, producing the FEXP model. The best technique is to compute autocovariances using the splitting method (Bertelli and Caporin 2002) (which involves the convolution of short- and long-memory autocovariances), since the autocovariance sequence for $|1-z|^{-2d}$ is known analytically and the autocovariance sequence for the short memory $g(\lambda) = \exp\{\sum_j g_j z^j\}$ decays at geometric rate:

$$\gamma_h = \frac{1}{2\pi}\int_{-\pi}^{\pi} |1-z|^{-2d} g(\lambda) z^{-h} d\lambda = \sum_k \gamma_k(g)\xi_{h-k}(d),$$
$$\gamma_k(g) = \frac{1}{2\pi}\int_{-\pi}^{\pi} g(\lambda) z^{-k} d\lambda,$$
$$\xi_j(d) = \frac{\Gamma(j+d)\Gamma(1-2d)}{\Gamma(j-d+1)\Gamma(d)\Gamma(1-d)}. \tag{17.2.3}$$

Here $\xi_j(d)$ is the autocovariance sequence for an ARFIMA$(0,d,0)$ as in Brockwell and Davis (1991), utilizing the Gamma function. The expression for γ_h involves an infinite sum that can be truncated safely, since $\gamma_k(g)$ will tend to decay rapidly (since g has no poles).

Secondly, suppose that $d = 0$ and $D > 0$ in Equation 17.2.2. Then rewrite the spectral density as $f(\lambda) = |1-z^{12}|^{-2D}|1-z|^{2D}g(\lambda)$. Observe that $k(\lambda) = |1-z|^{2D}g(\lambda)$ is a combination of negative-memory (hyperbolic zeroes in spectrum) and short-memory behavior and also has rapidly decaying autocovariance sequence. This autocovariance sequence need not decay geometrically, but will tend to decay rapidly nevertheless. The autocovariance function (acvf) of the spectrum $|1-z^s|^{-2D}$ is given by the following result.*

Proposition 17.1 *The autocovariance sequence of* $|1-z^s|^{-2D}$ *is*

$$\xi_j(D) = \frac{\Gamma(j/s+D)\Gamma(1-2D)}{\Gamma(j/s-D+1)\Gamma(D)\Gamma(1-D)} 1_{\{j\equiv 0 \ mod\ s\}}.$$

As a result, the desired autocovariance sequence is

$$\gamma_h = \sum_j \gamma_j(k)\xi_{h-j}(D) = \sum_j \gamma_{h-12j}(k)\frac{\Gamma(j+D)\Gamma(1-2D)}{\Gamma(j-D+1)\Gamma(D)\Gamma(1-D)}. \tag{17.2.4}$$

The calculation of these quantities is therefore fast and accurate.

If $D < 0$, the process exhibits negative memory and has a rapidly decaying autocovariance sequence. Therefore, $f(\lambda) = |1-z^{12}|^{-2D}|1-z|^{2D}g(\lambda) = |U(z)|^{-2D}g(\lambda)$ can be accurately and efficiently computed. In this case, several methods could be employed including McElroy and Holan (2011), a multiple splitting approach, or direct Fourier inversion of the spectral density using numerical integration.

---

* Proposition 17.1 is fairly common in the literature on long-memory time series and can be readily deduced from results found in Brockwell and Davis (1991). Thus, it is presented here without proof.

17.3 Long-Memory Unobserved Components Models and Seasonal Adjustment

In order to apply formulas for finite sample MMSE*, we need autocovariance generating functions for signal and noise. As previously alluded to, we take a structural approach, which posits models for signal and noise and, thus, an inferred autocovariance structure is obtained for the data process via summing the spectra of the component models. Specifically, we illustrate this for the SFEXP case.

Let Y_t equal the sum of two components S_t and N_t, the seasonal and non-seasonal, respectively. In terms of Equation 17.2.1, these have $\delta_N = 0$ for S_t and $\delta_S = 0$ for N_t, and potentially different orders m_S and m_N for the exponential model portions. These are working assumptions that are sensible, since we seek a seasonal component that has no trend dynamics and also a non-seasonal component with no seasonal dynamics. Including regression effects (i.e., TD and/or holiday effects), the two component model can be written as $Y_t = \mu_t + S_t + N_t$, where $\mu_t = X_t' \theta$ denotes a regression component. Thus, it follows that

$$W_t = \zeta_t + (1 - B)^{[\delta_N]} U_t + U(B)^{[\delta_S]} V_t,$$

where $\{U_t\}$ and $\{V_t\}$ are suitably differenced versions of $\{S_t\}$ and $\{N_t\}$ that are independent of one another, i.e., $U_t = U(B)^{[\delta_S]} S_t$ and $V_t = (1 - B)^{[\delta_N]} N_t$. Note that if we suppose that S_t and N_t follow Equation 17.2.1 then, in general, $Z_t = W_t - \zeta_t$ does not follow an exponential model. In particular, we have

$$f_S(\lambda) = |U(z)|^{-2[\delta_S]} f_U(\lambda) \qquad f_U(\lambda) = |U(z)|^{-2D} g_S(\lambda),$$
$$f_N(\lambda) = |1 - z|^{-2[\delta_N]} f_V(\lambda) \qquad f_V(\lambda) = |1 - z|^{-2d} g_N(\lambda)$$

for exponential models g_S and g_N given by $g_S(\lambda) = \exp\{\sum_{|j| \le m_S} u_j z^j\}$ and $g_N(\lambda) = \exp\{\sum_{|j| \le m_N} v_j z^j\}$. Thus it follows that the spectrum for the differenced, mean-centered process Z_t is

$$|1 - z|^{2[\delta_N]} |U(z)|^{-2D} g_S(\lambda) + |U(z)|^{2[\delta_S]} |1 - z|^{-2d} g_N(\lambda), \qquad (17.3.1)$$

which, in general, will not have the form of f given in Equation 17.2.1, as the exponential portion would have infinitely many nonzero coefficients. Nevertheless, Equation 17.3.1 can easily be used to construct a Gaussian likelihood function: given d, D, and the parameters of g_S and g_N (with $[\delta_N]$ and $[\delta_S]$ determined before-hand as in Section 17.2), we compute the autocovariances for each of the two terms and sum. Let $\Gamma(g)$ denote the (Toeplitz) covariance matrix associated with a stationary process having spectral density g.

* The described estimators are MMSE for Gaussian time series, or alternatively are MMSE among linear estimators in the data; this depends on certain signal extraction conditions described in McElroy (2008).

Then for a sample from $\{Y_t\}$ of size n, the autocovariance matrix associated with Z_t can be expressed as

$$\Sigma_Z = \underline{\Delta}_N \Gamma(f_U) \underline{\Delta}'_N + \underline{\Delta}_S \Gamma(f_V) \underline{\Delta}'_S,$$

where $\underline{\Delta}_N$ and $\underline{\Delta}_S$ are $(n - 12[\delta_S] - [\delta_N]) \times (n - 12[\delta_S])$ and $(n - 12[\delta_S] - [\delta_N]) \times (n - [\delta_N])$-dimensional differencing matrices with entries given by the coefficients of $(1 - B)^{[\delta_N]}$ and $U(B)^{[\delta_S]}$, respectively, appropriately shifted. Explicit examples of these matrices can be found in Bell (2004) and McElroy and Gagnon (2008).

Let ψ denote the full parameter vector for the model (excluding regression parameters); then $\psi = (d, u_0, u_1, \ldots, u_{m_S}, D, v_0, v_1, \ldots, v_{m_N})'$. Note that this vector partitions into the first $m_S + 2$ components corresponding to the seasonal component S and the latter $m_N + 2$ components for the nonseasonal component N. Using maximum likelihood, and the concepts of Section 17.2, the actual estimation of the structural model for the data is fast and accurate to compute. Conditional on the regression parameters, we only need to compute the autocovariance sequence associated with Equation 17.3.1 to obtain likelihood evaluations. The first term is a simple linear combination of autocovariances computed using Equation 17.2.4. The second term is another finite linear combination of autocovariances computed using Equation 17.2.3. Then one sums the autocovariance sequences to get the autocovariances for the differenced data.

If one utilizes this procedure in the heart of a maximum likelihood routine, the end result at convergence is parameter estimates for ψ (and θ – the vector of regression coefficients). This gives complete models for both the seasonal and nonseasonal as well as the autocovariance sequence for Z_t. Additionally, it is clear from the previous discussion that the data spectrum f will have stationary long-memory poles at the trend and seasonal frequencies, of order d and D, respectively, since it follows from Equation 17.3.1 that

$$f_\psi(\lambda) = \frac{|1 - z|^{2\delta_N} g_S(\lambda) + |U(z)|^{2\delta_S} g_N(\lambda)}{|1 - z|^{2d} |U(z)|^{2D}},$$

where $f_\psi(\lambda)$ denotes the spectral density associated with the parameters ψ. For the MMSE signal extraction formulas, we need the autocovariances associated with both components. Under the typical assumptions (given in Bell (1984b) and McElroy (2008)), we apply the matrix formula (17.3.2) to the finite sample of data $Y = (Y_1, Y_2, \ldots, Y_n)'$ (the presence of mean effects changes things slightly; see the discussion in the Appendix). Let Δ_S and Δ_N denote differencing matrices for seasonal and nonseasonal, such that when applied to the signal and noise vectors, yield U and V, respectively. Specifically, Δ_S and Δ_N are $(n - 12[\delta_S]) \times n$ and $(n - [\delta_N]) \times n$ differencing matrices, respectively, and are constructed similar to $\underline{\Delta}_N$ and $\underline{\Delta}_S$ (see McElroy (2008) for more details). Then the signal extraction matrix associated with ψ is given by

$$F(\psi) = \left(\Delta'_S \Gamma^{-1}(f_U) \Delta_S + \Delta'_N \Gamma^{-1}(f_V) \Delta_N\right)^{-1} \Delta'_S \Gamma^{-1}(f_U) \Delta_S. \qquad (17.3.2)$$

The dependence on the parameter vector ψ enters through f_U and f_V, whose reliance on ψ is suppressed in the notation.

Conditional on m_S and m_N being known, it is straightforward to write down the Gaussian likelihood associated with a sample of size n. Letting $W = (W_1, W_2, \ldots, W_{n'})'$, n' equal the length of the differenced series and $1_{n'}$ the vector of ones with length n' we have

$$p(W|\psi,\zeta) = (2\pi)^{-n/2}|\Sigma(f_\psi)|^{-1/2}\exp\left\{-\frac{1}{2}(W-\zeta 1_{n'})'\,\Sigma(f_\psi)^{-1}\,(W-\zeta 1_{n'})\right\}.$$

It is readily seen that our UC model naturally possesses a hierarchical structure. Ultimately, for signal extraction, we are interested in estimating the model parameters so that we can compute the necessary autocovariances. Specifically, the finite sample MMSE formulas will depend on ψ; the Appendix contains a comprehensive treatment of Bayesian finite sample MMSE. To this end, we use Bayes rule to obtain the posterior distribution of ψ and ζ (and ultimately the autocovariances, UC, and seasonal adjustments) given the data

$$\begin{aligned} p(\psi, \zeta|W) &= p(D, d, u, v, \sigma_u^2, \sigma_v^2, \zeta|W) \\ &\propto p(W|\psi,\zeta)p(u|\sigma_u^2)p(v|\sigma_v^2)p(\sigma_u^2)p(\sigma_v^2)p(d)p(D)p(\zeta), \end{aligned}$$

where $u = (u_0, u_1, \ldots, u_{m_S})'$, $v = (v_0, v_1, \ldots, v_{m_N})'$, $\sigma_u^2 = (\sigma_{u_0}^2, \ldots, \sigma_{u_{m_S}}^2)'$ and $\sigma_v^2 = (\sigma_{v_0}^2, \ldots, \sigma_{v_{m_N}}^2)'$ and we have assumed conditional independence between components. To completely specify a Bayesian model requires us to choose priors for $(d, u, \sigma_u^2, D, v, \sigma_v^2, \zeta)$. For ease of exposition, and to be consistent with our empirical case studies (cf. Section 17.4), we assume the differenced data to be mean-centered via ζ, noting that it is straightforward to include regression effects such as TD and holiday effects. Similar to Holan et al. (2009), for $j = 1, \ldots, m_S$ and $k = 1, \ldots, m_N$, we assign hierarchical priors on the unknown parameters as follows: $D \sim \text{Uniform}(-1/2, 1/2)$; $u_j|\sigma_{u_j}^2 \sim N(0, \sigma_{u_j}^2)$; $\sigma_{u_j}^2 \sim IG(A_u, B_u)$; $d \sim \text{Uniform}(-1/2, 1/2)$; $v_k|\sigma_{v_k}^2 \sim N(0, \sigma_{v_k}^2)$; $\sigma_{v_k}^2 \sim IG(A_v, B_v)$; $\zeta \sim N(\zeta_0, \sigma_\zeta^2)$. As usual IG denotes the inverse gamma distribution, so that σ_ℓ^2 has probability density function (pdf) $p(\sigma_\ell^2) \propto (\sigma_\ell^2)^{-(A+1)}\exp(-B/\sigma_\ell^2)$. Typically, as is the case in our illustrations, the hyperparameters A_u, B_u, A_v, B_v, ζ_0, and σ_ζ^2 are specified so that the prior distributions are vague or noninformative. Comprehensive details regarding the full conditional distributions and exact MCMC algorithm can be found in the Appendix.

17.4 Empirical Case Studies

In order to demonstrate the effectiveness and flexibility of our approach, we consider the seasonal adjustment of two time series. First, we consider a dataset from the Current Population Survey (CPS) (U.S. Bureau of Labor Statistics, http://www.bls.gov/data/) that consists of Employed Males, aged 16–19, dated 1/1976–6/2010; henceforth referred to as the "EM1619" series. Figure 17.1Aa provides a plot of the time series. Next, we consider data from the Current Employment Statistics Survey (CES) (U.S. Bureau of Labor Statistics, http://www.bls.gov/data/) that consists of U.S. Total Nonfarm Employment dated 1/1939–7/2009. Figure 17.2Aa provides a plot of the observed time series.

For both datasets, maximum likelihood is conducted using the *optim* command in R (R Development Core Team 2010) to numerically determine the maximum of the likelihood surface. Conversely, the Bayesian procedure uses the prior specification detailed in Section 17.3. Specifically, for both datasets we take $A_u = B_u = A_v = B_v = 0.1$, $\zeta_0 = 0$, and $\sigma_\zeta^2 = 10^3$ and implement the MCMC algorithm described in the Appendix. For model fitting, we run a single MCMC chain for 10,000 iterations discarding the first 1000 iterations for burn-in and keeping every third iteration for inference, leaving 3000 iterations in total. Convergence of the MCMC is verified through trace plots of the sample chains. All estimated parameters are taken as the posterior means.

In order to arrive at a model for illustration, we informally consider Akaike's information criterion (AIC) and Bayesian information criterion (BIC) for models estimated using maximum likelihood (Beran et al. 1998). In particular, Beran et al. (1998) provided formal justification for these criterion in the context of fractional autoregressive models. Nevertheless, we shall use these criteria here to narrow down the candidate models.

In the case of the Bayesian hierarchical approach, we use deviance information criterion (DIC) (Spiegelhalter et al. 2002) to evaluate candidate models. DIC has become commonplace in Bayesian model selection and, similar to AIC and BIC, models with smaller DIC are preferable. Ultimately, for each dataset, we choose a Bayesian model for illustration based on DIC. Again, since the goal of our illustration is to demonstrate effective seasonal adjustment, we have not conducted an exhaustive search to find an "optimal" model. Instead, we choose a competitive model and evaluate its effectiveness in seasonal adjustment.

In order to determine if a transformation or differencing is required for either dataset, we begin with an exploratory analysis. Figures 17.1 and 17.2 provide plots of the observed series, the first-differenced series, and the series obtained from taking the first difference and then applying the differencing operator $U(B)$. In addition, both figures display the associated acvfs, and AR(30) spectral densities. From an initial assessment of the plots in Figures 17.1 and 17.2, it seems reasonable to work with the data obtained from applying the $(1 - B)U(B) = 1 - B^{12}$ differencing operator to both observed series.

17.4.1 Current Population Survey—Employed Males

In seasonal adjustment applications, it is common to test for outliers, TD, and holiday effects in monthly time series such as the EM1619 series. Running

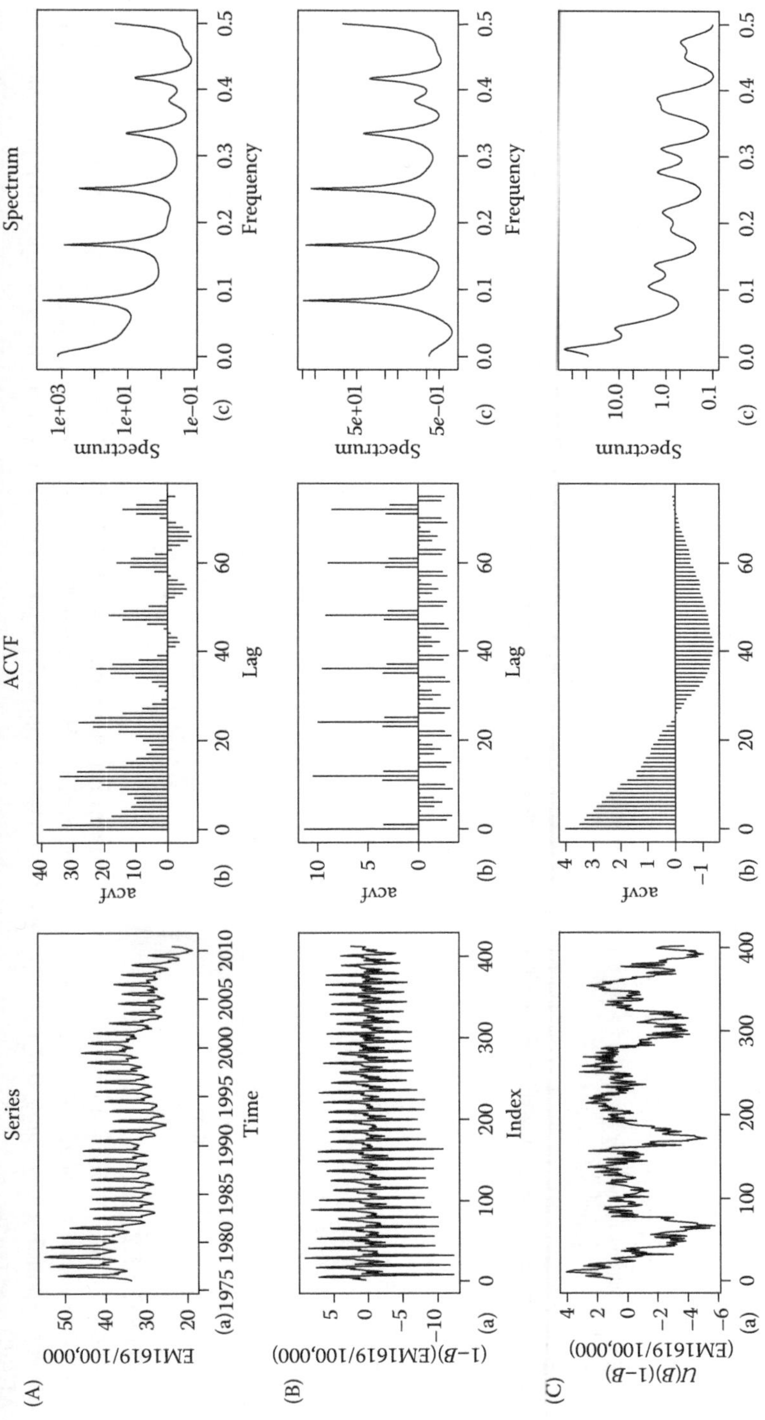

FIGURE 17.1
Exploratory data analysis plot for the Current Population Survey—Employed Males aged 16–19 from 1/1976–6/2010 (EM1619). (A) Displays the time series plot, the autocovariance (acvf) plot, and the AR(30) spectrum. (B) Displays the first differenced data (i.e., $(1 - B)Y_t$) along with the corresponding acvf plot and AR(30) spectrum. (C) Displays $U(B)(1 - B)Y_t$ along with the corresponding acvf plot and AR(30) spectrum.

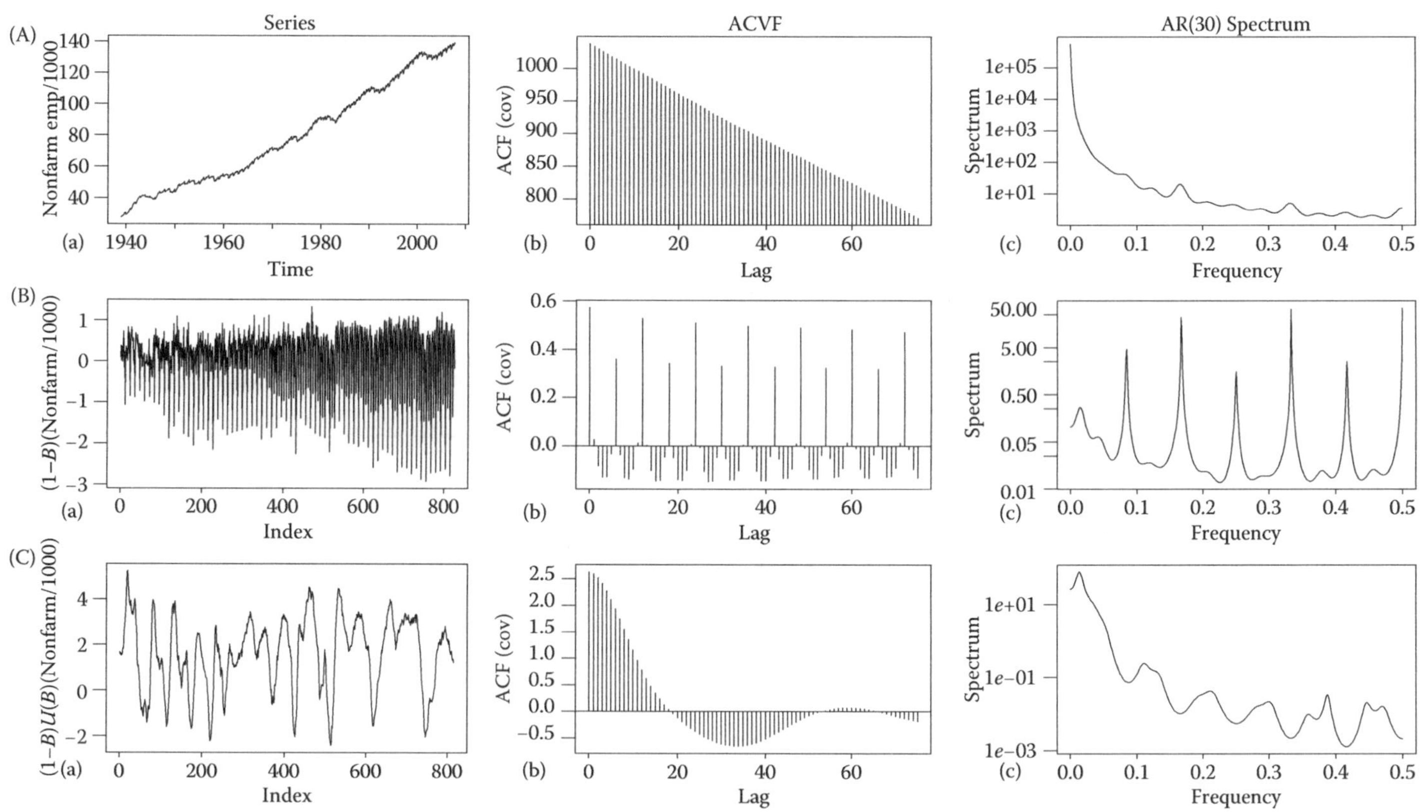

FIGURE 17.2
Exploratory data analysis plot for U.S. Total Nonfarm Employment from 1/1939 to 7/2009. (A) Displays the time series plot, the autocovariance (acvf) plot, and the AR(30) spectrum. (B) Displays the first differenced data (i.e., $(1 - B)Y_t$) along with the corresponding acvf plot and AR(30) spectrum. (C) Displays $U(B)(1 - B)Y_t$ along with the corresponding acvf plot and AR(30) spectrum.

different specifications through X-12 ARIMA, neither TD nor Easter holiday effects were found significant and thus no TD or holiday adjustments were made. The current model used at the Bureau of Labor Statistics involves removing three level shifts (LS). We fit models with both the three LS removed and retained and found no appreciable difference. Thus, in what follows, we detail the analysis with the three LS retained.

Several models were fit using maximum likelihood and although many models appeared to provide a good fit to the observed data, not all of these models provided adequate seasonal adjustment. One model identified for further consideration was a long-memory UC model with one seasonal and three nonseasonal short-memory coefficients (i.e., LM-UC(1,3)). The estimated long-memory parameters were $(\widehat{D}, \widehat{d}) = (0.460, 0.159)$ with standard errors of 0.032 and 0.084, respectively. The estimated seasonal short-memory coefficient, $\widehat{u}_0$, equals -4.719 with standard error 0.312. The estimated nonseasonal

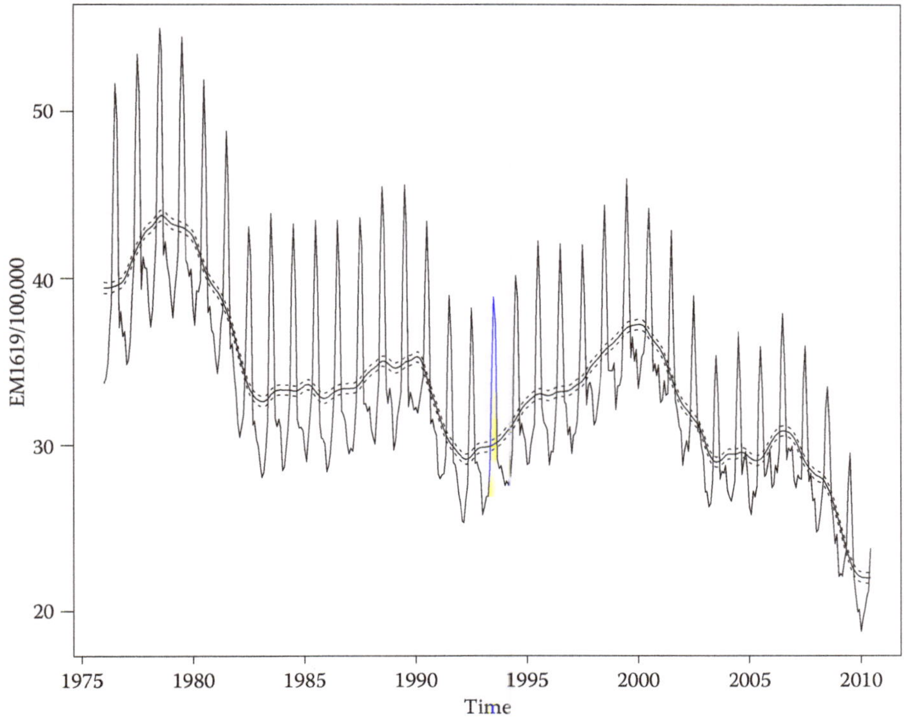

FIGURE 17.3
Time plot, for the Employed Males series (EM1619), with estimated nonseasonal component derived from an LM-UC(1,3) model using maximum likelihood. The dashed lines represent the estimated pointwise 95% confidence interval.

short-memory coefficients $(\widehat{v}_0, \widehat{v}_1, \widehat{v}_2) = (-0.751, -0.749, -0.420)$ with standard errors of 0.085, 0.204, and 0.157, respectively. Finally, $\widehat{\zeta}$, the estimated mean of the differenced data, equals -0.555 with standard error 0.579. Note that $\overline{x}_d$, the sample mean of the differenced data, equals -0.524 and closely agrees with our estimate.

Figure 17.3 displays the estimated nonseasonal component and associated pointwise 95% confidence band. To assess whether the seasonality has been removed, we plot the AR(30) spectral density for the first-differenced estimated trend (Figure 17.4). Figure 17.4 clearly illustrates that the seasonality has

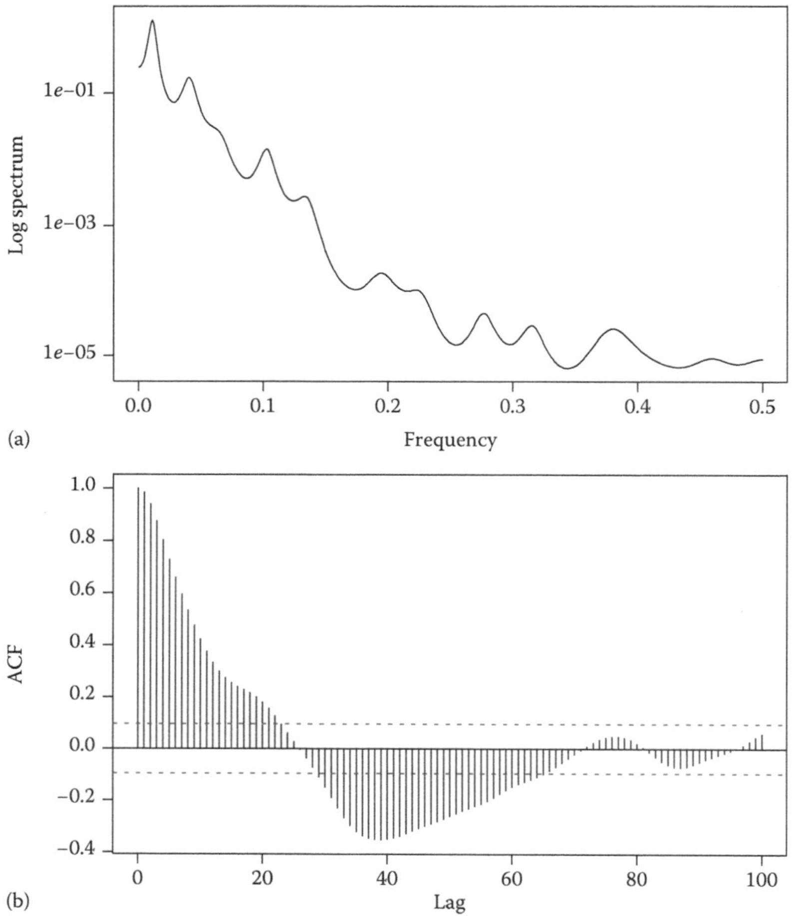

FIGURE 17.4
Employed Males series (EM1619)—maximum likelihood: (a) plots the AR(30) spectrum of the differenced estimated trend (nonseasonal) estimate. (b) Displays the sample autocorrelation function of the differenced trend (nonseasonal) estimate.

been satisfactorily removed. Finally, one can examine the seasonal adjustment filter through a plot of the gain function for the seasonal and nonseasonal components. As seen in Figure 17.5, the induced filters sensibly suppress the dynamics at the correct frequencies.

By contrast, we conducted seasonal adjustment using Bayesian methodology. Specifically, based on DIC, we estimated an LM-UC(1,5) model. It is important to emphasize that we have not conducted an exhaustive model selection, but rather chose a candidate model to illustrate Bayesian long-memory seasonal adjustment. The estimated model parameters were $(\widehat{D}, \widehat{d}) = (0.381, 0.097)$ with 95% credible intervals (CI) given by $(0.224, 0.471)$ and $(-0.143, 0.321)$, respectively. The estimated seasonal short-memory coefficient is -4.251 with 95% CI of $(-5.020, -3.246)$, whereas the estimated nonseasonal short-memory coefficients are given by $(-0.794, -0.491, -0.377, 0.233, -0.231)$ with 95% CIs given by $(-1.047, -0.570)$, $(-1.029, 0.009)$, $(-0.786,$

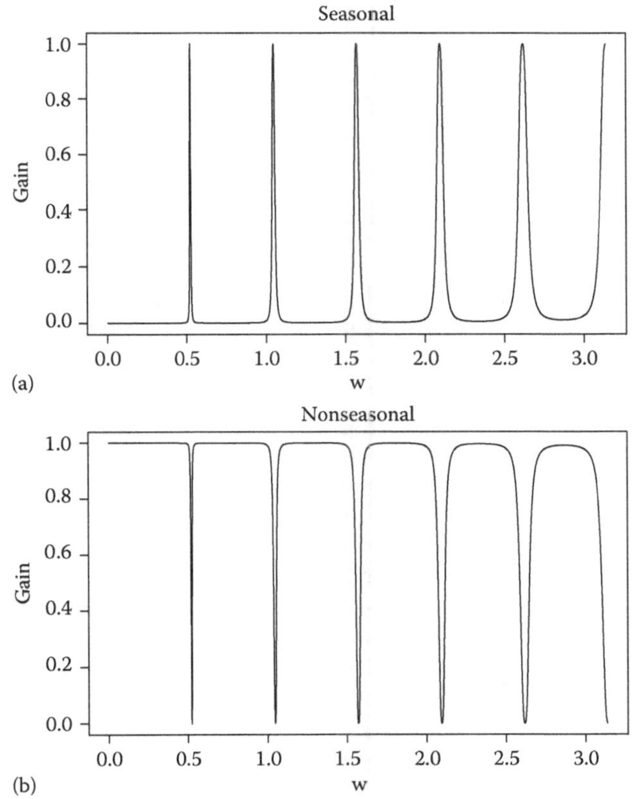

FIGURE 17.5
Employed Males series (EM1619): (a) plots the gain function for the seasonal filter. (b) Displays the gain function for the nonseasonal filter.

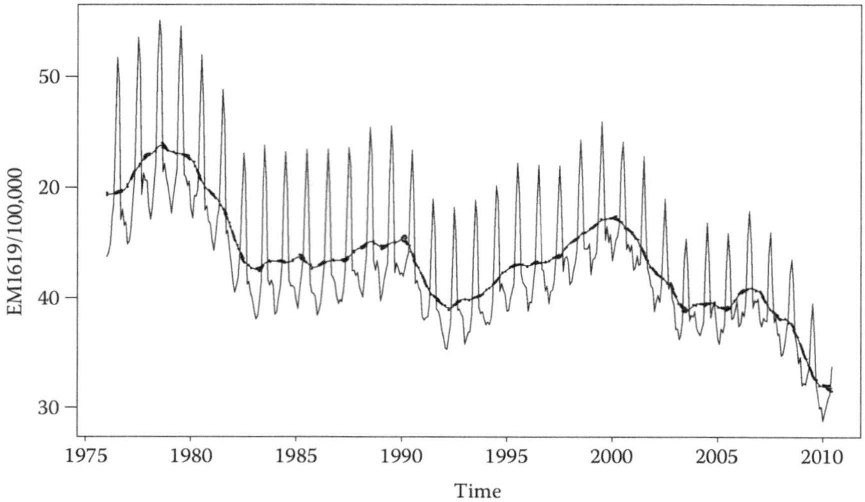

FIGURE 17.6
Employed Males series (EM1619): Time plot with estimated nonseasonal component derived from an LM-UC(1,5) model using Bayesian estimation. The dashed lines represent the estimated pointwise 95% credible interval.

0.007), (−0.066, 0.525), and (−0.546, 0.006) respectively. Finally, $\widehat{\zeta}$, the estimated mean of the differenced data, equals −0.542 with 95% CI equal to (−0.587, −0.495). Figure 17.6 displays the observed series along with the estimated nonseasonal component and pointwise 95% CIs. An AR(30) spectral density and acf plot identical to Figure 17.4 indicate that the induced filters sensibly suppress the dynamics at the correct frequencies (not displayed).

In both the maximum likelihood and Bayesian approaches, the estimated nonseasonal long-memory parameter is not statistically significant (at the 0.05 level). For comparison, we estimated a model (using classical and Bayesian methodology) with the nonseasonal long-memory parameter set identically equal to zero. We found that this produced qualitatively similar seasonal adjustments and, thus, is not presented here. In the Bayesian context, this parameter can be viewed as a nuisance parameter, since our target is an estimated trend component. The method we propose averages over the distribution of this parameter to produce a pointwise distribution of trend components. Therefore, it is advantageous to include this parameter in the model, since a significant portion of the distribution, for the model parameter, is located away from zero (see Figure 17.7). Importantly, the pointwise 95% CI for the estimated nonseasonal component takes into account parameter uncertainty and is narrower than the corresponding interval from maximum likelihood that appeals to large sample approximations (see Holan et al. 2009, for further discussion). Finally, we also estimated models with three components—trend, seasonal, and

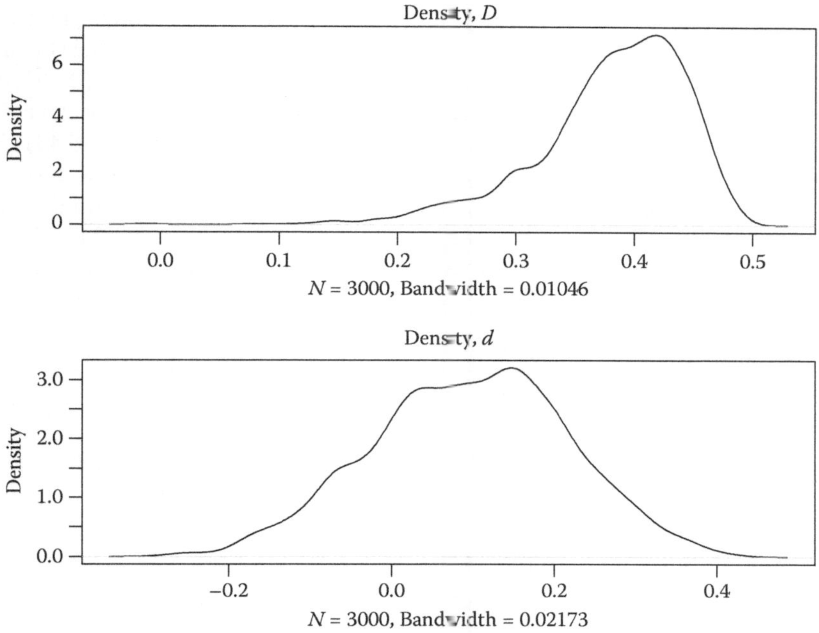

FIGURE 17.7
Employed Males series (EM1619): Kernel density estimate of the posterior distribution of the memory parameters D and d from a Bayesian LM-UC(1,5) (using the default *density* command in R).

irregular. The results for the seasonal adjustments were qualitatively similar in this case and thus are not presented here.

17.4.2 U.S. Total Nonfarm Employment

As previously discussed, preadjustment of economic time series in the context of seasonal adjustment is commonplace in practice. To assess the need for preadjustment, we ran several specifications in X-12 ARIMA; it was determined that no transformation was necessary but that stock-trading day effects were significant. Although stock-trading day effects could be directly incorporated into our model as a regression effect (cf., Section 17.3), and estimated using Bayesian methods, our focus is on illustrating the long-memory aspects of the model and thus we removed this effect prior to model estimation and seasonal adjustment. While this may not be preferred from a modeling perspective, this is also consistent with current seasonal adjustment practices in federal statistical agencies and advantageous from a computational viewpoint.

Similar to the EM1619 series, several candidate models were investigated. One model identified for further consideration (under both maximum likelihood and Bayesian estimation) was an LM-UC(2,3) model. Thus, using the Bayesian framework, we conducted seasonal adjustment under this model. In this case, the estimated long-memory parameters $(\widehat{D}, \widehat{d})$ equal $(0.053, 0.325)$ with 95% CIs equal to $(-0.061, 0.179)$ and $(0.208, 0.429)$, respectively. The estimated seasonal short-memory coefficients $(\widehat{u}_0, \widehat{u}_1)$, equal $(-6.431, 2.562)$ with 95% CIs equal to (−7.168, −5.832) and (2.041, 3.025), respectively. The estimated nonseasonal short-memory coefficients $(\widehat{v}_0, \widehat{v}_1, \widehat{v}_2)$ equal (−3.931, 0.278, 0.569) with 95% CIs equal to (−4.104, −3.771) and (0.004, 0.595) and (0.337, 0.828), respectively. Finally, $\widehat{\zeta}$ the estimated mean of the differenced data, equals 1.621 with 95% CI (1.609, 1.634). Figure 17.8 shows a plot of

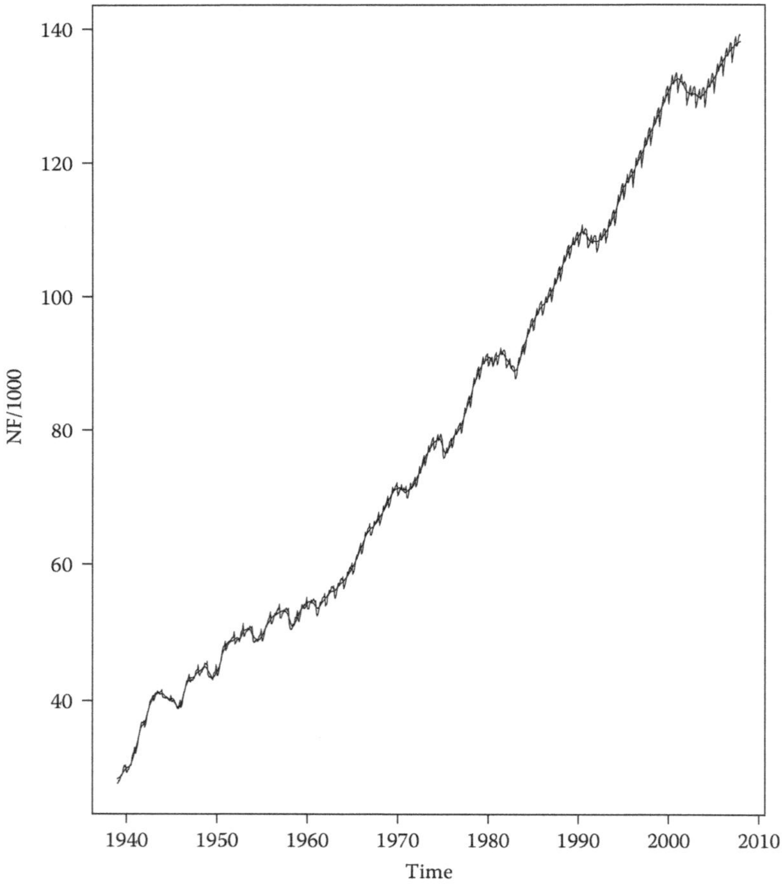

FIGURE 17.8
Nonfarm Employment series—Bayesian estimation: Time plot with estimated nonseasonal component derived from an LM-UC(2,3) model using Bayesian estimation. The estimated pointwise 95% CI has been suppressed since the width is uniformly less than 0.25.

the observed series along with the estimated nonseasonal component. The estimated pointwise 95% CI is intentionally suppressed since the width of this interval is uniformly less than 0.25. Finally, to assess whether the seasonality has been adequately removed, we plot the AR(30) spectral density for the first-differenced estimated trend (Figure 17.9). This figure clearly demonstrates that the seasonality has been removed. Again, similar to the EM1619 series,

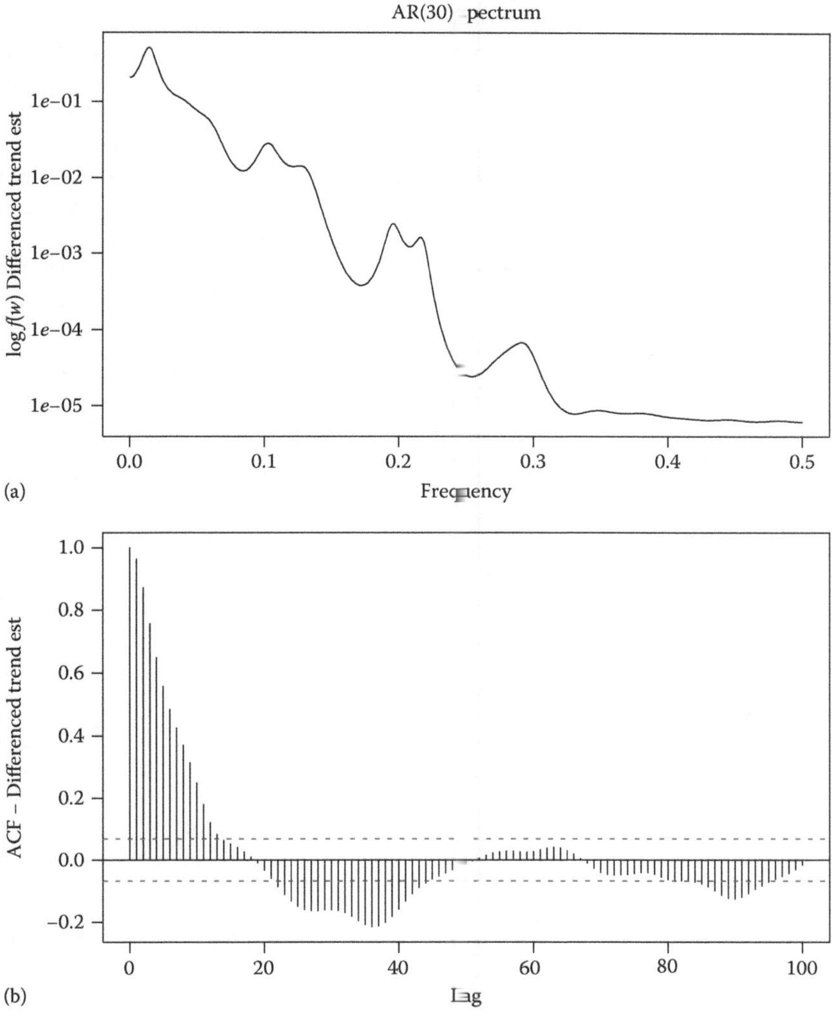

FIGURE 17.9
Nonfarm Employment series—Bayesian estimation: (a) plots the AR(30) spectrum of the differenced estimated trend (nonseasonal) estimate. (b) Displays the sample autocorrelation function of the differenced trend (nonseasonal) estimate.

one could study the properties of the seasonal adjustment filter through an investigation of the gain function. However, we defer such investigation here, noting that the investigation yields similar conclusions to the EM1619 series.

Alternatively, using maximum likelihood, the estimated long-memory parameters $(\widehat{D}, \widehat{d})$ equal $(0.064, 0.349)$ with standard errors of 0.062 and 0.069, respectively. The estimated seasonal short-memory coefficients $(\widehat{u}_0, \widehat{u}_1)$ equal $(-6.475,\ 2.583)$ with standard errors of (0.337, 0.260), respectively. The estimated nonseasonal short-memory coefficients $(\widehat{v}_0, \widehat{v}_1, \widehat{v}_2)$ equal $(-3.923, 0.231, 0.533)$ with standard errors of 0.082, 0.168, and 0.127, respectively. Finally, $\widehat{\zeta}$, the estimated mean of the differenced data, equals 1.613 with standard error 1.054 and agrees closely with $\overline{x}_d = 1.597$ (the sample mean of the differenced data). Plots of the estimated nonseasonal component, from maximum likelihood, and the AR(30) spectral density for the first differenced estimated trend demonstrate that the seasonality has been convincingly removed. These plots are similar to the Bayesian case (Figures 17.8 and 17.9) and, thus, are not displayed for the sake of brevity.

Similar to the EM1619 series, we could set $D \equiv 0$. However, our preference is to include this parameter in the model since its distribution has considerable

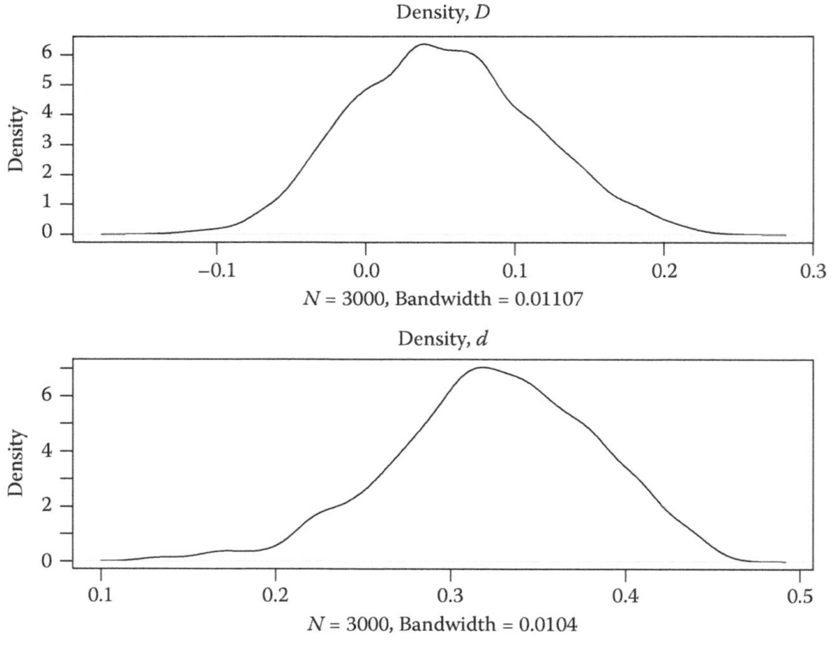

FIGURE 17.10
Nonfarm Employment series: Kernel density estimate of the posterior distribution of the memory parameters D and d from a Bayesian LM-UC(2,3) (using the default *density* command in R).

mass away from zero (see Figure 17.10). Additionally, our Bayesian approach views this parameter as a nuisance parameter and averages over the distribution of D to obtain the distribution of the UCs. To verify that this approach was reasonable, we fit a model with $D \equiv 0$ and found that the results were consistent with those reported here.

17.5 Discussion

Research into long-memory processes has recently spread to the modeling of seasonality through the use of generalized exponential time series models. This chapter considers the application of seasonal long-memory modeling to the problem of seasonal adjustment of economic time series. In particular, we introduced the new SFEXP model and explored its fit to economic time series data. Subsequently, we discussed a structural approach to obtaining component models for seasonal and trend in the context of long memory and use these models to obtain finite sample MMSE. The approach we propose is fully Bayesian, producing distributions for the UCs, and thus naturally quantifies the uncertainty in the signal extraction estimates.

One interesting direction for future research is to model the regressors (i.e., TD and Holiday effects) dynamically. In particular, in order to observe and effectively model long-range dependence typically requires a long time series, as was the case in our examples. Thus, it is conceivable that the regression coefficients might change over time. In principle, modeling these parameters dynamically at another level in the hierarchical model would constitute a relatively straightforward extension to the models we propose.

More specifically, the general modeling approach we propose extends seasonal adjustment methodology in several ways. First, our methodology provides the first attempt at exact finite sample MMSE signal extraction for long-memory time series. In addition, we propose a fully Bayesian framework for conducting finite sample MMSE seasonal adjustment, which extends the current methodology even when the differenced data does not present long-range dependence.

In order to facilitate Bayesian estimation, we develop an efficient block Metropolis–Hastings (M-H) sampler. The sampling algorithm provides efficient computation by minimizing the number of expensive evaluations of the likelihood. In addition, we propose an effective method for computing the necessary model autocovariances. These computational tools allow us to effectively estimate the SFEXP model and LM-UC models that were introduced in Sections 17.2 and 17.3.

The methodology is illustrated using two real economic time series, the CPS—Employed Males, aged 16–19, dated 1/1976–6/2010 and the CES—U.S. Total Nonfarm Employment dated 1/1939–7/2009. These empirical case studies demonstrate the flexibility and utility of our approach. In short, we have shown that our proposed methodology provides a necessary and timely extension to the current practice of seasonal adjustment.

17.6 Appendix

17.6.1 Full Conditionals and Markov Chain Monte Carlo

Estimation of the UC model presented in Section 17.3 is computationally demanding due to expensive likelihood evaluations. Thus, it is essential to minimize the number of likelihood evaluations in the MCMC algorithm. As in Section 17.3, we assume that the components U_t and V_t are uncorrelated. Therefore, it is natural to sample the parameters in blocks according to their respective components. Further, since some of the full conditionals are not of standard form, we have used a Metropolis within Gibbs algorithm (Gelman et al. 2003). We list the necessary full conditional distributions in the following.

First, since the prior for $\sigma^2_{u_j}$ $(j = 1, \ldots, m_S)$ does not depend on D, d, v, σ^2_v, or ζ and since u_j $(j = 1, \ldots, m_S)$ are independent of each other, it follows that

$$p(\sigma^2_{u_j}|d, D, u, v, \sigma^2_{u_{-j}}, \sigma^2_v, \zeta, W) \sim IG\left\{(A_u + 1/2), \quad (u_j^2/2 + B_u)\right\}, \quad (17.6.1)$$

where $\sigma^2_{u_{-j}}$ is the vector of variances for $u_0, u_1, \ldots, u_{j-1}, u_{j+1}, \ldots, u_{m_S}$. Similarly, for $k = 1, \ldots, m_N$, the full conditional of $\sigma^2_{v_k}$ is given by

$$p(\sigma^2_{v_k}|d, D, u, v, \sigma^2_u, \sigma^2_{v_{-k}}, \zeta, W) \sim IG\left\{(A_v + 1/2), \quad (v_k^2/2 + B_v)\right\}. \quad (17.6.2)$$

Furthermore, the joint full conditional of D and u is not conjugate under this model but is straightforward to derive

$$\begin{aligned} &p(D, u|d, v, \sigma^2_u, \sigma^2_v, \zeta, W) \\ &\quad \propto |\Sigma(f_\psi)|^{-1/2} \exp\{Z'\Sigma(f_\psi)^{-1}Z\} \times |\Sigma_u|^{-1/2} \exp\left\{u'\Sigma_u^{-1}u\right\} \\ &\quad \times I_{(-1/2,\, 1/2)}(D), \end{aligned} \quad (17.6.3)$$

where $Z = (W - \zeta 1_{n'})$, $\Sigma_u = \text{diag}(\sigma^2_{u_1}, \ldots, \sigma^2_{u_{m_S}})$ and $I_{(-1/2,\, 1/2)}(D)$ is the indicator function (i.e., equal to 1 if $D \in (-1/2,\, 1/2)$ and 0 otherwise). Similarly, the joint full conditional of d and v can be expressed as

$$\begin{aligned} &p(d, v|D, u, \sigma^2_u, \sigma^2_v, \zeta, W) \\ &\quad \propto |\Sigma(f_\psi)|^{-1/2} \exp\left\{Z'\Sigma(f_\psi)^{-1}Z\right\} \times |\Sigma_v|^{-1/2} \exp\left\{v'\Sigma_v^{-1}v\right\} \\ &\quad \times I_{(-1/2,\, 1/2)}(d). \end{aligned} \quad (17.6.4)$$

Finally, the full conditional of ζ is given by

$$p(\zeta|d, D, u, v, \sigma^2_u, \sigma^2_v, W) \sim N\left(\bar{\zeta}, \bar{\sigma}^2_\zeta\right), \quad (17.6.5)$$

where $\bar{\zeta} = c_2/c_1$ and $\bar{\sigma}_\zeta^2 = 1/c_1$, with $c_1 = \{1'_{n'}\Sigma^{-1}(f_\psi)1_{n'} + \sigma_\zeta^{-2}\}$ and $c_2 = \{W'\Sigma^{-1}(f_\psi)1_{n'} + \zeta_0\sigma_\zeta^{-2}\}$.

Given the calculated likelihood, implementation of the MCMC requires M-H updates in order to sample from the joint full conditional distributions of (D, u) and (d, v). To summarize, our MCMC algorithm proceeds as follows:

Step 1: Set initial values for all parameter values.

Step 2: For $j = 1, \ldots, m_S$, generate samples from Equation 17.6.1.

Step 3: For $k = 1, \ldots, m_N$, generate samples from Equation 17.6.2.

Step 4: Using a Random-Walk M-H step, jointly sample (D, u) from Equation 17.6.3.

Step 5: Using a Random-Walk M-H step, jointly sample (d, v) from Equation 17.6.4.

Step 6: Generate samples from Equation 17.6.5.

Step 7: Repeat until convergence.

In many cases, it is possible to estimate the parameters of the UC model using maximum likelihood. Under these circumstances, it is advantageous to use the maximum likelihood values for the initial values described in Step 1. In doing so, the MCMC algorithm essentially starts in the stationary distribution or at least close to it.

For implementation of the Random-Walk M-H (RW M-H) algorithm, one needs a candidate generating density. Chib and Greenberg (1995) have several proposals in this regard. However, since d and D both have bounded support, it is beneficial to take a transformation and work with a proposal distribution on the transformed space. Specifically, let $D_\infty = \text{logit}(D + 1/2)$, where $\text{logit}(r) = \log\{r/(1-r)\}$, and let d_∞ be defined analogously. For specificity, let $\mu_S^* = (D_\infty^*, u^*)$ denote the current state for the parameters $\mu_S = (D, u)$; we then draw a candidate value of μ_S^* using a $N(\mu_S, \Sigma_S)$ proposal distribution, where Σ_S is chosen as $\{2.4^2/(m_S + 1)\}C_S$ with C_S equal to the empirical covariance matrix of μ_S determined from a pilot simulation (Gelman et al. 2003). Choosing Σ_S in this manner produces a jumping rule shaped like an estimate of the target distribution and thus produces efficient simulation (i.e., acceptance rates around 25% with adequate mixing).

The algorithm accepts μ_S^* as a new value of μ_S with acceptance probability

$$\alpha_{\mu_S} = \min\left\{1, \frac{p(W|D^*, u^*, d, v, \sigma_u^2, \sigma_v^2, \zeta)p(u^*|\Sigma_u)|J^*|}{p(W|D, u, d, v, \sigma_u^2, \sigma_v^2, \zeta)p(u|\Sigma_u)|J|}\right\},$$

where $|J^*|$ and $|J|$ denote the necessary Jacobians for the transformation described above. Finally, a completely analogous RW M-H step is used to sample from the joint full conditional distribution of (d, v).

17.6.2 Derivation of Signal Extraction Estimator

Only for this section we reserve S for signal and N for noise, whereas in the remainder of this chapter, N is the nonseasonal—the actual signal of interest—and S is the seasonal noise. Our goal is estimation of the signal conditional on the data Y, which has mean vector μ. Suppose that the signal consists of a mean zero stochastic component S plus its mean effect μ^S. This fixed component is typically viewed as a regression component $X\theta$ for deterministic θ, though in the Bayesian framework, θ is just a subset of the full parameter vector ψ and, hence, is random as well. Likewise, the noise component is assumed to consist of stochastic N plus its mean μ^N, and $Y = S + N + \mu^S + \mu^N$, the sum of the signal and noise.

Note that conditional on ψ, the mean effects μ^S and μ^N are the expectations of the signal and noise, respectively. Write $S = \{S_1, S_2, \ldots, S_n\}'$. The MMSE solution to the estimation problem is given by conditional expectations

$$E(S + \mu^S|Y) = \int s \, p_{S+\mu^S|Y}(s) \, ds.$$

This equality is to be understood componentwise, i.e., that $E(S_j + \mu_j^S|Y) = \int s p_{S_j+\mu_j^S|Y}(s) \, ds$ for all $j = 1, 2, \ldots, n$. Integrals are over all the real numbers and $p_{S_j+\mu_j^S|Y}$ denotes the probability density function of $S_j + \mu_j^S$ conditional on Y. Further, this density can be expressed as

$$p_{S_j+\mu_j^S|Y}(s) = \int p_{S_j+\mu_j^S|Y,\Psi}(s) \, p_{\Psi|Y}(\psi) d\psi.$$

Here we represent multiple integration through a single integral sign, for economy of notation. This introduces the posterior for the parameter random vector Ψ, denoted as $p_{\Psi|Y}$. This function is assumed to be already known, being determined during the model estimation phase via usual sampling methods. If we substitute into the expression for the conditional expectation, we obtain

$$E(S_j + \mu_j^S|Y) = \int \int s \, p_{S_j+\mu_j^S|Y,\Psi}(s) \, ds \, p_{\Psi|Y}(\psi) \, d\psi.$$

The expression in the interior is equal to $E(S_j + \mu_j^S|Y, \psi)$, which is given by a simple formula. This is because, conditional on ψ, both S_j and Y are Gaussian, and μ_j^S and μ^N are deterministic. Simple extensions of McElroy (2008) to the case of fixed effects reveal that $E(S + \mu^S|Y, \psi) = F(\psi) \, [Y - \mu] + \mu^S$. That is, we first remove the fixed effects from Y (this is possible since they are known conditional on ψ), then apply the matrix $F(\psi)$, and then add μ^S back in. In some cases, $F(\psi)\mu = \mu^S$ so that we can just apply $F(\psi)$ to Y, but this need not always be the case (see as follows). So the final solution can be expressed as

$$E(S + \mu^S|Y) = \int (\mu^S + F(\psi) \, [Y - \mu]) \, p_{\Psi|Y}(\psi) \, d\psi,$$

interpreted componentwise. One way to approach this computation is to integrate the coefficients of the matrix $F(\psi)$ and the fixed effects. For example, component j can be written as

$$\mathrm{E}(S_j + \mu_j^S|Y) = \int \mu_j^S \, p_{\Psi|Y}(\psi)\, d\psi - \sum_{k=1}^{n} \int F_{jk}(\psi)\mu_k \, p_{\Psi|Y}(\psi)\, d\psi$$
$$+ \sum_{k=1}^{n} \int F_{jk}(\psi) p_{\Psi|Y}(\psi)\, d\psi \, Y_k.$$

So one could take simulations of ψ from its posterior distribution, plug these values into the formula for $F(\psi)$, μ^S, and μ^N, to get $F_{jk}(\psi)$ and the fixed effects for each $j, k = 1, 2, \ldots, n$, and average over the whole chain. This gives the Monte Carlo approximation to the above integrals. When this is finished, we apply the smoothed matrix to Y and add the appropriately smoothed fixed effects.

Application

We now discuss the particular application of the above exposition to the framework of this paper. To avoid confusion, we now let S denote the seasonal and N the nonseasonal once again. Consider the case of seasonal differencing $1 - B^{12}$ for data with no TD or other fixed effects (or assume they have been previously removed). Then the mean effects μ_t naturally break into two portions: a centered periodic effect μ_t^S and a linear trend effect μ_t^N (see Bell 1984a, 1995, and 2004, for discussion). The former is annihilated by $U(B)$, whereas the latter can be written as $\alpha_0 + \alpha_1 t$. Then it follows that $\zeta = 12\alpha_1$; thus when we estimate the mean from the differenced data, it is interpretable as being proportional to the slope in the trend mean effect. With F the signal extraction matrix for the nonseasonal, from Equation 17.3.2 we know that $F\mu^S$ is identically zero (essentially, F contains the $U(B)$ operator). Moreover, letting I_n denote the n-dimensional identity matrix, $I_n - F$ is the seasonal extraction matrix and hence contains a $1 - B$ factor; thus we can write $F\mu^N = \mu^N - (I_n - F)\mu^N = \mu^N - \alpha_1 \cdot H1_n$, where $I_n - F = H\Delta_N$ defines the matrix H. This is true because single differencing on the linear trend reduces it to constancy, represented through the vector $\alpha_1 1_n$. Hence it follows that $\mathrm{E}(N + \mu^N|Y, \psi) = FY + \alpha_1 H 1_n$, which we note does not depend on α_0. Finally, $\mathrm{E}(N + \mu^N|Y) = \int (\alpha_1 H(\psi) 1_n + F(\psi)Y) p_{\Psi|Y}(\psi)\, d\psi$.

Acknowledgments

The authors would like to thank the Editor, William Bell, and two anonymous referees for their useful comments, which helped improve this chapter.

References

Bell, W. (1984a). Seasonal decomposition of deterministic effects. Technical Report, Research Report No. 84/01, Statistical Research Division, U.S. Census Bureau.

Bell, W. (1984b). Signal extraction for nonstationary time series. *The Annals of Statistics*, 12:646–664.

Bell, W. (1995). Correction to seasonal decomposition of deterministic effects. Technical Report, Research Report No. 95/01, Statistical research division, U.S. Census Bureau.

Bell, W. R. (2004). On regcomponent time series models and their applications. In *State Space and Unobserved Component Models: Theory and Applications*, eds. A. Harvey, S. Koopman and N. Shephard. Cambridge: Cambridge University Press.

Beran, J., Bhansali, R. J., and Ocker, D. (1998). On unified model selection for stationary and nonstationary short- and long-memory autoregressive processes. *Biometrika*, 85:921–934.

Bertelli, S. and Caporin, M. (2002). A note on calculating autocovariances of long-memory processes. *Journal of Time Series Analysis*, 23(5):503–508.

Bisognin, C. and Lopes, S. R. C. (2009). Properties of seasonal long memory processes. *Mathematical and Computer Modelling*, 49:1837–1851.

Bloomfield, P. (1973). An exponential model for the spectrum of a scalar time series. *Biometrika*, 60:217–226.

Brockwell, P. J. and Davis, R. A. (1991). *Time Series: Theory and Methods.* New York: Springer-Verlag.

Carlin, J. B. and Dempster, A. P. (1989). Sensitivity analysis of seasonal adjustments: Empirical case studies. *Journal of the American Statistical Association*, 84:6–20.

Chib, S. and Greenberg, E. (1995). Understanding the metropolis-hastings algorithm. *American Statistician*, 49:327–335.

Dagum, E. B. (1980). *The X-11-ARIMA Seasonal Adjustment Method.* Catalogue No. 12–564E, Ottawa: Statistics Canada.

Gelman, A., Carlin, J., Stern, H., and Rubin, D. (2003). *Bayesian Data Analysis*, 2nd edition. Boca Raton: Chapman & Hall.

Granger, C. W. J. and Joyeux, R. (1980). An introduction to long-memory time series models and fractional differencing. *Journal of Time Series Analysis*, 1:15–29.

Harvey, A. C. (1990). *Forecasting, Structural Time Series Models, and the Kalman Filter.* Cambridge, UK: Cambridge University Press.

Hillmer, S. C. and Tiao, G. C. (1982). An ARIMA model-based approach to seasonal adjustment. *Journal of the American Statistical Association*, 77:63–70.

Holan, S., McElroy, T., and Chakraborty, S. (2009). A Bayesian approach to estimating the long memory parameter. *Bayesian Analysis*, 4:159–190.

Holan, S. H., Lund, R., and Davis, G. (2010). The ARMA alphabet soup: A tour of ARMA model variants. *Statistics Surveys*, 4:232–274.

Hosking, J. R. M. (1981). Fractional differencing. *Biometrika*, 68:165–176.

Hsu, N.-J. and Tsai, H. (2009). Semiparametric estimation for seasonal long-memory time series using generalized exponential models. *Journal of Statistical Planning and Inference*, 139(6):1992–2009.

McElroy, T. (2008). Matrix formulas for nonstationary ARIMA signal extraction. *Econometric Theory*, 24:1–22.

McElroy, T. and Gagnon, R. (2008). Finite sample revision variances for ARIMA model-based signal extraction. *Journal of Official Statistics*, 24(3):451.

McElroy, T. and Holan, S. (2011). On the computation of autocovariances for generalized Gegenbauer processes. Technical Report, Research Report No. RRS 2011/06, Center for Statistical Research and Methodology, U.S. Census Bureau.

Palma, W. (2007). *Long-Memory Time Series: Theory and Methods.* Hoboken, New Jersey: Wiley Interscience.

R Development Core Team (2010). *R: A Language and Environment for Statistical Computing.* R Foundation for Statistical Computing, Vienna, Austria. ISBN 3-900051-07-0.

Robinson, P. (2003). *Time Series With Long Memory.* New York: Oxford University Press.

Shiskin, J., Young, A., and Musgrave, J. (1967). The X-11 variant of the Census II Seasonal Adjustment Program. Technical Report, Bureau of the Census, Washington, DC.

Spiegelhalter, D. J., Best, N. G., Carlin, B. P., and van der Linde, A. (2002). Bayesian measures of model complexity and fit (Pkg: P583–639). *Journal of the Royal Statistical Society, Series B: Statistical Methodology*, 64(4): 583–616.

18

Bayesian Stochastic Model Specification Search for Seasonal and Calendar Effects

Tommaso Proietti and Stefano Grassi

CONTENTS

18.1 Introduction

Economic time series are typically available at the monthly frequency of observations. A key feature is the presence of seasonality and calendar effects, which account for much of the variation in the series. Modeling and extracting these components have thus constituted an important problem in the analysis of economic time series; see Zellner (1978, 1983), Nerlove et al. (1979), Hylleberg (1992), Peña et al. (2001), and Ghysels and Osborn (2001); Findley (2005) discusses some recent advances in seasonal adjustment.

Among the specification issues that have been debated by the literature on seasonality and its adjustment, a prominent one deals with characterizing the nature of the seasonal and calendar effects as deterministic or stochastically evolving over time; see, among others, Canova and Hansen (1995), Hylleberg and Pagan (1997), Haywood and Tunnicliffe Wilson (2000), Koop and van

Dijk (2000), Busetti and Harvey (2003), Dagum et al. (1993), Dagum and Quenneville (1993), and Bell and Martin (2004).

This chapter deals with two research areas to which David Findley contributed significantly: model selection and stochastic models of seasonality. We apply a recently proposed Bayesian model selection technique, known as stochastic model specification search (SMSS) (Frühwirth-Schnatter and Wagner 2010) to the problem of characterizing the nature of seasonality and calendar effects in macroeconomic time series. We illustrate that the methodology can be quite successfully applied to discriminate between stochastic and deterministic trends, seasonals, and trading day (TD) effects. In particular, we formulate stochastic models for the components of an economic time series and decide on whether a specific feature of the series, i.e., the underlying level and a seasonal cycle, is fixed or evolve.

The reference model is the unobserved component model known as the basic structural model (Harvey 1989, BSM henceforth), which is presented in Section 18.2. Section 18.3 discusses how SMSS can be applied for the selection of the components of the BSM. This hinges on the representation of the components in noncentered form and a convenient reparameterization of the standard deviation hyperparameters. Section 18.4 discusses the state-space representation of the noncentered model and Markov Chain Monte Carlo (MCMC) inference via Gibbs sampling (GS) for model selection and Bayesian estimation of the hyperparameters and the components. We apply SMSS to a set of monthly U.S. and Italian macroeconomic time series; the results are presented in Section 18.5. We draw our conclusions in Section 18.6.

18.2 Basic Structural Time Series Model

The BSM, proposed by Harvey and Todd (1983) for univariate time series and extended by Harvey (1989), postulates an additive decomposition of the series into a trend, a seasonal, and an irregular component; calendar effects are modeled as regression effects. The name stems from the fact that it provides a satisfactory fit to a wide range of seasonal time series, thereby playing a role analogous to the airline model in an unobserved components framework.

Let y_t denote a time series observed at $t = 1, 2, \ldots, n$; the BSM is formulated as follows:

$$y_t = \mu_t + S_t + C_t + \epsilon_t, \quad t = 1, \ldots, n, \tag{18.2.1}$$

where μ_t is the trend component, S_t is the seasonal component, C_t is the calendar component and, $\epsilon_t \sim \text{NID}(0, \sigma_\epsilon^2)$ is the irregular component.

The trend component has a local linear representation:

$$\begin{aligned} \mu_t &= \mu_{t-1} + q_{t-1} + \eta_t, & \eta_t &\sim \text{NID}(0, \sigma_\eta^2), \quad t = 1, \ldots, n, \\ q_t &= q_{t-1} + \zeta_t, & \zeta_t &\sim \text{NID}(0, \sigma_\zeta^2) \end{aligned} \tag{18.2.2}$$

where q_t is the slope component and we assume that η_t and ζ_t are mutually uncorrelated and independent of ϵ_t and S_t (see Harvey 1989; West and Harrison 1997).

The seasonal component has a trigonometric representation, such that S_t arises from the combination of six stochastic cycles defined at the seasonal frequencies $\lambda_j = 2\pi j/12$, $j = 1, \ldots, 6$, λ_1 representing the fundamental frequency (corresponding to a period of 12 monthly observations) and the remaining being the five harmonics (corresponding to periods of 6 months, i.e., two cycles in a year, 4 months, i.e., three cycles in a year, 3 months, i.e., four cycles in a year, 2.4, i.e., five cycles in a year, and 2 months)

$$S_t = \sum_{j=1}^{6} S_{jt}, \qquad \begin{bmatrix} S_{jt} \\ S^*_{jt} \end{bmatrix} = \begin{bmatrix} \cos\lambda_j & \sin\lambda_j \\ -\sin\lambda_j & \cos\lambda_j \end{bmatrix} \begin{bmatrix} S_{j,t-1} \\ S^*_{j,t-1} \end{bmatrix} + \begin{bmatrix} \varpi_{j,t} \\ \varpi^*_{j,t} \end{bmatrix}, \quad j = 1, \ldots, 5, \tag{18.2.3}$$

and $S_{6,t} = -S_{6,t-1} + \varpi_{6t}$. The disturbances ϖ_{jt} and ϖ^*_{jt} are normally and independently distributed with common variance σ^2_ω for $j = 1, \ldots, 5$, whereas $\mathrm{Var}(\varpi_{6t}) = 0.5\sigma^2_\omega$. While S_{jt} is interpreted as the jth seasonal cycle, the latent component S^*_{jt} is instrumental to casting the model in Markovian form. Alternatively, the variance of the seasonal disturbances can be allowed to vary with the frequency, i.e., $\varpi_{jt} \sim \mathrm{NID}(0, \sigma^2_j)$, $j = 1, \ldots, 6$, $\varpi^*_{jt} \sim \mathrm{NID}(0, \sigma^2_j)$, $j = 1, \ldots, 5$.

In the sequel, we will adopt an equivalent alternative representation for the seasonal component due to Hannan (1964), see also Hannan et al. (1970), known as the evolving seasonal model

$$\begin{aligned} S_t &= \sum_{j=1}^{5} (a_{jt}\cos\lambda_j t + b_{jt}\sin\lambda_j t) + a_{6t}\cos\pi t \\ a_{jt} &= a_{j,t-1} + \omega_{jt}, \quad \omega_{jt} \sim \mathrm{NID}(0, \sigma^2_j) \\ b_{jt} &= b_{j,t-1} + \omega^*_{jt}, \quad \omega^*_{jt} \sim \mathrm{NID}(0, \sigma^2_j) \end{aligned}, \tag{18.2.4}$$

and $E(\omega_{jt}\omega^*_{jt}) = 0$. This particular form can easily be represented in the non-centered form (see Section 18.3).

By trigonometric identities, it is possible to prove that there is a one-to-one mapping between the two representations; in particular,

$$\begin{bmatrix} a_{jt} \\ b_{jt} \end{bmatrix} = \begin{bmatrix} \cos\lambda_j t & -\sin\lambda_j t \\ \sin\lambda_j t & \cos\lambda_j t \end{bmatrix} \begin{bmatrix} S_{jt} \\ S^*_{jt} \end{bmatrix};$$

$$\begin{bmatrix} \omega_{jt} \\ \omega^*_{jt} \end{bmatrix} = \begin{bmatrix} \cos\lambda_j t & -\sin\lambda_j t \\ \sin\lambda_j t & \cos\lambda_j t \end{bmatrix} \begin{bmatrix} \varpi_{jt} \\ \varpi^*_{jt} \end{bmatrix}.$$

The random coefficients a_{jt} and b_{jt} are related to the amplitude of the jth seasonal cycle as S_{jt} can be rewritten: $S_{jt} = \varphi_t \cos(\lambda_j t - \vartheta_t)$, where

$\varphi_t = \sqrt{a_{jt}^2 + b_{jt}^2}$ is the time-varying amplitude and $\vartheta_t = \tan^{-1}(b_{jt}/a_{jt})$ is the phase shift.

Calendar effects are due to the differential effects of TDs and to moving festivals; see Cleveland and Devlin (1982). The former are modeled as $\text{TD}_t = \sum_k \phi_k x_{kt}$, where x_{kt} are deterministic regressors defined as follows: letting D_{jt} denote the number of days of type j, $j = 1, \ldots, 7$, occurring in month t, then $x_{kt} = D_{jt} - D_{7t}, k = 1, \ldots, 6$. The regressors are the differential number of days of type j, $j = 1 \ldots, 6$, compared to the number of Sundays, to which type 7 is conventionally assigned (see Bell and Hillmer 1983). If the effect of weekdays is the same, and Saturdays and Sundays are also the same, the TD component is captured by a single explanatory variable, i.e., $x_t = D_{1t} - 5D_{2t}/2$, where D_{1t} is the number of weekdays in the month and D_{2t} is the number of Saturdays and Sundays.

As far as moving festivals are concerned, we consider Easter and Labor Day (U.S. time series); their effects are modeled in terms of the proportion of seven days before Easter or Labor Day that fall in month t and subtracting their monthly long run average, computed over the first 400 years of the Gregorian calendar (1583–1982).

A time-varying TD component can be modeled by letting the coefficients ϕ_k evolve over time: $\text{TD}_t = \sum_{k=1}^{6} \phi_{kt} x_{kt}$, where x_{kt} were defined above and ϕ_{kt} are independent Gaussian random walks with common disturbance variance, $\phi_{kt} = \phi_{k,t-1} + \nu_{kt}, \nu_{kt} \sim \text{NID}(0, \sigma_\nu^2)$. Bell and Martin (2004) used this time-varying TD model with different disturbance variances.

18.3 Bayesian Stochastic Specification Search for the Bayesian Stochastic Model

This section illustrates how the SMSS proposed by Frühwirth-Schnatter and Wagner (2010, FS-W henceforth) can be applied for the selection of the components of the BSM. The different specifications for the trend and the seasonal components are nested inside a more general state-space model and are obtained by imposing exclusion restrictions, so that discriminating between deterministic and stochastic components amounts to performing variable selection within the regression framework considered by George and McCulloch (1993).

The SMSS methodology proposed by FS-W hinges on two basic ingredients: the first is the reparameterization of the unobserved components μ_t, S_t, and C_t, in noncentered form, with respect to location and scale (see also Gelfand et al. 1995, Frühwirth-Schnatter 2004, Strickland et al. 2007). The second is the reparameterization of the hyperparameters representing standard deviations as regression parameters with unrestricted support. The choice of the prior and the conditional independence structure of the reparameterized model enable the definition of a very efficient MCMC estimation strategy based on GS.

18.3.1 Noncentered Representation of the Random Components

The noncentered representation of the trend component is obtained as follows. Denoting by μ_0 and q_0 the initial values of the level and slope components, the trend (18.2.2) can be reparameterized as follows:

$$\begin{aligned} &\mu_t = \mu_0 + q_0 t + \sigma_\eta \tilde{\mu}_t + \sigma_\zeta \tilde{A}_t, && t = 1, \ldots, n, \\ &\tilde{\mu}_t = \tilde{\mu}_{t-1} + \tilde{\eta}_t, && \tilde{\eta}_t \sim \text{NID}(0,1), \\ &\tilde{A}_t = \tilde{A}_{t-1} + \tilde{q}_{t-1}, && \tilde{q}_t = \tilde{q}_{t-1} + \tilde{\zeta}_t, \tilde{\zeta}_t \sim \text{NID}(0,1), \end{aligned} \tag{18.3.1}$$

so that $\tilde{\mu}_0 = \tilde{A}_0 = \tilde{q}_0 = 0$ and $\tilde{\zeta}_t = \zeta_{t-1}/\sigma_\zeta$. Thus, in the noncentered representation, the mean function is explicitly written as a linear function of time and the stochastic part is the combination of a random walk and an integrated random walk, both starting off at the origin and driven by standardized independent disturbances.

The noncentered representation of the jth seasonal cycle is obtained as follows. Denoting by a_{j0} and b_{j0} the initial values of the coefficients,

$$\begin{aligned} S_{jt} &= a_{j0} \cos \lambda_j t + b_{j0} \sin \lambda_j t \\ &\quad + \sigma_j \left(\tilde{a}_{jt} \cos \lambda_j t + \tilde{b}_{jt} \sin \lambda_j t \right), && j = 1, \ldots, 5 \\ S_{6t} &= a_{j0}(-1)^t + \sigma_6 \tilde{a}_{6t}(-1)^t \\ \tilde{a}_{jt} &= \tilde{a}_{j,t-1} + \tilde{\omega}_{jt}, && \tilde{\omega}_{jt} \sim \text{NID}(0,1), \\ \tilde{b}_{jt} &= \tilde{b}_{j,t-1} + \tilde{\omega}^*_{jt}, && \tilde{\omega}^*_{jt} \sim \text{NID}(0,1). \end{aligned} \tag{18.3.2}$$

Hence, the noncentered representation of the seasonal component is obtained as $S_t = \sum_{j=1}^{6} S_{jt}$, with S_{jt} given as in Equation 18.3.2.

Alternatively, the noncentered representation of the jth seasonal cycle can be defined as

$$\begin{aligned} S_{jt} &= a_{j0} \cos \lambda_j t + b_{j0} \sin \lambda_j t + \sigma_j \tilde{S}_{jt}, && j = 1, \ldots, 5 \\ \tilde{S}_{jt} &= \cos \lambda_j \tilde{S}_{j,t-1} + \sin \lambda_j \tilde{S}^*_{j,t-1} + \tilde{\varpi}_{jt}, && \tilde{\varpi}_{jt} \sim \text{NID}(0,1), \\ \tilde{S}^*_{jt} &= -\sin \lambda_j \tilde{S}_{j,t-1} + \cos \lambda_j \tilde{S}^*_{j,t-1} + \tilde{\varpi}^*_t, && \tilde{\varpi}^*_{jt} \sim \text{NID}(0,1). \\ S_{6t} &= a_{j0}(-1)^t + \sigma_6 \tilde{S}_{6t}, \\ \tilde{S}_{6t} &= -\tilde{S}_{6,t-1} + \tilde{\varpi}_{6t}, && \tilde{\varpi}_{6t} \sim \text{NID}(0,1). \end{aligned} \tag{18.3.3}$$

The noncentered representation of the TDs component is

$$\begin{aligned} \text{TD}_t &= \sum_{k=1}^{6} \phi_{k0} x_{kt} + \sigma_\nu \left(\sum_{k=1}^{6} \tilde{\phi}_{kt} x_{kt} \right) \\ \tilde{\phi}_{kt} &= \tilde{\phi}_{k,t-1} + \tilde{\nu}_t, && \tilde{\nu}_t \sim \text{NID}(0,1). \end{aligned} \tag{18.3.4}$$

18.3.2 Reparameterization of the Bayesian Stochastic Model

The noncentered representation is useful not only for the efficiency of Bayesian estimation by MCMC methods (in particular, when e.g., σ_η^2 is small in comparison to σ_ϵ^2), but also since it paves the way to performing model selection in a regression framework via the stochastic search variable selection (SSVS) approach proposed by George and McCulloch (1993).

The noncentered representation of the components is identified up to sign switches that operate on both the standard deviations and on the underlying stochastic components. For instance, the trend component with $(-\sigma_\eta)(-\tilde{\mu}_t)$ replacing $\sigma_\eta\tilde{\mu}_t$ in Equation 18.3.1 is observationally equivalent, i.e., it has the same likelihood. The same can be said of the pairs $(-\sigma_\zeta)(-\tilde{A}_t)$ and $(\sigma_\zeta)(\tilde{A}_t)$, $(-\sigma_j)\{-(\tilde{a}_{jt}\cos\lambda_j t + \tilde{b}_{jt}\sin\lambda_j t)\}$, and $\sigma_j(\tilde{a}_{jt}\cos\lambda_j t + \tilde{b}_{jt}\sin\lambda_j t)$, and so forth. As a consequence, the likelihood function is symmetric around zero along the σ_η, σ_ζ, σ_j, and σ_ν dimensions and multimodal, if the true standard deviations are larger than zero. This fact can be exploited to quantify how far the posterior of σ_η, $\sigma_\zeta, \sigma_j, j = 1, \ldots, 6$, and σ_ν, is removed from zero.

As a matter of fact, defining independent Bernoulli random variables with success probability 0.5, $\mathsf{B}_\mu, \mathsf{B}_A, \mathsf{B}_{sj}, j = 1, \ldots, 6, \mathsf{B}_{\mathrm{TD}}$, we can equivalently write $\sigma_\eta\tilde{\mu}_t = \beta_\mu\mu_t^*$, where $\beta_\mu = (-1)^{\mathsf{B}_\mu}\sigma_\eta$, and $\mu_t^* = (-1)^{\mathsf{B}_\mu}\tilde{\mu}_t$,; similarly, $\sigma_\zeta\tilde{A}_t = \beta_A A_t^*$, where $\beta_A = (-1)^{\mathsf{B}_A}\sigma_\zeta$, $A_t^* = (-1)^{\mathsf{B}_A}\tilde{A}_t$,

$$\sigma_j\left(\tilde{a}_{jt}\cos\lambda_j t + \tilde{b}_{jt}\sin\lambda_j t\right)$$
$$= \beta_{sj}U_{jt}^*, \quad \beta_{sj} = (-1)^{\mathsf{B}_{sj}}\sigma_j, U_{jt}^* = (-1)^{\mathsf{B}_{sj}}\left(\tilde{a}_{jt}\cos\lambda_j t + \tilde{b}_{jt}\sin\lambda_j t\right),$$

for $j = 1, \ldots, 6$, and

$$\sigma_\nu\left(\sum_k \phi_{kt}x_{kt}\right) = \beta_{\mathrm{TD}}\Phi_t^*, \quad \beta_{\mathrm{TD}} = (-1)^{\mathsf{B}_{\mathrm{TD}}}\sigma_\nu, \Phi_t^* = (-1)^{\mathsf{B}_{\mathrm{TD}}}\left(\sum_k \phi_{kt}x_{kt}\right).$$

Substituting into the expressions for the components yields

$$y_t = \mu_t + S_t + C_t + \epsilon_t, \qquad \epsilon_t \sim \mathrm{NID}(0, \sigma_\epsilon^2),$$

$$\begin{aligned}
\mu_t &= \mu_0 + q_0 t + \beta_\mu\mu_t^* + \beta_A A_t^*, \\
\mu_t^* &= \mu_{t-1}^* + \tilde{\eta}_t, & \tilde{\eta}_t &\sim \mathrm{NID}(0,1), \\
A_t^* &= A_{t-1}^* + \tilde{q}_{t-1}, \\
\tilde{q}_t &= \tilde{q}_{t-1} + \tilde{\zeta}_t, & \tilde{\zeta}_t &\sim \mathrm{NID}(0,1),
\end{aligned}$$

$$S_t = \sum_{j=1}^{5}(a_{j0}\cos\lambda_j t + b_{j0}\sin\lambda_j t) + a_{60}(-1)^t + \sum_{j=1}^{6}\beta_{sj}U_{jt}^*,$$
$$U_{jt}^* = A_{jt}^*\cos\lambda_j t + B_{jt}^*\sin\lambda_j t, \;\; j = 1, \ldots, 5, \quad U_{6t}^* = A_{6t}^*\cos\pi t,$$

$$A_{jt}^* = A_{j,t-1}^* + \tilde{\omega}_{jt}, \quad \tilde{\omega}_{jt} \sim \mathrm{NID}(0,1),$$
$$B_{jt}^* = B_{j,t-1}^* + \tilde{\omega}_{jt}^*, \quad \tilde{\omega}_{jt}^* \sim \mathrm{NID}(0,1),$$
$$C_t = \sum_{k=1}^{6} \phi_{k0} x_{kt} + \beta_{\mathrm{TD}} \left(\sum_{k=1}^{6} \Phi_{kt}^* x_{kt} \right) + \phi_E x_{Et},$$
$$\Phi_{kt}^* = \Phi_{k,t-1}^* + \tilde{\nu}_t, \quad \tilde{\nu}_t \sim \mathrm{NID}(0,1). \tag{18.3.5}$$

where we have posited $A_{jt}^* = (-1)^{\mathsf{B}_{sj}} \tilde{a}_{jt}$, $B_{jt}^* = (-1)^{\mathsf{B}_{sj}} \tilde{B}_{jt}$, $\Phi_{kt}^* = (-1)^{\mathsf{B}_{\mathrm{TD}}} \phi_{kt}^*$.

By this reparameterization, a standard deviation is transformed into a regression coefficient and SSVS can be applied. Hence, the selection of a randomly evolving component is related to the inclusion of a particular regressor.

In principle, we could conduct variable selection for any of the explanatory variables; however, for the computational feasibility of the stochastic search, we consider specifications that always include as explanatory variables the constant term, the set of 11 sine and cosine terms at the seasonal frequencies, the six TD regressors, and the moving festivals regressors, so that the most elementary model is a model with a constant level, deterministic seasonals, and fixed calendar effects. Variable selection is carried out on the slope term $a_0 t$, on the random walk and integrated random walk components μ_t^*, A_t^*, on the six stochastic terms U_{jt}^*, and on $\left(\sum_{k=1}^{6} \Phi_{kt}^* x_{kt}\right)$.

We now introduce nine binary indicator variables $\gamma_\mu, \gamma_A, \gamma_{sj}, j = 1, \ldots, 6$, γ_{TD}, taking value 1 if the random effects $\mu_t^*, A_t^*, U_{jt}, j = 1, \ldots, 6, \left(\sum_{k=1}^{6} \Phi_{kt}^* x_{kt}\right)$ are present and 0 otherwise, along with a binary indicator for the linear trend component, δ, taking values (0,1) according to whether the term $a_0 t$ is included in the model. The 10 indicators can be further collected in the multinomial vector $\Upsilon = (\gamma_\mu, \gamma_A, \gamma_{sj}, j = 1, \ldots, 6, \gamma_{\mathrm{TD}}, \delta)$.

Hence, there are $K = 2^{10} = 1024$ possible models in competition. These are nested in the specification

$$\begin{aligned} y_t = \mu_0 + \delta q_0 t + \gamma_\mu \beta_\mu \mu_t^* + \gamma_A \beta_A A_t^* + \sum_{j=1}^{5} (a_{j0} \cos \lambda_j t + b_{j0} \sin \lambda_j t) \\ + a_{60}(-1)^t + \sum_{j=1}^{6} \gamma_{sj} \beta_{sj} U_{jt}^* + \sum_{k=1}^{6} \phi_{k0} x_{kt} \\ + \gamma_{\mathrm{TD}} \beta_{\mathrm{TD}} \left(\sum_{k=1}^{6} \Phi_{kt}^* x_{kt} \right) + \phi_E x_{Et} + \epsilon_t, \end{aligned}$$

The different models will be labeled by

$$M_k, \quad k = 1 + \sum_{u=1}^{U} 2^{U-u} \Upsilon_u,$$

where Υ_u is the uth element of the vector Υ, $u = 1, \ldots, U$.

18.3.3 Restricted Bayesian Stochastic Model with a Single Variance Parameter and Model Reparameterization

Deciding whether a single variance parameter should be used instead of six for the seasonal component is one of the most important specification issues in formulating a seasonal model.

The trigonometric seasonal model with a single variance parameter is nested within the model for S_t in Equation 18.3.5, as it arises when $\sigma_j = \sigma_\omega, j = 1, \ldots, 5$, and $\sigma_6 = 2^{-1/2}\sigma_\omega$. Under these restrictions, the noncentered representation for the seasonal component becomes

$$\begin{aligned}
S_t &= \sum_{j=1}^{5}(a_{j0}\cos\lambda_j t + b_{j0}\sin\lambda_j t) + a_{60}(-1)^t + \sigma_\omega U_t \\
U_t &= \sum_{j=1}^{5}\left(\tilde{a}_{jt}\cos\lambda_j t + \tilde{b}_{jt}\sin\lambda_j t\right) + 2^{-1/2}\tilde{a}_{6t}(-1)^t \\
\tilde{a}_{jt} &= \tilde{a}_{j,t-1} + \tilde{\omega}_{jt}, \qquad \tilde{\omega}_{jt} \sim \text{NID}(0,1), \\
\tilde{b}_{jt} &= \tilde{b}_{j,t-1} + \tilde{\omega}^*_{jt}, \qquad \tilde{\omega}^*_{jt} \sim \text{NID}(0,1).
\end{aligned} \tag{18.3.6}$$

where U_t is a single explanatory variable resulting from combining six noncentered orthogonal stochastic cycles.

More generally, this model can be nested within the more general specification that we have considered in the previous section, by decomposing the frequency specific variance parameters as follows:

$$\sigma_j = \sigma_\omega + (\sigma_j - \sigma_\omega), j = 1, \ldots, 5, \quad \sigma_6 = 2^{-1/2}\sigma_\omega + (\sigma_6 - 2^{-1/2}\sigma_\omega),$$

where

$$\sigma_\omega = \frac{\sum_{j=1}^{5}\sigma_j + \sqrt{2}\sigma_6}{5 + \sqrt{2}}$$

is a weighted average of the individual parameters. Further, we denote by $\sigma^*_j = \sigma_j - \sigma_\omega, j = 1, \ldots, 5, \sigma^*_6 = (\sigma_6 - 2^{-1/2}\sigma_\omega)$, the deviations from the mean. These coefficients are such that $\sum_{j=1}^{5}\sigma^*_j + \sqrt{2}\sigma^*_6 = 0$, and thus we can express the last coefficient σ^*_6 as a linear combination of the others, namely,

$$\sigma^*_6 = -2^{-1/2}\sum_{j=1}^{5}\sigma^*_j.$$

Replacing in Equation 18.3.3, we can reparameterize the seasonal component as follows:

$$\begin{aligned}
S_t &= \sum_{j=1}^{5}(a_{j0}\cos\lambda_j t + b_{j0}\sin\lambda_j t) + a_{60}(-1)^t + \sigma_\omega U_t + \sum_{j=1}^{5}\sigma^*_j U^\dagger_{jt} \\
U_t &= \sum_{j=1}^{5}\left(\tilde{a}_{jt}\cos\lambda_j t + \tilde{b}_{jt}\sin\lambda_j t\right) + 2^{-1/2}\tilde{a}_{6t}(-1)^t \\
U^\dagger_{jt} &= \tilde{a}_{jt}\cos\lambda_j t + \tilde{b}_{jt}\sin\lambda_j t - 2^{-1/2}\tilde{a}_{6t}(-1)^t.
\end{aligned} \tag{18.3.7}$$

Hence, the reparameterized noncentered form of the model features six random regressors, the first being a weighted average and the remaining five representing weighted contrasts between the j-th and the last noncentered stochastic cycles. If the restrictions were to hold, the coefficients σ_j^* would equal zero and the model reduces to Equation 18.3.6.

This treatment shows that deciding this specification issue can be considered as a model selection issue. Again, defining a suitable set of coefficients $\beta_s = \sigma_\omega(-1)^{\mathsf{B}_s}$ $\beta_{sj}^* = \sigma_j^*(-1)^{\mathsf{B}_{sj}}, j = 1, \ldots, 5$, where $\mathsf{B}_s, \mathsf{B}_{sj}$ are IID Bernoulli random variables, and indicators $\gamma_s, \gamma_{sj}^{\dagger}, j = 1, \ldots, 5,$, taking value 1 if the random effects $\tilde{U}_t = (-1)^{\mathsf{B}_s} U_t, \tilde{U}_{jt} = (-1)^{\mathsf{B}_{sj}} U_{jt}^{\dagger}, j = 1, \ldots, 5$, are present and 0 otherwise, we can write the 2^{10} possible models arising from the reparameterization as follows:

$$\begin{aligned} y_t = \mu_0 + \delta q_0 t + \gamma_\mu \beta_\mu \mu_t^* + \gamma_A \beta_A A_t^* + \sum_{j=1}^{5} (a_{j0} \cos \lambda_j t + b_{j0} \sin \lambda_j t) \\ + a_{60}(-1)^t + \gamma_s \beta_s \tilde{U}_t + \sum_{j=1}^{5} \gamma_{sj}^{\dagger} \beta_{sj}^* \tilde{U}_{jt}^* + \sum_{k=1}^{6} \phi_{k0} x_{kt} \\ + \gamma_{\mathrm{TD}} \beta_{\mathrm{TD}} \left(\sum_{k=1}^{6} \Phi_{kt}^* x_{kt} \right) + \phi_E x_{Et} + \epsilon_t. \end{aligned} \tag{18.3.8}$$

When the single variance parameter restriction is enforced ($\beta_{sj}^* = 0, j = 1, \ldots 5,$), the number of possible models reduces to $2^5 = 32$. For instance, model M_{32} has $\gamma_\mu = \gamma_A = \gamma_s = \gamma_{\mathrm{TD}} = \delta = 1$, which corresponds to the unrestricted local linear trend model with stochastic levels and slopes, stochastic seasonality with a single variance parameter, and time-varying TD effects.

18.4 Statistical Treatment

Depending on the value of Υ, the models nested in Equation 18.3.6 admit the following state-space representation

$$\begin{aligned} y_t &= x_{\delta,t}' \rho_\delta + z_{\gamma,t}' \alpha_{\gamma,t} + \epsilon_t, \quad \epsilon_t \sim \mathrm{NID}(0, \sigma_\epsilon^2), \quad t = 1, \ldots, n, \\ \alpha_{\gamma,t} &= T_\gamma \alpha_{\gamma,t-1} + R_\gamma u_{\gamma,t}, \quad u_{\gamma,t} \sim \mathrm{NID}(0, I), \end{aligned} \tag{18.4.1}$$

where $\alpha_{\gamma,0} = 0$, and

$$\begin{aligned} x_{\delta,t} &= (1, \delta t, \cos \lambda_1 t, \sin \lambda_1 t, \ldots, \cos \pi t, x_{1t}, \ldots, x_{6t}, x_{Et})' \\ \rho_\delta &= (\mu_0, q_0, a_{10}, b_{10}, \ldots, a_{60}, \phi_1, \ldots, \phi_6, \phi_E)', \\ z_{\gamma,t} &= (\gamma_\mu \beta_\mu, \gamma_A \beta_A, 0, \gamma_{s1} \beta_{s1} \cos \lambda_1 t, \gamma_{s1} \beta_{s1} \sin \lambda_1 t, \ldots, \\ &\quad \gamma_{s6} \beta_{s6} \cos \pi t, \gamma_{\mathrm{TD}} \beta_{\mathrm{TD}} x_{1t}, \ldots, \gamma_{\mathrm{TD}} \beta_{\mathrm{TD}} x_{6t})', \end{aligned}$$

$$\alpha_{\gamma,t} = (\mu_t^*, A_t^*, \tilde{q}_t, A_{1t}^*, B_{1t}^*, \ldots, A_{6t}^*, \Phi_{1t}^*, \ldots, \Phi_{6t}^*),$$

$$T_\gamma = \begin{pmatrix} 1 & 0 & 0 & 0 \\ 0 & 1 & 1 & 0 \\ 0 & 0 & 1 & 0 \\ 0 & 0 & 0 & I_{12} \end{pmatrix} \qquad R_\gamma = \begin{pmatrix} 1 & 0 & 0 \\ 0 & 0 & 0 \\ 0 & 1 & 0 \\ 0 & 0 & I_{12} \end{pmatrix}.$$

We will assume that the models $M_k, k = 1, \ldots, K$, are equally likely *a priori*, i.e., $p(M_k) \propto 1$, or equivalently $p(\Upsilon) = 2^{-U}$, where $p(\cdot)$ denotes the density or the probability function of the argument.

As far as model selection is concerned, it would be prohibitively expensive to compute the posterior model probabilities for each of the 2^U models and select the specification that has the largest marginal likelihood. The evaluation of the marginal likelihood for each model is computationally intensive and the accuracy may be poor (see the discussion in FS-W and the references therein). Rather than computing the posterior probabilities of all the possible models, it is computationally more attractive to simulate samples from their posterior distribution by MCMC methods. In particular, exploiting the conditional independence structure of the model, and given the availability of the full conditional posterior distribution of Υ in closed form, the multinomial vector Υ is sampled along with the model parameters by using a GS scheme and a stochastic search of the most likely explanation of the observed time series is sought. After the GS scheme has converged, model selection (and averaging, if one wishes) can be based on $p(\Upsilon|y)$, as estimated by the proportion of times a particular specification was drawn.

18.4.1 Prior Specification

Let y denote the collection of time series values $\{y_t, t = 1, \ldots, n\}$ and α denote that of the latent states $\{\alpha_{\gamma,t}, t = 0, 1, \ldots, n\}$; also let ψ_Υ collect the appropriate subset of the parameters $(\mu_0, q_0, a_{10}, b_{10}, \ldots, a_{60}, \phi_{10}, \ldots, \phi_{60}, \beta_\mu, \beta_A, \beta_{s1}, \ldots, \beta_{s6}, \beta_{\mathrm{TD}})$ that enter the model for a particular value of Υ.

The prior assumes a conditional independence structure between each block of variables, such that:

$$p(\Upsilon, \psi, \sigma_\epsilon^2, \alpha) = p(\Upsilon)p(\sigma_\epsilon^2)p(\psi|\Upsilon, \sigma_\epsilon^2)p(\alpha|\Upsilon).$$

As stated before, the prior distribution over the model space is uniform, that is $p(\Upsilon) = 2^{-U}$.

For the irregular variance, a hierarchical inverse Gamma prior (IG) is adopted, $\sigma_\epsilon^2 \sim IG(c_0, C_0)$, where $C_0 \sim Ga(g_0, G_0)$, $Ga(\cdot)$ denoting the Gamma distribution, $c_0 = 2.5$, $g_0 = 5$, and $G_0 = g_0/[0.75\mathrm{Var}(y_t)(c_0 - 1)]$, as in FS-W. The hierarchical prior makes the posterior distributions less sensitive to the choice of the hyperparameters of the IG distribution; it obviously requires an additional sampling step where C_0 is sampled conditional on σ_ϵ^2 from the conditional Gamma posterior $C_0|\sigma_\epsilon^2 \sim Ga(g_0 + c_0, G_0 + 1/\sigma_\epsilon^2)$ at each sweep of the sample.

For the parameter vector ψ_Υ, if we denote its generic element by $\psi_{\Upsilon i}$, $p(\psi_\Upsilon|\Upsilon,\sigma_\epsilon^2) = \prod_i p(\psi_i|\sigma_\epsilon^2)$, where all the priors are conjugate; for instance, $\beta_\mu|\sigma_\epsilon^2 \sim N(0,\kappa_\mu\sigma_\epsilon^2)$, $\beta_A|\sigma_\epsilon^2 \sim N(0,\kappa_A\sigma_\epsilon^2)$, $q_0|\sigma_\epsilon^2 \sim N(0,d_0\sigma_\epsilon^2)$, etc. For the constant term and the coefficients $a_{j0}, j = 1,\ldots,6, b_{j0}, j = 1,\ldots,5, \phi_{k0}, k = 1,\ldots,6$, we adopt the uninformative priors, e.g., $p(\mu_0|\sigma_\epsilon^2) \propto 1$.

A distinctive feature of the stochastic specification search methodology proposed by Frühwirth-Schnatter and Wagner (2010) is the adoption of Gaussian priors, centered at zero, for the parameters $\beta_\mu, \beta_A, \beta_{sj}$, and β_{TD}. Not only does this allow conjugate analysis, but FS-W show that inference will benefit substantially from the use of a normal prior, e.g., $\beta_\mu = \pm\sigma_\eta$, $\beta_\mu|\sigma_\epsilon^2 \sim N(0,\kappa_\mu\sigma_\epsilon^2)$, in lieu of the usual inverse Gamma prior for the variance parameter σ_η^2. In fact, a major problem arising when the IG prior is used is the high sensitivity of the posterior distribution of the variance parameters to the hyperparameters of the IG distribution, when the true variance is close to zero; as a result, the MCMC draws will mix very slowly or even lack convergence. On the contrary, the posterior distribution of the β coefficients is not too sensitive to the choice of the prior variance and Monte Carlo inference is much more efficient.

Notice that $\beta_\mu|\sigma_\eta, \gamma_\mu = 1$ is a random variable, which takes the values $-\sigma_\eta$ and σ_η with probabilities both equal to 1/2 so that a Gaussian prior centered at zero is reasonable; furthermore, this choice amounts to specifying a hierarchical mixture prior to the parameter β_μ, of the form $p(\beta_\mu) = (1-\gamma_1)I_0 + \gamma_1 N(0,\kappa\sigma_\epsilon^2)$, where I_0 is a degenerate density with point mass at zero; see Smith and Kohn (1996). As pointed out in George and McCulloch (1997), this prior entails that a stochastic trend will be included if β_μ can be distinguished from zero irrespective of its absolute size. Finally, the prior for α is provided by the Gaussian dynamic model (18.4.1), so that,

$$p(\alpha) = p(\alpha_{\gamma 0}) \prod_{t=1}^{n} p(\alpha_{\gamma t}|\alpha_{\gamma,t-1}),$$

with $\alpha_{\gamma t}|\alpha_{\gamma,t-1} \sim N(T_\gamma\alpha_{\gamma,t-1}, R_\gamma R_\gamma')$ and $\alpha_{\gamma,0} = 0$.

18.4.2 Markov Chain Monte Carlo Estimation

Model selection requires the evaluation of the posterior probability function of the multinomial vector Υ, denoted as $p(\Upsilon|y)$. Also, for the selected model, we are interested in the marginal posterior distributions of the parameters $p(\psi|y)$ and the states $p(\alpha|y)$. The required posteriors are not available in closed form, but we are capable of drawing samples from them by MCMC methods and, in particular, by a GS scheme that we now are going to discuss in some detail. The GS scheme produces correlated random draws from the posteriors by repeatedly sampling an ergodic Markov chain whose invariant distribution is the target density; see Robert and Casella (2004), and Gamerman and Lopes (2007). In essence, it defines a homogeneous Markov chain such that the transition kernel is formed by the full conditional distributions and the invariant distribution is the unavailable target density.

The GS scheme can be sketched as follows. Specify a set of initial values $\Upsilon^{(0)}, \sigma_\epsilon^{2(0)}, \alpha^{(0)}$, and $\psi^{(0)}$. For $i = 1, 2, \ldots, M$, iterate the following operations:

(a) Draw $\Upsilon^{(i)} \sim p(\Upsilon|\alpha^{(i-1)}, y)$

(b) Draw $\sigma_\epsilon^{2(i)} \sim p(\sigma_\epsilon^2|\Upsilon^{(i)}, \psi^{(i-1)}, \alpha^{(i-1)}, y)$

(c) Draw $\psi^{(i)} \sim p(\psi|\Upsilon^{(i)}, \sigma_\epsilon^{2(i)}, \alpha^{(i-1)}, y)$

(d) Draw $\alpha^{(i)} \sim p(\alpha|\Upsilon^{(i)}, \sigma_\epsilon^{2(i)}, \psi^{(i)}, y)$

The above complete conditional densities are available, up to a normalizing constant, from the form of the likelihood and the prior.

For the sake of notation, let us write the regression model as $y = Z_\Upsilon \psi_\Upsilon + \epsilon$, where y and ϵ are vectors stacking the values $\{y_t\}$ and $\{\epsilon_t\}$, respectively, and the generic row of matrix Z_Υ contains the relevant subset of the explanatory variables.

Step (a) is carried out by sampling the indicators with probabilities proportional to the conditional likelihood of the regression model, as

$$\begin{aligned} p(\Upsilon|\alpha, y) &\propto p(\Upsilon)p(y|\Upsilon, \alpha) \\ &\propto p(y|\Upsilon, \alpha), \end{aligned}$$

which is available in closed form (see the following).

Under the normal-inverse Gamma conjugate prior for $(\psi_\Upsilon, \sigma_\epsilon^2)$

$$\sigma_\epsilon^2 \sim IG(c_0, C_0), \quad \psi_\Upsilon|\sigma_\epsilon^2 \sim N(0, \sigma_\epsilon^2 D_\Upsilon),$$

where D_Υ is a diagonal matrix with elements κ_μ, κ_A, etc., steps (b) and (c) are carried out by sampling from the posteriors

$$\begin{aligned} \sigma_\epsilon^2|\Upsilon, \alpha, y &\sim IG(c_{T*}, C_{T*}) \\ \psi_\Upsilon|\Upsilon, \sigma_\epsilon^2, \alpha, y &\sim N(m, \sigma_\epsilon^2 S) \end{aligned}$$

where

$$\begin{aligned} S &= \left(Z'_\Upsilon Z_\Upsilon + D_\Upsilon^{-1}\right)^{-1}, & m &= S Z'_\Upsilon y \\ c_{T*} &= c_0 + T^*/2, & C_{T*} &= C_0 + \tfrac{1}{2}\left(y'y - m'S^{-1}m\right). \end{aligned}$$

Finally,

$$p(y|\Upsilon, \alpha) \propto \frac{|S|^{1/2}}{|D_\Upsilon|^{1/2}} \frac{\Gamma(c_{T^*})}{\Gamma(c_0)} \frac{C_0^{c_0}}{C_{T^*}^{c_{T^*}}},$$

see Geweke (2005), where $\Gamma(\cdot)$ denotes the Gamma function.

The sample from the posterior distribution of the latent states, conditional on the model and its parameters, in step (d), is obtained by the conditional simulation smoother proposed by Durbin and Koopman (2002) for linear and Gaussian state-space models.

Finally, the draws of the parameters β_μ, β_A, $\beta_{sj}, j = 1, \dots, 6$, β_{TD} are obtained by performing a final random sign permutation. This is achieved by drawing independent Bernoulli random variables B_μ, B_A, $\mathsf{B}_{sj}, j = 1, \dots, 6, \mathsf{B}_{TD}$ with probability 0.5 and recording $(-1)^{\mathsf{B}_\mu}(\sigma_\eta, \tilde{\mu}_t)$, $(-1)^{\mathsf{B}_A}(\sigma_\zeta, \tilde{A}_t, a_t)$.

18.5 Empirical Results

We apply Bayesian stochastic specification search to a set of U.S. and Italian macroeconomic time series, listed in Table 18.1, which were selected for their relevance in the measurement of the macroeconomy. All of the series are transformed into logarithms, except for the U.S. monthly inflation rate, which is computed as the logarithmic change of the consumer price index with respect to the previous month.

We start by discussing the results for the specifications with a single seasonal variance parameter, based on 60,000 MCMC draws, 20,000 of which constituted the burn-in sample. For this case, there are $K = 32$ models, as Υ is a vector of five indicator variables with elements $(\gamma_\mu, \gamma_A, \gamma_s, \gamma_{TD}, \delta)$.

Table 18.2 reports the percentage of MCMC replicates by which model $M_k, k = 1 + 16\gamma_\mu + 8\gamma_A + 4\gamma_s + 2\gamma_{TD} + \delta$, was selected. It also reports the value of the Deviance Information Criterion (DIC). The latter is a measure of model fit (see Gelman and Rubin 2004) computed as follows:

$$\text{DIC}_\Upsilon = \hat{D}_\Upsilon(y; \psi, \sigma_\epsilon^2) + \{\hat{D}_\Upsilon(y; \psi, \sigma_\epsilon^2) - D_\Upsilon(y; \hat{\psi}, \hat{\sigma}_\epsilon^2)\}, \qquad (18.5.1)$$

TABLE 18.1
Dataset Used in the Study

Series Description	Sample Period	Name
U.S. Housing Starts Total	1960.1–2010.2	US.HS
U.S. Industrial Product index	1986.1–2010.1	US.IP
U.S. Retail Sales Total	1960.1–2008.3	US.RSt
U.S. Retail with Food less Auto	1960.1–2008.3	US.RSla
U.S. Unemployment Rate	1960.1–2009.8	US.UR
U.S. Consumer Price Index	1960.1–2009.8	US.CPI
U.S. Monthly Inflation Rates	1960.2–2009.8	US.IR
U.S. Consumer Credit Total	1992.1–2009.12	US.CC
U.S. Imports of Crude Oil (Quantity)	1973.1–2009.7	US.Imp
Italian Industrial Production	1990.1–2010.1	IT.IP
Italian Tourist Arrivals	1990.1–2009.10	IT.TA

TABLE 18.2
BSM with Single Seasonal Variance Parameter

	Model											
Series	M_9	M_{10}	M_{13}	M_{14}	M_{17}	M_{18}	M_{21}	M_{22}	M_{25}	M_{26}	M_{29}	M_{30}
US.HS	0	0	0	0	4 (−1044.0)	5 (−1058.1)	82 (−1193.6)	9 (−1072.0)	0	0	0	0
US.IP	0	0	0	0	0	0	0	0	67 (−3579.2)	33 (−3557.3)	0	0
US.RSt	0	0	53 (−1028.6)	41 (−1009.3)	0	0	0	0	1 (−975.4)	1 (−974.2)	1 (−965.1)	2 (−1001.9)
US.RSla	0	0	30 (−1026.4)	68 (−1057.3)	0	0	0	0	0	0	0	2 (−1014.6)
US.UR	0	0	0	0	0	70 (−1944.1)	20 (−1851.9)	10 (−1850.9)	0	0	0	0
US.CPI	0	0	0	0	0	0	0	0	0	0	30 (−1818.0)	70 (−4739.7)
US.IR	0	0	0	0	0	0	65 (−5217.9)	35 (−5214.7)	0	0	0	0
US.CC	0	0	0	6 (−1017.1)	0	0	0	0	0	0	57 (−5101.0)	43 (−4595.9)
US.Imp	0	0	0	0	1 (−599.11)	0	70 (−689.34)	29 (−601.97)	0	0	0	0
IT.IP	0	0	0	10 (−914.89)	5 (−904.09)	5 (−905.40)	41 (−918.12)	34 (−914.65)	0	1 (−903.22)	4 (−905.70)	0
IT.TA	5 (−867.91)	3 (−868.33)	0	0	29 (−873.91)	59 (−877.05)	0	0	2 (−873.69)	1 (−872.35)	0	0

Note: Percentage by which model $M_k, k = 1 + 16\gamma_\mu + 8\gamma_A + 4\gamma_s + 2\gamma_{TD} + \delta$, is selected in 40,000 MCMC draws. DIC values are in parenthesis.

where

$$\hat{D}_\Upsilon(y; \psi, \sigma_\epsilon^2) = \frac{1}{R}\sum_{i=1}^{R} D_\Upsilon(y|\psi^{(i)}, \sigma_\epsilon^{2(i)}),$$

is the average value of the deviance

$$D_\Upsilon(y|\psi, \sigma_\epsilon^2) = -2\ln p(y|\psi, \sigma_\epsilon^2),$$

computed over the R posterior simulations of $(\psi, \sigma_\epsilon^2)$ for the specification Υ obtained by the GS scheme; the conditional likelihood $p(y|\psi, \sigma_\epsilon^2)$ is evaluated by the Kalman filter for the relevant state-space model with parameter values $(\psi, \sigma_\epsilon^2)$. The term in parenthesis in Equation 18.5.1, where $D_\Upsilon(y; \hat{\psi}, \hat{\sigma}_\epsilon^2)$ represents the deviance evaluated at the posterior means $\hat{\psi} = R^{-1}\sum_i \psi^{(i)}, \hat{\sigma}_\epsilon^2 = R^{-1}\sum_i \sigma_\epsilon^{2(i)}$, measures the number of effective parameters in the model.

The main evidence can be summarized as follows:

1. The specification with time-varying TDs is never selected.
2. The modal specification has $\Upsilon = (1, 0, 1, 0, 0)$ in four cases (US.HS, US.IR, US.Imp, and IT.IP): the trend is a driftless random walk and stochastic seasonals.
3. The specifications selected for the US.UR and IT.TA, and US.IP, M_{18} and M_{25}, respectively, do not feature stochastic seasonality. Model M_{18} features a random walk trend with constant drift and fixed seasonal and calendar effects; model M_{25} differs only for the trend model, which is local linear.
4. For US.CC and US.CPI models, the two most frequently selected specifications are M_{29} and M_{30}; they both feature a local linear trend and stochastic seasonal, the only difference relating to the fact that the slope component is nonzero at the beginning of the sample period only for the latter.
5. The models selected for US.CPI and its first differences, US.IR, can be easily reconciled as M_{21}, M_{22} are the same as M_{29}, M_{30}, but with a nonstochastic slope. However, notice that if $\sigma_\eta^2 > 0$, then the model for the irregular should be replaced by a moving average component of order 1.
6. The two U.S. retail sales series feature models M_{13} and M_{14} as modal specifications; they entail a fixed level, a stochastic slope, stochastic seasonality, and the initial slope is zero (M_{13}) or nonzero (M_{14}).
7. Models selected more frequently have lower DIC values.

Turning to the selection of seasonal models with variance parameters varying with the trigonometric components, we present in Table 18.3 the first three modal specifications that were selected, along with the posterior model probabilities $100 \times \hat{p}(\Upsilon|y)$ estimated by the GS scheme and the DIC.

TABLE 18.3

First Three Modal Specifications Selected by the GS Scheme, Estimated Posterior Probabilities $100 \times \hat{\pi}(\Upsilon|y)$ (in Parentheses)

Series	Fist Selected Model	%	DIC	Second Selected Model	%	DIC	Third Selected Model	%	DIC
US.HS	$\Upsilon = (1,0,1,1,0,0,0,0,0,0)$	35	−1208.7	$\Upsilon = (1,0,1,1,1,0,0,0,0,0)$	22	−1205.4	$\Upsilon = (1,0,1,0,0,0,0,0,0,0)$	15	−1185.3
US.IP	$\Upsilon = (1,1,0,1,1,1,1,0,0,0)$	30	−3822.5	$\Upsilon = (1,1,0,1,1,1,1,0,0,1)$	25	−3810.7	$\Upsilon = (1,1,0,1,1,1,0,0,0,0)$	10	−3769.9
US.RSt	$\Upsilon = (0,1,1,1,0,1,0,0,0,0)$	37	−1074.9	$\Upsilon = (0,1,1,1,0,0,0,0,0,0)$	31	−1020.1	$\Upsilon = (0,1,1,1,0,0,0,0,0,1)$	17	−1057.5
US.RSla	$\Upsilon = (0,1,1,1,1,1,1,1,0,1)$	30	−1153.5	$\Upsilon = (1,1,1,1,1,1,1,1,0,0)$	24	−1136.1	$\Upsilon = (0,1,1,1,1,1,1,1,0,1)$	15	−1146.1
US.UR	$\Upsilon = (1,0,0,1,1,1,1,1,0,0)$	40	−2115.3	$\Upsilon = (1,0,0,1,1,1,1,1,0,1)$	20	−2070.8	$\Upsilon = (1,1,0,1,1,1,1,1,0,0)$	16	−2068.7
US.CPI	$\Upsilon = (1,1,1,0,0,0,0,0,0,1)$	65	−5250.6	$\Upsilon = (1,1,1,1,0,0,0,0,0,1)$	34	−5249.2	$\Upsilon = (1,1,1,0,1,0,0,0,0,1)$	1	−5242.3
US.IR	$\Upsilon = (1,0,1,1,0,0,0,0,0,0)$	70	−7123.5	$\Upsilon = (1,0,1,1,1,0,0,0,0,0)$	24	−7113.2	$\Upsilon = (1,0,1,1,1,1,0,0,0,1)$	6	−7109.5
US.CC	$\Upsilon = (1,1,0,1,1,1,0,0,0,0)$	23	−4694.2	$\Upsilon = (1,1,0,1,1,1,0,1,0,0)$	17	−4685.4	$\Upsilon = (1,1,0,1,1,1,0,0,0,1)$	16	−4642.5
US.Imp	$\Upsilon = (1,0,1,0,0,0,0,0,0,0)$	38	−677.03	$\Upsilon = (1,0,0,0,0,0,0,0,0,0)$	31	−673.26	$\Upsilon = (1,0,1,1,0,0,0,0,0,0)$	17	−661.66
IT.IP	$\Upsilon = (1,0,1,1,1,1,1,0,0,0)$	30	−979.12	$\Upsilon = (1,0,1,1,1,1,1,1,0,0)$	24	−974.51	$\Upsilon = (1,0,1,1,1,1,0,0,0,0)$	10	−951.67
IT.TA	$\Upsilon = (1,0,1,1,0,0,0,0,0,1)$	45	−913.10	$\Upsilon = (1,0,1,1,1,0,0,0,0,1)$	28	−912.73	$\Upsilon = (1,1,1,1,0,0,0,0,0,0)$	10	−905.16

Note: The vector Υ has elements $(\gamma_\mu, \gamma_A, \gamma_{sj}, j = 1, \ldots, 6, \gamma_{TD}, \delta)$.

The results confirm that for the series considered in the application, TD effects can be safely considered as fixed, rather than evolving over time, the marginal probability $P(\gamma_{\mathrm{TD}} = 1)$ being virtually zero in all the cases. The main evidence arising from Table 18.3 can be summarized as follows:

- Trends and seasonals are better characterized as stochastic, rather than deterministic. The results are in broad agreement with the analysis of the restricted model, except for US.UR and IT.TA, and US.IP, for which some of the trigonometric cycles are not fixed when the variance parameters are allowed to vary with the frequency of the cycle.

- For US.IP and US.UR, the three modal models are such that the trigonometric component defined at the fundamental frequency $\lambda_1 = \pi/6$ is not stochastic. On the contrary, the only components that are stochastically evolving for IT.TA are the fundamental and the first harmonic.

- There is a lot of variation across the series as to which trigonometric cycles are time-varying or fixed. The broad evidence arising from Table 18.3 is that the number of occurrences in which the cycle at λ_j is selected as stochastically evolving decreases with j; quite often the cycle defined at the $\lambda_6 = \pi$ frequency (six cycles per year) is fixed.

- Model uncertainty often concerns marginal aspects, such as the presence of a nonzero slope term at the initial time, or a specific trigonometric component.

Hereby we provide a more detailed analysis of Italian IP series. Figure 18.1 displays the estimated posterior densities of some of the parameters of the saturated BSM model, which is Equation 18.3.6 with $\Upsilon = (1, 1, 1, 1, 1, 1, 1, 1, 1, 1)$. The estimates are based on MCMC draws obtained by running the Gibbs sampler for 40,000 iterations after a burn-in of 20,000.

When the posterior of the parameters $\beta_\Lambda, \Lambda = \{\mu, A, s_1, \ldots, s_6, \mathrm{TD}\}$ is bimodal and sufficiently removed from zero, the corresponding true variance parameter is different from zero and the associated random component contributes significantly to the evolution of the series. This is the case of β_μ (stochastic level) and the seasonal parameters $\beta_{sj}, j = 1, 2, 3, 4$, whereas β_{s5} and β_{s6} have some density around zero. On the contrary, the posterior of β_A is concentrated around zero, which points to a fixed slope; moreover, the distribution of q_0 is such that the initial slope is not significantly different from zero, so that the specification of the trend component reduces to a driftless random walk. Also, TD effects are fixed.

When SMSS is applied by running an MCMC sampling scheme that draws samples from the posterior distribution of the indicators, the specification with maximal estimated posterior probability is $\Upsilon = (1, 0, 1, 1, 1, 1, 1, 0, 0, 0)$, corresponding to M_{761}, which is a restricted BSM with no slope, a fixed trigonometric cycle at the Nyquist frequency, and fixed calendar effects. The estimated posterior model probability is 0.3. Figure 18.2 shows the estimated posterior means of the unobserved components (along with the 95% credible interval

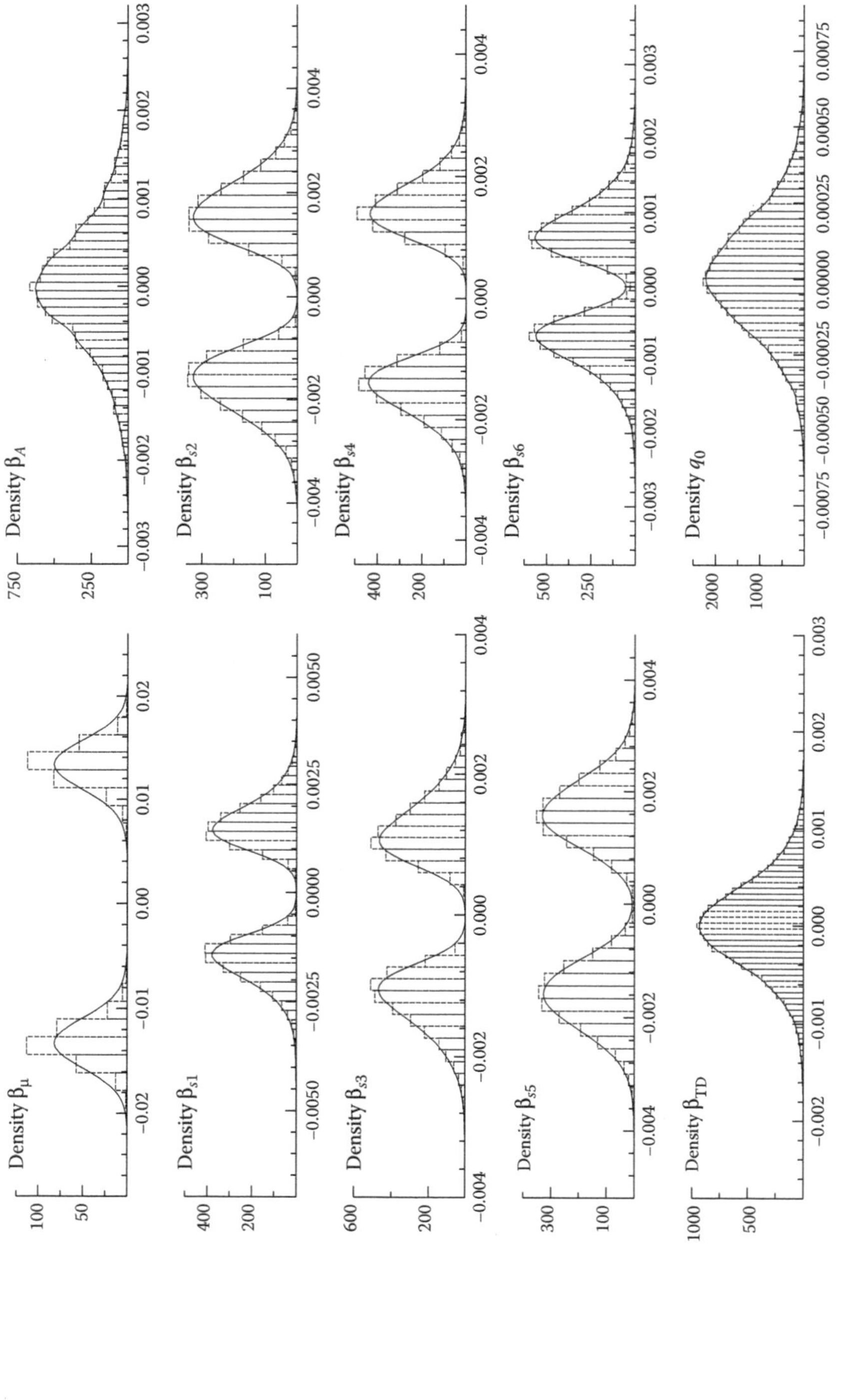

FIGURE 18.1
IT.IP series: estimated posterior densities of the parameters β_μ, β_A, $\beta_{sj}, j = 1, \ldots, 6$, β_{TD} and q_0.

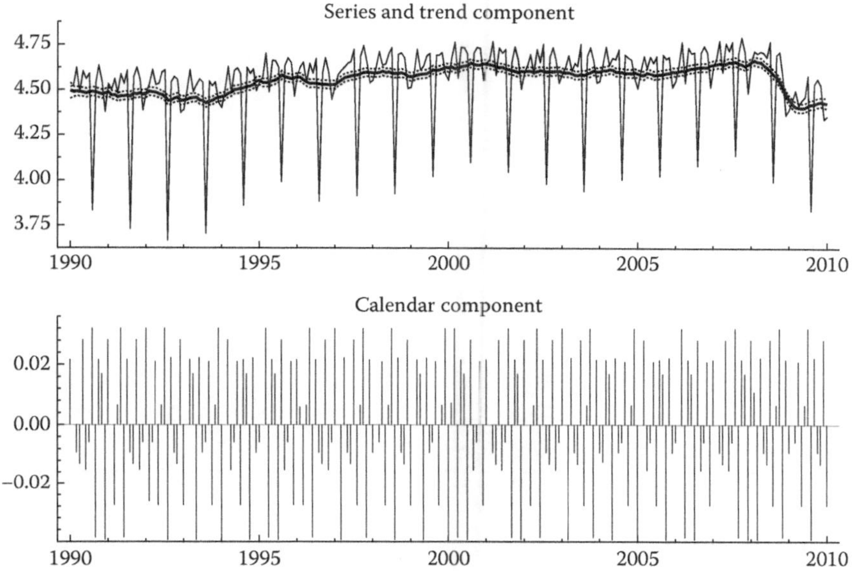

FIGURE 18.2
IT.IP series: posterior means of the unobserved components.

for the trend), whereas Figure 18.3 displays the estimated posteriors of the TD effects, $\phi_{k0}, k = 1, \ldots, 6$, along with the posterior of the Sunday effect, obtained as $\phi_{70} = -\sum_{j=1}^{6} \phi_{k0}$. Model uncertainty deals essentially with the time variation of the seasonal trigonometric cycles defined at the frequencies λ_5 and λ_6 (see Table 18.3).

The saturated BSM model can also be estimated using the reparameterization discussed in Section 18.3.2. In particular, pronounced bimodality of the posterior distribution of the parameter β_s (presented in the top left panel of figure 18.4) points out that seasonality is stochastic rather than deterministic. Also, the posterior distributions of the differential parameters $\beta^*_{sj}, j = 1, \ldots, 5$ point out that the variance parameters σ_j are likely to differ significantly from $\sqrt{2}\sigma_6$, except for σ_5. Hence, the seasonal model could be simplified by expressing the frequency specific variances in terms of five, rather than six, unrestricted parameters. Overall, the evidence is against the specification with a single variance parameter.

The model with frequency specific variance parameters is usually a substantial improvement over the specification with a single variance parameter σ^2_ω. To illustrate this point, Figure 18.5 compares the posterior distribution of the Easter regression coefficient ϕ_E for the unrestricted model (18.3.6) and the specification enforcing the restriction $\sigma^2_j = \sigma^2_\omega, j = 1, \ldots, 5, \sigma^2_6 = 0.5\sigma^2_\omega$. Similar considerations can be made for the precision by which the unobserved

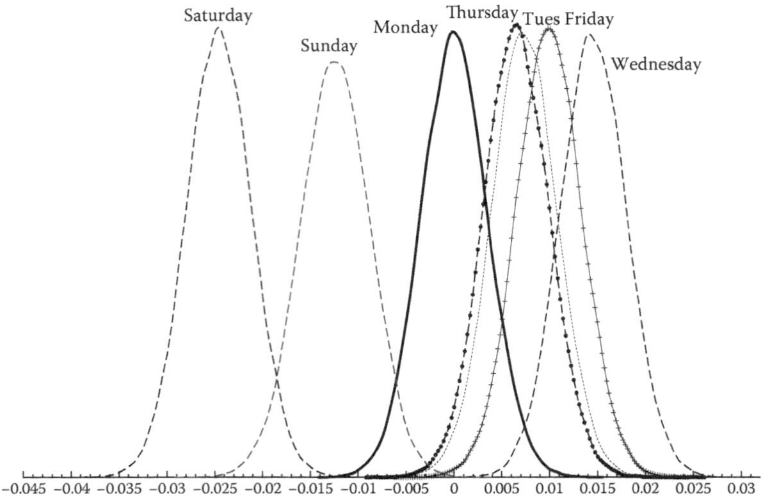

FIGURE 18.3
IT.IP series: estimated posterior densities of the TD coefficients ϕ_{k0}, $k = 1, \ldots, 6$. The Sunday effect has been obtained as $\phi_{70} = -\sum_1^6 \phi_{k0}$.

components are estimated: the bottom panel compares the 95% credible intervals of the trend component for the two specifications.

A final point deals with the comparison of the saturated model (M_{1024}) with the selected model (see Table 18.3). For the series investigated in this chapter, model selection has little effect on the estimation of the seasonally adjusted series, although it may affect the trend and the irregular or the seasonal and the calendar components, individually. However, after model selection has been carried out once, conditioning on the selected model may improve the efficiency and timeliness of the GS scheme (the convergence statistics, see, e.g., Geweke (2005), not reported for brevity, are always satisfactory for the restricted model, whereas they may fail for the unrestricted model).

18.6 Conclusions

We have applied a recent methodology, Bayesian SMSS (Frühwirth-Schnatter and Wagner 2010), for the selection of the unobserved components (level, slope, seasonal cycles, and TD effects) that are stochastically evolving over time.

SMSS hinges on two basic ingredients: the noncentered representation of the unobserved components, and the reparameterization of the hyperparameters representing standard deviations as regression parameters with

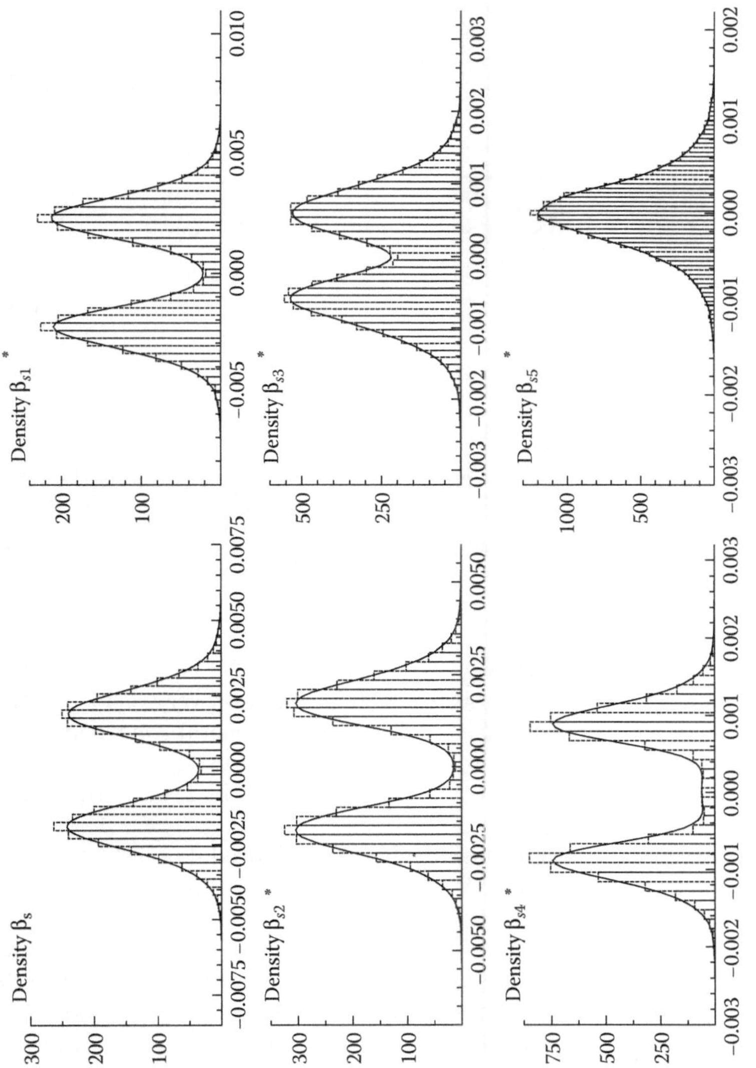

FIGURE 18.4
IT.IP series. Posterior densities of the seasonal parameters β_s and $\beta^*_{sj}, j = 1, \ldots, 5$, of the reparameterized model (18.3.8).

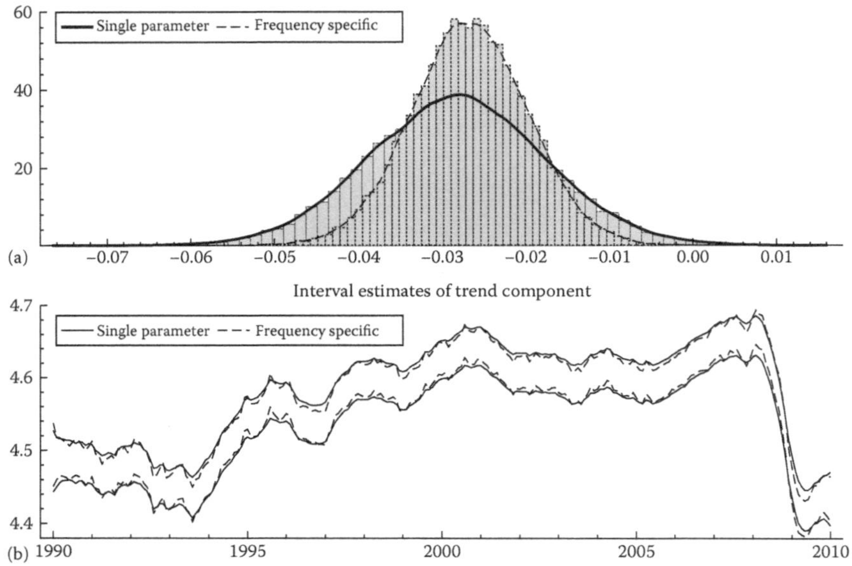

FIGURE 18.5
IT.IP series. (a) Posterior densities of the Easter coefficient for model (18.3.6) with frequency-specific coefficients and the restricted specification with $\sigma_j^2 = \sigma_\omega^2, j = 1, \ldots, 5, \sigma_6^2 = 0.5\sigma_\omega^2$ (single variance parameter). (b) Interval estimates of trend component.

unrestricted support. The choice of the prior and the conditional independence structure of the model enables the definition of a very efficient MCMC estimation strategy based on GS. Indeed, our first general conclusion is that, transcending the model selection problem, Bayesian estimation of the BSM should be carried out by using the approach suggested by Frühwirth-Schnatter and Wagner (2010).

Our empirical illustrations have dealt with a limited data set consisting of 11 time series, so that we can envisage an extension of this research that gathers further empirical evidence by processing a much larger set of data. However, there are some regularities that we have drawn from our case studies. The first is that, somewhat disappointingly, TD effects are time-invariant. A possible explanation is that the series available are possibly too short to enable us to detect small variations induced by the calendar; moreover, some of the TD variations may be absorbed by seasonal cycles defined at higher frequencies.

A second conclusion is that the specification with six frequency-specific variance parameters proves superior to that using a single parameter, yielding more precise estimates of the unobserved components and the regression effects. We also suspect that the latter can induce a bias toward selecting deterministic models of seasonality. We leave to future research discriminating between the two representations as a model selection problem, by comparing their posterior probabilities.

The selection of a BSM specification among the 2^{10} possible ones has led in all the cases to models with one or more seasonal cycles being characterized as deterministic. The overall result is that the set of time series analyzed display stochastically evolving trends and seasonality.

Finally, our stochastic model specification search was carried out for a version of the BSM with trigonometric seasonality. In the future, we would like to apply the methodology to alternative models for seasonal time series, featuring a stochastic dummy seasonal model (see West and Harrison 1997), where the individual monthly effects may be evolving over time.

Acknowledgments

The authors wish to thank the editors and the referees for their comments, which helped improve the paper. Financial support from CREATES, funded by the Danish National Research Foundation, is gratefully acknowledged by Stefano Grassi.

References

Bell, W. R. and Hillmer, S. C. (1983). Modeling time series with calendar variation. *Journal of the American Statistical Association*, 78:526–534.

Bell, W. R. and Martin, D. E. K. (2004). Modeling time-varying trading day effects in monthly time series. In *ASA Proceedings of the Joint Statistical Meetings*. Alexandria: American Statistical Association.

Busetti, F. and Harvey, A. (2003). Seasonality tests. *Journal of Business and Economic Statistics*, 21:420–436.

Canova, F. and Hansen, B. (1995). Are seasonal patterns constant over time? A test for seasonal stability. *Journal of Business and Economic Statistics*, 13:237–252.

Cleveland, W. and Devlin, J. (1982). Calendar effects in monthly time series: Modeling and adjustment. *Journal of of the American Statistical Association*, 77:520–528.

Dagum, E. and Quenneville, B. (1993). Dynamic linear models for time series components. *Journal of Econometrics*, 55:333–351.

Dagum, E., Quenneville, B., and Sutradhar, B. (1993). Trading-day variations multiple regression models with random parameters. *International Statistical Review*, 60:57–73.

Durbin, J. and Koopman, S. (2002). A simple and efficient simulation smoother for state space time series analysis. *Biometrika*, 89:603–615.

Findley, D. (2005). Some recent developments and directions in seasonal adjustment. *Journal of Official Statistics*, 21(2):343–365.

Frühwirth-Schnatter, S. (2004). Efficient bayesian parameter estimation for state space models based on reparameterizations. In *State Space and Unobserved Component Models: Theory and Applications*, eds. A. C. Harvey, S. J. Koopman, and N. Shephard, 123–151. Cambridge: Cambridge University Press.

Frühwirth-Schnatter, S. and Wagner, H. (2010). Stochastic model specification search for Gaussian and partial non-Gaussian state space models. *Journal of Econometrics*, 154(1):85–100.

Gamerman, D. and Lopes, F. H. (2007). *Markov Chain Monte Carlo: Stochastic Simulation for Bayesian Inference.* Boca Raton, Florida: Chapman and Hall/CRC.

Gelfand, A., Sahu, S., and Carlin, B. (1995). Efficient parameterizations for normal linear mixed models. *Biometrika*, 82:479–488.

Gelman, A., Carlin, J., Stern, H., and Rubin, D. (2004). *Bayesian Data Analysis*, 2nd edition. Boca Raton, Florida: Chapman and Hall/CRC.

George, E. I. and McCulloch, R. (1993). Variable selection via Gibbs sampling. *Journal of the American Statistical Association*, 88:881–889.

George, E. I. and McCulloch, R. (1997). Approaches for Bayesian variable selection. *Statistica Sinica*, 7:339–373.

Geweke, J. (2005). *Contemporary Bayesian Econometrics and Statistics.* Hoboken, New Jersey: Wiley Series in Probability and Statistics.

Ghysels, E. and Osborn, D. (2001). *The Econometric Analysis of Seasonal Time Series.* Cambridge: Cambridge University Press.

Hannan, E. J. (1964). The estimation of a changing seasonal pattern. *Journal of the American Statistical Association*, 59:1063–1077.

Hannan, E. J., Terrell, R. D., and Tuckwell, N. (1970). The seasonal adjustment of economic time series. *International Economic Review*, 11:24–52.

Harvey, A. (1989). *Forecasting, Structural Time Series and the Kalman Filter.* Cambridge: Cambridge University Press.

Harvey, A. C. and Todd, P. H. J. (1983). Forecasting economic time series with structural and Box–Jenkins models: A case study. *Journal of Business and Economic Statistics*, 1:299–307.

Haywood, J. and Tunnicliffe Wilson, G. (2000). Selection and estimation of component models for seasonal time series. *Journal of Forecasting*, 19:393–417.

Hylleberg, S. (1992). *Modelling Seasonality*. Oxford: Oxford University Press.

Hylleberg, S. and Pagan, A. (1997). Seasonal integration and the evolving seasonals model. *International Journal of Forecasting*, 13:329–340.

Koop, G. and van Dijk, H. (2000). Testing for integration using evolving trend and seasonals models: A Bayesian approach. *Journal of Econometrics*, 97:261–291.

Nerlove, M., Grether, D. M., and Carvalho, J. L. (1979). *Analysis of Economic Time Series: A Synthesis*. New York: Academic Press.

Peña, D., Tiao, G., and Tsay, R. (2001). *A Course in Time Series Analysis*. New York: John Wiley and Sons.

Robert, P. and Casella, G. (2004). *Monte Carlo Statistical Methods*. New York: Springer-Verlag.

Smith, M. and Kohn, R. (1996). Nonparametric regression using Bayesian variable selection. *Journal of Econometrics*, 75(2):317–343.

Strickland, C. M., Martin, G., and Forbes, C. (2007). Parameterisation and efficient MCMC estimation of non-Gaussian state space models. *Computational Statistical and Data Analysis*, 9‾(52):2911–2930.

West, M. and Harrison, J. (1997). *Bayesian Forecasting and Dynamic Models*. New York: Springer-Verlag.

Zellner, A. (1978). *Seasonal Analysis of Economic Time Series*. US Dept. of Commerce–Bureau of the Census, Washington, DC.

Zellner, A. (1983). *Applied Time Series Analysis of Economic Data*. US Dept. of Commerce–Bureau of the Census, Washington, DC.

Part VII

Modeling and Estimation for Nonseasonal Economic Time Series

19

Nonparametric Estimation of the Innovation Variance and Judging the Fit of ARMA Models

P. Kohli and M. Pourahmadi

CONTENTS

19.1 Introduction

The innovation (intrinsic, one-step-ahead prediction error) variance, σ^2, of a stationary process is of central importance in the theory and practice of time series analysis, and there are several time-domain parametric methods available for its estimation, cf. Brockwell and Davis (1991, §8.7) and Pourahmadi (2001). These estimators are useful in several statistical tasks such as constructing prediction intervals for the unknown future values and developing order selection criteria, such as the Akaike's information criteria (AIC). It is also a powerful tool for understanding the deeper aspects of time series models and data. For instance, Davis and Jones (1968) introduced a statistics based on the difference between the estimate of $\log \sigma^2$ and log of the estimated process variance, σ_X^2, for testing white noise. They showed equivalence of this test to the Bartlett's test for homogeneity of variances. Hannan and Nicholls (1977) suggested that a nonparametric estimator of σ^2 could provide useful information to judge the fits of various parametric models fitted to a time series data. Motivated by these findings, it is clearly of interest to estimate σ^2 subject to as few constraints on the time series or its spectrum as possible. In this chapter, we review various nonparametric estimators of σ^2 in the spectral domain using raw, smoothed, tapered, and multitapered periodograms for complete and incomplete time series data. Following Hannan and Nicholls' (1977) suggestion, we examine the role of these nonparametric estimators in judging the fits of eight autoregressive moving average (ARMA) models fitted to the well-known Wolfer's sunspot numbers.

For a stationary time series $\{X_t; t = 1, \ldots, n\}$, it is well-known that the Szegö–Kolmogorov–Wiener formula relates σ^2 to the spectrum, $f(\lambda)$, of the series by

$$\sigma^2 = \exp\left[\frac{1}{2\pi}\int_{-\pi}^{\pi} \log\{2\pi f(\lambda)\}\, d\lambda\right]. \tag{19.1.1}$$

It provides a lower bound for the variance, $\tilde{\sigma}^2$, of other competing linear predictors, in the sense that $\tilde{\sigma}^2 \geq \exp\left[1/2\pi \int_{-\pi}^{\pi} \log\{2\pi f(\lambda)\}\, d\lambda\right]$. This is similar to the Cramer–Rao lower bound for the variance of unbiased estimators for independently and identically distributed observations in the theory of statistics. Following the lead of Davis and Jones (1968), nonparametric estimators of σ^2 can be obtained by replacing the unknown $f(\lambda)$ in Equation 19.1.1 with its suitable nonparametric estimators such as the periodogram of the data and its smoothed/tapered versions.

Our approach to judging the fit of ARMA models proceeds as follows. For a given time series $\{X_t\}$, first we find a nonparametric estimator $\hat{\sigma}^2$ and say, a 95% confidence interval (CI) for σ^2. We then compute parametric one-step-ahead prediction error variances for the candidate ARMA models fitted to the data. An ARMA model is judged to be the most suitable model for prediction purposes if its prediction error variance falls in the CI for σ^2 and/or is closest to the point (nonparametric) estimate of σ^2.

We note that this approach is different from other standard methods of judging the fits of ARMA models, but it is conceptually related to the line of developments leading to the test statistics reviewed and studied in McElroy and Findley (2010). Their study is based on the difference between approximated asymptotic mean square forecast errors of different autoregressive integrated moving average (ARIMA) models to decide if one ARIMA model provides significantly better multistep-ahead forecasts than the other model. It is also related to McElroy and Holan (2009) who considered band-limited frequency-domain goodness-of-fit testing for stationary time series, without smoothing or tapering the periodogram, while taking into account the effects of parameter uncertainty.

Several modifications of the estimator of σ^2 using Equation 19.1.1 have been discussed in the literature (An, 1982; Bhansali, 1974; Bloomfield, 1973;

Jones, 1976; Mohanty and Pourahmadi, 1996; Taniguchi, 1980). We review some of these estimators of σ^2 in Section 19.2 with a focus on those having smaller biases and asymptotically normal distributions. The simulation study of Hannan and Nicholls (1977) indicates that the bias of the nonparametric estimator of σ^2 could be large in finite samples. For example, for a second-order moving average model in their study, a bias of 11.6% for a time series of length 100 and of 6.2% for a series of length 200 were observed. In many applications, such as economics and social sciences, the length of the time series is often short. Therefore, the bias in estimation of σ^2 may be considerable in these applications. We review the role of tapering and multitapering (MT) in removing the bias in estimation of σ^2 with a focus on the latter as it seems not to have received the attention it deserves. As a case study, in Section 19.3, we judge the fits of various ARMA models fitted to the Wolfer's sunspot numbers by comparing their estimated prediction error variances with the nonparametric estimators of σ^2 discussed in Section 19.2. In Section 19.4, a small simulation study is performed to show that MT methods offer significant improvements in the estimation of σ^2 over raw, smoothed, and tapered methods when the spectrum has high dynamic range, i.e., log of the ratio of highest to the lowest value of the spectra is large. In Section 19.5, we propose a nonparametric estimator of σ^2 for time series with missing values and provide simulation results in Section 19.6 to illustrate the effect of tapering on the proposed estimator of σ^2.

This nonparametric method of estimating σ^2 in Equation 19.1.1 and other smooth functionals of the spectrum of a stationary process like the *variance profile* (Luati et al., 2011)

$$\sigma_p^2 = \left[\frac{1}{2\pi}\int_{-\pi}^{\pi} \{2\pi f(\lambda)\}^p \, d\lambda\right]^{1/p}, \tag{19.1.2}$$

for $p \in R$ is broadly applicable in many areas of natural and social sciences, including business and economics. Note that for $p = 1, 0, -1, \sigma_p^2$ in Equation 19.1.2 reduces to the arithmetic, geometric, and harmonic mean of the spectrum, respectively. More precisely, $\lim_{p\to 0} \sigma_p^2 = \sigma^2$. The use of the variance profile in estimating the long-memory parameter in climatological, financial time series and assessing the structural change is discussed in Luati et al. (2011).

19.2 Review of the Existing Estimators of Innovation Variance

In this section, we review various nonparametric estimators of the innovation variance introduced using Szegö–Kolmogorov–Wiener formula (19.1.1).

19.2.1 Early Estimators

Davis and Jones (1968) were the first to propose a nonparametric estimator of σ^2 by approximating the integral in Equation 19.1.1 by a finite Riemann sum as

$$\sigma^2 = \exp\left\{\frac{1}{M}\sum_{j=1}^{M}\log f(\lambda_j)\right\},$$

where $M = [(n-1)/2]$ with $[x]$ as the integer part of x, and $\lambda_k = (2\pi k/n)$ is the Fourier frequency with $0 < k < (n/2)$ as an integer. Replacing $f(\lambda)$ with the periodogram, $I(\lambda)$, of the data $\{X_t\}$ to have

$$\hat{\sigma}^2 = \exp\left\{\frac{1}{M}\sum_{j=1}^{M}\log I(\lambda_j) + \gamma\right\}, \tag{19.2.1}$$

where

$$I(\lambda) = \frac{1}{n}\left|\sum_{t=1}^{n} X_t \exp(-i\lambda t)\right|^2, \tag{19.2.2}$$

and $\gamma \approx 0.57721$ (Euler's constant) is the bias in estimating $\log f(\lambda)$ with $\log I(\lambda)$. Davis and Jones (1968) showed that $\log\hat{\sigma}^2$ is asymptotically normal with mean $\log\sigma^2$ and variance $(\pi^2/6M)$.

Janacek (1975) investigated the Davis and Jones (1968) estimator in Equation 19.2.1 for small samples and proposed a modified estimator for σ^2 by using a trapezoidal approximation for the integral in Equation 19.1.1 as

$$\hat{\sigma}_J^2 = \exp\left[\frac{1}{M}\sum_{j=1}^{M-1}\log I(\lambda_j) + \frac{1}{2M}\{\log I(0) + \delta_n \log I(\pi)\} - \kappa\right], \tag{19.2.3}$$

where $\delta_n = 1$, when n is even and 0, otherwise. The quantity

$$\kappa = \left[\frac{(M-1)\gamma}{M} - \left\{(1+\delta_n)\frac{\Psi(1/2)}{2M}\right\}\right]$$

is the bias of the estimator of $\log(\sigma^2)$ and $\Psi(z) = d/dz(\log\Gamma(z))$ is the digamma or psi function. This approximation has two advantages. First, it includes both endpoints, i.e., $\lambda = 0$ and π, so that all available information is used. Second, the weight for these endpoints is 1/2, which adjusts for the double variance of the periodogram at these points.

The periodogram in Equation 19.2.2 is asymptotically unbiased but not a consistent estimator for the spectrum $f(\lambda)$, as its variance does not tend to zero for large n, cf. Brockwell and Davis (1991, §10.3). Hannan and Nicholls (1977) modified $\hat{\sigma}^2$ in Equation 19.2.1 by averaging over the periodogram of m adjacent frequencies and proposed a smoothed estimator for σ^2 as

$$\hat{\sigma}_s^2 = m\exp\left[\frac{1}{M'}\sum_{j=0}^{M'-1}\log\left\{\frac{1}{m}\sum_{k=1}^{m} I(\lambda_{jm+k})\right\} - \Psi(m)\right], \tag{19.2.4}$$

where $M' = [(n-1)/2m]$ and it reduces to Equation 19.2.1 when $m = 1$. This averaging of the periodograms across neighboring frequencies reduces the variance of the estimator of σ^2 in Equation 19.2.1. They also suggested a smoothed version of $\hat{\sigma}_J^2$ in Equation 19.2.3 by including terms for the end-points. Hannan and Nicholls (1977, §3) studied how increasing m affects bias and variance of $\hat{\sigma}_s^2$. For Gaussian processes, they reported $m = 3$ as a reasonable choice for bias/variance trade-off. They also pointed out that $m > 3$ leads to poor distributional approximations for $\hat{\sigma}_s^2$, even for a smooth spectrum.

Although smoothing reduces the variance of the raw periodogram in Equation 19.2.2, by averaging across a small neighborhood of λ, bias is introduced. This bias results from having the expectation of the periodogram values at neighboring frequencies similar but not identical to the frequency of interest. For spectrums with high dynamic range, smoothing can blur the spectrum estimator because peaks at certain frequencies can cause sidelobes (small peaks) when we average across neighboring frequencies. The influence of sidelobes introduced by smoothing can significantly be reduced by data tapering (Tukey, 1967), in which the original time series is transformed by multiplying it with a taper function $\{h(t); t = 1, \ldots, n\}$. Pukkila and Nyquist (1985), having noticed the bias of the smoothed estimator of σ^2 in Equation 19.2.4, suggested using the tapered series $\{Y_t\} = \{h(t)X_t\}$ and modified $\hat{\sigma}_s^2$ so that

$$\hat{\sigma}_T^2 = \exp\left\{\frac{1}{M}\sum_{j=1}^{M} \log I_T(\lambda_j) + \gamma\right\}, \qquad (19.2.5)$$

where

$$I_T(\lambda) = \frac{1}{n_1}\left|\sum_{t=1}^{n}(Y_t - \bar{y})\exp(-i\lambda t)\right|^2,$$

is the periodogram of the tapered data $\{Y_t\}$, $\bar{y} = \sum_{t=1}^{n}(Y_t/n_2)$, $n_1 = \sum_{t=1}^{n} h^2(t)$, and $n_2 = \sum_{t=1}^{n} h(t)$.

Hannan and Nicholls (1977, Table 1) and Pukkila and Nyquist (1985, Table 2) illustrate that some particular models, those with smooth spectrum, exhibited little difference between the estimators based on smoothed/tapered periodograms. However, the tapered estimator of σ^2 in Equation 19.2.5 shows significant reduction in the mean square error (MSE) as compared with the smoothed estimator of σ^2 in Equation 19.2.4 when the spectrum has a high dynamic range.

19.2.2 Multitapered Estimators

Tapering has the advantage of reducing the sidelobes but at the expense of increasing the variance of the spectrum estimator by a factor of $\sum_{t=1}^{n}(h^2(t)/n)$, (Brillinger, 1975). Walden (1995) employed the MT method of Thomson (1982) to diminish this variance increase. In the MT method, several orthogonal tapers are used instead of one taper and the spectrum estimator in its simplest form is the average of the estimators corresponding to each orthogonal taper. This averaging of the tapered periodograms results in reduction of the variance of the estimator of σ^2.

For further reading of the MT method, see Percival and Walden (1993, Ch. 7), and Walden (1995, 2000). For applications of the MT method in economics, see Gencay et al. (2002), Sella (2008, §4) and Sella et al. (2010).

A special class of orthogonal tapers effective in suppressing the sidelobes are called Slepian sequences or discrete prolate spheroidal sequences (DPSS). Since this is not discussed much in the statistics literature, a brief explanation of the construction of DPSS is given next.

Slepian (1978) introduced DPSS and showed their relation with continuous time functions. Let $\{v(t); t = 1, \ldots, n\}$ be a real-valued sequence such that $\sum_{t=1}^{n} v^2(t) = 1$. The Fourier transform of $\{v(t)\}$ is

$$V(\lambda) = \sum_{t=1}^{n} v(t) \exp(-i\lambda t). \tag{19.2.6}$$

From Parseval's theorem, we have

$$\int_{-\pi}^{\pi} |V(\lambda)|^2 d\lambda = 1,$$

i.e., V has unit spectral concentration in $[-\pi, \pi]$. Viewed as a taper function, this concentrates on suppressing the sidelobes by maximizing the spectral concentration in the band $[-W, W]$ for $0 < W < \pi$. The spectral concentration is given by

$$S(W) = \int_{-W}^{W} |V(\lambda)|^2 d\lambda = \int_{-W}^{W} V(\lambda)\overline{V(\lambda)} d\lambda, \tag{19.2.7}$$

where $\overline{V(\lambda)}$ is the complex conjugate of $V(\lambda)$. Substituting Equation 19.2.6 in 19.2.7 we have

$$\begin{aligned} S(W) &= \int_{-W}^{W} \sum_{t=1}^{n} v(t) \exp(-i\lambda t) \sum_{t'=1}^{n} v(t') \exp(i\lambda t') d\lambda \\ &= \sum_{t,t'=1}^{n} v(t)v(t') \int_{-W}^{W} \exp\{-i\lambda(t-t')\} d\lambda \\ &= \sum_{t,t'=1}^{n} v(t)v(t') \left\{ \frac{\sin 2\pi W(t-t')}{\pi(t-t')} \right\}. \end{aligned}$$

To maximize $S(W)$ subject to $\sum_{t=1}^{n} v^2(t) = 1$, we let

$$\beta = \sum_{t,t'=1}^{n} v(t)v(t') \left\{ \frac{\sin 2\pi W(t-t')}{\pi(t-t')} \right\} - \lambda \sum_{t=0}^{n-1} v^2(t).$$

Then solving the root of $\partial\beta/\partial v(t) = 0$ gives

$$\sum_{t'=1}^{n} \left\{ \frac{\sin 2\pi W(t-t')}{\pi(t-t')} \right\} v(t') = \lambda v(t).$$

This system represents a set of n eigenvalue equations expressed as

$$\sum_{t'=1}^{n} \left\{ \frac{\sin 2\pi W(t-t')}{\pi(t-t')} \right\} v_k(t') = \lambda_k(n, W) v_k(t). \qquad (19.2.8)$$

The first DPSS taper is the eigenvector $\{v_1(t)\}$, corresponding to the largest eigenvalue $\lambda_1(n, W)$. The second taper $\{v_2(t)\}$ is the eigenvector orthogonal to $\{v_1(t)\}$ and corresponds to the second largest eigenvalue $\lambda_2(n, W)$, and so on. The n eigenvectors $\{v_1(t), \ldots, v_n(t)\}$ form the required multitaper DPSS.

Walden (1995) employed the first K orthogonal DPSS tapers to modify the tapered estimator in Equation 19.2.5 as

$$\hat{\sigma}^2_{\text{MT}} = K \exp\left\{ \frac{1}{M} \sum_{j=1}^{M} \log I_{\text{MT}}(\lambda_j) - \Psi(K) \right\}, \qquad (19.2.9)$$

where

$$I_{\text{MT}}(\lambda) = \frac{1}{K} \sum_{k=1}^{K} \left| \sum_{t=1}^{n} X_t v_k(t) \exp(-i\lambda t) \right|^2$$

corresponds to the periodogram of $\{X_t\}$ after applying K orthogonal tapers.

The asymptotic distribution of $\hat{\sigma}^2_{\text{MT}}$ is based on the assumptions that there is no correlation among the periodograms obtained from orthogonal tapers and that $I_{\text{MT}}(\lambda_j)$ is approximately distributed as $f(\lambda_j)\chi^2_{2K}/2K$. Hence, Walden (1995, p. 184) suggested using only the first two or three tapers, i.e., $K = 2$ or 3 since otherwise these assumptions begin to break down. To select the multitaper bandwidth, W, Walden (1995, §5) suggested using either a heuristic or an automatic approach. To choose W for a given n, the heuristic approach selects nW corresponding to the lowest sidelobe bias. The automatic approach selects nW based on the smallest $\hat{\sigma}^2_{\text{MT}}$ when it is computed over a range of nW values. Walden (1995, §5) illustrated how to choose nW for two second-order autoregressive, AR(2), models with highly dynamic spectrum. He reported approximately 40% reduction in the MSE of the estimator of σ^2 obtained using the MT method over the tapering. One may further reduce the variance of the multitapered estimator of σ^2 in Equation 19.2.9 by smoothing the multitaper periodogram $I_{\text{MT}}(\lambda)$, using different weight functions and then taking their average, cf. Riedel and Sidorenko (1996).

19.2.3 Asymptotic Distribution

The asymptotic distributions of the log of the nonparametric estimators of σ^2, discussed in Section 19.2, are given in the following theorem. The results provide a way to improve the nonparametric estimators of σ^2 by reducing the bias; see Equations 19.2.10 through 19.2.13.

Theorem 19.1 *Let $\{X_t\}$ be a discrete time, real-valued and purely nondeterministic stationary process with an infinite moving average representation of the form $X_t = \sum_{j=0}^{\infty} \psi_j Z_{t-j}$, where $\psi_0 = 1$ and $\{Z_t\}$ is Gaussian white noise sequence with zero mean and variance σ^2. Then, under some regularity conditions on the spectrum of $\{X_t\}$(Hannan and Nicholls (1977, §2)) and for large n, we have the following results for the nonparametric estimators discussed in this section:*

$$\text{(a) } \log \hat{\sigma}^2 \sim N\left(\log \sigma^2, \frac{\pi^2}{6M} \right),$$

$$\text{(b) } \log \hat{\sigma}_s^2 \sim N\left(\log \sigma^2, \frac{m\Psi'(m)}{M'} \right),$$

$$\text{(c) } \log \hat{\sigma}_T^2 \sim N\left(\log \sigma^2, \frac{\pi^2}{6M} \right),$$

$$\text{(d) } \log \hat{\sigma}_{\text{MT}}^2 \sim N\left(\log \sigma^2, \frac{\Psi'(K)}{KM} \right),$$

where $\sim$ stands for asymptotically distributed and $\Psi'(m)$ is the trigamma function.

One can show result (a) using the central limit theorem and characteristic function of the log transform of a gamma random variable, cf. Davis and Jones (1968, 142–143). Hannan and Nicholls (1977, 835) proved the asymptotic distribution of the smoothed estimator of σ^2 given in (b). When the taper function $\{h(t)\}$ is normalized, i.e., $\sum h^2(t) = 1$, the asymptotic distribution of the tapered periodogram is the same as that of the raw periodogram (Brillinger, 1975, 128). Therefore, results (a) and (c) are asymptotically identical. Walden (1995, 184) suggested an approximate distribution of the multitapered periodogram, assuming no correlation among the periodograms obtained from orthogonal tapers. He also discussed the conditions under which this approximation fails. The result in (d) follows from the approximate distribution of the multitapered periodogram using log transformation.

Pukkila and Nyquist (1985) pointed out that one may further reduce the bias by using the fact that if $\log X \sim N(\mu, \sigma^2)$ for any random variable X then,

$$E(X) = \exp\left(\mu + \frac{\sigma^2}{2} \right).$$

Therefore, the above nonparametric estimators of σ^2 are modified to have reduced bias as

$$\hat{\sigma}^2 = \exp\left\{\frac{1}{M}\sum_{j=1}^{M}\log I(\lambda_j) + \gamma - \frac{\pi^2}{12M}\right\}, \tag{19.2.10}$$

$$\hat{\sigma}_s^2 = m\exp\left[\frac{1}{M'}\sum_{j=0}^{M'-1}\log\left\{\frac{1}{m}\sum_{k=1}^{m} I(\lambda_{jm+k})\right\} - \Psi(m) - \frac{m\Psi'(m)}{2M'}\right], \tag{19.2.11}$$

$$\hat{\sigma}_T^2 = \exp\left\{\frac{1}{M}\sum_{j=1}^{M}\log I_T(\lambda_j) + \gamma - \frac{\pi^2}{12M}\right\}, \tag{19.2.12}$$

$$\hat{\sigma}_{\mathrm{MT}}^2 = K\exp\left\{\frac{1}{M}\sum_{j=1}^{M}\log I_{\mathrm{MT}}(\lambda_j) - \Psi(K) - \frac{\Psi'(K)}{2KM}\right\}. \tag{19.2.13}$$

Theorem 19.1 is also used to construct approximate $100(1-\alpha)\%$ CIs for σ^2 using $\hat{\sigma}^2$, $\hat{\sigma}_s^2$, $\hat{\sigma}_T^2$, and $\hat{\sigma}_{\mathrm{MT}}^2$. These CIs are then used to judge the performance of various parametric models fitted to the time series data. Next, we demonstrate the use of nonparametric estimators of σ^2 in Equations 19.2.10 through 19.2.13 through real data analysis and a simulation study.

19.3 Case Study: Wolfer's Sunspot Numbers

In this section, we illustrate the use of nonparametric estimators of σ^2 in judging the fit of various ARMA models fitted to the famous Wolfer's sunspot data. This data consists of yearly averages of the number of sunspots and was first analyzed by Yule (1927). For historical details on sunspots data, see Izenman (1983). Woodward and Gray (1978) gave a partial list of ARMA models fitted to the sunspots data, see Table 19.1. Note that the models in Table 19.1 are not over the same time period. To compare the performance of the nonparametric estimators of σ^2 discussed in Section 19.2 and to assess their roles in judging the fit of ARMA models for sunspots data (1749–1924), we first compute the prediction error variance for each model listed in Table 19.1. We compare these variances to the nonparametric estimates of σ^2 computed using Equations 19.2.10 through 19.2.13 for the sunspots data (1749–1924).

We use the least squares estimator of the prediction error variance for the ARMA models in Table 19.1, cf. Brockwell and Davis (1991, §8.7) as

$$\tilde{\sigma}_{\mathrm{LS}}^2 = \frac{S(\tilde{\phi},\tilde{\theta})}{n-p-q}, \tag{19.3.1}$$

where (p,q) is the order of the ARMA model, $\tilde{\phi}$ and $\tilde{\theta}$ are the least squares estimates of the ARMA parameters ϕ and θ, and $S(\tilde{\phi},\tilde{\theta})$ is the unconditional sum of squares. Using the approximate distribution of $\tilde{\sigma}_{\mathrm{LS}}^2$, we compute

TABLE 19.1
ARMA Models for Wolfer's Sunspot Data

Model		Source in Literature
1	$(1 - 1.34B + 0.65B^2)X_t = Z_t$	Yule, Moran, Bailey
2	$(1 - 1.62B + B^2)X_t = Z_t$	Yule
3	$(1 - 1.30B + 0.54B^2 + 0.15B^3 - 0.19B^4$ $+0.24B^5 - 0.14B^6)X_t = Z_t$	Bailey
4	$(1 - 1.57B + 1.02B^2 - 0.21B^3)X_t = Z_t$	Box, Jenkins
5	$(1 - 1.42B + 0.72B^2)X_t = (1 - 0.15B)Z_t$	Phadke, Wu
6	$(1 - 1.25B + 0.54B^2 + 0.19B^3)X_t = Z_t$	Morris, Schaerf
7	$(1 - 0.64B + B^2)(1 - 0.29B^4 - 0.21B^5$ $-0.19B^6)X_t = (1 - 0.34B)Z_t$	Woodward, Gray
8	$(1 - 1.64B + 0.94B^2)(1 - 0.18B - 0.02B^2$ $-0.01B^3 - 0.6B^4 - 0.15B^5 - 0.16B^6)$ $X_t = (1 - 0.58B)Z_t$	Woodward, Gray

$100(1 - \alpha)\%$ CIs for the prediction error variances, cf. Brockwell and Davis (1991, §8.9) as

$$\left(\frac{S(\tilde{\phi}, \tilde{\theta})}{\chi^2_{n-p-q}(1 - \alpha/2)}, \frac{S(\tilde{\phi}, \tilde{\theta})}{\chi^2_{n-p-q}(\alpha/2)}\right). \qquad (19.3.2)$$

To compute the nonparametric estimators of σ^2 for the sunspot data, we use Equations 19.2.10 through 19.2.13. For the smoothed estimator of σ^2, we use $m = 3$, suggested by Hannan and Nicholls (1977). Following Pukkila (1979) and Pukkila and Nyquist (1985), we use the following trapezoidal taper function to compute the tapered estimator of σ^2:

$$h(t) = \begin{cases} \left(\dfrac{t}{n}\right) \Big/ c, & \text{if } 0 < t/n < c, \\ 1, & \text{if } c \le t/n < (1 - c), \\ \left\{1 - \dfrac{(t-1)}{n}\right\} \Big/ c, & \text{if } (1 - c) \le t/n \le 1, \\ 0, & \text{otherwise}, \end{cases}$$

where $c = 6.25/n$. This value of c was selected based on the Monte Carlo experiments performed in Pukkila (1977) to study the bias of the periodogram in estimating the spectrum for several different models. For the multitapered estimator of σ^2, we use DPSS tapers of order 3, i.e., $K = 3$, and choose nW from $\{1, 2, 2.5, 3, 3.5, 4, 6\}$, for which $\hat{\sigma}^2_{\text{MT}}$ is the smallest. For the sunspot data, $nW = 2$ and, using results in Theorem 19.1 (a)–(d), we construct 95% CIs for σ^2.

The results in Table 19.2 show that the multitapered estimator of σ^2 is smallest as compared with raw, tapered, and smoothed estimators. The $\tilde{\sigma}^2_{\text{LS}}$ for all eight ARMA models fitted to the sunspot data are higher than the nonparametric estimators of σ^2. Based on our approach, the most reasonable

TABLE 19.2
Parametric and Nonparametric Estimators of σ^2 for Wolfer's Sunspot Data

Model	$\tilde{\sigma}^2_{\text{LS}}$(95%CI)	Method	$\hat{\sigma}^2$ (95%CI)
1	242.31 (198.49, 302.53)	Raw	203.14 (195.98,210.57)
2	237.46 (194.51, 296.47)	Smoothed	199.92 (189.54, 210.87)
3	238.43 (194.87, 298.50)	Tapered	197.74 (190.77, 204.97)
4	233.89 (191.48, 292.21)	MT	181.50 (178.64, 184.41)
5	252.93 (207.07, 316.00)		
6	253.36 (207.42, 316.53)		
7	224.19 (183.03, 281.07)		
8	219.21 (178.86, 275.02)		

fit for the sunspot data is Model 8, since $\tilde{\sigma}^2_{\text{LS}}$ for Model 8 is closest to the four nonparametric estimates of σ^2 in Table 19.2. Furthermore, we note that the CI for prediction error variance of Model 8 contains the CIs of the four nonparametric estimators of σ^2 reported in Table 19.2.

19.4 Simulation Study for Spectrum with High Dynamic Range

In this section, we illustrate that the estimators of σ^2 based on the multitapered periodogram perform better than those based on raw, smoothed, and tapered periodograms when the spectrum has high dynamic range. We simulate from AR(2) models used in Pukkila and Nyquist (1985) for which the spectrum has high dynamic range

$$X_t = \left(1.25B - 0.75B^2\right) X_t + Z_t, \tag{19.4.1}$$

and

$$X_t = \left(1.8B - 0.9B^2\right) X_t + Z_t, \tag{19.4.2}$$

where B denotes the backshift operator and Z_t is Gaussian white noise with zero mean and unit variance. For each case, we generated series of lengths, $n = 100, 200$, and 500 and performed 1000 replications to compute the nonparametric estimates of σ^2 using Equations 19.2.10 through 19.2.13. For $\hat{\sigma}^2_s$ we used $m = 3$, as discussed in Section 19.2. The trapezoidal taper defined in Section 19.3 was used in computing $\hat{\sigma}^2_T$. For $\hat{\sigma}^2_{\text{MT}}$ we used DPSS tapers of order 3. Following Walden (1995, §5), we used $nW = 2.2$ for the AR model in Equation 19.4.1 and $nW = 2.6$ for the AR model in Equation 19.4.2. The nonparametric estimates of σ^2 and their MSEs are given in Table 19.3. The MSE for the multitapered estimator of σ^2 is smaller than its raw, smoothed, and tapered estimators. The MSEs for all four estimators of σ^2 decreases as n

TABLE 19.3
Nonparametric Estimators of σ^2 for AR(2) Models

n	$\hat{\sigma}^2$(MSE)	$\hat{\sigma}^2_s$(MSE)	$\hat{\sigma}^2_T$(MSE)	$\hat{\sigma}^2_{\text{MT}}(MSE)$
		$\phi_1 = 1.25$, $\phi_2 = -0.75$		
100	1.25 (0.17126)	1.26 (0.15125)	1.09 (0.09231)	1.11 (0.07024)
200	1.07 (0.01528)	0.92 (0.01426)	0.99 (0.00084)	1.02 (0.00054)
500	1.01 (0.00074)	1.02 (0.00061)	1.01 (0.00006)	0.99 (0.00004)
		$\phi_1 = 1.80$, $\phi_2 = -0.90$		
100	3.11 (9.57384)	2.84 (6.57317)	1.44 (0.36512)	1.62 (0.20674)
200	1.69 (1.38591)	1.88 (1.29828)	1.19 (0.03935)	1.07 (0.00815)
500	1.29 (0.26827)	1.33 (0.22964)	1.09 (0.00864)	1.06 (0.00459)

increases. MT method outperforms the raw, smoothed, and tapered methods in estimating σ^2, especially for spectrums with high dynamic range. These results are in agreement with the simulation results from Walden (1995).

19.5 Estimation of Innovation Variance for Time Series with Missing Values

An implicit assumption in all the nonparametric methods discussed in Section 19.2 for estimating σ^2 is that the observations are sampled at equally spaced time points. Unfortunately, it is often the case that some of the values are either missing or unavailable for certain dates in the sampling period of interest. If we simply ignore the missing values and treat the data as completely observed, this can introduce a significant amount of bias, which leads to incorrect predictions. The problem of missing data exists in many applications such as telemedicine, engineering, physics, economics, and astronomy. In this section, we propose a nonparametric estimator of σ^2 when there are missing values in the time series.

For time series with missing values, Bloomfield (1976, Ch. 10) proposed treating each uninterrupted segment of the time series as a separate series with equally spaced observations instead of calculating the periodogram of the whole time series. Each stretch is tapered and padded by zeros to a common length and the average of the periodograms of these parts is used. This method is reasonable when there are blocks of missing values. Whereas, if the missing values appear as isolated points, he suggested to interpolate each isolated missing value with a linear combination of its neighboring observations. In some situations, a combination of these two approaches may be used to divide the segments into blocks of missing values and interpolate the missing values at isolated points. He also pointed out that even the combined approach results in highly biased estimates when more than 20% of the data is missing because it may not be possible to divide the data into smaller segments with few blocks of missing values.

In Section 19.2, we used tapering to reduce sidelobes, especially for spectrums with high dynamic range. Interestingly, another important application of tapering is for the data with missing values where the taper function $\{h(t)\}$ is used as the indicator of the observed value at a given time point, i.e.,

$$h(t) = \begin{cases} 1, & \text{if } X_t \text{ is observed at time } t, \\ 0, & \text{if } X_t \text{ is missing at time } t. \end{cases}$$

This type of tapering used to deal with missing values in time series was first suggested by Jones (1962) for periodic sampling where a block of observed values is followed by a block of missing values. Parzen (1963) treated data with missing values as a special case of amplitude modulated processes and created tapered series $\{Y_t\} = \{h(t)X_t\}$ with zeros for the missing values. He proposed an estimator for the spectrum of $\{X_t\}$. Like Jones (1962) and Parzen (1963), Dalhaus (1987) proposed a smoothed estimator for the spectrum using the tapered series $\{Y_t\}$. He considered the percentage and pattern of missing values to study the effect of the structure of the taper function $\{h(t)\}$ on the behavior of the spectrum estimator.

Using the indicator taper function $\{h(t)\}$, we propose the following nonparametric estimator of σ^2 for missing data as a special case of the tapered estimator in Equation 19.2.5:

$$\hat{\sigma}^2_{miss} = \exp\left\{ \frac{1}{M} \sum_{j=1}^{M} \log I_{miss}(\lambda_j) + \gamma \right\}, \tag{19.5.1}$$

where

$$I_{miss}(\lambda) = \frac{1}{n_1} \left| \sum_{t=1}^{n} (Y_t - \bar{y}) \exp(-i\lambda t) \right|^2,$$

is the periodogram of the tapered data $\{Y_t\} = \{h(t)X_t\}$, $\bar{y} = \sum_{t=1}^{n}(Y_t/n_2)$, $n_1 = \sum_{t=1}^{n} h^2(t)$, and $n_2 = \sum_{t=1}^{n} h(t)$. For the indicator taper, $h(t) = h^2(t)$, for all t, therefore $n_1 = n_2 = n_{obs}$, say, is the total number of observed values in the data.

To apply the results from Theorem 19.1(c), we normalized $\{h(t)\}$ as

$$h_1(t) = \begin{cases} \dfrac{1}{\sqrt{n_{obs}}}, & \text{if } X_t \text{ is observed at time } t, \\ 0, & \text{if } X_t \text{ is missing at time } t, \end{cases}$$

so that the estimator for σ^2 in Equation 19.5.1 is modified to

$$\widehat{\sigma}^2_{miss_1} = \exp\left\{ \frac{1}{M} \sum_{j=1}^{M} \log I_{miss_1}(\lambda_j) + \gamma \right\}, \tag{19.5.2}$$

where

$$I_{miss_1}(\lambda) = \frac{1}{n_1} \left| \sum_{t=1}^{n} (Y_t - \bar{y}) \exp(-i\lambda t) \right|^2, \quad (19.5.3)$$

is the periodogram of the tapered data $\{Y_t\} = \{h_1(t)X_t\}$, $n_1 = \sum_{t=1}^{n} h_1^2(t) = 1$, $n_2 = \sum_{t=1}^{n} h_1(t) = \sqrt{n_{obs}}$, and $\bar{y} = \sum_{t=1}^{n}(Y_t/n_2)$.

Applying Theorem 19.1(c) to Equation 19.5.2, it follows that

$$\log \widehat{\sigma}^2_{miss_1} \sim N\left(\log \sigma^2, \frac{\pi^2}{6M}\right). \quad (19.5.4)$$

Our proposed nonparametric estimator of σ^2 for missing data with reduced bias is

$$\hat{\sigma}^2_{miss_1} = \exp\left\{ \frac{1}{M} \sum_{j=1}^{M} \log I_{miss_1}(\lambda_j) + \gamma - \frac{\pi^2}{12M} \right\}. \quad (19.5.5)$$

Due to sharp changes from 1 to 0, the indicator taper exhibits large sidelobes. This is worse when a large percentage of data is missing. Therefore, we suggest applying another taper function that goes from 1 to 0 more smoothly than the indicator taper function. Using a normalized smooth taper function $\{h_2(t)\}$ we construct the nonparametric estimator of σ^2 for data with missing values as

$$\widehat{\sigma}^2_{miss_2} = \exp\left\{ \frac{1}{M} \sum_{j=1}^{M} \log I_{miss_2}(\lambda_j) + \gamma - \frac{\pi^2}{12M} \right\}, \quad (19.5.6)$$

where

$$I_{miss_2}(\lambda) = \frac{1}{n_1} \left| \sum_{t=1}^{n} (Y_t - \bar{y}) \exp(-i\lambda t) \right|^2,$$

is the periodogram of tapered data $\{Y_t\} = \{h_2(t)Y_t\}$, $\bar{y} = \sum_{t=1}^{n}(Y_t/n_2)$, $n_1 = \sum_{t=1}^{n} h_2^2(t)$, and $n_2 = \sum_{t=1}^{n} h_2(t)$. We assessed the performance of the above estimators for different tapers through simulations.

19.6 Simulation Study

We generated data from the AR models in Equations 19.4.1 and 19.4.2 and then randomly selected time points at which the observations are missing. The pattern of missingness is known to have an impact on the estimation of the spectrum, cf. Sakai (1980) and Dalhaus (1987). We select the missing time points in a manner such that $T_i \subset T_j$, for $i < j$, where T_i is the set of random time points at which i% of the observations are missing. To illustrate the effect of taper functions smoother than the indicator taper in the estimation of σ^2,

TABLE 19.4
Nonparametric Estimators of σ^2 for AR(2) Models with Missing Values

	$\phi_1 = 1.25$, $\phi_2 = -0.75$			$\phi_1 = 1.8$, $\phi_2 = -0.9$		
$i\%$	$\hat{\sigma}_1^2(MSE)$	$\hat{\sigma}_2^2(MSE)$	$\hat{\sigma}_3^2(MSE)$	$\hat{\sigma}_1^2(MSE)$	$\hat{\sigma}_2^2(MSE)$	$\hat{\sigma}_3^2(MSE)$
				$n = 100$		
0	1.32(0.14)	1.13(0.024)	1.06(0.003)	2.82(7.862)	1.38(0.163)	1.24(0.0654)
10	2.57(2.47)	2.15(1.345)	1.76(0.584)	10.50(93.834)	8.66(59.394)	7.72(46.164)
20	3.76(7.66)	3.04(4.191)	2.54(2.375)	16.25(243.241)	12.82(144.671)	11.59(114.922)
				$n = 200$		
0	1.18(0.033)	1.09(0.008)	1.03(0.001)	1.77(1.317)	1.24(0.069)	1.22(0.0521)
10	1.82(0.681)	1.56(0.314)	1.45(0.215)	8.81(62.211)	7.82(48.610)	7.38(40.768)
20	2.80(3.264)	2.19(1.420)	1.98(0.966)	12.27(130.410)	10.11(82.151)	9.61(78.326)
				$n = 500$		
0	1.08(0.007)	1.06(0.006)	1.02(0.002)	1.22(0.125)	1.06(0.004)	1.02(0.001)
10	1.45(0.214)	1.28(0.087)	1.21(0.042)	4.35(11.278)	4.29(10.826)	3.88(8.281)
20	1.84(0.661)	1.56(0.324)	1.46(0.217)	8.41(54.937)	7.23(38.794)	6.71(32.585)

we use the trapezoidal taper defined in Section 19.3 and the cosine bell taper:

$$h(t) = \begin{cases} (1/2)\left[1 - \cos\left\{\dfrac{2\pi(t/n)}{\rho}\right\}\right], & \text{if } 0 \le t/n < \dfrac{\rho}{2}, \\ 1, & \text{if } \dfrac{\rho}{2} \le t/n \le 1/2, \\ (1/2)\left[1 - \cos\left\{\dfrac{2\pi(1-(t/n))}{\rho}\right\}\right], & \text{if } 1/2 < t/n \le 1, \\ 0, & \text{otherwise,} \end{cases}$$

where $\rho = n^{-k/2}$ for $0 \le k < 0.5$. We did 500 replications and for each case we used a fixed pattern of missingness with percentages of missing values, $i\% = 0, 10$, and 20. The estimators using indicator, trapezoidal, and cosine bell taper functions are denoted as $\hat{\sigma}_1^2$, $\hat{\sigma}_2^2$, and $\hat{\sigma}_3^2$, respectively, in Table 19.4. These estimates of σ^2 and their MSEs show that the MSE increase as the percentage of missing values in the dataset increases. The cosine bell taper function shows significant reduction in the MSE over the indicator and trapezoidal taper function in the estimation of σ^2, especially for large percentages of missing values. These results indicate that tapering can significantly influence the estimation of σ^2 for time series with missing values. Hence, careful choice of a taper function is recommended.

19.7 Summary

We compared the performance of four nonparametric estimators of the innovation variance based on raw, smoothed, tapered, and multitapered periodograms for spectrums with high dynamic range. They were compared in terms of MSEs of these estimators. We concluded that MT outperforms the other three methods of estimation of the innovation variance. Using these nonparametric estimators of innovation variance, we reviewed a general framework to judge the performance of different ARMA models for a given dataset in terms of their one-step-ahead prediction error variance. We illustrated this method on Wolfer's sunspot data (1749–1924) to choose an ARMA model from a partial list of models fitted to this data over the last eight decades. Further, we proposed a nonparametric estimator for the innovation variance for time series with missing values. The estimator performs better for smooth taper function, like the cosine bell taper used here. The results indicate that tapering can significantly influence the performance of the estimator of the innovation variance for time series with missing values.

Acknowledgments

The authors are grateful to the editor and two referees for their many useful and constructive comments, which led to a substantial improvement in the presentation of this chapter. This work was supported by the National Science Foundation grant DMS-0906252.

References

An, H. Z. (1982). Estimation of prediction error variance. *Stochastic Processes and their Applications*, 13(1):39–43.

Bhansali, R. J. (1974). Asymptotic properties of Wiener-Kolmogorov predictor, I. *Journal of the Royal Statistical Society B*, 36(1):61–73.

Bloomfield, P. (1973). An exponential model for the spectrum of a scalar time series. *Biometrika*, 60(2):217–226.

Bloomfield, P. (1976). *Fourier Analysis of Time Series: An Introduction.* New York: Wiley.

Brillinger, D. R. (1975). *Time Series: Data Analysis and Theory.* Philadelphia: SIAM.

Brockwell, P. J. and Davis, R. A. (1991). *Time Series: Theory and Methods.* New York: Springer-Verlag.

Dalhaus, R. (1987). Nonparametric spectral analysis with missing observations. *Sankhya, A*, 49(3):347–367.

Davis, H. T. and Jones, R. H. (1968). Estimation of the innovation variance of a stationary time series. *Journal of the American Statistical Association*, 63:141–149.

Gencay, R., Faruk, S., and Whitcher, B. (2002). *An Introduction to Wavelets and Other Filtering Methods in Finance and Economics*. California: Academic Press.

Hannan, E. J. and Nicholls, D. F. (1977). The estimation of the prediction error variance. *Journal of the American Statistical Association*, 72(360):834–840.

Izenman, A. J. (1983). J. R. Wolf and H. A. Wolfer: An historical note on the Zurich sunspot relative numbers. *Journal of the Royal Statistical Society A*, 146(3):311–318.

Janacek, G. (1975). Estimation of the minimum mean square error of prediction. *Biometrika*, 62(1):175–180.

Jones, R. H. (1962). Spectral analysis with regularly missed observations. *The Annals of Mathematical Statistics*, 33(2):455–461.

Jones, R. H. (1976). Estimation of the innovation generalized variance of a multivariate stationary time series. *Journal of the American Statistical Association*, 71(354):386–388.

Luati, A., Proietti, T., and Reale, M. (2011). The variance profile. MPRA-Paper 30378, Munich Personal RePEc Archive. See http://mpra.ub.uni-muenchen.de/30378/.

McElroy, T. S. and Findley, D. F. (2010). Selection between models through multi-step ahead forecasting. *Journal of Statistical Planning and Inference*, 140(12):3655–3675.

McElroy, T. S. and Holan, S. (2009). A local spectral approach for assessing time series model misspecification. *Journal of Multivariate Analysis*, 100(4):604–621.

Mohanty, R. and Pourahmadi, M. (1996). Estimation of the generalized prediction error variance of a multiple time series. *Journal of the American Statistical Association*, 91(433):294–299.

Parzen, E. (1963). On spectral analysis with missing observations and amplitude modulation. *Sankhya, A*, 25(4):383–392.

Percival, D. B. and Walden, A. T. (1993). *Spectral Analysis for Physical Applications*. Cambridge: Cambridge University Press.

Pourahmadi, M. (2001). *Foundations of Time Series Analysis and Prediction Theory*. New York: Wiley.

Pukkila, T. (1977). Fitting of autoregressive moving average models in the frequency domain. PhD thesis, Department of Mathematical Sciences, Tampere, Finland: University of Tampere.

Pukkila, T. (1979). The bias in periodogram ordinates and the estimation of ARMA models in the frequency domain. *Australian Journal of Statistics*, 21(2):121–128.

Pukkila, T. and Nyquist, H. (1985). On the frequency domain estimation of the innovation variance of a stationary univariate time series. *Biometrika*, 72(2):317–323.

Riedel, K. S. and Sidorenko, A. (1996). Adaptive smoothing of the log-spectrum with multiple tapering. *IEEE Transactions on Signal Processing*, 44(7):1794–800.

Sakai, H. (1980). Fitting autoregressive with regularly missed observations. *Annals of the Institute of Statistical Mathematics*, 32(1):393–400.

Sella, L. (2008). Old and new spectral techniques for economic time series. *Working Paper Series*, Department of Economics, Cognetti de Martiis, University of Tokyo, QR08:No 9.

Sella, L., Vivaldo, G., Ghil, M., and Groth, A. (2010). Economic cycles and their synchronization: Spectral analysis of macroeconomic series from Italy, the Netherlands, and the UK. EGU General Assembly, Vienna, Austria, 12:11847.

Slepian, D. (1978). Prolate spheroidal wave functions, Fourier analysis, and uncertainty: The discrete case. *Bell System Technical Journal*, 57:1371–1430.

Taniguchi, M. (1980). On estimation of the integrals of certain functions of spectral density. *Journal of Applied Probability*, 17(1):73–83.

Thomson, D. J. (1982). Spectrum estimation and harmonic analysis. *Proceedings of the IEEE*, 70(9):1055–1096.

Tukey, J. W. (1967). An introduction to the calculations of numerical spectrum analysis. *Advanced Seminar on Spectral Analysis of Time Series*, ed. B. Harris, 1:25–46. New York: Wiley.

Walden, A. T. (1995). Multitaper estimation of the innovation variance of a stationary time series. *IEEE Transactions on Signal Processing*, 43(1): 181–187.

Walden, A. T. (2000). A unified view of multitaper multivariate spectral estimation. *Biometrika*, 87(4):767–788.

Woodward, W. A. and Gray, H. L. (1978). New ARMA models for Wolfer's sunspot data. *Comunications in Statistics: Simulation and Computation*, 7(1):97–115.

Yule, G. U. (1927). On a method of investigating periodocities in disturbed time series, with special reference to Wolfers sunspot numbers. *Philosophical Transaction of the Royal Society A*, 226:267–298.

20

Functional Model Selection for Sparse Binary Time Series with Multiple Inputs

Catherine Y. Tu, Dong Song, F. Jay Breidt, Theodore W. Berger, and Haonan Wang

CONTENTS

20.1 Introduction

Consider an "output signal" recorded as a series of 0s and 1s, with 1 indicating that an event has occurred. An additional large set of observed "input signals" or potential covariates is available for modeling the probability of event occurrence. Of particular interest are binary input signals. Both input and output signals may be functions of either continuous or discrete time. Our analytic approach will treat time as continuous and employ tools from functional data analysis, though the actual data are usually recorded in discrete time.

In Equation 20.2.1, we propose a class of dynamic generalized linear models for such situations, with time-varying event probability $\theta(t)$ modeled through a known link function $g(\cdot)$ (such as logit or probit) as a linear combination

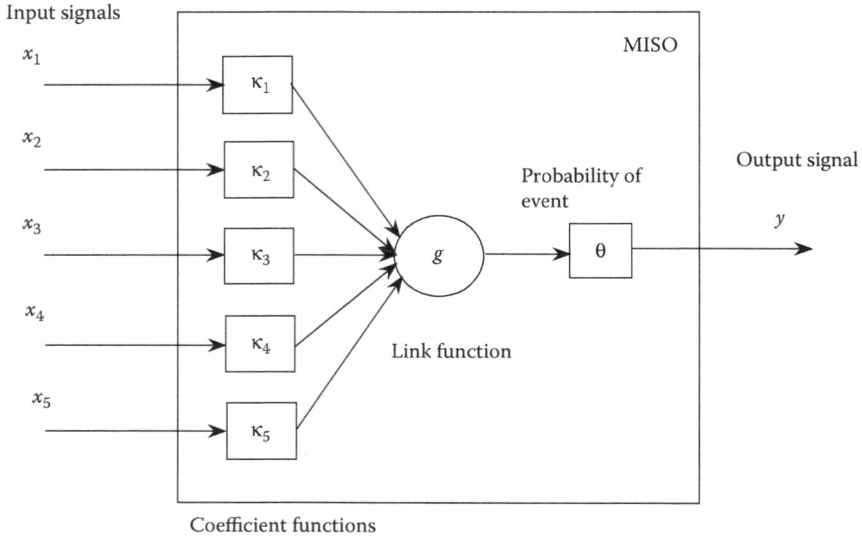

FIGURE 20.1
Structure of the multiple-input single-output (MISO) model, consisting of coefficient functions κ_i for each input signal x_i and link function $g(\cdot)$, which together determine the probability θ of an event in the binary output signal, y.

of the recent past of multiple input signals. Because our analysis treats each input signal x_i as a function of continuous time, it enters the model as an integral convolution with an unknown coefficient function $\kappa_i(\cdot)$, instead of as a sum with a finite set of coefficients. The model is depicted graphically in Figure 20.1.

It is possible that more input signals than necessary are considered in the model. It is also possible that not all of the information in the recent past of an input signal is transformed into output signal. These two possibilities raise the issue of model selection, both among input signals and within input signals. Our goal is to attain both: (1) *global sparsity:* among all input signals considered, those that are actually used in transformation to output signal are selected for the final model; and (2) *local sparsity:* within an important input signal, the periods within the recent past that are transformed into output signal (i.e., the periods with nonzero coefficient functions) are selected.

20.1.1 Motivating Applications

Two major application areas motivate this research. The first is in the context of neural science, in which events can represent neuron firings, stimulated by multiple recorded inputs in a designed study of brain regions undergoing cognitive function. Various cognitive functions rely on one or more brain regions. Each brain region contains a large number of neurons. Millions of axonal projections and synaptic connections extending from those neurons allow information communication between different brain regions. Information communication is coded through "neuron spikes," which are the ensemble firing of populations of neurons. A "spike train" is the time series of these spike signals. A brain region will transform incoming spike trains into outgoing spike trains, which enables information processing.

Actual data on cognitive function of an animal during the performance of a behavioral task can be collected from multiple implanted electrode arrays in a certain brain region of interest, allowing simultaneous recording of input and output signals. Binary input and output signals, as well as their associated neuron information, can be extracted from the recorded continuous signals.

As pointed out by Song et al. (2007a,b 2009), a brain region can be modeled as a multiple-input, multiple-output (MIMO), nonlinear dynamic system. This MIMO system can be further decomposed into several multiple-input, single-output (MISO) systems. One major research goal is then to model the causal relations between the input spike trains and the output spike trains in the MISO systems, facilitating the study of cognitive functions. In particular, understanding the mechanisms underlying cognition requires model selection and estimation from the set of potential explanatory input signals.

The second major area of application is in economic time series. In this context, events could represent transactions in a market, failures of institutions, interventions by government agencies, or almost any decision of an economic agent, large or small. Binary time series indicating occurrence of events might also be constructed from one or more underlying continuous variables (bull and bear markets, recessions, etc.; see Harding and Pagan (2011) and the references therein). The corresponding set of potential input signals is enormous, including lagged "news" of almost any kind, and again at essentially any scale. Understanding the behavior of the economic agents and processes requires model selection and estimation from this huge set of potential explanatory variables.

In both the neural science and economic applications, the major challenge is large-scale functional model selection with both global and local sparsity: we seek to choose the correct input signals and to estimate (as sparsely as possible) the coefficient functions for each input signal.

20.1.2 Review of Approaches to Model Selection

Model selection has a rich history, which we only touch upon here. For selecting individual variables, commonly used methods include Mallows-C_p (Mallows 1973), Akaike's Information Criterion (AIC) (Akaike 1973), and the Bayesian Information Criterion (BIC) (Schwarz 1978). In the context of time series modeling, the work of David Findley and co-authors is of particular note, including studies of the asymptotic properties of AIC (Findley 1985; Findley and Wei 2002), methods of model selection involving multistep-ahead forecasts (Findley 1983, 1991), and implementation of likelihood-based model selection methods in widely used seasonal adjustment software (Findley et al. 1998).

Another common technique in the fitting of large models is the use of a regularization method to improve estimation performance. Regularization typically involves imposing a penalty that increases with model dimension, and so is often closely tied to model selection. The classic example of regularization is ridge regression (Hoerl 1962). Some regularization methods with penalties can both improve estimation and select variables, as in LASSO/LARS (Tibshirani 1996; Efron et al. 2004), bridge (Frank and Friedman 1993), and smoothly clipped absolute deviation (Fan and Li 2001).

For selecting groups of variables, the techniques of group LASSO, group LARS, and group nonnegative garrote are introduced in Yuan and Lin (2006). In Huang et al. (2009), a group bridge approach has been proposed for both group variable selection and individual variable selection.

20.1.3 Overview

The contribution of this chapter is to consider both global and local sparsity in the functional model selection context. Global sparsity is similar to the notion of variable selection in a standard model selection problem, which has been widely studied. However, to the best of our knowledge, local sparsity has not been studied.

Our approach is to generalize the LASSO model selection methodology from the multivariate case to this functional model selection setting with binary input and output signals. We impose smoothness of the coefficient functions on each input signal by restricting attention to coefficient functions in the space spanned by B-splines. Other basis functions could of course be used, but we choose B-splines for their valuable properties, including computational stability (see Section 20.2.1). We then consider a penalized loglikelihood criterion, with likelihood conditioned on the covariates and with a LASSO-like penalty. The penalty is given as an overall tuning parameter multiplied by a linear combination of input-specific penalties. The input-specific penalties are powers of L_1 penalties on the B-spline coefficients. Rather than minimize the criterion directly, we propose an approximation from which we can readily obtain "one-step" estimates via the LARS algorithm.

This chapter is organized as follows. Section 20.2 gives detailed model setup and estimation criteria. The computational techniques used to obtain one-step estimates and the choice of tuning parameters are considered in Section 20.3. A simulation study comparing variable selection methods under three different scenarios is presented and discussed in Section 20.4. Simulation results demonstrate that the penalized likelihood methodology and the one-step estimators achieve the desired twofold sparsity, correctly selecting the number of nonzero components and the locations where the coefficient functions take value zero. We apply our method to binary series derived from a multivariate economic time series in Section 20.5. Finally, some concluding remarks are provided in Section 20.6.

20.2 Methodology

We begin our discussion with a brief introduction to B-spline basis functions and their properties.

20.2.1 B-Spline Polynomial Basis Functions

Polynomial splines are piecewise polynomials with smooth transitions between the adjacent pieces at a set of interior *knot* points. More specifically, a (polynomial) spline of degree $d \geq 0$ on $[0, M]$ with knot sequence

$$\eta_0 = 0 < \eta_1 < \cdots < \eta_m < \eta_{m+1} = M$$

is a function that is a polynomial of degree d between each pair of adjacent knots and has $d-1$ continuous derivatives for $d \geq 1$.

For a given knot sequence, the collection of spline functions with a particular degree form a linear space, denoted as $\mathbb{S}$. Any function $\beta(t)$, $t \in [0, M]$, can be approximated by an element in $\mathbb{S}$. Such an approximation will be exact if the function $\beta(\cdot)$ itself belongs to the linear space $\mathbb{S}$.

In our application, we use a B-spline basis for its valuable properties, especially computational stability. For more discussion on spline functions, see Schumaker (1980) and de Boor (2001). A B-spline basis function of degree d can be defined recursively using the Cox–de Boor recursion formula

$$B_{j,d}(u) = \frac{u - \eta_j}{\eta_{j+d-1} - \eta_j} B_{j,d-1}(u) + \frac{\eta_{j+d} - u}{\eta_{j+d} - \eta_{j+1}} B_{j+1,d-1}(u),$$

where

$$B_{j,0}(u) = \begin{cases} 1 & \text{if } \eta_j < u < \eta_{j+1}, \\ 0 & \text{otherwise.} \end{cases}$$

The total number of B-spline basis functions is $J = m + d + 1$. For purposes of illustration, a set of cubic ($d = 3$) B-spline basis functions defined on $[0, 1]$ is depicted in Figure 20.2. There are $m = 9$ interior knots evenly distributed on the entire domain, yielding a total of $J = 13$ basis functions.

Throughout this chapter, it is assumed without loss of generality that all B-spline basis functions are normalized to integrate to 1; i.e., we replace the basis functions defined above by the rescaled functions $B_j(u) = B_{j,d}(u) / \int_0^M B_{j,d}(u)du$.

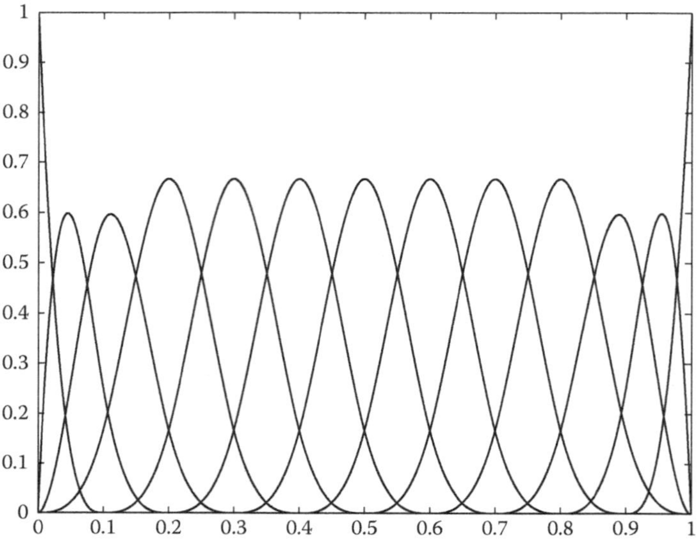

FIGURE 20.2
A set of 13 cubic ($d = 3$) B-spline basis functions based on 11 knots, including 2 endpoints and 9 interior knot points, evenly distributed on the interval.

20.2.2 Dynamic Multiple-Input, Single-Output Model

We now describe a dynamic MISO model with p input signals, denoted as $x_1(t), \ldots, x_p(t)$, and a single output signal, $y(t)$. Our primary goal is to model the probability of an event being observed for the output signal at any time t, given all information collected for all input signals. Write

$$\theta(t) = \Pr(y(t) = 1 \mid X(s), 0 \le s \le t) = \mathrm{E}(y(t) \mid X(s), 0 \le s \le t),$$

where $X(t) = (x_1(t), \ldots, x_p(t))'$. In addition, assume that at any given time t, the output signal only depends on the input signals within the past M time units. Here, M is called the *memory length* or *effective lag*. Note that we choose a single M sufficiently large for all input signals. In practice, M may be determined from subject-matter considerations.

We consider the following generalized functional additive model

$$g(\theta(t)) = \alpha_0 + \sum_{i=1}^{p} \int_{t-M}^{t} \kappa_i(u - t + M) x_i(u)\, du, \tag{20.2.1}$$

where $g(\cdot)$ is a known link function and $\kappa_i(\cdot)$, $i = 1, \ldots, p$ are unknown coefficient functions defined on $[0, M]$. To model binary output, probit and logit are two commonly used link functions. In this chapter, we use the logit link function.

Under the logit link, model (20.2.1) can be rewritten as

$$\theta(t) = \left[1 + \exp\left\{-\alpha_0 - \sum_{i=1}^{p} \int_{t-M}^{t} \kappa_i(u - t + M) x_i(u)\, du\right\}\right]^{-1}. \qquad (20.2.2)$$

Note that the coefficient functions $\kappa_i(\cdot)$ characterize the relationship between the output signal $y(t)$ and the i-th input signal.

In many applications, it seems intuitively sensible to assume some degree of smoothness for these coefficient functions. A natural approximation family for the coefficient functions is then the linear space spanned by the B-splines with given knot sequence and fixed degree. Even if the true coefficient functions have some nonsmooth behavior, like sharp transitions, the B-splines can approximate this behavior to some extent. In what follows, we use the cubic B-splines ($d = 3$), with the same knot sequence for all coefficient functions to reduce the complexity of the model. Consequently, all coefficient functions can be approximated as

$$\kappa_i(u) \approx \sum_{j=1}^{J} \alpha_{ij} B_j(u), u \in [0, M], \qquad (20.2.3)$$

for $i = 1, \ldots, p$, where $B_j(\cdot)$, $j = 1, \ldots, J$ are the normalized B-spline basis functions defined in Section 20.2.1.

Combining Equations 20.2.2 and 20.2.3, we have

$$\text{logit}\ \theta(t) \approx \alpha_0 + \sum_{i=1}^{p} \sum_{j=1}^{J} \alpha_{ij} D_{ij}(t) = \alpha_0 + \phi(t)^T \alpha, \qquad (20.2.4)$$

where

$$\alpha = (\alpha_{11}, \ldots, \alpha_{1J}, \ldots, \alpha_{pJ})', \quad \phi(t) = (D_{11}(t), \ldots, D_{1J}(t), \ldots, D_{pJ}(t))'$$

with

$$D_{ij}(t) = \int_{t-M}^{t} B_j(u - t + M) x_i(u)\, du.$$

It can be seen that the D_{ij}'s only depend on the B-spline basis functions and the observed input signals. In Section 20.2.3, we develop an estimation procedure for the α_{ij}'s.

20.2.3 Likelihood Function and Penalized Estimation

In practice, the continuous output signal is typically discretized. Suppose that the observed measurements are taken every $\delta = 1/h$ time unit. A 1 is recorded if an event occurs within a given time unit, otherwise 0 is recorded. Events are not instantaneous, but are of short duration relative to δ. In our motivating applications, events are fairly rare. This means that typical observed sequences

$y_n = (y(t_1), \ldots, y(t_n))'$, $(t_i = i/h)$, include many 0s, few 1s, and 1s tend to be isolated.

The continuous input signals may also be recorded in discrete time, but we continue to regard time as continuous by extending $x_j(\cdot)$, if necessary, to a piecewise constant function on each δ time increment.

For $i \leq n$, let $X_i = \{x_j(s) : 0 \leq s \leq t_i\}_{j=1}^{p}$. We assume that the elements of y_n are conditionally independent, given the present and past of the input signals so that the joint likelihood of the observations can be written as

$$L(y_n \mid X_n) = \prod_{i=1}^{n} f(y(t_i) \mid X_i) = \prod_{i=1}^{n} \theta(t_i)^{y(t_i)}(1 - \theta(t_i))^{1-y(t_i)}.$$

Thus, the log-likelihood is

$$l(y_n \mid X_n) = \sum_{i=1}^{n} \{y(t_i) \log \theta(t_i) + (1 - y(t_i)) \log(1 - \theta(t_i))\}. \tag{20.2.5}$$

Using Equation 20.2.4 to approximate $\theta(t)$ in Equation 20.2.5 yields an approximation of $l(y_n \mid X_n)$. This new criterion is a function of $\beta = (\alpha_0, \alpha')'$ and is denoted as $l(\beta)$. The maximizer of $l(\beta)$ is denoted as $\widehat{\beta}_{mle} = (\widehat{\alpha}_{0,mle}, \widehat{\alpha}'_{mle})'$.

By plugging $\widehat{\beta}_{mle}$ into Equation 20.2.3, we could obtain estimated coefficient functions using a likelihood-based method. However, these estimators would not take on zero values with positive probability. Therefore, they would not achieve the desired sparsity if some of the coefficient functions were zero over some part of the domain with positive Lebesgue measure.

Instead of the approximate loglikelihood criterion $l(\beta)$, we propose a penalized method to accomplish both global and local sparsity. More specifically, we generalize the idea of group variable selection (Huang et al. 2009) to the problem of sparse functional estimation, minimizing the criterion

$$W(\beta) = -l(\beta) + \lambda \sum_{i=1}^{p} c_i \left(\sum_{j=1}^{J} |\alpha_{ij}| \right)^{\gamma}. \tag{20.2.6}$$

Here, $\lambda > 0$ is a tuning parameter to balance the goodness-of-fit and model complexity/sparsity. Moreover, c_i's are positive constants to adjust the individual scales of different coefficient functions. In the case of $\gamma = 1$, Equation 20.2.6 is equivalent to the LASSO criterion, and only individual variable selection may be possible. In order to achieve both global and local sparsity, the value of γ is chosen between 0 and 1. See Section 20.3.3 for further discussion of the choice of γ.

20.3 Computational Aspects

Minimization of Equation 20.2.6 poses serious challenges since neither the log-likelihood function nor the penalty function is convex. In this section, we simplify the optimization problem by approximating the log-likelihood part of the objective function with a quadratic form, leading to "one-step estimators," which are approximations to the actual minimizers. Unlike the actual minimizers of Equation 20.2.6, these one-step estimators are readily computed. We then discuss tuning parameter selection.

20.3.1 Quadratic Approximation of the Criterion Function

Because α_0 does not appear in the penalty term, the minimizer of Equation 20.2.6 is of the form $(\widehat{\alpha}_{0,mle}, \alpha')$ for some α minimizing

$$W^*(\alpha) = -l(\alpha; \widehat{\alpha}_{0,mle}) + \lambda \sum_{i=1}^{p} c_i \left(\sum_{j=1}^{J} |\alpha_{ij}| \right)^{\gamma}, \qquad (20.3.1)$$

where $l(\alpha; \widehat{\alpha}_{0,mle})$ is the profile likelihood function evaluated at $\alpha_0 = \widehat{\alpha}_{0,mle}$. We write the profile likelihood more simply as $l(\alpha)$.

For a given initial value $\alpha^{(0)}$, $l(\alpha)$ can be locally approximated by

$$l(\alpha^{(0)}) + \nabla l(\alpha^{(0)})'(\alpha - \alpha^{(0)}) + \tfrac{1}{2}(\alpha - \alpha^{(0)})'\nabla^2 l(\alpha^{(0)})(\alpha - \alpha^{(0)}). \qquad (20.3.2)$$

Using $\widehat{\alpha}_{mle}$, the maximizer of the unpenalized log-likelihood (20.2.5), as an initial value, we have

$$l(\alpha) \approx l(\widehat{\alpha}_{mle}) + \tfrac{1}{2}(\alpha - \widehat{\alpha}_{mle})'\nabla^2 l(\widehat{\alpha}_{mle})(\alpha - \widehat{\alpha}_{mle}). \qquad (20.3.3)$$

Straightforward computation shows that $\nabla^2 l(\widehat{\alpha}_{mle}) = -\Phi' R \Phi$, where

$$R = \text{diag}\left\{ \widehat{\theta}(t_1)(1 - \widehat{\theta}(t_1)), \ldots, \widehat{\theta}(t_n)(1 - \widehat{\theta}(t_n)) \right\}$$

and

$$\Phi = (\phi(t_1), \ldots, \phi(t_n)).$$

Here, $\phi(t)$ is given following Equation 20.2.4, and $\widehat{\theta}(\cdot)$ is computed from Equation 20.2.4 by replacing α_0 and α by corresponding maximum likelihood estimates.

Combining Equations 20.3.1 and 20.3.3, the penalized likelihood criterion can be approximated by

$$Q(\alpha) = \frac{1}{2}\|z - \Psi\alpha\|_2^2 + \lambda \sum_{i=1}^{p} c_i \left(\sum_{j=1}^{J} |\alpha_{ij}| \right)^{\gamma}, \qquad (20.3.4)$$

where $z = R^{1/2}\Phi\widehat{\alpha}_{mle}$ and $\Psi = R^{1/2}\Phi$.

20.3.2 One-Step Estimation

We define the one-step estimate, $\widehat{\alpha}_{ose}$, as the minimizer of $Q(\alpha)$ in Equation 20.3.4. Note that in the case of $\gamma = 1$, this minimization can be carried out by the least angle regression (LARS) algorithm (Efron et al. 2004). For a given index $\gamma \in (0, 1)$, Huang et al. (2009) formulated an equivalent optimization problem and provided an efficient algorithm. In this chapter, we use the algorithm proposed by Huang et al. (2009) as the primary tool of our work. Their algorithm is outlined as follows.

First, consider the following minimization problem

$$Q^*(\alpha) = \frac{1}{2}\|z - \Psi\alpha\|_2^2 + \sum_{i=1}^{p} \xi_i^{1-1/\gamma} c_i^{1/\gamma} \left(\sum_{j=1}^{J} |\alpha_{ij}| \right) + \tau \sum_{i=1}^{p} \xi_i,$$

subject to $\xi_i \geq 0, i = 1, \ldots, p$. Huang et al. (2009) proved that minimization of $Q^*(\alpha)$ is equivalent to minimizing $Q(\alpha)$ if

$$\tau = \lambda^{1/(1-\gamma)} \gamma^{\gamma/(1-\gamma)} (1 - \gamma).$$

Next, optimization of $Q^*(\alpha)$ can be solved iteratively, until convergence, as

$$\xi_i^{new} = c_i \left(\frac{1-\gamma}{\tau\gamma} \right)^{\gamma} \left(\sum_{j=1}^{J} |\alpha_{ij}^{old}| \right)^{\gamma},$$

$$\alpha^{new} = \arg\min \left\{ \frac{1}{2}\|z - \Psi\alpha\|_2^2 + \sum_{i=1}^{p} (\xi_i^{new})^{1-1/\gamma} c_i^{1/\gamma} \left(\sum_{j=1}^{J} |\alpha_{ij}| \right) \right\},$$

which can be solved by the LARS algorithm to yield the one-step estimators.

20.3.3 Choice of Tuning Parameters

There are two tuning parameters, λ and γ, in the penalized likelihood function. The tuning parameter λ controls the trade-off between goodness-of-fit and sparsity of the resulting model. In particular, large values of λ often lead to a sparse fitted coefficient function with poor fit for nonzero values and small likelihood. On the other hand, small λ values lead to loose control on sparsity but better fit of coefficient functions and large likelihood. Thus, the choice of tuning parameter is very important. Here, we use the BIC to choose λ.

In principle, the regularization parameter γ can be any value in $(0, 1)$, but values close to 1 (the LASSO criterion) may fail to achieve local sparsity, while values close to 0 can lead to numerical troubles in the one-step estimation procedure. After some experimentation, we chose $\gamma = 0.5$ for the examples of this chapter as a good compromise value. The same choice was made by Huang et al. (2009). Further investigation of the effect of γ would be of interest, but is beyond the scope of this chapter.

For a fixed γ, let $\widehat{\alpha}(\lambda)$ denote the resulting one-step estimator. Write

$$\mathrm{BIC}(\lambda) = -2l(\widehat{\alpha}(\lambda); \widehat{\alpha}_0) + K(\lambda)\log(n),$$

where $K(\lambda)$ is the total number of nonzero estimates in $\widehat{\alpha}(\lambda)$. Thus, a data-dependent choice of λ is the minimizer of $\mathrm{BIC}(\lambda)$.

20.4 Simulation Study

In this section, the performance of the penalized likelihood strategy and the one-step estimators is examined through a simulation study. We consider a hypothetical system with five input signals and a single output. This could represent, e.g., the cognitive function of a small brain region with only five inputting neurons and a single output neuron.

We consider various possible coefficient functions for the input series. Three scenarios illustrate our methodology.

- *Scenario 1: Global sparsity only, without basis approximation error.* All coefficient functions live in the (same) linear space spanned by a set of B-spline basis functions. Some coefficient functions are identically zero through the entire domain, and the other functions are nonzero through the entire domain.

- *Scenario 2: Global and local sparsity, without basis approximation error.* In Scenario 1, for those coefficient functions that are not identically zero, local sparsity is allowed for some period of time.

- *Scenario 3: Global and local sparsity, with basis approximation error.* Similar to Scenario 2, but one coefficient function is not in the linear space spanned by the B-spline basis functions.

In each of the three scenarios, the length of effective lag for each input–output pair is fixed at $M = 1$ second and assumed known. Observations are collected for a period of 10 seconds, and there are $h = 100$ observations observed within each second. Input signals recorded from all five input neurons are randomly generated, at any time, as independent Bernoulli trials with a probability of success of 0.1.

The common set of basis functions used for constructing the coefficient functions (except for one coefficient function in Scenario 3) is the set of 13 basis functions shown in Figure 20.2. The output signal is generated according to the model specified in Section 20.2.2.

In each scenario, a Monte Carlo experiment is performed. About 10 seconds of input and output signals have been obtained. For each of the $R = 200$ iterations, estimates from three methods, maximum likelihood estimation (MLE), penalized MLE with L_1 penalty (LASSO), and our proposed method (PMLE_γ), are calculated. For each method, the following quantities are reported for comparison:

(a) average number of identically zero coefficient functions that are correctly identified, denoted as C_0.

(b) average number of identically zero coefficient functions that are incorrectly identified, denoted as I_0.

(c) average number of zero α_{ij}'s for the i-th coefficient function that are correctly identified, denoted as $C_{i,0}$.

(d) average number of zero α_{ij}'s for the i-th coefficient function that are incorrectly identified, denoted as $I_{i,0}$.

(e) estimated *estimation bias* for each $u \in [0, M]$ for the i-th signal, denoted as $\text{Bias}_i(u)$

$$\widehat{\text{Bias}}_i(u) = \frac{1}{R}\sum_{r=1}^{R} \widehat{\kappa}_i^{(r)}(u) - \kappa_i(u),$$

where $\widehat{\kappa}_i^{(r)}$ is the estimated coefficient function from the r-th iteration.

(f) estimated mean integrated squared error (MISE) for coefficient function $\kappa_i(\cdot)$, which is defined as

$$\widehat{\text{MISE}}_i = \frac{1}{R}\sum_{r=1}^{R} \int_0^1 \left(\widehat{\kappa}_i^{(r)}(u) - \kappa_i(u)\right)^2 du,$$

where a numerical method has been used for calculation of $\widehat{\text{MISE}}_i$.

Quantities (a)–(d) are used to compare model sparsity, both global and local, while quantities (e) and (f) are used to assess model fitting.

Scenario 1

We first consider a scenario with global sparsity only and without basis approximation error. Three of the five coefficient functions, κ_1, κ_2, and κ_3, are nonzero over the entire $[0, 1]$ interval, as shown in Figure 20.3. In particular, $\alpha_{ij} \neq 0$ for any $i = 1, 2, 3$, and $j = 1, \ldots, 13$. The remaining two coefficient functions, κ_4, κ_5, are identically zero.

In Table 20.1, the quantities defined in (a)–(d) are reported, and the MISEs for all coefficient functions are summarized. The estimated estimation bias for each function is depicted in Figure 20.4. Our proposed method with $\gamma = 0.5$, denoted as $\text{PMLE}_{0.5}$, outperforms the other two approaches in both model fitting and model sparsity. The coefficient functions estimated by MLE do not posses either global sparsity or local sparsity. The model fitted via the LASSO approach attempts to achieve sparsity by estimating several of the

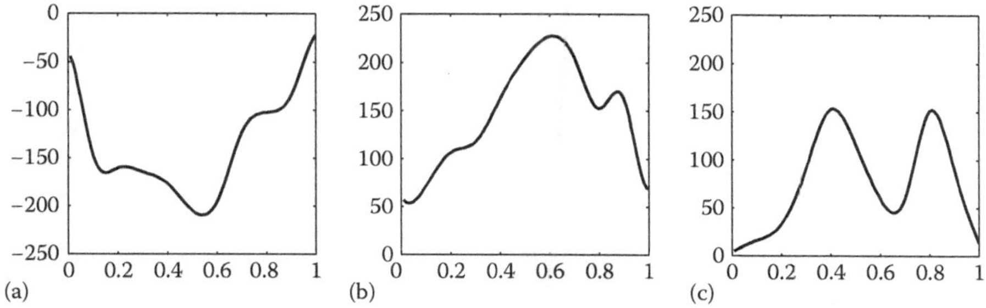

FIGURE 20.3
Coefficient functions κ_1 (a), κ_2 (b), and κ_3 (c) used in the Scenario 1 simulation experiment.

spline coefficients in functions $\kappa_4(\cdot)$ and $\kappa_5(\cdot)$ as equal to zero, but fails to achieve the appropriate global sparsity.

Scenario 2

Our second scenario illustrates both global and local sparsity, still without basis approximation error. As in Scenario 1, the two coefficient functions κ_4 and κ_5 are identically zero. The other three coefficient functions are not identically zero, but may take zero values for some interval of time on $[0, 1]$. Coefficient functions κ_1, κ_2, and κ_3 are displayed in Figure 20.5.

In Table 20.2, the quantities defined in (a)–(d) are reported, and the MISEs for all coefficient functions are summarized. The estimated estimation bias for

TABLE 20.1
Estimated MISE Values for Each Coefficient Function and Summary Quantities (a)–(d) for the Scenario 1 Simulation

	MISE				
Estimator	κ_1	κ_2	κ_3	κ_4	κ_5
MLE	485.84	489.73	280.76	185.93	173.38
LASSO	554.46	338.88	174.56	86.24	85.71
$\text{PMLE}_{0.5}$	530.44	264.88	153.61	6.05	5.01

	$C_{1,0}$	$I_{1,0}$	$C_{2,0}$	$I_{2,0}$	$C_{3,0}$	$I_{3,0}$	$C_{4,0}$	$I_{4,0}$	$C_{5,0}$	$I_{5,0}$	C_0	I_0
MLE	0	0	0	0	0	0	0	0	0	0	0	0
LASSO	0	0.48	0	0.12	0	1.06	4.26	0	4.26	0	0	0
$\text{PMLE}_{0.5}$	0	0.46	0	0.11	0	1.12	12.43	0	12.43	0	1.63	0
True model	0	13	0	13	0	13	13	0	13	0	2	3

Note: The row labeled "true model" gives the numbers of nonzero basis function coefficients $I_{i,0}$ for function κ_i, the number of zero basis function coefficients $C_{i,0}$ for function κ_i, the number of identically zero coefficient functions C_0, and the number of nonzero coefficient functions I_0.

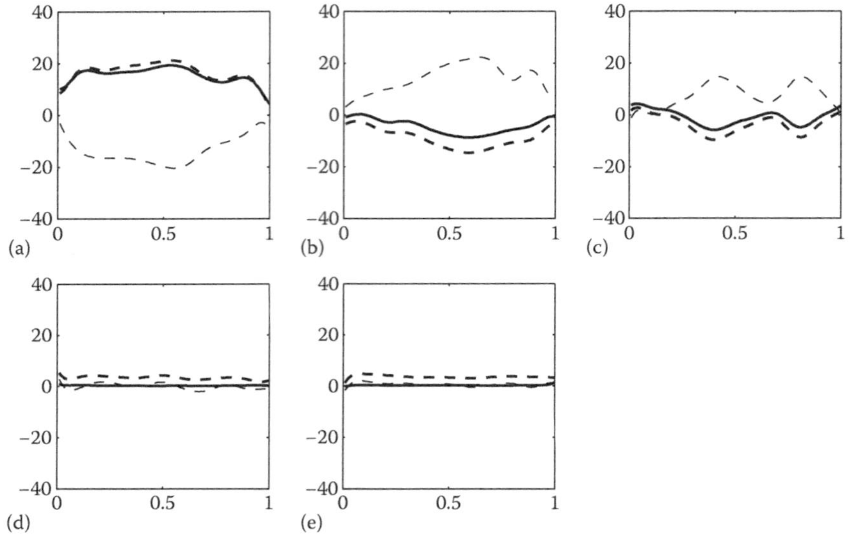

FIGURE 20.4
Scenario 1: Estimated estimation bias for all five coefficient functions (κ_1 (a), κ_2 (b), κ_3 (c), κ_4 (d), and κ_5 (e)) using MLE (dashed thin line), LASSO (dashed thick line), and $\text{PMLE}_{0.5}$ (solid line).

each function is depicted in Figure 20.6. When the coefficient functions are not identically zero, our proposed $\text{PMLE}_{0.5}$ method and the LASSO have similar performances in estimated MISEs, while the LASSO approach has estimated estimation bias of smaller magnitude. LASSO and $\text{PMLE}_{0.5}$ have similar performances on local sparsity, as measured by C_{i0}, I_{i0}. However, the C_0-values for $\text{PMLE}_{0.5}$ and LASSO are 2 and 0, respectively, indicating that the $\text{PMLE}_{0.5}$ method preserves the global sparsity. The LASSO method does not ensure any global sparsity.

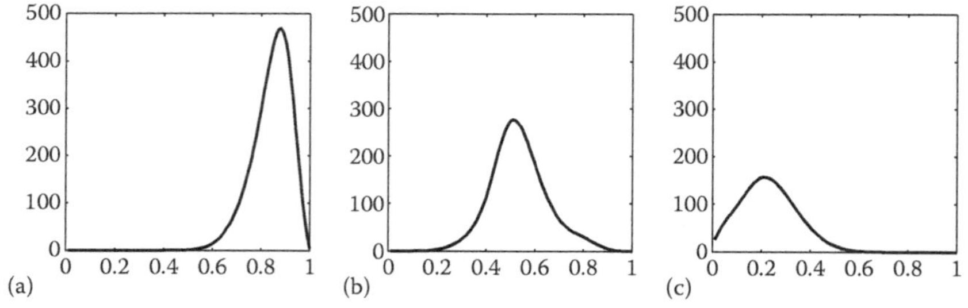

FIGURE 20.5
Coefficient functions κ_1 (a), κ_2 (b), and κ_3 (c) used in the Scenario 2 simulation experiment.

TABLE 20.2
Estimated MISE Values for Each Coefficient Function and Summary Quantities (a)–(d) for the Scenario 2 Simulation

	MISE				
Estimator	κ_1	κ_2	κ_3	κ_4	κ_5
MLE	393.81	248.29	190.31	139.57	142.85
LASSO	174.23	127.15	103.21	42.81	51.05
$\text{PMLE}_{0.5}$	231.34	137.57	92.67	0	0

	$C_{1,0}$	$I_{1,0}$	$C_{2,0}$	$I_{2,0}$	$C_{3,0}$	$I_{3,0}$	$C_{4,0}$	$I_{4,0}$	$C_{5,0}$	$I_{5,0}$	C_0	I_0
MLE	0	0	0	0	0	0	0	0	0	0	0	0
LASSO	4.48	0.96	4.39	0.31	3.79	0.86	8.16	0	8.31	0	0	0
$\text{PMLE}_{0.5}$	4.17	0.83	4.22	0.26	4.25	0.91	13	0	13	0	2	0
True model	7	6	7	6	6	7	13	0	13	0	2	3

Note: The row labeled "true model" gives the numbers of nonzero basis function coefficients $I_{i,0}$ for function κ_i, the number of zero basis function coefficients $C_{i,0}$ for function κ_i, the number of identically zero coefficient functions C_0, and the number of nonzero coefficient functions I_0.

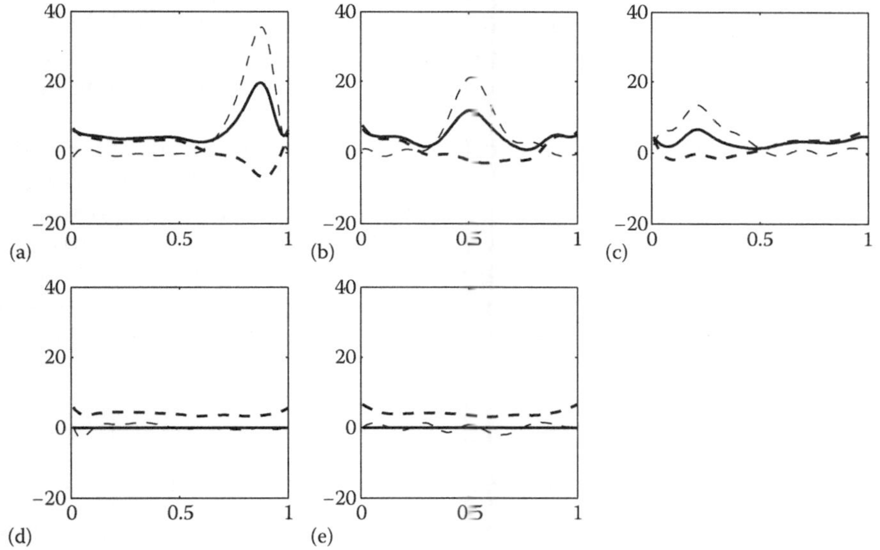

FIGURE 20.6
Scenario 2: Estimated estimation bias for all five coefficient functions (κ_1 (a), κ_2 (b), κ_3 (c), κ_4 (d), and κ_5 (e)) using MLE (dashed thin line), LASSO (dashed thick line), and $\text{PMLE}_{0.5}$ (solid line).

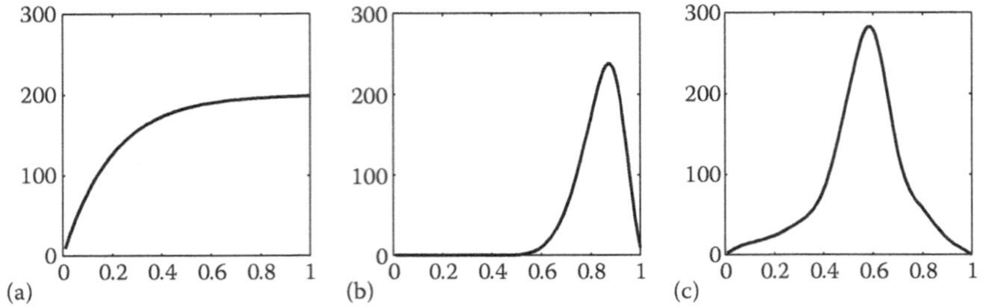

FIGURE 20.7
Coefficient functions κ_1 (a), κ_2 (b), and κ_3 (c) used in the Scenario 3 simulation experiment.

Scenario 3

Our final scenario has both global and local sparsity, as well as basis approximation error: one of the coefficient functions does not belong to the linear space spanned by the B-spline basis functions. Specifically, κ_1 is not in this linear space. As in the previous two scenarios, coefficient functions κ_4 and κ_5 are identically zero. Finally, κ_2 has local sparsity, taking zero values over some time interval, and κ_3 is not zero at any time. Coefficient functions κ_1, κ_2, and κ_3 are displayed in Figure 20.7. Since κ_1 is not in the linear space spanned by the B-spline basis functions, the true values of the coefficients α_{1j} are not well-defined.

In Table 20.3, the quantities defined in (a)–(d) are reported, and the MISEs for all coefficient functions are summarized. The estimated estimation bias for each function is depicted in Figure 20.8. As in the previous two scenarios, $\text{PMLE}_{0.5}$ performs satisfactorily in all aspects, including model fitting and global and local sparsity of the fitted model. The LASSO approach also performs satisfactorily, except for the lack of global sparsity. The model fitted via maximum likelihood is not as good as the other two competing methods.

20.5 Application to German Economic Data

We illustrate the methodology by applying it to a multivariate time series of German fixed investments, disposable income, and consumption expenditures in billions of Deutsche Marks. The data are recorded quarterly from 1960 to 1982 and are seasonally adjusted. See Chan (2002, § 10.5), for further discussion and data source. For illustration purposes, we construct a binary series b_t from each original time series o_t as follows: if $o_t - 1.01o_{t-1} > 0$, then $b_t = 1$; otherwise, $b_t = 0$. That is, each binary sequence records whether or not there is a 1% increase in the original sequence. While our motivation is purely illustrative, many binary economic time series are derived in similar ways (Harding and Pagan 2011).

TABLE 20.3

Estimated MISE Values for Each Coefficient Function and Summary Quantities (a)–(d) for the Scenario 3 Simulation

	MISE				
Estimator	κ_1	κ_2	κ_3	κ_4	κ_5
MLE	513.66	281.30	360.82	185.82	180.65
LASSO	336.34	137.89	217.93	50.51	47.14
$PMLE_{0.5}$	585.25	123.56	261.87	0	0

	$C_{1,0}$	$I_{1,0}$	$C_{2,0}$	$I_{2,0}$	$C_{3,0}$	$I_{3,0}$	$C_{4,0}$	$I_{4,0}$	$C_{5,0}$	$I_{5,0}$	C_0	I_0
MLE	0	0	0	0	0	0	0	0	0	0	0	0
LASSO	0	0.70	4.70	0.94	1.00	1.97	8.32	0	8.61	0	0.01	0
$PMLE_{0.5}$	0	0.69	6.22	1.46	1.20	2.12	13	0	13	0	2	0
True model	–	–	7	6	2	11	13	0	13	0	2	3

Note: The row labeled "true model" gives the numbers of nonzero basis function coefficients $I_{i,0}$ for function κ_i, the number of zero basis function coefficients $C_{i,0}$ for function κ_i, the number of identically zero coefficient functions C_0, and the number of nonzero coefficient functions I_0. These true values are not defined for coefficient function κ_1.

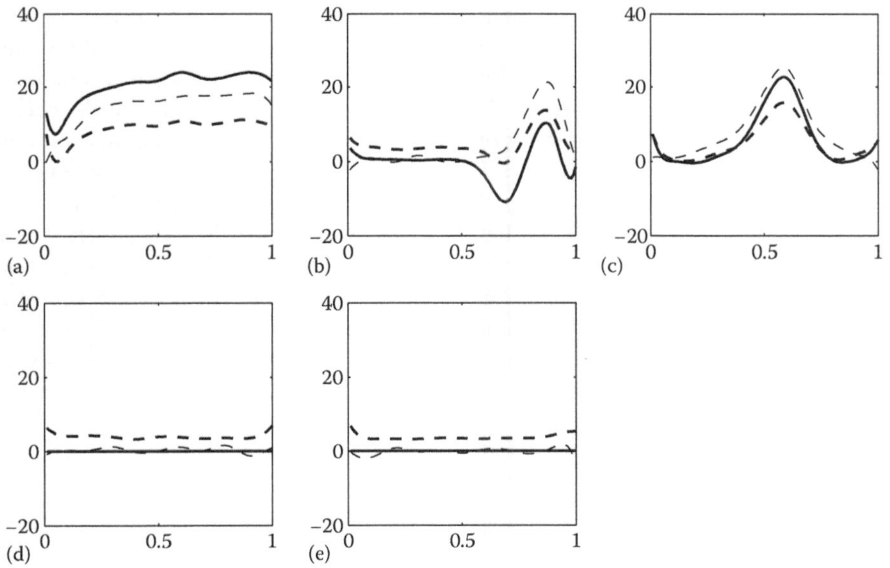

FIGURE 20.8

Scenario 3: Estimated estimation bias for all five coefficient functions (κ_1 (a), κ_2 (b), κ_3 (c), κ_4 (d), and κ_5 (e)) using MLE (dashed thin line), LASSO (dashed thick line), and $PMLE_{0.5}$ (solid line).

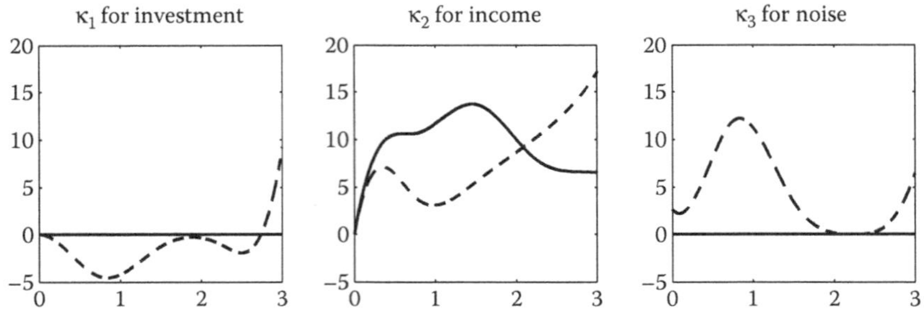

FIGURE 20.9
Fitted coefficient functions for German economic time series example using LASSO (dashed line) and $\text{PMLE}_{0.5}$ (solid line).

We are interested in regressing changes in consumption on changes in investments and income. We assume that the previous 3-year record of changes in investment and income could affect present change in consumption; i.e., we set the effective lag as $M = 12$ quarters.

In order to investigate the global sparsity of our variable selection method, another binary series constructed from a random noise is added to the set of covariates. We use the logit link function and choose a cubic B-spline space with three interior knots to approximate the coefficient functions. The set of basis functions is very small in this example due to the small sample size.

Figure 20.9 shows the fitting result of our proposed $\text{PMLE}_{0.5}$ method compared with the LASSO method. The MLEs are not shown because they are highly variable and would distort the scale of the plots. Our method chooses only changes in income to predict changes in consumption and correctly assigns zero predictive power to the random noise series. LASSO estimates a qualitatively similar coefficient function for changes in income. On the other hand, LASSO assigns mostly small negative weights to changes in investment and incorrectly assigns mostly positive weights to the noise. Because LASSO fails to achieve global sparsity in this example, we find the performance of $\text{PMLE}_{0.5}$ more satisfactory.

20.6 Conclusions

In this chapter, the problem of modeling sparse binary time series has been considered. We proposed a dynamic MISO model, in which the relationship between each input signal and the output signal is characterized by a smooth coefficient function. In this model, we extended the generalized linear model to a dynamic, functional generalized linear model, by specifying the conditional probability of an output event through an appropriate link. Functional model selection is of interest in the fitting of this model, ideally ensuring both global sparsity and local sparsity. Global sparsity identifies those coefficient functions that are identically zero, while local sparsity identifies intervals in the entire domain in which the individual coefficient functions are zero-valued. The functional estimation and model selection for the underlying coefficient functions can be carried out by optimizing a penalized likelihood criterion, where the penalty function used here is the group bridge penalty (Huang et al. 2009).

The optimization problem of the penalized likelihood function is rather challenging. It involves complicated functional optimization, and the objective function is nonconvex. Here, we considered a functional approximation approach, describing each coefficient function as a linear combination of B-spline basis functions of a given degree over a fixed sequence of knots. To circumvent the nonconvexity of the objective function, we implement a quadratic approximation and obtain a one-step estimate using a standard algorithm, built upon LARS.

In our simulation experiments, both LASSO and our proposed method perform satisfactorily in estimating coefficient functions with no global sparsity. When global sparsity exists, the performance of the LASSO method turns out to be worse than our proposed method. The MLE approach is outperformed by the other two methods in any scenario.

Acknowledgments

Part of this work was the master's thesis of Tu, written under the supervision of Wang, who was supported in part by NSF grants DMS-0706761, DMS-0854903, and DMS-1106975 and by the Air Force Office of Scientific Research under the contract number FA9550-10-1-0241. Breidt's research was supported in part by the U.S. National Science Foundation (SES-0922142). The work of Song and Berger was supported by the National Science Foundation (USC Biomimetic MicroElectronics Engineering Research Center), DARPA (USC REMIND Program), and NIBIB (USC Biomedical Simulations Resource). Any opinions, findings, and conclusions or recommendations expressed in this material are those of the author(s) and do not necessarily reflect the views of the National Science Foundation.

References

Akaike, H. (1973). Information theory and an extension of the maximum likelihood principle. In *Proceeding of the 2nd International Symposium on Information Theory*, eds. B. N. Petrov and F. Csaki, 267–281.

Chan, N. H. (2002). *Time Series: Applications to Finance.* New York: Wiley.

de Boor, C. (2001). *A Practical Guide to Splines.* New York: Springer-Verlag.

Efron, B., Hastie, T., Johnstone, I., and Tibshirani, R. (2004). Least angle regression. *The Annals of Statistics*, 32(2):407–499.

Fan, J. and Li, R. (2001). Variable selection via nonconcave penalized likelihood and its oracle properties. *Journal of the American Statistical Association*, 96:1348–1360.

Findley, D. F. (1983). On the use of multiple models for multi-period forecasting. *Proceedings of the Business and Economic Statistics Section of the American Statistical Association*, 528–531.

Findley, D. F. (1985). On the unbiasedness property of AIC for exact or approximating linear stochastic time series models. *Journal of Time Series Analysis*, 6:229–252.

Findley, D. F. (1991). Model selection for multistep-ahead forecasting. *Proceedings of the Business and Economic Statistics Section of the American Statistical Association*, 243–247.

Findley, D. F., Monsell, B. C., Bell, W. R., Otto, M. C., and Chen, B.-C. (1998). New capabilities and methods of the X-12-ARIMA seasonal-adjustment program. *Journal of Business and Economic Statistics*, 16(2): 127–152.

Findley, D. F. and Wei, C.-Z. (2002). AIC, overfitting principles, and the boundedness of moments of inverse matrices for vector autoregressions and related models. *Journal of Multivariate Analysis*, 83:415–450.

Frank, I. E. and Friedman, J. H. (1993). A statistical view of some chemometrics regression tools. *Technometrics*, 35(2):109–135.

Harding, D. and Pagan, A. (2011). An econometric analysis of some models for constructed binary time series. *Journal of Business and Economic Statistics*, 29:1–10.

Hoerl, A. E. (1962). Application of ridge analysis to regression problems. *Chemical Engineering Progress*, 58:54–59.

Huang, J., Ma, S., Xie, H., and Zhang, C.-H. (2009). A group bridge approach for variable selection. *Biometrika*, 96:339–355.

Mallows, C. (1973). Some comments on C_p. *Technometrics*, 15:661–675.

Schumaker, L. (1980). *Spline Functions: Basic Theory.* Cambridge: Cambridge University Press.

Schwarz, G. (1978). Estimating the dimension of a model. *The Annals of Statistics*, 6(2):461–464.

Song, D., Chan, R. H., Marmarelis, V. Z., Hampson, R. E., Deadwyler, S. A., and Berger, T. W. (2007a). Nonlinear dynamic modeling of spike train transformations for hippocampal-cortical prostheses. *IEEE Transactions on Biomedical Engineering*, 54:1053–1066.

Song, D., Chan, R. H., Marmarelis, V. Z., Hampson, R. E., Deadwyler, S. A., and Berger, T. W. (2007b). Statistical selection of multiple-input multiple-output nonlinear dynamic models of spike train transformation. *Proceedings of the 29th Annual International Conference of the IEEE EMBS.*

Song, D., Chan, R. H., Marmarelis, V. Z., Hampson, R. E., Deadwyler, S. A., and Berger, T. W. (2009). Nonlinear modeling of neural population dynamics for hippocampal prostheses. *Neural Networks*, 22:1340–1351.

Tibshirani, R. (1996). Regression shrinkage and selection via the LASSO. *Journal of the Royal Statistical Society, Series B*, 58:267–288.

Yuan, M. and Lin, Y. (2006). Model selection and estimation in regression with grouped variables. *Journal of the Royal Statistical Society, Series B*, 68:49–67.

21

Models for High Lead Time Prediction

G. Tunnicliffe Wilson and John Haywood

CONTENTS

21.1 Autoregressions and Long Range Prediction

The aim of this chapter is to illustrate the application of a class of linear time series models, called ZAR models, which have been introduced to the literature in recent years. They are a generalization of linear autoregressive (AR) models that have the potential to improve the long range prediction of time series by extending the dependence on past values to high lags. We will review earlier work on these models at the end of this section. We describe them in Section 21.3, and present their properties and estimation procedures in the following sections. A ZAR model is specified by its order, p, and a smoothing coefficient, θ, and reduces to an AR(p) model when $\theta = 0$. Standard AR (and ARIMA) models are widely and successfully used, but there are examples that suggest that we should be able to improve upon the predictions that they furnish. The specific example we use to illustrate the topics in this chapter is the series of the monthly USA unemployment rate from January 1968 to August 2009. In this section, we consider long range forecasting issues typified by this example series, and in the next section we present forecasts of the series which illustrate the ability of the ZAR model to address these issues.

The upper two plots in Figure 21.1 show the monthly and annual raw unemployment rates. The lower two plots show the seasonally adjusted (S-A) rate and its logarithms, which we use for most of our statistical analyses for reasons given at the start of the next section. We comment that the main features are the same in all these series: the slow rise and fall of the overall

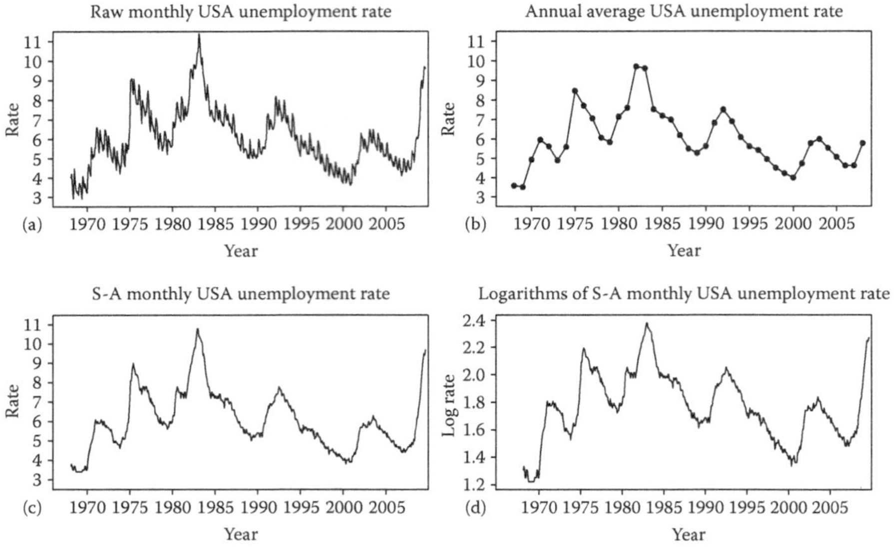

FIGURE 21.1
The USA unemployment rate: (a) raw values from January 1968 to August 2009, (b) the annual average rate from 1968 to 2008, (c) seasonally adjusted (S-A) values from January 1968 to August 2009, and (d) logarithms of S-A values from January 1968 to August 2009.

level similar to a random walk (we will call this the *walk* feature) and the approximate 5-year economic cycle (the *cycle* feature). Seasonal adjustment is carried out because the seasonality evident in the first series obscures the underlying level that is important for monitoring movements in the series from one month to the next. Forecasters are interested in predicting the series for periods of possibly several years ahead and it is usual to use S-A monthly data for this purpose. Two considerations that arise from the specific characteristics of this example are that:

1. The most notable features (walk and cycle) of the data are associated with low frequencies and long periods relative to the length of the series and the monthly sampling frequency.
2. Forecasts are desired to high lead times with respect to the monthly sampling frequency.

The first of these points raises the issue that standard AR models, selected using information criteria, do not have the flexibility to fit the features within the small fraction of the frequency range that is associated with these long period movements. The upper plots in Figure 21.2 show the (unsmoothed) log spectra of the logarithms of the raw and adjusted series. Evidence for the walk

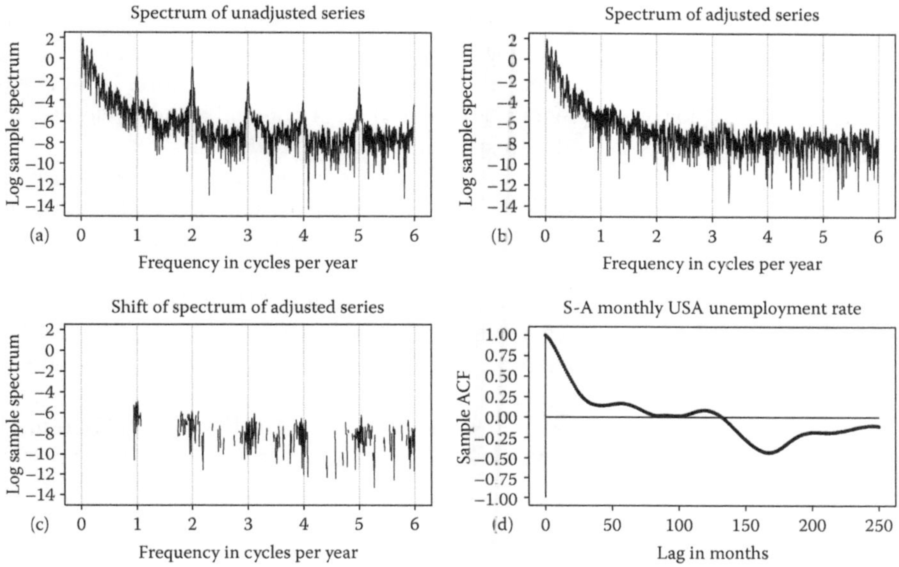

FIGURE 21.2
Log scale spectra of logarithms of the monthly unemployment rate: (a) for the unadjusted series, (b) for the S-A series, (c) those parts of the log spectrum of the adjusted series for which the spectrum is less than one half of that of the raw series, and (d) the sample autocorrelation function (ACF) of the adjusted series.

and cycle features in the series is only barely visible in a collection of narrow peaks below frequency 0.02 in both these plots, i.e., within 5% of the range shown. The second point is an issue because standard AR models are fitted to predict just one step ahead. A further consideration in this respect is the effect of seasonal adjustment on the series. Figure 21.2c shows those parts of the log spectrum of the adjusted series for which the spectrum is less than one half of that of the raw series. These illustrate that, in general, seasonal adjustment can introduce dips in the spectrum of the adjusted series around the frequencies of the seasonal harmonics.

The low frequency spectral peaks are strongly evident in the unlogged spectra (not shown). However, a model fitted to minimize the one-step-ahead error sum of squares is generally influenced by fluctuations of the series spectrum on the log scale. The structure associated with dips in the spectrum of the adjusted series at seasonal harmonic frequencies may then have an influence on the fitting of a parametric model that is comparable with that of the low frequency peaks. Given a sufficiently long series a standard AR model selected by the Akaike Information Criterion (AIC), Akaike (1973), will consistently estimate the whole spectrum (Shibata 1980). However, for the series we are considering, the selected model may be inadequate to provide a good fit both to the cyclical features in the lower 5% of the range and to the pattern over the remaining 95% that is affected by seasonal adjustment. Note, from Figure 21.2c, that the lower frequencies associated with the walk and cycle features are not affected by seasonal adjustment.

The time domain viewpoint is that the AR model essentially captures the lagged sample correlations (ACF) of a series up to the order of the model, and the order of the model required might be expected to be at least comparable with the time period of the cycles of about 60 months. Figure 21.2d shows the sample autocorrelations of the logarithms of the S-A series. Evidence for the approximate 5-year economic cycle in the ACF is obscured by the effect of the walk, and lags up to several multiples of the cycle period are needed to reveal it.

In Section 21.3, and those following, we describe the ZAR model and methods for fitting this model, which address the issues raised in the previous paragraphs as follows:

1. The form of the model provides flexibility in fitting features at low frequencies.
2. The method of fitting allows more weight to be placed on lower frequencies.

The corresponding time domain properties are that the model places weight on past data up to higher lags, and the fitting method also seeks to minimize the prediction error over high lead times.

For many years there has been an ongoing interest in methods for improved forecasting at higher lead times. This is based on the recognition that minimizing single-step forecast error variance, which is equivalent to maximum likelihood model estimation, can be far from optimal for higher lead time forecasting if the model is not correct. This may be true even if the misspecification may appear relatively minor in the sense that residual diagnostics do not readily reveal model inadequacy. Much ground-breaking work in this area was presented in Findley (1983, 1985, 1990, 1991), and discussion with Dr. Findley when he visited Lancaster led to the development of Haywood and Tunnicliffe Wilson (1997), on fitting models by minimizing squared multistep-ahead errors. Our extension of this idea to the construction of a test for improved multistep forecasting (Haywood and Tunnicliffe Wilson 2009) includes a review of more recent work by other authors in this general area. We showed that for commonly occurring models our approach implicitly gave greater weight to the lower frequencies in the data, but this weight was model-dependent.

The ZAR modeling approach is based on a very different idea, but is similar in that it has the capacity to give greater weight to lower frequencies in the data. However, this weighting is prescribed and not model-dependent. The ideas of ZAR modeling may be traced back to the generalized continuous time shift operator and Laguerre filters of Wiener (1949). Discrete time versions have, more recently, been used extensively in systems modeling (Wahlberg 1991). These ideas have been introduced by Wahlberg and Hannan (1993) in a class of time series models very closely related to the ZAR models of this chapter. Our formulation of the discrete time ZAR model developed from a continuous time model presented in Belcher et al. (1994). It is first found in Morton and Tunnicliffe Wilson (2004) where the model is equivalent to that in Wahlberg and Hannan (1993) and slightly different from the one presented in this chapter. Underlying the models is the idea of basis functions for the space of past observations, and an excellent mathematical background to these concepts can be found in Partington (1997). Multivariate time series applications are presented in Morton and Tunnicliffe Wilson (2001), Tunnicliffe Wilson et al. (2001), and Tunnicliffe Wilson and Morton (2004), as are continuous time versions of the model. The Ph.D. theses of Morton (2000), Ibañez (2005), and Lo (2008) study, respectively, the multivariate continuous time model, nonlinear ZAR models, and multistep prediction properties of ZAR models. The findings of the second thesis are summarized in Ibañez and Tunnicliffe Wilson (2007).

21.2 Some Forecast Comparisons

In this section, we compare predictions of the unemployment series using both the standard AR (and ARIMA) model and the ZAR model. All the models are fitted to the logarithms of the data and then transformed back to display forecasts. The results are not, however, particularly sensitive to this transformation. There is not a great difference in appearance between Figures 21.1c and d, but transformation does give a more similar appearance to the five or so peaks seen in the series. The asymmetry in the rise and fall of the peaks is evidence of some nonlinear behavior, which is not treated by the logarithmic transformation. The models presented in this chapter are all linear, but nevertheless have the capacity to reflect, in their predictions, the pattern of cycles evident in the past. All predictions are out of sample, i.e., the models are fitted to data up to the chosen origin and then forecasts made over the remaining period. The error limits shown on all forecasts are designed for 90% coverage at any given point.

Consider first the raw monthly series. A Box–Jenkins seasonal ARIMA model (Box and Jenkins 1970) fits this well with nonseasonal AR, differencing, and moving average orders set to $p = 2$, $d = 0$, and $q = 1$, corresponding seasonal orders $P = 0$, $D = 1$, and $Q = 1$, and seasonality set to $s = 12$. This model is encompassed by the default set of models used by the PICKMDL procedure of X-12-ARIMA. Residual diagnostics were good except for a hint of some calender effects. The estimated nonseasonal AR operator characterizes irregular cyclical behavior, and this is, to some extent, reflected in the forecasts from May 2001, shown in Figure 21.3a, which hint at the oscillation

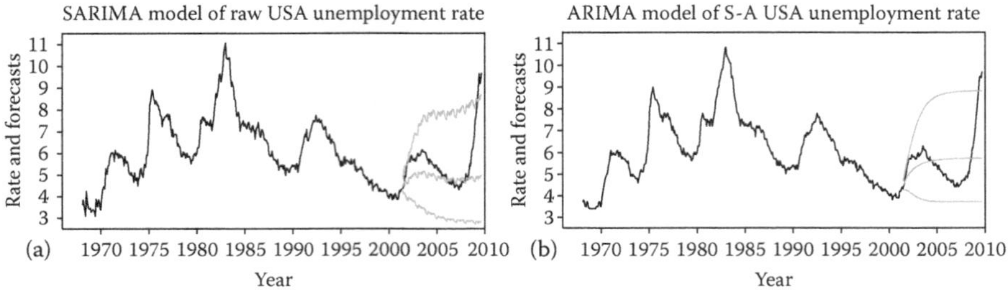

FIGURE 21.3
Forecasts of the USA unemployment rate from May 2001: (a) for the raw series with results corrected for a fixed annual cycle and (b) for the seasonally adjusted series.

observed in future values. In order to show the pattern of forecasts more clearly, we have subtracted from the series and forecasts displayed in this graph a fixed annual cycle, obtained by regression on the set of seasonal harmonics. Because the seasonality is not constant, some evidence of this remains in the figures.

Forecasts of the S-A series are shown, from the same origin, in Figure 21.3b. The nonseasonal ARIMA model used for this had orders $p = 3$, $d = 0$, and $q = 2$. All parameters were significant and residual diagnostics were very good. The forecasts from this model, shown in Figure 21.3b, are not very markedly different from those for the raw series, but fail to show any hint of the future cycle.

Illustrations of forecasts obtained by application of the ZAR model to the S-A series are shown in Figure 21.4, except that in Figure 21.4a the results are from the model restricted to the special case of the standard AR model for which AIC selects the order 6, and the forecasts are similar to those in Figure 21.3b from the ARMA model. The remaining frames of this figure show forecasts made using a ZAR model of order 14 from origins of May 2001, March 1997, and January 1993, which are, respectively, 400, 350, and 300 months from the start of the series. The forecast functions in all cases reflect the cyclical pattern in the future values with realistic error limits quite well, which is encouraging. However, on the logarithmic scale of the series, the forecast error sum of squares up to 6 years ahead for the ZAR(14) model is greater than that of the AR(6) model by a factor of 1.38 for the forecasts from May 2001 shown in Figure 21.4a and b. Simple models with forecast functions showing persistence or mean reversion as in Figure 21.4a can be hard to beat, though, overall, the more accurate forecast might be judged to be that of the ZAR(14) model in Figure 21.4b, when the much more precise error limits are taken into account. A similar comparison of forecasts from March 1997 and April 1993 results in ratios of, respectively, 0.79 and 0.33, strongly favoring the ZAR(14) model. This model, i.e., its order $p = 14$ and ZAR coefficient

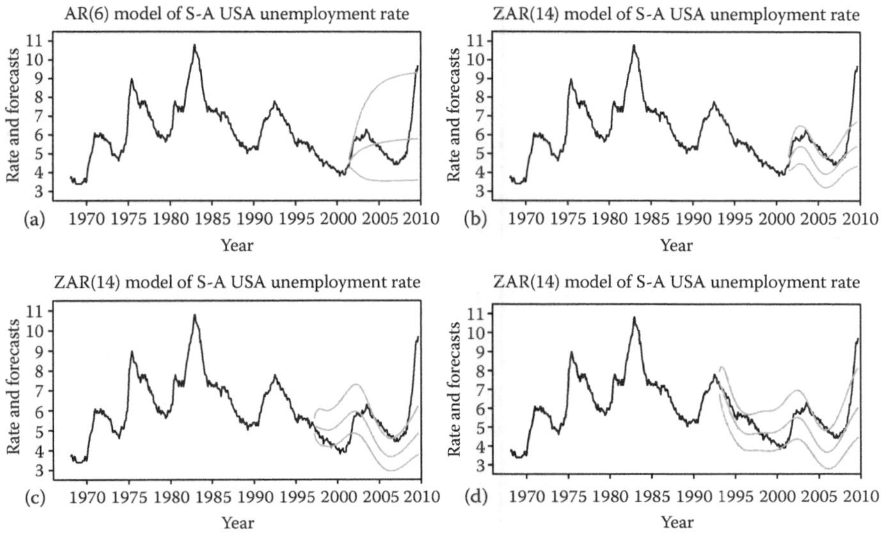

FIGURE 21.4
Forecasts of the S-A monthly USA unemployment: (a) from May 2001, using an AR(6) model; (b) from May 2001, using a ZAR(14) model; (c) from March 1997, using a ZAR(14) model; and (d) from January 1993, using a ZAR(14) model.

$\theta = 0.94$, was selected in preference to the mean-reverting AR(6) model, using an information criterion described in Section 21.6. This is an extension of the AIC, which provides protection against the overfitting of these more complex models. We recall the cautious advice of Tukey (1986) regarding attempts to extract too much structure from data, but he also makes a positive point that we should "look for appearances" in the data, and the cycles are quite apparent here, so a cautious attempt to include them in the results is recommended. Another point made in that article, specific to time series, is that one is fortunate if a sufficient length of data is available to determine its structure, without some change of structure occurring over that time span. For the unemployment series, it would not be surprising if structural breaks and lack of stationarity occurred over the 40-year span we are modeling: the last few points reflect the most recent dramatic break and lie well outside the forecast limits of the ZAR model. Nevertheless, substantial economic shocks have previously had their impacts on the recorded unemployment, and the dynamic behavior of the series seems to persist. The application to the unemployment series is very useful for illustrating the motivation and methodology, but it is a testing example, which we offer for critical reassessment by anyone who may wish to investigate these models further. We have used ZAR models and methods successfully in other contexts, including extensions to

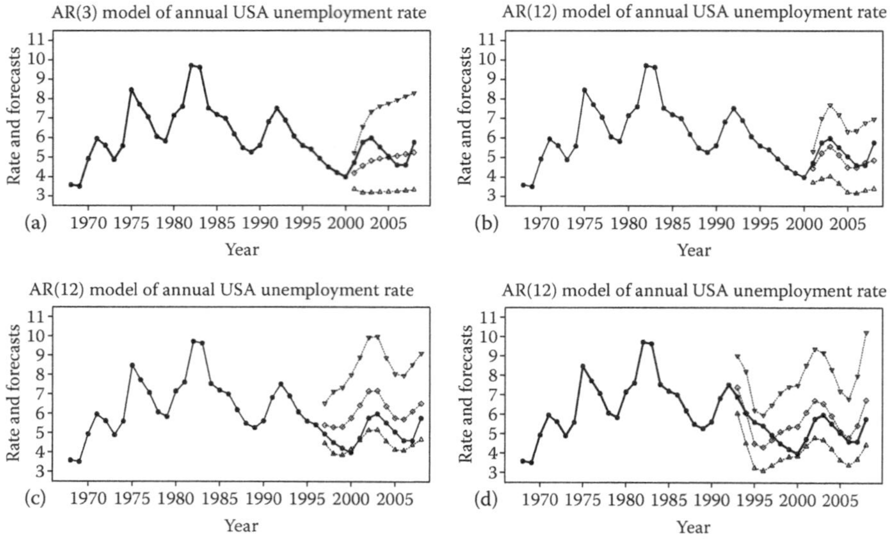

FIGURE 21.5
Forecasts of the average annual USA unemployment rate: (a) from the year 2000, using an AR(3) model; (b) from the year 2000, using an AR(12) model; (c) from the year 1996, using an AR(12) model; and (d) from the year 1992, using an AR(12) model.

vector time series and are confident of their value and potential in appropriate situations.

To complete this section, we consider the annual average series. Our point is to emphasize that our advocacy of the ZAR model is related to the higher monthly sampling frequency that makes it challenging for the standard AR to model the series parsimoniously. By contrast, the standard AR model can be applied to give annual forecasts that parallel those shown for the monthly ZAR model in Figure 21.4. Inspection of information criteria displayed in Figure 21.6 suggested two possible orders, 3 and 12. The modest forecasting performance of the AR(3) is shown in Figure 21.5a and is comparable with the forecast of the S-A monthly series in Figure 21.4a. Forecasts from the same origin for the AR(12) model are shown in Figure 21.5b. These are quite close to the actual, and comparable with those from the ZAR(14) model for the S-A monthly series in Figure 21.4b. Similarly, forecasts from the earlier origins of 1996 and 1992, shown in Figure 21.5c and d, though not so close, are comparable with those in Figure 21.4c and d; they reflect well the cyclical pattern of the future values.

The order 12 was determined by application of the AIC to the whole series. This is shown in Figure 21.6a together with three other criteria. The first is the modified AIC of Hurvich and Tsai (1989), which is appropriate to

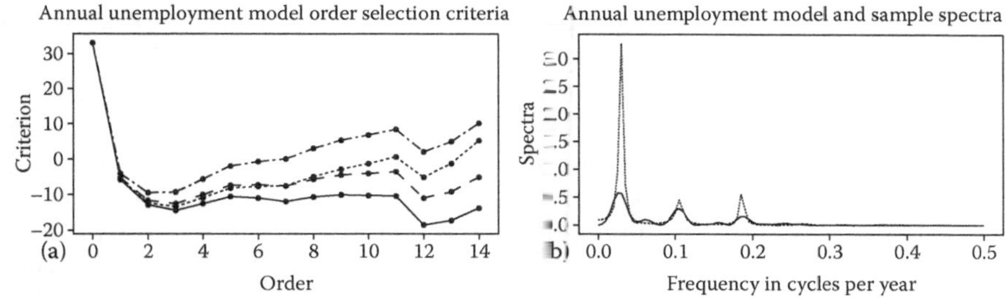

FIGURE 21.6
Autoregressive modeling of the average annual unemployment rate: (a) order selection criteria, respectively the AIC, the Hannan–Quinn, the Hurvich–Tsai, and the Schwarz criteria in increasing value at order 14 and (b) the sample (solid line) and model (dotted line) spectra of the series fitted by an AR(12).

consider when the order of the model is a substantial fraction of the series length, as in this application: an order 12 model is fitted to just 29 points in the example shown in Figure 21.5c. The second is the Hannan and Quinn (1979) criterion, and the third is the Schwarz (1978) criterion. All these select order 3 except the AIC, which selects order 12. Knowing the tendency of the AIC to over-estimate the true order of a model, one might hesitate to select the order 12 as overfitting the data. To avoid the loss of degrees of freedom suffered by simple lagged regression, which is serious for short series and high order models, we have used the exact likelihood for estimation and in the information criteria. However, the exact log-likelihood can be far from quadratic in its parameters, and care is needed to locate the maximum likelihood estimate.

The comparison between the AR model for the annual and the ZAR model for the monthly series is further illustrated by Figure 21.6b, which shows how the spectrum of the AR(12) model matches the sample spectrum of the annual series. This is the raw (unsmoothed) spectrum and the tallest peak is at the lowest harmonic frequency of the series. Such a peak is typical of a mean-corrected (near) random walk process, which gives the illusion of a cycle with a period close to the series length. Such behavior appears to be a component feature of the series. The fact that the spectral peaks of the fitted model are higher than those of the sample spectrum is due to the use of exact maximum likelihood estimation of the model. One would associate with the peak just below frequency 0.2 the economic cycle, which is the other main component feature with an approximate period of 5 years. The peak just above frequency 0.1 (period 10 years) corresponds to no immediately visually evident feature in the series. The testing of spectral peaks to avoid spurious detection of cycles has a long history, see Priestley (1981, 406), and we must interpret this apparent cycle with caution, even though supported by an AR model. The successful extrapolations from this model suggest, however, that the implied spectral peaks are important.

To return to the comparison with modeling the monthly S-A series, this is much longer, 500 instead of 41 values, but it does not contain much more information about the cycles. It just contains the extra 95% or so of higher frequency spectral components shown in Figure 21.2. One strategy for obtaining well-fitting AR models from high frequency data is subsampling as in this example, using annual averages of monthly values. But to forgo monthly records and monthly forecasts for such a reason is not desirable. ZAR models enable us to avoid the subsampling strategy while retaining well-fitting models.

21.3 ZAR Models

In the remainder of this chapter, we present the ZAR model, state and explain its properties including how it is fitted to data, and illustrate its application to the unemployment series. The reader is referred for derivations, proofs, and further explanations to the papers referenced earlier, and to the forthcoming book, Reale and Tunnicliffe Wilson (2012). The models are based on the generalized shift operator Z, acting on present and past values of a series and defined in terms of the backward shift (or lag) operator B as

$$Z = \frac{B - \theta}{1 - \theta B} = -\theta + (1 - \theta^2)(B + \theta\, B^2 + \theta^2\, B^3 + \cdots),$$

where θ is a specified smoothing coefficient, or discount factor, which lies in $[0, 1)$. We shall also write Z_θ to indicate the dependence of the operator upon θ, except that for convenience of notation we shall only use this form when some symbol other than θ is used, and will omit the subscript when the symbol is θ. The acronym ZAR is motivated by the use of this notation. In the case $\theta = 0$, we have $Z = B$. In practice, the calculation of $s_t = Z\, x_t$ is by the recursion:

$$s_t = x_{t-1} - \theta x_t + \theta s_{t-1}, \tag{21.3.1}$$

and Z may be applied repeatedly to construct a set of series that we will call ZAR states, $s_t^{(k)} = Z^k\, x_t$, including $s_t^{(0)} = x_t$. The effect of Z on a slowly varying series is similar to applying a lag of $\ell = (1 + \theta)/(1 - \theta)$. This is illustrated using $\theta = 0.9$ in Figure 21.7a, which shows the S-A unemployment series x_t with Zx_t and $Z^3 x_t$, for which the approximate lags are 19 and 57 months. Initial values of the states have to be assigned to start the recursions in Equation 21.3.1. In Section 21.5, we describe how these can be set to reduce the errors generated in subsequent states. However, these errors are transient, decaying, in general, like θ^t.

Algebraic manipulation shows that $Z^{-1} = (B^{-1} - \theta)/(1 - \theta B^{-1})$ and is an operator on present and future values. The operator Z is unimodular, i.e., if

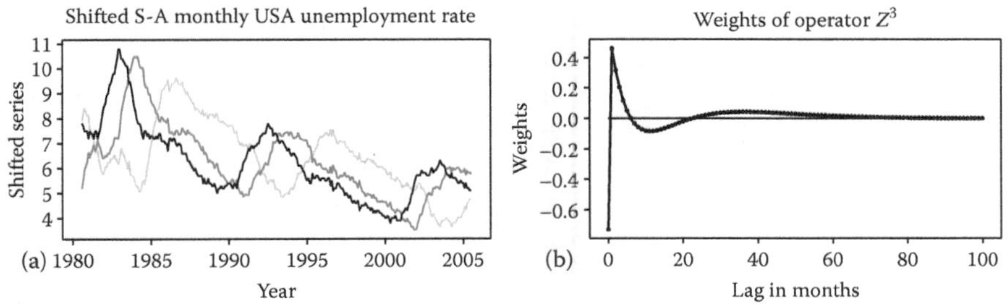

FIGURE 21.7
(a) The S-A monthly unemployment series x_t (solid line) with Zx_t (dark gray line) and $Z^3 x_t$ (light gray line) formed using the generalized shift operator with $\theta = 0.9$ and (b) the weights implicitly applied by Z^3 to lagged values of x_t in the construction of $Z^3 x_t$.

we take $B = \exp 2\pi i f$, a value on the unit circle $|B| = 1$, then $Z = \exp 2\pi i g$ is also a value on the unit circle $|Z| = 1$. A consequence is that for any k, $Z^k x_t$ has exactly the same lagged covariances and spectrum as x_t (just as is true for $B^k x_t$). The dependence of g on f is given by

$$\cos 2\pi g = \frac{(1+\theta^2)\cos 2\pi f - 2\theta}{1+\theta^2 - 2\theta \cos 2\pi f}, \tag{21.3.2}$$

and is illustrated later in Figure 21.8a for $\theta = 0.6$, where it is used to give insight into ZAR models. It is known as a *frequency warp*, a term that has a long history; see e.g., Braccini and Oppenheim (1974). We shall also find useful the expression for the derivatives

$$\frac{dg}{df} = \frac{1-\theta^2}{1+\theta^2 - 2\theta\cos 2\pi f} \quad \text{and} \quad \frac{df}{dg} = \frac{1-\theta^2}{1+\theta^2 + 2\theta\cos 2\pi g}. \tag{21.3.3}$$

Our ZAR models are motivated by expressing the predictor of the *future* value $Z_\rho^{-1} x_t$ as a linear combination of the finite set of present and *past* values $x_t, Z x_t, \ldots, Z^{p-1} x_t$, where we note that the operator Z_ρ^{-1} acting on the future may, in general, be chosen to have a different discount coefficient from that used to construct the predictors. In fact, $Z_\rho^{-1} x_t$ attaches the weight of $-\rho$ to the present value of x_t, but it is useful to consider it essentially as a function of the future. In constructing this predictor, the choice of the explicitly specified coefficient ρ provides a robust alternative to the choice of the simple one-step-ahead predicted value x_{t+1}, although this possibility can be included by setting $\rho = 0$. For a slowly varying series, $Z_\rho^{-1} x_t$ is an approximation to $x_{t+\ell}$, where $\ell = (1+\rho)/(1-\rho)$, and we shall see from our example that choosing a quite modest value of $\rho = 0.5$, for which $\ell = 3$, can substantially improve the accuracy of multistep forecasts generated by the ZAR model. The predictors $Z^k x_t$ in the ZAR model depend on the coefficient θ, which is not explicitly displayed. The choice of θ and the model order p allows the prediction to depend on values of x_t at lags up to and somewhat beyond $p(1+\theta)/(1-\theta)$, as illustrated in Figure 21.7b. We shall again see from our example that this is essential if the predictor is to use information from the past in an efficient manner. In Section 21.6, we will show how an information criterion that generalizes the AIC can be used to select both the coefficient θ and order p, but the choice of ρ remains to a large extent subjective. This is similar to the choice of lead time to use when fitting models for multistep prediction. As for classical ARMA modeling, if the specified model is correct, i.e., it does represent the series exactly, estimation is optimally achieved by minimizing the one-step-ahead squared forecast error, i.e., by setting $\rho = 0$. However, in a realistic situation, approximating a multistep predictor by using a value of $\rho > 0$ can give improved prediction over a range of lead times. Moreover, the loss of efficiency from using $\rho > 0$, even when the model is correct, is not necessarily substantial.

We now specify the ZAR(p, θ) model. We shall in fact set down three forms of the model: first the *general* form, with ρ unrestricted. The second is the *predictive* form, which is motivated by restricting $\rho = 0$, and the third is the *natural* form, in which ρ is set equal to θ. The important point is that these three forms are *exactly equivalent*—there is only one ZAR(p, θ) model, which is most sensibly expressed as the predictive form. The prediction coefficients in any one of these models can be algebraically transformed to those of any other form in quite a simple manner. The coefficient ρ is important for influencing the *fitting* of the model but is *not* included as a parameter of the model with p and θ. The coefficients of the general form of the model obtained by regression of $Z_\rho^{-1} x_t$ on x_t, $Z\,x_t, \ldots, Z^{p-1}\,x_t$, will depend on the choice of ρ, but can be transformed to those of the predictive form of the model, which would realize *exactly* the same prediction of $Z_\rho^{-1} x_t$.

For a mean-corrected stationary process, we express the models in the conventional manner, with the *present value* x_t given in terms of a set of predictors and an error term. To derive this from the motivating prediction of $Z_\rho^{-1} x_t$ by x_t, $Z\,x_t, \ldots, Z^{p-1}\,x_t$, we simply multiply all terms by Z_ρ. The general form of the model is then

$$x_t = Z_\rho\left(\zeta_1\,x_t + \zeta_2\,Z\,x_t + \cdots + \zeta_p\,Z^{p-1}\,x_t\right) + n_t. \tag{21.3.4}$$

We remark immediately that, except in the case of $\rho = 0$, the (so-called) predictors on the right hand side (RHS) of this model are linear functions of the present value x_t, as well as lagged values. Before considering further the implications of this fact, particularly regarding the error term n_t, we consider the predictive form of the model obtained by setting $\rho = 0$, so that $Z_\rho = B$:

$$x_t = \xi_1\,x_{t-1} + \xi_2\,Z\,x_{t-1} + \cdots + \xi_p\,Z^{p-1}\,x_{t-1} + e_t. \tag{21.3.5}$$

The predictors are now proper linear combinations of past values alone, and we assume e_t to be white noise uncorrelated with all past values x_{t-k} for

$k > 0$, i.e., the linear innovation process of x_t. We also write the predictive form of the model in operator notation as

$$\{1 - B\,\xi(Z)\}x_t = e_t,$$

where

$$\xi(Z) = \xi_1 + \xi_2\,Z + \cdots + \xi_p\,Z^{p-1}.$$

Returning to the general form of the model (21.3.4), the assumption that the prediction error in $Z_\rho^{-1}x_t$ is orthogonal to x_{t-k} for $k \geq 0$ implies that n_t follows the AR(1) model

$$n_t = \rho\,n_{t-1} + \varepsilon_t. \tag{21.3.6}$$

The process ε_t is white noise, proportional to the innovation series e_t of the predictive form:

$$\varepsilon_t = M e_t.$$

We can then express the general form of the model in operator notation as

$$(1 - \rho\,B)\{1 - Z_\rho\zeta(Z)\}x_t = \varepsilon_t,$$

from which the algebraic equivalence with the predictive form of the model is found as

$$(1 - \rho\,B)\{1 - Z_\rho\zeta(Z)\} = M\{1 - B\,\xi(Z)\}.$$

Depending on which of $\xi(Z)$ and $\zeta(Z)$ is to be derived from the other, we can determine $M = \{1 + \rho\,\zeta(-\theta)\}$ or $M = (1 - \rho^2)/\{1 - \rho\xi(-\tau)\}$, where $\tau = (\theta - \rho)/(1 - \theta\rho)$.

Finally, the natural form of the model is obtained by setting $\rho = \theta$ and, hence, $Z_\rho = Z$ in the general form, to give

$$x_t = \varphi_1 Z\,x_t + \varphi_2 Z^2\,x_t + \cdots + \varphi_p Z^p\,x_t + n_t,$$

where $(1 - \theta\,B)n_t = \varepsilon_t$. We will also write this model as $\varphi(Z)x_t = n_t$, where

$$\varphi(Z) = 1 - \varphi_1 Z - \varphi_2 Z^2 - \cdots - \varphi_p Z^p.$$

There are several important properties of these models that we now state.

1. Each model represents a stationary process if, when transformed to the natural form, the operator $\varphi(Z)$ satisfies the stationarity condition of the standard AR model, i.e., considering Z as a complex variable, $\varphi(Z)$ has no zeros inside or on the unit circle.
2. For any nondeterministic stationary process x_t, let coefficients of the model in the general form be determined for fixed ρ, θ, and p by projecting x_t on to the predicting variables $Z_\rho Z^k\,x_t$, $k = 0, 1, \ldots, p-1$, on the RHS of Equation 21.3.4. Then the ZAR model so derived will

satisfy the stationarity condition. Moreover, in the limit as $p \to \infty$, the projection error n_t will converge in mean square to a process that follows the AR(1) model (21.3.6) with ε_t proportional to the innovation series of x_t. In this sense, the models can approximate x_t to any arbitrary level of precision.

3. The model can be expressed as a restricted ARMA$(p, p-1)$ of the form

$$\phi(B)x_t = (1 - \phi_1 B - \phi_2 B^2 - \cdots - \phi_p B^p)x_t = (1 - \theta B)^{p-1} e_t.$$

This expression is useful for deriving some properties of the model, but is of little practical value because for models of reasonably high order, the parameterization typically leads to collinearity problems if used in model fitting. Note, however, that the reciprocal zeros r_k of $\phi(B)$, which characterize the dynamics of the process x_t, i.e., the decay rate and period of any cyclical component of the correlations, are related to the reciprocal zeros q_k of $\varphi(B)$ by $r_k = (\theta + q_k)/(1 + \theta\, q_k)$, and will generally be much closer to the unit circle. The ZAR model can therefore capture long-term dynamics with a parameterization that does not suffer the problems of zeros of $\varphi(B)$ close to the unit circle, which can lead to highly collinear estimates of model coefficients in standard AR models, due to the highly correlated predictors. The predictors of the ZAR model are, in general, less highly correlated.

4. There is a simple state-space representation of the predictive form of the model, in terms of the ZAR states. The state transition equation is

$$\begin{pmatrix} 1 & 0 & \cdots & 0 \\ \theta & 1 & 0 & \cdots \\ \ddots & \ddots & \ddots & \ddots \\ \cdots & 0 & \theta & 1 \end{pmatrix} \begin{pmatrix} s_t^{(0)} \\ s_t^{(1)} \\ \vdots \\ s_t^{(p-1)} \end{pmatrix} = \begin{pmatrix} \xi_1 & \xi_2 & \cdots & \xi_p \\ 1 & \theta & 0 & \cdots \\ \ddots & \ddots & \ddots & \ddots \\ \cdots & 0 & 1 & \theta \end{pmatrix} \begin{pmatrix} s_{t-1}^{(0)} \\ s_{t-1}^{(1)} \\ \vdots \\ s_{t-1}^{(p-1)} \end{pmatrix} + \begin{pmatrix} e_t \\ 0 \\ \vdots \\ 0 \end{pmatrix},$$

or $L\,S_t = R\,S_{t-1} + E_t$, where S_t is the state vector at time t. The first row of the equation is simply the predictive model and the remaining rows represent the recursive calculation of the states. The conventional form of a state-space representation is obtained on premultiplying through by L^{-1}, leading to the state transition matrix $T = L^{-1}R$. The observation equation is simply $x_t = s_t^{(0)}$.

This representation is useful for calculating model properties, constructing predictions, and model estimation. In particular, the covariance matrix V_S of the state vector S_t can be calculated using standard methods, and then $V_{S,k} = \text{Cov}(S_t, S_{t-k}) = T^k V_S$. The first element in this matrix is $\text{Cov}(x_t, x_{t-k})$.

21.4 Understanding the ZAR Model

Insight into the nature of the ZAR model for any stationary process x_t is given by defining, for any fixed t, a related process

$$X_k = s_t^{(-k)} = Z^{-k} x_t.$$

Then X_k, $k = \ldots, -1, 0, 1, 2, \ldots$ is also a stationary process, with the terms for $k \leq 0$ providing a basis for $x_s, s \leq t$, and the terms for $k \geq 0$ providing a basis for $x_s, s \geq t$. That X_k is stationary is verified by deriving its lagged covariances from the spectrum $S_x(f)$ of x_t:

$$\Gamma_{X,v} = \text{Cov}(X_k, X_{k+v}) = \int_{-0.5}^{0.5} Z^{-k} \bar{Z}^{-(k+v)} S_x(f) df = \int_{-0.5}^{0.5} Z^v S_x(f) df, \tag{21.4.1}$$

which depends only on v. To clarify this derivation, we have set $B = \exp 2\pi i f$ in $Z = (B - \theta)/(1 - \theta B)$ within the integral and used the property that $\bar{Z} = Z^{-1}$. Further insight is now obtained by transforming the integral (21.4.1) by substituting f in terms of g as defined in Equation 21.3.2. Then, on including the Jacobian of the transformation via Equation 21.3.3,

$$\Gamma_{X,v} = \int_{-0.5}^{0.5} \exp(2\pi i v g) S_x\{f(g)\} \frac{1 - \theta^2}{1 + \theta^2 + 2\theta \cos 2\pi g} dg$$

we deduce that the spectrum of X_k is given in terms of that of x_t by

$$S_X(g) = S_x\{f(g)\} \frac{1 - \theta^2}{1 + \theta^2 + 2\theta \cos 2\pi g}.$$

Figure 21.8 illustrates the effect of the frequency warp, shown in Figure 21.8a, on transforming the spectrum of a univariate process x_t, shown by the bimodal solid dark line plot in Figure 21.8b, into the (warped) spectrum of the corresponding process X_k, shown in Figure 21.8c. The process x_t used in this illustration is constructed as the sum of three independent components: an AR(1), which contributes the spectrum peak at frequency zero; an AR(2), which contributes the spectral peak close to frequency 0.07; and a uniform white noise. The value of $\theta = 0.6$ was used in this illustration. At zero frequency the gradient (21.3.3) of the transformation (21.3.2)

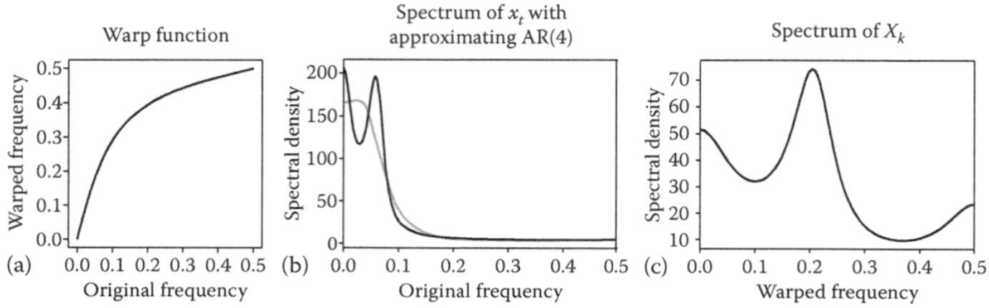

FIGURE 21.8
The frequency warp map shown in (a) transforms the bimodal spectrum in (b) of the process x_t into the spectrum in (c) of the process X_k. The gray line spectrum also shown in (b) is that of a Yule–Walker approximating AR(4) model; a ZAR(4,0.6) approximating spectrum is indistinguishable from that of x_t and is not plotted. The warped spectrum of this ZAR approximation is the Yule–Walker AR(4) approximation to the spectrum in (c) and is again not shown because it is almost indistinguishable from the spectrum of X_k.

is $(1+\theta)/(1-\theta) = 4.0$, so the frequency range of the main features of the spectrum in Figure 21.8b is expanded by a factor of approximately 4 in Figure 21.8c.

If x_t follows the natural ZAR(p, θ) model $\varphi(Z)x_t = n_t$, by applying Z^{-k} we obtain that X_k can be represented by $\varphi(Z)X_k = N_k$, where Z is the shift operator on k and $N_k = Z^{-k}n_t$. Moreover, the spectrum of n_t is warped into the spectrum of N_k, which is that of white noise. This representation of X_k is therefore a standard AR(p) model with the same coefficients as the natural ZAR model. The autocovariances of X_k, and hence the covariances between the ZAR states $s_t^{(k)}$ for fixed t, can then be derived as those of a standard AR(p). Furthermore, the approximation of a general process x_t by a natural ZAR(p, θ) model then corresponds exactly to the Yule–Walker approximation of the process X_k with the warped spectrum. This is also illustrated in Figure 21.8b and c. A Yule–Walker approximating AR(4) model spectrum for x_t fails to resolve the two peaks in Figure 21.8b. An approximating ZAR(4,0.6) model spectrum is, however, so close as to be indistinguishable and is not plotted. The warped spectrum of this ZAR approximation is the Yule–Walker AR(4) approximation to the warped spectrum in Figure 21.8c, and is again not shown because it is almost indistinguishable from the spectrum of X_k.

The concept of the frequency warp gives real insight into the capacity of the ZAR model to approximate certain processes much better than the standard AR model, as illustrated in Figure 21.8. There are two aspects to this, but both apply when the spectrum of x_t is generally confined to low frequencies. The first aspect is that the warp spreads out the low frequency features of the spectrum so that it is more readily approximated by a standard AR spectrum of relatively low order. Looked at in reverse, on the scale of the original frequencies, the ZAR model has much more flexibility for approximation at low frequencies. This is determined by the choice of θ. Secondly, the warp affects the weight applied at different frequencies in approximating the spectrum. It can be shown that fitting the general ZAR model corresponds to minimizing a weighted Whittle criterion on the original scale of frequencies

$$\int_{-0.5}^{0.5} w(f) \left\{ \log S_m(f) + \frac{S_x(f)}{S_m(f)} \right\} df. \tag{21.4.2}$$

Here $S_m(f)$ is the spectrum of the model to be fitted and $S_x(f)$ is the spectrum of the process to be approximated, or the sample spectrum of this process if it is required to fit to a sample series. The weight function $w(f)$ depends only on the choice of the coefficient ρ, which defines the future value $Z_\rho^{-1} x_t$ that is to be predicted in fitting the model. It is the spectrum of an AR(1) model with unit variance and coefficient ρ given by

$$w(f) = \frac{1-\rho^2}{1+\rho^2 - 2\rho\cos(2\pi f)}.$$

Even for the modest value of $\rho = 0.5$, which approximates a lead time of 3, almost 50% of the weight is attached to frequencies below 0.1, and for $\rho = 0.7$ the relative weight falls to nearly 25% at frequency 0.1. In particular, for an S-A monthly time series the parts of the spectrum close to the seasonal harmonic frequencies, which are generally depleted by seasonal adjustment, will carry much less weight in the fitting criterion. An inevitable consequence of using a value of $\rho > 0$ is some loss of efficiency in the estimation of a correct ZAR model, but this need not be large. A simple illustration is in the fitting of a standard AR(1) model, $x_t = \phi\, x_{t-1} + e_t$, but viewed as a ZAR(1,0.0) model. The coefficient ϕ can be recovered from the coefficent ζ of the regression of x_t on $Z_\rho x_t$ in the general model form, by $\phi = (\zeta + \rho)/(1 + \zeta\rho)$. It is left as an exercise for the reader to show that the relative efficiency of an estimate of ϕ found in this manner is $(1-\rho^2)/(1-\rho^2\phi^2)$, which has the value 94% for the quite realistic coefficients $\phi = 0.9$ and $\rho = 0.5$.

21.5 ZAR Model Estimation

We present, in outline, three approaches to estimation of the general form of the ZAR(p, θ) model for a process x_t, given observations from $t = 1$ to n. For simplicity, we will assume that the series has been mean-corrected. A major challenge is to handle the end effects, which are quite evident for ZAR models because the ZAR states $s_t^{(k)} = Z^k\, x_t$ at any given time depend to some extent on unobserved values of x_t for $t \le 0$. We will refer to the three approaches as the Yule–Walker, regression, and likelihood methods. The estimation methods are a prerequisite for constructing the criteria for selecting both the order p and discount factor θ of the model. These criteria will also depend on the value of the discount factor ρ of the general form of the model used for estimation. We do not propose any objective criterion for selecting ρ, but suggest that selection of p and θ be carried out for a small number of values of ρ, chosen to investigate the sensitivity of the selected model to values other than zero.

The Yule–Walker method for determining the parameters in the general form of the model is to project the variable $Y = Z_\rho^{-1} x_t$ on the variables $X_{-k} = Z^k x_t$ for $k = 0, 1, \ldots, p-1$. The equations for the coefficients in this projection involve the estimated covariances between these variables. We suggest that these are constructed numerically using frequency domain methods as

$$C_{Y,X,k} = \widehat{\mathrm{Cov}}(Z_\rho^{-1} x_t, Z^k x_t) = \int_{-0.5}^{0.5} Z_\rho Z^k S_x^*(f)df,$$

and

$$C_{X,v} = \widehat{\mathrm{Cov}}(Z^k x_t, Z^{k+v} x_t) = \int_{-0.5}^{0.5} Z^v S_x^*(f)df,$$

where

$$S_x^*(f) = (1/n)\left|\sum_{t=1}^{n} x_t \exp(2\pi i f t)\right|^2$$

is the sample spectrum of the observed series. The estimated coefficients are the solution of

$$C_{Y,X,k} = \zeta_1 C_{X,k} + \zeta_2 C_{X,k-1} + \cdots + \zeta_p C_{X,k-p+1} \quad \text{for} \quad k = 0, 1, \ldots, p-1,$$

and the variance of the error is

$$S_n^2 = C_{X,0} - \zeta_1 C_{Y,X,0} - \zeta_2 C_{Y,X,1} - \cdots - \zeta_p C_{Y,X,p-1}.$$

Note that in the case of the natural model for which $\rho = \theta$, we obtain $C_{Y,X,k} = C_{X,k+1}$ and the equations are identical in form to the classical Yule–Walker equations. If $\theta = 0$, they reduce to the standard Yule–Walker equations in the usual sample covariances. This spectral approach seemingly overcomes the end effect problem, but in fact, it implicitly substitutes zero for the unknown values of x_t for $t < 0$ and $t > n$. This results in estimation bias as in the case of classical Yule–Walker equations, but the bias can be substantially reduced if tapering is used in the construction of the sample spectrum, as in Zhang (1992). We could go further into the properties of the estimates obtained in this way, but our main point is that they are of value in providing rapidly estimated and consistent starting values for estimation by the likelihood method.

For the regression method, we first construct a response vector with elements $y_t = Z_\rho^{-1} x_t$ and regression vectors with elements $s_t^{(k)} = Z^k x_t$ by applying the respective operators to x_t, taking all unknown values of x_t for $t \leq 0$ and $t > n$ as zero. Thus we use $y_t = x_{t+1} - \rho x_t + \rho y_{t+1}$ for $t = n$,

$n-1, \dots, 1$, setting x_{n+1} and y_{n+1} to zero to start the recursions. Similarly, we use $s_t^{(1)} = x_{t-1} - \theta\, x_t + \theta\, s_{t-1}^{(1)}$ for $t = 1, 2, \dots, n$ setting x_0 and $s_0^{(1)}$ to zero, and similarly the recursions by which higher order states $s_t^{(k)}$ are generated are initialized by setting the values of the states to zero at time $t = 0$. We then introduce further regressors to compensate for the transient errors introduced by this treatment of the end effects. The transient error in y_t is $\rho^{n-t}(x_{n+1} + \rho y_{n+1})$, so we introduce the regressor ρ^{n-t} to allow for this. The transient errors in the regression vector $s_t^{(k)}$ depend on $s_0^{(j)}$ for $j \le k$ and span a space of dimension k. The space for $k = p-1$ contains the space for all lower values of k, so that the effect of these transient errors on the prediction also belongs to this space. To allow for these errors, we therefore include in the regression a further set of $p-1$ basis vectors of this space, which are easily generated as impulse responses of the unknown series value x_0 on $s_t^{(1)}, \dots, s_t^{(p-1)}$. If $\rho = 0$, the regressor for the transient error in y_t is simply an indicator for the last time point, and if $\theta = 0$, the regressors for the transient errors in the states are simply indicator variables for the time points $t = 1, \dots, p-1$. These time points are then effectively removed, and the effect is exactly the same as in lagged regression where the starting time point is taken as $t = p + 1$ so as to include only known values in lagged variables. The regression approach for the ZAR model is therefore a direct generalization of that for lagged regression.

The large sample properties of the estimates are that, under wide conditions, $n^{1/2}(\hat{\zeta} - \zeta) \sim N(0, V_\zeta)$, where V_ζ is defined in terms of the error variance σ_n^2, the variance V_S, and covariances $V_{S,k} = \mathrm{Cov}(S_t, S_{t-k})$ of the p dimensional state vector S_t and the transition matrix T:

$$\begin{aligned} V_\zeta &= \sigma_n^2\, V_S^{-1} \left(\sum_{k=-\infty}^{\infty} \rho^k V_{S,k} \right) V_S^{-1} \\ &= \sigma_n^2 \left\{ V_S^{-1}(I - \rho T)^{-1} + (I - \rho T')^{-1} V_S^{-1} - V_S^{-1} \right\}. \end{aligned} \tag{21.5.1}$$

This may be consistently estimated from the fitted model parameters. Note that V_ζ reduces to $\sigma_e^2\, V_S^{-1}$ for the predictive model with $\rho = 0$.

Lagged regression for the standard AR(p) model does, however, lose information if the order p is large, and the so-called exact likelihood estimation method has been developed to overcome this. We now generalize this method for the ZAR(p, θ) model, and first describe its form in the case $\rho = 0$ for which the likelihood of the observations is what we require. Important to the derivation is the idea that *given* the vector s of initial (unknown) states $s_t^{(0)}, \dots, s_t^{(p-1)}$ at $t = 0$, the vector $e = e_1, \dots, e_n$ of innovations may be directly constructed from the predictive form of the model after recursively generating the subsequent states from the observations up to time $n-1$. From this the initial state vector s may be estimated, i.e., its expected value $\tilde{s}$ found as a linear function of the known observations, and the *series innovations* vector $\tilde{e}$ regenerated using this initial vector. Furthermore, the initial state vector may be transformed to a set of *state innovations* $\tilde{f} = R\tilde{s}$, where R depends only on the model parameters through the natural form. The value of minus twice the log-likelihood, which we will call the deviance, $D(\xi)$, may then be expressed (up to a fixed constant) as

$$D(\xi) = SS/\sigma_e^2 + n\ \log(\sigma_e^2) - 2\log|R| + \log|W|,$$

where $SS = a'a$ is the sum of squares of a concatenated innovations vector $a = (\tilde{e}, \tilde{f})$, $\sigma_e^2 = \mathrm{Var}(e_t)$, and W is derived from the regression matrix used to estimate the initial state vector. Both R and W are functions of the model parameters only, excluding σ_e^2. The first term in the deviance is the dominant one, and maximum likelihood estimation by numerical minimization of the deviance is generally not difficult. One of the advantages of maximum likelihood, shared by the Yule–Walker method, though not by the regression method, is that the estimated parameters are constrained to satisfy the stationarity conditions, because $-2\log|R|$ diverges to infinity at the boundary of the stationarity region.

The extension of this approach to the general form of the model is to construct a modified or quasi-deviance, in which the vector $\tilde{e}$ is replaced by the vector with terms that approximate the prediction error in $Z_\rho^{-1}x_t$ of that model. These are generated as $\tilde{n}_t = \rho\tilde{n}_{t+1} + M\tilde{e}_t$ for $t = n, n-1, \ldots, 1$, where we recall that M is the factor relating the general model errors to the innovations. We take $\tilde{n}_t = 0$ for $t = n+1$ because there is no information about this term in the observed series. However, these modified errors must also be inversely weighted in the sum of squares by their relative standard deviations $d_t = M\{(1-\rho^{2(n-t+1)})/(1-\rho^2)\}^{1/2}$, and the corresponding term $\sum_{t=1}^{n} 2\log d_t$ added to the quasi-deviance. Because ρ is fixed, it is actually sufficient just to add the term $2n\log M$ to the deviance. We call this a quasi-deviance because the error terms in the sum of squares are now correlated. The sum of squares term, as a function of the model parameters, will be asymptotically equivalent to the sum of squares in the regression method. However, besides avoiding the loss of information suffered by the regression approach, the likelihood approach retains the contribution from the initial states, which adds the stability constraint on the parameters. The general model parameters ζ_k are not, however, directly estimated by this approach. Construction of the quasi-deviance is more conveniently implemented using the parameters of the predictive form.

21.6 ZAR Model Selection

We will use the quasi-deviance function of the likelihood approach in the selection of the order p and coefficient θ, given a fixed value of ρ in the general form of the model. We use the concept of the final prediction error (FPE) in constructing a penalty term to add to the minimized quasi-deviance to form a criterion for selecting p and θ. The FPE requires the calculation of two terms: the *bias correction* or underestimation of the error variance due to fitting the model, and the *excess variance* arising in the error from the use of estimated parameters for out-of-sample prediction. For the general ZAR(p, θ) model, the expected values of these two terms, as a proportion of the variance of the model error n_t, are both equal in large samples of size n to $n^{-1}b(p, \theta)$, where, from Equation 21.5.1,

$$b(p, \theta, \rho) = \sigma_n^2 \operatorname{tr} V_\zeta V_S = \operatorname{tr} \sum_{-\infty}^{\infty} \rho^{|k|} T^{|k|} = p\frac{(1+\rho\theta)}{(1-\rho\theta)} - 2\rho\frac{(1-\theta^2)}{(1-\rho\theta)^2}\frac{\varphi'(-\tau)}{\varphi(-\tau)}.$$

Here, $\varphi'(Z)$ is the derivative of the natural model form operator $\varphi(Z)$ and, as before, $\tau = (\theta - \rho)/(1 - \rho\theta)$. The relationship between the eigenvalues of T and the zeros of $\varphi(Z)$ is used to derive the final formula, which reduces to the standard value of p when $\rho = 0$. The model selection criterion is then

$$\text{ZIC}(p, \theta) = D(\hat{\zeta}) + 2\, b(p, \theta, \rho). \tag{21.6.1}$$

In practice, we have also applied a modification of Hurvich and Tsai (1989) to $b(p, \theta, \rho)$, which for smaller n gives a slight improvement in accuracy. Figure 21.9b shows a plot of the mean deviance bias of a ZAR(4,θ) model for a range of values of θ. The mean bias is the average from 1000 simulations of a series of length 500, of the difference between the deviance evaluated for the simulated series at the true and estimated model parameters. A value of $\rho = 0.7$ was used for fitting all the models. Also plotted are the mean bias correction evaluated for the fitted model parameters of the simulations and the bias correction evaluated for the true model parameters used in the simulation.

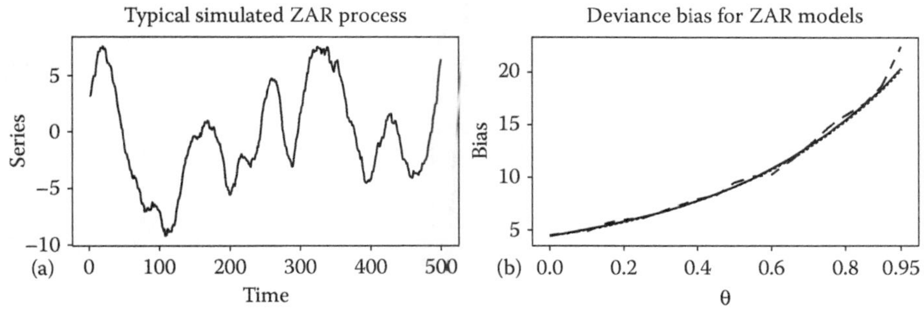

FIGURE 21.9
(a) A typical ZAR(4,0.9) series used in simulations with appearance broadly similar to that of the monthly S-A unemployment rate. (b) Mean deviance bias from 1000 simulated samples (dashed line) with large sample bias correction calculated from true model parameters (solid line) and the mean of the large sample bias correction calculated from estimated model parameters (dotted line, almost coincident with solid line). A value of $\rho = 0.7$ and the range of θ shown were used in the model simulation and estimation.

These two lines are so close that they are barely distinguishable. Figure 21.9a shows a typical sample series generated by the simulation model with a value of $\theta = 0.9$, with an appearance broadly similar to that of the monthly S-A unemployment rate. These simulations reassure us of the accuracy of the bias correction formula for use in model selection.

The bias correction formula is strictly only applicable to a valid model, i.e., one that is fitted with an order at least equal to that of the true model. The second term of the formula is therefore unreliable if evaluated for a model that is fitted with an order less than this. To avoid this difficulty, we advocate an initial strategy of selecting an order $p(\theta)$ for each of a range of values of θ using only the first term, $p(1 + \rho\theta)/(1 - \rho\theta)$. This is the only term that changes as the order of the fitted model is *increased* from that of the *true* model. For orders less than that of the true model and for sufficiently large sample sizes, ZIC will be decreasing with high probability. Figure 21.10 shows the results of a simulation exercise to illustrate the order selection for a fixed value of θ that was used in the ZAR(4,0.9) model from which the samples were generated. We investigated a further modification that is illustrated in the figure. This is the use of the extra factor $\log(\log(n))$ as a multiplier of the penalty term in the ZIC, motivated by the criterion of Hannan and Quinn (1979).

Figure 21.10a shows plots of the mean values from 1000 simulations of the deviance corrected only for the bias, i.e., $D(\zeta) + b(p, \theta, \rho)$, the ZIC as in Equation 21.6.1, and the ZIC with the Hannan and Quinn (1979) modification, i.e., $D(\zeta) + 2\log(\log(n))\, b(p, \theta, \rho)$. The first of these levels off from the true model order $p = 4$, the second has a minimum at the true model order, but the third has its minimum at $p = 3$. Figure 21.10b shows the distribution of model orders selected using the ZIC, and Figure 21.10c shows the distribution when

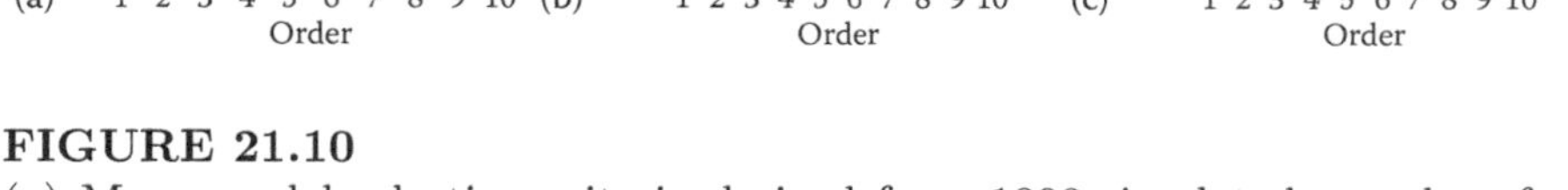

FIGURE 21.10
(a) Mean model selection criteria derived from 1000 simulated samples of a ZAR(4,0.9) process of length 500 estimated from the general model form with $\rho = 0.7$: the bias-corrected deviance (dashed line), AIC type penalized deviance (solid line), and Hannan–Quinn type penalized deviance (dotted line). (b) The distribution of the model orders selected using the AIC type criterion. (c) The distribution of the model orders selected using the Hannan–Quinn type criterion.

the Hannan and Quinn (1979) modification is applied. Order 3 is actually most frequently selected by both, which reflects the fact that the fourth order coefficient is quite small and would only be more certainly identified using a much larger sample. The use of the Hannan and Quinn (1979) modification would appear to be advantageous because it greatly reduces the instances of overestimation of the model order.

The final step of the model selection strategy is to plot the criterion ZIC over the chosen range of θ, using the order of the model selected for each of those values. The full bias formula (21.6.1) is used for this, applied to the parameters estimated for the selected order at each value of θ. The minimum of this plot is used to select θ. We have not yet carried out any simulation study to support this strategy, but show its outcome for the S-A unemployment series in Figure 21.11.

As advocated earlier, we applied this procedure for two values of ρ: $\rho = 0$ and $\rho = 0.5$. Figure 21.11a shows the model orders selected over the range of θ for each value of ρ, and Figure 21.11b shows the selection criteria over the range of θ. The range of θ is transformed to its equivalent lag $(1 + \theta)/(1 - \theta)$, so as to better understand the implications of the model. It is striking that for $\rho = 0.5$, the procedure selects models with equivalent lags for θ in the region of 30 to 50 months, with much higher orders. The model with $\theta = 0.94$ (equivalent lag 32) and order $p = 14$ is the one selected for the forecasts in Figure 21.4b, c, and d. For model selection, we did use the whole series, but all the forecasts were out of sample with the parameters re-estimated from past values alone. For $\rho = 0$, the selected model order remains relatively low

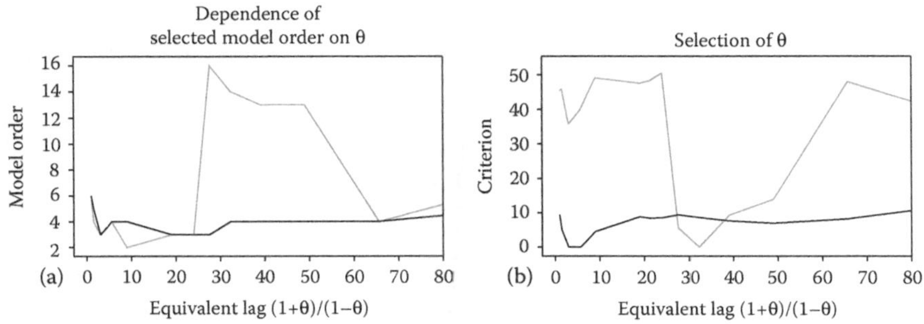

FIGURE 21.11
(a) The order p of the ZAR(p, θ) model selected by the Hannan–Quinn type criterion for the monthly unemployment rate series, for a range of values of θ. (b) The value of ZIC evaluated using the selected order and estimated parameters for each of a range of values of θ. The dark line shows results from setting $\rho = 0$, and the gray line the results for $\rho = 0.5$ in the general model form used for estimation. Each line in (b) is corrected to have its minimum value equal to zero.

over the range of θ with the selected parameters being $p = 3$ at $\theta = 0.5$. These resulted in rapidly mean-reverting forecast functions very close to that for the model with $p = 6$ at $\theta = 0$, shown in Figure 21.4a. The ZAR modeling methodology we have set out therefore appears to achieve its objectives in this example, and we hope that readers will be encouraged to apply it to their own modeling tasks.

References

Akaike, H. (1973). A new look at statistical model identification. *IEEE Transactions on Automatic Control*, AC–19(2):716–723.

Belcher, J., Hampton, J. S., and Tunnicliffe Wilson, G. (1994). Parameterisation of continuous time autoregressive models for irregularly sampled time series data. *Journal of the Royal Statistical Society Series B*, 56:141–155.

Box, G. E. P. and Jenkins, G. M. (1970). *Time Series Analysis: Forecasting and Control.* San Francisco: Holden-Day.

Braccini, C. and Oppenheim, A. (1974). Unequal bandwidth spectral analysis using digital frequency warping. *IEEE Transactions on Acoustics, Speech and Signal Processing*, 22:236–244.

Findley, D. (1983). On the use of multiple models for multi-period forecasting. In *Proceedings of the Business and Economic Statistics Section of the American Statistical Association*, 528–531. Alexandria: American Statistical Association.

Findley, D. (1985). Model selection for multi-step ahead forecasting. In *Proceedings of the 7th Symposium on Identification and System Parameter Estimation*, eds. H. A. Barker and P. C. Young, 1039–1044. Oxford: Pergamon.

Findley, D. (1990). Making difficult model comparisons graphically. In *Proceedings of the Survey Research Methods Section of the American Statistical Association*, 622–627. Alexandria: American Statistical Association.

Findley, D. (1991). Model selection for multistep forecasting. In *Proceedings of the Business and Economic Statistics Section of the American Statistical Association*, 243–247. Alexandria: American Statistical Association.

Hannan, E. J. and Quinn, B. G. (1979). The determination of the order of an autoregression. *Journal of the Royal Statistical Society Series B*, 41:190–195.

Haywood, J. and Tunnicliffe Wilson, G. (1997). Fitting time series models by minimizing multistep-ahead errors: A frequency domain approach. *Journal of the Royal Statistical Society Series B*, 59:237–254.

Haywood, J. and Tunnicliffe Wilson, G. (2009). A test for improved multi-step forecasting. *Journal of Time Series Analysis*, 30:682–707.

Hurvich, C. M. and Tsai, C.-L. (1989). Regression and time series model selection in small samples. *Biometrika*, 76(2):297–307.

Ibañez, J.-C. (2005). New tools for multi-step forecasting of non-linear time series. PhD thesis, Department of Mathematics and Statistics, Lancaster University.

Ibañez, J.-C. and Tunnicliffe Wilson, G. (2007). Multi-stage time series forecasting using Gaussian regression and generalised lags. In *European Symposium on Time Series Prediction, ESTSP'07*, ed. A. Lendasse, 49–58. Espoo, Finland: Multiprint Oy/Otamedia. ISBN: 978-951-22-8601-0.

Lo, M. T. (2008). Improvement in multi-step prediction by a class of extended autoregressive models. PhD thesis, Department of Mathematics and Statistics, Lancaster University.

Morton, A. and Tunnicliffe Wilson, G. (2001). Extracting economic cycles using modified autoregressions. *The Manchester School*, 69:574–585.

Morton, A. and Tunnicliffe Wilson, G. (2004). A class of modified high order autoregressive models with improved resolution of low frequency cycles. *Journal of Time Series Analysis*, 25:235–250.

Morton, A. S. (2000). Spectral analysis of irregularly sampled time series data using continuous-time autoregressions. PhD thesis, Department of Mathematics and Statistics, Lancaster University.

Partington, J. R. (1997). *Interpolation, Identification and Sampling.* Oxford: Clarendon Press.

Priestley, M. B. (1981). *Spectral Analysis and Time Series.* London: Academic Press.

Reale, M. and Tunnicliffe Wilson, G. (2012). *Models for Dependent Time Series.* Boca Raton: Chapman & Hall/CRC.

Schwarz, G. (1978). Estimating the dimension of a model. *Annals of Statistics*, 6:461–464.

Shibata, R. (1980). Asymptotically efficient selection of the order of the model for estimating parameters of a linear process. *Annals of Statistics*, 8:147–164.

Tukey, J. W. (1986). Sunset salvo. *The American Statistician*, 40(1):72–76.

Tunnicliffe Wilson, G. and Morton, A. (2004). Modelling multiple time series: Achieving the aims. In *Proceedings in Computational Statistics, 2004*, ed. J. Antoch, 527–538. Heidelberg: Physica Verlag.

Tunnicliffe Wilson, G., Reale, M., and Morton, A. (2001). Developments in multivariate time series modelling. *Estadistica*, 53:353–395.

Wahlberg, B. (1991). System identification using Laguerre filters. *IEEE Transactions on Automatic Control*, 36:551–562.

Wahlberg, B. and Hannan, E. (1993). Parametric signal modelling using Laguerre filters. *The Annals of Applied Probability*, 3:467–496.

Wiener, N. (1949). *Extrapolation, Interpolation and Smoothing of Stationary Time Series*. Cambridge, Massachusetts: MIT Press.

Zhang, H.-C. (1992). Reduction of asymptotic bias of AR and spectral estimators by tapering. *Journal of Time Series Analysis*, 13:451–469.

Index

B

C